STEVENS' HANDBOOK OF EXPERIMENTAL PSYCHOLOGY

THIRD EDITION

Volume 3:   Learning, Motivation, and Emotion

STEVENS' HANDBOOK OF EXPERIMENTAL PSYCHOLOGY

THIRD EDITION

Volume 3: Learning, Motivation, and Emotion

Editor-in-Chief

HAL PASHLER

Volume Editor

RANDY GALLISTEL

John Wiley & Sons, Inc.

Library of Congress Cataloging-in-Publication Data

Stevens' handbook of experimental psychology / Hal Pashler, editor-in-chief — 3rd ed.
    p. cm.
Includes bibliographical references and index.
Contents: v. 1. Sensation and perception — v. 2. Memory and cognitive processes — v. 3. Learning, motivation, and emotion — v. 4. Methodology in experimental psychology.

    ISBN 0-471-44333-6 (set) — ISBN 0–471–37777–5 (v. 1 : cloth : alk. paper) — ISBN 0–471–38030–X (v. 2 : cloth : alk. paper) — ISBN 0–471–38047–4 (v. 3 : cloth : alk. paper) — ISBN 0–471–37888–7 (v. 4 : cloth : alk. paper) — ISBN 0–471–44333–6 (set)
    1. Psychology, Experimental. I. Pashler, Harold E.

BF181.H336 2001
150—dc21   2001046809

Contributors

Anders Ågmo, PhD
University of Tromso, Norway

Bernard Balleine, PhD
University of California, Los Angeles

John T. Cacioppo, PhD
University of Chicago

Russell M. Church, PhD
Brown University

Thomas S. Collett, PhD
University of Sussex, England

L. Elizabeth Crawford, PhD
University of Chicago

Peter Dayan, PhD
Gatsby Computational Neuroscience Unit
London, England

Anthony Dickinson, PhD
University of Cambridge

Martha Escobar, PhD
SUNY Binghamton

Cynthia Fisher
University of Illinois

Rochel Gelman, PhD
Rutgers University

Lila R. Gleitman
University of Pennsylvania

James L. Gould, PhD
Princeton University

Geoffrey Hall, PhD
University of York, United Kingdom

Philip J. Kellman, PhD
University of California—Los Angeles

Frank Krasne, PhD
University of California—Los Angeles

Joseph E. LeDoux, PhD
New York University

Joan Lucariello
Boston College

Barbara Luka
University of Arizona

Louis D. Matzel, PhD
Rutgers University

Ralph Miller, PhD
SUNY Binghamton

Donald W. Pfaff, PhD
The Rockefeller University

Neil E. Rowland, PhD
University of Florida

Glenn E. Schafe, PhD
New York University

Randy J. Seeley, PhD
Univ. of Cincinnati Medical Center

Larry W. Swanson, PhD
Univ. of Southern California

Alan G. Watts, PhD
Univ. of Southern California

Roy A. Wise, PhD
National Institute on Drug Abuse

Stephen C. Woods, PhD
Univ. of Cincinnati Medical Center

Contents

Preface

The precise origins of experimental psychology can be debated, but by any count the field is more than a hundred years old. The past 10 years have been marked by tremendous progress: a honing of experimental strategies and clearer theoretical conceptualizations in many areas combined with a more vigorous cross-fertilization across neighboring fields.

Despite the undeniable progress, vigorous debate continues on many of the most fundamental questions. From the nature of learning to the psychophysical functions relating sensory stimuli to sensory experiences and from the underpinnings of emotion to the nature of attention, a good many of the questions posed in the late 19th century remain alive and in some cases highly controversial.

Although some have viewed this fact as discouraging, it should scarcely be surprising. As in the biological sciences generally, early hopes that a few simple laws and principles would explain everything that needed to be explained have gradually given way to a recognition of the vast complexity of human (and nonhuman) organisms in general, and of their mental faculties in particular. There is no contradiction between recognizing the magnitude of the progress that has been made and appreciating the gap between current understanding and the fuller understanding that we hope to achieve in the future.

Stanley Smith ("Smitty") Stevens' *Handbook of Experimental Psychology,* of which this is the third edition, has made notable contributions to the progress of the field. At the same time, from one edition to the next, the *Handbook* has changed in ways that reflect growing recognition of the complexity of its subject matter. The first edition was published in 1951 under the editorship of the great psychophysical pioneer himself. This single volume (described by some reviewers as the last successful single-volume handbook of psychology) contained a number of very influential contributions in the theory of learning, as well as important contributions to psychophysics for which Stevens was justly famous. The volume had a remarkably wide influence in the heyday of a period in which many researchers believed that principles of learning theory would provide the basic theoretical underpinning for psychology as a whole.

Published in 1988, the second edition was edited by a team comprised of Richard Atkinson, Richard J. Herrnstein, Gardner Lindzey, and Duncan Luce. The editors of the second edition adopted a narrower definition of the field, paring down material that overlapped with physics or physiology and reducing the role of applied psychology. The result was a set of two volumes, each of which was substantially smaller than the single volume in the first edition.

Discussions of a third edition of the *Stevens' Handbook* began in 1998. My fellow editors and I agreed that experimental psychology had broadened and deepened to such a point that two volumes could no longer reasonably encompass the major accomplishments that have occurred in the field since 1988. We also felt that a greatly enlarged treatment of methodology would make the *Handbook* particularly valuable to those seeking to undertake research in new areas, whether graduate students in training or researchers venturing into subfields that are new to them.

The past 10 years have seen a marked increase in efforts to link psychological phenomena to neurophysiological foundations. Rather than eschewing this approach, we have embraced it without whittling down the core content of traditional experimental psychology, which has been the primary focus of the *Handbook* since its inception.

The most notable change from the previous edition to this one is the addition of a new volume on methodology. This volume provides rigorous but comprehensible tutorials on the key methodological concepts of experimental psychology, and it should serve as a useful adjunct to graduate education in psychology.

I am most grateful to Wiley for its strong support of the project from the beginning. The development of the new *Handbook* was initially guided by Kelly Franklin, now Vice President and Director of Business Development at Wiley. Jennifer Simon, Associate Publisher, took over the project for Wiley in 1999. Jennifer combined a great measure of good sense, good humor, and the firmness essential for bringing the project to a timely completion. Although the project took somewhat longer than we initially envisioned, progress has been much faster than it was in the second edition, making for an up-to-date presentation of fast-moving fields. Both Isabel Pratt at Wiley and Noriko Coburn at University of California at San Diego made essential contributions to the smooth operation of the project. Finally, I am very grateful to the four distinguished volume editors, Randy Gallistel, Doug Medin, John Wixted, and Steve Yantis, for their enormous contributions to this project.

Hal Pashler

CHAPTER 1

Associative Structures in Pavlovian and Instrumental Conditioning

GEOFFREY HALL

INTRODUCTION

In the most basic of conditioning procedures, the experimental subject (usually an animal, but sometimes a human participant) experiences two events in close temporal conjunction. In Pavlovian conditioning, one stimulus (the unconditioned stimulus, US) occurs along with (usually shortly after) the presentation of some other (the conditioned stimulus, CS); in instrumental conditioning, a stimulus (or outcome, O) is forthcoming after the animal has emitted some specified pattern of behavior (or response, R). That is, in both procedures, the experimenter arranges an association between events in the world. What could be more natural then, than to attempt to explain the resulting changes in the animal's behavior in terms of a mechanism that allows the animal to form some central representation of the association between the events that it experiences? Indeed, the dominant account of conditioning over the last 100 years (since the pioneering work of Pavlov and of Thorndike at the turn of the 19th century) has been associative.

Specific accounts differ in many ways (as we shall see), but the central assumption of all associative analyses of conditioning has been that the effects observed can be explained in terms of the operation of a *conceptual nervous system* that consists of entities (to be referred to as *nodes*) among which links can form as a result of the training procedures employed in conditioning experiments. The existence of a link allows activity in one node to modify the activity occurring in another node to which it has become connected. My task in this chapter is to review what conditioning experiments have revealed about the structure of this conceptual nervous system. At the most general level, of course, the structure is assumed (i.e., we have assumed a set of nodes interconnected by links), but what characterizes the nodes involved in any given conditioning procedure and the pattern of interconnections that forms among them remains unspecified.

These questions concerning structure cannot be wholly divorced from consideration of the functional properties of the system. In particular, what is assumed about the nature of the activity engendered in a node (as a consequence of its being activated by way of an associative link) turns out to have important implications for interpretations of associative structure. My starting position will be the assumption that activity engendered in a stimulus node via an associative link is functionally identical to that produced by direct application of the relevant stimulus itself. It will

1

soon become evident, however, that this assumption can be hard to sustain (or at least that, in order to do so, it is necessary to postulate associative structures of possibly undue complexity). This issue will need to be dealt with in the course of my discussion. For the most part, however, it will be possible to sidestep any detailed discussion of a further question about the functioning of the system: What conditions must be met for an association to be formed? Many alternative answers have been given to this question, and debate about the relative merits of these alternatives has dominated the work of some associative learning theorists over the last 30 years. For present purposes, I will simply assume that an associative link between two nodes can form (or changes in strength can occur) when both nodes are concurrently activated. This is a gross oversimplification (as will be revealed by reading of Chap. 2, this volume); but it can be justified (see Hall, 1994), and it will serve to get the discussion of structural issues under way.

The rest of this chapter is divided into three main sections. The first is concerned with simple excitatory conditioning. "Simple" here refers not to the nature of the associative structures involved (which can be surprisingly involved) but to the basic experimental procedures employed. These are, for Pavlovian conditioning, the case in which a single CS reliably precedes the occurrence of a US and for instrumental conditioning, the case in which a given response reliably results in a given outcome. Unsurprisingly, it turns out to be necessary to consider more complex excitatory conditioning experiments in order to work out what is going on in these cases.

The second section deals with simple inhibitory conditioning. Again, the qualifier "simple" refers to the basic procedure, the effects of which are to be explained. This is the procedure in which the association between relevant events is discontinued—by presenting the CS without the US in the Pavlovian case, or by allowing the response to occur without outcome in the instrumental case (i.e., the procedure known as *extinction*). Again, it will be necessary to consider more elaborate procedures, including some that involve what I shall refer to as complex conditioning.

The third section directly addresses the issue of complex conditioning, in which the critical event (the CS or the response) cannot reliably predict what will follow (whether this be another event or its omission). Rather, the nature of the event that follows the CS (Pavlovian) or the response (instrumental) varies according to circumstances. Examples of such *conditional* training include procedures in which CS X is followed by the US only when it is presented in compound with CS A but not when it is presented alone (to be symbolized henceforth as AX+/X−) and those in which a response produces an outcome only when a given stimulus is present but not otherwise (instrumental discriminative training).

The final section of the chapter briefly reviews the ways in which the experimental work described in the other sections of the chapter requires us to modify or elaborate on those assumptions about the structure and functioning of the conceptual nervous system that we have taken as our starting point.

SIMPLE EXCITATORY CONDITIONING

Pavlovian Conditioning

In this procedure the experimenter manipulates two events (the CS and the US), of which the US commonly elicits some overt response, the unconditioned response (UR). Associative analysis begins by assuming a node for each event. Stimulus nodes will be activated by the presentation of the relevant stimulus;

(a)

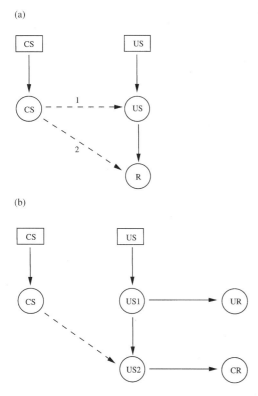

(b)

Figure 1.1 Excitatory Pavlovian conditioning. NOTE: (a) Possible associative structures for excitatory Pavlovian conditioning. (b) An elaboration expressing Wagner's (e.g., 1981) suggestion that conditioned and unconditioned stimuli might engender different states. Circles represent nodes in a conceptual nervous system; rectangles represent environmental events. Lines connecting nodes suggest how activity in one node can influence activity in another; solid lines indicate intrinsic links, and dashed lines indicate links that can be strengthened or weakened by experience. An arrow indicates that the action of the link is to engender activity in the target node. CS: conditioned stimulus; US: unconditioned stimulus; R: response; UR: unconditioned response; CR: conditioned response.

a response indicates activity in the node responsible for that behavior. These nodes are depicted in Figure 1.1a, in which the solid line indicates the presumed inherent excitatory link between the US node and the node responsible for organizing emission of the UR. The assumption that concurrent activation of

nodes allows the formation of links between them means that the connections indicated by the dashed lines could form during the course of conditioning. One (labeled 1 in the figure) allows presentation of the CS to activate the US node in the absence of the US itself; this may be described as an S-S theory of conditioning. The other (link 2) allows the CS directly to evoke the behavior that is otherwise called a UR (an S-R theory). The change that occurs in the properties of the CS (its acquired ability to evoke a conditioned response, CR) could reflect the operation of either or both of these links. The relevant experimental evidence, to be reviewed next, does not allow any simple choice between these alternatives but leads to the development of a more complex, but also more interesting, picture.

The Form of the Conditioned Response

Although widely discussed in this context, the form of the CR that develops with CS-US pairings turns out to supply little information about the underlying associative structure; accordingly, this matter can be dealt with very briefly here. It has been noted that the CR and UR are sometimes very similar (even, in some preparations, indistinguishable, e.g., Culler, Finch, Girden, & Brogden, 1935), a finding that has been taken to support the view that conditioning establishes link 2, which allows the CS direct access to the UR node. As will be evident from Figure 1.1a, however, link 1 also allows access to the UR node by a route that is only marginally less direct. Both interpretations can accommodate the fact that the form of the CR may match that of the UR. Furthermore, neither is much discomforted by those cases in which the CR differs from the UR. For example, in the Pavlovian training procedure widely used for pigeons (and known as autoshaping), the UR is pecking at food in a food tray, whereas the CR is pecking elsewhere (at a light that has previously signaled the delivery of food). This CR appears to be a blending of the UR with a (usually subthreshold) response tendency governed by the key light. Although the details need to be specified, it is clearly open to the theorist to postulate the existence of an output-controlling mechanism that takes its input not only from the UR node shown in the figure but also from any other response node that may be activated at the same time (see Holland, 1977, for a full discussion of this possibility).

Seemingly more problematic are cases in which the CR appears to be quite different from, even antagonistic to, the UR. A possible example is the ability of a CS that has signaled an injection of morphine to evoke hyperalgesia, the UR to morphine being analgesia (see, e.g., Siegel, 1975). Partly to deal with such effects, Wagner (e.g., 1981) introduced a version of the S-S theory that abandoned the assumption that the activation induced in a node by an associative link is functionally the same as that produced by direct application of the stimulus. The state evoked by the stimulus itself was referred to as being one of primary activation (the A1 state) and was assumed to be qualitatively different from the state of secondary activation (the A2 state) produced by the associative link. It is worth noting that it may be possible to express this general notion without the need to postulate that a given node can experience different types of activation. In the version shown in Figure 1.1b, the node directly activated by the US (US1) is assumed to activate a further node (US2), and it is with this latter node that the CS is assumed to form an association.

However it is formalized, Wagner's proposal turns out to have a range of far-reaching implications that are not discussed further here. For present purposes, its importance is that it allows the possibility that the CR and UR might differ in form. In some response systems, the response elicited by the A2 state (or by the US1 node) may be the same as that evoked by the A1 state (by the US2 node), but

in other systems, opponent principles may apply. What it does not do, however, is require us to accept the S-S account. Although no such theory has been explicitly developed, it would be quite possible for a proponent of the S-R account to adopt the analogous proposal that the activity evoked in the UR node by way of link 2 (Figure 1.1a) is qualitatively different from that evoked by the US itself. Choice between the alternative accounts requires evidence from other sources.

Conditioning with No UR

It is well established that classical conditioning can occur when the UR normally evoked by the US is prevented from occurring. For example, Zentall and Hogan (1975) reported that pigeons given pairings of a key-light CS and a food US would develop the CR of pecking at the key even when access to the food (and thus the normal UR of pecking and eating) was prevented by means of a transparent screen. This sort of observation argues against a literal interpretation of the S-R account but does not constitute decisive disproof of the general notion. Physically preventing the occurrence of the overt UR does not necessarily mean the absence of activity in the central node responsible for organizing the (attempted) emission of that response. Accordingly, an S-R connection (link 2 of Figure 1.1a) could still form in these circumstances. More informative on this matter are experiments that make use of the two-stage conditioning procedures depicted in Figures 1.2 and 1.3.

In the procedure known as *sensory preconditioning* (Brogden, 1939; see also Chap. 2, this volume), no attempt is made to suppress the UR; rather, evidence is sought for conditioning when the events involved are such that no overt UR is evident in the first place. In the first stage of this three-stage procedure, the subjects receive pairings of two stimuli (A and B in Figure 1.2a), as in standard classical conditioning, but both events are neutral (i.e.,

(a)

(b)

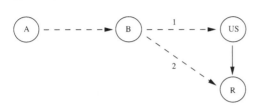

Figure 1.2   Sensory preconditioning.
NOTE: (a) Design of an experiment on sensory pre-conditioning; A and B represent stimuli. (b) Possible associative structures produced by this training procedure. Conventions and other abbreviations are as given for Figure 1.1.

neither evokes an obvious UR). Any association formed between these events may be assumed to be S-S in nature. The rest of the training procedure is designed to allow this association to show itself in behavior. In the second phase of training, one stimulus (B) is paired with an orthodox, motivationally sig-

(a)

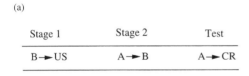

(b)

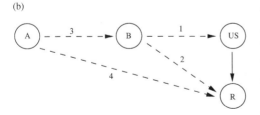

Figure 1.3   Second-order conditioning.
NOTE: (a) Design of an experiment on second-order conditioning; A and B represent stimuli. (b) Possible associative structures produced by this training procedure. Conventions and other abbreviations are as given for Figure 1.1.

nificant US so that a CR develops. Upon testing, it is found that stimulus A is also capable of evoking the CR to some degree (e.g., Brogden, 1939; Prewitt, 1967; Rescorla & Cunningham, 1978). This outcome is readily explained in terms of the *associative chain,* depicted in Figure 1.2b. By virtue of the (S-S) link between A and B, stimulus A, when presented during the test, is able to activate the node for stimulus B, which has itself acquired the power to evoke a CR. It may be noted that this procedure is silent about the mechanism by which B acquires this power; both S-R and S-S learning could occur during phase two, and both links 1 and 2 are shown in the figure. It does show, however, that S-S learning *can* occur (between A and B in phase 1); parsimony may justify the presumption that it will also occur (between B and US) in phase two.

In the *second-order conditioning* procedure of Figure 1.3, the order of the first two stages of sensory preconditioning is reversed. In stage one, subjects receive standard (first-order) conditioning, and as a result CS B may come to evoke a CR (either by way of an S-S connection, link 1, an S-R connection, link 2, or both; see Figure 1.3b). The second stage consists of pairing a new CS (A) with the pre-trained CS B. The outcome is that A acquires the power to evoke the CR. This result can be explained in both S-R and S-S terms. The former account assumes that during stage-two training a link is formed between stimulus A and the response that B is able to evoke, by virtue of its stage-one training (link 4 in the figure). According to the latter, an A-B link is formed during stage two (link 3 in the figure) so that A, when presented alone during the test, is able to activate the B representation and hence evoke the CR (by way of link 1, link 2, or both).

In itself, therefore, the phenomenon of second-order conditioning does not speak to the theoretical issue of concern here. Its importance in this context is that there are some instances of successful second-order conditioning in which the first-order stage does not establish a CR to stimulus B (or, at least, does not establish the CR finally elicited by A during the test). Nairne and Rescorla (1981) conducted a second-order conditioning experiment with pigeons in which stimulus B was a burst of noise paired with food in stage one, and stimulus A the illumination of a response key. The birds acquired the response of pecking at stimulus A, although the noise did not evoke a directed pecking response. It seems that link 4 cannot form in these circumstances (as link 2 is ineffective), prompting the conclusion that the critical link is directly between the representations of A and B. Before accepting this conclusion, however, we should acknowledge the viability of an alternative interpretation. Although the noise does not elicit overt pecking, it will undoubtedly acquire the ability to elicit other, covert, responses—the set of emotional or affective responses appropriate to the imminent delivery of food. An S-R link formed in stage two would allow stimulus A to evoke these same responses (although additional assumptions are needed to explain why these responses should come to show themselves in key pecking). The issue of the conditioning of emotional responses or states is taken up in the following sections.

Revaluation of the US

In the sensory preconditioning procedure, the first stage of training allows the formation of an association between two neutral stimuli. The second stage of training gives value to one of these stimuli (by pairing it with a motivationally significant event), and the consequences for the other are observed. This same general technique can be applied to give information about the nature of the association formed between an orthodox CS and US. For example, Holland and Straub (1979) gave rats pairings of a noise and food in a first stage of

training, sufficient to establish the CR of approaching the site of food delivery in the presence of the noise. In a second phase of training carried out in the home cage, the rats ate food pellets of the sort used as the US before receiving a nausea-inducing injection of a lithium salt (Li). This procedure was effective in devaluing the US, as evidenced by a reduction in the willingness of the rats to consume these pellets. A final test conducted in the original conditioning apparatus revealed a substantial reduction in the frequency of the CR to the noise, compared with the responding of rats that had not experienced the devaluation treatment. This outcome is not to be expected on the basis of the S-R analysis—there is no reason why an association between the CS and a response elicited by a US should be affected by a subsequent change in the value of that US. On the other hand, if conditioned responding depends on the ability of the CS to activate a representation of the US, then a sensitivity to changes in the nature of that representation is just what would be expected.

Sensitivity to postconditioning changes in the value of the US has been demonstrated a number of times in a variety of conditioning procedures (e.g., Fudim, 1978; Holland & Rescorla, 1975; Rescorla, 1973a, 1974), and it constitutes the best evidence for the widespread importance of the S-S association in classical conditioning. This is not to say, however, that an S-S link underlies all instances of conditioned responding or that it is the sole source of the CR in those preparations in which it is known to play a role. Holland and Straub's (1979) experiment is informative on both these points. With respect to the first, in addition to measuring food-cup approach, Holland Straub measured another CR: the increase in general activity that develops in the presence of an auditory signal for food. This response was present in full strength during the test and thus must depend on some mechanism that is not sensitive to the food devaluation procedure they used. With respect to the second point, it is noteworthy that in Holland and Straub's experiment, although the devaluation procedure appeared to be completely effective (several food-LiCl pairings were given and consumption of the pellets declined practically to zero), the conditioned food-cup approach in the test phase was not totally abolished. This observation prompts the conclusion that some mechanism other than that embodied in the S-S link plays a part in generating this CR—that an S-R link has also been established.

Further evidence supporting the view that no single associative structure is responsible for all cases of conditioning comes from a reconsideration of second-order conditioning. As we have already seen, the basic effect can be explained both in S-R terms (link 4 of Figure 1.3), or in S-S terms (link 3). A version of the devaluation procedure can again be used to choose between these possibilities. The S-S account implies that stimulus A is able to evoke the CR only because its associate, B, has previously acquired conditioned properties. Removing these should eliminate the CR to A; that is a phase of extinction, in which B is presented alone until its CR disappears, interposed between stage two and the test, should abolish a second-order conditioning effect based on an S-S association. For the S-R account, on the other hand, stimulus B will have done its job (by evoking a response) during stage one, and the ability of A to evoke the CR should be impervious to subsequent changes in the value of B.

The effects of extinguishing the first-order CS on the second-order CR have been investigated several times and the results have been mixed. Some (e.g., Leyland, 1977; Rashotte, Griffin, & Sisk, 1977; Rescorla, 1979a) have found significantly reduced responding to A after extinction of B; others (e.g., Nairne & Rescorla, 1981; Rizley & Rescorla, 1972) that responding to A is unaffected. We must con-

clude, following the logic of the argument set out in the preceding paragraph, that both S-S and S-R links can be formed; what remains to be determined is the nature of the circumstances that foster the formation of one type of link rather than the other. The full answer to this question is not yet clear, but it seems likely that the relative salience of the events involved will play a role (see Holland, 1985a). Consider the experiment by Rizley and Rescorla (1972) in which stimuli A and B were a light and a tone, and the US an electric shock. During stage two of the second-order conditioning procedure, therefore, the target stimulus A is paired with a B stimulus that lacks any salient immediate sensory properties but that, by virtue of its stage-one pairing with shock, is capable of evoking a powerful set of emotional (fear) responses. It is unsurprising then, that the S-R link should come to dominate in this training procedure. In the experiment by Leyland (1977), on the other hand, A and B were key lights, and the US the delivery of a small amount of food. If we may assume that for pigeons (Leyland's subjects), the presentation of a key light is a salient event, or at least, is more salient than the CRs it will evoke after being paired with food, then S-S learning can be expected to dominate in generating a second-order CR that is sensitive to devaluation of the first-order CS.

Sensory and Affective Aspects of the US

The analysis just offered for second-order conditioning provides a new perspective on the first-order case. The events used as traditional USs can also be seen as possessing both sensory and affective components (the latter being intrinsic, rather than acquired as a consequence of explicit training as in the second-order procedure). Thus the presentation of food must be assumed to activate not only a node or nodes representative of its visual properties, its taste, texture, and so on, but also some further node, in which activity corresponds to the presence of a positive affective state. Activation of each of these nodes can be assumed to elicit its own characteristic response—for instance, activation of a sensory node could result in a directed approach response whereas activation of the affective node might produce a state of enhanced autonomic activity. The simple picture of Figure 1.1a should be elaborated along the lines shown in Figure 1.4.

There are now four possible links to deal with and we must reconsider the evidence presented so far in light of this development. Interpretation of those cases in which US devaluation is effective is not much altered—this

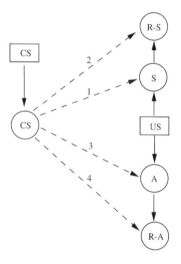

Figure 1.4   Associative structures for excitatory Pavlovian conditioning in which the sensory (S) and affective (A) properties of the US are represented by different nodes.
NOTE: R-S indicates a node responsible for generating responses specific to the particular sensory properties of the US; R-A indicates a node responsible for generating affective responses (an emotional state). Conventions and other abbreviations are as given for Figure 1.1. Although they are omitted from the figure for the sake of clarity, it may be supposed that links could also form between the various US nodes (e.g., a link between S and A would allow the sensory properties that characterize a foodstuff to evoke an affective state).

result tells us that an association has formed between the CS and some aspect of the US representation, meaning either or both of links 1 and 3 have been formed. For many of the procedures discussed so far, we cannot be sure which, although the nature of the CR can supply grounds for a plausible guess. In Rescorla's (1973a) experiment the CR that proved sensitive to US devaluation was the conditioned emotional response evoked by a signal for shock, a response that we may assume depends on learning about the affective properties of the US (i.e., on link 3). In the Holland and Straub (1979) experiment, however, the CR that was reduced by US devaluation was the response of approaching the food cup, a behavior that requires the animal to have encoded information about the sensory properties (location) of the US and thus implies the formation of link 1. (Sensory preconditioning provides even clearer evidence for the role of link 1—for an association between the CS and the sensory properties of the US—as the event that acts as the US does not possess affective properties.)

Complications arise, however, when it comes to cases in which US devaluation is ineffective; here the new possibilities introduced by Figure 1.4 render interpretation ambiguous. The persistence of responding after devaluation could indeed imply that the CR depends on one or both of the S-R links (links 2 and 4 in the figure). Alternatively, it could be that the devaluation manipulation affects only one aspect of the US representation, leaving the other still capable of evoking a response. If, for instance, food that has been associated with Li suffers a devaluation only of its sensory properties, then a CR based on link 1 in the figure would be lost, but a response controlled by the link between the CS and the affective node of the US (link 3 in the figure) would still be observable. The persistence of the general activity CR in the Holland and Straub (1979) experiment could thus reflect the operation of an S-S link rather than S-R learning. As evidence of S-R learning in this experiment, it should be recognized that food-cup responding was not totally abolished by a devaluation procedure hypothesized to have rendered link 1 ineffective. Such directed responding could not be generated by links 3 and 4—but is what would be expected if the (S-R) link 2 had acquired some strength during initial training.

The picture emerging from this analysis is that, under appropriate circumstances, each of the potential links shown in Figure 1.4 is capable of being formed. What remains to be determined, however, is which links do in fact form in the course of any given standard first-order procedure. The discussion of second-order conditioning introduced the proposal that there might be competition among aspects of the US for association with the CS, and that salient affective aspects of the US might dominate learning at the expense of potential associations involving sensory aspects of the US. Given that the events used as USs in standard conditioning procedures are chosen because of their motivational significance, it seems possible that these procedures might favor emotional or affective conditioning (i.e., the formation of links 3 and 4) and fail to generate learning about the sensory aspects of the US (links 1 and 2). Evidence relevant to this proposal comes from experiments using the *blocking* design in which subjects receive initial training with CS A signaling the US, followed by a phase of training in which a compound stimulus, AB, precedes the same US. Blocking of conditioning to B in these circumstances has been taken to indicate that learning fails to occur when the outcome of the trial is unsurprising (being fully predicted in this case by the pretrained CS A). In the variant of this design that is relevant to our present concern, the US used in the compound phase of training retains the same affective value as that used in the first phase, but its sensory proper-

ties are changed. In a number of experiments (e.g., Bakal, Johnson, & Rescorla, 1974, who switched from shock to a loud noise; Ganesan & Pearce, 1988, who switched from food to water), the blocking effect has still been obtained. This outcome prompts the conclusion that the change in the nature of the US was unsurprising to the animal, thus the association(s) established during the initial phase of training with A involved only the affective, not the sensory, properties of the US.

But whatever is true for the training procedures just considered, it is clear that in other procedures the specific sensory attributes of the US are learned about. That a rabbit given eye-blink conditioning shows a CR only with the eye to which the US has been applied, proves that one of the sensory properties of the US (its location) plays a role in the associative structure established during conditioning. Betts, Brandon, and Wagner (1996) made just this point and went on to demonstrate that blocking did not occur when the compound CS signaled a shock to the other eye—this sensitivity to the change of location confirms that the original location must have been learned in the first stage of training. Interestingly, however, blocking *was* obtained when the response measured was not the eye blink itself, but an index of a CS-induced heightening in the animal's general level of emotional responsiveness. Evidently the animal had also learned in the first stage about the affective properties of the US (properties that do not change, whether the shock is given to the left or the right eye). This result prompts two conclusions. First, the fact that transreinforcer blocking sometimes occurs (as in the experiment by Bakal et al., 1974) does not necessarily imply that the subjects had failed to learn about the sensory properties of the US—rather it may indicate that the response measure used is one that is sensitive only to the association between the CS and the US's affective properties. Second, the results of Betts et al. demonstrate that learning about the affective properties of a US does not preclude learning about its sensory properties (or vice versa). Indeed, according to the influential theory of conditioning proposed by Konorski (1967, and developed by Wagner & Brandon, 1989), dual association formation is the norm, and establishment of the affective link constitutes a necessary background for the development of specific CRs controlled by association with specific sensory aspects of the US. In first-order conditioning, at least, the two associations appear to cooperate rather than compete (see also Gewirtz, Brandon, & Wagner, 1998).

Instrumental Conditioning

The associative analysis of instrumental conditioning begins by assuming three nodes, in which activity will co-occur in a standard training procedure. One (S) represents a node sensitive to the cues impinging on the animal when a response is performed (e.g., the visual cues arising from the lever in a Skinner box); activity in the response node (R) equates to performance of the target response (e.g., pressing the lever); another stimulus node (O) is activated by the presentation of the outcome (e.g., the delivery of a food pellet) generated by that response. My present concern is to determine the nature of the association that the R node might enter into. Figure 1.5 shows the two most obvious possibilities—a link between the R and O nodes, and a link between the S and R nodes—and the bulk of the discussion in this section will be concerned with the role of these two links in determining instrumental performance. Also shown in the figure is the link between S and O that might also be expected to form on the basis of the Pavlovian conditioning principles described above (the O being construed as a Pavlovian US, and the set of stimuli that accompany it as a CS). The possible contribution of this

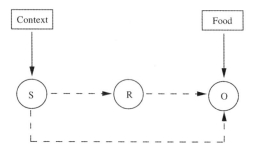

Figure 1.5   A possible associative structure for excitatory instrumental conditioning.
NOTE: S: stimulus; R: response; O: outcome. Conventions and other abbreviations are as given for Figure 1.1.

link to instrumental performance cannot be neglected.

Inadequacy of the S-R Interpretation

The strength of the notion that instrumental training establishes an S-R association lies in the fact that it provides a direct explanation for the behavior observed—once formed, the link ensures that perception of the relevant stimuli (e.g., lever cues) will automatically evoke the target response (the lever press). Additional theorizing is, of course, necessary to explain why it is that this S-R connection should form rather than some other, and the usual solution has been to adopt some version of Thorndike's law of effect, the principle that a rewarding outcome will *reinforce* an association that it immediately follows. It will be noted that, according to this account, the outcome does not itself enter any associative structure, and herein lies the weakness of the theory—for it is a simple matter to demonstrate that outcomes do more than simply reinforce S-R links. Two observations will suffice to make this point.

First, there is evidence suggesting that animals acquire information about the relationship between their response and the outcome. In particular, instrumental performance is sensitive to the validity of the response as a predictor of the outcome (the so-called *contingency* effect). The rate at which a thirsty rat will lever-press for the delivery of water will decline if "free" water deliveries are also available (e.g., Hammond, 1980). This makes sense if the rate of response is taken to depend on the strength of a R-O link (standard theories of association formation, e.g., Rescorla & Wagner, 1972, readily predict a weakened association in these conditions). According to S-R theory, however, what matters in establishing and maintaining performance is solely the contiguous occurrence of the response and the outcome, and, given that response-contingent outcomes continue to be available, the addition of the free outcomes should be without effect.

Second, there is evidence suggesting that animals acquire information about the nature of the outcome generated by their responding. It has long been known that if the outcome is changed during the course of training, say from a large to a small amount of food, the vigor of the animal's response will change immediately (as in Crespi's, 1942, negative contrast effect). Such sensitivity to change must mean that the properties (in this case, the size) of the original reward had been encoded in some way. Essentially the same conclusion is supported by more recent experiments that make use of the (now familiar) technique of postconditioning revaluation of the reinforcer. Rats trained to press a lever for a given type of food will, if that food is subsequently paired with an injection of Li, show a lowered rate of response on a test in which the lever is again made available (Adams & Dickinson, 1981; Colwill & Rescorla, 1985a). (No outcomes are delivered on the test, ensuring that the result is not a consequence of some direct response to the now-aversive food.) Other procedures for revaluing the outcome confirm the findings obtained with the food-aversion technique. Colwill and Rescorla (1985a; see also Dickinson, 1987) have shown that if, just

prior to the test, rats are given free access to the type of food that was used as the outcome in initial training, their willingness to make the response that had previously produced that outcome is significantly reduced. Also, Dickinson and Dawson (1987a, Experiment 1) found that rats trained to respond for food pellets when hungry showed a low rate of response when tested *thirsty* (as compared to a separate group of rats trained to respond for a sucrose solution, an event that presumably retains its value with the change from hunger to thirst). In all of these studies, responding appears to be determined by the current value of the outcome—which is consistent with the idea that information about the nature of the outcome has been encoded in the associative structure that determines performance, but is not consistent with an S-R theory that holds that the sole role of the outcome is to reinforce the S-R link in initial training.

The Role of the S-O Association

Establishing the inadequacy of the simple S-R account does not demonstrate the validity of the alternative R-O account. The analysis so far disregards the possibility that the S-O link of Figure 1.5 might also form during instrumental conditioning. Allowing that Pavlovian conditioning can go on alongside S-R learning may provide an explanation for the phenomena just discussed. The contingency effect would be explained if it was supposed that delivering free outcomes during instrumental training enhances the strength of a context-outcome association, and that an effect of this association is an increase in the likelihood of CRs (such as approaching the site at which the outcome is delivered) at the expense of lever pressing. The disruption of behavior evident in the Crespi effect could reflect the emotional response to an expectation about reward size, which is based on an association between the cues that constitute the training context and the reward presented in the first stage of training. Finally, devaluing an outcome will, as we have already seen, often reduce the effectiveness of a CS in evoking its CR. To the extent that a classically conditioned emotional state plays a role in energizing instrumental responding (a position adopted by many theorists, see Rescorla & Solomon, 1967), such devaluation might be predicted reduce the rate at which the instrumental response is performed.

This last suggestion is more than a theoretical possibility, as a further study (conducted by Dickinson and Dawson, 1987a, Experiment 2) of the effects of a motivational shift demonstrates. In this experiment, the rats were trained to perform (when hungry) two different responses in the same apparatus, one for a food pellet outcome, the other for sucrose solution. This within-subject procedure allows for the formation of associations between the contextual cues and both outcomes. When tested under thirst, the rats showed low rates of response, and these rates did not differ for the two responses. Thus, by this measure, the rats evidenced no knowledge of the relationship between a given response and its particular outcome; rather they simply showed an overall reduction in vigor, which is to be expected if a Pavlovian, or context-food, association was no longer contributing to the emotional state that energizes the behavior (see also Dickinson & Dawson, 1987b, and Chap. 12, this volume).

The Role of the R-O Association

For evidence that animals are sensitive to the R-O relation, it is necessary to demonstrate an effect that is selective to a particular R-O combination. Although the procedure used by Dickinson and Dawson (1987a) failed to reveal such selectivity, other procedures have been more successful. In a study of the contingency effect, Dickinson and Mulatero (1989; see also Colwill & Rescorla, 1986) trained rats to respond on two levers, each generating a different outcome. The introduction of free

outcomes of a given type resulted in a decline in responding that was particularly marked on the lever that was associated with that food-type. Colwill and Rescorla (1985a) report an analogous effect in a study using the outcome-devaluation technique. Again initial training was given in which two different responses (this time, pressing a lever and pulling a chain) produced different outcomes. Devaluing one of these outcomes by means of toxin injections produced a selective effect. When given access to the lever and the chain in a final test, given in extinction, the rats showed a reduced rate of response on the manipulandum that had been associated with the now-devalued outcome.

Although these results fit well with the proposal that instrumental training endows the animal with information about R-O relationships, an explanation in terms of S-O learning may still be possible. The training context does not constitute a single, simple stimulus, and it is possible that a range of S-O associations might be formed. For example, in the Colwill and Rescorla study, it is likely that cues arising from the chain, being closely associated with the outcome generated by the chain-pull, will form a particularly strong association with that outcome, whereas lever cues will be more closely associated with the outcome generated by the lever press. Devaluing one outcome could, therefore, according to standard Pavlovian principles, reduce the animal's tendency to emit the CR of approaching cues associated with that outcome. This, in itself, might be enough to reduce the likelihood of a particular response. Before we accept the notion of R-O learning, we should find reasons to discount this alternative interpretation of the results. Two lines of evidence will be considered.

Dickinson, Campos, Varga, and Balleine (1996; see also Colwill & Rescorla, 1986) adopted a strategy of looking for a response-selective devaluation effect that could not be explained in terms of associations between contextual cues and the outcome. They trained rats with a single manipulandum, a rod, which produced a food pellet when pushed in one direction and provided access to a starch solution when pushed in the other direction. Devaluing one of these outcomes (by allowing free access to it before the test) was found to have a selective effect—responses of the type that had previously produced the prefed outcome were suppressed. Given that the cues arising from the manipulandum will be equally associated with both the starch and the pellet outcomes, it is difficult for any straightforward interpretation of the S-O analysis to accommodate these results—any reduction in the tendency to approach the manipulandum would be expected to influence both of the trained responses.

The second line of evidence comes from studies that attempt a direct evaluation of the properties of the S-O association that is assumed to be formed during instrumental training. This is most readily done in experiments that employ an explicit *discriminative stimulus* (Sd), a cue in the presence of which generates responses that are effective in producing the outcome (responses in the absence of the cue being ineffective). The control acquired by such a stimulus (the animal will come to respond only when it is present) could, in principle, reflect the influence of an association between the discriminative stimulus and the outcome, but an experiment by Colwill and Rescorla (1988) provides reasons for doubting this. In this study, rats received training with two cues, one trained as an Sd, the other simply paired with an outcome without any response requirement (i.e., established as a Pavlovian CS). Presenting these cues in a subsequent test phase during which the rats were performing a new, separately trained, instrumental response produced changes in responding, but the pattern of change evoked by the Sd was different from that evoked by

the CS. This is not what would be expected if the Sd's influence depended on its direct, Pavlovian association with the outcome. Further evidence that Sds and CSs are not interchangeable (as the hypothesis under consideration requires) comes from a study by Holman and Mackintosh (1981) that made use of the blocking paradigm. They demonstrated that training stimulus A as an Sd would block the development of control by B when an AB compound was subsequently trained as the Sd, but that blocking did not occur when A was trained as a CS in the first stage. Similarly, when the compound (AB) training stage involved Pavlovian conditioning, blocking was found when A was trained initially as a CS, but not when it was trained as an Sd.

This evidence that instrumental conditioning will not endow an Sd with powerful Pavlovian properties is enough in itself to undermine the proposal that the effects described earlier in this section should be explained in terms of the operation of S-O associations, thus leaving the field open to acceptance of the R-O alternative. Consideration of why it should be that an Sd makes a poor CS offers a positive reason to adopt this alternative. However it is to be explained (see Chap. 2, this volume), the phenomenon of *cue competition* is well established in Pavlovian learning. When two events are available as potential CSs, conditioning will occur more readily to the one that correlates better with the reinforcer—and will do so at the expense of one that does not correlate as well. Instrumental conditioning may similarly be construed as involving two events in competition for association with the reinforcer. In this case, the two events are the response and the Sd; and since the former correlates more directly with the outcome than the latter (responses in the presence of the Sd regularly produce reinforcement whereas, should the animal fail to respond, the Sd will be experienced in the absence of reinforcement), a markedly strong association cannot be expected to form between Sd and outcome. Thus the failure of the Sd to function fully as a CS can be explained, provided we adopt a theoretical interpretation of instrumental learning that presupposes the reality of R-O learning. What remains to be explained is how Sds exert the control they do, given that it is not by way of their Pavlovian properties. This matter is taken up in the section on complex conditioning.

The Role of the S-R Association

An account in terms of S-R associations cannot explain the results described above (even if it is supplemented by the suggestion that S-O associations may also play a role). This does not mean, however, that S-R associations are not formed (alongside S-O and R-O associations) during instrumental training. In our discussion of Pavlovian conditioning, we allowed that the contiguous activation of a stimulus node and a response node might produce an S-R link, and since instrumental procedures also ensure the co-occurrence of activity in S and R nodes, it seems reasonable to presume that the S-R link will form in this case too. But direct evidence to support this presumption is hard to come by.

Seemingly the most obvious piece of supporting evidence is that devaluation procedures are not wholly effective, as was true for Pavlovian conditioning. Given a choice between two levers, rats will respond less readily on that associated with a now-devalued outcome, but responding does still occur (e.g., Colwill & Rescorla, 1985a). This residual responding could represent the contribution of a component (based on the S-R link) that will not be sensitive to devaluation procedures. It is a problem for this interpretation, however, that residual responding after reward devaluation is almost totally abolished by a small change in procedure (direct delivery of the reward into the rat's mouth; Colwill & Rescorla, 1990a) that does not affect the number of

S-R pairings. Colwill and Rescorla give reasons for thinking that this procedural change might make the devaluation procedure more effective, leaving open the possibility that residual responding, when it does occur, is a consequence of an inadequacy in the devaluation procedure employed in those experiments.

But devaluation procedures, even when proven to be totally effective in reducing the rat's willingness to consume a reward, have sometimes been found to be quite ineffective in selectively suppressing the response that has previously produced that reward as the outcome. The experiment by Dickinson and Dawson (1987a), described above, in which the value of the reward was changed by means of a motivational shift, supplies one example; similar failures to produce an effect have also been found in experiments that devalue the reward by means of a pairing with Li (e.g., Balleine & Dickinson, 1991). But before concluding that the responding seen in these experiments is controlled by an S-R association, we must again consider the possibility that the particular procedures used may have failed to modify the value of the outcome (and thus failed to influence behavior based on an R-O association). Dickinson and Balleine (e.g., 1994; see also Chap. 12, this volume) have argued that revaluation of an (instrumental) outcome depends on a process that they call incentive learning: only when the animal has had the opportunity to experience the outcome under appropriate conditions (to try food pellets when thirsty rather than hungry, to sample a sucrose solution after it has been paired with Li) will the effective value of the outcome be changed. And indeed, Balleine and Dickinson (1991) have demonstrated just such an effect for the case of devaluation by Li-induced aversion (see also Dickinson & Dawson, 1988).

Dependence of the outcome-devaluation effect on appropriate reexposure to the devalued outcome has not been a universal finding (e.g., Balleine & Dickinson, 1992; Rescorla, 1991a). But the source of this discrepancy is not our present concern. Rather, we need to ask if there are any cases of instrumental responding that show insensitivity to outcome devaluation even when every step has been taken (including reexposure to the devalued outcome) to ensure the effectiveness of the devaluation procedure. And the answer is that there are. An experiment by Adams (1982), which gave rats extended initial training on a continuous reinforcement schedule, found no effect of outcome devaluation on test responding, as did that by Dickinson, Nicholas, and Adams (1983), when initial training was given according to a variable interval schedule (the standard devaluation effect was seen when a ratio schedule was used in initial training). Dickinson's (e.g., 1989) interpretation of these experiments was that the training schedules they employed tended to minimize the extent to which the animal could experience a correlation between its responding and the occurrence of the outcome (on a variable interval schedule, for instance, rates of responding can vary over a wide range without producing variation in the rate of reinforcement). These conditions might be expected to work against the establishment of an R-O association and thus allow the S-R association to come to the fore. It should be acknowledged that other features of these experiments (in addition to the particular schedules used in training) must have contributed to their results (other experimenters, using somewhat different procedures, e.g., Colwill & Rescorla, 1985b, have found devaluation effects even in rats that are given extensive training on an interval schedule). However this may be, it is still legitimate to conclude that in some circumstances, even if these are rather special, it is possible to find evidence consistent with the assertion that instrumental training is capable of establishing an S-R association.

SIMPLE INHIBITORY CONDITIONING

In the standard Pavlovian *extinction* procedure, a pretrained CS is presented repeatedly in the absence of the US; in the instrumental case, the animal is allowed to perform the target response, but the previous outcome is no longer forthcoming. In both cases, the behavior established by initial conditioning disappears (the CS no longer evokes the CR; the probability of occurrence of the instrumental R falls toward zero). Since acquisition is referred to as excitatory conditioning, it seems only appropriate to refer to extinction as involving *inhibitory* conditioning—and this terminology has been widely adopted.

The issue to be addressed is what new associative structures are established by the extinction procedure and how might these structures explain the change in behavior that is observed. It will be immediately apparent, however, that structural considerations alone are unlikely to be sufficient to deal with extinction, and that some extension of our assumptions about the functioning of the system will be needed. So far we have made use of just two: Co-activation of a pair of nodes causes a link to form between them, and the existence of the link allows activity in one node to excite activity in the second. The fact that inhibitory learning occurs as a consequence of the presentation of just a single event seems, on the face of things, to present a challenge to the first of these assumptions. And the very use of the term inhibitory raises questions about the second—if acquisition deserves the label excitatory because it establishes a link that allows one node (e.g., the CS node) to excite activity in another (the US node), then the implication seems to be that the extinction procedure might have its effects because it establishes a link that has the opposite effect, in this example, inhibiting activity in the US node.

Most recent attempts to explain inhibitory learning suppose both that it involves the formation of new associative links and that the conditions under which these are formed and the effects that they exert might differ from what holds for the excitatory case. But before discussing these theories, it will be worthwhile to establish that such elaboration is necessary. In particular, to accept that some new process is engaged by the extinction procedure raises the possibility that this, in itself, might be enough to explain the phenomenon, making it redundant to suppose that a new associative structure is also established. Evidence relevant to this notion is discussed next.

Process Accounts of Extinction

Extinction as Unlearning

We have supposed that the co-occurrence of activity in two nodes, produced by the near simultaneous presentation of the relevant events (CS and US, R and O), will strengthen the link between these nodes. What if presentation of the CS alone or the occurrence of the R without the O produces a weakening of the link? The outcome would be the extinction effect, without any need to suppose that a new associative structure is formed. With sufficient extinction trials, the original learning would be undone and the animal would be restored to the *status quo ante*. Unfortunately, given the elegant simplicity of this account, there is a good deal of evidence (some admittedly, suggestive rather than conclusive) to indicate that it is wrong.

Recovery of Extinguished Responding. It has long been known (since, e.g., Pavlov, 1927) that a CR, extinguished by repeated, closely spaced presentations of the CS alone, will reappear if the CS is presented again after a substantial interval. More recent, and better

controlled, studies have confirmed the reliability of this Pavlovian *spontaneous recovery* effect (e.g., Rescorla, 1997a) and of its instrumental analogue (e.g., Rescorla, 1996a). In spontaneous recovery, the extinguished response returns after a retention interval. Other experimental manipulations can also generate recovery effects. The *renewal* effect involves manipulating the context in which training is given. If animals receive CS-US pairings in one experimental apparatus, followed by extinction trials in a discriminably different apparatus, the CR that has disappeared by the end of the extinction phase will return (be renewed) when the CS is again presented either in the original context or elsewhere (e.g., Bouton & Bolles, 1979a). In *reinstatement* (Rescorla & Heth, 1975; see also Bouton, 1984), animals given a "reminder" presentation of the US, after extinction has been completed, show recovery of the CR on a subsequent test session.

In none of these procedures can the experimental manipulation be expected to restore the strength of the original excitatory association, prompting the conclusion that this association must have been maintained during the extinction trials. What these observations do not allow us to conclude, however, is that the original link was maintained in full strength during extinction (i.e., that unlearning does not occur). An alternative interpretation is that the extinction procedure weakens the strength of the excitatory association to a point at which it falls below a threshold that must be surpassed if responding is to be evoked. Nonetheless, the original association may retain some strength that is able to show itself when the renewal or reinstatement procedure renders the test conditions more favorable. Perhaps, for example, the renewal effect reflects a summation of the weak CS-US association with the associative strength governed by the contextual cues of the original training context. Rather than discussing the

Table 1.1   Designs of Experiments by Rescorla (1993a, 1996b).

Training	Extinction	Retraining	Devaluation	Test
(a) Instrumental conditioning				
R1 → O1	R1−	R1 → O3		
&	&	&	O1 → Li	R2 > R1
R2 → O2	R2−	R2 → O3		
(b) Classical conditioning				
CS1 → US1	CS1−	CS1 → US3		
&	&	&	US1 → Li	CR2 > CR1
CS2 → US2	CS2−	CS2 → US3		

NOTE: R: instrumental response; CR: conditioned response; O: outcome in instrumental conditioning; US: unconditioned stimulus; CS: conditioned stimulus; Li: injection of lithium chloride.

experimental evidence directed at assessing the validity of this analysis (e.g., Bouton, 1991), we may turn to a different approach that attempts to demonstrate directly the permanence of excitatory associations.

The Persistence of Excitatory Associations. Table 1.1(a) presents a simplified version of the design of an experiment by Rescorla (1993a) investigating the effects of outcome devaluation on an extinguished instrumental response. In the first stage, two different responses were trained, each associated with a different reward. Both then underwent extinction. The final stages of the experiment assessed the effects of devaluing one of the outcomes used in original training (by associating it with Li). In order to see any effects of this procedure, it is necessary to reestablish some measure of responding. This was achieved by a retraining stage that immediately preceded outcome devaluation, in which both responses were reinforced by the delivery of a reward different from either of those used in the first stage. On tests, the animals readily performed R2 but rarely performed R1, the response associated in stage one with the outcome that had been devalued. Such a result could not have been obtained had information about the R1-O1 relationship been erased during the extinction phase. Rescorla's

experiment also included an assessment of the effect of outcome devaluation for a response that had not undergone extinction. The suppression of responding observed on the final test was no greater than that obtained for R1. According to this measure, therefore, the extinction procedure was quite without effect on the status or efficacy of the original R-O association.

Similarly, CS-US associations seem to be immune to the effects of extinction. Table 1.1(b) shows the design of a Pavlovian conditioning experiment (Rescorla, 1996b) analogous to that just described. Here the rats were first trained with two different CSs each associated with a different food US. Both CSs then underwent extinction until the CR (of approaching the site of food delivery) had disappeared. A retraining stage, using a different US, reestablished this response, allowing the effects of devaluation of one of the original USs to be assessed. The test showed a selective suppression of the CR to the CS that had been associated in the first stage of training with the now-devalued US. The size of this effect was comparable to that shown by animals treated equivalently but for the omission of the extinction stage, prompting the conclusion that the original CS-US association had been quite unaffected by the extinction treatment. Related experiments using a different procedure for assessing the strength of the original association (a transfer test procedure) have confirmed the reliability of this result for Pavlovian CSs (Delamater, 1996) and have demonstrated equivalent effects with stimuli trained as Sds (Rescorla, 1992).

Changes in Event Processing

The evidence discussed so far establishes that extinction is not to be explained as a process that simply dismantles the associative structure set up by excitatory training. This does not, however, force the conclusion that extinction must set up a new associative structure. It may simply mean that our first guess about the nature of the process engaged by extinction was wrong; instead, we should seek to explain the process as one that acts to prevent the intact excitatory link from fulfilling its normal function. Some possibilities emerge from the recovery effects described above.

One is suggested by the reinstatement effect. The interpretation originally offered by Rescorla and Heth (1975) was that the extinction procedure produces a change in the representation of the US, rendering it less easily excited by way of the CS-US link. According to this interpretation, the reminder trial is effective because it reestablishes the properties of the US node. There are several good reasons to reject this account. First, extinction will occur, albeit rather slowly, even when unsignaled presentations of the US are scheduled to occur, interspersed among the nonreinforced CS trials (e.g., Rescorla & Skucy, 1969). Such presentations might be expected to maintain the status of the US node, and thus prevent extinction from occurring. Second, nonreinforcement of one CS does not necessarily produce extinction of a second (e.g., Bouton & King, 1983). If extinction occurs because of change in the US node, then both CSs should be affected equally. Third,

although early work seemed to suggest otherwise, it now seems clear that reminder trials are ineffective in producing reinstatement if they are given in a context that is different from that used for the other phases of training (Bouton & Bolles, 1979b). Why this might be the case will not be considered here; for present purposes it is enough to note that the theory under consideration has no reason to predict such an effect.

Although extinction cannot be explained in terms of a change in the properties of the US node, there remains the possibility that it reflects a change in the CS node. Pavlov (1927) himself appears to have entertained this possibility, attributing spontaneous recovery to the dissipation of a labile inhibitory process that suppressed the excitability of the CS node (an idea taken up and developed more recently by Robbins, 1990). If the CS is no longer able to activate its central representation, then no CR can be expected, even if the CS-US link remains intact. Something similar was proposed for the instrumental case by Hull (1943), who explained extinction by suggesting that every response evoked a state (akin to fatigue and labeled *reactive inhibition*) that made it more difficult to activate the response node on subsequent occasions. Spontaneous recovery was taken to reflect the dissipation of this state.

Neither of these proposals has stood up well to experimental testing. As Robbins (1990) has shown, spontaneous recovery can still be obtained when presentations of a different stimulus that evokes the same target response occur during the recovery interval. Hull's (1943) account supposes, however, that reactive inhibition (which is specific to the response) will continue to accumulate in these circumstances, thus predicting that spontaneous recovery will not occur. Evidence that extinction cannot be due to a loss of CS effectiveness comes from the procedure sometimes known as *counterconditioning*. Bouton and Peck (1992) report a study in which rats were trained initially with a CS signaling a food US, followed by a second stage of training in which food deliveries were discontinued and replaced by the occurrence of a shock US. During this second stage, the CR typically supported by CS-food pairings disappeared; thus, at the behavioral level, extinction was observed to occur. Critically, however, during stage two the CS also acquired the ability to evoke a new CR indicative of the formation of a CS-shock association. This last observation implies that the CS must still have been effective in activating its central representation and thus permits rejection of the proposal that extinction of the food-related CR was a consequence of the loss of such effectiveness. This is not to assert that changes in CS effectiveness never occur—it is now widely accepted that repeated nonreinforced presentations of an event can reduce its ability to command some forms of processing (see Hall, 1991, for a review). But this effect is not the source of extinction: A fully familiar CS loses associability (becomes less good at entering into new associations), but its ability to evoke its CR still remains (Hall & Pearce, 1979; Pearce & Hall, 1980).

Structural Accounts of Extinction

Extinction does not erase the associative links formed during initial excitatory training; nor can it be explained in terms of nonassociative changes in the excitability or nature of the nodes connected by such links. Faced with these facts, theorists have turned to the alternative possibility of the extinction procedure engendering new associative learning—that it promotes the formation of a new associative structure that opposes or masks the effects of the original. Konorski was the first to clearly state this proposal (1948) and his formulation has set the agenda for most later discussions of the issue.

Konorski's Accounts

Konorski's (1948) approach to inhibitory Pavlovian conditioning was to treat it as being essentially parallel to the excitatory case, involving the formation of a new link between concurrently activated CS and US nodes. This link has different properties from those previously discussed—it allows presentation of the CS to inhibit activity in the US node (Konorski envisaged this as involving a raising of the threshold that the excitatory input must exceed to be effective). The pattern of coactivation that produces such a link must necessarily be assumed to be different in some way from that responsible for the formation of an excitatory link. Konorski suggested that the critical feature of the omission of the US was that it ensured that a high level of activity in the CS node would coincide with a rapid fall in (CS-generated) activity in the US node. These circumstances produce inhibitory learning, whereas the co-occurrence of increasing activity in both nodes (such as will happen when both CS and US are presented on the initial trials of acquisition) will produce excitatory learning. Wagner's (1981) model adopts much the same approach. It differs chiefly in its assumption that the activity induced in the US node by an excitatory CS (the A2 state) is different in nature from that produced by the US itself (the A1 state). Excitatory conditioning occurs when both nodes are in the A1 state; presenting the CS alone will ensure the co-occurrence of A1 activity in the CS node and A2 activity in the US node; this combination produces an inhibitory link, hence the extinction effect.

Konorski's (1948) scheme is shown in Figure 1.6a. During extinction training the inhibitory link is strengthened until the US threshold is sufficiently high that the excitatory link is incapable of generating any activity in the US node. Associative change will then stop and, of course, no CR will

(a)

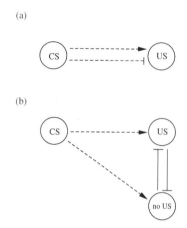

(b)

Figure 1.6   Alternative associative structures for inhibitory learning.
NOTE: (a) Konorski's 1948 theory. (b) Konorski's 1967 theory. A stopped link indicates that activity in one node can suppress activity in the target node; other conventions and abbreviations are as given for Figure 1.1.

be elicited. Adding the assumption that inhibitory links are inherently labile, or that first-learned associations are less susceptible to decay than later associations (or both of these), allows an explanation of at least some of the recovery phenomena described above.

In 1967 Konorski presented a radical extension and revision of his previous theorizing, one feature of which was the introduction of a conceptual nervous system more complex in its structure than any previously envisaged. In particular, it was suggested that representational nodes are frequently arranged in mutually antagonistic pairs—that, for example, the US node is connected by inhibitory links to a no-US node, and so on. The implication for extinction is the associative structure shown in Figure 1.6b. (In fact, the full picture is considerably more involved than this—since the US is assumed to have separable motivational and sensory properties, each of these should be shown separately with its own node and its own antinode.) As has of-

ten been noted (e.g., Rescorla, 1979b; but see also Mackintosh, 1983), the advantages bestowed by this new scheme seem to be only marginal—making the generation of inhibition in the US node a two-step process leaves the basic analysis unchanged. One possible advantage is that invoking a new structure makes it unnecessary to postulate a special inhibitory learning process—the conditions under which the CS–no-US link is formed are assumed to be the same (concurrent activation of the two nodes) as those that apply to standard excitatory conditioning. But this advantage is offset, to some extent, by the need to provide a precise specification of the conditions under which the no-US node is activated, a topic on which Konorski (1967) was less than forthcoming.

A further point is that the new structure makes it possible for the animal to have some knowledge about the nature of the event that had been omitted in inhibitory training. It is not obvious how a link that simply raises a US threshold could convey such information, but one that activates a node representing the absence of the sensory features of the US clearly has the potential to do so. The experimental evidence on this point is mixed. For example, Pearce, Montgomery, and Dickinson (1981) found that a CS that had signaled the omission of a shock US, otherwise applied to one eye of a rabbit, transferred its inhibitory properties perfectly well to a test in which shocks were applied to the other eye. This experiment thus supplied no evidence that the specific sensory properties of the omitted event had been learned about. By contrast, Kruse, Overmier, Konz, and Rokke (1983) found that a CS associated with the omission of a particular type of food would, when presented during instrumental responding, selectively reduce the vigor of a response that had previously been trained with that food-type as the outcome. Fortunately, we need not try to resolve this discrepancy here as Konorski's two theories make essentially the same predictions about the inhibitory learning phenomena that are our present concern.

The structures presented in Figure 1.6 are concerned solely with Pavlovian conditioning, but they may also be relevant to the instrumental case. Konorski's (1967) account of excitatory instrumental conditioning assumed the existence of two associations, S-R and S-O, and thus the inhibitory process shown in the figure, which would act to oppose the excitatory S-O association, could contribute to extinction of an instrumental response. In addition, Konorski postulated the existence of what he termed "motor act inhibition", the idea being that the discriminative stimulus could form an excitatory association with a motor node (perhaps, by analogy with the no-US node, to be regarded as a "no-response" node) that was antagonistic to the node controlling the response being measured. Konorski did not acknowledge the role of the R-O association (as we now do), but it is a straightforward matter to extend his general account to deal with this. Just as the omission of the US that follows a previously reinforced CS is held to generate an inhibitory CS-US link, we may suppose that the omission of the usual outcome following performance of a given instrumental response might generate an inhibitory R-O link.

Conditioned Inhibition

Konorski's theory (to take the 1948 version) states that a CS that is active at a time when there is a fall in activity in the US node will form an inhibitory connection with the US node. In extinction, it is the CS itself that generates (by way of the preexisting excitatory link) the necessary state of activity in the US node, but there is no requirement that this be so for inhibition to be established. If some neutral stimulus is presented at the same time as a pretrained CS is undergoing extinction, this stimulus too should be able to form an inhibitory link with the US node. Indeed, in a sense, such a stimulus should turn out to be an even more powerful inhibitor than the pretrained CS. The latter (referred to by Konorski as a secondary inhibitory stimulus) will be equipped both with excitatory and inhibitory links, the two matching each other in their effects on the US node. A stimulus introduced for the first time in the extinction phase (Konorski's primary inhibitory stimulus) will have only the inhibitory link.

The implication of this analysis is that (X+/AX−) discrimination training (in which animals receive reinforced trials when stimulus X is presented alone, but received extinction trials when X is presented in compound with some other stimulus, A) should be particularly effective in endowing A with inhibitory properties. Indeed, this training procedure, investigated by Pavlov (1927), was referred to by him as conditioned inhibition training. The conditioned inhibitor (A) showed its properties by suppressing the CR that X otherwise evoked. Figures 1.7a and 1.7b show how the associative structure postulated by Konorski's theories will generate such a result.

What Figure 1.7 also shows is a variety of other possibilities that might produce the same observed result. Stimulus A could, in principle, suppress the CR normally evoked by X by restricting the ability of X to excite its node (Figure 1.7c) or by directly inhibiting the CR itself (1.7d). A further possibility is that A might act on the link between X and the US (1.7e), gating the flow of activation from one node to the other. Confirmation of Konorski's account requires that these other possibilities be ruled out. The relevant evidence comes from an experiment by Rescorla and Holland (1977) in which the powers of a conditioned inhibitor were examined in a range of transfer tests. First they confirmed what had previously been shown in several other studies—that a shock-based conditioned inhibitor would suppress the CR not only of

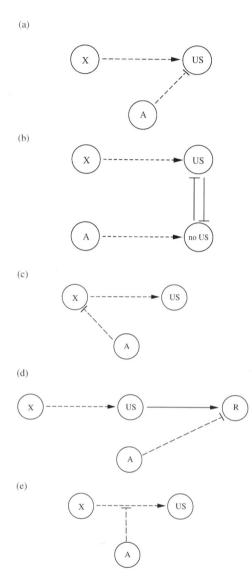

Figure 1.7 Alternative associative structures for conditioned inhibition.
NOTE: X represents an excitatory CS, and A represents a conditioned inhibitor. Conventions and other abbreviations are as given for Figure 1.1. (a) and (b): Structures for Konorski's proposal that the inhibitor acts on the US representation in terms of his 1948 theory (a) or his 1967 theory (b). (c) Structure in which the inhibitor acts on the excitatory CS. (d) Structure in which the inhibitor acts on the response node. (e) Structure in which the inhibitor acts on the link between CS and US.

stimulus X but also that normally evoked by a different excitatory CS separately trained as a signal for shock. The effect of the conditioned inhibitor is not specific to X, thus disconfirming, at least for this training preparation, options (c) and (e). They also showed that such a conditioned inhibitor was without effect on the CR evoked by an excitatory CS trained with a food US, adding support to the conclusion that the inhibition must operate either on the US node or on the CR itself (options (a) and (d)). In order to choose between the remaining alternatives, Rescorla and Holland made use of the fact that the CR evoked by an auditory CS signaling a food US is characteristically different from that evoked by a visual CS. They found that a conditioned inhibitor established for one of these CSs would transfer its power to the other, in spite of the difference in the form of the CR. The ability of a conditioned inhibitor to transfer across CSs and CRs but not across USs is what would be expected on the basis of the associative structure shown in Figure 1.7a.

Elaborations and Complications

Although consistent with most of the evidence cited so far, it remains to establish that the identification of extinction with US-specific inhibition can explain the full range of extinction phenomena. We will consider two lines of evidence that challenge the completeness of the account of extinction offered above. The first can be accommodated by an elaboration of the basic notion; the second requires a more radical revision of our assumptions about the nature of associations.

Sensory and Affective Properties of the US or Outcome. The experiments by Rescorla (1993a, 1996b), described above (see Table 1.1), appear to create some difficulties. These experiments showed, it will be recalled, that an extinguished response, reestablished by retraining with a different US or instrumental outcome, still shows sensitivity to the effects of devaluing the original US or outcome. Why should this be, if the original US (or outcome) representation has been fully inhibited as a result of the extinction procedure? One obvious possibility (given the reality of spontaneous recovery) is that the inhibitory association may have decayed in some way during the retraining phase, allowing the originally trained excitatory association to make a contribution to test performance (a contribution that would be eliminated by the devaluation procedure). A problem for this interpretation is that Rescorla found the magnitude of the devaluation effect to be as great for extinguished associations as for associations that had not undergone extinction, making it necessary to assume (what seems improbable) that the loss of inhibition in the former case had been total.

An explanation emerges, however, if we recall (what was discussed in our consideration of excitatory conditioning) that a US (or outcome) is likely to be represented by at least two nodes, one corresponding to its affective and another to its sensory properties. Initial training will establish excitatory associations with both these nodes (and will also, if it is not in existence already, establish a link between the sensory and affective properties of the US). The situation for the instrumental case is shown in Figure 1.8a. Now the omission of the expected outcome at the start of extinction produces a new and clearly salient affective state: A rat that presses the lever and fails to obtain the expected food pellet shows a characteristic set of vigorous emotional responses that have been taken to index a state of frustration. It is reasonable to assume that these responses or the state that produces them will be able to enter into associations. The absence of the specific sensory properties of the food pellet will be a much less salient event and is less likely to produce new learning. The consequence will be an associative structure of the

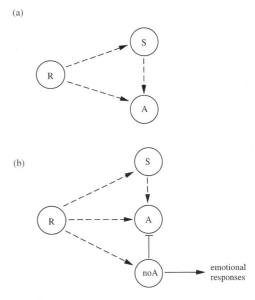

Figure 1.8 Associative structures for instrumental conditioning with separate nodes for affective (A) and sensory (S) properties of the outcome.
NOTE: (a) Structure produced by excitatory conditioning. (b) Structure produced by extinction employing the notion that the absence of affective properties (no A) is represented by its own node. Conventions are as given for Figure 1.1.

sort shown in Figure 1.8b. (The figure postulates a node of the sort proposed in Konorski's later, 1967, theory, although other formulations are possible—Rescorla, 2001, himself, suggests that the relevant association may be directly with the emotional responses themselves). The new learning produced by extinction could therefore inhibit the motivational state necessary for responding, although the animal's knowledge of the relationship between its response and certain sensory events and of the relationship between the latter and a positive affective state might remain more or less intact. Retraining with a different outcome of the same affective value as the original will restore responding because it restores the ability of the response to activate the positive emotional state. A devaluation procedure that associates the sensory properties of the outcome used in original training with an aversive consequence will then be able to act upon this positive state and produce a suppression of responding—the result obtained in the experiment by Rescorla (1993a).

Although seemingly complex, this account is no more than an elaboration of the basic principles that we have accepted so far. Indeed Rescorla's (2001) endorsement of the proposal that extinction involves new excitatory learning about the events that actually occur as a consequence of omission of the outcome (or US) has the advantage (shared with Konorski's later theory) of not requiring us to postulate a special inhibitory learning process. To this extent, it can be seen as a simplification. The next line of evidence to be considered, however, seems to require the introduction of a new associative principle.

Response-Specific Inhibition. The essence of the conclusion derived from the work of Rescorla and Holland (1977; see Figure 1.7) was that extinction operates on the US representation, not on the system responsible for generating the response. But a recent set of experiments by Rescorla himself has produced results that challenge this idea. These experiments, using instrumental training procedures for the most part, have evaluated the properties acquired by a stimulus in the presence of which extinction has occurred (e.g., Rescorla, 1993b, 1997b). The design of one such experiment (Rescorla, 1993b, Experiment 4) is shown in Table 1.2. Rats were trained initially to make two different responses, each of which generated a food pellet outcome; both then underwent extinction, one in the presence of a light, the other in the presence of a noise. A retraining phase reestablished some measure of responding, allowing the properties acquired by these stimuli to be assessed in a final test. Both showed evidence of having acquired inhibitory power, but their effects were specific to the response with which they had been trained: S1 (see Table 1.2) had no effect on the rate at which R2 occurred but suppressed performance of R1; S2 suppressed R2 but had no effect on R1.

The account of extinction that we have been developing to this point predicts no such response-specificity. As shown in Figure 1.9a, by the end of extinction, both stimuli (and both responses) should have acquired the power to inhibit the outcome representation (or, as shown, to excite an antagonistic no-outcome representation). Reestablishing the response-outcome associations through further reinforced training would permit the association governed by a stimulus to influence behavior by inhibiting activity in the outcome node, but since the outcome is common to both responses, both should be suppressed equally.

The most straightforward interpretation of this experimental result appears to be that the extinction phase of Rescorla's (1993b) experiment establishes an associative structure of the sort shown in Figure 1.9b, in which the stimulus comes to exert an inhibitory influence on the response node itself. But to adopt this interpretation creates as many problems as it solves. Chiefly, it now becomes necessary to specify what it is about the extinction procedure that causes such inhibitory links to form. So far we have assumed that the coactivation of a response node and a stimulus node will establish an excitatory link—and just such a coactivation is arranged in the extinction phase of Rescorla's (1993b)

Table 1.2   Design of Experiment by Rescorla (1993b).

Training	Extinction	Retraining	Test
R1 → O	S1: R1−	R1 → O	S1: R2 > R1
&	&	&	&
R2 → O	S2: R2−	R2 → O	S2: R1 > R2

NOTE: R: instrumental response; O: outcome; S: discriminative stimulus.

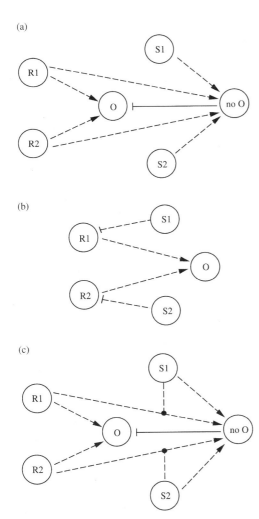

(a)

(b)

(c)

Figure 1.9 Possible associative structures generated by the training procedures outlined in Table 1.2.

NOTE: S1 and S2 represent two different discriminative stimuli in the presence of which two different responses, R1 and R2, have undergone extinction. No O represents the omission of a given outcome (O). In (c) a link that ends in a filled circle is assumed to be able to modulate activity in the associative link with which it makes contact. Other conventions are as given for Figure 1.1.

the response and what actually accompanies it. Figure 1.9c shows one way in which this advantage can be maintained while still providing an explanation for response-specificity in extinction. It supposes that the training given to the stimuli allows their nodes to form links, not (or not only) with the other nodes that are active when they are presented, but with other associations. Specifically the figure shows how each stimulus may come to activate the particular response-no outcome association that was formed in its presence. Such a stimulus can be expected to have a general effect on responding (the direct link with the no outcome node will still be formed), but in addition it will have a specific effect by selectively activating just one of the response-no outcome links.

This interpretation is one example of what has been referred to as a "hierarchical" account of conditioning in which higher-order associations operate on and determine the functioning of lower-order, simple associations of the sort that have dominated our discussion so far. To adopt this interpretation solves the immediate explanatory problem but raises a range of further questions. We have a clear rule specifying when one node will form a link with another, but what determines when a node will form a link with an association between two other nodes? (The experimental analysis of conditioned inhibition by Rescorla and Holland, 1977, for example, provided no support for the hierarchical structure depicted in Figure 1.7e.) We have a well formed idea of how activity in one node can generate activity in another with which it is linked, but by what process can a node influence the properties of an association? And, more basically, is there any independent evidence that would persuade us to take seriously what is, at this stage, merely an ad hoc assumption devised to explain a specific set of experimental results? These issues form the focus of the next section of the chapter.

experiment. The advantage of the structure shown in Figure 1.9a is that it accords perfectly well with our established principles, assuming that in extinction, as in acquisition, an orthodox association is formed between

COMPLEX CONDITIONING

Early in the study of instrumental learning it was demonstrated that responding can be brought under stimulus control: If a lever press results in a food pellet only when some external stimulus is presented, a rat will come to confine its responding to periods when the stimulus (the Sd) is present. Similarly, when food is available only in the absence of a given stimulus (known as an S-delta) the rat will learn to refrain from responding in the presence of the stimulus. Skinner (1938), who first investigated these effects in any detail, was insistent that the role of such discriminative stimuli was not to elicit (or suppress) the response directly; rather the stimuli were said to "set the occasion" on which the response would or would not be reinforced.

Parallel phenomena can be demonstrated in Pavlovian conditioning. In the procedure sometimes known as *feature positive* training, a CS (X) is paired with the US only when it is preceded or accompanied by some other stimulus (the so-called feature stimulus, A; the terminology reflects the fact that a distinctive element or feature is present on one of the two trial types, in this case on the reinforced, positive, trial). Animals given a mixture of AX+/X− trials come to show the CR to X only on trials when the feature is also present. In the *feature negative* case (AX−/X+), responding comes to be restricted to those trials on which the CS occurs in the absence of the feature. We have already met a version of this latter procedure in our discussion of conditioned inhibition, and it has been the subject of investigation since it was first introduced by Pavlov himself. Interest in the feature positive case has developed only in recent years (initiated by the pioneering study of Ross & Holland, 1981). Holland (e.g., 1983) made the parallel with the instrumental case quite explicit by labeling these Pavlovian procedures as occasion-setting and by referring to the feature stimulus as an occasion setter.

What characterizes these procedures is that they all involve a conditional relationship. In each, the response or target CS is sometimes followed by an outcome and sometimes not; what occurs is conditional on whether or not the discriminative stimulus or feature stimulus (the occasion setter) has also been presented. What makes them important is the suspicion (held as an article of faith by Skinner) that it may not be possible to explain them in terms of the associative principles and structures that have proved adequate for simple conditioning. The first part of this section of the chapter lays out the evidence that appears to confirm this suspicion. Later parts discuss those theories that have introduced new associative structures, new processes, or both, in order to explain complex, conditional conditioning.

The Role of Simple Associative Mechanisms

Instrumental Conditioning

The procedures used in rewarded instrumental conditioning permit the formation of simple excitatory associations between the Sd and the outcome and between the Sd and the response. In an earlier section of this chapter, we considered the possibility that the Sd might exert its effects by way of its association with the outcome; according to classical two-process theory (although other interpretations are possible; see Trapold & Overmier, 1972), such an association generates the motivational state that is necessary for the instrumental association to be expressed in behavior. But we also found reasons for doubting the adequacy of this interpretation. In particular, it was demonstrated that CSs and Sds are not interchangeable in the way that this account requires. And given the evidence (also discussed earlier in

Table 1.3   Design of Experiment by Colwill and Rescorla (1990b).

Training		Devaluation	Test
S1:	R1 → O1 & R2 → O2		S1: R2 > R
		O1 → Li	
S2:	R1 → O2 & R2 → O1		S2: R1 > R2

NOTE: R: instrumental response; O: outcome; S: discriminative stimulus; Li: injection of lithium chloride.

the chapter) supporting the view that S-R associations play no more than a minor role in generating instrumental responding, it would seem unwise to rely on this mechanism as an explanation of stimulus control.

In fact there is direct experimental evidence to show that Sds can exert control by means that are independent of any Sd-R or Sd-O associations that may be formed. An example comes from a study by Colwill and Rescorla (1990b), the design of which is summarized in Table 1.3. In a first stage of training, rats learned to perform two different responses for two different outcomes. Which response produced which outcome depended on which of two Sds was present. Such training could, potentially, establish direct links between each Sd and both responses and between each Sd and both outcomes. In the next stage of training, pairing with Li was used to devalue one of the outcomes. When the Sds were presented again in the test phase, the rats showed an unwillingness to perform the response that had previously produced the now-devalued outcome in the presence of that Sd. Simple associations cannot explain this result: The devaluation procedure should be without effect on S-R links; devaluing the outcome of an S-S link should have equivalent detrimental effects on both responses. Clearly what is critical is the specific combination of response and outcome; we may conclude that

what is learned about an Sd includes some information about the relationship between the response and the outcome that have occurred together in its presence.

What is true for Sds also hold for S-deltas. When responding is reinforced in the presence of stimulus X but not in the presence of the compound AX, it is possible that stimulus A (the S-delta) will acquire the properties of a Pavlovian conditioned inhibitor. The ability of A to suppress the animal's tendency to perform the target response might thus be attributed, in principle, to a capacity to inhibit the excitation of the outcome representation that the Sd, X, would otherwise evoke. Depending, as it does, on the questionable notion that the Sd works by way of a direct association with the outcome, such an interpretation may immediately be seen to be implausible. Experimental studies paralleling those described for the case of the Sd confirm this conclusion. The lack of interchangeability between an S-delta and a CS trained as a conditioned inhibitor has been demonstrated by Bonardi (1988). Two groups of rats were trained on the AX−/X+ task; for one group, responding was required for food to be delivered in the presence of X, that is, A was trained as an S-delta; for the other group, the animal's responses were irrelevant. The training given to the latter group might be expected to establish stimulus A as a Pavlovian conditioned inhibitor, and this was confirmed in a subsequent test in which A was paired with a US. The retardation of excitatory conditioning that was observed with this procedure is what would be expected of a CS having inhibitory properties. Significantly, however, inhibition was not evident in this test for the animals trained on the instrumental version of the initial discrimination. A further test examined the effects of presenting stimulus A while the animals were responding to the presentation of a separately trained Sd. On this test, the stimulus trained as an S-delta tended

Table 1.4   Design of Experiment by Bonardi and Hall (1994).

Stage 1	Stage 2	Test
X: R1 → O1		
&	Z: R1 → O1	AZ: lower response rate
AX: R1−		
&		
Y: R2 → O2		
&	Z: R1 → O2	AZ: higher response rate
AY: R2−		

NOTE: R: instrumental response; O: outcome; A, X, Y, and Z: different discriminative stimuli.

to suppress responding whereas the Pavlovian inhibitor did not. Evidently, an S-delta will not function as a conditioned inhibitor, nor will a conditioned inhibitor function as an S-delta.

Evidence that an S-delta can produce effects that are specific to the combination of response and outcome with which it has been trained comes from an experiment by Bonardi and Hall (1994). Table 1.4 presents a simplified version of the experimental design. In the first stage of training, rats learned to perform one response for a given outcome (a particular type of food) in the presence of one Sd and a different response for a different outcome in the presence of another. Responding was not rewarded when either of these Sds was presented in compound with the S-delta, stimulus A. In the second stage of training, a new Sd was established; for half the animals, this signaled one of the response-outcome relationships that had been used in stage one; for the remainder, the relationship was switched so that the response now produced the other type of food as its outcome. A final test showed that the S-delta was more effective in suppressing the responding governed by this new Sd in the former group than in the latter. In the first stage of training, stimulus A had the opportunity to become associated with the extinction of both responses and the omission of both types of food. But if this was all that

the animals learned about A, the way in which the responses and reinforcers are combined on the transfer test should be immaterial. The specificity of the effect obtained on the test suggests, rather, that the S-delta operates on the entire response-outcome association. This conclusion accords precisely with that drawn above on the basis of Rescorla's (1993b) study of simple extinction (see Figure 1.9).

The evidence discussed in this section confirms the suggestion that discriminative stimuli do not act (solely) by way of the simple associative properties they may acquire. An understanding of how they do act (whether by way of the hierarchical structure shown in Figure 1.9c, or in some other way) is best achieved in the light of information gained from the study of Pavlovian conditional discrimination tasks. As a preliminary, therefore, it is necessary to establish that these too cannot be explained in simple associative terms.

Feature Positive Discriminations

That animals can learn to respond to a reinforced compound stimulus (AX+) and not to presentations of a nonreinforced element (X−) requires no special assumptions. Standard accounts of the principles that govern the growth of associative strength (e.g., Rescorla & Wagner, 1972) predict that the more valid predictor, A, will readily gain strength whereas X will gain much less strength, eventually being rendered associatively neutral. The same patterns of associative strength might also be predicted for the case in which when a serial compound is used (i.e., when A precedes X, to be symbolized as A → X+), a procedure commonly used in studies of occasion setting (e.g., Holland, 1985b; Rescorla, 1985). Thus, it is of interest that animals trained with the serial procedure can develop a discrimination in which they come to respond to the supposedly weak or neutral X element on those trials in which it follows A. This result has been obtained when A itself generates no obvious CR (e.g., Rescorla, 1985) and when the CR to A is different from that generated by the stimulus used as X (e.g., Ross & Holland, 1981). It thus seems unlikely that the response to X, when it occurs, could simply reflect a carryover of the responding initiated by stimulus A. Rather, these results seem to suggest that a direct X-US association is indeed formed with this training procedure and that the role of A is to establish the conditions that allow this association to show in behavior.

Wagner and Brandon (1989) have developed an account of the role of stimulus A that requires no new principles additional to those used in the explanation of simple conditioning. We have already discussed the notion that in some circumstances CS-US pairings are likely to establish an association primarily between the CS and the affective properties of the US. Such a CS may not elicit a discrete CR, but it will evoke a motivational state (referred to by Konorski, 1967, as a *preparatory* CR), the presence of which will enhance the vigor of a discrete CR (Konorski's *consummatory* CR) controlled by some other CS. Wagner and Brandon argue that the specific temporal arrangement employed in many studies of serial (A → X+) feature positive training are such that stimulus A is likely to become associated with just the affective properties of the US, whereas X will become associated with the specific sensory properties of the US. Although A will not itself be capable of evoking the consummatory CR, it will supply the necessary motivational background that allows X to do so.

There is experimental evidence to confirm the validity of this analysis and to show that it operates in certain training preparations (see, e.g., Bombace, Brandon, & Wagner, 1991; Brandon & Wagner, 1991). But there are also good reasons for thinking that it cannot be the sole source of the occasion-setting effect. We shall briefly consider three

of these. First, there is considerable evidence (to be discussed in more detail below) showing that the effects of A are, to some extent, specific to the CS with which it has been trained. A separately trained CS that has been subject to the same schedule of reinforcement as cue X should, in principle, be just as susceptible to the effects of the emotional state engendered by A as the original cue. But although responding to the test CS may be boosted to some degree, the size of the effect is much less than that obtained with the original CS (e.g., Brandon & Wagner, 1991). Second, if the source of A's powers lies in its direct Pavlovian association with (the affective aspects of) the US, then a separately trained excitatory CS should have similar response-enhancing powers when presented before the target stimulus. Adequate tests of this proposition are hard to come by, as it proved difficult to arrange a training procedure that ensures that the simple CS and the stimulus trained as an occasion setter are exactly matched in their associative strength. With this caveat in mind, we may note that experiments that have investigated the matter have usually found that a simple excitatory CS is an inadequate substitute for a true occasion setter (e.g., Rescorla, 1985; Rescorla, 1987; Ross & Holland, 1981). Finally, if A's occasion-setting power depends on its ability to function as an excitatory CS, then extinction of A should eliminate this power. Although Holland (1989a) found just this result for rats trained with a simultaneous compound stimulus (AX+/X−), studies of the effect of nonreinforcement of A after serial feature positive training (A → X+/X−) have routinely found that A's powers are unaffected (e.g., Rescorla, 1986), or even enhanced (Holland, 1989a).

Feature Negative Discriminations

In our discussion of conditioned inhibition we considered the procedure in which an animal learns a discrimination between a reinforced element and a nonreinforced simultaneous compound (AX−/X+). Experimental analysis (Rescorla & Holland, 1977) led to the conclusion that the absence of responding to the compound reflected the ability of A to inhibit activation of the US node (see Figure 1.7a,b). Experiments analogous to those just described for the feature positive case give reason to doubt that this simple inhibitory mechanism can supply an explanation for all examples of feature negative discrimination, in particular, for those using a serial (A → X−/X+) training procedure.

Since the central observation is that responding to X is suppressed, the form of the CR can yield no information in this case. There are, however, very many studies looking at the extent to which A's powers will transfer to another separately trained CS. These will be discussed in more detail below; for the time being, it is sufficient to note that transfer may fail to occur although the same US has been involved in training both CSs (e.g., Holland, 1989b; interestingly, this study also included a demonstration of successful transfer in animals trained initially with simultaneous rather than a serial compound AX stimulus). The absence of transfer suggests that the serially trained A stimulus had not acquired the ability to inhibit the US representation. Further evidence to support this conclusion comes from studies showing that procedures designed to eliminate any direct inhibition that A may have acquired do not remove its occasion setting properties. Holland (1989b; see also Holland, 1984) gave rats reinforced trials with A after initial training on the serial feature negative discrimination. That A came to evoke the CR was evidence that any inhibitory properties had been effectively counteracted by this procedure. Nonetheless, the A stimulus still proved capable of suppressing responding to X on a subsequent test. (Again, different effects were obtained

after initial training with a simultaneous compound; here counterconditioning of the feature element abolished its ability to suppress the responding governed by the target.) Even more striking evidence of a dissociation between the simple associative properties of a feature stimulus and that feature's occasion-setting power comes from a study by Rescorla (1991b). In this experiment the subjects (pigeons) received reinforcement of the feature stimulus while concurrently learning a serial feature negative task (that is, they received A+/A → X−/X+ training). Not only did stimulus A suppress responding to X, it appeared to do so even more effectively than one that had not received such reinforced training.

Relationship between Occasion Setting and Simple Association Formation

A further reason for thinking that occasion setters do not exert their effects by way of any simple excitatory or inhibitory associations they may control comes from the observation that occasion setting effects are best obtained in circumstances that are likely to restrict the development of such associations.

As we have just noted, several of Holland's experiments allow a comparison of the effects of training with serial rather than simultaneous compound stimuli. These have found that the feature stimulus acquires occasion-setting properties more readily when the serial arrangement is used—an arrangement that would work against the formation of a strong association between the feature stimulus and the (temporally remote) outcome of the trial. Ross and Holland (1981; see also Holland, 1986) examined this issue in a study of serial feature positive training in which the interval between the feature stimulus and the reinforced CS was manipulated. As might be expected, the ability of the feature to evoke an overt CR declined somewhat as this interval (and thus the delay of reinforcement) was increased. Its ability to act as an occasion setter (to potentiate the elicitation of the CR by the target) showed no such effect, growing steadily more powerful as the interval was increased.

This is not to say that the serial procedure will always produce occasion setting and that the simultaneous procedure can never do so. An experiment by Rescorla (1989), looking at feature negative discrimination in pigeons, found the inhibitory properties acquired by the feature to be much the same after serial as after simultaneous training; conversely, Holland (1989c) found evidence for occasion setting in rats trained with a simultaneous feature positive procedure. It should be noted, however, that Rescorla used a training procedure in which presentation of the feature immediately preceded that of a relatively brief target CS—an arrangement likely to foster the development of a direct association between the feature and the outcome of the trial. Holland's experiment made use of a very salient target stimulus, and it is well known (from studies of the phenomenon of overshadowing) that the presence of such an element in a simultaneous compound will restrict the acquisition of associative strength by its less salient companion. The critical factor in producing occasion setting appears to be not so much that the compound is serial rather than simultaneous; instead, it is that the training procedure is one that does not allow the acquisition of direct associations by the feature (but see Holland, 1992, for a full discussion of other possible interpretations).

We may conclude that, although simple associations involving the feature stimulus and the US node may support the learning of some feature positive and feature negative discriminations, another mechanism comes into play when the circumstances are such that the relevant simple associations are unlikely to be formed. Consideration of why this should be so gives a hint as to what the other mechanism might be. When animals are trained on a simultaneous, AX+/X− feature positive discrimination, standard associative principles (e.g., Rescorla & Wagner, 1972) predict that A, being better correlated with reinforcement than X, should develop a particularly strong association with the US and do so at the expense of X. Similarly, for the AX−/X+ task, A, being uniquely correlated with nonreinforcement, will gain the lion's share of inhibitory strength. Only when the conditions are such that A is unable to gain much strength will X be able to do so. The critical feature of the experimental procedures described above may be not so much that they limit the acquisition of associative strength by stimulus A as that they allow the target CS X to acquire strength. The implication is that the feature may be able to acquire (or exhibit) occasion-setting properties only when its target stimulus has a reasonable amount of associative strength. This conclusion accords with the proposal that occasion setters work by *modulating* the effectiveness of standard excitatory or inhibitory associations. We examine this proposal in more detail next.

Modulatory Accounts of Occasion Setting

Associative Structures

The modulatory interpretation of occasion setting treats the target stimulus X as a standard CS that is subjected to a mixture of reinforced and nonreinforced trials. According to the analysis developed in previous sections of this chapter, this training will establish both excitatory and inhibitory links between the X node and that representing the US (see Figure 1.10). The exact schedule of reinforcement employed will determine the balance between the excitatory and inhibitory effects. We must assume that in the feature negative case the excitatory process predominates (X is capable of evoking the CR when A is not present); in the feature positive case (where

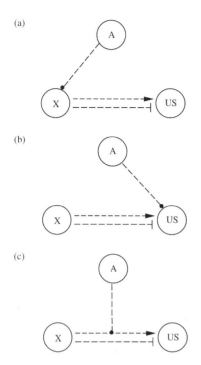

Figure 1.10 Possible associative structures according to modulatory accounts of occasion setting.
NOTE: A represents an occasion setter, and X represents a CS. The link ending in the filled circle is assumed to be able to modulate activity in the node or link with which it makes contact. Other conventions are as given for Figure 1.1. In (c) the modulation is shown as acting on the excitatory link between CS and US; it may also act on the inhibitory link or on both links.

X alone will not evoke the CR), we must assume that, even if the net effect of the CS is excitatory, the amount of excitation generated is not enough to pass the threshold necessary for the evocation of responding. Modulatory theories assume that occasion-setting training endows the feature stimulus with ability to modulate the effectiveness of one or other (or both) of these orthodox CS-US associations. In the feature positive case, it will be the excitatory effect that is enhanced, or the inhibitory one suppressed, or both; in the feature negative case, the reverse pattern must be assumed to operate.

Having adopted this general framework, it becomes necessary to specify where in the basic CS-US structure the occasion setter operates and exactly how it exerts its modulatory effect. Figure 1.10 shows three possibilities. All assume—in line with the theoretical position that has proved satisfactory so far—that the node representing the feature stimulus becomes linked to some other structure: to the CS node (Figure 1.10a), to the US node (Figure 1.10b), or to one or another of the associative links between the nodes (Figure 1.10c). The structures shown in the figure may seem simply to be elaborations of those already described for simple excitatory and inhibitory conditioning; it should be noted, however, that to adopt any of these also requires us to postulate the operation of a new process. The link running from the A node cannot have its effects (as, for example, an orthodox excitatory link is supposed to do) merely by engendering activity in a target node. This is most obvious for the structure shown in Figure 1.10c where the A node is connected not to another node but to the associative link between CS and US; but it also applies to the other two possibilities illustrated. With respect to the structure shown in 1.10b, we have already discussed evidence indicating that occasion setting is best obtained in circumstances that preclude the formation of a strong direct association between the feature and the US representation. With respect to that shown in Figure 1.10a, there is no reason to suppose that occasion-setting training will fail to establish a direct excitatory association between A and X, but there are good reasons to think that this link is not responsible for the occasion-setting effect (at least in the feature positive case). A direct association of this sort might allow stimulus A to "prime" excitatory activity in the X node prior to the presentation of X itself. But the evidence currently available suggests that the effect of such priming is to reduce, rather than enhance, the ability of the CS to excite activity in its node (Wagner, 1976; Hall & Mondragón, 1998). The effect would be the reverse of that observed in feature positive discrimination training. The link from A to X depicted in Figure 1.10a must have its occasion-setting effect in some other way.

One possibility is that the link enables activation of the A node to change the threshold for activation of the X node. Lowering the threshold would enhance the effectiveness of the CS and thus increase the likelihood that any low level of excitation it may control would activate the US node (the feature positive result); raising the threshold would make the CS less likely to activate the US (the feature negative result). A similar process might operate within the structure shown in Figure 1.10b: the feature positive effect would be obtained if A reduced the threshold for activation of the US node, and the feature negative result if A raised the threshold. (This is just the analysis of occasion setting developed by, e.g., Rescorla, 1985.) The notion that a link might be able to change the threshold associated with a node will already be familiar from our discussion of inhibitory learning (although the evidence, cited above, that a serially trained negative feature does not appear to act as a conditioned inhibitor raises doubts about its applicability in this particular case). The third possible structure (Figure 1.10c) requires a more radical theoretical step. Here the link from A is supposed to operate not on another node but on the associative link itself. Presumably, its effect must be to promote the passage of excitation (or hinder that of inhibition) in the feature positive case; to promote inhibition (or hinder excitation) in the feature negative case. This view of occasion setting, or a version of it, has been advanced by Holland (e.g., 1985b).

Clearly, to adopt any of the interpretations of occasion setting depicted in Figure 1.10 raises a number of questions about the processes implied by the structures they postulate. Our concern here, however, is to determine which, if any, of these structures is established by the occasion-setting procedure. Attempts to do this have made use of tests that examine the effects exerted by an occasion setter on a CS-US association other than that with which it was originally trained. Such transfer tests, it is suggested, can allow us to determine the target of occasion setter action.

Transfer Tests in Occasion Setting

If the feature stimulus in occasion setting operates by way of an effect on the CS node (as in Figure 1.10a) then this stimulus should be without effect on the responding controlled by a separately trained CS-US association. The alternative view (that the feature operates on the US node; Figure 1.10b) predicts that transfer will occur to a new CS, provided that the US remains the same. Experiments testing these seemingly simple predictions have been carried out on many occasions (see Swartzentruber, 1995, for a review) and have produced a varied pattern of results that defies any simple explanation. If we consider just the feature positive case, it is possible to find studies in which transfer to another CS appears to be complete (e.g., Rescorla, 1985), in which it fails to occur (e.g., Holland, 1986), and, quite commonly, studies in which the feature is able to boost the responding governed by the test CS to some degree, but to a lesser extent than is seen when the occasion setter is presented with its original CS (again, see Rescorla, 1985; Holland, 1986).

A close inspection of the details of the various experiments might help resolve these discrepancies (in particular, there is reason to think that the exact training history of the CS used in the transfer test may be a critical variable). But whatever the outcome of such a survey, it is important to appreciate that the result would not necessarily be theoretically decisive. Although the structure shown in Figure 1.10a seems to demand that occasion setters be target-specific, this is only so if we neglect the possibility that generalization is likely to occur between the test CS and that originally trained. To the extent that the animal fails to discriminate between the two CSs, transfer can be expected to occur. Similarly, a failure to find perfect transfer does not rule out the US-specific model of Figure 1.10b. Presenting the feature prior to the test CS could change the way in which the latter is perceived (that is, generalization decrement could occur)—the consequent disruption of conditioned responding would look like incomplete transfer even though the feature was fully capable of acting on the US representation.

An experiment by Bonardi (1996) goes some way toward resolving these issues. Pigeons were trained concurrently with two occasion-setting stimuli (A and B) and two CSs (X and Y) under the following contingencies, $A \rightarrow X+/X-$ and $B \rightarrow Y+/Y-$ (that is, X was reinforced when preceded by A but not when presented alone; similarly for Y and B). The subjects came to respond to the cues X and Y only when they were preceded by their occasion setters. They then received test trials in which each CS was preceded by the "wrong" occasion setter (i.e., $A \rightarrow Y$ and $B \rightarrow X$). The result was partial transfer—the pigeons responded to the CSs under these conditions but did so less vigorously than when the CSs were preceded by the "right" occasion setters. As we have seen, the view that the feature operates by way of the US representation explains this failure to obtain complete transfer by appealing to the effects of generalization decrement. In order to test this suggestion, we need some independent measure of the extent to which experiencing a novel combination of occasion setter and CS on the test does indeed produce generalization decrement. To achieve this, Bonardi included a condition in which the animals received ini-

tial training with cues (A and B) associated with continuously reinforced CSs (effectively, $A- > X+/X+/B- > Y+/Y+$). Such training would not be expected to establish occasion setting, but the novel test combinations, $A \rightarrow Y$ and $B \rightarrow X$, might still be expected to produce generalization decrement. No such effect was seen—after this form of training, test responding was as vigorous to the novel combinations as to those used in initial training. We may conclude that the decrement seen on the transfer test after occasion-setting training is not a product of generalization decrement; rather it indicates that the control exerted by the feature shows some degree of specificity to the target CS with which it was trained.

To demonstrate CS-specificity in occasion setting is only a first step, for this result is predicted not only by the structure shown in Figure 1.10a, but also by that in Figure 1.10c in which the feature acts on the CS-US combination. These accounts differ, however, in that the latter predicts that occasion setting should also show US-specificity—transfer should fail to occur when the test involves a separately trained association between the original CS and some new US. Such a test is technically difficult to arrange and, it should be noted, the result could still be ambiguous. A demonstration that occasion setting shows specificity both to the CS and US used in original training would not require us to accept the structure shown in Figure 1.10c. This pattern of result could be accommodated by supposing that the feature acts independently on both the CS and US representation (i.e., that the structures shown in Figures 1.10a and 1.10b are both correct). Confirmation of the accuracy of the structure of Figure 1.10c requires evidence that the occasion setter's action is specific to the association—to the *combination* of CS and US.

Table 1.5 shows a simplified version of the design of an experiment (Bonardi &

Table 1.5 Design of Experiment by Bonardi and Ward-Robinson (2001).

Stage 1	Stage 2	Test
A → X → f1/X−	A → XS → f1	
A → Y → f2/Y−	A → XD → f2	S: lower response rate
B → Y → f1/Y−	A → YS → f2	D: higher response rate
B → X → f2/X−	A → YD → f1	

NOTE: A, B, X, Y, S, and D: Pavlovian conditioned stimuli; f1 and f2: different types of food.

Ward-Robinson, 2001) intended to supply the relevant evidence. In the first stage, pigeons were trained with two CSs (X and Y) and two different types of food (f1 and f2) as the USs. The occasion setters (A and B) signaled which type of food would occur after a given CS. Thus A signaled that stimulus X would be followed by f1 whereas stimulus Y would be followed by a f2; B signaled the reverse relation between the CSs and the food types. In a second phase of training the occasion-setting stimuli continued to be followed by X and Y as in the first phase, but these two old CSs were now presented in compound with two new CSs (S and D). When S (for Same outcome predicted) was the new CS, the food given was the same as that previously predicted by the combination of occasion setter and old CS; when D (for Different outcome) was the added CS, the food given was of the "wrong" type (see Table 1.5 for a summary of the contingencies).

This experimental design constitutes a version of the blocking procedure in which a new CS is added to one that has already undergone reinforcement and the compound continues to be reinforced. It is well established that the added stimulus will fail to gain associative strength in these circumstances; blocking occurs because the outcome of the trial is already predicted by the pretrained CS. The question of interest was the extent to which the added

stimuli S and D would suffer from blocking. A final test phase, in which stimuli S and D were presented alone, showed that S controlled less responding than D, indicating blocking had been more effective for S than for D. The implication is that the outcome of the stage-two trials had been well predicted on those occasions on which S was the added stimulus, but less well predicted on those on which D was the added stimulus. As Table 1.5 shows, the other individual stimulus elements (A and B, X and Y), had all received equal training as predictors of both food types. What distinguished S trials from D trials was that in the former the *combination* of occasion setter and CS predicted what food type would occur in stage two, whereas in the latter it did not. We may conclude that the occasion-setting feature supplies information about what US will follow what CS—just what would be expected on the basis of the associative structure shown in Figure 1.10c.

Configural Accounts of Occasion Setting

Discriminating Stimulus Patterns

It has long been known (e.g., Woodbury, 1943) that animals can learn discriminations in which the critical stimulus is a pattern or configuration of events. For example, in the procedure referred to as negative patterning, the animal is required to discriminate between a compound stimulus and its elements—the elements A and X when presented separately are each reinforced, but the AX compound is not. With extended training, the animal comes to respond to A and to X but not to the compound. Such a discrimination could not be achieved if the response to the compound was determined simply by the sum of the associative strengths of its elements. In order to explain this result it has been suggested that the compound should be seen as constituting a further, configural cue, distinct from those provided by A and X alone (Rescorla, 1972, 1973b). This requires a conceptual nervous system in which the stimuli are represented by three nodes, one activated by A, one by X, and one by the combination of the two as in Figure 1.11a. Standard learning rules (e.g., Rescorla & Wagner, 1972) can then predict that the A and X nodes will each acquire excitatory links with the US node and that the configural (AX) node will acquire inhibition enough to counteract the excitatory influence of the individual element nodes (as depicted in Figure 1.11a).

Although adequate to meet the explanatory demands of this particular case, the structure shown in Figure 1.11a has some problems. At the empirical level, other, more complex patterning discriminations prove difficult to explain in these terms (see, e.g., Pearce, 1987, 1994). More generally, although one might allow that animals come equipped with a range of nodes sensitive to any and all of the events that experimenters might judge to be simple stimulus elements, it seems implausible to assume that they also have nodes available and ready to respond to all possible combinations of these elements. The response to these problems has been to depart from the simple associative structure that has served so far, in which all stimulus nodes are capable of being activated directly by environmental events, and to adopt instead a multilayer network incorporating what have been called *hidden units*. Figure 1.11b presents an example of such a network as it might apply to the negative patterning discrimination. Here the node marked AX represents a hidden unit, activated not by events in the world but by inputs from the element nodes, A and X. A network of this sort allows that conditioning procedures can change the effectiveness of links between the US node and other nodes in the usual way; but it also allows the possibility that experience might influence the links between simple stimulus nodes and hidden units—that

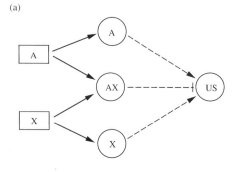

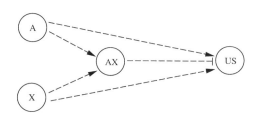

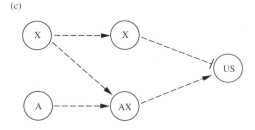

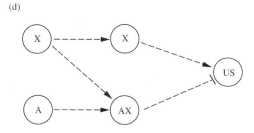

Figure 1.11 Possible associative structures for configural learning.

NOTE: In (a) the node sensitive to the configure A and X has the same status as the other nodes; in (b) this node is a hidden unit that is not accessed directly by events in the world. The multilayered structures (derived from Pearce, 1994) shown in (c) and (d) provide possible configural interpretations for feature-positive and feature-negative learning, respectively. Conventions are as given for Figure 1.1.

experience might "create" appropriate configural nodes.

Multilayer networks of the sort shown in Figure 1.11b come in many different versions. There are various views, for instance, as to what rules govern the activation of configural units and as to whether or not hidden units always mediate the connections between input units (even those corresponding to individual stimulus elements) and the US node (see, e.g., Brandon & Wagner, 1998; Pearce, 1994; Schamjuk & DiCarlo, 1992; Wagner & Brandon, 2001). It may be apparent, however, that the basic principle embodied by all these theories has the capacity to supply an explanation for occasion-setting effects. We have described feature positive and feature negative discriminations as involving conditional relationships, and the modulatory account developed above expresses this conditionality in the associative structure it employs (Figure 1.10c). But it is also possible to characterize these tasks as requiring a discrimination between stimulus patterns (with the AX pattern or configuration predicting one outcome and the X element alone another). Examples of the (rather different) associative structures generated by this latter perspective are presented in Figure 1.11. These structures (based on Pearce's, 1994, configural theory) postulate a hidden unit corresponding to each of the two patterns of stimulation (i.e., X alone and the AX compound) experienced by the animal. Standard associative learning rules then result in the formation of excitatory or inhibitory associations between the hidden units and the US unit. In the feature positive case (Figure 1.11c), the AX unit forms an excitatory link and the X unit an inhibitory link; in the feature negative case (Figure 1.11d), the reverse pattern is established.

Choosing between the Accounts

The modulatory and configural accounts of occasion setting are clearly saying different things. One way of characterizing the difference is to say that in the modulatory account the feature operates on the CS-US complex (for the feature positive case this may be symbolized as $A \rightarrow \{X\text{-}US\}$) whereas in the configural account a complex stimulus event operates on the US (symbolized as $\{AX\} \rightarrow US$). Nonetheless, it proves exceedingly difficult to devise an experimental test that allows choice between the alternatives. Both predict, for example, that the effect of the feature will be specific to the X-US combination with which it was trained (the transfer test results described above). Holland (1992) has carefully considered a range of other possible ways in which the rival theories might be distinguished, without reaching any decisive conclusion. It may be that the choice between the accounts will depend on consideration of data from procedures other than those employed for instrumental and Pavlovian conditioning. A particular strength of the configural account is its ability to explain the results from studies on complex discriminations in which subjects are required to categorize stimuli varying on a range of different dimensions—if it is necessary to use a configural theory to deal with these results, it may be deemed parsimonious to employ this same sort of theory when it comes to occasion setting.

But before discarding the modulatory account on these grounds, we should note two observations that indicate that it may still have a role to play. The first concerns the explanation of stimulus control in instrumental learning. Our analysis of this phenomenon, it will be recalled, led to the conclusion that the discriminative stimulus operates by modulating the effectiveness of the R-outcome association. No one has seriously suggested a configural interpretation of this phenomenon and accordingly we must acknowledge the reality of modulation in this case at least. And if modulation occurs in instrumental conditioning, might it not also occur in some

Table 1.6   Design of Experiment by Honey and Watt (1998).

Stage 1	Stage 2	Test
A: X → f/A:Y−		
B: X → f/B:Y−	A → shock	B > D
C: X−/C:Y → f	C−	
D: X−/D:Y → f		

NOTE: X and Y: Pavlovian conditioned stimuli; A, B, C, and D: occasion setters; f: food.

Pavlovian procedures? The second observation comes from an ingenious experiment by Honey and Watt (1998) designed to show such an effect.

The design of the experiment is outlined in Table 1.6. Rats were trained initially on a set of conditional discriminations in which two visual stimuli, X and Y, were followed by food on some trials but on others were nonreinforced. The outcome of the trial depended on the nature of the feature stimulus that preceded the auditory cue. When this was either A or B, X was reinforced and Y was not; when it was either C or D, Y was reinforced and X was not. This arrangement ensured that X, Y, and food all occurred equally often along with each of the feature stimuli. After extensive training, the animals learned to respond appropriately. The configural interpretation of this achievement holds that particular combinations of cues become associated with food or its omission; the animals learn {AX} → food, {CX} → no food, and so on. The modulatory account suggests that the feature stimuli acquire the power to control the effectiveness of particular CS-US associations (e.g., A → {X-food}; C → {X-no food}, and so on. To decide between these alternatives, Honey and Watt (1998) made use of the phenomenon known as acquired equivalence—the fact that generalization between quite different stimuli can be enhanced by initial training that establishes a common associate for them. (See, e.g., Honey & Hall, 1989; the effect is some-times referred to as mediated generalization, reflecting the assumption that the enhanced generalization is mediated by the acquisition of strength by the associate that is shared by the critical cues.) In a second phase of training, they gave trials in which feature A, presented alone, was paired with shock so that it acquired the power to suppress ongoing behavior; feature C was also presented but in the absence of shock. The final test phase showed that feature B was also able to elicit response suppression whereas D was not. Without special elaboration, the configural account has no grounds to predict such differential generalization. But if we assume that A and B hold in common the ability to activate a given CS-US combination (an ability not shared by C and D), then differential generalization from A to B and from C to D can be predicted. In short, the outcome is what would be expected on the basis of the modulatory account of the acquisition of the original discrimination.

CONCLUSION

We began this chapter by postulating a conceptual nervous system consisting of nodes that correspond to those events that the experimenter chooses to describe as "stimuli" and "responses." A stimulus in the external world is assumed to generate activity in its representative node; activity in a response node equates to the occurrence of a particular form of behavior. We further postulated that the training procedures employed in instrumental and Pavlovian conditioning result in the formation of new connections between nodes. Our central concern in this chapter has been to determine the pattern of connections (i.e., the associative structures) that are established by these procedures. Detailed discussion of process or function (as opposed to structure) has, accordingly, been outside the scope of this chapter. To get the analysis of structures under way we adopted only very minimal assumptions about the conditions in which associations are formed and the effects that they have on nodes. For the former we assumed that an association will be formed between two nodes when both are activated concurrently (i.e., we adopted a simple contiguity principle); for the latter, we assumed that the existence of an associative link allows activity in one node to generate activity in another. It is time now to review how these simple principles have fared in the light of the experimental data.

For simple excitatory conditioning these assumptions fare tolerably well. The basic features of excitatory Pavlovian conditioning can be explained in terms of the formation of an association between the CS node and the US node; for instrumental excitatory conditioning the association is between the response node and one representing the outcome. In both cases, an S-R connection may also play a role. For both cases it also proves necessary to allow that the sensory and affective properties of the US (or outcome) may be represented by separate nodes, each capable of entering into association with other nodes. This elaboration requires no new assumptions. More fundamental is the suggestion that the nature of the activity engendered in a US node by way of an associative link is different in kind from that produced by presentation of the US itself (although, as was shown in Figure 1.1b, it may be possible to express this notion in structural terms without the need to introduce a new type of nodal activity).

Our survey of experimental studies of extinction showed that the phenomena can again be accommodated by the assumption that extinction procedures result in the formation of new links between CS and US, or between response and outcome. But here it is necessary to postulate a new process. The effect of these links is not to excite but to inhibit activity in the target node (a process that we have identified with a raising of the node's threshold for sensitivity to excitatory influence). Again, it is possible to complicate the structure and maintain the assumption that conditioning consists solely of the formation of excitatory links between concurrently activated nodes. This is achieved by postulating the existence of a no-US node to which the extinguished CS forms an excitatory link (see Figure 1.6). But it still remains necessary to allow the existence of an inhibitory process (in this case, in the form of an intrinsic inhibitory connection between the no-US node and the US node).

Whichever of the rival accounts we adopt, explanation of the effects revealed in studies of complex (conditional) conditioning procedures requires a new degree of elaboration of our basic assumptions. The modulatory account requires quite a new process. Although the principle that the feature stimulus has its effects by way of an associative link is standard, the effect of this link is not to excite (or even inhibit) activity in another node—rather it is assumed that the link allows the feature to control the flow of activity along some other associative link. The configural account avoids the need to postulate a new process, but does so at the expense of creating an associative structure with a new level of complexity. The introduction of a new layer of hidden units serving a purely computational function means that nodes can no longer be directly identified with events in the external world and the simplicity of the original associative explanation of basic conditioning is lost. Neither of these accounts is wholly satisfactory and it is to be hoped that further research (and theorizing) may come up with some other associative structure in which the best features of both of the current rival accounts can be incorporated.

Finally, it is worth noting that, in spite of the need to add these elaborations, the basic explanatory scheme adopted by students of conditioning (in which learning consists of changes in the strength of connections between simple units) has proved to have very wide explanatory powers. The rediscovery of this scheme in recent years by advocates of connectionism (seemingly in ignorance, in some cases, of its long history in the conditioning laboratory) has extended the range of phenomena that the scheme is applied to and has brought it to the notice of a larger audience. But experimental studies using conditioning techniques and directed toward refining our understanding of basic associative principles still continue and we may hope, for the future, that the outcome of these studies will inform the work of those theorists who are attempting to provide an associative (or connectionist) account of cognition generally.

REFERENCES

Adams, C. D. (1982). Variations in the sensitivity of instrumental responding to reinforcer devaluation. *Quarterly Journal of Experimental Psychology, 34B,* 77–98.

Adams, C. D., & Dickinson, A. (1981). Instrumental responding following reinforcer devaluation. *Quarterly Journal of Experimental Psychology, 33B,* 109–121.

Bakal, C. W., Johnson, R. D., & Rescorla, R. A. (1974). The effect of a change in US quality on the blocking effect. *Pavlovian Journal of Biological Science, 9,* 97–103.

Balleine, B., & Dickinson, A. (1991). Instrumental performance following reinforcer devaluation depends upon incentive learning. *Quarterly Journal of Experimental Psychology, 43B,* 279–296.

Balleine, B., & Dickinson, A. (1992). Signalling and incentive processes in instrumental devaluation. *Quarterly Journal of Experimental Psychology, 45B,* 285–301.

Betts, S. L., Brandon, S. E., & Wagner, A. R. (1996). Differential blocking of the acquisition of conditioned eyeblink responding and conditioned fear with a shift in US locus. *Animal Learning & Behavior, 24,* 459–470.

Bombace, J. C., Brandon, S. E., & Wagner, A. R. (1991). Modulation of a conditioned eyeblink response by a putative emotive stimulus conditioned with hindleg shock. *Journal of Experimental Psychology: Animal Behavior Processes, 17,* 323–333.

Bonardi, C. (1988). Mechanisms of inhibitory stimulus control. *Animal Learning & Behavior, 16,* 445–450.

Bonardi, C. (1996). Transfer of occasion setting: The role of generalization decrement. *Animal Learning & Behavior, 24,* 277–289.

Bonardi, C., & Hall, G. (1994). Discriminative inhibition is specific to the response-reinforcer association but not to the discriminative stimulus. *Journal of Experimental Psychology: Animal Behavior Processes, 20,* 278–291.

Bonardi, C., & Ward-Robinson, J. (2001). Occasion setters: Specificity to the US and the CS-US association. *Learning and Motivation, 32,* 349–366.

Bouton, M. E. (1984). Differential control by context in the inflation and reinstatement paradigms. *Journal of Experimental Psychology: Animal Behavior Processes, 10,* 56–74.

Bouton, M. E. (1991). Context and retrieval in extinction and in other examples of interference in simple associative learning. In L. Dachowski & C. F. Flaherty (Eds.), *Current topics in animal learning: Brain, emotion, and cognition* (pp. 25–53). Hillsdale, NJ: Erlbaum.

Bouton, M. E., & Bolles, R. C. (1979a). Contextual control of the extinction of conditioned fear. *Learning and Motivation, 10,* 455–466.

Bouton, M. E., & Bolles, R. C. (1979b). Role of contextual stimuli in reinstatement of extinguished fear. *Journal of Experimental Psychology: Animal Behavior Processes, 5,* 368–378.

Bouton, M. E., & King, D. A. (1983). Effect of context with mixed histories of reinforcement and nonreinforcement. *Journal of Experimental*

Psychology: Animal Behavior Processes, 12, 4–15.

Bouton, M. E., & Peck, C. A. (1992). Spontaneous recovery in cross-motivational transfer (counterconditioning). *Animal Learning & Behavior, 20,* 313–321.

Brandon, S. E., & Wagner, A. R. (1991). Modulation of a discrete Pavlovian conditioned reflex by a putative emotive Pavlovian conditioned stimulus. *Journal of Experimental Psychology: Animal Behavior Processes, 17,* 299–311.

Brandon, S. E., & Wagner, A. R. (1998). Occasion setting: Influences of conditioned emotional responses and configural cues. In N. A. Schmajuk & P. C. Holland (Eds.), *Occasion setting: Associative learning and cognition in animals* (pp. 343–382). Washington, DC: American Psychological Association.

Brogden, W. J. (1939). Sensory pre-conditioning. *Journal of Experimental Psychology, 25,* 323–332.

Colwill, R. M., & Rescorla, R. A. (1985a). Postconditioning devaluation of a reinforcer affects instrumental responding. *Journal of Experimental Psychology: Animal Behavior Processes, 11,* 120–132.

Colwill, R. M., & Rescorla, R. A. (1985b). Instrumental responding remains sensitive to reinforcer devaluation after extensive training. *Journal of Experimental Psychology: Animal Behavior Processes, 11,* 520–536.

Colwill, R. M., & Rescorla, R. A. (1986). Associative structures in instrumental learning. In G. H. Bower (Ed.), *The psychology of learning and motivation* (Vol. 20, pp. 55–104). New York: Academic Press.

Colwill, R. M., & Rescorla, R. A. (1988). Associations between the discriminative stimulus and the reinforcer in instrumental learning. *Journal of Experimental Psychology: Animal Behavior Processes, 14,* 155–164.

Colwill, R. M., & Rescorla, R. A. (1990a). Effect of reinforcer devaluation on discriminative control of instrumental behavior. *Journal of Experimental Psychology: Animal Behavior Processes, 16,* 40–47.

Colwill, R. M., & Rescorla, R. A. (1990b). Evidence for the hierarchical structure of instrumental learning. *Animal Learning & Behavior, 18,* 71–82.

Crespi, L. P. (1942). Quantitative variation of incentive and performance in the white rat. *American Journal of Psychology, 55,* 467–517.

Culler, E., Finch, G., Girden, E., & Brogden, W. J. (1935). Measurements of acuity by the conditioned response technique. *Journal of General Psychology, 12,* 233–237.

Delamater, A. R. (1996). Effects of several extinction treatments upon the integrity of Pavlovian stimulus-outcome associations. *Animal Learning & Behavior, 24,* 437–449.

Dickinson, A. (1987). Instrumental performance following saccharin pre-feeding. *Behavioural Processes, 14,* 147–154.

Dickinson, A. (1989). Expectancy theory in animal conditioning. In S. B. Klein & R. R. Mowrer (Eds.), *Contemporary learning theories: Pavlovian conditioning and the status of traditional learning theory* (pp. 279–308). Hillsdale, NJ: Erlbaum.

Dickinson, A., & Balleine, B. (1994). Motivational control of goal-directed action. *Animal Learning & Behavior, 22,* 1–18.

Dickinson, A., Campos, J., Varga, Z. I., & Balleine, B. W. (1996). Bidirectional instrumental conditioning. *Quarterly Journal of Experimental Psychology, 49B,* 201–227.

Dickinson, A., & Dawson, G. R. (1987a). The role of the instrumental contingency in the motivational control of performance. *Quarterly Journal of Experimental Psychology, 39B,* 77–93.

Dickinson, A., & Dawson, G. R. (1987b). Pavlovian processes in the motivational control of instrumental performance. *Quarterly Journal of Experimental Psychology, 39B,* 201–227.

Dickinson, A., & Dawson, G. R. (1988). Motivational control of instrumental performance: The role of prior experience of the reinforcer. *Quarterly Journal of Experimental Psychology, 40B,* 113–134.

Dickinson, A., & Mulatero, C. W. (1989). Reinforcer specificity of the suppression of instrumental performance on a non-contingent schedule. *Behavioural Processes, 19,* 167–180.

Dickinson, A., Nicholas, D. J., & Adams, C. D. (1983). The effect of the instrumental training contingency on susceptibility to reinforcer devaluation. *Quarterly Journal of Experimental Psychology, 35B,* 35–51.

Fudim, O. K. (1978). Sensory preconditioning of flavors with a formalin-produced sodium need. *Journal of Experimental Psychology: Animal Behavior Processes, 4,* 276–285.

Ganesan, R., & Pearce, J. M. (1988). Effect of changing the unconditioned stimulus on appetitive blocking. *Journal of Experimental Psychology: Animal Behavior Processes, 14,* 280–291.

Gewirtz, J. C., Brandon, S. E., & Wagner, A. R. (1998). Modulation of the acquisition of the rabbit eyeblink conditioned response by conditioned contextual stimuli. *Journal of Experimental Psychology: Animal Behavior Processes, 24,* 106–117.

Hall, G. (1991). *Perceptual and associative learning.* Oxford: Clarendon Press.

Hall, G. (1994). Pavlovian conditioning: Laws of association. In N. J. Mackintosh (Ed.), *Handbook of perception and cognition. Vol. 9: Animal learning and cognition* (pp. 15–43). San Diego, CA: Academic Press.

Hall, G., & Mondragón, E. (1998). Contextual control as occasion setting. In N. A. Schmajuk & P. C. Holland (Eds.), *Occasion setting: Associative learning and cognition in animals* (pp. 199–222). Washington, DC: American Psychological Association.

Hall, G., & Pearce, J. M. (1979). Latent inhibition of a CS during CS-US pairings. *Journal of Experimental Psychology: Animal Behavior Processes, 5,* 31–42.

Hammond, L. J. (1980). The effects of contingencies upon appetitive conditioning of free-operant behavior. *Journal of the Experimental Analysis of Behavior, 34,* 297–304.

Holland, P. C. (1977). Conditioned stimulus as a determinant of the form of the Pavlovian conditioned response. *Journal of Experimental Psychology: Animal Behavior Processes, 3,* 77–104.

Holland, P. C. (1983). Occasion setting in Pavlovian feature positive discriminations. In M. L. Commons, R. J. Herrnstein, & A. R. Wagner (Eds.), *Quantitative analyses of behavior: Discrimination processes* (Vol. 4, pp. 183–206). New York: Ballinger.

Holland, P. C. (1984). Differential effects of reinforcement of an inhibitory feature after serial and simultaneous feature negative discrimination training. *Journal of Experimental Psychology: Animal Behavior Processes, 10,* 461–475.

Holland, P. C. (1985a). Element pretraining influences the content of appetitive serial compound conditioning in rats. *Journal of Experimental Psychology: Animal Behavior Processes, 11,* 367–387.

Holland, P. C. (1985b). The nature of conditioned inhibition in serial and simultaneous feature negative discriminations. In R. R. Miller & N. E. Spear (Eds.), *Information processing in animals: Conditioned inhibition* (pp. 267–297). Hillsdale, NJ: Erlbaum.

Holland, P. C. (1986). Temporal determinants of occasion setting in feature positive discriminations. *Animal Learning & Behavior, 14,* 111–120.

Holland, P. C. (1989a). Feature extinction enhances transfer of occasion setting. *Animal Learning & Behavior, 17,* 269–279.

Holland, P. C. (1989b). Transfer of negative occasion setting and conditioned inhibition across conditioned and unconditioned stimuli. *Journal of Experimental Psychology: Animal Behavior Processes, 15,* 311–328.

Holland, P. C. (1989c). Occasion setting with simultaneous compounds in rats. *Journal of Experimental Psychology: Animal Behavior Processes, 15,* 183–193.

Holland, P. C. (1992). Occasion setting in Pavlovian conditioning. In D. L. Medin (Ed.), *The psychology of learning and motivation* (Vol. 28, pp. 69–125). New York: Academic Press.

Holland, P. C., & Rescorla, R. A. (1975). The effects of two ways of devaluing the unconditioned stimulus after first- and second-order conditioning. *Journal of Experimental Psychology: Animal Behavior Processes, 1,* 355–363.

Holland, P. C., & Straub, J. J. (1979). Differential effects of two ways of devaluing the unconditioned stimulus after Pavlovian appetitive conditioning. *Journal of Experimental Psychology: Animal Behavior Processes, 5,* 65–78.

Holman, J. G., & Mackintosh, N. J. (1981). The control of appetitive instrumental responding does not depend on classical conditioning to the discriminative stimulus. *Quarterly Journal of Experimental Psychology, 33B,* 21–31.

Honey, R. C., & Hall, G. (1989). Acquired equivalence and distinctiveness of cues. *Journal of Experimental Psychology: Animal Behavior Processes, 16,* 178–184.

Honey, R. C., & Watt, A. (1998). Acquired relational equivalence: Implications for the nature of associative structures. *Journal of Experimental Psychology: Animal Behavior Processes, 24,* 325–334.

Hull, C. L. (1943). *Principles of behavior.* New York: Appleton-Century-Crofts.

Konorski, J. (1948). *Conditioned reflexes and neuron organization.* Cambridge: Cambridge University Press.

Konorski, J. (1967). *Integrative activity of the brain.* Chicago: University of Chicago Press.

Kruse, J. M., Overmier, J. B., Konz, W. A., & Rokke, E. (1983). Pavlovian conditioned stimulus effects upon instrumental choice behavior are reinforcer specific. *Learning and Motivation, 14,* 165–181.

Leyland, C. M. (1977). Higher-order autoshaping. *Quarterly Journal of Experimental Psychology, 29,* 607–619.

Mackintosh, N. J. (1983). *Conditioning and associative learning.* Oxford: Clarendon Press.

Nairne, J. S., & Rescorla, R. A. (1981). Second-order conditioning with diffuse auditory reinforcers in the pigeon. *Learning and Motivation, 12,* 65–91.

Pavlov, I. P. (1927). *Conditioned reflexes.* Oxford: Oxford University Press.

Pearce, J. M. (1987). A model of stimulus generalization for Pavlovian conditioning. *Psychological Review, 94,* 61–73.

Pearce, J. M. (1994). Similarity and discrimination: A selective review and a connectionist model. *Psychological Review, 101,* 587–607.

Pearce, J. M., & Hall, G. (1980). A model for Pavlovian learning: Variations in the effectiveness of conditioned but not of unconditioned stimuli. *Psychological Review, 87,* 532–552.

Pearce, J. M., Montgomery, A., & Dickinson, A. (1981). Contralateral transfer of inhibitory and excitatory eyelid conditioning in the rabbit. *Quarterly Journal of Experimental Psychology, 33B,* 45–61.

Prewitt, E. P. (1967). Number of preconditioning trials in sensory preconditioning with CER training. *Journal of Comparative and Physiological Psychology, 64,* 360–362.

Rashotte, M. E., Griffin, R. W., & Sisk, C. L. (1977). Second-order conditioning of the pigeon's key peck. *Animal Learning & Behavior, 5,* 25–38.

Rescorla, R. A. (1972). "Configural" conditioning in discrete-trial bar pressing. *Journal of Comparative and Physiological Psychology, 79,* 307–317.

Rescorla, R. A. (1973a). Effect of US habituation following conditioning. *Journal of Comparative and Physiological Psychology, 82,* 137–143.

Rescorla, R. A. (1973b). Evidence for "unique stimulus" account of configural conditioning. *Journal of Comparative and Physiological Psychology, 85,* 331–338.

Rescorla, R. A. (1974). Effect of inflation of the unconditioned stimulus value following conditioning. *Journal of Comparative and Physiological Psychology, 86,* 101–106.

Rescorla, R. A. (1979a). Aspects of the reinforcer learned in second-order Pavlovian conditioning. *Journal of Experimental Psychology: Animal Behavior Processes, 5,* 79–95.

Rescorla, R. A. (1979b). Conditioned inhibition and extinction. In A. Dickinson & R. A. Boakes (Eds.), *Mechanisms of learning and motivation* (pp. 83–110). Hillsdale, NJ: Erlbaum.

Rescorla, R. A. (1985). Conditioned inhibition and facilitation. In R. R. Miller & N. E. Spear (Eds.), *Information processing in animals: Conditioned inhibition* (pp. 299–326). Hillsdale, NJ: Erlbaum.

Rescorla, R. A. (1986). Extinction of facilitation. *Journal of Experimental Psychology: Animal Behavior Processes, 12,* 16–24.

Rescorla, R. A. (1987). Facilitation and inhibition. *Journal of Experimental Psychology: Animal Behavior Processes, 13,* 250–259.

Rescorla, R. A. (1989). Simultaneous and sequential conditioned inhibition in autoshaping. *Quarterly Journal of Experimental Psychology, 41B,* 275–286.

Rescorla, R. A. (1991a). Depression of an instrumental response by a single devaluation of its outcome. *Quarterly Journal of Experimental Psychology, 44B,* 123–136.

Rescorla, R. A. (1991b). Separate reinforcement can enhance the effectiveness of modulators. *Journal of Experimental Psychology: Animal Behavior Processes, 17,* 259–269.

Rescorla, R. A. (1992). Associations between an instrumental discriminative stimulus and multiple outcomes. *Journal of Experimental Psychology: Animal Behavior Processes, 18,* 95–104.

Rescorla, R. A. (1993a). Preservation of response-outcome associations through extinction. *Animal Learning & Behavior, 21,* 238–245.

Rescorla, R. A. (1993b). Inhibitory associations between S and R in extinction. *Animal Learning & Behavior, 21,* 327–336.

Rescorla, R. A. (1996a). Spontaneous recovery after training with multiple outcomes. *Animal Learning & Behavior, 25,* 11–18.

Rescorla, R. A. (1996b). Preservation of Pavlovian associations through extinction. *Quarterly Journal of Experimental Psychology, 49B,* 245–258.

Rescorla, R. A. (1997a). Spontaneous recovery after Pavlovian conditioning with multiple outcomes. *Animal Learning & Behavior, 25,* 99–107.

Rescorla, R. A. (1997b). Response-inhibition in extinction. *Quarterly Journal of Experimental Psychology, 50B,* 238–252.

Rescorla, R. A. (1998). Instrumental learning: Nature and persistence. In M. Sabourin, F. Craik, & M. Robert (Eds.), *Advances in psychological science* (Vol. 2, pp. 239–257). Hove, UK: Psychology Press.

Rescorla, R. A. (2001). Experimental extinction. In R. R. Mowrer & S. B. Klein (Eds.), *Handbook of contemporary learning theories* (pp. 119–154). Mahwah, NJ: Erlbaum.

Rescorla, R. A., & Cunningham, C. L. (1978). Within-compound flavor associations. *Journal of Experimental Psychology: Animal Behavior Processes, 4,* 267–275.

Rescorla, R. A., & Freberg, L. (1978). The extinction of within-compound flavor associations. *Learning and Motivation, 9,* 411–427.

Rescorla, R. A., & Heth, C. D. (1975). Reinstatement of fear to an extinguished conditioned stimulus. *Journal of Experimental Psychology: Animal Behavior Processes, 1,* 88–96.

Rescorla, R. A., & Holland, P. C. (1977). Associations in Pavlovian conditioned inhibition. *Learning and Motivation, 8,* 429–447.

Rescorla, R. A., & Skucy, J. C. (1969). Effect of response-independent reinforcers during extinction. *Journal of Comparative and Physiological Psychology, 67,* 381–389.

Rescorla, R. A., & Solomon, R. L. (1967). Two-process learning theory: Relationships between Pavlovian conditioning and instrumental learning. *Psychological Review, 74,* 151–182.

Rescorla, R. A., & Wagner, A. R. (1972). A theory of Pavlovian conditioning: Variations in the effectiveness of reinforcement and nonreinforcement. In A. H. Black & W. F. Prokasy (Eds.), *Classical conditioning, II: Current research and theory* (pp. 64–99). New York: Appleton-Century-Crofts.

Rizley, R. C., & Rescorla, R. A. (1972). Associations on second-order conditioning and sensory preconditioning. *Journal of Comparative and Physiological Psychology, 81,* 1–11.

Robbins, S. J. (1990). Mechanisms underlying spontaneous recovery in autoshaping. *Journal of Experimental Psychology: Animal Behavior Processes, 16,* 235–249.

Ross, R. T., & Holland, P. C. (1981). Conditioning of simultaneous and serial feature-positive discriminations. *Animal Learning & Behavior, 9,* 293–303.

Schmajuk, N. A., & DiCarlo, J. J. (1992). Stimulus configuration, occasion setting, and the hippocampus. *Psychological Review, 99,* 268–305.

Siegel, S. (1975). Evidence from rats that morphine tolerance is a learned response. *Journal of Comparative and Physiological Psychology, 89,* 498–506.

Skinner, B. F. (1938). *The behavior of organisms.* New York: Appleton-Century.

Swartzentruber, D. (1995). Modulatory mechanisms in Pavlovian conditioning. *Animal Learning & Behavior, 23,* 123–143.

Trapold, M. A., & Overmier, J. B. (1972). The second learning process in instrumental learning. In A. H. Black & W. F. Prokasy (Eds.), *Classical conditioning, II: Current research and theory* (pp. 427–452). New York: Appleton-Century-Crofts.

Wagner, A. R. (1976). Priming in STM: An information-processing mechanism for self-generated or retrieval-generated depression in performance. In T. J. Tighe & R. N. Leaton (Eds.), *Habituation: Perspectives from child development, animal behavior, and neurophysiology* (pp. 95–128). Hillsdale, NJ: Erlbaum.

Wagner, A. R. (1981). SOP: A model of automatic memory processing in animal behavior. In N. E. Spear & R. R. Miller (Eds.), *Information processing in animals: Memory mechanisms* (pp. 5–47). Hillsdale, NJ: Erlbaum.

Wagner, A. R., & Brandon, S. E. (1989). Evolution of a structured connectionist model of Pavlovian conditioning (AESOP). In S. B. Klein & R. R. Mowrer (Eds.), *Contemporary learning theories: Pavlovian conditioning and the status of traditional learning theory* (pp. 149–189). Hillsdale, NJ: Erlbaum.

Wagner, A. R., & Brandon, S. E. (2001). A componential theory of Pavlovian conditioning. In R. R. Mowrer & S. B. Klein (Eds.), *Handbook of contemporary learning theories* (pp. 23–64). Mahwah, NJ: Erlbaum.

Woodbury, C. B. (1943). The learning of stimulus patterns by dogs. *Journal of Comparative Psychology, 35,* 29–40.

Zentall, T. R., & Hogan, D. E. (1975). Key pecking in pigeons produced by pairing keylight with inaccessible grain. *Journal of the Experimental Analysis of Behavior, 23,* 199–206.

CHAPTER 2

Learning

Laws and Models of Basic Conditioning

RALPH MILLER AND MARTHA ESCOBAR

INTRODUCTION AND HISTORY

In the second edition of *Stevens' Handbook of Experimental Psychology,* Eliot Hearst (1988) provided an excellent detailed review of the fundamentals of conditioning and learning (for an older but even more comprehensive review, see Mackintosh, 1974). As there have been few changes in at least the fundamentals since that time and because Hearst did such a fine job, the present chapter is not centrally an update of Hearst's chapter, although some new findings are discussed. Rather, it is meant to complement Hearst's chapter by presenting some of the same material, but organized in a very different way that we hope will provide new insights into the nature of basic learning.

Ecological niches change over time, usually creating conditions that are less hospitable to current life-forms than are those that existed prior to the change. The earliest life-forms adjusted to these changes exclusively through mechanisms now collectively called evolution. Importantly, evolution improves a genetic lineage's functionality (i.e.,

its biological fitness, which is usually measured in terms of reproductive success) across generations, but it does nothing to enhance directly an organism's accommodation of changes in the environment within the organism's life span. However, animals did *evolve* a mechanism to improve their fit to their immediate ecological niche within each animal's life span (a capability clearly more advantageous to long-lived animals). Specifically, animals evolved the potential to modify their behavior as a consequence of experienced relationships between events, with events here including both their own behavior (i.e., responses) and events other than their own behavior (i.e., stimuli). Changing one's behavior as a function of prior experience is what we mean by conditioning and learning (used here synonymously). The acquired behavioral changes frequently appear to be preparatory for an impending, often biologically significant event that is contingent on (i.e., signaled by) immediately preceding stimuli. Animals seem to be able to use these stimuli as signals for the impending biologically significant event, and the behavioral changes serve to modify or cope with this event in an adaptive way.

In principle, there are many possible sets of rules by which an organism might modify

Parts of this chapter are based on R. Miller and Grace (2002). Manuscript preparation was supported by NIMH Grant 33881. The authors thank Francisco Arcediano, Raymond Chang, Randolph C. Grace, and Steven Stout for their critique of a draft of the manuscript.

its behavior to increase its biological fitness (preparing for and modifying impending events) as a result of prior exposure to specific event contingencies. However, animals are seen to use only a few of these sets of rules; these constitute what we call *biological intelligence*. Researchers who examine all possible sets of rules without regard for their occurrence in nature are said to be studying *artificial intelligence*. Here we summarize, at a psychological level of analysis, the basic principles of elementary biological intelligence: conditioning and elementary learning. Research has identified a set of rules, so-called *laws of learning,* that appear to apply quite broadly across many species, including humans. Moreover, these laws appear to apply across motivational systems and tasks, with only adjustments of parameters being required (e.g., Domjan, 1983; Logue, 1979). Indeed, as we look at more complex behavior, differences between species and between tasks become greater; however, we view these differences as reflecting interactions of the differing parameters mentioned earlier. That is, complex behaviors are built presumably with the process that underlies simple behaviors, and multiplication of parametric differences produces greater differences as the behavior in question becomes more complex. For example, after identical training experience, humans as well as dogs readily exhibit conditioned salivation or conditioned fear, whereas social behaviors differ far more between these species. However, the rules underlying acquisition and expression of these highly different behaviors appear to be the same. (Of course, we must recognize that some behaviors are specific to certain species, for example, language in humans and species-specific song in birds; these behaviors reflect strong predispositions that do not necessary depend on specific experience, as discussed later.)

Learning is the intervening process that mediates between an environmental experience and a change in behavior. More precisely, *learning* is ordinarily defined as a relatively permanent change in an organism's response potential, which results from experience, that (a) is under the control of the specific stimuli (or similar stimuli) that were present during the experience and (b) cannot be attributed to changes in receptors or effectors. The term *response potential* allows for learning that is not immediately expressed in behavior (i.e., latent learning), and the requirement that a stimulus from the training experience be present when the behavior is exhibited suggests that learning is a stimulus-specific phenomenon rather than a global change in behavior. Presumably, more complex changes in behavior are built from a constellation of elementary learned relationships (hereafter called *associations*), just as a house can be created through an assembly of many bricks.

Interest in the analysis of basic learning began over 100 years ago and has roots in several different controversies. Among these controversies was the dispute between *empiricism,* advanced in the 18th and 19th centuries by British empiricist philosophers such as David Hume and John Stuart Mill (whose orientation reaches back to Aristotle), and *rationalism,* advanced by philosophers such as Rene Descartes and Immanuel Kant (whose orientation reaches back at least as far as Plato). The empiricists assumed that knowledge about the world is acquired solely through experience with events in the external world, which result in both *mental representations* of these events and *associations* between representations of contiguous events. Through these associations, presentation of one event was assumed to activate the mental representations of associated events. In contrast, rationalists argued that *basic* knowledge (e.g., the dimensionality of space and the principle of causal relationship) is inborn and that experience merely provides the specifics that apply to this framework. Studies of learning were performed in part to determine the degree to which experience could modify representations of the world (and consequently behavior). Demonstrations of behavioral plasticity as a function of experience appeared to be more congruent with the empiricist position; however, the rationalists never denied that experience influenced knowledge and behavior. They simply asserted that most knowledge arises from within the organism, rather than directly from the experiencing of events; these innate principles (e.g., syntactic rules, the three-dimensionality of the space we inhabit) organize and make intelligible our sensory experience. Today, this controversy (reflected in more modern terms as part of the nature vs. nurture debate) has faded because of the realization that experience provides the content of knowledge about the world, but extracting relationships between events from experience requires a nervous system that is predisposed to extract these relationships. *Predispositions* to extract preferentially certain aspects from experience and encode (i.e., learn) preferentially certain relationships between events, although strongly modulated during development by experience, are surely influenced by genetic makeup (see Chap. 6, this volume). Hence, acquired knowledge, as revealed through a change in behavior, undoubtedly reflects an interaction of genes (rationalism/nature) and experience (empiricism/nurture).

A second controversy that motivated studies of learning was a desire to understand whether acquired thought and behavior could be better characterized by *mechanism,* which viewed the organism as a biological machine in which simple laws of learning operated, or by *mentalism,* which attributed to the organism some sort of conscious control of its thought and behavior. The experimental study of learning that began in the early 20th century was partly a reaction to the extreme mentalism implicit in the introspective approach to psy-

chology that prevailed until that time (Watson, 1913). Mechanism provided a more objective approach that was widely accepted as providing a compelling account of simple reflexes. However, the doctrine was not as compelling when accounting for behaviors that were more complex and seemingly volitional. Mechanism has been attacked for ignoring the (arguably obvious) active role of the organism in determining its behavior, whereas mentalism has been attacked for passing the problem of explaining behavior to some sort of homunculus (i.e., little person) residing within the organism. Mentalism starts out with a strong advantage in this dispute because human society, culture, and religion are all predicated on the assumption that people are free agents who have active (as opposed to passive) mental lives and are able to determine and control their behavior. In contrast, most traditional theoretical accounts of basic learning (Tolman, e.g., 1932, being a notable exception) are mechanistic and try to account for acquired behavior uniquely in terms of (a) past experience that is encoded in neural representations, (b) present stimulation, and (c) genetic predispositions (today, at least); notably, this list excludes any role for free will. To some degree, the mechanism/mentalism controversy has been confounded with level of analysis: Mechanistic accounts of learning tend to be more molecular, usually interested in simple behaviors, and mentalistic accounts tend to be more molar, often interested in complex behaviors. Obviously, different levels of analysis may be complementary, rather than contradictory, and mental experience (thoughts) may be an emergent consequence of a complex network of mechanistic associations.

A third controversy that stimulated interest in learning was the relationship of humans to other species. Human culture and religion have traditionally treated humans as superior to nonhuman animals on many dimensions. However, at the end of the 19th century, acceptance of Darwin's theory of evolution by natural selection challenged the uniqueness of humans. Defenders of tradition looked at learning capacity as a demonstration of the superiority of humans over animals, whereas Darwinians looked to basic learning to demonstrate (qualitative if not quantitative) continuity across species. A century of research has taught us that although species do differ appreciably in behavioral plasticity, a common set of laws of learning appears, with parametric adjustment, to apply at least across all warm-blooded animals (Domjan, 1983). Moreover, these parametric adjustments do not always reflect a greater learning capacity in humans than in other species. As a result of species-specific genes working in concert with species-specific experience during maturation, each species is adept at addressing the tasks that the environment commonly presents to that particular species in its ecological niche. For example, Clark's nutcrackers (birds that cache food) are able to remember where they have stored thousands of edible items (Kamil & Clements, 1990), a performance that humans would be hard pressed to match.

A fourth factor that stimulated an interest in the study of basic learning was a practical one. Researchers such as Thorndike (1949) and Guthrie (1938) were particularly concerned with identifying principles that might be applied in schools and toward other societal needs. Surely this goal has been fulfilled at least in part, as can be seen, for example, in contemporary application of procedures derived from the experimental study of learning to educational settings, behavior modification in clinical situations, drug testing, and advertising.

The question of whether humans and animals differed qualitatively in the ways in which they processed information (the third factor listed earlier) required that nonhuman animals be studied, but in principle the other questions did not. However, animal subjects were widely favored for two reasons. First, the behavior of nonhuman subjects was assumed by some researchers to be governed by the same basic laws that apply to human behavior, but in a simpler form that made these laws more readily observable. A problem with this approach is that although almost all researchers today accept the assumption of evolutionary continuity, research has demonstrated that the behavior of nonhumans is often far from simple. The second reason for studying learning in animals has fared better. When seeking general laws of learning (with its focus on commonalities across individuals), individual differences are an undesirable source of noise in the data. The use of animals permits greater efforts to minimize irrelevant differences in genes and prior experience, thereby reducing individual differences, than is ethically or practically possible with humans.

The study of learning in animals within simple situations in which two stimuli came to become associated had many parallels with the study of simple associative verbal learning in humans that was prevalent from the 1880s to the 1960s. The so-called cognitive revolution that began in the 1960s largely ended such research with humans and caused the study of basic learning in animals to be viewed by some as irrelevant to our understanding of human learning. The cognitive revolution was driven mainly by (a) a shift from trying to understand behavior with the assistance of hypothetical mental processes (preferably as few as possible) to trying to understand (often complex) mental processes through the study of behavior and (b) the view that the simple tasks that were being studied until that time told us little about the complex learning and memory observed outside of the laboratory in the real world (i.e., lacked ecological validity). However, many of today's cognitive psychologists have returned to constructs that were initially developed by students of basic learning before the advent of cognitive psychology (e.g., Horgan & Tienson, 1996; McClelland, 1988). There is still controversy about whether complex behavior in natural situations can be understood better by reducing the behavior into components that obey the laws of basic learning, or whether a more molar approach will be more successful; both approaches have their benefits and drawbacks. Clearly, the approach of this chapter is reductionist. For example, when we speak of *expectations,* we do not imply that we do something because of its future consequences (which would be a violation of the temporal order of causality). Rather, in our view expectations are representations of past relationships between behavior and its consequences, which make a behavior more likely to be emitted again under similar circumstances (without necessarily implying that the organism has knowledge about future consequences, introspection notwithstanding). With respect to ecological validity, the concern is a serious one. However, there are many instances in which the laws of basic learning, originally identified in the confines of the sterile laboratory, have been successfully applied to quasi-naturalistic studies of functional behaviors. For example, Domjan has demonstrated how Pavlovian conditioning improves the reproductive success of Japanese quail (reviewed in Domjan, Blesbois, & Williams, 1998; Domjan & Hollis, 1988); Kamil has shown how the laws of learning facilitate the feeding systems of different species of birds (reviewed in Kamil, 1983); and Timberlake has demonstrated how different spatiotemporal components of foraging behavior are organized, each subject to the basic laws of learning (reviewed in Timberlake & Lucas, 1989).

This chapter focuses on the conditions that favor the occurrence and expression of elementary learning, rather than its function. But one must never forget that the capacity for learning evolved because it enhances an animal's biological fitness (e.g., see Shettleworth, 1998). The vast majority of instances of learning are clearly functional. However, there are many documented cases in which specific instances of learned behavior are detrimental to the biological fitness of an organism. Typically, these arise in situations with imposed contingencies that are contrary to those that prevail in the animal's natural habitat (i.e., contrary to unlearned predispositions; e.g., Breland & Breland, 1961; D. Williams & Williams, 1969) or inconsistent with its past experience (i.e., contrary to prior learning; e.g., vicious circle behavior, Gwinn, 1949). Although behavior in these circumstances reflects the prior (ancestral or experiential) history of the organism, it is dysfunctional in the current circumstances. Better understanding of the circumstances under which learning results in dysfunctional behavior will contribute to designing improved forms of behavior therapy.

This chapter selectively reviews only the most basic findings concerning elementary learning. For purposes of illustration, our examples are couched in the cue-outcome language of Pavlovian conditioning (i.e., stimulus-stimulus learning, which refers to cues and outcomes, respectively) largely with nonhuman subjects. As we later conclude, however, the parallels between Pavlovian conditioning and instrumental learning (i.e., stimulus-response or response-outcome learning) are so great as to lead one to think that organisms store and link representations of events, regardless of whether the events are stimuli or responses. However, for reasons originating with the views of Skinner (1938), the study of instrumental learning has been both less theoretically driven than has the study of Pavlovian conditioning and highly focused on exploring changes in rate of responding as a function of reinforcement schedule (see Zeiler, 1977, 1984) and more recently on choice behavior (see Davison & McCarthy, 1988). We do not here describe the various tasks that have traditionally been used to study learning; however, an excellent review of them is provided by Hearst (1988).

EMPIRICAL LAWS OF CONDITIONING AND LEARNING

Given appropriate experience, a stimulus will come to elicit behavior that is not characteristic of responding to that stimulus but is characteristic for a second stimulus (hereafter called an *outcome*). For example, in Pavlov's (1927) classic studies, dogs salivated at the sound of a bell if previously the bell had been rung before food was presented. That is, the bell acquired *stimulus control* over the dogs' salivation, which is an initial (i.e., unconditioned) response to food seen prior to training. Because the salivation response to the bell presentation is conditional on its prior pairing with the food, the bell is called a conditioned stimulus (CS), and salivation to the bell's presentation is known as a conditioned (or conditional) response. In contrast, food (which unconditionally produces salivation) is called an unconditioned stimulus (US). In this section, we summarize the empirical relationships between stimuli that promote such acquired responding. For a review of (learned) changes in the unconditioned response to a single stimulus as a function of repeated exposures to it (i.e., *habituation*), see Groves and Thompson (1970), Hearst (1988), and Thompson and Spencer (1966).

Phenomena Involving a Single Cue and Single Outcome

Factors Influencing Acquisition of Stimulus Control of Behavior

Stimulus Salience.   The rate at which behavioral control by a CS (also known as cue or signal) is achieved (in terms of number of pairings with the unconditioned stimulus) and the asymptote of control attained by that CS are both positively related to the *salience* of both the CS (cue) and the outcome (e.g., Kamin, 1965). Salience as used here refers to a composite of stimulus attributes, such as intensity, size, contrast with background, motion, and stimulus change, among others. Salience is a function not only of the physical stimulus but also of the state of the subject (e.g., food is more salient to a hungry than to a sated person). Ordinarily, the salience of a cue has greater influence on the rate at which stimulus control of behavior develops (as a function of number of CS-US pairings; for a review, see Kamin, 1965), whereas the salience of the outcome has greater influence on the ultimate level of stimulus control that is reached over many trials (i.e., asymptotic level of conditioned responding; Kimble, 1955). The hybrid construct of salience as used here has much in common with *attention,* but we avoid that term because of its additional implications (attention has been used to refer to things other than salience—specifically, to certain cognitive processes occurring within the subject). Stimulus salience is not only important during training; conditioned responding is also directly influenced by the salience of the test stimulus, a point long ago noted by Hull (1952).

Predispositions (Genetic and Experiential).   The *salience* (sometimes equated to *associability*) of a specific cue refers to the ease with which that cue will come to control behavior as a result of its being paired with an outcome. By definition, salience is a function of the perceived attributes of the cue, independent of the nature of the outcome with which it is paired. Similarly, the salience (or associability) of a specific outcome refers to the ease with which a subject will come to respond to a cue as a result of its being paired with this outcome. Again, by definition, it is a function of the perceived attributes of the outcome, independent of the nature of the cue. Obviously, saliencies of the cue and outcome depend not only on the physical stimuli, but on the state of the subject (i.e., *predispositions* to perceive the specific stimuli and encode relationships concerning them). This common assumption, that each stimulus (cue and outcome) has its own independent salience, ignores the now well-established finding that rate of development of behavioral control is also a function of a predisposition to associate these two specific stimuli. That is, the rapidity with which behavioral control develops and the asymptote of control achieved not only is influenced by the subject's predispositions unique to the cue and by predispositions unique to the outcome, but also is strongly influenced by the subject's predisposition to associate this particular cue with this particular outcome. Garcia and Koelling (1966) provided the best know example of this predisposition to certain cue-outcome associations. In their experiment, thirsty rats were given access to flavored water that was accompanied by sound and light stimuli whenever drinking occurred. For half the animals, drinking was immediately followed by foot shock, whereas for the other half drinking was followed by an agent that induced gastric distress. Although all subjects received the same audiovisual + flavor compound cue, the subjects that received the footshock outcome subsequently exhibited greater avoidance of the audiovisual cues than of the flavor, whereas the subjects that received the gastric distress exhibited greater avoidance of the flavor than of the audiovisual cues. These so-called *cue-to-consequence* (or *belongingness*) *effects* cannot be explained in terms of the relative saliencies of the cues or the relative saliencies of the outcomes. Although Garcia and Koelling interpreted these observations in terms of genetic predispositions re-

flecting the importance both of flavor cues with respect to gastric consequences and of audiovisual cues with respect to cutaneous consequences, later research suggested that pretraining experience interacts with genetic factors in creating predispositions that allow stimulus control to develop more rapidly for some stimulus dyads than for others (e.g., Dalrymple & Galef, 1981). Thus, subjects' predispositions that are specific for the unique cue-outcome dyad join with their predispositions that are unique for the cue and unique for the outcome, and each of these predispositions is influenced by genetic and experiential factors.

Similarity (Including Spatiotemporal Contiguity). Stimulus control of acquired behavior by a cue is a strong direct function of the cue's proximity to an outcome in space (Rescorla & Cunningham, 1979) and time (Pavlov, 1927). Contiguity is so powerful a factor that some researchers have suggested that it is the central determinant of acquiring associations (or at least associative learning; e.g., Estes, 1950; Guthrie, 1935). However, several conditioning phenomena appear to violate this *law of contiguity*. Violations are of two types: failures to obtain stimulus control with contiguity and occurrences of stimulus control without contiguity. (The second type of violation is discussed in the section titled "Mediation.") One frequently cited failure of the first type is stimulus competition, in which a target cue paired with an outcome acquires less control of behavior if a second cue is present during the target cue-outcome pairings; however, stimulus competition appears to be an independent law (discussed later) that applies to behavioral control in addition to the law of contiguity.

A more challenging problem for the law of contiguity arises from the observation that simultaneous presentation of a cue and outcome results in weaker conditioned responding to the cue than when the cue slightly precedes the outcome. However, this *simultaneous conditioning deficit* has now been recognized as reflecting a failure to express information acquired during simultaneous pairings rather than a failure to encode the simultaneous relationship. As mentioned earlier, most conditioned responses are *anticipatory* of an outcome, and it is usually of little advantage to the organism to display an anticipatory response for an outcome that is already present. For example, Matzel, Held, and Miller (1988) demonstrated that simultaneous pairings do in fact result in robust learning, but that this information is behaviorally expressed only if an assessment procedure sensitive to simultaneous pairings is used. In their experiment, rats were first repeatedly exposed to Cue A leading to Cue B; then Cue B was presented simultaneously with a footshock outcome. When responding was assessed, Cue B elicited little fear (i.e., the simultaneous conditioning deficit), but Cue A (which served as an anticipatory signal for Cue B) elicited a strong fear response. Appropriate control groups demonstrated that responding to Cue A depended on Cue B's being paired with the outcome, despite the B-outcome association's being behaviorally silent in a direct test with Cue B. These results suggest that the rats had learned the simultaneous relationship between Cue B and the outcome, but they behaviorally expressed this learning only when a situation was created in which an anticipatory response was functional. Related to the simultaneous conditioning deficit is the asymmetry in behavioral control achieved with otherwise equivalent forward-paired (cue→outcome) and backward-paired (outcome→cue) events. Forward-paired cues become excitatory CSs that elicit conditioned responding, which increases with additional trials until a response asymptote is reached. In contrast, backward-paired cues become excitatory with few pairings and subsequently become inhibitory (i.e.,

in some sense a signal for the omission of the outcome; discussed later) with more backward pairings (Heth, 1976; discussed later). Thus, backward conditioning is not ineffectual relative to forward conditioning, but different behaviors are likely to result from the two situations. Again, the backward conditioning deficit appears to reflect the functional characteristics of acquired behavior. Anticipatory fear responses are functional only in situations in which the occurrence of shock can be predicted with some accuracy, a condition that is not met in the backward conditioning case. Later, we discuss the biphasic responding observed as a function of trials with backward conditioning.

A second challenge to the law of contiguity has been based on the observation that conditioned taste aversion training (i.e., flavor-internal malaise pairings) can yield stimulus control (i.e., aversion to the flavor) even when cues (flavor) and outcome (internal malaise) are separated by hours (e.g., Garcia, Ervin, & Koelling, 1966). However, even with conditioned taste aversions, stimulus control decreases as the interval between the flavor and internal malaise (the so-called interstimulus interval) increases. The only difference between conditioned taste aversion and other conditioning preparations is the rate at which stimulus control decreases as the interstimulus interval in training increases. Thus, conditioned taste aversion is merely a parametric variation of the law of contiguity, not a violation of it.

A third challenge to the law of contiguity that is not as readily dismissed is based on the observation that an increase in the interstimulus interval has less of a decremental effect on conditioned responding if the interval between outcomes (i.e., intertrial interval) is correspondingly increased. That is, stimulus control superficially appears to depend not as much on the absolute interval between a cue and an outcome (i.e., temporal proximity of the cue and outcome which we hereafter call absolute temporal contiguity) as on the comparison (ratio) of the cue-outcome interval to the interval between outcomes (i.e., relative contiguity; e.g., Gibbon, Baldock, Locurto, Gold, & Terrace, 1977). One might say that the cue and outcome are treated as being closer to one another if presentations of the outcome are farther apart. By relative contiguity of a cue and an outcome, we are referring to the inverse impact that the absolute contiguity of other cues (discrete and contextual present during target training) and the outcome have on the effectiveness of (absolute) contiguity of the target cue and outcome on stimulus control of behavior. That is, behavioral control by a target cue decreases as the contiguity of other (discrete or contextual) cues with the outcome increases; behavioral control by the target cue increases with increasing presentations of these competing cues far removed from the outcome (e.g., during the intertrial interval). One well-known manifestation of the impact of relative contiguity on responding is the *trial-spacing effect,* in which spaced trials yield better stimulus control of behavior than do massed trials, despite identical target cue-outcome contiguity. In the case of massed trials, both the cue and the context have relatively high contiguity with the outcome; thus, the context reduces the relative cue-outcome contiguity. In the case of spaced trials, the context-outcome contiguity is lower; hence, the relative cue-outcome contiguity more closely approximates the absolute cue-outcome contiguity. Consequently, rather than treat this relativity as a qualifier to the law of contiguity, it might be viewed as a direct result of the empirical law of cue competition (discussed later), which influences behavior orthogonally to contiguity. (A further challenge to the law of contiguity is discussed in the section titled "Mediation.")

According to the British empiricist philosophers, associations between events were more readily formed when the events were similar (Berkeley, 1710/1946). More recently, well-controlled experiments have confirmed that development of stimulus control is facilitated if paired cues and outcome are made more similar (e.g., Rescorla & Furrow, 1977). The neural representations of paired stimuli seemingly include many attributes of the stimuli, including their temporal and spatial locations. This is evident in the fact that conditioned responding reflects an *expectation* not only of a specific outcome but also of the outcome's occurring at a specific time and place (e.g., Chaps. 8 and 9, this volume; Saint Paul, 1982; Savastano & Miller, 1998). If temporal and spatial coordinates are viewed as stimulus attributes, *contiguity* can be viewed as *similarity* on the temporal and spatial dimensions, thereby subsuming spatiotemporal contiguity within a general construct of similarity. Thus, the *law of similarity* appears to be able to encompass the law of contiguity.

Objective Contingency. Ordinarily, when a cue is consistently followed by an outcome and these pairings are separated by intertrial intervals in which neither the cue nor the outcome occurs, the cue comes to control behavior over repeated trials. However, when cues or outcomes sometimes occur by themselves during the training sessions, conditioned responding to the cue is often slower to develop (measured in number of cue-outcome pairings required to observe asymptotic behavior; e.g., Fitzgerald, 1963) and is asymptotically weaker (e.g., Rescorla, 1968). *Contingency* refers to the probability that the cue and outcome occur together, compared to the probability that these events occur separately. Behavioral control is, in most cases, a positive function of the cue-outcome contingency.

Let us assume the existence of a cue and an outcome, each of which on any given trial can be either present or absent (i.e., dichotomous

Table 2.1   2 × 2 Contingency Table for a Dichotomous Cue (e.g., CS or Cause) and a Dichotomous Outcome (e.g., US or Effect).

	Outcome Present	Outcome Absent
Cue present	Type 1 (a)	Type 2 (b)
Cue absent	Type 3 (c)	Type 4 (d)

NOTE: a, b, c, and d are the frequencies of trial Types 1, 2, 3, and 4. See text for details.

variables). If the entire training session is segmented into trials, there are four possibilities for these events on each trial, as shown in Table 2.1: (1) cue-outcome, (2) cue-no outcome, (3) no cue-outcome, and (4) no cue-no outcome, where a, b, c, and d are the frequencies (number) of trials of Type 1, 2, 3, and 4, respectively. The objective contingency is usually defined in terms of the difference in conditional probabilities of the outcome occurring in the presence of the cue (p[O | C], calculated as a/[a + b]) and in the absence of the cue (p[O | ∼C], calculated as c/[c + d]). If the conditional probability of the outcome in the presence of the cue, p(O | C), is greater than in the absence of the cue, p(O | ∼C), the contingency is positive; conversely, if the conditional probability of the outcome is less in the presence than in the absence of the cue, the contingency is negative. Contingency is measured in terms of statistical probabilities, and probably the most widely used metric is that known as Δp, which is equal to p[O | C] − p[O | ∼C] (in terms of the Table 2.1 event frequencies, a/[a + b] − c/[c + d]). As is apparent from this formulation, contingency increases with the occurrence of a- and d-type trials and decreases with the occurrence of b- and c-type trials. Positive contingencies are associated with excitatory responding (i.e., seemingly reflecting expectation of occurrence of the outcome), whereas negative contingencies are associated with behavior indicative of conditioned inhibition (i.e., seemingly reflecting expec-

tations of outcome omission, as discussed later).

Empirically, the four types of trials are seen to have unequal influence on stimulus control; Type 1 (cue-outcome) trials have the greatest impact, and Type 4 (no cue-no outcome) trials have the least impact. This issue has been studied mostly in human causality judgments, in which an experimental situation that has the four trial types presented in Table 2.1 is created. A typical situation might involve the subject imagining a situation in which taking a fictitious medicine produces a fictitious side effect. Over reiterative trials, Type 1 trials are defined by taking the medicine and developing the side effect, Type 2 trials by taking the medicine without developing the side effect, Type 3 trials by not taking the medicine and developing the side effect, and Type 4 trials by neither taking the medicine nor developing the side effect. In such a situation, perceived contingency has been observed to change most with occurrences of Type 1 trials and least with the occurrence of Type 4 trials (e.g., Wasserman, Elek, Chatlosh, & Baker, 1993). Note that although we previously described the frequently observed beneficial effects on stimulus control of spaced over massed cue-outcome pairings as a qualifier of contiguity, such trial-spacing effects are readily subsumed under objective contingency because long intertrial intervals are effectively Type 4 trials, provided that these intertrial intervals occur in the training context (time outside the training context does not appear to contribute to the frequency of Type 4 trials). Thus, acceptance of the law of contingency obviates the need to qualify the law of contiguity to accommodate the trial-spacing effect.

Conditioned responding can be attenuated by presenting the cue alone before the cue-outcome pairings, intermingled with the pairings, or after the pairings. If the cue-alone presentations occur before the pairings, the attenuation is called the *CS-preexposure effect* (or *latent inhibition*; Lubow & Moore, 1959); if they occur during the pairings, the attenuation (in conjunction with the pairings) is described as a consequence of *partial reinforcement* (Pavlov, 1927); and if they occur after the pairings, the attenuation is called *extinction* (Pavlov, 1927). Notably, the operations that produce the CS-preexposure effect and habituation (i.e., repeated presentations of a single stimulus) are identical; the difference between the two phenomena is the behavior that is subsequently assessed. Habituation is assessed in terms of a reduction of unconditioned responding to the cue as a result of multiple cue-alone presentations, whereas the CS-preexposure effect is assessed in terms of a diminution in conditioned responding (the topology of which is determined largely by the unconditioned stimulus) to the cue during cue-outcome pairings that follow the multiple cue-alone presentations. To exemplify the difference between habituation and the CS-preexposure effect, imagine that you are having dinner at your parents' house. When you first sit down at the table, you can hear their old clock ticking very loudly; after a few minutes, however, you do not notice the clock's ticks anymore. That is, you have habituated to the sound of the clock. Now imagine that for dinner your mother cooks your favorite meal. The next day you suffer from food poisoning. Most likely, you will not attribute the food poisoning (outcome) to your favorite meal (cue) because previously you repeatedly ate it (i.e., you were exposed to it) without feeling sick (i.e., cue-no outcome exposures). At a more theoretical level, Hall (1991) has argued that habituation and the CS-preexposure effect arise from different underlying processes, due to the observation that these phenomena are doubly dissociable (i.e., a manipulation increases one of the two phenomena more than the other, whereas a second manipulation increases the other phenomenon

more than the first). The first dissociation discussed by Hall is context dependence. In the case of the CS-preexposure effect, a cue is repeatedly presented alone; then, when it is paired with an outcome, behavioral control by that cue develops slower than if the preexposure treatment had not occurred. However, if the cue-outcome pairings are given in a context different from the preexposure treatment, the retardation of behavioral control by the cue is greatly reduced. In contrast, habituation shows little context dependence; a cue habituated in one context will continue to produce little unconditioned responding in a new context. The second dissociation discussed by Hall is the effect of retention intervals. In the case of habituation, repeated exposures to the cue have much less of an effect if a long time interval is imposed between exposure to the cue and testing. In contrast, the CS-preexposure deficit is less affected by the imposition of intervals between preexposure and testing (and is sometimes actually enhanced; de la Casa & Lubow, 2000).

Conditioned responding can also be attenuated by presenting the outcome alone before the cue-outcome pairings, intermingled with the pairings, or after the pairings. If the outcome-alone presentations occur before the pairings, the attenuation is called the *US-preexposure effect* (Randich & LoLordo, 1979a, 1979b); if they occur during the pairings, the attenuation is called the *degraded contingency effect* (in the narrow sense, as any presentation of the cue or outcome alone degrades the objective contingency; Rescorla, 1968); and if they occur after the pairings, it is an instance of what is called *retrospective revaluation* (e.g., Denniston, Miller, & Matute, 1996). The retrospective revaluation effect has proven far more elusive than the other five means of attenuating excitatory conditioned responding through degraded contingency (e.g., Schweitzer & Green, 1982), but it occurs at least under select conditions

Table 2.2   Schematic Representation of Contingency-Degrading Procedures.

Procedure	Training
CS-preexposure	Cue-no outcome; then cue-outcome
Partial reinforcement	Cue-outcome intermixed with cue-no outcome
Extinction	Cue-outcome; then cue-no outcome
US preexposure	Outcome alone; then cue-outcome
Degraded contingency	Cue-outcome intermixed with outcome-alone
Retrospective revaluation	Cue-outcome; then outcome-alone

NOTE: The cue-outcome pairings that would normally result in conditioned responding are less effective in making the cue acquire behavioral control due to the cue-no outcome or outcome-alone trials. See text for details.

(e.g., R. Miller & Matute, 1996). Table 2.2 presents a summary of the different types of contingency-degrading treatments.

If compounded, these different types of contingency-degrading treatments have a cumulative effect on conditioned responding that is at least summative (Bonardi & Hall, 1996) and possibly greater than summative (Bennett, Wills, Oakeshott, & Mackintosh, 2000). A prime example of such a compound contingency-degrading treatment is *learned irrelevance* treatment, in which cue and outcome presentations that are truly random with respect to one another precede a series of cue-outcome pairings (Baker & Mackintosh, 1977). This pretraining treatment has a decremental effect on conditioned responding greater than either CS preexposure or US preexposure.

Contingency effects on responding are not uniquely a function of the frequency of different types of trials depicted in Table 2.1. Two important factors that also influence contingency effects are trial order and modulatory stimuli. When contingency-degrading Type 2 (cue-no outcome) and 3 (no cue-outcome) trials are administered in phases (rather than interspersed with Type 1 cue-outcome pairings), recency effects are pronounced. *Recency* refers to fact that trials that occur closest to testing have a relatively greater impact on responding. As the name suggests, such effects ordinarily fade with increasing retention intervals (however, one must not forget that the mere passage of time in long retention intervals is almost always confounded with an increasing number of intervening events). Additionally, if stimuli are present either during the cue-outcome pairings or the contingency-degrading (cue-alone or outcome-alone) treatments, presentation of these stimuli immediately prior to or during testing with the target cue causes conditioned responding to reflect better the events that occurred proximally to these stimuli (either the cue-outcome pairings or the contingency-degrading pairings). These *modulatory stimuli* can be either contextual stimuli (i.e., the static environmental cues present during training) or discrete stimuli. The so-called *renewal effect* (Bouton & Bolles, 1979) is an example of modulation by contextual stimuli. Renewal refers to the reoccurrence of a conditioned response produced by cue-outcome pairings after it has been experimentally extinguished (i.e., the cue-outcome contingency has been degraded by posttraining presentation of the cue alone). That is, extinction is observed to be specific to the context in which the extinction treatment occurred. For example, a man who has acquired a fear of dogs (cue) after having been bitten by the neighbor's dog (outcome) can be brought to tolerate dogs in the therapist's office by repeated interactions with dogs or dog-related stimuli (extinction). However, the fear might return when the man leaves the therapist's office and particularly in his neighbor's house (renewal). Similarly, discrete stimuli can modulate responding after extinction. In the previous example, the therapist may provide the man during extinction treatment with a certain object that he associates with the therapy sessions and then carries with him to activate the memory of therapy, thereby impeding renewal (for an experimental demonstration, see, e.g., Brooks & Bouton, 1993). Modulatory stimuli appear to have much in common with priming cues frequently used in cognitive research (e.g., Neely, 1977). For example, after learning two lists of words (e.g., one of fruits and the other of animals), presenting one of the components of one of the lists (e.g., orange) will facilitate retrieval of members of its list (e.g., banana) but will impair retrieval of members of the other list (e.g., dog).

Modulatory effects can be obtained even when the cue-outcome pairings are interspersed with the contingency-degrading events. For example, if Cue A always precedes pairings of Cue X and an outcome and does not precede presentations of Cue X alone, subjects will come to respond to X if and only if it is preceded by A; this effect is called *positive occasion setting* (or a feature-positive discrimination; Holland, 1983a). If A only precedes the X-alone presentations, subjects will come to respond to X only when it has not been preceded by A; this effect is called *negative occasion setting* (or a feature-negative discrimination). In other words, subjects behave as if the ambiguity concerning the occurrence of the outcome that is posed by partial reinforcement is resolved by the occasion setter (for further discussion of occasion setting, Chap. 1, this volume). Take, for example, the case of a woman who is afraid of being in a dark place during thunderstorms. If the woman has no fear of darkness at any other time, we can conclude that thunderstorms act as positive occasion setters for such fear. Now imagine that the woman feels no fear of darkness during thunderstorms if her husband is with her. We then can conclude that the husband acts as a negative occasion setter of fear during the thunderstorm situation. Surprisingly, behavioral modulation of conditioned responding by contexts that are present only on reinforced (or only on nonreinforced) tri-als appears to be acquired in far fewer trials than when the modulatory stimulus is a discrete cue, perhaps reflecting the important role that contextual modulation of behavior plays in the ecological niche of each species.

The attenuation of stimulus control through contingency-degrading events is often at least partially reversible without further cue-outcome pairings. This is most evident in the case of extinction, for which *spontaneous recovery* from extinction (i.e., a partial return of the conditioned response as time elapses after extinction treatment) and *external disinhibition* (i.e., temporary recovery of conditioned responding as a result of presenting an unrelated intense stimulus immediately prior to the extinguished test stimulus) are examples of restoration of behavioral control without the occurrence of further cue-outcome pairings (e.g., Pavlov, 1927). Similarly, spontaneous recovery from the CS-preexposure effect has been reported under select conditions (e.g., Kraemer, Randall, & Carbary, 1991). These phenomena suggest that the pairings of cue and outcome are encoded independent of the contingency-degrading events, but the behavioral expression of information concerning the pairings can be suppressed by additional learning during the contingency-degrading events.

Cue and Outcome Duration.   Cue and outcome durations have considerable impact on stimulus control of behavior. The effects are complex; generally speaking, however, increased cue or outcome duration reduces behavioral control, provided one controls for any changes in the value of the outcome due to its increased duration (i.e., increased hedonic value or habituation). What makes these variables complex is that different components of a stimulus can contribute differentially to stimulus control. The onset, presence, and termination of a cue can each influence behavior through its own relationship to the outcome.

This tendency toward fragmentation of behavioral control across different temporal components of a cue appears to increase with the length of the duration of the cue (e.g., Romaniuk & Williams, 2000). Similarly, the outcome can be fragmented with differential learning about each component, sometimes with surprising effects. For example, the termination of an aversive event is sometimes appetitive. Additionally, as an outcome is prolonged, its later components are further removed in time from the cue and presumably are less well associated to it.

Response Topology and Timing

The hallmark of conditioned responding is that the observed response to the cue reflects the nature of the outcome. For example, pigeons peck an illuminated key differently depending on whether the key cues delivery of food or water, and their manner of pecking is similar to that required to ingest the specific outcome (Jenkins & Moore, 1973). However, the nature of the cue also may qualitatively modulate the conditioned response. For instance, Holland (1977) has described how the conditioned responses to a light and to an auditory cue differ despite their having been paired with the same outcome.

Conditioned responding often closely resembles a diminished version of the subject's response to the unconditioned outcome (e.g., conditioned salivation with food as the outcome). Such a response topology is called *mimetic*. However, conditioned responding occasionally appears to be diametrically opposed to the unconditioned response (e.g., conditioned freezing with pain as the outcome, or a conditioned increase in pain sensitivity with delivery of morphine as the outcome; Siegel, 1989). Such a conditioned response topology is called *compensatory*. Even though there are many reports of both mimetic and compensatory conditioned responding, we are only beginning to understand when one or the other type of responding will occur (this is further discussed below).

Conditioned responding not only indicates that the cue and outcome have been paired but also reflects the spatial and temporal relationships that prevailed between the cue and outcome during those pairings (giving rise to the statement that subjects seemingly *anticipate* when and where the outcome will occur). If a cue has been paired with a rewarding outcome in a particular location, subjects are frequently observed to approach the location at which the outcome had been delivered (so-called *goal tracking*). For example, Burns and Domjan (1996) observed that Japanese quail, as part of their conditioned response to a signal for a potential mate, oriented to the location at which the mate had previously been introduced, independent of the subject's immediate location in the experimental apparatus. The temporal relationship between cue and outcome that existed in training is behaviorally evidenced in two ways. First, following training to a response asymptote, the conditioned response ordinarily is emitted just prior to the time at which the outcome would occur based on the prior pairings (Pavlov, 1927; see Chap. 9, this volume, for numerous examples of animal timing in instrumental situations). Second, the nature of the response often changes with different cue-outcome intervals. In some instances, when an outcome (e.g., food) occurs at regular intervals, during the intertrial interval subjects may emit a sequence of behaviors with a stereotypic temporal structure that is appropriate for that outcome in the species' ecological niche (e.g., Staddon & Simmelhag, 1970; Timberlake & Lucas, 1991).

Stimulus Generalization

No event is ever perceived exactly the same way twice because of continuous variation in both the environment and in one's nervous system. Thus, learning would be useless if

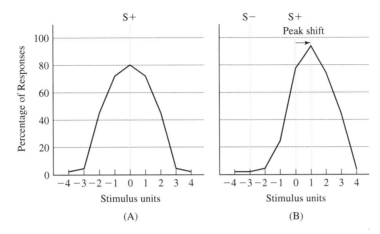

Figure 2.1   Hypothetical generalization gradients with a single stimulus (Panel A) and with two stimuli (differential reinforcement; Panel B).
NOTE: The x-axis represents values along a hypothetical stimulus dimension such as size. S+ represents the stimulus value reinforced during training, which for presentation purposes takes the value of zero stimulus units. S− represents the stimulus magnitude, which was not reinforced during discrimination training. The peak shift effect is evident in Panel B, in which the maximum response level is not observed to the training stimulus (S+), but in a different point along the stimulus dimension away from S−.

organisms did not generalize from stimuli encountered in training to test stimuli that are perceptually similar but not identical. Therefore, it is not surprising that conditioned responding is observed to decrease in an orderly fashion as the physical (and hence perceptual) difference between the training and test stimuli increases. This reduction in responding is called *stimulus generalization decrement*. Response magnitude or frequency plotted as a function of the physical similarity of the test stimulus to the training stimulus yields a symmetric curve that is called a *generalization gradient* (e.g., Guttman & Kalish, 1956). Gradients resulting from simple cue-outcome pairings can be made steeper by introducing trials with a second stimulus that is not paired with the outcome. Such *discrimination training* not only steepens the generalization gradient between the reinforced and nonreinforced stimuli but also often shifts the stimulus value at which maximum responding is observed from the reinforced cue in the direction away from the value of the nonreinforced stimulus (the so-called *peak shift;* e.g.,

Hanson, 1959; Weiss & Schindler, 1981). Figure 2.1 presents examples of hypothetical generalization gradients for training with a single stimulus (Panel A) and after discrimination training (Panel B). Note that after discrimination training, the most responses are observed in the presence of a test stimulus that is different from the training stimulus (peak shift). Another related observation is that with increasing retention intervals between the end of training and a test trial, stimulus generalization gradients tend to grow broader (e.g., Riccio, Ackil, & Burch-Vernon, 1992; Riccio, Richardson, & Ebner, 1984).

Phenomena Involving More Than Two Stimuli: Mediation, Competition, Interference, Facilitation, and Summation

When more than two stimuli are presented in close proximity during training, one might expect that each stimulus-outcome dyad would be processed independently according to the laws just described. Surely these laws do apply, but the situation becomes more complex because interactions between stimuli can occur. That is, when stimuli X and Y are presented together, behavioral control by X, based on X's relationship to Z, is often influenced by the presence of Y during training of X. When responding to X appears to depend causally on Y, we tend to say that Y *mediates* responding to X; otherwise we tend to say that Y *modulates* responding to X. A useful analogy to differentiate between mediation and modulation is to think of a mediating stimulus as an electrical wire that transmits energy (in this case, behavioral control) from one place (Cue 1) to the other (Cue 2) and of a modulator as an amplifier that can tone up or down responding to a related cue. This distinction between modulation and mediation, however, appears to rest empirically on baseline responding to X and theoretically on specific and arguable causal models. Hence, here we use "mediate" for any situation in which Y's influence on responding to X is stimulus-specific. If Y also influences responding to some other cue with which it has never been paired, we use "modulate." (Even this distinction is problematic because it assumes that stimulus specificity of stimulus Y's action on Stimulus X is dichotomous—all or none—whereas gradations of stimulus specificity are in fact observed as a function of the training paradigm.) Although all the cue interactions described next are often appreciable in effect size, they are neither as ubiquitous (i.e., they are more narrowly parameter-dependent) nor generally as robust as are any of the single cue-single outcome phenomena described earlier.

Multiple Cues with a Common Outcome

Cues Trained Together and Tested Apart (Competition and Enhancement). Over the last 30 years, considerable attention has been focused on *cue competition* (or *discounting*) between cues trained in compound. The two most frequently examined

Table 2.3   Schematic Representation of Two Common Procedures Used to Obtain Stimulus Competition (Overshadowing and Blocking).

Overshadowing Procedure		
Treatment	Training	Target Cue
Overshadowing	Yx-outcome	X
Control	x-outcome	X

Blocking Procedure		
	Training	
Treatment	Phase 1	Phase 2	Target Cue
---	---	---	---
Blocking	Y-outcome	YX-outcome	X
Control	Z-outcome	YX-outcome	X

NOTE: Cue salience is indicated by letter size. Stimulus competition is evidenced as less behavioral control by the target cue (X) in the blocking and overshadowing groups, relative to their respective control groups.

forms of cue competition are *overshadowing* and *blocking* (see Table 2.3). Imagine a situation in which a group of rats is trained to expect that a certain cue (e.g., a light) will be followed by the delivery of a certain outcome (e.g., a shock). Presentations of the light will likely result in a certain level of conditioned fear responding. Now imagine another group of rats in which the light is presented simultaneously with a tone and is followed by the shock. The usual observation is that in the latter group, responding to the light is greatly diminished by its having been presented in compound with the tone during training. That is, in this situation presentation of Cue X (light) in compound with Cue Y (tone) results in Cue Y overshadowing responding to Cue X (Pavlov, 1927). The degree to which Y will overshadow X depends on their relative salience; the more salient Y is relative to X, the greater the degree of overshadowing of X by Y (Mackintosh, 1976). When the two cues are equally salient, overshadowing is sometimes observed, but this is rarely a large effect. Now, imagine a similar situation in which one group of rats is presented with the compound of equally salient Cues X and Y followed by a shock. When X is presented at testing, it will likely elicit a high degree of conditioned responding. The observation is somewhat different for another group of rats, in which Y was repeatedly presented with the outcome before the XY-outcome pairings; in this situation, responding to X is greatly attenuated. That is, responding to X is blocked by the prior Y-outcome pairings (Kamin, 1968). Importantly, presentation of the XY compound in the former (control) group might result in some overshadowing between X and Y. Because observation of blocking requires good responding to X by the control group, the parameters selected must minimize overshadowing of X by Y in the control group; indeed, in many circumstances, it is preferred that X overshadows Y in the control group in order to ensure good responding to X.

Both overshadowing and blocking can sometimes be observed with a single compound training trial (e.g., Balaz, Kasprow, & Miller, 1982; Mackintosh & Reese, 1979); in addition, they are usually greatest with a few compound trials and tend to wane with many compound trials (e.g., Azorlosa & Cicala, 1988). Notably, recovery from each of these cue competition effects (i.e., increased conditioned responding to the overshadowed or blocked cue) can sometimes be obtained without further training trials through various treatments, including (a) lengthening the interval between training and testing (i.e., "spontaneous recovery"; Kraemer, Lariviere, & Spear, 1988); (b) administration of "reminder treatments," which consist of presentation of either the outcome alone, the cue alone, or the training context shortly before testing (e.g., Balaz, Gutsin, Cacheiro, & Miller, 1982); and (c) posttraining massive extinction of the overshadowing or blocking stimulus (e.g., Blaisdell, Gunther, & Miller, 1999; Kaufman & Bolles, 1981; Matzel, Schachtman, & Miller, 1985). The theoretical

implications of such recovery (paralleling the recovery often observed following the degradation of contingency in the one-stimulus situation) are discussed later in this chapter.

Although cue competition is the most frequent result of such experience, under select circumstances the presence of a second cue during training of the target cue has exactly the opposite effect; that is, it *enhances* (i.e., facilitates) responding to the target cue rather than attenuating it. When this effect is observed within the overshadowing procedure (i.e., XY-outcome trials, resulting in more responding to X than does X-outcome trials), it is called *potentiation* (Clarke, Westbrook, & Irwin, 1979); when it is seen in the blocking procedure (i.e., Y-outcome trials before the XY-outcome trials, resulting in more responding to X than if the Y-outcome pairings had not occurred), it is called *augmentation* (Batson & Batsell, 2000). Potentiation and augmentation are most readily observed when the outcome is an internal malaise (usually induced by a toxin), when the target cue is an odor, and when the modulating cue is a taste (this likely reflects animals' predisposition to associate odor and taste stimuli). However, enhancement is not restricted to these modalities (e.g., J. Miller, Scherer, & Jagielo, 1995).

Another example of enhancement, though possibly with a different underlying mechanism, is *superconditioning*. In a superconditioning situation, two cues (e.g., a tone and a light) are presented together and followed by an outcome; after this treatment, responding to one of the cues (e.g., the tone) is enhanced because the other cue (the light) has been trained as a conditioned inhibitor (i.e., a cue that signals outcome omission, as discussed later). The control group is treated comparably, except that the nontarget cue (the light) does not receive inhibitory training. Notably, in most instances enhancement effects are attenuated by posttraining extinction of the mediating stimulus that was present during training with the target (Durlach & Rescorla, 1980). This parallels the reduction in cue competition (i.e., more responding to a target cue) that is sometimes observed to result from post-training extinction of the competing cue.

Cues Trained Apart (with a Common Outcome) and Tested Apart (Interference and Facilitation). Although theory and research in learning over the past 30 years have focused on the interaction of cues trained together, there is an older literature concerning the interaction of cues with common outcomes that are trained apart (i.e., X→O, Y→O). This research was conducted largely in the tradition of associationist studies of human verbal learning that was popular in the mid-20th century. A paradigm used commonly in these experiments involved pairs of words (which can be considered analogous to cue-outcome pairings). For example, participants could be asked to memorize serially presented pairs of furniture→color words (e.g., chair→red) and then pairs of animal→color words (e.g., bird→red). Then, participants could be asked to retrieve the word associated with red. Retrieval of the word chair rather than bird in participants who were exposed to chair-red would suggest that retrieval of the word bird was diminished by the prior pairings of chair with red (i.e., *proactive interference*). In contrast, retrieval of the word bird would suggest that retrieval of chair is diminished by the subsequent pairings of bird with red (i.e., *retroactive interference*).

In more abstract terms, interference is defined as attenuated responding to cue X, which can be observed when X→O training is either preceded (proactive interference) or followed (retroactive interference) by Y→O training, relative to subjects receiving no training with cue Y (e.g., Slamecka & Ceraso, 1960). Although the stimuli used in these early verbal learning studies were usually pairs of consonant trigrams, nonsense syllables, or isolated

words, recent research using nonverbal preparations has found that such interference effects occur quite generally in both humans (Matute & Pineño, 1998) and nonhuman animals (Escobar, Matute, & Miller, 2001). Importantly, Y→O presentations during the second part of training can be viewed as degrading the X→O contingency established during the first part of training because they include presentations of O in the absence of X. This degradation does sometimes contribute to the attenuation of responding based on the X→O relationship (as seen in subjects who receive O-alone in the degraded contingency treatment). However, Y→O treatment sometimes produces a larger deficit than does the same number of presentations of the outcome alone, demonstrating that in addition to degraded contingency effects, associations with a common element can interact to reduce behavioral control by the target stimulus (e.g., Escobar et al., 2001). Additionally, although interference is the more frequent result of the X→O, Y→O design, facilitation is sometimes observed, most commonly when X and Y are similar. The extreme case occurs when X is equal to Y, which then reduces the Y→O pairings to more X→O pairings (e.g., Osgood, 1949; Robinson, 1927).

Cues Trained Apart (with a Common Outcome) and Tested Together (Summation). When two independently trained cues are compounded at test, responding is ordinarily at least as or more vigorous than responding to each cue when tested alone (see Kehoe & Gormezano, 1980). When the response to the compound is greater than that to either element, the phenomenon is called *response summation*. Presumably, a major factor limiting response summation is that compounding two cues trained apart creates a test situation that is different from that of training with either cue; thus, attenuated responding to the compound due to generalization decrement might be anticipated. (See Panel A of Figure 2.1. In this case, the training stimuli are equivalent to zero in the stimulus dimension, whereas testing with the compound can be viewed as a change in the stimulus dimension away from zero.) The question is under what circumstances will the attenuating effect of generalization decrement be sufficient to counteract or exceed the summation of the tendencies to respond to the two stimuli. Research suggests that when subjects treat the compound as a unique stimulus in itself, distinct from the original stimuli (i.e., *configuring*), summation will be minimized (e.g., Kehoe, Horne, Horne, & Macrae, 1994). Well-established rules of perception (e.g., Gestalt principles; Köhler, 1947) describe the conditions that favor and oppose configuring.

Multiple Outcomes with a Single Cue

Just as $Y\rightarrow O$ trials can interact with behavior based on $X\rightarrow O$ training, so too can $X\rightarrow O_1$ trials interact with behavior based on $X\rightarrow O_2$ training (with O_1 and O_2 representing two different outcomes).

Multiple Outcomes Trained Together with a Single Cue. When a cue X is paired with a compound of outcomes (i.e., $X\rightarrow O_1O_2$), responding on tests of the $X\rightarrow O_1$ relationship often yields less responding than does a control group for which O_2 was omitted, provided that O_1 and O_2 are sufficiently different. Such a result might be expected based on either distraction during training or response competition at test (e.g., conflicting approach and withdrawal tendencies when two outcomes are motivationally opposed), both of which are well-established phenomena. However, some studies have been designed to minimize these two potential sources of outcome competition. For example, Burger, Mallemat, and Miller (2000) administered to rats $X\rightarrow O_1O_2$ trials in which neither O_1 nor O_2 were biologically signif-

icant (i.e., they were innocuous audiovisual stimuli). The control group received the same number of $X\rightarrow O_1$ trials as did the experimental group. After this training, O_1 was paired with a biologically significant stimulus (foot shock) so that $X\rightarrow O_1$ learning could be assessed in terms of conditioned fear responding. As neither O_1 nor O_2 was biologically significant during training, (a) distraction from O_1 by O_2 was less likely to occur than if O_2 had been biologically significant during training (although it cannot be completely discounted) and (b) O_2 controlled no behavior that could have produced response competition at test. Despite minimization of distraction and response competition, Burger et al. still observed competition between outcomes: Responding consistent with the $X\rightarrow O_1$ pairings was weaker in the group that received $X\rightarrow O_1O_2$ training than in the group in which O_2 was omitted. To our knowledge, no one has reported enhancement from the presence of O_2 during training, but this possibility has not been extensively explored. Analogy with the multiple-cue case suggests that enhancement might occur if the two outcomes had strong within-compound links (i.e., O_1 and O_2 were similar or strongly associated to each other).

Multiple Outcomes Trained Apart with a Single Cue (Counterconditioning). Just as multiple cues trained apart with a common outcome can interact with each other in controlling behavior, so too can multiple outcomes trained apart with a common cue interact in terms of the responding elicited by the common cue. Returning to the example described above, participants asked to memorize pairs of color→furniture words (e.g., red→chair) and then pairs of color→animal words (e.g., red→bird), might show disrupted retrieval of chair due to the subsequent pairings of red and bird. Alternatively stated, responding based on $X\rightarrow O_1$ training can be influenced, and usually disrupted, by $X \rightarrow O_2$ training. The prototypical example of this type of interference is *counterconditioning,* in which conditioned responding consistent with $X \rightarrow O_1$ pairings is countered by subsequent $X \rightarrow O_2$ pairings. This principle has been widely used in behavior therapy of phobias and fears in a treatment known as systematic desensitization (e.g., Wolpe, 1969). For example, fear of dogs can be considered the result of a dog-bad experience ($X \rightarrow O_1$) pairing. Counterconditioning treatment would consist of pairing dog with an experience incompatible with fear (e.g., relaxation; i.e., $X \rightarrow O_2$). Although in counterconditioning, as usually defined, the interfering training occurs after the target training, more generally the interfering training ($X \rightarrow O_2$) can occur before, interspersed among, or after the target training trials ($X \rightarrow O_1$). A problem in regarding counterconditioning as a form of interference is that response competition (e.g., approach-withdrawal conflict) is often a contributing factor in counterconditioning. However, there is good evidence that such interference effects are due to more than simple response competition (e.g., Dearing & Dickinson, 1979). Moreover, degraded contingency of the $X \rightarrow O_1$ association can also be regarded as a contributing factor in counterconditioning because X is presented without O_1 during the $X \rightarrow O_2$ pairings (just as was discussed for interference between cues trained with a common outcome). Nevertheless, recent research has found that the response attenuation produced by the $X \rightarrow O_2$ trials is sometimes greater than that produced by X-alone presentations; hence, this sort of interference cannot be treated as simply an instance of degraded contingency (e.g., Escobar, Arcediano, & Miller, in press). Moreover, if the salience of cues and outcomes is equated, attenuation of responding to X in the $X \rightarrow O_1$, $X \rightarrow O_2$ situation appears to be symmetrical to response attenuation to X

in the $X \rightarrow O$, $Y \rightarrow O$ situation (Escobar et al., in press).

Behavior in the Face of Inconsistent Experiences

The magnitude of the interference effects just described is strongly influenced by conditions at the time of testing. Consider ambiguity created by experiencing competing elements that are trained apart (e.g., chair→red vs. bird→red). If the target (i.e., chair→red) and interfering (i.e., bird→red) treatments were administered in different contexts, presentation of contextual cues associated with the interfering treatment soon before testing of the target cue augments interference, whereas similarly timed presentation of contextual cues associated with target training attenuates interference. Thus, if the chair→red treatment is given in Context A and the bird→red treatment is given in Context B, testing for retrieval of the associate of red in Context B will enhance interference (i.e., reduce the probability that chair is retrieved), whereas similar testing in Context A will attenuate interference (i.e., increase the probability that chair is retrieved). In principle, contextual cues can be either diffuse background cues or discrete stimuli that were presented during the interference or target training sessions (Bidoleau & Schlosberg, 1951; Escobar et al., 2001). Additionally, recent training experience typically has a stronger effect on behavior than does earlier training (i.e., a recency effect), all other factors being equal. Thus, if training takes the form of learning chair-red and then bird-red and if testing is conducted immediately after training, participants are more likely to retrieve bird than chair when red is presented (i.e., retroactive interference with bird→red). However, recency effects fade with increasing retention intervals; consequently, retroactive interference fades, and proactive interference (with retrieval of 'chair→red') correspondingly increases as posttraining retention intervals are increased (e.g., Postman, Stark, & Fraser, 1968). Thus, if testing is conducted after a retention interval, participants will more likely retrieve chair than bird when presented with red.

Notably, the contextual and temporal modulation of interference effects is highly similar to the contextual and temporal modulation observed with the previously described degraded contingency effects. Thus, one might wonder whether interference effects are really different from degraded contingency effects. We previously cited reasons for rejecting the view that interference effects were no more than degraded contingency effects. That is, a contingency approach cannot account for all interference data. Consider now the question of whether an interference approach can account for all contingency effects. That is, if the training context is regarded as an element that can become associated with a cue on a cue-alone trial or with an outcome on an outcome-alone trial, contingency-degrading trials could be viewed as cue-context or context-outcome trials that interfere with behavior promoted by cue-outcome trials, much as interfering $Y \rightarrow O$ or cue$\rightarrow O_2$ trials do within the interference paradigm. In principle, this allows one to regard degraded contingency effects as a subset of interference effects. However, because of the vagueness of "context" as a stimulus and the consequent difficulties with experimentally manipulating the context, this approach has not received widespread acceptance.

Mediation

Although there are several different definitions of mediated behavior, we here define *mediated behavior* as responding to a target cue that is at least partially a function of the training history of a second cue that has at one time or another been paired with the target cue. Depending on the specific situation, the mediated interaction between the target and the companion cues can occur either at the time that they are paired during training (e.g., aversively motivated second-order conditioning; Holland & Rescorla, 1975) or at test (e.g., sensory preconditioning; Rizley & Rescorla, 1972). As discussed later, the mediated control transferred to the target can be either consistent with the status of the companion cue (hereafter called *positive mediation;* e.g., second-order conditioning) or inverse to the status of the companion cue (hereafter called *negative mediation;* e.g., conditioned inhibition or blocking). Testing whether a mediational relationship between two cues exists usually involves presenting the companion cue with or without the outcome in the absence of the target and seeing whether that treatment influences responding to the target. This manipulation of the companion cue can be done before, interspersed among, or after the target training trials. However, sometimes revaluation of the companion after target training does not alter responding to the target, suggesting that the mediational process in these instances occurs during training (e.g., aversively motivated second-order conditioning).

Second-Order Conditioning and Sensory Preconditioning

If Cue Y is paired with a biologically significant outcome (O) such that Y comes to control responding, and Cue X is subsequently paired with Y (i.e., Y-O, followed by X-Y), responding to X will ordinarily be observed. This phenomenon is called *second-order conditioning* (Pavlov, 1927). Thus, if an animal is trained to expect an electric shock immediately following presentation of a light, presentation of the light will produce a fear response. Subsequently, the light can be used as an outcome (e.g., in tone$\rightarrow$light pairings). The usual observation is that the tone also comes to produce a fear response. Usually, the light is called a first-order stimulus because it was paired with the outcome that unconditionally

Table 2.4   Schematic Representation of Two Procedures That Result in Mediated Learning (Second-Order Conditioning and Sensory Preconditioning).

Treatment	Training		Target Cue
	Phase 1	Phase 2	
Second-order conditioning	Y-outcome	X-Y	X
Sensory preconditioning	X-Y	Y-outcome	X

NOTE: In both procedures, responding is expected to the target cue (X) due conjointly to X's pairings with its mediating stimulus (Y) and the pairings of Y with the outcome.

elicits a response, whereas the tone is called a second-order stimulus because its relationship with the outcome is mediated by the light. A cue can similarly acquire behavioral control if the two phases of training are reversed (i.e., X-Y, followed by Y-O, or tone-light pairings followed by light-shock pairings). This latter phenomenon is called *sensory preconditioning* (Brogden, 1939; see Table 2.4) because sensory stimuli are paired before conditioning with the outcome occurs.

Second-order conditioning and sensory preconditioning are important for two reasons. First, these are examples of acquired behavior that depend on associations between stimuli that are not of inherent biological significance (in this context, biological significance refers to a stimulus's potential to elicit an unconditioned response). One might argue that in second-order conditioning, Y has acquired biological significance, so that one might conclude that associations are formed to stimuli that have biological significance, either inherent (e.g., food, a painful event) or acquired (a cue for food or a painful event). In sensory preconditioning, however, the association formed between X and Y is established before any biologically relevant event has occurred. Hence, we must conclude that associ-

ations are formed between neutral stimuli in sensory preconditioning. In earlier times, defenders of the view that biologically relevant events were necessary for learning to occur took refuge in the position that there is no such thing as a perceived stimulus that is totally lacking in biological significance; that is, they defined as biologically significant any stimulus to which there was an orienting response. This position was not categorically wrong, but it was sorely strained by the observation that the responding to X after sensory preconditioning training (i.e., X-Y followed by Y-US) does not decrease as rapidly as does the orienting (unconditioned) response to X and Y when these stimuli are presented in extinction.

Furthermore, second-order conditioning and sensory preconditioning are simple, clear examples of mediated responding, in that responding is observed to a cue that was never paired with a stimulus of inherent biological significance. As such, they pose a serious challenge to the previously discussed law of contiguity. However, given the enormous success of contiguity in generally describing the conditions that foster acquired behavior, researchers generally have elected to redefine contiguity explicitly or implicitly as spatiotemporal proximity between the cue *or its surrogate* and the outcome *or its surrogate,* thereby incorporating mediation within the principle of contiguity. In second-order conditioning (Y-O pairings followed by X-Y pairings), the mediating stimulus (Y) can be said to be serving as a surrogate for the outcome (i.e., O, which is often an unconditioned stimulus) with which it was previously paired; in sensory preconditioning (X-Y pairings followed by Y-O pairings), Y can be said to be serving as a surrogate for Cue X, with which it was previously paired.

Mediation appears to occur when two different sets of paired stimuli share a common element (e.g., Y in X-Y, Y-O). Importantly, the mediating stimulus ordinarily does not simply act as a (weak) substitute for the cue or outcome, as might be expected of a simple surrogate. Rather, the mediating stimulus (i.e., the first-order cue in the cases of second-order conditioning and sensory preconditioning) carries with its own spatiotemporal relationship to the outcome. Experimental data suggest that after X-Y, Y-O training, organisms integrate the spatiotemporal relationship between the mediating cue (Y) and the outcome (O) with the spatiotemporal relationship between the target cue (X) and the mediating cue (Y; for spatial summation, see Chap. 8, this volume; Etienne, Berlie, Georgakopoulos, & Maurer, 1998; for temporal summation, see Chap. 9, this volume; Matzel, Held, & Miller, 1988). In effect, subjects appear to integrate the two separately experienced relationships to create a spatiotemporal relationship between the second-order cue and the outcome, even though they have never been physically paired.

The mediating process that links two stimuli that were never paired could occur in principle either during training or testing. To address this issue, researchers have asked what happens to the response potential of a second-order conditioned cue when its first-order cue is extinguished between training and testing. Holland and Rescorla (1975) reported that such posttraining extinction of the first-order cue (Y) did not degrade responding to a second-order cue (X), but subsequent research has found that extinction of Y attenuates responding to X under some conditions (Cheatle & Rudy, 1978). The basis for this difference is not yet completely clear, but Nairne and Rescorla (1981) have suggested that it depends on the valence of the outcome—that is, appetitive (extinction of Y attenuates responding to X) or aversive (extinction of Y has no effect on responding to X). In sensory preconditioning, almost all researchers find that posttraining extinction of the first-order cue

attenuates responding to the second-order cue (e.g., Rizley & Rescorla, 1972).

Conditioned Inhibition

Conditioned inhibition refers to situations in which a subject behaves as if it has learned that a target stimulus (a so-called *conditioned inhibitor*) signals the omission of an outcome. Conditioned inhibition is ordinarily assessed by a combination of (a) a *summation test* in which the putative inhibitor is presented in compound with a known conditioned excitor (different from any excitor that was used in training the inhibitor) and is seen to reduce responding to that excitor and (b) a *retardation test* in which the inhibitor is seen to be slow (in terms of number of pairings with the outcome required to reach asymptote) in coming to act as a conditioned excitor (Rescorla, 1969). Both tests are required because passage of each test alone is subject to alternative noninhibitory accounts (e.g., increased attention to the target cue on the summation test and decreased attention to the target cue on the retardation test). However, these alternative accounts for the two different tests are mutually exclusive, so passage of both tests permits a conclusion that the target cue is inhibitory. Because the standard tests for conditioned excitation and conditioned inhibition are operationally distinct, stimuli sometimes can (weakly) pass tests for both excitatory and inhibitory status after identical treatment. For a given cue, then, conditioned inhibition and conditioned excitation are not mutually exclusive (Droungas & LoLordo, 1994; Matzel, Gladstein, & Miller, 1988; Tait & Saladin, 1986).

Several different procedures appear to produce conditioned inhibition to a given cue, X (LoLordo & Fairless, 1985). Among them are (a) Rescorla's (1968) procedure, in which the cue (inhibitor) and outcome are presented *explicitly unpaired* (outcome-alone trials intermixed with X-no outcome trials; described in the earlier section titled "Objective Contingency"); (b) Pavlov's (1927) procedure, in which trials that pair a training excitor (Y) with an outcome are interspersed with trials in which the training excitor and intended inhibitor (X) are presented in nonreinforced compound (Y-outcome trials intermixed with XY-no outcome trials); and (c) *backward pairings* of a cue with an outcome (outcome-X; Heth, 1976). What appears similar across these various procedures is that the inhibitor is present at a time when another cue (discrete or contextual) signals that the outcome is likely to occur, but in fact it does not occur. Pavlov (1927) also produced an inhibitor using the *differential inhibition procedure,* in which reinforced trials with Cue Y are interspersed with nonreinforced trials with the intended inhibitor, X (Y-outcome trials intermixed with X-no outcome trials), which superficially appears to violate the general rule for creating inhibitors presented earlier. However, R. Miller, Hallam, Hong, and Dufore (1991) have presented data suggesting that differential inhibition is supported by the expectation of the outcome based on the context in which the outcome has been administered. As the context is also present during the X-trials, the aforementioned rule appears to apply here as well. Table 2.5 presents a schematic representation of the procedures commonly used to produce conditioned inhibition.

Conditioned inhibition is stimulus-specific in that it generates relatively narrow generalization gradients, similar to or perhaps even narrower than those of conditioned excitation (Spence, 1936). Conditioned inhibition is also outcome-specific in that it transfers to excitors other than that with which it was trained, provided that this transfer excitor was trained with the same (or a similar) outcome (e.g., Colwill, 1991). Additionally, it is outcome-specific in that an inhibitor will transfer its response-attenuating influence on behavior between different cues for the same outcome, but not between cues for different outcomes (Rescorla & Holland, 1977). Hence, conditioned inhibition, like conditioned excitation, is a form of stimulus-specific learning about a relationship between a cue and an outcome. However, conditioned inhibition can be regarded as a form of mediated learning because it reflects encoding of a relationship between a cue and an outcome with which the cue has never been paired. From this perspective, conditioned inhibition is more similar to second-order conditioning than to simple (first-order) conditioning. However, it is important to note that many theorists regard conditioned inhibition as a direct result of the law of contingency, based on the assumption that if the cue-outcome contingency is negative, the cue becomes a conditioned inhibitor (see the earlier section titled "Objective Contingency"); this, however, ignores the need for some common stimulus, often the context, when the outcome is presented and when the cue is presented. Moreover, just as responding to a second-order conditioned cue not only appears as if the subject expects the outcome at a time and place specified conjointly by the spatiotemporal relationships between X and Y and between Y and the outcome (e.g., Barnet, Arnold, & Miller, 1991), so too does a conditioned inhibitor seemingly signal not only

Table 2.5   Schematic Representation of Some Procedures That Can Be Used to Obtain Conditioned Inhibition.

Procedure	Training	Inhibitor	Excitor
Explicitly unpaired trials	Outcome/X-no outcome	X	Context
Pavlov's procedure	Y-outcome/YX-no outcome	X	Y
Backward pairings	Outcome-X	X	Context
Differential procedure	Y-outcome/X-no outcome	X	Context

NOTE: See text for details.

the omission of the outcome but also the time and place of that omission (e.g., Denniston, Blaisdell, & Miller, 1998).

A phenomenon that is closely related to conditioned inhibition is negative occasion setting. Negative occasion setting often takes the form of Y→outcome trials interspersed with X→Y-no outcome trials, with X preceding Y by 5 s to 15 s (because of these serial presentations of Y and X, the procedure might be described as *serial* negative occasion setting). In contrast, most implementations of Pavlov's procedure for conditioned inhibition consist of Y→outcome trials interspersed with YX-no outcome trials, with Y and X being presented simultaneously. Thus, Pavlov's method might be regarded procedurally as *simultaneous* negative occasion setting. Calling both of these procedures occasion setting suggests a common or at least similar underlying process. The appropriateness of this hinges on whether the two phenomena have common attributes (R. Miller & Oberling, 1998). Indeed, they both appear to be stimulus-specific, outcome-specific, and specific to the temporal relationships prevailing during training (e.g., Barnet & Miller, 1996; Holland, Hamlin, & Parsons, 1997; see the earlier description of conditioned inhibition).

After negative occasion setting training (Y-outcome trials intermixed with X→Y-no outcome trials), Y elicits responding only when it is not preceded by X. Holland (e.g., Lamarre & Holland, 1987) has argued that occasion setting and conditioned inhibition are fundamentally different because X does not exhibit its occasion-setting properties if presented with a cue that has been paired with an outcome but has not been subject to occasion-setting treatment. Thus, if B has been experienced only within B-outcome pairings, X→B presentations will not attenuate responding to B. In contrast, if A has been experienced with both A-outcome and Z→A-no outcome trials, X→A presentations will attenuate responding

to A. In contrast with Holland's conclusion, Rescorla (1985) viewed negative occasion setting and conditioned inhibition as fundamentally similar because he observed attenuation of responding to both cues trained as excitors in an occasion setting situation (e.g., Cue A) and to excitors that have not been subject to occasion setting (e.g., Cue B). Indeed, Rescorla even refers to negative occasion setting as inhibition. Possibly, the seeming discrepancy here is a matter of emphasis (Holland obtained a nonsignificant tendency toward attenuation of responding to Cue B, and Rescorla obtained a nonsignificant tendency toward less attenuation when he tested with Cue B). Clearly, simultaneous negative occasion setters retain their response-attenuating properties better if tested in a serial fashion (i.e., occasion setter before excitor) than do serial negative occasion setters when tested in a simultaneous fashion (i.e., occasion setter simultaneous with the excitor).

One might ask about the behavioral consequences for conditioned inhibition of presentations of the mediating cue alone after completion of conditioned inhibition training (i.e., extinction of the excitor used during inhibition training; see Table 2.5). Similar to corresponding tests with second-order conditioning, the results have been mixed. For example, Rescorla and Holland (1977) found no alteration of behavior indicative of inhibition, whereas other researchers (e.g., Best, Dunn, Batson, Meachum, & Nash, 1985; Hallam, Grahame, Harris, & Miller, 1992; Lysle & Fowler, 1985) observed a decrease in inhibition. Yin, Grahame, and Miller (1993) suggested that the critical difference between these studies is that truly massive posttraining extinction of the mediating stimulus is necessary to obtain changes in behavioral control by an inhibitor.

Despite these operational and behavioral similarities of conditioned inhibition (Y-outcome trials intermixed with XY-no outcome trials) and second-order conditioning (Y-outcome trials followed by X-Y-no outcome trials), there is one most fundamental difference. Responding to a second-order cue is appropriate for the occurrence of the outcome, whereas responding to an inhibitor is appropriate for the omission of the outcome. In sharp contrast to second-order conditioning (and sensory preconditioning), which are examples of *positive mediation* (seemingly passing information concerning an outcome from the first-order cue to the second-order cue), conditioned inhibition is an example of what we would call *negative mediation* (seemingly inverting the expectation of the outcome conveyed by the first-order cue as the information is passed to the second-order cue). The important question of which variables determine whether positive mediation or negative mediation will occur in otherwise similar situations has yet to be fully answered. Rashotte, Marshall, and O'Connell (1981) and Yin, Barnet, and Miller (1994) have suggested that the critical variable may be the number of X-Y-no outcome trials, with few trials favoring positive mediation (i.e., resulting in conditioned responding—second-order conditioning) and many trials favoring negative mediation (i.e., resulting in no conditioned responding—conditioned inhibition). The observation that varying the number of trials in a certain paradigm can produce a change from excitatory to inhibitory conditioning is not unique to the Y-outcome, XY-no outcome treatment. Earlier we mentioned that backward outcome-cue pairings result in conditioned inhibition; however, few backward pairings actually yield excitatory responding, which diminishes and finally turns into inhibition as training progresses (Heth, 1976). A second difference between inhibition and second-order conditioning, which is likely related to the aforementioned distinction between negative and positive mediation, is that nonreinforced exposure to a second-order conditioned excitor produces extinction, whereas nonreinforced exposure to an inhibitor does not reduce its inhibitory potential but sometimes even increases it (e.g., DeVito & Fowler, 1987).

Retrospective Revaluation

As mentioned in the previous sections, when two cues are trained in compound, responding to one of those cues (i.e., the target cue) is often influenced (i.e., mediated) by training with the other (mediating) cue. Indeed, the mediating cue can be manipulated (by pairing it with the outcome or presenting it in the absence of the outcome) before, during, or after compound training. Thus, in the procedure for second-order conditioning (i.e., Y-outcome pairings followed by XY-no outcome), the mediating cue (Y) is manipulated (i.e., paired with the outcome) prior to the compound trials. In the procedure for conditioned inhibition (i.e., Y-outcome pairings interspersed with XY-no outcome), the mediating cue is manipulated during compound training. Recent interest has focused on manipulation of the mediating stimulus *after* completion of the compound trials because in this case the observed effects on responding to the target are particularly problematic to most conventional associative theories of learning, which assume that responding to a target cue cannot change if the cue is not presented for further training. A change in stimulus control following the termination of training with the target cue is called (empirical) *retrospective revaluation* (not to be confused with theoretical retrospective revaluation, in which the associative status of the target cue is assumed to be altered, as we discuss later).

Importantly, both positive and negative mediation effects have been observed with the retrospective revaluation procedure. Sensory preconditioning is a long-known but frequently ignored example of retrospective revaluation in its simplest form. It is an example of positive retrospective revaluation because the manipulation of the mediating stimulus after target training produces a change in responding to the target cue that mimics the change in control by the mediating stimulus (see Table 2.4). Other examples of positive retrospective revaluation include the decrease in responding sometimes seen to a target cue that was trained in compound with its mediating stimulus when the mediating stimulus is extinguished (i.e., YX-outcome, followed by Y-no outcome, resulting in decreased responding to X, sometimes called mediated extinction; Holland & Forbes, 1982). In contrast, there are also many reports of negative retrospective revaluation, in which the change in responding to the target cue is in the opposite direction to the change in direct behavioral control by the mediating stimulus. Examples of negative retrospective revaluation include recovery from cue competition as a result of extinction of the competing (e.g., overshadowing) stimulus (i.e., YX-outcome, followed by Y-no outcome, resulting in increased responding to X; e.g., Kaufman & Bolles, 1981; Matzel et al., 1985), decreases in Pavlovian conditioned inhibition as a result of extinction of the inhibitor's training excitor (i.e., Y-outcome/YX-no outcome, followed by Y-no outcome, resulting in increased responding to X; e.g., DeVito & Fowler, 1987; Lysle & Fowler, 1985), and backward blocking (i.e., YX-outcome, followed by Y-outcome; e.g., Denniston et al., 1996). Alternatively stated, a retrieved representation of an event can act either as a surrogate or as an antisurrogate for the event.

The occurrence of both positive and negative mediation in retrospective revaluation parallels the two opposing effects that are often observed when the companion cue is treated alone before or during the compound stimulus trials. We previously described not only overshadowing but also potentiation, which, although operationally similar to over-

shadowing, has the opposite behavioral result. Following AX-outcome training, the positive mediation apparent in potentiation can usually be reversed by posttraining extinction of the mediating (potentiating) cue (e.g., Durlach & Rescorla, 1980). Similarly, the negative mediation apparent in overshadowing can sometimes be reversed by massive posttraining extinction of the mediating (overshadowing) cue (e.g., Kaufman & Bolles, 1981; Matzel et al., 1985). However, the data are currently insufficient to specify a rule for the changes in control by a cue that will be observed when its mediating stimulus cue is reinforced or extinguished. That is, we do not know the critical variables that determine whether mediation will be positive or negative. As previously mentioned, two prime candidates for determining the direction of mediated change in responding are the number of pairings of the target with the mediating cue and whether these pairings are simultaneous or serial. Whatever the findings of future studies, recent research on retrospective revaluation has clearly demonstrated that there are events that can change the response potential of a cue even when that cue is not part of the event. As mentioned earlier, this observation is contrary to most conventional models of acquired behavior, which do not anticipate changes in behavioral control to cues that are not physically presented in a trial.

Instrumental Responding

Pavlovian conditioning is usually regarded as stimulus-stimulus learning: A conditioned stimulus (cue) is paired with an unconditioned stimulus (outcome) independent of the response of the subject, and presumably the subject forms an association between the two stimulus representations. In instrumental conditioning, some response of the subject influences the delivery of an outcome (reinforcer); that is, there is a response-outcome contingency. For example, a rat might press a bar (response) in order to obtain a food pellet (reinforcer). In this situation, the subject presumably forms an association between the response and the reinforcer. Often, a discriminative stimulus signals availability of reinforcement; in this case, the subject's behavior suggests encoding of a stimulus-response-reinforcement relationship (discussed later). Thus, the rat might be trained to press a bar, and reinforcement is delivered only if a light (discriminative stimulus) was on at the time the response was made. Although for simplicity the foregoing review has been couched largely in terms of cue-outcome relationships, most of the phenomena observed in Pavlovian conditioning have counterparts in instrumental learning. For instance, the basic relations of acquisition as a result of response-reinforcer pairings and extinction as a result of nonreinforcement of the response, as well as spontaneous recovery, are found in instrumental learning, closely paralleling what is observed with cues and outcomes in Pavlovian situations (for more detailed comparisons, see Dickinson, 1980; R. Miller & Balaz, 1981). Blocking and overshadowing may be obtained for instrumental responses (St. Claire-Smith, 1979; B. Williams, 1982). Stimulus generalization and discrimination characterize instrumental learning (Guttman & Kalish, 1956). Temporal contiguity is crucial to instrumental learning; response rate decreases rapidly as the response-reinforcer delay increases as long as an explicit stimulus does not fill the interval (e.g., B. Williams, 1976). If a stimulus does fill the interval, it facilitates responding, sometimes with the intervening stimulus functioning as a conditioned reinforcer with reinforcing power in its own right (e.g., Schaal & Branch, 1988); however, under some conditions it can attenuate (i.e., overshadow) the response (e.g., Pearce & Hall, 1978). This bridging procedure provides a parallel to second-order Pavlovian conditioning. Latent learning, in which learning occurs in the absence of explicit reinforcement (Tolman & Honzik, 1930), is analogous to sensory preconditioning. *Learned helplessness,* in which a subject first exposed to inescapable shock later fails to learn an escape response (Maier & Seligman, 1976), provides a parallel to learned irrelevance. Instrumental conditioning varies directly with the response-reinforcer contingency (e.g., Hammond, 1980). Cue-response-consequence specificity (Foree & LoLordo, 1973) is similar to cue-to-consequence predispositions in Pavlovian conditioning (discussed earlier). Overall, the number of parallels between Pavlovian and instrumental conditioning encourages the view that an organism's response can be mentally represented in a form analogous to a stimulus, and that learning fundamentally concerns the development of associative links between mental representations of *events* whether the events are stimuli or responses.

As previously mentioned, the 2×2 contingency between outcome and cue in Pavlovian situations (see Table 2.1) can be readily expanded to a $2 \times 2 \times 2$ contingency table in which the occurrence of an outcome now depends also on the emission of the target response. There are four basic types of instrumental contingencies, depending on whether the response either produces/enhances or prevents/eliminates the outcome and whether the outcome is of positive or negative hedonic value (see Table 2.6). *Positive reinforcement* (i.e., *reward*) is the contingency in which responding produces an outcome with the result that there is an increase in response frequency (e.g., when a pigeon's key peck results in food presentation or a student's studying before a quiz produces an A). Such outcomes are designated *appetitive reinforcers. Punishment* is the contingency in which responding results in the occurrence of an outcome with the result that there is a decrease in response frequency (e.g., when a child is scolded for reaching into the cookie jar or a rat's lever press pro-

Table 2.6 Response-outcome Contingencies That Operate in Instrumental Conditioning.

	Outcome of Positive Hedonic Value	Outcome of Negative Hedonic Value
Response produces outcome	Positive reinforcement	Punishment
Response eliminates outcome	Omission (negative punishment)	Escape/avoidance (negative reinforcement)

NOTE: See text for details.

duces foot shock). Such outcomes are designated *aversive events*. *Omission* (i.e., *negative punishment*) describes a situation in which responding cancels or prevents the occurrence of an outcome of positive hedonic value with the result that there is a decrease in response frequency (e.g., when a rat's bar pressing results in a period in which otherwise free food is not available or when a child is given time-out for misbehaving in the classroom). Finally, *escape* or *avoidance conditioning* (i.e., *negative reinforcement*) is the contingency in which responding leads to the termination of an ongoing—or prevention of an expected—aversive stimulus with the result that there is an increase in response frequency (e.g., when a rat learns to avoid a chamber in which a foot shock has been administered or when a man prefers to take the stairs to avoid entering an elevator in which he was previously trapped). By definition, both positive and negative reinforcement contingencies result in increases in the target response, whereas omission and punishment contingencies lead to decreases in the target response.

The contingency of reinforcement on a response, following Ferster and Skinner (1957), is ordinarily called a *schedule of reinforcement*. Historically, one of two criteria for reinforcement of a response has been used: the number of responses emitted since the last reinforced response (*ratio schedules*) and the

time since the last reinforced response (*interval schedules*). Frequently, these contingencies are conditional on the presence of a *discriminative stimulus* (i.e., a cue signaling whether the response-reinforcer contingency is in effect), which are analogous to Pavlovian occasion setters. Reinforcement schedules have been a major focus of research in instrumental conditioning (for reviews, see Zeiler, 1977, 1984). Because of the stable, reliable behaviors they produce, reinforcement schedules have been widely adopted for use in related disciplines as baseline controls (e.g., behavioral pharmacology, behavioral neuroscience).

Assessment of (Instrumental) Conditioning. How is one to assay the degree of learning that has occurred in a specific situation given that learning is an intervening variable and hence is not directly observable? One reasonable response to this question would be to describe the behavioral change (i.e., the experimental result) and not to discuss intervening variables such as learning; this is the solution advocated by Skinner (1938). However, this atheoretical position fails to suggest which independent and dependent variables are most worthy of examination; theories are often necessary to guide research. In his instrumental *free operant* (i.e., free-running rather than temporally segmented into trials) studies, Skinner focused largely on response-reinforcement contingencies as the independent variable and response frequencies as the dependent variable. In contrast with Skinner's position, researchers working in a discrete trial framework tend to favor the measurement of response magnitude over response frequency, largely because response frequency is usually a trivial function of the number of trials, which is controlled by the experimenter.

Despite the popularity of response frequency and magnitude, these measures are sometimes poorly correlated with independent variables that are intuitively thought to influence acquired behavior directly, such as percentage of responses (or trials) reinforced, reinforcement magnitude, and so on. For example, Bonem and Crossman (1988) found that response rate sometimes decreases as reward magnitude increases. Such paradoxical effects have prompted researchers to seek other measures of learning that are better correlated with independent variables intuitively thought to control acquired responding.

One such alternative measure of learning is *resistance to change* in the target behavior in the face of various disruptive treatments. Nevin (1974) conducted several experiments in which pigeons learned to respond in multiple schedules of reinforcement. After baseline training, he attempted to disrupt responding in both components of the schedule by either home-cage prefeeding or termination of reward (i.e., extinction). He found that responding in the component that had provided the richer schedule of reinforcement (in terms of greater rate, magnitude, or immediacy of reinforcement) decreased less than responding in the leaner component. Note that although Nevin was still measuring response frequency, percent change in response frequency rather than absolute frequency was being monitored. Based on these results and others, Nevin and his colleagues proposed *behavioral momentum theory,* which posits that resistance to change and response frequency are orthogonal independent variables of acquired behavior analogous to mass and velocity, respectively, in classical physics (Nevin, 1992; Nevin, Mandell, & Atak, 1983). According to this view, delivery of response-contingent reinforcement increases a mass-like aspect of behavior, which reflects knowledge of contingencies and can be assessed as resistance to change. Nevin, Tota, Torquato, and Shull (1990) suggested that behavioral mass depends primarily on (Pavlovian) stimulus-outcome contingencies. However, resistance to change as an index of learning has its own problems. For example, under certain conditions, responses that were inconsistently reinforced during training are slower to extinguish than are responses that were consistently reinforced (i.e., *the partial reinforcement extinction effect,* which is observed when subjects are exposed to a simple irregular schedule of reinforcement during training; e.g., Lewis, 1956), and sometimes subjects with a greater number of training trials cease responding in fewer extinction trials than do subjects that received fewer training trials (*overlearning extinction effect;* North & Stimmel, 1960; Tombaugh, 1967). Moreover, subjects given small rewards during training often persist in responding longer than do subjects given large rewards (Armus, 1959).

A distinction is sometimes made between *response energetics* (e.g., response frequency, resistance to change) and *response selection* (i.e., choice), with the latter, at least in some situations, being less influenced by performance variables such as the subject's motivational state. This distinction works well, say, for a rat running through a maze for food, when speed (response energetics) versus erroneous turns (response selection) are examined. The literature on instrumental choice behavior is enormous and has been reviewed frequently (e.g., B. Williams, 1988). Under some conditions, choice (i.e., preference) and resistance to change are highly correlated (e.g., Nevin & Grace, 2000), suggesting the existence of a single underlying construct.

Motivation

Acquired responding, whether Pavlovian or instrumental, requires motivation. Motivation is such a large and complex subject that we cannot review it here, beyond saying that all acquired behavior (not necessarily learning of relationships) involves a potential increase or decrease in the likelihood or magnitude of a biologically significant event (with the biological significance of an event being indexed by the degree of unconditioned responding that it elicits). Obviously, the biological significance of an event depends on both the physical nature of the outcome and the state of the subject (e.g., hungry or sated). Moreover, many experiments on contrast effects have demonstrated that the motivational value of an event is inversely influenced by the motivational value of other events in the same situation (i.e., contrast effects; e.g., Flaherty, 1996; Chap. 12, this volume).

PSYCHOLOGICAL MODELS OF ACQUIRED BEHAVIOR

We turn now from our review of variables that influence acquired behavior to a review of accounts of this acquired behavior, again staying largely within a Pavlovian framework. Here we contrast the major variables that differentiate among models and refer back to our list of empirical variables to ask how the different families of models account for the roles of these variables. Citations are provided for the interested reader wishing to pursue the specifics of any of these models.

Units of Analysis

What Is a Stimulus?

Before we review specific theories, we must briefly consider at the psychological level how an organism perceives and represents in mind a stimulus. Different models of acquired behavior use different definitions of stimuli. In some models the immediate perceptual field is composed of a vast number of microelements (e.g., we learn not about a tree, but about each branch, twig, and leaf; Estes & Burke, 1953; McLaren & Mackintosh, 2000). In other models the perceptual field consists at any given moment of a few integrated sources of receptor stimulation (e.g., the oak tree, the maple tree; Gallistel & Gibbon, 2000; Rescorla & Wagner, 1972). For yet other models the perceptual field at any given moment is fully integrated and contains only one configured stimulus, which consists of all that immediately impinges on the sensorium (the forest; Pearce, 1987). Although there are benefits and drawbacks to each approach, they have all proven viable. Generally speaking, the larger the number of elements assumed, the greater the complexity of the model and, consequently, the more readily behavior can be explained post hoc; however, it is also more difficult to make testable a priori predictions. By increasing in a defined physical situation the number of stimuli to be independently analyzed, each having its own associative status, one is necessarily increasing the number of variables and often the number of parameters. Thus, it may become difficult to distinguish between models that are correct in the sense that they faithfully represent some causal relationship between acquired behavior and events in the environment and models that succeed because there is enough flexibility in the model's parameters to account for virtually any result (i.e., curve fitting); only empirically supported a priori predictions differentiate these two possibilities. Most models take the middle ground and assume that subjects parse the immediate perceptual field into a small number of integrated stimuli representations. That is, the perceptual field might consist of discrete events such as a tone and a light and a tree, each separately represented as an integrated and inseparable whole.

Worthy of special note here is the McLaren and Mackintosh (2000) model with its elemental approach. This model not only addresses the fundamental phenomena of acquired behavior but also tries to account for perceptual learning (see Chap. 7, this volume), thereby providing an account of how and by what mechanism organisms weave the stimulation provided by many microelements into the perceptual fabric of lay usage. In other words, the model offers a learning account of how experience causes us to merge representations of branches, twigs, and leaves into a compound construct such as a tree.

The Nature of an Acquired Response

In Pavlovian learning, the conditioned response reflects the nature of the outcome, which is ordinarily a biologically significant unconditioned stimulus (but see Holland, 1977, who demonstrates that the physical nature of the cue also has some small influence on the topology of the response). However, this is not sufficient to predict the form of conditioned behavior. Although responding is often of the same form as the unconditioned response to the unconditioned stimulus (i.e., *mimetic*), it is sometimes in the opposite direction (i.e., *compensatory*). Examples of mimetic conditioned responding include eyelid conditioning, conditioned salivation, and conditioned release of endogenous endorphins with aversive stimulation as the unconditioned stimulus. Examples of compensatory conditioned responding include conditioned freezing with foot shock as the unconditioned stimulus and conditioned tolerance and withdrawal symptoms with opiates as the unconditioned stimulus. The question of the conditions under which acquired responding will be compensatory rather than mimetic has yet to be satisfactorily answered. Eikelboom and Stewart (1982) argued that all conditioned responding is mimetic and that seeming instances of compensatory responding simply reflect a misidentification of the effective unconditioned stimulus. That is, for unconditioned stimuli that impinge primarily on efferent neural pathways of the peripheral nervous system, the "real" reinforcer is the feedback to the central nervous system. Thus, what is often mistakenly viewed as the unconditioned response precedes a later behavior that constitutes the effective unconditioned response. For example, ethanol consumption decreases body temperature (i.e., it produces hypothermia), which has traditionally been considered to be an unconditioned response to ethanol. However, the conditioned response to a cue associated with ethanol is an increase in body temperature (i.e., hyperthermia); that is, conditioned responding to ethanol is compensatory in nature. Eikelboom and Stewart suggested that the effective unconditioned stimulus in this situation is not the ethanol, but the feedback that the ethanol-produced hypothermia sends to the central nervous system. Similarly, the unconditioned response is not the hypothermia, but the reaction of the system to counter the decrease in body temperature, namely, an increase in body temperature. Thus, both the unconditioned and the conditioned response would be of the same value (i.e., hyperthermia). This approach is stimulating, but it encounters problems in that most unconditioned stimuli impinge on both afferent and efferent pathways, and there are complex feedback loops at various anatomical levels between these two pathways.

Conditioned responding is not just a reflection of past experience with a cue indicating a change in the probability of an outcome; it reflects not only the likelihood that a reinforcer will occur, but also *when* and *where* the reinforcer will occur. This is evident in many learning situations (see the earlier section titled "Empirical Laws of Conditioning and Learning"). For instance, Clayton and Dickinson (1999) reported that scrub jays, which cache food, remember not only what food items have been stored but also where and when they were stored, as evidenced by their retrieving food from appropriate locations and doing so as a function of the previously experienced rate at which the specific type of food spoils and the length of the retention interval. Similarly, animals often orient to the place where reinforcement has been delivered in the past (goal tracking; e.g., Burns & Domjan, 1996). Additionally, there is evidence that subjects can integrate temporal and spatial information from different learning experiences to create spatiotemporal relationships between stimuli that were never paired in actual experience (e.g., Etienne et al., 1998; Savastano & Miller, 1998). Alternatively stated, in mediated learning, not only does the mediating stimulus become a surrogate for the occurrence of the outcome, but it also carries with it information concerning where and when the outcome will occur relative to the mediating stimulus.

What Mental Links Are Formed?

In the middle of the 20th century there was considerable controversy about whether stimulus-outcome (S-O), stimulus-response (S-R), or response-outcome (R-O) relationships (i.e., associations) were learned. The major strategies that were used to resolve this question concerning *associative structures* (i.e., the content of learning) were either (a) to use test conditions that differed from those of training by pitting one type of association against another (e.g., go toward a specific signal or respond by turning right), or (b) to degrade (or enhance) one or another type of association after training (e.g., satiation or habituation to the outcome or extinction of the eliciting cue) and observe its effect on acquired behavior. The results of such studies indicated that subjects could readily learn all three types of associations, and ordinarily the three different types of associations influenced acquired behavior to various degrees, depending on which allowed the easiest solution of the task confronting the subject (reviewed by Kimble, 1961). That is, subjects are versatile in their information-processing strategies; are opportunistic given the specific situation; learn

S-R, S-O, and R-O associations; and ordinarily use whichever combination of environmental relationships is most adaptive. The development of this view started with Tolman's (Tolman, Ritchie, & Kalish, 1946) studies of plus maze learning, in which response-outcome learning (turning in a specific direction determined by a learned sequence of muscular reactions to obtain reinforcement) was pitted against stimulus-outcome learning (turning toward a specific stimulus to obtain reinforcement) as a function of the availability of salient guiding stimuli. It was applied to *avoidance learning* by Mowrer (1947), who argued that subjects first learned an association between a stimulus and an aversive outcome (S-O), making the stimulus a potential second-order aversive reinforcer, and then learned to *escape* from the stimulus (R-O, with the stimulus now functioning as an outcome). Recent studies of associative structure are exemplified by Rescorla's (e.g., 1998) analysis of extinction of an instrumental response in which response-outcome associations appear to be deactivated during extinction treatment, leaving the cue-outcome association unaltered. Such studies demonstrate the utility of Skinner's (1938) *three-term* (X, Y, Z) *contingency* in analyzing learning tasks: Response Y in the presence of (discriminative) stimulus X is followed by outcome Z. A purely Pavlovian situation is defined as one in which Z is in no way dependent on Y (R-O contingency $= 0$). Starting from this complete independence, there are gradations of control of the outcome by the subjects' behavior, all conventionally defined as instrumental situations (R-O contingency $\neq 0$). For dichotomous stimulus X, response Y, and outcome Z (i.e., each present or absent on a given trial), it is instructive to imagine an extrapolation of the 2×2 contingency table in Table 2.1 into a three-dimensional $2 \times 2 \times 2$ contingency table in which responding is a function of the three-term contingency (for further discussion of the three-term contingency, see Chap. 1, this volume).

Although much stimulus control of behavior can be described in terms of simple associations among cues, responses, and outcomes, *occasion setting*—that is, the presentation of a contextual or discrete cue to signal whether (positive occasion setters) or not (negative occasion setters) the outcome will follow the target cue in that given trial—does not yield to such analyses. One view of how occasion setting works is that positive occasion setters serve to facilitate (and negative occasion setters inhibit) the retrieval of associations (e.g., Holland, 1983b). Thus, they might be viewed as stimuli with a higher-order association to a simple association, rather than an association to the representation of a stimulus or response. Such a view introduces a new type of learning, thereby adding complexity to the compendium of possible learned relationships. The leading alternative to the higher-order association view of occasion setting is that occasion setters join into configural units with the stimuli that they are modulating (Schmajuk, Lamoureux, & Holland, 1998). This latter approach suffices to explain behavior in most occasion-setting situations but to date has led to few novel testable predictions. Both approaches appear strained when used to account for transfer of the occasion-setting properties of an occasion setter from the association in which it was trained to another association. Empirically, such transfer is most successful if the transfer association itself was previously occasion-set (see the earlier section titled "Conditioned Inhibition"; Holland, 1989). For further discussion of occasion setting, see Hall (Chap. 1, this volume).

Acquisition-Focused (Associative) Models

All traditional models of acquired behavior have assumed that critical processing of information occurs exclusively when target stimuli are present, that is, during training, testing, or both. The processes that occur during training are mostly related to association formation (i.e., acquisition), whereas the processes that occur during testing are mostly related to behavior dictated by the learned associations (i.e., expression or performance). The various contemporary models of acquired behavior can be divided into those that emphasize processing that occurs during training (hereafter called *acquisition-focused* models) and those that emphasize processing that occurs during testing (hereafter called *expression-focused* models). (Note that we say "emphasize" here because all models at least pay lip service to the importance of information processing both at acquisition and at testing; later, we discuss hybrid models, but for immediate purposes of exposition we maintain the dichotomy.) For each of these two families of models in their simplest forms, some phenomena are readily explained, and other phenomena are problematic. However, theorists have managed to explain most observations within acquired behavior in either framework (see R. Miller & Escobar, 2001) when allowed to modify one or another model within that framework as new observations are reported.

The dominant tradition since Pavlov (1927) and Thorndike (1932) has been the acquisition-focused approach, which assumes that learning consists of the development of associations (i.e., connections between mental/neural representations of stimulus events). In theoretical terms, each association is characterized by an associative strength or value, which is a kind of *summary statistic* representing the subject's cumulative history with relationships (ordinarily pairings) between two events. Hull (1943) and Rescorla and Wagner (1972) provided two examples of acquisition-focused models, with the latter being the most influential model today (see R. Miller, Barnet, & Grahame, 1995, for a full description and critique of this model). Notably, in acquisition-focused models subjects are assumed not to recall specific experiences (i.e., training trials) at test; rather, they have access to only the current associative strength between events. At test, the presentation of one event (here called the cue) activates the mental representation of that event, which then activates the representation of the other (associated) event to a degree that is monotonically related to the strength of the association connecting the two representations. Activation of this latter representation in turn gives rise to conditioned responding. Models within this family differ primarily in the rules used to form (and calculate) associative strength, and whether or not they assume that additional summary statistics are computed. For example, Pearce and Hall (1980) proposed that on each training trial subjects not only update the associative strength between stimuli present on that trial but also recalculate the *associability* of each stimulus present on that trial (associability is defined as the readiness to associate a given stimulus). What all contemporary acquisition-focused models share is that new experience causes an updating of associative strength based on the current trial; hence, recent experience has greater impact on immediate behavior than does otherwise equivalent earlier experience, which is consistent with observations of stimulus control following opposing phases of training (e.g., reinforcement followed by nonreinforcement immediately results in behavior that is consistent with nonreinforcement). The result is that these models are quite adept at accounting for trial-order effects that ordinarily reflect *recency* (e.g., extinction, from which spontaneous recovery is often seen over increasing extinction-test retention periods); conversely, they are challenged by primacy effects in which early experience has greater influence on behavior than has later experience (generally speaking, primacy effects are far less frequent than are recency effects, but they do

occur; e.g., the CS-preexposure deficit). Next we discuss some of the major variables that differentiate among the various acquisition-focused models. Although we do not describe the specifics of each model of learning here, relevant citations are provided.

Acquisition-Focused Accounts of Critical Factors in Acquired Behavior

Stimulus Salience/Attention. Nearly all models (expression- as well as acquisition-focused) represent the saliencies of the cue and outcome through either one conjoint factor (e.g., Bush & Mosteller, 1951) or two independent factors (one for the cue and the other for the outcome; e.g., Rescorla & Wagner, 1972). This factor can be either a fixed parameter (e.g., Bush & Mosteller; Rescorla & Wagner) or a variable that changes as a function of experience (e.g., Mackintosh, 1975, in which the *associability* of a cue increases after each trial if it was the best predictor of the outcome on that trial; otherwise, it decreases). A significant departure from this standard treatment of salience/attention is Pearce and Hall's (1980) model, which posits two attentional variables: salience, which is a constant for each cue, and associability, which changes after each trial in proportion to the discrepancy between the outcome that was experienced and the outcome that was expected (based on all the cues present) on that trial. Hence, in this model associability is an additional summary statistic for each individual cue, in addition to associative strength, which is a summary statistic for each cue-outcome dyad.

Predispositions (Genetic and Experiential). Subjects enter each learning situation not only with existing response potentials given various cues but also with *predispositions* concerning the ease with which the underlying associations can be modified and with which new associations can be formed. These predispositions, which depend on evolutionary history and often on specific prior experience, have proven difficult to capture in models intended to have broad generality across tasks, across individuals within a species, and even across species. In the (perhaps misdirected) interests of generality, most models of acquired behavior (acquisition- and expression-focused) have ignored the issue of differential predispositions. However, those models that use a single parameter to describe the conjoint associability (a single associative growth parameter, as opposed to independent associabilities for each element) for both the cue and the outcome can readily incorporate predispositions within this parameter. For example, in the well-known Garcia and Koelling (1966) demonstration of flavors joining into association with gastric distress more readily than with electric shock, and audiovisual cues entering into association more readily with electric shock than gastric distress, separate (constant) associabilities for the flavor, audiovisual cue, electric shock, and gastric distress cannot explain the observed differences in predisposition to learn. In contrast, this example of cue-to-consequence effects is readily accounted for by high conjoint associabilities for flavor-gastric distress and audiovisual cues-electric shock, and low conjoint associabilities for flavor-electric shock and audiovisual cues-gastric distress. However, to require a separate associability parameter for every possible cue-outcome dyad creates a vastly greater number of parameters than does simply having a single parameter for each cue and each outcome (with changes in behavior being a function of these two parameters—usually their product). Hence, we see here the recurring tradeoff between a more tractable oversimplification (separate parameters for each cue and each outcome) and a less tractable reality (a unique parameter for each cue-outcome dyad).

An alternative to models of acquired behavior that aim for broad generality over tasks and species is to develop separate models for each family of biologically essential tasks (e.g., foraging, mating, defense, shelter from the elements) and species, consistent with the view that the mind is organized by modular-specific processes (e.g., Garcia, Lasiter, Bermudez-Rattoni, & Deems, 1985). This approach has been championed by some researchers (Cosmides & Tooby, 1994) but faces challenges because the resulting models can become very complex and are limited in their potential to generate unambiguous testable predictions. No doubt, organisms react to diverse motivational problems in different manners, which has supported the view that separate processes are responsible for addressing different environmental challenges (e.g., Gallistel, 1999). The question is whether one wishes to emphasize the differences or the similarities. In this chapter, we clearly emphasize the similarities.

Similarity (Including Spatiotemporal Contiguity). In light of the clear importance of cue-outcome temporal contiguity as a determinant of acquired behavior, it is surprising that many associative models give short shrift to this critical variable. One common tactic has been to incorporate contiguity indirectly through changes in the context-outcome association that are assumed to affect the cue-outcome association on subsequent trials, much as initial pairings of Cue Y with the outcome have an effect on how much responding Cue X elicits after YX-outcome pairings (i.e., blocking; e.g., Mackintosh, 1975; Pearce & Hall, 1980; Rescorla & Wagner, 1972). A different approach has been to assume that *relative* rather than *absolute* cue-outcome contiguity determines behavioral control by a cue (e.g., Gallistel & Gibbon, 2000; see the subsection titled "Similarity (Including Spatiotemporal

Contiguity)" under "Empirical Laws of Conditioning and Learning"). The only associative models that incorporate in their postulates the effects of temporal contiguity are the so-called real-time models (discussed later; e.g., McLaren & Mackintosh, 2000; Sutton & Barto, 1981; Wagner, 1981). No contemporary model centrally addresses the effects of cue-outcome similarity, although one might attempt to account for its effects in terms of stimulus generalization between the cue and outcome summating with the acquired cue-outcome association.

Objective Contingency. The attenuation of acquired behavior through degradation of contingency (see Table 2.2) has rarely been addressed as a unified problem. Most associative models of acquired behavior have accounted for extinction through either (a) the weakening of the cue-outcome association (e.g., Rescorla & Wagner, 1972) or (b) the development of an inhibitory relationship between the cue and outcome that opposes the initial excitatory association (e.g., Hull, 1952; Pearce & Hall, 1980; Wagner, 1981). Attenuated responding due to partial reinforcement (i.e., cue-alone presentations interspersed among the cue-outcome pairings) is ordinarily explained through mechanisms similar to those used to account for extinction. In contrast, the CS-preexposure effect (repeated exposures to the cue before cue-outcome pairings) has been explained both in terms of (a) a decrease in the associability (attention) to the cue as a result of non-reinforced pretraining exposure (e.g., Pearce & Hall, 1980) and (b) the development of a strong context-cue association that attenuates acquisition of the cue-outcome association (e.g., Wagner, 1981). The CS-preexposure effect is greatly attenuated if preexposure to the cue occurs in a context different from the context of the cue-outcome pairings. The context specificity of the CS-preexposure effect

seemingly lends support to this latter view, but some models that explain the effect in attentional terms can also accommodate it if the context is treated as a conditioned cue for inattention to the cue (e.g., Lubow, 1989). Notably, some prominent models simply fail to account for the CS-preexposure effect (e.g., Rescorla & Wagner, 1972).

Attenuated responding achieved by degrading contingency through unsignaled outcomes interspersed among the cue-outcome pairings and the US-preexposure effect are both explained by most associative models in terms of the development of context-outcome associations that then compete with the cue-outcome association on subsequent cue-outcome pairings in that context (as mentioned earlier, this view assumes that the context functions in a way similar to a discrete blocking stimulus). This is consistent with the context specificity of these effects (i.e., US-preexposure in one context retards subsequent stimulus control during cue-outcome pairings much less if the preexposure occurred outside of the training context). However, habituation to the outcome can also contribute to the effect in certain cases (Randich & LoLordo, 1979b). Only a few new associative models can account for reduced responding as a result of unsignaled outcome exposures after the termination of cue-outcome training (Dickinson & Burke, 1996; Van Hamme & Wasserman, 1994). However, this prediction is only partly successful because the effect is observed only under rather limited conditions (see Denniston et al., 1996).

Cue and Outcome Durations. Models that parse time into trials ordinarily account for the generally weaker stimulus control that is observed when cue duration is increased by changing the cue's associability/salience parameter (e.g., Rescorla & Wagner, 1972). A problem with studying this variable is that modifying it usually introduces a confound either with the cue-onset to outcome-onset interval (i.e., contiguity) or with the cue-termination to outcome-onset interval (i.e., the interstimulus gap), each of which has its own inverse effect on stimulus control by the target. In principle, changes in outcome duration also might be addressed through changes in the outcome's associability parameter, but they have received little attention because changes in the duration of the outcome ordinarily alter its reinforcing value as well (this issue would best be explored within a sensory preconditioning preparation in which an outcome could be used that has minimal reinforcing value). A far better account of cue and outcome durations is provided by real-time associative models (McLaren & Mackintosh, 2000; Sutton & Barto, 1981; Wagner, 1981). According to these models, the associative strength of a cue changes continuously when it is present, depending on the activity of the outcome representation.

Conditioned Inhibition.   The treatments and consequent changes in behavior indicative of conditioned inhibition (i.e., summation and retardation tests) were described earlier. At the theoretical level, acquisition-focused models have accounted for conditioned inhibition in at least three different ways. Konorski (1948) suggested that inhibitory cues elevate the activation threshold of the representation of the outcome required for generation of a conditioned response. Later, Konorski (1967) proposed that inhibitory cues activated a no-outcome representation that countered activation of an outcome representation by excitatory associations to that stimulus or to other stimuli present at test. Subsequently, Rescorla and Wagner (1972) proposed that conditioned inhibitors were cues with negative associative strength. For a given stimulus in this framework, conditioned inhibition and conditioned excitation are mutually exclusive. This posi-

tion has been widely adopted, perhaps in part because of its simplicity. However, as previously noted, considerable data (e.g., Droungas & LoLordo, 1994; Matzel et al., 1988; Tait & Saladin, 1986) demonstrate that inhibition and excitation are not mutually exclusive; that is, a given stimulus can pass tests for both excitation and inhibition without intervening training. Most acquisition-focused theories other than the Rescorla-Wagner model allow stimuli to possess both excitatory and inhibitory potential simultaneously (e.g., Pearce & Hall, 1980; Wagner, 1981). Notably, Denny (1971) completely avoided the issue of the nature of inhibitory processes that underlie inhibitory behavior by positing that inhibitory cues control overt behavior that is incompatible with the target excitatory behavior.

Response Rules.   Any model of acquired behavior must include both learning rules (to encode experience) and retrieval/response rules (to express this encoded information). The only things that we actually observe are changes in behavior as a function of experience. From these observations, we infer both learning (i.e., acquisition) and response rules. Historically, acquisition has been strongly emphasized, perhaps because introspection misleads us to think that whatever we see within our minds is available to influence behavior. Indeed, this bias has been so strong that the field has often been called *learning*, but rarely '*acquired behavior.*' Acquisition-focused models, by definition, have relatively simple response rules and leave accounts of behavioral phenomena largely to differences in what is learned during training. For example, the Rescorla-Wagner (1972) model simply stated that responding is a monotonic function of associative strength. In practice, most researchers who have tried to test the model quantitatively have gone further and assumed that response magnitude is proportional to associative strength. Thus, if

Cues A and B have associative strengths of 5 and 1, respectively, responding to A is expected to be five times greater than responding to B. The omission of a more specific response rule in the Rescorla-Wagner model was not an oversight. They wanted to focus attention on acquisition processes and did not want researchers to be distracted by concerns that were not central to their model. However, the lack of a specific response rule leaves the Rescorla-Wagner model and most other associative models less quantitative than they are often assumed to be. Typically, they make only ordinal predictions concerning responding following various treatments.

Reinforcement Theory.   For the first 60 years of the 20th century, various forms of reinforcement theory dominated the study of acquired behavior. The history of reinforcement theory can be traced from Thorndike's (1911) *strong law of effect* through Hull's several models (e.g., 1952). The basic premise of reinforcement theory was that learning (i.e., the formation of associations) did not occur without the presentation of a biologically significant stimulus because only such a *reinforcer* could engage the learning mechanism (i.e., it was assumed that reinforcement "stamped" the association into memory). Although this view was long dominant, as early as Tolman (1932) other theorists suggested that reinforcement had a greater impact on the expression of knowledge than on the encoding of it. Thus, learning could proceed without reinforcement, but reinforcement was necessary in order to translate that learning into behavior. Reinforcement was the first variable that was recognized to be primarily a performance variable, as opposed to an acquisition variable (subsequently, reinforcement has been joined by other performance variables, such as retrieval cues). Reinforcement during training may well accelerate the rate at which a relationship between two events is encoded, per-

haps by enhancing attention to task-relevant stimuli. However, encoding of event-event relationships has been shown to occur in the absence of reinforcement (unless one argues that every stimulus has some reinforcing value, an assumption that renders the principle so universal that it makes no testable predictions). Learning in the absence of reinforcement is readily demonstrated in Pavlovian situations by the sensory preconditioning effect (X-A training followed by A-US training, with a subsequent test on X; Brogden, 1939) and in instrumental situations by latent learning effects in which the subject is not motivated when exposed to the learning relationships. For example, rats allowed to explore a maze without reinforcement will show better performance than will rats not given the exposure when food reward is later introduced (Tolman & Honzik, 1930). Notably, Skinner (1938) circumvented the learning-performance distinction by speaking functionally only about changes in responding, rather than intervening variables such as learning. His approach works well in situations in which overt primary or secondary reinforcement occurs during training, but it is strained (although not refuted) in instances of latent learning.

Informational Hypothesis.   With the demise of reinforcement theory, the informational hypothesis was proposed as an alternative. The view that cues acquire associative strength to the extent that they are informative about (i.e., predict) an outcome was first suggested by Egger and Miller (1963), who observed less responding to X after A-X-US trials than after equivalent training in the absence of A (X-US), a phenomenon known as serial overshadowing. Kamin (1968) developed the informational hypothesis through his studies of cue competition and informal theorizing about the need for a *surprising* outcome for learning to occur. Kamin's concept of surprise was later formalized by Rescorla and Wagner (1972) as what has come to be known as the *delta rule*. Simply stated, the change in the associative strength of a cue in a given trial is proportional to the difference (delta) between the (value of the) outcome that actually occurred and the (value of the) outcome that was expected based on all cues present on that trial. Following Kamin's lead, their primary concern was competition between cues trained in compound (e.g., overshadowing and blocking). Rescorla and Wagner proposed that a target cue would acquire associative strength with respect to an outcome to the extent that the outcome was not fully predicted on that trial. If another cue that was present during training of the target already largely predicted the outcome, there was less new information about the outcome to be assigned to the target; hence, little learning to the target was predicted (i.e., they assumed that only a certain amount of outcome can be predicted; thus, different cues compete to predict the outcome). This position in one or another form held sway for several decades, became central to many subsequent models of learning (e.g., Pearce, 1987; Pearce & Hall, 1980; Wagner, 1981), and is still popular today. The informational hypothesis has been invoked to account for many observations, including the weak responding observed to cues presented simultaneously with an outcome (i.e., the simultaneous conditioning deficit). However, it has been criticized for failing to distinguish between learning (acquisition of associations) and expression of what was learned (behavioral expression of those associations; R. Miller et al., 1995). Treatments that result in recovery (without further training) from cue competition effects such as blocking and overshadowing challenge the informational hypothesis (e.g., reminder clues: Kasprow, Cacheiro, Balaz, & Miller, 1982; extinction of the competing cue: Kaufman & Bolles, 1981; spontaneous recovery: J. Miller, McKinzie, Kraebel, & Spear, 1996). Similarly

problematic is the observation that simultaneous presentations of a cue (X) and outcome appear to result in latent learning that can later be revealed by manipulations that create a forward relationship to a stimulus presented at test (e.g., presentation of X and a US simultaneously, followed by Y-X pairings result in strong conditioned responding to Y; Matzel, Held, & Miller, 1988). Thus, both cue competition and the simultaneous conditioning deficit appear to be, at least in part, deficits in expression of acquired knowledge rather than deficits in acquisition, contrary to the postulates of the informational hypothesis. Certainly, predictive power (the focus of the informational hypothesis) is the primary *function* of learning, but the *process* underlying learning appears to be dissociated from this important function. The wide acceptance of the informational hypothesis in the last quarter of the 20th century appears to have resulted from a failure to differentiate process from function. Notably, these acquisition-focused models can be restated to circumvent this issue by replacing the terms "discrepancy between anticipated and actual outcome" for the concepts of discrepancy between activation (of the representation of an outcome) from internal sources (i.e., retrieval activated) and activation from external sources (the physical outcome), as is done by McLaren and Mackintosh (2000).

Element of the Association Emphasized

Contemporary associative models of acquired behavior were developed in large part to account for cue competition (e.g., blocking) between cues trained in compound. Although there is considerable reason to think that cue competition is due at least in part to factors other than a deficit in acquisition (see the previous discussion), these models have attempted to account for cue competition through either the outcome's or the cue's becoming less effective in supporting new learning. *Outcome-limited* associative models are ordinarily based on the informational hypothesis and assume that in cue competition paradigms the outcome becomes less effective in entering into new associations because it is already predicted by the competing cues that are presented concurrently with the target (e.g., Rescorla & Wagner, 1972). In contrast, *cue-limited* models assume that attention to (or associability of) the target cue decreases as a result of the concurrent presence of other (competing) cues that also predict the outcome (e.g., Pearce & Hall, 1980).

As both outcome- and cue-limited models have their separate advantages, some theorists have been encouraged to create hybrid models that employ both mechanisms (e.g., Mackintosh, 1975; Wagner, 1981). Not surprisingly, such hybrid models tend to be more successful in providing post hoc accounts of phenomena. Because they incorporate relatively large numbers of different mechanisms, however, their a priori predictions tend to be dependent on specific parameters. Thus, in most cases their predictions are ambiguous unless extensive preliminary work is done to determine the appropriate parameters for the specific situation.

Temporal Window of Analysis

A central feature of any model of acquired behavior is the frequency with which new perceptual input is integrated with previously acquired knowledge. Most acquisition-focused models of learning are *discrete trial* models, which assume that acquired behavior on any trial depends on pretrial knowledge and that the information provided on the trial is integrated with this knowledge immediately after the trial (i.e., after the occurrence or nonoccurrence of the outcome; e.g., Mackintosh, 1975; Pearce & Hall, 1980; Rescorla & Wagner, 1972). Such an assumption contrasts with *real-time* models, which assume that new

information is integrated continuously (i.e., instant by instant) with prior knowledge and that behavior at any moment is a function of the subject's current knowledge and immediate impinging stimuli (e.g., McLaren & Mackintosh, 2000; Sutton & Barto, 1981; Wagner, 1981). In practice, most implementations of real-time models do not integrate information instantaneously, but rather do so after set periods of time (e.g., every 0.1 s) throughout each training session. A common weakness of all discrete trial models (expression- as well as acquisition-focused) is that they cannot account for the powerful effects of cue-outcome temporal contiguity. Parsing an experimental session into trials in which cues and outcomes each do or do not occur ordinarily results in the loss of temporal information. In contrast, real-time models (expression- as well as acquisition-focused) can readily account for temporal contiguity effects. Real-time models are clearly more realistic, but discrete trial models are more deterministic (less dependent on parameters for the direction of predicted effects) and consequently have stimulated more research.

Expression-Focused Models

In contrast to acquisition-focused models in which summary statistics representing prior experience are assumed to be all that is retained from prior experience, expression-focused models assume that a more or less veridical representation of the past is retained and that on each trial subjects process all (or a random or selective sample, depending on the model) of this large store of information to determine their immediate behavior (R. Miller & Escobar, 2001). Hence, these models can be regarded more as response rules than as rules for learning, per se. This approach makes far greater demands on memory, but there is actually little empirical reason to believe that limits on long-term memory capacity constrain how behavior is modified as a function of experience. In many respects, the summary statistic versus veridical representation approaches of acquisition- and expression-focused models, respectively, is analogous (perhaps homologous) to the distinction between prototype and exemplar models in category learning (e.g., Ross & Makin, 1999).

A consistent characteristic of contemporary expression-focused models of acquired behavior is that they all involve some sort of comparison between the likelihood of the outcome in the presence of the cue and the likelihood of the outcome in the absence of the cue. This feature is not essential for expression-focused models, but the assumption has proven so successful in accounting for behavioral phenomena of interest that it has been incorporated into all expression-focused accounts of acquired behavior.

Contingency Models

Contingency models are distinguished by their emphasis on event frequencies, which subjects are assumed to count, and behavior on each trial is determined by calculations based on the frequencies on the corresponding test trial. One of the earliest and best known expression-focused models is Rescorla's (1968; also see Kelley, 1967) contingency model. This discrete trial model posits that subjects behave as if they record the frequencies of (a) cue-outcome pairings, (b) cues alone, (c) outcomes alone, and (d) trials with neither cues nor outcomes (see Table 2.1). Based on these frequencies, conditioned responding reflects the difference between the conditional probability of the outcome given the presence of the cue and the conditional probability of the outcome in the absence of the cue (i.e., the base-rate of the outcome in the experimental context). Alternatively stated, stimulus control is assumed to be directly related to the change in outcome probability signaled by the cue. A conditioned excitor is presumed to be a cue that

signals an increase in the probability of the outcome, whereas a conditioned inhibitor is presumably a cue that signals a decrease in that probability. This model is often quite successful in describing conditioned responding (and causal inference, which appears to follow much the same rules as Pavlovian conditioning; see Shanks, 1994, for a review). Subsequently, researchers have found that differentially weighting the four types of trial frequencies (with Type 1 trials receiving the greatest weight and Type 4 trials the least) provides an improved fit to most data (e.g., Wasserman et al., 1993). However, even for a single task, the optimal weights are not constant, but a function of the outcome base rate (see, e.g., Baker, Murphy, & Vallée-Tourangeau, 1996).

Rescorla's contingency (1968) model is elegant in its simplicity. For example, contingency effects are explained as increases in trial Types 2 and 3 (see Table 2.1), and temporal contiguity effects are (somewhat less satisfactorily) explained as increases in the temporal window that defines a trial (necessarily increased to include proximate cues and outcomes on a single trial), thereby decreasing the number of Type 4 trials effectively occurring during the intertrial intervals. However, this model has several conspicuous failings. Unlike most performance-focused models, it cannot account for (a) the powerful effects of trial order (e.g., recency effects) because it simply records the occurrence of different trial types, ignoring the order in which they occur (i.e., recent trials receive the same weight as trials that occurred much earlier in time), or (b) cue competition effects (e.g., blocking) because it addresses only single cue situations. For these reasons, Rescorla abandoned his expression-focused contingency model in favor of the acquisition-focused Rescorla-Wagner (1972) model. However, other researchers have addressed these deficits by proposing variants of

Rescorla's contingency model. For example, Cheng and Novick (1992) developed their *focal set contingency model* that, rather than using information from all prior trials to generate immediate behavior, uses selection rules to determine which trials to incorporate into the calculation of the conditional probabilities. For example, in blocking (see Table 2.3), the presence of the blocking stimulus (Y) on both the Phase 1 (Y-outcome) trials and the Phase 2 (YX-outcome) trials causes the Phase 1 trials to be incorporated into the focal set (hence, all these trials are used to compute the conditional probabilities). In contrast, for control subjects that in Phase 1 receive Z-outcome trials and in Phase 2 receive XY-outcome trials, the only trials incorporated in the calculation of the conditional probabilities for X are the YX-outcome trials of Phase 2. Thus, Cheng and Novick's contingency model succeeds in accounting for blocking; it can account for overshadowing only by adding a salience ratio to the conditional probabilities, which is the same device used by most acquisition-focused models to account for overshadowing (e.g., Rescorla & Wagner, 1972). Additionally, if trials are differentially weighted as a function of recency or the number of relevant intervening trials, contingency models are able to address trial-order effects (e.g., Maldonado, Cátena, Cándido, & García, 1999).

Comparator Models

Comparator models constitute a second group of expression-focused models. Comparator models are similar to contingency models in emphasizing a comparison at the time of testing between the likelihood of the outcome in the presence and absence of the cue. However, these models do not focus on event frequencies, as do the contingency models. Currently, there are two types of comparator models. One focuses exclusively on comparisons of temporal relationships (e.g., rates of outcome occurrence), whereas the other assumes that

comparisons occur on many dimensions, with time being only one of them.

The best known timing model of acquired behavior is Gibbon and Balsam's (1981; see also Balsam, 1984) *scalar-expectancy theory* (SET). According to SET, conditioned responding is directly related to the average interval between outcomes during training (i.e., a measure of the prediction of the outcome based on the presence of the experimental context, abbreviated as C) and is inversely related to the interval between cue onset and the outcome (i.e., a measure of the prediction of the outcome based on the cue, abbreviated as T). (See Chap. 9, this volume, for models of how temporal information might be represented cognitively; here our concern is the use of temporal information in modulating behavior). Like all timing models (and in contrast to the other expression-focused models), SET is highly successful in explaining cue-outcome contiguity effects and also does well predicting the effects of contingency degradation that occur when the outcome is presented in the absence of the cue. However, the model has problems in accounting for the effect of contingency degradation produced by presenting the cue in the absence of the outcome. Although the model accounts for the CS-preexposure effect, it fails to explain extinction because C and T are assumed to be updated only when an outcome occurs, which does not happen during extinction. That is, SET predicts that extinction treatment should not attenuate responding until there is a reinforced trial because until then the extinction experience will not be incorporated. This counterintuitive prediction is incorrect; extinction treatment weakens responding, and one subsequent cue-outcome pairing is often seen to produce a resurgence of responding to the cue (it constitutes a reminder for the cue-outcome experience). SET also fails to account for stimulus competition/interference effects because, like Rescorla's (1968) contingency model, it has no mechanisms to address cue interactions.

A recent expression-focused timing model proposed by Gallistel and Gibbon (2000), called *rate expectancy theory* (RET), incorporates many of the principles of SET but emphasizes rates (number) of outcome occurrence (in the presence of the cue and separately in the experimental context without the cue present), rather than latencies (time) between outcomes. This inversion (from latencies to rates) allows the model to account for stimulus competition/interference effects because rates of reinforcement associated with different cues are assumed to summate. Consider the case of two cues, each of which predicts the outcome at rates A and B. If these two cues are presented together, the compound is assumed to predict the outcome at a rate equal to the sum of the separate rates ($C = A + B$), and the value of rates A and B will be decremented if the actual rate of reinforcement of the compound is less than the summed rate (C). In contrast to SET, which was developed to account for single cue-single outcome situations, RET attributes outcome rates to nontarget discrete cues that are paired with the outcome as well as background cues (which allows it to account for cue competition effects). Moreover, anticipated rates of outcome occurrence are assumed to change continuously with exposure to the cue or to the background stimuli in the absence as well as the presence of the outcome, thereby accounting for extinction as well as the CS-preexposure effect and partial reinforcement. Responding is predicted when the rate of outcome occurrence in the presence of the cue significantly exceeds the rate of outcome occurrence in the absence of the cue, where "significant" is determined as if the subject performed a statistical test. Thus, this model preserves the essence of SET and adds features that greatly improve its success, but at the cost of making it far more complex.

A comparator model that does not focus exclusively on timing is the *comparator hypothesis* of R. Miller and Matzel (1988; also see Denniston, Savastano, & Miller, 2001). Like SET, this model assumes that responding is directly related to the degree to which the target cue predicts the outcome and that it is inversely related to the degree to which the outcome is predicted by other (discrete and contextual) cues that were present when the cue was being *trained*. These latter cues are called comparator cues because expectation of the outcome based on the target cue is compared to the expectation of the outcome based on these cues. This comparison is presumed to occur anew on each test trial. The expectation of the outcome based on comparator cues is assumed to be a multiplicative function of the target cue-comparator cue association and the comparator cue-outcome association. Although this model is couched in terms of associations, the rules for forming these associations are assumed to follow a very simple contiguity principle (e.g., Bush & Mosteller, 1951). The down-modulating effect of the comparator cues on acquired responding depends on the similarity of the outcome (in all aspects including temporal and spatial attributes) that these cues predict relative to the outcome that the target cue predicts. Thus, this model (along with most other expression-focused models) brings to acquired responding the principle of relativity that is seen in many other subfields concerned with information processing by organisms (e.g., Fechner's law, the marginal value theorem of economics, contrast effects in motivational theory, the matching law of behavioral choice). SET also emphasizes relativity (so-called *time-scale invariance*), but only in the temporal domain. The comparator hypothesis accounts for both contingency degradation and cue competition effects through links between the target and comparator cues (discrete in the case of cue competition effect, and contextual in the case of contingency degradation) and links between these comparator cues and the outcome.

Conditioned Inhibition.   There is nothing inherent in either acquisition-focused or expression-focused models to demand one or another view of conditioned inhibition. Most acquisition-focused (i.e., associative) models have conceived of conditioned inhibition as an association to either expectation of no-outcome (e.g., Pearce & Hall, 1980) or a negative expectation of the outcome (e.g., Rescorla & Wagner, 1972). Some people (including the present authors) find these constructs hard to conceptualize; it seems difficult to conceive of how an animal can have a negative representation of, say, shock or how associations can be formed to a negated representation. With respect to performance-focused models, SET does not speak to conditioned inhibition, whereas RET treats conditioned inhibition as a negative rate of reinforcement, a view that is quite similar to the negative expectation view of the Rescorla-Wagner model. In the comparator hypothesis, a conditioned inhibitor is viewed as a stimulus that signals a reduction in the rate or probability of reinforcement relative to the baseline occurrence of the reinforcer during training in the absence of the cue (i.e., the expectation of the outcome based on the comparator cues exceeds the expectation of the outcome based on the target cue). This position appears to avoid the theoretical quandary of how no-outcome or a negative expectation could be represented (see also Denny, 1971).

Response Rules.   As previously stated, models of acquired behavior necessarily must include both acquisition rules and response rules. In contrast to acquisition-focused models that generally have simple, often implicit response rules and leave accounts of behavioral differences largely to differences in what is encoded during training, expression-focused models have simple, often implicit rules for acquisition and rely on response rules for an account of most behavioral differences. Thus, the attenuated responding to a target cue observed, for example, in a blocking or contingency-degrading treatment is assumed to arise not from a failure to encode the target cue-outcome pairings, but from a failure to express this information in behavior.

Accounts of Retrospection Revaluation

Previously, we described empirical retrospective revaluation of response potential, in which a target cue is trained in compound with other (discrete or contextual) cues in Phase 1 and then, in Phase 2, a companion cue is presented with or without the outcome. This treatment can alter responding to the target cue (relative to a situation in which the Phase 2 treatment does not occur), even though the target itself was not trained in Phase 2. The modification in responding to the target cue often takes the form of negative mediation; that is, responding to the target changes in a direction opposite from that of the companion cue. One example of such phenomena is the recovery from overshadowing that results from extinction of the overshadowing cue (e.g., Dickinson & Charnock, 1985; Kaufman & Bolles, 1981; Matzel et al., 1985). Expression-focused models that accommodate multiple cues (e.g., RET and the comparator hypothesis) generally have no difficulty accounting for retrospective revaluation because new experience with a companion cue changes the predictive value of the companion cue, and responding to the target cue is usually assumed to be inversely related to the response potential of companion cues. Thus, a retrospective change in the target cue's response potential does not represent new learning about the absent target, but rather new learning concerning the companion stimuli.

In contrast, empirical retrospective revaluation is problematic to most traditional acquisition-focused models. This is because these models assume that responding to the target cue uniquely reflects the associative status of the target, which is generally assumed not to change during retrospective revaluation trials (on which the target cue is absent). With growing evidence of empirical retrospective revaluation, however, several researchers have proposed models that permit changes in the associative status of a cue when it is absent. One of the first of these was a revision of the Rescorla-Wagner (1972) model by Van Hamme and Wasserman (1994), which allows changes in the associative strength of an absent target cue, provided that some associate of the target cue was present. This simple modification successfully accounts for most instances of retrospective revaluation but otherwise has the same failings and successes as the Rescorla-Wagner model (see R. Miller et al., 1995). An alternative associative approach to retrospective revaluation was provided by Dickinson and Burke (1996), who modified Wagner's (1981) SOP model to allow new learning about absent stimuli. As might be expected, the Dickinson and Burke model has many of the same successes and problems as Wagner's model has (discussed earlier).

A notable problem for these associative accounts of (negatively mediated) retrospective revaluation is that other researchers (Hall, 1996; Holland, 1981, 1983b) have used nearly identical models to explain positively mediated learning (e.g., sensory-preconditioning) and mediated extinction (i.e., decreased responding to a target stimulus that results from extinguishing the target's companion stimulus; see Chap. 1, this volume, for further discussion of mediated learning). The only difference between the models of Hall and Holland, of Van Hamme and Wasserman, and of Dickinson and Burke is that the Hall

and Holland models assume that the associability of the reactivated stimulus representation is positive, whereas the Van Hamme and Wasserman and Dickinson and Burke models assume that it is negative. This difference completely reverses most predictions. Without a principled rule for deciding when mediation will be positive (e.g., second-order conditioning) as opposed to negative (e.g., recovery from overshadowing achieved through extinction of the overshadowing cue), there seems to be an arbitrariness to this approach. In contrast to these different associative approaches to retrospective revaluation, all of the contemporary expression-focused models unambiguously predict negative mediation (and fail to account for positive mediation when it is observed). That is, a change in the response potential of a companion stimulus is always expected to be inversely related to the resulting change in the response potential of the target cue. As both positive and negative mediation surely occur, a major chore currently facing researchers is to further illuminate the conditions under which the presentation of a target's companion stimulus serves as a surrogate for the target, and under which the presentation of the companion serves as the negation of the target. As previously stated, the number of pairings of the target and the companion cue has been implicated (Yin et al., 1994), but there are still many other potential factors to examine.

Where Have the Models Taken Us?

As previously noted, theorists have been able to develop models of acquired behavior that can potentially account for many observations after the fact. Any *specific* model, in principle, can be refuted, but classes of models, such as the family of acquisition-focused models or the family of expression-focused models, allow nearly unlimited possibilities for future models within that family (R. Miller &

Escobar, 2001). If the goal is to determine precisely how the mind processes information at the psychological level, contemporary theories of learning have not been successful because viable post hoc alternatives are often possible and in retrospect often appear to be as plausible as does the a priori model that inspired the research.

Nevertheless, models have been highly successful in stimulating experiments that identify new empirical relationships. The models with the greatest success in this respect are often among the least successful in actually accounting for a broad range of changes in behavior that arise from experience because a model stimulates research only to the extent that it makes unambiguous predictions. Models with many parameters and variables (e.g., McLaren & Mackintosh, 2000; Wagner, 1981) can be tuned to account for almost any observation after the observation has been made; hence, few attempts are made to test such models, however plausible they might appear. In contrast, oversimplified models such as that of Rescorla and Wagner (1972) make unambiguous predictions that can be tested, with the result that the model is often refuted. For the foreseeable future, a dialectical path toward theory development in which relatively simple models are used to generate predictions that, when refuted, lead to the development of relatively complex models that are more difficult to test is likely to persist.

CONCLUSIONS

The study of conditioning and learning—basic information processing—is farther from the main stream of psychology today than it was 30 to 50 years ago. Yet progress continues; there are unanswered questions of considerable importance to many fields, including the treatment of psychopathology (particularly behavior modification), behavioral neuroscience, and education, to name but a few. Animal models of psychopathology are the starting points of many new forms of therapeutic psychopharmacology. In behavioral neuroscience, researchers are attempting to identify the neural substrate of behavior, a task that is predicated on an accurate description of the behavior to be explained. Thus, the study of basic behavior sets the agenda for much of the research in neuroscience. Additionally, the study of basic learning and information processing has important messages for educators. For example, research has repeatedly demonstrated that distractor events, changes in context during training, and spacing of training trials all make behavioral change proceed at a slower rate. But these very same procedures also result in improved retention over time and better transfer to new test situations. These are but a few of the enduring contributions stemming from the continued investigation of the principles of learning and basic information processing.

REFERENCES

Armus, H. L. (1959). Effect of magnitude of reinforcement on acquisition and extinction of a running response. *Journal of Experimental Psychology, 58,* 61–63.

Azorlosa, J. L., & Cicala, G. A. (1988). Increased conditioning in rats to a blocked CS after the first compound trial. *Bulletin of the Psychonomic Society, 26,* 254–257.

Baker, A. G., & Mackintosh, N. J. (1977). Excitatory and inhibitory conditioning following uncorrelated presentations of the CS and UCS. *Animal Learning & Behavior, 5,* 315–319.

Baker, A. G., Murphy, R. A., & Vallée-Tourangeau, F. (1996). Associative and normative models of causal induction: Reacting to versus understanding cause. In D. R. Shanks, K. J. Holyoak, & D. L. Medin (Eds.), *The psychology of learning and motivation* (Vol. 34, pp. 1–45). New York: Academic Press.

Balaz, M. A., Gutsin, P., Cacheiro, H., & Miller, R. R. (1982). Blocking as a retrieval failure: Reactivation of associations to a blocked stimulus. *Quarterly Journal of Experimental Psychology, 34B,* 99–113.

Balaz, M. A., Kasprow, W. J., & Miller, R. R. (1982). Blocking with a single compound trial. *Animal Learning & Behavior, 10,* 271–276.

Balsam, P. D. (1984). Relative time in trace conditioning. In J. Gibbon & L. Allan (Eds.), *Annals of the New York Academy of Sciences: Timing and Time Perception* (Vol. 243, pp. 211–227). Cambridge, MA: Ballinger.

Barnet, R. C., Arnold, H. M., & Miller, R. R. (1991). Simultaneous conditioning demonstrated in second-order conditioning: Evidence for similar associative structure in forward and simultaneous conditioning. *Learning and Motivation, 22,* 253–268.

Barnet, R. C., & Miller, R. R. (1996). Temporal encoding as a determinant of inhibitory control. *Learning and Motivation, 27,* 73–91.

Batson, J. D., & Batsell, W. R., Jr. (2000). Augmentation, not blocking, in an A+/AX+ flavor-conditioning procedure. *Psychonomic Bulletin & Review, 7,* 466–471.

Bennett, C. H., Wills, S. J., Oakeshott, S. M., & Mackintosh, N. J. (2000). Is the context specificity of latent inhibition a sufficient explanation of learned irrelevance? *Quarterly Journal of Experimental Psychology, 53B,* 239–253.

Berkeley, G. (1946). *A treatise concerning the principles of human knowledge.* La Salle, IL: Open Court Publication Co. (Original work published 1710)

Best, M. R., Dunn, D. P., Batson, J. D., Meachum, C. L., & Nash, S. M. (1985). Extinguishing conditioned inhibition in flavour-aversion learning: Effects of repeated testing and extinction of the excitatory element. *Quarterly Journal of Experimental Psychology, 37B,* 359–378.

Bidoleau, I., & Schlosberg, H. (1951). Similarity in stimulating conditions as a variable in retroactive inhibition. *Journal of Experimental Psychology, 41,* 199–204.

Blaisdell, A. P., Gunther, L. M., & Miller, R. R. (1999). Recovery from blocking achieved by extinguishing the blocking CS. *Animal Learning & Behavior, 27,* 63–76.

Bonardi, C., & Hall, G. (1996). Learned irrelevance: No more than the sum of CS and US preexposure effects? *Journal of Experimental Psychology: Animal Behavior Processes, 22,* 183–191.

Bonem, M., & Crossman, E. K. (1988). Elucidating the effects of reinforcement magnitude. *Psychological Bulletin, 104,* 348–362.

Bouton, M. E., & Bolles, R. C. (1979). Contextual control of the extinction of conditioned fear. *Learning and Motivation, 10,* 445–466.

Breland, K., & Breland, M. (1961). The misbehavior of organisms. *American Psychologist, 16,* 681–684.

Brogden, W. J. (1939). Sensory pre-conditioning. *Journal of Experimental Psychology, 25,* 323–332.

Brooks, D. C., & Bouton, M. E. (1993). A retrieval cue for extinction attenuates spontaneous recovery. *Journal of Experimental Psychology: Animal Behavior Processes, 19,* 77–89.

Burger, D. C., Mallemat, H., & Miller, R. R. (2000). Overshadowing of subsequent events and recovery thereafter. *Quarterly Journal of Experimental Psychology, 53B,* 149–171.

Burns, M., & Domjan, M. (1996). Sign tracking versus goal tracking in the sexual conditioning of male Japanese quail (*Coturnix japonica*). *Journal of Experimental Psychology: Animal Behavior Processes, 22,* 297–306.

Bush, R. R., & Mosteller, F. (1951). A mathematical model for simple learning. *Psychological Review, 58,* 313–323.

Casa, L. G. de la, & Lubow, R. E. (2000). Super-latent inhibition with delayed conditioned taste aversion testing. *Animal Learning & Behavior, 28,* 389–399.

Cheatle, M. D., & Rudy, J. W. (1978). Analysis of second-order odor-aversion conditioning in neonatal rats: Implications for Kamin's blocking effect. *Journal of Experimental Psychology: Animal Behavior Processes, 4,* 237–249.

Cheng, P. W., & Novick, L. R. (1992). Covariation in natural causal induction. *Psychological Review, 99,* 365–382.

Clarke, J. C., Westbrook, R. F., & Irwin, J. (1979). Potentiation instead of overshadowing in the pigeon. *Behavioral and Neural Biology, 25,* 18–29.

Clayton, N. S., & Dickinson, A. (1999). Scrub jays (*Aphelocoma coerulescens*) remember the relative time of caching as well as the location and content of their caches. *Journal of Comparative Psychology, 113,* 403–416.

Colwill, R. M. (1991). Negative discriminative stimuli provide information about the identity of omitted response-contingent outcomes. *Animal Learning & Behavior, 19,* 326–336.

Cosmides, K., & Tooby, J. (1994). Origins of domain-specificity: The evolution of functional organization. In L. A. Hirschfeld & S. A. Gelman (Eds.), *Mapping the mind: Domain specificity in cognition and culture* (pp. 85–116). New York: Cambridge University Press.

Dalrymple, A. J., & Galef, B. G., Jr. (1981). Visual discrimination pretraining facilitates subsequent visual cue/toxicosis conditioning in rats. *Bulletin of the Psychonomic Society, 18,* 267–270.

Davison, M., & McCarthy, D. (1988). *The matching law: A research review.* Hillsdale, NJ: Erlbaum.

Dearing, M. F., & Dickinson, A. (1979). Counterconditioning of shock by a water reinforcer in rabbits. *Animal Learning & Behavior, 7,* 360–366.

Denniston, J. C., Blaisdell, A. P., & Miller, R. R. (1998). Temporal coding affects transfer of serial and simultaneous inhibitors. *Animal Learning & Behavior, 26,* 336–350.

Denniston, J. C., Miller, R. R., & Matute, H. (1996). Biological significance as a determinant of cue competition. *Psychological Science, 7,* 235–331.

Denniston, J. C., Savastano, H. I., & Miller, R. R. (2001). The extended comparator hypothesis: Learning by contiguity, responding by relative strength. In R. R. Mowrer & S. B. Klein (Eds.), *Handbook of contemporary learning theories* (pp. 65–117). Hillsdale, NJ: Erlbaum.

Denny, M. R. (1971). Relaxation theory and experiments. In F. R. Brush (Ed.), *Aversive conditioning and learning* (pp. 235–295). New York: Academic Press.

DeVito, P. L., & Fowler, H. (1987). Enhancement of conditioned inhibition via an extinction treatment. *Animal Learning & Behavior, 15,* 448–454.

Dickinson, A. (1980). *Contemporary animal learning theory.* Cambridge, UK: Cambridge University Press.

Dickinson, A., & Burke, J. (1996). Within-compound associations mediate the retrospective revaluation of causality judgments. *Quarterly Journal of Experimental Psychology, 49B,* 60–80.

Dickinson, A., & Charnock, D. J. (1985). Contingency effects with maintained instrumental reinforcement. *Quarterly Journal of Experimental Psychology, 37B,* 397–416.

Domjan, M. (1983). Biological constraints on instrumental and classical conditioning: Implications for general process theory. In G. H. Bower (Ed.), *The psychology of learning and motivation* (Vol. 17, pp. 215–277). New York: Academic Press.

Domjan, M., Blesbois, E., & Williams, J. (1998). The adaptive significance of sexual conditioning: Pavlovian control of sperm release. *Psychological Science, 9,* 411–415.

Domjan, M., & Hollis, K. L. (1988). Reproductive behavior: A potential model system for adaptive specializations in learning. In R. C. Bolles & M. D. Beecher (Eds.), *Evolution and learning* (pp. 213–237). Hillsdale, NJ: Erlbaum.

Droungas, A., & LoLordo, V. M. (1994). Evidence for simultaneous excitatory and inhibitory associations in the explicitly unpaired procedure. *Learning and Motivation, 25,* 1–25.

Durlach, P. J., & Rescorla, R. A. (1980). Potentiation rather than overshadowing in flavor-aversion learning: An analysis in terms of within-compound associations. *Journal of Experimental Psychology: Animal Behavior Processes, 6,* 175–187.

Egger, M. D., & Miller, N. E. (1963). When is a reward reinforcing? An experimental study of the information hypothesis. *Journal of Comparative and Physiological Psychology, 56,* 132–137.

Eikelboom, R., & Stewart, J. (1982). Conditioning of drug-induced psychological responses. *Psychological Review, 89,* 507–528.

Escobar, M., Arcediano, F., & Miller, R. R. (in press). Conditions favoring retroactive interference between antecedent events and between subsequent events. *Psychonomic Bulletin & Review.*

Escobar, M., Matute, H., & Miller, R. R. (2001). Cues trained apart compete for behavioral control in rats: Convergence with the associative interference literature. *Journal of Experimental Psychology: General, 130,* 97–115.

Estes, W. K. (1950). Toward a statistical theory of learning. *Psychological Review, 57,* 94–170.

Estes, W. K., & Burke, C. J. (1953). A theory of stimulus variability in learning. *Psychological Review, 60,* 276–286.

Etienne, A. S., Berlie, J., Georgakopoulos, J., & Maurer, R. (1998). Role of dead reckoning in navigation. In S. Healy (Ed.), *Spatial representation in animals* (pp. 54–68). Oxford, UK: Oxford University Press.

Ferster, C. B., & Skinner, B. F. (1957). *Schedules of reinforcement.* New York: Appleton-Century-Crofts.

Fitzgerald, R. D. (1963). Effects of partial reinforcement with acid on the classically conditioned salivary response in dogs. *Journal of Comparative and Physiological Psychology, 56,* 1056–1060.

Flaherty, C. F. (1996). *Incentive relativity.* New York: Cambridge University Press.

Foree, D. D., & LoLordo, V. M. (1973). Relation of cue to consequence in avoidance learning. *Psychonomic Science, 4,* 123–124.

Gallistel, C. R. (1999). The replacement of general purpose learning models with adaptively specialized learning modules. In M. S. Gazzaniga (Ed.), *The new cognitive neurosciences* (2nd. ed.). Cambridge, MA: MIT Press.

Gallistel, C. R., & Gibbon, J. (2000). Time, rate and conditioning. *Psychological Review, 107,* 219–275.

Garcia, J., Ervin, F. R., & Koelling, R. A. (1966). Learning with prolonged delay of reinforcement. *Psychonomic Science, 5,* 121–122.

Garcia, J., & Koelling, R. A. (1966). Relation of cue to consequence in avoidance learning. *Psychonomic Science, 4,* 123–124.

Garcia, J., Lasiter, P. S., Bermudez-Rattoni, F., & Deems, D. A. (1985). A general theory of aversion learning. *Annals of the New York Academy of Sciences, 443,* 8–21.

Gibbon, J., Baldock, M. D., Locurto, C., Gold, L., & Terrace, H. S. (1977). Trial and intertrial durations in autoshaping. *Journal of Experimental Psychology: Animal Behavior Processes, 3,* 264–284.

Gibbon, J., & Balsam, P. (1981). Spreading association in time. In C. M. Locurto, H. S. Terrace & J. Gibbon (Eds.), *Autoshaping and conditioning theory* (pp. 219–253). New York: Academic Press.

Groves, P. M., & Thompson, R. F. (1970). Habituation: A dual-process theory. *Psychological Review, 77,* 419–450.

Guthrie, E. R. (1935). *The psychology of learning.* New York: Harper.

Guthrie, E. R. (1938). *The psychology of human conflict.* New York: Haprer.

Guttman, N., & Kalish, H. I. (1956). Discriminability and stimulus generalization. *Journal of Experimental Psychology, 51,* 79–88.

Gwinn, G. T. (1949). The effects of punishment on acts motivated by fear. *Journal of Experimental Psychology, 39,* 260–269.

Hall, G. (1991). *Perceptual and associative learning.* Oxford, UK: Oxford University Press.

Hall, G. (1996). Learning about associatively activated stimulus representations: Implications for acquired equivalence in perceptual learning. *Animal Learning & Behavior, 24,* 233–255.

Hallam, S. C., Grahame, N. J., Harris, K., & Miller, R. R. (1992). Associative structures underlying enhanced negative summation following operational extinction of a Pavlovian inhibitor. *Learning and Motivation, 23,* 43–62.

Hammond, L. J. (1980). The effect of contingency upon the appetitive conditioning of free-operant behavior. *Journal of the Experimental Analysis of Behavior, 34,* 297–304.

Hanson, H. M. (1959). Effects of discrimination training on stimulus generalization. *Journal of Experimental Psychology, 58,* 321–333.

Hearst, E. (1988). Fundamentals of learning and conditioning. In R. C. Atkinson, R. J. Herrnstein, G. Lindzey, & R. D. Luce (Eds.), *Stevens' handbook of experimental psychology, Vol. 2: Learning and cognition* (2nd ed., pp. 3–109). New York: Wiley.

Heth, C. D. (1976). Simultaneous and backward fear conditioning as a function of number of CS-UCS pairings. *Journal of Experimental Psychology: Animal Behavior Processes, 2,* 117–129.

Holland, P. C. (1977). Conditioned stimulus as a determinant of the form of the Pavlovian conditioned response. *Journal of Experimental Psychology: Animal Behavior Processes, 3,* 77–104.

Holland, P. C. (1981). Acquisition of representation-mediated conditioned food aversions. *Learning and Motivation, 12,* 1–18.

Holland, P. C. (1983a). Occasion setting in Pavlovian feature positive discriminations. In M. L. Commons, R. J. Herrnstein, & A. R. Wagner (Eds.), *Quantitative analyses of behavior: Discrimination processes* (pp. 183–206). Cambridge, MA: Ballinger.

Holland, P. C. (1983b). Representation-mediated overshadowing and potentiation of conditioned aversions. *Journal of Experimental Psychology: Animal Behavior Processes, 9,* 1–13.

Holland, P. C. (1989). Feature extinction enhances transfer of occasion setting. *Animal Learning & Behavior, 17,* 269–279.

Holland, P. C., & Forbes, D. T. (1982). Representation-mediated extinction of conditioned flavor aversions. *Learning and Motivation, 13,* 454–471.

Holland, P. C., Hamlin, P. A., & Parsons, J. P. (1997). Temporal specificity in serial feature positive discrimination learning. *Journal of Experimental Psychology: Animal Behavior Processes, 23,* 95–109.

Holland, P. C., & Rescorla, R. A. (1975). The effect of two ways of devaluing the unconditioned stimulus after first- and second-order appetitive conditioning. *Journal of Experimental Psychology: Animal Behavior Processes, 1,* 355–363.

Horgan, T., & Tienson, J. (Eds.). (1996). *Connectionism and the philosophy of psychology.* Cambridge, MA: MIT Press.

Hull, C. L. (1943). *Principles of behavior: An introduction to behavior theory.* New York: Appleton-Century.

Hull, C. L. (1952). *A behavior system: An introduction to behavior theory concerning the individual organism.* New Haven, CT: Yale University Press.

Jenkins, H. M., & Moore, B. R. (1973). The form of the autoshaped response with food or water reinforcers. *Journal of the Experimental Analysis of Behavior, 20,* 163–181.

Kamil, A. C. (1983). Optimal foraging theory and the psychology of learning. *American Zoologist, 23,* 291–302.

Kamil, A. C., & Clements, K. C. (1990). Learning, memory, and foraging behavior. In D. A. Dewsbury (Ed.), *Contemporary issues in comparative psychology* (pp. 7–30). Sunderland, MA: Sinauer.

Kamin, L. J. (1965). Temporal and intensity characteristics of the conditioned stimulus. In W. F. Prokasy (Ed.), *Classical conditioning* (pp. 118–147). New York: Appleton-Century-Crofts.

Kamin, L. J. (1968). "Attention-like" processes in classical conditioning. In M. R. Jones (Ed.), *Miami Symposium on the Prediction of Behavior: Aversive stimulation* (pp. 9–31). Miami, FL: University of Miami Press.

Kasprow, W. J., Cacheiro, H., Balaz, M. A., & Miller, R. R. (1982). Reminder-induced recovery of associations to an overshadowed stimulus. *Learning and Motivation, 13,* 155–166.

Kaufman, M. A., & Bolles, R. C. (1981). A nonassociative aspect of overshadowing. *Bulletin of the Psychonomic Society, 18,* 318–320.

Kehoe, E. J., & Gormezano, I. (1980). Configuration and combination laws in conditioning with compound stimuli. *Psychological Bulletin, 87,* 351–378.

Kehoe, E. J., Horne, A. J., Horne, P. S., & Macrae, M. (1994). Summation and configuration between and within sensory modalities in classical conditioning of the rabbit. *Animal Learning & Behavior, 22,* 19–26.

Kelley, H. H. (1967). Attribution theory in social psychology. In D. Levine (Ed.), *Nebraska Symposium on Motivation* (Vol. 15, pp. 192–240). Lincoln: University of Nebraska Press.

Kimble, G. A. (1955). Shock intensity and avoidance learning. *Journal of Comparative and Physiological Psychology, 48,* 281–284.

Kimble, G. A. (1961). *Hilgard and Marquis "Conditioning and Learning."* New York: Appleton-Century-Crofts.

Köhler, W. (1947). *Gestalt psychology: An introduction to new concepts in modern psychology.* New York: Liveright Publication Co.

Konorski, J. (1948). *Conditioned reflexes and neuron organization.* Cambridge, UK: Cambridge University Press.

Konorski, J. (1967). *Integrative activity of the brain: An interdisciplinary approach.* Chicago: University of Chicago Press.

Kraemer, P. J., Lariviere, N. A., & Spear, N. E. (1988). Expression of a taste aversion conditioned with an odor-taste compound: Overshadowing is relatively weak in weanlings and decreases over a retention interval in adults. *Animal Learning & Behavior, 16,* 164–168.

Kraemer, P. J., Randall, C. K., & Carbary, T. J. (1991). Release from latent inhibition with delayed testing. *Animal Learning & Behavior, 19,* 139–145.

Lamarre, J., & Holland, P. C. (1987). Transfer of inhibition after serial feature negative discrimination training. *Learning and Motivation, 18,* 319–342.

Lewis, D. J. (1956). Acquisition, extinction, and spontaneous recovery as a function of percentage of reinforcement and intertrial intervals. *Journal of Experimental Psychology, 51,* 45–53.

Logue, A. W. (1979). Taste aversion and the generality of the laws of learning. *Psychological Bulletin, 86,* 276–296.

LoLordo, V. M., & Fairless, J. L. (1985). Pavlovian conditioned inhibition: The literature since 1969. In R. R. Miller & N. E. Spear (Eds.), *Information processing in animals: Conditioned inhibition* (pp. 1–49). Hillsdale, NJ: Erlbaum.

Lubow, R. E. (1989). *Latent inhibition and conditioned attention theory.* Cambridge, UK: Cambridge University Press.

Lubow, R. E., & Moore, A. U. (1959). Latent inhibition: The effect of nonreinforced preexposure to the conditioned stimulus. *Journal of Comparative and Physiological Psychology, 52,* 415–419.

Lysle, D. T., & Fowler, H. (1985). Inhibition as a "slave" process: Deactivation of conditioned inhibition through extinction of conditioned excitation. *Journal of Experimental Psychology: Animal Behavior Processes, 11,* 71–94.

Mackintosh, N. J. (1974). *The psychology of animal learning.* London: Academic Press.

Mackintosh, N. J. (1975). A theory of attention: Variations in the associability of stimuli with reinforcement. *Psychological Review, 82,* 276–298.

Mackintosh, N. J. (1976). Overshadowing and stimulus intensity. *Animal Learning & Behavior, 4,* 186–192.

Mackintosh, N. J., & Reese, B. (1979). One-trial overshadowing. *Quarterly Journal of Experimental Psychology, 31,* 519–526.

Maier, S. F., & Seligman, M. E. P. (1976). Learned helplessness: Theory and evidence. *Journal of Experimental Psychology: General, 105,* 3–46.

Maldonado, A., Cátena, A., Cándido, A., & García, I. (1999). The belief revision model: Asymmetrical effects of noncontingency on human covariation learning. *Animal Learning & Behavior, 27,* 168–180.

Matute, H., & Pineño, O. (1998). Stimulus competition in the absence of compound conditioning. *Animal Learning & Behavior, 26,* 3–14.

Matzel, L. D., Gladstein, L., & Miller, R. R. (1988). Conditioned excitation and conditioned inhibition are not mutually exclusive. *Learning and Motivation, 19,* 99–121.

Matzel, L. D., Held, F. P., & Miller, R. R. (1988). Information and expression of simultaneous and backward associations: Implications for contiguity theory. *Learning and Motivation, 19,* 317–344.

Matzel, L. D., Schachtman, T. R., & Miller, R. R. (1985). Recovery of an overshadowed association achieved by extinction of the overshadowed stimulus. *Learning and Motivation, 16,* 398–412.

McClelland, J. L. (1988). Connectionist models and psychological evidence. *Journal of Memory and Language, 27,* 107–123.

McLaren, I. P. L., & Mackintosh, N. J. (2000). An elemental model of associative learning, I: Latent inhibition and perceptual learning. *Animal Learning & Behavior, 28,* 211–246.

Miller, J. S., McKinzie, D. L., Kraebel, K. S., & Spear, N. E. (1996). Changes in the expression of stimulus selection: Blocking represents selective memory retrieval rather than selective associations. *Learning and Motivation, 27,* 307–316.

Miller, J. S., Scherer, S. L., & Jagielo, J. A. (1995). Enhancement of conditioning by a nongustatory CS: Ontogenetic differences in the mechanisms underlying potentiation. *Learning and Motivation, 26,* 43–62.

Miller, R. R., & Balaz, M. A. (1981). Differences in adaptiveness between classically conditioned responses and instrumentally acquired responses. In N. E. Spear & R. R. Miller (Eds.), *Information processing in animals: Memory mechanisms* (pp. 49–80). Hillsdale, NJ: Erlbaum.

Miller, R. R., Barnet, R. C., & Grahame, N. J. (1995). Assessment of the Rescorla-Wagner model. *Psychological Bulletin, 117,* 363–386.

Miller, R. R., & Escobar, M. (2001). Contrasting acquisition-focused and performance-focused models of behavior change. *Current Directions in Psychological Science, 10,* 141–145.

Miller, R. R., & Grace, R. C. (2002). Conditioning and learning. In I. B. Weiner (Ed.), *Comprehensive handbook of psychology.* New York: Wiley.

Miller, R. R., Hallam, S. C., Hong, J. Y., & Dufore, D. S. (1991). Associative structure of differential inhibition: Implications for models of conditioned inhibition. *Journal of Experimental Psychology: Animal Behavior Processes, 17,* 141–150.

Miller, R. R., & Matute, H. (1996). Biological significance in forward and backward blocking: Resolution of a discrepancy between animal conditioning and human causal judgment. *Journal of Experimental Psychology: General, 125,* 370–386.

Miller, R. R., & Matzel, L. D. (1988). The comparator hypothesis: A response rule for the expression of associations. In G. H. Bower (Ed.), *The psychology of learning and motivation* (Vol. 22, pp. 51–92). San Diego: Academic Press.

Miller, R. R., & Oberling, P. (1998). Analogies between occasion setting and Pavlovian conditioning. In N. A. Schmajuk & P. C. Holland (Eds.), *Occasion setting: Associative learning and cognition in animals* (pp. 3–35). Washington, DC: American Psychological Association.

Mowrer, O. H. (1947). On the dual nature of learning: A reinterpretation of "conditioning" and "problem-solving." *Harvard Educational Review, 17,* 102–150.

Nairne, J. S., & Rescorla, R. A. (1981). Second-order conditioning with diffuse auditory reinforcers in the pigeon. *Learning and Motivation, 12,* 65–91.

Neely, J. H. (1977). Semantic priming and retrieval from lexical memory: Roles of inhibitionless spreading activation and limited-capacity attention. *Journal of Experimental Psychology: General, 106,* 226–254.

Nevin, J. A. (1974). Response strength in multiple schedules. *Journal of the Experimental Analysis of Behavior, 21,* 389–408.

Nevin, J. A. (1992). An integrative model for the study of behavioral momentum. *Journal of the Experimental Analysis of Behavior, 57,* 301–316.

Nevin, J. A., & Grace, R. C. (2000). Behavioral momentum and the law of effect [includes commentary]. *Behavioral and Brain Sciences, 23,* 73–130.

Nevin, J. A., Mandell, C., & Atak, J. R. (1983). The analysis of behavioral momentum. *Journal of the Experimental Analysis of Behavior, 39,* 49–59.

Nevin, J. A., Tota, M. E., Torquato, R. D., & Shull, R. L. (1990). Alternative reinforcement increases resistance to change: Pavlovian or operant contingencies? *Journal of the Experimental Analysis of Behavior, 53,* 359–379.

North, A. J., & Stimmel, D. T. (1960). Extinction of an instrumental response following a large number of reinforcements. *Psychological Reports, 6,* 227–234.

Osgood, C. E. (1949). The similarity paradox in human learning: A resolution. *Psychological Review, 56,* 132–143.

Pavlov, I. P. (1927). *Conditioned reflexes.* London: Oxford University Press.

Pearce, J. M. (1987). A model for stimulus generalization in Pavlovian conditioning. *Psychological Review, 94,* 61–73.

Pearce, J. M., & Hall, G. (1978). Overshadowing the instrumental conditioning of a lever press response by a more valid predictor of reinforcement. *Journal of Experimental Psychology: Animal Behavior Processes, 4,* 356–367.

Pearce, J. M., & Hall, G. (1980). A model for Pavlovian learning: Variations in the effectiveness of conditioned but not of unconditioned stimuli. *Psychological Review, 87,* 532–552.

Postman, L., Stark, K., & Fraser, J. (1968). Temporal changes in interference. *Journal of Verbal Learning and Verbal Behavior, 7,* 672–694.

Randich, A., & LoLordo, V. M. (1979a). Preconditioning exposure to the unconditioned stimulus affects the acquisition of a conditioned emotional response. *Learning and Motivation, 10,* 245–277.

Randich, A., & LoLordo, V. M. (1979b). Associative and nonassociative theories of the UCS preexposure phenomenon: Implications for Pavlovian conditioning. *Psychological Bulletin, 86,* 523–548.

Rashotte, M. E., Marshall, B. S., & O'Connell, J. M. (1981). Signaling functions of the second-order CS: Partial reinforcement during second-order conditioning of the pigeon's keypeck. *Animal Learning & Behavior, 9,* 253–260.

Rescorla, R. A. (1968). Probability of shock in the presence and absence of CS in fear conditioning. *Journal of Comparative and Physiological Psychology, 66,* 1–5.

Rescorla, R. A. (1969). Pavlovian conditioned inhibition. *Psychological Bulletin, 72,* 77–94.

Rescorla, R. A. (1985). Conditioned inhibition and facilitation. In R. R. Miller & N. E. Spear (Eds.), *Information processing in animals: Conditioned inhibition* (pp. 299–326). Hillsdale, NJ: Erlbaum.

Rescorla, R. A. (1998). Instrumental learning: Nature and persistence. In M. Sabourin, F. I. Craik, & M. Roberts (Eds.), *Advances in psychological science: Biological and cognitive aspects* (Vol. 2, pp. 239–257). London: Psychology Press.

Rescorla, R. A., & Cunningham, C. L. (1979). Spatial contiguity facilitates Pavlovian second-order conditioning. *Journal of Experimental Psychology: Animal Behavior Processes, 5,* 152–161.

Rescorla, R. A., & Furrow, D. R. (1977). Stimulus similarity as a determinant of Pavlovian conditioning. *Journal of Experimental Psychology: Animal Behavior Processes, 3,* 203–215.

Rescorla, R. A., & Holland, P. C. (1977). Associations in Pavlovian conditioned inhibition. *Learning and Motivation, 8,* 429–447.

Rescorla, R. A., & Wagner, A. R. (1972). A theory of Pavlovian conditioning: Variations in the effectiveness of reinforcement and nonreinforcement. In A. H. Black & W. F. Prokasy (Eds.), *Classical conditioning, II: Current theory and research* (pp. 64–99). New York: Appleton-Century-Crofts.

Riccio, D. C., Ackil, J. K., & Burch-Vernon, A. (1992). Forgetting of stimulus attributes: Methodological implications for assessing associative phenomena. *Psychological Bulletin, 112,* 433–445.

Riccio, D. C., Richardson, R., & Ebner, D. L. (1984). Memory retrieval deficits based upon altered contextual cues: A paradox. *Psychological Bulletin, 96,* 152–165.

Rizley, R. C., & Rescorla, R. A. (1972). Associations in second-order conditioning and sensory preconditioning. *Journal of Comparative and Physiological Psychology, 81,* 1–11.

Robinson, E. S. (1927). The "similarity" factor in retroaction. *American Journal of Psychology, 39,* 297–312.

Romaniuk, C. B., & Williams, D. A. (2000). Conditioning across the duration of a backward conditioned stimulus. *Journal of Experimental Psychology: Animal Behavior Processes, 26,* 454–461.

Ross, B. H., & Makin, V. S. (1999). Prototype versus exemplar models in cognition. In R. J. Sternberg (Ed.), *The nature of cognition* (pp. 206–241). Cambridge, MA: MIT Press.

Saint Paul, U. V. (1982). Do geese use path integration for walking home? In F. Papi & H. G. Wallraff (Eds.), *Avian navigation* (pp. 298–307). New York: Springer.

Savastano, H. I., & Miller, R. R. (1998). Time as content in Pavlovian conditioning. *Behavioural Processes, 44,* 147–162.

Schaal, D. W., & Branch, M. N. (1988). Responding of pigeons under variable-interval schedules of unsignaled, briefly signaled, and completely signaled delays to reinforcement. *Journal of the Experimental Analysis of Behavior, 50,* 33–54.

Schmajuk, N. A., Lamoureux, J. A., & Holland, P. C. (1998). Occasion setting: A neural network approach. *Psychological Review, 105,* 3–32.

Schweitzer, L., & Green, L. (1982). Reevaluation of things past: A test of the "retrospective hypothesis" using a CER procedure with rats. *Pavlovian Journal of Biological Science, 17,* 62–68.

Shanks, D. R. (1994). Human associative learning. In N. J. Mackintosh (Ed.), *Animal learning and cognition* (pp. 335–374). San Diego, CA: Academic Press.

Shettleworth, S. J. (1998). *Cognition, evolution, and behavior.* New York: Oxford University Press.

Siegel, S. (1989). Pharmacological conditioning and drug effects. In A. J. Goudie & M. W. Emmet-Oglesby (Eds.), *Psychoactive drugs: Tolerance and sensitization* (pp. 115–185). Clifton, NJ: Humana Press.

Skinner, B. F. (1938). *The behavior of organisms.* New York: Appleton-Century-Crofts.

Slamecka, N. J., & Ceraso, J. (1960). Retroactive and proactive inhibition of verbal learning. *Psychological Bulletin, 57,* 449–475.

Spence, K. W. (1936). The nature of discrimination learning in animals. *Psychological Review, 43,* 427–449.

Staddon, J. E., & Simmelhag, V. L. (1970). The "superstition" experiment: A reexamination of its implications for the principles of adaptive behavior. *Psychological Review, 78,* 3–43.

St. Claire-Smith, R. (1979). The overshadowing and blocking of punishment. *Quarterly Journal of Experimental Psychology, 31,* 51–61.

Sutton, R. S., & Barto, A. G. (1981). Toward a modern theory of adaptive networks: Expectation and prediction. *Psychological Review, 88,* 135–170.

Tait, R. W., & Saladin, M. E. (1986). Concurrent development of excitatory and inhibitory associations during backward conditioning. *Animal Learning & Behavior, 14,* 133–137.

Thompson, R. F., & Spencer, W. A. (1966). Habituation: A model phenomenon for the study of neuronal substrates of behavior. *Psychological Review, 73,* 16–43.

Thorndike, E. L. (1911). *Animal intelligence: Experimental studies.* New York: Macmillan.

Thorndike, E. L. (1932). *Fundamentals of learning.* New York: Columbia University.

Thorndike, E. L. (1949). *Selected writings from a connectionist's psychology.* East Norwalk, CT: Appleton-Century-Crofts.

Timberlake, W., & Lucas, G. A. (1989). Behavior systems and learning: From misbehavior to general principles. In S. B. Klein & R. R. Mowrer (Eds.), *Contemporary learning theories: Instrumental conditioning theory and the impact of biological constraints in learning* (pp. 237–275). Hillsdale, NJ: Erlbaum.

Timberlake, W., & Lucas, G. A. (1991). Periodic water, interwater interval, and adjunctive behavior in a 24-hour multiresponse environment. *Animal Learning & Behavior, 19,* 369–380.

Tolman, E. C. (1932). *Purposive behavior in animals and men.* London: Century/Random House.

Tolman, E. C., & Honzik, C. H. (1930). Introduction and removal of reward, and maze performance in rats. *University of California Publications in Psychology, 4,* 257–275.

Tolman, E. C., Ritchie, B. F., & Kalish, D. (1946). Studies in spatial learning, II: Place learning versus response learning. *Journal of Experimental Psychology, 36,* 221–229.

Tombaugh, T. N. (1967). The overtraining extinction effect with a discrete-trial bar-press procedure. *Journal of Experimental Psychology, 73,* 632–634.

Van Hamme, L. J., & Wasserman, E. A. (1994). Cue competition in causality judgments: The role of nonpresentation of compound stimulus elements. *Learning and Motivation, 25,* 127–151.

Wagner, A. R. (1981). SOP: A model of automatic memory processing in animal behavior. In N. E. Spear & R. R. Miller (Eds.), *Information processing in animals: Memory mechanisms* (pp. 5–47). Hillsdale, NJ: Erlbaum.

Wasserman, E. A., Elek, S. M., Chatlosh, D. L., & Baker, A. G. (1993). Rating causal relations: Role of probability in judgments of response-outcome contingency. *Journal of Experimental Psychology: Learning, Memory, and Cognition, 19,* 174–188.

Watson, J. B. (1913). Psychology as a behaviorist views it. *Psychological Review, 20,* 158–177.

Weiss, S. J., & Schindler, C. W. (1981). Generalization peak shift in rats under conditions of positive reinforcement and avoidance. *Journal of the Experimental Analysis of Behavior, 35,* 175–185.

Williams, B. A. (1976). The effects of unsignalled delayed reinforcement. *Journal of the Experimental Analysis of Behavior, 26,* 441–449.

Williams, B. A. (1982). Blocking the response-reinforcer association. In M. L. Commons, R. J. Herrnstein, & A. R. Wagner (Eds.), *Quantitative analyses of behavior: Acquisition* (Vol. 3, pp. 427–447). Cambridge, MA: Ballinger.

Williams, B. A. (1988). Reinforcement, choice, and response strength. In R. C. Atkinson, R. J. Herrnstein, G. Lindzey, & R. D. Luce (Eds.), *Stevens' Handbook of Experimental Psychology, Vol. 2: Learning and Cognition* (2nd ed., pp. 167–244). New York: Wiley.

Williams, D. R., & Williams, H. (1969). Automaintenance in the pigeon: Sustained pecking despite contingent non-reinforcement. *Journal of the Experimental Analysis of Behavior, 12,* 511–520.

Wolpe, J. (1969). *The practice of behavior therapy.* New York: Pergamon Press.

Yin, H., Barnet, R. C., & Miller, R. R. (1994). Second-order conditioning and Pavlovian conditioned inhibition: Operational similarities and differences. *Journal of Experimental Psychology: Animal Behavior Processes, 20,* 419–428.

Yin, H., Grahame, N. J., & Miller, R. R. (1993). Extinction of comparator stimuli during and after acquisition: Differential facilitative effects on Pavlovian responding. *Learning and Motivation, 24,* 219–241.

Zeiler, M. D. (1977). Schedules of reinforcement: The controlling variables. In W. K. Honig & J. E. R. Staddon (Eds.), *Handbook of operant behavior* (pp. 201–232). Englewood Cliffs, NJ: Prentice-Hall.

Zeiler, M. D. (1984). The sleeping giant: Reinforcement schedules. *Journal of the Experimental Analysis of Behavior, 42,* 485–493.

CHAPTER 3

Reinforcement Learning

PETER DAYAN

INTRODUCTION

Figure 3.1 shows a very simple maze problem that might be posed to a hungry rat, or even a robot, involving the choice of direction to run at three choice points A, B, and C. The rat repeatedly starts at location A, runs forward through the maze, and ends at one of the four shaded boxes. When it arrives at a termination position, it is awarded a random number of food pellets whose average is written in the box. Then the rat is replaced at A, only to start again.

This deceptively straightforward maze poses a sequential decision-making task in microcosm. We use it to discuss the standard techniques of reinforcement learning as well as their links with classical and instrumental conditioning. We seek to use formal mathematical and computational descriptions to model the nature and properties of behavior in such tasks. We use a navigation task because it is easy to visualize. Note, however, that navigation might engage specialized cognitive mechanisms (Gallistel, 1990).

First, consider the decision the rat has to make when it arrives at B or C. In either case, it faces a standard T-maze task with appeti-

tive outcomes. Such tasks are also known as stochastic two-armed bandit problems, where the equivalent of pulling one of the arms is choosing one of the directions, and the stochasticity comes from the randomness in the number of pellets actually delivered in each shaded box. The rat has to learn from its random experience that it gets more food on average if it runs left at B and right at C. Furthermore, it may need to consider the possibility that the experimenter might change the relative worths of the termination boxes, in which case it would have to explore the different possibilities continually.

Second, consider the more difficult case of the choice at location A. Whichever direction the rat chooses, it receives no direct reward;

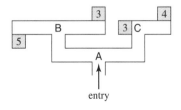

Figure 3.1 The maze task.
NOTE: The figure shows a simple maze task. The rat (or robot) enters from the bottom and is only allowed to run forwards. The shaded boxes are endpoints where the rat receieves food pellets. The average number of pellets is written in each box (with Poisson variability in our experiments). The potential choice points are at A, B, and C.
SOURCE: After Dayan & Abbott (2001).

Funding came from the Gatsby Charitable Foundation. The author is most grateful to Randy Gallistel for his trenchant comments on an earlier draft.

the only consequence is that it gets to location B or C. Information that location B is a better choice than C must somehow filter back to the choice of direction at A, in order that the rat can learn to go left. This is sometimes known as the *temporal credit assignment problem,* because if the rat goes left at A and right at B, how does it know that the first direction was good and the second bad, rather than vice versa? Credit (or, in this case, blame) must somehow be assigned to the second direction. In more challenging sequential decision tasks, there may be many steps before an actual reward is delivered.

Both these problems are familiar in a variety of fields, including psychology, statistics, and control theory. Reinforcement learning (see Bertsekas & Tsitsiklis, 1996; Sutton & Barto, 1998) has blended and adapted solutions that have been suggested in each. In summary, the essential idea for solving the first problem is to consider the model rat as adopting a parameterized stochastic *policy* at B and C, which specifies the probabilities with which it turns left or right at each location. The parameters of the policy are adjusted in the light of the rewards received by the rat, so that actions leading to larger average rewards come to be favored. This is essentially a formalization of Thorndike's (1898, 1911) famous law of effect. An alternative is to sample both directions in order to learn the average reward associated with each, and then choose whichever seems more lucrative. These methods are close to those suggested by Bush and Mosteller (1955; and, more distantly, Rescorla & Wagner, 1972), formalized in the engineering discipline of stochastic learning automata (Narendra & Thatachar, 1989), and analyzed in a reinforcement learning context by Williams (1992).

The essential idea for solving the second problem is to learn the attractiveness of locations B and C and to choose an action at A that leads to the more attractive outcome.

Here, the natural measure of attractiveness of the location, which is usually called its *value,* is the number of pellets that is expected to be delivered in the future path through the maze, starting from that location. Thus, going left at A, which leads to a location (B), from which a large number of pellets is expected in the future, should be favored over going right, which leads to a location (C), from which only a small number of pellets is expected. Of course, the values of B and C depend on the policies adopted there; as these policies change, the action that is preferred at A can change, too. However, provided that the policies are always getting better, so that the values of B and C only increase, then the policy at A will change for the better, too. In turn, the value of A, the expected number of pellets associated with starting from A, can also be learned, using information encountered about the expected number starting from B and C.

There has historically been great interest in psychology in the way that chains of behavior, like the successive choices of direction in the maze, are established and maintained by reinforcement, and this method for solving the second problem therefore has a large number of forebears. One is secondary conditioning—because the value of location A is acquired via a secondary association with the rewards that follow B and C. Values acquired during secondary conditioning are used to control instrumental choices of action (resulting in a form of two-factor conditioning theory; e.g., Mackintosh, 1974; Mowrer, 1956). A second link is to a method suggested by Deutsch (1960) as to how information about possible future rewards in the maze could come to influence present actions. There is a slightly more remote relationship with Hull's suggestion of goal gradients (Hull, 1943, 1952). Another link is to Samuel's (1959) checkerplaying program and Michie and Chambers' (1968) BOXES control system, since the expectation of future reward starting from A is determined by making it consistent with the expectations of future reward starting at the locations accessible from A, namely B and C. A further link, which we explain in more detail later, is to the engineering method of dynamic programming via policy iteration (Bellman, 1957). Finally, albeit in a slightly different setting, ethologists use dynamic programming to formalize behaviors such as these in the context of optimal foraging decisions (Mangel & Clark, 1988), and this provides a link between psychological and ethological ideas about learning. In reinforcement learning, the method was suggested and analyzed by Sutton (1988); Barto, Sutton, and Anderson (1983); and Sutton and Barto (1990), and was linked to dynamic programming by Watkins (1989) and Werbos (1990).

Many drugs of addiction hijack the mechanisms normally employed by animals to process appetitive information. This has led to the collection of a substantial body of experimental data in rats, monkeys, and humans on the neural underpinning of adaptive action choice, which bears directly on the neural basis of reinforcement learning. In particular, the neuromodulator dopamine is thought to play a critical role in the appetitive aspects of addictive drugs and thus is a natural candidate for the neural substrate for aspects of reinforcement learning. Consistent with this, as we will see, measurements of the activity of dopaminergic neurons during conditioning show that they exhibit some of the characteristic properties of the reinforcement learning signal involved in propagating information on prediction errors about future rewards to train present predictions and control present actions. Altogether, reinforcement learning melds neural, psychological, ethological, and computational constraints on a single problem.

In this chapter, we first consider the two control problems just described in the context of the maze and show the reinforcement learn-ing solution and its links with more standard accounts of classical and instrumental conditioning. In the fourth section, we discuss the putative neural basis, providing a model of the activity of dopamine cells. Finally, we consider some current efforts to model attentional aspects of conditioning. Whereas the standard reinforcement learning models are strongly influenced by engineering ideas about optimal control, the attentional models are influenced by statistical ideas about learning.

ACTION CHOICE

Choosing a direction at B or C is more straightforward than at A because immediate information is provided about the quality of the action in terms of the delivery of pellets of food. The main difficulty comes if the pellets are delivered in a stochastic manner at each termination point, so that averages must be taken over many trials, or if the experimenter actually changes the average values over time. These lead to a critical choice for the rat between *exploration* and *exploitation,* that is, between choosing the action that is currently believed to be worse in order to make sure that it really is, and choosing the action that is currently believed to be best in order to take advantage of its apparently superior characteristics. A fair wealth of theoretical work has been devoted to optimal tradeoffs between exploration and exploitation (e.g., Berry & Fristedt, 1985), and there is even some evidence of this sort of metaoptimization in animals (Krebs, Kacelnik, & Taylor, 1978). However, we confine ourselves to the simpler problem of learning which direction is best when the averages are fixed.

We consider two simple methods for choosing directions. One is based on parameterized stochastic policies, whose parameters are changed to increase the average number of pellets. This is sometimes called a *direct* method because the policy is directly specified and improved. The second is based on learning the average number of pellets provided by each direction and then preferring the direction associated with the greatest mean reward. This is called an *indirect* method because the policy is an indirect function of the estimated mean rewards. For convenience, we start by considering just location B, and therefore omit an argument or index indicating the location at which the choice is being made.

The Direct Actor

In the direct method, the choice between the directions is specified by a stochastic policy. Let π_L be the probability of turning left at B, and $\pi_R = 1 - \pi_L$ be the probability of turning right there. A natural way to parameterize these is to use the sigmoid rule

$$\pi_L = \sigma(\beta m), \qquad (1)$$

based on an action value m, where $\sigma(x) = 1/(1 + \exp(-x))$ is the standard logistic sigmoid function. This is actually a special form of the softmax or Luce choice rule (Luce, 1959). If m is positive, then the larger its magnitude, the more likely the rat is to go left at B. If m is negative, then the larger its magnitude, the more likely the rat is to go right at B. Here, the value of β sets the scale for the action value, and, by controlling the frequency with which the rat samples the alternative believed to be worse, controls the tradeoff between exploration and exploitation.

Say the rat chooses to go left on a particular trial and receives a reinforcement of r_L pellets of food. How should it use this information to change the parameter m to increase the expected number of pellets it will receive? Intuitively, if r_L is large, then m should be increased, since that makes π_L larger; if r_L is small, then m should be decreased, since that makes π_L smaller. One way to achieve this (Williams, 1992) is to change the parameter

according to

$$m \rightarrow m + \epsilon(r_L - \tilde{r})(1 - \pi_L), \qquad (2)$$

together with the equivalent expression if the rat chooses to go right instead

$$m \rightarrow m - \epsilon(r_R - \tilde{r})(1 - \pi_R) \qquad (3)$$

on receiving a reward of (r_R), then the number of pellets the rat can expect to receive will increase, at least on average. Here ϵ is a (small) *learning rate,* and $\tilde{r}$ is called a *reinforcement comparison* term, which sets a standard against which the actual number of reward is compared.

We should step back at this point to consider the implications of Equation (2). This is an algorithmic learning or adaptation rule for the parameter m, indicating how it should change in the light of experience. It was derived from the computationally sound intent of increasing the average reward. As we see in the rest of this chapter, in reinforcement learning many such algorithmic and computational proposals about the maximization of reward in more complicated circumstances are studied.

Rule 2 makes perfect sense: If the actual number of pellets delivered is greater than the comparison term, then m should be increased; if it is less than the comparison term, then m should be decreased. Oddly, provided the reinforcement comparison term $\tilde{r}$ does not depend on whether the rat chose to go left or right, then the fact that the average number of pellets increases does *not* depend on its actual value. For an intuition as to why this might be so, consider the case that $\tilde{r}$ is very large and positive. Then, if the rat goes left on a trial, m tends to decrease according to Equation (2), even if going left is better than going right. However, if the rat goes right on a trial, then, according to equation 3, m will increase by an even larger amount, so m will still tend to grow on average. The value of $\tilde{r}$ does not affect the average outcome of the learning rule.

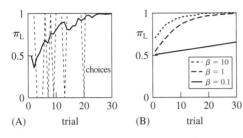

Figure 3.2 Simulation of the direct actor.
NOTE: A) The probability π_L of going left over 30 trials at location B (solid line) and the actual choices of direction (dotted line in a single session; 1 means left; 0 means right). Here $\beta = 1$, $\epsilon = 0.4$, $\tilde{r} = 4$, and the number of pellets has a Poisson distribution. B) The average probabilities (over 500 runs) of going left at B for $\beta = 0.1, 1, 10$.

Nevertheless, the value of $\tilde{r}$ does affect the variance of this learning rule and therefore can determine subsidiary factors such as the speed of learning. A natural value of $\tilde{r}$ is just the average reward across all directions.

Figure 3.2 shows the course of learning to go left at B using the direct actor. Here, the rewards have Poisson distributions, with means 5 and 3 for going left and right, respectively. Figure 3.2A shows π_L for one particular session; the randomness is clear. Figure 3.2B shows the average behavior for various values of β. For this simple problem, larger values of β lead to faster learning. However, if β (or indeed ϵ) is too large, then the rat can be overly tempted by the first reward it experiences, and it might never explore to find a better direction. The extent to which this is true depends on the actual mean and variance of the reward delivery, something about which the rat is likely to have only vague expectations at the start of learning.

Altogether, the direct actor is a very straightforward learning controller for which there is a relatively easy way of controlling the tradeoff between exploration and exploitation. We use it later for our full model for the maze, in which case we need different action

values for each location. We will call these $m(A)$, $m(B)$, and $m(C)$.

The Indirect Actor

The indirect actor uses the same action choice rule as the direct actor

$$\pi_L = \sigma(\beta(q_L - q_R)), \qquad (4)$$

but with two parameters q_L and q_R that have a completely different semantics from m in Equation (1). The idea is that q_L should come to be the average number of pellets provided for going left, and q_R the average number for going right. In this case, Equation (4) automatically favors the direction leading to the greater reward, where the size of the difference is judged according to β.

Say, as above, that the rat chooses from this distribution to go left, and receives a reinforcement of r_L pellets of food. How should the estimate of the average return of going left be altered? An obvious suggestion is to use

$$q_L \rightarrow q_L + \eta(r_L - q_L) \qquad (5)$$

where η is again a learning rate. This tends to increase q_L if the estimate is too low and increase it if the estimate is too high. Alternatively, it moves q_L toward a target value r_L by altering q_L according to the *prediction error* $\delta = r_L - q_L$. This learning rule is a simple form of the Rescorla-Wagner rule (Rescorla & Wagner, 1972). The only difference from standard applications of the Rescorla-Wagner rule is that the target value r_L here is stochastic, whereas in most standard cases it is deterministic (and is often written as λ, the asymptotic value to which the association tends over trials). In this case, the equivalent asymptotic value is the mean reward for going left, which we write as $\langle r_L \rangle$.

Sutton and Barto (1981) pointed out that this Rescorla-Wagner rule is a simple form of the least mean squares or delta rule in engineering (Widrow & Hoff, 1960). There is a substantial body of theory (see Widrow & Stearns, 1985) about how the delta rule will lead q_L to approximate the average value of the reward associated with going left, and which can be used for such tasks as understanding the consequences of different settings of η. An equivalent rule can be used to train q_R to estimate the average reward associated with going right. As for the direct actor, we later need different values q_L and q_R for each location. Where necessary, we write these *state-action* values as $q_L(X)$ and $q_R(X)$, where $X = A, B, C$ labels the location.

Later, we consider methods that use the average number of pellets $v(B)$ associated with starting from B, averaging over the randomness of the choice of direction as well as the outcome at each endpoint. This can also be learned using exactly the same learning rule

$$v(B) \to v(B) + \eta(r - v(B)) \qquad (6)$$

where r is the number of pellets received, whichever direction the rat chooses. Sometimes, $v(B)$ is called the *value* of B.

Although the direct and indirect actors look very similar, they actually have quite different interpretations and asymptotes. If, as in Figure 3.1 at B, going left is more lucrative on average than going right, then m for the direct actor should tend to increase without bound toward ∞, albeit extremely slowly because the increments are scaled by the ever-decreasing probability that the rat chooses to go right. However, $q_L - q_R$ for the indirect actor should come to take on the value of the average difference in worth between the two directions, even if this difference is very small. This makes the role for β very different in the two algorithms. For the direct actor, if β is fixed and $\tilde{r}$ is constant, then going left will generally be favored over going right to an arbitrary degree, even if left is only a little better than right. However, the indirect actor will tend to match its behavior more closely to the average outcomes. The preferred direc-

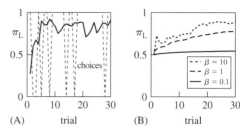

Figure 3.3 Simulation of the indirect actor. NOTE: A) The probability π_L of going left over 30 trials at location B (solid line) and the actual choices of direction (dotted line; 1 means left; 0 means right). Here $\beta = 1$, $\eta = 0.2$, and the number of pellets has a Poisson distribution. B) The average probabilities (over 500 runs) of going left at B for $\beta = 0.1, 1, 10$.

tion will only come to be chosen on every trial if β is set to be very large. Albeit in a rather more complicated reward context, Egelman, Person, and Montague (1998) showed that the propensity of this rule toward matching made it a good model of human choice behavior.

For the same task as Figure 3.2, Figure 3.3 shows the course of learning to go left at B using the indirect actor. As there, Figure 3.3A shows a sample of the randomness in a single run, and Figure 3.2B shows the mean effect over many runs for a few different values of β. The effect just described is at work in the persistently poor performance for small $\beta = 0.1$. Whereas for the direct actor in Figure 3.2B the probability of turning left continually increases, for the indirect actor it has an asymptotic value of $\pi_L = 0.55$. If β is too large, then, like the direct actor, the balance between exploration and exploitation can be disturbed.

SEQUENTIAL ACTION CHOICE

It is clear that neither direct nor indirect actors can explicitly be employed to choose which direction to take at A, since the equivalent of the reward terms r_L or r_R is always 0. The task here is closely analogous to the intensively studied case of sequential chains of behavior reinforced by a final goal. The investigations of this led to sophisticated, complicated, and contentious learning theories, such as those of Hull (1952) and Deutsch (1960). At the heart of the reinforcement learning solution to the temporal credit assignment problem is the very simple and old idea of using secondary reinforcement to learn values $v(B)$ and $v(C)$, which reflect the attractiveness of locations B and C, and then choosing the direction at A that leads to the more attractive location. Here, $v(B)$ acts like a surrogate reward for the choice of going left at A, and $v(C)$ acts like a surrogate reward for the choice of going right at A.

The main novelty (Sutton, 1988; Sutton & Barto 1990) in this approach lies in the way that secondary reinforcement is formalized and thus in the definition of the values. The suggestion is that the value of a location should come to be the total reward expected starting from that location, adding up over all future steps. The expectations of total future reward should be mutually consistent at successive steps; for instance, if the rat always chooses to go left at A, then the value of A should be the same as the value of B. The temporal difference learning rule is based on the discrepancy in the value estimates at successive steps.

Given these values, the actual reward term r_L in Equations (2) and (4) might simply be replaced by the expected future reward $v(B)$, and learning a policy at A using either direct or indirect actors could proceed. Of course, $v(B)$ and $v(C)$ will change as the policy at B and C improves, but this should only improve the choice of direction at A.

We first consider a more formal treatment of the problem of learning values, including what to do if pellets can be provided at any step. We then discuss how the information about values can be used to learn a good policy at A.

The Critic

The values of locations are the expected total number of pellets that will be received, starting from each location and following a fixed, though possibly stochastic, policy. Once the policy is fixed, the problem of learning the values can be seen as one for classical conditioning, that is, predicting the rewarding consequences of locations without reference to the actions actually adopted. This makes the link to secondary conditioning clearer: B is directly associated with the delivery of pellets; A is directly associated with getting to B; so A should be associated with the delivery of pellets, too. Indeed, the reinforcement learning method—called *temporal difference* learning (Sutton, 1988)—that we are about to describe for learning the values, was explicitly motivated by the failure of secondary conditioning to come under the umbrella of the Rescorla-Wagner rule. This failure comes about because the Rescorla-Wagner rule does not take account of the sequence of presentation of the stimuli (here, the sequence of locations in the maze).

Unfortunately, though the idea underlying temporal difference learning is simple, the notation is rather ugly. Starting from any location X, there are only two ways to get pellets. One is that some might be immediately provided for choosing a direction (as at B and C). These are called immediate rewards, and, as above, we write $\langle r_L(X)\rangle$ and $\langle r_R(X)\rangle$ for the average numbers of pellets provided for going left and right at location X. More generally, we write $\langle r_D(X)\rangle$ for the average number of pellets provided for choosing a direction D, and this allows for the possibility that pellets might be provided at intermediate locations in the maze on the way to the end points. The other way to get pellets is that they might be expected to be provided in the farther future, based on the location Y the rat gets to directly from X on account of its action. For instance, if the rat gets from A to B, then it can expect to get pellets in the future, following the action it takes at B. Once learning is complete, $v(Y)$ is exactly the number it can expect to get from Y. In fact, the expected future reward from X is simply the sum of these two contributions, averaged over the choice of action at X. Sutton and Barto's (1990) key insight was to introduce the idea of predicting the sum of all future rewards, rather than just the current reward, and this led directly to temporal difference learning.

To put this more concretely, we can write a formula for the value of A as

$$v(A) = \pi_L(A)(\langle r_L(A)\rangle + v(B))$$
$$+ \pi_R(A)(\langle r_R(A)\rangle + v(C)) \quad (7)$$
$$= \pi_L(A)v(B) + \pi_R(A)v(C). \quad (8)$$

In Equation (7), we have written out explicitly the two contributions mentioned earlier and averaged them over the probabilities of going left and right at A. Equation (8) follows because no pellets are immediately provided for the action at A. Similarly, we can write the value of B as

$$v(B) = \pi_L(B)\langle r_L(B)\rangle + \pi_R(B)\langle r_R(B)\rangle$$
$$= \pi_L\langle r_L\rangle + \pi_R\langle r_R\rangle$$
$$= \pi_L 5 + \pi_R 3 \quad (9)$$

where, in this case, the contributions to the number of pellets from the future steps in the maze (the equivalents of $v(B)$ and $v(C)$ in Equation [7]) are zero because the trial ends in one of the shaded boxes. We have also included the reduced notation of the previous section.

If we were to follow the Rescorla-Wagner rule of Equation (6) to learn $v(A)$, we might use the right-hand side of Equation (7) as the target for $v(A)$ (replacing the r), and use the difference between the target value and

the current value $v(A)$ to drive learning

$$v(A) \rightarrow v(A) + \eta([\pi_L(A)(\langle r_L(A)\rangle + v(B))$$
$$+ \pi_R(A)(\langle r_R(A)\rangle + v(C))] - v(A)). \quad (10)$$

There are three problems with Equation (10), all of which temporal difference learning addresses.

The first problem with Equation (10) is that the target value for $v(A)$ involves knowing the true values $v(B)$ or $v(C)$. Of course, at the beginning of learning, these are no better known than $v(A)$. Temporal difference learning ducks this concern by *bootstrapping* its estimates from each other. That is, learning proceeds for all locations simultaneously, and as $v(B)$ and $v(C)$ become more accurate, $v(A)$ becomes more accurate, too.

The second problem is that the learning rule involves an average over both possible directions that the rat could choose at A, rather than just the single direction that the rat can actually choose on a single trial. Gallistel (personal communication, 2001) calls this the problem of the road not taken. Fortunately, just as we use the random number of pellets r_L received for going left on a single trial in Equation (6) and still make q_L be the average number of pellets consequent on turning right $\langle r_L\rangle$, we can use the actual value $v(B)$ or $v(C)$ encountered by the rat on a single trial and still learn the average of Equation (8).

In order to have a slightly more general description of this, we need to use the more general way of describing a single step in the maze that we mentioned earlier. Consider the case that the rat starts at a location X, picks a random direction D according to $\pi_L(X)$ and $\pi_R(X)$, receives an immediate reward of $r_D(X)$ pellets, and moves to location Y. Here, $r_D(X) + v(Y)$ is a random quantity because both the choice of action D and the delivery of $r_D(X)$ pellets are random. Starting from X = A, if direction D is left, then Y is B; if direction D is right, then Y is C. Averaging over these sources of stochasticity, the mean value of $r_D(A) + v(Y)$ is

$$\pi_L(A)(\langle r_L(A) \rangle + v(B))$$
$$+ \pi_R(A)(\langle r_R(A) \rangle + v(C)) \quad (11)$$

which is just the right-hand side of Equation (7). This is also true for general moves in the maze. Thus, $r_D(X) + v(Y)$ can be thought of as a random sample of the value of $v(X)$ in the same way that r_L in Equation (5) is a random sample of $\langle r_L \rangle$. The overall learning rule uses this sample to replace the expression in the square brackets of Equation (10). That is, it uses the difference

$$\delta = r_D(X) + v(Y) - v(X) \quad (12)$$

between the sampled target $(r_D(X) + v(Y))$ and current $(v(X))$ values of X to drive learning, just as the Rescorla-Wagner rule of Equation (5) uses the difference between the sampled target (r_L) and current (q_L) state-action values. The final learning rule is

$$v(X) \rightarrow v(X) + \eta\delta. \quad (13)$$

The difference δ of Equation (12) is called the *temporal difference* and plays a central role in both biological and engineering aspects of reinforcement learning. Its name derives from the difference $v(Y) - v(X)$ between the estimates of the values of two successive states.

The third concern is that a straightforward implementation of Equation (13) seems to require that the rat have a very simple representation of each location, with a single parameter $v(X)$ for each location. As is completely standard in theories of conditioning, we might more reasonably expect X to be represented by the activity of a set of atomistic stimulus representation or cue units $(u_1, u_2, \ldots, u_n) = \mathbf{u}$, whose activity at X, called $\mathbf{u}(X)$ might be determined by the unique cues at each location in the maze, or perhaps the activity of place cells associated with the locations. Associated

with each cue unit u_i is a weight or parameter w_i that determines its contribution to the values of locations at which the cue is active. As in the Rescorla-Wagner rule in such circumstances, the value of location X, $v(X)$, is a sum over the weights of just the cues that are active at X, and only the weights associated with active cues are changed in the face of prediction errors.

An easy way to put this version of the Rescorla-Wagner rule more formally is to assume that a stimulus representation unit $u_i(X)$ takes the value 0, if the cue is not present at X, or 1 if the cue is present. Then, because of this simple binary form, the Rescorla-Wagner rule's assumption that the value of X is determined as a sum over the cues that are active there can be written

$$v(X) = \sum_i w_i u_i(X) = \mathbf{w} \cdot \mathbf{u}(X). \quad (14)$$

Further, the extension to the temporal difference learning rule of Equation (13) specifies changes to the weights for just the cues that are active at X

$$w_i \rightarrow w_i + \eta\delta u_i(X). \quad (15)$$

This rule shares most of the properties of the Rescorla-Wagner rule related to stimulus competition (such as blocking), and it also shares many of its faults. Figure 3.4 shows the learning architecture in a different way, where, in this case, there are just three cues and three weights $(n = 3)$.

The extensive theory of temporal difference learning (see Bertsekas & Tsitsiklis, 1996; Sutton & Barto, 1998) indicates circumstances under which this learning rule will make the values $v(X)$ come to satisfy Equation (8). More concretely, Figure 3.5 shows the course of learning of the values of A, B, and C (solid lines), together with their target values (dashed line) in a single session of 100 trials in the maze of Figure 3.1 for the case that the rat chooses left and right equally

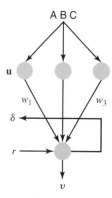

Figure 3.4   The architecture of the critic.
NOTE: The stimulus representation **u**, which here has one element for each location in the maze, maps to the value estimate v through a set of modifiable weights **w**. The prediction unit incorporates information about the delivered rewards r and calculates the temporal difference error δ, which is used to change the weights.

often. It is apparent that the values are learned quickly and accurately.

We have so far shown how to learn the values of the locations as the expected future rewards starting from those locations. How can we use this information to learn a good policy at location X? The idea, just as in Equations (12) and (13), is to use $r_D(X) + v(Y)$ as a sampled estimate of the value of performing action D. This sampled estimate can replace r_L in the learning rules for the direct and

indirect actor, as we discuss in the next two sections.

The Actor-Critic

In discussing the direct actor, we introduced the idea of the reinforcement comparison term $\tilde{r}$ and suggested that it might take on the value of the average reward. In this case, an estimate of the current average reward is just $v(X)$, and so, for instance, Equation (2) becomes

$$m(X) \to m(X) + \epsilon(r_L(X) + v(Y)$$
$$- v(X))(1 - \pi_L)$$
$$= m(X) + \epsilon\delta(1 - \pi_L) \qquad (16)$$

and depends on the values only through the temporal difference error δ of Equation (12). Therefore, the same temporal difference error term is used to train both the value of X *and* the policy at X. To put it another way, $\delta > 0$ means either that the estimate of the value $v(X)$ is too pessimistic or that the estimate is right on average, but the action D is better than average (or both). In the first case, the estimate should ideally be changed; in the second, the policy should be changed. Figure 3.6 shows the course of learning of actions at A, B, and C in the maze. The rat rapidly learns to turn left at A and B, and also to turn right at C. This combination of temporal difference learning and the direct actor was first suggested

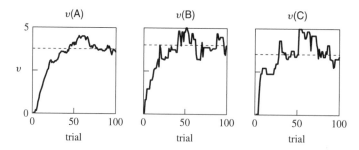

Figure 3.5   Learning the values.
NOTE: The solid lines show the course of learning of $v(A)$, $v(B)$, and $v(C)$ over a single session of 100 simulated runs through the maze. The dashed lines show the true values from Equation (8). Here, $\epsilon = 0.2$.

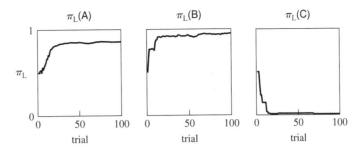

Figure 3.6   Learning the policies.
NOTE: The lines show the course of learning $\pi_L(A)$, $\pi_L(B)$, and $\pi_L(C)$ over a single session of 100 simulated runs through the maze using temporal difference learning and the direct actor. Here, $\epsilon = 0.4$.

by Barto, Sutton, and Anderson (1983) under the name of the actor-critic architecture.

In the case that stimulus units $u_i(X)$ represent the locations in the maze, then, as in Equation (14), a set of action weights m_i can be used to parameterize the action choice at X

$$m(X) = \sum_i m_i u_i(X). \qquad (17)$$

The equivalent of rule (16) is

$$m_i \rightarrow m_i + \epsilon\delta(1 - \pi_L)u_i(X). \qquad (18)$$

Q-Learning

It would be possible to use exactly the indirect actor as described in the first section in conjunction with the estimate $r_D(X) + v(Y)$ of the future rewards from a location. However, this is not done because of the redundancy between learning the average value of each action at each location $q_D(Y)$ and, *separately*, the average value of the location $v(Y)$ itself. Rather, the conventional alternative is to define $v(Y)$ in terms of the state-action values $q_D(Y)$. There are two ways to do this. Because the state-action values define an explicit policy, $\pi(Y)$, one way is to define $v(Y)$ as a weighted average of the state-action values, where the weights are determined by the policy. However, the object of learning is to find the actions that maximize the expected reward. Because the rat is free to choose which

direction to run at Y, it is appropriate to evaluate Y not according to the estimated average worth of all the possible directions at Y, but rather by the estimated worth of the *best* direction at Y. The second way to determine $v(Y)$ is thus

$$v(Y) = \max_D q_D(Y). \qquad (19)$$

Whichever form for the value of Y is used, given a choice of action D and a transition from location X to Y, the Q values should be updated as

$$q_D(X) \rightarrow q_D(X) + \eta(r_D(X) + v(Y). - q_D(X)). \qquad (20)$$

Rule (20) is almost the same as the standard temporal difference rule of Equation (13). This form of reinforcement learning is called Q-learning and was invented by Watkins (1989).

Dynamic Programming

Markov decision problems (Puterman, 1994) provide a rich theoretical context for understanding sequential action choice tasks such as the maze. Methods in engineering for solving Markov decision problems are generally forms of a technique called dynamic programming (Bellman, 1957), to which reinforcement learning algorithms are closely related. For instance, the actor-critic implements a dynamic programming technique called *policy iteration,* involving policy evaluation (finding the values $v[X]$ that satisfy Equation [8]) and policy improvement (using the values to find actions that are better). Q-learning implements a dynamic programming technique called *value iteration.*

The link with dynamic programming has led to comprehensive theory (see Bertsekas & Tsitsiklis, 1996; Sutton & Barto, 1998) about the circumstances under which Q-learning will find optimal policies in tasks such as the maze. It has also opened many lines of investigation extending and improving the basic methods outlined here.

DOPAMINE AND REINFORCEMENT LEARNING

Unfortunately, there has been no complete investigation of the neural basis of the learning behavior of rats or other animals in a maze such as that in Figure 3.1. However, as is evident in many other chapters in this volume, a substantial body of neurobiological data—based on drug addiction, self-stimulation, lesion studies, and neuropharmacology, bears on how animals actually learn about rewards. A venerable organizing focus of this work has been that the neuromodulator dopamine plays a central role (see, e.g., Chap. 19, this volume; Beninger, 1983; Koob, 1992; Robbins & Everitt, 1992; Simon & le Moal, 1998; Wise, 1982; Wise & Rompre, 1989). Note, however, that this is an active and controversial field of study, and there are also many recent challenges (see Berridge & Robinson, 1998; Ikemoto & Panksepp, 1999; Spanagel & Weiss, 1999). Temporal difference learning has been used to model the activity of dopamine cells during reward learning, a link we describe in this section. The relevant dopamine cells are both in the ventral tegmental area, which project to areas associated with the limbic system, including the nucleus accumbens or ventral striatum, and those in the substantia nigra pars compacta, which project to the dorsal striatum.

Figure 3.7 shows a histogram of the activity of dopamine cells of a thirsty macaque monkey in conditions before and after it learns a predictive association between a stimulus (which cues a motor response) and a reward (which is a drop of juice). These actually come from different experiments, but the qualitative pattern of results is robust. In Figure 3.7A, left and right plots show activity that is stimulus-locked to the cue and the reward, respectively. The cue is irrelevant before learning, and there is little response to it, whereas delivery of the reward induces a large and well-timed response from the cells. Figure 3.7B shows that after learning, the contingencies reverse: Now the activity is consequent on the early reliable predictor and not on the reward itself.

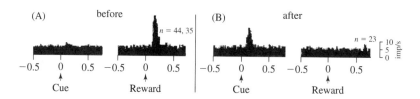

Figure 3.7　Histograms of population activity of dopamine cells stimulus-locked to a cue and to the reward during a conditioning task.
NOTE: A) Dopamine activity before learning shows response to the reward and not to the cue. B) Dopamine activity after learning shows response to the cue and not to the reward.
SOURCE: Adapted from Schultz (1998).

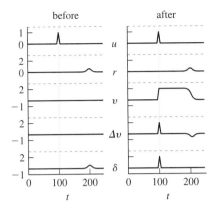

Figure 3.8 Model of the data of Figure 3.7.
NOTE: The series of graphs show the cue (u), the activity consequent on the reward (r), the learned prediction (v), the temporal difference in the learned prediction (Δv), and the temporal difference error signal ($\delta = r + \Delta v$). Left plots show "before" learning; right plots show "after" learning. δ should be matched to the data in Figure 3.7.
SOURCE: Adapted from Montague, Dayan, & Sejnowski (1996); Dayan & Abbott (2001).

Figure 3.8 describes the account of this activity that comes from temporal difference learning (Friston, Tononi, Reeke, Sporns, & Edelman, 1994; Houk, Adams, & Barto, 1995; Montague, Dayan, & Sejnowski, 1996; Schultz, Dayan, & Montague, 1997; Wickens, 1993). The idea is that the difference between the activity and the baseline activity reports the temporal difference prediction error δ (Equation [12]). In early trials the reward is unexpected, so the prediction error and the model dopamine activity follow the reward

signal r. In later trials the activity associated with the reward is expected and thus induces no prediction error and no nonbaseline dopamine activity. However, the stimulus is not expected. It provides a signal that reward will be delivered in the future and therefore is associated with a large and positive prediction error and thus a large and positive deflection above baseline of the dopamine activity. The way that this model accounts for secondary conditioning is clear. If another stimulus (e.g., a tone) is presented before the light, then the activity of the dopamine system consequent on the light (seen in "after") acts for the tone just as the activity consequent on the reward (seen in "before") originally acted for the light. Thus, learning about the relationship between tone and reward will proceed. In the figure, the signal Δv is the difference in successive predictions of the reward. This is 0 whenever the predictions are not changing (i.e., before the cue and between the cue and reward).

One facet of the temporal difference signal is shown by the plot of Δv in Figure 3.8 after learning is complete. If the monkey is not provided with a reward when it is expecting it, then the temporal difference signal $\delta = \Delta v$ will be exactly this. The below-baseline activity around the time of the reward is a mark of the reward prediction. The right-most plot in Figure 3.9 shows dopaminergic activity in the same circumstances. The well-timed, below-baseline activity is clear, just as in the model.

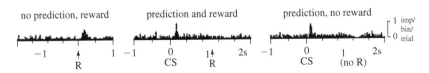

Figure 3.9 Activity of single dopamine cells to reward that is unexpected (left), predicted and delivered (center), or predicted and not delivered (right). The left and center plots match to Figures 3.7 and the lowest lines in Figure 3.8, the rightmost plot matches Δv "after" learning in Figure 3.8. The scale is in spikes per bin per trial.
SOURCE: Adapted from Schultz, Dayan, & Montague (1997).

Figure 3.8 embodies a crucial assumption that the monkey has a way of keeping time precisely between the stimulus and the reward. Each time step is individuated by a different stimulus (called a serial compound conditioned stimulus in Gormezano & Kehoe, 1989, or a spectral representation of time in Grossberg & Schmajuk, 1989) in just the same way that each location in the maze might be identified by a single stimulus. Because Figure 3.9 shows that the inhibition is well timed in the case that the reward is not provided, we know that this time must be represented somehow; however, the precise neural substrate is unclear. O'Reilly, Braver, and Cohen (1999) and Braver, Barch, and Cohen (1999) have suggested that one result of the dopamine response to the predictive stimulus is to gate the stimulus into working memory in prefrontal cortex. This would mean that information that the stimulus had recently been presented is available for prediction and control, and the complex developing pattern of population activity of neurons in the prefrontal working memory may individuate the time steps between the stimulus and reward, as in proposals for how timing information is represented in the cerebellum (Buonomano & Mauk, 1994; Medina & Mauk, 2000). Suggestions for the involvement of the hippocampus (Grossberg & Merrill, 1996) and intracellular processes in striatal cells (Brown, Bullock, & Grossberg, 1999) have also been made. In fact, the cerebellum has been suggested as another neural substrate for conditioning, particularly eye-blink conditioning, and Rescorla-Wagner (Gluck, Reifsnider, & Thompson, 1990) and temporal difference (Moore, Berthier, & Blazis, 1990) models of its involvement have been built. These lie outside the scope of this chapter. The subtleties of the timing behavior of animals in conditioning experiments are discussed in other chapters in this volume (e.g., Chap. 9). The substantial timing noise that is evident in many experiments and is the subject of substantial theory itself (e.g.,

Gibbon, 1977) may have a significant impact on the pattern of activity of the dopamine cells.

The original suggestion for a temporal difference account of conditioning (Sutton & Barto, 1990) did not employ a serial compound conditioned stimulus but instead relied on the earlier psychological notion of stimulus traces (Hull, 1943). The idea is that if u_i representing the cue is active at one time ($t = 100$ in Figure 3.8), then the associated weight w_i is *eligible* to be changed according to temporal difference prediction errors δ that occur at later times ($t = 200$ in the figure, around the time of the reward). This allows the model to account for phenomena such as secondary conditioning. However, short of a way of keeping time between the stimulus and the reward, it does not make correct predictions about the activity of the dopamine cells. Stimulus traces actually play an interesting computational role in the temporal difference model, as explored by Watkins (1989).

As mentioned, there is an active debate on the full link between dopamine and appetitive conditioning. For instance, we have focused on the phasic behavior of dopamine cells in response to surprising rewards; there is also evidence from dialysis that dopamine is released, and from neurophysiology that the dopamine cells are activated in a more persistent manner, by aversive contingencies (Abercrombie, Keefe, DiFrischia, & Zigmond, 1989; Claustre, Rivy, Dennis, & Scatton, 1986; Guarraci & Kapp, 1999; Herman et al., 1982). They are also activated by novel stimuli (Horvitz, Stewart, & Jacobs, 1997; Ljungberg, Apicella, & Schultz, 1992; although note that novelty can sometimes act as if it is itself rewarding: Reed, Mitchell, & Nokes, 1996) and by stimuli that resemble other stimuli that are associated with rewards (Schultz, 1998). Although extensions of the temporal difference model have been suggested to account for all these behaviors (e.g., Contreras-Vidal & Schultz, 1999; Daw & Touretzky, 2000;

Kakade & Dayan, 2001), more experiments and more theory are still required. These and other findings have led to suggestions about the role of dopamine other than prediction and reward learning, particularly focusing on orienting and the allocation of attention (Han, McMahan, Holland, & Gallagher, 1997; Redgrave, Prescott, & Gurney, 1999; Ward & Brown, 1996; Yamaguchi & Kobayashi, 1988). It is worth noting that it is not yet completely clear how activity of the dopamine cells translates into the release of dopamine at target sites.

It is also not clear exactly what is responsible for the activity of the dopamine cells, or which synapses change their values to reflect the predictions of reward associated with stimuli and to reflect the appropriate choice of actions. There is some evidence in both rats and monkeys that the basolateral nucleus of the amygdala and the orbitofrontal cortex play an important role in storing the values associated with stimuli (Gallagher, McMahan, & Schoenbaum, 1999; Hatfield, Han, Conley, Gallagher, & Holland, 1996; Robbins & Everitt, 1999; Rolls, 2000; Schoenbaum, Chiba, & Gallagher, 1998, 1999). However, exactly how this information translates into the activity of dopamine cells is open to speculation. Another critical piece for the model is the way that dopamine can control the selection—and particularly the learned selection—of actions. Early suggestions that this is a role for plasticity into the cortico-striatal afferents to the dorsal striatum are now under some question (see Houk, Davis, & Beiser, 1995; Kropotov & Etlinger, 1999).

STATISTICAL MODELS OF ATTENTION

The temporal difference model for learning values inherits a number of properties from the Rescorla-Wagner rule about how different possible cues interact to make predic-tions about expected future rewards and to have their predictive weights change. As in Equation (14), the predictions made by all the stimuli that are present are just summed, and, as in Equation (15), the weights of all stimuli present are changed by the same amount. The only competition between stimuli is as in blocking; that is, if one stimulus already predicts an outcome perfectly, then other stimuli that are simultaneously present will attract no learning because there is no prediction error.

The temporal difference model thus also inherits the problems that these assumptions make for the Rescorla-Wagner rule. What both leave out is *attention*. Attention is a complicated and multifaceted concept (see, for example, Parasuraman, 1998), with many different implications for different neural processes. In conditioning, there is a long history (for reviews, see Dickinson, 1980; Mackintosh, 1983) of the study of selective attention, originally sparked by the idea that there might be a limited-capacity learning processor that is responsible for relating stimuli to affective outcomes and that stimuli might compete to gain access to this processor. Even though the idea of limited-capacity explanations for attention now has rather less currency (Allport, 1993), substantial experimental results on selective attention in conditioning remain to be explained.

The Rescorla-Wagner and temporal difference models do not take account of the possibility that based on the past history of interaction, animals might accord more weight to the predictions made by some stimuli than by others, or that some stimuli might attract faster learning than others. Alternative models of conditioning, for which there is quite some evidence, place substantial emphasis on these stronger forms of competition between stimuli. One of the best studied alternatives is that due to Pearce and Hall (1980), who suggested that animals should learn more about stimuli whose consequences are more uncertain.

In fact, in its original form, the Pearce-Hall model explains even basic blocking by this mechanism, rather than by the lack of prediction error. Pearce and Hall also point out that stimuli about which an animal is uncertain are exactly the ones that should not be believed in making predictions about rewards. However, they did not suggest a quantitative account of how their predictions could be ignored. Grossberg (see 1982) suggests that all the stimuli that are present should compete to make predictions, although this competition is not, at least in a straightforward manner, based on uncertainty.

Holland and his colleagues (see Holland, 1997; Holland & Gallagher, 1999) have performed a wealth of tests of the neural basis of the Pearce-Hall model in appetitive conditioning. Primarily using selective lesions, they have identified a pathway in rats from the central nucleus of the amygdala through the cholinergic basal forebrain to the parietal cortex that is critically involved in the faster learning accorded to stimuli whose outcomes are made uncertain. They also identified a different pathway involved in the slower learning accorded to stimuli whose outcomes are perfectly predictable (as in latent inhibition; Lubow, 1989; see Baxter, Holland, & Gallagher, 1997). Baxter, Bucci, Holland, and Gallagher (1999) suggested that eliminating both these pathways leaves rats with an underlying learning behavior more consistent with the Rescorla-Wagner rule, confirming that a simple phenomenon such as blocking is likely to be multiply determined. As an aside, the involvement of cholinergic systems in processing uncertainty is striking because of evidence of the action of ACh in changing the balance in favor of stimulus-driven or bottom-up input against recurrent or top-down input in determining the activity of cells in both the hippocampus and the cortex (Hasselmo, 1999; Hasselmo, Anderson & Bower, 1992). In cases in which the animal knows itself to be uncertain, recurrent and top-down input is less likely to be correct.

From a computational point of view, these two rather different forms of attention should emerge naturally from statistical considerations. The models of this, such as Kruschke (1997, 2001); Gallistel and Gibbon (2000); Kakade and Dayan (2000); and Dayan, Kakade, and Montague (2000), are not yet completely integrated into the full reinforcement learning models for tasks such as the maze, so we describe them only briefly.

Competitive Combination

One way to generate competition between cues for making predictions about outcomes is to think of combining the views of multiple experts about the same event. In this circumstance, it is natural to weight each expert's view according to how reliable a predictor that expert has been in the past. Clearly, adding together the predictions made by all the experts, which is what Equation (14) suggests, would be rather strange. There are various ways to formalize competitive combination (Jacobs, 1995) from a statistical viewpoint. Understanding how these models fit conditioning data provides insight into the statistical assumptions embodied by animal learners.

Two statistical competitive models have been advocated for conditioning. Kruschke (1997, 2001) suggested using the standard mixture of experts architecture (Jacobs, Jordan, Nowlan, & Hinton, 1991), motivated partly by Mackintosh's (1975) attentional model, and Dayan and Long (1997) and Kakade and Dayan (2000) suggested the original mixture of experts model (Jacobs, Jordan & Barto, 1991) motivated by the experimental phenomenon of downwards unblocking (Mackintosh, Bygrave, & Picton, 1977; Holland, 1984, 1988) and results on the apparent sloth of learning in autoshaping (Gallistel & Gibbon, 2000). Although there

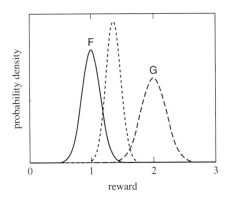

Figure 3.10   Unreliability model.

NOTE: Solid and dotted lines show the distributions of the predictions of reward made by two cues (F and G). These are Gaussian distributions with precisions (inverse variances) reflecting the reliabilities of the cues. The dot-dashed line shows the combined prediction, assuming that the individual predictions are statistically independent in an appropriate way.

SOURCE: After Dayan, Kakade & Montague (2000).

are substantial differences in the assumptions and behavior of these models, they share the characteristic of competitive combination.

Figure 3.10 shows an example of combination according to the Jacobs, Jordan, and Barto (1991) model. Here, competition is derived from unreliability. Two cues, F and G (e.g., a light and a tone) make unreliable predictions about the reward. The unreliability is shown on the plot in the terms of the whole distribution over the actual reward given each cue by itself. Cue F (the solid line) predicts a single pellet of reward; cue G (the dotted line), two pellets. However, F is more reliable than G as is evident from the fact that its distribution is sharper. That is, under cue F the reward is tightly constrained near 1 pellet, whereas under cue G the reward is more loosely constrained near 2 pellets. Given both cues, how should a net prediction be constructed? Under a model in which the unreliabilities of the cues are statistically independent, it turns out that these distributions should be multi-

plied together and then reweighted. The net prediction (the dot-dashed line) is therefore of an intermediate number of pellets, nearer 1 than 2 (because F, which predicts 1 pellet, is more reliable than G). The net prediction is more reliable than those of either F or G because it integrates information from both. By contrast, the standard additive combination model for temporal difference learning or the Rescorla-Wagner rule would predict 3 pellets of reward.

Purely additive models such as Equation (14) and purely competitive models such as Figure 3.10 both fail to account for some conditioning data. Competitive models have difficulty with circumstances such as overexpectation (see Lattal & Nakajima, 1998; Rescorla, 1999); additive models fail for phenomena such as downwards unblocking (see Dickinson, 1980). Providing a statistical basis for integrating these models is an important next step.

Competitive Adaptation

The opposite of a reliable predictor is a stimulus about whose consequences the animal is in substantial doubt. According to the Pearce-Hall model, this uncertainty should lead the animal to learn faster about the associated stimulus. In the context of the temporal difference model of Equation (15), this can be implemented simply by providing each stimulus unit with its own learning rate η_i. However, what is a computational account of how these learning rates should be set? Once again, a psychological intuition has a computational basis, in this case ideas about learning and adaptation in the face of uncertainty and change in the world. This basis was provided by Sutton (1992), who formalized an alternative way of thinking about the course of conditioning in terms of an engineering and statistical device called a Kalman filter (Anderson & Moore, 1979).

Sutton suggested that the conditioning behavior of animals is consistent with their trying to reverse-engineer the relationship between stimuli and rewards that is established by the experimenter (or, in more natural circumstances, by nature). The process of reverse-engineering consists of combining the information about the relationship that is provided by the sample stimuli and rewards provided on each trial. Initially, the animal will be quite uncertain about the relationship; given lots of trials, even noisy ones, it may become more certain. However, if the relationship continually changes (as it almost always does in both natural and experimental contexts), then very old trials may no longer be relevant to the current relationship, and therefore their information should be discarded. The Kalman filter is a statistically precise way of formulating the answer to this prob-

lem; Sutton (1992) and Dayan, Kakade, and Montague (2000) suggested an approximation to it as a way of modeling the phenomena that motivate the Pearce-Hall rule.

The approximate Kalman filter takes the prediction error δ of Equation (12) and distributes it among all the stimuli that are present in a trial, in proportion to their uncertainties. The more certain the animal is about the predictions based on a stimulus (i.e., the more past trials have been used to establish this prediction), the less responsibility that stimulus takes for any new prediction error. Conversely, stimuli about which the animal has learned little, and about which it is therefore very uncertain, have their weights changed substantially more.

Figure 3.11 shows a simple version of this model at work in a case in which three different stimuli (labelled u_1, u_2, and u_3) are

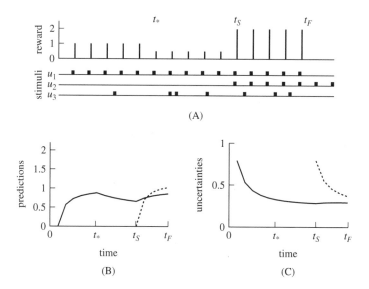

(A)

(B) (C)

Figure 3.11 Uncertainty model.
NOTE: A) Conditioning experiment involving three stimuli u_1, u_2, and u_3, whose presence on a trial is indicated by a small black square, and a variable number of pellets of reward. t_*, t_S, and t_F are particular times at which the stimulus or reward contingencies change. B) Net predictions for u_1 (solid) and u_2 (dashed) over the course of the experiment. C) Uncertainties associated with the same stimuli. The predictions change quickly (i.e., the weights change quickly) for stimuli whose predictions are highly uncertain.
SOURCE: After Dayan, Kakade, & Montague (2000).

provided in partial combination with a number of pellets of reward over an extended period. Stimulus u_3 is only randomly related to the reward and thus attracts no learning; stimuli u_1 and u_2 are closely related to the reward, but in different ways at different times during the experiment. Figure 3.11B shows the predictive weights w_1 (solid) and w_2 (dashed) for u_1 and u_2, respectively. The learning of these weights is based on the uncertainties shown in Figure 3.11C. Initially, the animal is highly uncertain about the associations of all the stimuli, so when u_1 is presented in close combination with one pellet of reward, learning of w_1 is swift. The animal then becomes more certain about the relationship, so at t_*, when it changes, the animal is rather slower to change its prediction. At time t_S, when u_2 is introduced in combination with a change in the number of pellets, the greater uncertainty of u_2 means that it learns much faster than u_1, and so establishes itself as a major predictor. This is exactly as expected from the Pearce-Hall model.

This model for the competitive allocation of learning is also rather preliminary and has yet to be integrated properly with the model of competitive combination. In particular, it does not capture Pearce-Hall's observation that the uncertainties change adaptively in response to prediction errors, both in predictions of reward and in predictions of other stimuli. For instance, the neural basis of attentional allocation has been studied using a task developed by Wilson, Boumphrey, and Pearce (1992), in which uncertainties in stimulus-stimulus predictions are explicitly manipulated. In this task, the predictive consequences of one conditioned stimulus for another change from one set of trials to the next. This change, which leads to an inevitable prediction error, makes for faster learning of the association between the first conditioned stimulus and a reward. Our simple account of the competitive allocation of

learning cannot model this more sophisticated experiment.

In general, reinforcement learning methods can be used to learn stimulus-stimulus predictions as well as stimulus-outcome predictions, (Dayan, 1993; Suri & Schultz, 2001; Sutton & Pinette, 1985), and this capacity has even been used to explain phenomena such as sensory preconditioning. However, the range of properties of such models has yet to be fully explored. Indeed, there is debate in both the psychological literature (Gallistel, 1990; Gallistel & Gibbon, 2000) and the theoretical reinforcement learning literature (Kearns & Singh, 1999) about the relative merits of model-free methods such as the actor-critic or Q-learning and model-based methods that build and use models of the stimulus-stimulus and stimulus-reward contingencies of environments.

DISCUSSION

Two areas of current work in reinforcement learning have a particular importance for psychological and neural modeling: eliminating the rather artificial definition of a trial and performing planning over larger spatial and temporal horizons.

First, as has been forcefully pointed out by Gallistel and Gibbon (2000) and others, the definition of a trial in tasks such as the maze is problematical. Even in the maze case, animals might integrate reward information over multiple runs if they are continually taken back to the start point when they reach one of the end boxes; further, many standard instrumental conditioning tasks involve extended series of repeated choices. Under such circumstances, the criterion of maximizing the sum total reward over a whole session is unreasonable, for instance, because this sum may get very large. In dynamic programming, two ways of handling such cases have been suggested, and both have been translated into reinforcement learning. The first is to consider summed *discounted* rewards. That is, rewards that are expected to be received in the future are down-weighted by an amount that reflects how long it takes them to arrive. The second is to consider the long-run average reward rate rather than the sum total reward.

The standard model of discounting in dynamic programming is exponential; that is, a reward of r pellets received t timesteps from now is treated as being worth only $\gamma^t r$, where $0 \leq \gamma < 1$ is the discount factor. If γ is near 0, only very proximal rewards have a significant impact on the sum discounted reward. Exponential discounting is standard in economic contexts over long times, in order to take account of inflation and interest rates. Exponential discounting is also easy to incorporate into the temporal difference model we described, for instance, changing Equation (12) to

$$\delta = r + \gamma v(\mathsf{Y}) - v(\mathsf{X}).$$

However, in direct tests humans and other animals do not appear to use exponential discounting. Rather, at least in many contexts, they discount rewards hyperbolically (Ainslie, 1975, 1992; Mazur, 1984; Rachlin, 1970, 1974), so the r pellets are worth $r/(\alpha + \beta t)$, where α and β are parameters. Hyperbolic discounting has a number of unexpected properties that have been experimentally confirmed. One example is preference reversals: Offered a choice between $10 now and $20 next week, subjects might prefer to get $10 now; whereas offered a choice between $10 in six weeks and $20 in seven weeks, subjects tend to be content to wait for the $20. Exponential discounting cannot generate preference reversals like this. Hyperbolic discounting is much harder to accommodate within a temporal difference framework because there is no equivalent to Equation (8)'s recursive definition of value.

The alternative to the discounted model for dynamic programming is the average-case model. In this case, the goal is to maximize the reward rate over time rather than the cumulative reward. Kacelnik (1997) argued that apparently hyperbolic discounting might really result from the average-case model, at least given the way that the preference experiments are run. There is an extensive body of dynamic programming (see Puterman, 1994) and reinforcement learning (Mahadevan, 1996; Schwartz, 1993; Tsitsiklis & Van Roy, 1999) theory on the average case, which turns out to require only a small modification to the temporal difference model we have discussed. The idea is to learn the overall average reward rate ρ, using a learning rule like the Rescorla-Wagner rule of Equation (6), and then to modify the temporal difference prediction error of Equation (12) by subtracting ρ from the expression there:

$$\delta = r + v(\mathsf{Y}) - v(\mathsf{X}) - \rho. \quad (21)$$

Daw and Touretzky (2000) suggested exactly this and showed that it makes essentially the same predictions as the standard temporal difference model for the experiments that have been used to probe the dopamine system.

Equation (21) has an interesting interpretation as the difference between a phasic signal (the original δ of Equation [12]) and a tonic signal (representing ρ). One possibility is that these signals are actually represented by different neuromodulators—in the appetitive case, perhaps dopamine for the phasic signal and serotonin for the tonic signal. Concomitantly, a tonic dopamine signal might represent the equivalent of ρ in the aversive case (i.e., the mean punishment rate). This has been suggested as an interpretation of the data that dopamine is released in cases of aversive conditioning. This way of looking at Equation (21) is a special case of an *opponent* interaction between appetitive and aversive systems, a longstanding psychological idea, which has been the subject of influential modeling by Solomon and Corbit (1974), Grossberg (1984), and Grossberg and Schmajuk (1987). Understanding the interactions between the various neuromodulators is a key current concern (Doya, 2000), as is incorporating the more sophisticated analysis of the involvement of dopamine in motivation and specifically motivational opponency, revealed in studies of incentive motivation and learning (Dickinson & Balleine, this volume; Wyvell & Berridge, 2000).

Another main area of investigation in reinforcement learning is the representation and manipulation of hierarchical structure. The idea is that many tasks are not best solved by considering only the simplest and shortest actions at every time (like a single step in the maze), but rather that planning can better proceed with longer spatial and temporal horizons. The expanded horizons might come from considering sets of actions, going by the names of chunks, options, macros, or subroutines (see Sutton, Precup, & Singh, 1999). These notions offer the prospect of going full circle back to some of the concerns that were central in the original study of sequential chains of behavior, such as the effects of multiple goals in an environment (stemming, e.g., from a sometimes hungry, sometimes thirsty, rat in a maze with both food and water rewards). They also offer mechanisms for integrating model-free and model-based methods of learning and control. In fact, there are even suggestions (Frank, Loughry, & O'Reilly, 2000) about how the interaction between the prefrontal cortex and the basal ganglia might implement such subroutines.

There is substantial theory about how to use hierarchical structure such as options within a reinforcement learning context, and indeed proofs that appropriate structure can make for much faster learning. However, there are rather fewer proposals about how such structure might be induced as tasks are being solved. One idea is that unsupervised learning methods, which are models for cortical plasticity (see Becker & Plumbley, 1996; Hinton & Sejnowski, 1999) and are designed to extract statistical structure from inputs, might be involved. Understanding this requires modeling the interactions between unsupervised and reinforcement learning, and between cortical and subcortical plasticity (Doya, 1999).

In conclusion, we have described the standard model of reinforcement learning for single and sequential action choice as well as its main relationships with classical and instrumental conditioning, dynamic programming, and the dopamine system. Reinforcement learning is thus one of the few areas in which constraints and ideas from many levels of computational analysis (computational, algorithmic, and implementational; Marr, 1982) and many sorts of experimental data (ethological, psychological, and neurobiological) can collectively be brought to bear.

REFERENCES

Abercrombie, E. D., Keefe, K. A., DiFrischia, D. S., & Zigmond, M. J. (1989). Differential effect of stress on in vivo dopamine release in striatum, nucleus accumbens, and medial frontal cortex. *Journal of Neurochemistry, 52,* 1655–1658.

Ainslie, G. (1975). Specious reward: A behavioral theory of impulsiveness and impulse control. *Psychological Bulletin, 82,* 463–496.

Ainslie, G. (1992). *Picoeconomics.* Cambridge: Cambridge University Press.

Allport, A. (1993). Attention and control: Have we been asking the wrong questions? A critical review of twenty-five years. In D. E. Meyer & S. Kornblum (Eds.), *Attention and performance 14* (pp. 183–218). Cambridge: MIT Press.

Anderson, B. D. O., & Moore, J. B. (1979). *Optimal filtering.* Englewood Cliffs, NJ: Prentice-Hall.

Barto, A. G., Sutton, R. S., & Anderson, C. W. (1983). Neuronlike elements that can solve difficult learning problems. *IEEE Transactions on Systems, Man, and Cybernetics, 13,* 834–846.

Baxter, M. G., Bucci, D. J., Holland, P. C., & Gallagher, M. (1999). Impairments in conditioned stimulus processing and conditioned responding after combined selective removal of hippocampal and neocortical cholinergic input. *Behavioral Neuroscience, 113,* 486–495.

Baxter, M. G., Holland, P. C., & Gallagher, M. (1997). Disruption of decrements in conditioned stimulus processing by selective removal of hippocampal cholinergic input. *Journal of Neuroscience, 17,* 5230–5236.

Becker, S., & Plumbley, M. (1996). Unsupervised neural network learning procedures for feature extraction and classification. *International Journal of Applied Intelligence, 6,* 185–203.

Bellman, R. E. (1957). *Dynamic programming.* Princeton, NJ: Princeton University Press.

Beninger, R. J. (1983). The role of dopamine in locomotor activity and learning. *Brain Research Reviews, 6,* 173–196.

Berridge, K. C., & Robinson, T. E. (1998). What is the role of dopamine in reward: Hedonic impact, reward learning, or incentive salience? *Brain Research Reviews, 28,* 309–369.

Berry, D. A., & Fristedt, B. (1985). *Bandit problems: Sequential allocation of experiments.* London: Chapman and Hall.

Bertsekas, D. P., & Tsitsiklis, J. N. (1996). *Neuro-dynamic programming.* Belmont, MA: Athena Scientific.

Braver, T. S., Barch, D. M., & Cohen, J. D. (1999). Cognition and control in schizophrenia: A computational model of dopamine and prefrontal function. *Biological Psychiatry, 46,* 312–328.

Brown, J., Bullock, D., & Grossberg, S. (1999). How the basal ganglia use parallel excitatory and inhibitory learning pathways to selectively respond to unexpected rewarding cues. *Journal of Neuroscience, 19,* 10502–10511.

Buonomano, D. V., & Mauk, M. (1994). Neural network model of the cerebellum: Temporal discrimination and the timing of motor responses. *Neural Computation, 6,* 38–55.

Bush, R. R., & Mosteller, F. (1955). *Stochastic models for learning.* New York: Wiley.

Claustre, Y., Rivy, J. P., Dennis, T., & Scatton, B. (1986). Pharmacological studies on stress-induced increase in frontal cortical dopamine metabolism in the rat. *Journal of Pharmacology and Experimental Therapeutics, 238,* 693–700.

Contreras-Vidal, J. L., & Schultz, W. (1999). A predictive reinforcement model of dopamine neurons for learning approach behavior. *Journal of Computational Neuroscience, 6,* 191–214.

Daw, N. D., & Touretzky, D. S. (2000). Behavioral considerations suggest an average reward TD model of the dopamine system. *Neurocomputing: An International Journal, 32,* 679–684.

Dayan, P. (1993). Improving generalisation for temporal difference learning: The successor representation. *Neural Computation, 5,* 613–624.

Dayan, P., & Abbott, L. F. (2001). *Theoretical neuroscience.* Cambridge: MIT Press.

Dayan, P., Kakade, S., & Montague, P. R. (2000). Learning and selective attention. *Nature Neuroscience, 3,* 1218–1223.

Dayan, P., & Long, T. (1997). Statistical models of conditioning. *Neural Information Processing Systems, 10,* 117–124.

Deutsch, J. A. (1960). *The structural basis of behavior.* Cambridge: Cambridge University Press.

Dickinson, A. (1980). *Contemporary animal learning theory.* Cambridge: Cambridge University Press.

Doya, K. (1999). What are the computations of the cerebellum, the basal ganglia and the cerebral cortex? *Neural Networks, 12,* 961–974.

Doya, K. (2000). Meta-learning, neuromodulation and emotion. In G. Hatano, N. Okada, & H. Tanabe (Eds.), *Proceedings of the 13th Toyota Conference on Affective Minds* (pp. 101–104). Amsterdam: Elsevier Science.

Egelman, D. M., Person, C., & Montague, P. R. (1998). A computational role for dopamine delivery in human decision-making. *Journal of Cognitive Neuroscience, 10,* 623–630.

Frank, M. J., Loughry, B., & O'Reilly, R. C. (2000). *Interactions between frontal cortex and basal ganglia in working memory: A computational model.* ICS Technical Report 00-01, Department of Psychology, University of Colorado at Boulder.

Friston, K. J., Tononi, G., Reeke, G. N., Jr., Sporns, O., & Edelman, G. M. (1994). Value-dependent selection in the brain: Simulation in a synthetic neural model. *Neuroscience, 59,* 229–243.

Gallagher, M., McMahan, R. W., & Schoenbaum, G. (1999). Orbitofrontal cortex and representation of incentive value in associative learning. *Journal of Neuroscience, 19,* 6610–6614.

Gallistel, C. R. (1990). *The Organization of Learning.* Cambridge, MA: Bradford Books/MIT Press.

Gallistel, C. R., & Gibbon, J. (2000). Time, rate, and conditioning. *Psychological Review, 107,* 289–344.

Gibbon, J. (1977). Scalar expectancy theory and Weber's Law in animal timing. *Psychological Review, 84,* 279–325.

Gluck, M. A., Reifsnider, E. S., & Thompson, R. F. (1990). Adaptive signal processing and the cerebellum: Models of classical conditioning and VOR adaptation. In M. A. Gluck & D. E. Rumelhart (Eds.), *Neuroscience and connectionist theory* (pp. 131–185). Hillsdale, NJ: Erlbaum.

Gormezano, I., & Kehoe, E. J. (1989). Classical conditioning with serial compound stimuli. In J. B. Sidowski (Ed.), *Conditioning, cognition, and methodology: Contemporary issues in experimental psychology* (pp. 31–61). Lanham, MD: University Press of America.

Grossberg, S. (1982). Processing of expected and unexpected events during conditioning and attention: A psychophysiological theory. *Psychological Review, 89,* 529–572.

Grossberg, S. (1984). Some normal and abnormal behavioral syndromes due to transmitter gating of opponent processes. *Biological Psychiatry, 19,* 1075–1118.

Grossberg, S., & Merrill, J. W. L. (1996). The hippocampus and cerebellum in adaptively timed learning, recognition, and movement. *Journal of Cognitive Neuroscience, 8,* 257–277.

Grossberg, S., & Schmajuk, N. A. (1987). Neural dynamics of attentionally modulated Pavlovian conditioning: Conditioned reinforcement, inhibition, and opponent processing. *Psychobiology, 15,* 195–240.

Grossberg, S., & Schmajuk, N. A. (1989). Neural dynamics of adaptive timing and temporal discrimination during associative learning. *Neural Networks, 2,* 79–102.

Guarraci, F. A., & Kapp, B. S. (1999). An electrophysiological characterization of ventral tegmental area dopaminergic neurons during differential Pavlovian fear conditioning in the awake rabbit. *Behavioural Brain Research, 99,* 169–179.

Han, J.-S., McMahan, R. W., Holland, P. C., & Gallagher, M. (1997). The role of an amygdalo-nigrostriatal pathway in associative learning. *Journal of Neuroscience, 17,* 3913–3919.

Hasselmo, M. E. (1999). Neuromodulation: Acetylcholine and memory consolidation. *Trends in Cognitive Science, 3,* 351–359.

Hasselmo, M. E., Anderson, B. P., & Bower, J. M. (1992). Cholinergic modulation of cortical associative memory function. *Journal of Neurophysiology, 67,* 1230–1246.

Hatfield, T., Han, J.-S., Conley, M., Gallagher, M., & Holland, P. C. (1996). Neurotoxic lesions of basolateral, but not central, amygdala interfere with Pavlovian second-order conditioning and reinforcer devaluation effects. *Journal of Neuroscience, 16,* 5256–5265.

Herman, J. P., Guillonneau, D., Dantzer, R., Scatton, B., Semerdjian-Rouquier, L., & le Moal, M. (1982). Differential effects of inescapable footshocks and of stimuli previously paired with inescapable footshocks on dopamine turnover in cortical and limbic areas of the rat. *Life Sciences, 30,* 2207–2214.

Hinton, G. E., & Sejnowski, T. J. (Eds.). (1999). *Unsupervised learning: Foundations of neural computation.* Cambridge, MA: MIT Press.

Holland, P. C. (1984). Unblocking in Pavlovian appetitive conditioning. *Journal of Experimental*

Psychology: Animal Behavior Processes, 10, 476–497.

Holland, P. C. (1988). Excitation and inhibition in unblocking. *Journal of Experimental Psychology: Animal Behavior Processes, 14,* 261–279.

Holland, P. C. (1997). Brain mechanisms for changes in processing of conditioned stimuli in Pavlovian conditioning: Implications for behavior theory. *Animal Learning & Behavior, 25,* 373–399.

Holland, P. C., & Gallagher, M. (1999). Amygdala circuitry in attentional and representational processes. *Trends In Cognitive Sciences, 3,* 65–73.

Horvitz, J. C., Stewart, T., & Jacobs, B. L. (1997). Burst activity of ventral tegmental dopamine neurons is elicited by sensory stimuli in the awake cat. *Brain Research, 759,* 251–258.

Houk, J. C., Adams, J. L., & Barto, A. G. (1995). A model of how the basal ganglia generate and use neural signals that predict reinforcement. In J. C. Houk, J. L. Davis, & D. G. Beiser (Eds.), *Models of information processing in the basal ganglia* (pp. 249–270). Cambridge, MA: MIT Press.

Houk, J. C., Davis, J. L., & Beiser, D. G. (Eds.). (1995). *Models of information processing in the basal ganglia.* Cambridge, MA: MIT Press.

Hull, C. L. (1943). *Principles of behavior.* New York, NY: Appleton-Century.

Hull, C. L. (1952). *A behavior system.* New Haven, CT: Yale University Press.

Ikemoto, S., & Panksepp, J. (1999). The role of nucleus accumbens dopamine in motivated behavior: A unifying interpretation with special reference to reward-seeking. *Brain Research Reviews, 31,* 6–41.

Jacobs, R. A. (1995). Methods for combining experts' probability assessments. *Neural Computation, 7,* 867–888.

Jacobs, R. A., Jordan, M. I., & Barto, A. G. (1991). Task decomposition through competition in a modular connectionist architecture: The what and where vision tasks. *Cognitive Science, 15,* 219–250.

Jacobs, R. A., Jordan, M. I., Nowlan, S. J., & Hinton, G. E. (1991). Adaptive mixtures of local experts. *Neural Computation, 3,* 79–87.

Kacelnik, A. (1997). Normative and descriptive models of decision making: Time discounting and risk sensitivity. In *Characterizing human psychological adaptations* (pp. 51–70). Chichester, England: Wiley.

Kakade, S., & Dayan, P. (2000). Acquisition in autoshaping. In S. A. Solla, T. K. Leen, & K.-R. Muller (Eds.), *Advances in neural information processing systems* (Vol. 12, pp. 24–30). Cambridge: MIT Press.

Kakade, S., & Dayan, P. (2001). Dopamine bonuses. In T. K. Leen, T. G. Dietterich, & V. Tresp (Eds.), *Advances in neural information processing systems* (Vol. 13, pp. 131–137). Cambridge: MIT Press.

Kearns, M., & Singh, S. (1999). Finite-sample convergence rates for Q-learning and indirect algorithms. In M. S. Kearns, S. A. Solla, & D. A. Cohn (Eds.), *Advances in neural information processing systems* (Vol. 11, pp. 996–1002). Cambridge: MIT Press.

Koob, G. F. (1992). Drugs of abuse: Anatomy, pharmacology and function of reward pathways. *Trends in Pharmacological Sciences, 13,* 177–184.

Krebs, J. R., Kacelnik, A., & Taylor, P. (1978). Test of optimal sampling by foraging great tits. *Nature, 275,* 27–31.

Kropotov, J. D., & Etlinger, S. C. (1999). Selection of actions in the basal ganglia-thalamocortical circuits: Review and model. *International Journal of Psychophysiology, 31,* 197–217.

Kruschke, J. K. (1997). Relating Mackintosh's (1975) theory to connectionist models and human categorization. Speech presented at the *Eighth Australasian Mathematical Psychology Conference.* Perth, Australia.

Kruschke, J. K. (2001). Toward a unified model of attention in associative learning. *Journal of Mathematical Psychology.* In press.

Lattal, K. M., & Nakajima, S. (1998). Overexpectation in appetitive Pavlovian and instrumental conditioning. *Animal Learning and Behavior, 26,* 351–360.

Ljungberg, T., Apicella, P., & Schultz, W. (1992). Responses of monkey dopamine neurons during learning of behavioral reactions. *Journal of Neurophysiology, 67,* 145–163.

Lubow, R. E. (1989). *Latent inhibition and conditioned attention theory.* New York: Cambridge University Press.

Luce, R. D. (1959). *Individual choice behavior.* New York: John Wiley & Sons.

Mackintosh, N. J. (1974). *The psychology of animal learning.* London: Academic Press.

Mackintosh, N. J. (1975). A theory of attention: Variations in the associability of stimuli with reinforcement. *Psychological Review, 82,* 276–298.

Mackintosh, N. J. (1983). *Conditioning and associative learning.* Oxford: Oxford University Press.

Mackintosh, N. J., Bygrave, D. J., & Picton, B. M. (1977). Locus of the effect of a surprising reinforcer in the attenuation of blocking. *Quarterly Journal of Experimental Psychology, 29,* 327–336.

Mahadevan, S. (1996). Average reward reinforcement learning: Foundations, algorithms, and empirical results. *Machine Learning, 22,* 159–195.

Mangel, M., & Clark, C. W. (1988). *Dynamic modeling in behavioral ecology.* Princeton, NJ: Princeton University Press.

Marr, D. (1982). *Vision.* New York: Freeman.

Mazur, J. E. (1984). Tests of an equivalence rule for fixed and variable reinforcer delays. *Journal of Experimental Psychology: Animal Behavior Processes, 10,* 426–436.

Medina, J. F., & Mauk, M. D. (2000). Computer simulation of cerebellar information processing. *Nature Neuroscience, 3,* 1205–1211.

Michie, D., & Chambers, R. A. (1968). BOXES: An experiment in adaptive control. *Machine Intelligence, 2,* 137–152.

Montague, P. R., Dayan, P., & Sejnowski, T. K. (1996). A framework for mesencephalic dopamine systems based on predictive Hebbian learning. *Journal of Neuroscience, 16,* 1936–1947.

Moore, J. W., Berthier, N. E., & Blazis, D. E. J. (1990). Classical eye-blink conditioning: Brain systems and implementation of a computational model. In M. Gabriel & J. Moore (Eds.), *Learn-*

ing and computational neuroscience: Foundations of adaptive networks (pp. 359–387). Cambridge: MIT Press.

Mowrer, O. H. (1956). Two-factor learning theory reconsidered, with special reference to secondary reinforcement and the concept of habit. *Psychological Review, 63,* 114–128.

Narendra, K. S., & Thatachar, M. A. L. (1989). *Learning Automata: An Introduction.* Englewood Cliffs, NJ: Prentice-Hall.

O'Reilly, R. C., Braver, T. S., & Cohen, J. D. (1999). A biologically based computational model of working memory. In A. Miyake & P. Shah (Eds.), *Models of working memory: Mechanisms of active maintenance and executive control* (pp. 375–411). New York, NY: Cambridge University Press.

Parasuraman, R. (Ed.). (1998). *The attentive brain.* Cambridge: MIT Press.

Pearce, J. M., & Hall, G. (1980). A model for Pavlovian learning: Variation in the effectiveness of conditioned but not unconditioned stimuli. *Psychological Review, 87,* 532–552.

Puterman, M. L. (1994). *Markov decision processes: Discrete stochastic dynamic programming.* New York: Wiley.

Rachlin, H. (1970). *Introduction to modern behaviorism.* San Francisco: Freeman.

Rachlin, H. (1974). Self control. *Behaviorism, 2,* 94–107.

Redgrave, P., Prescott, T. J., & Gurney, K. (1999). Is the short-latency dopamine response too short to signal reward error? *Trends in Neurosciences, 22,* 146–151.

Reed, P., Mitchell, C., & Nokes, T. (1996). Intrinsic reinforcing properties of putatively neutral stimuli in an instrumental two-lever discrimination task. *Animal Learning and Behavior, 24,* 38–45.

Rescorla, R. A. (1999). Summation and overexpectation with qualitatively different outcomes. *Animal Learning and Behavior, 27,* 50–62.

Rescorla, R. A., & Wagner, A. R. (1972). A theory of Pavlovian conditioning: The effectiveness of reinforcement and non-reinforcement. In A. H. Black & W. F. Prokasy (Eds.), *Classical* conditioning II: Current research and theory (pp. 64–69). New York: Appleton-Century-Crofts.

Robbins, R. W., & Everitt, B. J. (1992). Functions of dopamine in the dorsal and ventral striatum. *Seminars in Neuroscience, 4,* 119–127.

Robbins, T. W., & Everitt, B. J. (1999). Interaction of the dopaminergic system with mechanisms of associative learning and cognition: Implications for drug abuse. *Psychological Science, 10,* 199–202.

Rolls, E. T. (2000). Memory systems in the brain. *Annual Review of Psychology, 51,* 599–630.

Samuel, A. L. (1959). Some studies in machine learning using the game of checkers. *IBM Journal of Research and Development, 3,* 211–229.

Schoenbaum, G., Chiba, A. A., & Gallagher, M. (1998). Orbitofrontal cortex and basolateral amygdala encode expected outcomes during learning. *Nature Neuroscience, 1,* 155–159.

Schoenbaum, G., Chiba, A. A., & Gallagher, M. (1999). Neural encoding in orbitofrontal cortex and basolateral amygdala during olfactory discrimination learning. *Journal of Neuroscience, 19,* 1876–1884.

Schultz, W. (1998). Predictive reward signal of dopamine neurons. *Journal of Neurophysiology, 80,* 1–27.

Schultz, W., Dayan, P., & Montague, P. R. (1997). A neural substrate of prediction and reward. *Science, 275,* 1593–1599.

Schwartz, A. (1993). A reinforcement learning method for maximizing undiscounted rewards. In *Proceedings of the Tenth International Conference on Machine Learning* (pp. 298–305). San Mateo, CA: Kaufmann.

Simon, H., & le Moal, M. (1998). Mesencephalic dopaminergic neurons: Role in the general economy of the brain. *Annals of the New York Academy of Sciences, 537,* 235–253.

Solomon, R. L., & Corbit, J. D. (1974). An opponent-process theory of motivation: I. Temporal dynamics of affect. *Psychological Review, 81,* 119–145.

Spanagel, R., & Weiss, F. (1999). The dopamine hypothesis of reward: Past and current status. *Trends in Neurosciences, 22,* 521–527.

Suri, R. E., & Schultz, W. (2001). *Temporal difference model reproduces anticipatory neural activity. Neural Computation, 13,* 841–862.

Sutton, R. S. (1988). Learning to predict by the methods of temporal difference. *Machine Learning, 3,* 9–44.

Sutton, R. (1992). Gain adaptation beats least squares? In *Proceedings of the 7th Yale Workshop on Adaptive and Learning Systems,* 161–166.

Sutton, R. S., & Barto, A. G. (1981). Toward a modern theory of adaptive networks: Expectation and prediction. *Psychological Review, 88,* 135–170.

Sutton, R. S., & Barto, A. G. (1990). Time-derivative models of Pavlovian conditioning. In M. Gabriel & J. W. Moore (Eds.), *Learning and computational neuroscience* (pp. 497–537). Cambridge: MIT Press.

Sutton, R. S., & Barto, A. G. (1998). *Reinforcement learning: An introduction.* Cambridge: MIT Press.

Sutton, R. S., & Pinette, B. (1985). The learning of world models by connectionist networks. *In Proceedings of the Seventh Annual Conference of the Cognitive Science Society* (pp. 54–64). Irvine, CA: Erlbaum.

Sutton, R. S., Precup, D., & Singh, S. (1999). Between MDPs and semi-MDPs: A framework for temporal abstraction in reinforcement learning. *Artificial Intelligence, 112,* 181–211.

Thorndike, E. L. (1898). Animal intelligence: An experimental study of the associative processes in animals. *Psychological Monographs, 2* (4, Whole Number 8).

Thorndike, E. L. (1911). *Animal Intelligence.* New York: Macmillan.

Tsitsiklis, J. N., & Van Roy, B. (1999). Average cost temporal-difference learning. *Automatica, 35,* 1799–1808.

Ward, N. M., & Brown, V. J. (1996). Covert orienting of attention in the rat and the role of striatal dopamine. *Journal of Neuroscience, 16,* 3082–3088.

Watkins, C. J. C. H. (1989). *Learning from delayed rewards.* Unpublished doctoral dissertation, University of Cambridge, Cambridge, UK.

Werbos, P. J. (1990). A menu of designs for reinforcement learning over time. In W. T. Miller, III, & R. S. Sutton (Eds.), *Neural networks for control* (pp. 67–95). Cambridge: MIT Press.

Wickens, J. (1993). *A theory of the striatum.* Oxford: Pergamon Press.

Wickens, J., & Kötty, R. (1995). Cellular models of reinforcement. In J. C. Houk, J. L. Davis, & M. E. Hoff (Eds.), *Models of Information Processing in the Basal Ganglia.* Cambridge, MA: MIT Press, 187–214.

Widrow, B., & Hoff, M. E. (1960). Adaptive switching circuits. *WESCON Convention Report, 4,* 96–104.

Widrow, B., & Stearns, S. D. (1985). *Adaptive signal processing.* Englewood Cliffs, NJ: Prentice-Hall.

Williams, R. J. (1992). Simple statistical gradient-following algorithms for connectionist reinforcement learning. *Machine Learning, 8,* 229–256.

Wilson, P. N., Boumphrey, P., & Pearce, J. M. (1992). Restoration of the orienting response to a light by a change in its predictive accuracy. *Quarterly Journal of Experimental Psychology, 44B,* 17–36.

Wise, R. A. (1982). Neuroleptics and operant behavior: The anhedonia hypothesis. *Behavioral and Brain Sciences, 5,* 39–87.

Wise, R. A., & Bozarth, M. A. (1984). Brain reward circuitry: Four circuit elements "wired" in apparent series. *Brain Research Bulletin, 12,* 203–208.

Wise, R. A., & Rompre, P.-P. (1989). Brain dopamine and reward. *Annual Review of Psychology, 40,* 191–225.

Wyvell, C. L., & Berridge, K. C. (2000). Intra-accumbens amphetamine increases the conditioned incentive salience of sucrose reward: enhancement of reward "wanting" without enhanced "liking" or response reinforcement. *Journal of Neuroscience, 20,* 8122–8130.

Yamaguchi, S., & Kobayashi, S. (1988). Contributions of the dopaminergic system to voluntary and automatic orienting of visuospatial attention. *Journal of Neuroscience, 18,* 1869–1878.

CHAPTER 4

Neural Analysis of Learning in Simple Systems

FRANK KRASNE

INTRODUCTION

Learning has been center stage in psychology for longer than anyone reading this chapter can remember, but it is only within the past several decades that significant clues have emerged as to what may happen in nervous systems, at the level of neurons and synapses themselves, when animals (including humans) learn. This progress has occurred for a number of reasons. First, it has been the result of developing techniques and understanding within neuroscience generally. Second, it has derived from a gradually developing appreciation that the physiology of learning cannot be studied in the abstract, but rather it is necessary to focus on the mechanisms involved in particular learning tasks, and these tasks must be selected to have features that make them practical for study at a neural level. Finally, it has been the result of discoveries concerning activity-dependent plasticity of certain synapses within both vertebrate and invertebrate nervous systems.

The findings and ideas that we shall discuss have emerged partly from attempts to directly investigate the neural bases of particular kinds

The author wishes to thank Dean Buonomano, David Glanzman, and Tom Odell for helping him interpret literature in their respective areas of expertise. Writing of the chapter was supported by NIH Grant NS 08108 to the author.

of behavioral learning; we shall refer to this sort of analysis as *direct* neural analyses of learning. But without question, progress has also been the result of studying purely neural phenomena that have properties formally similar to important properties of actual (i.e., behavioral) learning. For example, the activity of neurons may lead to changes in the potency of synapses, and those changes may persist for very long periods of time providing models for some sort of acquisition of learning and for memory. We will refer to such purely neural analyses as the study of *neural analogs* or *models* of learning. It is often difficult to resist the assumption that such mechanisms provide the underpinnings for those kinds of behavioral learning that they mimic—but care must be exercised, for this need not be so. Of course, when neural analogs of learning are found, it is natural to try to show that the mechanisms underlying them are in fact relevant to behavioral learning, and we shall discuss research so directed. However, even when the relevance of a neural analog of learning to true (behavioral) learning has not been or cannot be established, the knowledge that the nervous system can produce learning-like phenomena in a given way can still be very important for furthering our thinking about the neural mechanisms of learning. Both direct analyses of learning and analyses of neural analogs are valuable.

Although work on a variety of kinds of learning or neural analogs have provided

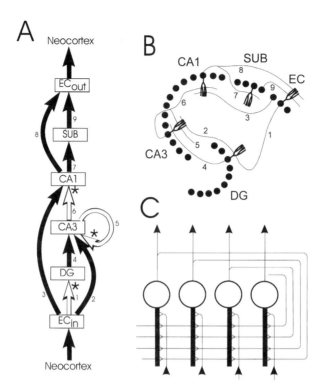

Figure 4.1 Outlines of hippocampal formation circuitry.
NOTE: A. Block diagram of major hippocampal formation cell groups [EC, entorhinal cortex; DG, dentate gyrus; CA3, CA1, regions of hippocampus proper; S, subiculum] and connecting tracts of axons (1–9) [perforant path, 1, 3; alvear path, 2; mossy fibers, 4; recurrent collaterals (association fibers), 5; Schaffer collaterals, 6]. Asterisks indicate pathways that are known to display associative LTP.

B. Sketch of a section perpendicular to the long axis of the banana-shaped hippocampal formation.

The recurrent collaterals of CA3 (5) form an often discussed positive feedback loop whereby any given CA3 neuron provides input to neurons all across CA3, as indicated schematically in C.

Broad arrows in A indicate pathways emphasized in one theory of hippocampal function. Open arrows indicate pathways considered by the theory to be ineffective unless strengthened by rapid by associative LTP; solid arrows indicate pathways proposed to be fixed (once established by development or early learning).

As commonly proposed by current theory, the function of hippocampus is to rapidly memorize patterns of activity occurring at ECin so that, subsequently, a subset of a learned pattern will evoke the whole at ECout. The EC patterns are in turn presumed to bear a 1:1 relationship to neocortical patterns. ECin activity can cause CA1 and hence ECout activity in either of two ways: via pathway 3, whose synaptic connections are already established, and via the right-hand set of pathways through DG and CA3, at several stages of which synapses must become potentiated before effective excitation of CA1 can occur. The organization of the right-hand pathway is such that the pattern evoked in CA3 at learning time, and reproduced during recall, bears no systematic relationship to the ECin pattern that is to be recalled. However, pathways 3 and 8 are so structured that, though ECin patterns bear no systematic relationship to the CA1 patterns they evoke, any CA1 pattern will reestablish in ECout a pattern identical to the ECin pattern that evoked it (i.e., the CA1-ECout pathway performs the inverse of the transformation caused by the ECin-CA1 pathway). Consequently, since the CA3-CA1 synapses are subject to associative LTP, the CA3 pattern that occurs during training will become associated with a CA1 pattern that evokes, in Ecout, the ECin pattern that was present at training time.

useful information, this observer believes that, at the time of writing, thinking in this field has been most influenced by work on (a) learned modifications of defensive withdrawal reflexes of the marine mollusk, *Aplysia,* (b) neural models showing various forms of the physiological phenomena of long-term potentiation (LTP) and long-term depression (LTD), (c) eyelid conditioning in rabbits, (d) odor aversion learning in the fruit fly, *Drosophila,* and (e) fear learning in rodents.

Fear learning is discussed extensively elsewhere in this volume (see Chap. 13). The focus of this chapter will be on the first three lines of work listed, with some reference to the fourth.

OVERVIEW OF THREE SYSTEMS

Hippocampal Long-Term Potentiation—a Neural Analog of Classical Conditioning

History and Basics

Discovery. In 1973 Bliss and Lomo (1973; Bliss and Collingridge, 1993) reported what has been probably the single most seminal discovery to date in attempts to understand the neural basis of learning and memory (equally important work concerned with the basis for simple forms of learning in the marine mollusk *Aplysia,* which is introduced in the next section, began earlier, but we defer its discussion for expository convenience). While investigating the properties of synaptic transmission in the mammalian hippocampus (a structure believed from the work of Scoville & Milner, 1957, to play some important role in learning), Bliss and Lomo found that if a group of axons whose terminals innervate cells of the dentate gyrus of the mammalian hippocampus (Figure 4.1) were made to fire at a rate of about 100 Hz for a few seconds (a *tetanic stimulation,* or *tetanus*—terms deriving from muscle physiology), the ability of those axons to excite their dentate target neurons was increased for the duration of the experiment, up to 10 hr. Seemingly similar procedures in other parts of the mammalian nervous system had often been seen to cause changes in synaptic potency, but these had typically lasted under 15 min. Bliss

---

Figure 4.1   The right-hand pathway works as follows: Each DG neuron is presumed to be innervated by a random subset of ECin neurons, and the population as a whole is subject to recurrent inhibition that limits to k the number of active DG neurons. Thus, the k most excited DG neurons fire (a k-winners-take-all rule). The plastic synapses of the DG neurons are conceived to be in an initially unpotentiated state but to be transiently functional at learning time; therefore the k most excited fire, and the synapses between them and the active ECin neurons undergo LTP. When a portion of a learned ECin pattern occurs, DG neurons that were active when it was learned are likely to receive more excitation than others and thus are likely to be included in the set of the k most excited. Thus most of the original DG pattern is likely to be reinstated. As more patterns are learned, cross talk between patterns becomes likely, but such confusion will be minimized if k is low and the number of DG neurons high (a sparse code). In fact, anatomy suggests that there are many more DG than ECin cells. Cross talk at subsequent stages would also be reduced if a sparse code is maintained, but actual numbers of neurons do not continue to be so high at later processing stages.

CA3 neurons also receive input from a random subset of the CA3 input population and are subject to the k-winners-take-all rule. At learning time, recurrent pathway connections from the k firing CA3 neurons to themselves are active in conjunction and undergo LTP. Thus, at recall, any of those neurons that becomes active will excite all of those that were active at training time, and thus the k most excited will be likely to be those that were coactive at training. Thus, both DG and CA3 independently (and somewhat redundantly) tend to pattern-complete. As already explained, completed CA3 patterns will evoke CA1 patterns that reinstate the full original EC pattern in ECout.

and Lomo therefore dubbed the hippocampal phenomenon *long-term potentiation*. It has gradually been discovered that apparently similar potentiation can be produced at many places in the brain; Using chronically implanted electrodes, it has been found that potentiation can still be detected at least three weeks after induction, but it is thought not to be permanent (Bliss & Lynch, 1988; Staubli & Lynch, 1987). To a neurophysiological community hungry for possible substrates for memory, this was an important discovery—but its full significance took some time to be generally appreciated.

In addition to longevity, two properties of LTP, as characterized by early experiments were of special importance. First, transmission was potentiated only at synapses that were activated by the tetanic stimulation used to induce the LTP (Andersen, Sundberg, Sveen, & Wigstrom, 1977; Bliss & Gardner-Medwin, 1973; Lynch, Dunwiddie, & Gribkoff, 1977), a property referred to as *homosynapticity* (but see Bonhoeffer, Staiger, & Aertsen, 1989, for limitations to homosynapticity). Second, LTP could not be induced by tetanizing only one or a few input fibers; the inducing train had to recruit the axons of many neurons innervating the recorded neuron (Bliss & Gardner-Medwin, 1973; McNaughton, Douglas, & Goddard, 1978). Thus it appeared that some sort of cooperative action of afferents was needed to induce LTP (a property referred to as *cooperativity*). Homosynapticity and cooperativity are also properties of LTP at synapses between cells of the CA3 and CA1 regions of the hippocampus (Andersen et al., 1977; Lynch et al., 1977) and at recurrent synapses that interconnect cells within area CA3 (discussed later; Debanne, Gahwiler, & Thompson, 1998) (Figure 4.1), but the properties of dentate-to-CA3 neurons are somewhat different (Nicoll & Malenka, 1995) and will not be further considered.

We must draw the reader's attention to one important technical point. The initial studies of LTP were carried out with stimulating and recording electrodes implanted deep within the brain. However, after 1975 (Schwartzkroin & Wester, 1975) more and more experiments were carried out on slices of brain kept alive in artificial media. Many new kinds of experiments become possible in the slice because, with proper optical arrangements, one can visualize neurons throughout an experiment and even see morphological changes occurring during the course of an experiment. While slices allow experiments that would be impossible without them, they lack normal input to hippocampal structures from other parts of the brain, including neuromodulatory influences that are probably needed for real learning. These attributes, both positive and negative, are even more the case for neurons and synapses grown in culture medium, which are utilized for many current experiments.

Associativity. Given homosynapticity and cooperativity one should be able to arrange an experiment in which one stimulating electrode (A; to be thought of as a fictional unconditioned stimulus, US) activates a group of fibers large enough to induce LTP while one or more other electrodes (B1, B2, etc.; to be thought of as fictional conditioned stimuli, CSs) each stimulate separate groups of fibers too small (due the requirement of cooperativity) to induce LTP. This done, the properties of cooperativity and homosynapticity allow one to predict that a tetanus to either A (the US stand-in) alone or any of B1, or the others, (the CS stand-ins) alone would not induce persisting increases in responsiveness to any of the CS stand-ins, whereas tetanic stimulation of A along with one of the Bs *would* lead to increased responding to that B. Thus this experimental arrangement should display a sort of analog of classical conditioning—in other words, homosynapticity and cooperativity together predict a capacity for what might be considered a form of *associativity*. By about 1986 several groups had carried out such demonstration experiments (Barrionuevo & Brown, 1983; Kelso & Brown, 1986; Levy & Steward, 1979), and gradually the associative property of LTP became generally appreciated, greatly increasing interest in LTP. It now appeared that LTP provided the basis for a neural model of classical conditioning.

Soon after, it became clear that what was crucial for the establishment of LTP was presynaptic activity coupled with sufficiently strong postsynaptic depolarization (Malinow, 1991; Malinow & Miller, 1986) and that the main reason that induction of LTP required high frequency stimulation of a large number of afferents was because such stimulation adequately depolarized postsynaptic neurons. In fact even modest numbers of separated firings of single presynaptic neurons will cause LTP if they occur while the postsynaptic neuron is sufficiently depolarized by any means, including direct injection of a depolarizing current via a microelectrode (illustrated in Figure 4.6, on page 158; Gustafsson & Wigstrom, 1986; Gustafsson, Wigstrom, Abraham, & Huang, 1987; Kelso, Ganong, & Brown, 1986; Sastry, Goh, & Auyeung, 1986; Wigstrom, Gustafsson, Huang, & Abraham, 1986). Once the crucial importance of pairing pre- and postsynaptic activity was recognized, it became apparent that these hippocampal synapses came close to obeying the rule that the psychological theoretician, Donald Hebb, had proposed many years previous: "When an axon of cell A is near enough to excite a cell B and repeatedly or persistently takes part in firing it, some growth process or metabolic change takes place in one or both cells such that A's efficiency, as one of the cells firing B, is increased" (1949, page 62). Thus, synapses showing associative LTP are often referred to as *Hebb synapses*. Hebb

had conjectured that both cells must actually fire for increases of synaptic strength to be induced. For some years it was believed that strong synaptic input that did not necessarily cause the postsynaptic cell to generate an action potential could provide adequate postsynaptic depolarization to permit development of LTP. However, it now appears that when hippocampal neurons generate action potentials that propagate down their axons, back-conduction of spikes into the neuron dendrites, which themselves have ion channels that allow generation of action potentials, also occurs, and it is thought that these back-propagating spikes are often crucial to producing significant amounts of LTP (see discussion of Figure 4.9b on page 178. Johnston, Magee, Colbert, & Cristie, 1996; Linden, 1999; Magee & Johnston, 1997; Markram, Lubke, Frotscher, & Sakmann, 1997; Paulsen & Sejnowski, 2000).

Role of Calcium Ions and NMDA Receptors. A crucial step in understanding the cellular events responsible for the induction of LTP was the discovery that procedures that would ordinarily induce LTP do not do so if agents that bind free calcium ions (*calcium chelators* such as EGTA and BAPTA) are injected into the postsynaptic cell (Lynch, Larson, Kelso, Barrionuevo, & Schottler, 1983; Malenka, Kauer, Zucker, & Nicoll, 1988).[1] This suggested that elevation of calcium ion concentration, which is often used by cells as an internal signal that controls important physiological activities, is crucial to the induction of LTP. It was then discovered that hippocampal neurons have several different classes of receptors for the common excitatory transmitter, glutamate. One class, which includes receptors that are defined by

---

[1] We will usually refer to organic chemicals by their commonly used abbreviations rather than their long chemical names.

the fact that they bind especially well to the artificial organic compound, AMPA, are channels that allow sodium ions to flow across the cell membrane when exposed to glutamate or to AMPA. In addition to these ordinary glutamate receptor/channels, a variety of central nervous system neurons, including hippocampal neurons, have been found to also have a kind of glutamate receptor that allows calcium ions to flow into the neurons when stimulated by glutamate—but only if the voltage across the postsynapic membrane is reduced (i.e., only if the postsynaptic neuron is partially depolarized"). These voltage-dependent glutamate receptors selectively bind and respond to the artificial agent, NMDA, for which they are named (Collingridge & Lester, 1989). These facts led to the conjecture that LTP induction might be the result of exposure of a depolarized hippocampal neuron to glutamate, causing the opening of the NMDA receptor channels, the entry of calcium ions, and the consequent induction of LTP. Subsequent work has verified this conjecture. Thus, pharmacological agents such as APV (also called AP5) that block the ability of glutamate (or NMDA) to bind to and open NMDA receptors prevent LTP induction (Collingridge, Kehl, & McLennan, 1983); a brief direct elevation of internal calcium ion concentration even without synaptic activity will induce LTP (Malenka et al., 1988); and using calcium-sensitive vital dyes whose fluorescent properties change in the presence of calcium ions allows one to actually see that calcium ion levels briefly rise in dendrites when pre- and postsynaptic stimulation that causes the development of LTP occurs (Muller & Connor, 1991; Regehr & Tank, 1990). Moreover, each excitatory synapse to a hippocampal neuron is established on a small bulb at the end of a stalk, a dendritic spine, that grows from the main dendritic shaft (one spine per synapse), and calcium imaging studies show that calcium ion becomes elevated mainly in those spines whose inputs were activated (Yuste & Denk, 1995; Yuste, Majewska, Cash, & Denk, 1999). This helps to explain the homosynapticity of LTP.

Neuronal Signaling Events Initiated by Transient Increase in Calcium Ion Level. The events that mediate between the brief postsynaptic elevations of calcium ion concentration that induce LTP and the resulting prolonged potentiation of transmission have been a matter of intensive study. One would expect that potentiated transmission would ultimately be due to a tendency for increased transmitter release presynaptically or increased reactivity to released transmitter postsynaptically, or both, either due to altered properties of existing synaptic contacts or to growth of additional synaptic contacts. It might be thought that because it is *postsynaptic* calcium elevation that is the triggering event, LTP must necessarily be due to a change in the properties of the *postsynaptic* neuron. However, since it is likely that properties of presynaptic neurons can be influenced by those of their postsynaptic targets, this does not necessarily follow.

Almost all control of cellular function is thought to be achieved by controlling the functional properties of biologically active proteins such as enzymes, receptors, ion channels, and so on; this in turn is normally done by adding or subtracting phosphate molecules at specific control sites on the proteins. Such phosphorylation is generally controlled by interacting systems of intracellular signaling molecules, or second messengers, that cause phosphorylation by activating various catalysts (protein kinases) that cause phosphates to be added at particular sites on specific proteins that are sensitive to that activated kinase. Thus, even prior to direct investigation, it could be surmised that such mechanisms would be involved in the production of LTP.

In fact, calcium ions in conjunction with a highly calcium-sensitive enzyme, calmodulin (CaM), themselves act as second messengers for a number of calcium- and calmodulin-dependent kinases such as calcium- and calmodulin-dependent protein kinase (CaMK II), which as we shall see, mediates between the elevation of calcium ion levels and alteration of synaptic properties.

Moreover, as direct investigation has progressed, it has become clear that the induction of LTP is at least a two-stage process. Initially calcium ion elevation leads, via a series of intracellular chemical messages, to the phosphorylation of preexisting proteins, including the AMPA receptors themselves, with effects that directly promote enlargement of excitatory postsynaptic potentials (EPSPs); the LTP caused in this way lasts a few hours. But additionally, through processes not yet elaborated, certain protein kinases enter the nucleus of the postsynaptic cell where they phosphoryalate proteins called *transcription factors* (the transcription factor called CREB seems to be especially important), which bind to genetic DNA and turn on the transcription of messenger RNAs. These are then subsequently translated into proteins. Transcription factor-dependent processes are required if LTP is to persist for much more than 3 hr (Bourtchuladze et al., 1994; Huang & Kandel, 1994; Nguyen, Abel, & Kandel, 1994).

Long-Term Depression. Finally, it is important to note that LTP is not the only possible consequence of postsynaptic calcium ion elevations produced by synaptic input to hippocampal neurons. Sometimes a long-term *depression* rather than potentiation is produced. A considerable amount of evidence suggests that depression rather than potentiation of transmission occurs in response to small, as opposed to large, elevations of calcium ion concentration (Artola & Singer, 1993; Bear & Malenka, 1994; Linden &

Connor, 1995; Malenka & Nicoll, 1993). It is believed that low levels of calcium activate a set of intracellular signaling molecules that cause depression, while higher levels activate a different set that suppress the activity of the depression-inducing molecules and also cause potentiation (Lisman, 1994; Linden & Connor, 1995).

We will discuss aspects of LTP in more detail later when we address recurring issues in evaluating and understanding the role of synaptic plasticity in learning.

Relationship to Behavioral Learning?

LTP has captured the attention of neuroscientists because it offers a rough cellular analog of associative learning in the form of a cellular model, or parody, of classical conditioning: Pairing of an initially weak stimulus, which cannot cause a target cell to initiate an action potential, with a separate strong stimulus, which can make the cell fire, induces a synaptic change that can make the initially weak stimulus capable of firing the postsynaptic neuron, and this change can last a great many hours and probably many days or weeks. But what of extinction, of blocking, of the capacity for producing a well timed response in delay and trace conditioning and of many other well known properties of true classical conditioning? Does the model share these with its behavioral cousin? And what of longevity? Nervous system changes lasting days or weeks are displaying a kind of memory that could be behaviorally significant, but does such memory provide a plausible model of behavioral memory that can be much longer? We will address some of these questions later.

Whatever the answers, the parallel between what Pavlov's dogs could do and what cells connected by synapses displaying LTP can do has been viewed by many minds as salient enough to raise the question of whether LTP might be the basis for at least some kinds of behavioral associative learning. This question has been raised for LTP-like phenomena in several kinds of synapses; for now we address it only for the mammalian hippocampus.

Hippocampus-Dependent Learning.
Obviously, it makes sense to evaluate the role of hippocampal LTP in learning only for kinds of learning that require the hippocampus. Discovery of a hippocampal role in learning was made in human patients with hippocampal damage.[2] It is widely agreed that the deficits resulting from such damage are limited to kinds of memory that have been described as declarative, explicit, and conscious including, in particular, episodic memory, the memory for one-time experiences of an observer (Squire, Knowlton, & Musen, 1993). Such memory has been defined as being called to consciousness as a proposition or an image. Learning and memory that have variously been referred to as procedural, implicit, and unconscious, which can be assessed only by an attempt at performance, such as motor skills and classical conditioning, occur normally in the absence of the hippocampus and associated circuitry. It is also agreed that the role of the hippocampus is time-limited; that is, the hippocampus is needed at the time of a to-be-remembered experience and for an extended period after, but eventually recall becomes independent of the hippocampus (Squire et al., 1993).

In animals, especially the rodents on which much of the relevant experimentation has been done, kinds of learning that are sensitive to hippocampal damage were at first difficult to find. However, when it was discovered that

many cells of the rat hippocampus become active when an animal is at a particular location relative to distal environmental cues (O'Keefe, 1976, 1979; Ranck, 1973), the ability of hippocampally damaged rats to learn the location of items (food, water, safety) in an environment was tested and found to be drastically compromised (O'Keefe, Nadel, Keightley, & Kill, 1975). This was found to be true both for the long-term learning of items that are always at a fixed location and for the transient recollection of where food has already been sought and found in a foraging situation, which perhaps is a parallel to episodic memory in humans (Olton, 1979; Olton & Feustle, 1981). Testing of long-term place-learning capacity now commonly uses an experimental situation known as the Morris water maze. Rats are placed in a pool of opaque water in which they must swim until they locate a platform hidden just under the surface of the water onto which they can climb and rest; normal rats learn the location of the hidden platform rapidly, as can be seen most convincingly in a test where the platform is omitted and the search patterns of the rat observed. Hippocampally compromised rats do not appear to learn the location of the platform (Schenk & Morris, 1985), nor do they remember its location if lesions are made soon after acquisition (Ramos, 1998). However, they do improve somewhat at finding the platform, presumably due to improving their search strategies; this can perhaps be viewed as an instance of the sort of procedural learning that does not require the hippocampus. If the location of a platform is marked by visible cues or if the platform is visible at the surface, then hippocampally compromised rats learn just as well as controls.

In animals, as in humans, most classical conditioning, though not trace conditioning (Kim, Clark, & Thompson, 1995), proceeds normally in the face of hippocampal damage (Caul, Jarrard, Miller, & Korn, 1969; Solomon

[2]Lesions intended to damage hippocampal system function may directly remove hippocampal tissue per se, may lesion tracts entering or leaving the hippocampus, or may lesion both the hippocampus and additional structures connected to it. For simplicity we will refer to all such lesions, which are certainly not fully equivalent, as "hippocampal"; the reader will have to refer to cited sources for particulars.

& Moore, 1975; see Thompson & Krupa, 1994; Chap. 13, this volume). Surprisingly, however, rats sustaining hippocampal damage soon after having been trained to fear a situation in which they have experienced foot shocks (contextual fear learning) show no signs of fearing the situation, although they continue to be afraid of a simple auditory cue that immediately preceded shock onset (Kim & Fanselow, 1992). As with human declarative learning, the role of the hippocampus in contextual fear learning is time-limited; hippocampal damage no longer causes deficits if sustained after 2-3 weeks. Given the robustness of these post-training effects (Fanselow, 2000), it comes as a surprise to find that animals lesioned *before* training may show only mild contextual learning deficits (Maren, Aharonov, & Fanselow, 1997). This may be taken to imply that, when present, the hippocampus holds in check the ability of other regions to acquire contextural fear memories (Fanselow, 1999, 2000). However, one may be reminded of Lashley's presumption, based on a similar difference between pre- and post-training cortical lesions, that the cortex suppresses the ability of midbrain structures to learn brightness discriminations (1950). In that case later experiments seemed to establish that the midbrain probably *did* acquire the brightness discriminations even with the cortex operative (Dru & Walker, 1975); probably, recall was merely very state-dependent and thus failed when cortex was removed.

Place learning in the water maze and contextual fear conditioning have both been frequently used paradigms in studying the role of hippocampal LTP in learning.

In the search for hippocampus-dependent learning in nonhumans, many kinds of visual discrimination tasks, which on the face of it might seem like plausible animal equivalents of human declarative learning, have been tested and found to be little affected by hippocampal damage (Douglas & Pribram, 1966;

Douglas, 1967; Kimble, 1963; Malamut, Saunders, & Mishkin, 1984; Stevens & Cowey, 1974; Zola-Morgan & Squire, 1984). However, there is an interesting exception in primates. Primates are particularly adept at learning when the discriminanda are three-dimensional objects rather than two-dimensional images, and many such discriminations can be learned simultaneously with remarkable rapidity. Surprisingly, *this* visual discrimination task *is* hippocampally dependent, and posttraining lesions show the role of the hippocampus to be time-limited to a period of about a month after training (Zola-Morgan & Squire, 1984, 1990). That the hippocampus seems to be important for this sort of relatively rapid learning but not for similar tasks where the learning is slow might be taken to suggest that the hippocampus plays some special role in rapid learning, a possibility that is consistent with its role in human episodic memory (see Mishkin, Malmut, & Bachovalier, 1984). Indeed, in rats contextual fear conditioning is quite rapid, and place learning usually is as well. On the other hand, fear of a tone that predicts shock is also rapid and does not seem to involve the hippocampus.

The attempt to understand what all the kinds of hippocampus-dependent learning in humans and other animals have in common and to establish criteria that will allow one to predict whether a task will require the hippocampus has been a difficult enterprise that has not at present come to any entirely satisfactory conclusion. However, it may be said that hippocampus-dependent learning tasks are often ones in which learning is rapid or ones in which subjects must learn to respond to unfamiliar combinations of simpler cues, as in contextual fear learning (see O'Reilly & Rudy, 2001).

Theories of Hippocampal Function. The observations that hippocampus-dependent learning is often rapid, that its role is time-limited, and that the synapses of the hippocampus are subject to LTP (which can be induced very rapidly and seems to be long-lasting but not permanent) have encouraged the hypothesis that, for those tasks that depend on the hippocampus, changes of strength in a stimulus-determined subset of the plastic hippocampal synapses constitute the initial record of experience that allows posttraining recall and performance (McClelland, McNaughton, & O'Reilly, 1995; Squire, 1992). However, over time the hippocampus, which is needed for recall only temporarily, exports this information. Because the cortex and hippocampus are richly and bidirectionally interconnected, it is often conjectured that the information that the hippocampus stores is received from the cortex and that it is to the cortex that the information is eventually exported. Commonly, it is proposed that the activity of cortical neurons that represent significant experiences alter hippocampal synapses in such a way that when some portion of the original cortical pattern subsequently recurs (e.g., a representation of the context in which an animal previously experienced shock), the rest of the original cortical pattern is automatically reinstated (e.g., a representation of the experience of being shocked). It is also often presumed that the transfer of information from hippocampus to cortex must involve hippocampal-cortical activity that occurs when neither the cortex nor the hippocampus is otherwise engaged (e.g., during sleep; Gluck & Myers, 1997; Marr, 1971; McClelland et al., 1995; O'Reilly & Rudy, 2001; Sutherland & McNaughton, 2000; Willshaw & Buckingham, 1990).

This working hypothesis, which has wide currency, has been motivated in part by many of the facts we have reviewed. However, it has also been enunciated on entirely theoretical grounds. The rationale has been that the cortex necessarily learns slowly for reasons related to the complexities of incorporating new knowledge in such a way that it becomes usefully integrated with extensive pre-existing cortical knowledge. It is argued that because the cortex learns slowly it requires as a partner some other part of the brain that can learn rapidly and can both mediate behavior until the cortex can learn and can also feed its new information repeatedly to the slowly learning cortex over an extended period of time to facilitate its eventual learning (Marr, 1971; McClelland et al., 1995; McNaughton & Morris, 1987).

The hippocampus has been identified as this temporary memory store both because of its rich interconnections with the cortex and because aspects of its structure have been seen as providing a basis for its conjectured ability to reinstate past cortical patterns of activity when probed by familiar but incomplete patterns. One of these features is the structure of the CA3 region (Figure 4.1). The neurons of this region receive input thought to be a random recoding of cortical activity patterns, as represented by the neurons of the dentate gyrus. The dentate in turn is thought to rerepresent cortical patterns with a much smaller percentage of active neurons than was the case for the original cortical representation (a sparse code). CA3 has attracted particular attention because the axons of its neurons, in addition to projecting information toward the cortex, have collateral branches (so-called *recurrent collaterals*) that provide synaptic input to great numbers of the CA3 neurons themselves. Theoretical analysis shows that if a pattern of CA3 activity has altered the CA3 recurrent collateral synapses according to Hebb's rule, then the subsequent activation of just a small fraction of the previously active neurons will cause reinstatement of the full initial pattern (Marr, 1971; McNaughton & Morris, 1987; O'Reilly & McClelland, 1994; O'Reilly & Rudy, 2001; Willshaw & Buckingham, 1990). Taken together with other known and hypothesized features of the hippocampus, this can cause reconstruction of a previously experienced cortical pattern of activity (see legend to Figure 4.1).

These briefly sketched theoretical ideas have formed a backdrop to many of the experiments that have been done.

Role of NMDA Receptors and LTP in Learning. What then of the role of hippocampal LTP? Perhaps the most obvious kind of experiment, and the first to have been attempted, asks whether rats, in which establishment of hippocampal LTP has been compromised by application of an NMDA antagonist such as APV, can still do hippocampus-dependent kinds of learning. The initial answers, both for place learning (Morris, 1989; Morris, Anderson, Lynch, & Baudry, 1986) and for contextual fear conditioning (Kim, DeCola, Landeira-Fernandez, & Fanselow, 1991), were no (Figure 4.2). Of course, such experiments raise issues such as whether the doses of NMDA antagonist that interfere with the behavioral learning are the same as those that prevent LTP and whether the NMDA antagonists affect learning or simply performance? Answering such questions

has not been straightforward (for reviews, see Holscher, 1999; Martin, Grimwod, & Morris, 2000; Shors & Matzel, 1997).

Thus, an early dose-response study found that the concentration of APV needed to affect LTP and water maze learning was about the same (Davis, Butcher, & Morris, 1992). But whether a given drug or other treatment will produce LTP can depend greatly on the particular induction protocol used and the particular class of synapses tested (Holscher, 1999; Holscher, McGlinchey, Anwyl, & Rowan, 1997; Lum-Ragan & Gribkoff, 1993; Meiri, Sun, Segal, & Alkon, 1998; Thomas, Moody, Makhinson, & O'Dell, 1996). Moreover, few of the induction protocols used bear much relationship to the activity patterns that one would conjecture might occur naturally in the context of hippocampus-dependent learning tasks. Furthermore, APV at effective doses does cause motor abnormalities that can affect the ability of a rat to get onto the platform in a Morris water maze (Cain, Saucier, Hall, Hargreaves, & Boon, 1996; Keith & Rudy, 1990), but the doses are not so great as to make it impossible for a well trained rat to

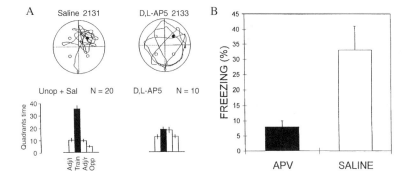

Figure 4.2 Effects of APV on hippocampus-sensitive learning.
NOTE: A. Search paths of rats trained to find a hidden platform in the Morris water maze. No platform is present during this test. Left: the search path of a control animal, which learned successfully. Right: search path of a rat trained under the influence of APV. Graphs show percent time in each quadrant of the maze for all animals (from Morris, 1989). B. Fear-produced freezing in rats previously given electric shocks in the testing chamber. Animals received either APV or a control solution directly into the hippocampus just before training, which was 24 hr before this test (re-drawn from Young et al., 1994).

perform correctly (Morris, 1989). Nor should the dosage affect performance on a test where the platform is omitted. Also, the ability of APV-treated rats to successfully learn a water maze task when the location of the platform is marked by a local cue might seem to rule out deficits due to motor impairment. However, it can be argued that a partial motor deficit might compromise learning more for the possibly more intellectually demanding task of learning the location of a platform relative to distal cues than when the platform location is marked by a flag. Although many appropriate controls have been done, it is difficult to lay these issues entirely to rest. Especially troubling for the hypothesis that hippocampal LTP mediates storage of platform location in the water maze is the finding that prior experience with either spatial or nonspatial tasks in a water maze can inoculate a rat against the effects of APV on location learning in a similar maze (Bannerman, Good, Butcher, Ramsay, & Morris, 1995; Saucier & Cain, 1995).

There has been less controversy about demonstrations that APV prevents learning of context fear. Here, APV appears to affect learning but not performance, and because no behavioral response appears to be needed for learning, motor impairments do not seem to be such an issue. But one might well imagine that APV could at the least distract animals and affect context learning by making them less attentive to their environments (see Fanselow, 2000). Therefore, the final word is probably not in.

In recent years the development of genetic engineering techniques have made it possible to create mice in which molecules such as NMDA receptors or protein kinases that are believed to be involved in the production of LTP can be altered. The study of such genetically engineered mice provides another means of evaluating the role of LTP in learning (Chap. 5, this volume, for detailed consideration of genetic issues). Thus, it has been

reported that mice with an abnormal NMDA receptor specifically in the CA1 region of the hippocampus are deficient in learning a water maze (Tsien, Huerta, & Tonegawa, 1996), whereas mice engineered to have a juvenile form of the receptor (in both hippocampus and cortex) as adults show heightened learning abilities (Tang et al., 1999).

The effects on learning (and LTP) of genes for signaling molecules that are downstream from the calcium ion elevation that is believed to trigger LTP have also begun to be investigated. Thus, it has been reported that mice lacking some forms of the protein kinases, CaMKII or PKC, are deficient in both LTP induction and water maze learning ability (Chen, Rainnie, Greene, & Tonegawa, 1994; Malenka, Kauer, Perkel, & Nicoll, 1989; Silva, Paylor, Wehner, & Tonegawa, 1992; Silva, Stevens, Tonegawa, & Wang, 1992). It has also been reported that in animals deficient throughout the brain in CREB, the signaling molecule that is suspected of initiating the protein synthesis needed for LTP and memory extending beyond a few hours (discussed later), hippocampal LTP can be induced but does not persist normally, and learning of a variety of tasks occurs normally but retention does not survive for even a day (Bourtchuladze et al., 1994). These findings are exciting demonstrations of the power of genetics in manipulating the chemistry of the nervous system. However, this approach has all the same complexities that plague the pharmacological manipulations discussed above, and similar questions are already beginning to arise (Huerta, Scearce, Farris, Empson, & Prusky, 1996; Miyakawa, Yagi, Kagiyama, & Niki, 1996; Silva, Paylor et al., 1992).

One powerful aspect of the molecular-genetic technology is that, in some cases, it is possible to alter molecules such as the NMDA receptor selectively in specific classes of cells (e.g., CA1 but not other parts of the hippocampus or elsewhere in the brain). In some cases, this should make possible powerful tests of specific theories. For example, in some theories of hippocampal memory storage plasticity of CA1 synapses is absolutely essential to hippocampus-dependent learning whereas in others loss of plasticity at CA1 synapses would be expected to cause deficits but not to totally prevent learning.

Are Memories Actually Stored within the Hippocampus?   The fact that the hippocampus is needed for the recall of newly learned material taken together with our awareness of hippocampal synaptic plasticity tends to seduce us into assuming that relevant types of newly acquired information are actually stored within the hippocampus. But this need not follow. At least in principle, the hippocampus could be essential for recall of newly formed memories, not because it is the site of information storage, but because it is somehow needed to effectively utilize information initially stored elsewhere. Eventually, and perhaps with the help of the hippocampus, information stored elsewhere might become recoded in such a way that the hippocampus is no longer needed for recall. Arguing against such interpretations, however, are experiments, which seem to show that animals trained on place learning or contextual fear tasks while hippocampal function is compromised by infusion of either NMDA or AMPA antagonists directly into the hippocampus, fail to show any signs of having learned (Figure 4.2b; see Riedel et al., 1999; Young, Bohenek, & Fanselow, 1994). This encourages the view that the hippocampus is actually needed for storage and not just for interpretation or utilization of information stored elsewhere. But such experiments are not without interpretive complications. Normal rats that have not been taught the location of a hidden platform in a Morris water maze, rats that have been trained while NMDA receptors were inhibited, and rats that were trained after sus-

taining hippocampal damage search *all over* the field for a way out of the water. In contrast, rats that have been trained during suppression of AMPA receptor function often search in a specific wrong location as though they think they know where the platform is, but they have it wrong (Riedel et al., 1999).

Very recently it has been reported that blockage of CA1 NMDA receptor function for about a week just *after* water maze training or contextual fear training prevents recollection as tested about two weeks after training (Shimizu, Tang, Rampon, & Tsien, 2000). According to the theories we have discussed, this period of NMDA receptor dysfunction should be one in which hippocampally stored information is being transferred to the cortex. If, as suggested by several lines of evidence (Judge & Quartermain, 1982; Misanin, Miller, & Lewis, 1968; Nader, Schafe, & Le Doux, 2000; Sara, 2000), recollection destabilizes memories, which must then be restored, the effects of posttraining NMDA receptor suppression might be taken as evidence for the sort of information transfer that theory predicts.

Saturation Studies.   If hippocampal circuitry stores information as suggested by the theoretical ideas sketched above, then massive and indiscriminate potentiation of hippocampal circuit synapses should obliterate recently stored information and prevent new learning in hippocampus-dependent tasks. This latter prediction has been tested by examining the learning abilities of animals in which an attempt has been made to potentiate (saturate) all available plastic synapses by direct high frequency activation of major input pathways to the hippocampus via implanted stimulating electrodes (Castro, Silbert, McNaughton, & Barnes, 1989; McNaughton, Barnes, Rao, Baldwin, & Rasmussen, 1986). While theoretically appealing, such experiments are problematical in practice because of the difficulty of effectively saturating all relevant synapses. Thus, it is perhaps not surprising that attempts to test this prediction have obtained rather variable results (Barnes et al., 1994; Jeffery & Morris, 1993; Moser & Moser, 1999; Robinson, 1992; Sutherland, Dringenberg, & Hoesing, 1993). But recently a study has been done in which special procedures were used to ensure successful saturation of synapses between cortical afferents to the hippocampus and their dentate gyrus targets and to evaluate the success of the procedures (Brun, Ytterbo, Morris, Moser, & Moser, 2001; Moser, Krobert, Moser, & Morris, 1998; but see Otnaess, Brun, Moser, & Moser, 1999). When this was done a rather good correlation between successful saturation and failure to learn the location of a hidden platform in the water maze was obtained. It is of some interest to note that according to most theories of hippocampal storage, saturation of LTP at cortical afferent-to-dentate gyrus synapses would be expected to have less severe effects on learning than saturation of both these synapses and the recurrent collateral synapses of the CA3 neurons (because plasticity at either level can implement some pattern learning and completion); the successful saturation experiments just described were designed to ensure saturation of the dentate gyrus synapses, but whether saturation of CA3 recurrent collateral synapses occurred is unknown.

Conclusion. A conclusive case for the hypothesis that LTP/LTD operating in the hippocampus is the means by which some kinds of behavioral memories are initially written would probably require demonstrations that (a) changes in the strength of particular hippocampal synapses be shown to be modified by training, that (b) the patterns of activity of the involved cells during the training be characterized and shown when duplicated in vitro to lead to the same sorts of synaptic

strength seen during the training, and that (c) undoing the changes occurring during the learning alter the learned behavior in plausible ways. Instead, what we have for the most part are demonstrations that a rather wide variety of treatments that should and do interfere with hippocampal LTP development often, though not always, interfere with new learning in hippocampus-dependent learning tasks. These findings are fairly convincing, but there are a number of observations that are not quite what one would expect under the hypothesis, and it seems not impossible that alternative explanations for the positive experiments will eventually be seen as valid.

Learning and Plasticity of the *Aplysia* Defensive Withdrawal Reflex

History and Basics

The first significant progress made in tracing real (behavioral) learning to its neural substrates was the result of experiments on an invertebrate animal, the sea hare (*Aplysia*), begun in the laboratory of Eric Kandel. There is a long tradition in neuroscience of physiologists finding within the great diversity of invertebrate animals characteristics convenient for a particular sort of analysis and exploiting these to great advantage. Most often the findings that emerge, while perhaps having some features special to the animals studied, generalize well to higher animals. Invertebrate nervous systems have many fewer neurons than those of vertebrates in part because they use neurons in a nonredundant fashion; processing tasks that in a vertebrate appear to involve massive numbers of neurons of rather similar function operating in parallel are often carried out in invertebrates by circuitry in which each individual neuron has a relatively unique role. Once a neuron's location, branching patterns, and role are found and characterized, the same identified neuron can be studied from one animal to another, greatly facilitating the task of functional analysis. In turning to invertebrates for the analysis of learning it was hoped that it would be possible to find behaviors subject to experience-produced change and yet mediated by neural circuitry simple enough to understand; for then, it should be possible to fathom the neural basis for the behavioral changes wrought by experience.

The gastropod mollusk, *Aplysia* (the sea hare) was picked for analysis because of the unusually large size of many of its nerve cells. *Aplysia* readily withdraws delicate exposed respiratory organs, the gill, siphon, and tail, in response to gentle mechanical stimulation at a variety of bodily loci[3] (Kandel, 1976; Kupfermann & Kandel, 1969; Walters, Byrne, Carew, & Kandel, 1983). Like most protective responses, even of protozoa, the gill/siphon protective reflex habituates with repeated stimulation and becomes enhanced following very strong ones (Carew, Castellucci, & Kandel, 1971; Pinsker, Kupfermann, Castellucci, & Kandel, 1970). The habituation is stimulus specific; stimulating a fresh location produces an unhabituated response. But the sensitization is generalized; a suitably strong stimulus will enhance responses to gentle mechanical stimulation anywhere on the body. Habituation normally develops with tens of stimulations and recovers within a few hours, and sensitization, usually induced by an electrical shock to the animals head or tail, usually lasts under an hour. But if habituation to a given stimulus is reestablished several times with adequate spacing between bouts of stimuli, the habituation persists for weeks rather than hours (Carew & Kandel, 1973; Carew, Pinsker, & Kandel, 1972). Similarly, if traumatic stimuli are repeated on several separate occasions sensitization can last for weeks (Pinsker, Hening, Carew, & Kandel, 1973).

These phenomena of short- and long-term habituation and sensitization of the gill/siphon protective reflex were the forms of simple learning that were initially analyzed in *Aplysia* and that may have given us our first glimpses of nervous system changes responsible for learning. A little more than a decade later, at about the same time that the associative properties of LTP were first becoming widely appreciated, it was discovered that gill/siphon withdrawal, and also a similar tail retraction response, can be classically conditioned, and this led rapidly to our first insights into mechanisms responsible for associative learning (Carew, Hawkins, & Kandel, 1983; Carew, Walters, & Kandel, 1981; Hawkins, Abrams, Carew, & Kandel, 1983; Walters & Byrne, 1983).

Analysis of Habituation and Sensitization. Neurophysiological analysis of the mechanisms of simple learning in *Aplysia* has been tremendously aided by the convenient fact that the sensory neurons activated by mechanical stimulation make synapses directly on motor neurons innervating muscles that produce protective withdrawal (Kupfermann & Kandel, 1969). When intracellular recordings from these motor neurons were carried out during repetitive mechanosensory stimulation (or during repetitive activation of sensory neurons by electrical stimulation, which has been used as a convenient and more controllable alternative to mechanical stimulation), it was immediately seen that the EPSPs evoked in the motor neurons by the activated sensory neurons decline roughly in parallel with the habituation of the motor response (see Figure 4.3) (Byrne et al., 1978; Castellucci et al., 1970; Castellucci et al., 1978; Kandel, 1976; Kupfermann et al.,

---

[3]Depending on the location of the stimulus, the tail, siphon, and/or gills may be withdrawn and slightly different reflex pathways utilized; however, we will here refer to all such reflexes, collectively, as withdrawal or protective reflexes.

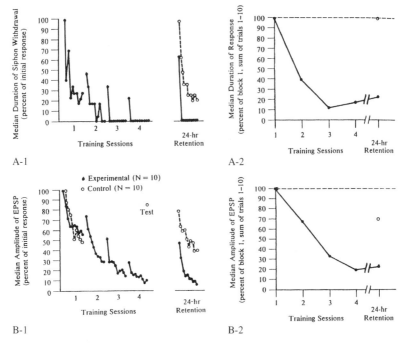

Figure 4.3   Comparison of reflex habituation and EPSP depression (from Kandel, 1976).
NOTE: Training and testing are the same in behavioral (A) and electrophysiological (B) experiments except for the differences described in the text. In A, open circles indicate responses to stimulation of a previously unstimulated sensory field. In B, open circles are responses to stimulation of a second nerve; comparison to the experimental points establishes that decline of response was not simply due to deterioration of the ganglion over time.

1970); this decline in synaptic efficacy is usually referred to as *synaptic* (or homosynaptic) *depression*. Similarly, strong, sensitization-causing stimulation causes an increase in EPSPs to test stimuli that roughly parallels behavioral sensitization (Castellucci & Kandel, 1976; Frost et al., 1985; Kandel, 1976; Kupfermann et al., 1970); the enlarged EPSPs are said to be facilitated. These observations seem to provide direct support for the widespread belief that when the neural bases of learning could be studied, it would be found that learning is due to changes in the efficacy of synaptic transmission. There are, however, caveats, which we will discuss later.

Further analysis of the synaptic depression that seems to be responsible for habituation was concerned with the relative roles of the pre- and postsynaptic neurons. Does the EPSP become smaller because the sensory neuron releases less chemical transmitter or does the motor neuron become less responsive to the transmitter that reaches it? Is it recurring activity of the sensory neuron or of the motor neuron that triggers the decline in synaptic efficacy? An experimental approach called *quantal analysis* (to be explained later) provided evidence that the synaptic depression in this reflex is due to decreased release and not to altered postsynaptic response (Castellucci & Kandel, 1974). The extent of this diminution of release from a given sensory neuron seems to depend entirely on the activity of the neuron itself and to be uninfluenced by whether the motor neuron does or does not fire in response to synaptic input (Kandel, 1976). Thus, synaptic depression at *Aplysia* sensory-motor synapses appears to be rather different from the long-term depression seen at hippocampal synapses.

Quantal analysis suggested that facilitation, too, is a presynaptic phenomenon (Castellucci & Kandel, 1976; Dale, Schacher, & Kandel, 1988). As we explain later, additional evidence of presynaptic changes was provided by an increase in the duration of spikes (spike broadening) in the cell body and presumably also in the terminals of sensory neurons under appropriate pharmacological conditions (Klein & Kandel, 1978), as well as by biochemical analyses of sensory neurons following induction of sensitization or facilitation provided further evidence. However, a very recent report on cells in culture suggests that serotonergic facilitation may have a more important postsynaptic component than has so far been thought (Chitwood, Li, & Glanzman, 2001).

Since a traumatic stimulus, typically applied to head or tail, alters the release properties of sensory neurons serving the entire receptive field of the protective reflex, it was apparent that traumatic stimulation causes the broadcast of a widely disseminated signal. The first hints as to the nature of this signal came when it was discovered that serotonin (5-HT) could mimic the effects of traumatic simulation, and it eventually emerged that a small set of facilitator neurons, some releasing serotonin and some releasing other less well investigated neuromodulatory agents, innervate the terminals of defensive reflex sensory neurons at their contacts with their motor neuronal targets and also on some interneurons (Brunelli, Castellucci, & Kandel, 1976; Glanzman et al., 1989; Hawkins, Castellucci, & Kandel, 1981; Hawkins & Schacher, 1989; Kistler et al., 1985; Longley & Longley, 1986; Mackey, Kandel, & Hawkins, 1989). The analysis of serotonin's effects on the sensory

neurons has been the subject of especially intensive research for which a recent Nobel Prize was awarded. Brief exposures to exogenously applied serotonin causes short-term facilitation of the sensory-motor synapse, lasting at most minutes and not nearly as long as facilitation produced by traumatic stimuli, while more prolonged application or repeated brief applications cause intermediate-term (hours long) and long-term facilitation (usually defined as persisting for more than a day; Ghirardi, Montarolo, & Kandel, 1995; Mauelshagen, Parker, & Carew, 1996; Mercer, Emptage, & Carew, 1991; Montarolo et al., 1986; Sutton & Carew, 2000; Walters et al., 1983).

Such experiments can be done in both the intact nervous system and at synapses between sensory and motor neurons grown in culture, where it is certain that only these two cells are involved. The use of the synapses of such sensory-motor cultures moves analysis even farther from behaving animals, but this further step away from behavior makes it possible to do many kinds of highly informative experiments that otherwise would be extremely difficult or impossible. As the distance between the behaving animal and the preparations used for analytical work grows, it becomes increasingly important to find predictions from the analytical work that can be tested on intact nervous systems or the behaving animal.

As with hippocampal LTP, protein phosphorylation was expected to play a major role in the alterations that underlie facilitation. In fact the initial publication of serotonin's facilitating effects also reported that the second messenger, cyclic AMP (cAMP), has similar effects (Brunelli et al., 1976), and it is now known that, as will be discussed in more detail later, phosphorylation caused by cAMP-dependent protein kinase (also known as protein kinase A, or PKA) plays a dominant and rather direct role in causing short-term facilitation as well as in causing new genetic transcription and protein synthesis, which are necessary for the production of long-term facilitation.

Classical Conditioning. Successful classical conditioning of protective withdrawal was first reported in 1981 (Carew et al., 1981), and a few years later two laboratories simultaneously reported the first neural analogs of this conditioning (Hawkins et al., 1983; Walters, Carew, & Kandel, 1981). In these experiments the US was an electric shock to *Aplysia*'s hind end (tail) and CSs were calibrated touches of specific points on the body surface for behavioral experiments, and in physiological experiments they were short trains of spikes in individual sensory neurons produced by intracellular depolarization. Tail shock (the US) alone caused generalized facilitation of withdrawal and of EPSPs in motor neurons that produce the withdrawal throughout the entire receptive field of the reflex, but the EPSPs produced by afferents that had served as the CS were enhanced much more.

An important observation was that under conditions where serotonin-dependent facilitation causes presynaptic spike broadening, *exaggerated* broadening was produced by classical conditioning protocols (Hawkins et al., 1983). This suggested the possibility that classical conditioning might be due to an amplified form of the same facilitation mechanism that causes sensitization. However, since the tail-shock US causes an unconditioned withdrawal reflex it was also possible that the extra enhancement was due to the coactivity of the CS-representing neurons and the US-driven motor neurons; in other words, these might be Hebb synapses. However, this possibility was rejected at the time because it was found that pairing CS-caused presynaptic activity with depolarizing current injection into withdrawal reflex motor neurons did

not cause enhancement of CS-evoked EPSPs, as would have been expected if the sensory-motor synapses were subject to LTP (Carew, Hawkins, Abrams, & Kandel, 1984; Hawkins et al., 1983). Nor did strongly hyperpolarizing motor neurons during the otherwise standard classical conditioning protocol prevent successful conditioning. The occurrence of LTP at these synapses was therefore rejected, prematurely as it turned out, and it was proposed that classical conditioning of protective withdrawal in *Aplysia* is due to an amplification of serotonergic facilitation of transmitter release by activity of the presynaptic neuron (activity-dependent facilitation). Subsequent experiments established that exposure to exogenously applied serotonin could substitute for the US both in the nervous system and sensory-motor synapse culture. Thus, it appeared that classical conditioning was due to a presynaptic activity-produced enhancement of serotonin-produced facilitation (or activity-dependent facilitation).

LTP in *Aplysia*. The development of this story was a landmark event. For the first time a physiological explanation for a simple form of classical conditioning had been offered. But there was an unsatisfactory feature to the explanation. It could easily explain how an animal learns to respond to a particular CS, but if the serotonergic facilitatory signal is really broadcast diffusely, activity-dependent facilitation could not explain how an animal can learn to produce a particular *response* to that stimulus. However animals can generally do just that. In *Aplysia* slightly different forms of withdrawal movement that can be evoked by differently located electric shocks can be specifically classically conditioned (Hawkins, Lalevic, Clark, & Kandel, 1989; Walters, 1989).

Of course LTP can in principle explain such stimulus and response-specific classical conditioning with ease. The first hints that the *Aplysia* sensory-motor synapses could in fact display a form of LTP came from experiments in culture in which a presynaptic tetanus was found to produce hours-long augmentation of EPSPs that could be prevented by postsynaptic hyperpolarization or by introducing the calcium chelator BAPTA into the postsynaptic cell or exposing the cell to APV. In addition, augmentation of EPSPs could be promoted by delivering depolarizing current into the postsynaptic neuron during a tetanus adjusted to produce little potentiation by itself (Lin & Glanzman, 1994a, 1994b). Subsequently, it was found that even in the intact nervous system the activity-dependent EPSP enhancements produced by pairing a CS with tail shock are greatly reduced by postsynaptic BAPTA or APV (Figure 4.4; Murphy & Glanzman, 1996, 1997, 1999). Thus, contrary to what was originally thought, classical conditioning in *Aplysia* does seem to depend on LTP.

What role if any does the widespread serotonin release produced by the tail shock play?

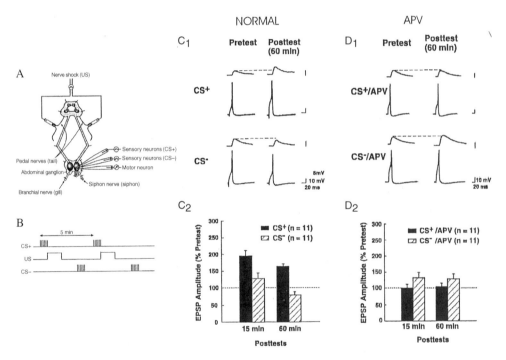

Figure 4.4   Changes in monosynaptic EPSPs and effect of APV in a ganglionic model of differential classical conditioning (from Murphy & Glanzman, 1999).

NOTE: Animals were trained as indicated in A and B. Conditional stimuli were brief trains of action potentials in single sensory neurons produced by intracellular current injection. Responses of a siphon motor neuron were recorded intracellularly. The US was a train of voltage pulses to nerves innervating the tail. During testing, but not during training, ionic composition of the medium bathing the ganglia was altered to greatly reduce interneuronal firing so that monosynaptic EPSPs could be observed uncontaminated by polysynaptic input to the recorded motor neuron. Under one condition, NMDA receptors were blocked by bathing the ganglia in an APV-containing solution during training. C and D show the effects of training with and without APV. In C1 and D1, the monosynaptic EPSPs and sensory neuron spikes that evoked them are shown for illustrative preparations. In C2 and D2, results for all experiments are averaged. Note that EPSPs would normally be expected to increase some if the US were given alone, not in association with CS+ or CS– due to simple serotonergic facilitation.

The answer is suggested by an investigation into the effects of serotonin on the LTP seen in culture: It was found that a presynaptic tetanus that was adjusted to produce only a moderate augmentation of EPSP amplitude (presumably due to LTP) produced a much larger one if the tetanus occurred in the presence of serotonin, and this large increase was prevented by postsynaptic hyperpolarization or BAPTA (Bao, Kandel, & Hawkins, 1998). In other words, it appears that serotonin enhances LTP. Thus, during classical conditioning it may be that effective conditioning is the result of cooperative interactions between contiguous firing of pre- and postsynaptic neurons *and* serotonin released by the facilitator neurons.

Relationship between Synaptic Plasticity and Simple Forms of Learning in Aplysia

In contrast to hippocampal LTP, the synaptic plasticities of *Aplysia*—synaptic depression, synaptic facilitation, activity-dependent facilitation, and *Aplysia* LTP—have considerable face-validity as mechanisms underlying habituation, sensitization, and classical conditioning of protective withdrawal behavior. The synaptic changes are at synapses between sensory neurons thought to be the normal afferents of the behavioral reflex (but see Hickie, Cohen, & Balaban, 1997) and motor neurons involved in producing the behavioral response. The protocols of sensory stimulation that cause the synaptic changes are similar to those that cause the corresponding forms of behavioral change, and the time course of the synaptic and behavioral changes seem comparable.

However, this face-validity is misleading. Physiological experiments are done with the nervous system removed from the animal, perhaps connected by sensory or motor nerves to a few bodily structures. Under such conditions intraganglionic polysynaptic pathways that parallel the monosynaptic one that is usually the focus of study are unlikely to be functioning normally; moreover, steps are commonly taken to minimize their influence so as to limit control of motor neuron activities to the well defined monosynaptic pathway. Yet it seems likely that, in the free animal, intraganglionic polysynaptic pathways contribute very significantly to the production of behavior (Fischer & Carew, 1993; Stopfer & Carew, 1996; Trudeau & Castellucci, 1992, 1993a, 1993b); according to one estimate, 75% of stimulus-evoked motor neuron excitation comes via polysynaptic routes (Trudeau & Castellucci, 1992). Furthermore, freely behaving *Aplysia* that have been shocked in a given context show heightened defensive withdrawal to constant test stimuli when exposed to that context (Colwill, Absher, & Roberts, 1988); this almost certainly means that the reflex is subject to control by higher ganglia whose influence is either likely to be highly abnormal or is totally absent under the conditions of the physiological experiments we have discussed.

Thus, what is being examined in most physiological experiments on *Aplysia* learning is not the detailed neural mechanism of the observed behavioral learning, but a *neural model* of that learning in which the neural elements chosen for analysis are hopefully representative fragments of the actually quite complex, and far from fully analyzed, complete circuit.

A case in point will be instructive: Figure 4.3 (from Kandel, 1976, after Carew & Kandel, 1973) shows the results of parallel behavioral and neurophysiological experiments on habituation lasting more than 24 hr. On the face of it, the results match strikingly. However, certain factors must be taken into consideration: (a) The behavioral experiments were done on intact, freely behaving animals; neurophysiological experiments were on isolated abdominal ganglia with all peripheral sensory and motor structures and the brain removed. (b) The behavioral response measured was the *duration* of *siphon* retraction; the neural response measured was the EPSP *amplitude* of a motor neuron L7, which innervates the *gill,* not the siphon (though gill and siphon responses do habituate roughly in parallel). (c) Stimuli in behavioral experiments were 800 ms water jets to the siphon; stimuli in neurophysiological experiments were 2 ms voltage pulses to siphon or branchial nerves adjusted to produce a synaptic potential in L7 similar to that produced by the mechanical stimulus used in behavioral experiments. These differences between behavioral and neural experiments were not accidental but were dictated by a range of practical considerations. It would be disingenuous to claim that in this study anyone was observing neural correlates of what was directly controlling siphon movements in the behavioral experiments. However, the study did establish the important point that synaptic mechanisms within the abdominal ganglion can produce, in a typical withdrawal reflex motor neuron, use-induced depression similar in extent and duration to behavioral habituation of protective withdrawal. And later experiments achieved a similar demonstration for direct sensory-to-motor neuron synapses. Increasingly, efforts are being made to rigorously evaluate the quantitative contribution of changes at various synaptic loci to learned changes in the movements produced by natural stimuli (e.g., Antonov, Antonova, Kandel, Hawkins, 2001; Antonov, Kandel, & Hawkins, 1999; Stopfer & Carew, 1996). Such work suggests that that mechanisms thought from earlier work to be responsible for behavioral change in some cases really do contribute to such change, but they are not always the whole story. Furthermore, the experiments are still necessarily done under conditions where the nervous system is surely operating far from normally.

It is a monumental accomplishment to have uncovered cellular mechanisms that may in principal be sufficient to account for the simple learning phenomena that have been studied in *Aplysia.* Considerable future effort will be required to determine the extent to which these or other mechanisms fully account for these learning phenomena as they occur in behaving animals.

Cerebellum-Mediated Classical Eye-Blink Conditioning

History and Basics

Sitting atop the brain stem just behind the midbrain, the cerebellum (little brain) is the most conspicuous externally visible structure of the mammalian brain aside from the cerebral hemispheres themselves. Like the cerebrum, it has a convoluted cortex and internal (deep) nuclei. It receives rich input from proprioceptors as well as from somatic, auditory, and visual centers of both the brain stem and cortex, and it provides rich output to motor and premotor cortices, to brain stem motor nuclei, and to spinal movement producing circuitry, suggesting that the cerebellum serves some sort of motor control function. Consistent with this, damage to the cerebellum results, though not in paralysis, in severe deficits of motor coordination. Given its apparent motor function and large size, it is hard not to entertain the possibility that it might play a role in the learning of skilled movements.

Cerebellar Organization. The cerebellum has a very regular and stereotyped cellular architecture that has been the focus of extensive anatomical and electrophysiological analysis (Eccles, Szentagothai, & Ito, 1967; Shepherd, 1990). The aspects of its organization that are essential to this account are summarized in Figure 4.5. The principal neurons of the cerebellar cortex, the Purkinje cells, are large neurons with huge dendritic arbors that branch extensively while running toward the outer surface of the cortex and with axons that

A.

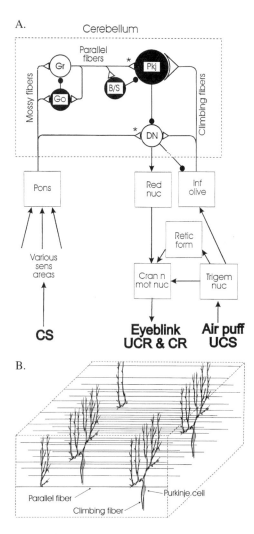

B.

Figure 4.5 Neural circuitry involved in conditioned and unconditioned blink reflex.
NOTE: A. Circuitry. Abbreviations: mf, mossy fibers; Gr, granule cells; pf, parallel fibers; Pkj, Purkinje cells; DN, deep nucleus neurons; cf, climbing fibers; B/S, basket and stellate cells; Go, Golgi cells; *, synapses whose plasticity has been implicated in eye-blink learning. B. Sketch of anatomical relationships of Purkinje cells, parallel fibers, and climbing fibers within a typical block of cerebellar cortex.

project in the opposite direction to neurons of the deep cerebellar nuclei on which they make inhibitory synapses. The deep-nucleus neurons project out of the cerebellum to reach a variety of movement-relevant targets, the

most relevant for our purposes being brain stem motor nuclei that in turn can cause excitation of motor neurons relatively directly.

Input reaches the cerebellum via two routes. (a) Information about all sorts of sensory events, as coded at various levels of the brain, are conveyed to the cerebellum via neurons that originate in the pons and send so-called mossy fibers to the cerebellum. There, they make direct excitatory contacts with the deep nucleus neurons, whose axons carry processed information out of the cerebellum, and also with a large population of small *granule cells*. The axons of the granule cells, the *parallel fibers,* run in parallel with one another and parallel to the surface of the cortex crossing and making synapses on the dendritic arbors of the Purkinje neurons as these ascend toward the cortical surface. The parallel fibers also excite a population of inhibitory neurons, the *Golgi cells,* that feed inhibition back to the granule cells, the cells of origin of the parallel fibers; this feedback inhibitory circuit is at the basis of a theory of conditioned response (CR) timing that we will later discuss. In addition to exciting granule cells, the mossy fibers also make excitatory connections with the Golgi cells as well as with a population of inhibitory neurons, the stellate and the basket cells (which we will not distinguish between), which in turn inhibit the Purkinje cells and the Golgi cells. So whenever a population of mossy fibers fires, the Purkinje neurons are influenced by a mix of excitation and inhibition. (b) The other source of input is via *climbing fibers* that arise from neurons of the inferior olivary nucleus in the hind brain and run to the cerebellar cortex giving off branches that directly excite the deep nucleus output cells along the way. At the cortex, each climbing fiber innervates a relatively small population of Purkinje neurons. As a climbing fiber reaches one of its Purkinje neuron targets, it runs toward the cortical surface branching and arborizing over the entire dendritic tree of the

Purkinje cell covering it like a vine and making great numbers of excitatory synaptic contacts with it all along the length of its branches. As one might expect from this description, climbing fibers provide a powerful excitatory input to their Purkinje targets. A single climbing fiber spike causes a huge Purkinje cell EPSP that in turn generates a burst of spikes in the Purkinje cell *dendrites* as well as in the axon. Unlike the ordinary action potentials of axons, which result from the movement of sodium ions into the axon through voltage-gated sodium ion channels, the dendritic spikes triggered by climbing fiber firings are produced by flow of calcium ions into the dendrites through voltage-gated calcium ion channels. This elevation of dendritic calcium ions has important consequences that we will discuss later.

Theories of Cerebellar Motor Learning. The general speculation that the cerebellum might be important for motor learning, together with the above picture of cerebellar organization prompted David Marr to develop an explicit conjectural theory of cerebellar learning (1969). In Marr's theory, the firing of Purkinje neurons is analogous to a response that can be classically conditioned. Climbing fiber activity, which innately produces this response, is analogous to the US, and a set of parallel fibers activated by an external stimulus event is analogous to the CS. Marr proposed that repeated pairing of a given pattern of parallel fiber activity (CS) with activity of a particular climbing fiber (US) would eventually strengthen the synapses of the active parallel fibers on the climbing fiber–driven Purkinje neuron (in essence an application of Hebb's hypothesis).

Marr's theory failed to consider the downstream consequences of Purkinje cell firing, which are *inhibition* of deep nucleus cerebellar output neurons and consequent *suppression* of the movements their activity can

cause. When this fact is considered, things get more complex. In order for Purkinje cell responses to a CS to cause a positive movement, it would be necessary to assume that the CS causes a *reduction* in the firing rate of otherwise continually active Purkinje neurons, thereby disinhibiting the deep nucleus neurons whose activity can cause the desired movement. Such a reduction could result if CS-US pairing were to weaken, rather than strengthen, active parallel fiber–Purkinje cell synapses, because then the inhibitory influence of the Golgi neurons that are activated by the mossy fiber input would be less opposed by excitation from the parallel fiber inputs. Thus, rather than the Hebb rule, one might postulate that pairing of parallel fiber and climbing fiber activity *reduces* the potency of the parallel fiber synapses on the excited Purkinje cell as proposed by Albus (1971) a few years after the publication of Marr's original theory.

Discovery of Cerebellar LTD and of Cerebellar Role in Classical Eye-Blink Conditioning. About a decade after the publication of these theoretical speculations two discoveries gave them empirical support: In 1982 Ito, Sakurai, and Tongroach (1982) reported that, just as Albus had proposed, parallel fiber–Purkinje synapses do in fact display a long-term decline in strength following parallel fiber–climbing fiber pairing, a now much studied form of synaptic plasticity commonly referred to as cerebellar long-term depression (LTD); for specificity we will refer to it as *Purkinje cell LTD*. In the same year Thompson and associates reported that damage to the cerebellum prevents performance of classically conditioned eye-blink responses without affecting responses to the US (McCormick, Clark, Lavond, & Thompson, 1982) and that neurons of the deep cerebellar nuclei could be found whose activity precedes and predicts the behavioral blink response

(McCormick et al., 1982; McCormick & Thompson, 1984a, 1984b), suggesting that the cerebellum might really mediate the classical conditioning of simple movements.

Subsequently a host of predictions made by the Marr/Albus theory were tested and verified. (a) Lesions of the deep nuclei (Clark, McCormick, Lavond, & Thompson, 1984; Lavond, Hembree, & Thompson, 1985; McCormick & Thompson, 1984a; Steinmetz, Lavond, Ivkovich, Logan, & Thompson, 1992) or lesions that prevent mossy fiber activity from reaching the cerebellum (Lewis et al., 1987) prevent conditioned eye blinks. (b) Lesions that abolish climbing fiber input to the cerebellum (theoretically preventing the possibility of reinforcement) prevent the development of conditioned eye blinks but do not prevent the performance of an already acquired conditioned blink. However, once the climbing fiber input to the cerebellum is abolished, a previously acquired conditioned blink response is gradually lost despite continued training, as would be expected if it were climbing fiber input to the Purkinje neurons that was the true reinforcer for the conditioned blink (McCormick et al., 1985; Mintz, Yun, & Lavond, 1988). (c) Electrical stimulation electrodes placed in the inferior olive at the origin of climbing fibers could be used in lieu of a natural US if placed so as to evoke an unconditioned blink. At other locations within the inferior olive other movements are elicited, and these too can be conditioned (Mauk, Steinmetz, & Thompson, 1986; Steinmetz, Lavond, & Thompson, 1989; Thompson, Swain, Clark, & Shinkman, 2000; Thompson, Thompson, Kim, Krupa, & Shinkman, 1998). (d) Electrical stimulation of mossy fibers can be used in lieu of a natural CS (Steinmetz, 1990; Steinmetz et al., 1989; Steinmetz, Rosen, Chapman, Lavond, & Thompson, 1986). (e) Lesions of the red nucleus, which is presumed to be a way station for signals from the cerebellar deep nuclei on their way to blink-producing motor neurons, prevents performance of conditioned eye blinks (Rosenfield, Dovydaitis, & Moore, 1985; Rosenfield & Moore, 1983), but training carried out during pharmacologically generated, reversible lesions of the red nucleus leads to normal acquisition, as can be shown by testing done after functioning of the red nucleus is restored (Chapman, Steinmetz, Sears, & Thompson, 1990; Clark & Lavond, 1993; Krupa, Thompson, & Thompson, 1993).

These and many further studies seem to provide convincing evidence that changes within the cerebellum are primary mediators of conditioned eye blinks (see Thompson & Krupa, 1994, for an excellent review), although there are those who question this conclusion (Harvey, Welsh, Yeo, & Romano, 1993; Llinas & Welsh, 1993; Welsh and Harvey, 1989, 1991). However, the Marr/Albus theory as an explanation of what goes on in the cerebellum during such learning seems not to be the whole story.

The Need for Revision of the Marr/Albus Theory. In the Marr/Albus theory learning is entirely due to changes at cortical synapses, and these changes are themselves entirely the result of cortical events. Thus, learning should not occur in the absence of cerebellar cortex, and CRs acquired before cortical ablation should be lost. Although it is difficult to remove cerebellar cortex extensively without also removing extra-cortical structures, when this aim is approximated, there are, as predicted, severe deficits of acquisition and retention. Nevertheless, it appears that CRs can sometimes be retained, albeit with abnormal timing, and that perhaps new learning can occur as well, though with difficulty (Garcia, Steele, & Mauk, 1999; Lavond, Steinmetz, Yokaitis, & Thompson, 1987; Logan, 1991; Medina, Garcia, Nores, Taylor, & Mauk, 2000; Perrett, Ruiz, & Mauk,

1993; Yeo & Hardiman, 1992; and see Thompson & Krupa, 1994). There are also a number of reports that temporary inactivation of the nucleus interpositus (the deep nucleus involved in producing eye blinks) during training can prevent learning, as determined by testing after removal of the inactivation (Clark, Zhang, & Lavond, 1992; Krupa et al., 1993; Nordholm, Thompson, Dersarkissian, & Thompson, 1993; and see discussion in Mauk & Donegan, 1997). This also should not occur under the original theory, but we will not consider these experiments further as it appears that in all of them partial inactivation of the cortex as well as the interpositus was a possibility.

Mauk and colleagues have offered an elaboration of the Marr/Albus theory (Mauk & Donegan, 1997) and a computational model (Kenyon et al., 1998; Medina et al., 2000; Medina & Mauk, 1999, 2000) that may account for these and a number of other difficult observations. In the face of what appears to be extracortical learning, they have postulated that mossy fiber–deep nucleus synapses are subject to a form of LTP. However, because it appears that, in the absence of cortex, eyeblink learning occurs at best with great difficulty and because there is some evidence that sudden cessation of Purkinje cell–produced inhibition of deep nucleus neurons may cause an influx of calcium ions into them (Llinas & Muhlethaler, 1988), they propose that development of LTP at a mossy fiber–deep nucleus synapse is contingent on the pairing of mossy fiber activity and calcium ion elevation due to cessation of Purkinje input to the postsynaptic neuron. Under that assumption training does not cause any development of deep nucleus LTP until the cortex learns (due to LTD) to silence the US-sensitive Purkinje cells in response to the CS; once this has happened CSs will cause interpositus cells to be released from Purkinje inhibition each time the CS activates mossy fiber inputs, with the result that

the mossy fiber synapses on the interpositus cells will become strengthened by deep nucleus LTP. Both the cortical and deep nucleus plasticity should contribute to production of a robust CR, but either alone could also cause some response. Little learning at the level of the interpositus should occur in the absence of cortical Purkinje cells (though the theory ignores possible effects of climbing fiber innervation of deep nucleus cells, which is present anatomically), and the interpositus LTP that develops during training in the normal animal and allows continued performance of CRs after cortical ablation will do so only with relatively extensive training. It is apparent that, at least in principle, this theory can account for some preserved learning and, if some LTP can develop in the absence of Purkinje cell input, possibly also for preservation of some learning ability in cortically damaged animals.

A theory of extinction, not addressed in the Marr/Albus formulation, is also proposed. Extinction is based on proposed synaptic-change rules that are more or less the obverse of those that account for acquisition: Purkinje synapses are hypothesized to undergo LTP if parallel fibers are active without climbing fiber reinforcement, and mossy fiber—deep nucleus synapses are hypothesized to undergo LTD if the mossy fibers fire in response to a CS but the ongoing Purkinje-caused inhibition does not shut off as it did during the advanced stages of acquisition. This theory of extinction predicts, apparently correctly, that any CRs that survive decortication will resist extinction because the Purkinje-caused inhibition on which deep nucleus LTD depends will be missing (Perrett & Mauk, 1995).

Is the Cerebellum Really the Locus of Eye-Blink Conditioning?

It seems to this observer that the experiments described above make a very strong case that synaptic plasticity in the cerebellar cortex and deep nuclei really do provide a major basis for classically conditioned eye-blink conditioning, though the exact locus and characteristics of this plasticity are still matters of conjecture and debate. However, the reader should be warned that this claim has met with hearty disagreement from some quarters, as mentioned before.

Analysis of the cellular mechanisms in this system seems less advanced than in the others we have discussed. As we will see, there is not yet a completely clear picture of the physiological mechanisms that make the development of Purkinje LTD contingent on the coincident occurrence of CS and US, and there are not yet widely discussed working hypotheses as to the basis for long-term retention, as there are for hippocampal LTP and for *Aplysia* synaptic plasticity. On the other hand, we believe that it is in this system that one can be most confident of a realistic connection between physiological findings and behavioral learning because more of the analysis has been carried out on behaving animals rather than surrogates such as the isolated ganglion, the slice, or cells in culture.

ISSUES AND GENERALITIES

We turn now to a discussion of some of the major questions that arise when one attempts to consider the neural basis of learning. However, before beginning, a few words of caution are in order.

We seek to understand learning, which is by definition a *behavioral* phenomenon, in terms of the neural properties and events that are responsible for it. If we find that what happens at the level of the nervous system has a certain formal similarity to what happens at the level of behavior, the findings will have considerable face-validity. For example, in *Aplysia* we can perhaps equate the CS, US, and withdrawal responses with their neural representations, and we can perhaps attribute successful learning to an increase in the strength of the synapse through which the neurons that represent the CS excite the neurons that represent the withdrawal response. But there is no a priori reason why such a direct isomorphism between behavior and the neural events should exist. Indeed, if we expect isomorphism, eye-blink conditioning might be said to get it all wrong, because the development of a positive conditioned eye blink may be the result of the *weakening* of synapses between parallel fibers and Purkinje cells. Similarly, there is no a priori reason why all of the many properties of learning that are known to students of behavior should be explainable by cellular mechanisms without recourse to the complex neural circuitry in which these mechanisms operate. For example, learning normally extinguishes when the CS is repeated without reinforcement. But even if explanations of classical conditioning in terms of Hebb's rule are valid, one should not necessarily expect that the occurrence of repeated (nontetanic) activation of a neuron that is part of the CS representation, without strong postsynaptic depolarization, should cause a loss of the potentiated state; instead development of extinction could perfectly well involve changes elsewhere that lead to inhibition of the previously learned response, a possibility that in fact is consistent with some behavioral explanations of extinction.

Virtually all of the discussion that follows concerns mechanisms of synaptic change. The current working assumption of the field is that learning is due to changes in the intrinsic efficacy of synapses *within* the neural pathways that mediate between stimuli and learned responses to those stimuli. Very little consideration has been given to the logical possibility that information flow in the neural pathways mediating between stimulus and response could be altered, not by changing the intrinsic efficacy of synapses within those pathways, but by alterations of ongoing modulation of those pathways by signals arising elsewhere in the nervous system. That this possibility should not be discounted is emphasized by evidence that such extrinsic modulation plays a major, actually dominant role, along with intrinsic synaptic change, in the habituation of escape behavior in crayfish, a model system in many ways very similar to the *Aplysia* withdrawal reflex (Krasne & Teshiba, 1995).

What Changes?

Sensitization, classical conditioning, and habituation in *Aplysia* as well as classical eyelid conditioning mediated by the cerebellum appear to be due to altered synaptic efficacy, while hippocampal LTP is itself a change in efficacy. But what about transmission is changing?

Anatomical and Physiological Change

One obvious possibility is that synapses might actually grow or atrophy in response to the factors that alter their physiological efficacy, and there is in fact increasing evidence that this is the case. As seen by the electron microscope (i.e., ultrastructurally), points of functional synaptic contact are marked by increases in density of the cell membrane both pre- and postsynaptically, by a dark fuzz on the intracellular side of the postsynaptic membrane, by a slight increase in the distance between the pre- and postsynaptic membrane, and by clusters of neurotransmitter-containing membrane-bound synaptic vesicles immediately adjacent to presynaptic membrane (sometimes all together referred to as the *active zone* of the synapse). When the presynaptic neuron releases the transmitter, a small pore forms where the vesicle contacts the membrane, the transmitter in the vesicle is all released into the space between the pre- and postsynaptic neuron, and the vesicle membrane, which is now fused to the cell membrane around the circumference of the pore, becomes incorporated into the neuron's membrane, an example of the general cellular phenomenon of *exocytosis*. Occasionally some of the various stages of this process are captured in an electron micrograph.

Electron micrographs of the sensory-motor synapses of the *Aplysia* defensive reflex taken under control conditions or after the induction of long-term sensitization, produced either by behavioral training or by exposure to serotonin, show increased numbers of active zones, increased zone size, and increased numbers of synaptic vesicles in the immediate vicinity of the membrane; more or less opposite changes are associated with habituation (Bailey, 1999; Bailey & Chen, 1988a, 1988b; Glanzman, Kandel, & Schacher, 1990; Schacher, Kandel, & Montarolo, 1993; Schacher & Montarolo, 1991). Such changes can develop very rapidly with some having been detected by about 30 min after suitable exposure to serotonin (Bailey, Chen, Kandel, & Schacher, 1993). Training or serotonin regimens that only produce short-term sensitization or facilitation (i.e., lasting less than 24 hr) do not lead to such morphological changes (though see Wu, Friedman, & Schacher, 1995). Even with a light microscope, one can see increased numbers of synaptic vesicle-containing swellings as well as growth of new presynaptic branchings in cultures of sensory and motor neurons after serotonin exposure (Casadio et al., 1999; Glanzman et al., 1990). Interestingly, in behaviorally trained animals elevated numbers of varicosities and active zones persist as long as does augmented transmission (>3 weeks), but active zone size and numbers of adjacent vesicles outlast training by only a few days (Bailey & Chen, 1989).

Early studies of hippocampal synapses subjected to LTP-producing stimulation suggested that dendritic spine and synapse characteristics change (Desmond & Levy, 1986a,

1986b; Lee, Schottler, Oliver, & Lynch, 1980). More recently, very convincing evidence of morphological change has arisen from experiments in which particular synapses likely to be ones at which transmission characteristics are changing can be identified by nonstructural criteria.

In one series of experiments (Engert & Bonhoeffer, 1999) on very thin cultured tissue slices, the possibility of transmitter release was restricted to an approximately 30-μm diameter spot by micro-control of the ionic composition of the tissue-bathing medium, and LTP was induced in that region by pairing 30 firings of presynaptic neurons (1 per 10 s) with postsynaptic depolarization through an intracellular electrode while the spot and adjacent regions were continuously visualized. LTP began to develop within the first few pre- and postsynaptic pairings. At about 30 min after the start of pairing the growth of new spines became evident in the region where synaptic transmission was permitted but not outside it (Figure 4.6). In cases in which pairing failed to cause LTP or in which an NMDA antagonist blocked its development, new spines did not develop. However, morphological change did not require stimulation. Spines often disappeared apparently spontaneously both in and out of the spot. Indeed, in culture, spine shape changes occur continually on a second time scale (Fischer, Kaech, Knutti, & Matus, 1998).

For electron microscopic analysis, postsynaptic spines in which LTP-induction protocols have caused calcium ion elevation can be identified by staining for calcium in subcellular structures that accumulate calcium as the result of its repeated transient elevation in the spine cytoplasm during LTP induction. By fixing tissue at various times after LTP-inducing protocols, a sense of the timecourse of morphological change can be obtained (Muller, Toni, & Buchs, 2000). Ordinarily, there is a single active zone at the point of contact between presynaptic swellings and

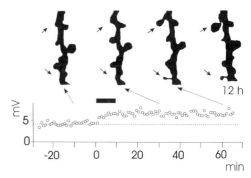

Figure 4.6   Associative LTP and its effects on dendritic spines of hippocampal CA1 neurons.
NOTE: The graph shows the intracellularly recorded amplitudes of EPSPs evoked in a CA1 neuron by electrical shocks to axons of the Schaffer collateral pathway (pathway 6 of Figure 4.1). Test shocks were given every 10 s throughout the experiment, and points are the averages of 5 responses. At the black bar 30 pairings at 1/10 s of such shocks, each during depolarizing current injection into the recorded neuron, were given. Silhouettes are shown of a small region of a dendritic branch receiving input from the stimulated afferents. These were imaged at the times indicated by the arrows and the last 12 hr later. The arrows pointing at the dendrite show where new spines later arose. In some experiments, new spines could first be seen at about 30 min postpairing, but in this case not until later (Redrawn from Engert & Boenhoffer, 1999).

dendritic spines. However, by about 30 min after induction procedures, about half of those spines showing signs of calcium ion entry display pairs of active zones with a short region of ordinary membrane apposition between them, so-called perforated synapses (Geinisman, deToledo-Morrell, & Morrell, 1991; Neuhoff, Roeper, & Schweizer, 1999). Perforated synapses are transient, being present only for about an hour. After they are gone, there is an elevated incidence of presynaptic swellings that make synaptic contact with two spines, which arise from next to each other on the same dendritic branch. It is suspected, but not established, that perforated synapses are a stage in the development of these multiple synapse arrangements.

Though major morphological change presumably requires new genetic transcription and translation, some morphological change, such as formation of new presynaptic swellings (Wu et al., 1995) and dendritic spines (Engert & Bonhoeffer, 1999) and shape changes in existing neuronal processes, may utilize mechanisms similar to those which allow an ameba to locomote by pseudopod extension and would be expected to occur without new protein synthesis (Fischer et al., 1998).

Functional changes of synaptic efficacy develop before morphological change becomes obvious, and it is these physiological changes that have received the greatest attention from neuroscientists attempting to probe the nature of learning.

The Method of Quantal Analysis

Before one can begin to identify and study physiological changes, one must identify the cells in which essential processes are occurring. Thus, a great amount of attention has been devoted to determining the relative roles of the cells on the two sides of a synapse. It would seem that the obvious way of doing this would be to measure both the amount of chemical transmitter released from the presynaptic side of the synapse and the effect of known amounts of exogenously applied transmitter on the postsynaptic neuron before and after inducing changes in efficacy. Although such experiments can sometimes be done (discussed later), there are usually considerable technical difficulties in actually carrying them out effectively; indeed, the chemical transmitter used at the changing synapse may not even be known.

Del Castillo and Katz, in their pioneering and Nobel Prize winning experiments on neuromuscular synapses, developed a generally applicable way of determining the extent to which changes in synaptic efficacy are due to altered release from the presynaptic neuron or altered response of the postsynaptic cell. This method, known as quantal analysis, depends on the fact that when transmitter is released from neurons, the release is from synaptic vesicles, each of which contains approximately the same amount of transmitter; all of this diffuses into the synaptic cleft when a vesicle forms a pore to the outside of the cell at its point of contact with the neuron membrane.

Vesicles release their contents probabilistically, each of the vesicles at the membrane is ready to release its contents randomly and independently of others. Even at rest there is a small probability of release, and the occasional spontaneous releases that occur produce tiny spontaneous, miniature synaptic potentials. Arrival of an action potential at the terminal greatly increases probability of release, but release nevertheless remains probabilistic. Thus, the amplitude of an evoked synaptic potential is always an integer multiple of the roughly constant amplitude of one spontaneous miniature (the so-called quantal size), the multiplier being the number of vesicles actually released (often referred to as the quantal content). The number of releases occurring in a given short period of time is in turn a random variable with a binomial distribution; consequently, the amplitude of spike-evoked synaptic potentials also has a binomial distribution, whose variance reflects the number of vesicles available for release (or release sites) and their individual probabilities of release. At many synapses the probability of release is low enough and the number of release sites small enough (or can be made so by pharmacological manipulations) that arrival of a spike at a terminal may cause only a few and sometimes no vesicles to release their contents. In such cases, relative frequency distributions of synaptic potential amplitude display visible peaks corresponding to no releases or one, two, and so on releases.

Quantitatively, if q is the amplitude of a spontaneous miniature, n the number of release sites, and p the probability of release at each site, then the mean evoked synaptic potential amplitude will be npq, the variance will be $nq^2 p(1 - p)$, the ratio of the standard deviation to the mean (the coefficient of variation) will be $\sqrt{[(1 - p)/np]}$, and the probability of a failure will be $(1 - p)^n$. These relationships provide a number of ways of determining whether changes in efficacy are attributable to the pre- or postsynaptic neuron. Thus, if changes in synaptic efficacy are due to altered reactivity of the postsynaptic neuron to a given amount of transmitter, then the size of spontaneous miniatures should change but measures such as the probability of release failures, the number of peaks in the relative frequency distribution of evoked synaptic potential amplitudes, and the coefficient of variation of amplitude should not. Conversely, if the per site probability of release or the number of release sites should change without postsynaptic responsiveness altering, coefficient of variation of evoked synaptic potentials, probability of failure, and the relative sizes of the various peaks in the frequency distribution of synaptic potential amplitudes will change, but the distance between peaks and the size of a spontaneous miniature will not.

Presynaptic and Postsynaptic Changes

Application of quantal analysis to *Aplysia* defense reflex sensory-motor synapses before and after inducing depression or facilitation of transmission gives results indicative of purely presynaptic change (Castellucci & Kandel, 1974, 1976; Dale et al., 1988), and a variety of experimental results, some of which we discuss in other contexts, support the occurrence of presynaptic change. However, when synapses grow and new points of synaptic contact form, new postsynaptic transmitter receptors and morphological specializations do develop (Trudeau & Castellucci, 1995; Zhu, Wu, & Schacher, 1997). It also seems pos-

sible that complexities that have arisen in the context of hippocampal synapse quantal analysis (discussed later) will eventually be seen as applying here as well.

Quantal analysis techniques have also been applied extensively to CA1 LTP. There, spontaneous miniature synaptic potentials do increase in amplitude after induction of LTP, and there is also some evidence of increased response of AMPA receptors to exogenously applied glutamate (Davies, Lester, Reymann, & Collingridge, 1989; Malenka & Nicoll, 1999; Manabe, Renner, & Nicoll, 1992; Oliet, Malenka, & Nicoll, 1996; Wyllie, Manabe, & Nicoll, 1994). Furthermore, LTP causes a greater percentage increase in the AMPA response than in the NMDA response (Kauer, Malenka, & Nicoll, 1988; Muller, Joly, & Lynch, 1988), which suggests that enhancement of transmission is not primarily a matter of increased release of transmitter, because at least on the face of it, increased release should cause commensurate increases in the responses produced by both types of glutamate receptor (unless the response of one receptor type saturates; see Perkel & Nicoll, 1993). Thus, it is widely believed that postsynaptic alterations are at least in part responsible for LTP (Malenka & Nicoll, 1999), and we will see further evidence of this shortly.

It is also found that failures decrease when LTP is induced at a CA1 synapse (Kullmann & Siegelbaum, 1995; Larkman & Jack, 1995; Nicoll & Malenka, 1995; Teyler & DiScenna, 1987), which would ordinarily be taken to imply that there must be changes in release as well. However, several studies using assays of released transmitter other than EPSP size itself, have indicated no increase whatsoever in transmitter release after induction of LTP (Diamond, Bergles, & Jahr, 1998; Luscher, Malenka, & Nicoll, 1998). How can this be rationalized with the reduction of failures? One much discussed possibility is that there are some release sites at which transmitter is released to regions of a postsynaptic neuron where there are essentially no functional AMPA receptors prior to LTP induction but where receptors get inserted (discussed later), or preexisting nonfunctional receptors get activated, when LTP is induced. In that event, releases at the postsynaptically insensitive sites would go undetected by the postsynaptic cell and be seen as failures of transmission before the induction of LTP but not after.

Currents produced by AMPA and NMDA receptors can be distinguished by sensitivity to different pharmacological receptor blockers and by other means. If one uses extracellular recording techniques to detect the currents flowing into very small regions of a postsynaptic neuron, one can find many sites that appear to be active zones (since presynaptic activity causes NMDA currents to flow into depolarized postsynaptic cells) but at which no AMPA currents whatsoever flow, implying the absence of functional AMPA receptors. However, after induction of LTP, AMPA currents are often seen at such sites (Isaac, Nicoll, & Malenka, 1995; Liao, Hessler, & Malinow, 1995). This provides strong support for the view that there are "silent" synapses that can be rapidly turned on by induction of LTP, and it provides a plausible postsynaptic explanation for failure analyses that would otherwise suggest presynaptic change.

Nature of Changes

Taking the findings from the systems we are discussing all together, it appears that alterations of synaptic efficacy can be due to physiological changes either pre- or postsynaptically. A variety of pre- and postsynaptic mechanisms can be involved.

Modulation of Presynaptic Ion Channel Properties.   The facilitation of transmitter release induced in *Aplysia* sensory neurons by 5-HT was the first learning-related

form of synaptic plasticity to be analyzed and the first for which a detailed mechanism was proposed. Release of neurotransmitter in all neurons is brought about by the entry of calcium ions into the nerve terminal; calcium entry occurs when depolarization of the terminal by arriving spikes causes the opening of the terminal's depolarization-gated calcium ion channels, which then allow extracellular calcium ions to flow down their electrochemical gradients into the terminal. Because the entry of the positively charged calcium ions itself depolarizes the terminals, a vicious cycle of depolarization-calcium ion entry-depolarization is established that tends to be self-perpetuating until the calcium channels inactivate, which they do only slowly. The opening of potassium ion channels that respond with a delay to the depolarization of the nerve terminal breaks this vicious cycle. Potassium ions then flow down their electrochemical gradients, out of the cell, terminating the terminal's depolarized state. Within a few years of the discovery of 5-HT as an inducer of presynaptic facilitation in *Aplysia* (Brunelli et al., 1976), it was found that 5-HT causes a reduction of transmembrane potassium currents that slows recovery from the terminal depolarization begun by the arrival of an action potential (Baxter, Canavier, Clark, & Byrne, 1999; Klein & Kandel, 1978, 1980; Klein, Shapiro, & Kandel, 1980). Because the repolarization occurs more slowly after exposure to 5-HT (i.e. the presynaptic spike is broadened), calcium ion levels remain high longer, and more transmitter can be released. It now appears that 5-HT actually causes the modification of a number of ionic currents through several kinds of calcium and potassium ion channels in these neurons, but probably the most important cause of presynaptic spike broadening is a reduction in the opening of potassium ion channels that open with a delay in response to depolarization (Baxter et al., 1999).

Soon after the identification of lowered potassium ion currents and consequent spike broadening as a cause of facilitation, evidence was presented that this is directly due to potassium channel phosphorylation (Shuster, Camardo, Siegelbaum, & Kandel, 1985; Siegelbaum, Camardo, & Kandel, 1982). This came from experiments in which a tiny glass, recording pipette was tightly sealed to the outside surface of a cell and the attached patch of membrane then pulled away from the parent cell. If the patch of membrane at the orifice of the recording pipette in such an experiment is sufficiently small, it will contain only a few ion channels of a any given species, each of which will independently open and close probabilistically. The basic open-state conductivity and the number of channels open can then be determined by monitoring the currents that flow into the electrode as a function of the voltage applied across the patch. In such experiments, the normal internal constituents of the cell are gone and the chemical composition on both sides of the membrane can be controlled; the extracellular surface can be accessed via the electrolyte solution in the lumen of the electrode and the intracellular surface via the medium outside the electrode. Using such an "inside-out" patch recording arrangement, it was shown that exposure of the intracellular surface of the membrane to PKA and a suitable source of phosphate lowered the opening probability of potassium ion channels in the patch. Since the rest of the cell's machinery was gone, it seemed likely that the change in channel behavior was due to direct phosphorylation catalyzed by the kinase, though it is conceivable that the effects were mediated indirectly via other chemical machinery still attached to the membrane.

It now appears that the species of potassium ion channels that were shown to be directly affected by PKA may not have been the species most responsible for spike broadening (Baxter et al., 1999). It should also be pointed out that in this and in many other experiments on *Aplysia* membrane events, cell body membrane has been used as a surrogate for the presynaptic terminal membrane, which is essentially assumed to have the same types of membrane channels. Nevertheless, these experiments came remarkably close to the extraordinary achievement of identifying a physical entity, the covalent bond between a phosphate and a particular protein, as the engram of a simple memory.

Modulation of the Pool of Synaptic Vesicles Ready for Immediate Release.   It has gradually become clear that while 5-HT-mediated spike broadening is probably an important cause of transmission enhancement at *Aplysia* sensory-motor synapses under some circumstances, such facilitation commonly occurs independent of spike broadening (Byrne & Kandel, 1996). Quantal analysis has indicated that serotonin-caused facilitation of release can often be attributed to an increase in n without an increase in p, suggesting that enhanced release may sometimes involve recruitment of new release sites (Royer, Coulson, & Klein, 2000). A similar conclusion can also be reached more directly. A technique often used to assess the number of synaptic vesicles ready for release is to observe the flurries of miniature synaptic potentials caused by exposure to hypertonic sucrose solution; the more miniatures produced by the sucrose exposure, the more vesicles in the pool readily available for release. Serotonin increases the number of miniatures produced by sucrose exposure, at least at synapses in which release is depressed by prior activity (Zhao & Klein, in press).

Modulation of Transmitter Receptor Properties.   Just as the properties of presynaptic depolarization-activated potassium channels can be modified by serotonin-stimulated phosphorylation in *Aplysia*, so too can the properties of postsynaptic transmitter-gated channels be altered by activity-stimulated phosphorylation. Thus, using a method of analyzing synaptic currents that allows single ion channel conductances to be estimated from statistical variations produced in dendritic currents by probabilistic channel openings and closings, the open-state conductance of AMPA receptors was shown to be increased by the induction of LTP (Benke, Luthi, Isaac, & Collingridge, 1998). That this change in basic open-state conductance was due to channel phosphorylation is indicated by several related findings: (a) Using radioactively labeled phosphate, it has been shown that AMPA channels do in fact become phosphorylated during LTP (Barria, Muller, Derkach, Griffith, & Soderling, 1997; Lee, Barbarosie, Kameyama, Bear, & Huganir, 2000). (b) Single-channel patch recording studies show that phosphorylation of AMPA receptors by activated CaMK II causes an increase in single-channel conductance comparable to that occurring during LTP (Derkach et al., 1999). (c) AMPA receptor phosphorylation is prevented by a pharmacological agent that specifically prevents CaMK II from being activated by calcium ions (Barria et al., 1997).

Receptors that let ions pass through the cell membrane when stimulated by transmitter are composed of a ring of subunits with the ion-passing channel in the center; typically, the ring is composed of several different types of subunits. By searching for point mutations that cause CaMK II to lose its effects on the AMPA channel, it has been shown that CaMK II phosphorylates serine 831 of the GluR1 subunits of AMPA receptors (Barria et al.,1997). Interestingly, LTD does not seem to be due simply to reducing phosphorylation at the same site phosphorylated by LTP. Rather, another site (serine-848 on the same subunit), which appears to be phosphorylated at "naive" synapses, looses its phosphate when LTD is induced (Lee et al., 2000).

This lowers EPSP amplitudes, not by reducing AMPA channel conductance, but by lowering the probability that glutamate will open channels (Banke et al., 2000). Thus, at the molecular level LTP and LTD may not be directly opposite effects; induction of one does not necessarily undo the other.

Adding and Subtracting Receptors.   In addition to causing changes in the functional properties of existing transmitter receptors, activity can also lead to the addition or subtraction of postsynaptic receptors. The most direct evidence for this comes from experiments in which GluR1 subunits of AMPA receptors that had been tagged with a green fluorescent protein were introduced into CA1 region neurons of cultured hippocampal slices by viral transfection (Shi et al., 1999). Several days later, the green fluorescent tag could be seen throughout the shafts of dendritic trees but not in synaptic spines. However, focal tetanic stimulation sufficient to produce LTP caused green label to appear within the spines receiving synaptic input within 15 min, where it was then incorporated into the surface membrane. This did not happen in the presence of the NMDA blocker, APV. Receptors are thought to be inserted into the cell membrane by first being incorporated into the membrane of internal vesicles via the cell's endoplasmic reticulum and Golgi apparatus, then fusing with the cell membrane in much the same way that synaptic vesicles do when they release transmitter (as mentioned before). Receptors are thought to be removed by a converse process wherein the receptor-containing membrane invaginates and then gets pinched off as an internal vesicle (endocytosis). Even at rest, there appears to be a steady removal by endocytosis and replenishment by vesicle mediated receptor insertion (Man, Ju, Ahmadian, & Wang, 2000). If various agents known to interfere with fusion of vesicles to the membrane are introduced into a neuron, the amount of LTP produced by a given induction procedure is greatly reduced compared to that produced in adjacent uninjected cells (Lledo, Zhang, Sudhof, & Malenka, 1998). Conversely both hippocampal (Luscher et al., 1999; Man, Lin, et al., 2000) and Purkinje neuron (Xia, Chung, Wihler, Huganir, & Linden, 2000) LTD induction are attenuated by agents that block endocytosis.

Intracellular Chemical Signaling Systems Involved in Producing Change

The role of intracellular chemical signaling systems in the production of synaptic change was first established when it was found that the cAMP/PKA signaling pathway mediates serotonergic facilitation of transmitter release in *Aplysia*. Thus, introduction of cAMP or the catalytic part of cAMP-dependent protein kinase (PKA) was found to mimic the facilitation of transmission caused by trauma or 5-HT; the introduction of an agent that prevents effective catalysis by PKA was found to prevent facilitation by 5-HT; and cAMP levels in sensory neurons were seen to rise when they were exposed to 5-HT or when animals received traumatic stimulation (Bernier, Castellucci, Kandel, & Schwartz, 1982; Brunelli et al., 1976; Castellucci et al., 1980; Castellucci, Nairn, Greengard, Schwartz, & Kandel, 1982).

As the signaling systems involved in producing synaptic change have continued to be studied, it has become clear that development of any given type of synaptic plasticity can be encouraged or discouraged by manipulations that affect any of quite a number of different intracellular signaling systems. This should come as no surprise, because, typically, any given signaling molecule affects not only chemical reactions within its own signaling pathway but also reactions within others. Indeed, the chemical signaling pathways of a

neuron (or any kind of cell for that matter) seem best thought of as complex *networks* of interacting molecules and chemical reactions that may well perform information processing tasks *within* neurons and other cells in a manner analogous to the processing done in the nervous system as a whole by *inter*cellular networks of neurons and synapses.

Figure 4.7a–c sketches one view of some of the signaling systems that seem to be involved in the synaptic plasticities that are the focus of this chapter. For now, we consider only the biochemical circuitry drawn with solid black lines (we discuss the circuitry indicated by dashed lines in the next section).

Facilitation of Transmitter Release in Aplysia Sensory Neurons

cAMP was the first signaling molecule implicated in control of synaptic function in *Aplysia*. The binding of 5-HT to a suitable 5-HT receptor causes the activation of the enzyme adenylate cyclase (via activation of a membrane G-protein), which then catalyzes the formation of cAMP. cAMP in turn causes the activation of PKA, which phosphorylates membrane potassium ion channels and also mobilizes transmitter for release, as described before (Figure 4.7a, pathway 1).

An interesting feature of this signaling pathway is that calcium ions amplify andenylate cyclase's catalysis of cAMP production. This feature led to the conjecture that the activity-dependence of presynaptic facilitation (the initially conjectured basis for classical conditioning) is due to amplification of cAMP production by the calcium ions that enter active presynaptic terminals (Figure 4.7a, pathway 2; Abrams, 1985; Abrams, Karl, & Kandel, 1991; Yovell & Abrams, 1992). Consistent with this explanation for activity dependence, activity no longer amplifies serotonin-caused facilitation if a calcium ion chelator has been infused into the sensory neuron (by using EGTA, a slowly acting chelator, it is possible to affect the activity dependence of facilitation while still allowing presynaptic calcium to cause transmitter release; Bao et al., 1998).

Subsequent work established that serotonin also causes the activation of another kinase, protein kinase C, or PKC (Figure 4.7a, pathway 3). PKA and PKC can each facilitate release by causing increases in the duration of spike-produced calcium entry via reductions in potassium ion currents (Figure 4.7a, pathway 4), and by mobilizing vesicles for release (Figure 4.7a, pathway 5). Both can also increase numbers of presynaptic transmitter containing varicosities along branches of a sensory neurons terminal arbor. Although the functional significance of using both PKA and PKC to recruit similar processes is not yet understood, it does not appear that these are simply redundant pathways because, with the use of selective inhibitors of each pathway, it can be shown that each exerts effective control over transmitter release under somewhat different circumstances. For example, PKA-mediation dominates when synapses are fresh whereas PKC becomes progressively more important when synapses are depressed due to use (all thoroughly reviewed in Byrne & Kandel, 1996).

Associative LTP in Hippocampal Neurons

In hippocampal neurons in which calcium ions have entered dendrites through NMDA channels in response to joint presynaptic activity and postsynaptic depolarization, the calcium causes activation of CaMK II (Figure 4.7b, pathway 1), which as we have already discussed, phosphorylates AMPA receptors at a site which alters their intrinsic open-state conductance. Generally, whatever means is used to elevate the amount of activated CaMK II, whether by direct injection (Lledo et al., 1995) or by viral tansfection (Pettit, Perlman, & Malinow, 1994), causes an increase in the efficacy of AMPA receptor-

mediated transmission, and treatments that block CaMK II activation or catalytic effect prevent induction of LTP (Malenka, Kauer, Perkel et al., 1989; Malinow, 1991). These findings obviously support a central role for CaMK II in the production of LTP, a view that is widely favored (Lisman, 1994; Lisman, Malenka, Nicoll, & Malinow, 2001; Malenka & Nicoll, 1999).

As we will discuss later, available evidence suggests that phosphate is rather rapidly removed from the targets of protein kinases. One would therefore expect that maintenance of LTP would depend on the persistent activation of whatever protein kinases induce it, and in fact when drugs that block CaMK II's catalytic action (but that are not all that selective) are added to the medium bathing a slice, potentiated EPSPs return to their pre-potentiated size (Malinow, Madison, & Tsien, 1988). Moreover, once LTP has been induced, extracts of CA1 neurons are able to catalyze phosphorylation of foreign targets of CaMK II for over an hour after LTP induction even in the absence of elevated calcium ion levels (Fukunaga, Stoppini, Miyamoto, & Muller, 1993). Thus, CaMK II appears to become constitutively activated. However, comparable experiments using very specific CaMK II blockers introduced only postsynaptically, which should have the same effect, do not necessarily do so (see Chen, Otmakhov, Strack, Colbran, & Lisman, 2001; Otmakhov, Griffith, & Lisman, 1997).

The reason for this is not understood. But PKC phosphorylates the same site on the GluR1 subunit of AMPA receptors as does CaMK II (Figure 4.7b, pathway 10; Roche, O'Brien, Mammen, Bernhardt, & Huganir, 1996), and PKC becomes constitutively activated following induction of LTP (Hrabetova & Sacktor, 1996; Klann, Chen, & Sweatt, 1993; Sacktor et al., 1993; Wang & Feng, 1992). Thus, one of several possibilities is that CaMK II may not act alone (Otmakhov et al.,

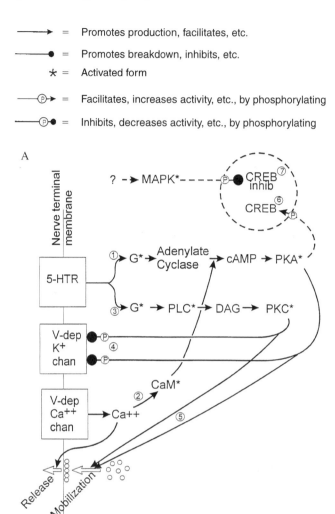

Figure 4.7   Intracellular signaling pathways involved in changing synaptic properties.
NOTE: The pathways shown are selected, and a few are not firmly established. To avoid unnecessary complexity, some intermediates are omitted. Most signaling molecules shown are discussed in the text; abbreviations not defined here are standard and can be found in any textbook of cellular physiology. Receptors (mGluR, NMDAR, AMPAR, and so on) and channels [V-dep K^+ chan (voltage-dependent calcium potassium ion channel) and V-dep Ca^{++} chan (voltage-dependent calcium ion channel)] are indicated at the membrane but no attempt was made to indicate which signaling molecules are membrane associated. Circled numbers are referred to in the text.

A. Pathways involved in presynaptic facilitation in *Aplysia*. See text for explanation. In this and subsequent parts of this figure, some signaling pathway molecules not mentioned in the text (e.g., PLC and DAG) are identified to help orient readers familiar with them; however, the identity of these molecules is irrelevant to the present discussion.

B. Pathways involved in hippocampal associative LTP and hippocampal LTD. See text for explanation. Three types of receptors that respond to glutamate are indicated at the membrane. The dotted line between calcium ions is intended to emphasize that it may be possible for calcium ions that enter the cell through NMDA receptors and the calcium ions that are released from internal stores within the cell by the second messenger IP_3 to summate their effects on downstream processes that are affected by calcium ions. TFs = unspecified transcription factors.

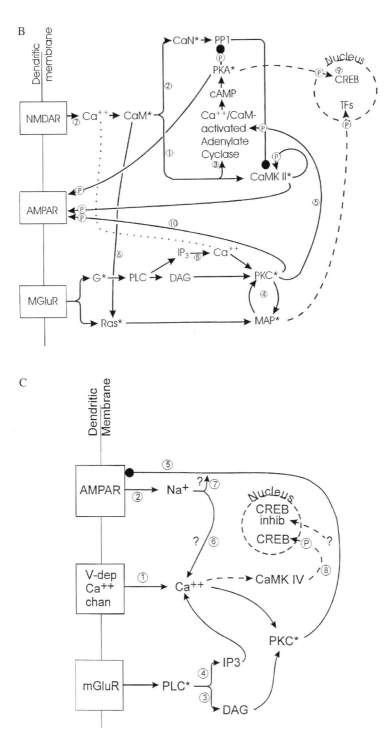

Figure 4.7 (Continued)   C. Pathways involved in Purkinje cell LTD. See text for explanation. The figure portrays a common pool of calcium ion to which both calcium entering through voltage-dependent calcium ion channels and calcium released from internal stores by IP_3 may contribute. Whether the latter source of calcium ion actually contributes to the activation of PKC is a matter of discussion.

1997). Another possibility is that once new AMPA receptors have been added (as mentioned earlier) CaMK II-catalyzed phosphorylation may no longer be needed to maintain enhanced transmission.

Later, we discuss the question of what maintains kinases in an activated state. However, it should be noted that one factor which has predisposed investigators to favor CaMK II mediation of LTP is that an appealing explanation for its constitutive activation is at hand.

The basic mechanism for induction of LTD is thought to be the calcium-stimulated activation of protein phosphatase-1, a molecule that when activated dephosphorylates CaMK II (Figure 4.7b, pathway 2; Bhalla & Iyengar, 1999; Lisman, 1994). There is however a complication. At least under some circumstances, the crucial stimulus triggering LTP and LTD is thought to be qualitatively the same, a transient elevation of calcium on the postsynaptic side of the synapse. A small calcium concentration increase is believed to cause depression whereas a large increase causes potentiation (Artola & Singer, 1993; Dudek & Bear, 1993; Lisman, 1994; Mulkey & Malenka, 1992). This creates a conundrum: Why do to the high calcium levels that are believed to cause potentiation not cause extensive activation of protein phosphatase-1 with a consequent competing depressive action? The answer appears to be provided by the presence of a cAMP pathway (Figure 4.7b, pathway 3) that begins with a particular variety of adenylate cyclase molecule that is calcium/calmodulin-activated (signaling molecules generally come in a variety of closely related isoforms, each having its own special properties). Calcium ion levels that are high enough to cause LTP rather than LTD are thought to activate this cAMP pathway, which causes the phosphorylation of protein phosphatase-1 at a site that renders it inactive (Bhalla & Iyengar, 1999; Lisman, 1994).

Thus, the biochemical circuitry indicated in Figure 4.7b essentially allows one level of a quantitative variable to produce one effect and a different level to produce a quite different effect.

Purkinje   Neuron   LTD.   Cerebellar Purkinje cell LTD develops when a set of parallel fibers and the one climbing fiber innervating a Purkinje cell are coactive. The climbing fiber activity causes calcium ions to enter the neuron throughout the entire dendritic arbor (Figure 4.7c, pathway 1). Active parallel fibers stimulate both AMPA receptors, which cause sodium ions to enter the dendrite (Figure 4.7c, pathway 2), and metabotropic glutamate receptors, which cause local production of the second messenger DAG (Figure 4.7c, pathway 3) and additional entry of calcium ions into the dendrite from internal stores (via production of the second messenger IP_3 (Figure 4.7c, pathway 4; Linden & Connor, 1995). DAG/calcium-dependent protein kinase (PKA) is thereby activated locally. PKC activation has been shown by use of PKC-activating agents (phorbol esters) to be sufficient to cause Purkinje LTD, and the use of a variety of manipulations that suppress PKC's catalytic effect show this to be necessary (Linden & Connor, 1991, 1995). Thus, the cell-wide dendritic calcium signal caused by a US (via climbing fiber activity) and synapse-specific DAG signal caused by the CS (via stimulation of metabotropic glutamate receptors) jointly establish the conditions normally needed for activation of PKC, which once activated causes changes leading to depression of transmission at the synapses of active parallel fibers (Figure 4.7c, pathway 5). Unfortunately, this story is not quite complete because, whereas it is known that the sodium ions that enter through AMPA channels are necessary for LTD induction, the biochemical reasons for this necessity remain obscure. Perhaps elevation of sodium ion concentration indirectly promotes calcium ion accumulation (Figure 4.7c, pathway 6) or perhaps sodium ions somehow enhance the ability of PKC to induce depression (Figure 4.7c, pathway 7; Linden and Connor, 1995; Linden, Smeyne, & Connor, 1993).

Memory

The basis for memory, especially very long-term memory, is one of the great mysteries of behavioral neuroscience. There is a natural tendency to assume that synaptic changes that are the basis for lifelong learning should themselves be intrinsically stable for a lifetime. But this is to make the error of assuming that cellular phenomenology must be isomorphic to behavioral phenomenology. We will see that stability of change at the cellular level may rely, not on intrinsically stable molecular changes, but on biochemical positive feedback loops in which intrinsically rather short-lived changes, once established, are continually reestablished. The same could hold at the systems level. At least in principle, the circuitry of the brain could encode algorithms for the periodic readout and reestablishment of synaptic change. Indeed, it has recently been reported that newly learned fear of a context is rapidly forgotten if NMDA receptor function in CA1 is knocked out *after* completion of training (Shimizu et al., 2000). Earlier, it was suggested that perhaps this was because hippocampal memories must be reestablished when they are read out in the process of transferring them out of the hippocampus. But it seems not inconceivable that they must be refreshed simply to be retained.

The Intrinsic Longevity of Synaptic Change

How long do the forms of plasticity under discussion here actually last? The longevity of LTP is typically studied by tetanizing input pathways to CA1 or dentate neurons via chronically implanted electrodes in waking animals, assessing it by means of extracellular field potential recording (Barnes, 1979; Bliss & Lynch, 1988; Buzsaki, 1980; de Jonge & Racine, 1985; Racine, Milgram, & Hafner, 1983; Staubli & Lynch, 1987). There has in fact been astoundingly little work of this sort done, given the prominence with which LTP is put forward as a memory mechanism. Based on the few studies that have been done, LTP is usually said to persist for perhaps weeks but to be far from permanent. However, as discussed by Staubli and Lynch, apparent lack of persistence could be a technical artifact; from their work one might be led to suspect that perhaps LTP can persist indefinitely. Much more work is needed on this important issue. Behavioral sensitization in *Aplysia,* presumed to be indicative of serotonergic facilitation, can persist with gradual decay for several weeks (Pinsker et al., 1973). Eye-blink conditioning itself persists a long time; however, it is difficult to estimate the duration of activity-dependent synaptic changes in the cerebellum, because all of the neurons involved display considerable spontaneous firing, which might itself produce new or reverse established change (see Medina & Mauk, 1999). In order to circumvent this problem, LTD has been studied in granule cell–Purkinje cell cocultures in which tetorodotoxin has been used to prevent all firing. LTD was produced by pairing glutamate exposure with Purkinje cell depolarization, and its duration was evaluated by measuring the amplitude of synaptic currents produced by spontaneous vesicular release. Under these circumstances LTD lasted only 2–3 days (Murashima & Hirano, 1999).

One might well have doubts as to the significance of Purkinje LTD longevity assessed under such abnormal conditions, and one might also wonder whether LTP established at synapses in the brain of a behaving animal is perhaps undone by LTD produced by uncontrolled experiences during the retention interval. Resolution of such uncertainties and an understanding of the basis for life-long or even months-long memory is still, alas, in the future. Nevertheless, it is a commonly held article of faith that what is learned by studying the manifestly day- and week-long plasticities that have been discovered will move us toward understanding more permanent memory.

Stages of Memory

It has long been known that memories of different age are stored differently. Thus, very recently acquired memory is disrupted by treatments like electroconvulsive shock that scramble or otherwise disrupt the ongoing activity of the brain, whereas older memories are not (McGaugh, 1966, 2000). Inhibition of gene transcription or translation does not seem to prevent new learning and does not prevent short periods of retention (hours), but does seem to prevent establishment of memories that last days, or more (see Davis & Squire, 1984). These older findings have had significant heuristic impact, but we have now entered an entirely new phase of inquiry. As the mechanisms involved in producing synaptic change have begun to be uncovered and the exact nature of the changes identified, it has become possible to investigate the bases of retention with a level of specificity previously unimagined.

Consistent with older behavioral findings, establishment of activity-dependent synaptic changes have generally been found to proceed normally and be retained for a short time, up to a few hours, even when translation of messenger RNAs into new protein or new messenger RNA transcription has been suppressed pharmacologically. However, transcription and translation are usually necessary if changes are to persist for 24 hr or more (Goelet, Castellucci, Schacher, & Kandel, 1986), and this is specifically the case for long-term facilitation in *Aplysia* (see Goelet et al., 1986), a late phase of hippocampal LTP

(Frey, Huang, & Kandel, 1993; Nguyen et al., 1994, 1996), and a late phase of Purkinje LTD (Linden, 1996). Thus, it is common to distinguish two forms of memory, short-term change, which does not depend on new transcription or translation and which persists for less than 24 hr, and long-term change, which does require new transcription and translation for its establishment and which persists for at least 24 hr and presumably considerably longer.

While these working definitions are convenient, it is becoming clear that their utility is limited. Thus, it is not always the case that new protein synthesis is required for 24 hr memory. In *Drosophila*, on which much important genetic analysis of learning has been done, massed training can result in protein synthesis-independent memory that is still strong at 24 hr, though it is gone by 4 days (Dubnau & Tully, 1998; Yin et al., 1994), and under certain circumstances, activity and 5-HT-dependent synaptic facilitation in *Aplysia* can persist for at least 24 hr, despite the suppression of protein synthesis (Bailey, Giustetto, Zhu, Chen, & Kandel, 2000).

Also, it is increasingly becoming clear that the division of memory into just two stages, short and long, is oversimplified. Thus, by varying regimens of 5-HT exposure or 5-HT exposure in combination with activity of the presynaptic cell, one can produce at least half a dozen distinguishable types of synaptic facilitation in *Aplysia:* (a) protein synthesis-independent facilitation perhaps lasting only a few minutes that appears to depend on activation of presynaptic PKA by persistently activated G-protein (Schwartz et al., 1983), (b) protein synthesis-independent facilitation that lasts over 24 hr (Bailey et al., 2000), (c) protein synthesis-independent facilitation lasting 1–3 hr that depends on persisting PKC activity (Sutton & Carew, 2000; see also Wu et al., 1995), (d) protein synthesis-dependent but transcription-independent facilitation that lasts 1–3 hr and that depends on persisting PKA activity (Sutton & Carew, 2000; Sutton et al., 2001; and see Ghirardi et al., 1995; Muller & Carew, 1998; Wu et al., 1995), (e) transcription-dependent facilitation that may begin within 30 min and persists beyond 24 hr without any apparent anatomical change (Casadio et al., 1999), (f) transcription-dependent facilitation that is present at 72 hr and is associated with formation of new branches, varicosities, and so on in the presynaptic neuron (Casadio et al., 1999). Study of classical conditioning in *Drosophila* (Dubnau & Tully, 1998) and of effects of fear learning in rats (McGaugh, 2000) also indicate the need to postulate more than two stages of memory formation. The very concept of stages of memory is also somewhat suspect because this term implies a process of serial transformation that may not hold (Emptage & Carew, 1993; Mauelshagen et al., 1996; and see McGaugh, 2000).

Mechanisms of Retention

Phosphorylation Seems Not to Be Intrinsically Stable.   We have seen that a crucial step in inducing the synaptic changes we have discussed is the activation of protein kinases, which produce change by phosphorylating various cellular proteins. The chemical bonds that form between these proteins and phosphate groups are covalent ones, and covalent bonds are essentially permanent; once formed, they do not get broken unless undone by specific chemical reactions designed to undo them. Thus, one might well be tempted to attribute at least protein synthesis-independent memory to the intrinsic stability of phosphate-protein bonds. However, though exceptions may yet be found, it seems to be the case that phosphorylation-dependent synaptic changes are generally undone by enzymes that are dedicated to that role (phosphatases) within a matter of seconds to minutes (however see Chen et al., 2001; Fukunaga et al., 2000).

The first test of the intrinsic stability of phosphorylation-dependent synaptic change was done on serotonin-induced facilitation at *Aplysia* sensory-motor synapses (Castellucci et al., 1982; Schwartz et al., 1983). Once facilitation had been established, a pharmacological inhibitor of PKA's catalytic activity was injected into the sensory neuron. If the phosphorylations that had been catalyzed by the serotonin-activated PKA were inherently stable, the synaptic facilitation should have persisted. But in fact it immediately declined. Similarly, CaMKII inhibitors have been shown to cause rapid loss of potentiated response after induction of LTP in hippocampal neurons (Malinow et al., 1988). PKC inhibitors do not cause reversal of Purkinje LTD (Linden & Connor, 1991), but this is presumably not because PKC-catalyzed phosphorylations persist but because AMPA receptors have been physically removed from the cell membrane by endocytosis (discussed earlier).

At least for some hours or even days after induction of synaptic change, functional memory can be based on the maintained activity of protein kinases. Thus, whereas LTP-enhanced EPSPs may be reduced to their prepotentiated size by drugs that block the catalytic activity of activated protein kinases, potentiation spontaneously returns when the drug is washed out, indicating that relevant kinases are still activated (Malinow et al., 1988). In *Aplysia,* it has been shown that extracts from sensory neurons that had been exposed to 5-HT some hours before would catalyze the addition of phosphate to a foreign protein that was an appropriate substrate for PKA, indicating that PKA was still activated (Muller and Carew, 1998), and following induction of LTP, hippocampal neurons can catalyze phosphorylation of foreign substrates of CaMK II (Fukunaga et al., 1993).

Kinase Activation May Be Maintained by Positive Feedback.   What keeps kinases active after removal of the original activating stimulus? One of the most interesting and most widely discussed, but not yet fully established, mechanisms is that of *autophosphorylation*. Autophosphorylation was at first suggested, purely hypothetically, as an ideal way of explaining memory (Crick, 1984; Lisman, 1985). It seemed plausible to suppose that synaptic strengths might be coded by the state of phosphorylation of proteins at each synapse, but known protein phosphorylation was generally unstable (due to the presence of phosphatases), and proteins themselves are subject to turnover. It was reasoned that persistent memory *could* be achieved if protein kinases were subject to their own catalytic effects, *and* phosphorylation rendered them active even in the absence of their normal activating second messenger. Once activated, a kinase with these properties would add phosphates to accessible molecules of its own kind and thereby maintain its activity despite molecular turnover and the action of phosphatases. Modeling of the conjectured chemical reactions indicated that the phosphorylated state of a local group of such kinases would indeed perpetuate itself (Lisman, 1985).

Soon after this proposal was offered, it was discovered that CaMK II has exactly the conjectured properties. When activated by calcium, CaMK II phosphorylates itself (as well as its other target proteins), and once this has happened, CaMK II remains active even in the absence of elevated calcium ion concentration. Thereafter, a variety of findings were made that seemed consistent with the view that autophosphorylation of CaMK II might be the basis for at least the early retention of LTP and even some learning. For example, it was found that, as mentioned earlier, extracts from cells in which LTP has been induced have heightened CaMK II activity for at least

an hour after induction in the absence of high calcium (Fukunaga et al., 1993), and CaMK II is in fact phosphorylated (Fukunaga et al., 1995). Furthermore, both LTP and a variety of forms of learning fail to persist if the site on CaMK II that is subject to autophosphorylation is mutated (Giese, Federov, Filipkowski, & Silva, 1998). Overall, a rather good case for the validity of this hypothesis can now be made (Lisman, 1994; Lisman et al., 2001). However, the hypothesis predicts that after an exposure to an inhibitor of CaMK II's catalytic action that is sufficient to cause return of EPSPs to their pre-LTP level (and thus presumably long enough for most of the kinase to become dephosphorylated), EPSPs should not recover their potentiated amplitude when the inhibitor is washed out. Unfortunately, there seems to be excellent recovery of potentiated response (Malinow et al., 1988) after inhibitor washout, leaving the validity of the hypothesis in doubt.

The autophosphorylation hypothesis amounts to storage based on a biochemical positive feedback loop. Another such loop involves *mitogen-associated protein* (MAP) *kinase,* a kinase that is involved in growth hormone-stimulated protein synthesis. PKC and MAP kinase mutually promote one another's activation (via several intermediate steps; Figure 4.7b, pathway 4). Computational modeling of the chemical reactions involved predicts that once sufficient concentrations of these kinases are transiently activated due to signals generated by suitable extracellular stimulation, both MAP and PKC will maintain their activation as the result of their mutual interaction. The other signaling systems we have already discussed interact with this MAP-PKC loop via pathway 5 and 6 in Figure 4.7b and by their common dependence on calcium ions, which becomes elevated both by passage into the cell through NMDA channels (Figure 4.6b, pathway 7) and by recruitment from intracellular stores by IP_3 (Figure 4.7b, pathway 8); the system as a whole is at least theoretically much more prone to show robust preservation of CaMK II activation after a transient exposure to glutamate plus postsynaptic cell depolarization than it would be if autophosphorylation were the only mechanism promoting persistent CaMK II activation (Bhalla & Iyengar, 1999).

Protein Synthesis-Dependent Stabilization of Kinase Activation. The above mechanisms do not involve new protein synthesis, but 24 hr-long serotonergic facilitation in *Aplysia* withdrawal sensory-motor synapses, which also involves the persistent activity of a kinase, PKA, requires new transcription and translation (Castellucci, Blumenfeld, Goelet, & Kandel, 1989; Goelet et al., 1986; Montarolo et al., 1986). The explanation is intriguing (Bergold et al., 1990; Chain et al., 1999; Greenberg, Castellucci, Bayley, & Schwartz, 1987; Hegde et al., 1997): PKA is composed of two loosely joined parts, a catalytic part and a regulatory part that when joined to the catalytic part suppresses its activity. cAMP activates PKA by binding to the regulatory part, thereby allowing it to dissociate from the catalytic portion and freeing it to act. Analysis of PKA from sensory neurons that have been exposed to 5-HT using regimens that produce long-term facilitation shows a reduction in the total amount of regulatory subunit, a reduction that does not occur if the sensory neuron was stimulated while exposed to drugs that inhibit genetic transcription or translation (Figure 4.8). No such reduction of regulatory subunit occurs if the 5-HT regimen was one that produces only short-term facilitation. Thus, it appears that in this case one function of genetic transcription and translation is to produce a protein that breaks down regulatory subunit and thereby frees the catalytic part of PKA to operate continuously. Of course, one must also explain why new regulatory subunits do not promptly

get synthesized to replace those that were degraded. Nevertheless, this provides us with an interesting model for the kind of role that protein synthesis may play in the development of long-term memory.

Morphological Change. Aside from what was mentioned earlier, not a lot can yet be said about what the new transcription and translation, which seem to be essential to long-term memory formation, actually do. At least in *Aplysia,* relatively major morphological alterations, such as the development of new terminal arbor branches, seem to require new transcription and translation (Bailey, Bartsch, & Kandel, 1996; Bailey, Montarolo, Chen, Kandel, & Schacher, 1992; Martin, Casadio et al., 1997). Sometimes investigators speak as though they believed that the basis for memory would have been found if it were shown that learning is due to morphological change. But of course this merely passes the problem on to the developmental biologist who must then explain the basis for the stability of anatomical form.

Initiation of Transcription-Dependent Stabilization: CREB and CREB Inhibitor. Whatever the exact functions of protein synthesis in establishing synaptic changes that will endure, the involvement of genetic transcription in stabilizing change raises two crucial questions: (a) How does the nucleus know to begin transcription? (b) Why do the translated proteins coded by the new transcripts affect only selected synapses? Significant progress is being made in answering both questions.

Transcription is controlled via proteins called *transcription factors* that when phosphorylated bind to DNA and turn on transcription of associated genes. The transcription factor called *cyclic AMP response element binding protein* (CREB), which when phosphorylated binds to a specific nucleotide

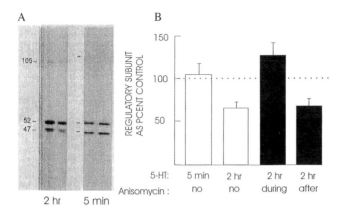

Figure 4.8   Effects of sensitization on amount of PKA regulatory subunit.

NOTE: A previous experiment (Greenberg et al., 1987) had demonstrated decreases in regulatory subunit after behavioral long-term sensitization training. In this study, sensitization was induced by directly exposing sensory neuron cell bodies to serotonin. Bilateral clusters of cell bodies were dissected out of pleural ganglia and maintained in sea water. Those of one side were exposed to 5-HT or the protein synthesis blocker, anisomysin, according to various schedules; those of the other side were used as controls (always processed along with the experimentally treated cells); the cells were then maintained in sea water for 24 hr. They were then homogenized and the homogenate mixed with an excess of radioactive cAMP, found only on regulatory subunits of PKA, that binds to all available cAMP binding sites, and thereby makes the regulatory subunit molecules identifiable. The material was finally separated according to molecular size by electrophoresis on polyacrylamide gels, the regulatory subunit molecules of which there are two major isoforms appearing as distinct bands, and exposed to a photographic emulsion to detect the presence of regulatory subunit. A. Gels for cells exposed to 5-HT for either 5 min, which induces only short-term facilitation in intact ganglia, or for 2 hr, which produces long-term facilitation. It will be seen that there is a decrease in the amount of regulatory subunit in both bands for the cell clusters that had been exposed to 5-HT for 2 hr but not those exposed for 5 min. B. Amount of radioactivity in both the 52,000 and 47,000 molecular weight bands is shown quantitatively for several 5-HT/anisomycin regimens. Note that 2-hr exposure causes a loss of radioactivity, also that this is prevented if protein synthesis is blocked during the 2-hr 5-HT exposure period, and that it is not prevented if protein synthesis is blocked after the 2-hr 5-HT exposure period SOURCE: Adapted from Borgold et al., 1990.

sequence (the *cAMP response element* or CRE) found in the regulatory region of certain genes, is currently believed to be the agent through which synaptic change-stabilizing protein synthesis is turned on in a variety of animals (Figure 4.7a, pathway 6; Figure 4.7b, pathway 9). CREB was so named because it binds to the regulatory region of and turns on transcription of those genes that can be turned on by cAMP. The first evidence for its involvement in synaptic plasticity came from experiments in which it was found that injecting an abundance of artificially synthesized CRE sequences into the nucleus of an *Aplysia* sensory neuron would prevent it from developing long-term facilitation (Dash, Hochner, & Kandel, 1990). The abundant CRE sequences presumably competed with native CRE of the genome for a limited amount of phosphorylated CREB. In later experiments, genetic engineering techniques were used to fuse CRE sequences to a bacterial lacZ gene that when active made an easily detectable product foreign to *Aplysia*. When sensory neurons into which these CRE-lacZ molecules had been injected were stimulated with 5-HT, the neurons made lacZ product when the neurons were stimulated by serotonin using protocols that would cause long-term facilitation but not when protocols that produce only short-term facilitation were utilized (Kaang, Kandel, & Grant, 1993). Injection of anti-CREB antibodies into *Aplysia* neurons also prevents the induction of long- but not short-term serotonergic facilitation (Martin, Casadio et al., 1997). A variety of experiments have also implicated CREB, and the cAMP pathway in the establishment of long-lasting (beyond a few hours) hippocampal LTP (Bourtchuladze et al., 1994; Frey et al., 1993; Huang & Kandel, 1994; Nguyen & Kandel, 1996), in various forms of hippocampus-dependent and hippocampus-independent long-term learning in mice (Bourtchuladze et al., 1994) and even in protein synthesis-dependent long-term learning in fruit flies (Dubnau & Tully, 1998; Yin, Del Vecchio, Zhou, & Tully, 1995; Yin et al., 1994). The protein synthesis-dependent late phase of Purkinje LTD also appears to be mediated via CREB, in this case phosphorylated by CaMK IV rather than via the cAMP pathway (Ahn et al., 1999).

In addition to CREB, a closely related protein, which we will call *CREB inhibitor*, is also found in *Aplysia,* humans, rodents, and fruit flies. Phosphorylated CREB inhibitor prevents CREB-induced transcription. The ratio of CREB to CREB inhibitor in a cell might influence its propensity to undergo long-lasting activity-dependent change (Yin et al., 1995), and the establishment of long-term change may well require suppression of CREB inhibitors as well as the activation of transcripton-inducing CREB (Bartsch et al., 1995; Martin, Michael et al., 1997). In fact, when the relative amounts of CREB and CREB inhibitor are altered experimentally, propensity for long-term learning does appear to be altered. Normally, single brief exposures of cultured *Aplysia* sensory-motor synapses to 5-HT induce only short-term facilitation of transmission; multiple spaced exposures are needed to induce 24 hr facilita-tion. However, if anti-CREB inhibitor antibodies are injected into the sensory neuron, a single pulse of serotonin causes 24 hr facilitation (Bartsch, Casadio, Karl, Serodio, & Kandel, 1998). In *Drosophila,* relatively transient classically conditioned odor aversions can be learned after a single association of an odor with electric shock, but long-term, protein synthesis-dependent retention normally requires multiple spaced epochs of training. However, genetic engineering techniques have been used to create mutants in which genes for producing extra CREB (but not CREB inhibitor) can be activated at will by exposing flies to a brief heat shock. After activating these genes, single pairings of odor with electric shock produce learning that has long-term persistence (Yin et al., 1995). Flies with "photographic memories" are thereby produced. Conversely, production of extra CREB inhibitor produces flies that fail to learn even with extensive training (Yin et al., 1994).

The Superiority of Spaced Practice; a Molecular Hypothesis.   The discovery in *Drosophila* of the effects on classical conditioning of CREB and CREB inhibitor has led to a hypothesis that may account for the well known superiority of spaced over massed training for producing learning that will endure, a superiority that holds dramatically for classical conditioning in flies (Tully et al., 1996). The suggestion is that under normal circumstances the balance of CREB and CREB inhibitor in the relevant neurons of *Drosophila* is such that immediately after a training trial, phosphorylated CREB inhibitor completely suppresses the transcription promoting effect of phosphorylated CREB. However over time, the dephosphorylation of CREB inhibitor proceeds more rapidly than that of CREB, with the result that a bit of protein synthesis is induced before both transcription factors become dephosphorylated to the point of inactivity. Therefore, if trials are spaced, each trial provides for a little bit more synthesis of the proteins that stabilize the changes on which long-term learned behavior depends; with sufficient spaced training long-term learning is thus established. But if trials are massed, CREB inhibitor becomes rephosphorylated too often to allow a pause in its effect, so no stabilization of learning is possible. If this hypothesis is correct, increasing the amount of CREB in a cell would make it possible for massed training to lead to long-term change, whereas increasing the amount of CREB inhibitor would prevent learning from occurring even with spaced training. Both predictions have been verified in *Drosophila* (Yin et al., 1995; Yin et al., 1994). The findings in *Drosophila* and *Aplysia* have led to comparable experiments in mammals. In mice, effects of underexpressing CREB are as predicted for several types of learning (Kogan et al., 1997), and overexpression of CREB, specifically within the amygdala, facilitates the long-term classical conditioning of fear to tones that predict shock (Josselyn et al., 2001).

Targeting Stabilization of Change. Once the nucleus has been signaled to transcribe mRNA coding for proteins needed to stabilize synaptic change and the proteins have been made, where do these proteins go? One might imagine that the signals received by the nucleus provide information about the location of the synapse from which the signal arose and that the nucleus is then able to direct its products back to that same synapse. But there is no known basis for such an arrangement, which would require precise targeting to each of thousands of the synapses of a neuron. A much simpler possibility would be for synapses that have undergone short-term alterations to send out a generic call for the production of whatever agents are needed to stabilize synaptic change; once made, these

agents could be broadcast widely but have an influence only at synapses prepared—by the establishment of short-term change locally—to use them. If this were the arrangement utilized, there might be circumstances under which stabilizing agents made in response to a call from one synapse could stabilize changes at a different synapse. The last few years have seen a number of experimental examples of just that. The first to be published was on hippocampal LTP (Frey & Morris, 1997). Sets of inputs to a group of CA1 neurons were tetanized in a pattern (three high frequency trains of 100 pulses separated by 10 min rests) that yielded LTP, which would persist without decline for over 9 hr. However, if protein synthesis were inhibited during and for an hour after the tetanus, LTP would be totally lost within 8 hr. In the critical experiments one set of input fibers, pathway A, was tetanized with protein synthesis intact; 35 min later a protein synthesis inhibitor was introduced and a second set of fibers, pathway B, then tetanized (1 hr after the tetanization of pathway A). The LTP produced in B would have declined within 8 hr had B alone been tetanized in this protein synthesis-deficient slice. However, because the tetanization of B followed that of A, the LTP in pathway B in fact persisted without decline for over 9 hr just as did that of pathway A. Presumably, *fixation protein,* made as the result of tetanizing A, was still present and able to stabilize the LTP produced a short time later in pathway B. It appears that the proteins involved in stabilizing change work anywhere in the cell that short-term change has been established.

A similar conclusion seems to hold for facilitation in *Aplysia,* as shown by an elegant series of experiments in which a single sensory neuron was made to establish synaptic contact with two widely separated motor neurons in cell culture (Martin, Casadio et al., 1997). One brief application of 5-HT to the sensory neuron synapses on one of the motor neurons produces short-term facilitation, and five spaced applications produces long-term (>24 hr) facilitation of transmission at the 5-HT-exposed synapse but not at the other. The long-term facilitation was prevented if either a transcription inhibitor was added to the bath or an aniti-CREB antibody was injected into the sensory neuron soma. Thus, the long-term synaptic facilitation was apparently dependent on CREB induced transcription. That the stabilizing protein made on the transcribed mRNA appears to spread throughout the sensory neuron, is indicated by the observation that a single pulse of 5-HT applied at one synapse would produce long-, rather than short-term facilitation if 5 pulses were also applied to the *other* synapse.

Change Rules

The discovery of associative LTP in hippocampus, supported by comparable findings in *Aplysia* in which LTP seems to play a major role in a rather compelling neural model of behavioral classical conditioning, encourages postulation of (associative) LTP as a possible basis for simple associative learning, with the presumption being that coactivity of the pre- and postsynaptic cells trigger potentiation. This neurophysiological hypothesis may be seen as parallel to the psychologist's law of contiguity (see Chap. 2, this volume). But on logical grounds, the hypothesis and the psychologist's law probably should not be, and on empirical grounds almost certainly are not a sufficient condition for learning to occur.

Neural Correlates of Contiguity and Effect?

One problem is that contiguity and its neural parallel seem too permissive as a condition for change. In *Aplysia,* for example, strong depolarization and firing of the motor neurons that cause the movements of protective withdrawal are driven to fire every several minutes by a circuit that generates respiratory pump-ing movements that clear the mantle cavity of debris (Byrne, 1983). If pre- and postsynaptic coactivity were the sole condition for synaptic change, then an animal that happened to brush against the side of a rock during a respiratory pumping movement would thereafter have an increased, and presumably maladaptive, tendency to retract its gill and siphon whenever the part of its body contacted the rock. The chances of such inappropriate learning would be greatly reduced if pre- and postsynaptic coactivity could trigger synaptic strengthening only if a traumatic US was responsible for the postsynaptic activity.

In fact, at the synapse between a sensory and motor neuron grown in culture, a tetanus, which by itself produces little lasting increase in synaptic strength, produces a sizeable increase in strength if paired with a squirt of serotonin that alone also has little lasting effect, and this increase has the LTP-like characteristics of being prevented by postsynaptic hyperpolarization or injection of calcium ion chelators. This experiment suggests that in *Aplysia* pre- and postsynaptic coactivity are much more likely to lead to LTP if they occur in the presence of the neuromodulator, serotonin, which in the intact animal would be released by facilitator neurons in response to a traumatic US (Bao et al., 1998). Thus, there may often be two important ingredients needed to precipitate associative change at synapses. One is coactivity of pre- and postsynaptic elements of the synapse, which in effect marks the synapse that is to change. The other is a widely broadcast chemical message, delivered by the brain's diffuse modulatory systems, that essentially gives "permission" for change to occur. A number of studies on mammals have also reported major effects of various neuromodulators such as norepinephrine, acetylcholine, and dopamine on development of hippocampal LTP (Frey & Morris, 1998; Huerta & Lisman, 1993; Thomas et al., 1996; Watabe, Zaki, & O'Dell, 2000).

Blocking

It is well known that unexpected events usually cause much more learning than expected ones, as shown by the well known behavioral phenomenon of blocking (see Chap. 2, this volume). If an animal has already learned that CS X predicts a US, Z, it will be difficult to establish an association to a new CS, Y, if X always accompanies Y as a predictor of Z. If blocking were a direct manifestation of basic cellular processes, then one might expect that following the development of LTP at the synapse made by a cell X on another cell Z, it would be difficult to establish LTP at the synapse between another Y and Z cell if X and Y, always firing together, were paired with firing of Z.

Such a synaptic blocking result could perhaps be predicted, at least in principle, from the known properties of LTP. There are two important properties: (a) As pointed out in the first part of this chapter, when hippocampal CA1 cells fire, their action potentials propagate back into the neuron's dendrites, which themselves have the capacity to generate spikes (Figure 4.9b). Dendritic spikes, like axonal spikes, have a refractory period during which a greater depolarization than normal is required to produce another action potential (Colbert, Magee, Hoffman, & Johnston, 1997). (b) As illustrated in Figure 4.9a, establishment of LTP is most effective when postsynaptic action potentials occur slightly after their occurrence presynaptically (Bi & Poo, 1998).

A thought experiment in which these two properties lead to a blocking effect is illustrated in Figure 4.9c. We assume two input pathways X and Y each containing enough axons so that once all the synapses on Z are potentiated the pathway can excite Z to firing level. The timing relationships are as indicated in the figure. For LTP to occur, a back-propagated dendritic spike must reach the dendrites at about 10 ms after glutamater-gic input to Z. After generating a spike, the dendrites are refractory for about 10 ms. Then if stimulation-produced activity of pathway X is followed by spike-producing somatic current injection timed so that the dendrites spike at 10 ms after glutamate from X reaches them, the X-Z synapses will be potentiated (Figure 4.9c, Pair X-Z). However, if *subsequently* simultaneous stimulation-produced activity of pathways X and Y is similarly followed by spike-producing somatic current injection (Figure 4.9c, Pair X, Y-Z), no potentiation of the Y-Z synapse will occur because the dendrites are refractory to spiking at the time when such spiking is required if potentiation is to be induced. This hypothetical cellular basis for blocking is essentially a biological implementation of much earlier theoretical ideas of Sutton and Barto (1981). Whether such an experiment could actually be carried out successfully, we don't know. But in fact, it may be that cellular processes are not immediately responsible for blocking anyway.

Attempts to determine the mechanism of blocking in eye-blink conditioning have implicated a mechanism that depends on the organization of cerebellar circuitry (Kim, Krupa, & Thompson, 1998). Firing of the deep nucleus neurons that leads to the eye-blink response also recruits GABA-ergic feedback inhibition of the olivary neurons that give rise to the climbing fibers (Figure 4.5). Consequently, once an animal has been conditioned to respond to the CS, the CR of the deep nucleus neurons causes the inhibition of the climbing fibers that would be recruited by the US in an untrained animal, preventing them from firing if the US occurs. This provides a very plausible explanation for blocking; in a blocking experiment, the CS A to which conditioning has already occurred should block the firing of climbing fibers excited by the US and thus prevents development of conditioned responding to another CS B that accompanies

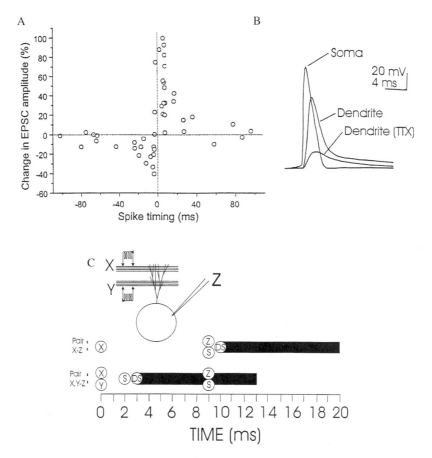

Figure 4.9   A thought experiment designed to demonstrate a neural analog of blocking.

NOTE: A. Dependence of synaptic change on delay between presynaptic and postsynaptic spike (pre- and postsynaptic hippocampal cells in culture were stimulated to fire 60 times at 1Hz at the abscissa interval) (from Big Poo, 1998). B. Response to a suprathreshold presynaptic volley of activity as seen in the soma and dendrite of a hippocampal paramidal cell (TTX shows the EPSP alone, as uncovered by blocking spikes with TTX) (from Stuart et al., 1997). C. Experimental design. X, Y = glutamate from pathways X and Y reaches dendritic receptors of postsynaptic neuron Z. Z = experimenter depolarizes Z to firing threshold via microelectrode. S = axon spike. DS = back-propagated dendritic spike (refractory period of dendrites shown by black bar).

it. This explanation of blocking predicts that injection of drugs that prevent GABA-ergic inhibition into the inferior olive would also abolish the blocking effect, a prediction that has been verified (Figure 4.10).

Blocking might also be accounted for as a corollary to findings that seem to show that the activity of brain stem neurons, which release dopamine (often conjectured as playing a role in reinforcement) to wide reaches of the

frontal cortex and striatum, fire in response only to *unexpected* rewards (Schultz, 1998). Thus, neuromodulatory enabling of synaptic plasticity might fail to occur if rewards are already expected. While such an explanation leaves many questions as to its mechanisms in need of explication, it shares with the earlier explanation of blocking during classical conditioning the property of being based on complex circuit properties of the nervous

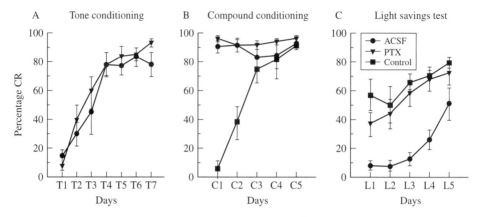

Figure 4.10   Evidence for a circuit-level explanation of blocking.
NOTE: A. Two groups of animals (ACSF and PTX) were given tone-airpuff conditioning; both learned to blink to tone. B. Both groups were then given light+tone-airpuff conditioning. The ACSF group received an infusion of artificial cerebro-spinal fluid into the olive; the PTX group received the GABA blocker, picrotoxin. Both groups, already conditioned to the tone, responded to the compound stimulus throughout training. A third group (control) began training during this period and acquired a conditioned blink response to the compound stimulus. C. All groups were now given further light-airpuff training. The control group, tested for the first time without tone, suffered some stimulus generalization decrement, but responded to the light alone from the outset. The ACSF group did not initially respond to the light at all, indicating that during period B no association between light and airpuff had formed. The PTX group, in which conditioned responses of deep nucleus neurons were unable to inhibit UCS-evoked climbing fiber activity, responded similarly to controls throughout; they had established a conditioned blink response to light during period B despite the fact that the previously conditioned tone always accompanied it (from Kim et al., 1998).

system rather than being directly due to the cellular mechanisms at the site of training-produced synaptic change.

Timing Issues

Classical CRs are generally well timed; if during acquisition the US occurs at a specific time after the start of the CS (the interstimulus interval or ISI), the CR will occur at approximately that time. Time also plays a role in the ease with which conditioning occurs: Under the conditions of most experiments, poor conditioning occurs with very short ISIs, and optimal conditioning occurs with intervals on the order of 0.2–0.5 s; past the optimum, conditioning becomes progressively poorer the longer the ISI (e.g., Schneiderman,

1966; Schneiderman & Gormezano, 1964). Gallistel and Gibbon (2000) have argued that it is not necessarily the ISI that affects rate of conditioning but the ratio of the ISI to the intertrial interval, and they have supported this view for eye-blink conditioning by an analysis that combines results from seemingly comparable experiments from several laboratories. The final word on this must await studies directed specifically to the matter, but whatever the final conclusions, a neural theory of classical conditioning cannot be said to be successful unless it can account for the effects of temporal factors on eye-blink conditioning.

We are aware of no information on whether the ISI influences the timing of classically conditioned defensive withdrawal in *Aplysia,* but CS–US interval has been reported to influence efficiency of learning, with learning falling off on either side of a 0.5-s optimum (Hawkins, Carew, & Kandel, 1986). If the activity-dependence of serotonergic facilitation is due to calcium ion facilitation of adenylate cyclase activity (discussed earlier), then one might try to account for the optimality of a 0.5-ms ISI by supposing that calcium ion levels (or levels of calcium-activated calmodulin) are maximal at this time. It seems more likely that they peak much earlier. The optimal interval between pre- and postsynaptic activity for induction of LTP (see Figure 4.9), though not studied specifically for *Aplysia* LTP, are also very short and seem unlikely to be able to explain an optimal CS-US interval of half a second. Thus, a cell-level explanation seems unlikely.

There has been a fair amount of effort expended in trying to understand how the timing of eye-blink responses is achieved. If relevant portions of cerebellar cortex are fully ablated after extensive training, animals continue to respond to the CS but emit their responses promptly after CS onset, rather than waiting until the time that the US occurred during training; subsequent attempts to reestablish responses at the previous or a new delay are unsuccessful (Garcia et al., 1999; Perrett & Mauk, 1995). This has been taken to indicate that an overall tendency to produce a response results from LTP of mossy fiber–deep nucleus synapses, whereas the timing of the response is sculpted by Purkinje cell inhibition of deep nucleus neurons, except at the proper time of response (Mauk & Donegan, 1997; Medina et al., 2000; Raymond, Lisberger, & Mauk, 1996). Attempts to explain timing have generally assumed, in one way or another, that the active population of parallel fibers representing the CS changes over time as the CS continues (Bullock, Fiala, & Grossberg, 1994; Buononmano & Mauk, 1994; Gluck, Reifsnider, & Thompson, 1990;

Mauk & Donegan, 1997; Medina et al., 2000; Moore, Desmond, & Berthier, 1989). Since LTD occurs at the synapses made by the particular population that is active at the time of the US, it is when that particular population is active on test trials of the CS alone that Purkinje cells fire least, suppress firing of deep nucleus neurons least, and thus produce the maximum response.

The most satisfying attempt to explain why different parallel fibers are active at different times after the start of the CS makes use of the inhibitory loop from granule cells to Golgi neurons and back to granules cells (Figure 4.5; Buononmano & Mauk, 1994). Because of this negative feedback loop, the population of granule cells (the parent cells of the parallel fibers) activated by a particular, constantly firing group of mossy fibers should continually shift over time, as proposed before. The degree of variation in the exact sequence of which cells fire when given inevitable noise of various kinds in the system has not been studied (though see Buononmano & Mauk, 1994), but it seems likely that the longer the CS-US interval, the more variability there will be in the time at which responses occur. Whether the coefficient of variation of latency will remain constant at different intervals, as occurs for a wide range of timing phenomena (Gallistel & Gibbon, 2000; Chap. 9, this volume), is unknown.

The likelihood that there would be more variation in which neurons are firing, as time after the start of the CS increases, might explain why it becomes more difficult to achieve successful conditioning at long ISIs (Mauk & Donegan, 1997). In effect, the population of neurons representing the CS at late intervals may be so variable that the development of LTD at any one parallel fiber–Purkinje synapse is extremely slow. The failure to condition at very short intervals cannot, as far as one can see, be explained by a similar mechanism. Nevertheless, it has been argued that some sort of inhibitory circuitry may create a need to delay climbing fiber activity to several hundred milliseconds after parallel fiber activation to produce effective LTD, since such a delay is said to hold in the slice under control conditions but not in the presence of GABA inhibitors (Chen & Thompson, 1995; Thompson and Krupa, 1994).

What Have We Really Got?

In a remarkably short number of years and in a literal frenzy of activity, our knowledge of learning has evolved from being a totally black box phenomenon to the possession of myriad hints as to what might be happening during learning, all the way from neural circuits to molecules. At the level of circuitry, we have gone from a mere conjecture that learning might be due to changing synapses to the rather surprising data-driven working hypothesis that learning is in fact due to changes in the efficacy of preexisting synapses. At the level of cellular mechanism, we have been able to see the possibility of understanding learning in terms of the molecular events that regulate the potency of synaptic connections. We even have the specter of a molecular level explanation of Ebbinghaus's principle of superior learning following well spaced practice.

This progress has come from attacking the problem at a wide variety of levels. It has necessarily involved jumping freely from the study of behavior to the study of isolated ganglia or brain slices to the study of neurons in culture to the study of neuronal enzymes working on substrates in a test-tube. However, the transition between levels has commonly been somewhat glib. Thus, analytical studies on *Aplysia* focus almost entirely on the monosynaptic part of the reflex arc, but there is good reason to believe that most of the action affecting behavior occurs in parallel, long

pathways via chains of interneurons. We are able to provide plausible accounts of sensitization and perhaps even classical conditioning in terms of changes in ion channels due to their phosphorylation, but important experiments are done on patches of membrane of the cell soma—not on the relevant presynaptic endings of neurons. The species of channels studied may well not always be the same species whose changes seem most likely to affect behavior, and there is even question that these changes are the most important cause of behavioral change. In the analysis of eyelid conditioning, we attempt to understand the synaptic changes occurring when CS and US are paired by experiments in which applying a squirt of glutamate to Purkinje cells in culture is a surrogate for parallel fiber activity, which is in turn thought to be the medium of CS representation, and direct depolarization of the Purkinje cell replaces the firing of climbing fibers whose activity is thought to be the neural representation of the US. Thus, we routinely study models of models of models of the learning process. At any jump between levels, we make assumptions that we know are only approximately valid, and there is the risk that we may often devote great time and energy to elucidating phenomena that in the end will turn out to be at best only minor players in the central story.

This is not to say that our apparent progress is a sham. However, we must be careful not to believe too firmly more than we have actually proved. Sooner or later we must do much more of the careful working back and forth between levels of analysis, testing predictions made about phenomenology at one level on the basis of findings made at a different one. But this is a slow painful business that takes time away from broader and deeper analysis. A reasonable balance between approaches is needed for optimal progress; we may hope that the current anarchy of approaches is not far from the optimal mix.

REFERENCES

Abrams, T. W. (1985). Activity-dependent presynaptic facilitation: An associative mechanism in *Aplysia*. *Cellular and Molecular Neurobiology, 5,* 123–145.

Abrams, T. W., Karl, K. A., & Kandel, E. R. (1991). Biochemical studies of stimulus convergence during classical conditioning in *Aplysia*: Dual regulation of adenylate cyclase by Ca2+/calmodulin and transmitter. *Journal of Neuroscience, 11,* 2655–2665.

Ahn, S., Ginty, D. D., & Linden, D. J. (1999). A late phase of cerebellar long-term depression requires activation of CaMKIV and CREB [see comments]. *Neuron, 23,* 559–568.

Albus, J. (1971). A theory of cerebellar function. *Mathematical Biosciences, 10,* 25–61.

Andersen, P., Sundberg, S. H., Sveen, O., & Wigstrom, H. (1977). Specific long-lasting potentiation of synaptic transmission in hippocampal slices. *Nature, 266,* 736–737.

Antonov, I., Antonova, I., Kandel, E. R., & Hawkins, R. D. (2001). The contribution of activity-dependent synaptic plasticity to classical conditioning in *Aplysia*. *Journal of Neuroscience 21,* 6413–6422.

Antonov, I., Kandel, E. R., & Hawkins, R. D. (1999). The contribution of facilitation of monosynaptic PSPs to dishabituation and sensitization of the *Aplysia* siphon withdrawal reflex. *Journal of Neuroscience 19,* 10438–10450.

Artola, A., & Singer, W. (1993). Long-term depression of excitatory synaptic transmission and its relationship to long-term potentiation. *Trends in Neurosciences, 16,* 480–487.

Bailey, C. H. (1999). Structural changes and the storage of long-term memory in *Aplysia*. *Canadian Journal of Physiology and Pharmacology, 77,* 738–747/

Bailey, C. H., Bartsch, D., & Kandel, E. R. (1996). Toward a molecular definition of long-term memory storage. *Proceedings of the National Academy of Sciences, USA, 93,* 13445–13452.

Bailey, C. H., & Chen, M. (1988a). Long-term memory in *Aplysia* modulates the total number of varicosities of single identified sensory neurons. *Proceedings of the National Academy of Sciences, USA, 85,* 2373–2377.

Bailey, C. H., & Chen, M. (1988b). Long-term sensitization in *Aplysia* increases the number of presynaptic contacts onto the identified gill motor neuron L7. *Proceedings of the National Academy of Sciences, USA, 85,* 9356–9359.

Bailey, C. H., & Chen, M. (1989). Time course of structural changes at identified sensory neuron synapses during long-term sensitization in *Aplysia*. *Journal of Neuroscience, 9,* 1774–1780.

Bailey, C. H., Chen, M., Kandel, E., & Schacher, S. (1993). Early structural chages associated with long-term presynaptic facilitation in *Aplysia* sensory neurons. *Society for Neuroscience Abstracts, 19,* 16.

Bailey, C. H., Giustetto, M., Zhu, H., Chen, M., & Kandel, E. R. (2000). A novel function for serotonin-mediated short-term facilitation in *Aplysia*: Conversion of a transient, cell-wide homosynaptic hebbian plasticity into a persistent, protein synthesis-independent synapse-specific enhancement. *Proceedings of the National Academy of Sciences, USA, 97,* 11581–11586.

Bailey, C. H., Montarolo, P., Chen, M., Kandel, E. R., & Schacher, S. (1992). Inhibitors of protein and RNA synthesis block structural changes that accompany long-term heterosynaptic plasticity in *Aplysia*. *Neuron, 9,* 749–758.

Banke, T. G., Bowie, D., Lee, H., Huganir, R. L., Schousboe, A., & Traynelis, S. F. (2000). Control of GluR1 AMPA receptor function by cAMP-dependent protein kinase. *Journal of Neuroscience, 20,* 89–102.

Bannerman, D. M., Good, M. A., Butcher, S. P., Ramsay, M., & Morris, R. G. (1995). Distinct components of spatial learning revealed by prior training and NMDA receptor blockade [see comments]. *Nature, 378,* 182–186.

Bao, J. X., Kandel, E. R., & Hawkins, R. D. (1998). Involvement of presynaptic and postsynaptic mechanisms in a cellular analog of classical conditioning at *Aplysia* sensory-motor neuron synapses in isolated cell culture. *Journal of Neuroscience, 18,* 458–466.

Barnes, C. A. (1979). Memory deficits associated with senescence: A neurophysiological and behavioral study in the rat. *Journal of Comparative and Physiological Psychology, 93,* 74–104.

Barnes, C. A., Jung, M. W., McNaughton, B. L., Korol, D. L., Andreasson, K., & Worley, P. F. (1994). LTP saturation and spatial learning disruption: Effects of task variables and saturation levels. *Journal of Neuroscience, 14,* 5793–5806.

Barria, A., Derkach, V., & Soderling, T. (1997). Identification of the Ca2+/calmodulin-dependent protein kinase II regulatory phosphorylation site in the alpha-amino-3-hydroxyl-5-methyl-4-isoxazole-propionate-type glutamate receptor. *Journal of Biological Chemistry, 272,* 32727–32730.

Barria, A., Muller, D., Derkach, V., Griffith, L. C., & Soderling, T. R. (1997). Regulatory phosphorylation of AMPA-type glutamate receptors by CaM-KII during long-term potentiation [see comments]. *Science, 276,* 2042–2045.

Barrionuevo, G., & Brown, T. H. (1983). Associative long-term potentiation in hippocampal slices. *Proceedings of the National Academy of Sciences, USA, 80,* 7347–7351.

Bartsch, D., Casadio, A., Karl, K. A., Serodio, P., & Kandel, E. R. (1998). CREB1 encodes a nuclear activator, a repressor, and a cytoplasmic modulator that form a regulatory unit critical for long-term facilitation. *Cell, 95,* 211–223.

Bartsch, D., Ghirardi, M., Skehel, P. A., Karl, K. A., Herder, S. P., Chen, M., Bailey, C. H., & Kandel, E. R. (1995). *Aplysia* CREB2 represses long-term facilitation: Relief of repression converts transient facilitation into long-term functional and structural change. *Cell, 83,* 979–992.

Baxter, D. A., Canavier, C. C., Clark, J. W., Jr., & Byrne, J. H. (1999). Computational model of the serotonergic modulation of sensory neurons in *Aplysia. Journal of Neurophysiology, 82,* 2914–2935.

Bear, M. F., & Malenka, R. C. (1994). Synaptic plasticity: LTP and LTD. *Current Opinion in Neurobiology, 4,* 389–399.

Benke, T. A., Luthi, A., Isaac, J. T., & Collingridge, G. L. (1998). Modulation of AMPA receptor unitary conductance by synaptic activity. *Nature, 393,* 793–797.

Bergold, P. J., Sweatt, J. D., Winicov, I., Weiss, K. R., Kandel, E. R., & Schwartz, J. H. (1990). Protein synthesis during acquisition of long-term facilitation is needed for the persistent loss of regulatory subunits of the *Aplysia* cAMP-dependent protein kinase. *Proceedings of the National Academy of Sciences, USA, 87(10),* 3788–3791.

Bernier, L., Castellucci, V. F., Kandel, E. R., & Schwartz, J. H. (1982). Facilitatory transmitter causes a selective and prolonged increase in adenosine 3':5'-monophosphate in sensory neurons mediating the gill and siphon withdrawal reflex in *Aplysia. Journal of Neuroscience, 2,* 1682–1691.

Bhalla, U. S., & Iyengar, R. (1999). Emergent properties of networks of biological signaling pathways [see comments]. *Science, 283,* 381–387.

Bi, G-q., & Poo, M-m. (1998). Synaptic modifications in cultured hippocampal neurons: Dependence on spike timing, synaptic strength, and postsynaptic cell type. *Journal of Neuroscience 18,* 10464–10472.

Bliss, T. V., & Lynch, M. (1988). Long-term potentiation of synaptic transmission in the hippocampus: Properties and mechanisms. In P. Landfield, & S. Deadwyler (Eds.), *Long-term potentiation: From biophysics to behavior* (pp. 3–72). New York: Alan R. Liss.

Bliss, T. V., & Collingridge, G. L. (1993). A synaptic model of memory: Long-term potentiation in the hippocampus. *Nature, 361,* 31–39.

Bliss, T. V., & Gardner-Medwin, A. R. (1973). Long-lasting potentiation of synaptic transmission in the dentate area of the unanaestetized rabbit following stimulation of the perforant path. *Journal of Physiology, 232,* 357–374.

Bliss, T. V., & Lomo, T. (1973). Long-lasting potentiation of synaptic transmission in the dentate area of the anaesthetized rabbit following stimulation of the perforant path. *Journal of Physiology, 232,* 331–356.

Bonhoeffer, T., Staiger, V., & Aertsen, A. (1989). Synaptic plasticity in rat hippocampal slice cultures: Local "Hebbian" conjunction of pre-

and postsynaptic stimulation leads to distributed synaptic enhancement. *Proceedings of the National Academy of Sciences, USA, 86,* 8113–8117.

Bourtchuladze, R., Frenguelli, B., Blendy, J., Cioffi, D., Schutz, G., & Silva, A. J. (1994). Deficient long-term memory in mice with a targeted mutation of the cAMP-responsive element-binding protein. *Cell, 79,* 59–68.

Brun, V. H., Ytterbo, K., Morris, R. G., Moser, M. B., & Moser, E. I. (2001). Retrograde amnesia for spatial memory induced by NMDA receptor-mediated long-term potentiation. *Journal of Neuroscience, 21,* 356–362.

Brunelli, M., Castellucci, V., & Kandel, E. R. (1976). Synaptic facilitation and behavioral sensitization in *Aplysia:* Possible role of serotonin and cyclic AMP. *Science, 194,* 1178–1181.

Bullock, D., Fiala, J., & Grossberg, S. (1994). A neural model of timed response learning in the cerebellum. *Neural Networks, 7,* 1101–1114.

Buonomano, D., & Mauk, M. (1994). Neural network model of the cerebellum: Temporal discrimination and timing of motor responses. *Neural Computation, 6,* 38–55.

Buzsaki, G. (1980). Long-term potentiation of the commissural path-CA1 pyramidal cell synapse in the hippocampus of the freely moving rat. *Neuroscience Letters, 19,* 293–296.

Byrne, J. H. (1983). Identification and initial characterization of a cluster of command and pattern-generating neurons underlying respiratory pumping in *Aplysia* californica. *Journal of Neurophysiology, 49,* 491–508.

Byrne, J. H., Castellucci, V. F., Carew, T. J., & Kandel, E. R. (1978). Stimulus-response relations and stability of mechanoreceptor and motor neurons mediating defensive gill-withdrawal reflex in *Aplysia. Journal of Neurophysiology 41,* 402–417.

Byrne, J. H., & Kandel, E. R. (1996). Presynaptic facilitation revisited: State and time dependence. *Journal of Neuroscience, 16,* 425–435.

Cain, D. P., Saucier, D., Hall, J., Hargreaves, E. L., & Boon, F. (1996). Detailed behavioral analysis of water maze acquisition under APV or CNQX: Contribution of sensorimotor disturbances to drug-induced acquisition deficits. *Behavioral Neuroscience, 110,* 86–102.

Carew, T. J., Castellucci, V. F., & Kandel, E. R. (1971). An analysis of dishabituation and sensitization of the gill-withdrawal reflex in *Aplysia. International Journal of Neuroscience, 2,* 79–98.

Carew, T. J., Hawkins, R. D., Abrams, T. W., & Kandel, E. R. (1984). A test of Hebb's postulate at identified synapses which mediate classical conditioning in *Aplysia. Journal of Neuroscience, 4,* 1217–1224.

Carew, T. J., Hawkins, R. D., & Kandel, E. R. (1983). Differential classical conditioning of a defensive withdrawal reflex in *Aplysia* californica. *Science, 219,* 397–400.

Carew, T. J., & Kandel, E. R. (1973). Acquisition and retention of long-term habituation in *Aplysia:* Correlation of behavioral and cellular processes. *Science, 182,* 1158–1160.

Carew, T. J., Pinsker, H., & Kandel, E. (1972). Long-term habituation of a defensive withdrawal reflex in *Aplysia. Science, 175,* 451–454.

Carew, T. J., Walters, E. T., & Kandel, E. R. (1981). Classical conditioning in a simple withdrawal reflex in *Aplysia* californica. *Journal of Neuroscience, 1,* 1426–1437.

Casadio, A., Martin, K. C., Giustetto, M., Zhu, H., Chen, M., Bartsch, D., Bailey, C. H., & Kandel, E. R. (1999). A transient, neuron-wide form of CREB-mediated long-term facilitation can be stabilized at specific synapses by local protein synthesis. *Cell, 99,* 221–237.

Castellucci, V. F., Blumenfeld, H., Goelet, P., & Kandel, E. R. (1989). Inhibitor of protein synthesis blocks long-term behavioral sensitization in the isolated gill-withdrawal reflex of *Aplysia. Journal of Neurobiology, 20,* 1–9.

Castellucci, V. F., Carew, T. J., & Kandel, E. R. (1978). Cellular analysis of long-term habituation of the gill-withdrawal reflex of *Aplysia californica. Science, 202,* 1306–1308.

Castellucci, V. F., & Kandel, E. R. (1974). A quantal analysis of the synaptic depression underlying habituation of the gill-withdrawal reflex in *Aplysia. Proceedings of the National Academy of Sciences, USA, 71,* 5004–5008.

Castellucci, V. F., & Kandel, E. R. (1976). Presynaptic facilitation as a mechanism for behavioral sensitization in *Aplysia. Science, 194,* 1176–1178.

Castellucci, V. F., Kandel, E. R., Schwartz, J. H., Wilson, F. D., Nairn, A. C., & Greengard, P. (1980). Intracellular injection of the catalytic subunit of cyclic AMP-dependent protein kinase simulates facilitation of transmitter release underlying behavioral sensitization in *Aplysia. Proceedings of the National Academy of Sciences, USA, 77,* 7492–7496.

Castellucci, V. F., Nairn, A., Greengard, P., Schwartz, J. H., & Kandel, E. R. (1982). Inhibitor of adenosine $3':5'$-monophosphate-dependent protein kinase blocks presynaptic facilitation in *Aplysia. Journal of Neuroscience, 2,* 1673–1681.

Castellucci, V., Pinsker, H., Kupfermann, I., & Kandel, E. R. (1970). Neuronal mechanisms of habituation and dishabituation of the gill-withdrawal reflex in *Aplysia. Science, 167,* 1745–1748.

Castro, C. A., Silbert, L. H., McNaughton, B. L., & Barnes, C. A. (1989). Recovery of spatial learning deficits after decay of electrically induced synaptic enhancement in the hippocampus. *Nature, 342,* 545–548.

Caul, W., Jarrard, L., Miller, R., & Korn, J. (1969). Effects of hippocampal lesions on heart rate in aversive classical conditioning. *Physiology and Behavior, 4,* 917–922.

Chain, D. G., Casadio, A., Schacher, S., Hegde, A. N., Valbrun, M., Yamamoto, N., Goldberg, A. L., Bartsch, D., Kandel, E. R., & Schwartz, J. H. (1999). Mechanisms for generating the autonomous cAMP-dependent protein kinase required for long-term facilitation in *Aplysia. Neuron, 22,* 147–156.

Chapman, P. F., Steinmetz, J. E., Sears, L. L., & Thompson, R. F. (1990). Effects of lidocaine injection in the interpositus nucleus and red nucleus on conditioned behavioral and neuronal responses. *Brain Research, 537,* 149–156.

Chen, C., Rainnie, D. G., Greene, R. W., & Tonegawa, S. (1994). Abnormal fear response and aggressive behavior in mutant mice deficient for alpha-calcium-calmodulin kinase II [see comments]. *Science, 266,* 291–294.

Chen, C., & Thompson, R. F. (1995). Temporal specificity of long-term depression in parallel fiber–Purkinje synapses in rat cerebellar slice. *Learning and Memory, 2,* 185–198.

Chen, H.-X., Otmakhov, N., Strack, S., Colbran, R., & Lisman, J. (2001). Is persistent activity of calcium/calmodulin-dependent kinase required for maintenance of LTP? *Journal of Neurophysiology, 85,* 1368–1376.

Chitwood, R. A., Li Q., & Glanzman, D. L. (2001). Serotonin facilitates AMPA-type responses in isolated siphon motor neurons of *Aplysia* in culture. *Journal of Physiology, 534,* 501–510.

Clark, G. A., McCormick, D. A., Lavond, D. G., & Thompson, R. F. (1984). Effects of lesions of cerebellar nuclei on conditioned behavioral and hippocampal neuronal responses. *Brain Research, 291,* 125–136.

Clark, R. E., & Lavond, D. G. (1993). Reversible lesions of the red nucleus during acquisition and retention of a classically conditioned behavior in rabbits. *Behavioral Neuroscience, 107,* 264–270.

Clark, R. E., Zhang, A. A., & Lavond, D. G. (1992). Reversible lesions of the cerebellar interpositus nucleus during acquisition and retention of a classically conditioned behavior. *Behavioral Neuroscience, 106,* 879–888.

Colbert, C. M., Magee, J. C., Hoffman, D. A., & Johnston, D. (1997). Slow recovery from inactivation of Na+ channels underlies the activity-dependent attenuation of dendritic action potentials in hippocampal CA1 pyramidal neurons. *Journal of Neuroscience, 17,* 6512–6521.

Collingridge, G. L., Kehl, S. J., & McLennan, H. (1983). Excitatory amino acids in synaptic transmission in the Schaffer collateral-commissural pathway of the rat hippocampus. *Journal of Physiology, 334,* 33–46.

Collingridge, G. L., & Lester, R. A. (1989). Excitatory amino acid receptors in the vertebrate central nervous system. *Pharmacological Reviews, 41,* 143–210.

Colwill, R. M., Absher, R. A., & Roberts, M. L. (1988). Context-US learning in *Aplysia* californica. *Journal of Neuroscience, 8,* 4434–4439.

Crick, F. (1984). Memory and molecular turnover [news]. *Nature, 312,* 101.

Dale, N., Schacher, S., & Kandel, E. R. (1988). Long-term facilitation in *Aplysia* involves increase in transmitter release. *Science, 239,* 282–285.

Dash, P. K., Hochner, B., & Kandel, E. R. (1990). Injection of the cAMP-responsive element into the nucleus of *Aplysia* sensory neurons blocks long-term facilitation. *Nature, 345,* 718–721.

Davies, S. N., Lester, R. A., Reymann, K. G., & Collingridge, G. L. (1989). Temporally distinct pre- and post-synaptic mechanisms maintain long-term potentiation. *Nature, 338,* 500–503.

Davis, H. P., & Squire, L. R. (1984). Protein synthesis and memory: A review. *Psychological Bulletin, 96,* 518–559.

Davis, S., Butcher, S. P., & Morris, R. G. (1992). The NMDA receptor antagonist D-2-amino-5-phosphonopentanoate (D-AP5) impairs spatial learning and LTP in vivo at intracerebral concentrations comparable to those that block LTP in vitro. *Journal of Neuroscience, 12,* 21–34.

Debanne, D., Gahwiler, B. H., & Thompson, S. M. (1998). Long-term synaptic plasticity between pairs of individual CA3 pyramidal cells in rat hippocampal slice cultures. *Journal of Physiology, 507,* 237–247.

de Jonge, M., & Racine, R. J. (1985). The effects of repeated induction of long-term potentiation in the dentate gyrus. *Brain Research, 328,* 181–185.

Derkach, V., Barria, A., & Soderling, T. R. (1999). Ca2+/calmodulin-kinase II enhances channel conductance of alpha-amino-3-hydroxy-5-methyl-4-isoxazolepropionate type glutamate receptors. *Proceedings of the National Academy of Sciences, USA, 96,* 3269–3274.

Desmond, N. L., & Levy, W. B. (1986a). Changes in the numerical density of synaptic contacts with long-term potentiation in the hippocampal dentate gyrus. *Journal of Comparative Neurology, 253,* 466–475.

Desmond, N. L., & Levy, W. B. (1986b). Changes in the postsynaptic density with long-term potentiation in the dentate gyrus. *Journal of Comparative Neurology, 253,* 476–482.

Diamond, J. S., Bergles, D. E., & Jahr, C. E. (1998). Glutamate release monitored with astrocyte transporter currents during LTP. *Neuron, 21,* 425–433.

Douglas, R., & Pribram, J. (1966). Learning and limbic lesions. *Neuropsychologia, 4,* 197–226.

Douglas, R. J. (1967). The hippocampus and behavior. *Psychological Bulletin, 67,* 416–442.

Dru, D., & Walker, J. B. (1975). Self-produced locomotion restores visual capacity after striate lesions. *Science, 187,* 265–266.

Dubnau, J., & Tully, T. (1998). Gene discovery in *Drosophila:* New insights for learning and memory. *Annual Review of Neuroscience, 21,* 407–444.

Dudek, S. M., & Bear, M. F. (1993). Bidirectional long-term modification of synaptic effectiveness in the adult and immature hippocampus. *Journal of Neuroscience, 13,* 2910–2918.

Eccles, J. C. S., Szentagothai, J., & Ito, M. (1967). *The cerebellum as a neuronal machine.* New York: Springer.

Emptage, N. J., & Carew, T. J. (1993). Long-term synaptic facilitation in the absence of short-term facilitation in *Aplysia* neurons. *Science, 262,* 253–256.

Engert, F., & Bonhoeffer, T. (1999). Dendritic spine changes associated with hippocampal long-term synaptic plasticity [see comments]. *Nature, 399,* 66–70.

Fanselow, M. (1999). Learing theory and neuropsychology: Configuring their disparate elements in the hippocampus. *Journal of Experimental Psychology: Animal Behavior Processes, 25,* 275–283.

Fanselow, M. (2000). Contextural fear, gestalt memories, and the hippocampus. *Behavioral Brain Research, 110,* 73–81.

Fischer, M., Kaech, S., Knutti, D., & Matus, A. (1998). Rapid actin-based plasticity in dendritic spines. *Neuron, 20,* 847–854.

Fischer, T. M., & Carew, T. J. (1993). Activity-dependent potentiation of recurrent inhibition:

A mechanism for dynamic gain control in the siphon withdrawal reflex of *Aplysia*. *Journal of Neuroscience, 13,* 1302–1314.

Frey, U., Huang, Y. Y., & Kandel, E. R. (1993). Effects of cAMP simulate a late stage of LTP in hippocampal CA1 neurons. *Science, 260,* 1661–1664.

Frey, U., & Morris, R. G. (1997). Synaptic tagging and long-term potentiation [see comments]. *Nature, 385,* 533–536.

Frey, U., & Morris, R. G. (1998). Synaptic tagging: Implications for late maintenance of hippocampal long-term potentiation [see comments]. *Trends in Neurosciences, 21,* 181–188.

Frost, W., Castellucci, V., Hawkins, R., & Kandel, E. (1985). Monosynaptic connections made by the sensory neurons of the gill- and siphon-withdrawal reflex in *Aplysia* participate in the storage oflong-term memory for sensitization. *Proceedings of the National Academy of Sciences, USA, 82,* 8266–8269.

Fukunaga, K., Muller, D., & Miyamoto, E. (1995). Increased phosphorylation of Ca2+/calmodulin-dependent protein kinase II and its endogenous substrates in the induction of long-term potentiation. *Journal of Biological Chemistry, 270,* 6119–6124.

Fukunaga, K., Muller, D., Ohmitsu, M., Bako, E., DePaoli-Roach, A., & Miyamoto, E. (2000). Decreased protein phosphatase 2A activity in hippocampal long-term potentiation. *J. Neurochem., 74,* 807–817.

Fukunaga, K., Stoppini, L., Miyamoto, E., & Muller, D. (1993). Long-term potentiation is associated with an increased activity of Ca2+/calmodulin-dependent protein kinase II. *Journal of Biological Chemistry, 268,* 7863–7867.

Gallistel, C., & Gibbon, J. (2000). Time, rate, and conditioning. *Psychology Review, 107,* 289–344.

Garcia, K. S., Steele, P. M., & Mauk, M. D. (1999). Cerebellar cortex lesions prevent acquisition of conditioned eyelid responses. *Journal of Neuroscience, 19,* 10940–10947.

Geinisman, Y., deToledo-Morrell, L., & Morrell, F. (1991). Induction of long-term potentiation is associated with an increase in the number of axospinous synapses with segmented postsynaptic densities. *Brain Research, 566,* 77–88.

Ghirardi, M., Montarolo, P. G., & Kandel, E. R. (1995). A novel intermediate stage in the transition between short- and long-term facilitation in the sensory to motor neuron synapse of *Aplysia*. *Neuron, 14,* 413–420.

Giese, K. P., Fedorov, N. B., Filipkowski, R. K., & Silva, A. J. (1998). Autophosphorylation at Thr286 of the alpha calcium-calmodulin kinase II in LTP and learning. *Science, 279,* 870–873.

Glanzman, D. L., Kandel, E. R., & Schacher, S. (1990). Target-dependent structural changes accompanying long-term synaptic facilitation in *Aplysia* neurons. *Science, 249,* 799–802.

Glanzman, D. L., Mackey, S. L., Hawkins, R. D., Dyke, A. M., Lloyd, P. E., & Kandel, E. R. (1989). Depletion of serotonin in the nervous system of *Aplysia* reduces the behavioral enhancement of gill withdrawal as well as the heterosynaptic facilitation produced by tail shock. *Journal of Neuroscience, 9,* 4200–4213.

Gluck, M. A., & Myers, C. E. (1997). Psychobiological models of hippocampal function in learning and memory. *Annual Review of Psychology, 48,* 481–514.

Gluck, M. A., Reifsnider, E., & Thompson, R. (1990). Adaptive signal processing and the cerebellum: Models of classical conditioning and VOR adaptation. In M. Gluck & D. Rumelhart (Eds.), *Neuroscience and connectionist theory* (pp. 131–185). Hillsdale, NJ: Earlbaum.

Goelet, P., Castellucci, V. F., Schacher, S., & Kandel, E. R. (1986). The long and the short of long-term memory—a molecular framework. *Nature, 322,* 419–422.

Greenberg, S. M., Castellucci, V. F., Bayley, H., & Schwartz, J. H. (1987). A molecular mechanism for long-term sensitization in *Aplysia*. *Nature, 329,* 62–65.

Gustafsson, B., & Wigstrom, H. (1986). Hippocampal long-lasting potentiation produced by pairing single volleys and brief conditioning tetani evoked in separate afferents. *Journal of Neuroscience, 6,* 1575–1582.

Gustafsson, B., Wigstrom, H., Abraham, W. C., & Huang, Y. Y. (1987). Long-term potentiation in the hippocampus using depolarizing current pulses as the conditioning stimulus to single volley synaptic potentials. *Journal of Neuroscience, 7,* 774–780.

Harvey, J. A., Welsh, J. P., Yeo, C. H., & Romano, A. G. (1993). Recoverable and nonrecoverable deficits in conditioned responses after cerebellar cortical lesions. *Journal of Neuroscience, 13,* 1624–1635.

Hawkins, R. D., Abrams, T. W., Carew, T. J., & Kandel, E. R. (1983). A cellular mechanism of classical conditioning in *Aplysia:* Activity-dependent amplification of presynaptic facilitation. *Science, 219,* 400–405.

Hawkins, R. D., Carew, T. J., & Kandel, E. R. (1986). Effects of interstimulus interval and contingency on classical conditioning of the *Aplysia* siphon withdrawal reflex. *Journal of Neuroscience, 6,* 1695–1701.

Hawkins, R. D., Castellucci, V. F., & Kandel, E. R. (1981). Interneurons involved in mediation and modulation of gill-withdrawal reflex in *Aplysia.* II. Identified neurons produce heterosynaptic facilitation contributing to behavioral sensitization. *Journal of Neurophysiology, 45,* 315–328.

Hawkins, R. D., Lalevic, N., Clark, G. A., & Kandel, E. R. (1989). Classical conditioning of the *Aplysia* siphon-withdrawal reflex exhibits response specificity. *Proceedings of the National Academy of Sciences, USA, 86,* 7620–7624.

Hawkins, R. D., & Schacher, S. (1989). Identified facilitator neurons L29 and L28 are excited by cutaneous stimuli used in dishabituation, sensitization, and classical conditioning of *Aplysia. Journal of Neuroscience, 9,* 4236–4245.

Hebb, D. (1949). *The organization of behavior.* New York: Wiley.

Hegde, A. N., Inokuchi, K., Pei, W., Casadio, A., Ghirardi, M., Chain, D. G., Martin, K. C., Kandel, E. R., & Schwartz, J. H. (1997). Ubiquitin C-terminal hydrolase is an immediate-early gene essential for long-term facilitation in *Aplysia. Cell, 89,* 115–126.

Hickie, C., Cohen, L. B., & Balaban, P. M. (1997). The synapse between LE sensory neurons and gill motoneurons makes only a small contribution to the *Aplysia* gill-withdrawal reflex. *European Journal of Neuroscience, 9,* 627–636.

Holscher, C. (1999). Synaptic plasticity and learning and memory: LTP and beyond. *Journal of Neuroscience Research, 58,* 62–75.

Holscher, C., McGlinchey, L., Anwyl, R., & Rowan, M. J. (1997). HFS-induced long-term potentiation and LFS-induced depotentiation in area CA1 of the hippocampus are not good models for learning. *Psychopharmacology, 130,* 174–182.

Hrabetova, S., & Sacktor, T. C. (1996). Bidirectional regulation of protein kinase M zeta in the maintenance of long-term potentiation and long-term depression. *Journal of Neuroscience, 16,* 5324–5333.

Huang, Y. Y., & Kandel, E. R. (1994). Recruitment of long-lasting and protein kinase A-dependent long-term potentiation in the CA1 region of hippocampus requires repeated tetanization. *Learning and Memory, 1,* 74–82.

Huerta, P. T., & Lisman, J. E. (1993). Heightened synaptic plasticity of hippocampal CA1 neurons during a cholinergically induced rhythmic state. *Nature, 364,* 723–725.

Huerta, P. T., Scearce, K. A., Farris, S. M., Empson, R. M., & Prusky, G. T. (1996). Preservation of spatial learning in fyn tyrosine kinase knockout mice. *Neuroreport, 7,* 1685–1689.

Isaac, J. T., Nicoll, R. A., & Malenka, R. C. (1995). Evidence for silent synapses: Implications for the expression of LTP. *Neuron, 15,* 427–434.

Ito, M., Sakurai, M., & Tongroach, P. (1982). Climbing fibre induced depression of both mossy fibre responsiveness and glutamate sensitivity of cerebellar Purkinje cells. *Journal of Physiology, 324,* 113–134.

Jeffery, K. J., & Morris, R. G. (1993). Cumulative long-term potentiation in the rat dentate gyrus correlates with, but does not modify, performance in the water maze [see comments]. *Hippocampus, 3,* 133–140.

Johnston, D., Magee, J. C., Colbert, C. M., & Cristie, B. R. (1996). Active properties of neuronal dendrites. *Annual Review of Neuroscience, 19,* 165–186.

Josselyn, S., Shi, C., Carlezon, W. J., Neve, R., Nestler, E., & Davis, M. (2001). Long-term memory is facilitated by cAMP response element-binding protein overexpression in the amygdala. *Journal of Neuroscience, 21,* 2404–2412.

Judge, M. E., & Quartermain, D. (1982). Characteristics of retrograde amnesia following reactivation of memory in mice. *Physiology and Behavior, 28,* 585–590.

Kaang, B. K., Kandel, E. R., & Grant, S. G. (1993). Activation of cAMP-responsive genes by stimuli that produce long-term facilitation in *Aplysia* sensory neurons. *Neuron, 10,* 427–435.

Kandel, E. R. (1976). *The Cellular Basis of Behavior: An Introduction to Behavioral Neurobiology.* San Francisco: Freeman.

Kauer, J. A., Malenka, R. C., & Nicoll, R. A. (1988). A persistent postsynaptic modification mediates long-term potentiation in the hippocampus. *Neuron, 1,* 911–917.

Keith, J., & Rudy, J. (1990). Why NMDA-receptor-dependent long-term potentiation may not be a mechanism of learning and memory: Reappraisal of the NMDA-receptor blockade strategy. *Psychobiology, 18,* 251–257.

Kelso, S. R., & Brown, T. H. (1986). Differential conditioning of associative synaptic enhancement in hippocampal brain slices. *Science, 232,* 85–87.

Kelso, S. R., Ganong, A. H., & Brown, T. H. (1986). Hebbian synapses in hippocampus. *Proceedings of the National Academy of Sciences, USA, 83,* 5326–5330.

Kenyon, G. T., Medina, J. F., & Mauk, M. D. (1998). A mathematical model of the cerebellar-olivary system I. Self-regulating equilibrium of climbing fiber activity. *Journal of Computational Neuroscience, 5,* 17–33.

Kim, J. J., Clark, R. E., & Thompson, R. F. (1995). Hippocampectomy impairs the memory of recently, but not remotely, acquired trace eyeblink conditioned responses. *Behavioral Neuroscience, 109,* 195–203.

Kim, J. J., DeCola, J. P., Landeira-Fernandez, J., & Fanselow, M. S. (1991). N-methyl-D-aspartate receptor antagonist APV blocks acquisition but not expression of fear conditioning. *Behavioral Neuroscience, 105,* 126–133.

Kim, J. J., & Fanselow, M. S. (1992). Modality-specific retrograde amnesia of fear. *Science, 256,* 675–677.

Kim, J. J., Krupa, D. J., & Thompson, R. F. (1998). Inhibitory cerebello-olivary projections and blocking effect in classical conditioning. *Science, 279,* 570–573.

Kimble, D. (1963). The effects of bilateral hippocampal lesions in rats. *Journal of Comparative and Physiological Psychology, 56,* 273–283.

Kimble, D., & Kimble, R. (1965). Hippocampectomy and response preservation in the rat. *Journal of Comparative and Physiological Psychology, 60,* 474–476.

Kistler, H. B., Jr., Hawkins, R. D., Koester, J., Steinbusch, H. W., Kandel, E. R., & Schwartz, J. H. (1985). Distribution of serotonin-immunoreactive cell bodies and processes in the abdominal ganglion of mature *Aplysia. Journal of Neuroscience, 5,* 72–80.

Klann, E., Chen, S. J., & Sweatt, J. D. (1993). Mechanism of protein kinase C activation during the induction and maintenance of long-term potentiation probed using a selective peptide substrate [see comments]. *Proceedings of the National Academy of Sciences, USA, 90,* 8337–8341.

Klein, M., & Kandel, E. R. (1978). Presynaptic modulation of voltage-dependent Ca2+ current: Mechanism for behavioral sensitization in *Aplysia* californica. *Proceedings of the National Academy of Sciences, USA, 75,* 3512–3516.

Klein, M., & Kandel, E. R. (1980). Mechanism of calcium current modulation underlying presynaptic facilitation and behavioral sensitization in *Aplysia. Proceedings of the National Academy of Sciences, USA, 77,* 6912–6916.

Klein, M., Shapiro, E., & Kandel, E. R. (1980). Synaptic plasticity and the modulation of the Ca2+ current. *Journal of Experimental Biology, 89,* 117–157.

Kogan, J. H., Frankland, P. W., Blendy, J. A., Coblentz, J., Marowitz, Z., Schutz, G., & Silva, A. J. (1997). Spaced training induces normal long-term memory in CREB mutant mice. *Current Biology, 7,* 1–11.

Krasne, F. B., & Teshiba, T. M. (1995). Habituation of an invertebrate escape reflex due to modulation by higher centers rather than local events. *Proceedings of the National Academy of Sciences, USA, 92,* 3362–3366.

Krupa, D. J., Thompson, J. K., & Thompson, R. F. (1993). Localization of a memory trace in the mammalian brain. *Science, 260,* 989–991.

Kullmann, D. M., & Siegelbaum, S. A. (1995). The site of expression of NMDA receptor-dependent LTP: New fuel for an old fire. *Neuron, 15,* 997–1002.

Kupfermann, I., Castellucci, V., Pinsker, H., & Kandel, E. (1970). Neuronal correlates of habituation and dishabituation of the gill-withdrawal reflex in *Aplysia. Science, 167,* 1743–1745.

Kupfermann, I., & Kandel, E. R. (1969). Neuronal controls of a behavioral response mediated by the abdominal ganglion of *Aplysia. Science, 164,* 847–850.

Larkman, A. U., & Jack, J. J. (1995). Synaptic plasticity: Hippocampal LTP. *Current Opinion in Neurobiology, 5,* 324–334.

Lashley, K. (1950). In search of the engram. In *Physiological mechanisms of animals behaviour* (pp. 4534–4482). Cambridge: Cambridge University Press.

Lavond, D. G., Hembree, T. L., & Thompson, R. F. (1985). Effect of kainic acid lesions of the cerebellar interpositus nucleus on eyelid conditioning in the rabbit. *Brain Research, 326,* 179–182.

Lavond, D. G., Steinmetz, J. E., Yokaitis, M. H., & Thompson, R. F. (1987). Reacquisition of classical conditioning after removal of cerebellar cortex. *Experimental Brain Research, 67,* 569–593.

Lee, H. K., Barbarosie, M., Kameyama, K., Bear, M. F., & Huganir, R. L. (2000). Regulation of distinct AMPA receptor phosphorylation sites during bidirectional synaptic plasticity. *Nature, 405,* 955–959.

Lee, K. S., Schottler, F., Oliver, M., & Lynch, G. (1980). Brief bursts of high-frequency stimulation produce two types of structural change in rat hippocampus. *Journal of Neurophysiology, 44,* 247–258.

Levy, W. B., & Steward, O. (1979). Synapses as associative memory elements in the hippocampal formation. *Brain Research, 175,* 233–245.

Lewis, J. L., Lo Turco, J. J., & Solomon, P. R. (1987). Lesions of the middle cerebellar peduncle disrupt acquisition and retention of the rabbit's classically conditioned nictitating membrane response. *Behavioral Neuroscience, 101,* 151–157.

Liao, D., Hessler, N. A., & Malinow, R. (1995). Activation of postsynaptically silent synapses during pairing-induced LTP in CA1 region of hippocampal slice. *Nature, 375,* 400–404.

Lin, X. Y., & Glanzman, D. L. (1994a). Hebbian induction of long-term potentiation of *Aplysia* sensorimotor synapses: Partial requirement for activation of an NMDA-related receptor. *Proceedings of the Royal Society of London: Series B, Biological Sciences, 255,* 215–221.

Lin, X. Y., & Glanzman D. L. (1994b). Long-term potentiation of *Aplysia* sensorimotor synapses in cell culture: Regulation by postsynaptic voltage. *Proceedings of the Royal Society of London: Series B, Biological Sciences, 255,* 113–118.

Linden, D. J. (1996). A protein synthesis-dependent late phase of cerebellar long-term depression. *Neuron, 17,* 483–490.

Linden, D. J. (1999). The return of the spike: Postsynaptic action potentials and the induction of LTP and LTD. *Neuron, 22,* 661–666.

Linden, D. J., & Connor, J. A. (1991). Participation of postsynaptic PKC in cerebellar long-term depression in culture. *Science, 254,* 1656–1659.

Linden, D. J., & Connor, J. A. (1995). Long-term synaptic depression. *Annual Review of Neuroscience, 18,* 319–357.

Linden, D. J., Smeyne, M., & Connor, J. A. (1993). Induction of cerebellar long-term depression in culture requires postsynaptic action of sodium ions. *Neuron, 11,* 1093–1100.

Lisman, J. E. (1985). A mechanism for memory storage insensitive to molecular turnover: A bistable autophosphorylating kinase. *Proceedings of the National Academy of Sciences, USA, 82,* 3055–3057.

Lisman, J. E. (1994). The CaM kinase II hypothesis for the storage of synaptic memory. *Trends in Neurosciences, 17,* 406–412.

Lisman, J. E., Malenka, R., Nicoll, R., & Malinow, R. (2001). Learning mechanisms: The case for CaMK-II. *Science, 276,* 5321–5325.

Lledo, P. M., Hjelmstad, G. O., Mukherji, S., Soderling, T. R., Malenka, R. C., & Nicoll, R. A. (1995). Calcium/calmodulin-dependent kinase II and long-term potentiation enhance synaptic transmission by the same mechanism. *Proceedings of the National Academy of Sciences, USA, 92,* 11175–11179.

Lledo, P. M., Zhang, X., Sudhof, T. C., Malenka, R. C., & Nicoll, R. A. (1998). Postsynaptic membrane fusion and long-term potentiation. *Science, 279,* 399–403.

Llinas, R., & Muhlethaler, M. (1988). An electrophysiological study of the in vitro, perfused brain stem-cerebellum of adult guinea-pig. *Journal of Physiology, 404,* 215–240.

Llinas, R., & Welsh, J. P. (1993). On the cerebellum and motor learning. *Current Opinion in Neurobiology, 3,* 958–965.

Logan, C. (1991). Cerebellar cortical involvement in excitatory and inhibitory classical conditioning. PhD dissertation, Stanford University, Stanford, California, unpublished.

Longley, R. D., & Longley, A. J. (1986). Serotonin immunoreactivity of neurons in the gastropod *Aplysia* californica. *Journal of Neurobiology, 17,* 339–358.

Lum-Ragan, J. T., & Gribkoff, V. K. (1993). The sensitivity of hippocampal long-term potentiation to nitric oxide synthase inhibitors is dependent upon the pattern of conditioning stimulation. *Neuroscience, 57,* 973–983.

Luscher, C., Malenka, R. C., & Nicoll, R. A. (1998). Monitoring glutamate release during LTP with glial transporter currents. *Neuron, 21,* 435–441.

Luscher, C., Xia, H., Beattie, E. C., Carroll, R. C., von Zastrow, M., Malenka, R. C., & Nicoll, R. A. (1999). Role of AMPA receptor cycling in synaptic transmission and plasticity. *Neuron, 24,* 649–658.

Lynch, G. S., Dunwiddie, T., & Gribkoff, V. (1977). Heterosynaptic depression: A postsynaptic correlate of long-term potentiation. *Nature, 266,* 737–739.

Lynch, G. S., Larson, J., Kelso, S., Barrionuevo, G., & Schottler, F. (1983). Intracellular injections of EGTA block induction of hippocampal long-term potentiation. *Nature, 305,* 719–721.

Mackey, S. L., Kandel, E. R., & Hawkins, R. D. (1989). Identified serotonergic neurons LCB1 and RCB1 in the cerebral ganglia of *Aplysia* produce presynaptic facilitation of siphon sensory neurons. *Journal of Neuroscience, 9,* 4227–4235.

Magee, J. C., & Johnston, D. (1997). A synaptically controlled, associative signal for Hebbian plasticity in hippocampal neurons [see comments]. *Science, 275,* 209–213.

Malamut, B. L., Saunders, R. C., & Mishkin, M. (1984). Monkeys with combined amygdalo-hippocampal lesions succeed in object discrimination learning despite 24-hour intertrial intervals. *Behavioral Neuroscience, 98,* 759–769.

Malenka, R. C., Kauer, J., Perkel, D., Mauk, M., Kelly, P., Nicoll, R., & Waxhaam, M. (1989). An essential role for postsynaptic calmodulin and protein kinase activity in long-term potentiation. *Nature, 340,* 554-557.

Malenka, R. C., Kauer, J. A., Perkel, D. J., & Nicoll, R. A. (1989). The impact of postsynaptic calcium on synaptic transmission—its role in long-term potentiation. *Trends in Neurosciences, 12,* 444–450.

Malenka, R. C., Kauer, J. A., Zucker, R. S., & Nicoll, R. A. (1988). Postsynaptic calcium is sufficient for potentiation of hippocampal synaptic transmission. *Science, 242,* 81–84.

Malenka, R. C., & Nicoll, R. A. (1993). NMDA-receptor-dependent synaptic plasticity: Multiple forms and mechanisms. *Trends in Neurosciences, 16,* 521–527.

Malenka, R. C., & Nicoll, R. A. (1999). Long-term potentiation—a decade of progress? *Science, 285,* 1870–1874.

Malinow, R. (1991). Transmission between pairs of hippocampal slice neurons: Quantal levels, oscillations, and LTP. *Science, 252,* 722–724.

Malinow, R., Madison, D. V., & Tsien, R. W. (1988). Persistent protein kinase activity underlying long-term potentiation. *Nature, 335,* 820–824.

Malinow, R., & Miller, J. P. (1986). Postsynaptic hyperpolarization during conditioning reversibly blocks induction of long-term potentiation. *Nature, 320,* 529–530.

Man, H. Y., Ju, W., Ahmadian, G., & Wang, Y. T. (2000). Intracellular trafficking of AMPA receptors in synaptic plasticity. *Cellular and Molecular Life Sciences, 57,* 1526–1534.

Man, H. Y., Lin, J. W., Ju, W. H., Ahmadian, G., Liu, L., Becker, L. E., Sheng, M., & Wang, Y. T. (2000). Regulation of AMPA receptor-mediated synaptic transmission by clathrin-dependent receptor internalization. *Neuron, 25,* 649–662.

Manabe, T., Renner, P., & Nicoll, R. A. (1992). Postsynaptic contribution to long-term potentiation revealed by the analysis of miniature synaptic currents. *Nature, 355,* 50–55.

Maren, S., Aharonov, G., & Fanselow, M. S. (1997). Neurotoxic lesions of the dorsal hippocampus and Pavlovian fear conditioning in rats. *Behavioural Brain Research, 88,* 261–274.

Markram, H., Lubke, J., Frotscher, M., & Sakmann, B. (1997). Regulation of synaptic efficacy by coincidence of postsynaptic APs and EPSPs [see comments]. *Science, 275,* 213–215.

Marr, D. (1969). A theory of cerebellar cortex. *Journal of Physiology, 202,* 437–470.

Marr, D. (1971). Simple memory: A theory for archicortex. *Philosophical Transactions of the Royal Society of London: Series B, Biological Sciences, 262,* 23–81.

Martin, K. C., Casadio, A., Zhu, H. E. Y., Rose, J. C., Chen, M., Bailey, C. H., & Kandel, E. R. (1997). Synapse-specific, long-term facilitation of *Aplysia* sensory to motor synapses: A function for local protein synthesis in memory storage. *Cell, 91,* 927–938.

Martin, K. C., Michael, D., Rose, J. C., Barad, M., Casadio, A., Zhu, H., & Kandel, E. R. (1997). MAP kinase translocates into the nucleus of the presynaptic cell and is required for long-term facilitation in *Aplysia. Neuron, 18,* 899–912.

Martin, S. J., Grimwood, P. D., & Morris, R. G. (2000). Synaptic plasticity and memory: An evaluation of the hypothesis. *Annual Review of Neuroscience, 23,* 649–711.

Mauelshagen, J., Parker, G. R., & Carew, T. J. (1996). Dynamics of induction and expression of long-term synaptic facilitation in *Aplysia. Journal of Neuroscience, 16,* 7099–7108.

Mauk, M. D., & Donegan, N. (1997). A model of Pavlovian eyelid conditioning based on the synaptic organization of the cerebellum. *Learning and Memory, 3,* 130–158.

Mauk, M. D., Steinmetz, J. E., & Thompson, R. F. (1986). Classical conditioning using stimulation of the inferior olive as the unconditioned stimulus. *Proceedings of the National Academy of Sciences, USA, 83,* 5349–5353.

McClelland, J. L., McNaughton, B. L., & O'Reilly, R. C. (1995). Why there are complementary learning systems in the hippocampus and neocortex: Insights from the successes and failures of connectionist models of learning and memory. *Psychological Review, 102,* 419–457.

McCormick, D. A., Clark, G. A., Lavond, D. G., & Thompson, R. F. (1982). Initial localization of the memory trace for a basic form of learning. *Proceedings of the National Academy of Sciences, USA, 79,* 2731–2735.

McCormick, D. A., Steinmetz, J. E., & Thompson, R. F. (1985). Lesions of the inferior olivary complex cause extinction of the classically conditioned eyeblink response. *Brain Research, 359,* 120–130.

McCormick, D. A., & Thompson, R. F. (1984a). Cerebellum: Essential involvement in the classically conditioned eyelid response. *Science, 223,* 296–299.

McCormick, D. A., & Thompson, R. F. (1984b). Neuronal responses of the rabbit cerebellum during acquisition and performance of a classically conditioned nictitating membrane-eyelid response. *Journal of Neuroscience, 4,* 2811–2822.

McGaugh, J. L. (1966). Time-dependent processes in memory storage. *Science, 153,* 1351–1358.

McGaugh, J. L. (2000). Memory—a century of consolidation. *Science, 287,* 248–251.

McNaughton, B., & Morris, R. (1987). Hippocampal synapticenhancement and information storage within a distributed memory system. *Trends in Neurosciences, 10,* 408–415.

McNaughton, B. L., Barnes, C. A., Rao, G., Baldwin, J., & Rasmussen, M. (1986). Long-term enhancement of hippocampal synaptic transmission and the acquisition of spatial information. *Journal of Neuroscience, 6,* 563–571.

McNaughton, B. L., Douglas, R. M., & Goddard, G. V. (1978). Synaptic enhancement in fascia dentata: Cooperativity among coactive afferents. *Brain Research, 157,* 277–293.

Medina, J. F., Garcia, K. S., Nores, W. L., Taylor, N. M., & Mauk, M. D. (2000). Timing mechanisms in the cerebellum: Testing predictions of a large-scale computer simulation. *Journal of Neuroscience, 20,* 5516–5525.

Medina, J. F., & Mauk, M. D. (1999). Simulations of cerebellar motor learning: Computational analysis of plasticity at the mossy fiber to deep nucleus synapse. *Journal of Neuroscience, 19,* 7140–7151.

Medina, J. F., & Mauk, M. D. (2000). Computer simulation of cerebellar information processing. *Nature Neuroscience, 3*(Suppl.), 1205–1211.

Meiri, N., Sun, M. K., Segal, Z., & Alkon, D. L. (1998). Memory and long-term potentiation (LTP) dissociated: Normal spatial memory despite CA1 LTP elimination with Kv1.4 antisense. *Proceedings of the National Academy of Sciences, USA, 95,* 15037–15042.

Mercer, A. R., Emptage, N. J., & Carew, T. J. (1991). Pharmacological dissociation of modulatory effects of serotonin in *Aplysia* sensory neurons. *Science, 254,* 1811–1813.

Mintz, M., Yun, Y., & Lavond, D. (1988). Unilateral inferior olive NMDA lesion leads to unilateral deficit in acquisition of NMR classical conditioning. *Society for Neuroscience Abstracts, 14,* 783.

Misanin, J. R., Miller, R. R., & Lewis, D. J. (1968). Retrograde amnesia produced by electroconvulsive shock after reactivation of a consolidated memory trace. *Science, 160,* 554–555.

Mishkin, M., Malmut, B., & Bachovalier, J. (1984). Memories and habits: Two neural systems. In J. Mcgaugh, G. Lynch, & N. Weinberger (Eds.), *The neurobiology of learning and memory* (pp. 65–77). New York: Guilford Press.

Miyakawa, T., Yagi, T., Kagiyama, A., & Niki, H. (1996). Radial maze performance, open-field and elevated plus-maze behaviors in Fyn-kinase deficient mice: Further evidence for increased fearfulness. *Brain Research: Molecular Brain Research, 37,* 145–150.

Montarolo, P. G., Goelet, P., Castellucci, V. F., Morgan, J., Kandel, E. R., & Schacher, S. (1986). A critical period for macromolecular synthesis in long-term heterosynaptic facilitation in *Aplysia*. *Science, 234,* 1249–1254.

Moore, J. W., Desmond, J. E., & Berthier, N. E. (1989). Adaptively timed conditioned responses and the cerebellum: A neural network approach. *Biological Cybernetics, 62,* 17–28.

Morris, R. G. (1989). Synaptic plasticity and learning: Selective impairment of learning rats and blockade of long-term potentiation in vivo by the N-methyl-D-aspartate receptor antagonist AP5. *Journal of Neuroscience, 9,* 3040–3057.

Morris, R. G., Anderson, E., Lynch, G. S., & Baudry, M. (1986). Selective impairment of learning and blockade of long-term potentiation by an N-methyl-D-aspartate receptor antagonist, AP5. *Nature, 319,* 774–776.

Moser, E. I., Krobert, K. A., Moser, M. B., & Morris, R. G. (1998). Impaired spatial learning after saturation of long-term potentiation [see comments]. *Science, 281,* 2038–2042.

Moser, E. I., & Moser, M. B. (1999). Is learning blocked by saturation of synaptic weights in the hippocampus? *Neuroscience and Biobehavioral Reviews, 23,* 661–672.

Mulkey, R. M., & Malenka, R. C. (1992). Mechanisms underlying induction of homosynaptic long-term depression in area CA1 of the hippocampus. *Neuron, 9,* 967–975.

Muller, D., Joly, M., & Lynch, G. (1988). Contributions of quisqualate and NMDA receptors to the induction and expression of LTP. *Science, 242,* 1694–1697.

Muller, D., Toni, N., & Buchs, P. A. (2000). Spine changes associated with long-term potentiation. *Hippocampus, 10,* 596–604.

Muller, U., & Carew, T. J. (1998). Serotonin induces temporally and mechanistically distinct phases of persistent PKA activity in *Aplysia* sensory neurons. *Neuron, 21,* 1423–1434.

Muller, W., & Connor, J. A. (1991). Dendritic spines as individual neuronal compartments for synaptic Ca2+ responses. *Nature, 354,* 73–76.

Murashima, M., & Hirano, T. (1999). Entire course and distinct phases of day-lasting depression of miniature EPSC amplitudes in cultured Purkinje neurons. *Journal of Neuroscience, 19,* 7326–7333.

Murphy, G. G., & Glanzman, D. L. (1996). Enhancement of sensorimotor connections by conditioning-related stimulation in *Aplysia* depends upon postsynaptic Ca2+. *Proceedings of the National Academy of Sciences, USA, 93,* 9931–9936.

Murphy, G. G., & Glanzman, D. L. (1997). Mediation of classical conditioning in *Aplysia* californica by long-term potentiation of sensorimotor synapses [see comments]. *Science, 278,* 467–471.

Murphy, G. G., & Glanzman, D. L. (1999). Cellular analog of differential classical conditioning in *Aplysia:* Disruption by the NMDA receptor antagonist DL-2-amino-5-phosphonovalerate. *Journal of Neuroscience, 19,* 10595–10602.

Nader, K., Schafe, G. E., & Le Doux, J. E. (2000). Fear memories require protein synthesis in the amygdala for reconsolidation after retrieval [see comments]. *Nature, 406,* 722–726.

Neuhoff, H., Roeper, J., & Schweizer, M. (1999). Activity-dependent formation of perforated synapses in cultured hippocampal neurons. *European Journal of Neuroscience, 11,* 4241–4250.

Nguyen, P. V., Abel, T., Kandel, E. R. (1994). Requirement of a critical period of transcription for induction of a late phase of LTP. *Science, 265,* 1104–1107.

Nguyen, P. V., & Kandel, E. R. (1996). A macromolecular synthesis-dependent late phase of long-term potentiation requiring cAMP in the medial perforant pathway of rat hippocampal slices. *Journal of Neuroscience, 16,* 3189–3198.

Nicoll, R. A., & Malenka, R. C. (1995). Contrasting properties of two forms of long-term potentiation in the hippocampus. *Nature, 377,* 115–118.

Nordholm, A. F., Thompson, J. K., Dersarkissian, C., & Thompson, R. F. (1993). Lidocaine infusion in a critical region of cerebellum completely prevents learning of the conditioned eyeblink response. *Behavioral Neuroscience, 107,* 882–886.

O'Keefe, J. (1976). Place units in the hippocampus of the freely moving rat. *Experimental Neurology, 51,* 78–109.

O'Keefe, J. (1979). A review of the hippocampal place cells. *Progress in Neurobiology, 13,* 419–439.

O'Keefe, J., Nadel, L., Keightley, S., & Kill, D. (1975). Fornix lesions selectively abolish place learning in the rat. *Experimental Neurology, 48,* 152–166.

Oliet, S. H., Malenka, R. C., & Nicoll, R. A. (1996). Bidirectional control of quantal size by synaptic activity in the hippocampus. *Science, 271,* 1294–1297.

Olton, D. S. (1979). Mazes, maps, and memory. *American Psychologist, 34,* 583–596.

Olton, D. S., & Feustle, W. A. (1981). Hippocampal function required for nonspatial working memory. *Experimental Brain Research, 41,* 380–389.

O'Reilly, R. C., & McClelland, J. L. (1994). Hippocampal conjunctive encoding, storage, and recall: Avoiding a trade-off. *Hippocampus, 4,* 661–682.

O'Reilly, R. C., & Rudy, J. W. (2001). Conjunctive representations in learning and memory: Principles of cortical and hippocampal function. *Psychological Review, 108,* 311–345.

Otmakhov, N., Griffith, L. C., & Lisman, J. E. (1997). Postsynaptic inhibitors of calcium/calmodulin-dependent protein kinase type II block induction but not maintenance of pairing-induced long-term potentiation. *Journal of Neuroscience, 17,* 5357–5365.

Otnaess, M. K., Brun, V. H., Moser, M. B., & Moser, E. I. (1999). Pretraining prevents spatial learning impairment after saturation of hippocampal long-term potentiation. *Journal of Neuroscience, 19,* RC49.

Paulsen, O., & Sejnowski, T. J. (2000). Natural patterns of activity and long-term synaptic plasticity. *Current Opinion in Neurobiology, 10,* 172–179.

Perkel, D. J., & Nicoll, R. A. (1993). evidence for all-or-none regulation of neurotransmitter release: Implications for long-term potentiation. *Journal of Physiology, 471,* 481–500.

Perrett, S. P., & Mauk, M. D. (1995). Extinction of conditioned eyelid responses requires the anterior lobe of cerebellar cortex. *Journal of Neuroscience, 15,* 2074–2080.

Perrett, S. P., Ruiz, B. P., & Mauk, M. D. (1993). Cerebellar cortex lesions disrupt learning-dependent timing of conditioned eyelid responses. *Journal of Neuroscience, 13,* 1708–1718.

Pettit, D. L., Perlman, S., & Malinow, R. (1994). Potentiated transmission and prevention of further LTP by increased CaMKII activity in postsynaptic hippocampal slice neurons. *Science, 266,* 1881–1885.

Pinsker, H. M., Hening, W. A., Carew, T. J., & Kandel, E. R. (1973). Long-term sensitization of a defensive withdrawal reflex in *Aplysia. Science, 182,* 1039–1042.

Pinsker, H. M., Kupfermann, I., Castellucci, V., & Kandel, E. (1970). Habituation and dishabituation of the gill-withdrawal reflex in *Aplysia. Science, 167,* 1740–1742.

Racine, R. J., Milgram, N. W., & Hafner, S. (1983). Long-term potentiation phenomena in the rat limbic forebrain. *Brain Research, 260,* 217–231.

Ramos, J. M. (1998). Retrograde amnesia for spatial information: A dissociation between intra and extramaze cues following hippocampus lesions in rats. *European Journal of Neuroscience, 10,* 3295–3301.

Ranck, J. B., Jr. (1973). Studies on single neurons in dorsal hippocampal formation and septum in unrestrained rats. I. Behavioral correlates and firing repertoires. *Experimental Neurology, 41,* 461–531.

Raymond, J. L., Lisberger, S. G., & Mauk, M. D. (1996). The cerebellum: A neuronal learning machine? *Science, 272,* 1126–1131.

Regehr, W. G., & Tank, D. W. (1990). Postsynaptic NMDA receptor-mediated calcium accumulation in hippocampal CA1 pyramidal cell dendrites. *Nature, 345,* 807–810.

Riedel, G., Micheau, J., Lam, A. G., Roloff, E., Martin, S. J., Bridge, H., Hoz, L., Poeschel,

B., McCulloch, J., & Morris, R. G. (1999). Reversible neural inactivation reveals hippocampal participation in several memory processes. *Nature Neuroscience, 2,* 898–905.

Robinson, G. B. (1992). Maintained saturation of hippocampal long-term potentiation does not disrupt acquisition of the eight-arm radial maze. *Hippocampus, 2,* 389–395.

Roche, K., O'Brien, R., Mammen, A., Bernhardt, J., & Huganir, R. (1996). Characterization of multiple phosphorylation sites on the AMPA receptor GluR1 subunit. *Neuron, 16,* 1179–1188.

Rosenfield, M. E., Dovydaitis, A., & Moore, J. W. (1985). Brachium conjunctivum and rubrobulbar tract: Brain stem projections of red nucleus essential for the conditioned nictitating membrane response. *Physiology and Behavior, 34,* 751–759.

Rosenfield, M. E., & Moore, J. W. (1983). Red nucleus lesions disrupt the classically conditioned nictitating membrane response in rabbits. *Behavioural Brain Research, 10,* 393–398.

Royer, S., Coulson, R. L., & Klein, M. (2000). Switching off and on of synaptic sites at *Aplysia* sensorimotor synapses. *Journal of Neuroscience, 20,* 626–638.

Sacktor, T. C., Osten, P., Valsamis, H., Jiang, X., Naik, M. U., & Sublette, E. (1993). Persistent activation of the zeta isoform of protein kinase C in the maintenance of long-term potentiation [see comments]. *Proceedings of the National Academy of Sciences, USA, 90,* 8342–8346.

Samuels, I. (1972). Hippocampal lesions in the rat: Effects on spatial and visual habits. *Physiology and Behavior, 8,* 1093–1097.

Sara, S. J. (2000). Retrieval and reconsolidation: toward a neurobiology of remembering. *Learning and Memory, 7,* 73–84.

Sastry, B. R., Goh, J. W., & Auyeung, A. (1986). Associative induction of posttetanic and long-term potentiation in CA1 neurons of rat hippocampus. *Science, 232,* 988–990.

Saucier, D., & Cain, D. P. (1995). Spatial learning without NMDA receptor-dependent long-term potentiation [see comments]. *Nature, 378,* 186–189.

Schacher, S., Kandel, E. R., & Montarolo, P. (1993). cAMP and arachidonic acid simulate long-term structural and functional changes produced by neurotransmitters in *Aplysia* sensory neurons. *Neuron, 10*, 1079–1088.

Schacher, S., & Montarolo, P. G. (1991). Target-dependent structural changes in sensory neurons of *Aplysia* accompany long-term heterosynaptic inhibition. *Neuron, 6*, 679–690.

Schenk, F., & Morris, R. G. (1985). Dissociation between components of spatial memory in rats after recovery from the effects of retrohippocampal lesions. *Experimental Brain Research, 58*, 11–28.

Schneiderman, N. (1966). Interstimulus interval function of the nictitating membrane response in the rabbit under delay versus trace conditioning. *Journal of Comparative and Physiological Psychology, 62*, 397–402.

Schneiderman, N., & Gormezano, I. (1964). Conditioning of the nictitating membrane of the rabbit as a function of CS-UCS interval. *Journal of Comparative and Physiological Psychology, 57*, 188–195.

Schultz, W. (1998). Predictive reward signal of dopamine neurons. *Journal of Neurophysiology, 80*, 1–27.

Schwartz, J. H., Bernier, L., Castellucci, V. F., Palazzolo, M., Saitoh, T., Stapleton, A., & Kandel, E. R. (1983). What molecular steps determine the time course of the memory for short-term sensitization in *Aplysia*? *Cold Spring Harbor Symposia on Quantitative Biology, 48*(Part 2) 811–819.

Schwartzkroin, P. A., & Wester, K. (1975). Long-lasting facilitation of a synaptic potential following tetanization in the in vitro hippocampal slice. *Brain Research, 89*, 107–119.

Scoville, W., & Milner, B. (1957). Loss of recent memory after bilateral hippocampal lesions. *Journal of Neurology, Neurosurgery, and Psychiatry, 20*, 11–21.

Shepherd, G. M. (1990). *The synaptic organization of the brain.* New York: Oxford University Press.

Shi, S. H., Hayashi, Y., Petralia, R. S., Zaman, S. H., Wenthold, R. J., Svoboda, K., & Malinow, R. (1999). Rapid spine delivery and redistribution of AMPA receptors after synaptic NMDA receptor activation [see comments]. *Science, 284*, 1811–1816.

Shimizu, E., Tang, Y. P., Rampon, C., & Tsien, J. Z. (2000). NMDA receptor-dependent synaptic reinforcement as a crucial process for memory consolidation. *Science, 290*, 1170–1174.

Shors, T. J., & Matzel, L. D. (1997). Long-term potentiation: What's learning got to do with it? *Behavioral and Brain Sciences, 20*, 597–614, 614–555.

Shuster, M. J., Camardo, J. S., Siegelbaum, S. A., & Kandel, E. R. (1985). Cyclic AMP-dependent protein kinase closes the serotonin-sensitive K+ channels of *Aplysia* sensory neurones in cell-free membrane patches. *Nature, 313*, 392–395.

Siegelbaum, S. A., Camardo, J. S., & Kandel, E. R. (1982). Serotonin and cyclic AMP close single K+ channels in *Aplysia* sensory neurones. *Nature, 299*, 413–417.

Silva, A. J., Paylor, R., Wehner, J. M., & Tonegawa, S. (1992). Impaired spatial learning in alpha-calcium-calmodulin kinase II mutant mice [see comments]. *Science, 257*, 206–211.

Silva, A. J., Stevens, C. F., Tonegawa, S., & Wang, Y. (1992). Deficient hippocampal long-term potentiation in alpha-calcium-calmodulin kinase II mutant mice [see comments]. *Science, 257*, 201–206.

Solomon, P. R., & Moore, J. W. (1975). Latent inhibition and stimulus generalization of the classically conditioned nictitating membrane response in rabbits (Oryctolagus cuniculus) following dorsal hippocampal ablation. *Journal of Comparative and Physiological Psychology, 89*, 1192–1203.

Squire, L. R. (1992). Memory and the hippocampus: A synthesis from findings with rats, monkeys, and humans [published erratum appears in *Psychological Review, 99*, 582]. *Psychological Review, 99*, 195–231.

Squire, L. R., Knowlton, B., & Musen, G. (1993). The structure and organization of memory. *Annual Review of Psychology, 44*, 453–495.

Staubli, U., & Lynch, G. (1987). Stable hippocampal long-term potentiation elicited by 'theta' pattern stimulation. *Brain Research, 435*, 227–234.

Steinmetz, J. E. (1990). Classical nictitating membrane conditioning in rabbits with varying interstimulus intervals and direct activation of cerebellar mossy fibers as the CS. *Behavioural Brain Research, 38,* 97–108.

Steinmetz, J. E., Lavond, D. G., Ivkovich, D., Logan, C. G., & Thompson, R. F. (1992). Disruption of classical eyelid conditioning after cerebellar lesions: Damage to a memory trace system or a simple performance deficit? *Journal of Neuroscience, 12,* 4403–4426.

Steinmetz, J. E., Lavond, D. G., & Thompson, R. F. (1989). Classical conditioning in rabbits using pontine nucleus stimulation as a conditioned stimulus and inferior olive stimulation as an unconditioned stimulus. *Synapse, 3,* 225–233.

Steinmetz, J. E., Rosen, D. J., Chapman, P. F., Lavond, D. G., & Thompson, R. F. (1986). Classical conditioning of the rabbit eyelid response with a mossy-fiber stimulation CS: I. Pontine nuclei and middle cerebellar peduncle stimulation. *Behavioral Neuroscience, 100,* 878–887.

Stevens, R., & Cowey, A. (1974). Visual discrimination learning and transfer in rats with hippocampal lesions. *Quarterly Journal of Experimental Psychology, 26,* 582–593.

Stopfer, M., & Carew, T. J. (1996). Heterosynaptic facilitation of tail sensory neuron synaptic transmission during habituation in tail-induced tail and siphon withdrawal reflexes of *Aplysia. Journal of Neuroscience, 16,* 4933–4948.

Stuart, G., Spruston, N., Sakmann, B., & Hausser, M. (1997). Action potential initiation and backpropagation in neurons of the mammalian CNS. *Trends in Neurosciences 20,* 125–131.

Sutherland, G. R., & McNaughton, B. (2000). Memory trace reactivation in hippocampal and neocortical neuronal ensembles. *Current Opinion in Neurobiology, 10,* 180–186.

Sutherland, R. J., Dringenberg, H. C., & Hoesing, J. M. (1993). Induction of long-term potentiation at perforant path dentate synapses does not affect place learning or memory [see comments]. *Hippocampus, 3,* 141–147.

Sutton, M. A., & Carew, T. J. (2000). Parallel molecular pathways mediate expression of distinct forms of intermediate-term facilitation at tail sensory-motor synapses in *Aplysia. Neuron, 26,* 219–231.

Sutton, M. A., Masters, S. E., Bagnall, M. W., & Carew, T. J. (2001). Molecular mechanisms underlying a unique intermediate phase of memory in aplysia. *Neuron, 31,* 143–154.

Sutton, R. S., & Barto, A. G. (1981). Toward a modern theory of adaptive networks: Expectation and prediction. *Psychological Review, 88,* 135–170.

Tang, Y. P., Shimizu, E., Dube, G. R., Rampon, C., Kerchner, G. A., Zhuo, M., Liu, G., & Tsien, J. Z. (1999). Genetic enhancement of learning and memory in mice [see comments]. *Nature, 401,* 63–69.

Teyler, T. J., & DiScenna, P. (1987). Long-term potentiation. *Annual Review of Neuroscience, 10,* 131–161.

Thomas, M. J., Moody, T. D., Makhinson, M., & O'Dell, T. J. (1996). Activity-dependent beta-adrenergic modulation of low frequency stimulation induced LTP in the hippocampal CA1 region. *Neuron, 17,* 475–482.

Thompson, R. F., & Krupa, D. J. (1994). Organization of memory traces in the mammalian brain. *Annual Review of Neuroscience, 17,* 519–549.

Thompson, R. F., Swain, R., Clark, R., & Shinkman, P. (2000). Intracerebellar conditioning—Brogden and Gantt revisited. *Behavioural Brain Research, 110,* 3–11.

Thompson, R. F., Thompson, J. K., Kim, J. J., Krupa, D. J., & Shinkman, P. G. (1998). The nature of reinforcement in cerebellar learning. *Neurobiology of Learning and Memory, 70,* 150–176.

Trudeau, L. E., & Castellucci, V. F. (1992). Contribution of polysynaptic pathways in the mediation and plasticity of *Aplysia* gill and siphon withdrawal reflex: Evidence for differential modulation. *Journal of Neuroscience, 12,* 3838–3848.

Trudeau, L. E., & Castellucci, V. F. (1993a). Functional uncoupling of inhibitory interneurons plays an important role in short-term sensitization of *Aplysia* gill and siphon withdrawal reflex. *Journal of Neuroscience, 13,* 2126–2135.

Trudeau, L. E., & Castellucci, V. F. (1993b). Sensitization of the gill and siphon withdrawal reflex of *Aplysia*: multiple sites of change in the neuronal network. *Journal of Neurophysiology, 70,* 1210–1220.

Trudeau, L. E., & Castellucci, V. F. (1995). Postsynaptic modifications in long-term facilitation in *Aplysia*: Upregulation of excitatory amino acid receptors. *Journal of Neuroscience, 15,* 1275–1284.

Tsien, J. Z., Huerta, P. T., & Tonegawa, S. (1996). The essential role of hippocampal CA1 NMDA receptor-dependent synaptic plasticity in spatial memory [see comments]. *Cell, 87,* 1327–1338.

Tully, T., Bolwig, G., Christensen, J., Connolly, J., DelVecchio, M., DeZazzo, J., Dubnau, J., Jones, C., Pinto, S., Regulski, M., Svedberg, B., & Velinzon, K. (1996). A return to genetic dissection of memory in *Drosophila. Cold Spring Harbor Symposia on Quantitative Biology, 61,* 207–218.

Walters, E. T. (1989). Transformation of siphon responses during conditioning of *Aplysia* suggests a model of primitive stimulus-response association. *Proceedings of the National Academy of Sciences, USA, 86,* 7616–7619.

Walters, E. T., & Byrne, J. H. (1983). Associative conditioning of single sensory neurons suggests a cellular mechanism for learning. *Science, 219,* 405–408.

Walters, E. T., Byrne, J. H., Carew, T. J., & Kandel, E. R. (1983). Mechanoafferent neurons innervating tail of *Aplysia:* II. Modulation by sensitizing stimulation. *Journal of Neurophysiology, 50,* 1543–1559.

Walters, E. T., Carew, T. J., & Kandel, E. R. (1981). Associative Learning in *Aplysia*: Evidence for conditioned fear in an invertebrate. *Science, 211,* 504–506.

Wang, J. H., & Feng, D. P. (1992). Postsynaptic protein kinase C essential to induction and maintenance of long-term potentiation in the hippocampal CA1 region. *Proceedings of the National Academy of Sciences, USA, 89,* 2576–2580.

Watabe, A. M., Zaki, P. A., & O'Dell, T. J. (2000). Coactivation of beta-adrenergic and cholinergic receptors enhances the induction of long-term potentiation and synergistically activates mitogen-activated protein kinase in the hippocampal CA1 region. *Journal of Neuroscience, 20,* 5924–5931.

Welsh, J. P., & Harvey, J. A. (1989). Cerebellar lesions and the nictitating membrane reflex: Performance deficits of the conditioned and unconditioned response. *Journal of Neuroscience, 9,* 299–311.

Welsh, J. P., & Harvey, J. A. (1991). Pavlovian conditioning in the rabbit during inactivation of the interpositus nucleus. *Journal of Physiology, 444,* 459–480.

Wigstrom, H., Gustafsson, B., Huang, Y. Y., & Abraham, W. C. (1986). Hippocampal long-term potentiation is induced by pairing single afferent volleys with intracellularly injected depolarizing current pulses. *Acta Physiologica Scandinavica, 126,* 317–319.

Wild, J. M., & Blampied, N. M. (1972). Hippocampal lesions and stimulus generalization in rats. *Physiology and Behavior, 9,* 505–511.

Willshaw, D. J., & Buckingham, J. T. (1990). An assessment of Marr's theory of the hippocampus as a temporary memory store. *Philosophical Transactions of the Royal Society of London: Series B, Biological Sciences, 329,* 205–215.

Wu, F., Friedman, L., & Schacher, S. (1995). Transient versus persistent functional and structural changes associated with facilitation of *Aplysia* sensorimotor synapses are second messenger dependent. *Journal of Neuroscience, 15,* 7517–7527.

Wyllie, D. J., Manabe, T., & Nicoll, R. A. (1994). A rise in postsynaptic Ca2+ potentiates miniature excitatory postsynaptic currents and AMPA responses in hippocampal neurons. *Neuron, 12,* 127–138.

Xia, J., Chung, H. J., Wihler, C., Huganir, R. L., & Linden, D. J. (2000). Cerebellar long-term depression requires PKC-regulated interactions between GluR2/3 and PDZ domain-containing proteins. *Neuron, 28,* 499–510.

Yeo, C. H., & Hardiman, M. J. (1992). Cerebellar cortex and eyeblink conditioning: A reexamination. *Experimental Brain Research, 88,* 623–638.

Yin, J. C., Del Vecchio, M., Zhou, H., & Tully, T. (1995). CREB as a memory modulator: Induced expression of a dCREB2 activator isoform enhances long-term memory in *Drosophila. Cell, 81,* 107–115.

Yin, J. C., Wallach, J. S., Del Vecchio, M., Wilder, E. L., Zhou, H., Quinn, W. G., & Tully, T. (1994). Induction of a dominant negative CREB transgene specifically blocks long-term memory in *Drosophila. Cell, 79,* 49–58.

Young, S. L., Bohenek, D. L., & Fanselow, M. S. (1994). NMDA processes mediate anterograde amnesia of contextual fear conditioning induced by hippocampal damage: Immunization against amnesia by context preexposure. *Behavioral Neuroscience, 108,* 19–29.

Yovell, Y., & Abrams, T. W. (1992). Temporal asymmetry in activation of *Aplysia* adenylyl cyclase by calcium and transmitter may explain temporal requirements of conditioning. *Proceedings of the National Academy of Sciences, USA, 89,* 6526–6530.

Yuste, R., & Denk, W. (1995). Dendritic spines as basic functional units of neuronal integration. *Nature, 375,* 682–684.

Yuste, R., Majewska, A., Cash, S. S., & Denk, W. (1999). Mechanisms of calcium influx into hippocampal spines: Heterogeneity among spines, coincidence detection by NMDA receptors, and optical quantal analysis. *Journal of Neuroscience, 19,* 1976–1987.

Zhao, Y., & Klein, M. (in press). Modulation of the readily releasable pool of transmitter and of exitation-secretion coupling by acitivty and serotonin at *Aplysia* sensorimotor synapses.

Zhu, H., Wu, F., & Schacher, S. (1997). Site-specific and sensory neuron-dependent increases in postsynaptic glutamate sensitivity accompany serotonin-induced long-term facilitation at *Aplysia* sensorimotor synapses. *Journal of Neuroscience, 17,* 4976–4986.

Zola-Morgan, S., & Squire, L. (1984). Preserved learning in monkeys with medial temporal lesions: Sparing of motor and cognitive skills. *Journal of Neuroscience 4,* 1072–1085.

Zola-Morgan, S. M., & Squire, L. R. (1990). The primate hippocampal formation: evidence for a time-limited role in memory storage. *Science, 250,* 288–290.

CHAPTER 5

Learning Mutants

LOUIS D. MATZEL

INTRODUCTION: THE CONCEPTUAL AND TECHNICAL EVOLUTION OF THE MODERN GENETIC APPROACH

Throughout recorded history, man has speculated on the physical substrates for memory. In his well-recited treatise, Socrates proposed that "there exists in the mind of man a block of wax . . . that when we wish to remember anything . . . we hold the wax to the perceptions and thoughts, and in that material receive the impression of them . . . ; we remember and know what is imprinted as long as the impression lasts" (Socrates, in Plato's *Theaetetus,* fourth century B.C.). In an insightful elaboration of this theory, Socrates asserted that his metaphoric tablet of wax was subject to variations, for instance, through the introduction of "impurities," such that the impression of new memories or the perception of old ones might be distorted. Furthermore, these impurities were said to accumulate over time but might also be present in different concentrations across individuals as a function of

age or heritage. In these classic speculations, Socrates foreshadowed central tenets of modern molecular/genetic descriptions of memory, that is, that memories are subserved by a physically delimited substrate, that this substrate (and its capacity to store memories) is subject to interactions with the environment and may mutate, and that properties of the substrate (and thus the parameters of memory) are in part determined by an individual's genetic blueprint.

The advent of Mendelian genetics engendered a more formal articulation of the genetic regulation of memory. Of particular note, Hering (1870) speculated on the basis of organic memory, proposing that heredity and memory were synonymous, subserved by a common underlying mechanism. A proponent of Hering, Ribot (1881) added that psychological memory differed from genetic memory only in that psychological memory interacted with the process of consciousness. While these (and related Lamarckian) conceptualizations of memory enjoyed enormous popularity during the later half of the 19th Century, the exploration of the genetic regulation of memory was largely restricted to statistical studies of recombination across generations, an approach that supported sophisticated

Thanks are extended to Chetan Gandhi and Tracey Shors for their helpful comments on an earlier version of this manuscript.

guesses about the characteristics of genetic material.

The description in 1953 by Watson and Crick (Watson & Crick, 1953) of the DNA molecule fostered a torrent of new strategies to address the mechanisms of genetics and, subsequently, a new interest in the role of genetics in memory storage. By 1960, the laboratory of Francois Jacob (e.g., Wollman, Jacob, & Hayes, 1956) had developed new methods to locate specific genes on chromosomal material and, moreover, a process by which genes could be excised or added into the DNA of single cells. These methods were the precursors to modern transgenic science, an approach that has recently revolutionized our approach to the elucidation of memory.

It is interesting to note that the rapid evolution of molecular genetics in the 1950s and 1960s brought with it expectations and questions that pervade colloquial discussions until this day. As a particularly striking example, in the preface of a text summarizing a three day symposium on the "chemistry of learning," Corning and Ratner (1967) write that one impetus for the symposium was the frequent request by nonscientists to be provided "'memory molecules' . . . to help some senile relative," a request familiar to many readers of this chapter. Despite the optimism of the early 1960s, our progress in satisfying these goals has been slow. However, during the prior decade we witnessed the emergence of a radically different approach to this problem, an approach that may at last provide answers to timeless questions, and in doing so, may render effective strategies to rescue those "senile relatives." In what follows, we will describe recent insights into the molecular constituents of memory. These insights have been derived from modern transgenic science, wherein it is possible to directly and specifically regulate mammalian genes so as to elucidate their influence on behavior. Although an extensive and complementary re-

search effort has been based on the analysis of generational recombinations and population statistics, the demands of brevity require that we not address that literature here although recent reviews are available (e.g., Dubnau & Tully, 1998).

LONG-TERM POTENTIATION: A PUTATIVE MECHANISM AND TARGET FOR GENETIC MANIPULATIONS

The search for the genetic substrates of memory was once delimited by the assumption that the genetic material might in itself serve to store memories, a hypothesis that has found little empirical support. While we return to this postulate later, the preponderance of recent research has been based on a different approach to this problem. Given its near complete dominance of the research effort, we will focus here on this contemporary approach, in which molecular/genetic technologies are employed to probe the underpinnings of the memory mechanism. However, this contemporary effort has itself been delimited by certain assumptions regarding the neurophysiological substrates for memory storage. Thus to appreciate fully these studies and their implications, it will first be necessary to understand the framework under which they were conceived. To a large extent, the transgenic approach in recent years has been restricted to the exploration of the relationship of long-term potentiation (LTP) to memory. LTP is a form of synaptic plasticity that is widely asserted to subserve the induction and storage of certain forms of memory. While it is far from certain that LTP is an adequate device to store memories (cf. Matzel & Shors, 2001; McEachern & Shaw, 1996; Saucier & Cain, 1995a; Shors & Matzel, 1997; Vanderwolf & Cain, 1994), the framework imposed by LTP has been a useful heuristic tool and has led to many insights into the molecular regulation of memory. Because of its central relevance to discussions of the molecular constituents of memory, it will first be necessary to briefly review concepts relevant to LTP. A more complete review of this literature is available in many sources (e.g., see Chap. 4, this volume; also see Hawkins, Kandel, & Siegelbaum, 1993; Martinez & Derrick, 1996; Matzel, Talk, Muzzio, & Rogers, 1998; Teyler & DiScenna, 1987), and the summary provided here can be disregarded entirely by those familiar with the phenomenon, its substrates, and its mechanisms.

The Phenomenon of LTP

Although the phenomenon of LTP had been alluded to for several years, its first formal description was reported by Bliss and Lomo in 1973 (also see Bliss & Gardner-Medwin, 1973). As it was then described, LTP reflected an increase in synaptic efficacy of hippocampal synapses that lasted from hours to days following brief high-frequency stimulation of an afferent pathway. Thus, LTP can be generally characterized as an activity-dependent potentiation of post-synaptic responses, that is, an increase in the amplitude and speed of evoked excitatory postsynaptic potentials (EPSPs).

Long-term potentiation, in various forms, can be induced at the three major synaptic connections of the hippocampus, a brain region considered critical to the acquisition or processing of some forms of memory (e.g., Scoville & Milner, 1957). LTP has been observed in dentate gyrus granule cells following strong stimulation of the perforant path (Bliss & Lomo, 1973), in CA3 pyramidal cells following stimulation of the mossy fibers (Alger & Teyler, 1976; Yamamoto & Chujo, 1978), and in CA1 pyramidal cells consequent to stimulation

of the Schaffer collateral branches of the CA3 neurons (Andersen, Sundberg, Sveen, & Wigstrom, 1977; Schwartzkroin & Wester, 1975). In addition to the hippocampus, various forms of LTP have been observed in other subcortical and cortical brain areas (see Shors & Matzel, 1997, for review) and thus can play a widespread role in modulating the flow of information throughout the brain.

It is beyond the scope of this article to describe the data which leads many to conclude that LTP subserves memory storage in the mammalian brain (for comprehensive reviews, see Martinez & Derrick, 1996; Shors & Matzel, 1997). For present purposes, suffice it to say that LTP can be induced under physiologically relevant conditions, it is relatively long-lasting (persisting for days to weeks), it may in some instances naturally occur coincident with memory induction, and it is sensitive to pharmacological agents that commensurately impair the formation of new memories.

The cellular and molecular events that underlie LTP induction at different synapses within the hippocampal formation and throughout the brain are not homogeneous, and no single mechanism is representative of the general phenomenon. Thus the term LTP has been suggested to have little descriptive value (Shors & Matzel, 1997). With that in mind, we will describe a *class* of features that are conserved across various forms of LTP and which have been the target of transgenic manipulations.

Postsynaptic Ca²⁺ and LTP Induction

We will focus here on two mechanistically similar and historically prototypical forms of hippocampal LTP which are observed in the dentate gyrus granule cells and CA1 pyramidal cells. For simplicity, we will often refer to these forms of LTP as hippocampal LTP, although it is clear that LTP in CA3 pyramidal cells is in some ways dissimilar (Jaffe & Johnston, 1990; Johnston, Williams, Jaffe, & Gray, 1992). Hippocampal granule and pyramidal cell LTP, as well as most other forms of LTP (cf. Salin, Malenka, & Nicoll, 1996), share a common requirement for a transient elevation of postsynaptic Ca^{2+}.

An elevation of intracellular Ca^{2+} is clearly necessary and may be sufficient to catalyze the induction of LTP. For example, induction of LTP between Schaffer collaterals and CA1 pyramidal cells is prevented by a pretetanus injection of Ca^{2+} chelators into the postsynaptic cell (Lynch, Larson, Kelso, Barrionuevo, & Schottler, 1983; Malenka, Kauer, Zucker, & Nicoll, 1988), and induction occurs when the postsynaptic cell is artificially loaded with the ion (Malenka et al., 1988). The elevation of intracellular Ca^{2+} during the induction of LTP may arise from several sources, including voltage-gated ion channels and via release of the ion from intracellular storage pools (Bortolotto & Collingridge, 1993, 1995). However, a more primary source of the Ca^{2+} signal during LTP induction reflects an influx of the ion through a channel pore coupled to the NMDA subtype of glutamate receptor (e.g., Collingridge, Kehl, & McLennan, 1983; Harris, Ganong, & Cotman, 1984). This receptor is unique in that stimulation of the channel requires glutamate binding as well as a moderate level of depolarization. At normal resting potentials (≈ -70 mV), the channel is blocked by magnesium ions, and glutamate binding is insufficient to open it. However, at depolarized membrane potentials (> -40 mV), magnesium is expelled from the channel, upon which glutamate binding will open the channel.

As stipulated above, the NMDA receptor complex is dually regulated by both glutamate and membrane voltage (i.e., depolarization). These cofactors can be recruited through several means, and the patterns of stimulation that are necessary are often said to reflect nonassociative and associative forms of LTP (see the section titled "Stimulus Convergence and LTP Induction" for further discussion).

Ca^{2+}-Dependent Biochemical Processes Underlying Potentiation

Since a rise in postsynaptic Ca^{2+} is presumed necessary for the induction of LTP, much emphasis has been placed on the signaling cascades consequent to this Ca^{2+} signal. A range of strategies have been used to determine the role of Ca^{2+} in the induction of LTP, including the pharmacological manipulation of Ca^{2+}-dependent enzymes, the direct stimulation of Ca^{2+}-dependent enzymes, and biochemical assays of Ca^{2+}-dependent enzyme activity and distribution. The convergence of evidence strongly implicates a role for Ca^{2+}-dependent enzymes in the induction of LTP. For instance, it has been demonstrated that introduction of activated Ca^{2+}/calmodulin-dependent kinase (CaMK) into the postsynaptic cell induces LTP and occludes the further induction of LTP by afferent stimulation (Pettit, Perlman, & Malinow, 1994), and also that peptidergic inhibition of calmodulin blocks LTP induction (Malenka et al., 1989). Roles analogous to that of CaMK have been found for cAMP-dependent kinases (Chavez-Noriega & Stevens, 1992; Frey, Huang, & Kandel, 1993; Qi et al., 1996) and protein kinase C (PKC; Abeliovich et al., 1993; Malenka, Madison, & Nicoll, 1986; Malinow, Schulman, & Tsien, 1989; Reymann, Schulzeck, Kase, & Matthies, 1988), among others (O'Dell, Kandel, & Grant, 1991; Zhuo, Hu, Schultz, Kandel, & Hawkins, 1994). Since these kinases contribute in complex ways to regulatory functions and signal transduction cascades, as well as to the regulation of neurotransmitter exocytosis, it is not entirely clear what *specific* role (if any) that each of these kinases plays in the induction of LTP. Likewise, it is not clear whether these kinases act on similar or independent substrates, although it has been suggested that they independently regulate the induction and maintenance phases of LTP (Huang & Kandel, 1994; Nguyen & Kandel, 1996). As will become apparent below, these ambiguities and controversies (symptomatic of a work in progress) will sometimes confound our attempts to interpret the effects of genetic manipulations on memory induction and storage.

Stimulus Convergence and LTP Induction

Forms of LTP that are normally induced by prolonged stimulation of the NMDA receptor do not necessarily require the convergence of multiple inputs onto a single target cell for induction and can be classified as nonassociative forms of plasticity. In their initial report of the phenomenon, Bliss and Lomo (1973) demonstrated that high frequency stimulation of a single afferent pathway was sufficient to induce LTP. This potentiation arises in large part from an influx of Ca^{2+} through NMDA receptor-coupled channels, and the resultant activation of Ca^{2+}-dependent kinases. However, the intense and prolonged afferent volley necessary to induce potentiation may not commonly occur under physiological conditions and may sometimes support a more rapidly decaying form of potentiation (Larson, Wong, & Lynch, 1986; Malenka, 1991a, 1991b). A more physiologically plausible form of LTP is induced using an associative stimulation protocol. Roughly contiguous, low intensity stimulation of two pathways that converge on a common postsynaptic target will often support LTP whereas stimulation of either pathway alone will not (Barrionuevo & Brown, 1983; Levy & Steward, 1983). Mechanistically, the convergence of stimulation from multiple sources of afferent activity promotes a depolarization that is sufficient to relieve the magnesium block from the NMDA receptor-coupled channel pore. The facilitation of LTP induction by the convergence of multiple sources of postsynaptic stimulation has

suggested to some that LTP might serve to record the relationship of temporally contiguous sensory events, and as such, might underlie the storage of associative memories (e.g., Brown, Kairiss, & Keenan, 1990; see Matzel & Shors, 2001, for a critical appraisal of this hypothesis).

Biophysical Mechanisms Underlying the Expression of LTP

The expression of LTP reflects both enhanced conductance at the synaptic terminals stimulated during the induction protocol, as well as a more general increase in excitability across the postsynaptic membrane (Bliss & Lomo, 1973). A consensus regarding the biophysical substrates of LTP expression has not emerged, although strong evidence indicates that LTP expression requires an increase in the number or sensitivity of postsynaptic AMPA-class glutamate receptors (Ambros-Ingerson, Xiao, Larson, & Lynch, 1993; Liao, Hessler, & Malinow, 1995; Staubli, Ambros-Ingerson, & Lynch, 1992). In addition, LTP expression may reflect the contribution or added influence of an increase in the number or quantal content of transmitter vesicles released from the presynaptic terminal (Stevens, 1993, but see Isaac, Nicoll, & Malenka, 1995; Stephane, Malenka, & Nicoll, 1996; for review, see Malinow, 1994).

For the present purposes, it is important to be aware that glutamatergic AMPA receptors make two distinct contributions to the expression of LTP. They promote LTP induction by subserving a depolarization of the postsynaptic membrane so as to repel magnesium from the NMDA receptor-coupled channel pore. Furthermore, they are likely to be a principal determinant of the potentiation of synaptic transmission that characterizes LTP expression; that is, they are modified by the LTP induction protocol in such a way that the postsynaptic response to glutamate is enhanced (i.e., the EPSP is potentiated).

Summary of the LTP Mechanism

A general summary of the mechanism of LTP induction and expression is provided in Figure 5.1. At this point, no complete description of the mechanism underlying LTP induction and expression is possible, owing both to certain ambiguous or conflicting observations, and the rapid rate at which the knowledge base is evolving. Nonetheless, certain ubiquitous principles have emerged. It can be safely stated that LTP requires a transient rise in postsynaptic Ca^{2+} levels and the resultant stimulation of some members of a class of Ca^{2+}-dependent protein kinases. The activation of these kinases subserve a postsynaptic phosphorylation event that results in increased AMPA receptor sensitivity, and consequently, a facilitation of the depolarizing

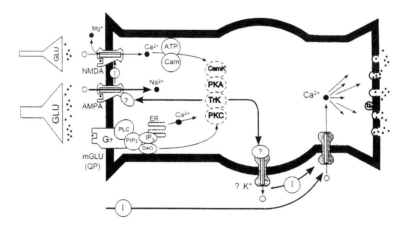

Figure 5.1 A gross illustration of the molecular constituents of hippocampal long-term potentiation (LTP).

NOTE: The large gray border represents (from left to right) the dendrites, soma, and axon of a generic cell (e.g., a hippocampal pyramidal cell). Glutamate (GLU) released from presynaptic terminals binds to three classes of receptors on the postsynaptic dendrites. Ionotropic AMPA receptors are directly coupled to Na^+ channels that mediate fast excitatory (depolarizing) postsynaptic potentials (EPSPs). When stimulated by glutamate, the isolated NMDA receptor will not conduct current owing to a block of the channel pore by Mg^{2+} ions. However, if glutamate binds to the NMDA receptor while the postsynaptic membrane is also depolarized (e.g., as in response to AMPA receptor stimulation), Mg^{2+} is expelled from the channel, and the open pore conducts a large Ca^{2+} current. The metabotropic glutamate receptor (mGLU) contributes little to postsynaptic current flow and voltage responses and instead stimulates an intracellular transduction cascade that ultimately promotes the release of Ca^{2+} from intracellular pools and the liberation of fatty acids (e.g., DAG) from the postsynaptic membrane, which can in turn interact with Ca^{2+} to stimulate protein kinases.

AMPA and mGLU receptors can contribute to the induction of LTP by promoting postsynaptic depolarization and the generation of coactivators of protein kinases. However, the principal catalyst for LTP induction is the NMDA receptor, which when stimulated promotes the accumulation of Ca^{2+} in the postsynaptic terminal. Subsequently, Ca^{2+} activates several classes of protein kinases (e.g., CaMK, PKA, TrK, and PKC) that phosphorylate AMPA receptors, causing an increase in the number of available receptors or in the sensitivity of existing receptors. Because of this phosphorylation event, subsequent episodes of glutamate binding to postsynaptic receptors produce an enhanced EPSP (postsynaptic depolarization); that is, LTP is expressed. Thus, while Ca^{2+} flux through the NMDA receptor channel plays a principal role in the induction of LTP, a resultant increase in Na^+ flux through the AMPA receptor channel underlies LTP expression.

SOURCE: Adapted from Matzel et al. (1998).

current flow through AMPA receptor-coupled ion channels. The net result of this enhancement of synaptic transmission is a modulation of the flow of information through the underlying neural network.

TRANSGENIC APPROACHES TO THE MODULATION OF LTP AND LEARNING

The General Transgenic Strategy, Its Limitations, and Its Advantages

Transgenic mice are generated in a process that begins with the injection of a DNA strand fragment (representing a gene) into the male pronucleus[1] of a newly fertilized mouse embryo, after which the DNA is incorporated into a random site on one of the chromosomes. Since the embryo is at the single-cell stage, the newly incorporated gene is replicated and ultimately is expressed in all of the animal's cells, including its germline. This heterologous expression of a DNA fragment is commonly referred to as a transgene, and the gene's product is made in *addition* to the endogenous gene expression pattern.

The manipulation of embryonic stem cells[2] may be used to induce more specific genetic modifications. When introduced into a host embryo, stem cells can contribute to all cell types as the embryo develops. By homologous

recombination[3] of stem cells maintained in culture, modifications can be introduced into specific genetic loci and introduced into the mouse germline to promote mutations of preexisting proteins. Depending on the nature of the recombination and its location on the DNA strand, these mutations can effect deletions (i.e., knockouts) or modifications of existing genes and the expression of novel proteins. Since the engineered strand of DNA replaces a strand that had been endogenously expressed, the effects of the new gene are "pure"; that is, they are not the summed product of the endogenous gene and the transgene.

Since their introduction, transgenic strategies have been employed to generate mice that lack, or express in a modified form, genes that contribute to molecular and biochemical processes that have been asserted to contribute in various ways to the induction, storage, and expression of memories in the mammalian brain. This approach may be recognized as a modern variant of more widely used pharmacological strategies that for many decades served as a mainstay in the arsenal of tools employed in attempts to elucidate the biochemical substrates of memory. Despite their wide use, pharmacological manipulations were widely acknowledged to be inadequate, owing to the lack of specificity of most (or all) pharmacological agents, the lack of agents for many targets, and the difficulty associated with specifying or restricting the site of action of a pharmacological manipulation. However, although the transgenic and pharmacological approaches are conceptually

---

[1]Upon its fertilization, an egg (the zygote) initially contains the nuclei of both the male and female (referred to as pronuclei). These nuclei join and combine their chromosomes in a single nucleus.

[2]During embryo development, stem cells (located in a larger set of cells known as the blastocyst) are reserved for the formation of the embryo itself. Embryonic stem cells can be removed and maintained in culture, where foreign genes can be introduced, after which they can be reinserted into the blastocyst to participate in the formation of the embryo. It should be noted that stem cells are considered precursor cells in that they have the ability to give rise to a variety of cell types.

[3]When expressed heterologously, DNA is incorporated into cells that do not normally express the gene, and thus a novel protein is generated and expressed in all affected cells. In contrast, through homologous recombination, a target gene is *replaced* by a new gene. Thus, with homologous recombination a novel protein replaces the native protein, and expression of the novel protein can be restricted to only those cells that normally express the target gene.

related, many of the complications incurred with pharmacological manipulations are circumvented with modern genetic techniques. In particular, for every gene there exists a specific target protein, and any protein of interest is coded for by a specific gene.

While superior in many respects to their pharmacological counterparts, the use of transgenic animals is not itself free from interpretative difficulties. Before describing the seminal attempts to employ transgenic animals in studies of memory, we should first describe the limitations of this approach (for a more detailed discussion, see Gerlai, 1996; Gingrich & Hen, 2000). First, genetic alterations dependent on a transgene are often expressed throughout an animal's development and can adversely impinge on a cascade of developmental processes. Thus, any unique properties of the adult phenotype (for instance, its capacity to learn) might reflect an acute influence of the genetic manipulation or, possibly, a consequence of an abnormal development of the nervous system and/or compensatory effects promoted by the gene deletion. In this regard, it should be noted that many gene deletions produce gross abnormalities (e.g., neuroanatomical or morphological) and in many instances are lethal. Hence, even transgenic animals which appear to be nominally normal can reasonably be expected to be abnormal at levels that escape detection. Second, a transgene is often expressed in every cell in the organism, confounding attempts to interpret the effect of the alteration in any specific brain region. Each of these first two complications have been at least partly overcome with recent advances in transgenic technology, and these modified techniques will be described in detail below in conjunction with the experiments in which they have been utilized. Third, the production of a mutant mouse requires several generations of inbreeding, and the inbreeding may introduce uncontrolled mutations that may themselves impinge on the

target behavior. Lastly, the genetic approach suffers from a major interpretative difficulty endemic to traditional pharmacologic manipulations. Specifically, a genetic mutation may impinge on a target behavior for reasons unrelated to that which was intended. To illustrate the analogy, a drug that impairs learning may do so via its disruption of a specific component of the learning mechanism, or may do so as a secondary or unintended effect of the drug, for instance, on the animal's state of alertness or its sensory acuity (as but two of many possibilities). Thus, while the transgenic approach has certain definite advantages over more traditional pharmacological interventions, the interpretation of results based on these genetic manipulations is not uncomplicated.

Global Gene Deletions, LTP, and Learning

Modern molecular/genetic attempts to discern the substrates for memory have been based on a specific (and limited) set of assumptions, and for the most part, have been delimited by the hypothesis that NMDA receptor-dependent LTP subserves memory storage in the mammalian brain. In addition to explicit attempts to critically evaluate this hypothesis, many relevant studies have been prompted by the presumption that a genetic manipulation impinging on the molecular cascade that regulates LTP will have a commensurate effect on memory. In this regard, the modulation of LTP is often offered as a hallmark of a manipulation's relevance to memory independent of any behavioral assessment of the phenomenon. For the present purposes, we will largely limit our discussion to those studies which make close contact with relevant behavioral endpoints.

Using gene deletions to assess the effects of a mutation on LTP and learning, a series of experiments from two laboratories introduced a new era in genetic research. In studies originating in the laboratory of Susumi

Tonegawa (a pioneer in the applications of transgenic techniques), Silva and colleagues (Silva, Paylor, Wehner, & Tonegawa, 1992; Silva, Stevens, Tonegawa, & Wang, 1992) assessed the effects of deletions of the gene coding CaMKIIα, a Ca^{2+}-sensitive protein kinase that is highly enriched in the post-synaptic densities of hippocampal neurons. Despite this gene deletion, the mice exhibited no gross neuroanatomical abnormalities and exhibited normal synaptic transmission. Moreover, the mutant animals were described as exhibiting "mostly normal" behaviors, although they were characterized as being generally "jumpy" and "nervous." As would be anticipated based on prior pharmacological evidence, the CaMKIIα deletion was associated with a reduced capacity for LTP maintenance in hippocampal CA1 neurons, presumably owing to the perturbation of a CaMKIIα-dependent phosphorylation[4] event necessary for the maintenance of LTP. Consistent with earlier pharmacologic evidence relating intact LTP to efficient spatial learning (Morris, Davis, & Butcher, 1991; Davis, Butcher, & Morris, 1992), the mutant mice exhibited impaired acquisition in the spatial version of the Morris water maze, a task in which animals must use distal environmental cues to guide their search for a submerged (hidden) escape platform. Silva, Paylor, Wehner, and Tonegawa (1992) concluded that a "mutation in a known gene [one associated with LTP maintenance] is linked to a specific mammalian learning deficit, and . . . can have a selective but drastic impact on learning and memory." Likewise, data from the Kandel

laboratory (Grant et al., 1992) indicated that the deletion of the fyn gene, which codes for tyrosine kinase (another kinase enriched in the postsynaptic densities of hippocampal neurons), impaired both LTP induction and learning in the water maze. These later results were somewhat complicated by the observation that the mutation was associated with neuroanatomical abnormalities unrelated to the LTP mechanism, such as an increased number of granule cells in the dentate gyrus and of pyramidal cells in the CA3 region. Nevertheless, similar to those of Silva, Stevens, et al., these results were interpreted as consistent with a role for LTP in the induction and storage of spatial memories in the hippocampus.

Despite the seminal nature of these early experiments with transgenic animals, they were fraught with interpretative difficulties, not the least of which was the "nervous" tendencies of some of the mutant mice. In a comment by Deutsch (1993), he notes that in the Silva, Paylor, et al. study, the mutant mice were impaired in unlearned aspects of performance in the water maze task, such as in the latency to swim to a visible escape platform (a test not conducted in the Grant et al., 1992, study). Among other possibilities, this deficit might reflect a mutation-induced alteration of motor function, vision, or motivation to escape the water. Likewise, in both the Silva and Grant studies, the mutant mice exhibited significantly longer latencies to locate the hidden platform on the *first* trial of water maze training, that is, before learning could have influenced their performance. Furthermore, the *rate* of learning of the mutant mice in each of these studies was actually accelerated relative to the wild-type control animals. That is, the latency to locate the hidden platform in both the mutant and wild-type animals asymptote at the same level, but the slope of the acquisition curves of the mutant animals is steeper (owing to their being significantly slower on the first training trial). Based on these factors

---

[4]A protein kinase is an enzyme. When stimulated (as CaMKIIα is by Ca^{2+}), the kinase adds a phosphate group to a target protein, a process referred to as phosphorylation. When phosphorylated, the protein's structure is modified such that its function is altered. In this way, protein kinases serve as a principal constituent of intracellular signaling cascades and can regulate a vast array of cellular processes and responses.

(and others), Deutsch concluded that there was "no evidence that the mutant mice in either set of studies suffered from a specific impairment of spatial memory" (1993, p. 761). Nevertheless, these reports were the impetus for dozens of the similarly motivated studies that would follow.

In a comprehensive and particularly relevant set of experiments, work in the Mishina laboratory focused on the effects of deletions of a subunit of the NMDA receptor on LTP and other neurophysiological responses, as well as the effects of this mutation on several forms of hippocampus-dependent learning. Recall that the flow of Ca^{2+} ions through NMDA receptor-coupled channels is of little consequence to basal synaptic transmission but is the principal catalyst for the induction of LTP. In their first experiments (Sakimura et al., 1995), it was reported that LTP induction was partially attenuated, and the rate of decay of LTP was accelerated, in mice lacking the gene coding the NMDA receptor $\varepsilon 1$ subunit. Furthermore, the mutant animals exhibited impaired acquisition of the spatial (hidden platform) version of the water maze and were less likely to swim in the vicinity of the platform when it was removed on a subsequent test of retention. (This later test is presumed to be indicative of perseveration, and it is assumed to be indicative of the strength of the underlying memory). Similarly, Kiyama et al. (1998) reported that the same mutation impaired animals' ability to form an association between a foot shock and a context (i.e., a contextual fear memory), a form of learning that is often asserted to depend on the hippocampus. However, formation of a presumably more "simple" association between a tone and shock, a task that does not require the hippocampus (and thus hippocampal LTP), was unaffected by the same mutation. Like the earlier results of Silva, Paylor, et al. (1992) and Grant et al. (1992), the data of Sakimura et al. and Kiyama et al. are difficult to inter-

pret. Again, animals expressing the NMDA $\varepsilon 1$ receptor mutation exhibited a significant reduction in their rates to simply swim to a visible platform in the water maze. Moreover, in subsequent studies, the Mishina laboratory found that these same mutants exhibit reduced pain sensitivity (Inoue, Mishina, & Ueda, 2000; Minami et al., 2000; Minami et al., 1997), a perceptual impairment that might influence an animal's learning about aversive stimulation (Matzel, Hallam, & Miller, 1988; Vigorito & Ayres, 1987) independent of the effect of the mutation on LTP.

In contrast to the NMDA-sensitive class of glutamate receptors, AMPA-class glutamate receptors are the principal mediators of fast excitatory transmission in the nervous system. However, the ion channel associated with the AMPA receptor displays a low permeability to Ca^{2+}. Although AMPA receptors can play a role in the induction of LTP (for instance, by providing a source of postsynaptic depolarization), these receptors are more clearly involved in the *expression* of LTP (see the section titled "Biophysical Mechanisms Underlying the Expression of LTP"). As described previously, LTP expression may reflect the phosphorylation of the GluR-A subunit of existing AMPA receptors or the insertion of new GluR-A receptors into the postsynaptic membrane (Shi et al., 1999). The differential roles of NMDA and AMPA receptors in the induction and expression of LTP was recently exploited in an attempt to further understand the maintenance of LTP and its role in learning. Zamanillo et al. (1999) generated mice lacking the GluR-A subunit AMPA receptor and found that hippocampal LTP in these animals decayed rapidly, such that no LTP could be detected within 40 min of its induction. This complete inhibition of LTP maintenance could not be attributed to inefficient synaptic transmission during the induction protocol since in mutant animals an *over-expression* of GluR-B receptors was observed, which apparently compensated for the absence of GluR-A receptors such that normal synaptic transmission was maintained. Moreover, a compendium of methods were used from which it was determined that the mutant animals exhibited no apparent abnormalities in the morphology, density, or distribution of synaptic spines in the hippocampus. This compensatory response and the absence of detectable neuroanatomical abnormalities renders this mutant quite useful as a tool to explore the link between LTP and learning, particularly given that no behavioral differences (in unlearned responses) could be detected between mutant and wild-type animals. It was thus surprising that when Zamanillo et al. trained animals in the spatial version of the water maze, the mutants learned in a manner that was indistinguishable from wild-type control subjects. Furthermore, relative to the wild-type controls, the mutants exhibited a similar propensity to search in the vicinity of the platform after it was removed during a later retention test, suggesting that the memory for the platform location was comparable in the two groups. Given that LTP maintenance was not supported in the hippocampus of the mutant animals, these results raise serious questions regarding what role, if any, that LTP plays in the storage of these spatial memories.

In total, the experiments described above reinforce our understanding of the molecular constituents of LTP and further elucidate the genetic regulation of this mechanism for synaptic modification. The results of Sakimura et al. (1995) and Kiyama et al. (1998) indicate that deletion of genes that code postsynaptic NMDA receptors (and thus current flow through the NMDA receptor channel) completely block the development of LTP, a result consistent with the view that NMDA receptor stimulation is the catalyst for the induction of some forms of LTP. Second, the deletion of genes coding

for Ca^{2+}-dependent kinases in the postsynaptic density impaired the induction of LTP, indicative of the necessity for a postsynaptic Ca^{2+}-dependent phosphorylation event in the induction of LTP. Lastly, Zamanillo et al. (1999) report that the absence of postsynaptic AMPA GluR-A receptors completely blocks the maintenance of LTP, a result consistent with the view that these receptors are the target of the aforementioned phosphorylation event. Despite this description of the genetic regulation of LTP, these studies do not support any definitive conclusion regarding the role of LTP in learning. The confounds associated with the studies of Silva, Paylor, et al. (1992), Grant et al. (1992), and Sakimura et al. complicate the interpretation of their results. Similarly, the demonstration by Zamanillo et al. that normal hippocampus-dependent learning occurs in the complete absence of hippocampal LTP casts at least a degree of doubt on the proposal that LTP serves as a memory storage device.

Regionally Restricted Gene Deletions, LTP, and Learning

The interpretative difficulties associated with the studies discussed thus far may originate in part from their use of regionally unrestricted gene deletions. Such deletions would necessarily impinge on brain regions that do not mediate the induction or storage of the target memory but which may nevertheless *influence* the induction, storage, or behavioral expression of the memory. A major advance in transgenic research occurred in 1996 and was reported in a series of articles from the Tonegawa laboratory (Tonegawa et al., 1996; Tsien, Chen, et al., 1996; Tsien, Huerta, & Tonegawa, 1996). In these papers, it was reported that a technique had been developed with which it was possible to restrict a gene deletion to a limited region of the brain, and in fact, to a single cell type. Homologous recombination (see notes 2 and 3) was used to insert *loxP* sequences into the genome of embryonic stem cells at a point where they flanked the target gene (referred to as a floxed gene). It had previously been reported that Cre recombinase would catalyze recombination between *loxP* recognition sequences and could thus be used to induce recombination of the floxed gene (Sauer & Henderson, 1988). Mice homozygous for the floxed gene were generated from these stem cells and were then crossed to a second mouse that harbored a *Cre* transgene under the control of a tissue-type specific transcriptional promoter. In progeny homozygous for the floxed gene and that carry the *Cre* transgene, the floxed gene will be deleted by the *Cre/loxP* recombination in those cells in which the *Cre* promoter is active. Although these molecular techniques may be unfamiliar to many readers, suffice it to say that such a strategy provides a means to delete a gene that codes for a single protein in a limited region of the brain. Using this strategy, the Tonegawa group used a promoter derived from the CaMKIIα gene to catalyze *Cre* gene expression, the result of which was mice with a localized and complete deletion of CaMKIIα in hippocampal CA1 pyramidal cells.

Based on the earlier work of Silva and colleagues (Silva, Paylor, et al., 1992; Silva, Stevens, et al., 1992), it is clear that the deletion of the gene coding CaMKIIα severely impairs the induction of hippocampal LTP and produces at least some impairment of hippocampus-dependent learning in the spatial water maze. As noted however, the observed learning deficits are difficult to interpret since the CaMKIIα deletion was regionally unrestricted and associated with a range of behavioral abnormalities that might themselves impinge on learning. The CA1-specific CaMKIIα mutants produced by the Tonegawa group (Tonegawa et al., 1996) were an appreciable advance over the mutant animals employed in the earlier studies and allay the complications arising from the more global gene deletions. Hence, there was a new opportunity with these mice to explore the role of CaMKIIα in the induction of hippocampal LTP and in hippocampus-dependent forms of learning. As expected, the CaMKIIα mutants exhibited a near complete absence of LTP. More importantly, the mutant animals exhibited only a slight impairment in reaching the visual-platform in the water maze (a hippocampus-independent task) but a more marked impairment in their ability to learn the location of the hidden platform (a hippocampus-dependent task). In additional experiments, mice exhibiting a regionally restricted deletion of the NMDA-1 receptor were generated, and a similar pattern of results was observed (Tsien, Huerta, et al., 1996). It is interesting to note that the mortality and growth rate of these animals was indistinguishable from the wild-type control animals, a marked improvement of the high perinatal mortality associated with conventional (global) NMDA receptor gene knockouts. In total, these sets of results were taken as evidence that the restricted deletion of the CaMKIIα or NMDA-1 gene in the hippocampus impaired LTP and had a commensurate effect on hippocampus-dependent learning.

While an improvement over previous approaches, results based on the use of regionally restricted gene knockouts were subject to many of the same interpretative difficulties inherent to the earlier studies of Silva, Paylor, et al. In the later studies, the animals' performance on the first training trial in the spatial maze is not reported; instead, performance is collapsed across four-trial blocks, and the NMDA mutants exhibit significantly worse performance than wild-type controls on the first block of trials. Since only a slight improvement in performance is typically observed between trial 1 and 4 in the water maze, it is likely that at least some of this deficit is attributable to poor performance on Trial 1. Moreover, the *relative* difference between the mutant and control animals is roughly maintained across 12 trial blocks; that is, the performance of both groups improve at approximately similar rates. Thus, while deletion of the gene coding the NMDA receptor *impairs* learning, substantial learning does occur despite the mutation. This is important to note given that *no* LTP could be induced in the mutant animals, again raising questions as to what the relationship actually is between LTP and learning.

Despite the caveats described, the site-restricted mutations produced by the Tonegawa group (Tonegawa et al., 1996) were a major advance for this line of research, and the experiments that they report do suggest at least some consequence of the deletion of genes coding CaMKIIα and of the NMDA receptor that is specific to learning. Nonetheless, it is not entirely clear what the nature of the relationship is between these genes and learning; that is, despite the complete absence of hippocampal LTP in mice lacking the genes coding the NMDA receptor, these mice still exhibited substantial hippocampus-dependent learning in the spatial water maze. This result is consistent with the previously described work of Zamanillo et al. (1999), wherein it was determined that the global deletion of AMPA receptors blocked the expression of hippocampal LTP but left spatial learning intact. So while it may be reasonable to conclude that the proteins targeted by these deletions play a role in the *modulation* of learning, it cannot be concluded that they are integral to the learning mechanism.

Inducible Gene Deletions, LTP, and Learning

As any student of animal learning will surely concede, learning *deficits* are easy to come by.

Seemingly insignificant (and often unnoticed) perturbations of an animal's "normal" state can markedly impact on the animal's capacity to acquire new information or to express what it has previously learned. As described above, conventional gene deletions are introduced prenatally and can alter the development of brain structures or neural circuits, and furthermore, may promote compensatory reactions in the nervous system. In fact, many global knockouts, including of NMDA receptors, can be perinatally lethal or may precipitate gross neuroanatomical and circuit abnormalities (Forrest et al., 1994; Li, Erzurumiu, Chen, Jhaveri, & Tonegawa, 1994). It should come as no surprise that such gross interventions can be associated with learning deficits (in those animals that survive). These complications were partially overcome in those studies described above in which site restrictions were placed on the gene deletion (Tonegawa et al., 1996; Tsien, Chen, et al., 1996; Tsien, Huerta, et al., 1996). First, the restricted deletion can be expected to have a lesser impact on the brain than a global deletion. More importantly, *Cre* recombination is developmentally delayed, such that the targeted gene is present until the middle of the third postnatal week, a time by which much (but not all) of the brain's development is complete (cf. Baudry, Arst, Oliver, & Lynch, 1994). As a consequence, the site-restricted deletion is not associated with such gross brain abnormalities or lethality and may promote no obvious changes in the behavioral phenotype of the adults (Tsien, Chen, et al., 1996). Of course this conclusion must be qualified because brain or behavioral abnormalities might be present that escaped detection or that were not explicitly examined. Moreover, these restricted deletions could still be reasonably expected to promote compensatory responses, even in the adult brain. For instance, chronic pharmacologic inhibition of excitatory synaptic transmission promotes a proliferation of postsynaptic glutamate receptors and dendritic spines (Turrigiano & Nelson, 2000). It is interesting to speculate that the normal learning that is observed in the absence of LTP following the AMPA receptor gene deletion reported by Zamanillo et al. (1999) might in fact represent such a compensatory response in the brain; that is, in the absence of NMDA receptor-dependent LTP, alternate brain mechanisms may have been recruited to incorporate forms of learning that might otherwise be subserved by LTP.

Were it possible to temporally control the expression of a particular transgene, the interpretative complications associated with these genetic manipulations could be at least partially nullified. To address this concern, methods have recently been developed with which it is possible to restrict the temporal expression of a transgene. To achieve such a restriction, a procedure is employed that exploits the antibiotic tetracycline (or its analogs) to repress or activate a specific transgene (Furth et al., 1994; Wang, O'Malley, Tsai, & O'Malley, 1994; Zhang et al., 1996). This "tetracycline transactivator" (tTA) system utilizes a protein that contains a portion of a repressor product that is encoded by a tetracycline-resistant operon. This transactivator binds to the operator site to initiate transcription of the target gene. Tetracycline binds to the transactivator protein so as to alter its conformation in such a manner that it can no longer bind its operator, resulting in the suppression of transcription of the operator-regulated genes. In an adult animal that harbors such a mutation, the transgene is normally active but can be repressed in response to the acute administration of tetracycline or its analogs. Conversely, the transgene can be habitually repressed if the mutant animal is chronically administered tetracyline (for instance, from the time of birth). In this latter instance, the transgene can be expressed at a particular time simply by withdrawing the animal from tetracycline. Thus, the expression of the transgene can be regulated by manipulating the animal's exposure to tetracycline, an operation that is easily accomplished by the addition or withdrawal of the antibiotic from the mutant animal's drinking water.

A recent study by Yamamoto, Lucas, and Hen (2000) is useful as an example of the efficacy and utility of the tTA system. Yamamoto et al. generated mice with a mutant form of the Huntington's gene, the expression of which was regulated by the tTA system. The animals were chronically administered doxycycline (an analog of tetracycline) and at 18 weeks of age exhibited none of the neuroanatomical or behavior abnormalities that normally characterize the Huntington's disorder. However, upon expression of the transgene pursuant to withdrawal of doxycycline from the animal's drinking water, neuroanatomical and movement pathologies characteristic of Huntington's disease emerged within four weeks. Surprisingly, these pathologies were found to be reversed shortly after the reintroduction of doxycycline to the animal's drinking water. The regression of these symptoms pursuant to the suppression of the transgene provides a striking repudiation of prevailing doctrine, that is, that once instantiated in the architecture of the brain, gross neurologic pathologies would not be reversed as a consequence of the suppression of the gene that had promoted them. Although of a preliminary nature, these data suggest the availability of important new directions for clinical research and may prove to be conceptually relevant to the development of strategies to overcome some forms of learning deficits.

Based on a conceptual framework similar to that which had guided earlier work with transgenic mice, temporally controlled gene expression has begun to be utilized as a tool to elucidate the genetic regulation of learning. An extensive and comprehensive series of experiments emanating from the Kandel laboratory (Mayford et al., 1996; Rotenberg et al., 1996) is emblematic of the systematic use of this strategy. In their first experiments, Mayford et al. (1996) combined the tTA system with a forebrain-specific transgene promoter to achieve both regional and temporal control of a gene coding an altered form of CaMKII, the postsynaptic Ca^{2+}-sensitive kinase previously implicated as integral to LTP induction (and possibly in spatial memory). In these studies, mice were generated in which the CaMKII kinase was expressed in a Ca^{2+}-independent (constituently active) form, resulting in a seven-fold increase in its activity (phosphorylation state) relative to that in wild-type animals. The transgene was expressed primarily in the CA1 and CA3 regions of the hippocampus, where the over-active form of the kinase exhibited impaired function (e.g., it was not available as a target of phosphorylation during LTP induction). However, when the animals were exposed to doxycycline for four weeks, the expression of the (mutant) Ca^{2+} independent form of CaMKII was suppressed such that the kinase's activity decreased to a level indistinguishable from that observed in wild-type animals. Upon withdrawal of doxycycline (and the resultant expression of abnormal CaMKII activity), the capacity for hippocampal LTP was assessed in the mutant animals, as well as in their wild-type counterparts. In wild-type animals, stimulation at 5, 10, or 100 Hz of the Schaffer collateral pathway that projects onto CA1 pyramidal cells each produced robust LTP. Relative to these animals, 100 Hz stimulation produced comparable LTP in the CaMKII mutants. However, no LTP was observed in the mutants in response to 5 or 10 Hz stimulation; in fact, these low rates of stimulation precipitated a *depression* of synaptic transmission, an effect referred to as long-term depression (LTD). Under normal conditions (i.e., in wild-type animals), LTD is typically induced with slow, repetitive stimulation in the range of 1 Hz. Thus, in the CaMKII mutants there

was a positive shift in the range of frequencies with which LTD was supported such that the synapses were biased toward the expression of LTD in response to stimulation protocols that normally support the formation of LTP. As an illustration of the utility of the tTA system, it should be noted that the responses to low-frequency stimulation recorded in the hippocampus of mutant animals were entirely normal throughout periods of doxycycline administration, indicative of the effective temporal control of transgene expression.

Endogenous (naturally occurring) oscillations in the range of 5–10 Hz are prevalent in the hippocampus of animals (e.g., rats and mice) engaged in the exploration of novel environments (Vanderwolf, Kramis, Gillespie, & Bland, 1975). Accordingly, it has been proposed that the induction of LTP by these slow oscillations may be particularly crucial to the storage of hippocampus-dependent spatial memories (Larson, Wong, & Lynch, 1986). To test their mutant animal's capacity for spatial learning, Mayford et al. (1996) trained animals in a maze in which 40 holes were evenly distributed along the circumference of a brightly illuminated circular field. Of the 40 available holes, one hole led to a darkened escape tunnel. Since mice exhibit an innate aversion to brightly lit open spaces, animals will normally learn to locate the hole that provides them with the opportunity to escape from the open field. (An animal's behavior in this maze can be guided by intramaze landmarks [the cued version of the task] wherein the escape hole is visibly flagged, or by extramaze landmarks [the spatial version], wherein the animal is said to rely on a cognitive map of its environment to locate the escape hole. In contrast to the cued version of the task, this later form of learning is severely impaired by lesions of the hippocampus [Barnes, 1988]; in this respect, it is comparable to the performance of animals in the spatial version of the Morris water maze.)

Based on a criterion in which an animal was said to have learned when it made three or fewer incorrect hole entries on five out of six trials (exposures to the maze), Mayford et al. (1996) found that none of the animals (0/6) expressing the CaMKII/hippocampus mutation were capable of solving the spatial version of this task, despite 40 training trials distributed across as many days. In contrast, approximately 60% of both wild-type and mutant animals administered doxycycline (to suppress the expression of the CaMKII transgene) attained this learning.

In a second assessment of their animal's capacity for learning, Mayford et al. (1996) delivered unsignaled foot-shocks to mice that were confined in a distinctive context. Following such treatment, animals will typically become immobile, or "freeze," when re-exposed to the training context, a response that is indicative of their acquisition of an associative fear memory. As with other forms of spatial learning, this contextual fear conditioning is believed to be dependent on the integrity of the hippocampus (LeDoux, 2000). Relative to doxycycline-treated mutants or wild-type animals, CaMKII/hippocampus mutants were found to be severely impaired in their acquisition of contextual fear.

In contrast to the impairment in the acquisition of hippocampus-dependent forms of spatial and contextual memories induced by the CaMKII mutation, Mayford et al. (1996) found that the mutant animals acquired hippocampus-independent forms of memory at a normal rate. For instance, the mutant animals exhibited normal acquisition of a tone-shock (conditioned stimulus-unconditioned stimulus; CS-US) association. This variant of classical conditioning is generally held to require an intact amygdala but is seemingly spared by perturbations of the hippocampus (LeDoux, 2000). It is important to note that the normal acquisition of learned fear in response to a punctate auditory stimulus indicates that the CaMKII/hippocampus mutant animals perceive shock and express fear in a manner that is comparable to wild-type animals. Thus, the deficits in contextual fear conditioning promoted by this same mutation is not easily attributable to simple sensory-motor deficits.

Mayford et al. (1996) generated a second line of mutant mice in which CaMKII over-expression was regulated in the amygdala, while CaMKII activity in the hippocampus was unaltered. In contrast to the CaMKII/hippocampus mutants, the CaMKII/amygdala mutants exhibited normal contextual fear conditioning but severely impaired conditioning to a punctate cue (i.e., a CS) paired with shock; this later learning deficit was absent in mutant animals treated with doxycycline. Moreover, the associative learning deficit exhibited by the CaMKII/amygdala mutants was not obviously attributable simply to an impairment of the animal's native fear, as the mutant mice displayed normal fear responses (freezing) when exposed to a rat.

The results of Mayford et al. (1996) were elaborated in a series of experiments reported by Rotenberg, Mayford, Hawkins, Kandel, and Muller (1996). Spatial location in a familiar open field appears to be encoded in the pattern of firing of individual hippocampal pyramidal cells; that is, cells fire preferentially depending upon an animal's location in its environment (O'Keefe & Dostrovsky, 1971). Moreover, new place cells are tuned within minutes of an animal's introduction into a novel environment and may exhibit a stable pattern of responding when the animal is returned to that environment after a retention interval of several months (Muller, Kubie, & Ranck, 1987). Thus, the patterned activity of hippocampal place cells is often asserted to act as a store of spatial memories and to aid the animal as it navigates within a familiar environment. As reported by Mayford et al., Rotenberg et al. generated mice that expressed the transgene coding the overexpression of the Ca^{2+}-independent form of CaMKII in the hippocampus. These mutant animals and their wild-type counterparts exhibited similar patterns, amplitudes, and waveforms of complex spike bursts and EEGs in the hippocampus, indicating that at least these fundamental neurophysiological properties of the hippocampal circuit were preserved in the mutant subjects. However, upon their introduction into a novel environment, several abnormalities in the activity of place cells were apparent in the transgenic animals. Relative to wild-type animals, place cells were less common in mutant animals and their tuning developed more slowly. The place-cell firing fields that did emerge were less precise (there was more overlap between adjacent place fields), and established place fields were less stable over time.

Relative to earlier work, this extensive and elegant set of experiments from the Kandel laboratory (Mayford et al., 1996; Rotenberg et al., 1996) provides a more clear picture of the learning phenotype of transgenic mice expressing a mutant form of CaMKII. If the abnormally active kinase was expressed in the hippocampus, animals exhibited a pattern of learning indicative of a specific impairment in their abilities to acquire information of a spatial nature: Their performance in the circular maze was impaired as was there ability to form associations to a particular context. Consistent with these learning deficits, synaptic plasticity in the form of LTP as well as the plasticity that is characteristic of hippocampal neurons during exploratory behavior in a novel environment was impaired in transgenic animals. In contrast, these same mutants exhibited no impairment in their capacity to form associations between punctate stimuli (i.e., tone and shock; CS-US), a form of learning that is widely thought to impinge more heavily on the amygdala formation. In contrast, if the abnormal expression of CaMKII was localized in the amygdala, the animals'

performance on spatial learning tasks was intact, while their ability to associate punctate cues was impaired. As these CaMKII mutations were associated with an impairment of LTP induction, it is convenient to conclude that LTP is the common denominator linking these observations, and by inference, that LTP is the substrate mechanism for memory storage. Regarding the role of LTP in learning, it was previously noted that Zamanillo et al. (1999) observed normal spatial learning in mice in which hippocampal LTP could not be maintained. However, the mutation employed by Zamanillo et al. was not spatially or temporally restricted as was the case in these more recent studies and consequently may have fostered the development of compensatory mechanisms of memory storage that might have otherwise been subserved by LTP. Nonetheless, these conflicting results forestall any definitive conclusion regarding the relationship between the genetic regulation of LTP to learning and memory storage.

Although the tTA system allows transgene expression to be suppressed (e.g., through the chronic administration of docycycline), a more recent variation of this system produces a transgene that is normally inactive and that can be transiently and precisely activated by the administration of an appropriate inducer. In the reverse tTA (rtTA) system, a mutant form of the tetracycline repressor is utilized that induces transcription only in the *presence* of docycycline. Mansuy, Winder, et al. (1998) have exploited this rtTA system to transiently induce the over-expression of calcineurin (a Ca^{2+}-sensitive phosphatase that can reverse kinase-induced protein phosphorylation) in the forebrain. Mansuy et al. hypothesized that the over-expression of an active form of calcineurin might interfere with the normal maintenance of LTP (by reversing Ca^{2+}-dependent phosphorylation events). In adult mice, Mansuy et al. induced the over-expression of calcineurin by administering docycycline to their mutant animals. In these mutants, hippocampal LTP could be induced only with excessive presynaptic stimulation, and the LTP that was induced decayed at an accelerated rate relative to that in wild-type control animals. In behavioral tests, it was determined that the mutant animals learned normally in the visible-platform version of the water maze task. However, these animals exhibited a severe impairment when tested on the spatial (hidden platform) version of this task. Similarly, these animals were later found to be deficient in their acquisition of the spatial version of the Barnes circular maze (Mansuy, Mayford, et al., 1998). Furthermore, if the over-expression of calcineurin was reversed by the withdrawal of doxycycline (i.e., suppression of the calcineurin transgene), this later spatial learning deficit was overcome such that mutant animals learned the location of the escape tunnel at a rate comparable to that of their wild-type counterparts. This result is a powerful rebuttal of the possibility that the transgene-induced learning deficits were the consequence of some developmental abnormality, or furthermore, that the learning deficit was a consequence of the inbreeding required for the generation of the mutant mice.

While the studies of Mansuy and colleagues (Mansuy, Mayford, et al., 1998; Mansuy, Winder, et al., 1998) are an impressive demonstration of the impact on learning of the transient expression of a transgene, those results must be interpreted cautiously. In their final experiment of the series, Mansuy, Winder, et al. (1998) expressed the calcineurin transgene in mice that had *previously* learned to locate the hidden platform the spatial version of the Morris water maze. While these animals learned normally (absent the transgene's influence), they exhibited severe memory deficits when retention was assessed subsequent to the induction of the transgene. Recall that these studies (as well as others that we have discussed) were

guided by the assumption that hippocampal LTP subserved the induction of certain forms of spatial memory. However, calcineurin over-expression should have no obvious effect on the stability of previously induced LTP, and by deduction, should spare previously established memories. Thus, the transgene-induced impairment of the *expression* of a previously stable memory suggests the possibility that calcineurin over-expression impinged on the mutant animal's performance in a manner that was unrelated to its effects on LTP. Alternatively, we must consider the possibility that the underlying assumption that LTP subserves the storage of spatial memories is in itself untenable.

Transgene-Induced Facilitation of LTP and Learning

As described earlier, LTP in a variety of forms is catalyzed by the stimulation of the NMDA class glutamate receptor and the consequent influx of Ca^{2+} across the postsynaptic membrane. Thus, the hypothesis that LTP subserves memory requires that the sensitivity of NMDA receptors be directly related to the efficacy with which memories are established. Were this the case, it would be reasonable to expect that the genetic up-regulation of the sensitivity of NMDA receptors might have a commensurately beneficial influence on the formation of new memories.

The NMDA receptor is a heteromeric complex comprised of a single NR1 subunit, which forms the channel pore, and several NR2 subunits, which regulate channel gating and the Mg^{2+} dependence of the response to glutamate. In the adult forebrain (including the hippocampus), the ·NMDA receptor channel is comprised of the NR1, NR2A, and NR2B subunits. In 1994, Monyer, Burnashev, Laurie, Sakmann, and Seeburg developed transgenic mice in which the NR2B subunit was overexpressed relative to the NR2A subunit. In CA1 and CA3 pyramidal cells of transgenic mice, EPSPs were prolonged relative to those in the hippocampus of wild-type animals. This enhancement of the EPSP arose as a consequence of a specific enhancement of the NMDA-receptor regulated Ca^{2+} current and reflected a shift in the voltage dependence of the release of the Mg^{2+} blocked of the NMDA receptor channel pore.

To test whether animal's overexpressing the NR2B subunit exhibited enhanced LTP and learning, Tang et al. (1999) developed a line of mutant mice (similar to those of Monyer et al., 1994) that exhibited a postnatal overexpression of this subunit in the forebrain. Relative to wild-type animals, these mice exhibited normal growth, body-weight gains, and exploratory behavior in an open field. However, the decay time of the NMDA receptor-dependent component of the EPSP in pyramidal cells was nearly doubled in the mutant mice, an effect associated with a fourfold increase in current through this channel. Moreover, following LTP induction, the amplitude of the potentiated EPSP was significantly longer and exhibited a considerably slower rate of decay in the mutant animals relative to the wild-type controls.

Having established that NR2B overexpression was associated with the facilitation of LTP induction and the prolongation of its maintenance, Tang et al. (1999) proceeded to assess the effects of this mutation on several different indices of learning. Relative to wild-type animals, the mutants displayed normal exploration of novel objects but enhanced recognition of a familiar objects (indicative of either better learning or prolonged retention). Moreover, when tested in retention, both contextual fear conditioning and fear-responses to a discrete CS paired with shock were elevated in the mutant animals, again suggestive of either superior learning or retention. Last, while mutant and wild-type animals exhibited similar latencies and strategies to escape onto a visible platform in the water maze, the mutant animals exhibited faster acquisition in the spatial (hidden platform) version of the task. In total, the overexpression of the NR2B subunit of the NMDA receptor complex was associated with a prolongation of transmitter-regulated current flow through the NMDA receptor channel and had a commensurate influence on a broad range of learning skills. Based on this pattern of results, it has been concluded that this mutation promotes a general enhancement of an animal's capacity to learn (Tsien, 2000).

As was noted earlier, perturbations of the brain (e.g., receptor sensitivity, current flow through postsynaptic channels, disruptions of protein kinase or phosphatase activity) are commonly associated with learning deficits. However, given that these perturbations can broadly impair brain function and are usually associated with deficits in motor or sensory function, the observation of a learning impairment following such a manipulation is difficult to interpret. Thus, the observation by Tsien and his colleagues (Tang et al., 1999) that a mutation can selectively *enhance* learning is a powerful demonstration of the influence of genetics on learning and of the potential utility of genetic methods as a tool to modulate learning. Despite the significance of these observations, it must be noted that the mechanism underlying the transgene's beneficial influence on learning in these studies is far from transparent. While it is appropriate to speculate that NR2B overexpression promoted better learning as a consequence of the facilitation of LTP induction, this mutation is likely to have effects that *secondarily* impact learning. For instance, Wei et al. (2001) report that mice overexpressing forebrain NR2B are significantly more sensitive to pain. As noted earlier, an increase in pain perception can facilitate learning about aversive (e.g., painful) stimuli (e.g., Vigorito & Ayres, 1987). Thus independent of any putative influence on learning via the modulation of LTP, it is equally plausible that NR2B overexpression promotes at least some forms of learning (e.g., fear conditioning, spatial navigation in the water maze) as a consequence of an animal's heightened sensitivity to aversive stimuli (e.g., shock or water immersion). Although we cannot at present know the exact route with which NR2B overexpression promoted learning, it cannot be denied that this transgene impacted learning in a manner that might generally be described as beneficial (see the following section for related results).

GENETIC REGULATION OF BRAIN DEVELOPMENT, DEGENERATION, AND LEARNING

Neurotrophins, Growth Factors, Synaptic Plasticity, and Learning

A large percentage of the neurons that are present at birth are lost in development during a period of genetically regulated cell death, usually occurring during the final stages of mitosis. Survival factors, or neurotrophins, can suppress programmed cell death, promoting or contributing to the survival of roughly 50% of cells of various classes. Moreover, these neurotrophins influence cell growth and morphology in ways that determine the interactions between synaptically coupled neurons.

A limited class of proteins are employed to regulate cell death and proliferation throughout the mammalian brain and are derived from cells that populate a particular brain region. These neurotrophic factors include nerve growth factor (NGF), brain-derived neurotrophic factor (BDNF), and neurotrophic factors 3, 4, and 6 (NT-3, NT-4, NT-6). These neurotrophic proteins act over very short distances as messengers between cells to induce rapid changes in synaptic transmission and

neuron morphology. Thus, it is not surprising that after the last stages of brain development are complete, the same neurotrophic factors can serve to stimulate the repair of cells following damage to the mature nervous system. Consistent with this role, neurotrophins may also contribute to the maintenance of brain cells throughout an animal's lifespan, and likewise, appear to serve as regulators of plasticity in the adult brain. For these reasons, the influence of neurotrophic factors on normal learning and learning in individuals suffering from various forms of neuronal degeneration has become an area of intense interest. To explore these latter influences of neurotrophins, lines of transgenic animals have been developed in which brain-derived neurotrophic factors have been suppressed or overexpressed, and the effects of these mutations on synaptic plasticity and learning have been assessed.

Studies aimed at the elucidation of the relationship between neurotrophins and learning are not so delimited by the LTP-learning hypothesis as were the studies of learning mechanisms described earlier. However, LTP has proven to be a convenient paradigm for assessing synaptic efficacy and plasticity, and consequently, most studies of neurotrophins and learning report measures of LTP. Kang and Schuman (1995a, 1995b) provided early evidence of an effect of neurotrophins on synaptic transmission and plasticity in the hippocampus of adult animals. Application of BDNF or NT-3 to hippocampal slices produced a dramatic and sustained (2 to 3 hrs) enhancement of synaptic strength at the Schaffer collateral-CA1 synapses. At synapses potentiated by exposure to the neurotrophic factors, LTP could still be induced via presynaptic stimulation, suggesting that these two forms of plasticity may use at least partially independent cellular mechanisms.

Based on observations like those of Kang and Schuman (1995a, 1995b), it has been speculated that neurotrophic factors might regulate the general fitness of synaptic transmission in a given brain area and thus might influence the form of learning that is dependent on those areas. To assess these roles of neurotrophins, a number of lines of mutant mice have been developed in which neurotrophins are suppressed or overexpressed in various brain regions.

Croll et al. (1999) generated transgenic mice to overexpress BDNF throughout the brain. Overexpression declined with age, presumably owing to endogenous compensatory processes, such that levels of BDNF were comparable in transgenic and wild-type animals by 6–9 months postnatal. Throughout the duration of overexpression, the transgenic mice exhibited no obvious deformities and exhibited a normal behavioral phenotype, displaying no obvious abnormalities. Likewise, the transgenic animals performed normally on tests of pain sensitivity, in tests of locomotion, and in entries into open arms in an elevated field (a presumed indication of anxiety levels). However, young transgenic mice (6–8 weeks postnatal) exhibited a significant deficit in the retention of a learned passive-avoidance response (wherein the animals remain stationary to avoid shock), indicating either a failure of memory or initial acquisition rate of learning. These apparent learning deficits were well correlated with the level of BDNF overexpression and were absent in 6–8 month-old mice, in which BDNF levels decreased to levels comparable to wild-type controls. This observation lessens the likelihood that the learning deficits exhibited by the transgenic animals arose as a consequence of neuroanatomical abnormalities originating during development. Recall that exposure of hippocampal slices to BDNF promoted an enhancement of synaptic transmission (Kang & Schuman, 1995a, 1995b), a result that suggested the possibility that BDNF overexpression might *facilitate* learning. Thus, the observations of Croll et al. are difficult to reconcile

within the framework of the LTP-memory hypothesis. Moreover, other observations complicate the interpretation of the Croll et al. results regarding learning. First, the BDNF transgenic mice exhibited a reduced threshold and increased severity of seizures in response to kainic acid, a result that supports the hypothesis that excess BDNF can have a pro-convulsant influence in the limbic system. Consistent with increased seizure activity, neuronal hyperexcitability was observed in area CA3 and the entorhinal cortex of the transgenic mice, and moreover, LTP induction was impaired in area CA1. These results suggest that the level of BDNF expression in the mutant animals was sufficiently high that it promoted a widespread increase in excitability, an effect that might in turn occlude normal plastic responses (such as LTP). This pattern of results clearly indicates that if an overexpression of neurotrophins were to have a facilitative influence on learning, it would do so within some limited range, beyond which, its effects can be detrimental. This conclusion will come as no surprise to many readers, as it is widely assumed that brain systems have been finely balanced by the evolutionary process. Furthermore, given the severity of these neurophysiological deviations, it is surprising that the animals appeared normal on a range of behavioral tests and suggests the possibility that the tests employed were not sensitive to real behavioral differences between the mutant and wild-type animals.

Results conceptually similar to those reported by Croll et al. (1999) have been reported elsewhere. For instance, Saarelainen et al. (2000) produced a line of mice that overexpress receptors for the neurotrophin NT-4. While normal hippocampal LTP was observed in these animals, they exhibited a severe deficit in their rate of learning in the spatial version of the water maze. Not only does this result raise concerns regarding the role of LTP in the storage of hippocampus-dependent memories, it again suggests that increasing levels of neurotrophins (or their receptors) can negatively impinge on learning.

Despite the paucity of evidence to support the hypothesis that increased levels of brain neurotrophins might commensurately impact learning, available evidence *does* suggest that the two are related, although in a nonlinear manner. For instance, Fiore et al. (2000) generated a line of mice that overexpressed tumor necrosis factor-α (TNFα), a cytokine that regulates neurotrophin levels in the brain. This mutation promoted a decrease in NGF in the hippocampus of the transgenic animals, and this decrease in NGF was associated with impaired learning in both the water maze and on a passive avoidance task. In a related and particularly illuminating series of experiments, Burrows, Levitt, and Shors (2000) identified a line of mice with a naturally occurring mutation that was associated with normal levels of TGFα through early adolescence but which prompted a decline in TGFα levels through adolescence and into adulthood. The decline in TGFα was associated with an enlargement of the mutant animal's ventricles, a reduction in vasculature in the region of the amygdala, and a reduction in size of the central nucleus. In adulthood, the mutant animals exhibited normal responsivity to auditory stimuli but were significantly less responsive to foot shock, and, moreover, were significantly *more* active in an open field. As the neuroanatomical abnormalities of the mutant animals progressed with age, a commensurate impairment of associative learning (fear conditioning) was observed, both in response to a punctate tone (CS) paired with shock and to a context in which shock had been administered. While these results suggest that deletion of the gene coding TGFα produces learning deficits, it is clear that these deficits are not specific or limited to learning. The behavioral and neuroanatomical phenotype of these animals is severely altered, and the brain abnormalities that impinge specifically on learning cannot be determined. To further complicate the interpretation of these results, Burrows et al. performed similar analyses on animals that were specifically engineered to express deficient levels of TGFα throughout development. Surprisingly, these transgenic animals exhibited none (or significantly reduced forms) of the neuroanatomical and behavioral abnormalities that characterized the animals expressing the natural mutation (and a depletion of TGFα only in adulthood). Of particular interest, the deficits in associative learning displayed in animals devoid of TGFα only in adulthood were *absent* in those animals devoid of the growth factor throughout development. This pattern of results is a further testament to the capacity of the mammalian brain to accommodate abnormalities (see the section titled "Global Gene Deletions, LTP, and Learning"). The insult inflicted on the adult brain by depletions of TGFα was associated with a marked impairment of learning. In contrast, adult animals absent TGFα since gestation exhibited normal learning, suggesting that the immature (and more labile) brain incorporated some compensatory mechanism(s) in response to the mutation.

Based on the above discussion, we might assume that the brain is regulated around some homeostatic set point, and furthermore, that deviations from this set point are influenced by the interactions of thousands of constituent proteins. If so, it is reasonable to wonder if we can *ever* specify with precision the impact of any single mutation on learning. Despite this cautionary note, the results of Fiore et al. (2000) and Burrows et al. (2000) indicate that depleted levels of brain neurotrophins or growth factors can profoundly impact brain neuroanatomy and an animal's behavioral repertoire. While the precise nature of the transgene's influence cannot be specified, one component of the altered behavioral repertoire may be reflected in an animal's ability to learn.

A more focused approach to delineating the relationship between brain growth-related proteins was reported by Routtenberg, Cantallops, Zaffuto, Serrano, and Namgung (2000). Synaptic morphology is widely presumed to influence the efficacy of synaptic transmission and may thus influence an animal's capacity to learn. Activation of the growth-associated protein 43 (GAP-43) is known to influence synaptic morphology in a way that promotes the facilitation of transmitter release, and thus GAP-43 regulation has been proposed as a means to modulate synaptic efficacy and possibly learning (Benowitz & Routtenberg, 1997). Importantly, GAP-43 is localized in presynaptic terminals and is stimulated by presynaptic activity (De Graan, Dekker, De Wit, Schrama, & Gispen, 1988; Dekker, De Graan, Versteeg, Oestreicher, & Gispen, 1989), and consequently has a restricted influence on gross neuroanatomical development relative to the neurotrophins and growth factors described above. Thus the expression of GAP-43 is particularly attractive for its potential as relatively specific modulator of learning. To test this relationship, Routtenberg et al. generated a line of mice that overexpressed a phosphorylatable form of GAP-43 (i.e., a form of GAP-43 that was responsive to stimulation by presynaptic activity). In adult mice, LTP was induced at the perforant path-granule cell synapse of the hippocampus. Relative to wild-type control animals, the transgenic animals exhibited nearly double the level of enhancement of the population EPSP following the LTP protocol. As anticipated, overexpression of GAP-43 was associated with an increased potential for LTP induction in the hippocampus.

The learning abilities of the GAP-43 transgenic animals was tested in an eight-arm radial maze, in which the animal's task is to collect food at the end of each arm. In this task, an efficient animal enters each arm only once, and so while navigating the maze, the animal must maintain some log of the arms that have already been visited. Since the maze contains no delimiting intramaze cues, spatial navigation is guided to a large extent by extramaze landmarks in a manner comparable to that which subserves performance in the Morris water maze. As with the water maze task, performance in this maze is reliant on the hippocampus and is severely impaired by hippocampus lesions (Wan, Pang, Olton, 1994). In a standard version of this task (1 min interval imposed between successive arm entries), the transgenic animals performed more efficiently than did the wild-type controls, committing slightly less than half of the number of errors. When the working memory component of the task was made more demanding by imposing a 20 min delay between successive arm entries (choices), the transgenic animal's superiority was further evident, committing only a third of the errors exhibited by wild-type animals. Based on these results, Routtenberg et al. (2000) concluded that "both learning and synaptic plasticity were enhanced by overexpression of a brain growth protein" (p. 7661). While the author's conclusions are warranted, the broader implications of these results are less clear. Routtenberg et al. report no other attempts to characterize these animals' behavioral phenotype or the neuroanatomical properties of their brains. Likewise, the hyperplasticity characteristic of the transgenic animals might predispose them to other cognitive impairments, such as in tasks that make rapidly shifting demands on the animals. Although Routenberg et al.'s results are intriguing, further work will be required to establish the extent to which their conclusions generalize beyond this one set of observations.

Genetic Regulation of Alzheimer's Disease and Learning

At the end of the spectrum from the regulation of development is the neurodegeneration characteristic of Alzheimer's Disease (AD) and its related family of dementias. The initial symptoms of AD include poor memory of recent experiences, and consequently, an impairment of learning and the ability to recall that which had been previously learned. AD is characterized by a number of pathologies of the hippocampus and its afferent cortical structures, and until recently, laboratory studies of AD were largely limited to pharmacological manipulations of these structures and their synaptic integration, both in attempt to produce animal models of the disorder and to assess the efficacy of treatment strategies (Bartus, 2000; Riekkinen, Schmidt, & van der Staay, 1998). Although fruitful, this approach has had limited success in describing the etiology or pathology of AD or as a tool for the development of effective treatments. However, recent advances in genetics and the development of transgenic technologies have made it possible to study alterations in brain morphology, synaptic transmission, and learning in strains of mice that carry genes associated with the human dementias characteristic of AD. Although this approach is being pursued in a variety of venues, we will focus on two that are particularly promising and which involve manipulations of the amyloid precursor protein and the family of proteins known as presenilins.

The amyloid precursor protein (APP) is the precursor to the β-amyloid peptide, the principal constituent of the senile plaques that are prevalent in the brains of human AD patients (Glenner & Wong, 1984). To determine the utility of APP in presenile animals, Zheng

et al. (1995) produced mice lacking the gene that codes APP. During early adulthood, a marked increase in reactive gliosis was observed in the brains of the transgenic animals. Behaviorally, the animals exhibited reduced locomotor activity and grip strength, as well as deficits in spatial water maze learning and a reduced capacity for hippocampal LTP (Dawson, Seabrook, & Zheng, 1998). This set of results indicates that under normal conditions, APP plays an essential role in the development of the nervous system and its regulation of behavioral function, suggesting that a disruption of ADD function may underlie or contribute to the expression of AD. However, it should be noted that transgenic animals that do not express APP do not *all* exhibit the deficits described above. Moreover, although APP deficient transgenic mice exhibit hippocampal neuron loss and declining synapse density in adulthood, only a subpopulation of these transgenic animals display lethargy or learning deficits (Phinney et al., 1999), suggesting that APP function or expression may alter the susceptibility to neuronal loss and dementia but may not itself underlie the behavioral or cognitive deficits that characterize AD.

Other APP transgenics have been generated that express mutations associated with early-onset familial AD, and these strains are characterized by accelerated deposition of β-amyloid protein (the constituent of senile plaques), a reduction in neuronal density in the hippocampus, and often, an impairment of LTP induction (Calhoun et al., 1998; Chen et al., 2000; Hsiao et al., 1995; Hsiao et al., 1996). Similarly, these mice often exhibit severe impairments in the rate at which they acquire escape responses in the spatial version of the water maze and choice performance in a t-maze. While some reports indicate that the emergence of these learning impairments correlate with the development of plaque formation (Chen et al., 2000;

Holcomb et al., 1998; Hsiao et al., 1996), in other instances, the development of plaques appears to be unrelated to learning deficits (Hsiao et al., 1995) or impairment of *in vitro* indices of learning-related synaptic plasticity, such as LTP (Larson, Lynch, Games, & Seubert, 1999). In all, variations in the expression of APP appear related to neuroanatomical abnormalities and behavioral deficits associated with AD, but its exact role in promoting these abnormalities is unclear and it does not appear sufficient in itself to underlie the dementia.

The early onset of AD is more highly correlated with mutations in one of two genes known as presenilins (PS-1 and PS-2) than with the APP gene itself. Proteolysis of presynilin proteins in turn stimulates the proteolysis of the APP (de Strooper et al., 1998), and downregulation of PS-1 is associated with a decrease in β-amyloid production (Saftig & de Strooper, 1998). Moreover, overexpression of the PS-1 gene leads to the overproduction of β-amyloid (Haass & Selkoe, 1998). Thus, variations in PS expression may precede irregularities in APP function and thus may be better suited as the determinant of the emergence of AD.

Targeted ablations of the PS-1 gene are lethal during development and are associated with abnormal development of the nervous system and thus electrophysiological recordings from mice lacking the PS-1 gene have been rare. In contrast, transgenic mice that overexpress the PS-1 gene have been developed, and these mice are amenable to electrophysiological and behavioral characterization in adulthood. In all such lines, increased levels of β-amyloid have been observed during middle adulthood (Borchelt et al., 1996; Citron et al., 1997; Duff et al., 1996; Janus et al., 2000; Parent, Lindon, Sisodia, & Borchelt, 1999). To examine whether the overexpression of PS-1 influences electrophysiological properties of the hippocampus implicated in

learning and memory storage, Parent et al. (1999) measured field EPSPs at the Schaffer collateral-CA1 synapse in hippocampal slices. Although basal indices of synaptic efficacy (e.g., EPSP slope and amplitude) were unaltered in the transgenic animals, input-specific LTP was more easily induced and was more persistent in the transgenic animals than in the respective wild-type control subjects. Thus, if LTP is a substrate mechanism for memory storage, it is difficult to reconcile these results with the proposal that PS-1 expression contributes to the learning deficits that are characteristic of AD. Even more problematic, Janus et al. (2000) found that expression of the human PS-1 gene was associated with a significant *improvement* in the performance of mice in the spatial version of the water maze task. Based on this pattern of observation, Janus et al. concluded that mutant PS1 alleles may require co-expression of human versions of other AD-associated genes in order to promote a behavioral phenotype indicative of AD.

Thus far, mice expressing single AD-related transgenes have been less than adequate as models for the elucidation of AD, prompting several attempts to generate mice carrying mutant ADD and PS-1 genes. Although in its infant stages, this "double-transgenic" approach has begun to yield promising results, including a line of mice that expresses neuropathologies in early adulthood (3 months), as well as a concomitant emergence of impaired choice performance in a t-maze (Holcomb et al., 1998). However, even at nine months of age, these same mice exhibit no impairment in spatial water maze learning (Holcomb et al., 1999), suggesting that even this double-transgenic manipulation is inadequate to capture the fundamental essence of the Alzheimer's pathology, even though it may more adequately model the etiology of the disorder. In total, it appears that a comprehensive description of the genetic regulation of AD will require the incorporation of the roles of as yet unidentified genes or interactions between known candidate genes and their protein targets.

THE LEARNING GENES: SUMMARY AND CONCEPTUAL FRAMEWORK

A diverse spectrum of genes have been identified that affect in various ways the processes involved in the induction, maintenance, and retrieval of normal memories, as well as those impacted by common dementias. As the reader may already have discerned, no single learning gene or even a class of genes has been identified, and few common denominators are evident from which we might construct a general description of the genetic regulation of learning. Were this the only conclusion to be drawn from the body of research summarized above, one might conclude that the effort has been less than fruitful. However, some ubiquitous principles *have* emerged from which significant insights into the mechanisms and modulation of the learning process are sure to be derived.

Attempts to characterize the genetic regulation of learning using modern transgenic techniques can be loosely segregated into two categories. First, there is that strategy with which attempts have been made to elucidate the biochemical and biophysical events that modify the brain in such a manner that memories are stored under normal conditions, that is, in the absence of brain insult, injury, or disease. These attempts to describe the memory mechanism can be contrasted with the broad effort underway to resolve the genetic regulation of common dementias, or brain disorders that impinge on an individual's capacity to learn and remember. Although insights into normal memory induction and storage are certain to be derived from this second approach, it is an approach that is necessarily more narrow in focus and one in which a prin-

cipal objective need not be to restrict manipulations to those that are specific to memory storage. For instance, currently useful models of Alzheimer's dementia employ transgenic animals which exhibit inflammation of brain tissue, increases in reactive gliosis, and plaque formations, as well as generally lethargic behavior compounded with motor impairments (Dawson et al., 1998; Zheng et al., 1995). While these (and similar) animals are sure to serve as useful tools for understanding many aspects of Alzheimer's disease and may facilitate the development of practical intervention and treatment strategies, they tell us less about the nature of memory storage itself, beyond the obvious conclusion that abnormal brains support abnormal behavior, one aspect of which is the animal's capacity for learning and ensuing memory.

Given the above considerations, general principles regarding the nature of memory storage are best extracted from those studies that were explicitly limited to manipulations of memory induction and storage in animals that were ostensibly normal with the single exception of a transgene thought to impinge on the substrate learning mechanism in the brain. Based on this more limited analysis, what lessons can we glean? First, it should be noted that the vast majority of learning studies employing transgenic animals have manipulated genes that impinge on various components of NMDA receptor-dependent LTP induction, maintenance, or expression. It is these studies that we have focused on throughout this review. This was not simply a convenience; in fact, the most systematic analyses of memory mechanisms in the vertebrate brain are overwhelmingly predicated on the assumption that LTP *is* the mechanism by which memories are stored. In some respects, this complicates our task, as it is not universally accepted that LTP is an adequate device to subserve memory storage (e.g., Matzel & Shors, 2001; Saucier & Cain, 1995a; Shors & Matzel, 1997; Vanderwolf & Cain, 1994).

Thus, any conclusions based on this governing approach will be subject to the same caveats levied against the broader assumption that LTP *is* the (or a) memory storage device. We should first address this issue, as despite our hesitancy to accept this assertion, the relevant work with transgenic mice is illuminating nonetheless. First, it should be noted that a vast body of research provides at least ostensible support for the LTP-memory hypothesis (for review, see Martinez & Derrick, 1996). However, even independent of work with transgenic mice, a large number of studies have reported dissociations between LTP and memory, for example, normal hippocampus-dependent memory despite a blockade or disruption of hippocampal LTP or the absence of hippocampus-dependent memory despite apparently normal LTP (e.g., Bannerman, Good, Butcher, Ramsay, & Morris, 1995; Cain, Hargreaves, Boon, & Dennison, 1993; Hoh, Beiko, Boon, Weiss, & Cain, 1999; Meiri, Sun, Segal, & Alkon, 1998; Nosten-Bertrand et al., 1996; Saucier & Cain, 1995a; Saucier & Cain, 1995b; Saucier, Hargreaves, Boon, Vanderwolf, & Cain, 1996; see Shors & Matzel, 1997, for review). Regarding the data obtained from studies of learning with transgenic mice, the picture is similarly complicated, and we will reiterate only several key points here. Recall that much of the data reviewed previously was difficult to interpret; for example, gene deletions or insertions do in many instances impair both LTP and learning, but these same genetic manipulations often affect brain processes that do not directly contribute to the mechanism of LTP but which might reasonably be assumed to impact on learning. Likewise, mutant animals often exhibit alterations in unlearned native behaviors, exhibiting such abnormalities as impaired motor control, altered pain sensitivity, and generally atypical behavior (that have been described, e.g., as jumpy or nervous). Thus, it is not surprising that in many studies, mutant animals appear to exhibit behavioral deficits early during training, before any appreciable learning could have occurred.

Although the pattern of results described in the prior paragraph makes it difficult to interpret the relationship between the influence of a transgene on LTP and learning, some of the studies reviewed here have been noteworthy in that it was possible to at least *partially* circumvent these interpretative difficulties. As examples, we will review two sets of data here. First, we will consider the effects of disrupting the activity of a postsynaptic protein kinase thought to be critical for the induction of NMDA receptor-dependent LTP in the hippocampus. Recall that Mayford et al. (1996) combined the tTA system with a forebrain-specific promoter to achieve both regional and temporal control of the transgene for CaMKII, the postsynaptic protein kinase that had previously been implicated in LTP induction (and possibly in spatial memory). When the kinase activity was acutely disrupted in the forebrain of adult animals, 5 or 10 Hz stimulation of the Shaeffer collaterals did not support normal LTP induction, but rather, promoted a *depression* of synaptic transmission, that is, LTD.

The shift from LTP to LTD induction by 5–10 Hz stimulation in the CaMKII/hippocampus mutants is quite important for the purposes of these experiments, given that 5–10 Hz oscillations are characteristic of the endogenous activity recorded in the hippocampus of animals engaged in the exploration of novel environments (Vanderwolf, Kramis, Gillespie, & Bland, 1975). Thus, it has been proposed that the induction of LTP by these slow rates of oscillation is particularly appropriate to subserve hippocampus-dependent spatial learning (Larson et al., 1986). Consistent with this proposal, Mayford et al. (Mayford et al., 1996) found that the mutant animals were severely retarded in the acquisition of spatial memories, and likewise, exhibited a severe deficit in contextual fear conditioning, another task that is dependent on the intact hippocampus. Since these learning deficits were observed in animals for which the CaMKII transgene was expressed only transiently in adulthood (i.e., not throughout development), it is difficult to attribute these deficits to developmental abnormalities or the promotion during development of compensatory mechanisms to subserve learning. Thus, it is not surprising that the mutant animals exhibited no impairment in the acquisition of learned fear responses (e.g., freezing) to a punctate stimulus (i.e., a conditioned stimulus; CS) paired with shock, a form of learning that is generally held to be dependent on the amygdala (LeDoux, 2000) but which does not impinge on the hippocampus. In all, this series of experiments provides good support for the conclusion that the disruption by genetic regulation of a normal postsynaptic molecular cascade (i.e., the stimulation of a CamKII-regulated cascade) can have a relatively specific and task-restricted influence on an animal's capacity to learn.

As a second example of the utility of the genetic approach to studies of learning, we return to studies in which the *overexpression* of a gene that promotes current flow through the NMDA receptor was found to have commensurately beneficial effects on LTP induction and memory formation. Tang et al. (1999) generated mice that overexpress the NR2B subunit of the NMDA receptor, a mutation that was associated with the facilitation of LTP induction and the prolongation of its maintenance. Relative to wild-type animals, these mutants displayed normal exploration of novel objects, but enhanced recognition of familiar objects (indicative of either better learning or prolonged retention). Moreover, when tested in retention, both contextual fear conditioning and fear responses to a discrete CS paired with shock were elevated in the mutant animals, again suggestive of either

superior learning or retention. Lastly, while mutant and wild-type animals exhibited similar latencies and strategies to escape onto a visible platform in the water maze, the mutant animals exhibited faster acquisition in the spatial (hidden platform) version of the task. Based on this pattern of results, it has been concluded that this mutation promotes a general enhancement of an animal's capacity to learn (Tsien, 2000).

As was noted earlier, perturbations of the brain (e.g., receptor sensitivity, current flow through postsynaptic channels, disruptions of protein kinase or phosphatase activity) are commonly associated with learning deficits. However, given that these perturbations can broadly impair brain function and are usually associated with deficits in motor or sensory function, the observation of a learning impairment following such a manipulation is difficult to interpret. Thus, the observation by Tsien and his colleagues (Tang et al., 1999) that a mutation can selectively *enhance* learning (but see Wei et al., 2001) is a powerful demonstration of the influence of genetics on learning and of the potential utility of genetic methods as a tool to modulate learning.

The studies by Mayford et al. (1996) and Tang et al. (1999) provide compelling support for the general conclusion that genetic perturbations can have a profound and relatively specific impact on learning, either to impair it, or in other instances, to facilitate it. This conclusion might at first glance strike the reader as manifestly obvious. In fact though, given the concerns raised earlier regarding the difficulties associated with interpretations of behavior consequent to transgene manipulations (see also Crawley, 1999; Gerlai, 1996), one goal of this approach should be to identify transgenes that impact on learning in the absence of any obvious sensory, motor, or motivational, abnormalities, that is, to isolate the genetic determinants of learning might reasonably be expected to have an impact *limited* to learning, sparing other functions of the nervous system. Although the studies of Mayford et al. and Tang et al. are an approach in this direction, it would be reasonable to conclude that they fall short of accomplishing this goal: The CaMKII kinase and NMDA receptors serve a multitude of functions in the nervous system, and it is unreasonable to expect that their regulation could have a limited and specific influence on learning. In this regard, it is entirely possible that no such learning-specific genes will ever be identified, because learning is itself a subset of the integrative processes subserved by the brain.

Despite the implications for this general approach, the data of Mayford et al. (1996) and Tang et al. (1999) do not allow us to draw any definitive conclusions regarding the actual nature of the learning mechanism, for instance, LTP. In particular, we must reconcile demonstrations by Mayford et al. and Tang et al. that a single mutation impinges on both LTP and memory formation (and by implication, that LTP is the underlying learning mechanism) with the multitude of pharmacological, electrophysiological, and genetic manipulations reviewed above that serve to dissociate LTP and learning. Is there another, more parsimonious interpretation of these results that can encompass *all* of these observations?

Although NMDA receptor-dependent LTP is most commonly heralded as the learning mechanism or as a memory storage device, many alternative mechanisms have been proposed to subserve memory storage (e.g., Alkon, 1989; Arancio, Kandel, & Hawkins, 1995; Disterhoft, Moyer, Thompson, & Kowalsk, 1993; Hawkins, Kandel, & Siegelbaum, 1993; Krasne & Glanzman, 1995), and these mechanisms share certain common elements (cf. Byrne, 1987; Matzel et al., 1998). Regardless of the *real* contribution of any of these purported mechanisms to the actual storage of memory,

all of these mechanisms make the same fundamental assumption that the synaptic interaction between relevant neural loci is the impetus for many forms of memory that require learning about stimulus relationships. Moreover, the biophysical modifications pursuant to this synaptic interaction are a consequence of a cascade of molecular events initiated by the synaptic response (i.e., transmitter binding). With this in mind, we have reported that the basal efficacy of synaptic transmission (at synapses relevant to learning) is strongly correlated with an animal's capacity to learn (Matzel, Gandhi, & Muzzio, 2000; Matzel, Muzzio, & Talk, 1996), and moreover, that the basal efficacy of synaptic transmission is homogeneously regulated throughout an individual's nervous system, such that it predicts individual differences in learning (Matzel et al., 2000). From this, we have argued that the level of synaptic efficacy that is characteristic of a nervous system may contribute to an animal's general capacity for learning and may serve as a common target for seemingly disparate manipulations that appear to impinge on an animal's learning performance (Matzel & Gandhi, 1999).

Can the framework described above encompass the data reviewed in this chapter? In large part, it does. Again, we return to studies by Mayford et al. (1996) and Tang et al. (1999). Mayford et al. report that disruption of the postsynaptic molecular cascade initiated by transmitter binding impairs learning that is presumed to be dependent on those synapses. Likewise, Tang et al. report that mutations that facilitate the postsynaptic response to transmitter binding have a commensurate affect on learning that is dependent on those synapses. Furthermore, the genetic stimulation of growth factors can promote an increase in the density of synaptic spines and may have a beneficial influence on learning (Routtenberg et al., 2000), and the impairment of synaptic transmission by the genetic implementation of dementia-related plaques is associated with learning impairments (Holcomb et al., 1998). It is important to note that we can account for these genetic influences on learning without any presumption as to the underlying learning mechanism. Thus, within the context of such a framework, it is of no concern that LTP has often been dissociated from learning or that genetic manipulations that impinge specifically on LTP do not always have a commensurate influence on an animal's capacity to learn.

Unencumbered by the interpretative restrictions imposed by the presumption of a *single* learning mechanism (e.g., LTP), a more parsimonious accounting of the genetic determinants of learning begins to emerge. To some, the conclusion that there exists no single learning gene will be less than satisfying. Absent a shift in the paradigm that guides this research effort (e.g., Pena de Ortiz & Arshavsky, 2001), it is unlikely that such a gene (or even small group of genes) will be identified. However, absent such a learning gene, it is clear that the genetic regulation of the constituents of synaptic plasticity and its biophysical substrates can broadly and profoundly impact on the learning process. From this vantage, it is clear that interventions to eradicate learning impairments and possibly to facilitate normal learning are within our grasp.

REFERENCES

Abeliovich, A., Chen, C., Goda, Y., Silva, A. J., Stevens, C. F., & Tonegawa, S. (1993). Modified hippocampal long-term potentiation in PKC gamma-mutant mice. *Cell, 75,* 1253–1262.

Alger, B. E., & Teyler, T. J. (1976). Long-term and short-term plasticity in the CA1, CA3, and dentate regions of the rat hippocampal slice. *Brain Research, 110,* 463–480.

Alkon, D. L. (1989). Memory storage and neural systems. *Scientific American, Vol. 260,* 42–50.

Alkon, D. L., & Rasmussen, H. (1988). A spatial-temporal model of cell activation. *Science, 239,* 998–1005.

Ambros-Ingerson, J., Xiao, P., Larson, J., & Lynch, G. (1993). Waveform analysis suggests that LTP alters the kinetics of synaptic receptor channels. *Brain Research, 620,* 237–244.

Andersen, P., Sundberg, S. H., Sveen, O., & Wigstrom, H. (1977). Specific long-lasting potentiation of synaptic transmission in hippocampal slices. *Nature, 266,* 736–737.

Arancio, O., Kandel, E. R., & Hawkins, R. D. (1995). Activity-dependent long-term enhancement of transmitter release by presynaptic 3′, 5′-cyclic GMP in cultured hippocampal neurons. *Nature, 376*(6535), 74–80.

Bannerman, D. M., Good, M. A., Butcher, S. P., Ramsay, M., & Morris, R. G. (1995). Distinct components of spatial learning revealed by prior training and NMDA receptor blockade [see comments]. *Nature, 378,* 182–186.

Barnes, C. A. (1988). Spatial learning and memory processes: The search for their neurobiological mechanisms in the rat. *Trends in Neuroscience, 11,* 163–169.

Barrionuevo, G., & Brown, T. H. (1983). Associative long-term potentiation in hippocampal slices. *Proceedings of the National Academy of Sciences, USA, 80,* 7347–7251.

Bartus, R. T. (2000). On neurodegenerative diseases, models, and treatment strategies: Lessons learned and lessons forgotten a generation following the cholinergic hypothesis. *Experimental Neurology, 163*(2), 495–529.

Baudry, M., Arst, O., Oliver, M., & Lynch, G. (1994). Development of glutamate binding sites and their regulation by calcium in rat hippocampus. *Developmental Brain Research, 1,* 37–48.

Benowitz, L. I., & Routtenberg, A. (1997). *Trends in Neuroscience, 20,* 84–91.

Bliss, T. V., & Gardner-Medwin, A. R. (1973). Long-lasting potentiation of synaptic transmission in the dentate area of the unanaestetized rabbit following stimulation of the perforant path. *Journal of Physiology (London), 232,* 357–374.

Bliss, T. V., & Lomo, T. (1973). Long-lasting potentiation of synaptic transmission in the dentate area of the anaesthetized rabbit following stimulation of the perforant path. *Journal of Physiology (London), 232,* 331–356.

Borchelt, D. R., Thinakaran, G., Eckman, C. B., Lee, M. K., Davenport, F., Ratovitsky, T., Prada, C. M., Kim, G., Seekins, S., Yager, D., Slunt, H. H., Wang, R., Seeger, M., Levey, A. I., Gandy, S. E., Copeland, N. G., Jenkins, N. A., Price, D. L., Younkin, S. G., & Sisodia, S. S. (1996). Familial Alzheimer's disease-linked presenilin 1 variants elevate Abeta1-42/1-40 ratio in vitro and in vivo. *Neuron, 17*(5), 1005–1013.

Bortolotto, Z. A., Bashir, Z. I., Davies, C. H., Taira, T., Kaila, K., & Collingridge, G. L. (1995). Studies on the role of metabotropic glutamate receptors in long-term potentiation: some methodological considerations. *Journal of Neuroscience Methods, 59,* 19–24.

Bortolotto, Z. A., & Collingridge, G. L. (1993). Characterisation of LTP induced by the activation of glutamate metabotropic receptors in area CA1 of the hippocampus. *Neuropharmacology, 32,* 1–9.

Bortolotto, Z. A., & Collingridge, G. L. (1995). On the mechanism of long-term potentiation induced by (1S,3R)-1-aminocyclopentane-1,3-dicarboxylic acid (ACPD) in rat hippocampal slices. *Neuropharmacology, 34,* 1003–1014.

Brown, T. H., Kairiss, E. W., & Keenan, C. L. (1990). Hebbian synapses: Biophysical mechanisms and algorithms. *Annual Review of Neuroscience, 13,* 475–511.

Burrows, R. C., Levitt, P., & Shors, T. J. (2000). Postnatal decrease in transforming growth factor alpha is associated with enlarged ventricles, deficient amygdaloid vasculature and performance deficits. *Neuroscience, 96*(4), 825–836.

Byrne, J. H. (1987). Cellular analysis of associative learning. *Physiological Reviews, 67,* 329–439.

Cain, D. P., Hargreaves, F., Boon, F., & Dennison, Z. (1993). An examination of the relations between hippocampal long-term potentiation, kindling, afterdischarge, and place learning in the watermaze. *Hippocampus, 3,* 153–164.

Calhoun, M. E., Wiederhold, K. H., Abramowski, D., Phinney, A. L., Probst, A., Sturchler-Pierrat, C., Staufenbiel, M., Sommer, B., & Jucker, M. (1998). Neuron loss in APP transgenic mice [letter]. *Nature, 395*(6704), 755–756.

Chavez-Noriega, L. E., & Stevens, C. F. (1992). Modulation of synaptic efficacy in field CA1 of the rat hippocampus by forskolin. *Brain Research, 574,* 85–92.

Chen, G., Chen, K. S., Knox, J., Inglis, J., Bernard, A., Martin, S. J., Justice, A., McConlogue, L., Games, D., Freedman, S. B., & Morris, R. G. (2000). A learning deficit related to age and beta-amyloid plaques in a mouse model of Alzheimer's disease. [In Process Citation]. *Nature, 408*(6815), 975–979.

Citron, M., Westaway, D., Xia, W., Carlson, G., Diehl, T., Levesque, G., Johnson-Wood, K., Lee, M., Seubert, P., Davis, A., Kholodenko, D., Motter, R., Sherrington, R., Perry, B., Yao, H., Strome, R., Lieberburg, I., Rommens, J., Kim, S., Schenk, D., Fraser, P., St George, H. P., & Selkoe, D. J. (1997). Mutant presenilins of Alzheimer's disease increase production of 42-residue amyloid beta-protein in both transfected cells and transgenic mice [see comments]. *Nature Medicine, 3*(1), 67–72.

Collingridge, G. L., Kehl, S. J., & McLennan, H. (1983). Excitatory amino acids in synaptic transmission in the Schaeffer-commissural pathway of the rat hippocampus. *Journal of Physiology (London), 443,* 33–46.

Corning, W. C., & Ratner, S. C. (1967). *Chemistry of learning.* New York: Plenum Press.

Crawley, J. N. (1999). Behavioral phenotyping of transgenic and knockout mice: Experimental design and evaluation of general health, sensory functions, motor abilities, and specific behavioral tests. *Brain Research, 835*(1), 18–26.

Croll, S. D., Suri, C., Compton, D. L., Simmons, M. V., Yancopoulos, G. D., Lindsay, R. M., Wiegand, S. J., Rudge, J. S., & Scharfman, H. E. (1999). Brain-derived neurotrophic factor transgenic mice exhibit passive avoidance deficits, increased seizure severity and in vitro hyperexcitability in the hippocampus and entorhinal cortex. *Neuroscience, 93*(4), 1491–1506.

Davis, S., Butcher, S. P., & Morris, R. G. M. (1992). The NMDA receptor antagonist D-2-amino-5-phosphonopentanoate (D-AP5) impairs spatial learning and LTP in vivo at intracerebral concentrations comperable to those that block LTP in vitro. *Journal of Neuroscience, 12,* 21–34.

Dawson, G. R., Seabrook, G. R., & Zheng, H. (1998). Age-related cognitive deficits, impaired long-term potentiation, and reductions in synaptic marker density in mice lacking the beta-amyloid precursor protein. *Neuroscience, 89,* 148–162.

De Graan, P. N., Dekker, L. V., De Wit, M., Schrama, L. H., & Gispen, W. H. (1988). Modulation of B-50 phosphorylation and polyphosphoinositide metabolism in synaptic plasma membranes by protein kinase C, phorbol diesters and ACTH. *Journal of Receptor Research, 8,* 345–361.

Dekker, L. V., De Graan, P. N., Versteeg, D. H., Oestreicher, A. B., & Gispen, W. H. (1989). Phosphorylation of B-50 (GAP43) is correlated with neurotransmitter release in rat hippocampal slices. *Journal of Neurochemistry, 52,* 24–30.

de Strooper, S. B., Saftig, P., Craessaerts, K., Vanderstichele, H., Guhde, G., Annaert, W., Von Figura, K., & Van Leuven, F. (1998). Deficiency of presenilin-1 inhibits the normal cleavage of amyloid precursor protein [see comments]. *Nature, 391*(6665), 387–390.

Deutsch, J. A. (1993). Spatial learning in mutant mice. *Science, 262,* 760–761.

Disterhoft, J. F., Moyer, J. R., Thompson, L. T., & Kowalsk, M. (1993). Functional aspects of calcium-channel modulation. *Clinical Neuropharmacology, 16,* s12–s24.

Dubnau, J., & Tully, T. (1998). Gene discovery in Drosophila: New insights for learning and memory. *Annual Review of Neuroscience, 21*(1), 407–444.

Duff, K., Eckman, C., Zehr, C., Yu, X., Prada, C. M., Perez-tur, J., Hutton, M., Buee, L., Harigaya, Y., Yager, D., Morgan, D., Gordon, M. N., Holcomb, L., Refolo, L., Zenk, B., Hardy, J., & Younkin, S. (1996). Increased amyloid-beta42(43) in brains of mice expressing mutant presenilin 1. *Nature, 383*(6602), 710–713.

Fiore, M., Angelucci, F., Alleva, E., Branchi, I., Probert, L., & Aloe, L. (2000). Learning performances, brain NGF distribution and NPY levels in transgenic mice expressing TNF-alpha. *Behavioral Brain Research, 112*(1–2), 165–175.

Forrest, D., Yuzaki, M., Soares, H. D., Ng, L., Luk, D. C., Sheng, M., Stewart, C. L., Morgan, J. I., Connor, J. A., & Curran, T. (1994). Targeted disruption of NMDA receptor 1 gene abolishes NMDA response and results in neonatal death. *Neuron, 13,* 325–338.

Frey, U., Huang, Y. Y., & Kandel, E. R. (1993). Effects of cAMP simulate a late stage of LTP in hippocampal CA1 neurons. *Science, 260,* 1661–1664.

Furth, P. A., St.Onge, L., Boger, H., Gruss, P., Gossen, M., Kistner, A., Bujard, H., & Hennighausen, L. (1994). Temporal control of gene expression in transgenic mice by a tetracycline-responsive promoter. *Proceedings of the National Academy of Sciences, USA, 93,* 10933–10938.

Gerlai, R. (1996). Gene-targeting studies of mammalian behavior: Is it the mutation or the background genotype? *Trends in Neuroscience, 19,* 177–181.

Gingrich, J. A., & Hen, R. (2000). The broken mouse: The role of development, plasticity, and environment in the interpretation of phenotypic changes in knockout mice. *Current Opinion in Neurobiology, 10,* 146–152.

Glenner, G. G., & Wong, C. W. (1984). Alzheimer's disease: Initial report of the purification and characterization of a novel cerebrovascular amyloid protein. *Biochemical and Biophysical Research Communications, 120,* 885–890.

Grant, S. G., O'Dell, T. J., Karl, K. A., Stein, P. L., Soriano, P., & Kandel, E. R. (1992). Impaired long-term potentiation, spatial learning, and hippocampal development in fyn mutant mice. *Science, 258,* 1903–1910.

Grover, L. M., & Teyler, T. J. (1990). Two components of long-term potentiation induced by different patterns of afferent activation. *Nature, 347,* 477–479.

Haass, C., & Selkoe, D. J. (1998). A technical KO of $-amyloid peptide. *Nature, 391,* 339–340.

Harris, E. W., Ganong, A. H., & Cotman, C. W. (1984). Long-term potentiation in the hippocampus involves activation of N-methyl-D-aspartate receptors. *Brain Research, 323,* 132–137.

Hawkins, R. D., Kandel, E. R., & Siegelbaum, S. A. (1993). Learning to modulate transmitter release: Themes and variations in synaptic plasticity. *Annual Review of Neuroscience, 16,* 625–665.

Hering, E. (1870). Uber das gedachtniss als eine allgemeine function der organisirten materie. *Almanach der kaiserlicheten Akademie der Wissenschaften, 20,* 253–278.

Hoh, T., Beiko, J., Boon, F., Weiss, S., & Cain, D. P. (1999). Complex behavioral strategy and reversal learning in the water maze without NMDA receptor-dependent long-term potentiation. *Journal of Neuroscience, 19,* 1–5.

Holcomb, L., Gordon, M. N., McGowan, E., Yu, X., Benkovic, S., Jantzen, P., Wright, K., Saad, I., Mueller, R., Morgan, D., Sanders, S., Zehr, C., O'Campo, K., Hardy, J., Prada, C. M., Eckman, C., Younkin, S., Hsiao, K., & Duff, K. (1998). Accelerated Alzheimer-type phenotype in transgenic mice carrying both mutant amyloid precursor protein and presenilin 1 transgenes. *Nature Medicine, 4*(1), 97–100.

Holcomb, L. A., Gordon, M. N., Jantzen, P., Hsiao, K., Duff, K., & Morgan, D. (1999). Behavioral changes in transgenic mice expressing both amyloid precursor protein and presenilin-1 mutations: Lack of association with amyloid deposits. *Behaviour Genetics, 29*(3), 177–185.

Hsiao, K., Chapman, P., Nilsen, S., Eckman, C., Harigaya, Y., Younkin, S., Yang, F., & Cole, G. (1996). Correlative memory deficits, Abeta elevation, and amyloid plaques in transgenic mice [see comments]. *Science, 274*(5284), 99–102.

Hsiao, K. K., Borchelt, D. R., Olson, K., Johannsdottir, R., Kitt, C., Yunis, W., Xu, S., Eckman, C., Younkin, S., & Price, D. (1995). Age-related CNS disorder and early death in transgenic FVB/N mice overexpressing Alzheimer amyloid precursor proteins. *Neuron, 15*(5), 1203–1218.

Huang, Y. Y., & Kandel, E. R. (1994). Recruitment of long-lasting and protein kinase A-dependent long-term potentiation in the CA1 region of hippocampus requires repeated tetanization. *Learning and Memory, 1*(1), 74–82.

Inoue, M., Mishina, M., & Ueda, H. (2000). Enhanced nociception by exogenous and endogenous substance P given into the spinal cord in mice lacking NR(2)A/epsilon(1), an NMDA receptor subunit. *British Journal of Pharmacology, 129*(2), 239–241.

Isaac, J. T., Nicoll, R. A., & Malenka, R. C. (1995). Evidence for silent synapses: Implications for the expression of LTP. *Neuron, 15,* 427–434.

Jaffe, D., & Johnston, D. (1990). Induction of long-term potentiation at hippocampal mossy fiber synapses follows a Hebbian rule. *Journal of Neurophysiology, 64,* 948–960.

Janus, C., D'Amelio, S., Amitay, O., Chishti, M. A., Strome, R., Fraser, P., Carlson, G. A., Roder, J. C., St George-Hyslop, P., & Westaway, D. (2000). Spatial learning in transgenic mice expressing human presenilin 1 (PS1) transgenes. *Neurobiology of Aging, 21*(4), 541–549.

Johnston, D., Williams, S., Jaffe, D., & Gray, R. (1992). NMDA-receptor-independent long-term potentiation. *Annual Review of Physiology, 54,* 489–505.

Kang, H. J., & Schuman, E. M. (1995a). Long-lasting neurotrophin-induced enhancement of synaptic transmission in the adult hippocampus. *Science, 267*(5204), 1658–1662.

Kang, H. J., & Schuman, E. M. (1995b). Neurotrophin-induced modulation of synaptic transmission in the adult hippocampus. *Journal of Physiology (Paris), 89*(1), 11–22.

Kiyama, Y., Manabe, T., Sakimura, K., Kawakami, F., Mori, H., & Mishina, M. (1998). Increased thresholds for long-term potentiation and contextual learning in mice lacking the NMDA-type glutamate receptor epsilon1 subunit. *Journal of Neuroscience, 18*(17), 6704–6712.

Krasne, F. B., & Glanzman, D. L. (1995). What can we learn from invertebrate learning. *Annual Review of Psychology, 46,* 585–624.

Kullmann, D. M., Perkel, D. J., Manabe, T., & Nicoll, R. A. (1992). Ca2+ entry via postsynaptic voltage-sensitive Ca2+ channels can transiently potentiate excitatory synaptic transmission in the hippocampus. *Neuron, 9,* 1175–1183.

Larson, J., & Lynch, G. (1986). Induction of synaptic potentiation in hippocampus by patterned stimulation involves two events. *Science, 232,* 985–988.

Larson, J., Lynch, G., Games, D., & Seubert, P. (1999). Alterations in synaptic transmission and long-term potentiation in hippocampal slices from young and aged PDAPP mice. *Brain Research, 840*(1–2), 23–35.

Larson, J., Wong, D., & Lynch, G. (1986). Patterned stimulation at the theta frequency is optimal for the induction of hippocampal long-term potentiation. *Brain Research, 368,* 347–350.

LeDoux, J. E. (2000). Emotion circuits in the brain. *Annual Review of Neuroscience, 23,* 155–184.

Levy, W. B., & Steward, O. (1983). Temporal contiguity requirements for long-term associative potentiation/depression in the hippocampus. *Neuroscience, 8,* 791–797.

Li, Y., Erzurumiu, R., Chen, C., Jhaveri, S., & Tonegawa, S. (1994). Whisker-related neuronal patterns fail to develop in the trigeminal brainstem nuclei of NMDAR1 knockout mice. *Cell, 76*(427), 437.

Liao, D., Hessler, N. A., & Malinow, R. (1995). Activation of postsynaptically silent synapses during pairing-induced LTP in CA1 region of hippocampal slice. *Nature, 375,* 400–404.

Lynch, G., Larson, J., Kelso, S., Barrionuevo, G., & Schottler, F. (1983). Intracellular injections of EGTA block induction of hippocampal long-term potentiation. *Nature, 305,* 719–721.

Malenka, R. C. (1991a). Postsynaptic factors control the duration of synaptic enhancement in area CA1 of the hippocampus. *Neuron, 6,* 53–60.

Malenka, R. C. (1991b). The role of postsynaptic calcium in the induction of long-term potentiation. *Molecular Neurobiology, 5,* 289–295.

Malenka, R. C., Kauer, J. A., Perkel, D. J., Mauk, M. D., Kelly, P. T., Nicoll, R. A., & Waxham, M. N. (1989). An essential role for postsynaptic calmodulin and protein kinase activity in long-term potentiation. *Nature, 340,* 554–557.

Malenka, R. C., Kauer, J. A., Zucker, R. S., & Nicoll, R. A. (1988). Postsynaptic calcium is sufficient for potentiation of hippocampal synaptic transmission. *Science, 242,* 81–84.

Malenka, R. C., Madison, D. V., & Nicoll, R. A. (1986). Potentiation of synaptic transmission in the hippocampus by phorbol esters. *Nature, 321,* 175–177.

Malinow, R. (1994). LTP: Desperately seeking resolution. *Science, 266,* 1195–1196.

Malinow, R., Schulman, H., & Tsien, R. W. (1989). Inhibition of postsynaptic PKC or CaMKII blocks induction but not expression of LTP. *Science, 245,* 862–869.

Mansuy, I. M., Mayford, M., Jacob, B., Kandel, E. R., & Bach, M. E. (1998). Restricted and regulated overexpression reveals calcineurin as a key component in the transition from short-term to long-term memory. *Cell, 92*(1), 39–49.

Mansuy, I. M., Winder, D. G., Moallem, T. M., Osman, M., Mayford, M., Hawkins, R. D., & Kandel, E. R. (1998). Inducible and reversible gene expression with the rtTA system for the study of memory. *Neuron, 21*(2), 257–265.

Martinez, J. L., & Derrick, B. E. (1996). Long-term potentiation and learning. *Annual Review of Psychology, 47,* 173–203.

Matzel, L. D., & Gandhi, C. C. (1999). The tractable contribution of synapses and their component molecules to individual differences in learning. *Behavioral Brain Research.*

Matzel, L. D., Gandhi, C. C., & Muzzio, I. A. (2000). A presynaptic influence on basal synaptic efficacy is homogeneously distributed and predicts individual differences in learning. *Neuroreport.*

Matzel, L. D., Hallam, S. C., & Miller, R. R. (1988). Contribution of conditioned opioid analgesia to the associative US preexposure deficit. *Animal Learning and Behavior, 16,* 486–492.

Matzel, L. D., Muzzio, I., & Talk, A. C. (1996). Variations in learning reflect individual differences in sensory function and synaptic integration. *Behavioral Neuroscience, 110*(5), 1084–1095.

Matzel, L. D., & Shors, T. J. (2001). Long-term potentiation and associative learning: Can the mechanism subserve the process? In C. Holscher (Ed.), *Neuronal mechanisms of memory formation: Long-term potentiation and beyond* (pp. 148–195). Cambridge: Cambridge University Press.

Matzel, L. D., Talk, A. C., Muzzio, I., & Rogers, R. F. (1998). Ubiquitous molecular substrates for associative learning and activity-dependent neuronal facilitation. *Reviews in the Neurosciences, 9,* 129–168.

Mayford, M., Bach, M. E., Huang, Y. Y., Wang, L., Hawkins, R. D., & Kandel, E. R. (1996). Control of memory formation through regulated expression of a CaMKII transgene. *Science, 274*(5293), 1678–1683.

McEachern, J. C., & Shaw, C. A. (1996). An alternative to the LTP orthodoxy: A plasticity-pathology continuum model. *Brain Research Reviews, 22*(1), 51–92.

Meiri, N., Sun, M. K., Segal, Z., & Alkon, D. L. (1998). Memory and long-term potentiation (LTP) dissociated: Normal spatial memory despite CA1 LTP elimination with Kv1.4 antisense. *Proceedings of the National Academy of Sciences, USA, 95*(25), 15037–15042.

Minami, T., Okuda-Ashitaka, E., Mori, H., Sakimura, K., Watanabe, M., Mishina, M., & Ito, S. (2000). Characterization of nociceptin/orphanin FQ-induced pain responses in conscious mice: neonatal capsaicin treatment and N-methyl-D-aspartate receptor GluRepsilon subunit knockout mice. *Neuroscience, 97*(1), 133–142.

Minami, T., Sugatani, J., Sakimura, K., Abe, M., Mishina, M., & Ito, S. (1997). Absence of prostaglandin E2-induced hyperalgesia in NMDA receptor epsilon subunit knockout mice. *British Journal of Pharmacology, 120*(8), 1522–1526.

Monyer, H., Burnashev, N., Laurie, D. J., Sakmann, B., & Seeburg, P. H. (1994). Developmental and regional expression in the rat brain and functional properties of four NMDA receptors. *Neuron, 12*(3), 529–540.

Morris, R. G. M., Davis, S., & Butcher, S. P. (1991). Hippocampal synaptic plasticity and NMDA receptors: A role in information storage. In J. R. Krebs & G. Horn (Eds.), *Behavioral and neural aspects of learning and memory* (pp. 89–106). Oxford: Clarendon Press.

Muller, R. U., Kubie, J. L., & Ranck, J. B. (1987). Spatial firing patterns of hippocampal complex-spike cells in a fixed environment. *Journal of Neuroscience, 7,* 1935–1950.

Nguyen, P. V., & Kandel, E. R. (1996). A macromolecular synthesis-dependent late phase of long-term potentiation requiring cAMP in the medial perforant pathway of rat hippocampal slices. *Journal of Neuroscience, 16*(10), 3189–3198.

Nishizuka, Y. (1992). Intracellular signalling by hydrolysis of phospholipids and activation of protein kinase C. *Science, 258,* 607–614.

Nosten-Bertrand, M., Errington, M. L., Murphy, K. P., Tokugawa, Y., Barboni, E., Kozlova, E., Michalovich, D., Morris, R. G., Silver, J., Stewart, C. L., Bliss, T. V., & Morris, R. J. (1996). Normal spatial learning despite regional inhibition of LTP in mice lacking Thy-1. *Nature, 379,* 826–829.

O'Dell, T. J., Kandel, E. R., & Grant, S. G. (1991). Long-term potentiation in the hippocampus is blocked by tyrosine kinase inhibitors. *Nature, 353,* 558–560.

O'Keefe, J., & Dostrovsky, J. (1971). The hippocampus as a spatial map. *Brain Research, 34,* 171–175.

Parent, A., Linden, D. J., Sisodia, S. S., & Borchelt, D. R. (1999). Synaptic transmission and hippocampal long-term potentiation in transgenic mice expressing FAD-linked presenilin 1. *Neurobiological Disorders, 6*(1), 56–62.

Pena de Ortiz, S., & Arshavsky, Y. I. (2001). DNA recombination as a possible mechanism in declarative memory: A hypothesis. *Journal of Neuroscience Research, 63,* 72–81.

Pettit, D. L., Perlman, S., & Malinow, R. (1994). Potentiated transmission and prevention of further LTP by increased CaMKII activity in postsynaptic hippocampal slice neurons. *Science, 266,* 1881–1885.

Phinney, A. L., Calhoun, M. E., Wolfer, D. P., Lipp, H. P., Zheng, H., & Jucker, M. (1999). No hippocampal neuron or synaptic bouton loss in learning-impaired aged beta-amyloid precursor protein-null mice. *Neuroscience, 90*(4), 1207–1216.

Qi, M., Zhuo, M., Skalhegg, B. S., Brandon, E. P., Kandel, E. R., McKnight, G. S., & Idzerda, R. L. (1996). Impaired hippocampal plasticity in mice lacking the Cbeta1 catalytic subunit of cAMP-dependent protein kinase. *Proceedings of the National Academy of Sciences, USA, 93,* 1571–1576.

Reymann, K. G., Schulzeck, K., Kase, H., & Matthies, H. (1988). Phorbol ester-induced hippocampal long-term potentiation is counteracted by inhibitors of protein kinase C. *Experimental Brain Research, 71,* 227–230.

Ribot, T. (1881). *Les Maladies de la Memoire.* Paris: J. B. Balliere.

Riekkinen, P. J., Schmidt, B. H., & van der Staay F. J. (1998). Animal models in the development of symptomatic and preventive drug therapies for Alzheimer's disease. *Annals of Medicine, 30*(6), 566–576.

Rotenberg, A., Mayford, M., Hawkins, R. D., Kandel, E. R., & Muller, R. U. (1996). Mice expressing activated CaMKII lack low frequency LTP and do not form stable place cells in the CA1 region of the hippocampus [see comments]. *Cell, 87*(7), 1351–1361.

Routtenberg, A., Cantallops, I., Zaffuto, S., Serrano, P., & Namgung, U. (2000). Enhanced learning after genetic overexpression of a brain growth protein. *Proceedings of the National Academy of Sciences, USA, 97*(13), 7657–7662.

Saarelainen, T., Pussinen, R., Koponen, E., Alhonen, L., Wong, G., Sirvio, J., & Castren, E. (2000). Transgenic mice overexpressing truncated trkB neurotrophin receptors in neurons have impaired long-term spatial memory but normal hippocampal LTP. *Synapse, 38*(1), 102–104.

Saftig, P., & de Strooper, S. B. (1998). Downregulation of PS1 expression in neurons decreases beta-amyloid production: A biochemical link between the two major familial Alzheimer's disease genes [news]. *Molecular Psychiatry, 3*(4), 287–289.

Sakimura, K., Kutsuwada, T., Ito, I., Manabe, T., Takayama, C., Kushiya, E., Yagi, T., Aizawa, S., Inoue, Y., & Sugiyama, H. (1995). Reduced hippocampal LTP and spatial learning in mice lacking NMDA receptor epsilon 1 subunit. *Nature, 373*(6510), 151–155.

Salin, P. A., Malenka, R. C., & Nicoll, R. A. (1996). Cyclic AMP mediates a presynaptic form of LTP at cerebellar parallel fiber synapses. *Neuron, 16,* 797–803.

Saucier, D., & Cain, D. P. (1995a). Spatial learning without NMDA receptor-dependent long-term potentiation [see comments]. *Nature, 378,* 186–189.

Saucier, D., & Cain, D. P. (1995b). Spatial learning without NMDA receptor-dependent long-term potentiation. *Nature, 378,* 186–189.

Saucier, D., Hargreaves, E. L., Boon, F., Vanderwolf, C. H., & Cain, D. P. (1996). Detailed behavioral analysis of water maze acquisition under systemic NMDA or muscarinic antagonism: Nonspatial pretraining eliminates spatial learning deficits. *Behavioral Neuroscience, 110,* 103–116.

Sauer, B., & Henderson, N. (1988). Site-specific DNA recombination in mammalian cells by the Cre recombinase of bacteriophage P1. *Proceedings of the National Academy of Sciences, USA, 85,* 5166–5170.

Schwartzkroin, P., & Wester, K. (1975). Long-lasting facilitation of a synaptic potential following tetenization in the in vitro hippocampal slice. *Brain Research, 89,* 107–119.

Scoville, W. B., & Milner, B. (1957). Loss of recent memory after bilateral hippocampal lesions. *Journal of Neurology, Neurosurgery, and Psychiatry, 20,* 11–21.

Shi, S. H., Hayashi, Y., Petralia, R. S., Zaman, S. H., Wenthold, R. J., Svoboda, K., & Malinow, R. (1999). Rapid spine delivery and redistribution of AMPA receptors after synaptic NMDA receptor activation [see comments]. *Science, 284*(5421), 1811–1816.

Shors, T. J., & Matzel, L. D. (1997). Long-term potentiation: What's learning got to do with it? *Behavioral and Brain Sciences, 20,* 597–655.

Silva, A. J., Paylor, R., Wehner, J. M., & Tonegawa, S. (1992). Impaired spatial learning in calcium-calmodulin kinase II mutant mice. *Science, 257,* 206–211.

Silva, A. J., Stevens, C. F., Tonegawa, S., & Wang, Y. (1992). Deficient hippocampal long-term potentiation in Calcium-Calmodulin kinase II mutant mice. *Science, 257,* 201–205.

Staubli, U., Ambros-Ingerson, J., & Lynch, G. (1992). Receptor changes and LTP: An analysis using aniracetam, a drug that reversibly modifies glutamate (AMPA) receptors. *Hippocampus, 2,* 49–57.

Stephane, H. R. O., Malenka, R. C., & Nicoll, R. A. (1996). Bidirectional control of quantal size by synaptic activity in the hippocampus. *Science, 271,* 1294–1297.

Stevens, C. F. (1993). Quantal release of neurotransmitter and long-term potentiation. *Cell, 72*(Suppl), 55–63.

Tang, Y. P., Shimizu, E., Dube, G. R., Rampon, C., Kerchner, G. A., Zhuo, M., Liu, G., & Tsien, J. Z. (1999). Genetic enhancement of learning and memory in mice [see comments]. *Nature, 401*(6748), 63–69.

Teyler, J. T., & DiScenna, P. (1987). Long-term potentiation. *Annual Review of Neuroscience, 10,* 131–161.

Tonegawa, S., Tsien, J. Z., McHugh, T. J., Huerta, P., Blum, K. I., & Wilson, M. A. (1996). Hippocampal CA1-region-restricted knockout of NMDAR1 gene disrupts synaptic plasticity, place fields, and spatial learning. *Cold Spring Harbor Symposium on Quantitative Biology, 61,* 225–238.

Tsien, J. Z. (2000). Building a brainier mouse. *Scientific American, 282*(4), 62–68.

Tsien, J. Z., Chen, D. F., Gerber, D., Tom, C., Mercer, E. H., Anderson, D. J., Mayford, M., Kandel, E. R., & Tonegawa, S. (1996).

Subregion- and cell type-restricted gene knockout in mouse brain [see comments]. *Cell, 87*(7), 1317–1326.

Tsien, J. Z., Huerta, P. T., & Tonegawa, S. (1996). The essential role of hippocampal CA1 NMDA receptor-dependent synaptic plasticity in spatial memory [see comments]. *Cell, 87*(7), 1327–1338.

Turrigiano, G., & Nelson, S. B. (2000). Hebb and homeostasis in neuronal plasticity. *Current Opinion in Neurobiology, 10,* 358–364.

Vanderwolf, C. H., & Cain, D. P. (1994). The behavioral neurobiology of learning and memory: A conceptual reorientation. *Brain Research Reviews, 19,* 264–297.

Vanderwolf, C. H., Kramis, R., Gillespie, L. A., & Bland, B. H. (1975). Hippocampal rhythmic slow activity and neocortical low-voltage fast activity: Relations to behavior. In R. L. Isaacson & K. H. Pribram (Eds.), *The Hippocampus, Vol. 2: Neurophysiology and Behavior* (pp. 101–128). New York: Plenum Press.

Vigorito, M., & Ayres, J. J. B. (1987). Effect of naloxone on conditioned suppression in rats. *Journal of Experimental Psychology: Animal Behavior Processes, 101,* 576–586.

Wan, R. Q., Pang, K., & Olton, D. S. (1994). Hippocampal and amygdaloid involvement in nonspatial and spatial working memory in rats: Effects of delay and interference. *Behavioral Neuroscience, 108*(5), 866–882.

Wang, Y., O'Malley Jr., B. W., Tsai, S. Y., & O'Malley, B. W. (1994). A regulatory system for use in gene transfer. *Proceedings of the National Academy of Sciences, USA, 91,* 8180–8184.

Watson, J. D., & Crick, F. H. C. (1953). A structure for deoxyribose nucleic acid. *Nature, 171,* 737–738.

Wei, F., Wang, G.-D., Kerchner, G. A., Kim, S. J., Xu, H.-M., Chen, Z.-F., & Zhou, M. (2001). Genetic enhancement of inflamatory pain by forebrain NR2B overexpression. *Nature Neuroscience, 4,* 164–170.

Wollman, E. L., Jacob, F., & Hayes, W. (1956). Conjugation and genetic recombination in

E-coli K-12. *Cold Spring Harbour Symposium on Quantitative Biology, XXI,* 141–148.

Yamamoto, A., Lucas, J. J., & Hen, R. (2000). Reversal of neuropathology and motor dysfunction in a conditional model of Huntington's disease. *Cell, 101,* 57–66.

Yamamoto, C., & Chujo, T. (1978). Long-term potentiation in thin hippocampal sections studied by intracellular and extracellular recordeings. *Experimental Neurology, 58,* 242–250.

Zamanillo, D., Sprengel, R., Hvalby, O., Jensen, V., Burnashev, N., Rozov, A., Kaiser, K. M., Koster, H. J., Borchardt, T., Worley, P., Lubke, J., Frotscher, M., Kelly, P. H., Sommer, B., Andersen, P., Seeburg, P. H., & Sakmann, B. (1999). Importance of AMPA receptors for hippocampal synaptic plasticity but not for spatial learning [see comments]. *Science, 284*(5421), 1805–1811.

Zhang, Y., Riesterer, C., Ayrall, A., Sablitzky, F., Littlewood, T., & Reth, M. (1996). Inducible site-directed recombination in mouse embryonic stem cells. *Nucleic Acid Research, 24,* 543–548.

Zheng, H., Jiang, M., Trumbauer, M. E., Sirinathsinghji, D. J., Hopkins, R., Smith, D. W., Heavens, R. P., Dawson, G. R., Boyce, S., & Conner, M. W. (1995). beta-Amyloid precursor protein-deficient mice show reactive gliosis and decreased locomotor activity. *Cell, 81*(4), 525–531.

Zhuo, M., Hu, Y., Schultz, C., Kandel, E. R., & Hawkins, R. D. (1994). Role of guanylyl cyclase and cGMP-dependent protein kinase in long-term potentiation. *Nature, 368,* 635–639.

CHAPTER 6

Learning Instincts

JAMES L. GOULD

INTRODUCTION

In the first two thirds of the twentieth century, when the Behaviorist school of psychology held sway, animals were imagined to have the ability of learning to associate any cues they were physically able to sense with any behavioral response, and of learning through trial and error any novel behavior of which they were physically capable. Instinct was considered an illusion; as Watson (1925), the founder of Behaviorism, succinctly put it, "There are for us no instincts—we no longer need the term in psychology." (p. 74).

At the same time, the ethological school of animal behavior focused largely on innate behavior under naturalistic conditions (Thorpe, 1979). Prominent exceptions included von Frisch's (1914; described in English in Gould, 1982 and Gould & Gould, 1995) explicit use of classical conditioning to study color sensitivity in honeybees, Tinbergen's study (1932/1972; Tinbergen & Kruyt, 1938/1972) of how hunting wasps remember the location of their nests, and Lorenz's work (1935/1957a) on imprinting in geese. This work was largely ignored by Behaviorists—excepting some fairly vicious attacks in the 1950s, the thrust of which was that all innate behaviors could be explained by learning (Lehrman, 1953). (This line of reasoning harks back to Watson's 1925 exhortation, "But try hardest of all to think of

each unlearned act as becoming conditioned shortly after birth—even our respiration and circulation.") (p. 105).

The resulting divide between psychology and ethology—students of learning and (mostly) instinct, respectively—mirrored the nature/nurture controversy that has been with us ever since humans began to think about the sources of behavior in humans and other animals. Behaviorism largely collapsed in the last decades of the twentieth century, in part a consequence of its increasing inability to explain even the narrow range of laboratory results on learning (e.g., Bolles, 1970, 1984; Breland & Breland, 1961; Hearst & Jenkins, 1974; LoLordo, 1979; LoLordo, McMillan, & Riley, 1974; Revusky, 1984; Wilcoxin, Dragoin, & Kral, 1971). The failure of Behaviorism to account for behavior in nature had been obvious for many, many years (reviewed by Gould, 1982). The completeness of its demise is indicated by its absence even from the index of the leading psychology texts by 1980 (e.g., Gleitman, 1981).

As the collapse of Behaviorism began, Gould and Marler (1984, 1987) sought to reconcile laboratory and field studies of learning. Our argument was that, as General Process Learning Theory (an apt term coined by one of its early critics; Seligman, 1970) was being abandoned, in fact the basic processes discovered by Behaviorists were probably at work outside of pigeons and rats, and could inform and enrich ethological studies of learning. At the same time, we guessed that ethological insights might help explain the growing list of learning anomalies that had brought down Behaviorism. We called the processes that link the two lines of research *instincts to learn*.

My object here is to reiterate and update that argument, and demonstrate that "innate learning" is not an oxymoron, but rather the inevitable consequence of natural selection. Several of the studies I will use in illustration were inspired by the idea of learning instincts.

ETHOLOGY

As essential background, I must start with the major concepts of both ethology and behaviorism. By the early 1950s, ethologists had formulated four major components to account for the behavior of animals (Tinbergen, 1951; reviewed by Gould, 1982). The first was the idea of sign stimuli. These are cues produced by objects or individuals which are specifically recognized by the nervous system of the animal. A newly hatched herring gull chick, for instance, is able to direct its food-begging pecks at the parent's bill because it responds (when hungry) to thin vertical objects, objects with one or more contrasting spots, and objects moving horizontally; these are three cues produced when a parent herring gull moves its beak over the nest (Alessandro, Dollinger, Gordon, Mariscal, & Gould, 1989; Griswold, Harrer, Sladkin, Alessandro, & Gould, 1995; Hailman, 1967; Margolis, Mariscal, Gordon, Dollinger, & Gould, 1987; Tinbergen & Perdeck, 1950). The chicks have no innate pecking response to any other component of the rich constellation of stimuli generated by parent gulls—the head shape for instance, or even the presence of a head attached to the bill. (By about a week of age, normal chicks have transferred response con-

trol to learned parent-specific cues. Sign stimuli are also sometimes called releasers.)

The second concept was that innate behavior is organized as endogenous motor programs. Thus, the pecking of gull chicks is an innate response generated by a prewired neural circuit when the nervous system calls for a peck. These endogenous circuits orchestrate the coordinated movement of several muscles, and thus are more complex than simple reflexes. Originally, these behavior units were known as fixed-action patterns (Lorenz & Tinbergen, 1938/1957), a name that fell into disfavor because it seemed to exclude the role of feedback control evident in even the first studies of the phenomenon. Subsequent work has shown that even complex behavioral sequences like nest building are organized as a series of independent motor programs, each of which is performed until some criteria is reached that transfers the animal into the hands of the next motor program in the series (e.g., Smith, 1978).

The third concept involves the pathway from sign stimuli to motor program. Ethologists inferred that there must be some control circuit—an innate releasing mechanism—which compares the strength of the stimuli against the degree of drive or motivation for performing the response in question, and thus determines whether the behavior will be triggered (Lorenz, 1952/1957b; Tinbergen, 1951). In the case of the gull chick, hunger would gate the chick's responsiveness to adult beaks, as would (indirectly) the drive to release competing behavioral pathways such as responses to danger.

The final concept touches on learning: Ethologists believed that learning in the wild is generally organized along the lines of imprinting, in which context-specific cues trigger learning as a special kind of behavioral response analogous to a motor program. Imprinting itself is characterized by a critical or sensitive period during which learning is possible, and a high degree of irreversibility

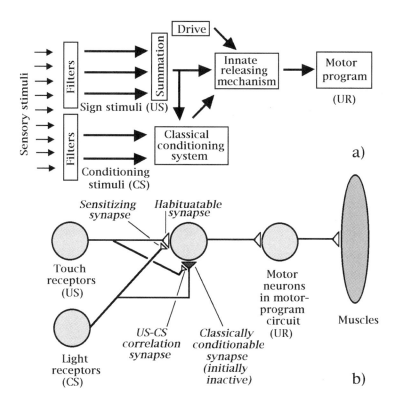

Figure 6.1   A schematic view of the ethological model of behavior and learning.
NOTE: a) Stimuli from the world are sorted, and sign stimuli are filtered out by the nervous system. These are combined through heterogeneous summation, and if they are sufficiently powerful given the behavior-specific drive, they release the behavior. b) Equally schematic view of the gill-withdrawal circuitry in *Aplysia,* along with the sensitization circuit that allows classical conditioning of the behavior. The similarity of the two diagrams is obvious.

once the learning has taken place. In the case of ducklings, for instance, the cues that trigger imprinting include movement away, an exodus call, and the color of the speculum on the wing; the critical period extends from 6–30 hours after hatching, with peak sensitivity at about 16–18 hours (reviewed by Hess, 1973).

Figure 6.1a illustrates how these four components can be arranged to account for the control of innate behavior, including learning of novel cues to substitute for innate ones. This model does not account for learning novel behaviors. In essence, it is identical to the neural pathway now known to underlie the control of gill withdrawal in *Aplysia* (Hawkins, Abrams,

Carew, & Kandel, 1983), where presynaptic facilitation mediated by the sensory and sensitization circuitry mediate learning (Figure 6.1b).

BEHAVIORISM

Watson (1925) imagined that all behavior could be explained in terms of the associative learning first described by Pavlov (reviewed by 1927)—the process now usually called classical conditioning. For Watson there was no innate behavior beyond simple reflexes. In Pavlov's (often mistranslated) terminology, animals are sensitive to innately recognized cues known as unconditioned stimuli (US), and respond to them with innate behavioral units called unconditioned responses (UR). Thus, the innate stimulus-response chain is

$$US \rightarrow UR.$$

Watson (1925) called the UR an unconditioned reflex, reflecting his view that innate behavior consists entirely of simple reflexes rather than the more complex behavioral units ethologists inferred. Pavlov showed that if a novel stimulus—one that does not initially trigger the response in question—is added as a conditioning stimulus (CS) that precedes the US by a second or two, the animal will in time come to respond to the CS alone:

$$CS + US \rightarrow UR; \quad \text{then, after many repetitions,}$$
$$CS \rightarrow UR.$$

(Some formulations changed UR to CR—conditioned response—because the form of the behavior may change slightly during learning. Some workers preferred to call the CS a conditioned stimulus—thus emphasizing its ultimate rather than original status.) This is considered a form of associative learning because the animal must learn to associate the CS with the US. (See Chaps. 1 and 2, this volume, for extensive treatment of associative learning.)

Watson (1925) accounted for the development of complex behavior in terms of reflex chaining, which is behavior developed by using the stimulus generated by one UR as the CS for triggering the next UR:

Skinner (1938) rejected the idea of reflex chaining, and instead explained complex behavior in terms of trial-and-error learning. This way of accounting for all behavior beyond the level of reflexes—called operant conditioning, in which the novel behavior is the operant—requires that feedback from an animal's actions serves to shape the behavior into an evermore efficient form. This optimization process necessitates associating cause and effect at the level of overt behavior, and thus is also considered associative learning. It seems ironic that operant-conditioning theory was developed to account for complex, novel learned behavior, and yet most of the studies involved operants no more elaborate than pushing a lever and pecking (which is innate).

Intensive study of laboratory-based learning on pigeons and rodents led researchers to note enough similarities to propose that a General Process might underlie all learning (reviewed by Schwartz, 1984; Terrace, 1984; see also the introduction to Chap. 2, this volume). For instance, all lab species tested undergo blocking: After training that

$$CS_1 + US_1 \rightarrow UR_1$$

the animals are exposed to the condition

$$CS_2 + US_1 \rightarrow UR_1.$$

When tested, they are unresponsive to CS_2. But the animals are perfectly able to learn CS_2 when that relationship is taught first, or at the same time:

$$CS_1 + CS_2 + US_1 \rightarrow UR_1.$$

$$CS_1 + US_1 \rightarrow UR_1 \qquad (UR_1 \text{ becomes/creates } CS_2)$$
$$CS_2 + US_2 \rightarrow UR_2 \qquad (UR_2 \text{ becomes/creates } CS_3)$$
$$CS_3 + US_3 \rightarrow UR_3 \qquad (UR_3 \text{ becomes/creates } CS_4)$$
$$CS_4 + US_4 \rightarrow UR_4; \quad \text{leading to}$$
$$CS_1 \rightarrow UR_1 \rightarrow UR_2 \rightarrow UR_3 \rightarrow UR_4$$

Other similarities include evidence for both short-term and long-term memory, conditioned inhibition (the ability to learn that a CS predicts the *absence* of the US), generalization, extinction (loss of a response), and so on. Rescorla and Wagner (1972) showed that the classical-conditioning system of animals is basically an automatic probability analyzer, which computes the degree to which a CS predicts the arrival of a US, producing in turn a corresponding degree of conditioning or conditioned inhibition. Work on species as phylogenetically remote as honey bees and sea slugs has often (but not always) turned up similar phenomenology.

ANOMALIES

While these similarities in learning suggest there is something to the idea of a General Process, other problems led to the decline of the field. One class of problems was the mounting list of anomalies (i.e., contradictions) to the Behaviorist model. For instance, in rapid food-avoidance conditioning the CS and US can be separated by several hours rather than a few seconds (Garcia & Koelling, 1966).

Take another telling example: In classical conditioning of rats, the animals will readily learn to associate an olfactory stimulus with a food reward US, but are slow to associate a sound; but to a punishment US (like a mild electric shock), they readily learn an auditory stimulus but are slow to associate the shock with an odor (reviewed by Bolles, 1984; Revusky, 1984; Schwartz, 1984). Similarly, pigeons will learn to peck at a visual stimulus (an illuminated disc) but not at the source of a sound during classical conditioning for a food reward; when a punishment is the US, the sound is learned far more readily than the light. Since the animals can clearly sense and, in at least one context, readily learn either cue, the dogma that any CS can equally well be connected to any US is violated. At the same time, these learning biases make sense in terms of the natural history of the species: Pigeons, as diurnal seed eaters, do well to pay little attention to sounds (seeds being mute) and concentrate on visual cues when learning about food, while rats (nocturnal scavengers) are better off concentrating on odor cues.

An analogous asymmetry exist in operant conditioning: Rats can readily learn to press a lever with a forepaw as an operant rewarded by food, but do not learn to jump over a barrier for the same reward; but to avoid a shock, rats can be operantly conditioned to leap over a barrier but not (or only rarely and with great difficulty) to press a lever (reviewed by Bolles, 1984; Revusky, 1984; Schwartz, 1984). Similarly, pigeons can be taught to peck for food, but not to avoid a shock; they can be taught to hop on a treadle to avoid shock, but not to obtain food. These biases seem related to autoshaping, the unexpected, spontaneous, and reliable production of unconditioned operants by animals during classical conditioning—as when birds being taught that an illuminated key predicts the arrival of food begin to insist on pecking the key. Once again, the observed biases make sense: A pigeon does well to experiment with its beak rather than feet in the context of food learning, whereas the legs (and wings) are better employed in escape; rats will learn faster if they concentrate on their forepaws in their behavioral experimentation aimed at obtaining food, but experiment with the potential of their hind legs for leaping when danger is the context they find themselves in.

One axiom of operant conditioning is that animals cannot learn from what they have not experienced in the context of a reward. Thus when rats exploring a radial-arm maze were found not to revisit arms (even when removed from the maze after having explored only some of the arms, and then reintroduced hours or days later), the behavior suggested the expression of unconditioned strategy formation: planning (Olton & Samuelson, 1976). Results like these had been reported (and largely ignored) years earlier by Tolman (1948), who called the ability to plan a behavior, in the absence of rewarded experimentation, a cognitive map.

Seeds of doubt were also sown by neurobiologists looking for the wiring underlying reflex chains. Wilson (1961), for instance, examined the neural basis of flight in locusts, assuming that it was a reflex chain—raising of the wings (UR_1) activates a wings-up stretch receptor (US_2), which triggers lowering of the wings (UR_2), which activates a wings-down stretch receptor (US_1), and so on ad infinitum:

But when Wilson cut the stretch receptors, the insects continued to fly. (The wing-beat frequency declined slightly, and the coordination suffered a bit.) Further investigation revealed an endogenous complex of neurons that orchestrate flight. Analogous circuits have been found in a wide variety of organisms.

Behaviorists were given fair warning of the shortcomings in their picture of the world, at least when applied to nonlab species, by two of Skinner's former graduate students (Breland & Breland, 1961). Kavanau's analysis of mouse behavior was far more devastating. Kavanau (1969) showed most behavior exhibited by mice kept under typical laboratory behavior is aberrant, and driven by a powerful urge to explore, control, and modify the environment and to practice skills useful in nature. For instance, mice will spend hours running in wheels without reinforcement, and prefer more challenging wheels (ones with internal barriers or a square shape) over ordinary ones. Lab-reared mice will work to create a natural day cycle (gradual changes in light levels, and night-time levels of about the intensity of starlight in preference to complete darkness). The mice spontaneously explore mazes without reinforcement, learning an optimum 96-meter path, with 1205 turns and 445 blind alleys to avoid, through a three-dimensional maze 427 meters in extent. (This was the largest maze tried; Kavanau comments that the mice could probably master far more complex tasks.) Kavanau concluded that the mice are driven by inborn needs ordinarily ignored (and denied) by Behaviorists.

Finally, the strained variety of ad hoc explanations that accumulated to explain how apparently innate behavior could actually be a result of conditioning simply could not keep pace with the increasing evidence for inborn behavior. Moreover, tests of these ad hoc hypotheses were almost inevitably failures. And yet, dumping the General-Process approach simply because much of behavior is innate and much of learning is species specific was a serious mistake: The Behaviorist approach was simply far too narrow, but not wholly wrong. It seems obvious that USs are sign stimuli, URs are motor programs, CSs are what ethologists once called search images, and that even imprinting is just a very special kind of classical conditioning (the cues (USs) that induce following and learning (URs) of the individual features of the parent (CSs) are limited to a narrow but appropriate range, and the drive to perform the behavior rises and falls at a single ideal time in the organism's life) (Gould & Marler, 1984).

WHY LEARN?

Once one admits the reality and ubiquity of innate behavior, it is learning that seems to be the exception rather than the rule in many species. This is particularly obvious in the context of specialized and often complex behavior, such as prey selection and capture by hunting wasps or nest building by birds. Where the task is predictable, selection should favor innate instructions over trial-and-error learning, because the former is far more efficient and less prone to error. And when the task is also complex, the pressure to prewire the behavior will be even greater because of the long learning period that would otherwise be required (Gould & Marler, 1984). Indeed, it is not obvious that most animals can learn any novel behavior from observation: Most cases seem instead to involve local enhancement— attraction of animals to others, where they independently discover the techniques being used (Galef, 1988).

What, then, would select for learning? One possibility is contexts in which there is time for optimization (Gould & Marler, 1984); thus, though materials, site type, and design of bird nests appear to be innate, individuals in many species clearly improve with experience. The innate components provide an enormous jump start to the behavior, which would take forever to learn otherwise. Thus, the learning serves as a kind of calibration to local contingencies and programming omissions: It optimizes both recognition (a classical task) and performance (an operant task).

Another possibility is that in contexts where animals are not specialists, there is bound to be variability in the relevant cues— be they related to food sources, nesting materials, mates, territorial boundaries, or what have you (Gould & Marler, 1984). Thus, though digger wasps are generally species specific in their prey preferences (and come equipped with a highly specialized stinging behavior adapted to the locations of the ganglia in the one species of victims that need to be attacked), and can learn nothing about prey recognition or the capture behavior, the same wasps are capable of impressive degrees of learning about the location of multiple nests and (in the case of progressive provision-

ers) the condition of the offspring in each (Baerends, 1941). But, flexible as the learning is, it has adaptive biases that focus the wasp's attention on the cues that are likely to the most useful.

One of the reasons pigeons and rats proved such fruitful species for study (beyond their willingness to live and breed in laboratory cages) is probably that they are relative generalists in regard to both food and danger recognition. On the other hand, in the context of courtship, mating, nest building, and the rearing of young, they are much less flexible. Still, they learn nest location and individual recognition of both mates and offspring—just the things that are important and unpredictable in these contexts. Cross-species comparisons of offspring learning provide some of the best examples of the match between learning and natural history (see below).

Psychologists and some others often talk now of constraints on learning (e.g., Hinde & Stevenson-Hinde, 1973; Schwartz, 1984; Terrace, 1984). This has a slightly off-key sound to many ethologists. In some sense, the term reflects the progression of psychological perspective: In the early twentieth century, animals could learn anything; by the end of the century, they could learn a much more limited set of associations. Clearly their learning ability became quite constrained during the intervening decades. In discussions of the evolution of learning, this constraint perspective creeps in to suggest that selection has acted to make animals selectively stupid.

To ethologists, for whom animal learning has always appeared species specific, the term with the right feel is *enabling biases* in learning. For many of them, the evolutionary model they are most drawn to is one in which innate behavior is the starting point, and learning programs evolve to solve particular problems. Without innate mechanisms to guide learning, to sort out the relevant features of the world and reduce the overwhelming ambiguity of sensory experience, reliable learning would be impossible. At the neural level (Figure 6.1b), the difference is that from the psychological perspective all possible CSs were originally wired into the interneuron, and then selection pruned out the useless connections; the alternative view is that selection led to the creation of appropriate modality-specific sensitization connections, and then to modifications of the synaptic connections to allow some sensitization stimuli to serve as CSs.

Studies of neural development (reviewed by Delcomyn, 1998) offer some comfort to both views. Sensory systems (e.g., the visual system) wire themselves by sending axons to the approximately correct location and forming synapses with many cells in the target area. During development or early experience after birth, synaptic competition takes place. During this period, correlated discharge of one synapse with those nearby tends to strengthen its connection; uncorrelated discharge tends to weaken and finally eliminate it. Thus synapses responding to the same or adjacent parts of the sensory world tend to cluster on the same target cells, refining an overall pattern that was set by the specificity of the molecules and gradients involved in axonal migration.

The correlated discharge is analogous to classical conditioning; uncorrelated discharge is analogous to conditioned inhibition; indeed, they may represent the neural precursors of associative learning (Gould & Marler, 1984). Thus at the outset, the general pattern is set by genetically controlled developmental mechanisms (reviewed by Gould, 1996), but the fine tuning (calibration) is accomplished by experience. At the level of motor programs, however, the wiring must be in place from the outset, since there is often no opportunity for practice, and no improvement in (at least certain aspects) of the behavior when it appears (matures; e.g., Bentley & Hoy, 1970;

Ewer, 1965; Fentris, 1973; Hess, 1956); in these cases, calibration is often mediated by prewired feedback circuits.

Thus one could imagine that learning develops from a loosely (or perhaps randomly) wired ancestor, with selection operating to make the wiring sensible (in a manner analogous to sensory sharpening); or one could picture that learning evolves from a strictly wired ancestor, with selection operating to add neural routes for feedback correction (in a manner analogous to motor-program circuits). Given that the first model would start with an animal basically responding maladaptively to everything, it cannot be correct in its extreme form. The real-world examples described below, depending on species comparisons and/or the known evolutionary history of the species in question, suggest that the latter model—evolution of enabling biases to make learning possible—is more plausible.

LEARNING PROGRAMS

Offspring Learning

By learning program, I mean an endogenous circuit that orchestrates a specific learning task. The program specifies when and on what learning can take place, how the relevant memory (classical, operant, or—most often—both working together) is to be stored, and how and when the information is to be used. Parental imprinting is one such example already covered (reviewed by Hess, 1973; Immelmann, 1975), as is sexual imprinting in the many species that use it (Immelmann, 1972). Since, as we saw earlier, the classical conditioning of food-related versus danger-avoidance-related are clearly independent in both rats (and also in pigeons) given the different modality-specific responsiveness, and the same is true for both species with regard to context-specific operant learning, we can infer that there must be at least one learning program for each context. And, as suggested above, there must be programs for learning about mates and offspring in many species as well.

Cross-species comparisons of egg and offspring learning suggest the extent to which the programming is tailored to the needs of each kind of animal (Cullen, 1957; Rothstein, 1978, 1982; Tinbergen, 1960; Tschanz, 1959). Imagine a cliff with a narrow beach at the bottom and trees at the top, adjacent to a cove with extended dunes. At the base of the cliff we might find the closely packed nests of guillemots; on narrow ledges of the otherwise sheer cliff, we might see nesting shags and kittiwake gulls. In the trees at the top we might find robins, while on the dunes we could well see a colony of herring gulls, with their nests spaced perhaps 10 m apart on average.

When we look for egg learning, which we might do by exchanging eggs between nests after incubation has begun, or replacing an egg with one from another species, of a different size and color, we will find that only the guillemots notice the change and eject or eat the imposter. Guillemots are programmed to memorize what their eggs look like; the other species are not. A look at their natural history reveals the evolutionary logic: Most birds rotate their eggs several times a day (which helps prevent the embryo from sticking to the inside of the shell); sometimes an egg rolls out. The ground-nesting guillemots and herring gulls have an egg-rolling response that recovers the egg; the others do not, because an egg that leaves the nest falls to its destruction. When there is an egg near the nest, the spacing of the nests is such that there is no ambiguity about which parents it belongs to in the case of herring gulls, but for guillemots, there is considerable uncertainty. Since rearing offspring other than its own lowers a bird's reproductive fitness, it makes sense that selection has operated to create a egg-learning program in the

one species that faces this challenge and has omitted to do so in all of the others. (Some species parasitized by cuckoos also learn to recognize their eggs; the selective logic is obvious.)

One might suppose that the other species are poor learners, but when we look at offspring learning, a different pattern emerges. Guillemots and herring gulls both learn to recognize their young as individuals by 5 days of age (about the time the chicks become mobile enough to wander into other nests); robins learn to recognize their chicks the day before or the day of fledging—the point at which the young can safely stray from the nest. Kittiwake gulls (which are white) and shags (which are black) learn nothing about their chicks—indeed, they can be exchanged across species without the parents seeming to notice (reviewed by Gould & Marler, 1984). Of course, for these species any chick that wanders off inevitably falls to its death. Again, the learning programs have evolved in the species that need them, and the timing matches the contingencies of the natural history almost exactly.

If we consider these examples in light of the alternative models for the evolution of learning, we have to ask what selective pressure would have operated to eliminate egg and offspring learning in the species that lack it. Similarly, we must wonder why some species that have been parasitized by cuckoos do memorize their eggs while related species do not (Rothstein, 1978, 1982): Parasitism is evolutionarily recent compared with nesting; thus, the once-smart hypothesis would have to posit that the capacity remained in birds until relatively recently, then vanished from many species (including some subject to heavy nest parasitism). The alternative view—that learning programs can evolve to meet new needs—has rather less trouble with this pattern: The species that are parasitized and learn to recognize their eggs evolved that behavior after cuckoos began preying on them; the other parasitized species have simply not evolved the behavior—not surprising since evolution depends on mutations and chance to create the variation it needs to work on.

Song Learning

Bird-song learning is a special case of sexual imprinting (Marler, 1984). I should begin by pointing out that most if not all species of birds have a substantial innate repertoire of calls—the mobbing call, distress call, and begging call, to mention but three. Moreover, many species have innate courtship calls: Doves, pheasants, and ducks represent three of the large groups that do not learn songs. Songbirds, on the other hand, normally sing songs involving a substantial degree of learning. Even so, hand-reared birds without access to the normal songs of their species ultimately produce a simple innate song with some of the features of the learned songs—enough appropriate cues that females of the species recognize the song as being from a conspecific male, though a less desirable one than those that produce more typically complex songs (Marler, 1984).

Extensive tests show that most songbirds learn best (or even only) from conspecific songs, and then during a limited sensitive period beginning while they are nestlings (reviewed by Gould & Marler, 1987; Marler, 1984). In most cases this critical period is over long before the chicks begin to produce their first attempts at song. Deafening studies reveal that the young bird must hear its own voice to be able to create a reasonable match to the song it heard as a nestling (or even to generate the innate song when it was deprived of a suitable acoustic model). Thus, since chicks presented only acoustic stimuli during their critical period select the correct species song to commit to memory, the first step in the process of song learning is a kind of association-based learning: Cues (sign stimuli, or USs) embedded in the species song trigger learning of the rest of the model song (CS). The need for later behavioral experimentation to match the vocal output with this memory represents an operant phase in the process. (In normal classical conditioning, there is an overt UR; if song learning is to be interpreted as a variant of classical conditioning, then memorization of the song for later reference must be the UR.)

The structure of the learning in some songbirds (like the swamp sparrow, which sings a single syllable repeated at a constant rate for about two seconds) illustrates some important features of the learning process. (Concentrating on a simple and convenient example should not lead us to forget that males in many species learn several species-typical songs—dozens in some species—while in a very few species, song is relearned each year; in a few others, some or even most of the songs are copied from other species or even nonbiological sounds.) If swamp sparrow chicks reared in isolation are played a medley of songs, they select the swamp sparrow song to memorize. If they are played the same medley without a swamp sparrow song in the collection, they then sing an innate song. If they are played artificial songs made up of swamp sparrow syllables, but with two or more parts rather than one, or with increasing or decreasing syllable repetition rates, they learn one of the syllables, but sing it at a constant rate and for the species-typical duration. Songs made up of syllables from other species but scored like swamp sparrow songs, on the other hand, are ignored (Marler, 1984). The greater variability in the songs of other bird species makes such analyses more difficult, but the same general mixture of innate biases and individual learning seems to hold.

The ontogeny of swamp sparrow song is also intriguing (Marler, 1984). Song development goes through a series of steps beginning with the production of brief individual sounds (subsong), followed by the organization of these sounds into crude song-like melodies (plastic song), followed by the appearance of stable mature songs. When songbirds first begin subsong, they produce an apparently wide variety of different sounds, rather in the manner of infants babbling before they create speech sounds. But close analysis reveals that the subsong elements of different swamp sparrows, exposed to different model songs of their species, are strikingly similar. There is a limited repertoire of syllable-element types, the varied combining of which generates true syllables. One is tempted to suppose that these elements might be innate motor programs.

As subsong progresses into plastic song, the birds begin to concentrate on recreating the syllable they heard during the sensitive period (and, often, similar syllables), and repeating them in brief runs analogous to short sections of full song. Finally, mature song crystallizes into a single train of a single syllable (the one most like the model) repeated for the duration typical of the species (Marler, 1984).

A striking feature of the ontogeny of swamp sparrow song learning is its apparent similarity to Watson's (1925) model of reflex chaining, in which we replace reflex with motor program. Is it possible that some or all of the operants that animals readily learn in nature are constructed of preexisting motor-program elements arranged through shaping into the optimal order (Marler, 1984)? If so, the set of elements available in one context might be somewhat or even entirely different from those available in another. On the surface, it would seem a more efficient way to program operant learning, supplying the animal with a set of prewired behavioral building blocks, and perhaps biasing it toward trying some in preference to others. This idea had been suggested earlier by Schiller (1957)

to explain the formation of novel behavior in chimpanzees first observed by Köhler (1927). The same idea is suggested by the work of Jenkins and Moore (1973): When conditioned to associate an illuminated key with a food reward, pigeons deliver a wholly unnecessary biting peck, whereas when water is the US, the pigeons produce a drinking peck. When the US is a potential mate, pigeons court the illuminated key and coo at it (Hearst & Jenkins, 1974).

Danger

Enemy-learning programs (to the extent they have been studied) seem equally well adapted. The most exhaustively studied species is the European blackbird. Like most birds, it will mob potential nest predators (like crows), producing an innately generated and innately recognized mobbing call. But how does it distinguish between predators and harmless species, so that the parents are not continually leaving their eggs to cool off while they mob anything that moves? Some species (like owls) are innately recognized on the basis of paired forward-looking eyes; in fact, a number of ground-living birds have death-feigning behaviors which are used to inhibit attack (Arduino & Gould, 1984; Gallup, 1974). For others the flying silhouette is recognized by some kinds of birds (Canty & Gould, 1995; Tinbergen, 1951). Other species do not provide innate cues.

In a crisp set of experiments, Curio, Ernst, and Vieth (1978) showed that the learning about other species is cultural: Birds learn from each other. Thus when he showed a stuffed harmless species (unlike anything in Europe) to his birds, there was no reaction. Then he would show birds in one cage an owl while birds in an adjacent cage were exposed to the harmless model. The mobbing calls produced by the birds seeing the owl induced the other birds to try to mob the harmless species.

These birds were then used to teach the aversion to the first group.

This looks like a highly customized case of classical conditioning: The US is the mobbing call, the CS is the model, and the UR is mobbing and learning. There is obviously no blocking in this circuit, because new enemies can always be added to the list. Since the tests were done without any reference to conditioning theory, none of the other familiar components of classical conditioning were looked for.

A potentially more complex (though less well-studied) case of enemy learning is found in vervet monkeys (Cheney & Seyfarth, 1990). These primates have not just one but four distinct alarm calls: one for aerial threats (certain eagles), one for dangerous snakes, one for ambush hunters (leopards), and one for terrestrial group hunters. (The latter call has not been much studied.) Each type of call leads to a quite different escape behavior: for eagles, vervets on the ground move under the protection of trees while monkeys in the canopy drop like stones into the inner branches; for leopards, monkeys in trees move out to the tips of the limbs, while those under trees move into the open; for snakes, animals in the open stand and scan the ground for the snake.

Without laboratory tests, the way enemy learning is programmed in vervets must be inferred from its ontogeny and the results of playback test using recorded alarm calls broadcast from hidden loudspeakers. It seems clear that both production and recognition of these calls is innate. The reactions seem to have an innate bias, though escape improves with time. And while the young learn which species are dangerous, the process is less mechanical than what is seen in birds. For one thing, naive vervet infants will give the alarm calls, but only to a limited variety of potential enemies. For instance, an infant might give the eagle alarm for a stork or a falling leaf, but never for a snake, leopard, or other terrestrial hunter. Adults react instantly to the calls of other adults, but for infants, they look for themselves first, and then continue foraging, grooming, or whatever they were doing if it is a false alarm. The youngsters become more accurate with time, presumably by observing which species elicit escape behavior in the adults and which do not. In short, this appears to be a set of four learning programs which calibrate themselves to the local predators based on social cues from within the group.

Food Acquisition

Food learning is usually important to generalist species, where innate encoding of the full range of safe and acceptable foods seems impossible. Among vertebrates, the best understood system for learning about foods is seen in rats (reviewed by Galef, 1996). Rats learn from the odors on the whiskers and in the breath of other rats. Thus one rat from a group can be fed on a novel food (flavored, for instance, with cinnamon or cocoa), and then returned to a group of naive rats. When one of the naive rats is later removed and offered a choice between the food the first rat had fed on and a one with a different novel odor, the test rat will consume the food with the flavor its colleague had consumed.

Probably the most thoroughly studied case of food learning involves honey bees (reviewed by Gould & Gould, 1995). Individuals of this species specialize on particular kinds of flowers during various parts of the day. The benefit of this specialization is that the individual foragers become highly efficient at recognizing and harvesting specific blossom morphologies. Solitary bees and other nectar- and pollen-gathering insects are rarely flower-constant, probably reflecting the need of these species to balance the diets of their larvae by collecting food from different source. For highly social insects, the independent choices of thousands of foragers, bringing in and mixing food from perhaps a dozen species, allows individuals (and thus the colony) to benefit from more efficient foraging while providing more balance automatically.

Because many species of flowers offer food only during a restricted part of the day, honey bee foragers may specialize on as many as four different species each day. To perform this task, honey bees must be able to learn how to recognize several different species of flowers at once. By 1920, von Frisch (1967) had shown that honey bees can learn colors and odors, though he did not gather any information of rates of acquisition and degree of specificity. He did show, however, that food odors are picked up by naive bees from the waxy hairs on the body of foragers, allowing the recruited bee to select the same odor from a large selection (in one case, more than 700) alternatives. Later, his student Hertz (1930) reported a primitive ability to learn shapes—far cruder than the 20/2000 vision of these insects ought to permit.

More recent work has greatly expanded on this beginning. Color learning has been explored in great detail (Menzel, Erber, & Mashur, 1974), and the ability to learn complex shapes has been demonstrated and defined (Gould, 1985, 1986a, 1988). Honey bees have also been shown to learn landmarks—which are used to triangulate the location of food sources (Anderson, 1977a; Cartwright & Collett, 1983; Gould, 1986c, 1987a, 1987d, 1989, 1990)—time of day, location, and hive appearance, and then shape their own flower-handling operants (Gould, 1987b). The details of the learning in each context reveal a complex but logical network of biases and preadaptations (Gould, 1991, 1993).

Color learning is a good example of the balance between bias and flexibility. In modern learning tests, the bee is trained (or recruited by the dancing of another bee) to a testing device offering two alternatives. Naive bees have

strong biases that lead them to experiment by landing on targets that are more likely to be flowers. For example, they will approach blue targets more often than green or black ones, though in time they try them all. Thus to perform a two-choice test, the experimenter must either balance the attractiveness of the targets (by varying cue size and saturation) or perform the tests in reciprocal pairs (that is, the positive target is blue in one test against the negative green target; in the next, the green target is the positive one; for analysis, the two sets of data are combined).

Menzel et al. (1974) showed that even after balancing a set of color targets so that spontaneous choice frequencies were 50:50, after a single reinforced trial bees would return to a violet positive stimulus about 80:20, whereas a positive green stimulus yields a performance ratio of 60:40. By the tenth trial, the ratio is better than 90:10 for all colors, with no significant difference between the performance for violet relative to green. So, though bees can learn any color, they find violet and blue somehow easier. (This is not a simple consequence of color-receptor numbers: Bees are equally sensitive to green and blue but about ten times as sensitive to UV—a color they learn at only an average rate.) Of course, flowers are more often blue and violet than green.

Odor, in general, is learned at a faster rate than color. For a variety of floral odors, choice ratios of 90:10 after a single trial are typical, and after ten trials ratios of 95:5 are often observed (Menzel et al., 1974). However, bees are slow to learn nonfloral odors (Menzel, 1985). Again, this is not a simple result of receptor bias: One of the odors they are most sensitive to, butyric acid, is also one of the odors they learn (in the context of foraging) most slowly. This makes sense: Butyric acid is an odor commonly produced by animals rather than plants—especially dead animals. Thus both spontaneous approach and learning rates mimic the contingencies of the natural world.

Shape and pattern are learned more slowly than floral odor. Bees spontaneously approach busier patterns—targets with a higher spatial frequency (Hertz, 1930). Even when two targets with different spatial frequencies are made equally attractive (by altering relative size, or using differentially attractive colors to compensate), subsequent learning mirrors the initial biases: Complex patterns are learned faster than simple ones (Schnetter, 1972). Again, this reflects the reality that natural flowers tend to be visually complex. Another concession of the flower-learning program to natural selection is the long list of cues bees can sense but *not* use as CSs— among them polarization and movement, two features of the visual world to which honey bees are highly sensitive in other circumstances (Menzel, 1985).

Color and pattern are learned on a bee's approach to the target (Gould, 1986a; Menzel et al., 1974). This is not unexpected, since these CS cues ought reliably to precede the US of sweet taste to enable conditioning. (As we will see, another aspect of flower learning has a quite different timing.) Careful tests also show that conditioned inhibition is an important component: Bees in a two-choice learning paradigm remember the positive target better than those trained to a single rewarding target; in fact, bees show a strong bias against the unrewarded target after training (Gould, 1986a). Finally, exhausting experiments reveal that the memory of shape and pattern is effectively stored at about $7°$ resolution—far below the $1.5°$ resolution of honey bee vision (Gould, 1986a, 1988). Despite earlier work that presumed that bees must have $1.5°$ visual memory (e.g., Anderson, 1977b), this lower memory resolution is typical of animals; memory at real-time resolution—so called eidetic memory—is exceedingly rare in animals, if it exists at all.

These three cues, once learned to saturation, are not equally weighted by returning foragers (Bogdany, 1978). Cue separation experiments show that bees will choose a target with the training odor but the wrong shape and color over an alternative with the correct shape and color but the wrong odor. Similar tests reveal that color is more important than shape. As with all of the tests described, these biases are innate; bees reared in closed rooms show the same preferences. Once again, the biases seem to reflect the realities of the natural world: Odor is the most reliable guide to flowers, while perceived shape varies greatly depending on angle of approach; color is intermediate in value as a predictor in the wild.

Landmark learning serves the useful function of allowing an insect with poor vision to use large cues to localize flowers that are not visible until the forager gets quite close (by human standards). Bees learn the color, shape, and relative location of landmarks. One might suppose this process is actually part of flower learning (indeed, by placing cues too far from the food and calling them flower-learning cues, it is possible to completely muddy the waters on the nature of flower learning and reach wholly incorrect conclusions (e.g., Bitterman & Couvillon, 1991)). The evidence that it is a separate system comes from many directions. For one thing, the most easily learned cues are complex in shape and violet in color, as opposed to simple and green (reviewed by Gould; Gould, 1995); for another, the cues are learned on departure from the flower rather than upon approach (one of the rare cases of backwards conditioning observed in nature—and considered impossible by most Behaviorists; Gould, 1989); finally, the resolution of landmark memory is $3°$ rather than $7°$ (Gould, 1987a). Another innate bias is the preference to use widely separated landmarks rather than closely spaced ones: When both are available in training, but only a subset is offered during testing, bees invariably assume the remaining landmarks to be the ones most widely spaced (and thus most useful) ones observed during training (1987a). (See Chap. 8, this volume, for more on landmark learning by bees and other animals.)

Because a bee can approach flowers as closely as it likes to see if they match its memory of the blossom being sought, but necessarily must use landmarks at whatever distance and visual angle they happen to be as seen from the flower, the higher investment in landmark memory makes sense (Gould, 1987c). The other biases in landmark memory and use are equally logical in terms of natural contingencies. There is one bias, however, that is less obviously a product of natural selection. When pitting landmarks against target shape, Lindauer (1976) found that one subspecies of honey bee (*Apis mellifera carnica*) uses landmarks in preference to shape, whereas another (*A. m. ligustica*) has the opposite bias. The two also differ slightly in their odor biases (Lindauer, 1976). These two examples remind us that some predispositions in learning programs may either have subtle bases in natural history, be a consequence of genetic drift (chance), or reflect a secondary consequence of some other aspect of selection. Other specializations that differ between subspecies of honey bees are well known (Gould, 1986b; Gould & Gould, 1995).

Honey bees also learn different flower-approach and flower-handling techniques via trial and error—that is, through operant conditioning (Gould, 1987b). Thus it is possible to train bees to land on only the lower-right petal of one color of flower, and the lower-left petal of a flower of the same shape but a different color. (The innate bias is to land on the bottom petal; teaching a bee to land on an upper petal takes much longer than for a lower petal, but is not impossible.) This is perhaps also a good place to mention that the probability of a forager dancing to communicate

the location of the target from which it is collecting food varies with certain aspects of the target and its position. Everything else being equal, dancing is more probable for flowers that are easier to land on and nearer sources, and that have particular qualities: Targets with low to moderate amounts of odor, nectar that is higher in sugar content than the average being collected by other foragers at the moment, targets that enclose the bee while feeding, feeders with narrow tubes through which the sugar solution is extracted (even if this slows the net rate of food acquisition), targets that have innately desirable colors, odors, and high spatial frequencies, and feeders that have a soft or rough (as opposed to slick) texture (von Frisch, 1967; Gould, unpublished; Gould & Gould, 1995).

Bees also learn the time of day associated with food availability at a target. Thus the same group of foragers can be trained to a single site that provides one combination of cues during one hour of the day and another during the next (Bogdany, 1978). After a few days of training, both feeders can be presented simultaneously and, so long as they do not become overcrowded, the foragers will select the feeder that had food at that time on previous days. The same is true for landing and handling techniques even if the two flowers have the same shape, odor, and color, so that only the handling technique differed between the two times of day during training (Gould, 1987b). In fact, bees seem to learn about flowers as a time-linked set, with information relevant to one hour of the day unavailable at another (Bogdany, 1978; Gould, 1987b). This appointment-book system reflects the realities of flower behavior.

Another curious but appropriate feature of flower learning is that the cues are learned as a time-linked set, such that when a previously missing cue (like odor) is added, it is learned (and thus there is no blocking), but when the same cue is *changed,* the forager forgets the other cues and relearns them all together (Bogdany, 1978). In the natural context, a dramatic change in one cue would mean that the bee is encountering a new kind of blossom, and it makes sense to discard the previous information, which would otherwise tend to lead to errors and prejudices. It is troubling that some workers insist on training bees to a target that systematically alternates the odor, color, or pattern of the artificial flower between visits (e.g., Bitterman & Couvillon, 1991); little wonder that research carried out under such conditions paints a very different picture of learning, and leads these researchers to conclude that honey bees are not very good or reliable at various learning tasks. Studying learning without regard to the natural history of the species in question is worse than foolish.

CONCLUSION

Depending on the context and the contingencies of their life history and niche, the optimum balance between innate responses, innate learning biases, and (if it exists) unfettered learning ought to (and apparently does) vary from one species to another. Selection should invariably lead to programming that focuses animals on the most plausible cues and behavioral experimentation. Thus the idea that there is one learning system that underlies all behavior, or even just all learned behavior, is absurd in the light of the enormous force of evolutionary adaptation. On the other hand, there is nothing intrinsically implausible about the idea that a limited set of processes, customized through selection, underlies most or all of learning among animals. In short, both psychologists and ethologists have, at least potentially, much to learn from each other.

REFERENCES

Alessandro, D., Dollinger, J., Gordon, J., Mariscal, S., & Gould, J. L. (1989). The ontogeny of the pecking response in herring gull chicks. *Animal Behaviour, 37,* 372–382.

Anderson, A. M. (1977a). A model for landmark learning in the honey bee. *Journal of Comparative Physiology, 114,* 335–355.

Anderson, A. M. (1977b). Shape perception in the honey bee. *Animal Behaviour, 25,* 67–69.

Arduino, P., & Gould, J. L. (1984). Is tonic immobility adaptive? *Animal Behaviour, 32,* 921–922.

Baerends, G. P. (1941). Fortpflanzungsverhalten und Orientierung in der Grabwespe. *Tijdschrift voor Entomologie, 84,* 68–275.

Bentley, D. R., & Hoy, R. R. (1970). Postembryonic development of adult motor programs in crickets. *Science, 170,* 1409–1411.

Bitterman, M. E., & Couvillon, P. A. (1991). Failures to find adaptive specialization in the learning of honeybees. In L. J. Goodman & R. C. Fisher (Eds.), *The behaviour and physiology of bees* (pp. 288–305). Wallingford, UK: CAB International.

Bogdany, F. J. (1978). Linking of learning signals in honey bee orientation. *Behavioral Ecology and Sociobiology, 3,* 323–336.

Bolles, R. C. (1970). Species-specific defense reactions and avoidance learning. *Psychological Review, 77,* 32–48.

Bolles, R. C. (1984). Species-typical response predispositions. In P. Marler & H. Terrace (Eds.), *The biology of learning* (pp. 435–446). Berlin: Springer.

Breland, K., & Breland, M. (1961). The misbehavior of organisms. *American Psychologist, 16,* 681–684.

Canty, N., & Gould, J. L. (1995). The hawk-goose experiment: Sources of variability. *Animal Behaviour, 50,* 1091–1095.

Cartwright, B. A., & Collett, T. S. (1983). Landmark learning in bees. *Journal of Comparative Physiology, 151,* 521–543.

Cheney, D. L., & Seyfarth, R. M. (1990). *How monkeys see the world*. Chicago: University of Chicago Press.

Cullen, E. (1957). Adaptations in the kittiwake to cliff-nesting. *Ibis, 99,* 275–302.

Curio, E., Ernst, U., & Vieth, W. (1978). Cultural transmission of enemy recognition: One function of mobbing. *Science, 202,* 899–901.

Delcomyn, F. (1998). *Foundations of neurobiology*. New York: W. H. Freeman.

Ewer, R. F. (1965). Food burying in the South African ground squirrel. *Zeitschrift für Tierpsychologie, 22,* 321–317.

Fentris, J. C. (1973). Development of grooming in mice with amputated forelimbs. *Science, 179,* 704–705.

Frisch, K. von. (1914). Der Farbensinn und Fromensinn der Bienen. *Zoologische Jahrbuch (Physiologie), 35,* 1–188.

Frisch, K. von. (1967). *The dance language and orientation of bees*. Cambridge, MA: Harvard University Press.

Galef, B. G. (1988). Imitation in animals. In T. R. Sentall & B. G. Galef (Eds.), *Social learning: Psychological and biological perspectives* (pp. 3–28). Hillsdale, NJ: Erlbaum.

Galef, B. G. (1996). Social enhancement of food preferences in Norway rats: A brief review. In C. M. Heyes & B. G. Galef (Eds.), *Social learning and imitation in animals* (pp. 49–64). New York: Academic Press.

Gallup, G. G. (1974). Animal hypnosis: Factual status of a fictional concept. *Psychological Bulletin, 81,* 836–853.

Garcia, J., & Koelling, R. A. (1966). The relation of cue to consequence in avoidance learning. *Psychonomic Science, 4,* 123–124.

Gleitman, H. (1981). *Psychology*. New York: W. W. Norton.

Gould, J. L. (1982). *Ethology*. New York: W. W. Norton.

Gould, J. L. (1985). How do bees remember flower shape? *Science, 227,* 1492–1494.

Gould, J. L. (1986a). Pattern learning in honey bees. *Animal Behaviour, 34,* 990–997.

Gould, J. L. (1986b). The biology of learning. *Annual Review of Psychology, 37,* 163–192.

Gould, J. L. (1986c). The locale map of honey bees: Do insects have cognitive maps? *Science, 232,* 861–863.

Gould, J. L. (1987a). Landmark learning in honey bees. *Animal Behaviour, 35,* 26–34.

Gould, J. L. (1987b). Honey bees store learned flower-landing behaviour according to time of day. *Animal Behaviour, 35,* 1579–1581.

Gould, J. L. (1987c). Instinct and learning in honey bee foraging. In A. C. Kamil, J. R. Krebs, & H. R. Pulliam (Eds.), *Foraging behavior* (pp. 479–496). New York: Plenum.

Gould, J. L. (1987d). Memory and maps in honey bees. In R. Menzel & A. Mercer (Eds.), *Neurobiology and behaviour of honey bees* (pp. 298–309). Berlin: Springer.

Gould, J. L. (1988). Resolution of pattern learning in honey bees. *Journal of Insect Behavior, 1,* 225–233.

Gould, J. L. (1989). Timing of landmark learning in honey bees. *Journal of Insect Behavior, 1,* 373–378.

Gould, J. L. (1990). Honey bee cognition. *Cognition, 37,* 83–103.

Gould, J. L. (1991). The ecology of honey bee learning. In L. J. Goodman & R. C. Fisher (Eds.), *The behaviour and physiology of bees* (pp. 306–322). Wallingford, UK: CAB International.

Gould, J. L. (1993). Ethological and comparative aspects of honey bee learning. In A. C. Lewis & D. R. Papaj (Eds.), *Insect learning: Ecological and evolutionary perspectives* (pp. 19–50). New York: Chapman & Hall.

Gould, J. L. (1996). *Biological Science* (6th ed.). New York: W. W. Norton.

Gould, J. L., & Gould, C. G. (1995). *The Honey Bee* (2nd ed.). New York: W. H. Freeman.

Gould, J. L., & Marler, P. (1984). Ethology and the natural history of learning. In P. Marler & H. Terrace (Eds.), *The biology of learning* (pp. 47–74). Berlin: Springer.

Gould, J. L., & Marler, P. (1987). Learning by instinct. *Scientific American, 256*(1), 74–85.

Griswold, D. A., Harrer, M. F., Sladkin, C., Alessandro, D., & Gould, J. L. (1995). Intraspecific recognition by laughing gull chicks. *Animal Behaviour, 50,* 1341–1348.

Hailman, J. (1967). The ontogeny of an instinct. *Behaviour Supplements, 15,* 1–159.

Hawkins, R. D., Abrams, S. W., Carew, T. J., & Kandel, E. R. (1983). A cellular mechanism of classical conditioning in *Aplysia. Science, 219,* 400–403.

Hearst, E., & Jenkins, H. M. (1974). *Sign-Tracking: The stimulus-reinforcer relation and directed action.* Austin, TX: Psychonomic Society.

Hertz, M. (1930). Die Organisation des optischen Feldes bei der Biene. *Zeitschrift für vergleichend Physiologie, 11,* 107–145.

Hess, E. H. (1956). Space perception in the chick. *Scientific American, 195*(1), 71–80.

Hess, E. H. (1973). *Imprinting.* New York: Van Nostrand Reinhold.

Hinde, R. A., & Stevenson-Hinde, J. (1973). *Constraints on learning.* New York: Academic Press.

Immelmann, K. (1972). Sexual and other long-term aspects of imprinting in birds and other species. *Advances in the Study of Behavior, 4,* 147–174.

Immelmann, K. (1975). Ecological significance of imprinting and early learning. *Annual Review of Ecology and Systematics, 6,* 15–37.

Jenkins, H. M., & Moore, B. R. (1973). The form of the autoshaped response with food or water reinforcers. *Journal of the Experimental Analysis of Behavior, 20,* 163–181.

Kavanau, J. L. (1969). Behaviour of captive white-footed mice. In E. R. Willems & H. L. Raush (Eds.), *Naturalistic viewpoints in psychology* (pp. 221–270). New York: Holt, Rinehart, Winston.

Köhler, W. (1927). *The mentality of apes.* New York: Harcourt Brace.

Lehrman, D. S. (1953). A critique of Konrad Lorenz' theory of instinctive behavior. *Quarterly Review of Biology, 28,* 337–363.

Lindauer, M. (1976). Recent advances in the orientation and learning of honey bees. In *Proceedings of the XV International Congress on Entomology* (pp. 450–460).

LoLordo, V. M. (1979). Selective associations. In A. Dickenson & R. A. Boakes (Eds.), *Mechanisms of learning and motivation* (pp. 367–398). Hillside, NJ: Earlbaum.

LoLordo, V. M., McMillan, J. C., & Riley, A. L. (1974). The effects upon food reinforced pecking and treadle pressing of auditory and visual signals for response-independent food. *Learning and Motivation, 5,* 24–41.

Lorenz, K. Z. (1957a). Companionship in bird life. In P. H. Schiller (Ed.), *Instinctive behavior* (pp. 83–128). New York: International Universities Press. (Originally published in 1935)

Lorenz, K. Z. (1957b). The past twelve years in the comparative study of behavior. In P. H. Schiller (Ed.), *Instinctive behavior* (pp. 288–310). New York: International Universities Press. (Originally published in 1952)

Lorenz, K. Z., & Tinbergen, N. (1957). Taxis and instinct. In P. H. Schiller (Ed.), *Instinctive behavior* (pp. 176–208). New York: International Universities Press. (Originally published in 1938)

Margolis, R. A., Mariscal, S., Gordon, J., Dollinger, J., & Gould, J. L. (1987). The ontogeny of the pecking response in laughing gull chicks. *Animal Behaviour, 35,* 191–202.

Marler, P. (1984). Song learning: Innate species differences in the learning process. In P. Marler & H. Terrace (Eds.), *The biology of learning* (pp. 289–310). Berlin: Springer.

Menzel, R. (1985). Learning in honeybees in and ecological and behavioral context. In B. Holldobler & M. Lindauer (Eds.), *Experimental behavioral ecology and sociobiology* (pp. 55–74). Stuttgart: Gustav Fischer.

Menzel, R., Erber, J., & Mashur, T. (1974). Learning and memory in the honeybee. In L. Barton-Browne (Ed.), *Experimental analysis of insect behaviour* (pp. 195–217). Berlin: Springer.

Olton, D. S., & Samuelson, R. J. (1976). Remembrance of places passed: Spatial memory in rate. *Journal of Experimental Psychology: Animal Behaviour Processes, 2,* 97–116.

Pavlov, I. (1927). *Conditioned reflexes.* Oxford: Oxford University Press.

Rescorla, R. A., & Wagner, A. R. (1972). A theory of Pavlovian conditioning. In A. H. Black &

W. F. Prokasy (Eds.), *Classical conditioning II*. New York: Appleton-Century-Crofts.

Revusky, S. (1984). Adaptive predispositions. In P. Marler & H. Terrace (Eds.), *The biology of learning* (pp. 447–460). Berlin: Springer.

Rothstein, S. I. (1978). Mechanisms of avian egg-recognition: Additional evidence for learned components. *Animal Behaviour, 26,* 671–677.

Rothstein, S. I. (1982). Successes and failures in avian egg and nestling recognition. *American Zoologist, 22,* 547–560.

Schiller, P. H. (1957). Innate motor action as a basis of learning. In P. H. Schiller (Ed.), *Instinctive behavior* (pp. 264–287). New York: International Universities Press.

Schneirla, T. C. (1956). Interrelationships of the "innate" and the "acquired" in instinctive behavior. In P. P. Grassé (Ed.), *L'Instinct dans le domportment des animaux* (pp. 387–452). Foundation Singer-Polignac, Masson et Cie Editeurs: Paris.

Schnetter, B. (1972). Experiments on pattern discrimination in honey bees. In R. Wehner (Ed.), *Information processing in the visual system of arthropods* (pp. 195–200). Berlin: Springer.

Schwartz, B. (1984). *Psychology of learning and behavior* (2nd ed.). New York: W. W. Norton.

Seligman, M. E. P. (1970). On the generality of the laws of learning. *Psychological Review, 77,* 406–418.

Skinner, B. F. (1938). *The behavior of organisms*. New York: Appleton-Century-Crofts.

Smith, A. W. (1978). Investigation of the mechanisms underlying nest construction in the mud wasp. *Animal Behaviour, 26,* 232–240.

Terrace, H. S. (1984). Animal learning, ethology, and biological constraints. In P. Marler & H. Terrace (Eds.), *The biology of learning* (pp. 15–46). Berlin: Springer.

Thorpe, W. H. (1979). *Origins and rise of ethology*. New York: Praeger.

Tinbergen, N. (1951). *The study of instinct*. Oxford: Oxford University Press.

Tinbergen, N. (1960). *The herring gull's world*. New York: Basic Books.

Tinbergen, N. (1972). On the orientation of the digger wasp. In N. Tinbergen (Ed.), *The animal in its world* (pp. 103–127). Oxford: Oxford University Press. (Originally published in 1932)

Tinbergen, N., & Kruyt, W. (1972). On the orientation of the digger wasp III. In N. Tinbergen (Ed.), *The animal in its world* (pp. 146–196). Oxford: Oxford University Press. (Originally published in 1938)

Tinbergen, N., & Perdeck, A. C. (1950). On the stimulus situation releasing the begging response in the newly hatched herring gull chick. *Behaviour, 3,* 1–38.

Tolman, E. C. (1948). Cognitive maps in rats and men. *Psychological Review, 55,* 189–208.

Tschanz, B. (1959). Sur brutbiolgie der trottellumme. *Behaviour, 14,* 1–100.

Watson, J. B. (1925). *Behaviorism*. New York: People's Institute.

Wilson, D. M. (1961). Central nervous control of flight in the locust. *Journal of Experimental Biology, 38,* 401–490.

Wolcoxin, H. C., Dragoin, W. B., & Kral, P. A. (1971). Illness-induced aversions in rat and quail. *Science, 171,* 826–828.

CHAPTER 7

Perceptual Learning

PHILIP J. KELLMAN

INTRODUCTION AND BACKGROUND

When we think of learning, several prototypical ideas come to mind: the encoding of an item in memory, the connecting of one idea to another, the connecting of a response to a stimulus, or the learning of a motor sequence or procedure. Less commonly considered, both in ordinary intuition and in research, is *perceptual learning*. Perceptual learning refers to experience-induced changes in the way information is extracted. A large and growing set of research results indicates that such changes are not only possible but pervasive in human information processing. On a full spectrum of tasks, from processing the most basic sensory discriminations to apprehending the most complex spatial and temporal patterns and relations, experience improves the pickup of information, often by orders of magnitude. These improvements affect almost all skilled behavior, form important foundations of higher cognitive processes (such as language; see Chap. 11, this volume), interact with other kinds of learning in important ways, and furnish one of the most important components of high-level expertise.

Preparation of this chapter was supported in part by research grant R01 EY13518-01 from the National Eye Institute and by a grant from the MURI Program at the Office of Naval Research. The author thanks Randy Gallistel and John Hummel for helpful discussions.

Yet perceptual learning is not well understood. What are the mechanisms that enable information-extraction systems to change their operation? Is there one basic process or several in perceptual learning? What are the conditions that lead to perceptual learning? How does this kind of learning relate to plasticity at various levels of the nervous system?

These questions have cycled in and out of scientific concern for more than a century. William James, in his *Principles of Psychology* (1890/1950), noted several examples of extraordinary perceptual skills and emphasized the importance of perceptual learning for expertise, including achievements that we often think of as motor skills. A flurry of research in the mid-1960s put perceptual learning firmly on the scientific map. The field owes a great debt to the work of Eleanor Gibson and her collaborators around this time, culminating in a classic review (E. Gibson, 1969). For about a decade or so afterward, few papers were published in perceptual learning with human adults, for reasons that are obscure. Perhaps the focus in this period on perceptual development in infancy occupied many of the relevant investigators. Another factor may have been de facto boundaries between different research communities. Perceptual learning has often been omitted from or poorly integrated with research on both animal learning and human cognition.

Beginning in the mid-1980s and still accelerating, there has been a new wave of interest in perceptual learning. Much interest has been sparked by findings at the lowest sensory levels of sensory systems, that is, improvements in basic sensory acuities previously assumed to be relatively fixed. Interest in linking these changes to phenomena of neural plasticity has also helped to spotlight, and inform, studies of perceptual learning.

Definitions of Perceptual Learning

Over the years, the phrase "perceptual learning" has been used to refer to various ideas. Some are restrictive in implicating a particular process or mechanism, or in labeling particular kinds of experimental effects. For example, some have suggested that we consider as perceptual learning only those effects that can be shown to be specific to low levels of the sensory nervous system. If subjects' improvements in an orientation discrimination task proves specific to the trained eye, the trained retinal position, or the trained orientation, these characteristics would argue against explanations in terms of high-level cognitive strategies. Hence, one can be on safe ground in calling these "perceptual" changes.

As we will see, research has revealed a variety of effects in perceptual learning, and the theoretical situation is still in flux. This situation suggests that we be more eclectic and functional regarding definitions. Although it is reasonable to seek criteria to distinguish perceptual learning from other types of learning, it is premature to limit the domain in advance of a better understanding of the processes involved. The case of specificity in low-level perceptual learning is instructive. As we see later, it turns out that the specificity of learning varies substantially with relatively minor alterations in learning procedures, and apparently low-level effects are modulated by higher-level factors. It is possible that rather than engaging wholly differ-ent processes with minor paradigm changes, we are discovering characteristics of perceptual learning processes that are multilevel and flexible. In addition, taking a broad view allows us to consider significant improvements in information extraction that do not involve the most basic sensory elements. Perception involves the extraction of structure from the environment by means of the senses (e.g., J. Gibson, 1966, 1979). This structure may be relational and complex. As with perception, perceptual learning may involve not merely low-level sensory coding but also apprehension of relatively abstract structure, such as relationships in time and space.

For a broad and functional definition, it is hard to improve on that given by E. Gibson (1969, p. 3):

"Perceptual learning then refers to an increase in the ability to extract information from the environment, as a result of experience and practice with stimulation coming from it."

As my purpose is not to be vague but inclusive, I explore a number of more specific ideas about perceptual improvement. These are set out next, and they comprise a tool kit for interpreting experimental evidence throughout the chapter. Eventually, these particular notions about how experience changes information extraction will attain sufficient clarity to help adjudicate questions about different learning processes and the relation of perceptual learning to other forms of learning.

Perceptual Learning and Perceptual Development

One other definitional matter is worth mentioning. Sometimes the phrase "perceptual learning" is used to refer broadly to the many and substantial changes in perceptual capacities that occur in infancy. This view was an especially snug fit to classical empiricist ideas about the nature of perception. Learning to construct reality must be high on the agenda of a new perceiver, if his or her innate endowment includes only the ability to have sensations, and meaningful perception of objects and events must be constructed from combining sensations (Locke, 1857; Titchener, 1896), or sensations and actions (e.g., Piaget, 1954). In such a scheme, all meaningful perception and most of perceptual development must be perceptual learning. The reason is that from this perspective, sometimes termed *enrichment* (J. Gibson & Gibson, 1955), the initial connections between stimulus variables and perceptual representations of environmental properties necessarily arise by learning.

Improved understanding of early human perception does not sustain the overall view that initial perceptual competencies are established by learning (for a review, see Kellman & Arterberry, 1998). Many appear prior to learning, and many others arrive via maturation after birth. Some experience-induced attunements and improvements in perception also occur early in life. For some abilities, such as pictorial depth perception, maturational and enrichment learning explanations still compete to explain the original connections between stimulus variables and meaningful perceptual representations.

Accordingly, in this review, we do not define perceptual development as synonymous with perceptual learning. We are concerned with learning processes that appear to occur throughout the life span, including infancy. Most of what we know about these processes to date comes from experiments outside the infancy period. As we will consider, however, some experiments with young infants are also beginning to shed light on the nature of the learning processes, as well as on their role in perceptual development.

Discovery and Fluency

Progress in understanding perceptual learning will come from refining our conceptions of particular processes and mechanisms. Many different ideas have been proposed. These ideas about how perception improves with practice fall into two general categories. Some involve *discovery:* how perceivers uncover, select, or amplify the particular information, features, or relations required for some discrimination or classification. The second category of change might be called *fluency.* Fluency effects involve changes, not in the content of information extracted, but in the ease of extraction. At its extreme, practice in information pickup has been argued to lead to *automaticity:* processing that is fast and relatively insensitive to attentional load (Schneider & Shiffrin, 1977).

Although the distinction between discovery and fluency is conceptually clear, some phenomena may be difficult to classify. First, discovery and fluency effects often arise together in learning. Second, the dependent variables associated with discovery and fluency are not fixed. Sensitivity (a measure of detection or discrimination ability in signal detection theory) would seem the best indicator of discovery of new bases of response, whereas improvement in speed of processing tends to indicate fluency. However, this mapping can be misleading. Not every paradigm in which perceivers become faster with practice implies an improvement in fluency. An improvement in speed, for example, may reflect discovery of a better basis for response. Likewise, under time constraints, sensitivity may improve because the same information can be extracted more quickly.

COMPONENTS OF PERCEPTUAL LEARNING

In what follows, I explore perceptual learning in terms of (a) ideas about processes and mechanisms and (b) illustrations of phenomena at different levels of sensation, perception, and cognition. The strategy will be as follows.

First, I set out a few ideas about processes and mechanisms. Later, I examine them in greater detail in connection with specific experimental findings. These will be addressed in a progression from early sensory sensitivities, including work in several senses, to work in middle vision (perception of contours, objects, and surfaces) through higher level vision. The review is selective; my aim is to consider a variety of explanatory ideas in perceptual learning in connection with useful examples from the research literature.

Some Discovery Processes

The most remarkable fact about perceptual learning is that it can lead to new bases of response. In an extreme case, an observer may appear not to encode or register a feature or relation that after practice becomes the basis for reliable classification. It is often said about wine-tasting skill that a novice may be unable to distinguish two different wines on any basis. As expertise grows, it may become obvious that one of the two previously indistinguishable wines is a prized delicacy, whereas the other is a cheap, barely drinkable embarrassment. (Suffice it to say, learning to discern such differences can have expensive consequences.)

There are several useful ways to think about the nature of discovery effects. How is it possible for perceptual systems to discover previously unnoticed information?

Sensitivity Change versus Noise Reduction

Perhaps the most basic question in this regard is whether it is possible to show rigorously that learning truly improves sensitivity. If perceptual learning improves sensitivity in detection or discrimination, different kinds of explanations are required than if it merely changes response biases or leads to the attachment of a label or response to an already-encoded attribute. Several investigators have

examined perceptual learning to ask this question using procedures of signal detection theory. They have sought to learn whether sensitivity changes occur and how these might be more precisely characterized in terms of biases, signal enhancement, or noise reduction (Dosher & Lu, 1999; Gold, Bennett, & Sekuler, 1999). I examine these approaches next. The evidence indicates that perceptual learning involves true increases in sensitivity. Such findings certainly make perceptual learning worth explaining, but they do not in and of themselves furnish the explanations.

Selection and Differentiation

An influential notion of perceptual learning is E. Gibson's (1969) notion of perceptual learning as *differentiation* learning. Differentiation involves the selection of relevant features or relationships in stimulation that are useful in making particular classifications or discriminations. Unlike the attaching of significance to information (so-called enrichment learning), the function of differentiation learning is to allow selection of relevant information from among the abundance of available information, most of which may be irrelevant to a particular task. Gibson put forth the specific hypothesis that what is learned in perceptual learning are *distinguishing features:* those properties that make the difference in a particular task in which the observer must classify a stimulus as being one kind of thing or another. This notion may be contrasted with the idea that experience with certain objects leads us to form general structural descriptions. In the latter case, learning might lead to more detailed representations for all object attributes. On the distinguishing features hypothesis, learning will specifically affect key contrasts. Some evidence supports the idea that we do preferentially extract task-relevant dimensions of difference (e.g., Pick, 1965).

The distinguishing features hypothesis can be applied to learning at different levels of complexity. In complex classification tasks, this may involve some kind of search among complex relationships to find invariant bases of classification. Basic sensory tasks may include overlap in the sets of elementary analyzers activated by two similar stimuli. With discrimination practice, one relies more heavily on the most relevant analyzers for making the discrimination, whereas those that are activated equally by both categories may be suppressed.

In recent years it has been suggested that some aspects of differentiation learning—selection of relevant inputs and suppression of irrelevant ones—can be modeled using neural-style network learning models (Dosher & Lu, 1999; Goldstone, 1998; Poggio, Fahle, & Edelman, 1992). The stimulus is encoded as an input vector, that is, as values along a number of stimulus dimensions or an array of analyzers varying, for instance, in terms of sensitivity to retinal position, orientation, and spatial frequency. An output layer contains nodes that correspond to the different response categories for a task. There may be one or more hidden layers between the input and output layers. Nodes at one layer are connected to all nodes at the next layer. These connections pass activation along according to the weights of their connection (connection strength) and the activation of the nodes themselves. At the beginning of learning, all nodes at one layer are connected to all nodes in the succeeding layer with random weights. Across learning trials, weights change, either by back-propagation of an error signal (supervised learning) or by unsupervised learning schemes (e.g., Hebbian learning, in which weights increase between units activated at the same time). This kind of model can apply to selection of relevant analyzers for basic sensory tasks. It can also encompass some relations among features, most obviously conjunctive ones, in networks with hidden units. Conventional networks may be limited, however, in dealing with abstract or symbolic relations (see the section titled "Perceptual Learning of Abstract Relations").

Attentional Weighting

A particular hypothesis about improved selectivity in perceptual learning is the notion that selective attention guides the pickup of relevant information (and possibly suppresses irrelevant information). Attention can be allocated to particular dimensions, such as color, or to particular features, such as red. This notion that learning involves a selection of relevant dimensions and the connection of particular values on dimensions to behavioral outcomes has a long tradition in learning research on animals and humans (Lawrence, 1949; Trabasso & Bower, 1968). The attentional weighting hypothesis is formally similar to the hypothesis of selection and suppression of analyzers in sensory discrimination learning. The processes may differ in the involvement of explicit attentional or strategic components. Ahissar (1999) suggested that these higher and lower level selective processes interact to produce perceptual learning.

Discovery of New Relationships or Features

Some examples of perceptual learning appear to involve the discovery of features or relationships that were not initially encoded at all. To make clear what is intended here, compare two learning situations. First, consider problems in which learners must figure out which of two patterns fits in the experimenter-defined category (or which pattern leads to a reward in some task). Suppose that the two choices always have stimuli that are circles or triangles that are red or black and large or small. Across trials, the learner can test hypotheses about what determines the correct choice. Trabasso and Bower (1968) considered problems of this sort in detail, both in human and animal learning, and found that performance could be accurately modeled by learning processes in which trials altered two parameters: the relevance of a given dimension (e.g., shape) and the reward value of particular values on relevant dimensions (e.g., red connected to correct choices). Although learning in such paradigms involves important issues, the most commonly studied problems raise only minimally the issues of discovery of potentially relevant dimensions and features. The ways in which stimuli differ are salient and obvious from the start.

For contrast, consider a trainee in art appraisal. When confronted with an authentic van Gogh painting and a clever forgery, the trainee may not be able to detect any difference at all, nor indicate what dimensions might be relevant. The expert, on the other hand, may find the differences in brushstrokes obvious. In this example, the expert's enhanced sensitivity arguably involves noticing details to which the novice is oblivious. Learning must somehow allow unnoticed information to become salient or at least efficacious in guiding classification. Discovery of new information also seems to apply to higher order patterns and relationships, including abstract ones. A chess grandmaster, for example, may notice at a glance that white's position is lost, due not to an imminent loss of a piece, but to a structural defect that will take many moves to prove fatal. The novice may be completely blind to the structural information enabling the grandmaster's diagnosis. Here, the relevant information is relational and abstract, involving relations of shape, color, and spatial position.

Whether it involves fine detail or complex relations, discovery of information to which the observer has initially zero sensitivity (in a signal detection sense) is perhaps the most mysterious aspect of perceptual learning. For basic features, one possibility (elaborated later) is that experience leads to isolating particular sensory analyzers most relevant to a task. Initially, responses may be heavily influenced by analyzers that are activated by stimuli in both of two categories to be discriminated. These overlapping responses are weeded out with learning, leaving performance to depend on the analyzers that discriminate best. For higher level relational information, a possibility is that new sorts of information are synthesized by conjoining features that are initially encoded, a notion referred to as *chunking* (e.g., Chase & Simon, 1973) or unitization (e.g., Goldstone, 1998). A different idea is that expert classification depends sometimes on discovery of new, higher order invariants that underlie some classification (E. Gibson, 1969). Such invariants may involve relations that go beyond mere conjunction of already encoded information; the relevant relationships may involve structural relations of many kinds, including highly abstract information. Abstracting grammatical relations from speech signals in language learning is a good, albeit possibly special, example. In language, the realm of possibly relevant relations may be more constrained by specialized learning mechanisms than in the general case of perceptual learning.

How can higher order relations involving rich structure be discovered in perceptual learning? Another parallel to language may provide a clue. Novel sentences are routinely produced and comprehended in natural language use, presumably because they are synthesized from sets of basic elements and relations. It is possible that perceptual learning proceeds from a set of basic encodings and a set of operators that can connect basic features and properties to form relationships of higher order. For example, learning what kinds of things are squares may involve encoding edge lengths and relations among edge lengths as registered by equal/different operators (Kellman, Burke, & Hummel, 1999). Our current understanding of such learning processes is modest. Understanding phenomena in which perceptual learning appears to depend on the discovery or synthesis of new relations is an important challenge for researchers.

Remapping of Perceptual Dimensions

Another idea about perceptual learning is that the mapping between different stimulus dimensions, or between stimulus dimensions and perceptual representations, may be shifted by experience. In this category are experiments using rearranged optical stimulation, such as the shifting of visual directions laterally via prism goggles (Bedford, 1989; Harris, 1965) or, more radically, the inversion of scenes using inverting prisms (e.g., Kohler, 1964).

The remapping of perceptual dimensions is an important but special category of perceptual learning. Most often, remapping involves relations between two channels through which the same environmental property is perceived. For example, it is important that the felt position and visible position of one's arm correspond, because the world contains not a haptic space and a visual space, but space. Accordingly, remapping or recalibration occurs for perceptual inputs that are intrinsically linked in this manner. The obvious function of remapping is to maintain proper coordination among the senses and between perceptual and motor activity. One clear application of remapping processes involves changes that occur during growth and development. For example, the radial localization of sounds depends on time, phase, and intensity differences given to the two ears. The specific mapping between interaural differences and radial direction depends on the size of the head, which changes as a child grows. Remapping processes sensitive to discrepancies across modalities may serve to maintain sensory and

motor coordination (Knudsen & Knudsen, 1985). For adults, the need for remapping processes is less obvious; nonetheless, the capability for remapping when adults are subjected to altered stimulus inputs is dramatic. Perhaps such phenomena imply some ongoing need for recalibration, even in adults.

As the focus of this review is primarily on learning processes that lead to improvements in the pickup of information, I will not do justice to the literature or issues on remapping processes. The section titled "Spatial Intervals" elaborates one example. For a more comprehensive discussion of the issues in remapping, see Bedford (1995).

Fluency Processes

Automaticity

A classic example of improved fluency as a result of perceptual learning is the work of Schneider and Shiffrin (1977). In a series of studies, subjects judged whether certain letters in a target set appeared at the corners of rectangular arrays. Attentional load was manipulated by varying the number of items in the target set and the number of items on each card in a series of frames. Early in learning, performance was highly load-sensitive, but with extensive training subjects came to perform the task equally well within a range of target set sizes and array sizes. These results led Shiffrin and Schneider (1977; Schneider & Shiffrin, 1977) to claim that a transition occurred from *controlled* to *automatic* processing.

Item Storage

A wide variety of evidence indicates that experience with particular items facilitates subsequent performance on those items in classification tasks. This effect occurs even in cases in which subjects have extracted a clear classification rule and in cases in which the familiarity is based on aspects that are irrelevant (for a review, see Goldstone, 1998). The effects of instance learning may diminish over days or weeks in comparison to effects of learning some rule or invariant (Posner & Keele, 1967).

The fluency improvements from item storage appear to lie at the margin of what we would label perceptual learning. Such improvements have been described as a form of "imprinting" in which the stored trace may be functionally described as a new "receptor" or "detector" (Goldstone, 1998). A reasonable alternative is that these improvements in fluency derive from the associative connection of a particular stimulus representation to a particular categorization response (Hall, 1991). A useful criterion may be whether the perceptual representation itself changes as learning progresses or whether learning consists of the connection of a given representation to responses or other representations (see Chaps. 1 and 2, this volume).

Unitization

In contrast to processes of differentiation that occur from experience, unitization refers to the combining or connecting of encoded features to create chunks or units that make perceptual classification faster or more accurate. Evidence suggests that stimulus features that co-occur tend to become encoded as units. Such a process has often been invoked to account for fluent processing of letters (e.g., LaBerge, 1973) and words (e.g., Salasoo, Shiffrin, & Feustel, 1985). Such chunking processes may also come into play for spatially separated entities, including separated line segments (Shiffrin, 1996) and complex spatial configurations in chess (Chase & Simon, 1973).

Several ideas have been proposed to account for unitization. One is that items or parts that are simultaneously activated in short-term memory become integrated units in long-term

memory (Shiffrin & Schneider, 1977). Computational models using neural-style units have also used synchrony of activation as the basis for chunking (Mozer, 1991). Some physiological evidence suggests that training leads to the development of specific neural responses that depend on configural relations (Logothetis, Pauls, & Poggio, 1995).

Interaction of Fluency and Discovery Processes. Fluency and discovery processes may interact in the development of expertise. Writing in *Psychological Review* in 1899, Bryan and Harter proposed that automatizing the processing of basic information was a foundation for discovering higher order relationships. These investigators studied learning in the task of telegraphic receiving. When the measure of words (in Morse code) received per minute was plotted against weeks of practice, a typical, negatively accelerated learning curve appeared, reaching asymptote after some weeks. With continued practice, however, many subjects produced a new learning curve, rising from the plateau of the first. For some subjects, a third learning curve ultimately emerged after even more practice. Each learning curve raised performance to substantially higher levels than before.

What could account for this remarkable topography of learning? When Bryan and Harter asked their subjects to describe their activity at different points in learning, responses suggested that the information being processed differed considerably at different stages. Those on the first learning curve reported that they were concentrating on the way letters of English mapped onto the dots and dashes of Morse code. Those on the second learning curve reported that dots and dashes making letters had become automatic for them; now they were focusing on word structure. Finally, learners at the highest level reported that common words had become automatic; they were now focusing on message structure. To test these introspective reports, Bryan and Harter presented learners in the second phase with sequences of letters that did not make words. Under these conditions, performance returned to the asymptotic level of the first learning curve. When the most advanced learners were presented with sequences of words that did not make messages, their performance returned to the asymptotic levels of the second learning curve. These results confirmed the subjects' self-reports.

Although the robustness of the phenomenon of three separable learning curves in telegraphic receiving has been questioned (Keller, 1958), Bryan and Harter's (1899) ideas about improvement, as well as the tests indicating use of higher order structure by advanced learners, remain important. Specifically, they argued that discovery of structure is a limited-capacity process. Automatizing the processing of basic structure at one level frees attentional capacity to discover higher level structure, which can in turn be automatized, allowing discovery of even higher level information, and so on. This continuing cycle—discovering and automatizing of higher and higher levels of structure—may account for the seemingly magical levels of human expertise that sometimes arise from years of sustained experience, as in chess, mathematics, music, and science. Bryan and Harter's study offers one of the most intriguing suggestions about how discovery and fluency processes interact and complement each other. Their 1897 article ends with a memorable claim: "Automaticity is not genius, but it is the hands and feet of genius."

Cortical Plasticity

Underlying changes in discovery and fluency in perceptual learning are changes in neural circuitry. Although linking particular changes to particular information-processing functions remains a difficult challenge

(Buonomano & Merzenich, 1998; Edeline, 1999), much evidence suggests that modifications of neural circuitry accompany perceptual learning. As research progresses, a number of the discovery and fluency processes enumerated earlier may turn out to be connected directly to types of neural changes. Some of these possibilities are considered later.

Perceptual Learning and Other Concepts of Learning

What is the relation of perceptual learning to other concepts of learning? A compelling answer probably awaits a more precise understanding of process and mechanism. One relationship that is not fully clear is the connection of perceptual learning to the notion of *implicit learning* (defined as learning without awareness). Many tasks used to study implicit learning are perceptual learning tasks. Consistent with implicit learning, in complex perceptual learning tasks (e.g., sorting of newborn chicks by sex, chess playing), experts are often unable to explain what stimulus relationships they are using in classification. Also, in some kinds of amnesic patients, explicit learning processes appear to be disrupted, whereas performance on perceptual and implicit tasks remains intact. Yet it is not at all clear that perceptual learning and implicit learning are synonymous. Some perceptual learning may in fact be explicit; in some pattern-classification learning subjects can indeed point out what information they are using. Moreover, neuropsychological data may suggest more than one type of implicit learning.

Many other questions exist regarding the boundaries and relations between perceptual learning and other notions of learning. One issue is whether some aspects of perceptual learning can be understood in terms of more familiar associative learning concepts (Hall, 1991). Another is the involvement of perceptual learning in what are usually regarded as motor skills. When a baseball batter successfully hits a pitch, perceptual learning may account for the skill that allowed him to detect early in its flight that the pitch was a curveball. However, perceptual differentiation of the feel of swinging the bat in various ways may also have been involved in learning the muscle commands that produced the smooth swing.

Other questions involve not so much boundaries between types of learning, but components of information processing that are common to, or analogous among, different forms of learning. One is automaticity. Some aspects of information extraction become automatic with practice, but the same appears to be true of habitual motor sequences and reasoning patterns. The notion of automatization seems to crosscut several forms of learning. Another family resemblance involves the conditions for perceptual learning. Perceptual skill seems unlikely to be subsumed by the dichotomy of declarative and procedural knowledge, yet the conditions under which perceptual learning occurs appear to have much in common with procedural learning (see the section titled "Conditions Affecting Perceptual Learning").

PERCEPTUAL LEARNING IN BASIC VISUAL DISCRIMINATIONS

Physical devices designed to detect energy or to make simple pattern discriminations will have fixed limits of sensitivity. An extraordinary fact about human perceptual learning is that many of our most basic sensory thresholds are modifiable by experience. In examining psychophysical evidence for this claim, I focus on vision. In recent years studies have shown that this conclusion is true for discriminations involving virtually all basic dimensions of early visual encoding, including, for example, orientation (Dosher & Lu, 1999;

Shiu & Pashler, 1992; Vogels & Orban, 1985), motion direction (Ball & Sekuler, 1982) and stereoacuity (Fendick & Westheimer, 1983). I sample the literature selectively, highlighting studies that raise interesting issues or point toward explanatory mechanisms. Much of the work attempting to connect learning effects to specific sites of cortical plasticity has involved senses other than vision; I explore some of this work at the end of this section.

Vernier Acuity

Vernier acuity—the ability to detect deviations from collinearity of two lines—is a basic measure of visual resolution. It is often labeled as a *hyperacuity;* the term refers to the fact that sensitivity to a particular spatial difference is smaller than the diameter of individual photoreceptors. In Vernier acuity tasks, thresholds for reliable detection of misalignment may be 10 arc sec of visual angle, about a third of the diameter of a photoreceptor.

This level of precision is perhaps one reason that researchers have often considered basic sensory acuities to be relatively fixed operating limits. Remarkably, as research has revealed in recent years, these operating limits can be strikingly improved by training. McKee and Westheimer (1978) carried out an early training study using a Vernier task in foveal vision. After about 2,000 trials, subjects' thresholds decreased about 40% on average. These results have been replicated and extended for both foveal vision (Saarinen & Levi, 1995) and parafoveal vision (Beard, Levi, & Reich, 1995). The effects appear to be resilient; tests carried out 4 months later showed no decline in the improvement.

Curiously, little improvement was found in a variant of the Vernier task, the three-point Vernier task (Bennett & Westheimer, 1991). In the three-point task, two vertically aligned dots are presented, and the subject must judge whether a third dot midway between them is displaced to the left or the right of the imaginary line connecting the upper and lower dots. Despite practice for more than 10,000 trials, no reliable threshold changes were found. The difference in outcome from the standard Vernier task could be due to the difference between stimuli. Additionally, a procedural difference could be relevant. Bennett and Westheimer gave 300 practice trials prior to measuring learning effects. Learning could have occurred rapidly during these practice trials. Other reports suggest that Vernier learning occurs rather rapidly, with most of the effects attained within 300 or so trials (e.g., Fahle, Poggio, & Edelman, 1992). The three-dot results are nonetheless discrepant with the slower course of learning found by McKee and Westheimer (1978). Adding to the confusion, Fahle and Edelman (1993) did find a long-term learning effect for the three-dot acuity task. It is not clear how to resolve these discrepancies.

Learning effects on Vernier tasks are highly specific to the stimulus orientation used in training (e.g., Fahle et al., 1992). This fact has motivated explanations emphasizing changes at relatively early levels of the visual system. For example, Fahle et al. proposed that task-specific modules are set up based on retinal or early cortical inputs. Specifically, they suggested that the set of analyzer responses (photoreceptor outputs in their model but orientation-sensitive cells in a more plausible realization) to an individual stimulus are stored as a vector. Each such template is connected to a response output ("left" or "right" in a Vernier task), obtained through supervised learning. After storage of a number of such examples, new stimuli can be classified by comparison to the templates. The templates are used as *radial basis functions* in that each template's response to the new pattern is determined by a Gaussian function of its Euclidean distance from the pattern in the multidimensional space that encodes the templates. The

responses of the several templates are linked by weights to the response categories. In the extreme case in which all stimuli match stored templates, this model amounts to a look-up table. Models of this type show learning effects of a magnitude similar to that shown for human subjects (Fahle et al., 1992). On the other hand, this kind of model seems an unlikely account of other features of perceptual learning in hyperacuity. One is the fact that learning can occur without explicit feedback (i.e., without supervised learning). The other is that radial basis function models predict specificity in learning in terms of retinal location, eye, and orientation, yet learning effects transfer at least partially across these dimensions (Fahle, Edelman, & Poggio, 1995).

Findings about specificity have also been examined in attempts to localize learning effects anatomically. Because only certain layers of cortical area V1 and earlier parts of the visual pathway have significant numbers of monocularly driven cells (cells sensitive to inputs from only one eye), one strategy has been to train in one eye and test in another. For Vernier acuity, results have been inconsistent (Fahle, 1994, 1995), except for a fairly clear effect that learning transfers across eyes when the inputs for both are given to the same hemiretina (Beard et al., 1995). (The left hemiretina—right visual field—of each eye sends its information to the left hemisphere of the cortex.) This result is consistent with the idea that learning effects involve binocular cells in the trained hemiretina. Results involving specificity of location within a single visual field have been inconsistent (Fahle, 1994, 1995).

Orientation Discrimination

Orientation tuning is a basic feature of early visual analyzers which first appears at the cortical level. Cells in V1, the earliest cortical visual area, tend to have small receptive fields sensitive to particular retinal locations, with clear orientation selectivity. Except in the earliest layers of V1, most cells are driven binocularly. These facts make orientation sensitivity especially interesting in efforts to connect learning effects to particular cortical loci. For example, a learning effect that was specific to orientation and to the trained eye would suggest the involvement of monocular V1 cells.

Orientation sensitivity has been shown to improve with practice (Shiu & Pashler, 1992; Vogels & Orban, 1985). In Shiu and Pashler's study, reliable improvement was shown over nine blocks of 44 trials each, all conducted at specific retinal locations. When lines appeared in new locations (either in the opposite hemifield or in the other quadrant of the same hemifield), little or no transfer of learning was observed. Learning was also specific to the orientations used. Such effects are consistent with learning mechanisms that are specific to particular retinal locations, perhaps orientation-selective cells in early cortical areas.

A separate experiment by Shiu and Pashler (1992) indicated that when subjects judged brightness differences in the same set of stimuli, they did not gain improved discrimination abilities for orientation. The latter result suggests the importance of cognitive set, attention, or active task engagement in perceptual learning. Such factors, however, would seem to involve much higher levels of the nervous system. Thus, even perceptual learning effects involving basic visual dimensions may depend on an interplay of higher and lower levels of processing.

Orientation and Visual Search

Studies in which visual search depends on an orientation difference between a target and other items in an array also show substantial practice effects (Ahissar & Hochstein, 1997; Fiorentini & Berardi, 1981; Karni & Sagi,

1991, 1993). Karni and Sagi (1991, 1993) tested visual search for a set of three parallel oblique lines that could be aligned vertically or horizontally in an array of horizontal lines. The stimulus onset asynchrony (time between the display onset and a pattern mask) needed to achieve a given accuracy (e.g., 80% correct) decreased rapidly from the beginning of training. (After 3 sessions of about 1,000 trials each, it had decreased 50% for some subjects.) Improvements continued more slowly for many sessions afterward.

Some aspects of their data led Karni and Sagi (1991, 1993) to argue that learning consists of two components. One is a fast component that is noticeable within sessions. This learning fully transfers across eyes. The other component arises more slowly, appears to require some period of consolidation or sleep after learning (as discussed later), and is specific to the trained eye. Karni and Sagi reported that both kinds of learning are specific to the stimulus orientations used and the specific quadrant of the visual field. (Targets always appeared in the same quadrant during training.) The idea that different learning processes have both differing time courses and specificity characteristics is appealing for distinguishing underlying mechanisms. Unfortunately, it is not clear how consistently these effects occur. Schoups and Orban (1996), for example, used the same task as Karni and Sagi and found that learning of both types transferred fully across eyes.

Motion Perception

Discrimination of motion direction improves substantially with practice. Discriminating two directions differing by 3 deg is initially quite difficult but becomes highly accurate with extended practice. When training involves only a difficult discrimination, the effects are found to be largely specific to the training direction (e.g., Ball & Sekuler, 1982). Such specificity suggests alteration in the sensitivity of specific neural channels selective for that direction.

Results differ, however, if training utilizes an easier discrimination. Liu (1999) had observers perform a forced-choice discrimination between two directions differing by 8 deg. After training, performance improved at directions that differed by 90 deg from the training directions. Liu and Weinshall (2000) reported another interesting result. For direction discriminations involving stimuli 4 deg apart, there was little transfer when performance was tested at new orientations (90 deg different). A different measure of transfer, however, produced some evidence that learning does generalize. During the second discrimination task, the learning *rate* was almost twice as fast as that in the original task.

These results mandate some caution in inferring the neural locus of learning effects from specificity of learning effects. If the same learning processes are at work in the difficult and easier problems, there may be some differences in the way they are engaged by slightly different tasks. If so, varying levels of specificity may reflect more about the task than about the mechanism. Alternatively, the results may indicate different kinds of learning processes—one involving improved selectivity of particular neural channels and another utilizing higher level processes. These issues are considered further in the section titled "Task Difficulty" below.

Specificity in Perceptual Learning

At this point, it is fair to say that attempts to use anatomical or stimulus specificity to infer the locus of learning in the nervous system have not yielded any clear generalizations. This conclusion comes both from inconsistent results on nearly identical tasks and from differences across tasks. The situation may reflect the fact that multiple types of learning effects (involving multiple loci) are strongly

affected by small task differences. An alternative conception is that perceptual learning ordinarily involves a coordinated interaction of higher level processes, such as attention, and lower level ones, such as tuning of receptors sensitive to particular stimulus properties (e.g., Ahissar & Hochstein, 1997).

Sensitivity versus Noise Reduction in Perceptual Learning

Applications of concepts of signal detection theory have led to recent progress in understanding perceptual learning. A fundamental question about changes in detection and discrimination performance is whether these effects entail true improvements in sensitivity. Sensitivity might increase, for example, if learning somehow amplifies the relevant internal signals used in a task. Another possible account of improved performance is that internal noise—departures from ideal processing within the observer—is somehow reduced. Dosher and Lu (1999) described a framework for studying these questions, illustrated in Figure 7.1.

The framework begins with the assumption that processing of a sensory discrimination may be thought of as assessing a signal's match to one or another internal templates. Matching accuracy may be affected by external noise (in the stimulus) or by internal noise. Internal noise may be of two types: additive (constant) or multiplicative with the stimulus (in which the stimulus equals the signal plus external noise). By testing performance with different amounts of external noise, different notions of improvement can be tested. In Figure 7.1a, the effect of practice is to enhance or amplify the stimulus; perhaps a better description is that calculation efficiency improves. Associated with this effect is a characteristic set of curves shown in Figure 7.1b. These curves show the signal contrast required to achieve a certain performance threshold. In

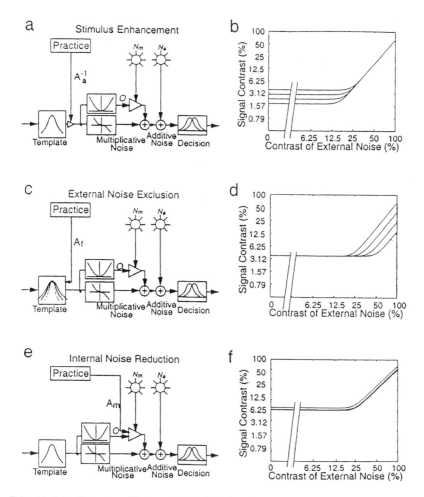

Figure 7.1   Models of learning effects and their data signatures.
NOTE: a) Practice turns up the gain on the stimulus, corresponding to stimulus enhancement. (N_m and N_a indicate multiplicative and additive noise, respectively; A_a indicates multipliers on internal additive noise, leading to stimulus enhancement.) b) Stimulus enhancement is associated with improvements in performance in the lower noise limb of the contrast threshold functions. c) Practice affects the amount of external noise processed through the perceptual template by narrowing the filter tuning, corresponding to external noise exclusion. (A_f indicates multipliers on the output of the perceptual filter applied to external noise, corresponding to external noise reduction.) d) External noise exclusion improves performance only in the high noise limb of the contrast threshold functions. e) Practice reduces the gain on multiplicative internal noise, or internal multiplicative noise reduction. (A_m indicates multipliers on internal multiplicative noise.) f) Internal (multiplicative) noise reduction improves performance somewhat over both limbs of the contrast threshold functions.
SOURCE: Reprinted from *Vision Research, 39,* B. A. Dosher and Z.-L. Lu, "Mechanisms of perceptual learning," pp. 3197–3221. Copyright © 1999, with permission from Elsevier Science.

the flat part of the curve, changes in external noise have little effect, as performance is limited by internal noise. Beyond a certain point, increases in external noise increase the contrast required to attain threshold performance. Practice has the effect of lowering contrast thresholds (shifting the performance curve downward) in the lower limb of the curve, while not affecting the higher limb.

Figure 7.1c illustrates the case in which learning reduces only external noise. (This is shown in the figure by the increasingly narrow tuning of the template.) The effect of practice on the data is schematized in Figure 7.1d. There is no change in the required contrast to attain threshold in the flat part of the curves. However, the range within which performance is limited by external noise (the rising portion of the curve) moves rightward with practice. Finally, the possibility of reduction of the multiplicative component (gain) of internal noise is shown in Figure 7.1e. Practice has the effect of improving performance in both parts of the curves, as shown in Figure 7.1f.

Dosher and Lu (1999) tested these predictions in a series of experiments in which observers judged on each trial whether a Gabor patch embedded in noise tilted to the left or right of vertical. A staircase procedure was used to find a contrast threshold in each condition. To distinguish different mixtures of the possible kinds of effects, experiments were carried out in which data were collected at more than one threshold level. This manipulation provided more detailed information on shifts in performance curves from practice.

Fitting the model predictions to their subjects' data, Dosher and Lu found evidence for both stimulus enhancement and external noise exclusion. There was no evidence of an effect of decreased gain of internal multiplicative noise. They discussed these effects in terms of changes with practice in the weights given to particular analyzers. Among a set of analyzers that are initially engaged by a task, some turn out to be less relevant than others. Learning is conceived of as a reduction of the contributions of less relevant analyzers to decisions.

One limitation in Dosher and Lu's analysis is the difficulty of distinguishing stimulus enhancement from reduction of additive internal noise, as these make similar predictions. Using similar methods, Gold, Bennett, and Sekuler (1999) found signal enhancement in perceptual learning tasks. They tested learning in a face identification and texture identification task. Subjects made a 10-alternative, forced-choice decision about which stimulus was presented on each trial in varying amounts of external noise. To assess the effect of internal noise, they used a double-pass response consistency measure, in which subjects judged a specific set of stimuli twice. Given that the signal plus external noise combinations in the stimulus set were held constant, any inconsistencies in responding must be due to internal variability. From the observer's consistency, it is possible to obtain an estimate of total internal noise (additive plus multiplicative). Gold et al.'s results suggested no change in internal noise.

Although the tasks in these studies have varied, all have indicated effects of signal enhancement and perhaps improved external noise exclusion. Changes in internal noise have not been found. It is not clear how general these findings are across different learning tasks.

Cortical Plasticity

The rapidity of perceptual learning in some studies is consistent with some known phenomena of neural changes in the brain. The activity of single neurons in sensory areas of the cerebral cortex is often characterized by their *receptive fields*—the description of the range of values on some relevant stimulus dimensions that influence the firing rate of the neuron. The receptive field of a visual neuron, for example, could describe the locations on the retina that, if stimulated, influence that cell's responding.

Visual receptive fields of cortical neurons can be changed rapidly by creating an artificial scotoma (blank area) in the cell's original receptive field while stimulation (e.g., moving gratings or dynamic noise dots) are presented in the surround. Pettet and Gilbert (1992) observed large increases in receptive field sizes within as little as 10 min of exposure to the artificial scotoma. It is not completely clear that increased receptive field size is the accurate description of the changes; an increased responsivity in the entire receptive field, including previously subthreshold areas, might explain the data (Das & Gilbert, 1995). Either kind of change might represent a cortical basis of perceptual learning. Contrary to behavioral studies of perceptual learning, however, such receptive field changes appear to be short-lived. It is possible that the difference in duration of the receptive field and perceptual learning effects are due to differences in training protocols.

A variety of studies have found evidence consistent with the specific idea of Hebbian learning mechanisms, in which co-occurring activations of units result in the strengthening of their connections. For example, the orientation sensitivity of V1 cells in cats can be experimentally altered by pairing presentation of selected orientations at the retina with applications to single cells of electrical current (Frégnac, Schulz, Thorpe, & Bienenstock, 1988) or neurotransmitter substances, such as GABA or glutamate (McLean & Palmer, 1998). Hebbian learning appears to be one mechanism of change in neural circuitry that could contribute to perceptual learning phenomena.

Plasticity in the Somatosensory System

Changes in cortical neurons, and indeed in whole cortical areas, are also characteristic of learning in other sensory modalities. For example, Wang, Merzenich, Sameshima, and Jenkins (1995) trained owl monkeys on a tactile task in which two bars were attached across three fingers at either their bases (proximal end) or their tips (distal end). Stimulation of all three fingers from one bar and the other generally alternated, and the monkey was required to respond whenever two consecutive stimuli were applied through the same bar. Normally, receptive fields in somatosensory area 3b are specific to individual digits; multidigit receptive fields are extremely rare. As shown in Figure 7.2, after prolonged training many cells exhibited multidigit receptive fields. The investigators noted that the development of these receptive fields is consistent with Hebbian learning.

Plasticity in the Auditory System

Whereas the organization of both early visual and somatosensory cortical areas involve topological maps of the space on the receptor surfaces (retina or skin), early auditory areas are *tonotopic,* organized in terms of frequency responses. The receptive field of a neuron in primary auditory cortex consists of the range of frequencies that influence its firing. Learning tasks have been shown to cause changes in the frequency responses of cells in auditory cortex of monkeys. Recanzone, Schreiner, and Merzenich (1993) showed that monkeys trained on a difficult frequency discrimination showed improvement over several weeks. Subsequent mapping of the receptive fields of cortical cells indicated that areas responding to frequencies relevant to the task were substantially enlarged. Weinberger and colleagues have found similar evidence of plasticity in guinea pigs and other species using a classical conditioning paradigm (Edeline & Weinberger, 1993; Weinberger, Javid, & Lepan, 1995). In most experiments a particular frequency was used as a conditioned stimulus (CS) and was paired with an electrical shock. Responses of cells in primary auditory cortex and also in the thalamus showed an enhancement of responses to the frequency used as the CS as well as a general alteration of many receptive fields such that they tended to become more centered on that frequency.

A   Cortical Map of Trained
     Digit Surfaces

B   Receptive Fields in Different
     Area 3b Zones

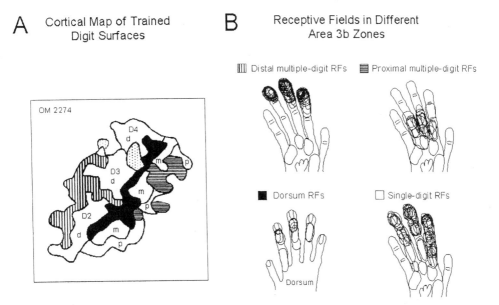

Figure 7.2 Training-dependent cortical map reorganization in primary somatosensory cortex. Map and receptive fields of the hand and representations of area 3b from the monkey that underwent behavioral training. Training involved extensive simultaneous stimulation across the proximal and distal portions of digits D2-D4. (A) The map shows that in contrast to normal maps, there was a significant portion of the map that exhibited multiple digit receptive fields, which were specific to either the proximal (horizontal striping) or distal (vertical striping) phalanges. (B) The receptive fields of the map shown in A, sorted according to the four observed classes; distal multiple-digit, proximal multiple-digit, dorsum, and single-digit receptive fields.
SOURCE: Buonomano and Merzenich (1998). Reprinted with permission.

Understanding the relations between particular kinds of neural plasticity and learning processes is a complicated task that will occupy researchers for a long time to come. One reason the task is so complicated is that the answers depend on other basic, unresolved issues, such as the precise nature of the learning processes themselves and how these processes and the information which they utilize are represented in the brain. An interesting discussion of specific issues confronting the effort to connect plasticity and learning phenomena may be found in Edeline (1999). One specific issue he raised is that we have as yet little understanding of how groups of neurons work together; yet clearly, circuitry encompassing more than the coding done by single cells is of fundamental importance.

PERCEPTUAL LEARNING IN MIDDLE VISION

Shape: Differentiation

A classic perceptual learning study (J. Gibson & Gibson, 1955) still serves as a good example of the idea of differentiation processes in perceptual learning. Figure 7.3 shows a coiled scribble pattern in the center, surrounded by a number of other patterns that differ along dimensions of compression, orientation, or left-right reversal. These patterns were combined with 12 others that were quite looked quite different from these scribbles and also varied greatly among themselves. In the experiments, cards containing individual patterns were shown. The standard stimulus (center

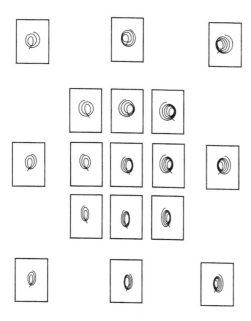

Figure 7.3 Scribble stimuli redrawn from Gibson and Gibson (1955).
NOTE: All patterns other than the one in the center are derived from the central pattern by compression, scaling, and/or left-right reversal. See text for additional details.

scribble) was shown for 5 s, and subjects were told that some items in the other cards to be presented would match the standard. They were instructed to make a same/different judgment about whether each card matched the previously shown standard. The dependent variable was the number of times through the pack of cards required to achieve perfect performance. Gibson and Gibson found that subjects tended to say "same" to similar items, but this tendency decreased across runs. Adults reached criterion (saying "same" only to the single matching stimulus) in fewer runs than did older (8.5- to 11-year-old) children, who learned faster than younger (6- to 8-year-old) children. Learning in this study proceeded without any explicit feedback. In general, errors involved overinclusion at the start, and exposure to the displays led to differentiation—the noticing of differences within the set.

Differentiation phenomena have a mysterious character. If, initially, the perceptual representations created by two or more stimuli are identical, how could they ever come to be discriminated? Perceptual representations of particular stimuli must somehow change with repeated exposure. Such changes may occur because of sampling or search processes. Of the many potentially encodable attributes of a pattern, only some are sampled and encoded in any one encounter (Trabasso & Bower, 1968). With repeated exposures, either some probabilistic element in the sampling process or a systematic search for dimensions of difference in a given task could lead to discovery of differences that were not initially noticed.

Whether initial stimulus encodings are followed by a search process that leads to differentiation may depend on the task in which the perceiver is engaged (E. Gibson, 1969). In the experiment with squiggles, the different patterns may initially have been encoded similarly as line drawings of roughly a certain size resembling coils of wire. In an experiment in which subjects were asked to judge members of this set to be the same or different, differentiation occurred. If the same patterns occurred incidentally on the sides of cars in a task where the observer was to classify the manufacturer of the car, these coils may have remained undifferentiated. The question of whether performance of an active classification is important in engaging perceptual learning mechanisms is discussed in the section titled "Active Classification, Attention, and Effort."

Shape: Unitization

The idea of unitization is that practice in a task allows features that were originally encoded separately to be combined into a larger unit. The term is synonymous with some uses of the term *chunking* (Chase & Simon, 1973). Goldstone (2000) reported a series of studies designed to examine unitization. He used

Category 1 | Category 2

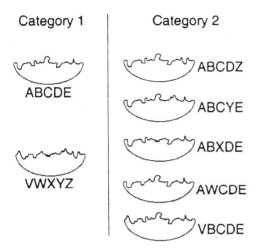

ABCDE

VWXYZ

ABCDZ

ABCYE

ABXDE

AWCDE

VBCDE

Figure 7.4 Stimuli used by Goldstone (2000). NOTE: Each top contour is composed of five contour segments. See text for additional details. SOURCE: Goldstone (2000). Copyright © 2000 by the American Psychological Association. Reprinted with permission.

stimuli like those shown in Figure 7.4. The top contours of these stimuli are composed of five separate shape fragments.

After extensive familiarization with the category assignments for the stimuli, subjects were given practice in sorting exemplars into categories 1 and 2 (shown in Figure 7.4). Reaction times were measured over four blocks of 80 trials. In one experiment, four conditions were compared. Categorization was based on (a) a conjunction of five parts in a particular order (as in Figure 7.4), (b) a conjunction of five parts with variable order, (c) a single component in a constant position, or (d) a single component in a randomly varying position. Responses showed that categorization based on a single component was faster than for those requiring multiple components. More important, the most learning was shown when categorization involved five parts in a consistent relationship. Goldstone interpreted the results to indicate that learners are developing a chunked representation that comes to function as a unit.

An important issue in Goldstone's studies of unitization, as in earlier work invoking unitization or chunking effects, is that there are at least two possible explanations for changes in performance. One is that a number of previously separate features come to be aggregated into a unit. The other is that processing of features gives way to categorization based on discovery of a higher-order relationship. The difference in these possibilities is that the higher-order relation is a new basis for response, not a collection of the lower level features. An example of a higher-order relation can be observed in display VWXYZ in Figure 7.4. If an imaginary curve connected the three highest peaks of the contour of VWXYZ, the curve would be nearly flat, perhaps slightly concave upward. In the other displays, such a curve would be convex upward. Thus, VWXYZ might be efficiently placed into category 1 based on this stimulus relationship. The relationship is not definable from the individual elements or from the mere fact that they occur together. This example is not meant to be a specific claim about the information that subjects used in Goldstone's studies; the point is that such higher-order relations are available. Goldstone explicitly indicated that his studies are unable to reveal the specific relations or units that the subjects actually use. His results appear consistent with either of these possibilities. One piece of evidence that true unitization is occurring is that learning effects also occurred in a condition in which the five contour fragments were separated and stacked in a vertical arrangement. The issue of stimulus redescription (discovery of higher-order relations) persists, however, as even a stack has invariant relations to be discovered. If discovery of higher order relationships is occurring, one might expect it to occur more readily for connected segments. Indeed, Goldstone's data indicate that learning was significantly better in the connected case.

Spatial Intervals

Perception of spatial extents is an important part of comprehending any environment. Spatial intervals can be signaled by a variety of information sources, and it appears that perceptual learning can function to maintain accurate perception from these sources. An example comes from research by Wallach, Moore, and Davidson (1963). They equipped observers with a telestereoscope, a viewing device that effectively changed the interocular distance (distance between the two eyes). In ordinary stereoscopic perception, the use of binocular disparity to specify depth involves a computation requiring the egocentric distance to at least one point in the scene. This distance to a point allows disparities to be converted into perceived depth intervals in the scene. Changing the interocular distance alters the magnitude of binocular disparities. When this occurs, the normal computation of depth intervals from distance and disparity is incorrect.

In the experiment of Wallach, Moore, and Davidson (1963), the observers viewed a rotating cube through the telestereoscope. Because all depth intervals were exaggerated, an edge of the cube that appeared to have a certain length when viewed horizontally appeared to grow in length as it rotated away to become more oriented in depth. With prolonged viewing, however, adaptation occurred, such that a new relation between disparity and depth obtained; this relation reestablished accurate perception of depth intervals. Wallach et al. argued that the basis of learning or adaptation in this situation is the assumption of physical invariance. The system adjusts the relation between depth and disparity (essentially learning a new interocular distance) in order to allow rotating object to have unchanging shape. A cogent elaboration of this type of argument, and further examples of this kind of perceptual recalibration, may be found in Bedford (1995).

As mentioned earlier, this kind of perceptual learning—remapping of the relationships across information sources—may differ in kind from most examples of perceptual learning that we have considered here. In adaptation research, including the large literature on adaptation to distorted optical input due to prism glasses and other devices, altered inputs lead to a new relation between perceptual dimensions, or between perceptual and motoric dimensions. Although involving multiple processes, a commonality of perceptual learning cases we have examined is that they involve improved information extraction with ordinary (unaltered) stimulation. Both kinds of learning are important.

Size Perception

Perceptual learning in size perception was tested by Goldstone (1994). In a pretest, subjects made forced choice, same/different judgments about the sizes of successively presented squares. Categorization training was then carried out in which four different sizes of squares had to be judged one at a time as "large" (the two largest squares) or "small" (the two smallest). After categorization, subjects were given a posttest that was identical to the pretest. They showed reliably improved sensitivity to size differences; enhancement was greatest around the category boundary. Some evidence suggests that these effects may be mediated by category labels and that they may not be truly perceptual effects, as evidenced by the lack of positive results when the same/different tests are carried out with simultaneously presented displays (Choplin, Huttenlocher, & Kellman, 2001). The roles of improved perceptual sensitivity, category labelling, and their possible interactions deserve further investigation, in this and other contexts.

Visual Search

As mentioned earlier, some researchers have argued that perceptual learning involves discovery of distinguishing features (E. Gibson, 1969), that is, those attributes or contrasts that govern some classification. An important question is how the learning of contrasts relates to the basic encodings that are unlearned. What kinds of features are naturally encoded prior to learning, and how can we tell? Treisman and colleagues (Treisman & Gelade, 1980; Treisman & Gormican, 1988) have attempted to characterize the basic inputs in vision as functionally separable *feature maps,* involving inputs such as orientation, size, color, closure of lines, and so on. Several criteria have been used to identify such features, which are said to be automatically encoded. One involves search times for an item having a certain feature in an array of items lacking that feature (distractors). If search times for a single item having the feature are insensitive to the number of distractors, that featural contrast is considered to be encoded in basic feature maps. Effortless segregation of textural regions based on the featural differences is another criterion. A third criterion relates to the converse idea: If information processing based on separately encoded features is relatively easy, processing of items that proves difficult may indicate that contrasts in single, automatically encoded features are not sufficient to do that task. One example involves conjunctions of basic features. Connecting information in separate feature maps to a unitary object is hypothesized to require attention. Accordingly, observers shown brief exposures of object arrays may experience *illusory conjunctions*—inaccurate conjunctions of features. Likewise, search for an item in an array whose difference from distractors is defined by a conjunction of features is slow, and it increases with the number of distractors (Treisman, 1991).

The idea that perceptual learning involves discovery or synthesis of new features suggests that this architecture may be modifiable. Some evidence indeed shows that the information-processing criteria used to identify basic features may be achievable for some classification tasks with practice. For example, Sireteanu and Rettenbach (1995) studied visual search tasks using feature contrasts that initially required serial search. These included searching for a plain circle among circles with gaps or with small intersecting line segments and searching for a pair of parallel edges among pairs of converging edges. Initially, performance indicated positive slopes relating reaction times to set size (1, 4, 8, or 16 items). A subject given extended practice achieved flat (approximately zero-slope) functions of set size for all search tasks. Some subjects who were tested for only a few hundred trials approached similar performance. A separate experiment showed that learning that achieved apparently parallel search on one task transferred fully to another search task and also transferred from the trained eye to the untrained eye. The tasks used in the transfer experiment involved searching for a circle target against distractors of circles with intersecting line segments and searching for a pair of parallel lines amid diverging line pairs. Transfer between these search tasks seems unlikely to depend on use of the same low-level analyzers. Instead, the results suggest that practice may lead to general search strategies that allow new feature contrasts to be processed as efficiently as those governed by basic feature maps.

The results of Schneider and Shiffrin (1977) may be related. Recall that in a task requiring search for target letters in a sequence of frames, each containing one or more letters, they found a transition from controlled to automatic processing, indicated by the fact that performance became insensitive to attentional load (number of target items times number of search items per frame). Shiffrin and Schneider (1977) interpreted their results in terms of connecting letter features in the target set to automatic attention responses.

The meaning of this account of improvement—attaching automatic attention responses to features—depends heavily on what can be a feature. One diagnostic criterion for identifying basic features, used by Treisman and others, has been asymmetry of search performance. Searching for a Q among Os allows "pop-out," because the system can distinguish, in theory, whether the feature map that registers straight line segments has some activation or none. Searching for an O among Qs, however, is slow and serial because both the feature map for closed loops and for segments have activation. To find the odd O requires attentive processes that examine particular locations. Taken at face value, the results of Sireteanu and Rettenbach (1995) appear difficult to fit with this overall scheme because practice led to parallel search for an O among what were essentially Qs. In this case, no feature is attached to an automatic attention response; rather, the location having the absence of the feature is what becomes easier to find. The results are similar to those involving conjunctive features (see the section titled "The Word Superiority Effect") in that they appear to require modification of our notions about basic input features or new ideas about what is learned with practice.

Implicit Learning in Visual Search

Earlier I noted that perceptual learning is sometimes considered to be closely related to the notion of implicit learning, that is, learning without conscious awareness. Implicit learning is often demonstrated by presenting certain stimulus regularities in the context of an irrelevant task and later testing to detect whether sensitivity to the regularities has been incidentally acquired (e.g., Reber, 1993). In recent years research has suggested that in certain populations of amnesics, explicit learning processes are impaired while implicit or perceptual learning processes are spared.

However, the precise relation between so-called implicit learning and perceptual learning remains unclear. It seems probable that multiple processes are encompassed by the conditions to which these terms have been applied. An example of the difficulty can be seen in research by Chun and Phelps (1999). They tested normal subjects and amnesic patients with hippocampal and surrounding medial temporal lobe system damage on a visual search task. The main experimental question involved the use of 12 stimulus arrays that repeated on half of the experimental trials. If subjects were able to encode the specific arrays, then over the 480 experimental trials, performance in locating the target should have become faster (because it always appeared in the same place in each of those 12 arrays). Results showed that both groups improved in overall visual search performance. However, only the normal subjects showed faster performance for repeated arrays after practice. Thus, what the authors call "contextual" learning in this paradigm appears to be impaired in amnesics, who can perform other implicit and perceptual learning tasks. Such results support neither a unitary notion of implicit learning nor an identification of perceptual learning with implicit (or explicit) learning.

PERCEPTUAL LEARNING IN HIGH-LEVEL PERCEPTION AND VISUAL COGNITION

Although some treatments of perceptual learning focus on changes in basic sensory function, even as a matter of definition, some of the most interesting and exciting phenomena and implications of perceptual learning involve relatively high-level information and tasks. These also pose some of the greatest challenges for understanding the processes and mechanisms involved.

Chess

One well studied example is expertise in chess. In 1997 the best human chess player, Gary Kasparov, defeated the best chess-playing computer, Deep Blue, in a 12-game match. There were some differences in the way the human and machine played. Deep Blue searched broadly and deeply through the space of possible moves and sequences at a rate of about 125 million moves per second. Skilled human players examine a smaller number of moves: about 4 per turn, with each followed about 4 plies deep (a ply is a pair of turns by white and black).

Given this difference in the scope of search, how could the human match the computer? The answer lies in human abilities to extract patterns from the board. These abilities were studied by DeGroot (1965, 1966), who tested both chess masters and less skilled players. Players at different levels differed not in terms of conceptual knowledge, search heuristics, or number of possible moves considered, but in their ability to encode and reconstruct a chess position after seeing it briefly. Grandmasters were able to reconstruct nearly perfectly a 25-piece position with a single 5-s exposure. This ability decreased substantially for players below the master level. It might be conjectured that chess masters and grandmasters happen to be individuals with exceptional visual memories, but that turns out not to be the case. When chess masters and ordinary individuals were tested for board positions that are not meaningful chess games, they showed equivalent performance in reconstructing the positions. It appears that chess masters and average individuals have about the same short-term memory capacities (Chase & Simon, 1973).

Chase and Simon (1973) hypothesized that experience with chess changes perception such that experts pick up chunks—sets of pieces in particular relations to each other. Following de Groot's work, they used a method in which subjects reconstructed viewed chess positions. Masters' overall performance (pieces reconstructed per view, number of views needed to reconstruct the whole position) was better than the overall performance of A-level chess players, which in turn exceeded that of beginners. Chase and Simon also measured the latencies with which subjects placed the pieces. Their data indicated that several related pieces—chunks—were placed in quick succession, followed by a pause and another set of related pieces, and so on. Masters had larger chunks than middle-level or novice players.

Chase and Simon concluded that most of the differences in chess skill related to changes in the way information is picked up that have occurred through practice. Their description involves both the concepts of discovery and fluency that we described earlier and is worth quoting:

> One key to understanding chess mastery, then, seems to lie in immediate perceptual processing, for it is here that the game is structured, and it is here in the static analysis that the good moves are generated for subsequent processing. What was once accomplished by slow, conscious deductive reasoning is now arrived at by fast, unconscious perceptual processing. It is no mistake of language for the chess master to say that he "sees" the right move; and it is for good reason that students of complex problem solving are interested in perceptual processes. (1973)

Similar comments may apply to almost any domain in which humans attain high levels of expertise. I use chess as an example partly because the value of perceptual learning can be quantified. Subsequent to his 1997 victory, Kasparov lost a close match with an improved Deep Blue that examined over 200 million moves per second. We can estimate that this human's ability to extract important pattern structure in chess is worth upwards of 125 million moves per second in raw search—an awesome equivalent computing power.

The Word Superiority Effect

Master-level chess skill is the province of very few; highlighting it as an example of complex perceptual learning may make such learning appear to be exotic and remote from ordinary cognition. The impression would be misleading. As an illustration, consider a phenomenon shown by almost every skilled reader of English: the word superiority effect.

Late in the 1960s, researchers discovered a remarkable fact. Exposure time required to identify which of two letters was presented on a trial was lower if the letter appeared in the context of a word than if the letter appeared alone (Reicher, 1969; Wheeler, 1970; see Baron, 1978, for a thorough review). In other words, subjects could more easily distinguish between WORK and WORD than they could judge whether a K or a D had been presented on a given trial. Detailed studies of the word superiority effect have revealed several other intriguing aspects. For one, the effect is not explained merely by rapid processing of familiar words as units. In fact, a substantial effect occurs for pronounceable nonsense (E. Gibson, J. Gibson, Pick, & Osser, 1962). Baron and Thurston (1973), among others, found that pronounceable nonsense produced effects of the same magnitude as did actual words. These results indicate that general knowledge of some sort, perhaps the spelling or pronunciation patterns of English, facilitates letter recognition. One might predict that this kind of fluent processing of word-like strings would emerge from practice and skill at reading, and the prediction would be correct (Baron, 1978).

What kinds of mechanisms can explain the word superiority effect? Several detailed pos-

sibilities remain open (Baron, 1978; Noice & Hock, 1987). The effect may involve aspects of both discovery and fluency. Experience with English orthography seems to lead to detection of useful structures involving more than single letters. With practice these come to be rapidly extracted, so much so that the path from these higher structures to a decision about the presence of a particular letter ends up being faster than the time needed to detect the letter alone. The fact that the effect occurs for novel strings, not just for recurring words, suggests that the discovery of relations among letters generally characteristic of English spelling or pronunciation is involved. The fact that such units come to be processed rapidly and automatically provides a clue to the mechanisms of fluent reading. More specific understanding of what the relevant structures are and how they are learned remains to be discovered.

Unitization in Auditory and Speech Perception

Although this review has focused primarily on vision, processes of perceptual learning characterize information extraction in other sensory modalities as well. One conspicuous example, with some parallels to the word superiority effect in vision, is the learning of relationships in spoken words. Learning to segment the speech stream into words is a conceptually difficult problem, yet doing so is crucial for language learning (see Chap. 11, this volume). Saffran, Aslin, and Newport (1996) found evidence that learning can occur, even in 8-month-old infants, based on statistical relations among syllables. They used nonsense words comprised of three syllables and presented them in unbroken, monotone streams of 270 syllables per minute. Transitional probabilities between syllables X and Y (transitional probability = frequency of XY/frequency of X) were manipulated so that these were always high within words ($p = 1.0$ for syllables 1-2 and 2-3) and lower across "word" boundaries ($p = .33$). After familiarization for 2 min, infants were tested with sequences that either preserved words intact or changed the sequences of syllables. The showed a novelty response (longer attention) to the novel sequences. Follow-up studies (Aslin, Saffran, & Newport, 1998) showed that learning effects depend specifically on transition probabilities as opposed to more general frequency of exposure effects.

These findings provide dramatic evidence that forming of units based on statistical relations of sequential units is an early capacity of human learners, one that works in remarkably short periods of exposure. Is this capacity for early statistical learning specific to language learning? Saffran, Johnson, Aslin, and Newport (1999) explored this question by testing learning of statistical dependencies in tone sequences. Learning effects were similar, suggesting that these learning capacities may serve language acquisition but may also operate more generally.

Feature Conjunctions

A basic question in high-level perceptual learning is how new bases of response may be discovered. One natural source of such information is to make new combinations out of stimulus features that can already be encoded. Implicit in this idea is that perceptual learning may be something like a grammar—an open-ended class of new relations can be synthesized from a finite set of basic encodings and some means for combining these. Pursuing this general approach requires investigating both the vocabulary of basic encodings and the ways in which information can be combined.

Earlier I described some efforts to characterize features that are automatically encoded

in vision (e.g., Treisman & Gelade, 1980). Feature contrasts that are basic (automatically encoded) may be the ones that allow efficient (e.g., load-insensitive or parallel processing) performance on certain kinds of tasks, such as visual search. Conversely, information that is not basic may require selective attention or serial processing. One prediction from this perspective is that search for conjunctions of features must utilize attention and must be sequential (across items) in nature. Numerous experimental tests have supported this conjecture. For example, Treisman and Gelade (1980) found that extensive experience did not reduce set size effects when subjects searched for a blue O among blue Ts and red Os.

Yet the relatively fixed architecture that allows us to discover basic features (i.e., ease of processing features and difficulty with conjunctions) seems intuitively to be at variance with phenomena of perceptual learning and proficient performance. Various examples of expertise seem consistent with the idea that perceptual learning can lead to efficient processing of feature conjunctions. In chess, for example, knowing whether one piece is attacking another requires conjoining positions on the board, color, and shape. It is hard to imagine how grandmasters grasp whole board positions from a 2-s glance without being able to extract feature conjunctions efficiently, if not automatically.

The suspicion that feature conjunctions are learnable under some conditions is borne out by a small amount of experimental evidence. Shiffrin and Lightfoot (cited in Shiffrin, 1996) tested visual search for target patterns defined by conjunctions of spatially separated line segments and found that search slopes (average response time per element in the search arrays) decreased substantially with practice. Wang, Cavanagh, and Green (1994) found popout effects with the characters N or Z, shown in an array of backward Ns or Zs. The target was rapidly detected with little effect of the array size (number of distractors). The converse search task—searching for a backward N or Z in an array of Ns or Zs showed clear increases in response time with number of distractors. It appears that distractors can be rejected in parallel when these are highly familiar characters. The asymmetry in search performance suggests that the conjunctions of the several edges in the familiar characters have become encoded as unitary features (at least for purposes of rapid rejection in search).

Artificial Grammar Learning

Reber developed an important paradigm for testing the learning of structure: artificial grammars (Reber, 1967; for a review, see Reber, 1993). In his paradigm, letter strings were generated based on a grammar expressed as a transition network: Possible elements of the grammar (letters) were connected by directional paths, constraining the ways in which strings could be constructed. Although letter strings not permitted could look quite similar to those generated by a given grammar, evidence indicates that humans can, under certain conditions, learn the structural relations of the grammar allowing them to classify new strings correctly. Two issues that have been contested by researchers are whether the learning really consists of abstracting structure, as opposed to classifying new instances based on analogies to stored instances, and whether learning is implicit (i.e., without awareness). It appears that the learning can indeed consist of abstracting structure; it can also be based on analogies with stored instances, depending on the learning conditions (Reber & Allen, 1978). Evidence also clearly supports the idea that learning can be implicit. Structure can be detected from exposure to stimuli from a given generating grammar even when the structural relations are not directly relevant to an assigned task.

Implicit learning of artificial grammars is hardly ever discussed as an example of perceptual learning. Perhaps perceptual learning is too often interpreted as sensory learning (e.g., dealing with elementary sensory dimensions such as color) as opposed to the learning of structure in the input. Perhaps, because of their connection to linguistic material, artificial grammars may be thought of as too symbolic or abstract for perceptual learning. (For a discussion of these issues in the context of language acquisition, see Chap. 11, this volume). Recalling our earlier discussion of definitions, it is plausible to consider learning perceptual if it makes use of information in the stimulus. Structural relations in letter strings are fair game; if the learning arrives at an economical description (a grammar, for instance), that result might be better interpreted as indicating the nature of perceptual learning rather than indicating that the task is nonperceptual. Of course, some symbolic learning cannot be perceptual if the relevant information is not available in the stimulus. For example, in trigonometry one can learn from looking at graphs what a cosine function looks like, but one could not learn from looking that the function is ordinarily defined by a construction involving a triangle. In work with artificial grammars, there does not seem to be an extrastimulus component of this sort (i.e., the bases for learning are relations available in the stimuli). In a similar manner, although words have a primarily symbolic function, the fact that pronounceable nonsense strings show the "word" superiority effect implicates processes that pick up on stimulus relationships apart from the symbolic meaning in these kinds of representations. Integrating findings from implicit learning tasks used by cognitive psychologists with those in more commonly designated perceptual learning tasks may reveal commonalities and insights for modeling of processes that extract stimulus structure.

Object Recognition

Some evidence suggests that learning processes may specially engage object-specific representations. Furmanski and Engel (2000) measured exposure durations required for subjects to name low-contrast, gray-scale images of 60 common objects. Exposure durations needed to obtain 63% accuracy decreased 20% to 25% across five days of training. Transfer tests with a new object set showed partial transfer, indicating that effects involved both some generalizable learning and some specific component. A follow-up experiment indicated that learning for trained objects was fully maintained when half of them were mixed with an equal number of new object displays. Moreover, changes in size did not disrupt learning effects. These results differ from what would be predicted if subjects had learned primarily distinguishing features within the training set. The reason is that relevant contrasts for distinguishing objects should vary for different object sets. Results of this type suggest that perceptual learning may involve specific object descriptions as well as distinguishing features.

Perceptual Learning of Abstract Relations

An important characteristic of human perceptual learning is that it can involve abstract relations. Such an idea is consistent with theories of perception that emphasize abstract or higher order relationships (J. Gibson, 1979; Koffka, 1935) and the idea that perception produces abstract descriptions of reality (Marr, 1982), that is, descriptions of physical objects, shapes, spatial relations, and events, rather than, for instance, records of visual sensations. The idea that perceptual learning involves abstract relations is thus connected to the idea that perception itself involves abstract information and output.

What does it mean for perceptual learning to be abstract? It may help to provide a working definition, or at least a clear example, of what is abstract. Abstract information is information that necessarily involves *relations* among certain inputs, rather than collections of the inputs themselves. These ideas were central in Gestalt psychology (e.g., Koffka, 1935; Wertheimer, 1923). Their example of a melody serves as well today. Suppose you hear a melody and learn to recognize it. What is it that you have learned? At a concrete sensory level, the melody consists of a sequence of certain particular frequencies of sound. For most human listeners, however, learning the melody will not involve retaining the particular frequencies (or more properly, the sensed pitches corresponding to those frequencies). If you hear the same melody a day later, this time transposed into a different key, you will recognize it as the same melody. Your encoding of the melody involves *relations* among the pitches, not the particular pitches themselves. We often hear this fact mentioned in a disparaging light, namely, that few humans have "perfect pitch." In fact, the example makes a marvelous point about ordinary perceptual learning. The extraction and encoding of relations in the stimulus is fundamental. (Of course, musicians with perfect pitch are still better off in that they undoubtedly encode relations as well as particular pitches.)

The Gestalt psychologists argued that this response to patterns, rather than to concrete sensory elements, is pervasive in perception. In attaining the most important and behaviorally relevant descriptions of our environment, encoding relations is more crucial than is encoding sensory particulars (J. Gibson, 1979; Koffka, 1935; von Hornbostel, 1927). Whether this holds true depends on the task and environment, of course.

That encoding of abstract relations is a basic characteristic of human perceptual learning is suggested by recent research with human infants. Marcus, Vijayan, Bandi Rao, and Vishton (1999) familiarized 7-month-old infants with syllable sequences in which the first and last elements matched, such as "li na li" or "ga ti ga." Afterwards, infants showed a novelty response (longer attention) to a new string such as "wo fe fe" but showed less attention to a new string that fit the abstract pattern of earlier items, such as "wo fe wo." Similar results have been obtained in somewhat older infants (Gomez & Gerken, 1999). These findings indicate an early capacity for learning of abstract relationships. It is possible that these results are special in that they involve speech stimuli (Saffran & Griepentrog, 2001).

Mechanisms of Abstract Perceptual Learning

For a number of learning phenomena involving basic sensory dimensions, we considered how perceptual templates may be refined through practice. In a two-choice orientation discrimination, for example, the "template" for each orientation may consist of responses from a set of analyzers (e.g., orientation-sensitive units spanning some range of orientations, spatial frequencies, and positions). In a network-style learning model, these input units may be connected, perhaps through a middle layer of "hidden" units, with identification responses. Learning consists of the strengthening of weights of the most relevant analyzers with particular responses. This type of model is consistent with a wide range of results in perceptual learning (e.g., Dosher & Lu, 1999; Fahle et al., 1992; Goldstone, 1997). Such models are concrete in the sense that the output responses are determined by weighted combinations of the elements of the input vectors, consisting of the responses of analyzers at some point in the sensory pathway (e.g., V1 cells in the orientation example).

These concrete models are inadequate to explain more abstract examples of perceptual learning. Consider a simple example. In a con-

cept learning experiment you are given the task of learning to classify letter strings as to whether they are in category A. You are told that the strings "VXV" and "DLD" are in the category. Additionally, you are told that the strings "ABC" and "MRH" are not in category A. Now, suppose you are tested with the string "KSK." Is this string in category A? In the many times I have done this demonstration, I have yet to encounter anyone who did not answer "yes" with high confidence.

There are several important implications of this and similar examples. First, humans readily discover structure in these items. Second, the structure is abstract. The classification of a novel item "KSK" does not match any of the training items in terms of the specific letters at each position. Rather, the learner apprehends a higher order structure: the relation that the first and last elements of the strings in category A are identical.

Standard neural network models are concrete in a way that makes them incapable of this kind of learning. Such a model would have an input layer, possibly one or more hidden layers, and an output layer. The nodes in each layer would be connected to all those in the prior and succeeding layers. Learning would change the weights of these connections between layers, such that certain inputs would lead to certain outputs. For our example, the input layer might have 26 possible nodes to be activated in position one of a three-letter string; there would also be 26 possible input activations for the middle position and 26 for the last position. Training on an example such as "DLD" would strengthen the connections between the letter D in first position and the output response "category A." The L and final D in their respective positions would also be weighted toward this categorization response.

The abstraction problem is simply that after training with the examples given, the network would know nothing about the test string

"KSK." The reason is that not one of those input letters had previously appeared in those positions (or any positions, in our example).

In an analysis of a related problem—a device that takes strings such as "1010" as inputs and gives an identical output ("1010" in this case)—Marcus (2001) concluded that they are not solvable by conventional statistical learning methods. Nonetheless, only a few examples are sufficient to allow human learners to learn this input-output rule.

Discovery of abstract, higher order relations seems to be a natural and important feature of human perceptual learning. A key challenge is to characterize the processes and mechanisms of this kind of perceptual learning. These problems are very general. They apply to the learning of shapes and relations in vision, to melodies, phonemes, and words in audition, and to a great many other things.

There has not been much work on learning abstract relations. One possibility is that such learning combines statistical learning processes with early extraction of relational information. Kellman et al., (1999) demonstrated the plausibility of such an approach in modeling the learning of shape categories for quadrilateral figures (e.g., square, rhombus, parallelogram, trapezoid). They assumed that these categorizations are not built into visual processors but must be learnable at least via supervised learning (as, e.g., when a child sees someone point to certain objects in the world and hears a word such as "square"). Learning, moreover, must draw only on inputs that are *generic,* that is, that are known or can be assumed to be available from ordinary visual processing. Specifically, they assumed that the visual system (a) can locate vertices or points of very high edge curvature in a figure, (b) can encode intervertex distances on the retina (or real distances when adequate information for size constancy is present), and (c) that the learning system contains operators that can compare ex-

tents for equality (and produce a graded response as departures from equality—e.g., of two extents—increase). Simulations showed that the model could learn almost all of the planar shape names tested from one or two examples. The network generalized its classifications to novel exemplars that were rotated, scaled, or distorted versions of the training exemplars. It also handled certain distortions in ways similar to human classifiers (e.g., tolerance for applying a term such as "square" to shapes with minor deviations given by unequal sides or misplacement of one vertex). Both the domain and the model are simplified in a number of respects, but this general approach of combining early relational recoding of inputs with later stages of connectionist learning processes may hold a great deal of promise.

CONDITIONS AFFECTING PERCEPTUAL LEARNING

Research to date has yielded useful clues about the processes and mechanisms of perceptual learning, but we by no means have a thorough understanding. Even in the absence of a complete understanding of process, however, we can say a fair amount about the conditions that lead to perceptual learning.

Contrast

Perceptual learning is facilitated by comparison of positive and negative instances of some category, or by contrasting instances that fit into differing categories. In E. Gibson's (1969) view, contrast is the very essence of this kind of learning: What is learned are distinguishing features—those attributes that govern the classifications that are important to the task. Hence, perceptual learning is often described as differentiation learning. The notion that differentiation learning is facilitated by presentation of negative instances is at least as old as Pavlov, who wrote,

> The question can now be discussed as to how the specialization of the conditioned reflex, or, in other words, the discrimination of external agencies, arises. Formerly we were inclined to think that this effect could be obtained by two different methods: the first method consisted in repeating the definite conditioned stimulus a great many times always accompanied by reinforcement, and the second method consisted in contrasting the single definite conditioned stimulus, which was always accompanied by reinforcement, with different neighboring stimuli which were never reinforced. At present, however, we are inclined to regard this second method as more probably the only efficacious one, since it was observed that no absolute differentiation was ever obtained by use of the first method, even though the stimulus was repeated with reinforcement over a thousand times. On the other hand, it was found that contrast by even a single unreinforced application of an allied stimulus, or by a number of single unreinforced applications of different members of a series of allied stimuli at infrequent intervals of days or weeks, led to a rapid development of differentiation. (Pavlov (1927), p. 117, cited in E. Gibson, 1969, p. 117).

One way of thinking about the effects of contrast is to view perceptual learning as a filtering process. In a given task a wealth of information may be available. Learning consists of selecting those features or relationships that are crucial for some classification (E. Gibson, 1969). In this process, those stimulus attributes that do not govern the classification must be rejected or filtered out. The presentation of negative instances (or members of an alternate category) allows decorrelation of the irrelevant attributes with the classification being made.

Task Difficulty

Specificity of perceptual learning depends on task difficulty in training. Ahissar and Hochstein (1997) undertook a systematic approach to this issue. The researchers used a visual search task in which subjects had to decide whether a line having a unique orientation appeared in an array of uniformly oriented background lines. Two dimensions of difficulty were manipulated. One was positional uncertainty: The unique orientation could occur anywhere in the array on positive trials, or, in an easier version, it could occur in only one of two locations in the array (indicated at the start of the experiment). The other dimension was the difference in orientation between the target and background lines; differences of 16, 30, and 90 deg were used. Figure 7.5 shows the conditions and data.

The task was considered to be easy either if the orientation difference was 90 deg or if the difference was 30 deg but targets were limited to two positions. Similarly, the task was considered difficult for 30-deg differences with all positions possible or for 16-deg differences and two possible positions.

These categorizations showed utility in predicting transfer data. Transfer to new orientations and new retinal positions was substantial for subjects in the easy conditions, but transfer was minimal for subjects trained in difficult conditions.

Learning easy examples first may lead not only to better transfer but also to better learning of hard cases. In fact, a single clear or easy trial can lead to rapid improvement in classification performance on difficult problems, a result termed the *Eureka effect* by Ahissar and Hochstein (1997). These investigators suggested that the effect indicates an interaction between high- and low-level mechanisms, with the high-level mechanisms directing the search for distinguishing information, followed by the attunement and selection of relevant low-level analyzers.

The connection between difficulty of training problems and specificity of learning has

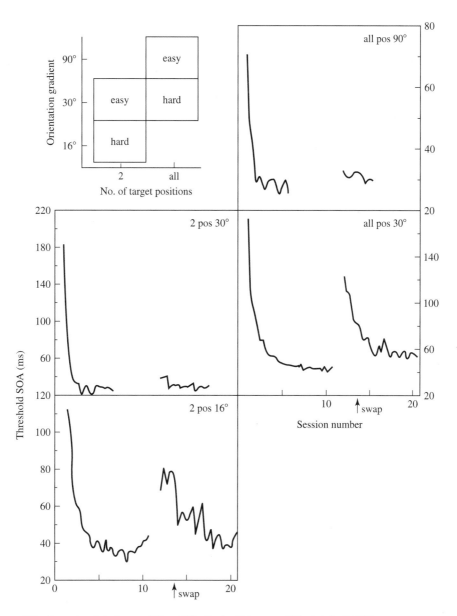

Figure 7.5   Learning data by condition difficulty in Ahissar and Hochstein (1999).
NOTE: SOA: Stimulus onset asynchrony. See text for additional details.
SOURCE: Ahissar and Hochstein (1999). Reprinted with permission.

been found in other learning tasks, for example, in Liu's (1999) studies of motion discrimination. Several investigators (Liu & Weinshall, 2000; Nakayama, Rubin, & Shapley, 1997), however, have suggested interpretations of difficulty effects—and rapid learning from clear examples—that do not involve communication between higher strategic processes and lower level analyzers. Instead, they propose that difficulty effects may reflect a single process. Recall that Liu and Weinshall (2000) found that learning a difficult motion discrimination did not transfer immediately to an orthogonal direction of motion, but it improved the learning rate for the second discrimination. Liu and Weinshall suggested that these results, and the results showing transfer across directions of easier discriminations, can be explained without invoking processes at multiple levels. They proposed that stimuli in a discrimination learning task initially activate populations of informative and uninformative analyzers. Because of computational capacity limits, on each trial the learning system samples only a subset of analyzers to assess their informativeness, an assumption proposed and supported in much earlier research (Trabasso & Bower, 1968). Over trials, learning effects of two types occur. Not only are individual analyzers found to be informative or uninformative, but also *classes* of analyzers are assessed. Outputs of analyzers signaling particular spatial orientations, for example, may be irrelevant to a task in which motion direction must be discriminated.

These assumptions can be used to explain different kinds of learning and transfer effects (Weinshall & Liu, 2000). For difficult discriminations, only a few analyzers have high sensitivity for doing the task, and it takes longer to find these than in easy discriminations, in which many analyzers may have high sensitivity. Also, in the learning of one task, whole classes of analyzers may be discovered to be uninformative. Applying this logic to the transfer results for motion direction discrimination goes as follows. In learning the first problem, particular motion analyzers prove to be informative. These analyzers are not very helpful when a new direction of motion is tested. However, another effect of learning the first problem was that whole classes of analyzers (such as those for spatial orientation) have been learned to be uninformative. Therefore, particular members of such classes do not have to be sampled during the learning of

the second problem; hence the faster learning rate for the second problem.

Consolidation and Sleep

Some evidence suggests that perceptual learning effects do not take hold until a consolidation or sleep period occurs. Data from Karni and Sagi (1993) suggest that learning effects from a particular session reach their peak after a consolidation period of about 8 hr. Stickgold, LaTanya, and Hobson (2000) used the same discrimination task as Karni and Sagi and found that maximal improvement occurred when subjects were tested 48 hr to 96 hr after a learning session. Their data also suggested the importance of sleep in consolidating perceptual learning effects. When subjects were deprived of sleep for 30 hr after the learning session, and then given two full nights of sleep recovery, they showed no improvement from initial levels.

The consolidation hypothesis has not been established beyond doubt. One alternative is that learning effects at the end of a learning session may be masked by fatigue effects. After a suitable interval, when fatigue effects have dissipated, learning effects are more visible (Shiu & Pashler, 1992).

Active Classification, Attention, and Effort

Studies in which the observer processes one stimulus dimension in an assigned task while stimulus variation on another dimension is simultaneously present find learning effects specific to the task-relevant dimension (Goldstone, 1994; Shiu & Pashler, 1992). Such results suggest the importance of attention in generating perceptual learning effects. Attentional effects were also suggested by Bennett and Westheimer (1991), who found no improvement in a grating acuity task tested in the fovea. One of their four subjects showed improvement for targets presented at 7.5 deg from the fovea, an effect they attributed to learning to make relatively large attentional shifts from the central visual field. Consistent with this idea, the reduction in threshold transferred fully from the horizontal training stimulus to a vertical stimulus. Unlike explanations invoking reweighting of low-level receptors, an attentional shift notion would predict transfer to a new orientation.

It is unfortunately difficult to untangle several conceptually different ideas here. One is that perceptual learning depends on attention. Another is that perceptual learning depends on the subject's active engagement in some kind of classification task. These possibilities may be hard to distinguish because any experimental manipulation that would involve assigning subjects an active task would also elicit their attention to the stimuli. The converse is easier to imagine: There are ways of arranging subjects' attention to stimuli without assigning a task. In some studies, mere exposure to certain stimulus variation during a task involving another stimulus dimension does not lead to learning (e.g., Shiu & Pashler, 1992). On the other hand, implicit learning of structure that is not specifically task-relevant is known to occur (e.g., Reber, 1993; Tolman, 1948). The inconsistency of results regarding learning from incidental exposure may be due to the possibility that carrying out some tasks involves active suppression of irrelevant information. In other words, learning incidentally while doing no task may be better than learning while doing some conflicting task. These issues of the roles of attention and assignment of active classification tasks in perceptual learning are ripe for further research.

Feedback

An intriguing characteristic of perceptual learning emphasized by E. Gibson (1969) is that in many cases it does not require feedback. Improved discrimination can come from mere exposure. In J. Gibson and Gibson's (1955) scribbles experiment (discussed earlier and shown in Figure 7.3), subjects judged whether a number of curved line patterns were the same or different from a sample pattern. If we describe the task as detecting differences, subjects initially made many errors that were misses (e.g., they labeled patterns that were physically different as "same"). Although no feedback was given, after several runs through the set of patterns, adult subjects achieved virtually perfect discrimination performance.

Models of statistical learning that work without feedback—unsupervised learning—may account for some aspects of exposure-based learning. In unsupervised schemes, the weights in a network change because of correlations in the inputs themselves (Hebbian learning), or they develop under certain constraints, such as the constraint that units in a hidden layer should be maximally uncorrelated with each other. A number of more sophisticated statistical techniques can be applied to unsupervised learning as well (for discussion of such methods applied to the problems of language acquisition, see Chap. 11, this volume).

Some studies indicate that perceptual learning of basic visual discriminations improves in similar fashion with and without feedback (Fahle & Edelman, 1993; Fahle et al., 1995; McKee & Westheimer, 1978). In Shiu and Pashler's (1992) study of learning in orientation discrimination, trial and block feedback (feedback only after each block of numerous trials) had similar effects on learning. A condition with no feedback showed smaller learning effects. Block feedback has also proved effective in other studies of perceptual learning (Herzog & Fahle, 1998; Kellman & Kaiser, 1994).

Herzog and Fahle (1998) pointed out that the effectiveness of block feedback, as well as a number of other commonly observed features of perceptual learning, are incompatible with conventional neural network architectures. They proposed a number of higher level (recurrent) mechanisms that guide learning via the allocation of attention and the use of feedback to modulate learning rates. One motivation for these suggestions consists of quantitative arguments indicating that learning occurs too efficiently to involve merely the gradual adjustment of weights in a network-style model. Higher level mechanisms that are sensitive to performance level and that perhaps incorporate knowledge of connectivity patterns in the nervous system may be implicated (Herzog & Fahle, 1998).

APPLICATIONS OF PERCEPTUAL LEARNING

There are numerous reasons to be interested in perceptual learning. As a somewhat neglected topic, its study adds new dimensionality to our ideas about learning. Many contemporary researchers view it, justifiably, as a window into processes of plasticity in the nervous system. As has been evident in this review, it is also a topic that connects various levels of information processing and neural activity in interesting and revealing ways.

Another reason for interest in perceptual learning is that it has great practical import. It is likely that changes in the way information is picked up—both in terms of discovery and fluency—form some of the most important foundations of human expertise. In an early section of her 1969 book, Eleanor Gibson included a section entitled "Perceptual Learning in Industry and Defense." Her examples included not only the grading of cheese and cloth, sexing of chicks, and wine tasting, but also some higher level skills such as landing an aircraft, interpreting maps and infrared photographs, and radiological diagnosis.

Although the grading of products, like William James' earlier comments about experts in Madeira and wheat, are not inconsequential examples, Gibson's other examples are perhaps of greater interest in indicating that the scope of perceptual learning applications may extend further into complex cognitive tasks than has generally been realized. Perceptual learning may underwrite abilities to discover complex, relational structures and become fluent in using them. The example of grandmasters in chess is instructive, as we saw. As argued by deGroot and by Chase and Simon, the most important distinguishing component of exceptional chess-playing ability involves learned skills for extracting patterns. It is not far-fetched to believe that such skills may be a major contributor also to the expertise of radiologists, pilots, financial analysts, mathematicians, and scientists.

Cognitive scientists and psychologists, however, have done much more to document the performance of experts than to apply perceptual learning concepts to develop expertise. In educational settings, one finds strong emphases on declarative facts and concepts and little attention to the development of expert apprehension of structure. One explanation may be the lack of any obvious method for bringing about expert information-extraction skills. For most advanced skills, from reading a financial spreadsheet to interpreting aircraft instruments, there are accepted methods of conveying facts and concepts, but the expert's intuitions about patterns and structure are believed to arise mysteriously from time and experience.

The view is too limited, however. Not only is the passage of time a suspect explanatory notion for perceptual skill, but also—strikingly—researchers have routinely been able to improve perceptual classifications in relatively brief laboratory experiments. As we have seen, these investigations have been carried out to address basic scientific questions, but they give hints as to methods by which advanced skills might be directly trained.

In recent years there have been attempts to apply perceptual learning methods to both basic and complex skills. Like experimental procedures, these ordinarily use training situations in which the subject receives many short classification trials. Successful efforts have been made to adapt auditory discrimination paradigms to address speech and language difficulties (Merzenich et al., 1996; Tallal, Merzenich, Miller, & Jenkins, 1998). For example, Tallal et al. reported that auditory discrimination training in language learning impaired children, using specially enhanced and extended speech signals, improved not only auditory discrimination performance but speech and language comprehension as well. Similar methods may be applied also to complex visual displays. Kellman and Kaiser (1994) designed perceptual learning methods to study pilots' classification of aircraft attitude (e.g., climbing, turning) from primary attitude displays (used by pilots to fly in instrument flight conditions). They found that an hour of training allowed novices to process displays as quickly and accurately as did civil aviators averaging 1,000 hours of flight time. Experienced pilots also showed substantial gains, paring 60% off their response times required for accurate classification. Studies of applications to the learning of structure in mathematics and science domains, such as the mapping between graphs and equations, apprehending molecular structure in chemistry, have also yielded successful results (Silva & Kellman, 1999; Wise, Kubose, Chang, Russell, & Kellman, 2000).

Efforts to improve directly the discovery of structure and its fluent processing are relatively new in educational and training contexts. Available evidence suggests that these have substantial promise, for both basic sensory discriminations and for processing of structure in complex and abstract cognitive domains. Much remains to be learned about the conditions that optimize learning, however. A number of lines of research have already suggested some of the conditions that affect the amount and durability of learning. To some extent, these can be investigated even in the absence of precise process models of perceptual learning. Understanding the variables that affect learning, of course, will have benefits beyond the practical. Clear accounts of when and how much learning occurs may be among the most important contributors to efforts to develop better models of process and mechanism.

SUMMARY

It has been more than 100 years since William James called attention to the phenomena of perceptual learning and over 30 years since the publication of Eleanor Gibson's synthesis of the field. What have we learned?

In several respects, progress is evident. More exacting tests of what changes in perceptual learning have been possible through the application of signal detection methods. Our tool kit of explanatory concepts has expanded and has also become more detailed in the form of computational modeling of notions such as analyzer weighting, differentiation, and unitization. At the level of biological mechanism, research is revealing types of plasticity that seem likely to relate to the implementation of perceptual learning processes in the brain.

However, most of these developments serve to sharpen our questions and to indicate how much remains to be learned. Accordingly, our answers to key questions, a few of which follow, must be necessarily provisional.

Is Perceptual Learning a Separable Form of Learning?

The evidence is persuasive that the general idea of improvements in the pickup of information deserves its own place among concepts of learning. Clearly, processes of information pickup do change with experience, and the representations that they produce change as well. These phenomena are not encompassed by other learning concepts, and their common involvement with information extraction allows them to form a natural grouping. At the margins are phenomena that may involve other forms of learning, such as associative or procedural learning. However, at the same margins, some phenomena thought to consist of the learning of procedures or connections between stimuli and responses no doubt involve changes in the way information is picked up and represented.

That said, clarification of the relationship between perceptual learning and other taxonomic categories of learning remains a high priority. The ways in which concepts such as implicit learning and automaticity crosscut several different forms of learning should be explored. Likewise, the relations among associative, procedural, and perceptual learning need to be further elaborated.

Is There One Process of Perceptual Learning, or Many?

The evidence seems clear that several processes are involved in perceptual learning. For example, the distinction between discovery and fluency processes may mark a difference in the kinds of improvement in perception. Discovering new bases of response may occur through the weighting of analyzers, the synthesis of new relation detectors, or the sampling of many information sources to locate the relevant ones. In all of these processes, changes occur in the content that is

extracted. Improvements in fluency, on the other hand, can occur without changes in what is extracted; practice in particular information pickup tasks seems to increase speed and decrease attentional load and effort. Possible mechanisms include automaticity and unitization. At the borderline between discovery and fluency processes is the possibility that speed increases, not because of more rapid linking of existing representations but because of the discovery of higher order invariants that make classification more efficient. Distinguishing the operation of these processes is an important priority for research.

Does Perceptual Learning Involve a Single Level in the Nervous System, or Multiple Levels?

Both the existence of multiple processes in perceptual learning and our review of particular phenomena suggest that adaptive improvement in perceptual tasks involves multiple levels of neural activity. Despite the lack of consistency across tasks and procedures, in visual tasks with humans the existence of results indicating specificity of learning to a single eye, stimulus value, or retinal location strongly suggests involvement of cells at relatively early locations in the cortical visual streams. Physiological measurements of receptive fields in several senses and a variety of species directly implicate changes in other primary sensory cortices.

Meanwhile, a number of other findings indicate the involvement of higher level (including attentional and strategic) processes. In some paradigms, or with minor procedural changes from those showing specificity, learning does transfer: across eyes, across retinal positions, or across motion directions. Engagement of attention for a specific task affects learning, and initial presentation of easier examples facilitates it. Effects of trial-by-trial feedback do not indicate much about the locus of learning, but when block feedback produces effects on a par with trial feedback, the existence of higher level processes supervising and directing learning is intimated.

Finally, though not as often explored as yet by researchers, much of human perceptual learning involves abstract relationships. Little is known about the mechanisms of this sort of learning, but it cannot arise exclusively from modifications of receptive fields in primary sensory cortical areas. Attaining a computational and physiological account of high-level perceptual learning is among the many challenges remaining for researchers.

REFERENCES

Ahissar, M. (1999). Perceptual learning. *Current Directions in Psychological Science, 8*(4), 124–128.

Ahissar, M., & Hochstein, S. (1997). Task difficulty and learning specificity. *Nature, 387,* 401–406.

Aslin, R. N., Saffran, J. R., & Newport, E. L. (1998). Computation of conditional probability statistics by 8-month-old infants. *Psychological Science, 9*(4), 321–324.

Ball, K., & Sekuler, R. (1982). A specific and enduring improvement in visual motion discrimination. *Science, 218,* 697–698

Baron, J. (1978). The word-superiority effect: Perceptual learning from reading. In W. K. Estes (Ed.), *Handbook of learning and cognitive processes.* Hillsdale, N.J.: Erlbaum.

Baron, J., & Thurston, I. (1973). An analysis of the word-superiority effect. *Cognitive Psychology, 4*(2), 207–228.

Beard, B. L., Levi, D. M., & Reich, L. N. (1995). Perceptual learning in parafoveal vision. *Vision Research, 35*(12), 1679–1690.

Bedford, F. L. (1989). Constraints on learning new mappings between perceptual dimensions. *Journal of Experimental Psychology: Human Perception & Performance, 15,* 232–248.

Bedford, F. L. (1995). Constraints on perceptual learning: Objects and dimensions. *Cognition, 54,* 253–297.

Bennett, R. G., & Westheimer, G. (1991). The effect of training on visual alignment discrimination and grating resolution. *Perception & Psychophysics, 49*(6), 541–546.

Bryan, W. L., & Harter, N. (1899). Studies in the physiology and psychology of the telegraphic language. *Psychological Review, 6*(4), 345–375.

Buonomano, D. V., & Merzenich, M. M. (1998). Cortical plasticity: From synapses to maps. *Annual Review of Neuroscience, 21,* 149–186.

Chase, W. G., & Simon, H. A. (1973). Perception in chess. *Cognitive Psychology, 4*(1), 55–81.

Choplin, J., Huttenlocher, J., & Kellman, P. (2001, May). Perceptual discrimination and memory. Paper presented at the First Annual Meeting of the Vision Sciences Society, Sarasota, FL.

Chun, M. M., & Phelps, E. A. (1999). Memory deficits for implicit contextual information in amnesic subjects with hippocampal damage [see comments]. *Nature Neuroscience, 2*(9), 844–847.

Das, A., & Gilbert, C. D. (1995) Long-range horizontal connections and their role in cortical reorganization revealed by optical recording of cat primary visual cortex. *Nature, 375*(6534), 780–784.

deGroot, A. D. (1965). *Thought and choice in chess.* The Hague, Netherlands: Mouton.

deGroot, A. D. (1966). Perception and memory vs. thought: Some old ideas and recent findings. In B. Kleinmuntz (Ed.), *Problem solving* (pp. 19–50). New York: Wiley.

Dosher, B. A., & Lu, Z.-L. (1999). Mechanisms of perceptual learning. *Vision Research, 39,* 3197–3221.

Edeline, J. M. (1999). Learning-induced physiological plasticity in the thalamo-cortical sensory systems: A critical evaluation of receptive field plasticity, map changes and their potential mechanisms. *Progress in Neurobiology, 57*(2), 165–224.

Edeline, J. M., & Weinberger, N. M. (1993). Receptive field plasticity in the auditory cortex during frequency discrimination training: Selective retuning independent of task difficulty. *Behavioral Neuroscience, 107*(1), 82–103.

Fahle, M. (1994). Human pattern recognition: Parallel processing and perceptual learning. *Perception, 23*(4), 411–427.

Fahle, M. (1995). Perception of oppositely moving verniers and spatio-temporal interpolation. *Vision Research, 35*(7), 925–937.

Fahle, M., & Edelman, S. (1993). Long-term learning in vernier acuity: Effects of stimulus orientation, range and of feedback. *Vision Research, 33*(3), 397–412.

Fahle, M., Edelman, S., & Poggio, T. (1995). Fast perceptual learning in hyperacuity. *Vision Research, 35*(21), 3003–3013.

Fendick, M., & Westheimer, G. (1983). Effects of practice and the separation of test targets on foveal and peripheral stereoacuity. *Vision Research, 23*(2), 145–150.

Fiorentini, A., & Berardi, N. (1981). Learning in grating waveform discrimination: Specificity for orientation and spatial frequency. *Vision Research 21,* 1149–1158.

Frégnac, Y., Shulz, D., Thorpe, S., & Bienenstock, E. (1988). A cellular analogue of visual cortical plasticity. *Nature, 333*(6171), 367–370.

Furmanski, C. S., & Engel, S. A. (2000). Perceptual learning in object recognition: Object specificity and size invariance. *Vision Research, 40*(5), 473–484.

Gibson, E. J. (1969). *Principles of perceptual learning and development.* New York: Appleton-Century-Crofts.

Gibson, E. J., Gibson, J. J., Pick, A. D., & Osser, H. A. (1962). A developmental study of the discrimination of letter-like forms. *Journal of Comparative & Physiological Psychology, 55*(6), 897–906.

Gibson, J. (1966). *The senses considered as perceptual systems.* Boston: Houghton Mifflin.

Gibson, J. (1979). *The ecological approach to vision perception.* Boston: Houghton Mifflin.

Gibson, J. J., & Gibson, E. J. (1955). Perceptual learning: Differentiation or enrichment? *Psychological Review, 62,* 32–41.

Gold, J., Bennett, P. J., & Sekuler, A. B. (1999). Signal but not noise changes with perceptual learning. *Nature, 402*(11), 176–178.

Goldstone, R. L. (1994). Influences of categorization on perceptual discrimination. *Journal of Experimental Psychology: General, 123*(2), 178–200.

Goldstone, R. L. (1998). Perceptual learning. *Annual Review of Psychology, 49,* 585–612.

Goldstone, R. L. (2000). Unitization during category learning. *Journal of Experimental Psychology: Human Perception & Performance, 26*(1), 86–112.

Gomez, R. L., & Gerken, L. (1999). Artificial grammar learning by 1-year-olds leads to specific and abstract knowledge. *Cognition, 70*(2), 109–135.

Hall, G. (1991). *Perceptual and associative learning.* Oxford: Clarendon Press.

Harris, C. S. (1965). Perceptual adaptation to inverted, reversed and displaced vision. *Psychological Review, 72,* 419–444.

Herzog, M. H., & Fahle, M. (1998). Modeling perceptual learning: Difficulties and how they can be overcome. *Biological Cybernetics, 78*(2), 107–117.

Hornbostel, E. M. von. (1927). The unity of the senses (E. Koffka & W. Vinton, Trans.). *Psyche, 7*(28), 83–89.

James, W. (1950). *The principles of psychology.* New York: Dover Publications. (Original work published 1890)

Karni A., & Sagi, D. (1991). Where practice makes perfect in texture discrimination: Evidence for primary visual cortex plasticity. *Proceedings of the National Academy of Sciences, USA, 88,* 4966–4970.

Karni, A., & Sagi, D. (1993). The time course of learning a visual skill. *Nature, 365*(6443), 250–252.

Keller, F. S. (1958). The phantom plateau. *Journal of the Experimental Analysis of Behavior. 1,* 1–13.

Kellman, P. J., Arterberry, & M. E. (1998*). The cradle of knowledge: Development of perception in infancy.* Cambridge, MA: MIT Press.

Kellman, P. J., Burke, T., & Hummel, J. (1999). Modelling perceptual learning of abstract invariants. In M. Hahn & S. C. Stoness (Eds.), *Proceedings of the Twenty-First Annual Conference of the Cognitive Science Society* (pp. 264–269). Mahwah, NJ: Erlbaum.

Kellman, P. J., & Kaiser, M. K. (1994). Perceptual learning modules in flight training. *Proceedings of the 38th Annual Meeting of the Human Factors and Ergonomics Society* (pp. 1183–1187). Santa Monica, CA: Human Factors and Ergonomics Society.

Knudsen, E. I., & Knudsen, P. F. (1985). Vision guides the adjustment of auditory localization in young barn owls. *Science, 230*(4725), 545–548.

Koffka, K. (1935). *Principles of Gestalt psychology.* New York: Harcourt, Brace.

Kohler, Ivo. (1964). *The formation and transformation of the perceptual world.* New York: International Universities Press.

LaBerge, D. (1973). Attention and the measurement of perceptual learning. *Memory & Cognition, 1*(3), 268–276.

Lawrence, D. H. (1949). Acquired distinctiveness of cues, I: Transfer between discriminations on the basis of familiarity with the stimulus. *Journal of Experimental Psychology, 39,* 770–784.

Liu, Z. (1999). Perceptual learning in motion discriminatioin that generalizes across motion directions. *Proceedings of the National Academy of Sciences, USA, 96*(24), 14085–14087.

Liu, Z., & Weinshall, D. (2000). Mechanisms of generalization in perceptual learning. *Vision Research, 40*(1), 97–109.

Locke, John. (1857). *An essay on human understanding.* Philadelphia: Hayes & Zell.

Logothetis, N. K., Pauls, J., & Poggio, T. (1995). Shape representation in the inferior temporal cortex of monkeys. *Current Biology, 5*(5), 552–563.

Marcus, G. F. (2001). *The algebraic mind.* Cambridge, MA: MIT Press.

Marcus, G. F., Vijayan, S., Bandi Rao, S., & Vishton, P. M. (1999). Rule learning by seven-month-old infants. *Science, 283*(5398), 77–80.

Marr, D. (1982). *Vision.* San Francisco: W. H. Freeman.

McKee, S. P., & Westheimer, G. (1978). Improvement in vernier acuity with practice. *Perception & Psychophysics, 24*(3), 258–262.

McLean, J., & Palmer, L. A. (1998). Plasticity of neuronal response properties in adult cat striate cortex. *Visual Neuroscience, 15*(1), 177–196.

Merzenich, M. M., Jenkins, W. M., Johnston, P., Schreiner, C., Miller, S., & Tallal, P. (1996). Temporal processing deficits of language-learning impaired children ameliorated by training. *Science, 271*(5245), 77–81.

Mozer, M. C. (1991). *The perception of multiple objects: A connectionist approach.* Cambridge, MA: MIT Press.

Noice, H., & Hock, H. S. (1987). A word superiority effect with nonorthographic acronyms: Testing for unitizedvisual codes. *Perception and Psychophysics, 42*(5), 485–490.

Pavlov, I. P. (1927). *Conditioned reflexes: An investigation of the physiological activity of the cerebral cortex.* London: Oxford University Press.

Pettet, M. W., & Gilbert, C. D. (1992). Dynamic changes in receptive-field size in cat primary visual cortex. *Proceedings of the National Academy of Sciences, USA, 89*(17), 8366–8370.

Piaget, J. (1954). *The construction of reality in the child.* New York: Basic Books.

Pick, A. D. (1965). Improvement of visual and tactual form discrimination. *Journal of Experimental Psychology, 69*(4), 331–339.

Poggio, T., Fahle, M., & Edelman, S. (1992). Fast perceptual learning in visual hyperacuity. *Science, 256,* 1018–1021.

Posner, M. I., & Keele, S. W. (1967). Decay of visual information from a single letter. *Science, 158*(3797), 137–139.

Reber, A. S. (1967). Implicit learning of artificial grammars. *Journal of Verbal Learning & Verbal Behavior, 6*(6), 855–863.

Reber, A. S. (1993). *Implicit learning and tacit knowledge.* New York: Oxford University Press.

Reber, A. S., & Allen, R. (1978). Analogic and abstraction strategies in synthetic grammar learning: A functionalist interpretation. *Cognition,* *6*(3), 189–221.

Recanzone, G. H., Schreiner, C. E., & Merzenich, M. M. (1993). Plasticity in the frequency representation of primary auditory cortex following discrimination training in adult owl monkeys. *Journal of Neuroscience, 13*(1), 87–103.

Reicher, G. M. (1969). Perceptual recognition as a function of meaningfulness of stimulus material. *Journal of Experimental Psychology, 81*(2), 275–280.

Rubin, N., Nakayama, K., & Shapley, R. (1997). Abrupt learning and retinal size specificity in illusory-contour perception. *Current Biology, 7*(7), 461–467.

Saarinen J., & Levi, D. M. (1995). Perceptual learning in vernier acuity: What is learned? *Vision Research, 35,* 519–527.

Saffran, J. R., Aslin, R. N., & Newport, E. L. (1996). Statistical learning by 8-month-old infants [see comments]. *Science, 274*(5294), 1926–1928.

Saffran, J. R., & Griepentrog, G. J. (2001). Absolute pitch in infant auditory learning: Evidence for developmental reorganization. *Developmental Psychology, 37*(1), 74–85.

Saffran, J. R., Johnson, E. K., Aslin, R. N., & Newport, E. L. (1999). Statistical learning of tone sequences by human infants and adults. *Cognition, 70*(1), 27–52.

Salasoo, A., Shiffrin, R. M., & Feustel, T. C. (1985). Building permanent memory codes: Codification and repetition effects in word identification. *Journal of Experimental Psychology: General, 114*(1), 50–77.

Schneider, W., & Shiffrin, R. M. (1977). Controlled and automatic human information processing, I: Detection, search, and attention. *Psychological Review. 84*(1), 1–66.

Schoups, A. A., & Orban, G. A. (1996). Interocular transfer in perceptual learning of a pop-out discrimination task. *Proceedings of the National Academy of Sciences, USA, 93,* 7358–7362.

Shiffrin, R. M. (1996). Laboratory experimentation on the genesis of expertise. In K. A. Er-

icsson (Ed.), *The road to excellence: The acquisition of expert performance in the arts and sciences, sports, and games.* Hillsdale, NJ: Erlbaum.

Shiffrin, R. M., & Schneider, W. (1977). Controlled and automatic human information processing, II: Perceptual learning, automatic attending and a general theory. *Psychological Review, 84,* 7, 127–190.

Shiu, L., & Pashler, H. (1992). Improvement in line orientation discrimination is retinally local but dependent on cognitive set. *Perception & Psychophysics, 52,* 582–588.

Silva, A., & Kellman, P. J. (1999). Perceptual learning in mathematics: The algebra-geometry connection. In M. Hahn & S. C. Stoness (Eds.), *Proceedings of the Twenty First Annual Conference of the Cognitive Science Society,* Mahwah, NJ: Erlbaum.

Sireteanu R., & Rettenbach R. (1995). Perceptual learning in visual search: Fast, enduring, but nonspecific. *Vision Research, 35,* 2037–2043.

Stickgold, R., LaTanya, J., & Hobson, J. A. (2000). Visual discrimination learning requires sleep after training. *Nature Neuroscience, 3*(12), 1237–1238.

Tallal, P., Merzenich, M., Miller, S., & Jenkins, W. (1998). Language learning impairment: Integrating research and remediation. *Scandinavian Journal of Psychology, 39*(3), 197–199.

Titchener, E. B. (1896). *An outline of psychology.* New York: Macmillan.

Tolman, E. C. (1948). Cognitive maps in rats and men. *Psychological Review, 55,* 189–208.

Trabasso, T., & Bower, G. (1968). *Attention in learning, theory, and research.* New York: Wiley.

Treisman, A. M. (1991). Search, similarity, and integration of features between and within dimensions. *Journal of Experimental Psychology: Human Perception & Performance, 17*(3), 652–676.

Treisman, A. M., & Gelade, G. (1980). A feature-integration theory of attention. *Cognitive Psychology, 12,* 97–136.

Treisman, A. M., & Gormican, S. (1988). Feature analysis in early vision: Evidence from search asymmetries. *Psychological Review, 95*(1), 15–48.

Vogels, R., & Orban, G. A. (1985). The effect of practice on the oblique effect in line orientation judgments. *Vision Research, 25*(11), 1679–1687.

Wallach, H., Moore, M. E., & Davidson, L. (1963). Modification of stereoscopic depth-perception. *American Journal of Psychology, 76*(2), 191–204.

Wang, Q., Cavanagh, P., & Green, M. (1994). Familiarity and pop-out in visual search. *Perception & Psychophysics, 56,* 495–500.

Wang, X., Merzenich, M. M., Sameshima, K., & Jenkins, W. M. (1995). Remodelling of hand representation in adult cortex determined by timing of tactile stimulation. *Nature, 378*(6552), 71–75.

Weinberger, N. M., Javid, R., & Lepan, B. (1995). Heterosynaptic long-term facilitation of sensory-evoked responses in the auditory cortex by stimulation of the magnocellular medial geniculate body in guinea pigs. *Behavioral Neuroscience, 109*(1), 10–17.

Wertheimer, M. (1923). Untersunchungen zur Lehre der Gestalt. *Psychologische Forschung, 4,* 301–350.

Wheeler, D. D. (1970). Processes in the visual recognition of words (Doctoral dissertation, University of Michigan, 1970). *Dissertation Abstracts International, 31*(2), 940B.

Wise, J. A., Kubose, T., Chang, N., Russell, A., & Kellman, P. J. (2000). Perceptual learning modules in mathematics and science instruction. In D. Lemke (Ed.), *Proceedings of the TechEd 2000 Conference,* Amsterdam: IOS Press.

CHAPTER 8

Spatial Learning

THOMAS S. COLLETT

INTRODUCTION

"The great aim of life is not knowledge but action." Though perhaps unappealing to academics, this aphorism of T. H. Huxley helps emphasize that spatial learning is more about learning to act effectively in a complex spatial environment than about acquiring knowledge of space and its furnishings. Guthrie (1952) made a similar point in his comment that a rat with a cognitive map may still be buried in thought: Maps are worthless without some principled means of applying the information that they hold to guiding actions.

Animals move both their appendages and themselves in a purposive manner. They point their eyes, heads, or bodies at objects in the environment, and they grasp those objects with their mouths, beaks, or limbs either reaching directly or around obstacles to do so. They move themselves toward a desirable object or away from a threatening one, and they are able to plan routes to remembered places that are invisible from their starting point. The panoply of different skills that underpin an animal's spatial behavior means that learning occurs for many different reasons and in many different systems within the central nervous system. Plastic adjustments are needed to ensure that movements are accurate and that distances and directions can be estimated with precision. Information must be acquired to allow animals to return to significant places and to follow routes, and more generally for them to exploit changing resources within familiar territory.

Underlying this diversity are common synaptic mechanisms of learning that probably involve strengthening or weakening connections between abutting neural processes that are simultaneously active. One problem that we will encounter is that although learning is mostly local, somehow large-scale flexible spatial behavior emerges out of such local processes. An important feature of spatial learning that may account for some of this flexibility is that it occurs on different spatial scales. Memories for circumscribed places are embedded in a larger context so that an animal returning to a specific site is often primed by the context to recognize the landmarks defining that site. Similarly, when following a route, an animal's state at one stage along the route sets its expectations for the next stage. Nested memories—particularly if associative links are bidirectional with small-scale memories priming

The author is very grateful to Neil Burgess, Fred Dyer, Michael Huffman, Kate Jeffrey, Al Kamil, Charles Menzel, Bruno Poucet, David Redish, David Sherry, Jeff Taube and Giorgio Vallortigara for sending him information, manuscripts, or illustrations. Neil Burgess, Randy Gallistel, David Redish, and Josh Wallman very kindly read and tactfully criticized sections of the manuscript.

large-scale ones, and vice versa—give versatile memory architecture.

Another important feature of much spatial learning is that it is anticipatory. Animals equip themselves with navigational skills and information about the world before they ever set out on a journey. For example, a young bird watching the night sky has innate mechanisms that allow it to learn the shape of constellations of stars around the North Star. Later, when it migrates and flies at night, it can use this knowledge to control the compass direction of its path. A bee first leaving the shelter of its hive needs to be able to return there, and it is programmed to learn the immediate visual surroundings of the hive during special orientation flights that it performs before it embarks on its foraging career. Rodents gradually explore a new environment, ranging farther and learning progressively more about the disposition of resources in it. The characteristic common to these examples is what Gould and Marler (1987) called an instinct to learn, or more properly instincts, since each example depends on its own preadapted mechanisms. Learning mechanisms that are discussed in the context of spatial behavior may, however, be used more generally. The sophisticated control of movement in space is likely to have occurred early in the evolution of vertebrate lines, and learning mechanisms that developed primarily for spatial control may in the course of time be co-opted by other systems as well.

COMPONENTS OF SPATIAL BEHAVIOR AND THEIR CALIBRATION

Precision of action is important to much spatial behavior. Fingers grasp tiny fruit at arm's length. A chameleon extends its tongue to pluck an insect off a twig. Animals of many kinds can judge the distances and sizes of objects. The scale over which distances and sizes can be measured accurately turns out to be quite large, as a number of recent studies of blindfolded walking in humans have shown (e.g., Loomis, Da Silva, Fujita, & Fukusima, 1992; Thomson 1983). In such studies a subject is led to an open space to view a target. The subject is then blindfolded and given earmuffs or earphones emitting white noise to mask any acoustic cues and is asked to walk to the target. Performance is accurate over distances of at least 25 m (Figure 8.1). This ability implies not only that distance is measured using visual cues but also that the distance walked can be monitored using nonvisual cues and that these two different measures correspond to each other.

The mutual calibration of visual and nonvisual cues to distance can be seen in a variant of the blind walking test. Subjects are again blindfolded after viewing a target. However, instead of walking toward the target, they are asked to walk in another direction. At some unexpected moment, they are told either to point at the target or to turn and walk toward it. Their success in doing this task means that while they are walking, they continuously revise their estimate of their distance and direction from that target (Loomis, Da Silva, Philbeck, & Fukusima, 1996). Experiments on scene recognition suggest that humans update what they expect to see as they move around (Rieser, 1989). Wang and Simons (1999) found that a scene is identified more easily from a new viewpoint if the (blindfolded) subject moves to the new viewpoint than if the same changed viewpoint is generated by rotating the environment about the subject. Analogous experiments in which stationary subjects view the simulated optic flow generated by virtual movement around a virtual scene that is curtained off during the motion show that vision can be used interchangeably with idiothetic cues to update a subject's expectations (Christou & Bülthoff, 1999).

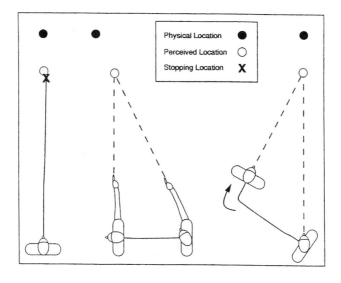

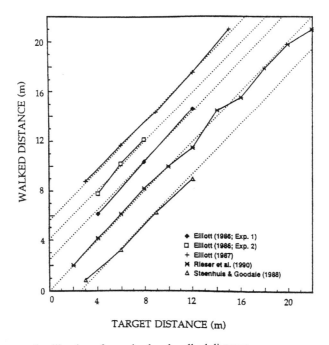

Figure 8.1   The mutual calibration of perceived and walked distance.

NOTE: Top: Experimental methods. Solid lines show distances walked; dashed lines show indicated directions. SOURCE: From Loomis et al. (1996). Copyright © by the American Psychological Association. Bottom: Data from five experiments by different authors in which subjects walked to a previously viewed target with their eyes closed. Walked distance is plotted against target distance. Data are shifted vertically for clarity. Dotted lines show perfect performance. SOURCE: After Loomis et al. (1992). Copyright © 1992 by the American Psychological Association. Adapted with permission.

Such a close interaction between vision and locomotion is possible only if the metrics of both are well calibrated relative to each other. The major concern of this chapter is the learning that sustains animal navigation. To date, however, the mechanisms of calibration have been best analyzed not in the locomotion of whole animals, but rather in the movements of the eyes.

Saccadic Calibration

Saccades are the rapid eye movements made by many animals in order to redirect a high acuity fovea at some desired part of the visual scene. Saccades are so rapid—movements of 10° degrees are completed within about 50 ms—that they are open loop. Time is too short for the movement to be controlled by visual feedback. Saccade amplitude is determined principally by the angular distance of the desired target from the fovea at the time that the programming of the saccade starts.

Thus, there must be an accurate correspondence between movement amplitude and target distance. In most sensorimotor systems rough correspondence is hardwired. Its precision is refined through a process of continuous calibration that reduces an error signal, in this case the distance of the target from the fovea of the eye after the saccade has been completed. Natural selection acts, of course, not only on the accuracy of the initial hardwiring but also on the subsequent process of error correction so that learning mechanisms are in a sense also hardwired.

Saccadic calibration can be studied by perturbing the relation between saccade amplitude and target position. In the method introduced by McLaughlin (1967), the target is shifted to a new position while a saccade is underway and vision is poor (Figure 8.2, top panel). Suppose that the eye begins a 10° saccade to fixate a target at 10° to the right. During the saccade, the target is stepped 5° left

toward the fovea. The saccade will then overshoot the target position by a factor of two. After about 100 such experiences in man, or 1,000 in monkey, the amplitude of a saccade generated by a target 10° from the fovea has decreased considerably so that the fovea lands near the back-shifted target.

In principle, the error signal driving the adjustment could be derived either visually from the angular position of the target relative to the fovea at the end of the saccade or by the amplitude of the subsequent saccade made to correct the visual error. Wallman and Fuchs (1998) showed that the adjusting signal is likely to be the visual error. They distinguished between the two possibilities using an ingenious manipulation. Instead of leaving the target in its displaced position for the duration of the saccade, they returned it to its original peripheral position after about 200 ms. Consequently, a corrective saccade was not needed. Nonetheless, adaptation, driven by the momentary visual error, still occurred, even though under these circumstances it was maladaptive. After adaptation the eye has not moved far enough, and the target has to be fixated by a second corrective saccade in the same direction (Figure 8.2, bottom panel). An important lesson from this experiment is that the mechanism of calibration has evolved to cope with a restricted range of behaviors. If the system must handle unusual conditions, the result of calibration may be to degrade rather than to improve the overall performance of the system.

Saccadic changes induced by this technique are limited to movements that have a similar direction and distance to the saccades that have been adapted (Frens & van Opstal, 1994). Thus, if the gain (saccade amplitude/ angular distance of target from fovea) has been adapted to a target at one retinal location that is stepped to another, the ensuing change in gain is greatest for the trained amplitude and direction and falls as saccade parameters

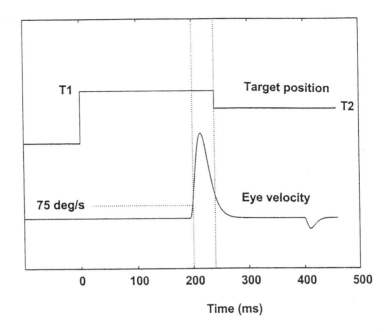

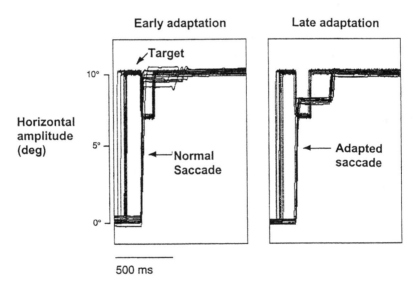

Figure 8.2   Calibration of saccades using Deubel's brief back-step procedure.

NOTE: Top: McLaughlin's method of recalibrating saccades. The target, a spot of light, is stepped to 10° (T1). At the onset of the saccade toward it, the target, triggered by the eye velocity signal, is stepped back to 7° (T2) (adapted from Frens & van Opstal, 1994). Bottom: Deubel's variant of this method begins the same way, then, after a short interval of about 130 ms, the back-stepped target is returned to 10°. Early in adaptation, the monkey's saccade is about 10°. B: Late in adaptation the monkey has adapted to the brief back-step, and its saccade is reduced in size. It must now make a correction saccade to foveate the target. Adaptation occurs although the monkey makes few backward saccades, implying that the error signal is visual.

SOURCE: Wallman & Fuchs (1998). Reprinted with permission.

depart from those training values. The local nature of the adaptation is also seen if the system is adapted to a gain decrease for saccades of one amplitude and a gain increase for saccades of another amplitude. This double training does not lead to any interference: The gain change for each saccade amplitude is similar to what it would be if it were adapted in isolation (Noto, Watanabe, & Fuchs, 1999). It is usually supposed that adaptation is local because it occurs within a neural sheet on which saccade direction and distance are mapped spatially. For any given saccade, a relatively small area of the sheet is active, and adaptation is restricted to the active area. Current guesses are that the site of adaptation lies within the cerebellum (for a review, see Houk, Buckingham, & Barto, 1996).

Saccadic adaptation is local in another way. The calibration considered so far is reflexively driven: The animal moves its eyes to fixate a stimulus that because of its novelty or sudden appearance grabs attention. Saccades are also performed volitionally, as when scanning a stationary scene or when moving the eye to fixate a remembered target. These three types of saccades (reflexive, scanning, and memory) probably employ somewhat different cortical and subcortical pathways and have their own adaptive mechanisms, such that adapting one type of saccade may leave unchanged saccades of the same amplitude and direction that are performed in other behavioral circumstances (Deubel, 1999). Saccadic calibration illustrates well how plastic changes are restricted to particular predetermined locations within complex neural circuits and how the changes are steered in predetermined ways.

Learning and Calibrating Navigational Tools

Biological compasses are essential for navigation and must be well tuned before they can be trusted for guiding long journeys. The learning that is needed to produce a service-able compass tends to be preprogrammed and to anticipate the animal's requirements. In addition, it often makes use of elaborate in-built structures for extracting essential information or for providing a skeleton that is molded and fleshed out during learning.

Sun Compass in Birds

Birds and insects use the sun as a compass. They derive compass direction by noting the sun's azimuth (i.e., the direction of the point on the horizon that lies directly below the sun's current position). Obtaining direction from the sun is not straightforward because the sun's azimuth changes from east to west during the course of the day. Matters would be relatively simple if the rate of change of azimuth were a constant 15° per hour. But it is not. The solar ephemeris, the function that relates the sun's azimuth to time of day, varies in a complex way, depending on latitude and season. Animals cope with this complexity by learning their local solar ephemeris and relating it to a more stable directional cue (Figure 8.3).

Pigeons seem to learn the behavior of the solar ephemeris in relation to their innate magnetic compass. A commonly used method for investigating the acquisition of the sun compass is clock shifting (Schmidt-Koenig, 1958). Birds are kept for some days in an artificially lit environment where dawn and dusk are advanced or retarded by a few hours with respect to the world outside. This treatment leads to phase advances or delays in the birds' internal clocks. The bird is then mistaken in its expectations about the sun's compass direction and makes predictable directional errors when attempting to home from a release site.

W. Wiltschko, Wiltschko, & Keeton (1976) used clock shifting to test whether young pigeons learn the solar ephemeris. Pigeons reared from the egg with their clocks permanently retarded by six hours were allowed to fly from their loft in the afternoon. This limited experience gave them some opportunity

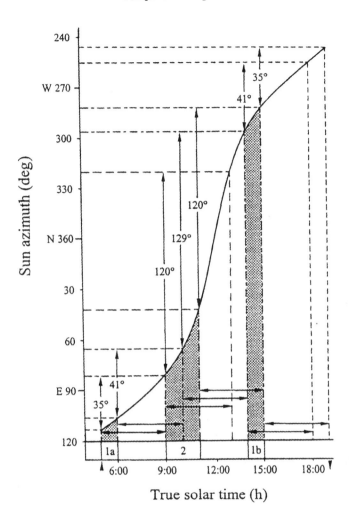

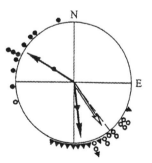

▲ 4-hr shifted
early release

● 4-hr shifted
midday release

○ no clock shift

Figure 8.3   Learning the local ephemeris function.
NOTE: Top: Sun's azimuth during the course of a day in Auckland, New Zealand (37° S), on January 25. The azimuth changes more steeply around the middle of the day than early in the morning. Bottom: Circular histogram of clockshifted and control pigeon's vanishing bearings on release. Dashed line indicates direction of home. Symbols show the bearings of individual birds. Control birds are accurate. The errors of clock-shifted birds vary predictably with release time.
SOURCE: R. Wiltschko et al. (2000). Reprinted with permission. Copyright Company of Biologists.

of linking the sun's azimuth to a reference bearing. When these pigeons were taken to a site in the afternoon and released, their homing direction was normal. This result by itself says nothing; direction could, for instance, be specified by a magnetic compass. When the internal clock was set back to normal, however, the young pigeons made errors similar to those of adult birds with their clocks advanced by 6 hours. The young pigeons must therefore have used their retarded clocks to associate the position of the sun to a reference bearing.

The precision with which birds learn the ephemeris function can most easily be examined in relatively low latitudes using birds whose clocks have been shifted by just a few hours. In these latitudes the sun lies to the east most of the morning so that directional errors measured at this time are small. At midday the sun shifts rapidly from east to west, and directional errors caused by small clock shifts are much larger. In the afternoon, with the sun remaining in the west, errors are again small (Figure 8.3). R. Wiltschko, Walker, and Wiltschko (2000) measured the homing directions of adult pigeons in Auckland, New Zealand (37°S), after the birds' internal clocks had been advanced by 4 hours. Pigeons were taken from their loft to a release site, either early in the morning or at midday. Early morning releases were associated with directional errors of approximately 40° east of the loft direction. The errors for releases around midday were, as predicted, much greater (approximately 120°). The magnitude of these errors is consistent with pigeons tuning their ephemeris function accurately to local conditions by learning the association between the sun and a reference bearing throughout the day.

Young pigeons rely initially on their magnetic compass for guidance, and their compass direction is disturbed whenever they fly with magnets attached to their heads (Keeton, 1971). Adult pigeons, on the other hand, pre-fer to use the sun compass: Magnets attached to their heads do not cause directional errors on sunny days, but only when the sky is overcast (Keeton, 1971). The response of young pigeons to a shifted clock indicates that the sun compass develops around 3 months, provided that the birds have a view of the sun (R. Wiltschko & Wiltschko, 1981). If pigeons are raised so that they only see the sun in the afternoon, they will home accurately both morning and afternoon. If their clock is shifted, the predicted directional errors occur in the afternoon, but the birds remain accurate in the morning (R. Wiltschko & Wiltschko, 1980). Conversely, on sunny days magnets induce directional errors in the morning but not in the afternoon. These birds seem to rely on the sun in the afternoon, but in the morning, when they have had no experience of the sun's movements, they depend on a magnetic compass (R. Wiltschko, Nohr, & Wiltschko, 1981).

By rearing young pigeons in a magnetic field that was rotated 120° clockwise with respect to the Earth's field, W. Wiltschko, Wiltschko, Keeton, and Madden (1983) showed that the sun compass is calibrated relative to the magnetic compass. Pigeons grew up in a loft in which the magnetic field was rotated and from which they had a view of the sun throughout the day. Flight experience outside the loft was restricted to overcast days. When first released on a sunny day, the pigeons made large directional errors corresponding roughly to the difference between earth north and magnetic north in the loft. The pigeons had learned that in the morning the sun lies in their magnetically defined east and in the afternoon in their magnetically defined west. Taken together, this series of experiments shows that pigeons have an innate tendency to calibrate their ephemeris function by referring the sun's direction during the course of the day to a magnetically defined compass direction.

The Sky Compass in Bees

Bees have an innate component to their solar ephemeris. Lindauer (1959) first spotted this feature when he limited the foraging experience of naive bees to the late afternoon so that the bees never encountered the morning sun. Nonetheless, their behavior in the morning indicated that they expected the sun to rise in the east (i.e., 180° from where they had seen it the previous evening).

Dyer and Dickinson (1994) went on to plot the full ephemeris function of bees that had also only viewed the sun in the late afternoon. When bees with normal experience return from a familiar foraging site, their waggle dance in the dark hive signals the direction of the site with respect to the sun. The bees know the sun's arc through the sky so well that they will dance normally, indicating the sun's changing position when they forage at a familiar site in total overcast. On such a cloudy day, Dyer and Dickinson observed

the waggle dances of bees that knew only the sun's position in the afternoon. In agreement with Lindauer's results, these bees thought that the early morning sun should be in the east. Over the rest of the day the untutored solar ephemeris differed significantly from the real, local one (Figure 8.4). Bees behaved as if the sun remained in the east until about midday, when it switched abruptly to the west. Learning involves both anchoring this simplified solar ephemeris to some reference bearing and adjusting the shape of the function to match local conditions.

This section is headed sky compass, rather than sun compass, to emphasize the remarkable fact that bees and ants can still obtain compass cues from the sky when the sun is screened from their view. As long as they can see an area of blue sky and detect the polarization gradients that are caused by Rayleigh scattering of sunlight, they can navigate by the sky's characteristic polarization pattern (for a review, see Wehner, 1994).

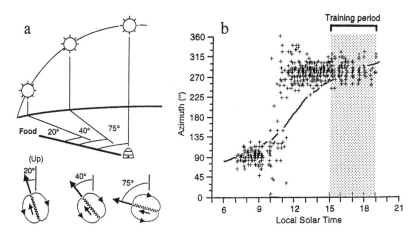

Figure 8.4   The honeybee's intrinsic ephemeris function.
NOTE: a: Food direction signaled by the waggle dance. The angle between the vertical and the straight run on the vertical comb indicates the angle between the food, the hive, and the sun's azimuth. b: The changing direction of the straight run during the course of the day reveals the intrinsic ephemeris function of bees that have experienced the sun only in the late afternoon. Each cross shows the direction of the dance in a bee foraging under complete overcast. Solid line shows local ephemeris.
SOURCE: Dyer & Dickinson (1994). Copyright ©1994 National Academy of Sciences, U.S.A.

Star Compass

Birds often migrate at night by obtaining direction from the stars in the sky. Instead of a single visible star, the sun, many can be seen, and they move across the sky at different angular speeds. Birds have hit upon an ingeniously simple method of learning direction from the rotating night sky. The details were unraveled by Emlen (1975), who worked with indigo buntings that migrate south in the autumn and north in the spring. He found that young buntings learn to identify the constellations close to the North Star. As the Earth rotates, the stars appear to move through circles with a radius and speed that increases with their angular distance from the Earth's axis of rotation. Because it is on this axis, the North Star remains stationary. Buntings are programmed to learn the appearance of slowly moving constellations that are close to the center of rotation and to use them to determine north.

Emlen demonstrated this to be the case by rearing birds under a planetarium sky. He could then rotate the planetarium sky around any star he wished. Buntings reared with Betelgeuse as the center of rotation treated Betelgeuse as their North Star. Motion of the celestial sphere was needed only for learning what constellation was relevant. Once acquisition was complete, the buntings oriented successfully under a stationary sky, indicating that they had used image speed to pick out and learn the particular configuration that lay close to the axis of rotation.

BEHAVIORAL ROUTINES FOR PLACE LEARNING

Learning Flights in Bees and Wasps

Before leaving a significant place, bees and wasps take the precaution to learn enough about the spatial relationships between the place and surrounding landmarks so that they can return there. Learning on departure makes it easy for an animal to focus on the exact spot that it wants to relocate. In a rough sense, animals also know what they should learn. They have a priori expectations about what makes a good landmark, such as its proximity to the goal and its size as well as whether it protrudes above the ground.

On its first departure from a nest (Tinbergen, 1932) or a foraging site (Lehrer, 1993), a wasp or bee performs a structured and stereotyped learning flight. The flights recur when insects have difficulties in relocating the site, as may happen when the surroundings are altered or when there has been a long interval since an insect's previous survey of the site. And bees fail to return if they leave a new place without a learning flight. Wagner (1907), for instance, moved a bumblebee colony indoors and after a few day's confinement allowed the insects to leave their nest. One bumblebee in the colony made a mistake and, unlike the rest, delayed the start of its learning flight until it had just passed through the window. This bee never returned home and searched fruitlessly for its nest at the origin of its learning flight near the window. When a beekeeper shifts a hive to a new location, he has various stratagems to ensure that experienced foragers will also perform learning flights. One trick is to leave the hive closed for a couple of days; another is to stuff grass into the entrance so that bees must remove the grass and are forcibly told that something has changed.

Learning flights can typically be divided into distinct phases. They begin with circumscribed movements close to the nest or food source, continue with the insect circling high above it, and may end with a trip of several hundred meters—the ensemble enabling the insect to navigate with increasing precision as it approaches its goal.

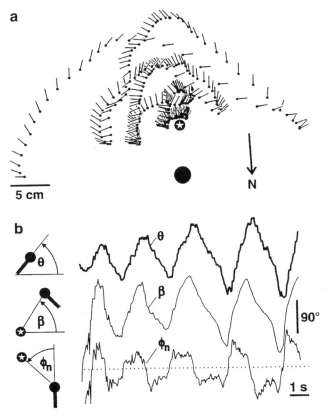

Figure 8.5 Learning flight of a solitary wasp (*Cerceris rybyensis*) as it leaves the nest.
NOTE: The top panel shows the flight viewed from above. Circles with tails denote the wasp's position and orientation every 20 ms. The star shows the nest entrance, and the filled black circle indicates a small cylinder placed upright on the ground. The time course of various parameters of the flight is plotted in the bottom panel. θ is the direction in which the wasp faces; β is the direction of the line segment connecting the wasp to the nest; and Φ_n is the horizontal position of the nest on the wasp's retina.
SOURCE: Replotted from Zeil (1993a). Copyright © 1993 Springer-Verlag.

Pivoting and Distance Measurement

The most striking characteristic of the first phase near the nest or feeding site is that the insect pivots about the site to which it will return. This design feature is found whether the insect is learning the location of its nest (Zeil, 1993a; Zeil & Kelber, 1991) or of a foraging site (T. S. Collett, 1995; T. S. Collett & Lehrer, 1993). Pivoting has been particularly well studied in *Cerceris,* a solitary wasp that digs a nest in which it rears larvae. Every morning, on first leaving its nest, the wasp refreshes its memory of the location of the nest hole by performing a new learning flight. It emerges from the nest hole, turns to face it, and then backs away in a series of sideways zigzags or arcs that are roughly centered on the hole (Figure 8.5, top). As the insect flies, its body axis (θ in Figure 8.5) rotates at an angular velocity that matches the angular velocity at which the arc (β in Figure 8.5) is described. Consequently, the nest hole is viewed by roughly the same area of retina (φ_n in Figure 8.5) throughout each arc. The nest hole falls on an area about 45° left of the midline during arcs to the left and 45° to the right of the midline during arcs to the right. The insect increases its translational velocity as the radius of the arc grows so that the angular speed of pivoting about the nest remains constant and independent of the wasp's distance from it.

This pattern of movement makes it easy to pick out landmarks that are close to the goal site. During pivoting, the images of objects near the goal move slowly over the retina, whereas the image speeds of objects beyond it grow with increasing separation between object and goal to a maximum that equals the insect's turning speed. The slow image speeds of objects close to the goal make them especially salient. Their images are not blurred, and they contrast strongly with the moving background. Pivoting provides an automatic filter for selecting and emphasizing those close landmarks that best pinpoint a goal.

If insects were to guide their approach to a nest or feeder using the distance information picked up during learning flights, their approach flight would need to incorporate similar arcs in order to generate the same parallax information that was available from learning flights. The first few return flights of a wasp to a goal do indeed mimic several features of its learning flight. The returning insect flies through segments of arcs, thus recapturing the optic flow and distance information that it experienced on departure (T. S. Collett & Lehrer, 1993; Zeil, 1993b). After a few visits, however, the wasp's return flights are straight (Figure 8.6).

Experiments with honeybees show that on their first few returns to a new feeding site, they search for food at the real distance of the food from a nearby landmark, even if the latter's size has been altered (Lehrer & Collett, 1994). After more experience, bees are guided by the apparent size of the landmark, flying to where the current image of the landmark matches in size a remembered view, even though with a landmark of changed size they position themselves at the wrong distance

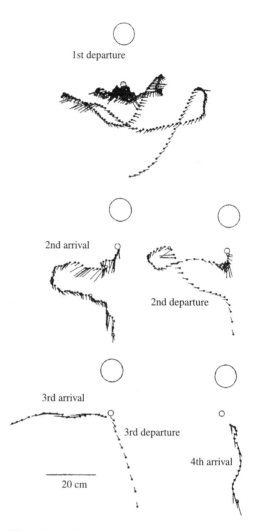

Figure 8.6   The geometry of approach and departure flights becomes simpler with experience.
NOTE: A wasp (*Vespula vulgaris*) has just discovered a feeder. The sequence shows its first few departures from and approaches to the feeder. Small circle shows feeder; large circle shows a nearby black cylinder. Position and orientation of the wasp is shown every 20 ms in the first departure from the feeder (learning flight) and at 40 ms intervals in all subsequent flights. Tails are elongated when the wasp faces within 10° of the feeder. SOURCE: Adapted from T. S. Collett & Lehrer (1993).

from it. The same phenomenon is seen in the wasp, *Cerceris*. Search flights made by a wasp early in the day, soon after it has performed its daily learning flight, are governed by the absolute distance of the cylinder, and its search pattern is unaffected by changes to the landmark's size. However, later in the day after several returns to the nest, its search is guided by the landmark's apparent size (Zeil, 1993b). This assumed switch in cue use, from motion parallax to apparent size, suggests that the primary function of pivoting is to flag those landmarks that are close to the goal and thus worth remembering. The provision of information about the distance between landmark and goal for path guidance is only a transient phenomenon (see Brünnert, Kelber, & Zeil, 1994, for an exception).

Retinotopic Learning

A second notable feature of learning flights is the direction in which the insect faces while it backs away. The insect's viewing direction tends to match its subsequent approach direction on later returns (T. S. Collett, 1995; Vollbehr 1975; Zeil, 1993b), thus simplifying the acquisition of retinotopically organized views and their control of return flights. Viewpoint consistency seems to be achieved differently in different wasps. The orientation of *Cerceris* during learning flights is determined by the position of a landmark close to the nest. When the wasp emerges from the nest, it looks back toward the nest, facing in the direction of the landmark, and it continues to back away in roughly the same direction so that the nest hole lies between it and the landmark, as in Figure 8.5. On its return, it approaches facing in the same direction, so that it can be guided by the landmark all the way back to the nest (Zeil, 1993a, 1993b). *Vespula*'s learning flights on leaving a feeder are a little different. The wasp looks back at the feeder toward the end of the arcs, often with the landmark on lateral retina. It seems likely to store views at these times: It tends to face the feeder from one or two fairly constant viewing directions over several learning flights (Figure 8.7) and to adopt the same viewing direction on its later

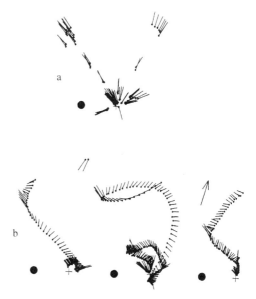

Figure 8.7   An individual wasp views its goal from preferred directions during leaning flights.
NOTE: A sequence of six departure flights was recorded from a wasp (*Vespula vulgaris*) as it left a recently discovered feeder to return home. During these flights the wasp turned back to look at the feeder. a: Superimposition of the wasp's position and orientation in those frames collected from all six flights in which the wasp faced within +/−10° of the feeder. b: Three of the six departure flights shown in full. SOURCE: From T. S. Collett (1995).

return flights, when it is close to the feeder (T. S. Collett, 1995).

The learning flights of tropical bees can vary widely with a species' lifestyle and habitat (Jander, 1997). Some bees hover in one spot at particular moments during learning flights, suggesting the capture of static views that can guide the final stages of their return. The orchid bee, *Euglossa cyanipes,* for example, alternates between stationary periods of hovering close to the nest and abrupt lateral or vertical displacements that take the bee to a new vantage point where it hovers again. Similar behavior has been seen in arboreal stingless bees, which begin their learning flight by hovering briefly at the four corners of a square centered on the nest (Richard Friebe, personal communication, 1998).

Large-Scale Learning Flights

New radar techniques now make it possible to follow the paths of individual honeybees or bumblebees over hundreds of meters (Riley et al., 1996). In the last phase of their orientation flights, bees fly a long way from the hive and seem to learn landmarks that can guide their subsequent returns from a distant site. In honeybees, this phase consists of a relatively straight outward path from the hive of between 10 m and 300 m. The bee then loops around and returns directly home along a route that is often close to the outward one (Capaldi et al., 2000).

Bees make a variable number of these flights (mean about 6) before beginning to collect food. Later orientation flights tend to be longer and to be flown at higher speeds than earlier ones. Because bees adjust their flight speed to keep image speed on their retina constant, it is likely that bees fly higher on their longer flights. A strategy of increasing height with distance from the hive enables bees to learn smaller landmarks close to the ground when they are nearer to the hive and larger features of the landscape when they are farther away, giving them geographical knowledge that is fine-grained close to home and coarse-grained further away.

Even a single orientation flight is enough to teach a bee something about the landscape near home. Capaldi and Dyer (1999), following Becker (1958), caught bees after their first orientation flight and transported them to one of several release sites a few hundred meters from the hive. On release, the bees flew directly toward the hive from those release sites that gave an unobstructed view of the landscape around the hive. Enough landmark information had been acquired during the orientation flight to guide a short homeward trip.

A general lesson to emerge from detailed studies of learning flights is that the flights seem designed to pick up the information that supports particular strategies for navigating between nest and food site, rather than for learning the overall topography of the terrain.

Food Caching in Birds

Some bird species cache food in times of plenty and then recover it when food is less available. Jays, for instance, cache acorns in the autumn and retrieve them in the winter (Bossema, 1979). There is abundant evidence that birds learn and remember their caching sites (for a review, see Sherry, 1984).

Although wasps and bees cannot choose where a particular nest hole or patch of flowers is located, caching birds have the opportunity to select the most appropriate sites for hiding food. Some birds pick sites that are easy to remember and that can be located even when covered with snow. Bossema found that jays, in their natural habitat, tend to cache acorns near conspicuous objects such as saplings or at the boundary between vegetation types (e.g., heather and grass). When retrieving food in winter, the jays search preferentially within half a meter of conspicuous objects, such as tree trunks, that protrude above the snow (see also Bennett, 1993). Bossema and Pot (quoted in Vander Wall, 1990) observed that jays in the laboratory faced in the same direction when recovering acorns that they had adopted when hiding them, thus making recognition easier. Clark's nutcrackers have a similar preference for caching seeds and for probing for them close to conspicuous objects (Vander Wall, 1982). Nutcrackers also adopt similar orientations when caching and recovering seeds. However, the correlation is not close, and cache recovery does not seem to require a consistent orientation (Kamil, Balda, & Good, 1999).

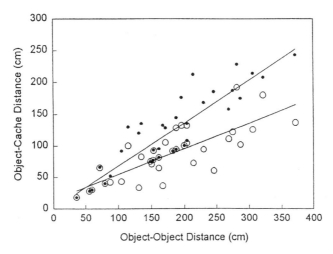

Figure 8.8   13-lined ground squirrels cache seeds away from prominent objects.
NOTE: For each cache site, the distance from it to the two closest objects is plotted against the distance between the objects. Open circle shows closest object to cache site. Filled circle shows next-closest object.
SOURCE: Devenport et al. (2000). Reprinted with permission.

A real danger of using a conspicuous object as an aide-mémoire is that pilferers come to learn that such landmarks signal the proximity of food. Ground squirrels (*Spermophilus tridecemlineatus*) actively avoid caching seeds close to conspicuous objects that may be unsafe. Devenport, Luna, and Devenport (2000) found that squirrels in natural environments tend to select sites that are equidistant from the two closest landmarks, leading to a strong correlation between landmark separation and the distance of the cache from the nearest of those landmarks (Figure 8.8). This behavior lessens the risk of plunder but does not prevent the squirrels from relocating their cache.

Rooks and crows avoid caching food when in the presence of conspecifics that are themselves not caching (Källander, 1978; James & Verbeek, 1985; reviewed by Vander Wall 1990). Such precautions are necessary. Laboratory experiments on piñon jays and Mexican jays show that birds can learn the caching site used by a conspecific while watching the caching bird from a distance

(Bednekoff & Balda, 1996a, 1996b). The observing bird was placed in a cage on a stool 1 m high in the center of a laboratory while a second bird cached seeds in 20 clusters of holes that were drilled into a plywood floor. All holes in each cluster except one were plugged, thus preventing a caching bird from choosing a preferred site and also preventing any bias in favor of correct choices by the observing bird. The latter turned to follow the cacher's movements, frequently sticking its head through the bars of the cage when doing so. Both observers and cachers were allowed to recover seeds one day later when all the holes were open and any possible surface cues had been removed. Both cacher and observer did significantly better than chance in choosing the correct hole within a cluster. This important result suggests that in some way the bird extrapolates its view from the stool to the situation of finding the seed on the ground. A view from a goal may not be an essential prerequisite for learning a place.

Given that birds select their sites, it is curious that laboratory experiments give no indication that learning is preferentially triggered by the act of caching. Shettleworth and Krebs (1986) had marsh tits cache seeds in holes drilled into a vertical board so that caching sites were selected by the experimenter, rather than by the bird. The ability to recover a cache was the same, whether the bird cached the seed itself or whether it encountered a previously placed seed while inspecting a potential caching site. The probability of later recovery also did not change if a bird approached the previously filled hole with a seed in its beak rather than with its beak empty.

Learning about a caching site seems to happen without the elaborate movement patterns found in insects. Tits and chickadees cock their heads briefly after caching as though looking at the site with the temporal fovea of each eye (Sherry, Krebs, & Cowie, 1981). Nutcrackers cache seeds quickly, just glancing at nearby objects while doing so, and spending no more than 10 to 12 s when hiding several seeds at a single cache site (Kamil et al., 1999; Vander Wall, 1990). Recovery is equally swift: Finding each seed requires no more than 3 to 4 s (Kamil et al., 1999). Nonetheless, the possibility should not be dismissed that a finer-grained analysis of caching in natural situations may yet reveal evidence of in-built sensorimotor patterns that aid learning and recall.

Exploration in Rodents

Rodents explore unfamiliar surroundings and re-explore familiar ones if they notice changes. Information about the layout of environmental cues seems to be acquired during exploration, but the detailed behavioral strategies underlying rodent spatial learning are not yet well understood. Leonard and McNaughton (1990) give a vivid account of the evolving behavior of a group of rats as they become familiar with new surroundings. A small number of laboratory rats was released

for three consecutive nights into a large cluttered room. When first put in the room, the rats made numerous small excursions from their initial release site. Over some hours they gradually explored further afield. During that first night they found a tunnel that became their home base and from which they made frequent exploratory trips. On the second night they began to cache food, carrying it from a pile to preferred caching sites. By the third night they had become familiar enough with the room to treat it as living space: They began to engage in aggressive social and territorial interactions, to establish latrine sites, and to build nests. Their knowledge of the layout of objects in the room rapidly improved. After the first morning, rats became increasingly difficult to catch as they dashed from one familiar shelter to another. As with bees, exploration and the associated spatial learning proceed outward from a home base. If rats were to use landmarks to improve the precision of path integration (discussed later), such progressive learning over an increasingly wide area would mean that the coordinates derived from path integration could be corrected using landmark information. Such bootstrapping would allow accurate path integration coordinates to be attached to landmarks over long distances (Gallistel, 1990; Poucet, 1993; Touretzky & Redish, 1996).

Rodents will also re-explore a familiar environment when old objects in it are displaced or new objects are introduced, focusing on the new or rearranged objects (Poucet et al., 1986, Thinus-Blanc et al., 1987). Not all changes induce exploration. A uniform expansion or contraction of a square array of cylindrical objects is ignored, suggesting some scale invariance in the rat's memory, but if a single cylinder is moved outward, transforming the square array into a kite, exploration is restricted to the outlier. If a single cylinder is moved inward toward the others, all the cylinders in the array are examined. The general conclusion from such findings is that exploration,

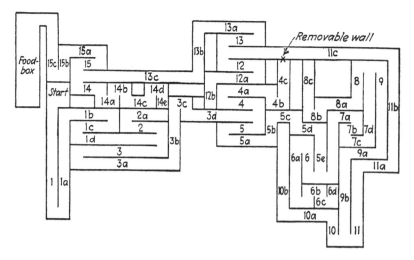

Figure 8.9 The discovery of a shortcut through a complex maze.
NOTE: The odd numbers indicate the open path, and the even numbers indicate the blind alleys. After rats had learned the maze, a wall was unblocked at the point indicated by the cross (4c). Rats detected the unblocked wall as they passed through 11c and briefly explored 4c and beyond. They returned to 11c and continued to the exit. Next trial they took the new shortcut. SOURCE: From Shepard, 1933, illustration Fig 1.3 in Maier and Schneirla (1935). Reprinted with permission.

like learning in general, happens when there is a discrepancy between an animal's expectations and what it encounters.

Many maze studies have shown that when rats explore a maze, they learn much about its spatial structure and the visual cues within it. Their exploration can lead to dramatic changes in their subsequent behavior. Shepard (1933) trained rats to negotiate an intricate maze with many blind passages (Figure 8.9). Once rats were experienced at running the maze with no errors, a hole was made in the maze wall that allowed a new short cut. Rats on their first trial through the altered maze detected and entered the newly opened hole, backtracking through what had been a blind end. Two of the rats on their next trip took the new short cut, showing that they adjusted their route as a result of information picked up during their short exploration. Whether scent marking assisted with this improved path is unclear.

More controlled studies have been performed with simpler mazes (Woodworth &

Schlosberg, 1955). In one such experiment, rats explored a T maze with two visually distinct goal boxes and with all extra-maze cues screened off (Seward, 1949). After three half-hour sessions of exploration with no food, rats were placed singly in one of the goal boxes and were allowed to eat a few bites there. When replaced at the entrance, 28 out of 32 rats returned directly to the box where they had been fed. A control group fed in one goal box without prior exploration of that particular maze showed no tendency to return to the same box. In a similar study (Tolman & Gleitman, 1949), rats learned to feed in the two goal boxes of a T maze made distinguishable by cues within them. The goal boxes were then detached and taken to another room. Rats were shocked in one of these displaced goal boxes and fed in the other. On their later return to the maze, they consistently turned away from the box in which they had been shocked and toward that in which they had been fed. Exploration has allowed them to learn the path to different recognized locations that can later be assigned a positive or a negative valence. Intriguingly, although rats find it easy to learn to go to one place in a maze for food and another for water, they find it very difficult to learn to take different routes to the same place for these rewards, reaching the same goal box by one path for food and by another for water (Woodworth & Schlosberg, 1955).

FINDING PLACES

A particular location in space can come to act as an attractor for a particular animal when it is in a certain internal state, drawing the animal toward it. Picture a downtown subway station some early weekday evening and commuters streaming inward. Early in the morning the stream goes the other way, stemming from the station, whereas on weekends there is little flow at all. What does a commuter need to know about the place to find the subway station? There is no set answer. A stranger need have no geographical knowledge. Weekdays in mid-twentieth century London, it would have been enough to follow the bowler hats and furled umbrellas. Others able to navigate by themselves could use any of a variety of strategies. The spatial knowledge needed depends upon the particular strategy deployed and may only be properly describable in the context of that strategy.

The learning flights of bees and wasps, for example, can be interpreted as a means of acquiring information to support particular guidance mechanisms. Three distinct mechanisms are involved in the final stages of approaching a goal that is close to a visual landmark. The first step is to aim straight at the landmark (von Frisch, 1967). Provided that it can be identified from different vantage points, such beacon aiming is a robust strategy that allows the insect to be drawn to the landmark from a wide area. The problem of viewpoint-independent recognition, however, is far from trivial. One solution adopted by

wood ants is to learn a landmark's appearance from several viewpoints (Judd & Collett, 1998). Another solution is seen in walking *Drosophila* (Straus & Pichler, 1998). Once the fly has begun to approach an object, it ignores artificial changes in the object's appearance. The fly continues for a while in the same direction after the object has been transformed and even after it vanishes. In using this mix of open and closed loop guidance, the fly relies on the usually safe assumption that landmarks are stationary.

When the insect is near the beacon, the beacon plays a different role. It becomes a visual cue for pinpointing the goal. The transition between these different phases is probably not under immediate visual control. The insect must relinquish fixation of the beacon and move in the direction of the goal. It is likely that it escapes from the beacon by performing a learned "local vector" that is triggered by a close-up view of the landmark (T. S. Collett & Rees, 1997). In the last stage of pinpointing the goal, the insect moves so that the view on its retina resembles the surrounding landmarks that it had stored earlier at the goal. When the match is correct, the insect will have arrived at its goal. The mechanism works well if current and stored views are reasonably similar. In a complex landscape this condition is usually true only near the goal. As we have seen, other strategies are employed to bring the insect within this catchment area.

Flying wasps and bees tend to maintain a constant orientation during the last phase of their approach (Figure 8.10). They can adjust the retinal position of a landmark without changing orientation because they are able to fly sideways or even backwards. This allows them to uncouple their direction of flight from their viewing direction. Any mismatch between a current and stored view can thus be corrected by translational movements. The insect's landmark guidance system need not be concerned with the control of rotation.

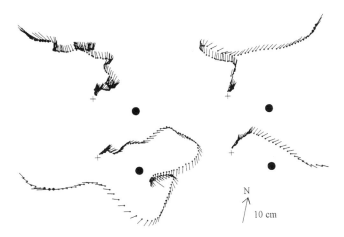

Figure 8.10   Consistency of viewing direction during approaches to a feeder.
NOTE: a: Records of four approach flights to a feeder performed by a single wasp (*Vespula vulgaris*). The feeder (+) was on the ground with an upright cylinder (•) placed nearby. The arrow points north, and its length represents 10 cm on the ground. The wasp's position and orientation are plotted every 20 ms. The wasp generally aims at the cylinder before approaching the feeder. Once close to the feeder, the wasp tends to adopt a preferred orientation that is constant over many flights. SOURCE: From T. S. Collett (1995).

Evolving Networks for Navigation

How should one rate a set of navigational strategies? Are those used by bees and wasps particularly well suited for reaching a goal, or are they constrained severely by the animal's evolutionary history and the properties of pre-existing control circuits? One way to explore such issues is to evolve artificial neural networks that are given a similar task of finding a goal near one or more landmarks. The artificial evolutionary process is free to explore the space of possible solutions and is limited only by the building blocks that the system is given. When evolutionary modeling of this kind is tried, the strategies reached by artificial networks are remarkably similar to those of flying insects (Dale & Collett, 2001).

The whole system—including the environment, the artificial neural network (ANN), and the artificial animal (or animat) in which the ANN is embedded—was simulated on computer. The ANN had input from a one-dimensional circular retina with 36 equally spaced sensors sampling the visual world. It was fed also by four compass neurons, each of which responded maximally to a different cardinal direction. Movement was through thrust generators, and in the example given in Figure 8.11, the direction of thrust was evolvable. At the start of the selection procedure, all motors were oriented in parallel, delivering thrust in a forward direction. The virtual axles were free to rotate during evolution, allowing a sideways component to appear. The number of neurons and their interconnections and links to sensors and motors were also determined by artificial selection. The evolvable part of the system was encoded on a single string of 0s and 1s that constituted an animat's genome (Figure 8.11, left).

The animat's task was to find its way from a starting area to a goal that was at a specific distance and direction from a fixed visual landmark. The animat's fitness score was determined by how close to the goal it stopped. A starting cohort of animats with randomly and sparsely connected ANNs all performed badly and had low scores. Offspring contributing to the next generation were produced by combining the bit strings of relatively fit pairs of animats. Genetic variation was introduced

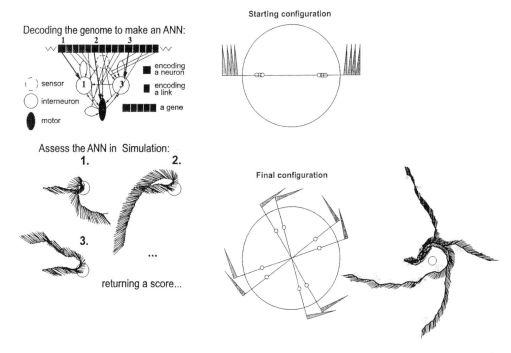

Figure 8.11   Evolving models of insect navigation.

NOTE: Left: A string of 1s and 0s encodes an artificial neural network (ANN) that is embedded in a simulated animat moving within a simulated environment. Over many generations animats are selected for their ability to navigate to a goal that is close to a circular landmark. Animats have visual and compass sensors and move by means of thrust generators. Right: Four superimposed paths from start to goal performed by a successfully evolved animat with four pairs of thrust generators (shaded arrows). At the start of the evolutionary run, the virtual axles of the thrust generators are aligned. The angles of the motors are evolvable, and the outcome is for the angles to diverge, allowing the animat to develop a sideways as well as a forward thrust component. The paths of animats moving to the goal resemble strongly those of real wasps (Figure 8.10). Animats first aim at the landmark and then keep to a constant orientation as they follow a line from the landmark to the goal, keeping one landmark edge on a fixed retinal position. SOURCE: From Dale & Collett (2001).

through mutation and through gene insertion and deletion. New offspring replaced animats with relatively low scores. Over several hundred thousand life cycles of selection, animats came to perform the task accurately and robustly, despite simulated winds and sensory and motor noise.

In many independent evolutionary runs with different starting conditions, animats hit upon the same set of navigational strategies to reach the goal as had wasps and bees. The initial phase of the trajectory was a direct, visually guided approach to a landmark. After leaving the landmark, the animat followed a direct line to the goal. During this phase it kept to a fixed orientation that was governed by a compass-driven feedback loop, and it held the landmark on a fixed retinal position using a visual-driven feedback loop. Like wasps and bees, it evolved an ability to move sideways and thus could decouple its visual- and compass-driven control loops.

One message to be taken from these simulations is that the overriding constraints determining the insect's solutions are imposed by the task rather than by the insect's evolutionary history. The simulations also stress that navigational control involves separate control loops, each of which is engaged in the right context and requires only limited information. The appropriate questions to ask about spatial behavior may be less about an animal's internal representations of the world and more about what control mechanisms exist and what is needed for them to operate.

Places as Views

Reaching a site by moving so as to place particular visual features on particular retinal positions means that in some sense the site is defined by the view of the relevant parts of the scene from that vantage point (Cartwright & Collett, 1983; T. S. Collett

& Land, 1975; Wehner & Räber, 1979). Landmarks in this two-dimensional pattern may appear as patches that differ from the background in shape, in color, or in texture, and the patches will vary in retinal size and motion according to the landmark's size and distance.

Evidence for such a two-dimensional representation is found when insects search for a goal within an array that has been distorted from its usual arrangement. The insects spend the most time looking where the distorted array generates, as far as possible, the same two-dimensional pattern on the retina that the normal array does when the insect is at the goal. In the experiment illustrated in Figure 8.12, bees were trained to collect sucrose from a small bottle top on the floor of a room. The position

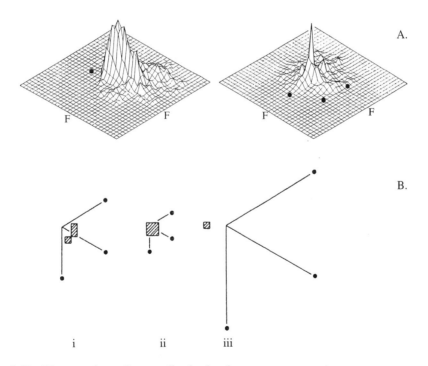

Figure 8.12 Places as views of surrounding landmarks.

NOTE: Honeybees search for a missing source of sucrose at a site defined by one or by three black upright cylinders. A. Relative time spent by one bee in each cell of an imaginary grid. Position of sucrose during training is marked by Fs on axes. Grid-lines are 8.7 cm apart. B. Single bee's search when distance between three landmarks is increased or reduced from the training situation. Bee searches where landmarks have same bearings (shown by lines) as those experienced at the feeder during training. Hatched areas show where search density is at least 80% of the maximum. SOURCE: From Cartwright & Collett (1983).

of this feeder in the room was marked by one or by three black cylinders on the floor. When the feeder was removed, bees spent most time searching for it at the location defined by the position of the cylinders. If the three cylinders were moved closer together or farther apart, bees searched where the positions of the cylinders on their eye would match those seen from the feeder during training. They continued to match retinal positions even though the consequence of doing so was that the bees' distances from the cylinders were grossly abnormal.

Water striders maintaining station in an artificial stream provide another example of a control system that operates by keeping images in particular retinal positions (Junger, 1991a). The swimming insect can keep station when the only visual cue is a single small light bulb seen in its frontal, dorsal visual field in an otherwise darkened room. The insect compensates for its drift downstream by discrete jumps against the direction of water flow, so that it holds the light bulb at a constant retinal elevation. If the bulb is suddenly raised, the bug allows itself to drift with the stream until the bulb is returned to its original position on the retina (Figure 8.13, top). If the bulb is lowered, the insect jumps forward. It remembers the bulb's desired retinal position and moves in the appropriate direction to restore the bulb to that position.

With a slightly more elaborate visual stimulus, one can monitor the water strider while it adjusts its stored template to cope with new circumstances (Junger, 1991b). Instead of a single bulb, five bulbs were arranged symmetrically along a horizontal arc. The water strider soon stabilized itself with respect to this array (Figure 8.13a). The leftmost lamp was then switched off, and an additional lamp at the right end of the row was turned on. The bug turned to its right, as though the change on its retina were caused by its own unwanted rotation (Figure 8.13b). The consequence of the turn was that the stored tem-

plate of the array was again occupied by five bulbs. However, when the bug jumped forward, it no longer moved exactly upstream. About 30 s later, it has adjusted the direction of its jump so that it again faced upstream (Figure 8.13c). During this time, the bug has adapted its template to match the new situation on its retina: It truncated the left end of the stored image and added to it on the right. To test whether the stored template had really been updated, the leftmost bulb was relit, and the rightmost bulb was extinguished. The bug now turned to the left, keeping the bulbs in the position demanded by the revised template (Figure 8.13d). Learning new views can happen very rapidly.

Reference Bearings and Place Learning

There is a transient but powerful feeling of disorientation when one emerges above ground from a subway station by the wrong exit. Even if the place is very familiar, it is hard to recognize where one is until one has "got one's bearings." One expects the world outside the subway station to be in a particular configuration, and the view from the wrong exit is confusing until one's internal bearings and the external world are aligned.

The use of reference bearings can be seen when animals search in the correct position relative to a single symmetrical landmark (e.g., Figure 8.12). In such cases, something other than the landmark must provide a directional reference. Reference bearings can come from compass cues, visual cues, or idiothetic cues. The water strider's orientation is fixed by the direction of the stream in which it swims. Bees and wasps use solar and magnetic compasses to maintain a consistent bearing when searching for a goal (Figure 8.10) so that the surrounding view is automatically placed in its proper orientation on the retina (T. S. Collett & Baron, 1994; Frier, Edwards, Neal, Smith, & Collett, 1996).

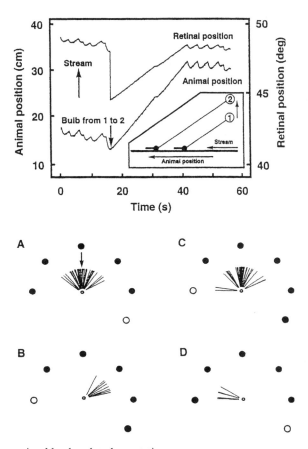

Figure 8.13 Using a visual landmark to keep station.
NOTE: Top: A water strider remains in a stable position on an artificial stream flowing at 0.75 cm/s⁻¹. A small bulb located 115 cm from the bug was moved from position 1 to position 2. The insect compensated for the change in the bulb's height by allowing itself to drift backwards until the bulb regained its initial retinal position. Graph plots the insect's position on the stream and the retinal elevation of the bulb over time. SOURCE: Modified from Junger (1991b). Copyright © 1991 Springer-Verlag. Bottom: Amending a stored image. A water strider uses a semicircular array of small light bulbs to keep its position on the stream. A: Five bulbs are illuminated, and the bug tends to jump upstream, as shown by the fan of straight lines pointing away from the center. Each line represents the direction of one jump, and the arrow shows the direction of water flow. B: Directions of jumps after the leftmost lamp is switched off and an additional light is switched on at the right side of the array. C: Stable distribution of jump directions that is reached 30 s after the switch. D: Initial direction of jumps immediately after the bulbs are switched back to the original arrangement. SOURCE: Modified from Junger (1991a). Copyright ©1991 W. Junger.

One of the prettiest demonstrations that bees set landmarks within a compass-based coordinate frame comes from Lindauer (1960). Honeybees were trained in a single afternoon to collect sucrose from the southern corner of a black square on top of a large circular table placed to the east of their hive. After this training, hive and table were moved overnight to a new location; the table was placed to the south of the hive, and bees were tested the following morning. Thus, the positions of the sun, the hive, and the distant landmarks were all changed from the training conditions. Nonetheless, the trained bees searched predominantly at the southern corner of the square. The position of the food on the table must have been learned with respect to compass bearings (Figure 8.14).

Rodents exploit reference bearings more flexibly. Like humans, they can use a variety of cues to update their perceived location and orientation while navigating through an environment. A fruitful approach to exploring what visual cues a rat uses to regain its bearings within a familiar scene has been to

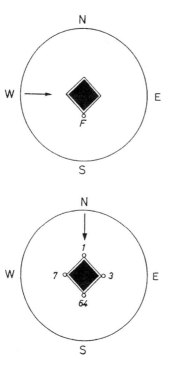

Figure 8.14 Landmarks learned in relation to a compass.

NOTE: Top: Afternoon training to a feeder at the south corner of a black square table. Bees flew from a hive that was positioned to the west of the table. Bottom: Morning test after table and hive have been moved to a new area and hive is to the north of the table. Empty dishes are placed at all corners of the table. Most approach flights are to the southern corner.

SOURCE: After Lindauer (1960) from Von Frisch (1967). Reprinted with permission.

analyze its behavior after it has been disoriented. In a small indoor environment, rats focus primarily on the overall geometry of the environment when reestablishing their bearings (Cheng, 1986). Rats were trained to find food that was always in a rectangular box but that from trial to trial was buried in a different location on the floor. The rat was allowed to discover the food and to eat a small portion before being removed from the box. The rat was then rotated in the dark to disorient it and replaced in the box. Where did it look for the residue of its meal? With no cues, apart from the shape of the box, there is a 180° degree ambiguity. For each possible food site in the box there is an equivalent site that can be specified by rotating the box 180° about the center. Disoriented rats replaced in the box searched equally in both the correct site and the rotationally equivalent one.

Rotational errors persisted even when each corner of the box was labeled conspicuously by color, odor, and texture. The rats seem to ignore these strong featural cues when reestablishing their reference bearing and rely just upon the global geometry of the surroundings. Reestablishing a reference bearing is likely a separate process from determining position relative to a landmark. Thus, if rats pick the wrong reference bearing, the featural cues are not in the expected location and so cannot help in locating the food. Humans share this reliance on geometric rather than featural cues. In analogous tests, both prelinguistic children (Hermer & Spelke, 1996) and adults, when they perform a concurrent task that interferes with their linguistic coding of the scene (Hermer-Vazquez, Spelke, & Katsnelson, 1999), behave in an astonishingly rat-like manner. In an outdoor environment, it makes sense to obtain direction from a global panorama of distant cues with small parallax effects. It could well be that these laboratory manipulations tap into such a system.

Disoriented rats that are unable to place landmarks in a global framework are bad at long-term spatial learning. Disoriented rats found it difficult to learn to find food that was always placed in the same arm of a radial maze. Without disorientation, however, the task was acquired reliably. Very similar results were obtained whether the maze was in an open laboratory furnished with many cues (Martin, Harley, Smith, Hoyles, & Hynes, 1997) or screened with a large black sheet on white curtains providing the sole visual cue (Dudchenko, Goodridge, Seiterle, & Taube, 1997). Learning the spatial relationships between a landmark and a feeding site specified by that landmark is also hard when the landmark's global position is made unstable by moving the landmark and feeding site within a larger reference frame (Biegler & Morris, 1993).

Curiously, disorientation is less debilitating when the task is to find a submerged platform in a constant position within a water maze (Morris, 1981). Two independent sets of experiments have shown that such water mazes are learned despite disorientation before each training trial (Dudchenko et al., 1997; Martin et al., 1997). These differences might result because rats have higher motivational levels when they must swim to find a safe landing place than when approaching a reward. Or it might be that disorientation on dry land does not transfer to the very different context of swimming.

Collections of Landmarks

A significant place is often surrounded by a complex array of nearby and more distant landmarks. Though it might be supposed that multiple landmarks provide redundant information for locating a place and that animals could economize by learning just a small subset of the array, there are two obvious benefits to learning more. First, landmarks can gain their identity by being embedded in a landscape; second, the use of multiple landmarks enhances the precision and flexibility of navigation.

Landmarks in Context

An animal's responses after an array has been rearranged, or after the removal of one or more landmarks from the array, makes it clear that animals can learn and identify individual landmarks by their idiosyncratic visual features. But animals can also recognize a landmark by its relation to other landmarks in the array. Indeed, a small stone marking a wasp's nest site may be insufficiently distinctive to be recognized without extra cues: It can only be identified when it is seen in its spatial context.

An experiment on gerbils shows that identity can be conferred by a landmark's position in an array. A gerbil was trained to find sunflower seeds at a location defined by two similar-looking landmarks. When the gerbil was tested with the array pulled apart, it searched at two locations, corresponding to the distances and directions of the goal from each landmark (Figure 8.15). That the landmarks' identity comes from the geometry of the array is confirmed by removing one of the landmarks: The gerbil cannot then identify the remaining landmark and searches at two locations, corresponding to the distance and direction of the goal from each of the possible landmarks.

Contextual cues can be very diverse. An animal arrives in a location expecting to encounter a particular landmark or array of landmarks that will help it find its goal. Its expectations are cued not only by the distant panorama seen from near the goal location but also by its motivational state, the path it has taken, the time of day, and so forth. Contextual signals enable the same local cues to be

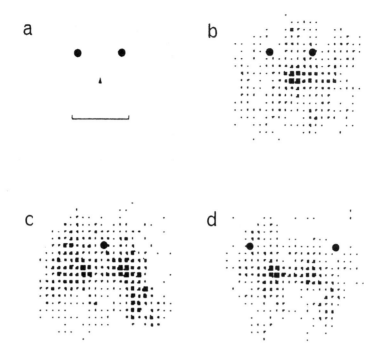

Figure 8.15 Gerbils can recognize landmarks by their position in an array.
NOTE: a: Animals are trained to find a seed at the position marked by the small triangle. This goal is fixed relative to two black cylinders that are shifted en bloc from trial to trial. b: Animals' search pattern with training configuration and no seed. The larger the black square in the grid, the more time the animal spent there. c: Tests with one cylinder. Two search clusters: one appropriate to the left cylinder, one to the right cylinder. d: Tests with distance between two cylinders doubled. Each cylinder now has a single peak associated with it. Calibration bar is 100 cm. SOURCE: From T. S. Collett et al. (1996).

treated in different ways. Gould (1987) trained a bee to land on one petal of an artificial flower at one time of day and on another at another time of day (Figure 8.16). The artificial flower presents essentially the same visual information throughout the day. However, particular features of the flower are primed differentially and attract the bee's approach according to the changing signal from the bees' internal clocks.

More distant contextual cues can play a significant supporting role in the recognition of local landmarks. For obvious geometrical reasons, the landmarks that best aid the pinpointing of a goal are those that are close to that goal. For similar geometrical reasons, the appearance of such close landmarks will change

markedly as the insect moves in their vicinity, so that both learning and recognizing them can be problematic. Evidence from more distant contextual cues that change more slowly with viewing position can thus make recognition more robust to variation in viewing position and direction.

When bees learn to respond to a particular stimulus that is set in one context, they will accept a broad range of stimuli as equivalent to that stimulus (T. S. Collett, Fauria, Dale, & Baron, 1997; T. S. Collett & Kelber, 1988). In one experiment, bees collected food in two places. In place A they flew through a maze in which they learned to fly left on seeing a 45° diagonal grating of black and white stripes on the back wall of the maze, and to fly right

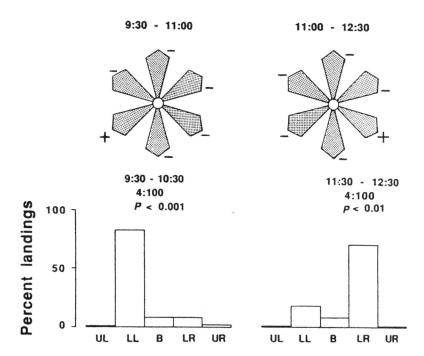

Figure 8.16   Bees' spatial memories can be linked to a temporal context.
NOTE: Bees were trained to land on the lower left petal of an artificial flower in the early morning (top-left panel) and at the bottom right around midday (top-right panel). Bees were flipped off the flower if they landed incorrectly. Lower panels show distributions of landings on test days with no punishment for incorrect landings.
SOURCE: Gould (1987). Reprinted with permission.

on seeing blue (Figure 8.17). In place B the same bees encountered a similar maze, but in this case they had to fly right on seeing a 135° striped grating and left on seeing yellow. After this training, they responded correctly to both gratings in both contexts, showing that they were sensitive to grating orientation. But they treated a vertical (90°) grating differently in the two contexts. In context A, they flew left as though it were a 45° grating, and in context B they flew right as if it were a 135° grating. The vertical grating is categorized according to the context in which it is set.

With training in a single place, such contextual capturing does not occur. A somewhat similar experiment was performed in which bees flew through a two-compartment maze that was located in one site (Figure 8.18). Each

compartment of the maze was again decorated with stripes of different orientations (45° or 135°), and the correct trajectory was to the left in one compartment and to the right in the other. Tests with vertical stripes now gave very different results. With the two compartments in a very similar context, bees flew in a compromise direction neither left nor right (T. S. Collett, Baron, & Sellen, 1996).

More generally, a variety of contextual cues (the pattern of more distant landmarks, distance from hive) change gradually with location. These contextual cues enable a bee to arrive with strong a priori expectations of what it will see. They can be used as supporting evidence for recognizing a fixed local landmark. Weaker local evidence is thus needed so that the bee can be somewhat sloppy in its looking

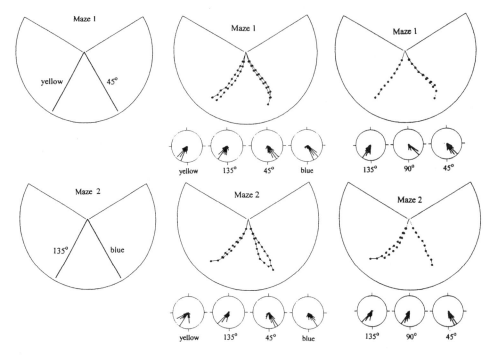

Figure 8.17   Pattern recognition and spatial context in honeybees.
NOTE: Left column sketches the task. Bees learn over successive periods to find sucrose in two mazes, each in a different place. The direction to be taken, shown by radial labeled lines, depends on the orientation of the stripe pattern or on the color decorating the back wall of the semicircular arena (radius 70 cm). In maze 1 bees fly through a hole to their left to reach sucrose when the wall is covered with 45° black and white stripes and to their right when the wall is plain yellow. In maze 2 bees fly to the left when the back wall is blue and to the right when it is covered with stripes oriented at 135°. Middle column: Bees behave appropriately with all training patterns in both mazes, flying to their left for blue or 45° stripes and to their right for yellow and 135° stripes. Dotted line plots mean trajectories. Circular distributions below plot directions of individual vectors at 40 cm from entry hole to maze. The ordering of labeled distributions corresponds to the ordering of mean trajectories through the maze. Right column shows that 90° stripes are treated differently in the two mazes. In maze 1 they are treated like 45° stripes and in maze 2 like 135° stripes. SOURCE: From T. S. Collett et al. (1997).

strategies when learning and recognizing local cues.

Conversely, when bees have little contextual background, they become fussier about what constitutes the right landmark. In one experiment bees were trained to search in the center of a square array of blue cylinders. Training took place either on a white platform in an outside environment with a surrounding panorama of trees and buildings or inside a featureless white hut. Trained bees were tested with a square array of the same sized yellow cylinders. Bees trained on the platform and cued by the panorama treated the yellow and blue cylinders equivalently and searched in the center of the array. The search pattern of bees trained in the hut, where there were few features apart from the cylinders, was disrupted when the colors were switched (Figure 8.19).

Contextual cues carve up the world into separate regions along many dimensions (space, time, internal states, behavioral sequences). They allow learning in one context

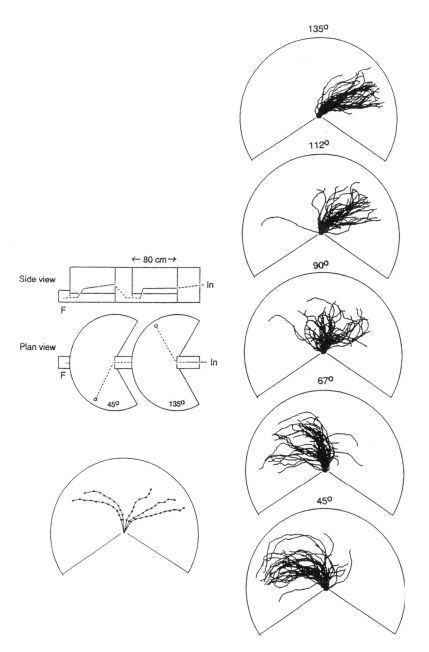

Figure 8.18   Behavior in a two-compartment maze in one place.

NOTE: Bees are trained to fly to their right in the first compartment that has 135° stripes on the back semicircular wall and to fly to the left in the second compartment, where there are 45° stripes on the back wall. In tests, the first compartment is covered with stripes of one of several different orientations. The direction of the bees' trajectories recorded in the first compartment changes with stripe orientation in a graded manner. Top left: Sketch of maze and training conditions. Right column: Superimposed trajectories for different stripe orientations. Bottom left: Mean trajectories for data in right column.

SOURCE: From T. S. Collett et al. (1996).

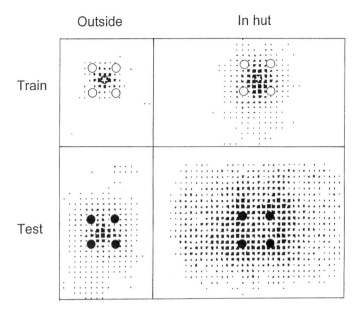

Figure 8.19   Contextual cues and landmark recognition.
NOTE: One group of bees is trained to find food in the center of a square array of yellow cylinders that is placed on a platform in the open. The other is trained with the same array placed in a uniform white hut. The bees' search pattern is recorded when the feeder is absent, either with the training array or with the color of the cylinders switched to blue. The changed color perturbs the search behavior of bees trained in the hut but not of bees trained on the platform, where the distant panorama provides supporting cues for recognizing local landmarks. SOURCE: From T. S. Collett & Kelber (1988).

to be independent of (and therefore not to interfere with) what is learned in another context. A number of studies have shown that insects will learn potentially competing associations in different contexts. To gain access to a feeder, a honeybee or bumblebee will learn to choose a hole surrounded by stripes of one diagonal and to avoid a hole surrounded by stripes of the opposite diagonal. At the same time it will learn to choose a hole that is labeled by the opposite diagonal to gain access to its nest (Colborn, Ahmad-Annuar, Fauria, & Collett, 1999; Srinivasan, Zhang, & Gadakar, 1998).

The learning of such potentially competing associations is easier if the associations are acquired sequentially. If bees are already trained to approach one diagonal to reach the feeder, acquiring the opposite association to

reach the nest is quick and interferes only marginally with the acquired association at the feeder. Learning in both contexts is slowed if the two associations must be acquired at the same time. This interference is not prevented by prior familiarity with the two contexts. An association is insulated from interference only after it has been acquired within the context (Fauria, Dale, Colborn, & Collett, in press).

Enhanced Precision from Multiple Landmarks

Provided that an animal has compass information, the bearing and distance from a single landmark is enough to define a location. However, errors in measuring bearings and distances mean that precision will increase if more landmarks are used and estimates from them are combined (Figure 8.12;

Kamil & Cheng, 2000). Parallax effects imply that errors will be smaller the closer the landmarks are to the location. These two considerations suggest that animals should be programmed to learn about and use several landmarks surrounding a goal and that they should weight preferentially information from landmarks that are close to the goal.

A standard method for investigating how information from different landmarks is used has been to train an animal to find food in a position that is specified by a given array. The array is then truncated or transformed, and the animal's search distribution is recorded when no food is present. Thus, nutcrackers presented with different subsets of an array of landmarks to which they have been trained search in the correct location relative to each subset, showing that many landmarks in the array contribute to guiding their search (see Basil, quoted in Kamil & Cheng, 2000). If the array is expanded by a large amount, a winner-takes-all mechanism often comes into play so that at any one time the animal's search is determined by just one member of the array. If one landmark is normally much closer to the goal than are the rest, that landmark tends to dictate the animal's search. In other cases the search is distributed over several sites, each site corresponding to the usual bearing and distance of the food from one or more of the landmarks in the array (e.g., Figure 8.16). Such data show that animals learn about multiple landmarks, but they reveal little about how information from different landmarks is combined. Smaller transformations of an array should be more informative, but have not been much used.

Combining Distance Information.
Kamil and Jones (1997, 2000) have developed a new approach for analyzing how nutcrackers combine guidance information from different landmarks. To examine the interaction of distance cues, they trained nutcrackers to search

for buried seeds along a line segment that connected two cylindrical landmarks of different colors. The seeds were always one quarter of the line segment from one cylinder and three quarters of the segment from the other. The absolute distance between cylinders varied from trial to trial during training, between 38 cm and 98 cm, but the 1:3 ratio of the two distances from the seed to the cylinders remained constant. This procedure may accustom birds to transformations of the array so that their behavior is less likely to be disrupted when they are tested with changes that go beyond the training range. Birds readily mastered the problem and searched on the line segment at a point where the ratio of the two distances to the cylinders was the required 1:3. The birds' performance was not impaired when the separation of landmarks was decreased or slightly increased beyond the range of training separations to 28 cm or 108 cm. The search position must therefore be governed by the birds' distances from both landmarks (Figure 8.20, top).

A simple model (T. S. Collett, 2000) suggests how information from the landmarks is combined. Suppose that the bird is at a short distance from a learned food site or goal. A restoring force brings the bird back to that goal. The strength of this force increases linearly with the bird's distance from the goal, pushing the bird away from the landmark if the bird is on the near side of the goal, and pulling it toward the landmark if it is on the far side. The goal is an equilibrium point where the restoring force, or error signal, is zero. If we suppose that birds learn some visual cue to the distance of the landmark from the site, then the amplitude of the restoring force can be envisaged as the magnitude of the difference between the stored and the current value of that cue.

We need two further assumptions to explain the bird's behavior. The first is that the strength of the restoring force due to each

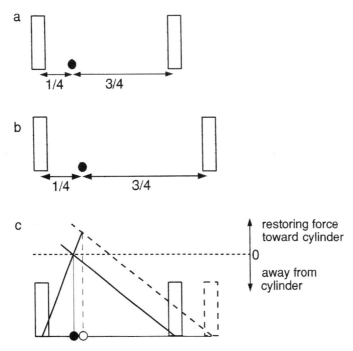

Figure 8.20 Clark's nutcracker uses the relative distances from two landmarks to specify a goal. NOTE: a: Bird's search position (•) after learning to find seeds at a site located between two landmarks. Birds are trained with multiple separations, with the seed always placed a quarter of the landmark separation from one landmark and three quarters of the separation from the other landmark. b: Bird searches at the correct ratio when the separation between landmarks is expanded beyond the training range (data from Kamil & Jones, 2000). c: Model to account for these results. Associated with each landmark is a restoring force that increases with the distance of the bird from the expected seed site (•), pushing the bird away from the landmark if it is too close and pulling the bird toward the landmark if it is too far. The rate of change of the force (slopes of diagonal lines) depends on the proximity of the seed to the landmark. When the separation between landmarks is enlarged beyond training values, the bird searches at the equilibrium point where the sum of the restoring forces due to the two landmarks is zero. Dotted lines show that there is no change in the ratio of the distances between search point (○) and landmarks. Further details in text. SOURCE: From T. S. Collett (2000).

landmark varies inversely as the distance of that landmark from the goal. Specifically, the slope of the line that relates restoring force to distance from the equilibrium point varies as the reciprocal of the distance of the landmark from the goal. The empirical basis of this assumption is the finding that landmarks near a goal control a bird's search more strongly than do distant ones. In terms of visual cues to distance, cues from close landmarks change more rapidly with distance and therefore can provide a larger error signal than can cues

from more remote landmarks. The second assumption is that when several landmarks define a goal, the net restoring force is just the linear sum of the component forces contributed by each landmark.

Figure 8.20 shows the outcome of applying these assumptions to tests with two landmarks for a bird that has been trained to a site located one quarter of the landmark separation from one of the landmarks and three quarters from the other. In this example only one training separation has been used, but this model behaves similarly when there are several training separations. The net restoring force is zero at the training site. If tests are given with the separation increased from the training value, the component restoring forces will be in equilibrium, with a net value of zero, at a point where the ratio of the distances to the two landmarks is 1:3. This model shows that the nutcracker's ability to take ratios need not imply complex interactions between landmarks. Distance estimates may be combined simply by summing the component forces contributed by each landmark.

Combining Directions.   Laboratory experiments show that both honeybees (Figure 8.12) and nutcrackers can specify a place by the compass bearings of several landmarks viewed from that place. Birds were able to learn to find buried seeds at the corner of a triangle formed by the food site and two cylinders when the bearing from each cylinder to the food site remained constant, but the size of the triangle varied from trial to trial (Kamil & Jones, 2000). In principle, bearings can be combined using a model equivalent to that proposed for distances. The bird would attempt to minimize the individual differences between the learned and actual bearing of each landmark from the goal site. If estimates were errorless, this process would bring the bird to the food site where all landmark bearings intersected. Errors in estimating actual bearings or errors in stored bearings would tend to pull the birds away from this site.

Consider a bird that is a short way from the goal site. As with distance measurements, we assume that a restoring force acting perpendicularly to the learned bearing of each landmark minimizes the difference between the current and learned estimates of the bearings. We also assume that the amplitude of the force increases linearly with the angular difference between the two estimates. The bird is then driven in the direction defined by the sum

of the forces associated with each landmark in the array to an equilibrium point that will tend to average the errors. Again, information is combined simply by linear summation.

Proximity Weighting and Landmark Selection

In many species, from insects to mammals, landmarks close to a goal are weighted preferentially over more distant ones. This bias can be demonstrated by training animals with an array that contains landmarks at different distances and then giving tests with the array expanded or transformed. The animal's search in these tests is driven principally, and sometimes exclusively, by those landmarks that are normally close to the goal (Bennett, 1993; Cheng, Collett, Pickhard, & Wehner, 1987; Vander Wall, 1982). Such data suggest that identifiable close landmarks are weighted more heavily in memory and can in some way capture the animal's search. The model just outlined emphasizes that another factor also contributes to this bias: As an animal moves away from the goal, the error signals from landmarks close to the goal are stronger than are signals from more distant ones.

A different method of demonstrating proximity weighting has been to exploit overshadowing (i.e., an animal's propensity to learn little about a cue if another cue is more salient and grabs the animal's attention). Spetch (1995) demonstrated the overshadowing caused by a close landmark in pigeons that viewed a vertical touch screen. The birds' task was to peck at a site that was defined relative to an array of landmarks on the screen. Each pigeon learned two arrays, both of which contained a landmark (the letter T) at the same distance from the goal but in a different direction and with different features. In one array T was the closest landmark to the goal, and in the second array another landmark was even closer. When T was shown by itself, search was more accurate when the T had been the

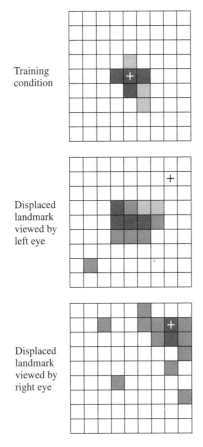

Training
condition

Displaced
landmark
viewed by
left eye

Displaced
landmark
viewed by
right eye

Figure 8.21   Chicks attend to different aspects of
a scene through each eye.
NOTE: Chicks learn to search in the center of a
square arena (70 cm sides) close to a landmark.
In tests, the landmark (a red plastic stick 15 cm
by 0.5 cm) is shifted to the right corner. Chicks
ignore the shift and guide their search relative to
the cues provided by the walls of the arena if they
look through their left eye (middle), but they search
close to the landmark when observing the scene
through their right eye. Landmark is shown by the
cross; search density is proportional to blackness
of the squares.
SOURCE: Vallortigara (2000). Reprinted with permission.

closest one to the goal than when it had been
overshadowed by an even closer landmark.

Landmark selection can depend also on
which intrinsic neural circuits an animal focuses on a landmark array. For reasons that

are unclear, a bird using its left eye attends to
different landmark features than does a bird
using its right eye (Vallortigara, 2000). Week-
old chicks were trained to search for buried
food at the center of a circular arena (95 cm
across with 30 cm high walls). A red plastic stick placed close to the food also marked
the food's location. On probe tests the landmark was moved toward the edge of the arena.
Binocular chicks ignored the displaced landmark and searched in the center of the arena,
as did chicks with eye patches over their
right eyes. Chicks which were patched on the
left eye so that vision was restricted to the
right eye searched at the location of the red
stick and not in the center (Figure 8.21). The
brain systems fed by the two eyes seem to
be structured to encode, learn, or respond to
different features of the visual world.

ROUTE LEARNING IN INSECTS

Ants, bees, and wasps readily learn routes
between their nests and a feeding site, and
there is much evidence that these insects guide
themselves through familiar territory with the
aid of visual landmarks (for reviews, see T. S.
Collett & Zeil, 1998; Wehner, 1992). Consider
the foraging career of a desert ant that forages
individually for many tens of meters over the
sand with no chemical trails to help it keep to
its route. A young forager leaves its nest for
the first time. It looks back at its nest and learns
features of the surrounding landmarks so that
it can find its nest hole again. Until it becomes
familiar with the more distant landscape, its
principal means of guidance can only be path
integration (PI; for reviews, see M. Collett
& Collett, 2000; Wehner & Wehner, 1990).
Throughout its journey, the ant, using its sky
compass (for a review, see Wehner, 1994),
monitors the direction in which it walks, continuously updating an accumulator that keeps
a record of its current distance and direction

from its nest. At any point the insect can use this vector information to return directly home, navigating by PI until it has reached its nest. When the ant encounters a food item, such as a dead insect, it records the coordinates of the site as given by the accumulator and goes back to the nest. Using these stored coordinates, it (like honeybees; von Frisch, 1967) is able to return to its previous food site, again by PI.

Path integration enables the ant to cope with voluntary or enforced detours. With an estimate of its current PI coordinates always available, the ant can at any point subtract these coordinates from those of the goal to obtain the direction to the goal. The outcome of this process is seen in operation in Figure 8.22. Ants ran up and down a channel between their nest and a feeding site. The walls of the channel obscured the surrounding

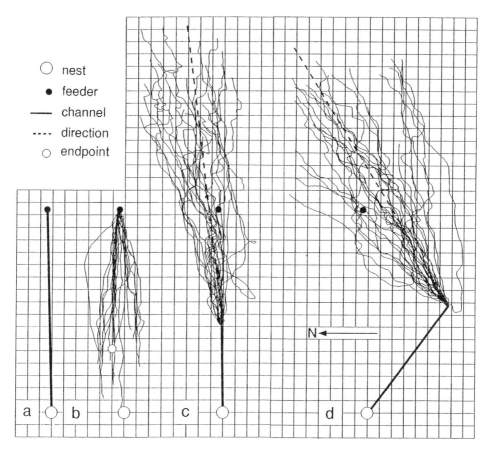

Figure 8.22   A route to a feeder controlled by path integration in a desert ant.
NOTE: a: Training route. Ants travel 15 m from their nest along an eastward pointing channel to a feeder. b: Homing trajectories of ants taken from the feeder and released in a test area. Large open circle shows position of fictive nest. Small circle indicates mean endpoint at 11.1 m from the nest. c: Individual foraging trajectories of ants on open ground after they have left a shortened channel connected to the nest. Filled circle marks the usual position of food, which is absent in these tests. d: Individual foraging trajectories of ants after leaving a channel pointing 38° to the east of the training channel. Grid lines are spaced at 1 m. SOURCE: From M. Collett et al. (1999).

landscape but allowed the ants a view of the sky. In tests, the channel from the nest was shortened and rotated so that ants hunting for food emerged on open ground in an unfamiliar location. The ants guided by their PI system immediately turned in the rough direction of the goal, running through an unfamiliar landscape to reach it.

On arrival at the previous food site, the ant will often fail to find more food. It then searches nearby or in the same direction beyond its previous find (Schmid-Hempel, 1984). This strategy tends to keep the ant within a constant sector that is centered on the nest (Wehner, Harkness, & Schmid-Hempel, 1983), giving the ant the opportunity to become familiar with landmarks along the route. After a few trips the ant's knowledge of the visual landscape becomes evident in that the ant follows a fixed path to and from its foraging site (T. S. Collett, Dillmann, Giger, & Wehner, 1992; Santschi, 1913; Wehner, Michel, & Antonsen, 1996) and may then no longer rely on PI, except as a backup. Different ants may take the same fixed route, even though they normally forage singly, indicating that they must pick up the same visual information and operate using the same visuo-motor rules (T. S. Collett et al., 1992).

Fixed routes involve associations between individual landmarks along the route and a variety of actions linked to them. These landmark-directed actions keep insects within a narrow corridor and restore them to the corridor if they are outside it. Landmarks are used as attractive beacons that can pull the insect back to the route (Chittka, Kunze, Shipman, & Buchmann, 1995; von Frisch, 1967). Ants detour around landmarks consistently to the left or to the right as appropriate for a given part of the route (T. S. Collett et al., 1992). Bees and ants follow extended edges like a shoreline or the margin of a forest direction (T. S. Collett, Collett, & Wehner, 2001; Dyer, 1987; von Frisch, 1967). They also link local vec-

tors to landmarks so that on leaving one landmark they move in the appropriate direction, and sometimes distance, to the next subgoal of their route (Collett et al., 1996; M. Collett, Collett, Bisch, & Wehner, 1998; T. S. Collett, Fry, & Wehner, 1993; R. Menzel, Geiger, Joerges, Müller, & Chittka, 1998, Srinivasan, Zhang, & Bidwell, 1997). Dividing routes into segments with vectors carrying insects between subgoals makes route following more precise than navigation by PI. The inevitable errors in distance and direction associated with PI or with performing a local vector increase with the distance traveled so that dividing a route into segments defined by reliable landmarks that allow a vector to be reset will necessarily lessen the overall error (Srinivasan et al., 1997).

An ant's performance of a fixed route seems to operate largely independently of PI. One sign of this independence is that ants follow very similar routes whether they are homing normally or whether they are allowed to reach the vicinity of the nest before being carried back and replaced near the food (Figure 8.23). Unless the accumulator were to be reset at the familiar release site, it would be in different states in the two homing conditions so that a significant contribution from PI should be easily visible in differences between the paths taken in the two situations.

In fact, the PI accumulator is unlikely to be reset at subgoals marked by landmarks. It seems, instead, that responses to landmarks transiently suppress the output of the PI system (M. Collett et al., 1998). Evidence comes from training desert ants along an L-shaped route to a feeder. The first leg of the route was 8 m north over open ground followed by 8 m west along a channel to a feeder at the end of the channel (Figure 8.24, top). Both the channel and feeder were sunk into the ground so as to be invisible to ants walking over ground. When the ant emerged from the channel on its normal homeward route, it traveled south to

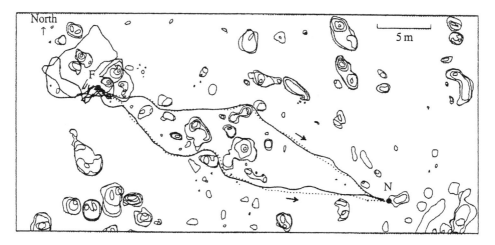

Figure 8.23   Fixed routes in desert ants may be unaffected by the state of the path-integration accumulator.

NOTE: Routes followed by two desert ants returning from a feeding site (F) through desert scrub to their nest (N). Shrubs are marked by contour lines at 15 cm height intervals. Dotted lines show the normal idiosyncratic path of each ant. Solid lines show the very similar paths followed by the same two ants when they were carried back to the feeding site after they had almost reached the nest.

SOURCE: Wehner et al. (1996). Reprinted with permission. Copyright © 1996 Company of Biologists.

the nest. An identical feeder and channel were set up in a test area. Ants were taken to the test feeder, either from the training feeder, before they started returning home, or when they had almost reached the nest. Ants taken from the training feeder went south on exiting the channel (Figure 8.24a), in agreement with the direction set by local vectors and by PI. When ants taken from the training feeder were released at the west end of a shortened 4 m channel, the directions predicted by PI and local vectors conflicted. Some (35%) trajectories were directed southeast, as though driven entirely by PI (Figure 8.24b). In the majority of cases (65%), PI was initially overridden, and the ants first went south for approximately 3 m (Figure 8.24c). The same south-directed local vector was also performed when ants were taken on their return trip from a point close to the nest and placed at the end of the 4 m test channel (Figure 8.24d). This vector must be associated with the channel and recalled in the context of leaving it. Had the ants taken

from the nest been governed by the PI system, their trajectories would be directed back along the channel to the test feeder. Had the ants' familiarity with the channel caused the accumulator to be reset to its accustomed state, either at the feeder or on leaving the channel, their trajectories would have been like those in Figure 8.24b or in Figure 8.24a, respectively, instead of like those in Figure 8.24d.

The strategy of following a local vector takes precedence over PI. When the response indicated by PI disagrees with that linked to a landmark, ants temporarily place their bets on the landmark information. The current information supplied by PI is not ignored but is relegated to the background: The accumulator continues to be updated so that it can be used if landmarks fail.

Route learning must be fast to be useful. A desert ant may have a foraging career of about 6 days before it falls prey to a spider or a robber fly or is caught and blown away by a sudden gust of wind (Schmid-Hempel &

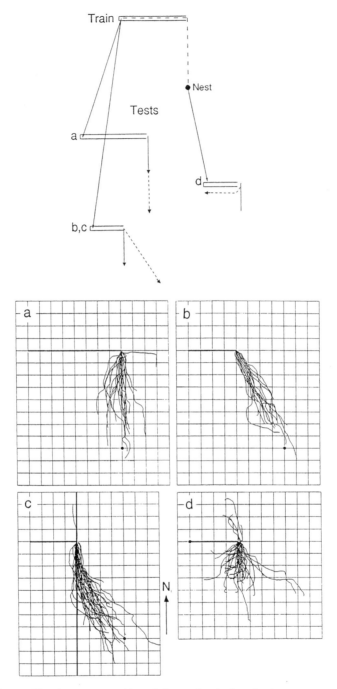

Figure 8.24   Learned local vectors override path integration in desert ants.

NOTE: Top: Schematic of experimental design. Ants were trained from the nest (filled circle) to travel 8 m north over open ground and then along an 8 m channel (double line) to a feeder at its west end. They returned along the same path to the nest (dotted line). Trained ants were taken either from the training feeder or from the nest to a test field where they were placed in a test feeder at the end of 8 m or 4 m channels similar to the training channel. Trajectories were recorded when ants left the channel until they

Schmid-Hempel, 1984). Each day a typical ant performs no more than four or five foraging trips from its nest (Wehner et al., 1983), so its lifetime experience may be limited to 30 foraging excursions. Learned routes can be long, involving the acquisition of many views and of path segments associated with these views. Moreover, because the sequence of views will generally differ on inward and outward trips, the two journeys are presumably learned independently. How can insects acquire long sequences of views rapidly?

Sequence learning is often thought to involve some variant of reinforcement learning, with the sequence acquired backwards from the goal. The reinforcement signal begins by strengthening actions and events that lead immediately to the goal. These reinforced events then become secondary reinforcers of the preceding step in the sequence, and reinforcement propagates recursively to the beginning of the sequence. Consequently, with long sequences the process will be relatively slow. One way in which insects could speed up the process and learn events simultaneously along the whole route is by using PI information as a learning signal (Collett, 1998). When an ant is guided by PI, the vector signaling the direction and distance to home becomes smaller throughout the journey. The ant could exploit a decrementing vector as a sign that an appropriate landmark should be learned.

Another scaffold for route learning is provided by chemical trails. Many species of ants lay trails between their nests and a foraging site, and nest mates may be recruited to a site by these trails. Following trails is slow because the ant must sniff out the trail with its antennae close to the ground. Guidance by visual landmarks increases walking speed twofold, and experienced ants may switch from relying on chemical trails to visual landmarks (Figure 8.25). Again, the chemical trail can act as a guidance signal for learning the whole route.

An ant following a route may see numerous objects that could be learned as landmarks. The ant's home or food vector might also help restrict its learning to the most useful of these and prevent the acquisition of views of objects that are far off the path between feeder and nest. Figure 8.26 illustrates an experiment in which ants were trained along a route with a single, large cylinder placed at one point to the right of the direct homeward path (Figure 8.26a). An ant's knowledge of the landmark was probed in tests in which it was caught at the feeder as it was about to depart for home and then taken to a test area (Figure 8.26b). Here it was released on the ground, where it faced a similar cylinder that was placed in the direct path of its home vector. Ants demonstrated their familiarity with the cylinder by detouring around it in a consistent direction. With the training landmark to the right of their homeward route, ants detoured to the left of the cylinder, thus viewing it on the right as they would on normal homeward trips.

Figure 8.24 started searching. Dotted line and arrow shows the ant's predicted path on the assumption that it is guided by path integration (PI). Solid line and arrow show the ant's path on the assumption that it follows a local vector associated with the channel. a: Ants taken from the training feeder to an 8 m channel. The ants' trajectories on leaving the channel point south. Filled circles in this and panels b to d represent the predicted goal of PI. b,c: Ants taken from the training feeder to a 4 m test channel. The trajectories were divided into two categories. A minority of trajectories (b) followed PI from the outset. Most trajectories (c) followed a local vector south for about 3 m and then followed PI. d: Ants taken at the end of the return journey when they have almost reached the nest to the end of a 4 m test channel. On exiting the channel, their trajectories are directed south following the local vector.
SOURCE: Data from M. Collett et al. (1998).

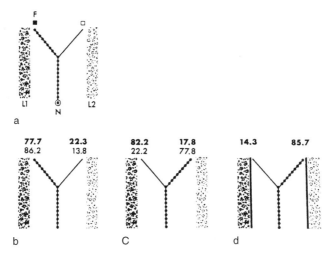

Figure 8.25   The ponerine ant, *Paraponera clavata,* learns to favor visual over chemical cues.
NOTE: Sucrose (F) is available at the end of the left branch of a Y-shaped platform. L1 and L2 are natural landmarks on either side of the platform. Dotted lines show pheromone trail left by ants when returning to their nest (N). b: Feeder removed. c: Pheromone trail is switched to right fork. d: Pheromone trail is switched to right fork, and the visual landmarks are screened. Percentage choices for each fork are separated for experienced ants (bold figures in upper row) that follow visual cues and for naive ants (lower row) that follow pheromone trails. SOURCE: Wehner, 1992 (data from Harrison, Fewell, Stiller, & Breed [1989]). Copyright ©1992 Kluwer Academic Publishers.

Different groups of ants were trained with the cylinder in different positions. Figure 8.26c plots the proportion of ants that detoured in this expected direction for the different positions of the cylinder on the training ground. Evidence of learning was stronger when the cylinder was close to the direct path between feeder and nest. The acceptable offset was greater the further the cylinder was positioned from the start of the homeward path. For acquisition to occur, the landmark needs to be viewed along a bearing that is near that of the home vector. Such a rule would provide a simple way to filter out objects that are off to one side and thus not useful guideposts. Additionally, if the ant were to set a minimum time over which the landmark must be viewed before acquisition occurs, it could screen out the learning of small landmarks that are visible only briefly.

INSIGHTS FROM HIPPOCAMPAL PLACE CELLS AND HEAD DIRECTION CELLS

Over the past few decades study of the hippocampus in freely behaving rats has contributed greatly to a better understanding of spatial learning and navigation. It is now possible to record simultaneously the individual signals from tens of neurons (e.g., Wilson & McNaughton, 1993) while rats are learning a route, foraging, or solving a maze. The fine-grained analysis of the neural mechanisms of navigation that this methodology allows is putting flesh on concepts derived from behavioral observations and giving new insights into the processes involved. Intriguing and important as the hippocampus is, it is, as many authors have stressed, only one part of the central nervous system that is concerned

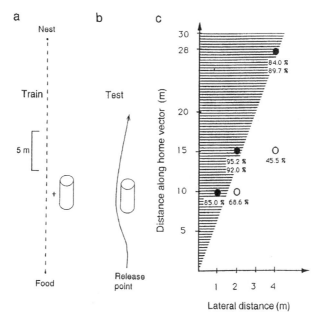

Figure 8.26   Desert ants that have learned a homeward route seem ignorant of a landmark unless its bearing from the route is relatively close to the direct line between food and nest.

NOTE: a: During training, ants foraged for several days at a feeder 30 m distant from their nest on a patch of sand that was bare apart from an oil barrel that was fixed in one position. Separate training sessions were conducted with the barrel in different places. b: In tests, ants were carried to another area where they were released with a second barrel in the direct path of their home vector. Ants showed that they were familiar with this object by detouring consistently to its left. c: Percentage detours to the left for different training positions of the barrel. Circles mark training positions. When more than 80% of detours are to the left, the circles are filled. Hatched area marks roughly the region within which it is supposed that views of landmarks are acquired. SOURCE: Data from T. S. Collett et al. (1992).

with navigation (e.g., McNaughton, Leonard, & Chen, 1989; Redish & Touretzky, 1997; Save & Poucet, 2000).

Place Cells and Place Fields

The discovery of place cells (O'Keefe & Dostrovsky, 1971) has stimulated numerous studies on the role of the hippocampus in navigation. These remarkable cells specify particular places within a circumscribed environment. A given place cell has a low level of activity until the animal comes within a small area. The cell's firing rate then increases significantly. The location associated with en-

hanced firing (the cell's place field) remains stable over long periods. A population of cells with different overlapping place fields carpets an area of a few square meters so that position within this small-scale environment can, in principle, be computed precisely from the activity of the population (Wilson & McNaughton, 1993). It is unknown whether coverage would be equally complete over a rat's normal home range extending for hundreds of meters or whether place fields would be restricted to certain significant regions within it.

Nonuniform coverage is already seen in laboratory environments of a few meters square. Vacant areas without significant land-marks are represented less well in the firing of place cells than are regions that are more cluttered. Hetherington and Shapiro (1997) recorded fewer place fields in the center of a rectangular arena than near the walls. Place fields were particularly prevalent close to prominent visual cues that were fixed to the walls, and several studies suggest that the position of the field is linked to such cues. O'Keefe and Burgess (1996) recorded place cells in an area enclosed by an open square box. In tests, the box was enlarged in one or two dimensions. The location of a place field within the enlarged area often shifted in con-cert with the closest wall, suggesting that the field is at a fixed distance from that wall. Similarly, Gothard, Skaggs, Moore, and McNaughton (1996b) showed that fields can be attached to a start box or to a goal that is specified by local landmarks that are shifted together relative to a larger environment. The density of place cells may also be higher at significant goal sites that are not marked by

nearby landmarks. In the water maze (Morris, 1981), rats swimming in a bath of murky wa-ter can escape by climbing onto a platform just below the surface. The platform itself is invisible; its location is only defined relative to cues external to the water bath. Hollup, Molden, Donnett, Moser, and Moser (2001) found that an unexpectedly high percentage of place cells have fields close to the site of the platform.

Place Cells and Visual Cues

Place cells are especially intriguing in that their firing is determined by many different spatial cues, so that their behavior reflects some of the complexity of the whole ani-mal. If stable visual cues are displaced, place fields shift in accord (e.g., Muller & Kubie, 1987; O'Keefe & Conway, 1978). The ex-ample in Figure 8.27 is notable in showing that place cells are influenced by the features of individual landmarks as well as by their spatial arrangement. Three similarly sized

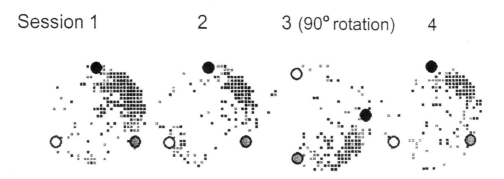

Figure 8.27   Place cells: Field stability and its control by visual objects.
NOTE: Maps of firing rate for one cell over four consecutive 16 min sessions. Rat wears a light-emitting diode on its head so that its position in the cylinder and the firing of the cells can be correlated. Dark areas show where the firing rate is greatest. A black cone, a white cylinder, and a French wine bottle (full), all about the same height, were placed at the edge of the 76 cm diameter recording cylinder arranged in an equilateral triangle. On the third session the triangle was rotated through 90°. On the fourth session the objects were rotated back. The place fields of 23 out of 29 cells rotated with the triangle. In the example shown, the field remained between the wine bottle and the cone in all sessions.
SOURCE: Cressant et al. (1999). Copyright © 2000 John Wiley & Sons, Inc. Reprinted by permission of Wiley-Liss, Inc., a subsidiary of John Wiley & Sons, Inc.

objects—a bottle, a cone, and a cylinder—were placed against the wall of the cylinder equidistantly from each other. When the array was rotated about the center of the cylinder, the place fields rotated by the same amount.

Place cells employ visual cues in a sophisticated manner. A place cell is recorded from a rat in an open arena with a prominent visual landmark and with food scattered evenly over the floor, making all positions and paths within the arena equally significant. In such circumstances, the cell fires within its place field in whatever direction the rat faces (Muller, Kubie, & Ranck, 1987), implying that place cell firing depends on more than matching a single local view. Place cells can lose this ability, if structures outside the hippocampus that contain head direction cells (discussed later) are lesioned. A frequent consequence of such lesions is to make cells more directional: They then respond best when the rat faces in a particular direction within the field (Archey, Stackman, Goodridge, Dudchenko, & Taube, 1997, see also Taube 1998). One possible interpretation of this finding is that place cells respond to an assemblage of local views (P. A. Sharp, 1991), each view tagged with a directional signal, or, more broadly, that directional signals modulate the input to which a place cell responds. Place cells also become increasingly directional when rats follow fixed routes, either in mazes (McNaughton, Barnes, & O'Keefe, 1983) or in an open arena (Markus et al., 1995), firing most when the rat moves in one direction through the field.

Place Fields and Nonvisual Cues

Rodents can use PI to return to their nest when the journey is performed in total darkness and when all external cues to direction are eliminated (hamsters: Etienne, 1980; gerbils: Mittelstaedt & Mittelstaedt, 1980). Place fields also remain stable for a while when an-

imals run in the dark, suggesting that path-related idiothetic cues or local olfactory and tactile cues contribute to specifying place fields. Initial evidence for a contribution from path-related cues came from O'Keefe and Speakman (1987; see also P. E. Sharp, Kubie, & Muller, 1990). The fields of place cells were recorded in a cross maze where the location of the goal arm varied from trial to trial. The goal was labeled by surrounding spatial cues that rotated together with the goal arm. On probe trials the cues were removed after the rat was in the start arm and had viewed the maze. Many place fields maintained their relative position to the start arm when the rat was released after the cues were removed.

Although odor cues were eliminated by O'Keefe and Speakman's procedure, they are nonetheless likely to assist in stabilizing place fields. In the absence of a visual cue card, or in the dark, place fields become more variable after the floor of the recording arena has been cleaned (Save, Nerad, & Poucet, 2000). Stable and precisely delimited place fields were even found in rats that were blinded shortly after birth. As in sighted animals, fields tend to be clustered close to landmarks, and the fields rotate with the landmarks. Stable fields are found away from landmarks (Save, Cressant, Thinus-Blanc, & Poucet, 1998). The long-term positional stability of such fields may be helped by the rat's habit of frequently contacting landmarks, as well as by odor cues.

Sometimes in the absence of a useful visual cue, the fields of a set of simultaneously recorded place cells in a circular arena rotate as a coherent group over many minutes (Knierim, Kudrimoti, & McNaughton, 1998). The cells are decoupled from external input, but their relative mapping remains stable, probably through interconnections between the place cells and inputs from idiothetic cues.

Interactions between Visual and Path Integration Cues

Path integration is of limited precision (Etienne et al., 1988). Stuchlick, Fenton, and Bures (2001) demonstrated this fact using an ingenious method to force rats to rely solely on idiothetic cues in avoiding an unpleasant place in a circular arena. The rats remained accurate for a path length of no more than about 7 m to 8 m (or about 2 min), whereas with additional visual cues they performed the task stably over a long time. Unless discrepancies are very large, hamsters tend to navigate by visual cues rather than by PI when the two are placed in conflict (for a review, see Etienne, Maurer, & Séguinot, 1996). If a hamster is given brief exposure to visual landmarks during an otherwise dark outward trip, the animal's later homeward path in the dark shows that it was strongly influenced by its earlier visual fix (Etienne, Boulens, Maurer, Rowe, & Siegrist, 2000).

The primacy of visual cues over idiothetic cues is also found in the responses of place cells. For instance, Jeffrey and O'Keefe (1999) rotated a rat so slowly that its vestibular system was unaware of the rotation, and at the same time they rotated visual cues in the opposite direction. Place fields were then anchored to the visual cue. This preference is limited to stable visual cues. With repeated experience of a visual cue that moved relative to idiothetic cues, the place cells came to ignore the unstable visual information, and instead their fields were tied to the rats' internal senses of direction (see also Knierim, Kudrimoto, & McNaughton, 1995). Over the short term, then, visual cues dominate idiothetic ones, but over the longer term visual cues need to be perceived as stable relative to other locational cues for the animal (Biegler & Morris, 1993) and its place cells to rely on them.

By what mechanism do PI and landmark cues interact? One frequently mentioned pos-sibility that requires elaborate circuitry for its realization is for the accumulator to be reset by visual information. According to this hypothesis, an animal stores the PI coordinates of multiple sites in its environment, each of which is also specified by visual landmarks, so that landmark and PI information can be associated together. When the animal recognizes a site from the arrangement of landmarks, it adjusts its accumulator so that its current PI coordinates match the stored ones associated with that site (e.g., Etienne et al., 2000; Gallistel, 1990, McNaughton et al., 1996; Redish & Toureztky, 1997). A simpler possibility is for the accumulator to be reinitialized frequently at familiar sites that are defined by landmarks. Such a mechanism could account for the stability of a rat's place cells, but perhaps not for the hamster's ability to adjust its homeward path after a brief visual fix. A third possibility, due to Mittelstaedt (Etienne et al., 2000), is that visual information does not influence the state of the accumulator but simply resets the animal's internal compass.

If place cells were an intimate part of the mechanism of PI, their behavior would suggest that the accumulator is indeed reset by visual input. So far, however, the neural basis of the accumulator is not understood. If the accumulator is implemented outside the hippocampus, the known response of place cells to inconsistent landmark and PI stimuli is perhaps explained more simply by independent visual and PI inputs to the cells.

Head Direction Cells

Head direction (HD) cells (Ranck, 1984) behave in a way that is complementary to place cells (for a review, see Taube, 1998). Whereas place cells can register location independently of the direction in which the rat faces, HD cells are sensitive to direction irrespective of location. Their discharge varies systematically with the horizontal direction of the rat's head.

Some cells, for instance, respond maximally when the rat faces north, and their response drops linearly as the rat's heading departs from north. Cells differ in their preferred direction with the population spanning all compass directions. Although HD cells are not found in the hippocampus, their behavior is intimately related to that of place cells (see the following section).

If experiments are performed with the rat in a uniform circular arena with a contrasting card in one position on the wall, then, as with place cells, this cue card comes to control the responses of the population of HD cells. Should, for instance, the card be shifted through 90° while the rat has been removed from the cylinder, the preferred direction of all head direction cells shifts by a little less than that amount when the rat is replaced (Taube, Muller, & Ranck, 1990). An exposure of 8 min suffices for the activity of HD cells to become bound to a visual cue of this kind (Goodridge, Dudchenko, Worboys, Golob, & Taube, 1998).

The response of HD cells to the cue card presents an interesting computational problem. The direction associated with the peak firing rate of an HD cell is independent of the rat's position in the cylinder. However, the cue card on the wall is very close to the rat. Unlike the distant sun, the bearing of the cue card from the rat varies strongly with the rat's position. Despite this parallax the rat is able to abstract direction. An important unanswered question is whether (and, if so, how) place cells play a role in this computation. Although HD cells can obtain direction from close landmarks, it is not their preferred mode of operation. HD cells ignore cues from close landmarks when there is a larger and more distant panorama (Wiener, Berthoz, & Zugaro, 2000).

As with place cells, the directional properties of HD cells persist for several minutes when the rat moves in the dark (Taube, 1998), suggesting that idiothetic cues update the direction reported by the population of HD cells. Similarly, HD cells maintain their directional response when rats explore a new environment. Taube and Burton (1995) had rats walk from a familiar cylindrical compartment through a corridor into an unfamiliar rectangular compartment. HD cells kept the same directional preference in this new environment as they had in the cylinder (Figure 8.28). When idiothetic and landmark cues were put in conflict in this two-compartment setup, the cells' firing was controlled by landmark cues. The rat was replaced in the cylinder after the cue card had been rotated through 90°, and, as expected, the preferred direction of the HD cells rotated through 90°. When the rat left the cylinder and entered the corridor, it experienced a conflict between the rotated reference bearing that it carried from the cylinder and the one that it met in the corridor. The current visual signals prevailed and the preferred directions of the HD cells rotated back to their former values (Figure 8.28). Cue conflict experiments often give more variable and complex results (e.g., Knierem et al., 1998). By and large it seems that with small conflicts whole animals, place cells and their HD cells tend to trust visual cues whereas with large discrepancies they rely on idiothetic information.

Place Cells, HD Cells, and the Rat's Sense of Direction

O'Keefe and Speakman (1987) discovered that the behavior of place cells mirrors the behavior of the whole animal. They trained rats to find food at the end of one arm of an open cross maze, with the arms distinguishable by visual cues near the maze. When the cues were removed, the rats were sometimes mistaken about which arm led to the goal, and the positions of their place fields then shifted corresponding to the rats' errors. A close

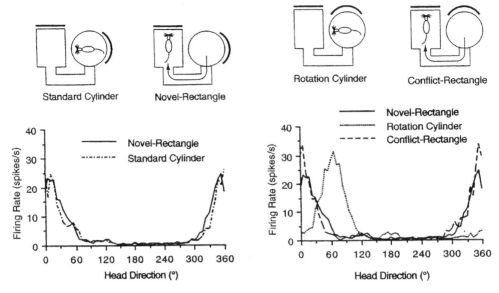

Figure 8.28   Behavior of a postsubiculum head direction (HD) cell in a complex environment showing that firing rate depends on both idiothetic and visual cues.

NOTE: A cylinder, 76 cm in diameter, led through a door via a corridor to a rectangle. White cards provided polarizing visual cues in both containers. Graphs show firing rate of HD cell plotted against the rat's head direction. Left: The preferred direction of cells remained almost constant as the rat moved for the first time from the cylinder through the newly opened door to the rectangle that it had never entered before. Right: The rat was removed from the cylinder and the cue card rotated through 90°. When the rat was replaced, the preferred direction rotated to match the new orientation of the card (dotted line). When the rat was allowed to reenter the rectangle, the preferred direction instantly switched to its previous value (dashed line).

SOURCE: Taube & Burton (1995). Reprinted with permission.

correlation thus exists between the moment-by-moment behavior of the whole rat and its place cells. Similar experiments suggest that HD cells also reflect the rat's current sense of direction. If rats are induced to make errors in a radial maze, the firing of HD cells tends to be correlated with these directional errors. If the rat thinks one direction is north, so do its HD cells (Dudchenko & Taube, 1997).

Knierim et al. (1995) showed directly that both place cells and HD cells agree on the same reference bearing. Rats were disoriented before and after they were placed in a circular arena that was bare except for a prominent cue card hung on the wall. Consequently, from trial to trial the perceived direction of the card differed with respect to any directional or positional cues from path integration. Collections of place cells and HD cells were recorded together from rats undergoing this treatment, and the place fields and directional responses shifted in concert from trial to trial regardless of the card. This experiment yielded the important finding that the fields of all the simultaneously recorded place cells and HD cells rotated as a group. The coherence may come in part from common idiothetic input to the cells and in part from interconnections between place cells and between HD cells. It is difficult to resolve whether these global interactions are part of the rat's decision-making process, helping, the rat decide upon its orientation in the world, or whether they reflect decisions made elsewhere.

A Patchwork of Places

Our spatial knowledge seems to be composed of a patchwork of disconnected regions; laboratory and home, for example, that may be separated by a subway ride. The rat hippocampus also seems to contain multiple and independent representations of distinct neighborhoods. If place cells are recorded from a rat in different laboratory arenas, some cells are found in both arenas, but some are limited to just one (Muller & Kubie, 1987). Place cells recorded in a gray walled cylinder with a cue card that was sometimes black and sometimes white developed different representations in the two situations (Bostock, Muller, & Kubie, 1991). The hallmark of such independent representations is that correlations between cells in one environment do not transfer to the second environment (Redish, 1999). One suggested reason for multiple maps is that each map requires both PI and landmark information, so that map size is limited by the distance over which the rat's PI system can operate (Redish & Touretzky, 1997). Interpretation is, however, complicated by the finding that multiple maps in different arenas may take a long time to develop (see discussion in Hartley, Burgess, Lever, Cacucci, & O'Keefe, 2000).

The dynamics of switching between two acquired representations (or reference frames) was studied by Gothard et al. (1996b) and by Redish, Rosenzweig, Bohanick, McNaughton, and Barnes (2000). Rats were accustomed to local cues provided by a start box that from trial to trial was shifted with respect to the room. When the rat was close to the local cue, its hippocampal cells were tied to that reference frame. As the rat moved away, the population of active cells changed to ones in the room-based reference frame. The system seemed to switch between two distinct attractors, each associated with its own reference frame.

How does a place cell acquire its field in a particular environment, and what determines whether a particular cell is active in any given environment? McNaughton et al. (1996) proposed a bold model that was attractive in that it answered both questions in a neat way. They suggested that the hippocampus is the PI accumulator and that different collections of cells in it represent different environments. As a consequence of its intrinsic connections, each cell in such a collection signals a particular PI coordinate. Idiothetic inputs update the rat's current position as it walks through a given environment so that activity progresses through the collection of cells. According to this model, the PI input is the primary determinant of a cell's activity. Particular cells, which are active at particular points in the environment, become linked to the values of the sensory cues at that place. After this association has been made, the cells can be activated either by PI input or by the appropriate visual cues.

Other models of place field assignment focus on a cell's visual input. Hartley et al. (2000) have used a hardwired, feedforward network to simulate the complex properties of place cells when they are recorded in several environments of different shapes. A given place cell is fed by a random sample of input cells taken from a larger set, each of which is sensitive to a surface or an object at a specific distance and allothetic direction from the animal. This simple scheme is astonishingly good at mimicking the way in which place fields transform as the environment is changed. Other models of this general type incorporate learning in the formation of place fields and adjustable connections between place cells (e.g., Brunel & Trullier, 1998; Kali & Dayan, 2000; Touretzky & Redish, 1996). Kali and Dayan employed Hebbian learning to enable input cells to associate particular views with particular head directions. The directional invariance of place cells then depends on the animal's experiencing many directions during the learning process. On the assumption that the PI accumulator is implemented outside the hippocampus, it is easiest to suppose that place cells modeled this way obtain idiothetic input from the direction and velocity signals that provide inputs to the PI system rather than from the output of the PI accumulator.

Evidence bearing on these models has come from recording place cells in two rectangular arenas connected by a corridor (Skaggs & McNaughton, 1998). Many but not all cells had equivalent place fields in the two arenas even though the rats moved frequently to and fro between the two (Figure 8.29). A single path integrator acting through both

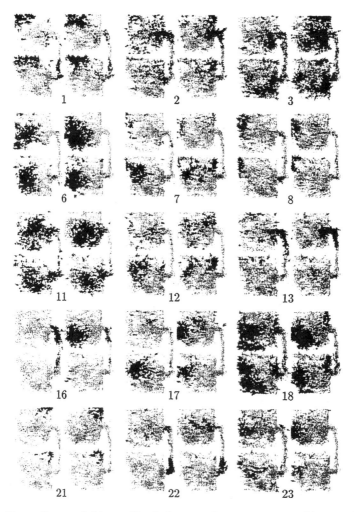

Figure 8.29   Place cells recorded in two identical rectangular arenas connected by a corridor.
NOTE: Between 10 and 39 cells were recorded simultaneously. The figure shows the fields of 15 cells out of a total sample of 25 recorded in two consecutive 15 min sessions. Black points represent the rat's position when the cell fires. Some cells had equivalent fields in the two arenas, and some had very different fields.
SOURCE: From Skaggs & McNaughton (1998). Copyright ©1998 Society for Neuroscience.

compartments would register different coordinates for the two place fields of one cell. These data are not easy to reconcile with the model of McNaughton et al. (1996); they are more consistent with a place field that is defined jointly by a cell's intrinsic visual sensitivity and the spatial arrangement of cues in a given environment.

Place Cells and Route Learning

Recent studies on place cells hint that route learning may be accompanied by an enhancement of the connections between place cells that have fields along the route. Suppose that a rat learns a route in which it passes through place fields A, B, C, and D in that order. After the rat has performed the route about five times, the fields come to develop a tail that extends backwards along the route (Mehta, Barnes, & McNaughton, 1997; Mehta, Quirk, & Wilson, 2000). A plausible interpretation of such skewed place fields is that with experience of the route, the firing of cell A provides an enhanced input to cell B so that cell B fires earlier along the route than before, and so on with other pairs along the route.

Extensive asymmetric connections of this kind might in part account for the route-dependent place fields described by Frank, Brown, and Wilson (2000) and Wood, Dudchenko, Robitsek, and Eichenbaum (2000). In Wood et al's experiments, rats ran along a modified T maze. The end of each arm of the T was visited in turn for a water reward. A trained rat returned from the reward along a connecting link to the bottom of the T. It then traveled up the stem and turned into the other arm. Some place cells with fields in the stem were active primarily when the trajectory up the stem was preceded by a return down the left connecting link and followed by a right turn. They were silent when the rat passed through the field when on the opposite route.

Other route-dependent place cells behaved in the reverse manner.

ROUTE PLANNING

Some animals learn enough about the large-scale environment around them that they are able to reach any one of many possible goal sites from a multitude of starting points. Because it is relatively easy to communicate with chimpanzees reared in a language-rich environment, their capacities are accessible to a human observer. A recent study (C. R. Menzel, Savage-Rumbaugh, & Menzel, 2002) involved a 4-year-old Bonobo named Kanzi. Before this study began, Kanzi was accustomed to taking daily excursions within a 20-hectare wood and had learned to associate particular places with particular lexigrams (abstract signs representing a word). Kanzi's human companions on these excursions had touched lexigrams and pointed at the represented place (often out of sight), but there had been no fixed link between a lexigram and moving toward a place. Despite the lack of any formal training, tests showed that Kanzi could guide a person to the place labeled by a particular lexigram. Fifteen food containers were scattered around the wood at a maximum distance of 170 m from Kanzi's enclosure. Most of the food sites were invisible from outside the enclosure. Morning and afternoon, with Kanzi indoors, one container was baited with Kanzi's rations, and two lexigrams were hung on a board outside the laboratory. One lexigram indicated food, and the other indicated its location. Kanzi could initiate a food search at will and on 99 out of 127 trials successfully led a human companion who was ignorant of the food's location straight to the indicated site.

In a second series of tests, Kanzi performed equally well on 12 trials spread over many months when he was led into the woods to an arbitrary starting point and then given a lexigram signaling a location that harbored food or some other desirable item. On all occasions Kanzi successfully reached and led a human companion to the correct location (Figure 8.30). Sometimes Kanzi took new and direct trails, and sometimes he followed a more indirect path.

Human data of a broadly similar kind were collected by Thorndyke and Hayes-Roth (1982). They measured how well subjects could indicate different destinations within a large and complex building. Subjects with at least one month's experience of working in the Rand Corporation Building were led by an experimenter to each one of six start rooms, and in each room they were asked to indicate the direction of seven different destination rooms. Directional errors averaged about 30° for subjects with one to two months of experience and dropped to 22° after one to two years of experience of the building. Given such results and the paucity of equivalent tests on other mammals, it would be easy to exaggerate the unusualness of the spatial abilities of apes. Once suitable tests have been designed, it would not

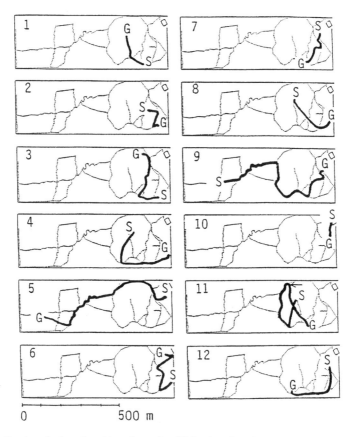

Figure 8.30   Routes of a bonobo chimp through a 20-hectare forest.
NOTE: The chimp set out from one of various stating points (S) where he was shown a lexigram representing one of several goal sites that was always out of sight from S. The chimp then traveled (route shown by solid line) to the indicated goal (G). Sometimes he followed regular paths (dotted lines), and sometimes he chose a new route.
SOURCE: C. R. Menzel et al. (2002). Reprinted with permission.

be surprising to find that many other mammals possess similar navigational abilities.

How are paths planned from an arbitrary starting point to a goal? Two broad classes of models have been discussed. The first involves path integration and is easy to explain but perhaps hard to implement. If an animal knows the PI coordinates of its goal and of its current position, it can elaborate a direct path to the goal (as seen in Figure 8.22). Suppose that the animal also learns the coordinates of many sites that it can recognize and that (unlike desert ants) it can reset its accumulator to those coordinates when it finds itself in such a site. The animal then has the means to plan a route between any two places, provided that it has the PI coordinates of both. The hallmark of this method of route planning should be that an animal picks out the correct direction to the goal from its starting point.

An alternative theoretical approach to route planning is more topological. It can be described concretely in terms of networks of interconnected place cells that can link a starting position to a goal site. Connections between place cells may change not only as a consequence of traveling the same route several times (Mehta et al., 1997, 2000) but also, perhaps, during exploration. In both cases, connections between place cells along feasible paths will be enhanced. Activity propagating through such a network could in principle determine an animal's route in terms of existing links between place cells. The shortest route can be found in terms of the path of least resistance between known and activated start and end points.

The known properties of place cells reveal how adaptable such a method of path planning could be. A classic problem in path planning is incorporating a method of detouring around obstacles. When barriers are introduced into an arena, place cells with fields close to the barrier become silent (Muller & Kubie, 1987), effectively removing themselves from the network of interconnected cells and thus from the planning process. The rat would in consequence automatically detour around the barrier (Muller, Stead, & Pach, 1996). Several detailed models of this general kind have been worked out (e.g., Franz et al., 1998; Gerstner & Abbott, 1997; Matarić, 1991; Muller et al., 1996; Trullier & Meyer, 2000).

The ability to point to goals from arbitrary starting points indicates that directional information is explicitly incorporated in route planning and that purely topological models may not be sufficient to account for a real animal's behavior. Hybrid models could take directional information from PI or from learned routes that have local vectors attached to them and that crisscross familiar terrain.

A more complex form of route planning is picking an efficient order when visiting a sequence of places. Given several possible goals to be visited in a self-selected order, what determines the sequence that the animal chooses? E. W. Menzel's (1973) famous study of chimpanzees in a one-acre field was the first to examine this question. An animal was carried on an extensive tour through the field during which it watched an experimenter hide as many as 16 pieces of food in 16 different places in a haphazard order. The animal was then allowed to retrieve the food in any order. It did not follow the roundabout path of the experimenter but rather took a more efficient route with a shorter path length.

One possible explanation of this result that is relatively simple to simulate is that the chimpanzee chooses its next goal by recalling the memory that is visually most similar to its current goal: the nearest neighbor in memory space. Gallistel and Cramer (1996) have begun to examine plausible algorithms of this process in vervet monkeys performing a similar task in a 9 m by 9 m outdoor enclosure. Like E. W. Menzel's chimpanzees, the monkeys were more efficient at finding food than was the experimenter at hiding it. The

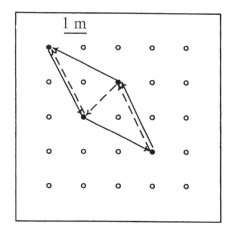

1 m

Figure 8.31 Route planning and looking ahead. NOTE: A vervet monkey is presented with rewards placed around a diamond-shaped route. The best route depends on the location of the final reward. The dashed route is optimal if the monkey starts at one acute vertex and find its final reward at the other. The solid route is optimal if the monkey must make a round trip to reach its final reward. Monkeys making the round trip generally followed the solid line, and those ending at the far vertex followed the dashed line. This evidence suggests that the monkey's strategy is more complex than just going to the nearest rewarded site. SOURCE: Gallistel & Cramer (1996). Reprinted with permission. Copyright © 1996 Company of Biologists.

results of two experiments hint that the monkeys might be doing something more subtle than following a nearest-neighbor stratagem of locating one food site and then going to the closest, still unvisited site. In one test, three corners of a diamond were baited with food, and one acute corner was used as a starting point. On some trials, after the monkey was en route to its first destination, a grape was placed at the starting point to ensure that the monkey returned to that point. If the monkey were using a nearest-neighbor routine, it should move to one site at the center of the diamond and then make for the opposite one. Instead, on those occasions when the

start was baited, it tended to make its way around the periphery of the diamond, suggesting that it looked ahead to beyond the next goal (Figure 8.31).

REWARDS AND PLACES

Places are significant because of the resources, like nests, food, building materials, tools, or mates, that they contain. Some resources, such as a water hole, are relatively permanent. Others may be periodic, such as those associated with a fruiting tree. Others may be transient: A cache containing a single food item is visited usefully just once. Proper timing of a visit means knowing the properties of the contents: Perishable items should be retrieved before they rot. Resources may even move around. Animals do well to keep track of the locations and the conditions of a variety of resources.

Knowing What Is Where

Chimpanzees naturally remember the locations of many specific objects. C. R. Menzel (1999) worked with an 11-year-old chimpanzee that had previously been trained to learn symbols representing different objects. No additional training was needed for her to demonstrate her knowledge in a new situation. She watched a human experimenter hide a desirable object on the ground 2.5 m to 8 m away in the woods outside her outdoor enclosure. After a delay of up to 16 hours she interacted with a second person indoors who did not know what the object was or where it had been hidden. Fifty-seven such trials with different objects and locations were distributed irregularly over 268 days. On 34 of these days the chimpanzee first attracted the person's attention, pressed the key symbolizing the object, led the person outside, and pointed with her index finger extended at the object until the person retrieved it. On only three occasions did she recruit someone when there was no object to retrieve. The chimp thus knew both the location and the identity of the object and could retain this information for many hours.

Without the benefit of interspecific communication, more indirect methods are needed to show that an animal knows what is where. Clayton and Dickinson (1999a) used an ingenious method to show that scrub jays know what food they have cached in a particular site. They allowed birds to cache two different types of food. Just before recovery, the cache sites were all emptied to remove olfactory cues, and the birds were prefed with one of the two foods. Prefeeding caused a relative devaluation of that food. The birds then preferred to search in those sites that had contained the other food type, demonstrating that they knew which food was where.

Using perishable food items, Clayton and Dickinson (1999b) went on to show that scrub jays also know when they cached a particular food item. Birds were given two food items to cache: peanuts with a long shelf life and wax worms that become unpalatable within a few days. Again, the caches were emptied before the birds were allowed to search for food. After a 4-hour delay between caching and recovery, birds chose sites where they had cached wax worms. After a 124-hour delay during which the wax worms would have had time to rot birds preferred sites that had contained peanuts. Control birds were trained to cache and retrieve wax worms that had been frequently replaced so that the birds had no opportunity to learn that over time wax worms lose their appeal. These birds preferred wax worm sites after both a 4 hour and a 124 hour delay. Birds in some way tag their memories of caches with a time stamp so that the memory decays or is ignored after an appropriate interval.

Periodic Exploitation

Long-lived mammals can draw on long-held knowledge to cope with environmental fluctuations. They may remember several locations of a given resource, some that are easily available and some that are more difficult to reach but may be essential for surviving occasional shortages. Kummer (1995) described how baboons exploit hidden or distant sources of water during periods of drought. Some favored foods may only be found briefly at certain times of year. Altman (1998) saw baboons respond to ripe berries on an isolated bush in the center of their home range as though they were a sign of the availability of this fruit elsewhere. The baboons then trekked to a remote and rarely visited location at the edge of their home range to reach an extensive patch of bushes bearing that fruit.

A similar example comes from C. R. Menzel (1991), who showed that on seeing ripe fruit, Japanese macaques look in the appropriate place for more. He placed ripe akebi fruit on the ground out of season; monkeys on the forest floor noticed the fruit then stared upward and climbed trees with akebi vines growing on them, responding in a generically correct manner. The macaques behaved differently when Menzel placed pieces of chocolate on the ground. This food had no expected spatial context, and the monkeys restricted their search to a small area close to where they had come across the chocolate.

Comfort and longevity can be improved by the occasional consumption of plants for medicinal purposes. For self-administered medication, animals must know what plant to eat and where to find it. A fully documented case is the use of *Veronia amygdalina* by wild chimpanzees in Tanzania (for a review, see Huffman, 1997). Like humans, chimpanzees ingest this unpleasantly bitter plant specifically to clear infestations of intestinal parasites. The trees are sparsely distributed within the chimpanzee's home range and seem to be targeted when required. It is plausible, but not proven, that young chimpanzees learn the function and location of this plant by observing and imitating their elders (M. A. Huffman, personal communication, 2000). *Veronia amygdalina* acts pharmacologically to clear parasites. Populations of chimpanzees have also developed the habit of swallowing without chewing a variety of bristly leaves in the early morning, when their stomachs are empty. The whole leaves pass undigested through the intestinal tract, causing increased gut motility and diarrhea, and by their scouring action help eliminate parasite infestations (Huffman & Caton, 2001; Wrangham, 1995).

Keeping Track of Resources

The locations and states of resources may change rapidly. Examples are accumulating of the ability of various animals to keep track of changing resources in their environment. Female cowbirds lay eggs in heterospecific nests to be reared by foster mothers. To find suitable nests for their eggs, they explore potential nests and monitor their states of readiness. A good nest to parasitize is one that has eggs in an early stage of development so that the nestlings will not have fledged before the foreign egg hatches (Sherry, Forbes, Khurgel, & Ivy, 1993). Similarly, male squirrels pick out potential mates that will ovulate in a day or two and return to the sites where they spotted a likely female the previous day (Shwagmeyer, 1995).

Flowers depleted of nectar replenish slowly, and nectar-feeding birds leave an interval for the nectar to recover before revisiting a flower. Kamil (1978) observed the visits of marked Hawaiian honeycreepers to flowering mamani trees in Hawaii. Individual birds avoided returning to the same cluster of flowers for 1 to 2 hours after each visit. Using an artificial array of eight flowers in a natural environment, Healy and Hurly (1995) showed that rufous hummingbirds that were scared away after visiting four of the flowers in the array came back later to sample the undepleted flowers. It is clear that birds learn the location of flowers (for a review, see Healy & Hurly, 2001) and that they time repeated visits to allow the flowers to replenish. The interval between visits represents a fine balance between a short interval to lessen the danger of competition from other birds and a long interval to allow a flower to refill. Hummingbirds adjust visiting times to match the filling of an artificial flower at fixed intervals, but they visit more frequently if they find evidence of competition (Gill, 1988).

Chimpanzees use stones as hammers (0.5 kg to 18 kg in weight) for cracking open panda nuts. Panda trees are widely scattered and often out of site of each other. Stones are a scarce commodity and are transported from tree to tree. Boesch and Boesch (1984) followed the journeys of stones that they had marked, and concluded that a chimpanzee on finding a nut recalls the location of the closest stone to the tree. After a chimpanzee has opened the nut, it leaves the stone at the anvil site, and for future use it must remember where it last deposited the stone.

Forgetting and Erasure

The counterpart to remembering the updated location of a resource is forgetting an old location that is no longer relevant. Cache retrieval is especially interesting because it highlights the need for birds to tag or in some way erase their memories of sites they have already emptied and so prevent fruitless visits. Marsh tits, black-capped chickadees and Clark's nutcrackers (Kamil, Balda, Olson, & Good, 1993) have all been reported to avoid revisiting sites that they have emptied. Clark's nutcrackers avoid with equal accuracy sites that they have found to be plundered so that the act of finding a seed may not be a particularly effective trigger for inducing forgetting.

Rats trained on radial mazes are typically given the task of retrieving a single food item from each arm of the maze. They avoid revisiting arms that they have already depleted. Analysis of the revisiting errors that are made shows that the errors tend to be to arms that were visited early in the sequence. One interpretation of this result has been that rats keep a list of which arms they have already visited and that items at the head of the list are forgotten (Roitblat, 1987). This task differs in many ways from caching, especially in that the memory task is short-term and one that is performed repeatedly in the same maze. Indeed, it is rare in birds to find any correlation between the order of caching and the order of recovery. An interesting exception comes from Northwestern crows, which cache clams that soon decompose. For good reason the crows search first for the oldest caches (James & Verbeek, 1985).

CODA

This chapter has emphasized the specialized learning that is associated with the many special purpose devices that participate in guiding an animal's movements through familiar surroundings. However, spatial learning is also a general tool that is appropriated by other cognitive faculties. Before humans had the luxury of written notes, overheads, or teleprompts as memory aids when giving speeches, people remembered long arguments by exploiting their natural ability to recall places and routes. Cicero would imagine himself wandering through a hall with many alcoves along the walls, each containing a different memorable statue, and in each alcove he would place a paragraph of his speech. Later, walking through this memory palace, he could

look in each alcove, find the paragraph placed there, and so retrieve his speech in the desired order.

Over time the best way to develop and make use of this skill was codified. It had an ancient and allegedly dramatic beginning (Yates, 1966). At a banquet, the poet Simonides of Ceo received a message to meet two young men outside the banqueting hall. He left but could find no one outside. During his absence the roof of the hall caved in, crushing and mangling the guests so that their relatives could not identify the corpses. Simonides was able to recall who sat where and so could point the relatives to their dead. The tale goes that this experience inspired Simonides to develop this mnemonic trick into a full-blown system. In Cicero's words: "He inferred that persons desiring to train this faculty of memory must select places and form mental images of the things they wish to remember and store those images in the places so that the order of the places will preserve the order of the things, and the images of the things will denote the things themselves" Cicero De oratore, II, lxxxvii, 355 (translation Yates, 1966). As memory loci, buildings are recommended with clearly recognized locations within them. They should not be too cluttered or brightly lit, and individual loci should be spaced about 30 feet apart. The images placed in these loci must be striking and vivid. This memory palace, once built, can be reused because the images placed in it will fade away. To recall a sequence, walk through the palace and see the images pop up in the correct order, and the words or thoughts denoted by the images will also come to mind. By reversing the tour, a skilled mnemonist could recall Virgil's *Aeneid* backwards.

Whereas fixed routes through internal models allow sequences to be recalled, more flexible navigation within a spatial model or manipulation of a spatial model can aid reasoning. Johnson-Laird and Byrne (1991) summarized evidence that deductive reasoning relies on transforming a series of verbal statements into mental models, usually spatial ones. They find that when the translation between discourse and model is hard to make, arriving at legitimate conclusions becomes difficult. How this more general faculty of spatial reasoning and memory might mesh with the multitude of special-purpose modules studied in current research is an intriguing question that still needs proper formulation.

REFERENCES

Altman, S. A. (1998). *Foraging for survival.* Chicago: University of Chicago Press.

Archey, W. B., Stackman, R. W., Goodridge, J. P., Dudchenko, P. A., & Taube, J. S. (1997). Place cells show directionality in an open field following lesions of the head direction cell system. *Society for Neuroscience Abstracts, 23,* 504.

Becker, L. (1958). Untersuchungen über das Heimfindevermögen der Bienen. (Studies of homing in bees.) *Zeitschrift für vergeichende Physiologie, 41,* 1–25.

Bednekoff, P. A., & Balda, R. P. (1996a). Social caching and observational spatial memory in pinyon jays. *Behavior, 33,* 807–826.

Bednekoff, P. A., & Balda, R. P. (1996b). Observational spatial memory in Clark's nutcracker and Mexican jays. *Animal Behavior, 52,* 833–839.

Bennett, A. T. D. (1993). Spatial memory in a food-storing corvid. 1. Near tall landmarks are primarily used. *Journal of Comparative Physiology, A*(173), 193–207.

Biegler, R., & Morris, R. G. M. (1993). Landmark stability is a prerequisite for spatial but not discrimination learning. *Nature, 361,* 631–633.

Boesch, C., & Boesch, H. (1984). Mental map in wild chimpanzees: An analysis of hammer transports for nut cracking. *Primates, 25,* 160–170.

Bossema, I. (1979). Jays and oaks: An eco-ethological study of a symbiosis. *Behavior, 70,* 1–117.

Bostock, E., Muller, R. U., & Kubie, J. L. (1991). Experience-dependent modifications of hippocampal place cell firing. *Hippocampus, 1,* 193–206.

Brunel, N., & Trullier, O. (1998). Plasticity of directional place fields in a model of rodent CA3. *Hippocampus, 8,* 651–665.

Brünnert, U., Kelber, A., & Zeil, J. (1994). Ground-nesting bees determine the location of their nest relative to a landmark by other than angular size cues. *Journal of Comparative Physiology, A*(175), 363–369.

Capaldi, E. A., & Dyer, F. C. (1999). The role of orientation flights on homing performance in honeybees. *Journal of Experimental Biology, 202,* 1655–1666.

Capaldi, E. A., Smith, A. D., Osborne, J. L., Fahrbach, S. E., Farris, S. M., Reynolds, D. R., Edwards, A. S., Martin, A., Robinson, G. E., Poppy, G. M., & Riley, J. R. (2000). Ontogeny of orientation flight in the honeybee revealed by harmonic radar. *Nature, 403,* 537–540.

Cartwright, B. A., & Collett, T. S. (1983). Landmark learning in bees: Experiments and models. *Journal of Comparative Physiology, 151,* 521–543.

Cheng, K. (1986). A purely geometric module in the rat's spatial representation. *Cognition, 23,* 149–178.

Cheng, K., Collett, T. S., Pickhard, A., & Wehner, R. (1987). The use of visual landmarks by honeybees: Bees weight landmarks according to their distance from the goal. *Journal of Comparative Physiology, A*(161), 469–475.

Chittka, L., Kunze, J., Shipman, C., & Buchmann, S. L. (1995). The significance of landmarks for path integration of homing honey bee foragers. *Naturwissenschaften, 82,* 341–342.

Christou, C. G., & Bülthoff, H. H. (1999). *The perception of spatial layout in a virtual world* (Tech. Rep. No. 75). Tübingen, Germany: Max-Planck Institut für biologische Kybernetik.

Clayton, N. S., & Dickinson, A. (1999a). Memory for the content of caches by scrub jays (*Aphelocoma coerulescens*). *Journal of Experimental Psychology: Animal Behavior Processes, 25,* 82–91.

Clayton, N. S., & Dickinson, A. (1999b). Scrub jays (*Aphelocoma coerulescens*) remember the relative time of caching as well as the location and content of their caches. *Journal of Comparative Psychology, 113,* 403–416.

Colborn, M., Ahmad-Annuar, A., Fauria, K., & Collett, T. S. (1999). Contextual modulation of visuo-motor associations in bumblebees. *Proceedings of the Royal Society of London: Series B, 266,* 2413–2418.

Collett, M., & Collett, T. S. (2000). How do insects use path integration for their navigation? *Biological Cybernetics, 83,* 245–259.

Collett, M., Collett, T. S., Bisch, S., & Wehner, R. (1998). Local and global vectors in desert ant navigation. *Nature, 394,* 269–272.

Collett, M., Collett, T. S., & Wehner, R. (1999). Calibration of vector navigation in desert ants. *Current Biology, 9,* 1031–1034.

Collett, T. S. (1995). Making learning easy: The acquisition of visual information during the orientation flights of social wasps. *Journal of Comparative Physiology, A*(177), 737–747.

Collett, T. S. (1998). Rapid navigational learning in insects with a short lifespan. *Connection Sciences, 10,* 255–270.

Collett, T. S. (2000). Birds as geometers? *Current Biology, 10,* R718–R721.

Collett, T. S., & Baron, J. (1994). Biological compasses and the coordinate frame of landmark memories in honeybees. *Nature, 368,* 137–140.

Collett, T. S., Baron, J., & Sellen, K. (1996). On the encoding of movement vectors by honeybees. Are distance and direction represented independently? *Journal of Comparative Physiology, A*(179), 395–406.

Collett, T. S., Cartwright, B. A., & Smith, B. A. (1986). Landmark learning and visuo-spatial memories in gerbils. *Journal of Comparative Physiology, 158,* 835–851.

Collett, T. S., Collett, M., & Wehner, R. (2001). The guidance of desert ants by extended landmarks. *Journal of Experimental Biology, 204,* 1635–1639.

Collett, T. S., Dillmann, E., Giger, A., & Wehner, R. (1992). Visual landmarks and route following in desert ants. *Journal of Comparative Physiology, A*(170), 435–442.

Collett, T. S., Fauria K., Dale, K., & Baron J. (1997). Places and patterns—Study of context learning in honeybees. *Journal of Comparative Physiology, A*(181), 343–353.

Collett, T. S., Fry, S. N., & Wehner, R. (1993). Sequence learning by honey bees. *Journal of Comparative Physiology, A*(172), 693–706.

Collett, T. S., & Kelber, A. (1988). The retrieval of visuo-spatial memories by honeybees. *Journal of Comparative Physiology, A*(163), 145–150.

Collett, T. S., & Land, M. F. (1975). Visual spatial memory in a hoverfly. *Journal of Comparative Physiology, 100,* 59–84.

Collett, T. S., & Lehrer, M. (1993). Looking and learning: A spatial pattern in the orientation flight of the wasp *Vespula vulgaris. Proceedings of the Royal Society of London: Series B, 252,* 129–134.

Collett, T. S., & Rees, J. A. (1997). View-based navigation in hymenoptera: Multiple strategies of landmark guidance in the approach to a feeder. *Journal of Comparative Physiology, A*(181), 47–58.

Collett, T. S., & Zeil, J. (1998). Places and landmarks: An arthropod perspective. In S. Healy (Ed.), *Spatial representation in animals* (pp. 18–53). Oxford: Oxford University Press.

Cressant, A., Muller, R. U., & Poucet, B. (1999). Further study of the control of place cell firing by intra-apparatus objects. *Hippocampus, 9,* 423–431.

Dale, K., & Collett, T. S. (2001). Using artificial evolution and selection to model insect navigation. *Current Biology, 11,* 1305–1316.

Deubel, H. (1999). Separate mechanisms for the adaptive control of reactive, volitional and memory-guided saccadic eye movements. In D. Gopher & A. Koriat (Eds.), *Attention and performance* (Vol. 17, pp. 697–721). Cambridge, MA: MIT Press.

Devenport, J. A., Luna, L. D., & Devenport, L. D. (2000). Placement, retrieval and memory of caches by thirteen-lined ground squirrels. *Ethology, 106,* 171–183.

Dudchenko, P. A., Goodridge, J. P., Seiterle, D. A., & Taube, J. S. (1997). Effects of repeated disorientation on the acquisition of spatial tasks in rats: Dissociation between the appetitive radial arm maze and aversive water maze. *Journal of Experimental Psychology: Animal Behviour Processes, 23,* 194–210.

Dudchenko, P. A., & Taube, J. S. (1997). Correlation between head direction cell activity and spatial behavior on a radial arm maze. *Behavioral Neuroscience, 111,* 3–19.

Dyer, F. C. (1987). Memory and sun compensation in honey bees. *Journal of Comparative Physiology, A*(160), 261–633.

Dyer, F. C., & Dickinson, J. A. (1994). Development of sun-compensation by honey bees: How partially experienced bees estimate the sun's course. *Proceedings of the National Academy of Sciences, USA, 91,* 4471–4474.

Emlen, S. T. (1975). The stellar-orientation system of a migratory bird. *Scientific American, 233*(2) 102–111.

Etienne, A. S. (1980). The orientation of the golden hamster to its nest site after the elimination of various sensory cues. *Experientia, 36,* 1048–1050.

Etienne, A. S., Boulens, V., Maurer, R., Rowe, T., & Siegrist, C. (2000). A brief view of known landmarks reorientates path integration in hamsters. *Naturwissenschaften, 87,* 494–498.

Etienne, A. S., Maurer, R., & Saucy, F. (1988). Limitations in the assessment of path dependent information. *Behavior, 106,* 81–111.

Etienne, A. S., Maurer, R., & Séguinot, V. (1996). Path integration in mammals and its interaction with visual landmarks. *Journal of Experimental Biology, 199,* 201–209.

Fauria, K., Dale, K., Colborn, M., & Collett, T. S. Learning speed and contextual isolation in bumblebees. *Journal of Experimental Biology.* (In press).

Frank, L. M., Brown, E. N., & Wilson, M. (2000). Trajectory encoding in the hippocampus and enthorhinal cortex. *Neuron, 27,* 169–178.

Franz, M. O., Schöllkopf, H. A., Mallot, H.-P., & Bülthoff, H. H. (1998). Learning view graphs for robot navigation. *Autonomous Robots, 5,* 111–125.

Frens, M. A., & van Opstal, A. J. (1994). Transfer of short-term adaptation in human saccadic eye movements. *Experimental Brain Research, 100,* 293–306.

Frier, H. J., Edwards, E., Neal, S., Smith, C., & Collett, T. S. (1996). Magnetic compasses and visual pattern learning in honey bees. *Journal of Experimental Biology, 199,* 1353–1361.

Frisch, K. von (1967). *The dance language and orientation of bees.* London: Oxford University Press.

Gallistel, C. R. (1990). *The organization of learning.* Cambridge, MA: MIT Press.

Gallistel, C. R., & Cramer, A. E. (1996). Computations on metric maps in mammals: Getting oriented and choosing a multi-destination route. *Journal of Experimental Biology, 199,* 211–217.

Gerstner, W., & Abbott, L. F. (1997). Learning navigational maps through potentiation and modulation of hippocampal place cells. *Journal of Computational Neuroscience, 4,* 79–94.

Gill, F. B. (1988). Trapline foraging by hermit hummingbirds: Competition for an undefended renewable resource. *Ecology, 69,* 1933–1942.

Goodridge, J. P., Dudchenko, P. A., Worboys, K. A., Golob, E. J., & Taube, J. S. (1998). Cue control and head direction cells. *Behavioral Neuroscience, 112,* 749–761.

Gothard, K. M., Skaggs, W. E., & McNaughton, B. L. (1996a). Dynamics of mismatch correction in the hippocampal ensemble code for space: Interaction between path integration and environmental cues. *Journal of Neuroscience, 16,* 8027–8040.

Gothard, K. M., Skaggs, W. E., Moore, K. M., & McNaughton, B. L. (1996b). Binding of hippocampal CA1 neural activity to multiple reference frames in a landmark-based navigation task. *Journal of Neuroscience, 16,* 823–835.

Gould, J. L. (1987). Honey bees store learned flower-landing behavior according to time of day. *Animal Behavior, 35,* 1579–1581.

Gould, J. L., & Marler, P. (1987). Learning by instinct. *Scientific American, 256*(1), 74–85.

Guthrie, E. R. (1952). *The psychology of learning.* New York: Harper and Rowe.

Harrison, J. F., Fewell, J. H., Stiller, T. M., & Breed, M. D. (1989). Effects of experience on use of orientation cues in the giant tropical ant. *Animal Behavior, 37,* 869–871.

Hartley, T., Burgess, N., Lever, C., Cacucci, F., & O'Keefe, J. (2000). Modeling place fields in terms of the cortical inputs to the hippocampus. *Hippocampus, 10,* 369–379.

Healy, S. D., & Hurly, T. A. (1995). Spatial memory in rufous hummingbirds (*Selasphorus rufus*): A field test. *Animal Learning and Behavior, 23,* 63–68.

Healy, S. D., & Hurly, T. A. (2001). Foraging and spatial learning in hummingbirds. In L. Chittka & J. Thomson (Eds.), *Cognitive ecology of pollination* (pp. 127–147). Cambridge: Cambridge University Press.

Hermer, L., & Spelke, E. S. (1996). Modularity and development. The case of spatial reorientation. *Cognition, 61,* 195–232.

Hermer-Vazquez, L., Spelke, E. S., & Katsnelson, A. S. (1999). Sources of flexibility in human cognition: Dual task studies of space and language. *Cognitive Psychology, 39,* 3–36.

Hetherington, P. A., & Shapiro, M. L. (1997). Hippocampal place fields are altered by the removal of single visual cues in a distance-dependent manner. *Behavioral Neuroscience, 111,* 20–34.

Hollup, S. A., Molden, S., Donnett, J. G., Moser, M.-B., & Moser, E. I. (2001). An accumulation of hippocampal place fields at the goal location in an annular watermaze task. *Journal of Neuroscience, 21,* 1635–1644.

Houk, J. C., Buckingham, J. T., & Barto, A. G. (1996). Models of the cerebellum and motor learning. *Behavioral Brain Science, 19,* 368–383.

Huffman, M. A. (1997). Current evidence for self-medication in primates: a multidisciplinary perspective. *Year Book of Physical Anthropology, 40,* 171–200.

Huffman, M. A., & Caton, J. M. (2001). Self-induced increase of gut motility and the control of parasite infections in wild chimpanzees. *International Journal of Primatology, 22,* 329–346.

James, P. C., & Verbeek, N. A. M. (1985). Clam storage in a northwestern crow (*Corvus caurinus*): Dispersion and sequencing. *Canadian Journal of Zoology, 63,* 857–860.

Jander, R. (1997). Macroevolution of a fixed action pattern for learning: The exploration flights of bees and wasps. In G. Greenberg & E. Tobach (Eds.), *Comparative psychology of invertebrates: The field and laboratory study of insect behavior.* New York: Garland.

Jeffrey, K. J., & O'Keefe, J. M. (1999). Learned interaction of visual and idiothetic cues in the control of place field orientation. *Experimental Brain Research, 127,* 151–161.

Johnson-Laird, P. N., & Byrne, R. M. J. (1991). *Deduction.* Hove, UK: Erlbaum.

Judd, S. P. D., & Collett, T. S. (1998). Multiple stored views and landmark guidance in ants. *Nature, 392,* 710–714.

Junger, W. (1991a). Waterstriders (*Gerris paludum* F.) compensate for drift with a discontinuously working visual position servo. *Journal of Comparative Physiology, A*(169), 633–639.

Junger, W. (1991b). Die sensorischen und neuronalen Grundlagen der Driftkompensation beim Wasserläufer *Gerris paludum.* Unpublished doctoral dissertation, University of Tübingen, Tübingen, Germany.

Kali, S., & Dayan, P. (2000). The involvement of recurrent connections in area CA3 in establishing the properties of place fields: A model. *Journal of Neuroscience, 20,* 7463–7477.

Källander, H. (1978). Hoarding in the rook, *Corvus frugilegus.* Anser Suppl. 3, 124–128.

Källander, H., & Smith, H. G. (1990). Food storing in birds: An evolutionary perspective. In D. M. Power (Ed.), *Current ornithology* (Vol. 7, pp. 147–207). New York: Plenum Press.

Kamil, A. C. (1978). Systematic foraging by a nectar-feeding bird the amakihi (*Loxops virens*). *Journal of Comparative and Physiological Psychology, 92,* 388–396.

Kamil, A. C., Balda, R. P., & Good, S. (1999). Patterns of movement and orientation during caching and recovery by Clark's nutcrackers (*Nucifraga columbiana*). *Animal Behavior, 57,* 1327–1335.

Kamil, A. C., Balda, R. P., Olson, D. J., & Good, S. (1993). Returns to emptied cache sites by Clark's nutcrackers (*Nucifraga columbiana*): A puzzle revisited. *Animal Behavior, 45,* 241–252.

Kamil, A. C., & Cheng, K. (2000). Way-finding and landmarks: The multiple bearings hypothesis. *Journal of Experimental Biology, 204,* 103–113.

Kamil, A. C., & Jones, J. E. (1997). The seed-storing Corvid Clark's nutcracker learns geometric relationships among landmarks. *Nature, 390,* 276–279.

Kamil, A. C., & Jones, J. E. (2000). Geometric rule learning by Clark's nutcrackers (*Nucifruga columbiana*). *Journal of Experimental Psychology: Animal Behavior Processes, 26,* 439–453.

Keeton, W. T. (1971). Magnets interfere with pigeon homing. *Proceedings of the National Academy of Sciences, USA, 68,* 102–106.

Knierim, J. J., Kudrimoti, H. S., & McNaughton, B. L. (1995). Place cells, head direction cells, and the learning of landmark stability. *Journal of Neuroscience, 15,* 1648–1659.

Knierim, J. J., Kudrimoti, H. S., & McNaughton, B. L. (1998). Interaction between idiothetic cues and external landmarks in the control of place cells, head direction cells. *Journal of Neurophysiology, 80,* 425–446.

Kummer, H. (1995). *In search of the sacred baboon.* Princeton, NJ: Princeton University Press.

Lehrer, M. (1993). Why do bees turn back and look? *Journal of Comparative Physiology, A*(172), 549–563.

Lehrer, M., & Collett, T. S. (1994). Approaching and departing bees learn different cues to the distance of a landmark. *Journal of Comparative Physiology, A*(175), 171–177.

Leonard, B., & McNaughton, B. L. (1990). Spatial representation in the rat: Conceptual, behavioral and neurophysiological perspectives. In R. P. Kesner & D. S. Olton (Eds.), *Neurobiology of comparative cognition* (pp. 363–422). Hillsdale, NJ: Erlbaum.

Lindauer, M. (1959). Angeborene und erlente Komponenten in der Sonnenorientierung der Bienen. (Innote and acquired components of the bee's sun compass.) *Zeitschrift für vergeichende Physiologie, 42,* 43–62.

Lindauer, M. (1960). Time-compensated sun orientation in bees. *Cold Spring Harbor Symposia on Quantitative Biology, 25,* 371–377.

Loomis, J. M., Da Silva, J. A., Fujita, N., & Fukusima, S. S. (1992). Visual space perception and visually directed action. *Journal of Experimental Psychology: Human Perception and Performance, 18,* 906–921.

Loomis, J. M., Da Silva, J. A., Philbeck, J. W., & Fukusima, S. S. (1996). Visual perception of location and distance. *Current Directions in Psychological Science, 5,* 72–77.

McLaughlin, S. (1967). Parametric adjusment in saccadic eye movements. *Perception and Psychophysics, 2,* 359–362.

McNaughton, B. L., Barnes, C. A., Gerrard, J. L., Gothard, K., Jung, M. W., Knierim, J. J., Kudrimoti, H., Quin, Y., Skaggs, W. E., Suster, M., & Weaver, K. L. (1996). Deciphering the hippocampal polyglot: The hippocampus as a path integration system. *Journal of Experimental Biology, 199,* 173–185.

McNaughton, B. L., Barnes, C. A., & O'Keefe, J. (1983). The contribution of position, direction and velocity to single unit activity in the hippocampus of freely moving rats. *Experimental Brain Research, 52,* 41–49.

McNaughton, B. L., Leonard, B., & Chen, L. (1989). Cortical-hippocampal interactions and cognitive mapping: A hypothesis based on reintegration of the parietal and inferotemporal pathways for visual processing. *Psychobiology, 17,* 230–235.

Maier, N. R. F., & Schneirla, T. C. (1935). *Principles of Animal Psychology.* New York: McGraw-Hill.

Markus, E. J., Quin, Y., Leonard, B., Skaggs, W. E., McNaughton, B. L., & Barnes, C. A. (1995). Interactions between location and task affect the spatial and directional firing of hippocampal neurons. *Journal of Neuroscience, 15,* 7079–7094.

Martin, G. M., Harley, C. W., Smith, A. R., Hoyles, E. S., & Hynes, C. A. (1997). Spatial disorientation blocks reliable goal localization on a plus maze but does not prevent goal localization in the Morris maze. *Journal of Experimental Psychology: Animal Behavior Processes, 23,* 183–193.

Matarić, M. (1991). Navigating with a rat brain: A neurobiologically-inpsired model for robot spatial representation. In J.-A. Meyer & S. W. Wilson (Eds.), *Proceedings of the First International Conference on Adaptive Behavior: From animals to animats* (pp. 169–175). Cambridge, MA: MIT Press.

Mehta, M. R., Barnes, C. A., & McNaughton, B. L. (1997). Experience dependent asymmetric expansion of hippocampal place fields. *Proceedings of the National Academy of Sciences, USA, 94,* 8918–8921.

Mehta, M. R., Quirk, M. C., & Wilson, M. A. (2000). Experience-dependent asymmetric shape of hippocampal receptive fields. *Neuron, 25,* 705–715.

Menzel, C. R. (1991). Cognitive aspects of foraging in Japanese monkeys. *Animal Behavior, 41,* 387–402.

Menzel, C. R. (1999). Unprompted recall and reporting of hidden objects by a chimpanzee (*Pan troglodytes*) after extended delays. *Journal of Comparative Psychology, 113,* 426–434.

Menzel, C. R., Savage-Rumbaugh, E. S., & Menzel, E. W. (2002). Bonobo (*Pan paniscus*) spatial memory and communication in a 20-hectare wood. *International Journal of Primatology.*

Menzel, E. W. (1973). Chimpanzee spatial memory organization. *Science, 182,* 943–945.

Menzel, R., Geiger, K., Joerges, J., Müller, U., & Chittka, L. (1998). Bees travel novel homeward routes by integrating separately acquired vector memories. *Animal Behavior, 55,* 139–152.

Mittelstaedt, M. L., & Mittelstaedt, H. (1980). Homing by path integration in a mammal. *Naturwissenschaften, 67,* 566–567.

Morris, R. G. M. (1981). Spatial localization does not require the presence of local cues. *Learning and motivation, 12,* 239–260.

Muller, R. U., & Kubie, J. L. (1987). The effects of changes in the environment on the spatial firing of hippocampal place cells. *Journal of Neuroscience, 7,* 1951–1968.

Muller, R. U., Kubie, J. L., & Ranck, J. B., Jr. (1987). Spatial firing of hippocampal complex-spike cells in a fixed environment. *Journal of Neuroscience, 7,* 1935–1950.

Muller, R. U., Stead, M., & Pach, J. (1996). The hippocampus as a cognitive graph. *Journal of General Physiology, 107,* 663–694.

Noto, C. T., Watanabe, S., & Fuchs, A. F. (1999). Characteristics of simian adaptation fields produced by behavioral changes in saccade size and direction. *Journal of Neurophysiology, 81,* 2798–2813.

O'Keefe, J., & Burgess, N. (1996). Geometric determinants of the place fields of hippocampal neurons. *Nature, 381,* 425–428.

O'Keefe, J., & Conway, D. H. (1978). Hippocampal place units in the freely moving rat: Why they fire where they fire. *Experimental Brain Research, 31,* 573–590.

O'Keefe, J., & Dostrovsky, J. (1971). The hippocampus as a spatial map. Preliminary evidence from unit activity in the freely-moving rat. *Brain Research, 34,* 171–175.

O'Keefe, J., & Speakman, A. (1987). Single unit activity in the rat hippocampus during a spatial memory task. *Experimental Brain Research, 68,* 1–27.

Poucet, B. (1993). Spatial cognitive maps in animals: New hypotheses on their structure and neural mechanisms. *Psychological Review, 100,* 163–182.

Poucet, B., Chapuis, N., Durup, M., & Thinus-Blanc, C. (1986). Exploratory behavior as an index of spatial knowledge in hamsters. *Animal Learning and Behavior, 14,* 93–100.

Ranck, J. B., Jr. (1984). Head-direction cells in the deep cell layers of dorsal presubiculum in freely moving rats. *Society for Neuroscience Abstracts, 10,* 599.

Redish, A. D. (1999). *Beyond the cognitive map—From place cells to episodic memory.* Cambridge, MA: MIT Press.

Redish, A. D., Rosenzweig, E. S., Bohanick, J. D., McNaughton, B. L., & Barnes, C. A. (2000). Dynamics of hippocampal ensemble activity realignment: Time versus space. *Journal of Neuroscience, 20,* 9298–9309.

Redish, A. D., & Touretzky, D. S. (1997). Cognitive maps beyond the hippocampus. *Hippocampus, 7,* 15–35.

Rieser, J. J. (1989). Access to knowledge of spatial structure at novel points of observation. *Journal of Experimental Psychology: Learning, Memory and Cognition, 15,* 1157–1165.

Riley, J. R., Smith, A. D., Reynolds, D. R., Edwards, A. S., Osborne, J. L., Williams, I. H., Carreck, N. L., & Poppy, G. M. (1996). Tracking bees with harmonic radar. *Nature, 379,* 29–30.

Roitblat, H. L. (1987). *Introduction to comparative cognition.* New York: Freeman.

Santschi, F. (1913). Comment s'orientent les fourmis. (How do ants find their way?) *Revue Suisse de Zoologie, 21,* 347–425.

Save, E., Cressant, A., Thinus-Blanc, C., & Poucet, B. (1998). Spatial firing of hippocampal place cells in blind rats. *Journal of Neuroscience, 18,* 1818–1826.

Save, E., Nerad, L., & Poucet, B. (2000). Contribution of multiple sensory information to place field stability in hippocampal place cells. *Hippocampus, 10,* 64–76.

Save, E., & Poucet, B. (2000). Hippocampal-parietal cortical interactions in spatial cognition. *Hippocampus, 10,* 491–499.

Schmid-Hempel, P. (1984). Individually different foraging methods in the desert ant *Cataglyphis bicolor* (Hymenoptera, Formicidae). *Behavioral Ecology Sociobiology, 14,* 263–271.

Schmid-Hempel, P., & Schmid-Hempel, R. (1984). Life duration and turnover of foragers in the ant *Cataglyphis bicolor* (Hymenoptera, Formicidae). *Insectes Sociaux, 31,* 345–360.

Schmidt-Koenig, K. (1958). Experimentelle Einflussnahme auf die 24-Stunden-Periodik bei Brieftauben und deren Auswirkung unter besonderer Berüchsichtigung des Heimfindevermögens. (The effect of perturbing the pigeon's 24 hour clock on its homing ability.) *Zeitschrift für Tierpsychologie, 15,* 301–331.

Seward, J. P. (1949). An experimental analysis of latent learning. *Journal of Experimental Psychology, 39,* 177–186.

Sharp, P. A. (1991). Computer simulation of hippocampal place cells. *Psychobiology, 19,* 103–115.

Sharp, P. E., Kubie, J. L., & Muller, R. U. (1990). Firing properties of hippocampal neurons in a visually symmetrical environment: Contribu-

tions of multiple sensory cues and mnemonic processes. *Journal of Neuroscience, 10,* 3093–3105.

Shepard, J. F. (1933). Higher processes in the behavior of rats. *Proceedings of the National Academy of Sciences, USA, 19,* 149–152.

Sherry, D. F. (1984). What food storing birds remember. *Canadian Journal of Psychology, 38,* 304–321.

Sherry, D. F., Forbes, M. R. L., Khurgel, M., & Ivy, G. O. (1993). Females have a larger hippocampus than males in the brood-parasitic brown-headed cowbird. *Proceedings of the National Academy Sciences, USA, 90,* 7839–7843.

Sherry, D. F., Krebs, J. R., & Cowie, R. J. (1981). Memory for the location of stored food in marsh tits. *Animal Behavior, 29,* 1260–1266.

Shettleworth, S. J., & Krebs, J. R. (1986). Stored and encountered seeds: A comparison of two spatial memory tasks in marsh tits and chickadees. *Journal of Experimental Psychology: Animal Behavior Processes, 12,* 248–257.

Shwagmeyer, P. L. (1995). Searching for tomorrow's mates. *Animal Behavior, 50,* 759–767.

Skaggs, W. E., & McNaughton, B. L. (1998). Spatial firing properties of hippocampal CA1 populations in an experiment containing two visually identical regions. *Journal of Neuroscience, 18,* 8455–8466.

Spetch, M. L. (1995). Overshadowing in landmark learning: Touch-screen studies with pigeons and humans. *Journal of Experimental Psychology: Animal Behavior Processes, 21,* 166–181.

Srinivasan, M. V., Zhang, S. W., & Bidwell, N. J. (1997). Visually mediated odometry in honeybees navigation en route to the goal: Visual flight control and odometry. *Journal of Experimental Biology, 200,* 2513–2522.

Srinivasan, M. V., Zhang, S. W., & Gadakar, R. (1998). Context-dependent learning in honeybees. *Proceedings of the 26th Göttingen Neurobiology Conference* (p. 521). Stuttgart: Thieme.

Straus, R., & Pichler, J. (1998). Persistence of orientation toward a temporarily invisible landmark in *Drosophila melanogaster. Journal of Comparative Physiology, A*(182), 411–423.

Stuchlik, A., Fenton, A. A., & Bures, J. (2001). Substratal idiothetic navigation of rats is impaired by removal or devaluation of extramaze and intramaze cues. *Proceedings of the National Academy of Sciences, USA, 98,* 3537–3542.

Taube, J. S. (1998). Head direction cells and the neurophysiological basis for a sense of direction. *Progress in Neurobiology, 55,* 225–256.

Taube, J. S., & Burton, H. L. (1995). Head direction cell activity monitored in a novel environment and during a cue conflict situation. *Journal of Neurophysiology, 74,* 1953–1971.

Taube, J. S., Muller, R. U., & Ranck, J. B., Jr. (1990). Head direction cells recorded from the postsubiculum in freely moving rats: II. Effects of environmental manipulations. *Journal of Neuroscience, 10,* 436–447.

Thinus-Blanc, C., Bouzouba, L., Chaix, K., Chapuis, N., Durup, M., & Poucet, B. (1987). A study of spatial parameters encoded during exploration in hamsters. *Journal of Experimental Psychology: Animal Behavior Processes, 13,* 418–427.

Thorndyke, P. W., & Hayes-Roth, B. (1982). Differences in spatial knowledge acquired from maps and navigation. *Cognitive Psychology, 14,* 560–589.

Thomson, J. A. (1983). Is continuous visual monitoring necessary in visually guided locomotion? *Journal of Experimental Psychology: Human Perception and Performance, 9,* 427–443.

Tinbergen, N. (1932). Über die Orientierung des Bienenwolfes. (On the orientation of the bee-wasp.) (*Philanthus triangulum* Fabr.) *Zeitschrift für vergleichende Physiologie, 16,* 305–334.

Tolman, E. C., & Gleitman, H. (1949). Studies in learning and motivation: 1. Equal reinforcement in both end-boxes, followed by a shock in one end-box. *Journal of Experimental Psychology, 39,* 810–819.

Touretzky, D. S., & Redish, A. D. (1996). A theory of rodent navigation based on interacting representations of space. *Hippocampus, 6,* 247–270.

Trullier, O., & Meyer, J.-A. (2000). Animal navigation using a cognitive graph. *Biological Cybernetics, 83,* 271–285.

Vallortigara, G. (2000). Comparative neuropsychology of the dual brain: A stroll through animal's left and right perceptual worlds. *Brain and Language, 73,* 189–219.

Vander Wall, S. B. (1982). An experimental analysis of cache recovery in Clark's nutcracker. *Animal Behavior, 30,* 84–94.

Vander Wall, S. B. (1990). *Food hoarding in animals.* Chicago: University of Chicago Press.

Vollbehr, J. (1975). Zur Orientierung junger Honigbienen bei ihrem: 1. Orientierungsflug. (On the orientation of young honeybees on their first orientation flight.) *Zoologisches Jahrbuch Physiologie, 79,* 33–69.

Wagner, W. (1907). *Psycho-biologische Untersuchungen an Hummeln.* Stuttgart, Germany: Schweizerbartsche Verlagsbuchhandlung.

Wang, R. F., & Simons, D. J. (1999). Active and passive scene recognition across views. *Cognition, 70,* 191–210.

Wallman, J., & Fuchs, A. F. (1998). Saccadic gain modification: Visual error drives motor adaptation. *Journal of Neurophysiology, 80,* 2405–2416.

Wehner, R. (1992). Arthropods. In F. Papi (Ed.), *Animal homing* (pp. 45–144). New York: Chapman and Hall.

Wehner, R. (1994). The polarization-vision project: Championing organismic biology. *Fortschritte der Zoologie, 39,* 103–143.

Wehner, R., Harkness, R. D., & Schmid-Hempel, P. (1983). Foraging strategies in individually searching ants, *Cataglyphis bicolor* (Hymenoptera, Formicidae). *Akademie der Wissenschaften und der Literatur, mathematisch-naturwissenschaftliche Klasse.* Stuttgart: Fischer.

Wehner, R., Michel, B., & Antonsen, P. (1996). Visual navigation in insects: Coupling of egocentric and geocentric information. *Journal of Exerimental Biology, 199,* 129–140.

Wehner, R., & Räber, F. (1979). Visual spatial memory in desert ants, *Cataglyphis fortis* (Hymenoptera, Formicidae). *Experientia, 35,* 1569–1571.

Wehner, R., & Wehner, S. (1990). Insect navigation: Use of maps or Ariadne's thread? *Ethology, Ecolology and Evolution, 2,* 27–48.

Wiener, S. I., Berthoz, A., & Zugaro, M. B. (2000). Preferred directions of thalamic head direction cells are controlled by 3D objects only when they are the most distant visual cues in the periphery. *Society of Neuroscience Abstracts, 26,* 983.

Wilson, M. A., & McNaughton, B. L. (1993). Dynamics of the hippocampal ensemble code for space. *Science, 265,* 676–679.

Wiltschko, R., Nohr, D., & Wiltschko, W. (1981) Pigeons with a deficient sun compass use the magnetic compass. *Science, 214,* 343–345.

Wiltschko, R., Walker, M., & Wiltschko, W. (2000) Sun-compass orientation in homing pigeons: Compensation for different rates of change in azimuth? *Journal of Experimental Biology, 203,* 889–894.

Wiltschko, R., & Wiltschko, W. (1980). The process of learning sun compass orientation in young homing pigeons. *Naturwissenschaften, 67,* 512–513.

Wiltschko, R., & Wiltschko, W. (1981). The development of sun compass orientation in young homing pigeons. *Behavior Ecology and Sociobiology, 9,* 135–141.

Wiltschko, W., Wiltschko, R., & Keeton, W. T. (1976). Effects of a 'permanent' clock-shift on the orientation of young homing pigeons. *Behavior Ecology and Sociobiology, 1,* 229–243.

Wiltschko, W., Wiltschko, R., Keeton, W. T., & Madden, R. (1983). Growing up in an altered magnetic field affects the initial orientation of young homing pigeons. *Behavior Ecology and Sociobiology, 12,* 135–142.

Wood, E. R., Dudchenko, P. A., Robitsek, R. J., & Eichenbaum H. (2000). Hippocampal neurons encode information about different types of memory episodes occurring in the same location. *Neuron, 27,* 623–633.

Woodworth, R. S., & Schlosberg, H. (1955). *Experimental Psychology.* London: Methuen.

Wrangham, R. W. (1995) Relationship of chimpanzee leaf-swallowing to a tapeworm infection. *American Journal of Primatology, 37,* 297–303.

Yates, F. A. (1966). *The art of memory.* London: Routledge and Paul.

Zeil, J. (1993a). Orientation flights of solitary wasps (*Cerceris*; Sphecidae; Hymenoptera): I. Description of flight. *Journal of Comparative Physiology, A*(172), 189–205.

Zeil, J. (1993b). Orientation flights of solitary wasps (*Cerceris*; Sphecidae; Hymenoptera): II. Similarities between orientation and return flights and the use of motion parallax. *Journal of Comparative Physiology, A*(172), 207–222.

Zeil, J., & Kelber, A. (1991). Orientation flights in ground-nesting wasps and bees share a common organisation. *Verhandlungen Deutschen Zoologischen Gesellschaft, 84,* 371–372.

CHAPTER 9

Temporal Learning

RUSSELL M. CHURCH

Humans and other animals are adapted to a physical world that can be described in terms of events that occur at some time and in some location. The events are changes in physical stimuli, such as the onset or termination of a noise, that usually can be localized in time and space. This chapter concerns the ability of animals to learn about the dimension of time, a topic that includes questions about temporal perception and temporal memory as well as decisions about temporal intervals. Most of the data come from asymptotic levels of performance, but some come from the initial learning and subsequent adjustment to new temporal intervals. The history of the study of behavioral adjustment to the temporal dimension of the physical world has three origins: human psychophysics, biological rhythms, and animal learning.

HISTORICAL BACKGROUND

In a chapter on the perception of time, William James (1890) reviewed the psychophysical and introspective evidence available primarily from laboratories in Germany. James' chapter contains many ideas that are worth the attention of a modern reader. These include chunking (p. 612), span of temporal attention (p. 613), particular intervals that are judged with maximal accuracy (p. 616), context effects (p. 618), effect of filled versus empty intervals (p. 618), prospective versus retrospective timing (p. 624), the effect of age on time perception (p. 625), neural processes in time perception (p. 635), and the effect of hashish intoxication on time perception (p. 639). In the first edition of his handbook, Woodrow (1951) reviewed knowledge about time perception. That chapter, based primarily on psychophysical research in the first half of the twentieth century, dealt with many of the problems described by James. Both of these treatments of temporal perception were focused on humans, and many of the testing methods required the use of language. The central problem of the psychophysical approach to the study of human timing was to understand temporal perception, particularly the relationship between subjective time and physical time.

The daily cycles of activity of animals were studied for over 50 years by Richter (1922, 1965, 1977). He developed methods used in the study of these rhythms and studied factors controlling the circadian clock. Although the phase of a circadian clock provides information about the time since an entraining event (such as onset of light or food), this clock did not seem to have properties useful for timing short intervals from an arbitrary event. The central problem of the study of biological rhythms was to describe the animals' adaptations to cyclical regularities in the physical environment, and their neural mechanisms (Moore-Ede, Sulzman, & Fuller, 1982).

In his lectures on conditioned reflexes, Pavlov (1927) reported the results of many experiments with dogs in which conditioned and unconditioned stimuli were presented and salivary responses were measured. The procedures were described in terms of the type of stimulus (e.g., rotating object, tone) and of the time intervals between the onset or termination of the stimulus and the delivery of the unconditioned stimulus (usually food powder or acid). The tables of results typically included information about the time of occurrence as well as the nature of the event. Pavlov studied *temporal conditioning,* in which there was a fixed interval between successive deliveries of the unconditioned stimulus; he also studied *delayed conditioning,* in which a stimulus onset occurred a fixed time prior to the delivery of the unconditioned stimulus and terminated with it; and he studied *trace conditioning,* which was the same as delayed conditioning except that the stimulus terminated a fixed time before the delivery of the unconditioned stimulus (see Figure 9.1). In all cases there was an increasing amount of salivary responding as a function of time since an event that had a fixed time relation to the unconditioned stimulus. The event that marked the onset of an interval terminating in an unconditioned stimulus was either the previous un-

conditioned stimulus (in temporal conditioning), a conditioned stimulus onset (in delayed conditioning), or both the conditioned stimulus onset and termination (in trace conditioning). Pavlov noted the functional value of the anticipatory salivary response for digestion. He wrote, "When we come to seek an interpretation of these results, it seems pretty evident that the duration of time has acquired the properties of a conditioned stimulus" (p. 41).

The early animal-learning studies of behavioral adjustment to temporal intervals between events included not only the classical conditioning research of Pavlov and others, but also instrumental learning research. (By definition, a classical conditioning procedure is one in which the interval between stimulus and reinforcement is specified and the interval between the response and reinforcement is not; an instrumental learning procedure is one in which the interval between a response and reinforcement is specified.) The instrumental (operant) procedures and results of B. F. Skinner have had the greatest influence on contemporary research. The research on schedules of reinforcement by Skinner (1938) featured the importance of temporal intervals, as described later in the section on fixed-interval reinforcement schedules. A good review of the role of time in animal behavior is provided by Richelle and Lejeune (1980).

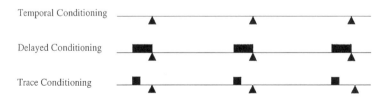

Figure 9.1   Three timing procedures used by Pavlov.

NOTE: The filled rectangles indicate the presence of a stimulus; the filled triangles indicate the time of a reinforcer. In temporal conditioning there was a constant interval between successive reinforcers; in delayed conditioning there was also a constant interval between the onset of a stimulus and a reinforcer; and in trace conditioning there was also a constant (nonzero) interval between the termination of a stimulus and a reinforcer.

The central problem of the study of animal learning was to understand the effect of arbitrary intervals of time between stimuli on the behavior of animals.

During most of the twentieth century the studies of the temporal dimension of the physical world by investigators of human psychophysics, biological rhythms, and animal learning progressed independently. The extensive experimental research in each of these fields typically was conducted by different investigators using different methods and different theories. Articles based on studies in these three fields typically were published in different journals, and they rarely cited each other. The secondary literature also typically treated these three fields as separate topics. An exception is the monograph of Fraisse (1963) that contained sections on biological rhythms, classical and operant conditioning, introspection, and psychophysics. Though eclectic, this monograph did not develop the connections among the approaches to the study of temporal learning.

An edited volume that was based on a symposium sponsored by the New York Academy of Sciences (Gibbon & Allan, 1984) undoubtedly encouraged many investigators to examine connections between the study of timing based on human psychophysics, biological rhythms, and animal learning. This symposium was organized by an active investigator of animal timing (John Gibbon) and an active investigator of human timing (Lorraine Allan), and Gibbon and Allan were able to obtain participation from established investigators of both human and animal timing. This may have led to an increasing use of more similar experimental methods, as well as an increasing use of the same theories of time perception and timed performance (Allan, 1998). When similar methods are used for the study of timing by humans and other animals, similar results often occur (Church, 1993).

This chapter describes temporal learning from the viewpoint of animal learning but notes various influences based on research in human psychophysics and biological rhythms.

TIME AS A STIMULUS ATTRIBUTE

A starting point for the analysis of time as a stimulus attribute is to determine whether an animal can discriminate between stimuli that differ only in duration. For example, can a rat be trained to make a lever response following a 4-s auditory stimulus, but not following shorter or longer intervals? A temporal generalization procedure may be used that is equivalent to a generalization procedure for auditory intensity or auditory frequency. The only difference is that the manipulated dimension is the duration of the auditory stimulus, rather than its intensity or frequency.

Discrimination of a Temporal Interval: A Temporal Generalization Procedure

An example of a temporal generalization procedure for a rat in a lever box, based on an experiment by Church and Gibbon (1982), is as follows: After a 30-s interval, a house light was turned off for 0.8, 1.6, 2.4, 3.2, 4.0, 4.8, 5.6, 6.4, or 7.2 s. A random half of the durations were 4.0 s; the remaining durations were randomly selected from the remaining eight durations. When the house light came back on, a lever was inserted into the box. If the stimulus duration had been 4.0 s, and the rat pressed the lever within 5 s, food was delivered, and the lever was withdrawn. If the stimulus duration had not been 4.0 s, and the rat pressed the lever within 5 s, no food was delivered, and the lever was withdrawn. If the rat did not press the lever within 5 s, the lever was withdrawn, and another cycle began. This cycle was repeated throughout sessions lasting 1 hr 50 min.

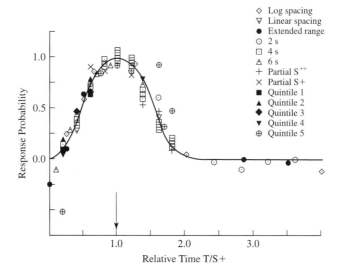

Figure 9.2 Temporal generalization procedure.

NOTE: Probability of a response given attention to time as a function of stimulus duration relative to reinforced stimulus duration.

SOURCE: From Church and Gibbon (1982).

The probability of a lever response was greatest following the reinforced stimulus duration (4 s) and was lower at shorter or longer durations. This temporal generalization gradient was not affected by a logarithmic spacing of the intervals or by an extension of the range from 0.8 s to 7.2 s to 0 s to 32 s, but it was affected by many experimental manipulations. For example, it was affected by the duration of the reinforced stimulus: The maximum response probability and the spread of the gradient increased with increases in the reinforced duration. The temporal generalization gradient was also affected by partial reinforcement and by a reduction in the probability of presentation of the reinforced stimulus: Both led to an overall lowering and flattening of the gradient. There were also large individual differences in the temporal gradient that were related to overall responsiveness. Some rats had steep generalization gradients that began and ended near zero; others had flatter generalization gradients that began and ended at higher response probabilities.

The essential similarity of performance under all of these conditions was revealed when "attention to time" was separated from "sensitivity to time." The assumption was that, with some probability, the rat attended to the duration of the stimulus and its behavior was affected by the duration of the stimulus, or that it did not attend to the duration of the stimulus and its behavior was not affected by the duration of the stimulus. Figure 9.2 shows the probability of a response given attention to time as a function of relative duration of the stimulus. (The relative duration is the duration of the stimulus, T, divided by the duration of the reinforced stimulus, $S+$.) Most of the data from the various experimental manipulations and individual differences fall approximately on the same function. This analysis of general attention, developed by Heinemann, Avin, Sullivan, and Chase (1969), suggests that the various procedures affected the probability of attention to stimulus duration rather than the sensitivity to stimulus duration.

The results of experiments with the temporal generalization procedure provided evidence that animals can discriminate between stimuli that differ in duration, and the analysis of these data suggests that a single timing mechanism may be used under various conditions. This procedure has also been used with human participants (Wearden, Denovan, & Haworth, 1997), but it has not been used extensively, probably because of the asymmetrical (biased) nature of the two elements used for a calculation of a probability (a response and a nonresponse in a 5-s interval). Much more evidence regarding the ability of animals to discriminate between stimuli that differ in duration, as well as evidence regarding the characteristics of the psychophysical function relating response probability to stimulus duration, has come from a somewhat more complex procedure known as the bisection procedure.

Discrimination between Temporal Intervals: A Bisection Procedure

In a duration discrimination procedure, one response is reinforced following a short-duration stimulus (such as 2 s) and another response is reinforced following a long-duration stimulus (such as 8 s). Animals learn to make one of the responses following the short-duration stimulus (called the "short response") and to make the other response following the long-duration stimulus (the "long response"). In the bisection procedure, stimuli of various intermediate durations are also presented, but neither the long nor the short response is reinforced. The results of a bisection procedure are often reported as a psychophysical function that relates the probability of a long response to the duration of the stimuli. This function usually has the S-shaped form of an ogive that increases from a probability close to 0.0 to a probability close to 1.0. This procedure provides a way to define the psy-

chological middle of the two reinforced time intervals: It is the time at which it is equally probable that the animal will make a short or long response. This psychological middle is called the point of bisection, or the point of subjective equality (PSE).

Such a bisection procedure, modified from a temporal discrimination procedure developed by Stubbs (1968), was conducted by Church and Deluty (1977) with rats in lever boxes. A cycle consisted of (a) the termination of the house light for some duration, (b) the insertion of both levers, (c) the pressing of one of the levers (and, possibly, delivery of food), (d) the retraction of both levers, and (e) the turning on of the house light for 30 s. Food was delivered following a response on one of the levers after the shortest stimulus in a series, and it was delivered following a response on the other lever after the longest stimulus in a series. Food was not delivered following either response after a stimulus of intermediate duration. Rats were trained under different ranges of durations (1–4 s, 2–8 s, 3–12 s, and 4–16 s).

Some results are shown in Figure 9.3, redrawn from data from individual rats included in the appendix of Church and Deluty (1977). The probability of a long response is shown as a function of the stimulus duration in seconds for the four ranges of intervals. These functions were slightly asymmetrical and rose more rapidly for the shorter ranges of intervals (upper-left panel). The probability of a long response is also plotted in relative logarithmic units; these functions were more symmetrical, and they superposed (upper-right panel). The point of bisection was near the geometric mean (middle-left panel), and the difference limen (the semi-interquartile range of the functions shown in the upper-left panel) was a linear function of the geometric mean (middle-right panel). Thus, an estimate of the coefficient of variation (the difference limen divided by the point of bisection) was

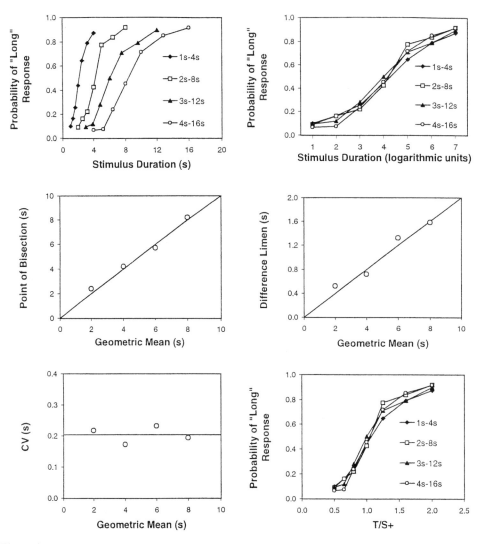

Figure 9.3   Bisection procedure.

NOTE: Upper left: Probability of long response as a function of stimulus duration in seconds. Upper right: Probability of long response as a function of stimulus duration in logarithmic units. Middle left: Point of bisection as a function of geometric mean of reinforced stimulus durations. Middle right: Difference limen as a function of geometric mean of reinforced stimulus durations. Bottom left: Coefficient of variation (CV) as a function of geometric mean of reinforced stimulus durations. Bottom right: Probability of long response as a function of stimulus duration divided by the point of bisection.

SOURCE: From Church and Deluty (1977).

approximately constant (bottom-left panel). Superposition was also obtained when the probability of a long response was plotted as a function of the stimulus duration in seconds (T) divided by the geometric mean ($S+$), as shown in the bottom-right panel.

Such bisection experiments have provided evidence for the following six principles:

1. *Symmetry.* The psychophysical function relating the proportion of long responses to stimulus duration is an ogive that is

approximately symmetrical on a logarithmic scale of time.

2. *Geometric mean.* The point of bisection is near the geometric mean of the reinforced short interval and the reinforced long interval.

3. *Proportional timing.* The point of bisection increases approximately linearly with the geometric mean of the reinforced short interval and the reinforced long interval.

4. *Scalar variability.* The standard deviation of the point of bisection increases approximately linearly with stimulus duration.

5. *Weber's law.* The coefficient of variation (the standard deviation divided by the mean) of the point of bisection is approximately constant.

6. *Superposition.* The psychophysical functions at all ranges superpose when the duration of a stimulus is divided by the point of bisection (which is often approximated by the geometric mean).

These principles are not all independent. For example, proportional timing and scalar variability imply that Weber's law applies to timing (Gibbon, 1977). Superposition is probably the most fundamental principle because it applies to all of the data points in a psychophysical function and not just to a measure of central tendency or variability.

The regularities in the results of the bisection procedure by pigeons and rats are also observed in similar experiments with human participants (Allan & Gibbon, 1991). The stimuli were 1000-Hz tones with durations to be discriminated. In one experiment described in this article, each participant was given five sessions at each of four different ranges (1–2 s, 1–1.5 s, 1.4–2.1 s, and .75–1 s). Results of the six individual participants at these four different ranges is shown in Figure 9.4. These psychophysical functions show the probability of a long response as a function of

the ratio of the duration of the stimulus to the point of bisection. The six principles described for the rats apply also to human participants.

Although the coefficient of variation of the point of bisection is approximately constant (Gibbon, 1977), there are some small systematic deviations from constancy. The important features of these deviations is that (a) they are systematic rather than random, (b) they are local (i.e., the coefficient of variation is lower at some time intervals than at shorter or longer intervals), and (c) there are multiple local minima. Evidence for such systematic, multiple local deviations from a constant coefficient of variation require that animals be tested at a large number of closely spaced time intervals. Using a temporal discrimination method in which many different short intervals were used and in which the duration of the long stimulus was adjusted until the rat responded correctly on approximately 75% of the stimuli, intervals of particular sensitivity have been located in the range of 100 ms to 2 s and 2 s to 50 s (Crystal, 1999, 2001). These small departures from Weber's law may provide evidence about the mechanism involved in temporal perception.

The results from both the temporal generalization and the temporal bisection procedures have provided evidence that animals can discriminate stimuli that differ in duration. The question arises whether the discrimination is based on some modality-specific mechanism (such as light adaptation) rather than on an attribute of duration characteristic of stimuli of different modalities. A cross-modal transfer of training procedure can provide evidence about this. In one experiment 16 rats were trained in a 1-s versus 4-s temporal discrimination procedure (Roberts, 1982). Half of them were trained with durations of light and others with durations of noise. Then the stimulus modalities were switched. The rats trained with light were tested with noise, and vice

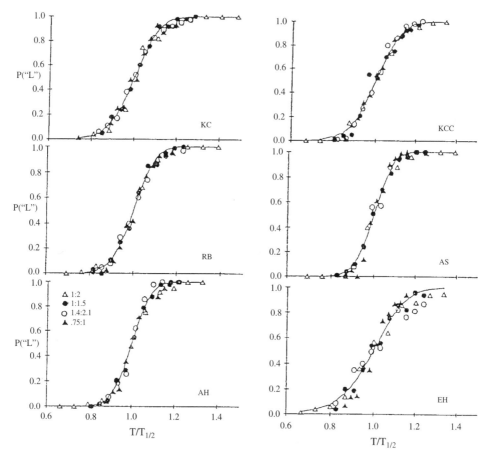

Figure 9.4 Bisection procedure with six human participants.
NOTE: Probability of a long response as a function of duration of the stimulus (T) divided by the geometric mean of the shortest and longest stimulus ($T_{1/2}$).
SOURCE: From Allan and Gibbon (1991).

versa. Rats in a random half of each of these groups were trained with the same response for the short and long stimulus, and the others were trained with the opposite response for the short and long stimulus. An empirical question was whether the speed that a rat would learn to press the left lever for a 1-s light and the right lever for a 4-s light would be affected by whether it had learned to press the left lever for the 1-s noise and the right lever for the 4-s noise, or the reverse. The essential idea was to determine if there were something common between a 1-s light and a 1-s noise. The results clearly indicated that percentage correct was much higher in retraining with the same as-

sociation of stimulus duration and response than in the reversed association of stimulus duration and response. The same conclusions were reached in other related cross-modal transfer experiments (Meck & Church, 1982a, 1982b).

The empirical effects of a retention interval on the psychophysical function relating the probability of a long response to the presented stimulus duration are quite clear. Under most conditions the function flattens, with a bias toward reporting the stimuli as being short. Both of these factors increase with an increase in the retention interval between the presentation of the stimulus and the opportunity to make a response (Spetch & Wilkie, 1983). The retention intervals that have been studied are primarily in the range of 0 s to 20 s. The flattening of the function is presumably due to forgetting or interference that results in a decrease in overall stimulus control, but the cause of the bias to respond "short" is still uncertain.

The phenomenon of choosing the short response as the retention interval is increased is often called *subjective shortening*. This suggests that the forgetting of a temporal duration, in contrast to forgetting of other features of a stimulus, occurs on the time dimension. Based on the stability of the point of bisection with retention intervals of 0 s, 0.5 s, 2 s, and 8 s, the probability of .79 of classifying an absent stimulus as "short," and the high probability of classifying both a 2-s and an 8-s stimulus after a 32-s retention interval as "short," Church (1980) concluded that "there was no evidence that forgetting of a signal duration occurred on the time dimension." p. 219.

An alternative to subjective shortening as a mechanism is that forgetting of temporal intervals, like forgetting of other features of a stimulus, occurs on a general strength dimension and that a weak memory is more similar to a short stimulus than to a long stimulus (Kraemer, Mazmanian, & Roberts, 1985). Another alternative is that animals typically report the presence or absence of the most salient stimulus, that the long stimulus is the salient one, and that it weakens during the retention interval (Gaitan & Wixted, 2000). No consensus has been reached on whether the perceived duration of an interval shortens during a retention interval.

Time as an Attribute of Stimuli: The Temporal Coding Hypothesis

Classical conditioning procedures involve the presentation of stimuli at particular times. For example, the interval between the onset of a conditioned stimulus and the onset of the unconditioned stimulus (the CS-US interval) affects performance. There is general agreement about the profound effects of such temporal independent variables on behavior, but there is no common agreement about the content of learning. One type of interpretation of the results is that the shorter CS-US interval leads to a stronger association; another type of interpretation of the results is that the interval between the onset of the CS and the onset of the US is stored as a temporal interval. This distinction was clearly described by Logan (1960), but there is still no general agreement about whether classical conditioning requires both a strength and a timing dimension, and if not, which of the two is fundamental.

The temporal coding hypothesis has led to a series of experiments that provide substantial support for the view that animals learn the specific temporal intervals that are used in classical conditioning experiments. Most of these have been conducted in a lick suppression paradigm for rats in which the unconditioned reinforcement was an electric shock, and the measured response was the latency to begin to drink. The latency to respond is usually reported in logarithmic units (base 10), so that a 1.0 refers to 10 s and a 2.0 refers to 100 s.

An application of the temporal coding hypothesis is shown in the upper two panels of Figure 9.5, which are based on an experiment by Matzel, Held, and Miller (1988). In the first phase a sensory preconditioning procedure was used in which two 5-s neutral stimuli were presented sequentially. This may lead to an association between the two neutral stimuli, but one that may produce only subtle behavioral manifestations or, perhaps, none at all. In the second phase an electric shock preceded the second neutral stimulus. This backward conditioning procedure also may not produce any obvious manifestations of learning. According to the temporal coding hypothesis, however, the rats in Phase 1 learned the temporal

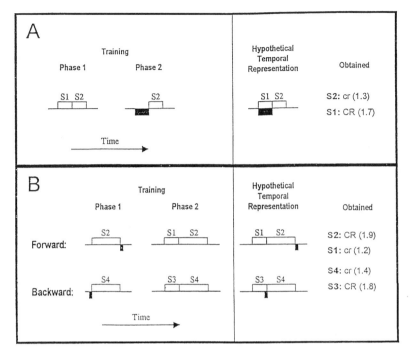

Figure 9.5 Temporal maps for two experimental procedures.
NOTE: A: The left panel shows the procedure used by Matzel, Held, and Miller (1988); the right panel shows the temporal map as well as predicted and obtained results. B: The left panel shows the procedure used by Barnet, Cole, and Miller (1997); the right panel shows the temporal map as well as predicted and obtained results.
SOURCE: From Arcediano and Miller (in press).

intervals between the two neutral stimuli, and in Phase 2 they learned the temporal intervals between the electric shock and the second neutral stimulus. This temporal coding hypothesis becomes testable because it also includes the assumption that animals can integrate the temporal maps formed in the two phases. The nature of the integration is shown in the top-right panel of Figure 9.5. The assumptions are that the animals identify the common element (in this case, the second neutral stimulus), that they know the temporal relationship between the common element and the first neutral stimulus (from Phase 1), and that they know the temporal relationship between the common element and the second neutral stimulus (from Phase 2). This leads to the hypothetical temporal representation shown in the top-right panel of Figure 9.4. The prediction is that if the second stimulus is presented, there would be only slight suppression (as indicated by the lowercase letters used for the conditioned response); if the first stimulus is presented, however, there would be substantial suppression (as indicated by the uppercase letters used for the conditioned response). These predictions were supported by the results, which showed that the latency to drink was about 20.0 s ($10^{1.3}$ s) to the second stimulus and about 50.1 s ($10^{1.7}$ s) to the first stimulus.

A similar analysis is shown in the two lower panels of Figure 9.5, which are based on a secondary conditioning procedure (Barnet,

Cole, & Miller, 1997). The reader can follow the procedures in Phase 1 and Phase 2, recognize that the hypothetical temporal representation is based on precisely the same temporal hypothesis used in the interpretation of the results of the previous experiment, and appreciate why lick suppression in the forward group should be greater in the second stimulus than in the first stimulus used in Phase 2, as well as why lick suppression in the backward group should have the reverse pattern. Finally, the figures show that the results support the predictions of the temporal coding hypothesis.

The assumptions of the temporal coding hypothesis appear to apply also in experiments in blocking (Barnet, Grahame, & Miller, 1993), overshadowing (Blaisdell, Denniston, & Miller, 1998), and conditioned inhibition (Denniston, Cole, & Miller, 1998). These experiments support the view that the temporal relationships between stimuli are learned during conditioning procedures and that intervals that are learned separately may be integrated into the same temporal map. Other experiments have provided evidence that the intervals are learned bidirectionally. For example, if a light has been followed by a tone after a 10-s interval, then when the light occurs, the animal expects the tone to occur in 10 s; when the tone occurs, the animal remembers that the light typically occurred 10 s earlier (Arcediano & Miller, in press).

Typically, conditioning theories have focused on states, such as the presence or absence of a noise. Timing theories have focused on state transitions, which may also be referred to as events or time markers. They include the onset and termination of a stimulus, a response, and a reinforcer. The time interval between any of these events can be learned. In the temporal generalization and bisection procedures, the relevant interval is from stimulus onset to termination. In other procedures animals demonstrate their ability to perceive the

causal efficacy of their responses. For example, a pigeon can learn to discriminate whether a peck on the center key was followed immediately by two side key lights or whether they went on independently of the pigeon's responses (Killeen, 1978; Killeen & Smith, 1984).

Preferences among Distributions of Time Intervals

Not only can animals use time intervals between events as discriminative stimuli; they can also indicate a preference among alternative distributions of intervals. They prefer short intervals to long ones, variable intervals to fixed intervals of the same arithmetic mean, and signaled intervals to unsignaled ones. Such preferences may be based on local expected time to reinforcement on the two alternatives, rather than overall relative reinforcement rate.

In a concurrent schedule of reinforcement, animals distribute their responding between two continuously available response alternatives that lead to two distributions of reinforcement. The relative response rate on the two alternatives is a measure of relative preference. The matching law states that the relative response rates are equal to the relative reinforcement rates, and the generalized matching law states that the logarithm of the relative responses rates is a linear function of the logarithm of the relative reinforcement rate (Davison & McCarthy, 1988; Herrnstein, 1997). Both of these are called molar laws because they make predictions about the average response rate as a function of the average reinforcement rate. The generalized matching law provides a good fit to behavior in the concurrent variable-interval schedules of reinforcement, as well as in other schedules. A local maximizing account may do so also (Shimp, 1969). A related approach that makes use of current understanding of response timing has been developed by Gallistel and Gibbon (2000).

In the concurrent schedule of reinforcement, the relative response rate is used as a measure of preference. In some cases, different response rates may be due to reactions to reinforcers, to selective reinforcement of particular response patterns, and to other factors not normally considered to be involved in a concept of preference. To separate the act of choice from its consequences, Autor (1969) developed the concurrent chains procedure. In this procedure a pigeon is presented with two illuminated keys in an initial link; after a random interval of time, the next peck on one of the keys leads to a terminal link with one time to reinforcement and the next peck on the other key leads to a terminal link with a different time to reinforcement. The relative response rate is approximated by the matching rule

$$R_L/(R_L + R_R) = 1/t_{2L}/(1/t_{2L} + 1/t_{2R}) \quad (1)$$

where R_L and R_R refer to the response rate on the left and right keys of the initial link, respectively. It is also approximated by the delay reduction hypothesis (Fantino, 1969, 1977):

$$R_L/(R_L + R_R)$$
$$= (T - t_{2L})/[(T - t_{2L}) + (T - T_{2R})],$$
$$t_{2L} < T, \quad t_{2R} < T \quad (2)$$

where T refers to the mean time to reinforcement from the onset of the initial links, and t_{2L} and t_{2R} refer to the mean time to reinforcement from the onset of the left and right terminal links, respectively. The essence of the idea is that the value of an alternative is related to the reduction in the delay of reinforcement (in seconds) rather than, for example, to the reduction in the delay of reinforcement as a proportion. The delay reduction hypothesis has been successfully applied to many other procedures (Fantino, Preston, & Dunn, 1993), but the equation that involves only mean values does not account for the preference for

variable over constant intervals with the same mean durations (Mazur, 1997).

The relative preference for two delays of reinforcement may be derived from an assumption about the mathematical form of this gradient. One particularly successful equation is the hyperbolic-decay hypothesis:

$$V = A/(1 + KD) \quad (3)$$

where V is the value, A is the amount of reinforcement, D is the delay of reinforcement, and K is a parameter to be estimated from the data. In an extensive program of research on factors affecting choice, Mazur (1997) has used a simple adjusting-delay procedure with pigeons. A single peck on the side key illuminated with a red light led to a fixed delay to food; a single peck on the side key illuminated with a green light led to a delay that could be adjusted. An adjustment rule led to increases or decreases of the duration of the adjusting delay until a stability criterion was achieved. This is the point at which the value (V) on the two alternatives is approximately equal. The hyperbolic decay hypothesis provided quantitative fits to experiments in which amounts, probabilities, and distribution of reinforcements were varied. Figure 9.6 shows

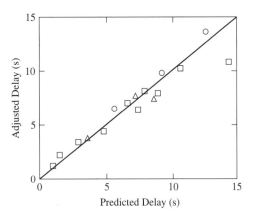

Figure 9.6 Adjusting delay choice procedure.
NOTE: Adjusted delay as a function of predicted delay. Predictions were based on the hyperbolic decay hypothesis shown in Equation (3).
SOURCE: From Mazur (1997).

the adjusted delay in seconds (the indifference points) as a function of the durations predicted from the hyperbolic decay hypothesis. This equation accounted for 96% of the variance of the adjusted delay measure.

TIME AS A RESPONSE ATTRIBUTE

The latency of a response refers to the interval between the onset of a stimulus and the occurrence of the response. The latency of a response has been used to measure three different psychological processes. First, it has been used to measure the time required for psychological processes such as memory search speed (Sternberg, 1966). It has also been used as a measure of response strength (Hull, 1943). Finally, it has been used as a measure of the expected time of a reinforcing event (Pavlov, 1927). The problem is how to interpret a response latency. If substantial time passes between the presentation of a stimulus and the occurrence of a response, is this an indication that (a) a great deal of mental effort was required to make the decision to respond, (b) the strength of the response was low, or (c) a response does not occur until the expected time to reinforcement has declined to some critical value? Empirical studies support each of these interpretation of response latencies: (a) Response latency usually increases as the number of required mental operations increases; (b) response latency usually decreases as a function of the amount of training; and (c) response latency usually is related to the time between stimulus onset and reinforcer availability. A theory of response times should make correct predictions when the independent variable is task complexity, amount of training, or time of reinforcement.

Studies of time as a stimulus attribute are often regarded as investigations of temporal perception, whereas studies of time as a response attribute are regarded as temporal performance. They clearly differ in what the investigator measures. In studies of time as a stimulus attribute, the measure is a categorical one such as a left- or right-lever response; in studies of time as a response attribute, the measure is a quantitative one on the temporal dimension. However, both types of studies provide information about perception, memory, and decision processes.

Platt and Davis (1983) developed a bisection procedure in which the important dependent variable is the time of occurrence of the two responses. In contrast to the bisection procedure previously described, in this procedure the animal can respond at any time during the interval. In Platt and Davis's procedure, two side keys were turned on, and (with equal probability) either (a) after a short interval of time, the first peck to left key was followed by food or (b) after a long interval of time, the first peck to the right key was followed by food. (The left and right keys were counterbalanced across pigeons.) In one condition the short interval was 40 s and the long interval was 200 s. As a result of this training, the response rate on the left key increased to a maximum near 40 s and then declined, and the response rate on the right key increased throughout the 200 s. The point of bisection was defined in two ways— from the time at which the response rates on the two keys was equal ("rate"), and from the median time of a switch from one key to the other ("switch"). Both of these are measures of the time at which the animal has equal preference for the two alternatives (i.e., is indifferent toward them). With both definitions, the point of bisection was approximately equal to the geometric mean of the short and long reinforced intervals (see Figure 9.7). Thus, the results of an experiment in which the animal is free to respond throughout the interval (such as Platt & Davis, 1983) is similar to one in which the animal is exposed to the stimulus and is permitted to make only a single response (Church & Deluty, 1977). Studies of time as a response attribute may be accounted

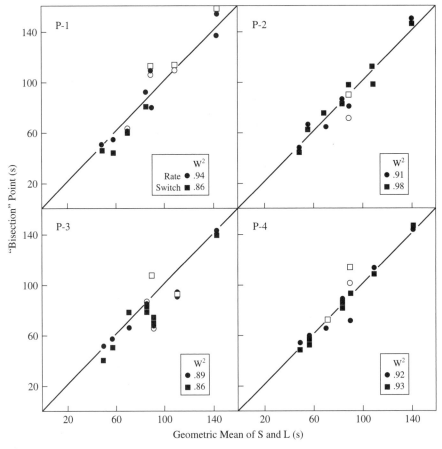

Figure 9.7　The point of bisection as a function of the geometric mean of the short and long intervals of four pigeons.

NOTE: The two measures of the point of bisection (rate and switch) are described in the text. The percentage of variance accounted for (ω^2) is shown.

SOURCE: From Platt and Davis (1983).

for by the same processes as studies of time as a stimulus attribute.

Fixed-Interval Schedule of Reinforcement

A fixed-interval schedule of food reinforcement is one in which there is a fixed time from delivery of a food until the availability of the next food; food is delivered immediately after the next response. Thus, a cycle consists of a fixed interval of time followed by reinforcement of the next response. Skinner referred to this as *periodic recondi-*

tioning because there was a fixed interval of extinction followed by continuous reinforcement. He identified four sources of variability in the response rates of rats in a fixed-interval schedule of reinforcement (Skinner, 1938, 123–126). There were differences among sessions, differences among intervals, and differences as a function of time since an interval began, and the responses tended to appear in clusters.

From the standpoint of temporal learning, the change in the response rate as a function of time since the previous delivery of food is the most diagnostic source of variability in a fixed-interval schedule of reinforcement. The increase in response rate is similar at fixed intervals of quite different durations. In one experiment, pigeons were trained on fixed intervals of 30 s, 300 s, and 3,000 s; the response rate was reported in successive fifths of the interval as a fraction of the response rate in the final fifth of the interval (Dews, 1970). This normalized response rate is shown in Figure 9.8 as a fraction of the interval; the functions for the three fixed intervals of very different durations is approximately the same. Similar results, although usually with a much smaller range of fixed intervals, have been obtained with different species, intervals, response measures, and reinforcers (Gibbon, 1991).

The increase in rate as a function of time since the previous reinforcement has been described as a gradual increase (a scalloped pattern) and also as an abrupt increase (break-run pattern). This is an important distinction because the theoretical processes necessary to generate these two patterns are different. Although extensive research by Skinner (1938), Ferster and Skinner (1957), and Dews (1970) has indicated that gradual increases often occur on individual cycles, quantitative analyses based on fitting of a two-state model has accounted for most of the variance (Church, Meck, & Gibbon, 1994; Schneider, 1969). The two-state model assumes that the response rate is constant at some low rate on each cycle until a point of transition, when it becomes constant at some high rate. Further, it is assumed that the point of transition is a random variable with a mean that is proportional to the fixed interval. The average response rate of many such step functions with the variable point of transition is a gradually increasing function.

To test the two-state hypothesis of fixed-interval performance, it is necessary to identify a point of transition on each cycle. This classification can be done with a formal definition of the temporal criterion that provides the largest difference in response rate between the early and later parts of the interval. Then cycles can be averaged, not with respect to the time of the last food, but with respect to the temporal criterion. These average functions are characterized by a rather steady low rate prior to the criterion, followed by a rather steady high rate after the criterion (Schneider, 1969). An example from one pigeon on a fixed interval of 256 s is shown in the top panel of Figure 9.9. Before the breakpoint criterion (shown by the vertical dashed line) the response rate was low and approximately constant; after the breakpoint criterion it was high and approximately constant. There are systematic deviations from a step function,

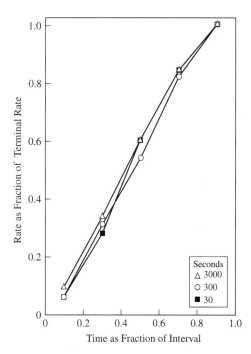

Figure 9.8   Fixed interval procedure.
NOTE: Response rate (as a fraction of terminal rate) as a function of time since food (as a fraction of the interval).
SOURCE: From Dews (1970).

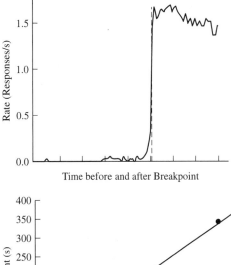

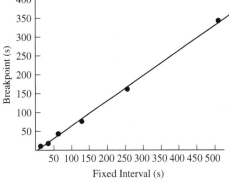

Time before and after Breakpoint

Fixed Interval (s)

Figure 9.9 Fixed interval procedure.
NOTE: Top panel: Response rate as a function of time relative to the breakpoint. Bottom panel: Time of the breakpoint as a function of the duration of the fixed interval.
SOURCE: From Schneider (1969).

but they are small. If this analysis were done on an increasing function, the increase should be detectable both in the period prior to the criterion and in the period after the criterion.

Schneider (1969) tested pigeons on fixed-interval schedules of 16 s, 32 s, 64 s, 128 s, 256 s, and 512 s. He found the breakpoint criterion occurred at approximately a constant proportion of the fixed interval over this range of intervals; the response rate changed from a low state to a high state at about two thirds of the interval (see the bottom panel of Figure 9.9). This is another example of approximately proportional timing.

To determine if there are systematic deviations from approximately proportional timing, it is necessary to investigate a large number of closely spaced fixed intervals. A ramped fixed-interval procedure is an efficient way to determine the functional relationship between the time of starting to respond and the length of the fixed interval (see Figure 9.10). In two experiments, rats were tested on a fixed interval that varied between 10 s and 140 s in 2-s steps (Crystal, Church, & Broadbent, 1997). Each successive interval was 2 s longer than the previous interval, until the maximum interval of 140 s was presented, and then each successive interval was 2 s shorter than the previous interval, until the minimum interval of 10 s was presented. The median start times (solid points in the top panels) and the interquartile range of the start times (open points in the top panel) were approximately proportion to the interval. The residuals of these two measures from the best-fitting straight line are shown in the bottom panels. These showed, relative to the linear rule, that particular intervals were overestimated, that others were underestimated, and that particular intervals were estimated with more or less variability. Tests at slightly different ranges indicated that the systematic residuals were related to the absolute values of the intervals, rather than to the relative values. As in the case of systemic deviations from proportionality in the temporal discrimination task, the important features of these deviations are that (a) they are systematic rather than random, (b) they are local, (i.e., the dependent measure is lower at some time intervals than at shorter or longer intervals), and (c) there are multiple local minima. These small departures from Weber's law in the fixed-interval task may provide evidence about the mechanism involved in temporal perception.

In a standard fixed-interval procedure, the delivery of the food marks the beginning of an interval that culminates in the next delivery of

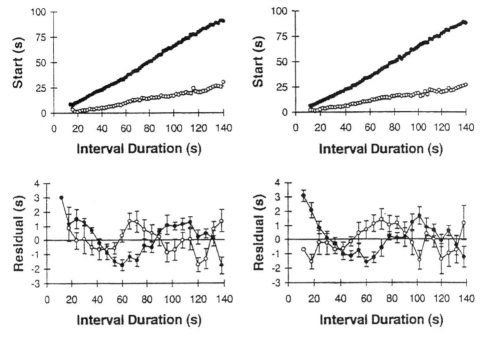

Figure 9.10 Ramped interval procedure.
NOTE: The top panels show the median start times (closed circles) and interquartile range of the start times as a function of interval duration in seconds. The bottom panels show the residuals of these two measures from the best-fitting straight line.
SOURCE: From Crystal, Church, and Broadbent (1997).

food. In a discriminative fixed-interval procedure, the onset of a stimulus is a time marker. A cycle consists of an interval without a stimulus, the onset of a stimulus (the time marker), the availability of food after a fixed interval after the onset of the stimulus, a response, and delivery of food. The same regularities described for the standard fixed-interval procedure apply to the discriminative fixed-interval procedure, especially if measures are taken to minimize the effect of food delivery as an additional time marker. With a short and fixed interval between the delivery of food and the onset of the stimulus, the delivery of food can be an additional time marker. Typically, investigators use a long random interval between the delivery of food and the onset of the stimulus to minimize this effect (Church, Miller, Meck, & Gibbon, 1991).

The Peak Procedure

In the discriminative fixed-interval procedure, the mean response rate increases as a function of time from stimulus onset to food. The peak procedure randomly intermixes with these food cycles other cycles in which the stimulus lasts much longer and in which there is no food. On these nonfood cycles, the mean response rate can be examined as a function of time from stimulus onset to a time much later than the time that food is sometimes delivered. Catania (1970) trained a pigeon on a peak procedure in which there were food and nonfood cycles. On a food cycle, the key light and house light were turned on, and food was delivered following the first response after a 10-s interval. On a nonfood cycle the lights remained on for 38 s, and no food was delivered.

On nonfood cycles the response rate increased as a function of time to a maximum near the time of reinforcement and then declined. The overall response rate was influenced by the probability of a food cycle ($p = .9$ or $.1$), but this did not influence the time of the maximum response rate, which was near 10 s in both conditions.

This procedure was used effectively by Roberts (1981) to determine factors affecting the peak time and the peak rate. For example, the peak time is approximately equal to the time at which food is sometimes delivered (Figure 9.11, top panel), and the peak rate is positively related to the probability of food (Figure 9.11, bottom panel). The distinction between factors that produce a horizontal shift in the function (on the time axis) and factors that produce a vertical shift in the function (on the response axis) can be made easily from the nonfood cycles of a peak procedure that increase to a maximum and then decrease. This distinction is much more difficult to make on the basis of the food cycles of a peak procedure (or with a fixed-interval procedure) because the distinction between vertical and horizontal shifts of a rising function is more subtle. Experiments with the peak procedure have provided evidence for six principles that are similar to those based on investigations of temporal bisection:

1. *Symmetry.* The function-relation response rate as a function of time since stimulus onset (the peak function) is approximately on an arithmetic scale of time, often with some positive skew.

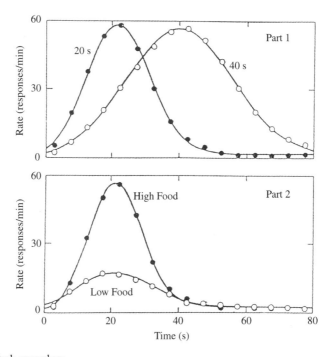

Figure 9.11   Peak procedure.
NOTE: Response rate as a function of time since stimulus onset. Top panel: Time of food availability was 20 s or 40 s. Bottom panel: Probability of food availability was .8 (high food) or .2 (low food).
SOURCE: From Roberts (1981).

2. *Peak time.* The maximum response rate is near the reinforced interval.

3. *Proportional timing.* The peak time increases approximately linearly with the time of the reinforced interval.

4. *Scalar variability.* The standard deviation of the peak time increases approximately linearly with stimulus duration.

5. *Weber's law.* The coefficient of variation (the standard deviation divided by the mean) of the peak location is approximately constant.

6. *Superposition.* The peak functions at all ranges superpose when the duration of a stimulus is divided by the peak time (which is often approximated by the time of reinforcement).

The superposition result is normally obtained by training different animals at different intervals, or by training the same animals for many sessions on one interval and then many sessions on another interval. It can, however, be obtained also by training animals on two different intervals (such as 10 s and 30 s) that are marked by different stimuli (such as light and noise) and intermixed on each session (Gibbon, Church, & Meck, 1984). In this experiment, the peak response rates were somewhat greater than 10 s and somewhat less than 30 s when the times of scheduled reinforcement were 10 s and 30 s, respectively. The functions did not superimpose when normalized by the time of scheduled reinforcement, but they did superimpose when normalized by the peak time. This suggests that the relative subjective time, rather than the relative physical time, is used in determining the times to respond.

The mean response functions obtained with the peak procedure gradually increase to a maximum near the time that reinforcement sometimes occurs, followed by a slightly asymmetrical decrease. This is not characteristic of individual cycles. Cycles that end in food typically have no responding until some point after stimulus onset, and then they have responding at a fairly steady rate until the food is received. (This is the same pattern typically obtained in fixed-interval schedules of reinforcement.) Cycles that do not end in food typically have no responding until some point after stimulus onset, and then they have a fairly steady rate until some point after the time that that food is sometimes received, and finally no responding until the next stimulus onset. This is a low-high-low pattern of responding in which the period of high response rate generally brackets the time that food is sometimes received. On each cycle it is possible to define a start and stop of the high response rate, and from these to define a center (halfway between the start and stop) and a spread (the difference between the start and stop). The patterns of correlations among these measures are quite consistent, and they have been used in the development of quantitative theories of timing (Cheng & Westwood, 1993; Church et al., 1994; Gibbon & Church, 1990, 1992).

Differential Reinforcement of Low Response Rates

Reinforcers, stimuli, and responses can all be used as time markers. Animals learn to adjust to the interval between reinforcers in temporal conditioning and in fixed-interval schedules of reinforcement; they learn to adjust to the interval between a stimulus and reinforcer in discriminated fixed-interval schedules of reinforcement and in the peak procedure; and they learn to adjust to the interval between a response and a reinforcement in the differential reinforcement of low response rate schedules (DRL; Harzem, 1969; Skinner, 1938). In the DRL schedule of reinforcement, a response that is separated by more than t seconds from the previous response will be reinforced. For example, in a DRL-20 schedule, the first response that is spaced more than 20 s from the previous response will be reinforced. This leads to a low response rate and many interresponse intervals that are near 20 s. The mean response rate is inversely related to the duration of the DRL schedule; the interresponse intervals are typically bimodal, with one very short mode and the other near the duration of the DRL schedule.

Dynamics of Temporal Learning

Most research on temporal learning has concerned the asymptotic performance under steady-state conditions. The study of initial acquisition of temporal learning is more difficult because the amount of data that can be recorded at each stage of acquisition from each animal is limited. An analysis of the development of a temporal gradient by pigeons trained on 40-s and 80-s fixed-interval schedules of reinforcements (Machado & Cevik, 1998) suggested that training led to an increase in the slope of a nonlinear increasing gradient without markedly affecting either the mean response rate or the response rate at some intermediate time (a fixed pivot point). This might mean that the mean density of food (leading to the mean response rate) and the temporal interval (leading to the fixed pivot point was learned rapidly, but that the quantitative features of the temporal gradient were developed only with considerable training.

The study of transitions in the temporal schedules of reinforcement has shown that the effects may be very rapid. A single, short interfood interval in a series of longer interfood intervals leads to an immediate shortening of the waiting time on the next interval (Higa, Wynne, & Staddon, 1991). Even changes in the schedule of random interval

reinforcements can have a rapid effect on behavior, as shown by Mark and Gallistel (1994) in their studies of transitions in the relative rates of brain-stimulation reward of rats.

Temporal Pattern Learning

Considerable research has been done with repeating sequences of interfood intervals by Staddon and his colleagues. In these experiments pigeons have been exposed to a repeating series of food-food intervals, and the time from food delivery until the next response was measured (Staddon & Higa, 1991). The effects of many different series were explored, and under many of them the pigeons appeared to track the series. This was often due to an immediate reaction to the previous interval. Staddon and his colleagues proposed the one-back hypothesis, in which the wait time on a particular interval was a linear function of the previous interfood interval. Thus, if the series changed gradually, a linear function of the previous interfood interval would approximate a linear function of the next interfood interval. In some of the research by Staddon and his colleagues, the wait times of the pigeons were accounted for better by the duration of the current interval than by the duration of the previous interval. In a procedure for rats in which a 10-step ramp function of intervals was used, the wait time was more closely related to the duration of the present or next interval than to the duration of the previous interval (Church & Lacourse, 1998). This indicates that under conditions that have not yet been clearly specified, animals anticipate subsequent intervals in a repeating series.

Classical Conditioning

Many classical conditioning experiments involve variations in the distribution of time intervals between stimuli and reinforcers. These include the three procedures diagrammed in Figure 9.1 (temporal conditioning, delayed conditioning, and trace conditions), as well as many others. In some cases, more than one temporal interval can be shown to be affecting behavior simultaneously. For example, in autoshaping of pigeons (a delayed conditioning procedure in which the stimulus is a lighted key, the reinforcer is food, and the conditioned response is a peck on the key), the interval from stimulus to food and the interval from one food to the next may both be constant. Under these conditions the number of reinforcers necessary for a pigeon to achieve a criterion of acquisition is negatively related to the ratio of the stimulus-food interval to the food-food interval (Gibbon & Balsam, 1981). Investigations of these two time intervals have been done in an appetitive conditioning experiment with rats in which the stimulus is usually a noise, the reinforcer is food, and the conditioned response is a head entry into the food cup (Holland, 2000; Kirkpatrick & Church, 2000; Lattal, 1999). A plausible interpretation of the results is that the two time intervals have independent effects and that simultaneous timing of the two intervals leads to the observed response gradients, discrimination ratios, and number of responses to achieve an acquisition criterion (Kirkpatrick & Church, 2000).

The ability of animals to time intervals is not restricted to constant intervals. If the time between food reinforcements is constant, rats have an increasing tendency to make a head entry into the food cup as a function of time since the last food; if the time between food reinforcements is random, rats have a relatively constant tendency to make a head entry as a function of time since the last food; and if the time between foods is the sum of a fixed and random time, the head-entry gradient reflects the expected time to next food as a function of time since food. In these experiments,

the overall response rate was determined by the mean reinforcement rate in the fixed, random, and combined conditions (Kirkpatrick & Church, in press).

The control of behavior by random intervals between shocks was established in an important experiment by Rescorla (1968). Rats were trained in a conditioned suppression procedure in which they were given five sessions of training to press a lever for food reinforcers, given five sessions with occasional shocks in the presence or absence of a stimulus, and then given five sessions in the lever box in which the stimulus was presented but no food was delivered (extinction). During the shock-conditioning phase, there were 2-min presentations of the stimulus and a mean interstimulus interval of 8 min. Shocks were administered during the stimulus and in the absence of the stimulus according to random interval schedules. The schedules used were random intervals of 5 min, 10 min, or 20 min (or no shock). All of the combinations were used in which the shock rate in the stimulus was greater or equal to the shock rate in the absence of the stimulus (10 groups). The results are shown in Figure 9.12. (The probabilities given in the figure are for the expected number of shocks in a 2-min interval.) The figure shows that the relative response rate in the presence of the stimulus (the suppression ratio) was affected by the shock rate in the presence of the stimulus relative to the shock rate in the absence of the stimulus.

Most interpretations of the contingency experiments of Rescorla (1968) emphasize the instantaneous probability of a shock in determining the amount of suppression. However, if shock is delivered at the end of a fixed-duration stimulus, fear increases during the stimulus; if it is delivered at random during the stimulus, fear decreases during the stimulus (Libby & Church, 1975). This was interpreted to mean that "fear at a given

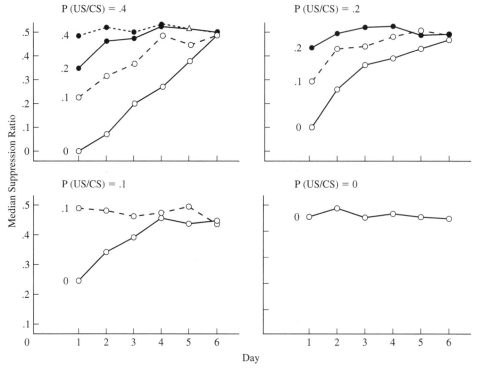

Figure 9.12 Conditioned suppression procedure.

NOTE: Median suppression ratio as a function of days of extinction. The expected rate of shock in the presence of the stimulus was the same for all the functions in a panel; the expected rate of shock in the absence of the stimulus was different for each of the functions in a panel.

SOURCE: From Rescorla (1968).

time after signal onset depends upon the expected time to the next shock" (p. 915). The decrease in fear when shock is delivered at random during a fixed-duration stimulus (with a lower shock rate in the absence of the stimulus) may occur because the expected time to the next shock does decrease as a function of time since stimulus onset. In a condition in which all shocks occurred at random during the stimulus, Rescorla (1968) found that fear decreased markedly as a function of time during the conditioned stimulus. The conditional expected time to reinforcement is also a critical determinant of behavior in classical conditioning experiments with positive reinforcement (Kirkpatrick & Church, in press).

Learning of Circadian Phase

There is no general consensus regarding the relationship between the circadian clock (Moore-Ede et al., 1982) and the various temporal abilities of animals that have been described in this chapter.

One possibility is that they are separate mechanisms used for entirely different purposes. A major function of a circadian clock is to coordinate the behavior of an animal with its external environment; the major function of an interval clock is to measure short intervals of time from an arbitrary stimulus that occurs at an arbitrary time. Of course, this does not preclude some influences that the circadian system may have on an interval timing system.

Another possibility is that the phase of the circadian clock serves as a time marker. Both interval and circadian may be involved in daily meal anticipation (Terman, Gibbon, Fairhurst, & Waring, 1984) and in incubation of eggs by male and female ringdoves (Gibbon, Morrell, & Silver, 1984). Animals readily learn to go to different places at different times of day, a well-studied phenomenon known as time-place learning (Bieback, Gordijn, & Krebs, 1989; Carr & Wilkie, 1999), and often there are alternative bases for making that discrimination.

The most interesting possibility is that there is a fundamental connection between circadian and interval timing. The most thorough analysis of this possibility is contained in the three chapters on timing in Gallistel's 1990 book, *The Organization of Learning*. A periodic clock can serve for the perception of duration if the animal is able to subtract the current phase from a previously remembered phase. In a study of meal anticipation of rats, Crystal (1999) found that rats anticipated the time of food availability with greater precision in the circadian range (22–26 hr) than at shorter or longer intervals (see Figure 9.13). Such privileged intervals

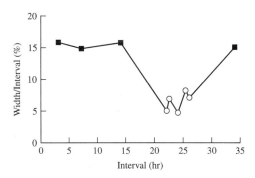

Figure 9.13 Circadian time perception.
NOTE: The relative precision of food anticipation was greater in the circadian range (open circles) than at shorter or longer intervals (closed circles).
SOURCE: From Crystal (2001).

of low variability have also been identified in shorter time ranges, as described earlier in the chapter.

QUANTITATIVE MODELS OF TIMING

Most research on temporal learning concerns the ways in which intervals between stimuli, responses, and outcomes affect response probability and response time. These facts have led to the descriptive generalizations that have been described in this chapter. These are sometimes referred to as general principles because they may apply to many different stimuli, reinforcers, procedures, and species. In many cases these general principles can be described in terms of quantitative functions.

Some investigators have attempted to identify reliable differences in the timing behavior of different species, with the goal of relating these differences to evolutionary pressures, ecology, and brain structure. This approach is clearly described in Shettleworth's (1998) book, *Cognition, Evolution, and Behavior*. Other investigators have proposed that no general principles of timing apply to all stimuli, reinforcers, procedures, and species. The present chapter has emphasized similarities rather than differences, but any complete understanding of temporal learning must include an appreciation of reliable differences also.

One way to explain behavior is in terms of general principles, such as the scalar property. Thus, in a new procedure with a new measure of timing, one may hypothesize that the standard deviation (rather than the variance) of that measure will increase linearly with the mean of the measure. This kind of explanation, which may also be regarded as an organization of the facts, was important in the development of theoretical understanding of temporal learning.

Another way to explain behavior is in terms of a process model, such as the scalar timing theory described next. In a process model there are input, intermediate, and output states; connections between the states may be described with quantitative rules. A process model provides a way to generate output than can be compared with the data.

Scalar Timing Theory

Scalar timing theory refers both to a set of general principles and to a process model. The distinction between the development of general principles and of a process model is described clearly by Gibbon (1991) for scalar timing theory. The former is described in the section on the historical origins of the scalar property, and the latter is described in the section on the causal origins of scalar timing.

In the historical section, Gibbon (1991) referred to Dews' (1970) finding of superposition in the temporal gradients produced by a fixed-interval procedure with very different interval lengths, which is reproduced as Figure 9.8. He then replotted Catania's (1970) finding—the constancy of the coefficient of variation of the temporal gradients produced by a differential reinforcement of low response rates procedure with very different response-to-reinforcer intervals. Other examples came from studies of avoidance learning in the 1950s, choice studies, and classical conditioning. Gibbon's (1977) influential article titled "Scalar Expectancy Theory and Weber's Law in Animal Timing" served to organize such empirical generalizations into a more general principle.

In the causal section, Gibbon (1991) referred to an information-processing model of the timing process that was introduced by Gibbon and Church (1984) for the analysis of animal timing behavior (see Figure 9.14). (This was similar to Treisman's 1963 model of the internal clock.) It included an internal

clock (which included a pacemaker, a switch, and an accumulator), a memory, and a decision process. Gibbon and Church described the effects of variance at several places in this system and the effects of two different response decision rules.

A diagrammatic representation of the theory applied to the temporal generalization procedure is shown in Figure 9.14. The top panel shows subjective time as a function of signal duration. After a latency (T_0) the mean subjective time (X_T) increases linearly with signal duration (T). Because of numerous sources of variability, a particular signal duration does not always produce exactly the same

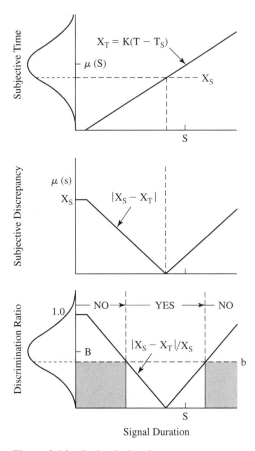

Figure 9.14 Scalar timing theory.
SOURCE: From Church and Gibbon (1982).

subjective time; a normal distribution of subjective times for a particular reinforced signal duration is shown on the vertical axis of the top panel. The middle panel shows the absolute difference between the subjective time and a random sample of one element from the distribution of remembered times of reinforcement (the subjective discrepancy). The bottom panel shows this measure of subjective discrepency expressed as a ratio of the sampled element (the discrimination ratio). Finally, a normal distribution of thresholds is postulated with a mean of B. A random sample of one element from this threshold distribution (b) is used to predict the occurrence of a response. If the discrimination ratio is above the threshold, no response will be made; if it is below the threshold a response will be made.

The appendix of Gibbon, Church et al. 1984 article provides an explicit solution of the theory for three timing procedures (temporal generalization, the peak procedure, and the time-left procedure). For example, a two-parameter version of scalar timing theory involving sensitivity to time and a bias parameter led to the smooth functions near the data points in Figure 9.2. A two-parameter version of scalar timing theory involving the coefficient of variation of clock speed and bias parameter led to the smooth functions near the data points in Figure 9.4.

In practice, most of the tests of the model have been conducted with simulations. Scalar timing theory has been particularly effective in accounting for well-trained behavior on a wide range of temporal discrimination and performance tasks; it was not developed to account for acquisition of temporal performance or for adaptation to new temporal intervals. This is primarily due to the assumptions about memory storage and retrieval: Each reinforced interval is stored as an example, and retrieval is based on a random sample of one of these examples.

A Behavioral Theory of Timing

An alternative theory of timing, proposed by Killeen and Fetterman (1988), was based on the possibility that the animal's behavior might itself serve as a clock. For example, Killeen and Fetterman referred to results from rats on a 30-s fixed-interval schedule of lever pressing in which measures were taken of eating, drinking, general activity, activity in a running wheel, and lever responses (Roper, 1978). The rats typically began the interval eating activity, then the drinking activity, and then lever responding. Such behavioral states, rather than a hypothetical accumulator mechanism, could serve as a clock. Machado (1997) presented a fully specified version of a behavioral theory of timing. Although it is described in behavioristic terms—whereas the information-processing version of scalar timing theory is described in cognitive terms—it is not clear that this is an essential distinction. Process theories of timing and conditioning can be described in terms of processes such as perception, memory, and decision (Church & Kirkpatrick, 2001).

Many other quantitative models of timing and conditioning have been proposed. These include the multiple-oscillator model (Church & Broadbent, 1990), the spectral theory of timing, the multiple time-scale model of time (Staddon & Higa, 1999), and real-time models of conditioning. They differ in their perceptual representations of time, in memory representations, and in their decision processes. All of them have unique merits, but not one would be able to pass a Turing test (Church, 2001).

REFERENCES

Allan, L. G. (1998). The influence of the scalar timing model on human timing research. *Behavioural Processes, 44,* 101–117.

Allan, L. G., & Gibbon, J. (1991). Human bisection at the geometric mean. *Learning and Motivation, 22,* 39–58.

Arcediano, F., & Miller, R. R. (in press). Some constraints for models of timing: A temporal coding hypothesis perspective. *Learning and Motivation.*

Autor, S. M. (1969). The strength of conditioned reinforcers as a function of frequency and probability of reinforcement. In D. P. Hendry (Ed.), *Conditioned reinforcement* (pp. 127–162). Homewood, Ill: Dorsey Press.

Barnet, R. C., Cole, R. P., & Miller, R. R. (1997). Temporal integration in second-order conditioning and sensory preconditioning. *Animal Learning & Behavior, 25,* 221–233.

Barnet, R. C., Grahame, N. J., & Miller, R. R. (1993). Temporal encoding as a determinant of blocking. *Journal of Experimental Psychology: Animal Behavior Processes, 19,* 327–341.

Bieback, H., Gordijn, M., & Krebs, J. R. (1989). Time-and-place learning by garden warblers. Sylvia borin. *Animal Behaviour, 37,* 353–360.

Blaisdell, A. P., Denniston, J. C., & Miller, R. R. (1998). Temporal encoding as a determinant of overshadowing. *Journal of Experimental Psychology: Animal Behavior Processes, 24,* 72–83.

Carr, J. A. R., & Wilkie, D. M. (1999). Rats are relunctant to use circadian timing in a daily time-place task. *Behavioural Processes, 44,* 287–299.

Catania, A. C. (1970). Reinforcement schedules and psychophysical judgments: A study of some temporal properties of behavior. In W. N. Schoenfeld (Ed.), *The theory of reinforcement schedules* (pp. 1–42). New York: Appleton-Century-Crofts.

Cheng, K., & Westwood, R. (1993). Analysis of single trials in pigeons' timing performance. *Journal of Experimental Psychology: Animal Behavior Processes, 19,* 56–67.

Church, R. M. (1980). Short-term memory for time intervals. *Learning and Motivation, 11,* 208–219.

Church, R. M. (1993). Human models of animal behavior. *Psychological Science, 4,* 170–173.

Church, R. M. (2001). A Turing test of computational and association theories. *Current Directions in Psychological Science, 10,* 132–136.

Church, R. M., & Broadbent, H. A. (1990). Alternative representations of time, number, and rate. *Cognition, 37,* 55–81.

Church, R. M., & Deluty, M. Z. (1977). Bisection of temporal intervals. *Journal of Experimental Psychology: Animal Behavior Processes, 3,* 216–228.

Church, R. M., & Gibbon, J. (1982). Temporal generalization. *Journal of Experimental Psychology: Animal Behavior Processes, 8,* 165–186.

Church, R. M., & Kirkpatrick, K. (2001). Theories of conditioning and timing. In R. R. Mowrer & S. B. Klein (Eds.), *Handbook of Contemporary Learning Theories* (pp. 211–253). Mahwah, NJ: Erlbaum Associates.

Church, R. M., & Lacourse, D. M. (1998). Serial pattern learning of temporal intervals. *Animal Learning & Behavior, 26,* 272–289.

Church, R. M., Meck, W. H., & Gibbon, J. (1994). Application of scalar timing theory to individual trials. *Journal of Experimental Psychology: Animal Behavior Processes, 2,* 135–155.

Church, R. M., Miller, K. D., Meck, W. H., & Gibbon, J. (1991). Sources of symmetric and asymmetric variance in temporal generalization. *Animal Learning & Behavior, 19,* 207–214.

Crystal, J. D. (1999). Systematic nonlinearities in the perception of temporal intervals. *Journal of Experimental Psychology: Animal Behavior Processes, 25,* 3–17.

Crystal, J. D. (2001). Circadian time perception. *Journal of Experimental Psychology: Animal Behavior Processes, 27,* 68–78.

Crystal, J. D., Church, R. M., & Broadbent, H. A. (1997). Systematic nonlinearities in the memory representation of time. *Journal of experimental Psychology: Animal Behavior Processes, 23,* 267–282.

Davison, M., & McCarthy, D. (1988). *The matching law: A research review.* Hillsdale, NJ: Erlbaum.

Denniston, J. C., Cole, R. P., & Miller, R. R. (1998). The role of temporal relationships in the transfer of conditioned inhibition. *Journal of Experimental Psychology: Animal Behavior Processes, 24,* 200–214.

Dews, P. B. (1970). The theory of fixed-interval responding. In W. N. Schoenfeld (Ed.), *The theory of reinforcement schedules* (pp. 43–61). New York: Appleton-Century-Crofts.

Fantino, E. (1969). Choice and rate of reinforcement. *Journal of the Experimental Analysis of Behavior, 12,* 723–730.

Fantino, E. (1977). Conditioned reinforcement: choice and information. In W. K. Honig & J. E. R. Staddon (Eds.), *Handbook of operant behavior.* Englewood Cliffs, NJ: Prentice-Hall.

Fantino, E., Preston, R. A., & Dunn, R. (1993). Delay reduction: Current status. *Journal of the Experimental Analysis of Behavior, 60,* 159–169.

Ferster, C. B., & Skinner, B. F. (1957). *Schedules of reinforcement.* New York: Appleton-Century-Crofts.

Fraisse, P. (1963). *The psychology of time.* New York: Harper.

Gaitan, S. C., & Wixted, J. T. (2000). The role of "nothing" in memory for event duration in pigeons. *Animal Learning & Behavior, 28,* 147–161.

Gallistel, C. R. (1990). *The organization of learning.* Cambridge, MA: MIT Press.

Gallistel, C. R., & Gibbon, J. (2000). Time, rate, and conditioning. *Psychological Review, 107,* 289–344.

Gibbon, J. (1977). Scalar expectancy theory and Weber's Law in animal timing. *Psychological Review, 84,* 279–325.

Gibbon, J. (1991). Origins of scalar timing. *Learning and Motivation, 22,* 3–38.

Gibbon, J., & Allan, J. G. (Eds.). (1984). *Timing and time perception.* New York: New York Academy of Sciences.

Gibbon, J., & Balsam, P. (1981). Spreading association in time. In C. M. Locurto, H. S. Terrace, & J. Gibbon (Eds.), *Autoshaping and conditioning theory* (pp. 219–254). New York: Academic Press.

Gibbon, J., & Church, R. M. (1984). Sources of variance in an information theory of timing.

In H. L. Roitblat, T. G. Bever, & H. S. Terrace (Eds.), *Animal cognition* (pp. 465–488). Hillsdale, NJ: Erlbaum.

Gibbon, J., & Church, R. M. (1990). Representation of time. *Cognition, 37,* 23–54.

Gibbon, J., & Church, R. M. (1992). Comparison of variance and covariance patterns in parallel and serial theories of timing. *Journal of the Experimental Analysis of Behavior, 57,* 393–406.

Gibbon, J., Church, R. M., & Meck, W. H. (1984). Scalar timing in memory. In J. Gibbon & L. G. Allan (Eds.), *Annals of the New York Academy of Sciences: Timing and time perception* (pp. 52–77). New York: New York Academy of Sciences.

Gibbon, J., Morrell, M., & Silver, R. (1984). Two kinds of timing in circadian incubation rhythm of ring doves. *American Journal of Physiology: Regulatory, Integrative and Comparative Physiology, 237,* 1083–1087.

Harzem, P. (1969). Temporal discrimination. In R. M. Gilbert & N. S. Sutherland (Eds.), *Animal discrimination learning* (pp. 299–334). London, Academic Press.

Heinemann, E. G., Avin, E., Sullivan, M. A., & Chase, S. (1969). Analysis of stimulus generalization with a psychophysical method. *Journal of Experimental Psychology, 80,* 215–224.

Herrnstein, R. J. (1997). *The matching law: Papers in psychology and economics* (H. Rachlin & D. I. Laibson (Eds.). Cambridge, MA: Harvard University Press.

Higa, J. J., Wynne, C. D., & Staddon, J. E. (1991). Dynamics of time discrimination. *Journal of Experimental Psychology: Animal Behavior Processes, 17,* 281–291.

Holland, P. C. (2000). Trial and intertrial durations in appetitive conditioning in rats. *Journal of Experimental Psychology: Animal Behavior Processes, 28,* 121–135.

Hull, C. L. (1943). *Principles of behavior.* New York: Appleton-Century-Crofts.

James, W. (1890). *The principles of psychology.* London: Macmillan.

Killeen, P. R. (1978). Superstition: A matter of bias, not detectability. *Science, 199,* 88–90.

Killeen, P. R., & Fetterman, J. G. (1988). A behavioral theory of timing. *Psychological Review, 95,* 274–295.

Killeen, P. R., & Smith, J. P. (1984). Perception of contingency in conditioning: Scalar timing, response bias, and erasure of memory by reinforcement. *Journal of Experimental Psychology: Animal Behavior Processes, 10,* 333–345.

Kirkpatrick, K., & Church, R. M. (2000). Independent effects of conditioning and cycle duration in conditioning: The role of timing processes. *Animal Learning & Behavior, 28,* 373–388.

Kirkpatrick, K., & Church, R. M. (in press). Tracking of expected times in classical conditioning. *Animal Learning & Behavior.*

Kraemer, P. J., Mazmanian, D. S., & Roberts, W. A. (1985). The choose-short effect in pigeon memory for stimulus duration: Subjective shortening versus coding models. *Animal Learning & Behavior, 13,* 349–354.

Lattal, K. M. (1999). Trial and intertrial durations in Pavlovian conditioning: Issues of learning and performance. *Journal of Experimental Psychology: Animal Behavior Processes, 25,* 433–450.

Libby, M. E., & Church, R. M. (1975). Fear gradients as a function of the temporal interval between signal and aversive event in the rat. *Journal of Comparative and Physiological Psychology, 88,* 911–916.

Logan, F. A. (1960). *Incentive.* New Haven: Yale University Press.

Machado, A. (1997). Learning the temporal dynamics of behavior. *Psychological Review, 104,* 241–265.

Machado, A., & Cevik, M. (1998). Acquisition and extinction under periodic reinforcement. *Behavioural Processes, 44,* 237–262.

Mark, T. A., & Gallistel, C. R. (1994). Kinetics of matching. *Journal of Experimental Psychology: Animal Behavior Processes, 20,* 79–95.

Matzel, L. D., Held, F. P., & Miller, R. R. (1988). Information and expression of simultaneous and backward associations: Implications for contiguity theory. *Learning and Motivation, 19,* 317–344.

Mazur, J. E. (1997). Choice, delay, probability, and conditioned reinforcement. *Animal Learning & Behavior, 25,* 131–147.

Meck, W. H., & Church, R. M. (1982a). Abstraction of temporal attributes. *Journal of Experimental Psychology: Animal Behavior Processes, 8,* 226–243.

Meck, W. H., & Church, R. M. (1982b). Discrimination of intertrial intervals in cross-modal transfer of duration. *Bulletin of the Psychonomic Society, 19,* 234–236.

Moore-Ede, M. C., Sulzman, F. M., & Fuller, C. A. (1982). *The clocks that time us.* Cambridge, MA: Harvard University Press.

Pavlov, I. P. (1927). *Conditioned reflexes* (G. V. Anrep, Trans.). London: Oxford University Press.

Platt, J. R., & Davis, E. R. (1983). Bisection of temporal intervals by pigeons. *Journal of Experimental Psychology: Animal Behavior Processes, 9,* 160–170.

Rescorla, R. A. (1968). Probability of shock in the presence and absence of CS in fear conditioning. *Journal of Comparative and Physiological Psychology, 66,* 1–5.

Richelle, M., & Lejeune, H. (1980). *Time in animal behaviour.* Oxford: Pergammon.

Richter, C. P. (1922). A behavioristic study of the activity of the rat. *Comparative Psychology Monographs, 1,* 1–55.

Richter, C. P. (1965). *Biological clocks in medicine and psychiatry.* Springfield, IL: C. C. Thomas.

Richter, C. P. (1977). Heavy water as a tool for study of the forces that control the length of period of the 24-hour clock of the hamster. *Proceedings of the National Academy of Sciences, USA, 74,* 1295–1299.

Roberts, S. (1981). Isolation of an internal clock. *Journal of Experimental Psychology: Animal Behavior Processes, 7,* 242–268.

Roberts, S. (1982). Cross-modal use of an internal clock. *Journal of Experimental Psychology: Animal Behavior Processes, 8,* 2–22.

Roeckelein, J. E. (2000). *The concept of time in psychology: A resource book and annotated bibliography.* Westport, CT: Greenwood.

Roper, T. J. (1978). Diversity and substitutability of adjunctive activities under fixed-interval schedules of food reinforcement. *Journal of the Experimental Analysis of Behavior, 30,* 83–96.

Schneider, B. A. (1969). A two-state analysis of fixed-interval responding in the pigeon. *Journal of the Experimental Analysis of Behavior, 12,* 677–687.

Shettleworth, S. J. (1998). *Cognition, evolution, and behavior.* New York: Oxford University Press.

Shimp, C. P. (1969). Optimal behavior in free-operant experiments. *Psychological Review, 76,* 97–112.

Skinner, B. F. (1938). *The behavior of organisms.* New York: Appleton-Century-Crofts.

Spetch, M. L., & Wilkie, D. M. (1983). Subjective shortening: A model of pigeons' memory for event duration. *Journal of Experimental Psychology: Animal Behavior Processes, 9,* 14–30.

Staddon, J. E. R., & Higa, J. J. (1991). Temporal learning. *The Psychology of Learning and Motivation, 27,* 265–294.

Staddon, J. E. R., & Higa, J. J. (1999). Time and memory: Toward a pacemaker-free theory of interval timing. *Journal of the Experimental Analysis of Behavior, 71,* 215–251.

Sternberg, S. (1966). High-speed scanning in human memory. *Science, 153,* 652–654.

Stubbs, A. (1968). The duration of stimulus duration by pigeons. *Journal of the Experimental Analysis of Behavior, 11,* 223–238.

Terman, M., Gibbon, J., Fairhurst, S., & Waring, A. (1984). Daily meal anticipation: Interaction of circadian and interval timing. In J. Gibbon & L. Allan (Eds.), *Timing and time perception* (pp. 470–487). New York: New York Academy of Sciences.

Treisman, M. (1963). Temporal discrimination and the indifference interval: Implications for a model of the "Internal clock." *Psychological Monographs, 7* (13, Whole No. 576).

Wearden, J. H., Denovan, L., & Haworth, R. (1997). Scalar timing in temporal generalization in humans with longer stimulus durations. *Journal of Experimental Psychology: Animal Behavior Processes, 23,* 502–511.

Woodrow, H. (1951). Time perception. In S. S. Stevens (Ed.), *Handbook of experimental psychology.* New York: Wiley, pp. 1224–1236.

CHAPTER 10

Role of Learning in Cognitive Development

ROCHEL GELMAN AND JOAN LUCARIELLO

The role of learning in cognitive development has been conceptualized in three different ways. From a purely empiricist perspective, cognitive development *is* learning. A general-purpose learning process—association formation—is the process through which the structure of experience forms the structure of the mind. The only developmental constraints on knowledge acquisition are whether the capacity to form associations between elementary sensations, or between sensations and responses, is in place. If one's sensory systems are immature or not functioning, or the capacity to form associations is weak, then little or no cognitive development can occur. The structure of the associative learning process is independent of the structure of the material being learned. There are no a priori data-organizing principles. The mind of the infant is a blank slate (tabula rasa), and "The senses at first let in *particular* ideas, and furnish the yet empty cabinet...." (p. 72; Locke, 1690). The same learning process operates throughout development and for all domains of understanding. This assumption is shared by a range

of theories grounded on general processes (Rumelhart & McClelland, 1986; Siegler, 1991; Skinner, 1938, 1950).

Stage theories, on the other hand, assume that the structure of the child's mind passes through a sequence of qualitatively different stages and that the structure at a given stage determines what can be learned at that stage (Bruner, 1964; Piaget, 1970). In stage theories, the mind is active and constructs reality. It goes in quest of particular experiences, rather than passively registering the associations that it happens to encounter. The experiences it seeks are those that will nurture its development to the next structural stage through the processes of assimilation and accommodation.

Although the structure of the mind at a given stage determines what can be learned, the structures of the successive stages are not domain-specific. They govern what can be extracted from experience in any domain. For example, Piaget's stages are about sensorimotor schemata during infancy and concrete logical operations during the school-aged years. Within this theoretical framework, infants at the beginning of the sensorimotor period of development cannot form stable perceptions of objects, social or otherwise. A fortiori, they cannot form concepts about objects within domains, such as physical objects or social objects. Instead, they start

Authors are listed in alphabetical order. The preparation of this chapter was partially supported by NSF grants DFS-9209741 and SRB-97209741 to Rochel Gelman. The authors are especially grateful to their editor for his input and editing suggestions.

responding reflexively to particular stimuli; then, with continued use, these reflexes are gradually adapted to form what are called primary circular reactions as opposed to reflexive ones to these stimuli. These in turn are used repeatedly and become interrelated and coordinated, and so on.

Although infants actively engage whatever objects are placed before them, it is assumed that they have no memory for these. The idea is, if out of sight (or touch or hearing range), out of mind. Thus, Piagetian theory shares with the general learning theory the position that it will take a great deal of time before infants can be granted the concept of an object that exists in a three-dimensional space and independently of the infants' own actions. Even after several years of mental development, preschool-aged children are assumed to be perception-bound and unable to form consistent classifications. The result is that they are unable to form abstract concepts. Thus, the stage theory perspective shares with the general learning theory the assumption that cognitive development proceeds from elementary experiences to abstractions, and that this progression takes a long time. Haith and Benson (1998) recent treatment of infant cognition has much in common with this position.

In recent decades, a third perspective has come to the fore; this may be called the rational-constructivist perspective. It assumes that learning is guided from the outset by domain-specific principles (hence, the "rationalism"). These principles enable the child to construct a representation of the world from experience (hence, the "constructivism"). This perspective explains a range of new experimental findings, which is a key reason for our discussion to focus on this approach and its account of cognitive development and learning.

The rational-constructivist perspective recognizes a fundamental truth at the heart of the Piagetian perspective, which is that children are active participants in the construction of their own cognitive development. However, learning is not a homogeneous or content-neutral process. Rather, it is made possible, at least to start, by different sets of core or domain-specific skeletal principles that direct the infant's attention to relevant aspects of experience and organize the resulting experiences (Baillargeon, 1995; Carey, 1985; Cosmides & Tooby, 1994; Fodor, 1975, 1983; Gallistel & Gibbon 2000; Gardner, 1992; Hirschfeld & S. Gelman, 1994; Keil and Wilson, 2000; Leslie, 1995; Spelke, 2000). Hence these principles foster domain-based early learning (even in infancy). Such learning is rapid, universal, and non-reliant on instruction (cf. Chap. 11 this volume for a documentation of this in connection with the learning of language).

The rational constructivist perspective, moreover, can account for a developmental function in learning. This developmental function is evident in three kinds of later learning that contrast with early core learnings in terms of rapidity, ease, universality, and reliance on instruction. One kind of later learning can be characterized as "core-consistent knowledge extension." This later learning is domain-based because what is to be learned is consistent with and hence builds on the core knowledge or skeletal principles in a domain. It is very similar to initial learning in being relatively rapid and easy. This kind of later learning will be considered in this chapter. Second, later learning can represent "core-inconsistent knowledge acquisition." In these cases, what is to be learned might appear to be related to core knowledge in a domain, but is inconsistent with one or more core principles. Hence, while domain-related, the learning is not based on a known knowledge structure. This learning is very dissimilar to early learning in being effortful, protracted, and non-universal. Examples of this kind of later learning also will be discussed in this chapter. Finally, there are those cases where later learning involves totally new domains, ones unrelated to core domains of knowledge. Learning sushi-making and air traffic control are cases of such later learning. This chapter does not address later learning of this kind.

This discussion of learning in cognitive development, based on the rational constructivist perspective, presumes a variety of learning tools that the mind recruits in the service of knowledge acquisition. The kind of tools that are recruited, be it for early or later learning, can vary depending primarily on whether what is to be learned is consistent or inconsistent with the skeletal principles in a domain.

We move first to a general discussion and overview of the rational-constructivist view of cognitive development and learning. This entails review of the concepts of domain (core and noncore), of the skeletal nature of early principles, and of the description of mental learning tools. We follow this with a discussion of learning in three domains—physical objects, number, and sociality—with more emphasis on the latter. Early and later learning will be examined. Cases of later learning that are "core-consistent" will be contrasted with cases that are "core-inconsistent."

WHAT IS A DOMAIN?

A given set of principles, the rules of their application, and the entities to which they apply together constitute a domain (e.g., R. Gelman, 1993; see also Gallistel, 1990). Different domains are defined by different sets of principles. Therefore, we can say that a body of knowledge constitutes a domain of knowledge if we can show that a set of interrelated principles organizes its rules of operation and entities. Sets of principles carve the psychological world at its joints, producing distinctions that guide and organize our reasoning about entities in one domain versus

another. In this way, available domain-specific structures encourage attention to inputs that have a privileged status because they have the potential to nurture learning about that domain; they help learners find inputs that are relevant for knowledge acquisition and problem solving within that domain.

Core and Noncore Domains

Nothing in the above definition of domain-specific knowledge structures speaks to their origin. Although some knowledge domains benefit from foundational skeletal structures, many do not (Bransford, Brown, & Cocking, 1999; Karmiloff-Smith, 1992). To emphasize this, R. Gelman and Williams (1998) distinguished between *core* and *noncore* domains. The class of core domains is simply those that are universally learnable with relative ease.

The distinction between core and noncore domains is analogous to the linguistic distinction between closed and open class morphemes. All who acquire language as young children share knowledge of the small set of closed class of morphemes in that language. These morphemes serve the capacity to generate utterances that honor the combinatorial rules underlying the syntax of the language. The open class of morphemes includes all learned and to-be-learned nouns, verbs, adjectives, and adverbs—potentially an infinitely large class. Different individuals can master different examples and different numbers of entries in the open class. Similarly, the set of noncore domains is potentially very large and can vary from individual to individual. In contrast, the set of core conceptual domains is relatively small, and their underlying structures are shared by all (R. Gelman & Williams, 1998).

As in the case of different languages, there are some underlying common structures even though different cultures might differ in the particulars that make up the domain-relevant knowledge. For example, as far as we can tell, everyone all over the world makes a distinction between animate and inanimate objects that are separably movable. Still, there exist notable differences in how rich a knowledge structure about animals a given culture achieves (Hatano & Inagaki, 1999).

Early Learning/Competencies

The idea that core domains serve as learning devices provides an account of the fact that young learners respond to structured data as opposed to simple punctate sensations. The reason is that application of even skeletal structures means that the class of relevant data will be relational and overlap with the abstract principles that lime the domain. This means that those infants need not be confronted with William James' "blooming buzzing" confusion of punctate bits of uninterpretable sensations. Instead, they can behave as if there were an environment with physical and social things "out there"—things to find, interact with, and learn about. Different implicit knowledge structures should encourage attention to and exploration of different kinds of structured data, and assimilating these helps nourish the coherent growth of these nascent structures.

The metaphor of a skeleton helps to clarify the notion of innate principles. If there were no skeletons to outline the shape and contents of the bodies of the pertinent mental structures, then there would be no reason for young learners to select domain-relevant experiences, let alone store those experiences in a coherent way. Just as different skeletal structures are assembled according to different principles, so too are different coherent bodies of knowledge. Skeletons need not be evident on the surface of a body. Similarly, the underlying axiom-like principles, which enable the acquisition of coherent knowledge, need never be explicitly accessible. Many principles that

organize language learning, for example, are deeply inaccessible (see Chap. 11, this volume). Most importantly, skeletons lack flesh and some relevant body structures. Thus, they are not full-blown explanatory theories, as suggested by Gopnik and Meltzoff (1997). They are information-structuring principles that need to interact with the kinds of environments that nourish and support domain-relevant conceptual development.

In the history of developmental biology, this kind of account of development is called epigenetic, in contrast to the preformistic account that it superseded. In epigenetic development the final structure is not present at the outset (preformed); it develops through an interaction between an initial genetic structure and relevant environments. Eyes are not preformed in embryos. They emerge through an epigenetic process that is guided by a hierarchy of genes specific to eye formation. Similarly, the grammar of a specific language is not preformed in the mind of the newborn baby. It develops in the mind of the young child from its experience with its linguistic environment, guided by a hierarchy of language-specific principles (see Chap. 11, this volume). In a related way, skeletal structures for different core domains serve to guide the epigenesis of the domain (cf. Scholl & Leslie, 1999). Like language, the surface structure of the knowledge that emerges differs from one locale to another, but these different surface structures share underlying domain-specific principles. For an explanation of how this perspective accounts for the development of religious beliefs, see Pascal Boyer (2001).

Later Learning

It helps to distinguish between three kinds of later learning in development. The first constitutes those cases in which learning is about structurally consistent acquisitions. Hartnett and Gelman's (1998) treatment of the successor principle for natural numbers—that every natural number has a successor—is an example of this kind of learning. This is an example of *core-based* knowledge extension. Two kinds of later learning do not readily build off existing core knowledge structures. One involves those concept acquisitions that appear related to what is known but upon careful consideration are not. This is because the "structures" of what is to be learned differ or even contradict the structures of already acquired concepts. Rational numbers constitute an example of the former because the principles that organize their domain are different from those for natural numbers. For example, because there is an infinite number of numbers between any pair of natural numbers, a rational number (e.g., a fraction such as 1/4) has no specifiable successor number. We dub this kind of subsequent learning *core-inconsistent*. The learning that occurs here is clearly built on the easily mastered core knowledge, but it depends on the mounting of a new structure. In the same vein, the counterscript structures for representing ironic situations violate the principles of social scripts (that is why they are counterscripts). Hence, the mastering counterscripts for the understanding of ironic events is another example of core-inconsistent learning and development.

Finally, there are the cases in which people must master bodies of knowledge that seem unrelated to any core domains. These kinds of later learning are often discussed in the expert-novice literature on chess, history, algebra, economics, literature, and so on.

Both of the latter kinds of subsequent learning present comparable challenges to individuals because there is no domain-relevant skeletal structure to start the learning ball rolling. The relevant mental structures must be acquired de novo, which means that learners acquire domain-relevant structures as well as a coherent base of domain-relevant knowledge about the content of that domain (see also Brown, 1990). It is far from easy to assemble truly new conceptual structures (Bransford et al., 1999; Carey, 1991; Chi, 1992; Kuhn, 1970), and it usually takes a very long time. Something resembling formal instructions is often required, and even still this is not effective unless there is extended practice and effort on the part of the learner (Bransford et al., 1999). In both cases, the later learning might even be at risk because learners may assimilate inputs to existing conceptual structures even when those inputs are intended to force accommodation and conceptual change (R. Gelman, 1993, 1994; Slotta, Chi, & Joram, 1995). That is, learners may fail to interpret novel inputs as intended and instead treat the data as further examples of the kinds of understanding that they have available.

The theoretical account of how later learning can occur should cover both core-inconsistent and noncore kinds of domains because in both cases a new conceptual structure must be mastered. A theory that involves learning tools for structural learning can accomplish this goal.

LEARNING TOOLS

Structure Mapping

Within the associationist framework, elementary sense data are the primary data for early concept learning. By contrast, within the rational-constructivist framework, basic experiences are defined in structural terms, by the relations exhibited. A domain's organizing principles lead learners to attend to relations when interacting with the world. This is not to say that sensory data are irrelevant but rather to say that, by themselves, they do not serve to get learning about concepts off the ground. Instead, babies and young children use the abstract principles from a domain to find, organize, and assimilate domain-relevant, organized inputs. This follows from the assumption that principles of a domain encourage attention to domain-relevant data, that is, data that share a common structure with the domain's principles. In core domains, the skeletal principles themselves define initial representations that become the repository of all data whose structure can be mapped to them. Structure mapping serves learners' abilities to identify relevant inputs when going beyond old learnings, given the ever-present tendency to apply existing mental structures to new learning.

Like others, we assume that learning leads to the buildup of a richer conceptual structure within a domain. R. Gelman and Williams (1998) couched their account of learning in terms of the kinds of mental learning tools that can contribute to the active construction of knowledge. They argue that the mind favors *structure mapping* as the fundamental learning process. Given that the mind actively applies its existing structures to find examples of structured data in the environments with which it interacts, learning in core domains is privileged. Skeletal structures provide the beginning learner with the wherewithal to find and map inputs that are examples to available structures. This leads to the enrichment of those structures.

Analogical Reasoning: A Variant of Structure Mapping

Learning by analogy involves finding a correspondence between two events, domains, or examples and then transferring what is given or understood about one case to the other case. For example, Inagaki and Sugiyama (1988) asked children ranging in age from 5 years to 10 years about a number of biological characteristics of living kinds. They first obtained similarity-to-people judgments. The children rank-ordered rabbits, pigeons, fish, grasshoppers, trees, tulips, and rocks and used

this similarity ranking to assign predicates such as "breathes," "has a heart," "can think." Obviously, analogical reasoning by itself will not suffice to guarantee acquisition of correct knowledge. For example, a grasshopper—no matter how small and different looking when compared with a person—does breathe. A key consideration in the success of analogical reasoning is the choice of the analogy.

There is an emerging consensus that successful analogical transfer depends on the extent to which structure mapping is possible. The probability that transfer will occur is very high if learners achieve representations that are structural isomorphs but very low if learners must rely on surface cues of perceptual similarity (Brown, 1990; Gentner, Rattermann, & Forbus, 1993; Goswami, 1995; Holyoak & Thagard, 1995). For instance, by taking advantage of very young children's principled knowledge about causality, Goswami and Brown (1990) were able to illustrate that children solve analogies of the a:b::c:d form when a common causal transformation forms the basis of the analogy. In another example of analogical reasoning and transfer, Catrambone and Holyoak (1989) presented subjects with multiple analogous word problems and measured transfer to the solution of a superficially different word problem; transfer was facilitated when the problems were worded to emphasize their structural similarities.

Imitation and Template Matching

Imitation is a way to learn by watching and listening to others. It clearly depends on an ability to form a representation of a model that embodies key aspects of what is being done. Meltzoff and Moore's (1983, 1989) work on imitation makes it clear that even infants learn new event sequences by watching others perform them. It is hard to overestimate the significance of this learning tool. It provides learners a way to acquire new knowledge schemas at negligible cost and then to use these to monitor the quality of their output. This phenomenon is well known to piano players. Often, they listen to a record by a great master to get a better model of how a particular piece can be played. Then follow hours of practice, with the pianists stopping, starting over again, stopping, and so on, often shaking their heads and indicating that their performances are not matching the models in their heads. Significantly, the fact that the mind monitors the output generated by a given mental structure means that there is an on-line way to get feedback about the degree to which learners have achieved their learning goals—a match of their knowledge and skill to what their models set as the standard.

In some cases it is reasonable to conclude that a young learner starts with a template, that is, a sketchy model of the kind of data and performance opportunities that are needed to tune the given template. Marler's (1991) work on birdsong learning in the male song sparrow provides an excellent example. Songbird-learning mechanisms are specific adaptations that are designed to operate in environmentally specific contexts to ensure the uptake of information that is essential to the later reproductive success. Innately determined song templates guide selection of what is to be remembered to serve as the model for later practice. Of major interest here is the fact that song sparrows that grow up in different places sing different songs, namely, songs with the characteristics of the local dialect to which they are exposed plus individual signature elements. White-crowned sparrows, like many songbirds, have a sensitive period somewhere during the first year of their life. If they do not get to hear the song of an adult sparrow during this time, the song they sing will be decidedly odd when they grow up. The sensitive period has the effect of tuning the bird's template for a particular class of song.

Exposure during an early period of life does not, however, suffice to guarantee that the young bird will grow up to sing the represented song, or that its adult song will be normal. The bird must go through periods of subsong learning and crystallization, again during the first year of life. The subsong learning period is especially interesting for us because only at this time (after the sensitive period for exposure) does the young bird start to sing. The initial efforts in this period look very much like a trial-and-error series and in some ways are like an infant's babbling; the song sounds not at all like the adult target model. The data gathered by Marler and colleagues suggest that the bird is working at converging on a particular output plan, which generates a song that is consistent with the song template that is mentally represented. Without any more input than what the young bird produces at this point, the bird gradually moves toward singing a song that contains more and more notes and phrasal units of the adult song (Marler, 1991; D. Nelson & Marler, 1993). It is hard to resist comparing the young white-crowned sparrow's learning path with examples of children's learning. A case that we take up later comes from beginning language learners' efforts to master the count list of their language.

Pattern Detection and Learning

Work on perceptual learning (see Chap. 7, this volume) highlights another learning tool: pattern detection across multiple, different examples of the target. Kellman (1996) shows that this kind of perceptual learning can facilitate the acquisition of knowledge about mathematics and airplane controls. In Kellman's studies, individuals are not drilled with repeated exposure to the same examples; instead, numerous and *different* instantiations of a complex situation are presented. There are theoretical reasons for this choice. By presenting different examples of the same structure, individuals encounter opportunities to separate relevant from irrelevant aspects of the display. This is related to the fact that there are opportunities to compare and contrast examples. Such considerations are well known to students of Gibson's (1969, 1984) theory of perceptual learning. They also were important in R. Gelman's (1969) choice of conservation training materials. Together, the different examples provide learners with an opportunity to rule out the irrelevant features of any one particular example and abstract the conceptual structure that generates the examples.

The foregoing description shares many of the ideas regarding the centrality of structure in new learning. For this reason, one should expect individuals to recruit pattern detection abilities when the data for new learning constitute multiple and different examples of the principles that organize a domain.

Contingent Frequency Computing

Skeletal principles in core domains draw attention to the class of relevant inputs and organize the assimilation and early representation of noticed cases. Skeletal structures start to accumulate flesh as structured examples are assimilated. In addition, they take advantage of an automatic (i.e., nonconscious) ability to keep a running frequency count of encountered exemplars and their relevant aspects. Such a learning tool contributes to the buildup of knowledge of the predictive validity of the different attributes of encountered exemplars. For example, certain surface properties and form attributes characterize animate objects, as opposed to different properties and attributes, which characterize inanimate objects (R. Gelman, 1990; S. Gelman & Opfer, 2001).

The registration of attribute frequencies and the computation of their predictiveness (i.e., of the contingency between a given concept and the possession of a given surface attribute) are carried out by what we call a frequency/contingency learning tool. It is a good example of the middle ground, described earlier, between domain generality and domain specificity; it operates specifically on frequency data, but it also performs the same frequency-computing function in many different conceptual domains.

There is good evidence that animals and humans of all ages keep track *automatically* of the frequency of relevant events, objects, words, and grammatical units (Aslin, Saffran, & Newport, 1998; Gallistel, 1990; Marcus, Pinker, Ullman, Hollander, Rosen, & Xu, 1992; Saffran, Aslin, & Newport, 1996; Watson and Ramey, 1987; Zacks & Hasher, 2001; see Chap. 11, this volume, for the fundamental role this plays in the learning of language).

For example, Hasher and Zacks (1979) showed children ages 5 through 8 a series of pictures, in which each picture appeared zero to four times. Afterward, children in all age groups were highly and equally successful at reporting how many times a picture had been shown, even though they received no instructions to keep track of this information. Similarly robust abilities to pick up frequency information about objects or events abound. Marcus et al. (1992) document people's ability to keep track of the different frequencies of irregular past tense and plural words. Infants keep track of frequencies of items or events of interest, including the number of times they have to suck on a pacifier or turn their head to achieve presentations of sounds, well-focused photographs, and the movement of a mobile (Rovee-Collier & Bhatt, 1993; Watson and Ramey, 1987).

People know that black is the most frequent color of limousines, that red is the preferred color for fire engines, that white and green are the colors commonly worn by people who work in hospitals, and so on. Perhaps more surprising is Macario's (1991) finding that preschool children who could play his "what will we take on a picnic" game were able to generate possible foods on the basis of a color cue. All of these examples feed Zacks & Hasher's (2001) proposal that learning about the frequency of *noticed* objects and events is ubiquitous and well as and Tversky and Kahneman's assumption (1973) that we can use base rate information in making judgments.

These lines of evidence contribute to our assumption that humans and animals make use of an implicit frequency computational device as an extremely potent learning tool. Gallistel (1990; Gallistel & Gibbon, 2000) reviewed evidence that animals in classical and instrumental conditioning paradigms are learning the rate/frequency of reinforcement and its contingency on available cues, rather than the ever stronger associative pairings predicted by associationist theory. From raw frequencies the animals are computing contingencies, that is, the extent to which the frequency of reinforcement in the presence of a conditioned stimulus is different from the frequency observed in its absence. As with humans, these computations are automatic and continuous.

Some readers may misunderstand the idea that contingent frequency computation is a learning tool. Indeed, the report of infants using statistical information about language has been erroneously taken to mean that language learning is not based on an innate domain-specific structure. The claim is that the ability to register frequency information supports a general learning mechanism, one that is indifferent to the structure of different domains (e.g., Elman et al., 1996), in the spirit of the general-purpose learning process of radical empiricism (as elaborated, e.g., in Chap. 2, this volume). This is an unwarranted conclusion. It fails to recognize the significance of granting the mind the ability to represent frequency and do so selectively, that is, with respect to whether such information is recruited for a given type of knowledge acquisition.

If it is, the mind must have a way to recognize that it would help to learn the frequency with which certain kinds of events or objects occur. There is nothing about frequency information itself that says "I am here to tell you about animal kinds and their colors," "I am here to tell you about events forming a script about them," or "I am here to enable you to extract the grammatical function of this word." Whether a frequency-tracking device should be engaged depends on the nature of the mental structure guiding the learning. Hence, *contingent* frequencies are stored.

There is another reason that it is an error to slip from the fact that the mind records frequency to a variant of an associationist, rule-free model of acquisition. Within the framework of an association model, frequency is one condition for the accrual of association strength. It is the associative strength (or weight of a connection) that is represented, not the condition that led to its strength. That is, there is nothing in the association that preserves the conditions that influence its strength, be these frequency or contiguity of pairings. In our view, the foundational structure in core domains always comes from the skeletal principles embodied in enabling constraints; frequency data about relevant encounters are *subsequently* recorded and attached to that existing framework. Frequency information does not help the learner to recognize encounters in the first place. How such frequency information is used depends on the domain in question. Individuals will not say that an irregular verb that has a high frequency is a better example of verb than is a relatively novel example of a verb with a regular past tense (Marcus, 1996; Pinker, 1991). Many different factors combine to determine associative strength, but the factors contributing to that strength (e.g., frequency) are not represented by associative strength and therefore are not recoverable as inputs for learning.

In sum, the frequency-counting computational device is a mental learning tool and not a variant of the law of frequency governing the learning of associations. If learners take advantage of a frequency-computing device, they have a way of learning that some features of objects have predictive validity, even though they are not defining (Macario, 1991). For example, although the color red has high predictive validity for a tomato, it is not defining. There are yellow tomatoes. Worse yet, there are other foods that have a high probability of being red. Similarly, the distinction between a rigid versus malleable form is strongly correlated with the animate-inanimate distinction, but does not determine it. To be sure, the rigidity cue has considerable predictive validity for animacy/inanimacy, as do attributes such as uniform versus variable surface textures, motion paths, and the presence or absence of limbs, eyes, ears, and so on. Although not one of these is defining, it is still helps to learn their relative frequencies and related contingencies. Such computations allow us to make informed guesses about the animacy status of a novel or unidentified item, and then check to see if the guess is consistent with the requirements of the domain. Informed guesses can be disconfirmed by subsequent information, which violates core principles about a domain; no matter how much something looks like a rock, we will no longer believe it to be a rock if it gets up and walks away. And no matter how unlikely a particular example of a category might be, we can accept it if it can be assimilated to the domain's principles. Thus, a green lemon with writing on it is still a lemon, and a three-legged cat is still a cat.

The proposal that a mental learning tool computes the frequency of relevant encounters converges with conclusions drawn by other authors. Schwartz and Reisberg (1991) suggested that we may need a three-part theory of concepts in which "concepts are represented by a prototype, some set of specifically remembered cases, and some further abstract information" (p. 391), where all parts interact to accomplish correct similarity judgments and inferences. In our account, the recorded knowledge of frequencies and contingencies underlies subjects' abilities to answer questions in ways that make them look like they learn prototypes and some salient domain-relevant exemplars. Armstrong, Gleitman, and Gleitman (1983) concluded that we know the difference between saying an object is an instance of a concept versus characterizing it as a good or bad instance. More generally, our account provides a way to reconcile these response patterns with the compelling arguments against the idea that our concepts are based on prototypes (Fodor & Lepore, 1996).

Converging lines of thought exist with respect to children's understanding of causality. Bullock, Gelman, and Baillargeon (1982) argued that causal principles lead children to search for causal mechanisms and assimilate causally relevant information about events, including the cue value of spatial and temporal cues. Ahn, Kalish, Medin, and Gelman (1995) concluded that information about covariation and causal mechanisms plays complementary roles in our decisions about causes. Cheng (1997) showed that people relate their computations of contingency to their beliefs in causal principles.

Metacognition

The term "metacognition" is used to refer to a host of processes, including monitoring, self-correction, planning, thinking about ones knowledge, engaging in thought experiments, and so on (for further discussion see Brown, Bransford, Ferrara, & Campione, 1983; Bransford et al., 1999). We agree with

Brown et al. (1983). It is a mistake to lump all these processes under one umbrella.

Monitoring and self-correction can be seen in very young children; indeed they are expected given a constructivist theory of learning and therefore the active involvement of even young learners in their own cognitive development. Very young children have potent tendencies to keep at an act, be it throwing a cup off the table, climbing steps, 'rehearsing' the language they are starting to acquire, self-correct their counts, and so on. These activities are best thought of as on-line monitoring and self-correction. As crucial as they are, they surely are of a different kind than are those that involve active planning or pondering the nature of one's knowledge of about language, sociality, mathematics, etc. We therefore follow the convention of treating meta-cognition as a process that cannot be engaged unless the individual already has acquired either a knowledge base and (or) some problem-solving strategies.

Our emphasis on the difference between domain-specific and domain-general learning tools has implications for a discussion of meta-cognition. First, there should be different kinds of meta-cognition, for example, ones that are domain-relevant and ones that are domain-independent. Problem-solving strategies like "take the problem apart" are examples of the latter. Thinking about one's domain-based knowledge is a case of the former. Thus, whether there is another natural number after a googol requires pondering the consequences of addition and whether one can make up new count-words. This involves an ability to reason about the domain-specific consequences of arithmetic. Similarly, when we turn to thinking about the domain of sociality, we are thinking about social rules. Now the meta-cognition involves thinking about social rules and different ways to violate or play with them. As we shall see, there are different kinds

of meta-cognition—even within the sociality domain.

Re-Representational and Technological Tools

Human knowledge acquisition benefits from the ability to create and use re-representations. A re-representation represents in a culturally determined format something that has a more basic or more primitive, purely mental representation. Examples of re-representational tools are spoken and written language, drawings, maps, mathematical and musical notations, and so on. Similarly, man-made tools of both simple and complex varieties offer rich opportunities to go beyond what is based on core domains. Not only do young children benefit from the ability to develop language, but they quickly start to catch on to the role of tools and some re-representational formats as well, including those involved in television and computers. Given a supporting culture, young children catch on to the fact that there are different rules for different notation systems, even though they have much to learn about the details and conventions for these (Brenneman et al., 1996).

Learners' proclivities to map available structures to environments help to explain what might seem like a rather precocious ability in young children. Before they are taught to write, they can generate different plans of action in response to a request either to write a word or to draw a picture for a given line drawing (Brenneman, Massey, Machado, & Gelman, 1996); they can develop writing systems (Tolchinsky-Landsmann, 1990); and they can distinguish between a string of marks on paper that are "good for writing" as opposed to "good for numbers" (e.g., Lee & Karmiloff-Smith, 1996). How do the young even begin to sort out the fact that there are different kinds of "marks on paper"?

Gelman and Brenneman (1994) argued that young children's structure-mapping tendencies serve them in this case as well as those discussed already. The idea is that each of the symbol systems has its own structure and related constraints. For example, we know that young children have implicit knowledge about the structure of inanimate objects and language. The latter have bounded surfaces and are solid (as discussed later). Drawings of objects map these characteristics, at least often enough. An orange is drawn as a continuous circle and is filled in with the color orange. Language is represented as a sequence of sound units; print (at least in the cultures studied) consists of a sequence of marks with spaces between them, and so on. Such differences in structural relations do not begin to define the full range of our implicit knowledge about objects and speech, on the one hand, and drawing and writing conventions, on the other. Still, they might suffice from the viewpoint of young learners whose goal is likely to be limited to an attempt to distinguish between the kinds of marks on paper that they encounter. This goal can be served by their omnipresent tendency to engage in structure mapping. These young children's beginning representations of the difference between drawing and writing are hardly adequate. No matter. What matters is that they exist at all. Once they do, a learning path opens up. In the case of writing, they will encounter many adults who are eager to encourage and support their movement along it.

The tools of the information age have expanded the representational and communication formats that children live with. There can be no question that these influence children's learning paths; however, how they do this is very much an open question. We do not take up their potential as learning tools, it is clear that such cognitive amplifiers (Bruner, 1964) in this chapter, can open a host of learning paths.

Summary

Together, these structural tools can be viewed as learning tools for identifying what aspects of new information are relevant and what information about different domains should be treated as coming from different categories, events, and so on. They afford the mind ways of identifying relevant novel data sets and setting up new memory drawers in which to collect and keep together in memory the new domain-relevant knowledge. Over time, these memory drawers will start to fill up—most likely in an unorderly way given the lack of understanding about them. With continued interaction with inputs and informal or formal instruction about these, however, there will come a point where we will, so to speak, look into our messy memory drawers and organize them in a systematic way. How and when this happens are key research questions that are especially likely to inform understanding about the shift from novice to expert levels of knowledge.

THREE DOMAINS

Central to the rational constructivist perspective is the assumption that different knowledge structures derive from the different principles that guide learning in different domains. Tables 10.1 and 10.2 highlight this central assumption by making it clear that different entities, principles, and structures are involved in the three domains that we will now consider: the domain of physical objects, the domain of number, and the domain of social objects. Physical objects move only when acted on, whereas social objects move spontaneously. Agency is a key principle for reasoning in the sociality domain, but it plays no role in understanding the interactions between inanimate physical objects. Cardinal values (the numerosities of sets) are elementary

Table 10.1 The Different Principles and Entities Forming the Skeletal Structure of the Domains of Physical Objects, Sociality, and Number.

Domain	Objects		Number		Sociality
Entities	Objects		Cardinality		Persons
Principles	For object identification	For causal relations	For counting	For arithmetic operations	For person identification and social interaction
	Solidity: One object in a given place (in 3-D space) Connectedness in place and through most motions	External energy source (contact) No action at a distance (implicit mechanism) Order (cause before effect)	One-one stable ordering Cardinal item indifference Tagging-order indifference	Addition Subtraction Ordering	Agency Contingency Emotional evaluation Mental states Fittingness

objects of thought in the number domain. Solidity and inanimacy are irrelevant.

Inanimate Physical Objects

Spelke, Breinlinger, Macomber, and Jacobson (1992) suggested that infants begin with the assumption that their environment is three-dimensional and composed of things that occupy space, persist, move as units independently of one another, and maintain their coherence and boundaries as they move. Two principles of object perception follow: Two surfaces will be perceived as bounding the same object if they appear continuous with one another or if they move together at the same time and speed along parallel paths in three-dimensional space, even if their connection is occluded. She also proposed that the principle of solidity was a fundamental organizing principle: Because the surfaces bounding an object are inviolate, one object cannot pass through another.

Five-month-old infants respond in ways that are consistent with the belief that one solid object, a rotating screen, cannot pass through another solid object, a block hidden behind the screen (Baillargeon, Spelke, & Wasserman, 1985). Spelke (1991) provided similar evidence with 3- and 4-month-old infants. In her initial habituation phase, a ball was held above a screen and then dropped behind it, after which the screen was removed to reveal the ball resting on the surface of the table. This event sequence was repeated until infants habituated, that is, looked less than half as long as on the first trial. During the posthabituation test trials, the ball was again dropped, but when the screen was removed after the drop, the object was resting either on top of or underneath a novel shelf that had been placed surreptitiously into the display. For the latter case, the ball ended up in a familiar position, on top of the table. To get there, however, the ball would have had to pass through the shelf interposed between the dropping point and the table. Therefore, both of the post-habituation events were novel, but only the latter one (ball-on-the-table) was impossible. Infants looked longer at the impossible event.

A series of related studies conducted in the laboratories of Baillargeon and Leslie showed that infants' understanding of physical phenomena involves the principles that objects need support to keep them from falling, that objects are displaced when one moves into contact with another, and that objects need to be propelled into motion (Baillargeon, 1995, 1998; Baillargeon, Kotovsky, & Needham, 1995; Leslie, 1994).

Given the above findings from infants, it is not surprising that toddlers and preschool

Table 10.2 Event Structure for Sociocultural Events by Event-Kind.

Event-Kinds	Event Structure				Example
	Causal Relations	Emotive Structure	Person and Interpersonal Relations	Temporal-Spatial Relations	
Script	$A_g \to G_o \to Act \to Out_W$	Pos/Happy	Concordance & Reciprocity	Delimited context	Mary is having a birthday party. Her friends have come and brought gifts. She opens her presents and blows out the candles, and they eat cake. They play games, and then the kids go home.
Counterscripts: Fluke-Win	$A_g \to G_o \to Act \to Out_L \to$ Non-G_o Act $\to Out_W$	Pos/Happy	Concordance	Delimited context	Clown practices his trick, where cream pie hits him in face. At show, the trick doesn't work, and the kids boo him. Clown sadly walks away, when he slips on the cream into a bucket of water. Kids love the clown.
Planned-Loss	$A_g \to G_o \to Act \to$ self-inflicted Out_L	Neg/Sad	Concordance	Delimited context	Billy gets a telescope at his birthday. He wants to be sure nothing happens to it. So he leaves his party to put it in his closet. On the way, he trips and falls, breaking the telescope.
Fruitless Win-Double Outcome	$A_g \to G_o \to Act \to Out_L \to$ Out now irrelevant $\to$ Out attainable$_{L\&W}$	Neg/Sad Neg/Sad	Concordance	Delimited context	The Smiths wake to a great day and decide to have a picnic. They do lots of preparing and then go all the way to the park. Just then clouds come up, and it starts storming. They drive home. Then the sky clears and the sun comes out.
Temporal-Imbalance	—	—	Mismatch	Across contexts (temporal)	Clumsy child grows up to be prima ballerina.

NOTE: A_g = Agent; G_o = Goal; Act = Goal-based actions; Out = Outcome (W = Win or L = Loss); Pos = Positive; Neg = Negative.

children learn about cause-effect sequences more readily than they learn about other sequences (Brown, Kane, & Echols, 1986; Mandler & McDonough, 1996). They can apply their skeletal principles about the nature of inanimate physical causation to learn about particular cause and effect sequences (Bullock, Gelman, & Baillargeon, 1982; R. Gelman, Durgin, & Kaufman, 1995). For example, young children postulate a hidden mechanism when confronting what looks like a possible case of "action at a distance"—an effect of one inanimate object on another located some distance away. When Bullock and Gelman (1979) showed 3- and 4-year-old children an event that had a gap between the cause and the outcome (cf., Leslie & Keeble, 1987), they either inferred a mechanism ("when I wasn't looking, the ball slided over"), talked about magic, or made it clear that something was not quite right ("What? How did that happen? It's a trick, right?"). Young children produced predominantly external causal attributions for the motion of familiar inanimate objects but not for the motion of familiar animate objects (Massey & Gelman, 1988; S. Gelman & Gottfried, 1996). They are also rather good at making predictions about the effects of transformations (Bullock, Gelman, & Baillargeon, 1982; Wilson & Keil, 1998; Zur & Gelman, 2001).

The foregoing kinds of results about preschool competencies contrast dramatically with the children's explanations of causal mechanisms and the makeup of physical objects. Explanations of physical mechanisms require knowledge about electricity, mechanics, properties of different materials, and so on. All of these involve conceptual structures that are not among those at the core of the domain. And many require conceptual change or the acquisition of noncore domains (Carey, 1991; Gelman, Romo, & Francis, in press; Keil & Wilson, 2000). It is therefore no surprise that even undergraduates attending top

universities in the United States provide shallow explanations of causal mechanisms (Keil & Wilson, 2000). Indeed, it is likely that most of us would do the same even for cases that we live with every day. Unless one is a trained automobile mechanic, it is a fair bet that most adults can predict that their car will start without being able to explain why. All of this goes to make the point that early principles about physical objects do not guarantee that one will acquire scientific explanations of how these interact in complex systems.

For recent reviews of the extensive work in this domain from several different laboratories, see Keil and Wilson (2000).

Number

Rapid Initial Learning

There is some evidence that infants abstract discrete and continuous quantities. Such findings serve as one line of evidence cited in favor of the idea that principles of number and quantity make up a core domain. Importantly, there are other lines of converging evidence in favor of this conclusion. Cross-cultural findings about "street arithmetic," studies with developmentally delayed or disabled children, and comparative animal data all contribute to the conclusion that humans are endowed with skeletal principles that support attention to number and quantity as well as their role in arithmetic reasoning principles.

By 6 to 9 months of age, infants look preferentially at a 2-item or 3-item heterogeneous visual display depending on whether they hear 2 or 3 drum beats (Starkey, Spelke, & Gelman, 1990). Xu and Spelke (2000) reported that 6-month-old infants discriminate 8 versus 16 items, even when the density, size, and area of the displays vary. These quantity abstraction abilities are related to implicit principles of addition and subtraction. Wynn (1992) reported that 4-month-old infants are surprised when the number of objects they expect (1 or 2) is different as a result of un-seen, surreptitious additions and subtractions (Wynn, 1992, 1995). Keochlin, Dehaene, and Mehler (1997) replicated and extended the Wynn findings to show that it held even when the objects in a display were changing location.

Evidence that these effects of addition and subtraction are treated as number-relevant comes from Brannon's finding that 11-month-old infants make use of an ordering relation. To demonstrate infants' ability to attend to and learn about numerical ordering, Brannon (2001) first habituated infants to ascending or descending sequences of set sizes (e.g., 1, 2, and 4 and 2, 4, and 8, etc.). When tested with the novel values of 3, 6, and 12 items over six alternating ascending and descending tri-als, they showed a reliable tendency to detect the reversal in order. It remains to be seen whether younger infants will show a similar sensitivity to an arithmetic ordering. Whether they will or not, it is becoming clear that pre-verbal infants respond to abstract properties such as number and quantity as well as some simple arithmetic relations. This conclusion gains strength from studies showing that an-imals and adult humans probably share the same nonverbal mathematical structures for generating cardinal values and the effects of combining these with the operations of ad-dition and subtraction (Gallistel & Gelman, 2000).

As illustrated in Table 10.1, nonverbal counting is part of a number-specific do-main because the representatives of numeros-ity (what Gelman and Gallistel, 1978, dubbed numerons) generated by counting are oper-ated on by mechanisms informed by, or obe-dient to, arithmetic principles. For counting to provide the input for arithmetic reasoning, the principles governing counting must com-plement the principles governing arithmetic reasoning. For example, the counting princi-ples must be such that sets assigned the same

numeron are in fact numerically equal and that the set assigned a greater numeron is more nu-merous than a set assigned a lesser numeron. Importantly, there is nothing in this formula-tion that requires that counting be done with words. As long as the process that generates symbols for numerosity honors the one-one, stable, and cardinal principles and tolerates a wide range of item types, we can say that it is a candidate counting device. A pulse generator and a computer are examples of such entities. Data from children who have developmental disorders reinforce the idea that normal chil-dren benefit from a nonverbal core domain that involves counting and arithmetic princi-ples that operate on their output.

Absence of Initial Learning in Some Impaired Populations

R. Gelman and Cohen (1988) compared the ability of preschool children and (older) chil-dren with Down syndrome who had similar mental ages to solve a novel counting prob-lem. The use of a novel (unusual) counting task was motivated by considerations about the nature of transfer. Transfer is unlikely to occur if the original acquisition task did not yield understanding of the underlying concep-tual structure. Even after intensive instruction, children with Down's syndrome have consid-erable difficulty with simple arithmetic tasks, including adding and subtracting, telling time, and shopping. From the core domain per-spective, this suggests that these children lack the organizing principles that enable them to profit from relevant experience—even exten-sive experience. If so, despite repeated drill in counting, adding, subtracting, and ordering numbers, they might not achieve learning with understanding. R. Gelman and Cohen found that six of the eight children with Down's syn-drome failed to solve the order-irrelevance task, a test of whether children behave as if they know that any item in an array can be tagged with any of the 1 . . . N tags that can be placed in one-one correspondence as long as one and only one tag is assigned to each item (Gelman & Gallistel, 1978). The performance of the comparison group of preschool children far outstripped that of the Down's syndrome sample, both in terms of their ability to invent strategies and in terms of the ease with which they engaged the task.

Many of the children with Down's syndrome in the R. Gelman and Cohen (1988) study had a considerable amount of syntax (Fowler, Gelman, & Gleitman, 1993). Thus, one should be cautious about arguments that treat the mastery of semantic and syntactic rules as conditions of verbal counting (e.g., Carey, 1998; Bloom, 2000). This is especially so given that some individuals with low IQs have almost no syntax but are very good with numbers, as contrasted to others, who have extremely complex syntax but cannot count systematically (Grinstead, Swann, Curtiss, & Gelman, 2001). This kind of double dissociation in selected populations of impaired subjects is another reason to treat number as a core domain that is independent of language.

The children with Down's syndrome in the R. Gelman and Cohen study lived at home and attended an excellent school. They received extensive training in counting, money, time, and other numerical and arithmetic tasks. Nevertheless, they did not induce the counting principles. By contrast, there are normal children who do not go to school who engage in what is called street arithmetic (Nunes, Schliemann, & Carraher, 1993) or intuitive mathematics. Liberian tailors who have no schooling can solve arithmetic problems by putting out and counting familiar objects, such as buttons (Reed & Lave, 1979). Taxicab drivers and child fruit vendors in Brazil invent solutions that involve different ways of putting together (adding) and decomposing count numbers (Nunes et al., 1993). Such data fit well with the idea that individuals have a number-relevant skeletal structure of the kind presented in Table 10.1.

Facilitate Re-Representational Learning

If one assumes that humans start out with a domain-specific set of numerical/quantity principles, a key question arises. To what extent, if any, does this facilitate acquisition of verbal and notational instantiations of counting and arithmetic principles? If structure mapping serves as a major learning tool, then nonverbal counting principles should facilitate children's ability to identify and start to learn to use the count list of their language. Preverbal counting principles provide a conceptual framework for helping beginning language learners identify and render intelligible the individual tags that are part of a list that is initially meaningless. It also provides a structure against which to self-rehearse counting trials as well as build an understanding of the words (R. Gelman, 1993). On the matter of self-rehearsal, because mastery of the verbal list involves committing to memory a specific, long ordered sequence, it is unlikely that beginning learners will accomplish this task in one trial. If they indeed attempt to match input to a given structure, the structure can serve as a checkpoint against which to compare the output sequence with that required for counting. By analogy to Marler's young birds, the nonverbal structure is like a template against which one can determine whether the output is correct or wrong. Given that young counters do self-correct (Gelman & Gallistel, 1978), this is a plausible hypothesis regarding the way young children start to learn the count list of their language. It also fits with data indicating that beginning counters are far from perfect (Wynn, 1992) as well as the data presented above regarding children with developmental disorders. The reader should consult other accounts of the acquisition of verbal counting, ones that do not appeal to the idea that there is a mapping between nonverbal and verbal counting (e.g., Bloom, 2000; Carey, 2000; Fuson, 1988).

It is one thing to master the language rules of a culture that make it possible to generate successive next numerals forever. First, even adults, unlike computers, do not readily memorize long lists of sounds that are not intrinsically organized. There is nothing about the sound "two" that predicts the next sound will be "three," or about the sound "three" that predicts that the next sound will be "four," and so on. This is a nonmathematical, information-processing reason to expect the task of committing even the first nine count words to memory to take a considerable amount of time, and it does—as much as 2 to 4 years (Miller, Smith, Zhu, & Zhang, 1995).

The nonverbal counting process allows for the generation of a successor for each representation (the mind never runs out of numerons). To achieve the same in the verbal re-representation of number, the child has to confront a further serial learning problem. This is to master the often-complex base rules that are embedded in a particular language's counting system. The English count list lacks a transparent decade rule for at least the first 40 entries, and probably for the first 130 count words. Learning this rule takes a surprisingly long time. Hartnett (1991) found that a number of kindergarten and first grade students had yet to catch on to the procedure for generating the count words in the hundreds, most probably because many English-speaking children think that *one hundred* is the next decade word after *ninety*. In order for them to induce the hundreds rules in English, they need to encounter relevant examples of "hundreds."

Cross-cultural findings are consistent with this argument. Chinese has a more transparent base-10 count rule for generating subsequent count words, even for the tens and decades. Although the rate at which English- and Chinese-speaking children learn the first

nine count words is comparable, Chinese-speaking children learn the subsequent entries at a much faster rate (Miller et al., 1995).

This does not mean that English-speaking children are slower to recognize that every natural number has a successor; many 5-year-old children who have yet to master the base-10 generative rule acknowledge that nonverbal iterative processes can continue "forever" (Hartnett, 1991). A related phenomena was reported by Hartnett and Gelman (1998). They engaged children in kindergarten as well as in first and second grade in a thought experiment designed to encourage them to reach an explicit induction of the successor principle.

Ease of Learning Domain-Consistent Concepts

Hartnett and Gelman (1998) proposed that learning the natural number successor principle would take place with relative ease. In contrast, they expected children to have difficulty learning to understand the mathematical nature of fractions. These predictions were based on a consideration of whether children's principled understanding of counting and its role in addition and subtraction mapped to the principles that organize the to-be-learned concepts. In the case of the successor principle, the structure is completely consistent with those that make up the counting and arithmetic ones that organize their knowledge about natural numbers. This is not so for rational numbers.

Difficulty of Learning Domain-Inconsistent Numerical Concepts

The mathematical principles underlying the numberhood of fractions are not consistent with the principles of counting and the child's idea that numbers are rendered when sets of things are counted and that addition involves "putting together" two sets. One cannot count things to generate a fraction. Formally, a fraction is defined as the division of one cardinal number by another. This definition solves the problem that there is a lack of closure of the integers under division. That is, if only integers are numbers, then, in general, it is not possible to divide one integer by another, because the result will not be an integer. To complicate matters further, some counting-number principles do not apply to fractions. Rational numbers (fractions) do not have unique successors; there is an infinite number of numbers between any two rational numbers. Thus, one cannot use counting based algorithms for ordering fractions, for example, 1/4 is *not* more than 1/2.

Neither the nonverbal nor the verbal counting principles map to a tripartite symbolic representations of fractions (two cardinal numbers X and Y separated by a line), but the formal definition of a fraction does. Related mapping problems have been noted by others (e.g., Behr, Lesh, Post, & Silver, 1983). Therefore, if children bring to their early school mathematics lessons their theory of number that is grounded in counting principles and related rules of addition and subtraction, their constructivist tendencies could lead them to distort fraction inputs to fit their counting based number theory. Early knowledge of number might therefore serve as a barrier to learning about fractions.

The Hartnett and Gelman findings were as expected. Even though the children did not receive lessons in school about the successor principle, they were relatively quick to take up the offered data and reach the conclusion that there always is a next natural number. The pertinent studies that were involved asked children to ponder a very larger number, then add 1 to that, then again add 1, and so on. Periodically, a child was asked if the number she or he was thinking about was the largest there could be or whether there were more numbers. Then, depending on children's answers, they were asked what the biggest number was

and whether they could add to it or what was the next number. Note that the interview does more than commandeer an existing knowledge structure. It encourages meta-cognition about the arithmetic principles and the generation of number words. No wonder that the children ended up talking to their friends and their parents about their new knowledge. The results regarding rational numbers make for a very different story, even though the children are taught about fractional representations and how to manipulate these arithmetically.

In one study reported in Hartnett and Gelman, children were asked to place number cards in order, on an "ordering cloth." After a pretest that included experience placing sticks of different lengths, demonstrations that some sticks could go at the same place, that it was okay to move items around, and naming of the numbers on each of the separate experimental cards, children were given the test items and then told to place these in order. The different cards had 1/4, 1/3, 1/2, 1 1/2, 2 1/2, 2/3, 2/4, 2/2, 3/3, 0, 1, 2, and 3 on them. The results were striking: Not one child placed all cards correctly. They did not lack for inventiveness; they constructed a number of novel solutions. However, all of these involved treating the fractions as novel exemplars of counting numbers. For example, one child placed the fractional notations as follows: 1/2, 1/3, 2/3, 2/4. Some children separated the whole numbers into one category. No children recognized 2/2 and 3/3 as mathematical wholes (i.e., as equal to 1). Yet, it is essential that they eventually understand that this is the case and that they thus realize that the rational numbers include such entities. When put this way, it becomes clear that the everyday language of numbers does not provide the relevant stepping stone to learning. We do not go around saying, "You have two halves and I have three thirds, so we have equal shares." It is only in the language of mathematics that $2/2 = 3/3 = 1$. Of course, some children do go on to master the arithmetic of rational numbers, but it is not difficult to find college students who lack an understanding of fractions (R. Gelman, 2000). The pedagogical task is to find learning tools that facilitate movement onto the relevant learning path, this being one involving mastery of the language and concepts of mathematics. In the next section we expand on the idea that learning tools can move cognitive development toward the goal.

SOCIALITY

This domain pertains to persons in social interactions. Hence, persons are the entities in this domain. As such, they are analogous to numbers and objects, which are entities in the domains of numerical reasoning (R. Gelman, 1998) and physical object knowledge (e.g., Spelke, Breinlinger, Macomber, & Jacobson, 1992), respectively.

Five principles guide the acquisition of social understanding: *contingency, agency, mental states, emotional evaluation,* and *fittingness.* These guiding principles are evident in the behavior of even very young infants. This is analogous to the principles of continuity and solidity guiding the infant's understanding of the world of inanimate objects and the principles of counting and integer arithmetic guiding children's understanding of number.

It is important to emphasize the skeletal nature of these principles. They are only implicit in the structure of the child's information processing system. The operation of these principles is tied to the input, that is, to the social interactions of the world. The young child is not thought to represent these principles conceptually any more than it conceptualizes the principles of a universal grammar (see Chap. 11, this volume). Put another way, the baby does not have conceptual command of these principles. One might best think of

the principles through a notation system of noncapital letters, such as the agency principle with a small "a" or mental states principle with a small "m" and "s."

The Privileged Status of Persons

Recognition of persons qua persons is fundamental. As in the other domains, evidence of the operation of this foundational abstraction appears very early in development. Persons tend to be imitated. Neonates imitate certain facial displays (Field, Woodson, Greenberg, & Cohen, 1983) as well as tongue protrusions, mouth openings, and head movements (Meltzoff & Moore, 1983, 1989).

Moreover, babies recognize persons as distinct from inanimate objects (Bonatti, Frot, Zangl, & Mehler, in press; Legerstee, Barna, & DiAdamo, 2000; Poulin-Dubois, 1999). For example, by two months of age in face-to-face interactions, infants respond differently to people (e.g., gazing, smiling, vocalizing) and objects (see Legerstee, 1992, for review). In addition, imitation is selective to persons. Five- to eight-week old infants imitate tongue protrusions and mouth openings modeled by an adult but not by an object (Legerstee, 1991). By ten months, differential exploratory behavior for novel objects and novel persons has also been demonstrated (Eckerman & Rheingold, 1974; Ricard & Gouin-Decarie, 1989). In exploring novel objects and novel persons (strangers), infant behaviors include longer approach time and more smiling and looking for the people.

Importantly, infants distinguish persons from other animals (Bonatti et al., in press). Hence, the distinction between humans and all other species of animals is as fundamental as the animate-inanimate distinction. Persons then are the basic entities in the sociality domain.

Also fundamental in this domain is an understanding of persons as social objects, hence engaged with others. Persons participate in social interaction from the outset of life. Considerable data indicate that babies are social and that they engage in and respond to interaction with others from the start. Indeed, infants seem predisposed to social interaction.

Attachment behavior is a case in point. On ethological attachment theory, attachment arises from one of several species-typical behavioral systems evolved to promote infant survival (see Bowlby, 1969, 1973). This system motivates infants to seek the protective proximity of adults, especially when infants are distressed, alarmed, or in danger.

By 6 months of age, infants, at least on occasion, are influenced by the distal and proximal actions of their peers (Hay, Pederson, & Nash, 1982) and engage in successful attempts to interact, through vocalizations, smiles, and touches (Vandell, Wilson, & Buchanan, 1980). Infants, between 10- and 24-months of age, interact with their peers, exchanging smiles, vocalizations, and toys and imitating each other's actions (Eckerman, Whatley, & Kutz, 1975).

A biological preparedness for empathy has been proposed (Hoffman, 1975). The reflexive crying of infants in response to the crying of other infants has been interpreted as a primitive precursor of empathic arousal (Sagi & Hoffman, 1976; Simner, 1971). Furthermore, infants respond to the emotions of others: Certain emotion signals can elicit corresponding emotional states in infants, even in newborn infants. Sagi & Hoffman (1976) found that newborns cry in response to the sound of another newborn's cry and do so significantly more often then when they are exposed to silence or a synthetic newborn cry. Such responding has been found to be both peer and species-specific. Neonates are more likely to cry in response to a tape recording of another neonate's cry than in response to a tape recording of their own cry, an older infant's cry, or a chimp's cry (Martin & Clark, 1982).

Infants, nearly from birth, exhibit emotional responsiveness to other persons. Infants can perceive the emotions of others. Nine-month-olds express more joy and look longer at their mothers' joy expression and express more sadness, anger, and gaze aversion when watching an expression of sadness (Termine & Izard, 1988). Similarly, babies as young as 10 weeks discriminate between mothers' presentations of happy/joy, sad, and angry faces and match their mothers' emotions under some conditions (Haviland & Lelwica, 1987). Moreover, more than just simple matching of maternal expressions is evident in infant behavior. For instance, infants' responses to mothers' happy expressions represented a change in infants' affect state, rather than simple imitation. While infants' initial response to their mother's happy expression was to match or mirror that expression, infants became increasingly expressive of interest in the still positive interaction and less expressive of joy. Infants' responses to a maternal sad expression also demonstrated a change in infant state. Rather than matching the expression, infants showed more mouthing behavior, which is thought to be self-soothing.

Infants also show preferential attention to faces (J. Johnson & Morton, 1991; L. Nelson, 1987). Moreover, it has been proposed that facial expressions evolved specifically to convey social intentions and contingencies relevant to a specific audience (Darwin, 1859/1991; Fridlund, 1994). Indeed, facial expressions of emotion have been found to convey social messages with about as much consensus as they convey emotional ones (Yik & Russell, 1999).

Finally, the basic sociality of persons is evident in the universality of four social relationship types that people use to generate, understand, coordinate, and evaluate most social interaction (Fiske, 1991, 1992, 1993). These four basic types of social relationships are:

communal sharing; authority ranking; equality matching; market pricing. These relational categories are presumed to be intrinsic to the nature of mind.

These lines of data taken together make a compelling case for the basic sociality of persons. Granting social interaction as intrinsic to human functioning, the next section discusses evidence about the nature of its organization.

Evidence for Core Principles of Social Interaction

Five principles guide the acquisition of social understanding and represent initial albeit skeletal knowledge in the sociality domain. These are: *contingency, agency, mental states, emotional evaluation,* and *fittingness.* Although these are discussed sequentially, they are neither independent nor additive. Rather, the final principle is superordinate to the others in that it specifies an interrelation of the other principles. Hence, these principles exhibit a hierarchic organization.

Contingency

The principle of contingency concerns the relation between persons. It specifies that when two or more people are interacting, the actions of each should be contingent on the actions of the others. Role knowledge and role relations subsequently emerge from this early understanding of contingency and reciprocity in interpersonal interaction.

The game-like, formulaic routines of infancy, such as "peek-a-boo" and "wave bye-bye" are an indication of babies' understanding of and participation in reciprocal and contingent interactions.

Early mother-child interactive exchanges are contingent (Stern, 1985). Moreover, actions or behaviors of babies are time-linked to an object/person that moves or vocalizes in response to a baby's movement or vocaliza-

tions (Gergely & Watson, 1999; S. Johnson, Slaughter, & Carey, 1998; Watson, 1972).

Indeed, disruptions in social interaction, such as nonreciprocal or noncontingent interactions distress infants. In the first year, infants get upset when people do not behave actively and contingently or when they maintain a "still face" (Ellsworth, Muir, & Hains, 1993; Muir & Hains, 1993).

Toddlers coordinate behavior with that of a play partner (Baudonierre, Garcia-Werebe, Michel & Liegois, 1989), engage in communicative overtures in dyadic play (Ross, Lollis, & Elliot, 1982), and show interactional skills, such as coordination and alternation of turns, during games (Goldman & Ross, 1978). Moreover, toddlers show evidence of relationships, with reciprocal relationships predominating (Ross, Conant, Cheyne, & Alevizos, 1992). Further, toddlers engage in friendship patterns defined as complementary or reciprocal dyadic exchange and shared positive affect (Howes, 1983, 1988).

Contingency is also intrinsic to linguistic communication. It is apparent in the early linguistic exchanges between caretakers and children. Caretakers respond vocally to sounds, even such as burps, from babies (Snow, 1986). Moreover language use is guided by a contingency principle. Such a principle underlies Grice's (1975, 1978) maxim to be relevant and Sperber and Wilson's (1986) "relevance principle."

Agency

The principle of agency concerns the relation between persons and actions. It specifies that the actions of persons are goal-directed. Hence, persons are agents. Agents are described as decision makers, improvisers, or executive overseers (Russell, 1995) or as able to adapt, respond, and adjust to environments (R. Gelman, in press; R. Gelman et al., 1995) and to unforeseeable changes in circumstances (Gallistel, 1980).

An understanding of agency is not thought to develop from the abstraction of different types of motion characteristics, as proposed by Poulin-Dubois (1999). Indeed, R. Gelman (in press) has shown that the abstraction of motion characteristics alone is not sufficient for an understanding of agency. Rather, agency seems fundamental. An appropriate interpretation of motion characteristics requires that a concept of agency be in place already.

A notion of agency may be part of our biological endowment (R. Gelman, 1998; Leslie, 1995). Alternatively, or additionally, it may originate in social interaction. Such interaction is unpredictable or novel (Glick, 1978; Russell, 1995). According to Russell, agency originates in social interaction precisely because it is unpredictable. To deal successfully with others, the child must be a prodigious decision maker and must be on guard to select new but appropriate behaviors in light of what the other has done. The claim is that the most crucial ability for social life is the ability to improvise. Russell invokes the Norman and Shallice (1986) distinction between routine-action "scripts" and "supervising attentional systems." The latter, the executive overseer, takes control in novel situations. In social interaction there is constant novelty; new things are constantly being done. Hence, the supervisory system is in constant use.

Evolutionary arguments support the link between the complexity of the social world and the calculations to be done by an agent. The Machiavellian intelligence hypothesis notes that primates appear to have a surplus intelligence for their everyday wants of feeding and ranging, but that the social complexity inherent in many primate groups might have been a significant selective pressure for primate intelligence (Byrne & Whiten, 1997; Humphrey, 1976; Whiten & Byrne, 1988). Group living must be beneficial overall to each member, or it would not occur; however, only individual (and kin) benefits drive evolution. For each individual primate, this sets up an environment favoring the use of social manipulation to achieve individual benefits at the expense of other group members, but without causing such disruption that the individual's membership of the group is put in jeopardy. Particularly useful to this end would be manipulations in which the losers are unaware of their loss, as in some kinds of deception, or in which there are compensatory gains, as in some kinds of cooperation. Intelligence is thereby favored as a trait. This selective pressure applies to all group members. It leads to spiraling increases in intelligence.

That the principle of agency is implicitly known or available early to infants is indicated in a variety of data. Infants are sensitive to the difference between self and externally caused motion (Leslie, 1982, 1988; Leslie & Keeble, 1987; Oakes & Cohen 1995; Premack, 1990). For example, Leslie and Keeble (1987) habituated one group of infants (causal group) to a direct launching event (one object hits another causing the hit-object to move), as in Michotte (1963). A second group (non-causal group) was habituated to a short time delay or spatial gap inserted between the impact of the first object and the movement of the second object. Accordingly, in this latter condition, there is no reason to assign causal roles to perceived objects. In post-habituation trials, the causal group experienced its reverse (film backwards). This represents both a perceptual and conceptual reversal. The non-causal group also experienced its reverse. Here, however, this represents only a perceptual reversal. If infants do not understand the perception of launching with respect to causal roles, no differences across groups would be expected in their reaction to the respective reversals. By 27 weeks, the causal group, however, produced more recovery of attention when viewing the reversal of an apparently caused event.

Infants apparently understand that only animate objects can move independently, that is, act as agents. Infants discriminate between reactive motion at a distance (an action characteristic of agents) and motion induced by direct physical contact. As indicated above, the principle of contact aids reasoning about inanimate objects; objects act on each other only if they come into physical contact (Golinkoff, Harding, Carlson, & Sexton, 1984; Leslie 1988; Oakes & Cohen 1995; Poulin-Dubois, Lepage, & Ferland, 1996). For example, 8- and 13-month-olds were habituated to novel events of a person (female stranger) or inanimate object (ball or chair) moving without any forces action on them (Poulin-Dubois & Shultz, 1988). Thirteen-month-olds showed significant decrease in fixation time in the person-as-agent condition but not in the ball-as-agent condition. The eight-month-olds exhibited the opposite pattern. In a follow-up study using unfamiliar objects, 9- and 12-month-olds were shown a stationary unfamiliar object followed by the same object moving around the room without any impetus. The unfamiliar object was a self-propelled robot with some human-like facial features. A female stranger was presented in the same way. The self-propelled robot was considered incongruous by infants of both ages as indicated in an increase in their negative affect.

The contact principle appears to be suspended by infants in reasoning about human action (Spelke, Philips, & Woodward, 1995). Seven-month-olds were habituated to objects or people disappearing at one end of screen, while a second object or person appeared at the other end. In post-habituation trials, with the occluder removed, one of the objects or people is shown moving toward the other, who starts to move after either a collision or no collision. In the inanimate object condition, the majority of infants looked longer at the test films that did not show a collision. They did not show this tendency in the person

condition. Hence by 7 months infants assume inanimate objects require contact to cause the other to move whereas people do not.

Infants are also sensitive to goal-directed, as opposed to random, action by the end of their first year. From about 3 months, infants discriminate aminate-biological motions versus random or mechanical ones (Bertenthal, 1993). Moreover, by 3 months of age, infants are sensitive to information specifying social contingencies and agent intentionality (Rochat, Morgan, & Carpenter, 1997). To show this, 3- and 6-month-olds' visual preferences for 2 different dynamic events were compared. One event showed a pair of discs moving around a screen independently. The second showed a "chase" event, in which the same pair of objects is displayed in a systematic interaction of chasing (an intentional social event). Three-month-olds prefer the chase event. Infant sensitivity to intentional events was demonstrated also by Gergely, Nadasdy, Csibra, & Biro (1995). These authors habituated 12-month-olds to the event that adults interpret as goal-directed. A small computer-animated circle/ball repeatedly approached a large circle by jumping over a rectangular figure separating them. This event is interpretable as the rational action of avoiding an obstacle to reach a goal. In post-habituation trials, the obstacle was removed. Infants saw either of two events. An "indirect" event made-up of the old/familiar (now non-rational) jumping action, which is not justified in the current context. A new, rational action, a "direct" event, which showed a small circle moving directly toward a large circle. Infants looked longer at the indirect test event, indicating they had perceived the moving ball as intentional. They expected it to go directly for its object (the second ball). This discrimination ability shows up between 6 and 9 months (Csibra, Gergely, Biro, Koos, & Brockbank, 1999).

Infants also perceive goal-directed action in reaching behavior. Woodward (1998) found 6- and 9-month-olds sensitive to the goal-related, in contrast to spatio-temporal, properties, of a reach act. She habituated infants to the sight of a hand reaching to and grasping 1 of 2 toys. In one test event, "new object-old path," the arm-hand reached to the old location and grasped a different object. In a second test event, "old object-new path," the arm-hand grasped the same object, but in a new location. If infants simply perceived the habituation event in terms of the arm's spatial movement, then the "new object-old path" would seem familiar. However, if they perceived the habituation movement as an arm grasping a particular target object, then the "old object-new path" would be familiar. Babies looked longer when the actor grasped a new toy than when she moved through a new path.

Infants, moreover, consider the human hand as an agent of functional actions (Leslie, 1984). Infants were habituated to a hand picking up a doll. In posthabituation trials, infants were tested on a sequence showing a hand picking up a doll again, but with a small gap between the hand and object. Seven-month-olds recover attention to this change. They do not to a similar change, when there was no hand but only another object making the same movements.

An early understanding of agency is indicated in children's language use as well. Use of the agentive case, which expresses the notion of an animate being initiating some action, is pervasive in children just starting to use language (Bloom, Lightbown, & Hood, 1975; Bowerman, 1976). By 18 months, infants typically attend to the agent in an observed agent-action-recipient sequence both during and after the action (Robertson & Suci, 1980). Moreover, syntactically, young children consistently place agents before the verb (Bloom et al., 1975; Bowerman, 1976; Chap. 11, this volume).

Mental States

The principle of mental states concerns the relation between persons, their internal states, and behavior. It specifies that persons are not understood on the plane of action alone, but that mental states underlie and determine their actions. Mental states include emotional states.

Social interaction relies on an understanding of one's own and other's mental states. This is all the more true to the extent that social interaction is novel and unpredictable. Indeed, the existence of predictable behavior mitigates against the need to know and talk about others' mental states (Vinden & Astington, 2000). Hence awareness that mental states underlie behavior may originate in social interaction to the extent that such interaction is unpredictable.

That the behavior of persons is mediated by mental states appears to be understood very early in life. Infants show an understanding of persons as intentional agents. For instance, infants' imitative acts are often focused on objects and represent first evidence of shared meaning between peers (Mueller & Silverman, 1989). Moreover, even babies as young as 6 months expect people's actions to be related to objects in ways that are continuous with more mature, intentional understandings (Legerstee et al., 2000). In experimental conditions, infants were habituated to an actor who either talked with or reached for and swiped something hidden behind an occluder. In the test events, the actor was occluded, but the infants were shown either a person or an object. Infants who had been habituated to the talking actor looked longer at the object, whereas infants who had been habituated to the actor who reached and swiped looked longer at the person. Hence, infants associated communicative acts with people and manipulative acts with objects.

In early interactions, infants engage in behaviors, such as teasing, that require an understanding of the mental states of others (Reddy, 1991). Between 8 and 14 months, social interaction seems infused with mental state understanding. Trevarthen and Hubley (1978) describe secondary intersubjectivity in interpersonal interaction. Intentional communication emerges (Bates, Benigni, Bretherton, Camaioni, & Volterra, 1979). Such social tool use is seen in deictic gestures, such as pointing, to request adult help in getting an object. Indeed, pointing to reference objects, accompanied by gaze alternation, indicates that children expect adults to behave autonomously after seeing such signals (Murphy & Messer, 1977). Adamson and Bakeman (1985) document triadic awareness, joint reference and affect being expressed in these periods of shared object play. Joint visual attention (i.e., understanding others' gazes) also develops during this time (Butterworth, 1991; Scaife & Bruner, 1975). Indeed, 12- to 18-months-olds can use information about focus of attention to disambiguate the referent of another's emotional message when at least two potential referents are available (Baldwin & Moses, 1994, 1996). Finally, social referencing indicates understanding of mental states in self and others (Feinman, 1982; Sorce, Emde, Campos, & Klinnert, 1985).

At about 17 months infants begin to turn toward other people to request help in recreating an interesting event (Sexton, 1983) and begin to restrict their communicative overtures to people (Bates, Camaioni, & Volterra, 1975). From about 18 months to 2 years of age, children's understanding of intentional states is manifest in symbolic behaviors. They engage in pretense (Leslie, 1987). Further, word learning during this time is based on the intentional states of the child (Bloom, 1993) and on the child's discernment of the intentional states of the

adult (in terms of referential intent with respect to an object-focus; Baldwin, 1993, 1995; Tomasello & Barton, 1994; Tomasello, Strosberg, & Akhtar, 1996). Moreover, words for mental states begin to appear in children's vocabulary (Bretherton, McNew, & Beeghly-Smith, 1981; Wellman & Bartsch, 1994). Additionally, in child language, agents appear as experiencers of mental states (Bruner & Lucariello, 1989).

In addition, toddlers can reason about desire. For example, 18-month-olds understand desires as subjective as shown by demonstrations that they know you might want broccoli, as compared to their own preference for crackers (Repacholi & Gopnik, 1997). Two-year-olds can predict actions and reactions related to simple desires and they pass desire reasoning tasks (Wellman & Woolley, 1990). In addition, they show cognitive-perspective taking ability and the ability to understand others' feelings (Denham, 1986). Moreover, preschoolers show an understanding of the nature of mental states or entities, for example, that thoughts are nonmaterial, subjective, or mental things in contrast with substantial, objective, physical objects (Wellman, Hollander, & Schult, 1996).

Emotional Evaluation

The principle of emotional evaluation concerns the presumptive outcome for contingent, agency-directed social interaction. It specifies that contingent, goal-directed social interaction succeeds. Hence, the default or unmarked emotional assessment or interpretation of such interaction is neutral to positive.

The primacy of neutral-positive emotional interpretation or assessment is evident in a variety of data. Early mother-infant interaction is disrupted and is less positive and more negative arousal is caused in infants by maternal depression (Cohn & Tronick, 1983; Cohn, Campbell, Matias, & Hopkins, 1990).

In ontogenetic development, positive emotion affords development. When the two expressive systems of affect (already in place) and language/word learning (being acquired) are first integrated, this integration is restricted to positive affect. Words, when first said with emotion, are said with positive emotion only (Bloom, 1993). Similarly, simpler narrative structures are associated with positive experiences, while negative emotional experiences lead to more complicated narrative structure (Dunn, 1999). This suggests again that positive affect undergirds the integration of the expressive systems of language (here in terms of base narrative structure) and affect.

Positive or emotionally gratifying evaluation or assessment appears to be the default condition of normative cognitive processing in healthy subjects. For example, when memories are reconstructed, they are shifted in emotionally gratifying and self-enhancing directions (Bahrick, Hall, & Berger, 1996; Greenwald, 1980). Bahrick et al. (1996) showed college students to make errors that inflate their grades, when remembering their high school grades. Further, people remember their choices in an emotionally gratifying way (Mather & Johnson, 2000; Mather, Shafir, & Johnson, 2000).

Reciprocally, nondepressed individuals at high cognitive risk for depression process information about themselves more negatively than do those with positive cognitive styles (Alloy, Abramson, Murray, Whitehouse, & Hogan (1997). This preferential processing of self-referent negative depression-relevant information is revealed in greater endorsement, faster processing, greater accessibility, and better recall of content involving themes of incompetence, worthlessness, and low motivation. These high cognitive risk participants also are less likely to process positive depression-relevant stimuli than are low cognitive risk participants. Of course, such negatively toned self-relevant information processing is characteristic of depressed individuals as well (Segal, 1988).

Fittingness

Finally, there is the fittingness principle. This principle concerns the relation among the other four principles. It binds these together. The fittingness principle states that the normative relation for the operation of these principles is that of synchrony. Specifically, agents in given social interactive exchanges perform actions that are pursuant to their goals and persons/identities. These goal-directed actions achieve the goal (intended outcome). Agents and their interactants engage in contingent interaction, fulfilling and complementing roles. This presumes mutual understanding of one another's mental states.

Learning Paths in the Sociality Domain

Learning related to the sociality domain consists in acquisition of those knowledge structures that we use to participate in and understand social interaction. Three to-be-learned structures will be treated in this section. Two of these are event knowledge structures: *scripts* and *counterscripts*. The third is the *intentionalist causal framework* (*folk psychology*).

These three are chosen to illustrate three developmental levels of learning. Scripts represent domain-based early learning. Acquisition of the intentionalist causal framework represents domain-based later learning that is core-consistent knowledge extension. The to-be-acquired knowledge accords with core domain knowledge and represents an extension of such. Counterscript learning is illustrative of domain-related (but not based) later learning that is core-inconsistent knowledge acquisition. The to-be-acquired knowledge is inconsistent with or contradicts the skeletal, core knowledge in the domain.

Domain-Based Early Learning

To be a competent, full-fledged member of the culture, we must understand, participate in, and even predict social interactive events. Hence, we must acquire knowledge of the many kinds of sociocultural events that we experience. Scripts are our knowledge or representations for expected, commonplace, sociocultural activities. These include caretaking activities (e.g., getting dressed; mealtimes) and other activities, such as going to school, restaurants, stores, and the doctor's office. Also considered to be script events are ritualized occasions, such as birthdays and holidays.

Defining sociocultural events and understanding how they are learned requires an analysis of their structure. Four aspects of event structure are discerned: causal relations, emotive structure, person and interpersonal relations, and temporal-spatial relations. Each event structure we learn (with scripts and counterscripts considered in this chapter), can be analyzed in terms of its degree of consistency with the principles organizing the sociality domain.

Script-event structure, with respect to its instantiation of the four aspects of event structure, is consistent with the five skeletal principles representing initial knowledge in the sociality domain (see Table 10.2).

In script representations, causal relations are based in an agent who undertakes appropriate, goal-directed actions that achieve the goal. An essential feature of script knowledge is that causal relations are successful (see also Trabasso & Stein, 1996, and Trabasso, van den Broek, & Suh, 1989, for a related analysis of events in terms of their causal relations). Hence, the agency principle is honored in script events. The result is that script events embrace a neutral to positive/happy emotive structure. This in turn is consistent with the emotional evaluation principle.

Further, in script structure, interpersonal role relations are contingent and reciprocal. For example, the diner orders the food, the waitress takes the order and brings the food, and the diner then eats the food. At birthday parties, the guests bring the gifts; the birthday honoree receives them. Hence, the contingency principle also is honored. The smooth coordination of script role relations is strong indication that participants are cognizant of one another's mental states. Additionally, relative to temporal-spatial relations, script events occur in discrete or delimited time-place contexts. They occur, for example, at McDonald's, at school, at the grocery store, at the birthday party. Finally, scripts embody the fittingness principle. The principles of agency, contingency, mental states, and emotion evaluation operate in synchrony in script events.

As noted, on an epigenetic view of learning and cognitive development, learning is a function of the degree to which existing mental structures overlap with the structure of the input. Assimilation of inputs is more likely where a structure map exists between what is to be learned and what is already known. The structure of script events is consonant with the initial skeletal principles in the sociality domain. Accordingly, script learning occurs through structure mapping. This leads to two predictions. One is that script learning should be early, easy, and non-dependent on instruction. Second, script learning should be universal.

With respect to the timing and ease of learning, it is now well documented that scripts can be acquired by very young children. Learning begins as early as the second year, and scripts become a predominant knowledge structure for children (Bauer & Mandler, 1990, 1992; Bauer, Wenner, Dropik, Wewerka, 2000; K. Nelson, 1986; K. Nelson & Gruendel, 1981; Ratner, Smith,

& Dion, 1986). Children amass a substantial knowledge base of commonplace events. These include activities such as caretaking, conventional organizational structures, such as school, restaurants, stores, and ritualized occasions such as birthdays and holidays.

That script knowledge is robust in young children is evident also in the cognitive competencies afforded by scripts. Scripts lead to the development of taxonomic categorization through a script-based categorical organization known as the slot-filler category (Lucariello, 1998; Lucariello, Kyratzis, & Nelson, 1992; Lucariello & Nelson, 1985). Slot-filler categories represent the items that fill the slot created by a script-based action. Symbolic behaviors of language and play are also supported by script knowledge (Lucariello, 1987; Lucariello, 1990; Lucariello, Kyratzis, & Engel, 1986; Lucariello & Nelson, 1987). Moreover, scripts support inferential reasoning (Hudson & Slackman, 1990), the understanding of temporal (Carni & French, 1984) and causal (French, 1988), relations planning (Hudson & Fivush, 1991; Hudson, Shapiro, & Sosa, 1995; Hudson, Sosa, & Shapiro, 1997), self-understanding (K. Nelson, 1997, 2000), and autobiographical memory (Fivush, Hudson, & Nelson, 1984; Hudson, Fivush, & Kuebli, 1992).

Since script knowledge is consistent with initial domain knowledge, scripts are presumed to be universal. Although little empirical work has been conducted to examine this point, some data can be relied on. For example, the script-based slot-filler categories documented by Lucariello and colleagues (Lucariello & Nelson, 1985; Lucariello et al., 1992) in young children's knowledge bases have been documented in other cultures (Nelson & Nelson, 1990; Yu & Nelson, 1993). This provides indirect evidence that script knowledge is universal. Moreover, several studies show culture-specific script effects on information processing. Americans better summarize and recall stories when these fit their own cultural scripts (Forgas & Bond, 1985; Kintsch & Greene, 1978), and they misremember stories based on foreign scripts as being more like stories based on American scripts (Harris, Lee, Hensley, & Schoen, 1988). More strikingly, distinct cultural groups interpret the same event, such as a wedding or a game or a fight, differently based on their own cultural script knowledge (Carrell, 1983; Reynolds, Taylor, Steffensen, Shirey, & Anderson, 1982; Steffensen, Joag-dev, & Anderson, 1979).

Hence, the data reveal domain-based early learning to consist in script acquisition. They show script learning to be early, easy, non-reliant on instruction, and likely universal.

Later Learning: Core-Consistent Knowledge Extension

An *intentionalist causal framework* entails the explanation and prediction of behavior by appeal to internal, mental (including emotional) states. It involves interpreting behavior through psychological causes. This framework is very similar, if not identical to, what is meant by "folk psychology."

For the past decade, considerable attention has been paid to one behavior emblematic of the intentionalist causal framework: *false belief*. False belief refers to one's understanding that another has a false belief—an incorrect or erroneous belief with respect to reality. Accordingly, false belief provides evidence for mental state understanding (i.e., understanding the distinction between mind (internal mental states) and real-world events and situations.

False belief is commonly assessed through one of three kinds of tasks. In a "surprising contents" task, the child is presented with a familiar object (e.g., crayon box) and states what it normally contains (crayons). Then the child discovers the object to hold other things instead (e.g., candies). The child is then asked what someone else, who hasn't looked inside, will think is in the object (e.g., crayon box). False belief is indicated by an answer stipulating the normal contents (e.g., crayons). The "surprising identity" task relies on a deceptive object to engender a false belief. For example, in the rock-sponge task, the child sees, without touching, a sponge painted to look like a rock. The child presumably believes it to be a rock. Then the child handles the object. The child is then asked what it is and answers "sponge." The object is then placed back in its original location. In the test of false belief, the child is asked what another child, who will only see the object, will think it is. The answer "rock" gives evidence of false belief. The third task entails "change in location," and the Maxi task is most commonly relied on here. The child is presented with a scenario in which Maxi puts his chocolate in the kitchen cupboard and leaves the room to play. While he is away (and cannot see), his mother moves the chocolate from the cupboard to a drawer. Maxi returns. The false belief question has been asked in terms of action (where will Maxi look for his chocolate), thoughts (where does Maxi think his chocolate is), and language (where will Maxi say his chocolate is).

Clearly then, false belief is grounded in the intentionalist causal framework, just the ability to explain the behavior of self and others by appeal to mental states. Acquisition of this framework represents domain-based later learning of the "core-consistent knowledge extension" variety. The intentionalist causal framework is consistent with initial, skeletal knowledge in the sociality domain. The principles of contingency, agency, mental states, emotional evaluation, and fittingness are recruited in this framework. Accordingly, these principles afford assimilation of the relevant inputs, making structure mapping operative in acquisition.

Yet, the intentionalist causal framework requires a more enriched and a more controlled understanding of these principles than is inherent in their skeletal form. It requires that these principles be re-represented conceptually. The outcome is the development of the *concepts* of belief and false belief, for example. Reliance on the intentionalist causal framework to explain and predict behavior requires, in addition, a metacognitive understanding of these principles as well. Put differently, folk psychology entails being *meta-social*. Indeed, tasks such as false belief force a meta-use of these principles. To capture the more conceptual and more meta-understanding of these principles entailed in the intentionalist causal framework, we return to the notation system used earlier in this chapter. It can be said that, in the intentionalist causal framework, these principles are operative *in capital letters* (e.g., agency with a capital "A"). The difference in knowledge of these principles across their skeletal and "conceptual plus meta" form is analogous to the difference in knowledge of counting across the nonverbal and verbal counting principles.

Because conceptual and meta-knowledge, not simply skeletal knowledge, of these domain principles is required in the intentionalist causal framework, structure mapping alone will not be sufficient for its learning. These principles will need to be exercised, practiced, mined, honed. One's culture has to provide multiple, indeed ubiquitous, examples of the framework. In this way, culture can be said to amplify cognitive development (Greenfield & Bruner, 1966). Many, but not all, cultures provide such data, particularly those of agency and mental states, leading to their conceptual and meta-development.

Two predictions follow from this discussion of how the intentionalist causal framework is learned. One is developmental. Because learning is based on more than structure mapping alone, learning will occur later, ontogenetically, than knowledge acquisitions based only on structure mapping. Accordingly, learning of the causal intentionalist causal framework should be later and more effortful than script learning. The latter occurs on the basis of structure mapping. The second prediction is that this learning is unlikely to be universal. Since learning depends also on recruiting the multiple lines of evidence in the sociocultural environment, and these environments are not the same everywhere, it is not expected that the intentionalist causal framework would be a universal acquisition. The data on the acquisition of false belief bear out both these predictions.

With respect to development, all indications are that learning the intentionalist framework is a case of later learning. Scripts are learned beginning in the second year and are well established by age three. This, however, is the modal age at which learning of the intentionalist causal framework is just beginning. False belief tasks are generally failed by the 3-year-old and are not passed until the child is between 4 and 5 years of age (Gopnik & Astington, 1988). A recent meta-analysis of 178 separate studies indicates that false belief develops between the ages of 3 and 5 years (Wellman, Cross, & Watson, 2001). The method of assessment (i.e., the three kinds of tasks) does not affect this pattern.

Other data support the view that a folk psychology begins to be established around 3 years of age. Understanding of mental states—in terms of distinguishing intentional acts and outcomes from accidents, mistakes, and passive movements—does not appear before about 3 years of age (T. Shultz, 1980; T. Shultz, Wells, & Sarda, 1980). Additionally, Lucariello (1990) explored the kindergarten-aged children's abilities to explain behavior through an intentionalist causal framework. Even at this age, children generally did not invoke psychological causes for behavior. Indeed, such invocations seemed to

require a trigger, consisting in the presentation of incongruous behavior. Other data similarly show that psychological explanations of human actions and emotional reactions, where such are explained in terms of actors' mental states, are not apparent prior to age 3 years (Bartsch & Wellman, 1989; Lillard & Flavell, 1990; Schult & Wellman, 1997; Wellman & Banerjee, 1991).

Interestingly, Wellman et al.'s (2001) meta-analysis of theory of mind development uncovered four task variables that independently contribute to (i.e., enhance) children's performance. Three of these are consistent with the initial principles in the sociality domain, which is likely why they emerged as relevant. Indeed, the present account of initial knowledge in the sociality domain provides an explanation for these findings on the effects of task variables. These findings are left unexplained by Wellman et al. (2001).

One variable, motive, refers to a task variation in which a deceptive motive is explicitly stated for a change of location or unexpected contents (e.g., the chocolate was moved to trick the protagonist Maxi). This manipulation accords with—in fact, exploits—the agency principle. A second variable, salience of the protagonist's mental state, refers to manipulations in which the protagonist's belief is clearly stated or pictured (e.g., "Maxi thinks his chocolate is in the cupboard/drawer," and the false belief question, "Where will Maxi look for his chocolate/think that it is?"). This manipulation is consistent with and indeed relies on the mental states principle. The third variable, participation, refers to the child's setting up or manipulating the initial task situation. In some cases, it refers also to the child's performing the essential transformation (e.g., moving Maxi's chocolate; substituting the candies for the crayons in the crayon box). That the child's participation in the social situation of the experimental task improves task performance would be predicted from our claim that humans are prone to sociality. Moreover, in participating, the child's social interaction is following many of the initial principles of the domain: contingency, agency, and mental states.

As noted, learning the intentionalist causal framework was thought to be a non-universal acquisition. Here again the data support the prediction. Children from the Peruvian Andes who speak Quechua (a language with no separate lexical items for many mental states) found questions about mental states very difficult and did poorly on false belief (and representational change) tasks (Vinden, 1966). More recently, Vinden (1999) studied, in Africa and New Guinea, three different indigenous groups. Also studied were three groups of Western children (North American, Australian, and European). In this method, children were involved in creating a false belief in another person. Moreover, in assessment, there was a component concerning the prediction of emotion in the other. Two of the three indigenous groups showed a delay of several years in mental state understanding (understanding that people will act on the basis of what they believe, rather than merely reacting to the way the world is). However, one of these groups—Tainae of Papua, New Guinea—found the direct question about the other's thoughts much more difficult than the question about where the other would look. This was true even in children as old as 15 years of age who did not perform above chance on the direct question about another's thoughts. On other tasks, only the oldest children performed above chance on false belief (and representational change) questions using their word for "think."

With regard to the ability of predicting an emotion based on false belief, the English-speaking children appeared to follow the usual path from a situation-desire to belief-desire understanding of emotion. Almost all children from the three indigenous groups had difficulty predicting an emotion based on a false belief about the world. Hence, the non-western children did not show a clear progression toward a mentalistic understanding of emotion.

In thinking about sources of data in Western culture that are both salient and that seem particularly related to learning the intentionalist causal framework, three seem very relevant. These are: "intentionalist" model of language socialization, self-reflective schooling practices, and an "independent" self-concept.

The intentionality model of language socialization is typical of Western middle-class culture (see Snow, 1986). It reflects the skeletal principles of agency and mental states and hence can lead to conceptual and meta-knowledge of them. Herein the child is seen as an intentional agent, with mental states, from the outset of life. Children are treated as intentional communicative partners, and speech is directed *to* them from infancy. Moreover, characteristics of child-directed speech, such as expansions and requests for clarification, focus on the child's intentional states. Further, much of parent-child conversation, such as teasing, joking, and joint pretense, is relevant to mental states (Cutting & Dunn, 1999; Dunn, 1999; Dunn & Brown, 1993). Dunn (1999) describes parental attributions of intentionality to child behavior as typical in the second year. Moreover, she finds four kinds of interaction to be common in the third and fourth years. These kinds—mindreading, joint pretending, early narratives, and early deception—are thought to assist theory of mind learning.

Schooling experiences as well can reflect and exercise the skeletal principles of agency and mental states. Such can lead to conceptual and metaknowledge of these principles. Discourse practices are a particularly important feature of Western schooling in this regard. These include practices in which pupils are routinely asked to explain and justify their thinking and answers (Scribner & Cole, 1981). In cross-cultural research examining effects of literacy practices and schooling on cognition, the most pervasive schooling effect was on the ability to explain one's cognitive performance (Scribner & Cole, 1981). Naturally, this entails thinking about one's own mental states and knowledge. These discourse practices also include the related practice of teacher test questions (questions for which the teacher already knows the answer; Brice Heath, 1983). Test questions focus on the child's mental states and knowledge and would presumably foster conceptual and metaknowledge about mental states.

Finally, regarding self-concept, the independent self-concept, which is emphasized in some cultures, recruits the principles of agency and mental states. Such would foster conceptual knowledge and meta-use of each. Relevant effects on cognition of an independent self-concept have been found (Greenfield & Bruner, 1966; Markus & Kitayama, 1991; Vinden & Astington, 2000). For example, Greenfield and Bruner (1966) found self-consciousness to result from the independent value orientation. Self-consciousness is a facility in reasoning about mental states. Indeed, self-consciousness was lacking in their Wolof subjects in Senegal. In their conservation studies, Greenfield and Bruner were unable to use the traditional subjective form of justification questions (e.g., Why do you think there is more water in this glass than in that glass?). These subjects had difficulty with this type of question. It was necessary to transform the question to an objective form (e.g., Why is there more water in this glass than in that one?). More recently, an independent self-concept was found to facilitate such cognitive activity as hypothetical and counter-factual reasoning (Markus & Kitayama, 1991). These forms of thinking demand complex reasoning about mental states.

Later Learning: Core-Inconsistent Knowledge Acquisition

To be full-fledged participants in our culture, we must have some structured understanding about unexpected events. Script event structures cannot be the only ones acquired. Counterscripts constitute an important class of event structures (Lucariello, 1994; Lucariello & Mindolovich, 1995, in press). These structures capture much of our understanding of the irregularity of events as well as how to "play" with the irregularities. Classic among counterscript representations are those for situationally ironic events (Lucariello, 1994; Lucariello & Mindolovich, 1995, in press).

An analysis of counterscript events in terms of elements of event structure shows these events to violate the initial, skeletal principles in the core domain of sociality. In particular, the principles of agency, emotional evaluation, and fittingness are violated. Four of the most prototypical counterscript ironic event kinds will be treated here. Three of these—"Wins," "Losses," and "Double Outcome"—exhibit aberrancy in causal relations. In contrast to script events, the successful and straightforward links among agency, goal-directed action, and outcome do not hold. The aberrancies in causal relations show a failure of the agency principle in that the goal-directed action of an agent is rendered impotent. In this, except for Wins events, the emotional evaluation principle is also violated. The default emotional assessment of neutral-positive cannot hold.

Wins counterscript events are the most similar to script-event structure. A major type of Win is Fluke-Win. In these events, inadvertent, non-goal-directed actions, rather than goal-directed ones, secure the outcome. Such is the aberrancy in causal relations. Nonetheless, the intended goal is achieved in the outcome making these events very similar to script events. Moreover, because the desired outcome is attained, the emotive structure of Fluke-Win counterscript events is, like that of scripted events, positive/happy.

Losses and Double Outcomes also exhibit aberrant causal relations. These relations, however, lead to loss outcomes and hence to script-contradictory negative/sad emotive structure. Loss events entail a single loss outcome. Planned-Loss ironic events refer to backfired plans. The agent has a goal and takes appropriate actions. Rather than securing the intended outcome, as in script causal relations, these actions achieve the outcome opposite to that intended. The result is that the loss outcome is also self-inflicted.

Double Outcome ironic events entail two opposing outcomes, win and loss. In Fruitless Win–Double Outcome events, the agent has a goal and takes appropriate actions, but the outcome is lost (not achieved). Subsequently, when the outcome is no longer relevant or desired, it actually becomes attainable. This final outcome constitutes a bittersweet experience. It represents a loss because it arrived too late, but it reminds one of the win that it could have been.

A different variety of counterscript ironic events also violate the initial skeletal principles of the sociality domain, in particular the agency and fittingness principles. In these events, however, this is accomplished through aberrancy, not in the causal relations, but in the temporal-spatial relations in conjunction with person-interpersonal relations. Imbalance counter-script ironics capture contradiction in person relations, such as agent-action or agent-goal, across contexts. In Temporal-Imbalance, person relations are contradicted across distinct temporal contexts, generally past versus present (e.g., the clumsy classmate who becomes the prima ballerina; the inmate who later becomes a lawyer). Apparent here is a weakened or diluted sense of agency. The agent is not steady or constant.

Counterscript ironic events may be distinguished from other unexpected, script-aberrant events that do not qualify as counterscript events. These nonscript events exhibit idiosyncratic anomalies. Hence, they show no common instantiation of the four aspects of event structure. For example, in a deviation of the Planned-Loss example (Table 10.2), let us say that while Billy is putting away his telescope for safekeeping, he does not drop it. Rather, he has to run back to his party because his friends are fighting. In this case, an anomalous, nonscript event has occurred. However, a counterscript ironic event has not. Presumably, we do not acquire general, semantic representations for these events. They are not learned.

How are counterscript events learned? Several learning tools will be needed. As noted, because counter-script event structure violates the initial skeletal principles of the sociality domain, structure mapping will not play much of a role in learning. To the extent that it operates at all, it would pertain to the Wins event kind, which represents the greatest structural match, among all counterscript ironic kinds, with script events.

Accordingly, for the most part, counterscript learning occurs in the absence of potential structural maps. Indeed, a new structure has to be mounted. Moreover, prior script knowledge has to be overcome in learning because its inconsistency with the relevant inputs renders it a barrier to new learning. In scripts, one's clumsy classmate becomes a clumsy waitress; in counterscripts, one's clumsy classmate arrives at a contradictory state of prima ballerina. In scripts, one's plans work out; in counterscripts, plans backfire. Prior script knowledge is also a barrier to learning in the apparent tendency to resist changing the knowledge base. Data are simply assimilated to the existing structure. Indeed, learners often fail to realize that they do not understand a new concept. Due to these conditions, counterscript learning will be effortful and protracted. In addition, it will require learning tools other than structure mapping.

Of the learning tools described earlier, some are particularly important for counterscript learning. These include pattern analysis, frequency computing, and metacognition.

Learning counterscript event structures relies on pattern matching. All event inputs—typical and atypical—must be compared against script structure to determine matches and nonmatches. Moreover, among the mismatches (the input of atypical events), the child must detect the event structure (e.g., causal relations as well as temporal-spatial and person-relation patterns) that distinguishes counterscript ironic events from other unexpected (nonscript) events that exhibit idiosyncratic anomalies. These latter events show no common instantiation of event structure. Recall the example cited earlier of the fight suddenly breaking out at Billy's birthday party. Representations for these latter events must not be learned as if they were counterscript ironic structures, and perhaps not learned at all. Hence, the child must make such distinctions among atypical events.

This process is made more complicated by prior knowledge. Prior knowledge can impede interpretation of the input. Because the child's knowledge about doing daily things is contradicted in the experience of counterscript ironic events, the input of counterscript atypical events contradicts available mental structures. Experiencing inputs contradictory to prior domain knowledge can prevent the learner from moving onto the appropriate learning path. Or it can cause misconceptions in learning, based on misinterpretation of or failure to distinguish among inputs (Hartnett & Gelman, 1998). Learning problems such as ignoring input or wrongly assimilating it into existing structure are possible (R. Gelman, 1991; R. Gelman & Williams, 1998).

Additional learning tools can help the child distinguish among atypical events. One is contingent frequency computing. Presumably, the counterscript patterns occur more frequently than do idiosyncratic ones. This gives learners an opportunity to keep track of cases that eventually can be organized.

Learning is also facilitated by the ability discussed earlier to create and use re-representations, including spoken and written language. Counterscript ironic patterns, in contrast to anomalous, idiosyncratic unexpected events, are more likely to be re-represented culturally. Counterscript ironic events are often, if not always, labeled as such when referenced (e.g., the newscaster who heads a story, "Ironically . . ."). Moreover, ironic events are commonly rendered in texts, such as children's books (Dyer, Shatz, & Wellman, 2000). The re-representation serves to increase the salience of counterscript patterns among the input of atypical events. Put differently, children are offered ubiquitous and redundant examples of inputs relevant for acquiring these new event structures.

Because learning counterscript event structures entails acquiring a second tier of event knowledge contradictory to the first, advanced metacognitive skills will also be needed. They are advanced in that their operation is dependent on, though not automatically precipitated by, the learner already having some related knowledge (script knowledge).

One metacognitive skill required for counter-script learning may be defined as a *skeptical frame of mind*. This frame consists in a critical stance or detachment toward one's knowledge, on which knowledge is not viewed as fact, but is subject to question. On this frame, one's knowledge structures or categories are understood as limited—insufficient and inaccurate in accounting for all the relevant inputs (see Goffman, 1974, for discussion of frames of mind). This orientation to one's knowledge enables the learner to overcome the constraints of prior knowledge to acquire and process structures inconsistent with or contradictory to related prior knowledge. In counterscript learning, the learner must transcend prior, related script knowledge because the new knowledge contradicts the prior knowledge. If children stick with their primary base of event structures, even in the face of contradictory input, learning will not occur. Rigid adherence to one's current categories of knowledge can prevent learning.

A second metacognitive skill needed is *dialectical metarepresentation*. This is reasoning about contradictions in one's own thought and relative to metarepresentations. In learning counterscripts, contradictory (not simply inconsistent) tiers of event knowledge must be maintained in the knowledge base. These tiers are the primary representations, scripts, and the secondary or metarepresentations, counterscripts. Although scripts are transcended in learning counterscripts, scripts must also be maintained during and after acquisition of counterscripts. Scripts, although inadequate in accounting for all event inputs, nonetheless account for a significant share of event inputs. Accordingly, in acquiring and processing counterscript representations ("not A"), which render how events are "not supposed" to occur, one must necessarily understand script representations ("A"), which specify how they are "supposed" to occur. Dialectical metarepresentation is required for managing such contradictory tiers of event knowledge.

The very challenging nature of learning counter-scripts, due to their being about core-inconsistent knowledge acquisition, leads to two predictions about their acquisition. It is likely to be protracted and effortful, hence a relatively late-accomplishment. Moreover, this learning is likely non-universal.

To date, two studies have examined children's counter-script learning and they reveal it to be late-emerging and difficult

(Lucariello & Mindolovich, 1995; Lucariello, Mindolovich, & Le Donne, 2001). In a story completion task, 6- and 8-year-olds were presented with story stems and asked them to complete the stories (Lucariello & Mindolovich, 1995). Endings were analyzed for counterscript ironic status (Lucariello & Mindolovich, 1995). Results showed that even at 8 years of age children do not easily produce counterscript ironic events. Half of these children never did so. These data reveal the effortful nature of counter-script acquisition. Moreover, they point to the role of metacognition, in terms of a skeptical frame of mind, in counterscript learning. Children at both ages spontaneously preferred to end their stories as scripts (i.e., with endings that meet the agent's goal or that add an appropriate action in the event sequence). Counterscript production generally occurred after an intervention from the experimenter requesting a "sad" ending. These data illustrate the tendency to stick with one's prior knowledge/categories in learning. They underscore the necessity of developing a skeptical frame of mind.

In a follow-up study, child counterscript learning was assessed through a comprehension methodology using a story recall task (Lucariello et al., 2001). Kindergarten and third grade children's recall of script, counterscript ironic, and anomalous (idiosyncratic) unexpected event stories was studied. With respect to counterscripts, learning of the four structures already described was assessed. These were: Fluke-Win, Planned-Loss, Fruitless Win-Double Outcome, and Temporal-Imbalance. The premise of this methodology is that better recall is elicited by stimuli that tap underlying knowledge structures. Accordingly, completed counterscript learning would be evident in a recall pattern wherein script and counterscript stories are well recalled and comparably so, while anomaly stories are less well recalled. Script and counterscript events are to be learned and hence stories about these events should tap underlying knowledge structures. In contrast, anomaly events are not to be learned; hence we should not have knowledge structures for these events. Thus, stories depicting these events should not be well recalled. Here again the data show the challenge of counterscript learning. Even older children showed only partial learning and this for only two of the four counterscript structures whose learning was assessed.

As noted, counterscript learning, as a case of later leaning inconsistent with core domain knowledge, is thought to be non-universal. To our knowledge there are not yet cross-cultural studies on counterscript learning.

CONCLUSION

The demonstrated abilities of infants and young children to use abstract information and acquire abstract concepts about objects, numbers, and people are inconsistent with the long-standing view that they are preconceptual, perception-bound, and limited to concrete reasoning or stimulus-response pairings. Such findings have motivated the development of the rational-constructivist class of theories of cognitive development. Even though appeal is made to innate contributions to development, it is a mistake to conclude that this is paired with the idea that cognitive development does not involve learning. Instead, the problem of learning in development has to be restated as follows: What kind of learning theory fits the developmental facts? This was the central question addressed in this chapter—hence the focus on mental learning tools that the mind can recruit in the name of finding and gathering data that can nurture, develop, and even create mental structures. What emerges is that an account of learning in cognitive development is likely to involve

devices that seek out and create structures. This is obviously not a traditional learning theory with its commitment to the buildup of associations. In many respects it is a learning theory that is Piagetian in spirit. In the end it differs from Piaget's because of its emphasis on innate skeletal principles and domain specificity.

REFERENCES

Adamson, L. B., & Bakeman, R. (1985). Affect and attention: Infants observed with mothers and peers. *Child Development, 56,* 582–593.

Ahn, W., Kalish, C. W., Medin, D. L., & Gelman, S. A. (1995). The role of covariation versus mechanism information in causal attribution. *Cognition, 54*(3), 299–352.

Alloy, L. B., Abramson, L. Y., Murray, L. A., Whitehouse, W. G., & Hogan, M. E. (1997). Self-referent information-processing in individuals at high and low cognitive risk for depression. *Cognition and Emotion, 11,* 539–568.

Armstrong, S. L., Gleitman, L. R., & Gleitman, H. (1983). What some concepts might not be. *Cognition, 13,* 263–308.

Aslin, R. N., Saffran, J. R., & Newport, E. L. (1998). Computation of conditional probability statistics by 8-month-old infants. *Psychological Science, 9,* 321–324.

Bahrick, H. P., Hall, L. K., & Berger, S. A. (1996). Accuracy and distortion in memory for high school grades. *Psychological Science, 7,* 265–271.

Baillargeon, R. (1995). Physical reasoning in infancy. In M. S. Gazzaniga (Ed.), *The cognitive neurosciences* (pp. 181–204). Cambridge, MA: MIT Press.

Baillargeon, R. (1998). Infants' understanding of the physical world. In E. M. Sabourin, E. F. Craik, & M. Robert (Eds.), *Advances in psychological science, Vol. 2: Biological and cognitive aspects* (pp. 503–529). Hove, UK.

Baillargeon, R., Kotovsky, L., & Needham, A. (1995). The acquisition of physical knowledge in infancy. In D. Sperber, D. Premack, & A. J. Premack (Eds.), *Causal cognition: A multidisciplinary approach* (pp. 79–116). Oxford, England: Clarendon Press.

Baillargeon, R., Spelke, E. S., & Wasserman, S. (1985). Object permanence in 5-month-old infants. *Cognition, 20,* 191–208.

Baldwin, D. A. (1993). Early referential understanding: Infants' ability to recognize referential acts for what they are. *Developmental Psychology, 29,* 832–843.

Baldwin, D. A. (1995). Understanding the link between joint attention and language. In C. Moore & P. Dunham (Eds.), *Joint attention: Its origin and role in development* (pp. 131–158). Hillsdale, NJ: Erlbaum.

Baldwin, D. A., & Moses, L. J. (1994). Early understanding of referential intent and attentional focus: Evidence from language and emotion. In C. Lewis & P. Mitchell (Eds.), *Children's early understanding of mind* (pp. 133–156). Hillsdale, NJ: Erlbaum.

Baldwin, D. A., & Moses, L. J. (1996). The ontogeny of social information gathering. *Child Development, 67,* 1915–1939.

Bartsch, K., & Wellman, H. M. (1989). Young children's attribution of actions to beliefs and desires. *Child Development, 60,* 946–964.

Bates, E., Benigni, L., Bretherton, I., Camaioni, L., & Volterra, V. (1979). *The emergence of symbols: Cognition and communication in infancy.* New York: Academic Press.

Bates, E., Camaioni, L., & Volterra, V. (1975). The acquisition of performatives prior to speech. *Merrill-Palmer Quarterly, 21,* 205–226.

Baudonniere, P., Garcia-Werebe, M., Michel, J., & Liegois, J. (1989). Development of communicative competencies in early childhood: A model and results. In B. H. Schnieder, G. Attili, J. Nadel, & R. P. Weissberg (Eds.), *Social competence in developmental perspective* (pp. 175–193). Boston: Kluwer Academic.

Bauer, P. J., & Mandler, J. M. (1990). Remembering what happened next: Very young children's recall of event sequences. In R. Fivush & J. A. Hudson (Eds.), *Knowing and remembering in young children. Emory symposia in cognition* (Vol. 3, pp. 9–29). New York: Cambridge University Press.

Bauer, P. J., & Mandler, J. M. (1992). Putting the horse before the cart: The use of temporal order in recall of events by one-year-old children. *Developmental Psychology, 28,* 441–452.

Bauer, P. J., Wenner, J. A., Dropik, P. L., & Wewerka, S. S. (2000). Parameters of remembering and forgetting in the transition from infancy to early childhood. *Monographs of the Society for Research in Child Development, 65*(4, Serial No. 263).

Behr, M. J., Lesh, R., Post, T. R., & Silver, E. A. (1983). Rational-number concepts. In R. Lesh & M. Landua (Eds.), *Acquisition of mathematics concepts and processes* (pp. 91–126). New York: Academic Press.

Bertenthal, B. I. (1993). Infants' perception of biomechanical motions: Intrinsic image and knowledge-based constraints. In C. Granrud (Ed.), *Visual perception and cognition in infancy* (pp. 175–214). Hillside, NJ: Erlbaum.

Bloom, L. (1993). *The transition from infancy to language.* Cambridge: Cambridge University Press.

Bloom, L., Lightbown, P., & Hood, L. (1975). Structure and variation in child language. *Monographs of the Society for Research in Child Development, 40*(1).

Bloom, P. (2000). *How children learn the meanings of words.* Cambridge, MA: MIT Press.

Bonatti, L., Frot, E., Zangl, R., & Mehler, J. (in press). The human first hypothesis: Identification of conspecifics in the young infant. *Cognition.*

Bowerman, M. (1976). Semantic factors in the acquisition of rules for word use and sentence construction. In D. M. Morehead & A. E. Morehead (Eds.), *Normal and deficient child language* (pp. 30). Baltimore: University Park Press.

Bowlby, J. (1969). *Attachment and loss, Vol. 1: Attachment.* New York: Basic Books.

Bowlby, J. (1973). *Attachment and loss, Vol. 2: Separation, anxiety, and anger.* New York: Basic Books.

Boyer, P. (2001). *Religion explained.* Cambridge, MA: MIT Press.

Brannon, E. M. (2001). *The development of ordinal numerical knowledge in infancy.* Manuscript submitted for publication.

Bransford, J. D., Brown, A. L., & Cocking, R. R. (Eds). (1999). *How people learn: Brain, mind, experience and school.* Washington, DC, National Academy of Sciences.

Brenneman, K., Massey, C., Machado, S., & Gelman, R. (1996). Notating knowledge about words and objects: Preschoolers' plans differ for "writing" and drawing. *Cognitive Development, 11,* 397–419.

Bretherton, I., McNew, S., & Beeghly-Smith, M. (1981). Early person knowledge as expressed in gestural and verbal communication: When do infants acquire a "theory of mind?" In M. E. Lamb & L. R. Sherrod (Eds.), *Infant social cognition* (pp. 333–373). Hillsdale, NJ: Erlbaum.

Brice Heath, S. (1983). *Ways with words.* Cambridge, MA: Cambridge University Press.

Brown, A. L. (1990). Domain specific principles affect learning and transfer in children. *Cognitive Science, 14,* 107–133.

Brown, A. L., Bransford, J. D., Ferrara, R. A., & Campione, J. C. (1983). *Learning, remembering, and understanding.* In J. H. Flavell & E. M. Markman (Eds.). *Cognitive development. Vol. 3.* (pp. 78–166). New York: Wiley.

Brown, A. L., Kane, M. J., & Echols, C. H. (1986). Young children's mental models determine analogical transfer across problems with a common goal structure. *Cognitive Development, 1,* 103–121.

Bruner, J. S. (1964). The course of cognitive growth. *American Psychologist, 19* (pp. 1–15).

Bruner, J. S., & Lucariello, J. (1989). Monologue as narrative recreation of the world. In K. Nelson (Ed.), *Narratives from the crib* (pp. 73–97). Cambridge, MA: Harvard University Press.

Bullock, M., & Gelman, R. (1979). Preschool children's assumptions about cause and effect: Temporal ordering. *Child Development, 50,* 89–96.

Bullock, M., Gelman, R., & Baillargeon., R. (1982). The development of causal reasoning.

In W. J. Friedman (Ed.), *The developmental psychology of time* (pp. 209–253). New York, Academic Press.

Butterworth, George (1991). The ontogeny and phylogeny of joint visual attention. In A. Whiten (Ed.), *Natural theories of mind: Evolution, development and simulation of every day mindreading* (pp. 223–232). Cambridge, MA: Basil Blackwell, Inc.

Byrne, R. W., & Whiten, A. (1997). Machiavellian intelligence. In A. Whiten & R. W. Byrne (Eds.), *Machiavellian Intelligence, II: Extensions and evaluations* (pp. 1–23). Oxford: Oxford University Press.

Carey, S. (1985). *Conceptual change in childhood.* Cambridge, MA: Cambridge University Press.

Carey, S. (1991). Knowledge acquisition: Enrichment or conceptual change? In S. Carey & R. Gelman (Eds.), *Epigenesis of the mind: Studies in biology and cognition.* Hillsdale, NJ: Erlbaum.

Carey, S. (1998). Knowledge of number: Its evolution and ontogeny. *Science, 282,* 53–89.

Carni, E., & French, L. (1984). The acquisition of before and after reconsidered: What develops? *Journal of Experimental Child Psychology, 37,* 394–403.

Carrell, P. K. (1983). Background knowledge in second language comprehension. *Language Learning and Communication, 2,* 25–33.

Catrambone, T. N., & Holyoak, K. (1989). Overcoming contextual limitation on problem solving transfer. *Journal of Experimental Psychology: Learning, Memory, and Cognition, 15,* 1147–1156.

Cheng, P. W. (1997). From covariation to causation: A causal power theory. *Psychological Review, 104,* 367–405.

Chi, M. (1992). Conceptual change within and across ontological categories: Examples from learning and discovery in science. In R. Giere. (Ed.), *Cognitive models of science: Minnesota studies in the philosophy of science.* Minneapolis: University of Minnesota Press.

Cohn, J. F., Campbell, S. B., Matias, R., & Hopkins, J. (1990). Face-to-face interactions of postpartum depressed and nondepressed mother-infant pairs at 2 months. *Developmental Psychology, 26,* 15–23.

Cohn, J. F., & Tronick, E. Z. (1983). Three-month-old infants' reaction to simulated maternal depression. *Child Development, 54,* 185–193.

Cosmides, L., & Tooby, J. (1994). Origins of domain specificity: The evolution of functional organization. In S. A. G. Lawrence & A. Hirschfeld (Eds.), *Mapping the mind: Domain specificity in cognition and culture* (pp. 85–116). New York: Cambridge University Press.

Csibra, G., Gergely, G., Biro, S., Koos, O., & Brockbank, M. (1999). Goal attribution without agency cues: The perception of "pure reason" in infancy. *Cognition, 72,* 237–267.

Cutting, A. L., & Dunn, J. (1999). Theory of mind, emotion understanding, language and family background: Individual differences and interrelations. *Child Development, 70,* 853–865.

Darwin, C. (1991). *On the origin of species* (G. Beer, Ed.). Buffalo, NY: Prometheus Books. (Original work published 1859)

Denham, S. A. (1986). Social cognition, prosocial behavior, and emotion in preschoolers: Contextual validation. *Child Development, 57,* 194–201.

Dunn, J. (1999). Making sense of the social world: Mindreading, emotion, and relationships. In P. Zelazo, J. W. Astingon, & D. R. Olson (Eds.), *Developing theories of intention: Social understanding and self-control* (pp. 229–242). Mahwah, NJ: Erlbaum.

Dunn, J., & Brown, J. R. (1993). Early conversations about causality: Content, pragmatics and developmental change. *British Journal of Developmental Psychology, 11,* 107–23.

Dyer, J., Shatz, M., & Wellman, H. M. (2000). Young children's story books as a source of mental state information. *Cognitive Development, 15,* 17–37.

Eckerman, C. O. (1979). The human infant in social interaction. In R. B. Cairns (Ed.), *The analysis of social interactions: Methods, issues, and illustrations* (pp. 163–178). Hillsdale, NJ: Erlbaum.

Eckerman, C. O., & Rheingold, H. L. (1974). Infants' exploratory responses to toys and people. *Developmental Psychology, 10,* 255–259.

Eckerman, C. O., Whatley, J. L., & Kutz, S. L. (1975). Growth of social play with peers during the second year of life. *Developmental Psychology, 11,* 42–49.

Ellsworth, C. P., Muir, D. W., & Hains, S. M. J. (1993). Social competence and person-object differentiation: An analysis of the still-face effect. *Developmental Psychology, 29,* 63–73.

Elman, J. L., Bates, E., Johnson, M. H., Karmiloff-Smith, A., Parisi, D., & Plunkett, K. (1996). *Rethinking innateness: A connectionist perspective on development.* Cambridge, MA: MIT Press.

Feinman, S. (1982). Social referencing in infancy. *Merrill-Palmer Quarterly, 28,* 445–70.

Field, T. M., Woodson, R., Greenberg, R., & Cohen, D. (1982). Discrimination and imitation of facial expressions by neonates. *Science, 218,* 179–81.

Fiske, A. P. (1991). *Structures of social life: The four elementary forms of human relations: Communal sharing, authority ranking, equality matching, market pricing.* New York: Free Press.

Fiske, A. P. (1992). The four elementary forms of sociality: Framework for a unified theory of social relations. *Psychological Review, 99,* 689–723.

Fiske, A. P. (1993). Social errors in four cultures: Evidence about universal forms of social relations. *Journal of Cross-Cultural Psychology, 24,* 463–494.

Fivush, R., Hudson, J., & Nelson, K. (1984). Children's long term memory for a novel event: An exploratory study. *Merrill-Palmer Quarterly, 30,* 303–316.

Fodor, J. A. (1975). *The language of thought.* New York: Thomas Y. Crowell.

Fodor, J. A. (1983). *The modularity of thought.* Cambridge, MA: MIT Press.

Fodor, J. A., & Lepore, E. (1996). The red herring and the pet fish: Why concepts still can't be prototypes. *Cognition, 58,* 253–270.

Forgas, J. P., & Bond, M. H. (1985). Cultural influences on the perception of interaction episodes. *Personality & Social Psychology Bulletin, 11,* 75–88.

Fowler, A. E., Gelman, R., & Gleitman, L. R. (1993). The course of language learning in children with Down Syndrome. In H. Tager-Flusberg (Ed.), *Constraints on language acquisition: studies of atypical populations* (pp. 91–140). Hillsdale, NJ: Erlbaum.

French, L. A. (1988). The development of children's understanding of "because" and "so." *Journal of Experimental Child Psychology, 45,* 262–279.

Fridlund, A. J. (1994). *Human facial expression: An evolutionary view.* San Diego: Academic Press.

Fuson, K. C. (1988). *Children's counting and concepts of number.* New York: Springer-Verlag.

Gallistel, C. R. (1980). From muscles to motivation. *American Scientist, 68,* 398–409.

Gallistel, C. R. (1990). *The organization of learning.* Cambridge, MA: MIT Press.

Gallistel, C. R., & Gelman, R. (2000). Non-verbal cognition: From reals to integers. *Trends in Cognitive Science, 4,* 59–65.

Gallistel, C. R., & Gibbon, J. (2000). Time, rate and conditioning. *Psychological Review, 107,* 289–344.

Gardner, H. (1992). *Frames of mind.* New York: Basic Books.

Gelman, R. (1969). Conservation acquisition: A problem of learning to attend to relevant attributes. *Journal of Experimental Psychology, 7,* 167–187.

Gelman, R. (1990). First principles organize attention to and learning about relevant data: Number and the animate-inanimate distinction as examples. *Cognitive Science, 14*(1), 79–106.

Gelman, R. (1991). Epigenetic foundations of knowledge structures: Initial transcendent constructions. In S. Carey & R. Gelman (Eds.), *The epigenesis of mind: Biology and knowledge* (pp. 293–338). Hillsdale, NJ: Erlbaum.

Gelman, R. (1993). A Rational-constructivist account of early learning about numbers and objects. In D. Medin (Ed.), *Learning and motivation* (pp. 61–96). New York: Academic Press.

Gelman, R. (1994). Constructivism and supporting environments. In D. Tirosh (Ed.), *Implicit and explicit knowledge: An educational approach* (pp. 55–82). Norwood, NJ: Ablex.

Gelman, R. (1998). Domain specificity in cognitive development: Universals and nonuniversals. In M. Sabourin, F. Craik, & M. Robert (Eds.), *Advances in psychological science, Vol. 2: Biological and cognitive aspects* (pp. 557–580). Hove, UK: Psychology Press.

Gelman, R. (2000). The epigenesis of mathematical thinking. *Journal of Applied Developmental Psychology, 21,* 27–37.

Gelman, R. (in press). Animates and other worldly things. In N. Stein, P. Bauer, & M. Rabinowitz (Eds.), *Representation, memory, and development: Essays in honor of Jean Mandler.* Mahwah, NJ: Erlbaum.

Gelman, R., & Brenneman, K. (1994). First principles can support both universal and culture-specific learning about number and music. In L. A. Hirschfeld & S. A. Gelman (Eds.). *Mapping the mind: Domains, culture and cognition* (pp. 369–390). Cambridge, England, New York: Cambridge University Press.

Gelman, R., & Cohen, M. (1988). Qualitative differences in the way Down Syndrome and normal children solve a novel counting problem. In L. Nadel (Ed.), *The psychobiology of Down Syndrome* (pp. 51–99). Cambridge, MA: MIT Press.

Gelman, R., Durgin, F., & Kaufman, L. (1995). Distinguishing between animates and inanimates: Not by motion alone. In D. Sperber, D. Premack, & A. J. Premack (Eds.), *Causal cognition: A multidisciplinary debate* (pp. 150–184). New York: Clarendon Press/Oxford University Press.

Gelman, R., & Gallistel, C. R. (1978). *The child's understanding of number.* Cambridge, Mass: Harvard University Press.

Gelman, R. Romo, L., & Francis, W. (in press). Notebooks as windows on learning: The case of a science-into-ESL program. In N. Granott & J. Parziale (Eds.), *Microdevelopment.* Cambridge, Eng: Cambridge University Press.

Gelman, R., & Williams, E. (1998). Enabling constraints for cognitive development and learning: Domain specificity and epigenesis. In W. Damon (Series Ed.), D. Kuhn, & R. S. Siegler (Volume Eds.), *Handbook of child psychology, Vol. 2: Cognition, perception, and language* (pp. 575–630). New York: Wiley.

Gelman, S. A., & Gottfried, A. (1996). Children's causal explanations of animate and inanimate motion. *Child Development, 67,* 1970–1987.

Gelman, S. A., & Opfer, J. E. (2001). Development of the animate-inanimate distinction. In U. Goswami (Ed.), *Handbook of childhood cognitive development.* London, Eng: Blackwell.

Gentner, D., Rattermann, M. J., & Forbus, K. (1993). The roles of similarity in transfer: Separating retrievability from inferential soundness. *Cognitive Science, 25,* 524–575.

Gergely, G., Nadasdy, Z., Csibra, G., & Biro, S. (1995). Taking the intentional stance at 12 months of age. *Cognition, 56,* 165–193.

Gergely, G., & Watson, J. S. (1999). Early socioemotional development: Contingency perception and the social-biofeedback model. In P. Rochat (Ed.), *Early social cognition: Understanding others in the first months of life* (pp. 101–136). Mahwah, NJ: Erlbaum.

Gibson, E. J. (1969). *Principles of learning and development.* New York: Appleton-Century-Crofts.

Gibson, E. J. (1984). Perceptual development from the ecological approach. In M. C. Lamb, A. L. Brown, & B. Rogoff (Eds.), *Advances in development* (pp. 243–286). Hildsale, NJ: Erlbaum.

Glick, J. (1978). Cognition and social cognition: An introduction. In J. Glick & K. A. Clarke-Stewart (Eds.), *The development of social understanding* (pp. 1–9). New York: Gardner.

Goffman, E. (1974). Frame analysis: An essay on the organization of experience. New York: Harper and Row.

Goldman, B. D., & Ross, H. S. (1978). Social skills in action: An analysis of early peer games. In J. Glick & K. A. Clarke-Stewart (Eds.), *The Development of Social Understanding* (pp. 177–212). New York: Gardner.

Golinkoff, R. M., Harding, C. G., Carlson, V., & Sexton, M. E. (1984). The infant's perception of causal events: The distinction between animate and inanimate objects. In L. P. Lipsitt & C. Rovee-Collier (Eds.), *Advances in infancy research* (Vol. 3, pp. 145–151). Norwood, NJ: Ablex.

Gopnik, A., & Astington, J. W. (1988). Children's understanding of representational change and its relation to the understanding of false belief and the appearance-reality distinction. *Child Development, 59,* 26–37.

Gopnik, A., & Meltzoff, A. N. (1997). *Words, thoughts and theories.* Cambridge, MA: MIT Press.

Goswami, U. (1995). Analogical reasoning and cognitive development. In H. Reese (Ed.), *Advances in child development and behavior* (p. 26). New York: Academic Press.

Goswami, U., & Brown, A. (1990). Melting chocolate and melting snowmen: Anological reasoning and causal relations. *Cognition, 35,* 69–95.

Greenfield, P. M., & Bruner, J. S. (1966). Culture and cognitive growth. *International Journal of Psychology, 1,* 89–107.

Greenwald, A. G. (1980). The totalitarian ego: Fabrication and revision of personal history. *American Psychologist, 35,* 603–618.

Grice, H. P. (1975). Logic and conversation. In P. Cole & J. Morgan (Eds.), *Syntax and semantics:* (Vol. 3, *Speech Acts,* pp. 41–58). New York: Academic Press.

Grice, H. P. (1978). Some further notes on logic and conversation. In P. Cole (Ed.), *Syntax and Semantics: Vol. 9. Pragmatics* (pp. 113–128). New York: Academic Press.

Grinstead, J., Swann, J., Curtiss, S. & Gelman, R. (2001). *The independence of language and number.* Manuscript under review.

Haith, M., & Benson, J. B. (1998). Infant cognition. In W. Damon (Series Ed.). *Handbook of child psychology. Vol. 2: Infancy and developmental psychology.* (pp. 199–254). New York: Wiley.

Harris, R. J., Lee, D. J., Hensley, D. L., & Schoen, L. M. (1988). The effect of cultural script knowledge on memory for stories over time. *Discourse Processes, 11,* 413–431.

Hartnett, P. M. (1991). *The development of mathematical insight: From one, two, three to infinity.* Unpublished doctoral dissertation. University of Pennsylvania, Philadelphia.

Hartnett, P. M., & Gelman, R. (1998). Early understandings of numbers: Paths or barriers to the construction of new understandings? *Learning and Instruction: The Journal of the European Association for Research in Learning and Instruction, 8,* 341–374.

Hasher, L., & Zacks, R. T. (1979). Automatic and effortful processes in memory. *Journal of Experimental Psychology, 108*(3), 356–388.

Hatano, G., & Inagaki, K. (1999). A developmental perspective on informal biology. In D. L. Medin & S. Atran (Eds.), *Folkbiology* (pp. 321–354). Cambridge, MA: MIT Press.

Haviland, J. M., & Lelwica, M. (1987). The induced affect response: 10-week old infants' responses to three emotion expressions. *Developmental Psychology, 23,* 97–104.

Hay, D. F., Pedersen, J., & Nash, A. (1982). Dyadil interaction in the first year of life. In K. H. Rubin & H. S. Ross (Eds.), *Peer Relationships and Social Skills in Childhood* (pp. 11–39). New York: Springer-Verlag.

Hirschfeld, L. A., & Gelman, S. A. (Eds.). (1994). *Mapping the mind: Domain specificity in cognition and culture.* New York: Cambridge University Press.

Hoffman, M. L. (1975). Development of prosocial motivation: Empathy and guilt. In N. Eisenberg (Ed.), *The Development of Prosocial Behavior* (pp. 281–313). New York: Academic Press.

Holyoak, K., & P. Thagard (1995). *Mental leaps: Analogy in creative thought.* Cambridge, MA, MIT Press.

Howes, C. (1983). Patterns of friendship. *Child Development, 54,* 1041–1053.

Howes, C. (1988). Peer interaction of young children. *Monographs of the Society for Research in Child Development, 53* (Serial No. 217).

Hudson, J., & Fivush, R. (1991). Planning in the preschool years: The emergence of plans from general event knowledge. *Cognitive Development, 6,* 393–415.

Hudson, J., Fivush, R., & Kuebli, J. (1992). Scripts and episodes: The development of event memory. *Applied Cognitive Psychology. Special Issue: Memory in everyday settings, 6,* 483–505.

Hudson, J., Shapiro, L., & Sosa, B. (1995). Planning in the real world: Preschool children's scripts and plans for familiar events. *Child Development, 66,* 984–998.

Hudson, J., & Slackman, E. A. (1990). Children's use of scripts in inferential text processing. *Discourse Processes, 13,* 375–385.

Hudson, J., Sosa, B., & Shapiro, L. (1997). Scripts and plans: The development of preschool children's event knowledge and event planning. In S. L. Friedman & E. L. Scholnick (Eds.), *The developmental psychology of planning: Why, how and when do we plan?* (pp. 77–102). Mahwah, NJ: Erlbaum.

Humphrey, N. K. (1976). The social function of intellect. In P. P. G. Bateson & R. A. Hinde (Eds.), *Growing points in ethology* (pp. 303–317). Cambridge: Cambridge University Press.

Inagaki, K., & Sugiyama, K. (1988). Attributing human characteristics: Development changes in over- and underattribution. *Cognitive Development, 3,* 55–70.

Johnson, J. S., & Morton, J. (1991). *Biology and cognitive development: The case of face recognition* Cambridge, UK: Blackwell.

Johnson, S., Slaughter, V., & Carey, S. (1998). Whose gaze will infants follow? The elicitation of gaze-following in 12-month-olds. *Developmental Science, 1,* 233–238.

Karmiloff-Smith, A. (1992). *Beyond modularity: A developmental perspective on cognitive science.* Cambridge, MA: MIT Press.

Keil, F. C., & R. A. Wilson (Eds.). (2000). *Explanation and cognition.* Cambridge, MA: MIT Press.

Kellman, P. (1996). The origins of object perception. In R. Gelman & T. Au (Eds.), *Perceptual and cognitive development* (pp. 3–48). New York: Academic Press.

Kintsch, W., & Greene, E. (1978). The role of culture-specific schemata in the comprehension and recall of stories. *Discourse Processes, 1,* 1–13.

Koechlin, E., Dehaene, S., & Mehler, J. (1997). Numerical transformations in five-month-old human infants. *Mathematical Cognition, 3*(3), 89–104.

Kuhn, T. S. (1970). *The structure of scientific resolutions.* Chicago: University of Chicago Press.

Lee, K., & Karmiloff-Smith, A. (1996). The development of external symbol systems: The child as notator. In R. Gelman & T. Au (Eds.), *Perceptual and cognitive development. Handbook of perception and cognition* (2nd ed., pp. 185–211). New York: Academic Press.

Legerstee, M. (1991). The role of person and object in eliciting early imitation. *Journal of Experimental Child Psychology, 51,* 423–433.

Legerstee, M. (1992). A review of the animate-inanimate distinction in infancy. *Early Development and Parenting, 1,* 59–67.

Legerstee, M., Barna, J., & DiAdamo, C. (2000). Precursors to the development of intention at 6 months: Understanding people and their actions. *Developmental Psychology, 36,* 627–634.

Leslie, A. M. (1982). The perception of causality in infants. *Perception, 11,* 173–186.

Leslie, A. M. (1984). Infant perception of a manual pick-up event. *British Journal of Developmental Psychology, 2,* 19–32.

Leslie, A. M. (1987). Pretense and representation: The origins of "theory of mind." *Psychological Review, 94,* 412–426.

Leslie, A. M. (1988). The necessity of illusion: Perception and thought in infancy. In L. Weiskrantz (Ed.), *Thought without language* (pp. 185–210). Oxford: Clarendon.

Leslie, A. M. (1994). ToMM, ToBy, and Agency: Core architecture and domain specificity. In A. L. A. Hirschfeld, & S. A. Gelman (Eds.), *Mapping the mind: Domain specificity in cognition and culture* (pp. 119–148). New York: Cambridge University Press.

Leslie, A. M. (1995). A theory of agency. In D. S. Sperber, D. P. Premack, & A. J. Premack (Eds.), *Causal cognition: A multidisciplinary approach* (pp. 121–141). New York: Clarendon Press/Oxford University Press.

Leslie, A. M., & Keeble, S. (1987). Do six month-old infants perceive causality? *Cognition, 25,* 265–288.

Lillard, A. S., & Flavell, J. H. (1990). Young children's preference for mental state versus behavioral descriptions of human action. *Child Development, 61,* 731–741.

Locke, J. (1690). *An essay concerning human understanding.* A. D. Woozley (Ed.), Cleveland: Meridian Books, 1964.

Lucariello, J. (1987). Spinning fantasy: Themes, structure, and the knowledge base. *Child Development, 58,* 434–442.

Lucariello, J. (1990). Canonicality and consciousness in child narrative. In B. Britton & A. Pellegrini (Eds.), *Narrative thought and narrative language* (pp. 131–149). Hillsdale, NJ: Erlbaum.

Lucariello, J. (1994). Situational irony: A concept of events gone awry. *Journal of Experimental Psychology: General, 123,* 129–145.

Lucariello, J. (1998). Together wherever we go: The ethnographic child and the developmentalist. *Child Development, 69,* 355–358.

Lucariello, J., Kyratzis, A., & Engel, S. (1986). Context effects on lexical specificity in maternal and child discourse. *Journal of Child Language, 13,* 507–522.

Lucariello, J., Kyratzis, A., & Nelson, K. (1992). Taxonomic knowledge: What kind and when? *Child Development, 63,* 978–998.

Lucariello, J., & Mindolovich, C. (1995). The development of complex metarepresentational reasoning: The case of situational irony. *Cognitive Development, 10,* 551–576.

Lucariello, J., & Mindolovich, C. (in press). The best laid plans...: Beyond scripts are counter-scripts. *Journal of Cognition and Development.*

Lucariello, J., Mindolovich, C., & LeDonne, M. (2001). *Learning about sociocultural events: Defining the learning path and mental learning tools.* Manuscript submitted for publication.

Lucariello, J., & Nelson, K. (1985). Slot-filler categories as memory organizers for young children. *Developmental Psychology, 21,* 272–282.

Lucariello, J., & Nelson, K. (1986). Context effects on lexical specificity in maternal and child discourse. *Journal of Child Language, 13,* 507–522.

Lucariello, J., & Nelson, K. (1987). Remembering and planning talk between mothers and children. *Discourse Processes, 10,* 219–235.

Macario, J. F. (1991). Young children's use of color and classification: Foods and canonically colored objects. *Cognitive Development, 6,* 17–46.

Mandler, J. M., & McDonough, L. (1996). Drinking and driving don't mix: Inductive generalization in infancy. *Cognition, 59,* 307–335.

Marcus, G. F. (1996). Why do children say "breaked"? *Current Directions in Psychological Science, 5*(3), 81–85.

Marcus, G. F., Pinker, S., Ullman, M., Hollander, M., Rosen, T. J., & Xu, F. (1992). Overregularization in language acquisition. *Monographs of the Society for Research in Child Development, 57*(4, Serial No. 228), 1–182.

Markus, H. R., & Kitayama, S. (1991). Culture and the self: Implications for cognition, emotion, and motivation. *Psychological Review, 98,* 224–253.

Marler, P. (1991). The instinct to learn. In S. Carey & R. Gelman (Eds.), *The epigenesis of mind* (pp. 37–66). Hillsdale, NJ: Erlbaum.

Martin, G. B., & Clark, R. D. (1982). Distress crying in neonates: Species and peer specificity. *Developmental Psychology, 18,* 3–9.

Massey, C., & Gelman, R. (1988). Preschoolers' ability to decide whether a photographed unfamiliar object can move itself. *Developmental Psychology, 24*(3), 307–317.

Mather, M., & Johnson, M. K. (2000). Choice-supportive source monitoring: Do our decisions seem better to us as we age? *Psychology and Aging, 15,* 596–606.

Mather, M., Shafir, E., & Johnson, M. K. (2000). Misrembrance of options past: Source monitoring and choice. *Psychological Science, 11,* 132–138.

Meltzoff, A. N., & Moore, M. K. (1983). Newborn infants imitate adult facial gestures. *Child Development, 54,* 702–719.

Meltzoff, A. N., & Moore, M. K. (1989). Imitation in newborn infants: Exploring the range of gestures imitated and the underlying mechanisms. *Developmental Psychology, 25,* 954–962.

Michotte, A. (1963). *The perception of causality.* London: Methuen.

Miller, K. F., Smith, C. M., Zhu, J. & Zhang, H. (1995). Preschool origins of cross-national differences in mathematical competence: The role of number-naming systems. *Psychological Science, 1,* 56–60.

Mueller, E., & Silverman, N. (1989). Peer relations in maltreated children. In D. Cicchetti & V. Carlson (Eds.), *Child maltreatment: Theory and research on the causes and consequences of child abuse and neglect* (pp. 529–578). New York: Cambridge University Press.

Muir, D., & Hains, S. M. J. (1993). Infant sensitivity to perturbations in adult facial, vocal, tactile, and contingent stimulation during face-to-face interactions. In B. de Boysson-Bardies & S. de Schonen (Eds.), *Developmental neurocognition: Speech and face processing in the first year of life. NATO ASI series D: Behavioural and social sciences.* Vol. 69 (pp. 171–185). Netherlands, Kluwer Academic Publishers.

Murphy, C. M., & Messer, D. J. (1977). Mothers, infants and pointing: A study of gesture. In H. R. Schaffer (Ed.), *Studies in mother-infant interaction* (pp. 323–354). New York: Academic Press.

Nelson, D. A., & P. Marler (1993). Innate recognition of song in white-crowned sparrows: A role in selective vocal learning? *46,* 806–808.

Nelson, K. (1986). *Event knowledge: Structure and function in development.* Hillsdale, NJ: Erlbaum.

Nelson, K. (1997). Finding one's self in time. In J. G. Snodgrass & R. L. Thompson (Eds.), *The self across psychology: Self-recognition, self-awareness, and the self-concept. Annals of the New York Academy of Sciences* (Vol. 818, pp. 103–116). New York: New York Academy of Sciences.

Nelson, K. (2000). Narrative, time and the emergence of the encultured self. *Culture and*

Psychology, Special Issue: Changing times: Reflections on the development of self and culture, 6, 183–196.

Nelson, K., & Gruendel, J. (1981). Generalized event representations: Basic building blocks of cognitive development. In M. E. Lamb & A. L. Brown (Eds.), *Advances in developmental psychology* (Vol. 1, pp. 131–158). Hillsdale, NJ: Erlbaum.

Nelson, K., & Nelson, A. P. (1990). Category production in response to script and category cues by kindergarten and second-grade children. *Journal of Applied Developmental Psychology, 11,* 431–446.

Nelson, L. A. (1987). The recognition of facial expressions in the first two years of life: Mechanisms of development. *Child Development, 58,* 889–909.

Norman, D. A., & Shallice, T. (1986). Attention to action: Willed and automatic control of behavior. In R. J. Davidson, G. E. Schwartz, & D. Shapiro (Eds.), *Consciousness and self-regulation* (Vol. 4). New York: Plenum.

Nunes, T., Schliemann, A. D., & Carraher, D. W. (1993). *Street mathematics and school mathematics.* Cambridge: Cambridge University Press.

Oakes, L. M., & Cohen, L. B. (1995). Infant causal perception. In C. Rovee-Collier & L. P. Lipsitt (Eds.), *Advances in infancy research* (Vol. 9, pp. 1–54). Norwood, NJ: Ablex.

Ochs, E., & Schieffelin, B. (1984). Language acquisition and socialization: Three developmental stories and their implications. In R. Saweder & R. LeVine (Eds.), *Culture theory* (pp. 276–320). Cambridge: Cambridge University Press.

Piaget, J. (1970). Piaget's theory. In P. H. Mussen (Ed.), *Carmichael's manual of child psychology* (Vol. 1). New York: Wiley.

Pinker, S. (1991). Rules of language. *Science, 253,* 530–544.

Poulin-Dubois, D. (1999). Infants' distinction between animate and inanimate objects: The origins of naïve psychology. In P. Rochat (Ed.), *Early social cognition: Understanding others in*

the first months of life (pp. 257–280). Mahwah, NJ: Erlbaum.

Poulin Dubois, D., Lepage, A., & Ferland, D. (1996). Infants' concept of animacy. *Cognitive Development, 11,* 19–36.

Poulin-Dubois, D., & Shultz, T. R. (1988). The development of the understanding of human behavior: From agency to intentionality. In J. W. Astington, D. R. Olson, & P. L. Harris (Eds.), *Developing theories of mind* (pp. 109–125). Cambridge: Cambridge University Press.

Premack, D. (1990). The infants' theory of self-propelled objects. *Cognition, 36,* 1–16.

Ratner, H. H., Smith, B. S., & Dion, S. A. (1986). Development of memory for events. *Journal of Experimental Child Psychology, 41,* 411–428.

Reddy, V. (1991). Playing with others' expectations: Teasing and mucking around in the first year. In A. Whiten (Ed.), *Natural theories of mind: Evolution, development and simulation of everyday mindreading* (pp. 143–158). Cambridge, MA: Basil Blackwell.

Reed, H. J., & Lave, J. (1979). Arithmetic as a tool for investigating relations between culture and cognition. *American Ethnologist, 6,* 568–582.

Repacholi, B. M., & Gopnik, A. (1997). Early reasoning about desires: Evidence from 14- and 18-month olds. *Developmental Psychology, 33,* 12–21.

Reynolds, R. E., Taylor, M. A., Steffensen, M. S., Shirey, L. L., & Anderson, R. C. (1982). Cultural schemata and reading comprehension. *Reading Research Quarterly, 17,* 353–366.

Ricard, M., & Gouin-Decarie, T. (1989). Strategies of 9-10 month-old infants with a stranger and a novel object. *Revue Internationale de Psychologie Sociale, 2,* 97–111.

Robertson, S. S., & Suci, G. J. (1980). Event perception by children in the early stages of language production. *Child Development, 51,* 89–96.

Rochat, P., Morgan, R., & Carpenter, M. (1997). Young infants' sensitivity to movement information specifying social causality. *Cognitive Development, 12,* 441–465.

Ross, H. S., Conant, C., Cheyne, J. A., & Alevizos, E. (1992). Relationships and alliances in the social interaction of kibbutz toddlers. *Social Development, 1,* 1–17.

Ross, H. S., Lollis, S. P., & Elliott, C. (1982). Toddler-peer communication. In K. H. Rubin & H. S. Ross (Eds.), *Peer relationships and social skills in childhood* (pp. 73–98). New York: Springer-Verlag.

Rovee-Collier, C., & Bhatt, R. S. (1993). Evidence of long-term memory in infancy. In R. Vasta (Ed.), *Annals of child development* (pp. 1–45). London: Jessica Kingsley Publishers.

Rumelhart, D. E., & McClelland, J. L. (Eds.). (1986). *Parallel distributed processing.* Cambridge, MA: MIT Press.

Russell, J. (1995). At two with nature: Agency and the development of self-world dualism. In J. L. Bermudez & A. J. Marcel (Eds.), *The body and the self* (pp. 127–151). Cambridge, MA: MIT Press.

Saffran, J. R., Aslin, R. N., & Newport, E. L. (1996). Statistical learning by 8-month-old infants. *Science, 274,* 1926–1928.

Sagi, A., & Hoffman, M. L. (1976). Empathic distress in the newborn. *Developmental Psychology, 12,* 175–176.

Scaife, M., & Bruner, J. S. (1975). The capacity for joint visual attention in the infant. *Nature, 253,* (5489), 265–266.

Scholl, B. J., & Leslie, A. M. (1999). Explaining the infant's object concept: Beyond the perception/cognition dichotomy. In E. Lepore & Z. Pylyshyn (Eds.), *What is Cognitive Science?* (pp. 26–73). Oxford: blackwell.

Schult, C. A., & Wellman, H. M. (1997). Explaining human movements and actions: Children's understanding of the limits of psychological explanation. *Cognition, 62,* 291–324.

Schwartz, B., & Reisberg, D. (1991). *Learning and Memory.* New York: Norton.

Scribner, S., & Cole, M. (1981). *The psychology of literacy.* Cambridge, MA: Harvard University Press.

Segal, Z. V. (1988). Appraisal of the self-schema construction in cognitive models of depression. *Psychological Bulletin, 103,* 147–162.

Sexton, M. E. (1983). The development of the understanding of causality in infancy. *Infant Behavior and Development, 6,* 201–210.

Shultz, T. R. (1980). Development of the concept of intention. In W. A. Collins (Ed.), *Development of cognition, affect, and social relations. The Minnesota Symposia on Child Psychology* (Vol. 13, pp. 131–164). Hillsdale, NJ: Erlbaum.

Shultz, T. R., Wells, D., & Sarda, M. (1980). Development of the ability to distinguish intended actions from mistakes, reflexes, and passive movements. *British Journal of Social and Clinical Psychology, 19,* 301–310.

Siegler, R. S. (1991). *Children's thinking.* Englewood Cliffs, NJ, Prentice Hall.

Simner, M. L. (1971). Newborn's response to the cry of another infant. *Developmental Psychology, 5,* 136–150.

Skinner, B. F. (1938). *The behavior of organisms.* New York: Appleton-Century-Crofts.

Skinner, B. F. (1950). Are theories of learning necessary? *Psychological Review, 57,* 193–216.

Slotta, J. D., Chi, M. T. H., & Joram, E. (1995). Assessing students' misclassifications of physics concepts: An ontological basis for conceptual change. *Cognition and Instruction, 13,* 373–400.

Snow, C. E. (1986). Conversation with children. In P. Fletcher and M. Garman (Eds.), *Language acquisition* (pp. 69–89). Cambridge: Cambridge University Press.

Sorce, J. F., Emde, R. N., Campos, J. J., & Klinnert, M. D. (1985). Maternal emotional signaling: Its effect on the visual cliff behavior of 1-year olds. *Developmental Psychology, 21,* 195–200.

Spelke, E. S. (1991). Physical knowledge in infancy: Reflections on Piaget's theory. In S. Carey & R. Gelman (Eds.), *The epigenesis of mind: Essays on biology and cognition* (pp. 133–169). Hillsdale, NJ: Erlbaum.

Spelke, E. S. (2000). Core knowledge. *American Psychologist, 55*(11), 1233–1243.

Spelke, E. S., Breinlinger, K., Macomber, J., & Jacobson, K. (1992). Origins of knowledge. *Psychological Review, 99,* 605–632.

Spelke, E. S., & Hermer, L. (1995). Early cognitive development: Objects and space. In R. Gelman

& Au, T. (Eds.), *Perceptual and cognitive development* (pp. 72–114). San Diego, CA: Academic Press.

Spelke, E. S., Phillips, A., & Woodward, A. L. (1995). Infants' knowledge of object motion and human action. In D. Sperber, D. Premack, & A. J. Premack (Eds.), *Causal cognition: A multidisciplinary debate* (pp. 44–78). New York: Clarendon Press/Oxford University Press.

Sperber, D., & Wilson, D. (1986). *Relevance: Communication and cognition.* Cambridge, MA: Harvard University Press.

Starkey, P., Spelke, E. S., & Gelman, R. (1990). Numerical abstraction by human infants. *Cognition, 36*(2), 97–127.

Steffensen, M. S., Joag-dev, C., & Anderson, R. C. (1979). A cross-cultural perspective on reading comprehension. *Reading Research Quarterly, 15,* 10–29.

Stern, D. N. (1985). *The interpersonal world of the infant.* New York: Basic Books.

Termine, N. T., & Izard, C. E. (1988). Infants' responses to their mothers' expressions of joy and sadness. *Developmental Psychology, 24,* 223–229.

Tolchinsky-Landsmann, L. (1990). Early writing development: Evidence from different orthographic systems. In M. Spoolders (Ed.), *Literacy acquisition.* Norwood, NJ: Ablex.

Tomasello, M., & Barton, M. E. (1994). Learning words in nonostensive contexts. *Developmental Psychology, 30,* 639–650.

Tomasello, M., Strosberg, R., & Akhtar, N. (1996). Eighteen-month old children learn words in nonostensive contexts. *Journal of Child Language, 23,* 157–176.

Trabasso, T., & Stein, N. L. (1996). Narrating, representing, and remembering event sequences. In P. van den Broek, P. J. Bauer, & T. Bourg (Eds.), *Event comprehension and representation* (pp. 237–270). Hillsdale, NJ: Erlbaum.

Trabasso, T., van den Broek, P., & Suh, S. (1989). Logical necessity and transitivity of causal relations in stories. *Discourse Processes, 12,* 1–25.

Trevarthen, C., & Hubley, P. (1978). Secondary intersubjectivity: Confidence, confiding, and acts of meaning in the first year. In A. Lock (Ed.), *Action, gesture and symbol: The emergence of language* (pp. 183–229). New York: Academic Press.

Tversky, A., & D. Kahneman (1973). Availability: A heuristic for judging frequency and probability. *Cognitive Psychology, 5*(2), 207–232.

Vandell, D. L., Wilson, K. S., & Buchanan, N. R. (1980). Peer interaction in the first year of life: An examination of its structure, content, and sensitivity to toys. *Child Development, 51,* 481–488.

Vinden, P. G. (1996). Junin Quechua children's understanding of mind. *Child Development, 67,* 1707–1716.

Vinden, P. G. (1999). Children's understanding of mind and emotion: A multi-cultural study. *Cognition and Emotion, 13,* 19–48.

Vinden, P. G., & Astington, J. W. (2000). Culture and understanding other minds. In S. Baron-Cohen, H. Tager-Flusberg, & D. J. Cohen (Eds.), *Understanding other minds: Perspectives from developmental cognitive neuroscience* (pp. 503–519). Oxford: Oxford University Press.

Watson, J. S. (1972). Smiling, cooing, and "the game." *Merrill-Palmer Quarterly, 18,* 323–339.

Watson, J. S., & Ramey, C. T. (1987). Reactions to response-contingent stimulation in early infancy. In J. Oates & S. Sheldon (Eds.), *Cognitive development in infancy* (pp. 77–85). Hillsdale, NJ: Erlbaum.

Wellman, H. M., & Banerjee, M. (1991). Mind and emotion: Children's understanding of the emotional consequences of beliefs and desires. *British Journal of Developmental Psychology, Special Issue: Perspectives on the child's theory of mind, 9,* 191–214.

Wellman, H. M., & Bartsch, K. (1994). Before belief: Children's early psychological theory. In C. Lewis & P. Mitchell (Eds.), *Children's early understanding of mind: Origins and development* (pp. 331–354). Hillsdale, NJ: Erlbaum.

Wellman, H. M., Cross, D., & Watson, J. (2001). Meta-analysis of theory-of-mind development: The truth about false belief. *Child Development, 3,* 655–684.

Wellman, H. M., Hollander, M., & Schult, C. A. (1996). Young children's understanding of thought bubbles and of thoughts. *Child Development, 67,* 768–788.

Wellman, H. M., & Woolley, J. D. (1990). From simple desires to ordinary beliefs: The early development of everyday psychology. *Cognition, 35,* 245–275.

Whiten, A., & Byrne, R. W. (1988). Tactical deception in primates. *Behavioural and Brain Sciences, 11,* 233–273.

Wilson, R. A., & Keil, F. C. (1998). The shadows and shallows of explanation. *Minds and Machines, 8,* 137–159.

Wilson, R. A., & Keil, F. C. (2000). Shadows and shallows of explanation. In F. C. Keil & R. A. Wilson (Eds.), *Explanation and cognition* (pp. 87–114). Cambridge, MA: MIT Press.

Woodward, A. L. (1998). Infants selectively encode the goal object of an actor's reach. *Cognition, 69,* 1–34.

Wynn, K. (1992). Addition and subtraction by human infants. *Nature, 358,* 749–750.

Wynn, K. (1995). Infants possess a system of numerical knowledge. *Current Directions in Psychological Science, 4,* 172–177.

Xu, F., & Spelke, E. S. (2000). Large number discrimination in 6-month-old infants. *Cognition, 74,* B1–B11.

Yik, M. S. M., & Russell, J. A. (1999). Interpretation of faces: A cross-cultural study of a prediction from Fridlund's thoery. *Cognition and Emotion, 1,* 93–104.

Yu, Y., & Nelson, K. (1993). Slot-filler and conventional category organization in young Korean children. *International Journal of Behavioral Development, 16,* 1–14.

Zacks, R., & Hasher, L. (2001). Frequency processing: A twenty-five year perspective. In P. Sedlmeier & T. Betsch (Eds.), *Frequency processing and cognition.* New York: Oxford University Press.

Zur, O., & Gelman, R. (2001, April). Young children's understanding of the inverse relation between addition and subtraction. Poster session presented at the Bi-Annual Meeting of the Society for Research in Child Development. Minneapolis, MN.

CHAPTER 11

Language Acquisition

CYNTHIA FISHER AND LILA R. GLEITMAN

INTRODUCTION: OUTLINE OF THE TASK

Language learning begins with a perceptual task of startling complexity. Faced with the continuous flow of speech, infants during the first months of life learn about the sound structure of their language and begin to identify words. A number of intricate problems must be solved along the way, including compensation for many sources of systematic variability in the speech stream. The infant's task is to segment relevant units (of many sizes) from the continuous flow and to store and categorize these—implicitly, of course. The child learning English, for example, must discover that this language is built out of such sound segments as t, p, and a and that these occur within such larger units as *tap, apt,* and *pat.* This achievement sets the stage for other aspects of language acquisition. Armed with even a few recognizable words, a child can begin to observe how those words are distributed in sentences and relative to communicative contexts. These observations are the primary data for the acquisition of the syntactic and semantic organization of the native language.

Issues of category discovery and labeling arise at every level of linguistic organization. The learner cannot know in advance whether *tap* or *apt* will be permitted sound sequences; whether 'dog' is to be pronounced *dog, chien,* or *perro;* which words are nouns (*lightning*), verbs (*flee*), or both (*storm*); how these words are grouped into phrases; whether the subject will precede or follow the verb; or whether word order (rather than case-marking morphology) is used to signal semantic roles in sentences. Moreover, not all learners get the same fair shot at data for these discoveries. Owing to preexisting differences in their life circumstances, children receive systematically differing samples of the exposure language in extralinguistic contexts that also vary. Language learning is not only robust over such environmental differences; it is rapid, accurate, and efficient. As a first indication of this, average children all over the world have acquired a vocabulary of roughly 10,000 words by the fifth birthday (Carey, 1978); by this age, virtuoso sentences like "Remember the game that you told me last night on the phone you would buy me?" are routine accomplishments.

How do children accomplish this learning? Three fundamental components of this problem structure this review: First, children must find the particular linguistic forms used in their community. Second, they must be able to entertain concepts of the kind that are expressed in languages. Third, they must accomplish a specific mapping between these linguistic elements and the ideas that they are used to evoke. Despite this tripartite partitioning of the learning problem for language, its tasks really cannot be separated so simply. Our discussions of the linguistic-formal and conceptual bases of language learning necessarily engage with questions about word and structure mapping at every level. But in each part of the discussion, we will ask about the learner's initial states. That is, what can children find in the environment before learning a particular language? The need to understand these primitives is obvious to all commentators, whatever their other theoretical disagreements. In Chomsky's words,

> One has to try to find the set of primitives which have the empirical property that the child can more or less tell in the data itself whether they apply before it knows the grammar. . . . So now take grammatical relations, say the notion *subject*. The question is: is it plausible to believe that in the flow of speech, in the noises that are presented, it is possible to pick out something of which one can say: here is the subject? That seems wildly implausible. Rather it seems that somehow you must be able to identify the subject on the basis of other things you've identified, maybe configurational notions which are somehow constructed out of accessible materials or maybe out of semantic notions, which are primitive for the language faculty. (Chomsky, 1982, 118–119)

These primitives, whatever they turn out to be, are part of the human child's endowment for language learning—the set of capacities, mechanisms, and limitations that permit children to find structure in the linguistic input or, if need be, to impose structure on their own invented gestural systems for expressing their ideas. Theories of language learning are distinguished in no small way by what they take these primitives to be, just as are theories of learning in other domains (see Chaps. 6 and 10, this volume).

To learn a language is, by definition, to acquire a set of pairings between sounds or more abstract linguistic structures and their meanings. Thus for English it must be learned that the phonological sequence /siy/ is paired with the meaning 'apprehend visually,' for Spanish that it is paired with 'yes,' and for French 'if.' The seven properties of language listed next are basic to language knowledge and use, and so set the minimal agenda to which any viable theory of acquisition must answer.

1. *Novelty.* Each language provides an infinite set of form-meaning pairings. Therefore, children learn a language "creatively," developing an understanding of the structure of their language that is abstract enough to produce and understand new sentences.

2. *Compositionality.* Language accomplishes its unbounded communicative goals without overrunning the limitations of memory and categorization by composing each message out of lawfully recombinatory elements at several levels of complexity, arranged hierarchically. The lowest levels in this hierarchy are speech-sound categories, and the highest are sentences and discourses. For example, languages decompose unitary events (say, that of a kangaroo jumping) into parts (e.g., the doer, the action) which then are combined in a sentence ("The kangaroo jumps").

3. *Expressiveness.* Toddlers bother to learn a language not (or not solely) because of its pleasing formal character but because it is a vehicle supporting the planning and organization of cognitive life, and for communicating with others. Language is meaningful and referential, expressing no end of messages about the things, stuff, properties, acts, states, processes, relations, and abstractions of which human minds can conceive.

4. *Sketchiness.* To be useable, language is necessarily sketchy in its conveyance of thought, proceeding in broad brushstrokes, by hints and partial clues. For instance, we refer to a complex observed motion, say of a baseball, with a restricted description of its path and manner of motion, for example, "He bounced out to third" or "looped one to short left." We make reference by catch-as-catch-can methods, as the waiter who famously told another that "The ham sandwich wants his check" (Lakoff, 1987). We organize discourse via successive utterances whose interconnections the listener must reconstruct by flights of inference (SHE: "I'm leaving you"; HE: "Who *is* he?"; Sperber & Wilson, 1986).

5. *Ambiguity.* Overt clues to how sentences' parts fit together are often missing or subtle, or unavailable early in the linear transmittal of the sentence. We notice these ambiguities mainly on occasions where the competing outcomes are amusing or bizarre, such as in the ambiguous headlines that linguists use to liven up their classes: *Drunk gets nine months in violin case, Prostitutes appeal to Pope,* or *British left waffles on Falkland Islands* (Pinker, 1994). In most cases, the alternative interpretations that pop up in the course of listening go unnoticed by fluent adults. This points to the next crucial property of language.

6. *Sociality.* Language use of any kind requires implicit understanding of the goals and intents of others. When a speaker says *I had my car washed,* one must understand plausibilities in the world enough to guess that this was a voluntary act. The same structure is interpreted differently in *I had my car stolen* but must be *re*interpreted if the speaker is a shady character trying to cheat the insurance company. Words and sentences are used intentionally and symbolically with the goal of directing another's attention toward the ideas that the speaker has in mind. Therefore, some communality, some shared "theory of mind" and shared social context are necessary to get language learning and use off the ground.

7. *Transmissability.* Language is instantiated in processing systems that allow messages to be transmitted between speaker and listener rapidly and relatively errorlessly. This efficiency of transmission is achieved because the interpretive options made available as the sentence unfolds in time are resolved "on-line" by the human listener integrating across several convergent sources of evidence, including situational, lexical, and syntactic (see Trueswell, Tanenhaus, & Garnsey, 1994, among others).

WHERE LEARNING BEGINS: FINDING LANGUAGE IN THE SPEECH STREAM

Faced with the unbroken flow of language use in the environment, infants discover the sound structure of their native language. The analysis of speech is a daunting problem. Every acoustic cue used to identify speech sounds is influenced by many other factors, including the identity of upcoming sounds, overall utterance prosody, speech rate, and even the speaker's voice. Identifying words requires disentangling these interacting sources of information. As we see next, the infant begins to solve these problems using a formidable capacity for taking in and remembering information about the details and distributions of speech sounds, even before they are assigned any meaning.

Some analysis of speech is logically and temporally prior to the tasks of learning the lexical items and syntactic structures of the language. But learning about sound is by no means irrelevant to other tasks of language acquisition. One connection is obvious: The child's detection of phonological systematicity *creates* the higher-level linguistic units whose distribution relative to one another and to things and events in the world constitutes the primary data for syntactic and semantic learning. In addition, processes involved in the identification of speech sounds interact with other levels of linguistic knowledge. Word identification processes make use of various partially predictive top-down cues to help reduce uncertainty, and the sound patterns of words and utterances play a role (for better and for worse) in the classification of words into grammatical categories and the grouping of linguistic elements in memory (Kelly & Martin, 1994; Morgan & Demuth, 1995). Work in this area provides some of the most compelling evidence for the opportunistic and formal nature of language acquisition: Learners are influenced by multiple types of systematicity in languages and allow information at one level of linguistic analysis to affect other levels.

Categorization of Speech Sounds

The Starting Point

Infants are born with a variety of phonetically relevant perceptual capacities. Early in the first year, they readily discriminate speech sounds that fall into different phonetic categories (e.g., discriminating the syllable /ba/ from /pa/) but typically fail to discriminate differences within phonetic categories (e.g., discriminating acoustically different tokens of the syllable /ba/; see Werker & Lalonde, 1988, for a review). The boundaries of young infants' phonetic categories are the same as those commonly found in studies of adult speech perception.

Infants show this sensitivity to phonetic contrasts even for distinctions that are not honored in the language that they are learning.

Each language's sound system relies on only some of the possible phonetic contrasts; other possible phonetic distinctions are ignored, that is, not used *contrastively* to differentiate words in the language. For example, Hindi distinguishes two t-like sounds, a dental [t] and a retroflex [T]. In English both of these sounds are heard as instances of the same category /t/, and English-speaking adults have difficulty discriminating the two. English-exposed 8-month-olds, on the other hand, readily discriminate the dental and retroflex /t/s (Werker & Lalonde, 1988; see Eimas, 1975; Trehub, 1976; Werker & Tees, 1984, for related findings). Infants' ability to discriminate categories not used contrastively in their languages, and not reliably controlled by their parents, tells us that these speech sound categories are a built-in part of the auditory perceptual capacities of the infant. The initial set of phonetic categories is not unique to humans: Other mammals, including chinchillas and macaques (Kuhl & Miller, 1975; Kuhl & Padden, 1982, 1983), exhibit the same peaks of discriminability along dimensions of phonetically relevant variation. Human languages are made out of the perceptual categories that young humans (and other mammals) find easy to discriminate.

Effects of Language Experience

Language experience reduces the set of phonetic distinctions to those used contrastively in a particular language. By 10 to 12 months, infants' ability to discriminate nonnative contrasts is sharply reduced (Werker & Tees, 1984).[1] In a few short months, infants redirect their attention to contrasts relevant to their native language phonology (Jusczyk, 1997; Liberman, Harris, Hoffman, & Griffith,

---

[1] The irrelevant contrasts are not entirely destroyed: Adults are not completely hopeless at relearning nonnative contrasts when acquiring a second language, although they rarely achieve native competence in discriminating them (e.g., Pisoni, Aslin, Perey, Hennessy, 1982).

1957; Pisoni, Lively, & Logan, 1994). A traditional assumption is that semantic learning could drive this reorganization: Infants could learn to ignore phonetic differences that do not signal meaning differences (e.g., Bloomfield, 1933), using pairs of words that differ minimally in sound but contrast in meaning (*bear/pear, rent/lent*) to determine the phonemic inventory of their native language. This notion has some initial plausibility to the extent that infants begin to attach meanings to some words before their first birthdays.

However, there are reasons to believe that semantic learning is not the initial force that drives the creation of phonological categories. First, although it is hard to estimate infant comprehension vocabularies, it seems unlikely that the word comprehension skills of 10-month-olds are sufficient to fix the phonemic inventory of their language in such a short time. Word recognition is hard, and young listeners are notoriously prone to error (Gerken, Murphy, & Aslin, 1995; Stager & Werker, 1997); yet infants uniformly move to a language-specific pattern in consonant perception between 10 and 12 months of age. Second, some migrations toward native-language targets happen before infants learn the meanings of any words. Kuhl, Williams, Lacerda, Stevens, and Lindblom (1992) found that 6-month-olds learning English and Swedish showed systematically different patterns of discrimination among synthetic vowels and that these differences were predictable from English and Swedish speakers' judgments of vowel typicality. Such an early effect of language experience suggests that pre-semantic perceptual learning changes the child's phonetic inventory. Third, the adult consonant inventory is not simply a subset of the infant's. Languages differ not only in which of a built-in set of possible speech sounds are contrastive in their phonologies, but also in the detailed phonetic realization of each category (Farnetani, 1997; Keating, 1985; Lisker & Abramson, 1964; Pierrehumbert, 1990). Learning a language's phonological categories involves adjusting the weighting of various acoustic cues and the boundaries between phonetic categories to coincide with the category structure used by its speakers. These considerations suggest that the discovery of native-language phonology relies heavily on perceptual learning about native-language sounds, without early feedback from the semantic system. Kellman (Chap. 7, this volume) argues that much perceptual learning across domains occurs as a result of simple exposure and requires no feedback.

The Role of Distributional Information

What information, other than word meaning, could drive the change in speech sound categorization? It might be that infants could learn about the functional significance of various sound properties by observing their distribution in the speech that they hear, without initial recourse to meaning. This could happen in at least two ways.

First, consonant and vowel tokens in different languages differ in their distributions along various acoustic dimensions. Sounds common in some languages are rare in others, and areas of the phonetic space in which different languages make different numbers of distinctions (e.g., one category versus two or three) will differ correspondingly in whether speech sound tokens cluster around one, two, or three frequency modes (Lisker & Abramson, 1964). Infants listening to different languages thus hear different distributions of acoustic tokens; this information could help to redistribute their attention within the phonetic perceptual space (e.g., Guenther & Gjaja, 1996; Jusczyk, 1997; Kuhl, 1994; Maye & Gerken, 2000).

Second, sounds that are not contrastive can be defined not only as those never used to differentiate semantically distinct words but also as phonetically similar sounds that occur in *complementary distributions* in the language being learned (e.g., Chomsky & Halle, 1968). Such sounds become *allophones* of the same language-specific phonemic category. For example, in English we do not use nasal and nonnasal vowels contrastively (although other languages do). Instead, vowel nasalization in English is predictable from context. Vowels preceding nasal consonants (e.g., the /i/ in *bean*) are nasalized, and vowels in other contexts are not (e.g., the /i/ in *bead*). Vowel nasalization is not contrastive in English because its occurrence is redundant with a following nasal consonant. Systematic phonetic variation that is not contextually predictable is contrastive in the language being learned. Distributional learning—about what sounds occur frequently in one's language and where they occur—is thus directly relevant to the categorization of speech sounds (Guenther & Gjaja, 1996; Jusczyk, 1997; Kuhl & Meltzoff, 1996; Lotto, 2000; McClelland & Elman, 1986; Werker & Tees, 1999).

More generally, the *phonotactic* patterns that describe how speech sounds can be ordered in a particular language interact with speech sound categorization. For example, in English, words never begin with the sequence /tl/, although it occurs elsewhere (e.g., *little*). By 9 months, English-listening infants prefer to listen to sequences of unknown words from their own language than to Dutch words that violate the phonotactic rules of English (Jusczyk, Friederici, Wessels, Svenkerud, & Jusczyk, 1993; see also Friederici & Wessels, 1993). Infants also pick up phonotactic regularities that are less absolute than the proscription of initial /tl/ in English: By 9 months they listen longer to made-up words with frequent rather than infrequent (though legal) sequences of segments (Jusczyk, Luce, & Charles-Luce, 1994). The language processing system remains sensitive

to phonotactic probabilities throughout life; thus adults pick up new sequencing regularities through speaking practice (Dell, Reed, Adams, & Meyer, 2000) or listening practice (Chambers & Onishi, 2001).

Adults use phonotactic patterns to help identify speech sounds. Because /tl/ never begins English words, for example, a sound ambiguous between an /l/ and an /r/ will be heard as an /r/ if it follows an initial /t/ (e.g., Elman & McClelland, 1988). Given a highly constraining context, listeners hear sounds with no acoustic basis at all; this includes the phoneme restoration effect which allows us to interpret white noise as a consonant in the context of a familiar word (Samuels, 1997). Such context effects characterize language processing systems at every level of linguistic analysis: Wherever possible, information about how elements are combined into higher-level units plays a role in the identification of those elements. As infants acquire the phonotactic regularities of a language, knowledge of what sequences are possible or frequent should influence their ability to identify speech sounds. Top-down effects on perceptual identification accuracy are not unique to human speech perception. Perceptual category learning in many domains affects our perception of the categorized objects: Objects in the same category are judged more similar; objects in different categories are judged less similar, whether the stimuli are faces, nonsense objects, or speech sounds (Goldstone, Lippa, & Shiffrin, 2001; Chap. 7, this volume).

Segmentation and Spoken Word Identification

The foregoing discussion of distributional learning about speech has already invoked higher-level linguistic units. Phonotactic regularities depend on position in syllables and words, for example. This suggests the kind of chicken-and-egg learning problem that plagues every area of language acquisition: To learn the phoneme categories, infants must learn about the distributions of phonetically relevant sounds; to learn the relevant distributional facts, infants must identify the boundaries of syllables and words. But how could anybody identify words without having a phoneme inventory to begin with? Where do these units come from?

The Starting Point

Segmentation of continuous speech into any sort of units is more problematic than it might seem. Even the syllable is not acoustically well defined (see Brent & Cartwright, 1996; Eimas, 1999; Lass, 1984; Vroomen, van den Bosch, & de Gelder, 1998). Vowels have more acoustic energy (i.e., are louder) than consonants, and this profile creates a salient alternation between high- and low-energy sounds in speech. The difficulty lies in how to syllabify consonants at the edges of syllables. Different languages have different rules about where syllable boundaries fall. Sub-lexical units like the syllable also play different roles in the on-line processing of different languages by adults, depending on the rhythmic structure of the language (Cutler, Mehler, Norris, & Segui, 1986). The real perceptual obscurity of syllable boundaries can be seen in word-perception errors that sometimes violate the presumed boundaries of syllables (as in "This guy is falling" heard instead of "The sky is falling").

Despite the perceptual pitfalls and cross-linguistic variability of syllabification, it is likely that something like the syllable is a fundamental unit of speech perception for young infants. This conclusion is based partly on failures to find evidence of segmentation into smaller, phoneme-like units (Eimas, 1999; Jusczyk, 1997; Mehler, Segui, & Frauenfelder, 1981) but also on evidence that newborn infants categorize speech sequences by syllable number (e.g., 2 versus 3;

Bijeljac-Babic, Bertoncini, & Mehler, 1993), stress pattern (Sansavini, Bertoncini, & Giovanelli, 1997), and shared syllables (Eimas, 1999; Jusczyk, Jusczyk, Kennedy, Schomberg, & Koenig, 1995). Infants' representations of speech contain information that allows them to detect its rhythmic structure. Finding the edges of syllables may depend on language-specific phonotactic learning (Brent & Cartwright, 1996; Church, 1987; Smith & Pitt, 1999; Vroomen et al., 1998).

Finding Words

The perceptual problems involved in finding words have been canvassed many times. Spoken words are not separated by silences or other obvious cues to their boundaries, as written words are separated by white spaces on the page. There are some cues to the location of word boundaries, including word-position effects on the duration of segments (Klatt, 1976), allophonic variations unique to beginnings or endings of words or syllables (Gow & Gordon, 1995; Jusczyk, 1997; Nakatani & Dukes, 1977), stress patterns (Cutler, 1990), and the phonotactic regularities discussed earlier. These prelexical cues are language-specific; thus they have to be learned. Even once learned, moreover, such cues leave considerable ambiguity about the location of word boundaries. For this reason, theories of adult spoken word recognition typically assume that identification of word boundaries is in part a result of the identification of a familiar word, rather than a prerequisite to it (Lively, Pisoni, & Goldinger, 1994).

Distributional Evidence for Word Boundaries. Evidence now suggests that infants, like adults, may identify word boundaries by recognizing words as familiar sound sequences. Eight-month-olds listened to an uninterrupted sequence of nonsense syllables constructed by randomly concatenating four nonsense words (e.g., *bidaku*padotigolabu*bidaku*...; Saffran, Aslin, & Newport, 1996). The stimuli were presented with no pauses or variations in stress, so as to offer no clues to word boundaries other than the high transitional probability linking syllables within but not across word boundaries. In test trials, infants heard words from this artificial language on some trials and "part-words" on other trials. Part-words were sequences that had occurred during the familiarization phase, by chance concatenation of the four words that formed the basis of the training language. Infants listened longer to the relatively novel part-words. Later experiments controlled the frequency of word and part-word test items, to ensure that transitional probability, and not simple frequency, was responsible for infants' preference for part-words (Aslin, Saffran & Newport, 1998). These findings are akin to the use of kinetic cues in segmenting coherent objects in the visual world: An object whose parts move together against a variable background is readily perceived as a single object (e.g., Kellman & Spelke, 1983). Similarly, the infants in these listening experiments detected repeating sequences whose syllabic parts remained in the same relationship to one another across different speech contexts.

This ability to pick up on contingencies in the input is specific neither to language nor to human learning: Infants show the same ability to learn sequential patterns among musical notes (Saffran, Johnson, Aslin, & Newport, 1999), and tamarin monkeys carve internally coherent "words" from a stream of syllables (Hauser, Newport, & Aslin, 2001). Younger infants, however, are probably unable to find words as repeating sound patterns in the speech stream: 7.5-month-olds, but not younger infants, preferred to listen to isolated words that they recently heard presented in connected speech over words not recently presented (Jusczyk & Aslin, 1995).

Six-month-olds also show no sensitivity to the phonotactic regularities of their native language (Jusczyk et al., 1993). Such findings suggest that the ability to identify and remember a sequence of phonological segments—well enough to identify a word—does not become reliable until after 7 months of age.

Rhythmic Cues for Word Segmentation. Despite their inability to recognize particular sequences of phonemes or syllables reliably, younger infants are not at a loss to detect familiar units of any kind when presented with continuous speech. Six-month-olds use consistent metrical or rhythmic patterns in speech to create coherent word-like units (Morgan & Saffran, 1995; Morgan, 1996). Six- and 9-month-old infants were trained to turn their heads whenever they heard a buzz, to catch sight of a visual reward. These buzzes were presented against a background of syllable sequences varying in segmental consistency and stress pattern. Six-month-olds were slower to detect the buzzes if they interrupted two-syllable sequences presented with a consistent trochaic (strong-weak, as in *baby*) or iambic (weak-strong, as in *delay*) stress pattern than if the buzzes occurred at the boundaries of such units. This was true even if the syllables picked out by the consistent pattern varied in their order (e.g., *KOgati*...*GAkoti*...); 9-month-olds required both consistent ordering and consistent stress to hear these nonsense syllables as a word-like, uninterruptible unit. Before they can reliably identify and remember a sequence of phonemes, infants can hear a repeating stress pattern. This rough analysis of the speech stream would provide infants with some starting units that could make possible a finer-grained analysis of words.

Infants quickly pick up the typical stress patterns of words in their language. By 9 months, infants have figured out that strong syllables tend to begin words in English and therefore prefer to listen to sets of unfamiliar words with a strong-weak stress pattern rather than a weak-strong pattern (Jusczyk, Cutler, & Redanz, 1993), and find novel trochaic bi-syllables more cohesive in the buzz-detection task just mentioned (Morgan, 1996). Infants aged 7.5 months old are better able to detect words in continuous speech if the words have a strong-weak stress pattern, and they can be fooled by chance repetitions of adjacent strong and weak syllables that happen not to constitute a word (Jusczyk, 1997). The advantage for strong-weak words in word-detection experiments suggests that infants use their knowledge of the frequency of strong-weak bisyllabic words in English as a heuristic to find new words. This is the metrical segmentation strategy proposed by Cutler (1990) as a bias in English word identification. Early input would support this heuristic: Investigations of spontaneous child-directed speech show that the vast majority of bisyllabic English words have a trochaic stress pattern (Morgan, 1996; Swingley, 2000).

Phonotactic Cues to Word Boundaries. By 9 months, infants use phonotactic regularities to help carve words out of continuous speech. For example, the consonant sequence /ft/ occurs relatively frequently within English words (e.g., *lift, after*); /vt/ is rare within words but common across word boundaries (e.g., *love to*). Mattys and Jusczyk (2001) embedded nonsense words in texts so that their edges were marked by phonotactic sequences either common within words (therefore bad for word segmentation) or rare within words (therefore good for word segmentation). Nine-month-olds detected the words, later showing a listening preference for the familiarized nonwords presented in isolation, only if the new words were edged with good phonotactic word segmentation cues. Infants, like adults (McQueen, 1998), use phonotactic rules and probabilities in word segmentation.

How do infants learn about phonotactic regularities? One possibility is that they learn which sound sequences can begin and end words by observing what sound sequences begin and end whole utterances (Brent & Cartwright, 1996). As we next discuss, utterance boundaries are well marked by reliable prosodic cues; these boundaries display many (though not all) of the possible word onsets and offsets. Another possibility is that infants detect regularities in the sound patterns of words or syllables by detecting repeating sequences of phonemes, just as by 8 months they can detect repeating sequences of syllables.

Summary: Multiple Constraints. The picture that emerges is one of a perceptual learning process sensitive to interacting distributional regularities at many levels of analysis. Infants detect and make use of a variety of probabilistic cues that make some analyses of a speech sequence into words more likely than others. These cues include the internal consistency of phoneme or syllable sequences within familiar words, the typical stress patterns of native language words, and probabilistic phonotactic regularities.

The Role of Sound in Syntactic Analysis

As soon as some words can be identified, children can begin learning how those words are used, both syntactically (how they are distributed with respect to other words and phrases) and semantically (how they function to convey meaning). These facts feed back into the word identification process, allowing word selection to profit from knowledge of semantic and syntactic constraints. In this section we see that the sound patterns of words and phrases are relevant to syntactic processing as well. Just as English-learning infants (and adults) find it easier to identify the boundaries of bisyllabic words with a trochaic (strong-weak) than with an iambic (weak-strong) metrical pattern, sound-pattern information contributes probabilistically to the identification of a word's grammatical category and the grouping of words within phrases and clauses.

Prosodic Bootstrapping

Utterances have a characteristic rhythmic and intonational structure known as prosodic structure. Prosodic phonology proposes a hierarchy of phonological units (e.g., utterances, phrases, words) that define the domains of phonological rules (Selkirk, 1984). These prosodic units tend to correspond to syntactic units. The prosodic bootstrapping hypothesis proposes that infants' perception of the familiar rhythmic and intonational structure of phrases and utterances in their language guides analysis of the syntax of the native language (Gleitman, Gleitman, Landau, & Wanner, 1988; Gleitman & Wanner, 1982; Morgan, 1986; Morgan & Demuth, 1995; Morgan, Meier, & Newport, 1987; Morgan & Newport, 1981).

Acoustic Bracketing of the Utterance. The usefulness of prosodic bracketing of speech is most obvious at the level of the whole utterance. The boundaries of utterances are well marked by salient acoustic cues, both in adult- and infant-directed speech. In adult-directed English, words tend to be lengthened at the ends of utterances or major phrases (Cooper & Paccia-Cooper, 1980; Klatt, 1976); pitch tends to fall near the end of an utterance (Cooper & Sorenson, 1977); and pauses occur at utterance or major phrase boundaries (Gee & Grosjean, 1983; Scott, 1982). The same kinds of features are readily measured in spontaneous speech to infants (Bernstein Ratner, 1986; Fisher & Tokura, 1996; Morgan, 1986). These acoustic properties help utterances to cohere as perceptual units for adult listeners. Lengthening and pitch changes cause adults to perceive a subjective pause in speech in the absence of a silent pause (Duez, 1993; Wightman, Shattuck-Hufnagel, Ostendorf, & Price, 1992) and can disambiguate syntactically ambiguous sentences (Beach, 1991; Kjelgaard & Speer, 1999; Klatt, 1976; Lehiste, 1973; Scott, 1982).

Infants are also sensitive to these prosodic contours: 6- to 9-month-olds listened longer to samples of infant-directed speech with pauses inserted at sentence boundaries rather than within these constituents (Hirsh-Pasek et al., 1987; Kemler-Nelson, Hirsh-Pasek, Jusczyk, & Wright-Cassidy, 1989). Apparently, infants detect pitch and timing changes that predict upcoming pauses, and pauses not preceded by these changes sound unnatural to them. In a habituation task, 2-month-olds were better able to remember the phonetic content of words produced as a single utterance than of the same words produced in a list or as two sentence fragments (Mandel, Jusczyk, & Kemler-Nelson, 1994; Mandel, Kemler-Nelson, & Jusczyk, 1996). The familiar rhythm and melody of utterances helps infants to organize speech in memory, serving the perceptual grouping function proposed by Morgan et al. (1987).

Acoustic Bracketing of Phrases within Utterances. Can prosody hint at the boundaries of within-utterance phrases? Evidence suggests it can, but this evidence also suggests important limitations on prosody as a source of information about syntactic structure. Sentences in speech to infants and toddlers are short (Newport, Gleitman, & Gleitman, 1977; Snow, 1972) and so offer few opportunities for clear acoustic markings of within-utterance phrase boundaries. But where there are multiple syllables preceding a major phrase boundary, some acoustic cues to boundary location can be detected (Fisher & Tokura, 1996; Gerken, Jusczyk, & Mandel, 1994). Infants are sensitive to these subtle within-sentence cues as well as to the grosser prosodic patterns that group words into utterances. In several studies, 9-month-olds listened longer to sentences with pauses inserted between the subject and the verb phrase than to sentences with pauses inserted after the verb (Jusczyk et al., 1992; Gerken et al., 1994), though only when these sentences had relatively long, full noun phrase subjects (*the caterpillar;* see also Read & Schreiber, 1982).

The Discovery of Prosody and Syntax. A number of problems arise in developing an account of the role of prosody in early syntactic analysis of input speech. The first is that prosody and syntax do not always coincide, and some syntactic boundaries have no prosodic marking at all. This suggests that prosody can serve only as one among many kinds of data that could guide analysis of linguistic elements. As Morgan et al. (1987) suggested, prosodic contours could help to group elements within likely syntactic boundaries, but so could concord morphology, which places rhyming affixes on words within a phrase (e.g., *los niños pequeños*), and so could semantic information (e.g., if *red* is true of the *cup,* then the two words are probably in the same phrase; Pinker, 1984). The second problem is the discovery of prosody itself. Prosodic structure is abstract, and its identification based on acoustic properties of sentences is knowledge-driven enough to complicate its role as a bottom-up cue to other levels of linguistic structure. The very same features of duration, pitch, and amplitude of syllables that are used to identify prosodic structure are also affected by particular segments and words, and by the idiosyncrasies and emotional state of the speaker (Fisher & Tokura, 1996). The acoustic expression of prosodic structure also varies across languages. Infants therefore must develop quantitative estimates of the acoustic shape of utterances and phrases in their own language.

How might this work? Infants pick up abstract rhythmic properties of speech very readily. Newborns can discriminate sets of sentences spoken in different languages (Mehler et al., 1988; Nazzi, Bertoncini, & Mehler, 1998). This ability is based on a sensitivity to the rhythmic basis of speech, even in languages that the infants have never heard before. Languages can be classified in terms of their basic unit of timing: English and Dutch are stress-timed languages, characterized by alternation between strong and weak syllables, with a (rough) tendency to equate intervals between stressed syllables. Other language classes select different units to mete out the regular timing of sentences. Japanese is mora-timed (morae are subsyllabic units), and Spanish and French are syllable-timed. Nazzi et al. (1998) habituated newborn infants to samples of speech in one of two unfamiliar languages and found that the infants could detect a change to the other language only if the two differed in their fundamental rhythmic basis. Ramus, Nespor, and Mehler (1999) found that stress-, syllable-, and mora-timed languages differed categorically along a dimension defined by the proportion of each utterance devoted to vowels. This phonetic dimension could be used to predict language discrimination by newborn infants. Other factors such as variability in vowel duration across utterances may permit more detailed prediction· of the perception of linguistic rhythm. Robust sensitivity to rhythmic structure is also found in adult's and infants' perception of music (Trehub, 1987), even though music, like speech, provides only very complex evidence for a regular beat.

Infants become able to discriminate their own language from another language in the same rhythmic class by 4 or 5 months of age (American vs. British English: Nazzi, Jusczyk, & Johnson, 2000; Spanish and Catalan: Bosch & Sebastian-Galles, 1997). Given the tender age of these listeners, it is most likely that this new ability is due to learning about prosody rather than phonotactic structure or recognition of particular words. Consistent with this possibility, 4-month-olds who listened to Spanish or Catalan could still tell those two languages apart when the materials were filtered to hide such details; the result sounds much like the muffled speech that one sometimes hears through hotel room walls (Bosch & Sebastian-Galles, 1997).

The Coincidence of Sound and Grammatical Category

Words within grammatical categories tend to share phonological similarity, and both adults and children use this information in categorizing words (e.g., Kelly, 1992; Kelly & Martin, 1994). One of the most obvious differences is the phonological distinction between open-class or content words (the nouns, verbs, adjectives) and the closed-class or function words (affixes, determiners, etc.). Because function words provide major clues to boundaries between phrases, being able to recognize them by their sound patterns would aid the discovery of syntactic structure. Across languages, content and function words differ in ways that would support such a procedure: in all the acoustic correlates of stress (duration, pitch change, amplitude), in syllable weight (function words possess minimal syllable structures and short vowels), and in their positions in phrases (function words tend to appear at phrase edges). These two clusters of correlated phonological properties permit a very accurate division of words into content and function word sets (Shi, Morgan, & Allopenna, 1998). The phonological difference between these two sets is so large that even newborns can categorize words this way, reorienting to sets of content words after habituating to isolated function words, and the reverse (Shi, Werker, & Morgan, 1999).

Surprisingly, there are also probabilistic phonological differences between syntactic categories of content words, though these are specific to particular languages. English nouns tend to have more syllables than verbs. Even though most words in English (nouns and verbs alike) have first-syllable stress, this generalization is much stronger for nouns than for verbs. Adults are more likely to identify a nonsense word as a verb than a noun if it has second-syllable stress (Kelly, 1988; 1992). Similar effects have been shown for 3-year-olds (Wright-Cassidy & Kelly, 1991). Such phonological similarities within grammatical categories are common across languages (Kelly, 1992) and may support the discovery of these categories during acquisition.

Distributional Analysis and the Discovery of Syntax

Although phonological similarity influences syntactic categorization, these sound-organizational properties are partial and probabilistic and vary across languages. Similarly, semantic evidence for word classification is also probabilistic (why is *thunder* but not *lightning* a verb?) and enormously abstract: Although our teachers said that a noun was "a person, place, or thing," it was no great trick to find counterexamples (*fun, mile, thought, nothing, green*). For these familiar reasons, every theory of grammar acquisition presumes that children put their money primarily on a more reliable database: Different kinds of words are distributed differently across the sentence. We already saw that young infants efficiently extract the patterned distribution of syllable types in nonsense sequences like "*bidaku*padoti ... "; presumably, this laboratory demonstration is related to the way infants segment continuous speech into words in real life. Next we see such a procedure repeat itself at the next linguistic level: A formal analysis of the relative distribution of linguistic forms yields their classification as nouns, verbs, and so forth, and thus is fundamental to syntax acquisition.

The most familiar modern statement of a distributional learning algorithm for grammatical categories is from Maratsos and Chalkley (1980). Following the structural linguists Bloomfield (1933) and Harris (1951), they proposed that children could sort words into grammatical categories by noting their co-occurrences with other morphemes and their privileges of occurrence in sentences. *Morphemes* include words and smaller meaningful elements that attach to words (e.g., the English past tense *-ed*). Nouns and verbs occur with different classes of function morphemes (*the, a, -s* versus *is, will, -ing, -ed*); noun phrases serve as subjects of sentences and as objects of various predicates (the verbs, the prepositions). Maratsos and Chalkley's (1980; see also Maratsos, 1998) original argument for the necessity and power of distributional analysis in the acquisition of grammatical categories and phrase structure was based on the existence of the meaningless or nearly meaningless grammatical gender classes within the category noun. The distinction between masculine and feminine nouns in many languages is notorious for its lack of a reasonable semantic basis; what makes a noun "feminine" is its co-occurrence with feminine determiners, case markers, and agreement markers on adjectives and verbs. Thus the existence and extension of these categories must be acquired via an analysis that detects these predictive dependencies. Children learn the grammatical gender classes at about the same rate that they pick up other grammatical categories in their language. Why not distributional learning, all the way down?

Many reviews of the field of language acquisition since the publication of Maratsos and Chalkley's work were skeptical. Several commentators (Gleitman & Wanner, 1982; Pinker, 1984) objected that the useful correlations on which Maratsos and Chalkley's analysis relied were between open-class (nouns, verbs, adjectives) and closed-class items (determiners, tense, case, or agreement markers). Function morphology is conspicuously lacking in young children's language use (R. Brown, 1973). If children are late to discover function morphology, it would seem perilous to build an initial acquisition procedure on the distribution of function morphemes. In addition, the procedure seemed too unconstrained. How would children ever find the useful dependencies between open- and closed-class morphemes amid the unbounded set of irrelevant or misleading co-occurrences that they might track? The empirical foundation of theories of language acquisition has changed in some fundamental ways in the past 20 years, robbing these objections of much of their force. First, as we showed earlier, the content-word/function-word distinction can be discovered by noting the differing phonological properties characteristic of these classes (Shi, Morgan, & Allopenna, 1998, Shi et al., 1999). Second, there is now evidence that very young children are sensitive to the distribution of function morphemes, in the way required. Gerken, Landau, and Remez (1990) found that young 2-year-olds, when asked to imitate long sequences of real and nonsense words, omitted real function words more often than unstressed nonsense syllables. The selective preservation of unfamiliar unstressed syllables suggested that these toddlers knew more about the sound patterns and distribution of function words than their own speech would suggest. Gerken and McIntosh (1993) also showed that two-year-olds more accurately comprehended familiar nouns preceded by grammatical (*the bird*) rather than ungrammatical (*was bird*) function words (see also Santelmann & Jusczyk, 1998, for related findings with verb-phrase morphology in 18-month-olds). These studies do not exhaust what we need to know about young children's detection and use of function morphology in language comprehension, or their use of dependencies among words to construct grammatical categories and build phrase structure; but they put our theories of the role of distributional analysis in early syntax acquisition on a very different empirical footing.

There was a final objection to distributional analysis as a foundation for category discovery and syntax acquisition (Pinker, 1984, 1987; Gleitman & Wanner, 1982), which can still be found in the introductions of papers that take a more optimistic stance toward distributional analysis by infants (e.g., Cartwright & Brent, 1997; Mintz, Newport, & Bever, 1995): Strings of morphemes are full of ambiguity. Nouns occur with a plural *-s*, but verbs occur with a second-person present-tense singular *-s*. Active verbs take the progressive ending *-ing,* but verbs so marked can be used as adjectives (*astonishing*) or as nouns (*Jogging exhausts Bill*). The English morpheme *-ed* has the same fate, often marking verbs (e.g., *admired, hot-footed*) but also marking attributive adjectives that are not verbs at all (*redheaded, light-fingered, widely-admired*). Sentence templates pose the same problem: The sentences *I like fish* and *I can fish* form a distributional minimal pair that might falsely license the categorization of *like* and *can* as the same sort of word.

The status of this objection, 20 years later, is still unclear. Such examples tell us that the distributional analysis carried out by language learners must be a protracted process of integrating multiple predictive dependencies across many sentences, bolstered by the semantic cues that are part of every theory of syntax acquisition as well as by phonological grouping and within-category similarity, and strongly influenced by progress in morpheme segmentation. Chiefly through research on infant learning of phonology, the field has gained a greater respect for the statistical learning abilities of young infants and

for the wealth of detail that learners can hold in memory and bring to bear on new experience. The preschoolers who show instance-specific as well as abstract long-term priming for the sounds of new words (Fisher, Hunt, Chambers, & Church, 2001), the 10-month-olds who recognize a particular musical performance (Palmer, Jungers, & Jusczyk, 2001), the 9-month-olds who are sensitive to the phonotactic probabilities of the native language (Jusczyk et al., 1994), and the 8-month-olds who learn words based only on transitional probabilities (Aslin et al., 1998) are clearly no slouches when it comes to taking in, remembering, and abstracting over huge quantities of data.

Computational work on distributional learning has begun to examine explicit models of how distributional analysis of linguistic forms might work. The general finding is that fairly simple assumptions and algorithms can go some distance toward sorting words into grammatical categories, even unaided by semantic and phonological cues. For example, Cartwright and Brent (1997) generalized the notion of sentential minimal pairs (as in the earlier misleading example, but also in *That's a cat* and *That's a cup*) to produce a distributional learning algorithm that groups words based on appearance in similar templates. The algorithm seeks the most compact description of the input sentences in terms of few, short, and frequent sentence templates and few, uniform word groups. Simulations demonstrated that, assuming preexisting knowledge only of word boundaries, co-occurrences of sets of words provide considerable information about grammatical categories. Mintz et al. (1995) clustered together words based on similarity in distributional context defined as the preceding and following word. They found that this restricted analysis of co-occurrence among words yielded a similarity space that permitted good separation of nouns and verbs. Similar results were obtained when unstressed monosyllabic function words (e.g., *a, the, is*) were left out of the analysis altogether or when they were all treated as an undifferentiated weak syllable. These computational analyses and simulations lead to an important class of conclusions: On various sets of simple assumptions, a tractable analysis of the probabilistic distributional patterns in language can provide a bootstrap for the discovery of the linguistic category structure that produced those patterns (see also Redington, Chater, & Finch, 1998). Similar arguments are made for the discovery of morphology. For example, Goldsmith (2001) proposed an algorithm that learns a probabilistic morphological system from text input, dividing words into roots and affixes to minimize the number and maximize the frequency of the component morphemes. Finally, Brent (1994) presented a similar computational treatment of subcategorization frames for verbs. Individual verbs are choosy about what sentence structures they can occur in; for example, some can be transitive (as in *John eats fish*), while others may be only intransitive (as in *John fishes*). Again, based on very little syntactic knowledge (in this case a few function words), an analysis of the lexical contexts of verbs provides useful information for distinguishing among those that are transitive or intransitive or that take verbal or sentential complements (as in *John likes to fish*).

Many fundamental questions remain about the role of distributional analysis in syntax acquisition. However, the preponderance of recent evidence suggests that human learners—including and maybe especially the very young—are intricately attuned to the details of their experience and that in many domains they show great facility in sorting out and trading off multiple probabilistic indicators of the same underlying structure in the world (see Kelly & Martin, 1994). The view that substantial aspects of language acquisition, from phonology to syntax and semantics, might submit to similar kinds of explanation has benefited in recent years from the wealth of research on phonological learning in infancy, from advances in computational modeling and analyses of large linguistic corpora, and from the study of the constraints, at many levels of analysis, that influence adult (Garnsey, Perlmutter, Myers, & Lotocky, 1997; Trueswell et al., 1994) and child (Hurewitz, Brown-Schmidt, Thorpe, Gleitman, & Trueswell, 2000; Trueswell, Sekerina, Hill, & Logrip, 1999) language processing.

THE MEANINGS

Accounts of word and syntax learning are usually accounts of *mapping*. They concern the ways that conceptual entities (concepts of objects, properties, and relations) match up with linguistic entities (words, syntactic categories, and structures). Insofar as this task analysis is correct, it suggests an initial procedure for language learning. Although "meanings" are not the sorts of object that one can directly observe, aspects of the observed world are often assumed to offer up meanings transparently, and therefore to set language learning into motion. In John Locke's (1690/1964) famous description,

> "If we will observe how children learn languages, we shall find that . . . people ordinarily show them the thing whereof they would have them have the idea, and then repeat to them the name that stands for it, as 'white', 'sweet', 'milk', 'sugar', 'cat', 'dog' " (Book 3, IX, 9).

Locke's stance seems warranted. Even at 9 months of age, uttering a word helps to direct infants' attention to objects in a way that emphasizes to them similarity among category members (Balaban & Waxman, 1997). Children only a few months older apparently begin to map more complicated relational aspects of sentences (e.g., some infant approximation of the category *subject*) onto more abstract relational concepts (e.g., some infant approximation of the category *causal agent;* Hirsh-Pasek & Golinkoff, 1996).

Where do these meanings come from? It would not help the learning infant to show it a dog (and say "dog") if this infant could not, by its native abilities to observe the world, tell dogs from shoes or ships or sealing wax. We approach these issues by discussing some particularly relevant aspects of the literature on infant cognition (see Chap. 10, this volume, for an extensive review). In this section we briefly defend the claim that prelinguistic infants' primitive categories of experience include rudimentary concepts of objects and events, sufficiently robust and accessible for them to begin to make sense of linguistic reference.

Primitive Categories of Experience

The Shape of Things ... : Whole Objects and Object Kinds

Before the first word is acquired, infants have acquired a good deal of knowledge about the kinds of objects that exist in their world. The notion *object* itself seems to be based on a primitive set of notions about physical cohesion and a core set of learning mechanisms dedicated to representing and learning about objects. Infants first find coherent objects in the world by assuming that visible surfaces moving together against a variable background are parts of the same thing (Jusczyk, Johnson, Spelke, & Kennedy, 1999; Kellman & Spelke, 1983). The assumptions that objects are solid and exist continuously in space and time are fundamental in this domain and apply generally across different types of events and objects (e.g., Spelke, Breinlinger, Macomber, & Jacobson, 1992). Even 2.5-month-olds detect violations of object solidity or continuity as long as the events are simple enough that

they can represent all the required information (e.g., Aguiar & Baillargeon, 1999).

Like adults, young infants come to use disparities in shape as a cue to the boundaries of objects, and they also rely on knowledge of particular familiar objects and categories of familiar objects to segment objects out of a complex environment (Needham & Baillargeon, 2000). Prelinguistic infants do not possess the same rich concepts of objects that an adult has: A 7.5-month-old may think of keys as something delightful to jingle and chew on; the 14-month-old has figured out that they have something to do with big artifacts like cars (Mandler, 2000); and the adult (in most modern environments) attains an enlightened view of keys that specifies their relationship to locks. Despite all the knowledge that we know must be gained by specific experience with the ambient world of things, the infant literature suggests the early appearance of something like kind categories. Infants' object concepts depend on physical similarity (Hume, 1739/1978; Mandler, 2000; Quinn & Eimas, 1997; Smith, Jones, & Landau, 1992) but also support inductive inferences about currently invisible properties of the objects (Baldwin, Markman, & Melartin, 1993; Needham & Baillargeon, 2000). The prelinguistic appearance of object-kind concepts takes at least part of the mystery out of a topic that we discuss presently: that when infants at the ages of 10 to 15 months begin to understand and utter words, these first vocabularies include a heavy dose of concrete nouns.

... To Come: Categories of Events

Some of the best evidence for knowledge-rich categories in early infancy comes from the study of event categories (see Baillargeon, 1998, for a review). Beginning with core representational constraints including object continuity and solidity, infants articulate categories of physical events—such as support, occlusion, containment, and collision—and gradually add knowledge within each category. To account for infants' early expectations about collision events, for example, a primitive notion of force has been proposed as part of the infant's built-in representational vocabulary (Leslie, 1995). Equipped with an ability to attend to and represent solid moving objects and with this notion of force, infants expect objects to move when struck by other objects (Kotovsky & Baillargeon, 1998; Leslie & Keeble, 1987). They gradually elaborate their concept of collision events by adding knowledge about the role of the relative sizes of the striking object and the object it strikes (Kotovsky & Baillargeon, 1998). These infant concepts of physical events really are categories in the usual sense: They are readily applied to new instances of the event type and can support inferences about event outcomes (Baillargeon, 1998). Evidently, then, event categories serve as tractable domains within which infants work out the intricate consequences of physical causality. These event categories interact complexly with abstract object-kind categories. For example, as they elaborate their developing concept of collision events, infants learn that not all objects move when hit. Some things are movable objects, while others are fixed barriers that stop the motion of objects that strike them. At 8 months, infants seem to base this categorization on a fairly strict geometric criterion: Anything with a salient vertical dimension is a barrier; anything else is an object (Baillargeon, 1998).

These event categories imply a very useful kind of conceptual structure. Each event category is defined over some set of participants that play different roles in the event, and the participants must be of the correct abstract type to play those roles (e.g., moving object and movable object for collision, container and movable object for containment). Infants' developing event categories provide exactly the sort of relational concepts that will eventually be mapped onto relational terms in their language. The infant's conceptual

repertoire appears to entail an early (possibly unlearned) distinction between the *relations* between objects that define event type and the *objects* or conceptual entities that participate in those events—about "in-ness" apart from particular containers and "hitting" apart from the particular objects involved. This amounts to a distinction between conceptual predicates and arguments, of just the type needed to describe the semantics of sentences (Bierwisch & Schreuder, 1992; L. Bloom, 1970; Braine, 1992; Fodor, 1975).

One strong suggestion that prelinguistic infants factor their experience into relations and participant roles comes from Alan Leslie's work on the perception of causality. Six-month-olds appear to have an appropriately asymmetrical view of causality: After habituating to a simple computer-generated event in which one shape strikes and launches another, infants found a reversed version of the same event more interesting (Leslie & Keeble, 1987). The infants did not show the same recovery of interest to a reversed event if they had been habituated to an event in which there had been either a spatial or temporal gap between the striking and launched objects. Such gaps interfere with adults' perception of causality in similar events (Michotte, 1946/1963; Scholl & Tremoulet, 2000). Leslie and Keeble concluded that the infants detected the change in mechanical-causal role in the reversed film, in exactly the circumstances where adults would readily perceive the display as causal. The difference between the launching events when played normally or in reverse is in the assignment of participant roles to particular objects: When the film is played backwards, the hitter becomes the hittee.

Animacy, Agency, and Intention

The event types just discussed concern relationships among things qua physical objects and mechanical causality. Recent work also suggests that prelinguistic infants develop the right kind of conceptual vocabulary to be mapped onto talk about intentions. Seminal studies concerning infants' understanding of reaching come from Woodward (1998). She showed 6- and 9-month-olds a simple event in which a hand reached for and grasped one of two toys visible on a stage. After the infants habituated to the repeated presentation of the hand reaching for the bear (not the ball), Woodward presented a test in which, on alternate trials, the hand now reached for and grasped either the same toy in a new location or the other toy in the old location. These events pitted two aspects of event similarity against each other by changing either the goal object (bear vs. ball) or the goal location and trajectory of reach. Both 6- and 9-month-olds looked longer at the reach to the new goal object, suggesting that they found a reach for a different object more novel than a reach to a different location. When watching a hand reach for an object, young infants apparently focused on the object reached for; infants did not show the same preference when the "reach" was enacted by an inanimate object. These and other findings testify to the power of a notion of intentional agency in interpreting events. Just as adults are prone to perceive intentionality when watching the apparently contingent, "social" motions of flat geometric shapes (Heider & Simmel, 1944), young infants appear ready to interpret interactions in the same way. Intentional agents have goals; they perceive objects and events at a distance and react to them; self-moving objects can initiate actions and apply or resist forces (Csibra, Gergely, Bíró, Koós, & Brockbank, 1999; Leslie, 1995; Luo, 2000).

In related tasks, infants between about 9 and 12 months of age show signs of understanding the intent to refer: They can follow a pointing finger to its destination and follow others' line of gaze (Baldwin & Moses, 1996, for a review). These nonverbal indicators of attention play a role in early word learning.

Young children are better able to learn new object names if an adult labels whatever the child is attending to than if the adult tries to shift the child's attention to another object (Tomasello & Farrar, 1986). Even very young learners need not be fooled into word-mapping errors by these officiously directive acts of labeling, however. A nascent understanding of the intent to refer is engaged in children's early word interpretations: Toddlers glance up as if to check the speaker's intent when they hear a new word produced, and they seek the speaker's referent (Baldwin, 1991). Baldwin (1993) found that 19-month-olds attached a new word to whatever the experimenter looked at when she spoke, even if the named object was hidden at the time of labeling and another object (the wrong object) was made available first. Similar evidence of early sophistication in the interpretation of others' goals emerges from studies of imitation in toddlers: 18-month-olds watched an actor try and fail to (for example) drop an object into a cup or insert a peg into a hole, and they then inferred and imitated the apparent goal of the failed attempts, rather than the actions that they observed (Meltzoff, 1995; see also Carpenter, Akhtar, & Tomasello, 1998).

Compositional Meaning

Prelinguistic infants and very young word learners develop implicit notions of objects and events, agents and patients, and intentions and goals. These conceptual primitives have the right properties to provide the initial conceptual vocabulary onto which the basic linguistic elements (words and structures) are mapped. Language systematically pulls apart unitary states of affairs in the world into separate pieces: It assigns a word to each entity (*kangaroo, gnu*), another for whether that entity is uniquely identifiable in context (*the, a*), and yet another for the relation holding between the entities (*kicked, tickled*). These words are composed into a sentence, for example, *The kangaroo kicked a gnu*. The meaning of a sentence is greater than the sum of its parts, for aspects of the semantics are contributed by their arrangement: *A gnu kicked the kangaroo* means something quite different from the original sequence even though it consists of all and only the same words. A simple sentence (borrowing a metaphor from Healy & Miller, 1970) can be seen as a kind of mystery story whose plot (or *predication*) is the verb, *kick* in this case. The nouns ranged around the verb play varying roles with respect to the predication: The *kangaroo* is the agent or doer; the *gnu* is the done-to or patient. These nouns are thus the *arguments* of the predicate.

Language partitions and structures the descriptions of entities and events in its basic sentences. We have argued that infants, before language learning, also naturally factor their representations of events into conceptual predicates and arguments. This suggests that prelinguistic human cognition provides conceptual structure of the right type to be mapped onto linguistic expressions. In our view, the best evidence that the structure of human cognition yields a language-appropriate division into predicates and arguments comes from learners who are isolated from ordinary exposure to a language and so have to invent one on their own. No child has to be taught by specific language experience to abstract conceptual predicates away from the arguments that they relate.

The clearest cases of language invention involve deaf children, whose acquisition of a conventional signed language takes place under widely varying input conditions and at different learner ages. The great majority of deaf children are born to hearing parents who do not sign, and therefore the children do not come into contact with gestural languages for years, sometimes for half a lifetime or more (Newport, 1990). Deaf children with

no available language model spontaneously invent gesture systems called "home sign" (Feldman, Goldin-Meadow, & Gleitman, 1978; Goldin-Meadow, 1982, 2000; Goldin-Meadow & Mylander, 1984, 1998). Remarkably, although these children are isolated from exposure to any conventional language, their home sign systems factor their experience into the same pieces that characterize the elements of sentences in Latin, Punjabi, and English. Home sign systems have nouns and verbs, distinguishable from each other by their positions in the children's gesture sequences and by their distinctive iconic properties. Sequences of these gestures vary in the number and positioning of the nouns as a function of what their verbs mean (Feldman et al., 1978). Before unpacking this idea, we want to introduce a new data source that spectacularly rounds out the picture of language learning without a model: This case is the emergence of Nicaraguan Sign Language (NSL).

In the late 1970s the Sandinista government of Nicaragua opened a school for the deaf, thus bringing together a group of heretofore isolated deaf children of hearing parents. The school advocated an "oralist" (nonsigning) approach to deaf education, but the deaf children immediately began gesturing to each other in the playgrounds of the school, using their spontaneously developed and varying home sign systems. This signing, and its evolution at the hands of continuously arriving new deaf students, has been intensively studied ever since (Kegl, Senghas, & Coppola, 1999; Senghas, 1995; Senghas & Coppola, 2001; Senghas, Coppola, Newport, & Supalla, 1997). Taken at their broadest, the results of that work suggest that, while Rome surely wasn't built in a day, Latin might have been: Born in the mimetic gesturing of linguistically isolated children, NSL exhibits both fundamental organization and certain specialized elaborative choices familiar from the received languages of the world.

The systems that first emerge in home sign systems and in early stages of NSL represent the logic of predicate-argument structure, mapped onto an utterance unit that we might as well call "the basic sentence." This unit can be established both in terms of its universal prosodic correlates, and by its interpretation in context. Each clause typically contains an action or state word with iconic properties so transparent as to convince even the most skeptical observer (e.g., swooping motions of the arm and hand to represent flying, downward fluttering fingers to represent snowing). Now matters really get interesting: Ranged around the verb are other, also recognizable linguistic entities (call them "the nouns") playing the thematic roles required by the logic of the verb—the *agent* or initiator of the act, the *patient* or thing affected, the *goal* of the action, and so forth. "Grape-give-me" signs a 3-year-old home signer; "Man—cry," "Man-tap-cup," gesture the NSL users. Not only are there nouns and verbs, detectable both phonetically and positionally, organized into sentence-like sequences, but *the number of noun-phrases in these sentences is a systematic function of the logic of the particular verb.*

The nature of this relationship is easy to see from the examples just given: Because 'crying' involves only a single participant (the crier), a verb with this meaning surfaces intransitively not only in English and Bengali and Navaho, but also in the speech of young language learners—both those who hear or see a received language and those who perforce must invent it for themselves. Because 'tapping' has two participants, the tapper and the thing tapped, such verbs surface transitively (with two nominal phrases). Because 'giving' requires a giver, a getter, and a thing exchanged between them, this verb shows up with three nominal phrases. The semantic

functions of the nouns vis-à-vis the verb are known as their *thematic* (or *semantic*) *roles* (Chomsky, 1981). Thus the primitive structure of the clause in both self-generated and more established communication systems derives from the nonlinguistic conceptual structures by which humans represent events. This cognitivist interpretation of the origin of language in child conceptual structure motivates all modern linguistic treatments of verb semantics that we know of (for important statements, see Chomsky, 1981; Dowty, 1991; Fillmore, 1968; Goldberg, 1995; Grimshaw, 1990; Gruber, 1967; Jackendoff, 1983; 1985; Rappaport Hovav & Levin, 1988). The same cognitivist approach figures in most psychological theories about learning of both structure and lexicon, whatever their other disagreements (L. Bloom, 1970; Bowerman, 1990; Braine, 1992; Fisher, 1996; Fisher, Hall, Rakowitz, & Gleitman, 1994; Gentner, 1982; Gleitman, Gleitman, Landau, & Wanner, 1988; Pinker, 1984, 1989; Schlesinger, 1988; Slobin, 1996; Tomasello, 2000).

So far we have emphasized the one-to-one relation between the number of participants implied by a verb's meaning and the number of noun-phrases associated with it. One further feature discernable in these invented manual languages, and in toddlers' use of a received language as well, is *a formal means for distinguishing among the participants in the act*—for instance, between the agent and the thing affected in a causal act (Goldin-Meadow & Mylander, 1998; Senghas et al., 1997). Established languages employ some combination of local markings on nouns (morphology) and word order to achieve these distinctions, usually emphasizing one of these machineries over the other. For instance, modern English and Chinese are inflectionally impoverished languages that rely on word order, lexical choice, and pragmatics to achieve distinctions that are morphologically rendered (case-marked) in many other languages such as Latin and Finnish.

Nothing being as simple as it seems, we should mention provisos and complications here. The first is that the very youngest child learners (roughly, between 12 and 24 months), whether learning or inventing a language, at first produce only single words, usually followed by a period of several more months where they seem to be limited to two words in the clause. During these earliest periods the full complement of participant roles cannot surface in any single sentence in the child's speech or signing (but even for these early productions the regular mapping between thematic roles and noun-phrase number can sometimes be reconstructed inferentially; L. Bloom, 1970; see also Feldman et al., 1978). Second, even novice speech often allows or requires omission of the *agent* role in certain environments, as in the deaf isolate's imperative "Grape-give-me!" (and its English equivalent), and in many of the world's languages whenever the pragmatics of the situation permit (e.g., Spanish "Hablo Espanol" rather than "Yo hablo Espanol").

In sum, linguistically isolated children construct, out of their own thoughts and communicative needs, systems that resemble the languages of the world in at least the following regards: All such systems have words, and words of more than one kind, at minimum the nouns and the verbs organized into sentences expressing predicate-argument relations. The number and positioning of the nouns express their semantic roles relative to the verb. Both "nativist" and "learning-functionalist" wings of the language-learning investigative community have seized upon the transparency and universality of form-to-meaning correspondence in language acquisition as supporting their learning positions in particular. (After the battle, the opposing generals retreated to their tents to celebrate their victory).

Interactions between Linguistic and Conceptual Categories

We have just discussed certain primitive conceptual categories that constitute a humanly universal grounding for language acquisition. This is in keeping with a *linguistic universalist* approach maintained by many linguists and developmental psycholinguists who have their attention fixed squarely on the difficulty of explaining language learning (Chomsky, 1965, 1995; R. Clark, 1992; Dresher, 1999; Pinker, 1987; Wexler & Culicover, 1980). These commentators have usually pinned their hopes on their certainty that a well-articulated conceptual structure predates language and is (one of) its required causal engines: "to study semantics of natural language *is* to study cognitive psychology" (Jackendoff, 1983, pp. 3); "if . . . [you] couldn't pick pieces of meaning out of the world in advance, before you learned a language, then language couldn't be learnt" (Chomsky, 1982). But now suppose instead that the driving investigative question had been how to "explain concept acquisition" or how to "explain culture" rather than how to "explain language acquisition." When explanatory aims are reversed, so, often, are the certainties about original causes. Psychologists whose problem is to explain the growth of concepts and anthropologists whose problem is to explain culture often turn to language itself as a grounding explanatory idea. The intellectual collision of these two traditions has generated a stimulating, but sometimes uneasy, revival of the *linguistic relativity* tradition that had lain submerged for most of the second half of the twentieth century. Perhaps language explains cognition in some way, instead of or in addition to cognition explaining language.

The recent literature points again and again to pervasive behavioral correlates of speaking a particular language. But the basis for such correlational findings is much in doubt and hotly debated. It could be that different peoples speak somewhat differently because as a practical matter—that is, despite their shared mentality—their life circumstances and cultural practices lead them to think somewhat differently and so to choose differently among the available conceptual and linguistic resources. (It could be, for example, that Eskimos talk in such refined ways about snow because they live under conditions where snow and snow types are a big factor in everyday existence). Or perhaps peoples think somewhat differently because they talk somewhat differently. (It could be, that is, that having so many words for snow is what enables the Eskimos to think so precisely about their snowy circumstances—which would be a lucky coincidence for the Eskimos). This idea at its strongest (including the Eskimo example) is the Whorf-Sapir Hypothesis concerning the linguistic shaping of thought (Whorf, 1956).[2]

In Whorf's words,

"The categories and types that we isolate from the world of phenomena we do not find there because they stare every observer in the face; on the contrary, the world is presented as a kaleidoscopic flux of impressions which has to be organized by our minds—and this means largely by the linguistic systems in our minds" (1956, p. 213).

And relatedly, Sapir says,

"Human beings do not live in the objective world alone, . . . but are very much at the mercy of the particular language which has become the medium of expression for their society. . . . The fact of the matter is that the 'real world' is to a large extent unconsciously built upon the language habits of the group" (as cited in Whorf, 1941, p. 75).

We now consider several examples from the recent literature of language acquisition that have been taken to bear on the possibility of the linguistic shaping of thought. In every such case, languages differ in how they divide up the same semantic space into linguistic expressions. These differences naturally affect how speakers of these languages speak; after cataloging some of these cross-linguistic variations, we consider whether such differences have deeper effects on the way we perceive the world.

Categorizing Things and Stuff

The problem of reference to *stuff* versus *objects* has attracted considerable attention because it starkly displays the indeterminacy in how language refers to the world (Chomsky, 1957; Quine, 1960). Whenever we indicate some physical object, we necessarily indicate some portion of a substance as well; the reverse is also true. In light of this general problem, investigators have considered how linguistic and situational clues interact in the linguistic discovery of words for stuff and things. Some languages make a grammatical distinction that roughly distinguishes object from substance reference. Count nouns in such languages refer to objects as individuals. These are marked in English with determiners like *a* and are subject to counting and pluralization (*forty thieves; two turtledoves*). Mass nouns typically refer to substance rather than object kinds; these are marked in English with a different set of determiners (*more porridge*) and require an additional term that specifies quantity to be counted and pluralized (*a tube of toothpaste* rather than *a toothpaste*).

Soja, Carey, and Spelke (1991) asked whether children approach this aspect of

---

[2] According to Pullam (1991), citing a study by L. Martin, Whorf was incorrect in thinking that such Eskimo languages as Inuit or Yupik are rich in snow words: Various morphological and translation confusions and unchecked references led to the gross inflation of a snow vocabulary no more extensive than that found in English. Still, the well-known snow case is a handy example of the way that Whorf and his various intellectual descendents have thought about the relations between language and thought.

language learning already equipped with the ontological distinction between things and substances or whether they are led to make this distinction through learning count/mass syntax. They taught English-speaking 2-year-olds words in reference to various types of displays: Some were solid objects, and others were nonsolid substances arranged in an interesting shape. The children were shown a sample, named with a term presented in a syntactically neutral frame that marked it neither as a count nor as a mass noun (e.g., "This is my *blicket*"). In extending these words to new displays, 2-year-olds honored the distinction between solid object and nonsolid substance displays: When the sample was a solid object, they extended the new word to objects of the same shape and of different material. When the sample was a nonsolid substance (e.g., hand cream with sparkles), they went for substance rather than shape. Soja et al. took this as evidence of a conceptual distinction between coherent objects and stuff, independent of (prior to) the syntactic distinction made in English.

This interpretation was put to a stronger test by Imai and Gentner (1997) by extending Soja et al.'s task to a new language, Japanese. Japanese does not have the same count-mass distinction found in English. Speaking somewhat metaphorically, we might say that all of this language's nouns start life as mass terms, requiring a special marker to be counted. One might claim, then, that substance is in some sense linguistically basic for Japanese, whereas objecthood is basic for English speakers (see Lucy & Gaskins, 2001, for this position for Yucatec Mayan). If children are led to differentiate object and substance reference by the language forms themselves, the resulting abstract semantic distinction should differ for Japanese and English speakers. Imai and Gentner replicated Soja et al.'s original result by demonstrating that both American and Japanese children (even 2-year-olds) extended names for

complex nonsense objects on the basis of shape rather than substance; thus the lack of separate grammatical marking did not put the Japanese children at a disadvantage in this regard. However, the Japanese children extended names for the mushy hand-cream displays according to their substance, whereas the American children were at chance for these items. There were also language effects on word extension for very simple object stimuli (e.g., a kidney-bean-shaped piece of colored wax). While the Japanese children at ages 2 and 4 were at chance on these items, the English speakers showed a tendency to extend words for them by shape. These findings strengthen the evidence for the universal prelinguistic ontology that permits us to think both about objects and about portions of stuff. But another aspect of the results hints at a role for language itself in categorization—at least where categorization is tested through extension of a new name. Reference to objects that do not clearly demand one or the other construal—that fall near the midline between "obviously an object" and "obviously some stuff"—tends to be interpreted as a function of the language spoken.

Categorizing Motion Events

Talmy (1985) famously described two styles of motion expression characterizing different languages: Some languages, including English, typically use a verb plus a separate path expression to describe motion events. In such languages the verb is often used to express manner of motion (as in *crawl, clamber, swagger, float,* and *slide*), and the path of that motion is expressed in a prepositional phrase (*out of the room, from the front door to the sidewalk*). In a language like Greek or Spanish (and most other Romance languages), the dominant pattern is to include path information within the verb itself (as in *salir* "exit" and *entrar* "enter"). The manner of motion often goes unmentioned or appears as an optional adverbial phrase (*flotando*). These patterns are not absolute. Spanish has motion verbs that express manner, and English has motion verbs that express path (*enter, exit, cross*). However, several studies have shown that children and adults have learned these dominance patterns. Slobin (1996) showed that child and adult Spanish and English speakers vary in this regard in the terms that they typically use to describe the very same picture-book stories. Papafragou, Massey, and Gleitman (2001) showed the same effects for the description of motion scenes by Greek- versus English-speaking children and, much more strongly, for Greek- versus English-speaking adults.

Categorizing Spatial Relationships (In-ness and Out-ness)

Choi and Bowerman (1991) studied the ways in which common motion verbs in Korean differ from their counterparts in English. First, Korean motion verbs often contain locative or geometric information that is more typically specified separately by a spatial preposition in English. For example, to describe a scene in which a cassette tape is placed into its case, English speakers would say "We put the tape *in the case*." Korean speakers typically use a verb *kkita* to express the *put in* relation for this scene. Second, *kkita* does not have the same extension as English *put in*. Both *put in* and *kkita* describe an act of putting an object in a location; but *put in* is used for all cases of containment (fruit in a bowl, flowers in a vase), while *kkita* is used only in case the outcome is a tight fit between two matching shapes (tape in its case, one Lego piece on another, glove on hand). Quite young learners of these two languages have already worked out the language-specific classification of motion events in their language (Choi & Bowerman, 1991). Indeed Hespos and Spelke (2000) showed that 5-month-old infants exposed only to English are sensitive to this distinction.

Explaining Language-Specific Categorization

As we have just seen, languages differ to some degree in how they package up conceptual categories inside words and sentence structures. Moreover, manifestly the language users have acquired these language-specific patterns and can use them when called upon to do so in experimental settings. What should we make of these findings vis-à-vis the relationship between language and thought?

Effects of Language on Language.   One kind of interpretation appeals to effects of language on the interpretation and use of language: Slobin (1996, 2001), P. Brown (2001), and Bowerman (1996) have proposed that native speakers not only learn and use the individual lexical items their language offers, but they also learn the *kinds* of meanings typically expressed by a particular grammatical category in their language and come to expect that new members of that category will have similar meanings. Languages differ strikingly in their commonest forms and locutions—preferred "fashions of speaking," to use Whorf's phrase. These probabilistic patterns could bias the interpretation of new words. Such effects come about when subjects are offered language input (usually nonsense words) under conditions where implicitly known form-to-meaning patterns in the language might hint at how the new word is to be interpreted. As one example, consider again the Imai and Gentner effects for objects and substances. When the displays themselves were of nonaccidental-looking hard-edged objects, subjects in both language groups opted for the object interpretation. But when the world was less blatantly informative (e.g., for waxy lima-bean shapes), the listeners fell back upon linguistic cues if available. No relevant morphological clues exist in Japanese (object terms and substance terms have no separate special markers, so Japanese subjects chose at random for these indeterminate stimuli). For the English subjects, the linguistic cue was in some formal sense interpretively neutral: "This is *my* blicket" is a template that accepts both mass and count nouns ("This is my horse/toothpaste"). Here, however, principle and probability part company. Any English speaker equipped with the roughest subjective probability counter should consider the massive preponderance of count nouns to mass nouns in English and so conclude that a new word "blicket," referring to some indeterminate display, is probably a count noun with shape predictivity.

Such effects of language on language have been shown again and again. Naigles and Terrazas (1998) found that Spanish- and English-speaking adults differed in their preferred interpretations of new (nonsense) motion verbs in manner-biasing (*She's kradding toward the tree* or *Ella esta mecando hacio el árbol*) or path-biasing (*She's kradding the tree* or *Ella esta mecando el árbol*) sentence structures, used to describe videotaped scenes (e.g., of a girl skipping toward a tree). The interpretations were heavily influenced by syntactic structure (see the section titled "Mapping Forms to Meanings" for further discussion). However, judgments also reflected the preponderance of verbs in each language: Spanish speakers gave more path interpretations, and English speakers gave more manner interpretations. Similar effects of language-specific lexical practices on presumed word extension have been found for adjectives (Waxman, Senghas & Beneviste, 1997).

This notion that children develop language-specific expectations for how to interpret words of different grammatical categories can be reached via another inferential route as well. The grammatical categories themselves are not the same across languages. For example, not all languages have distinct categories of prepositions that

convey spatial meanings, or of adjectives that name (roughly) stable attributes. Instead, they may use items more like main verbs to convey these meanings (e.g., Croft, 1990; Maratsos, 1990, 1998). If languages have different sets of grammatical categories, they must have different mappings from grammatical categories to semantic ones. If there is no preposition category, then verbs or perhaps nouns must have more spatial information packaged into them; if there is no adjective category, then property meanings will end up being encoded in words grammatically more like verbs or nouns as well. This, in turn, predicts that when speakers of these various languages are taught a new word and are asked to infer its meaning based on its grammatical category, they will have (for some categories) slightly different views of the options. There are differences in the language patterns, and the speakers use them as a probabilistic basis for inferring how new words will relate to new objects and events.

Does It Matter? Linguistic and Nonlinguistic Classifications. Another question is the extent to which acquisition of these language patterns influences the structure of our concepts, and hence our nonlinguistic categorization, as Whorf and Sapir would have it. The answer to this further question is not so obvious. For example, Hespos and Spelke's demonstration of American 5-month-old infants' sensitivity to the tight fit/loose fit distinction vitiates the claim that this distinction "arose from language." The fact that English speakers learn and readily use verbs like *jam, pack,* and *wedge* weakens any claim that the lack of commonest terms like *kkita/nohta* seriously diminishes the availability of categorization in terms of tightness of fit. Despite these provisos, some psychologists have speculated, with Whorf, that these speech fashions in turn influence the salience of differing categorizations of the world (see, e.g., Bowerman & Levinson, 2001).

Rather different results concerning the influence (or noninfluence) of learned linguistic categories on nonlinguistic cognition come from studies that explicitly compare performance when subjects from each language group are instructed to classify objects or pictures by *name*, versus when they are instructed to classify the same objects by *similarity*. In one such study, Li, Gleitman, Landau, and Gleitman (1997) showed Korean- and English-speaking subjects pictures of events such as putting a suitcase on a table (an example of *on* in English, and of *nohta*, "loose fit," in Korean). For half the subjects from each language group, these training stimuli were labeled by the experimenter ("See? Miss Picky likes to put things *on* things"), and for the other subjects the stimuli were described more vaguely ("See? Miss Picky likes to do things *like this*"). Later categorization followed language in the labeling condition: English speakers identified new pictures showing tight fits (e.g., a cap put on a pen) as well as the original loose-fitting ones as belonging to the category "that Miss Picky likes," but Korean speakers generalized only to new instances of loose fits. These language-driven differences disappeared in the similarity sorting condition, in which the word (*on* or *nohta*) was not invoked; in this case, the categorization choices of the two language groups were the same.

Another example was reported by Malt, Sloman, Gennari, Shi, and Wang (1999). They examined the vocabulary used by their subjects to label the various containers we bring home from the grocery store full of milk, juice, ice cream, bleach, or medicine (e.g., *jugs, bottles, cartons, juice boxes*). English, Spanish, and Chinese differ in the set of terms available for this domain and in how these terms are extended to group diverse containers as "the same kind." Speakers of these languages

therefore differed strikingly in which objects they classified together by name: For example, a set of objects distributed across the sets of *jugs, containers,* and *jars* by English speakers were unified by the single label *frasco* by Spanish speakers. Yet Malt et al.'s subjects did not differ much (if at all) from each other in their classification of these containers by overall similarity rather than by name.

Let us return to the path-manner distinction. Papafragou, Massey, and Gleitman (2001) showed English and Greek speakers series of pictures of motion events, and asked them to (a) describe these events (i.e., to label them linguistically), and either (b) to remember which pictures they had already seen, or (c) to choose a new event "most similar" to the original event. One of the choices in the categorization task shared manner of motion but not path with the original, and the other shared path but not manner. Though subjects showed language-specific preferences for manner or path in *labeling* these events linguistically, they showed no differences in *similarity* categorization or *memory* for path and manner.

Even more surprising is that within-language choice of manner versus path verb neither predicted nor reflected memory or categorization performance *within* language. Papafragou et al. divided their Greek- and English-speaking subjects' verbal descriptions of motion events according to the path/manner distinction, now regardless of native language. Though English speakers usually chose manner verbs, sometimes they produced path verbs; the Greek speakers varied, too, but with the preponderances reversed. The particular label provided by each subject did not predict classification of the same event. Subjects were not more likely to name events that they had just categorized together as most similar by labeling them with the same verb, and subjects were no more likely, two days later, to correctly reject path changes for an event that they had previously labeled with a path (rather than manner) verb, or to more readily detect manner changes for events that they had previously labeled with manner verbs.

Sketchiness: Language Is No True Mirror of Our Thoughts.   These three sets of experiments show an important dissociation between naming on the one hand, and perception and cognition on the other. Naming is a social or conventional act, influenced not only by our perceptions of similarity among objects and events but also by the somewhat arbitrary details of our linguistic experience. Words are extended, in part by happenstance, to objects or events sharing only partial similarity; thus, in English we use *paper* to refer to a pulped-wood substance, to various objects made of that substance (the daily paper), and to collected ideas expressed on paper (a paper about word extension; see Lakoff, 1987, for many such examples of the vagaries of word extension). Examples like these suggest that we cannot take the details and semi-arbitrary choices of our own words too seriously. As Malt et al. pointed out, a child may readily call a plastic bear with a straw in its head "a juice box" simply because that's what it's called in the local community. One infant and his parents were perfectly content to use the label "Thank you" to describe all acts of giving and getting. The reason was that this was the only word in the infant's productive vocabulary, yet it served the purpose of making reference to their exchange games perfectly well.

A fair conclusion from this and related evidence is that verbal descriptions are under the control of many factors that are related to accessibility, including the simple frequency of a word's use, as well as of faithfulness as a description of the scene. Often, given the heavy information-processing demands of rapid conversation, faithfulness is sacrificed to accessibility. For these and other reasons, verbal reports do not come anywhere near

exhausting the observers' mental representations of events. Language use is in this sense "sketchy." Rather than "thinking in words," humans seem to make easy linguistic choices that, for competent listeners, serve as rough pointers to those ideas.

In introductory remarks, we pointed out that language users make reference by whatever catch-as-catch-can methods they find handy, leading to some potentially misleading locutions like "Chomsky and Socrates are both on the top shelf" or "The ham sandwich wants his check." What chiefly matters to talkers and listeners is that successful reference be made. If one tried to say all and exactly what one meant, conversation couldn't happen; speakers would be lost in thought as they struggled to get things stated just so, like a population of orators-in-training. Because this is obviously so, listeners would be in quite a pickle if they took their conversational partners' words and structures as precisely indexing the thoughts expressed.

MAPPING FORMS TO MEANINGS

The Mapping Problem

Thus far we have discussed the conceptual underpinnings of language acquisition, arguing that prelinguistic infants are in possession of usefully structured concepts that offer up the conceptual vocabulary onto which linguistic elements are mapped. We also reviewed evidence for the infant's impressive abilities in the formal analysis of linguistic elements. During the first year, infants learn an enormous amount about objects and events in the world and about the distributions of sounds and words in their native language. Apparently, when infants approach 1 year of age—at about the time that word mapping gets underway—they are capable of representing both linguistic and conceptual entities in ways that are conducive to language learning. Moreover, we have seen that young children invent their own home sign systems, and that these systems are fundamentally similar to more established languages.

This may sound like it solves all problems: Toddlers starting to learn language are "creatures like us" in many respects. But richness of representation is a double-edged sword. On the one hand, surely nobody could learn language without the ability to conceive of objects and events in the many and various respects encoded by any language (and all languages). On the other hand, this essential multiplicity and flexibility of cognitive life makes word mapping seem less tractable. How does the child figure out which of the many ways in which she can think about objects and events is meant by a particular word? Or, given that a toddler can factor a complex event into its participants and the relations among them, how is he or she to know which word maps onto which element of the scene representation?

Recent evidence suggests that observation of words' extralinguistic contexts, across multiple uses, does provide the kind of information needed to identify some words. The evidence suggests, however, that simple observation of word-world contingencies works better for learning some words than others. Gillette, Gleitman, Gleitman, and Lederer (1999) carried out "human simulations" of observational word learning: They showed adult observers silenced video clips of mothers talking to their toddlers and asked the observers to guess what word the mother said to her child whenever a beep occurred on the tape. The beeps were positioned at just the points at which the mothers had uttered one of the 24 most common nouns, or 24 most common verbs, found in the sample of child-directed speech from which these video clips were drawn. Subjects saw six clips for each word, presented in a row, and were told that

each series of six beeps marked utterances of the same word. Thus they had an opportunity for some cross-situational observation to guide the interpretation of each word; in the initial studies they were told whether the words were nouns or verbs; in a replication by Snedeker and Gleitman (in press) the beeps were not identified by lexical class. In both experiments, adults were much better able to guess the mothers' nouns than their verbs.

Success rates in this task could be predicted by other subjects' judgments of the concreteness of each word. On average, the common nouns in the mothers' speech were judged more concrete than the common verbs. Variability in judged concreteness was a better predictor than the noun/verb distinction of which words were successfully inferred from observation of the scenes. The most concrete verbs (e.g., *throw*) were identified relatively frequently, while the most abstract verbs (e.g., *think, know*) were never guessed correctly by any subject. This suggests a fairly simple account of which words will be most efficiently learned based on simple observation of scenes in which they are used: The most concrete words, including a useful vocabulary of concrete nouns, are just those for which linguistically unaided observation is likely to be informative.

The Gillette et al. data suggest that the solution to the mapping problem may not be as simple as suggested by Locke's sanguine expression quoted earlier: "We ... show them the thing ...." Observation of "the thing" appears to be sufficient for the acquisition of some but not all of our vocabulary. The trouble with verbs and other predicate terms is that they are abstract: Verb meanings depend not only on the event, but also on a choice of perspectives on events (Gleitman, 1990; see also Bowerman, 1985; Choi & Bowerman, 1991; E. V. Clark, 1990; Fillmore, 1977; Fisher, 1996, 2000a; Fisher et al., 1994; Goldberg, 1995; Grimshaw, 1994; Landau &

Gleitman, 1985; Pinker, 1989; Rispoli, 1989; Slobin, 2001; Talmy, 1985). This perspective can be surprisingly unpredictable from observations of the events themselves. For example, perspective-changing verbs like *chase* and *flee* describe the same class of events but differ in their focus on the perspective of one or the other participant in the event. Similarly, one cannot say *give* if nobody *gets,* and every time one *puts* the cup on the table, the cup also *goes* on the table. Linguistic perspective on an event is influenced by many factors, including the words and structures that the language makes available (e.g., Bowerman, 1990; Choi & Bowerman, 1991; Talmy, 1985) and the momentary accessibility of particular words and syntactic structures (e.g., Bock, Loebell, & Morey, 1992).

Responding to Locke's analysis of the mapping problem, Landau and Gleitman (1985) examined word and syntax acquisition in congenitally blind children. From the purest of empiricist perspectives, the consequences of sensory deficits like blindness for relevant conceptualizations should be fatal. Here is Hume on this topic:

> "wherever by any accident the faculties which give rise to any impression are obstructed in their operations, as when one is born blind or deaf, not only the impressions are lost, but also their correspondent ideas; so that there never appear in the mind the least trace of either of them" (1739/1978, p. 49).

Descriptively, the outcome of Landau and Gleitman's investigation was that blind and sighted children were remarkably alike both in the rate and the content of their language learning. Correcting for neurological problems often associated with congenital blindness, the two populations started to talk at about the same time; the semantic content of their early vocabularies was alike; and they proceeded in the same steps toward the acquisition of the structures of the exposure language.

Of particular interest in the present context is the acquisition of words that Locke called "of one sense only," that is, items whose experiential basis would appear to come uniquely from vision. Two cases studied by Landau and Gleitman were vision verbs (*look, see,* etc.) and color terminology (*color, green, red*). Sighted blindfolded 3-year-olds told to "Look up!" turned their faces skyward, suggesting that they interpreted 'look' to implicate vision in particular. A blind 3-year-old given the same command raised her hands skyward instead, suggesting that for her the term was connected to the manual sense. Thus, the difference in observational opportunities led the two populations to different interpretations of the same term, just as Locke would have expected: Successful communication from mother to blind child using this term often occurred just when the objects to be looked at were in the learner's hands, licensing a physical contact interpretation of blind looking. However, as these investigators also showed, several common verbs used by the mother to the blind child shared the property of being uttered—and proportionally much more often than *look*—when the child had a relevant object in hand; namely, *hold, give, put,* and *play.* Moreover, the blind child's interpretation of *look* went beyond manual contact. When told "You can touch that table but don't look at it!" the blind child gave a gingerly tap or scratch at the table. Then told "Now you can look at it," the child explored the surfaces of the table manually. Based on this kind of evidence, Landau and Gleitman concluded that blind *look* (a) semantically differed from sighted *look* by implicating a different sense modality but (b) semantically resembled sighted *look* and differed from *hold, touch,* etc., in being a term of perception. In sum, we can easily account for the blind child's failure to map *look* onto the visual modality from an orthodox associative perspective on word learning that focuses on the necessity of extralinguistic observation. However, this perspective cannot so easily explain how blind (and sighted) learners hit upon looking as a perceptual rather than contact term. Again, these findings suggest that extralinguistic observation is insufficient as a full explanation of word learning.

The blind child's understanding of color terms offers a similar insight: The blind subject of Landau and Gleitman's case study knew (a) that *color* is the supernym for a subset of adjectival terms including *green* and *red* but not *clean* and *happy* and (b) that these terms apply only to concrete objects. To illustrate, although children (blind or sighted) have no experience of either *blue dogs* or *yellow ideas,* their responses to these two types of property violation were systematically different. Asked "Can a dog be blue?" the blind child at 5 years of age responded with different color terms: "A dog is not even blue. It's gold or brown or something else." Asked "Can an idea be yellow?" the child responded, "Really isn't yellow; really talked about—no color but we think about it in our mind." These findings display the remarkable resilience of semantic acquisition over variations of input: Lacking the ordinarily relevant observations that support the learning of visual terms, a blind child nevertheless detected some information in the use of these words that told her *what kinds of concept* they denoted.

How should we explain the robustness of semantic aspects of language learning in the face of the ordinary variability of experience and the vast array of reasonable semantic alternatives? The hypothesis we consider here is that vocabulary acquisition can get off the ground because some set of lexical items— mostly concrete nouns—can be learned by observation of the world alone. As Gillette et al. demonstrated, this kind of learning (word-to-world pairing) yields a limited concrete vocabulary even for adults. These items provide required scaffolding for the interpretation of more abstract words, including predicate terms (verbs, adjectives, prepositions). This linguistic information helps in a variety of ways, some of which are more helpful for some terms than others. First, known words can narrow the meanings of new ones via some form of lexical contrast. Second, a stock of known words can aid the acquisition of new words of the same grammatical category by giving semantic consequences to the morphological or syntactic cues that pick out new members of that category (R. Brown, 1957); we have already alluded to this influence in discussing apparent effects of language on cueing the intended interpretation of events. Third, the nouns constitute arguments for predicate terms and so serve as a foundation on which the children build a rudimentary representation of the phrase structure of the input language (Fisher, 1996; Fisher et al., 1994; Gillette et al., 1999; Snedeker & Gleitman, in press).

Concrete Words First

Many studies show that children's early production vocabulary is dominated by concrete nouns—names for objects and people, in particular (see Gentner & Boroditsky, 2001, and Woodward & Markman, 1998, for reviews). This is true in languages other than English, even in languages like Italian (Caselli et al., 1995), Mandarin Chinese (Tardif, Gelman, & Xu, 1999), Korean (Au, Dapretto, & Song, 1994; cf. Choi & Gopnik, 1995), and Japanese (Fernald & Morikawa, 1993), which possess surface properties conducive to verb learning, including the omission of noun phrases when they can be inferred. Such factors do affect productive verb vocabularies: A checklist study of early vocabularies in Mandarin Chinese revealed a significantly smaller noun advantage for Chinese- than for English-speaking children, suggesting that the frequent appearance of isolated verbs in speech to children creates enhanced opportunities for learning verbs (Tardif et al., 1999; but see also Snedeker and Li, 2000, who have data suggesting that the most potent factor may be that Chinese mothers are far less likely than are American mothers to use abstract verbs such as *think* and *like* to their toddlers). Despite all these countervailing influences, to a greater or lesser degree, object terms predominate in the early production vocabulary cross-linguistically.

A bias toward learning object names is present in the earliest language comprehension as well. As noted earlier in this review, novel words presented in object-manipulation contexts cause 9- to 13-month-olds, as well as older children, to focus on the kinds of similarity across objects that can indicate shared category membership (Balaban & Waxman, 1997; Markman & Hutchinson, 1984; Waxman & Markow, 1995; Woodward & Markman, 1998). When a new word is presented, the object-kind interpretation is often so salient that it is difficult to get children to arrive at any other interpretation (P. Bloom, 2000; Gentner, 1982; Maratsos, 1990).

Other things being equal, children prefer object categories at the relatively concrete, "basic" level of categorization (the ordinarily used "bird" level of categorization in the *robin-bird-animal* hierarchy; e.g., Hall & Waxman, 1993). This preference on the part of the child maps neatly onto the naming practices of adults, at least in English parent-child conversations: Parents tend to give things their basic-level names before naming their parts, before invoking a superordinate label, or before using a situation-limited label like *passenger* (e.g., Callanan, 1985; Hall, 1994; Ninio, 1980; Shipley, Kuhn, & Madden, 1983).

The object-naming preference in early word learning is not an absolute bias. Although names for things predominate in early production and comprehension vocabularies,

very young children also learn property terms (*hot, dirty*), action words (*walk, kiss*), directional particles (*up, out*), terms for substances (*milk, juice*), and other oddments (*bath, noise;* e.g., Caselli et al., 1995; Nelson, Hampson, & Shaw, 1993). Children as young as 15 months old understand some verbs in sentences (e.g., Hirsh-Pasek & Golinkoff, 1996); children learn and produce verbs during the second year (e.g., Tomasello, 1992).

The Gillette et al. (1999) evidence reviewed earlier yields a simple explanation for the probabilistic noun dominance of the earliest vocabulary. The adult subjects in Gillette et al.'s studies had already grasped the concepts lexicalized by all the English words to be guessed in the study. Nevertheless, only the most concrete words were successfully identified from observing the extralinguistic contexts alone. Children's first words are determined by the tools available for word learning. The true beginner can only try to observe elements in the world that systematically occur with the use of particular words. This leads to success in those cases in which the word's meaning is concrete enough to be readily observable in the flow of events: mostly nouns, but also a heterogeneous set of other words. To learn less concrete (less observable) terms, the learner needs other kinds of evidence: linguistic evidence, bootstrapped from the previously acquired vocabulary of concrete words.

Another proposal that has much in common with ours is that of Gentner (1982; Gentner & Boroditsky, 2001). Gentner also argues that nouns fall toward the concrete, easy-to-grasp end of a conceptual-linguistic continuum along which word categories vary in their appearance across languages. Names for people and objects uniformly surface as nouns across languages, while words for properties, locations, substances, actions, and so forth, vary both in what kinds of information are conflated into the same word and in their organization into grammatical categories (e.g., Bowerman, 1990; Maratsos, 1998; Talmy, 1985). The less concrete terms thus are more dependant on linguistic learning. The only aspect of this argument as expressed by Gentner and Boroditsky (2001) that we cannot agree with is stated in the first paragraph of their paper: "The world presents perceptual bits whose clumping is not pre-ordained, and language has a say in how the bits get conflated into concepts" (pp. 215). We would amend: "Language has a say in how the conceptual bits get conflated into *words*." As we have already testified at some length, *the semantic organization of the lexicon is surely language-specific, but the meanings of our words do not exhaust our knowledge.*

Old Words Make New Words Easier to Learn

The true linguistic novice can pick up a small stock of concrete words, learned via word-to-world mapping unaided by prior linguistic knowledge but aided by all the conceptual apparatus and nascent understanding of human intentions described in the section titled "Primitive Categories of Experience." This step boosts the child into a better position to learn other words and to begin to work out the phrase structure of the exposure language.

Mutual Exclusivity, Lexical Contrast, Suppletion

Some notion of a simple contrast between words is widely assumed as an explanatory force in lexical acquisition. The most familiar demonstration was reported by Markman and Wachtel (1988): 3-year-olds were presented with two objects, one familiar (e.g., a cup), and one that they could not name (e.g., a wire whisk). Asked to give the experimenter "the blicket," the children handed over the whisk, appearing to assume that the new word did not apply to an already-named

object. Children also use their knowledge of familiar words to overcome the preference for object-category interpretations: In another of Markman and Wachtel's experiments, 3-year-olds interpreted a novel word applied to a familiar object as a name for a salient part—for example, the boom on a fire truck. Effects like these have been demonstrated in many different settings and with different categories of words (e.g., substance terms, property terms, verbs; see P. Bloom, 2000, and Woodward & Markman, 1998, for reviews). Old words seem to repel new ones, directing inferences toward conceivable interpretations that have not yet been picked out by a word. Once any set of word meanings is known, it provides a new source of bias in word interpretation.

Accounts of how children achieve this useful behavior vary. Markman and Wachtel proposed a mutual exclusivity principle, which holds that each object has exactly one name. This is a preference or a bias, not an absolute constraint; thus, it permits the acquisition of second names for things based on strong linguistic evidence (Liittschwager & Markman, 1994). Clark (1987) proposed a principle of contrast, which holds that any two linguistic forms (words, but also syntactic formats) differ in their meanings, and a principle of conventionality, which holds that there is a preferred, ordinary way of making reference to each thing. This permits the hearer to make the pragmatic inference that if the conventional name was not used, something else must have been meant. On either view, old words influence the induction of meanings for new words. Some form of contrast between lexical items, also known as suppletion, plays a role in virtually every theory of word and syntax acquisition. The child's existing knowledge of language (or whatever part of it can be retrieved at the moment) is used to interpret each utterance by boosting the salience of interpretations for which the child does not already have a word.

Differentiating Grammatical Categories

We earlier reviewed evidence that children make progress in the creation of grammatical categories via a distributional analysis over linguistic forms. This analysis, however, proceeds at the same time that children are learning the meanings of words. Distributional analysis gives children an enormously powerful source of information for grouping words into semantic as well as grammatical categories: Even though the grade-school definitions of parts of speech are inadequate in detail, grammatical categories are probabilistically related to abstract semantic categories across languages (L. Bloom, 1998; Gleitman, 1990; Grimshaw, 1981; Macnamara, 1982; Maratsos, 1998; Pinker, 1984; Schlesinger, 1988). The abstract semantic coherence of grammatical categories has at least two effects: (a) Once a category has been formed, even in part, learners can determine the grammatical categories of new words whose meanings they know; and (b) if the grammatical category of a word can be inferred from its distributional signature, its meaning can be inferred with less error.

The differentiation of grammatical categories begins early. By 13 months of age infants infer a property interpretation of a new word (e.g., 'yellow' things) if the set of objects that the infants are shown does not support an object-category interpretation and if the new word is presented as an adjective, not as a count noun (e.g., "a daxish one," not "a dax"; Waxman, 1999); count nouns are interpreted as object-category names by 12-month-olds (Waxman & Markow, 1995). These infants have apparently already picked up some of the morphological cues that identify count nouns in English, and they use them to guide word mapping (see also Waxman & Hall, 1993). By 18 months to 2.5 years, children extend a novel count noun ("a dax") to other, similar objects but restrict their extension of a novel noun with no determiner to the named individual (a proper name, "Dax"; Katz, Baker, & Macnamara, 1974; Gelman & Taylor, 1984; Hall, 1991). Two- and 3-year-olds use count- and mass-noun syntax ("a dax" vs. "some dax") to choose between substance and object interpretations of new words (Soja, 1992). This process culminates in the performance of preschoolers in Roger Brown's famous experiment (1957), who indicated that "a dax" was an object, "some dax" was a nonsolid substance, and "daxing" meant an action.

The morphological markers of grammatical class are language-specific and must be learned. This learning depends on the formal analysis required to achieve word and morpheme segmentation and on the acquisition of a sufficiently large set of words within a category to identify its morphological signature. In addition, as mentioned earlier, the grammatical categories themselves are not quite the same across languages (e.g., Croft, 1990; Maratsos, 1998). Children must achieve a language-specific differentiation of predicate types (verbs, prepositions, adjectives). On the current view, this differentiation is based on the distributional, semantic, and phonological similarity of items within grammatical categories. These categories, perforce, have language-specific semantic consequences. Learners of a language that does not have the same split between noun and adjective meanings should not show the same word-interpretive preferences when given new members of these categories (see Waxman et al., 1997).

Inference from language-specific grammatical categories provides a way for early vocabulary learning to guide further word learning. Closed-class cues to grammatical class are not all-powerful, however, for a variety of reasons. First, to the extent that the child's earliest vocabulary consists mostly of elements from one class (nouns), other linguistic evidence will be required to begin to interpret and identify other word types. Second, assignment of a novel word to a specific grammatical category depends on the identification of function morphemes. These short and unstressed items should be relatively hard to detect in connected speech. Although very young children are sensitive to some of the function morphology found in noun and verb phrases (Gerken et al., 1990; Santelmann & Jusczyk, 1998; Waxman, 1999), this surely does not mean that they identify these elements without error. Like any linguistic cue, morphological cues to grammatical category will influence interpretation only to the extent that children correctly analyze the given string of morphemes (see Gleitman et al., 1988). Third, correct assignment to a grammatical category offers quite abstract evidence about the meaning of a new word. Even the youngest child's nouns are not all object-names (e.g., Caselli et al., 1995; Nelson, 1988). Apparently, the child is not forced by morphology to interpret *bath* or *sky* as an object category name just because it is presented as a count noun. Finally, and relatedly, in any instance of mapping a word form (guided by the available syntactic hints) onto some interpretation of the world context, what is available and most salient in the child's conception of the context will also constrain interpretation. For all these reasons, even though preschoolers can use closed-class cues to grammatical form class in interpreting new words, they do not always manage to do so. The presence or absence of closed-class markers can persuade children to arrive at property or substance interpretations of a new word (e.g., "This is a zavish one" rather than "This is a zav" or "This is pewter"), but preschoolers are more likely to show sensitivity to such cues if the new word is presented in the context of objects whose basic-level names are already familiar (Hall, Waxman, & Hurwitz, 1993; Markman & Wachtel, 1988) or provided ("a zav horse"; Mintz & Gleitman, 2001).

Nouns as Scaffolding for Sentence Interpretation

How does the child move beyond an initial concrete vocabulary (mostly nouns) and begin to learn words of other classes? The indirect relationship between verb meaning and world events makes verb learning in particular somewhat mysterious. The view known as *syntactic bootstrapping* (Gleitman, 1990) proposes that the interpretation of verbs and other predicate terms is guided by information about the structure of the sentence in which the verb appears (see also Fisher, 1996, 2000a; Fisher et al., 1994; Gleitman & Gleitman, 1997; Naigles, 1990). Most generally, this view proposes that word learning after the first primitive steps proceeds by sentence-to-world pairing rather than merely by word-to-world pairing.

To illustrate, let us return to Gillette et al.'s (1999) human simulations, described earlier. Gillette et al. repeated their experiment, asking adults to guess verbs spoken to young children based on various combinations of linguistic and extralinguistic information. Adults were much more accurate in guessing which verb the mother said to her child when given information about the sentence in which the verb occurred. When given a list of the nouns that occurred in the sentence (alphabetized to remove word-order information), along with the scene in which the verb was produced, subjects' guesses were significantly more accurate than when given the scene alone. More elaborated syntactic information made subjects' guesses still more accurate: When presented with the complete sentence with the verb replaced by a nonsense word (much as in Lewis Carroll's poem, "Jabberwocky"), subjects' guesses were quite accurate even without access to the scenes and were nearly perfect with both sentence and scene.

Why would syntactic information so strongly guide semantic inferences? These effects stem from the same fundamental links between syntax and semantics which we earlier discussed in the context of the invention of languages. Verbs vary in their syntactic privileges (i.e., the number, type, and positioning of their associated phrases). Quirks and exceptions aside, these variations are systematically related to the semantic argument-taking properties of the verbs (e.g., L. Bloom, 1970; Croft, 1990; Fillmore, 1968; Fisher, Gleitman, & Gleitman, 1991; Gleitman, 1990; Goldberg, 1995; Grimshaw, 1981, 1994; Gruber, 1967; Levin & Rappaport Hovav, 1995; Pinker, 1989). A verb that describes the motion of an object will tend to occur with a noun phrase that specifies the object; a verb that describes action on an object will typically accept two noun phrases (i.e., be transitive), one for the actor and one for the object; a verb that describes transfer of an object from one person to another will take three arguments. Similarly sensible patterns appear for argument type: A verb like *see* can take a noun phrase as its complement (because we can see objects), but it also can take a sentence as its complement because we can perceive states of affairs. To the adults in Gillette et al.'s studies, therefore, or to a suitably constructed young learner, sentences can provide information about the semantic structure of the verb in that sentence, providing a kind of "linguistic zoom lens" to help the learner detect the verb's perspective on the event. The evidence from language invention reviewed earlier sharply focuses our understanding of these syntax-semantic correspondences and how they feed the language-learning process. Certain of these fundamental correspondences between the argument-taking aspects of predicates and their realizations in syntactic structure need not be learned, but in some skeletal form come for free, as shown in the sentence forms of Goldin-Meadow's isolates and the child inventors of NSL. Landau and Gleitman (1985) conjectured that just such linguistic systematicity accounts for how the blind learner concludes that *see* is a perceptual term.

According to syntactic bootstrapping theory, what goes for these special populations goes for more normally circumstanced learners as well. Learning of words takes place in situations of massive variability and ambiguity. As for the structures, however, they too provide only partial evidence as to the meaning of the words that they contain. Verbs that share a syntactic structure can vary greatly in their semantic content: Transitive verbs include *see, like,* and *break;* intransitive verbs include *sleep* and *dance.* The semantic information that might be inferred from sentence structure could be described as relevant to the sentence's semantic structure—how many and what participants are involved—rather than the event-dependent semantic content (sleeping vs. dancing; see Fisher et al., 1991; Grimshaw, 1994). But this abstract information is precisely what is not routinely available in observations of events. Taken together, the data of event observation and linguistic observation converge in an efficient learning procedure for vocabulary and syntax.

Children's Use of Syntactic Evidence in Sentence Interpretation

Many studies show that children between about 2 and 5 years old use syntactic cues in sentence interpretation, arriving at different interpretations of verbs presented in different sentence structures (e.g., Fisher, 1996, in press; Fisher et al., 1994; Naigles, 1990; Naigles & Kako, 1993). Naigles (1990) showed 25-month-olds a videotape depicting two concurrent events. In one case, a duck bent a bunny into a bowing posture while both duck and rabbit made arm circles. Children heard a new verb used to describe this composite scene; half of the children heard a transitive verb, as in (1), and half of the children heard an intransitive verb, as in (2). Following this introduction, the two parts of the composite event were separated onto two video screens. Now one screen showed the causal action of the duck on the bunny (causing-to-bow, but no arm-waving), while the other showed the simultaneous action of the duck and the bunny (arm-waving, but no causing-to-bow). When exhorted to "Find kradding!" the children who had heard the transitive sentence (1) looked longer at the causal scene, whereas those who had heard the intransitive sentence (2) looked longer at the simultaneous action scene. These 2-year-olds used syntactic evidence to infer which event in a complex scene was described by a new verb.

(1)   The duck is kradding the bunny!

(2)   The duck and the bunny are kradding!

Similar syntactic evidence can persuade young children to alter their interpretations of a familiar verb. Naigles, Gleitman, and Gleitman (1993) asked preschoolers to act out sentences using a toy Noah's Ark and its associated characters. The informative trials were those in which a verb was offered in a new syntactic environment, as in "Noah brings to the ark" or "Noah goes the elephant to the ark." Young children adjusted the interpretation of the verb to fit its new syntactic frame, for example acting out *go* as "cause to go" when it was presented as a transitive verb. Sentence evidence can also cause preschoolers to focus on different aspects of the same event in interpreting a novel verb (Fisher et al., 1994).

The sentences in these studies provided many language-specific sources of evidence: the set of familiar nouns in the sentence, their order relative to each other and relative to the new verb, and English functional elements like *and* and *to* that specified how particular noun phrases were to be linked into the

sentence structure. A recent series of studies was designed to isolate particular features of a sentence's structure, asking what aspects of the structure young children find meaningful. In several studies, 2.5, 3-, and 5-year-olds (Fisher, 1996, in press) heard novel verbs used to describe unfamiliar causal events; the verbs were presented either transitively or intransitively. The sentences contained only ambiguous pronouns, as in (3); thus the sentences differed only in their number of noun phrases. The children's interpretations of the novel verbs were tested by asking them to point out, in a still picture of the event, which character's role the verb described ("Who's pilking [her] over there?"). Both adults and children at all three ages were more likely to select the causal agent in the event as the subject of a transitive verb rather than that of an intransitive verb. Just as for the adult judges in the Gillette et al. studies, these findings provide evidence that the *set of noun phrases* in the sentence—even without information about which is the subject—influences young children's interpretations of verbs. Even 2.5-year-olds interpret the subject's role differently depending on the overall structure of the sentence.

(3)   She's pilking her over there.
      She's pilking over there.

Compare these results with the innovations of the deaf home signers who invented their own manual communication systems. In both cases, children seem to be biased to map participants in a conceptual representation of an event one to one onto noun arguments in sentences. Elsewhere we have proposed (Fisher, 1996, 2000a; Fisher et al., 1994; Gillette et al., 1999) that children might arrive at this structure-sensitive interpretation of a sentence in a simple way: by aligning a representation of a sentence with a structured conceptual representation of a relevant situation. In this way a child might infer that a sentence with two noun arguments must mean something about a conceptual relationship between the referents of the two nouns, while a sentence with only one noun argument might describe a state, property, or act of the single participant. This simple structure mapping could take place as soon as the child can identify some nouns and represent them as parts of a larger utterance. The familiar nouns in the sentence might provide a partial or skeletal sentence structure that would constrain interpretation.

Arguments and Adjuncts. Immediate objections to this "counting the nouns" procedure might come to mind. First, *nouns in the sentence* are not the same thing as *arguments of the verb*. In many languages, sentence subjects can be freely omitted if they are recoverable from context and prior discourse; in some languages, including Chinese, Japanese, and Korean, verbs' direct objects can be omitted as well (e.g., Clancy, 1985; Rispoli, 1989). These well-known facts guarantee that many individual sentences in casual speech will not display the complete set of the verb's arguments. In addition, sentences can contain more noun phrases than argument positions. The distinction between arguments of a verb and adjunct phrases ("with Ginger," "in the morning") that can be added to almost any sentence is a notoriously slippery one, difficult to define across languages (e.g., Croft, 1990).

Despite the somewhat messy relationship between nouns in sentences and the syntactically subcategorized arguments of the verb, several sources of evidence suggest that ordinary sentences provide strong probabilistic information about the participant structures of verbs. Brent's (1994) simulations of verb-subcategorization frame learning from spontaneous child-directed speech, described earlier, testified to the robustness of information about verb subcategorization in input sentences. Lederer, Gleitman, and Gleitman (1995) showed that the syntactic contexts of verbs in speech to young children powerfully predicted judged verb-semantic similarity. In the "human simulations" of Gillette et al. (1999), adults benefited from simply being given an alphabetized list of the nouns in each sentence in which the mothers had produced a particular verb. In this case the adults (like the hypothetical learner) could not tell which nouns were arguments of a verb and which were adjuncts, yet this linguistic hint aided recovery of verb meanings from scenes. Li (1994) analyzed speech to young children in Mandarin Chinese and found that although mothers did omit noun phrases in sentences, maternal utterances still supported a strong differentiation among semantically and syntactically distinct classes of verbs. Although arguments can be omitted, transitive verbs still occur with two nouns in the sentence more often than intransitive verbs do. Considerable evidence tells us that young children are quite good at learning about the sentence structures in which particular verbs occur (e.g., Gordon & Chafetz, 1990; Tomasello, 2000); such findings suggest that young children may well be capable of taking advantage of probabilistic evidence, presented across multiple sentences, for the range of sentence structures assigned to each verb.

Learned Correspondences between Syntax and Meaning. A second objection is essentially the reverse of the first: The findings reported so far are consistent with the view that there is a bias to map one to one between the set of arguments of the verb and the set of participants in the event, in children acquiring an established language as well as for linguistic isolates inventing their own sign systems. Perhaps, however, in the case of children learning an established language, the early honoring of this simple mapping from participant number to noun-phrase number is an effect of language learning rather than the reflection of some unlearned bias.

Language-specific aspects of the mapping between syntax and meaning affect sentence interpretation from an early age: Hirsh-Pasek and Golinkoff (1996) showed English-learning 17- to 19-month-olds two videos displaying the same familiar action, differing only in which participants were the doer and done-to in each. The infants' attention to the two screens revealed sensitivity to word order (e.g., "Cookie Monster is tickling Big Bird" vs. "Big Bird is tickling Cookie Monster"): They looked longer at the screen on which the subject of the test sentence was the agent of the action. Children aged 26 and 21 months showed the same sensitivity to English word order when presented with made-up verbs and unfamiliar actions (Fisher, 2000b). Very young children acquiring a free word-order language acquire the semantic implications of case-marking morphology by age two (e.g., results for Turkish learners reported in Slobin, 1982). Do children simply exploit the most stable cues to mapping made available in the language that they hear, rather than relying on an unlearned bias for one-to-one mapping?

To investigate this issue, Lidz, Gleitman, and Gleitman (2000) asked preschoolers to act out novel combinations of verbs and syntactic structures in two languages: English (as in Naigles et al., 1993) and Kannada, a language spoken in Western India. Kannada permits pervasive argument dropping, rendering the relationship between argument number and noun-phrase number relatively variable in typical input sentences. Kannada also has, however, a causative morpheme that only occurs with causative verbs. The critical sentences pitted argument number (two nouns vs. one) against causative morphology (explicitly marked as causal or not). Kannada-speaking 3-year-olds ignored the presence or absence of the causative morpheme, relying only on the number of noun phrases in the sentence they heard. In contrast, Kannada-speaking adults'

enactments were influenced by both morphology and argument number. The adult findings again demonstrate that language learners ultimately acquire whatever cues to sentence meaning the exposure language makes available. But strikingly, they also show that children are not totally open-minded: They appear to find some formal devices (argument number) more potent than others (inflectional morphology).

Summary: Consequences of One-to-One Mapping. Given the inevitable mismatches between number of nouns in a sentence and number of arguments of a verb, the structural alignment procedure yields a number of interesting consequences for learning, predicting both useful properties and errors that the learner will need to overcome (see Fisher, 2000a). One advantage of structural alignment is that it could guide the interpretation of any argument-taking predicate term. A one-to-one mapping of nouns in sentences onto participants in conceptual representations of scenes provides no basis for distinguishing between different classes of argument-taking words like verbs, adjectives, and prepositions. This lack of specificity could be useful given the cross-linguistic variability in categories of predicate terms (e.g., Croft, 1990). Maratsos (1990; see also Braine, 1992) has suggested that children might approach language acquisition expecting a basic syntactic distinction between referential and relational words, analogous to the semantic distinction between arguments and predicates.

The notion that children can interpret sentence structure as a general analog of predicate-argument semantics could help to explain how the child figures out which words are argument-taking predicates in the first place: Landau and Stecker (1990) taught 3-year-olds a novel word that the experimenter introduced as she placed an unfamiliar object on top of a box. The word was presented either as a noun ("This is a corp") or as a preposition ("This is acorp my box"). Children who heard the word presented as a noun considered that an object in any location relative to the box could be "a corp," but they resisted changes in the object's shape. Children who heard the word presented as a preposition accepted shape changes but maintained that only objects in certain locations could be "acorp the box." Having arguments, "is acorp" was taken to refer to a relation between the referents of those arguments.

WHERE LEARNING ENDS

We have tried in this review to bring together some of what is currently known about the spectacular and species-uniform programmed learning capacity for language. We have reviewed evidence for the infant's remarkable capacity for learning about the idiosyncrasies of particular languages, but also for powerful constraints that structure the mapping of ideas onto linguistic expressions. One matter we have left aside until now is that this capacity does not persist forever and unchanged in species members. Sufficient witness are the heavy accents and fractured grammars characteristic of many brilliant foreign-born adults, be they architects, physicists, philosophers, and even linguists. Adults who may solve quadratic equations cannot equal the achievements of the most ordinary native-born 5-year-old in mastering the relative clause and verbal auxiliary.

Much of our knowledge on this topic has traditionally come from studies of second-language learning, for the obvious reason that it is hard to find adults who have not been exposed to a language early in life. In general, the findings are these: In the first stages of learning a second language's morphology, syntax, and semantics, adults appear

to be more efficient than children (Snow & Hoefnagel-Hoehle, 1978). But the long-range outcome is just the reverse. After a few years' exposure, young children speak the new language fluently. Differences between native-born and very young second-language learners typically cannot be detected except under stringent laboratory tests (e.g., for phonetic discrimination; Pallier, Bosch, & Sebastian-Galles, 1997). This contrast has been drawn by investigators who studied the outcome of second-language learning as a function of age at first exposure (Johnson & Newport, 1989; Oyama, 1978). In the Johnson and Newport study, the subjects were native Chinese and Korean speakers who came to the United States and were immersed in English at varying ages. These subjects were tested after a minimum of 3 years living in the English-speaking American community. Subjects listened to English sentences, half of which were ungrammatical, the other half being the grammatical counterparts of these. Correct assignment of these sentences as grammatical versus ungrammatical was native-like for those exposed to English before about age 7. Thereafter, there was an increasing decrement in performance as a function of age at first exposure. These results have usually been interpreted as suggesting a critical period for language acquisition—an effect attributable to the mental status of the learner rather than to the environmental conditions for learning.

However, based on the data just discussed, an entirely different kind of explanation is possible: Perhaps exposure to Mandarin or Greek affects learning or organizational biases relevant to language and so interferes with the later learning of a different language. There must be some merit to this alternative hypothesis; otherwise there would be no explaining why Greeks and Chinese and Germans have different accents and different grammatical difficulties in acquiring English. The analysis of speech is context- and knowledge-dependent; therefore, having the wrong knowledge should cause trouble with the analysis of foreign linguistic data.

Over the past decade and a half Newport, Supalla, and their colleagues have studied populations that permit a disentangling of age or critical period effects from the effects of prior language learning. The subjects are the language-isolated deaf children of hearing parents who were discussed earlier. Although these children generate idiosyncratic home sign systems that reveal the skeletal hallmarks of all human languages, this situation is by no means equivalent to acquiring a fully elaborated language from native-speaking or -signing adults. As they grow up, most of these children eventually come into contact with a formal sign language; at that point they ordinarily enter the deaf community and use sign language daily and habitually for the rest of their lives. Newport (1990) studied the production and comprehension of American Sign Language (ASL) by adults who had been using ASL as their primary means of communication for at least 30 years, but whose first exposure was either from birth (children of deaf, signing parents), early in life (between ages 4 and 6), or late (after age 12). Only the early learners showed native competence 30 years later. Later learners had particular trouble with the ASL equivalents of function morphemes and the embedding structures of complex sentences. The same pattern emerges in the acquisition of NSL by its first generations of speaker/inventors as discussed earlier: Senghas and Coppola (in press) found effects of signers' age of entry into the signing community on their use of aspects of NSL morphology. During NSL's development as a language, learners who started young were more likely to acquire the spatial morphological resources of this emerging system.

In short, late learning, whether of a first or a second language, leads to nonnative competence. In both cases, the universal skeletal forms of language—the meanings of content words and their combination in spelling out basic predicate argument structures—are acquired, but the frills and grace notes of elaborated languages are evidently more fragile and grow progressively harder to attain with the passage of time. Language learning, as we have tried to show, is robust to all the environmental variation compatible with the maintenance of human life but reaches its apogee in the very young human learner.

REFERENCES

Aguiar, A., & Baillargeon, R. (1999). 2.5-month-old infants' reasoning about when objects should and should not be occluded. *Cognitive Psychology, 39,* 116–157.

Aslin, R. N., Saffran, J. R., & Newport, E. L. (1998). Computation of conditional probability statistics by 8-month-old infants. *Psychological Science, 9,* 321–324.

Au, T. K., Dapretto, M., & Song, Y. (1994). Input vs constraints: Early word acquisition in Korean and English. *Journal of Memory & Language, 33,* 567–582.

Baillargeon, R. (1998). Infants' understanding of the physical world. In M. Sabourin, F. Craik, & M. Robert (Eds.), *Advances in psychological science* (Vol. 2, pp. 503–529). London: Psychology Press.

Balaban, M. T., & Waxman, S. R. (1997). Do words facilitate object categorization in 9-month-old infants? *Journal of Experimental Child Psychology, 64,* 3–26.

Baldwin, D. A. (1991). Infants' contribution to the achievement of joint reference. *Child Development, 62,* 875–890.

Baldwin, D. A. (1993). Early referential understanding: Infants' ability to recognize referential acts for what they are. *Developmental Psychology, 29,* 832–843.

Baldwin, D. A., Markman, E. M., & Melartin, R. L. (1993). Infants' ability to draw inferences about nonobvious object properties: Evidence from exploratory play. *Child Development, 64,* 711–728.

Baldwin, D. A., & Moses, L. J. (1996). The ontogeny of social information gathering. *Child Development, 67,* 1915–1939.

Beach, C. M. (1991). The interpretation of prosodic patterns at points of syntactic structure ambiguity: Evidence for cue trading relations. *Journal of Memory & Language, 30,* 644–663.

Bernstein Ratner, N. (1986). Durational cues which mark clause boundaries in mother-child speech. *Journal of Phonetics, 14,* 303–309.

Bierwisch, M., & Schreuder, R. (1992). From concepts to lexical items. *Cognition, 42,* 23–60.

Bijeljac-Babic, R., Bertoncini, J., & Mehler, J. (1993). How do 4-day-old infants categorize multisyllabic utterances? *Developmental Psychology, 29,* 711–721.

Bloom, L. (1970). *Language development: Form and function in emerging grammars.* Cambridge, MA: MIT Press.

Bloom, L. (1998). Language acquisition in its developmental context. In W. Damon (Series Ed.), D. Kuhn & R. S. Siegler (Vol. Eds.), *Handbook of child psychology, Vol. 2: Cognition, perception, and language* (pp. 309–370). New York: Wiley.

Bloom, P. (2000). *How children learn the meanings of words.* Cambridge, MA: MIT Press.

Bloomfield, L. (1933). *Language.* New York: Holt.

Bock, K., Loebell, H., & Morey, R. (1992). From conceptual roles to structural relations: Bridging the syntactic cleft. *Psychological Review, 99,* 150–171.

Bosch, L., & Sebastian-Galles, N. (1997). Native-language recognition abilities in 4-month-old infants from monolingual and bilingual environments. *Cognition, 65,* 33–69.

Bowerman, M. (1985). What shapes children's grammars? In D. I. Slobin (Ed.), *The cross-linguistic study of language acquisition, Vol. 2: Theoretical Issues* (pp. 1257–1319). Hillsdale, NJ: Erlbaum.

Bowerman, M. (1990). Mapping thematic roles onto syntactic functions: Are children helped by innate linking rules? *Linguistics, 28,* 1253–1289.

Bowerman, M. (1996). Learning how to structure space for language: A cross-linguistic perspective. In P. Bloom, M. A. Peterson, L. Nadel, & M. F. Garrett (Eds.), *Language and space* (pp. 385–436). Cambridge, MA: MIT Press.

Bowerman, M., & Levinson, S. C. (2001). Introduction. In M. Bowerman & S. C. Levinson (Eds.), *Language acquisition and conceptual development* (pp. 1–16). Cambridge: Cambridge University Press.

Braine, M. D. S. (1992). What sort of innate structure is needed to "bootstrap" into syntax? *Cognition, 45,* 77–100.

Brent, M. R. (1994). Surface cues and robust inference as a basis for the early acquisition of subcategorization frames. In L. R. Gleitman & B. Landau (Eds.), *The acquisition of the lexicon* (pp. 433–470). Cambridge, MA: MIT Press.

Brent, M. R., & Cartwright, T. A. (1996). Distributional regularity and phonotactic constraints are useful for segmentation. *Cognition, 61,* 93–125.

Brown, P. (2001). Learning to talk about motion UP and DOWN in Tzeltal: Is there a language-specific bias for verb learning? In M. Bowerman & S. C. Levinson (Eds.), *Language acquisition and conceptual development* (pp. 512–543). New York: Cambridge University Press.

Brown, R. (1957). Linguistic determinism and the part of speech. *Journal of Abnormal and Social Psychology, 55,* 1–5.

Brown, R. (1973). *A first language.* Cambridge, MA: Harvard University Press.

Callanan, M. A. (1985). How parents label objects for young children: The role of input in the acquisition of category hierarchies. *Child Development, 56,* 508–523.

Carey, S. (1978). The child as word learner. In M. Halle, J. Bresnan & G. A. Miller (Eds.), *Linguistic theory and psychological reality* (pp. 264–293). Cambridge, MA: MIT Press.

Carpenter, M., Akhtar, N., & Tomasello, M. (1998). Fourteen- through 18-month-old infants differentially imitate intentional and accidental actions. *Infant Behavior & Development, 21,* 315–330.

Cartwright, T. A., & Brent, M. R. (1997). Syntactic categorization in early language acquisition:

Formalizing the role of distributional analysis. *Cognition, 63,* 121–170.

Caselli, M. C., Bates, E., Casadio, P., Fenson, J., Fenson, L., Sanderl, L., & Weir, J. (1995). A cross-linguistic study of early lexical development. *Cognitive Development, 10,* 159–199.

Chambers, K. E., & Onishi, K. H. (2001, April). *Distributional learning of phonotactic constraints.* Paper presented at the Biennial Meeting of the Society for Research on Child Development, Minneapolis, MN.

Choi, S., & Bowerman, M. (1991). Learning to express motion events in English and Korean: The influence of language-specific lexicalization patterns. *Cognition, 41,* 83–121.

Choi, S., & Gopnik, A. (1995). Early acquisition of verbs in Korean: A cross-linguistic study. *Journal of Child Language, 22,* 497–529.

Chomsky, N. (1957). *Syntactic structures.* The Hague: Mouton & Co.

Chomsky, N. (1965). *Aspects of the theory of syntax.* Cambridge, MA: MIT Press.

Chomsky, N. (1981). *Lectures on government and binding.* Dordrecht: Foris.

Chomsky, N. (1982). *Noam Chomsky on the generative enterprise: A discussion with Riny Huybregts and Henk van Riemsdijk.* Dordrecht: Foris.

Chomsky, N. (1995). *The minimalist program.* Cambridge, MA: MIT Press.

Chomsky, N., & Halle, M. (1968). *The sound pattern of English.* New York: Harper & Row.

Church, K. W. (1987). Phonological parsing and lexical retrieval. In U. H. Frauenfelder & L. K. Tyler (Eds.), *Spoken word recognition* (pp. 53–69). Boston: MIT Press.

Clancy, P. M. (1985). The acquisition of Japanese. In D. I. Slobin (Ed.), *The crosslinguistic study of language acquisition, Vol. 1: The data* (pp. 373–524). Hillsdale, NJ: Erlbaum.

Clark, E. V. (1987). The principle of contrast: A constraint on language acquisition. In B. MacWhinney (Ed.), *Mechanisms of language acquisition* (pp. 1–33). Hillsdale, NJ: Erlbaum.

Clark, E. V. (1990). Speaker perspective in language acquisition. *Linguistics, 28,* 1201–1220.

Clark, R. (1992). The selection of syntactic knowledge. *Language Acquisition, 2,* 83–149.

Cooper, W. E., & Paccia-Cooper, J. (1980). *Syntax and speech.* Cambridge, MA: Harvard University Press.

Cooper, W. E., & Sorenson, J. M. (1977). Fundamental frequency contours at syntactic boundaries. *Journal of the Acoustical Society of America, 62,* 683–692.

Croft, W. (1990). *Typology and universals.* New York: Cambridge University Press.

Csibra, G., Gergely, G., Bíró, S., Koós, O., & Brockbank, M. (1999). Goal attribution without agency cues: The perception of "pure reason" in infancy. *Cognition, 72,* 237–267.

Cutler, A. (1990). Exploiting prosodic probabilities in speech segmentation. In G. T. M. Altmann (Ed.), *Cognitive models of speech processing: Psycholinguistic and computational perspectives* (pp. 105–121). Cambridge, MA: MIT Press.

Cutler, A., Mehler, J., Norris, D., & Segui, J. (1986). The syllable's differing role in the segmentation of French and English. *Journal of Memory & Language, 25,* 385–400.

Dell, G. S., Reed, K. D., Adams, D. R., & Meyer, A. S. (2000). Speech errors, phonotactic constraints, and implicit learning: A study of the role of experience in language production. *Journal of Experimental Psychology: Learning, Memory, & Cognition, 26,* 1355–1367.

Dowty, D. (1991). Thematic proto-roles and argument selection. *Language, 67,* 547–619.

Dresher, B. E. (1999). Charting the learning path: Cues to parameter setting. *Linguistic Inquiry, 30,* 27–67.

Duez, D. (1993). Acoustic correlates of subjective pauses. *Journal of Psycholinguistic Research, 22,* 21–39.

Eimas, P. D. (1975). Auditory and phonetic coding of the cues for speech: Discrimination of the [r-l] distinction by young infants. *Perception & Psychophysics, 18,* 341–347.

Eimas, P. D. (1999). Segmental and syllabic representations in the perception of speech by young infants. *Journal of the Acoustical Society of America, 105,* 1901–1911.

Elman, J. L., & McClelland, J. L. (1988). Cognitive penetration of the mechanisms of perception: Compensation for coarticulation of lexically restored phonemes. *Journal of Memory & Language, 27,* 143–165.

Farnetani, E. (1997). Coarticulation and connected speech processes. In W. J. Hardcastle & J. Laver (Eds.), *The handbook of phonetic sciences* (pp. 371–404). Cambridge, MA: Blackwell.

Feldman, H., Goldin-Meadow, S., & Gleitman, L. R. (1978). Beyond Herodotus: The creation of language by linguistically deprived deaf children. In A. Lock (Ed.), *Action, symbol, and gesture: The emergence of language* (pp. 351–414). New York: Academic Press.

Fernald, A., & Morikawa, H. (1993). Common themes and cultural variations in Japanese and American mothers' speech to infants. *Child Development, 64,* 637–656.

Fillmore, C. J. (1968). The case for case. In E. Bach & R. T. Harms (Eds.), *Universals in linguistic theory* (pp. 1–88). New York: Holt, Rinehart and Winston.

Fillmore, C. J. (1977). The case for case reopened. In P. Cole & J. M. Sadock (Eds.), *Syntax and semantics, Vol. 8: Grammatical relations* (pp. 59–81). New York: Academic Press.

Fisher, C. (1996). Structural limits on verb mapping: The role of analogy in children's interpretations of sentences. *Cognitive Psychology, 31,* 41–81.

Fisher, C. (2000a). From form to meaning: A role for structural analogy in the acquisition of language. In H. W. Reese (Ed.), *Advances in child development and behavior* (Vol. 27, pp. 1–53). New York: Academic Press.

Fisher, C. (2000b, July). *Who's blicking whom? Word order influences toddlers' interpretations of novel verbs.* Paper presented at the 11th International Conference on Infant Studies, Brighton, England.

Fisher, C. (in press). Structural limits on verb mapping: The role of abstract structure in 2.5-year-olds' interpretations of novel verbs. *Developmental Science.*

Fisher, C., Gleitman, H., & Gleitman, L. R. (1991). On the semantic content of subcategorization frames. *Cognitive Psychology, 23,* 331–392.

Fisher, C., Hall, D. G., Rakowitz, S., & Gleitman, L. (1994). When it is better to receive than to give: Syntactic and conceptual constraints on vocabulary growth. *Lingua, 92,* 333–375.

Fisher, C., Hunt, C. M., Chambers, K., & Church, B. A. (2001). Abstraction and specificity in preschoolers' representations of novel spoken words. *Journal of Memory & Language, 45,* 665–687.

Fisher, C., & Tokura, H. (1996). Acoustic cues to grammatical structure in infant-directed speech: Cross-linguistic evidence. *Child Development, 67,* 3192–3218.

Fodor, J. A. (1975). *The language of thought.* Cambridge, MA: Harvard University Press.

Friederici, A. D., & Wessels, J. M. I. (1993). Phonotactic knowledge of word boundaries and its use in infant speech perception. *Perception & Psychophysics, 54,* 287–295.

Garnsey, S. M., Perlmutter, N. J., Myers, E., & Lotocky, M. A. (1997). The contributions of verb bias and plausibility to the comprehension of temporarily ambiguous sentences. *Journal of Memory & Language, 37,* 58–93.

Gee, J. P., & Grosjean, F. (1983). Performance structures: A psycholinguistic and linguistic appraisal. *Cognitive Psychology, 15,* 411–458.

Gelman, S. A., & Taylor, M. (1984). How two-year-old children interpret proper and common names for unfamiliar objects. *Child Development, 55,* 1535–1540.

Gentner, D. (1982). Why nouns are learned before verbs: Linguistic relativity versus natural partitioning. In K. Bean (Ed.), *Language, thought, & culture* (pp. 301–334). Hillsdale, NJ: Erlbaum.

Gentner, D., & Boroditsky, L. (2001). Individuation, relativity and early word learning. In M. Bowerman & S. C. Levinson (Eds.), *Language acquisition and conceptual development* (pp. 215–256). New York: Cambridge University Press.

Gerken, L., Jusczyk, P. W., & Mandel, D. R. (1994). When prosody fails to cue syntactic structure: 9-month-olds' sensitivity to phonological versus syntactic phrases. *Cognition, 51,* 237–265.

Gerken, L., Landau, B., & Remez, R. E. (1990). Function morphemes in young children's speech perception and production. *Developmental Psychology, 26,* 204–216.

Gerken, L., & McIntosh, B. J. (1993). Interplay of function morphemes and prosody in early language. *Developmental Psychology, 29,* 448–457.

Gerken, L., Murphy, W. D., & Aslin, R. N. (1995). Three- and four-year-olds' perceptual confusions for spoken words. *Perception & Psychophysics, 57,* 475–486.

Gillette, J., Gleitman, H., Gleitman, L. R., & Lederer, A. (1999). Human simulations of vocabulary learning. *Cognition, 73,* 135–176.

Gleitman, L. R. (1990). The structural sources of verb meanings. *Language Acquisition, 1,* 3–55.

Gleitman, L. R., & Gleitman, H. (1997). What is a language made out of? *Lingua, 100,* 29–55.

Gleitman, L. R., Gleitman, H., Landau, B., & Wanner, E. (1988). Where learning begins: Initial representations for language learning. In F. J. Newmeyer (Ed.), *Linguistics: The Cambridge survey, Vol. 3. Language: Psychological and biological aspects* (pp. 150–193). New York: Cambridge University Press.

Gleitman, L. R., & Wanner, E. (1982). Language acquisition: The state of the state of the art. In E. Wanner & L. R. Gleitman (Eds.), *Language acquisition: State of the art* (pp. 3–48). New York: Cambridge University Press.

Goldberg, A. E. (1995). *Constructions: A construction grammar approach to argument structure.* Chicago: Chicago University Press.

Goldin-Meadow, S. (1982). The resilience of recursion: A study of a communication system developed without a conventional language model. In E. Wanner & L. R. Gleitman (Eds.), *Language acquisition: The state of the art* (pp. 51–77). New York: Cambridge University Press.

Goldin-Meadow, S. (2000). Learning with and without a helping hand. In B. Landau, J. Sabini, J. Jonides, & E. L. Newport (Eds.), *Perception, cognition, and language: Essays in honor of Henry and Lila Gleitman* (pp. 121–138). Cambridge, MA: MIT Press.

Goldin-Meadow, S., & Mylander, C. (1984). Gestural communication in deaf children: The effects and noneffects of parental input on early language development. *Monographs of the Society for Research in Child Development, 49.*

Goldin-Meadow, S., & Mylander, C. (1998). Spontaneous sign systems created by deaf children in two cultures. *Nature, 291,* 279–281.

Goldsmith, J. (2001). Unsupervised learning of the morphology of a natural language. *Computational Linguistics, 27,* 153–198.

Goldstone, R. L., Lippa, Y., & Shiffrin, R. M. (2001). Altering object representations through category learning. *Cognition, 78,* 27–43.

Gordon, P., & Chafetz, J. (1990). Verb-based versus class-based accounts of actionality effects in children's comprehension of passives. *Cognition, 36,* 227–254.

Gow, D. W., & Gordon, P. C. (1995). Lexical and prelexical influences on word segmentation: Evidence from priming. *Journal of Experimental Psychology: Human Perception & Performance, 21,* 344–359.

Grimshaw, J. (1981). Form, function, and the language acquisition device. In C. L. Baker & J. J. McCarthy (Eds.), *The logical problem of language acquisition* (pp. 165–182). Cambridge, MA: MIT Press.

Grimshaw, J. (1990). *Argument structure.* Cambridge, MA: MIT Press.

Grimshaw, J. (1994). Lexical reconciliation. *Lingua, 92,* 411–430.

Gruber, J. S. (1967). Look and see. *Language, 43,* 937–947.

Guenther, F. H., & Gjaja, M. N. (1996). The perceptual magnet effect as an emergent property of neural map formation. *Journal of the Acoustical Society of America, 100,* 1111–1121.

Hall, D. G. (1991). Acquiring proper nouns for familiar and unfamiliar animate objects:

Two-year-olds' word-learning biases. *Child Development, 62,* 1142–1154.

Hall, D. G. (1994). How mothers teach basic-level and situation-restricted count nouns. *Journal of Child Language, 21,* 391–414.

Hall, D. G., & Waxman, S. R. (1993). Assumptions about word meaning: Individuation and basic-level kinds. *Child Development, 64,* 1550–1570.

Hall, D. G., Waxman, S. R., & Hurwitz, W. M. (1993). How two- and four-year-old children interpret adjectives and count nouns. *Child Development, 64,* 1651–1664.

Harris, Z. (1951). *Methods in structural linguistics.* Chicago: Chicago University Press.

Hauser, M. D., Newport, E. L., & Aslin, R. N. (2001). Segmentation of the speech stream in a non-human primate: Statistical learning in cotton-top tamarins. *Cognition, 78,* B53–B64.

Healy, A. F., & Miller, G. A. (1970). The verb as the main determinant of sentence meaning. *Psychonomic Science, 20,* 372.

Heider, F., & Simmel, S. (1944). An experimental study of apparent behavior. *American Journal of Psychology, 57,* 243–259.

Hespos, S. J., & Spelke, E. S. (2000). *Conceptual precursors to spatial language: Categories of containment.* Paper presented at the biennial meeting of the International Society on Infant Studies, Brighton, England.

Hirsh-Pasek, K., & Golinkoff, R. M. (1996). *The origins of grammar: Evidence from early language comprehension.* Cambridge, MA: MIT Press.

Hirsh-Pasek, K., Kemler Nelson, D. G., Jusczyk, P. W., Wright-Cassidy, K., Druss, B., & Kennedy, L. (1987). Clauses are perceptual units for young infants. *Cognition, 26,* 269–286.

Hume, D. (1978). *A treatise on human nature.* Oxford: Clarendon. (Originally published in 1739)

Hurewitz, F., Brown-Schmidt, S., Thorpe, K., Gleitman, L. R., Trueswell, J. (2000). One frog, two frog, red frog, blue frog: Factors affecting children's syntactic choices in production and comprehension. *Journal of Psycholinguistic Research, 29,* 597–626.

Imai, M., & Gentner, D. (1997). A cross-linguistic study of early word meaning: Universal ontology and linguistic influence. *Cognition, 62,* 169–200.

Jackendoff, R. (1983). *Semantics and cognition.* Cambridge, MA: MIT Press.

Jackendoff, R. (1985). Multiple subcategorization and the (theta)-criterion: The case of climb. *Natural Language & Linguistic Theory, 3,* 271–295.

Johnson, J. S., & Newport, E. L. (1989). Critical period effects in second language learning: The influence of maturational state on the acquisition of English as a second language. *Cognitive Psychology, 21,* 60–99.

Jusczyk, P. W. (1997). *The discovery of spoken language.* Cambridge, MA: MIT Press.

Jusczyk, P. W., & Aslin, R. N. (1995). Infants' detection of the sound patterns of words in fluent speech. *Cognitive Psychology, 29,* 1–23.

Jusczyk, P. W., Cutler, A., & Redanz, N. J. (1993). Infants' preference for the predominant stress patterns of English words. *Child Development, 64,* 675–687.

Jusczyk, P. W., Friederici, A. D., Wessels, J. M., Svenkerud, V. Y., & Jusczyk, A. M. (1993). Infants' sensitivity to the sound patterns of native language words. *Journal of Memory & Language, 32,* 402–420.

Jusczyk, P. W., Hirsh-Pasek, K., Kemler-Nelson, D. G., Kennedy, L. J., Woodward, A., & Piwoz, J. (1992). Perception of acoustic correlates of major phrasal units by young infants. *Cognitive Psychology, 24,* 252–293.

Jusczyk, P. W., Johnson, S. P., Spelke, E. S., & Kennedy, L. J. (1999). Synchronous change and perception of object unity: Evidence from adults and infants. *Cognition, 71,* 257–288.

Jusczyk, P. W., Jusczyk, A. M., Kennedy, L. J., Schomberg, T., & Koenig, N. (1995). Young infants' retention of information about bisyllabic utterances. *Journal of Experimental Psychology: Human Perception and Performance, 21,* 822–836.

Jusczyk, P. W., Luce, P. A., & Charles-Luce, J. (1994). Infants' sensitivity to phonotactic patterns in the native language. *Journal of Memory & Language, 33,* 630–645.

Katz, N., Baker, E., & Macnamara, J. (1974). What's in a name? A study of how children learn common and proper names. *Child Development, 45,* 469–473.

Keating, P. A. (1985). Universal phonetics and the organization of grammars. In V. Fromkin (Ed.), *Phonetic linguistics: Essays in honor of Peter Ladefoged* (pp. 115–132). Orlando, FL: Academic Press.

Kegl, J., Senghas, A., & Coppola, M. (1999). Creation through contact: Sign language emergence and sign language change in Nicaragua. In M. Degraff (Ed.), *Language creation and language change: Creolization, diachrony, and development* (pp. 179–237). Cambridge, MA: MIT Press.

Kellman, P. J., & Spelke, E. S. (1983). Perception of partly occluded objects in infancy. *Cognitive Psychology, 15,* 483–524.

Kelly, M. H. (1988). Phonological biases in grammatical category shifts. *Journal of Memory & Language, 27,* 343–358.

Kelly, M. H. (1992). Using sound to solve syntactic problems: The role of phonology in grammatical category assignments. *Psychological Review, 99,* 349–364.

Kelly, M. H., & Martin, S. (1994). Domain-general abilities applied to domain-specific tasks: Sensitivity to probabilities in perception, cognition, and language. *Lingua, 92,* 105–140.

Kemler-Nelson, D. G., Hirsh-Pasek, K., Jusczyk, P. W., & Wright-Cassidy, K. (1989). How the prosodic cues in motherese might assist language learning. *Journal of Child Language, 16,* 55–68.

Kjelgaard, M. M., & Speer, S. R. (1999). Prosodic facilitation and interference in the resolution of temporary syntactic closure ambiguity. *Journal of Memory & Language, 40,* 153–194.

Klatt, D. H. (1976). Linguistic uses of segmental duration in English: Acoustic and perceptual evidence. *Journal of the Acoustical Society of America, 59,* 1208–1221.

Kotovsky, L., & Baillargeon, R. (1998). The development of calibration-based reasoning about collision events in young infants. *Cognition, 67,* 311–351.

Kuhl, P. K. (1994). Learning and representation in speech and language. *Current Opinion in Neurobiology, 4,* 812–822.

Kuhl, P. K., & Meltzoff, A. N. (1996). Infant vocalizations in response to speech: Vocal imitation and developmental change. *Journal of the Acoustical Society of America, 100,* 2425–2438.

Kuhl, P. K., & Miller, J. D. (1975). Speech perception by the chinchilla: Voiced-voiceless distinction in alveolar plosive consonants. *Science, 190,* 69–72.

Kuhl, P. K., & Padden, D. M. (1982). Enhanced discriminability at the phonetic boundaries for the voicing feature in macaques. *Perception & Psychophysics, 32,* 542–550.

Kuhl, P. K., & Padden, D. M. (1983). Enhanced discriminability at the phonetic boundaries for the place feature in macaques. *Journal of the Acoustical Society of America, 73,* 1003–1010.

Kuhl, P. K., Williams, K. A., Lacerda, F., Stevens, K. N., & Lindblom, B. (1992). Linguistic experience alters phonetic perception in infants by 6 months of age. *Science, 255,* 606–608.

Lakoff, G. (1987). *Women, fire, and dangerous things.* Chicago: University of Chicago Press.

Landau, B., & Gleitman, L. R. (1985). *Language and experience: Evidence from the blind child.* Cambridge, MA: Harvard University Press.

Landau, B., & Stecker, D. (1990). Objects and places: Geometric and syntactic representations in early lexical learning. *Cognitive Development, 5,* 287–312.

Lass, R. (1984). *Phonology.* Boston: Cambridge University Press.

Lederer, A., Gleitman, H., & Gleitman, L. (1995). Verbs of a feather flock together: Semantic information in the structure of maternal speech. In M. Tomasello & W. E. Merriman (Eds.), *Beyond names for things: Young children's acquisition of verbs* (pp. 277–297). Hillsdale, NJ: Erlbaum.

Lehiste, I. (1973). Rhythmic units and syntactic units in production and perception. *The Journal of the Acoustical Society of America, 54,* 1228–1234.

Leslie, A. M. (1995). A theory of agency. In D. Sperber, D. Premack, & A. J. Premack (Eds.), *Causal cognition: A multidisciplinary debate* (pp. 121–141). Oxford: Oxford University Press.

Leslie, A. M., & Keeble, S. (1987). Do six-month-old infants perceive causality? *Cognition, 25,* 265–288.

Levin, B., & Rappaport Hovav, M. (1995). *Unaccusativity: At the syntax-lexical semantics interface.* Cambridge, MA: MIT Press.

Li, P. (1994). *Subcategorization as a predictor of verb meaning: Cross-language study in Mandarin.* Unpublished manuscript, University of Pennsylvania.

Li, P., Gleitman, L. R., Landau, B., & Gleitman, H. (1997, November). *Space for thought.* Paper presented at the 22nd Boston University Conference on Language Development, Boston, MA.

Liberman, A. M., Harris, K. S., Hoffman, H., & Griffith, B. (1957). The discrimination of speech sounds within and across phoneme boundaries. *Journal of Experimental Psychology, 54,* 358–368.

Lidz, J., Gleitman, H., & Gleitman, L. R. (2000, November). *Morphological causativity and the robustness of syntactic bootstrapping.* Paper presented at the 25th Annual Boston University Conference on Language Development, Boston, MA.

Liittschwager, J. C., & Markman, E. M. (1994). Sixteen- and 24-month-olds' use of mutual exclusivity as a default assumption in second-label learning. *Developmental Psychology, 30,* 955–968.

Lisker, L., & Abramson, A. (1964). A cross-language study of voicing in initial stops: Acoustical measurements. *Word, 20,* 384–422.

Lively, S. E., Pisoni, D. B., & Goldinger, S. D. (1994). Spoken word recognition. In M. A. Gernsbacher (Ed.), *Handbook of Psycholinguistics* (pp. 265–301). New York: Academic Press.

Locke, J. (1964). *An essay concerning human understanding* (A. D. Woozley, Ed.). Cleveland, OH: Meridian Books. (Originally published in 1690)

Lotto, A. J. (2000). Language acquisition as complex category formation. *Phonetica, 57,* 189–196.

Lucy, J. A., & Gaskins, S. (2001). Grammatical categories and the development of classification preferences: A comparative approach. In M. Bowerman & S. C. Levinson (Eds.), *Language acquisition and conceptual development* (pp. 257–283). Cambridge: Cambridge University Press.

Luo, Y. (2000, July). *6-month-old infants expect inert but not self-moving objects to move when hit.* Paper presented at the 12th Biennial International Conference on Infant Studies, Brighton, UK.

Macnamara, J. (1982). *Names for things.* Cambridge, MA: MIT Press.

Malt, B. C., Sloman, S. A., Gennari, S., Shi, M., & Wang, Y. (1999). Knowing versus naming: Similarity and the linguistic categorization of artifacts. *Journal of Memory & Language, 40,* 230–262.

Mandel, D. R., Jusczyk, P. W., & Kemler-Nelson, D. G. (1994). Does sentential prosody help infants organize and remember speech information? *Cognition, 53,* 155–180.

Mandel, D. R., Kemler-Nelson, D. G., & Jusczyk, P. W. (1996). Infants remember the order of words in a spoken sentence. *Cognitive Development, 11,* 181–196.

Mandler, J. M. (2000). Perceptual and conceptual processes in infancy. *Journal of Cognition and Development, 1,* 3–36.

Maratsos, M. (1990). Are actions to verbs as objects are to nouns? On the differential semantic bases of form, class, category. *Linguistics, 28,* 1351–1379.

Maratsos, M. (1998). The acquisition of grammar. In W. Damon (Series Ed.), D. Kuhn, & R. S. Siegler (Vol. Eds.), *Handbook of child psychology, Vol. 2: Cognition, perception, and language* (pp. 421–466). New York: Wiley.

Maratsos, M., & Chalkley, M. A. (1980). The internal language of children's syntax. In K. Nelson (Ed.), *Children's language* (pp. 1–28). New York: Gardner Press.

Markman, E. M., & Hutchinson, J. E. (1984). Children's sensitivity to constraints on word meaning: Taxonomic versus thematic relations. *Cognitive Psychology, 16,* 1–27.

Markman, E. M., & Wachtel, G. F. (1988). Children's use of mutual exclusivity to constrain the meanings of words. *Cognitive Psychology, 20,* 121–157.

Mattys, S. L., & Jusczyk, P. W. (2001). Phonotactic cues for segmentation of fluent speech by infants. *Cognition, 78,* 91–121.

Maye, J., & Gerken, L. (2000). Learning phonemes without minimal pairs. In S. C. Howell, S. A. Fish, & T. Keith-Louis (Eds.), *Proceedings of the Boston University Conference on Language Development* (Vol. 24, pp. 522–533). Boston: Cascadilla Press.

McClelland, J. L., & Elman, J. L. (1986). Interactive processes in speech recognition: The TRACE model. In J. L. McClelland & D. E. Rumelhart (Eds.), *Parallel distributed processing: Explorations in the microstructure of cognition* (pp. 58–121). Cambridge, MA: MIT Press.

McQueen, J. M. (1998). Segmentation of continuous speech using phonotactics. *Journal of Memory & Language, 39,* 21–46.

Mehler, J., Jusczyk, P., Lambertz, G., Halsted, N., Bertoncini, J., & Amiel-Tison, C. (1988). A precursor of language acquisition in young infants. *Cognition, 29,* 143–178.

Mehler, J., Segui, J., & Frauenfelder, U. (1981). The role of the syllable in language acquisition and perception. In T. F. Myers, J. Laver, & J. Anderson (Eds.), *The cognitive representation of speech.* Amsterdam: North-Holland.

Meltzoff, A. N. (1995). Understanding the intentions of others: Re-enactment of intended acts by 18-month-old children. *Developmental Psychology, 31,* 838–850.

Michotte, A. (1963). *The perception of causality.* New York: Basic Books. (Originally published in 1946)

Mintz, T. H., & Gleitman, L. R. (2001). *Adjectives really do modify nouns: The incremental and restricted nature of early adjective acquisition.* Manuscript submitted for publication.

Mintz, T. H., Newport, E. L., & Bever, T. G. (1995). Distributional regularities of form class in speech to young children. *Proceedings of NELS, 25.* Amherst, MA: GLSA.

Morgan, J. L. (1986). *From simple input to complex grammar.* Cambridge, MA: MIT Press.

Morgan, J. L. (1996). A rhythmic bias in preverbal speech segmentation. *Journal of Memory & Language, 35,* 666–688.

Morgan, J. L., & Demuth, K. (1995). Signal to syntax: An overview. In J. L. Morgan & K. Demuth (Eds.), *Signal to syntax* (pp. 1–24). Hillsdale, NJ: Erlbaum.

Morgan, J. L., Meier, R. P., & Newport, E. L. (1987). Structural packaging in the input to language learning: Contributions of prosodic and morphological marking of phrases to the acquisition of language. *Cognitive Psychology, 19,* 498–550.

Morgan, J. L., & Newport, E. L. (1981). The role of constituent structure in the induction of an artificial language. *Journal of Verbal Learning & Verbal Behavior, 20,* 67–85.

Morgan, J. L., & Saffran, J. R. (1995). Emerging integration of sequential and suprasegmental information in preverbal speech segmentation. *Child Development, 66,* 911–936.

Naigles, L. G. (1990). Children use syntax to learn verb meanings. *Journal of Child Language, 17,* 357–374.

Naigles, L. G., Gleitman, H., & Gleitman, L. R. (1993). Children acquire word meaning components from syntactic evidence. In E. Dromi (Ed.), *Language and cognition: A developmental perspective* (pp. 104–140). Norwood, NJ: Ablex.

Naigles, L. G., & Kako, E. T. (1993). First contact in verb acquisition: Defining a role for syntax. *Child Development, 64,* 1665–1687.

Naigles, L. G., & Terrazas, P. (1998). Motion-verb generalizations in English and Spanish: Influences of language and syntax. *Psychological Science, 9,* 363–369.

Nakatani, L. H., & Dukes, K. D. (1977). Locus of segmental cues for word juncture. *Journal of the Acoustical Society of America, 62,* 714–719.

Nazzi, T., Bertoncini, J., & Mehler, J. (1998). Language discrimination by newborns: Toward an understanding of the role of rhythm. *Journal of Experimental Psychology: Human Perception & Performance, 24,* 756–766.

Nazzi, T., Jusczyk, P. W., & Johnson, E. K. (2000). Language discrimination by English-learning 5-month-olds: Effects of rhythm and familiarity. *Journal of Memory & Language, 43,* 1–19.

Needham, A., & Baillargeon, R. (2000). Infants' use of featural and experiential information in segregating and individuating objects: A reply to Xu, Carey and Welch. *Cognition, 74,* 255–284.

Nelson, K. (1988). Constraints on word learning? *Cognitive Development, 3,* 221–246.

Nelson, K., Hampson, J., & Shaw, L. K. (1993). Nouns in early lexicons: Evidence, explanations, and implications. *Journal of Child Language, 20,* 61–84.

Newport, E. L. (1990). Maturational constraints on language learning. *Cognitive Science, 14,* 11–28.

Newport, E. L., Gleitman, H., & Gleitman, L. R. (1977). Mother, I'd rather do it myself: Some effects and non-effects of maternal speech style. In C. E. Snow & C. A. Ferguson (Eds.), *Talking to children: Language input and acquisition* (pp. 109–149). New York: Cambridge University Press.

Ninio, A. (1980). Ostensive definition in vocabulary teaching. *Journal of Child Language, 7,* 565–573.

Oyama, S. (1978). The sensitive period and comprehension of speech. *Working Papers on Bilingualism, 16,* 1–17.

Pallier, C., Bosch, L., & Sebastian-Galles, N. (1997). A limit on behavioral plasticity in speech perception. *Cognition, 64,* B9–B17.

Palmer, C., Jungers, M. K., & Jusczyk, P. W. (2001). Episodic memory for musical prosody. *Journal of Memory & Language, 45,* 526–545.

Papafragou, A., Massey, C., & Gleitman, L. R. (2001). *Shake, rattle, 'n' roll: The representation of motion in language and cognition.* Manuscript submitted for publication.

Pierrehumbert, J. (1990). Phonological and phonetic representation. *Journal of Phonetics, 18,* 375–394.

Pinker, S. (1984). *Language learnability and language development.* Cambridge, MA: Harvard University Press.

Pinker, S. (1987). The bootstrapping problem in language acquisition. In B. MacWhinney (Ed.), *Mechanisms of language acquisition* (pp. 399–441). Hillsdale, NJ: Erlbaum.

Pinker, S. (1989). *Learnability and cognition.* Cambridge, MA: MIT Press.

Pinker, S. (1994). *The language instinct.* New York: Harper-Collins.

Pisoni, D. B., Aslin, R. N., Perey, A. J., & Hennessy, B. L. (1982). Some effects of laboratory training on identification and discrimination of voicing contrasts in stop consonants. *Journal of Experimental Psychology: Human Perception & Performance, 8,* 297–314.

Pisoni, D. B., Lively, S. E., & Logan, J. S. (1994). Perceptual learning of nonnative speech contrasts: Implications for theories of speech perception. In J. C. Goodman & H. C. Nusbaum (Eds.), *The development of speech perception* (pp. 121–166). Cambridge, MA: MIT Press.

Pullam, G. K. (1991). *The great Eskimo vocabulary hoax and other irreverent essays on the study of language.* Chicago: University of Chicago Press.

Quine, W. (1960). *Word and object.* New York: Wiley.

Quinn, P. C., & Eimas, P. D. (1997). A reexamination of the perceptual-to-conceptual shift in mental representations. *Review of General Psychology, 1,* 271–287.

Ramus, F., Nespor, M., & Mehler, J. (1999). Correlates of linguistic rhythm in the speech signal. *Cognition, 73,* 265–292.

Rappaport Hovav, M., & Levin, B. (1988). What to do with theta-roles. In W. Wilkins (Ed.), *Syntax and semantics, Volume 21: Thematic relations* (pp. 7–36). New York: Academic Press.

Read, C., & Schreiber, P. (1982). Why short subjects are harder to find than long ones. In E. Wanner & L. R. Gleitman (Eds.), *Language* acquisition: The state of the art (pp. 78–101). New York: Cambridge University Press.

Redington, M., Chater, N., & Finch, S. (1998). Distributional information: A powerful cue for acquiring syntactic categories. Cognitive Science, 22, 425–469.

Rispoli, M. (1989). Encounters with Japanese verbs: Caregiver sentences and the categorization of transitive and intransitive sentences. First Language, 9, 57–80.

Saffran, J. R., Aslin, R. N., & Newport, E. L. (1996). Statistical learning by 8-month-old infants. Science, 274, 1926–1928.

Saffran, J. R., Johnson, E. K., Aslin, R. N., & Newport, E. L. (1999). Statistical learning of tone sequences by human infants and adults. Cognition, 70, 27–52.

Samuels, A. G. (1997). Lexical activation produces potent phonemic percepts. Cognitive Psychology, 32, 97–127.

Sansavini, A., Bertoncini, J., & Giovanelli, G. (1997). Newborns discriminate the rhythm of multisyllabic stressed words. Developmental Psychology, 33, 3–11.

Santelmann, L. M., & Jusczyk, P. W. (1998). Sensitivity to discontinuous dependencies in language learners: Evidence for limitations in processing space. Cognition, 69, 105–134.

Schlesinger, I. M. (1988). The origin of relational categories. In Y. Levy, I. M. Schlesinger, & M. D. S. Braine (Eds.), Categories and processes in language acquisition (pp. 121–178). Hillsdale, NJ: Erlbaum.

Scholl, B. J., & Tremoulet, P. D. (2000). Perceptual causality and animacy. Trends in Cognitive Science, 4, 299–309.

Scott, D. R. (1982). Duration as a cue to the perception of a phrase boundary. Journal of the Acoustical Society of America, 71, 996–1007.

Selkirk, E. (1984). Phonology and syntax: The relation between sound and structure. Cambridge, MA: MIT Press.

Senghas, A. (1995). Conventionalization in the first generation: A community acquires a language. Journal of Contemporary Legal Issues, 6, 501–519.

Senghas, A., & Coppola, M. (2001). Children creating language: How Nicaraguan Sign Language acquired a spatial grammar. Psychological Science, 12, 323-328.

Senghas, A., Coppola, M., Newport, E. L., & Supalla, T. (1997). Argument structure in Nicaraguan Sign Language: The emergence of grammatical devices. In E. Hughes, M. Hughes, & A. Greenhill (Eds.), Proceedings of the Boston University Conference on Language Development (pp. 550–561). Boston: Cascadilla Press.

Shi, R., Morgan, J. L., & Allopenna, P. (1998). Phonological and acoustic bases for earliest grammatical category assignment: A cross-linguistic perspective. Journal of Child Language, 25, 169–201.

Shi, R., Werker, J. F., & Morgan, J. L. (1999). Newborn infants' sensitivity to perceptual cues to lexical and grammatical words. Cognition, 72, B11–B21.

Shipley, E. F., Kuhn, I. F., & Madden, E. C. (1983). Mothers' use of superordinate category terms. Journal of Child Language, 10, 571–588.

Slobin, D. I. (1982). Universal and particular in the acquisition of language. In E. Wanner & L. R. Gleitman (Eds.), Language acquisition: The state of the art (pp. 128–172). New York: Cambridge University Press.

Slobin, D. I. (1996). From "thought and language" to "thinking for speaking". In J. J. Gumperz & S. C. Levinson (Eds.), Rethinking linguistic relativity (pp. 70–96). New York: Cambridge University Press.

Slobin, D. I. (2001). Form-function relations: How do children find out what they are? In M. Bowerman & S. C. Levinson (Eds.), Language acquisition and conceptual development (pp. 406–449). New York: Cambridge University Press.

Smith, K. L., & Pitt, M. A. (1999). Phonological and morphological influences in the syllabification of spoken words. Journal of Memory & Language, 41, 199–222.

Smith, L. B., Jones, S. S., & Landau, B. (1992). Count nouns, adjectives, and perceptual properties in children's novel word interpretations. Developmental Psychology, 28, 273–286.

Snedeker, J., & Gleitman, L. (in press). Why it is hard to label our concepts. To appear in D. G. Hall & S. R. Waxman (Eds.), *Weaving a lexicon*. Cambridge, MA: MIT Press.

Snedeker, J., & Li, P. (2000). Can the situations in which words occur account for cross-linguistic variation in vocabulary composition? In J. Tai & Y. Chang (Eds.), *Proceedings of the Seventh International Symposium on Chinese Languages and Linguistics*.

Snow, C. E. (1972). Mothers' speech to children learning language. *Child Development, 43*, 549–565.

Snow, C. E., & Hoefnagel-Hoehle, M. (1978). The critical period for language acquisition: Evidence from second language learning. *Child Development, 49*, 1114–1128.

Soja, N. N. (1992). Inferences about the meanings of nouns: The relationship between perception and syntax. *Cognitive Development, 7*, 29–45.

Soja, N. N., Carey, S., & Spelke, E. S. (1991). Ontological categories guide young children's inductions of word meaning: Object terms and substance terms. *Cognition, 38*, 179–211.

Spelke, E. S., Breinlinger, K., Macomber, J., & Jacobson, K. (1992). Origins of knowledge. *Psychological Review, 99*, 605–632.

Sperber, D., & Wilson, D. (1986). *Relevance: Communication and cognition*. Oxford, UK: Blackwell.

Stager, C. L., & Werker, J. F. (1997). Infants listen for more phonetic detail in speech perception than in word-learning tasks. *Nature, 388*, 381–382.

Swingley, D. (2000, November). *On the origins of infants' lexical parsing preferences*. Paper presented at the 25th Annual Boston University Conference on Language Development, Boston, MA.

Talmy, L. (1985). Lexicalization patterns: Semantic structure in lexical forms. In T. Shopen (Ed.), *Language typology and syntactic description* (pp. 57–149). New York: Cambridge University Press.

Tardif, T., Gelman, S. A., & Xu, F. (1999). Putting the "noun bias" in context: A comparison of English and Mandarin. *Child Development, 70*, 620–635.

Tomasello, M. (1992). *First verbs: A case study of early grammatical development*. New York: Cambridge University Press.

Tomasello, M. (2000). Do young children have adult syntactic competence? *Cognition, 74*, 209–253.

Tomasello, M., & Farrar, M. J. (1986). Joint attention and early language. *Child Development, 57*, 1454–1463.

Trehub, S. E. (1976). The discrimination of foreign speech contrasts by infants and adults. *Child Development, 47*, 466–472.

Trehub, S. E. (1987). Infants' perception of musical patterns. *Perception & Psychophysics, 41*, 635–641.

Trueswell, J. C., Sekerina, I., Hill, N. M., & Logrip, M. L. (1999). The kindergarten-path effect: Studying on-line sentence processing in young children. *Cognition, 73*, 89–134.

Trueswell, J. C., Tanenhaus, M. K., & Garnsey, S. M. (1994). Semantic influences on parsing: Use of thematic role information in syntactic ambiguity resolution. *Journal of Memory & Language, 33*, 285–318.

Vroomen, J., van den Bosch, A., & de Gelder, B. (1998). A connectionist model for bootstrap learning of syllabic structure. *Language & Cognitive Processes, 13*, 193–220.

Waxman, S. R. (1999). Specifying the scope of 13-month-olds' expectations for novel words. *Cognition, 70*, B35–B50.

Waxman, S. R., & Hall, D. G. (1993). The development of a linkage between count nouns and object categories: Evidence from fifteen- to twenty-one-month-old infants. *Child Development, 64*, 1224–1241.

Waxman, S. R., & Markow, D. B. (1995). Words as invitations to form categories: Evidence from 12- to 13-month-old infants. *Cognitive Psychology, 29*, 257–302.

Waxman, S. R., Senghas, A., & Beneviste, S. (1997). A cross-linguistic examination of the noun-category bias: Its existence and specificity in French- and Spanish-speaking preschool-aged children. *Cognitive Psychology, 32,* 183–218.

Werker, J. F., & Lalonde, C. E. (1988). Cross-language speech perception: Initial capabilities and developmental change. *Developmental Psychology, 24,* 72–683.

Werker, J. F., & Tees, R. C. (1984). Cross-language speech perception: Evidence for perceptual reorganization during the first year of life. *Infant Behavior & Development, 7,* 49–63.

Werker, J. F., & Tees, R. C. (1999). Influences on infant speech processing: Toward a new synthesis. *Annual Review of Psychology, 50,* 509–535.

Wexler, K., & Culicover, P. (1980). *Formal principles of language acquisition.* Cambridge, MA: MIT Press.

Whorf, B. (1941). The relation of habitual thought and behavior to language. In L. Spier, A. I. Hallowell, & S. S. Newman (Eds.) *Language, culture and personality: Essays in memory of Edward Sapir* (pp. 75–93). Menasha, WI: Sapir Memorial Publication Fund.

Whorf, B. (1956). *Language, thought, and reality: Selected writings of Benjamin Lee Whorf.* New York: Wiley.

Wightman, C. W., Shattuck-Hufnagel, S., Ostendorf, M., & Price, P. J. (1992). Segmental durations in the vicinity of prosodic phrase boundaries. *Journal of the Acoustical Society of America, 91,* 1707–1717.

Woodward, A. L. (1998). Infants selectively encode the goal object of an actor's reach. *Cognition, 69,* 1–34.

Woodward, A. L., & Markman, E. M. (1998). Early word learning. In W. Damon (Series Ed.), D. Kuhn, & R. S. Siegler (Vol. Eds.), *Handbook of child psychology: Vol . 2. Cognition, perception, and language* (5th ed., pp. 371–420). New York: Wiley.

Wright-Cassidy, K., & Kelly, M. H. (1991). Phonological information for grammatical category assignment. *Journal of Memory & Language, 30,* 348–369.

CHAPTER 12

The Role of Learning in the Operation of Motivational Systems

ANTHONY DICKINSON AND BERNARD BALLEINE

INTRODUCTION

Over half a century ago, Neal Miller (1951) set the agenda for the present chapter in his contribution titled "Learnable Drives and Reward" to the first edition of Stevens' *Handbook of Experimental Psychology*. Miller introduced his chapter with the claim that "People are not born with a tendency to strive for money, for discovery of scientific truth, or for symbols of social status. Such motives are learned during socialization.... Even primary drives themselves may be modified by learning, so that hunger becomes a desire for a particular type of food appetizingly prepared" (p. 435). The essence of Miller's claim is that behavior is not driven by some energetic-like state but rather is motivated by the desire for specific commodities, resources, and states of affairs and, moreover, that desires are learned rather than being an automatic consequence of even basic biological motivational states. Miller's claim was surprising; not only was it out of kilter with the contemporary theories of motivation, but it also lacked empirical foundation at the time. Our aim in this chapter is to marshal evidence gathered over the last 50 years to substantiate that behavior is motivated by desires and that desires, even for the most basic and primary commodities (food, water, warmth, and sex), are learned. In this respect, therefore, the present chapter can be viewed as an extended addendum to Miller's original claim about the role of learning in motivation.

Before embarking on this enterprise, however, we must be clear about why the analysis of behavior requires a concept of motivation. The term was developed and applied to human behavior in the nineteenth century by the German philosopher Schopenhauer in an attempt to equate the forces controlling human action with physical forces, such as gravitation. However, motivational explanations have been with us for much longer. Descartes (1649/1911), for example, claimed that motivational states, which he referred to as "the passions," are the basis of action, both initiating a desire for specific objects and providing a force that impels behavior to the fulfillment of desire. For Descartes, the passions "dispose the soul to desire those things which nature tells us are of use, and to persist in this desire, and also bring about that same agitation of spirits which customarily causes them to dispose the body to movement which serves for the carrying into effect of

The authors thank Nicola Clayton, Dominic Dywer, Felicity Miles, and especially Kent Berridge for their comments on the manuscript.

these things" (1649/1911, article 52, p. 358). The two functions that Descartes identified for "passions"—the determination of the current goal of our actions and the activation or energization of these actions—capture an important distinction that is honored by contemporary analyses of motivation.

Perhaps the simplest demonstration of motivational processes in action comes from studies of shifts in motivational state. For example, Mollenauer (1971) fed her rats for 1 hr per day while training them to run from the start box of an alleyway to the goal box for a food reward. The animals in Group DEP received two trials 22 h after each daily meal so that they were hungry at the time of training. By contrast, those in Group NON were effectively nondeprived at the time of training because they received their pair of daily trials only 1 hr after each meal. Figure 12.1A shows performance during a series of test trials after 74 prior training trials. Not surprisingly, Group DEP ran consistently faster than did Group NON. Although an obvious explanation is that hungry rats are more motivated to seek food than are sated ones, an alternative account is that rats learn to run faster for food when hungry than when sated. Put simply, the issue is whether food is a more effective reinforcer under hunger with the result that animals learn to run faster in the deprived state. The motivational alternative is that Mollenauer's rats learned the same behavior under the two levels of deprivation but were simply more motivated to perform when hungry.

It was thought that these alternatives could be distinguished by shifting the deprivation state. Consider the case of the rats trained in the food-deprived state but then suddenly shifted to the nondeprived state. If the rats have simply learned to run faster when hungry, we should expect them to require a number of trials with the less effective reward in the nondeprived state before they learned to

run more slowly. By contrast, if varying the deprivation state acts by changing the motivation to perform food-seeking behavior, a reduction in the level of deprivation should have an immediate impact on performance. The performance of a third group of rats in the Mollenauer (1971) study, Group dep/NON, favors the motivation account. These rats, like Group DEP, were trained for 74 trials in the deprived state but were then suddenly tested in the nondeprived state. As Figure 12.1A shows, Group dep/NON ran slower than did Group DEP on the very first pair of trials after the shift in deprivation state. Mollenauer also observed a comparable performance shift by Group non/DEP in which the rats were initially trained in the nondeprived state but then were tested hungry. Although the performance shift was delayed by one pair of trials, by the second pair of postshift trials these rats were running faster than those trained and tested in the nondeprived state, Group NON, and as fast as the rats in Group DEP, which had been hungry throughout.[1]

Although the rapid impact of deprivation shifts suggests that states such as hunger can exert a direct effect on behavior, the nature of the underlying motivational process is less clear. Theories of motivation are, of necessity, tightly constrained by theories of learning. An action can be motivated by a desire for its outcome only if the agent has learned about the consequences of acting. In the absence of

---

[1] The role of generalization decrement complicates the interpretation of shifts in motivational state. Not only did the shift from the deprived to the nondeprived state in Group dep/NON reduce the animals' motivational state, but it also changed the conditions from those present when the animals learned to run during training. Consequently, the immediate reduction in performance may, at least in part, have been due to generalization decrement, which would have summed with any motivational effect. In the up-shift case, by contrast, the motivating effect of increased hunger and generalization decrement would have worked against each other, thus producing the delayed shift in performance observed in Group non/DEP.

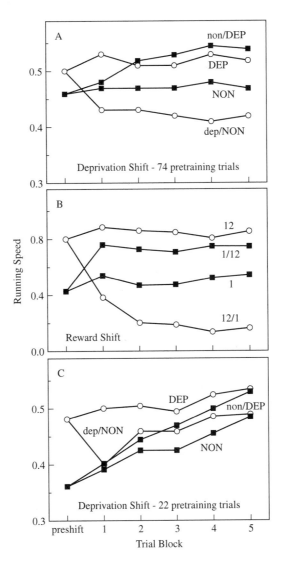

Figure 12.1   Mean running speed on the final preshift trial block and on the postshift trial blocks.
NOTE: The data in Panels A and C were estimated graphically from Figures 1 and 2 of Mollenauer (1971) for rats that received 74 and 22 preshift training trials, respectively, and are reproduced by permission of Academic Press. Each trial block consisted of a pair of daily trials. During the preshift training, Groups DEP and dep/NON were tested 22 hr after a feeding period, and Groups NON and non/DEP were tested 1 hr after a feeding period. Correspondingly, during the postshift training, Groups DEP and non/DEP were tested 22 hr after a feeding period, and Group NON and dep/NON were tested 1 hr after a feeding period. The data in Panel B were estimated graphically from the N panel of Figure 1 of Franchina and Brown (1971) and are reproduced by permission of the American Psychological Association. Each trial block consisted of six daily trials. During the preshift training, Groups 12 and 12/1 received 12 food pellets per trial, and Groups 1 and 1/12 received 1 food pellet per trial. Correspondingly, during the postshift training, Group 12 and 1/12 received 12 food pellets per trial, and Groups 1 and 12/1 received 1 food pellet per trial.
SOURCE: Panels A and C from Mollenauer (1971). Reprinted with permission. Panel B from Franchina and Brown (1971). Copyright © 1971 by the American Psychological Association. Reprinted with permission.

action-outcome knowledge, the desire is behaviorally impotent, unable to select and motivate the appropriate action. However, such
action-outcome knowledge was denied by the
stimulus-response (S-R) theories that dominated the analysis of learning at the time of
Miller's chapter. According to S-R habit theory, the outcome of an action simply serves to
reinforce a connection between the stimulus
context and the response (Thorndike, 1911),
an associative structure that does not encode
any information about the outcome; as a consequence, habit theory cannot support the
selection of a response on the basis of the relevance of its outcome to the agent's motivational state. In other words, S-R theory does
not permit, for example, nutritional need to
motivate selectively a particular response because the agent has learned that this behavior
has yielded food in the past.

Within S-R habit theory, therefore, there
can be no motivational role for specific desires or drives, whether they be for "food appetizingly prepared" or for one's heart's desire; for this reason, S-R theorists (e.g., Hull,
1943) had to marry their theory of learning
to a general drive theory of motivation. According to general drive theory, all primary
motivational states funnel into one general
motivational process that simply serves to energize any predominant habits. Consequently,
a drive theorist would argue that this energization was most simply reflected in the immediate impact of the downshift in food deprivation on the running speed of Group dep/
NON. General drive theory thus captures
Descartes' "agitation of spirits" but not the
soul's desires.

Despite the apparent success of drive theory, by the time Miller (1951) wrote his
Stevens' chapter, it was well established that
drive states could not be the sole motivational process. By investigating variations and
shifts in magnitude of a food reward, Crespi
(1942) discovered that rewards, like deprivation states, exert a motivational-like effect on

performance. Figure 12.1B illustrates the effect of shifts in reward magnitude in a study
by Franchina and Brown (1971) that used
a design analogous to that employed by
Mollenauer (1971) to study deprivation shifts.
In this experiment, Franchina and Brown also
trained four groups of rats to run down a
straight runway when food-deprived. Rather
than varying the number of hours of food deprivation, however, they manipulated the size
of the reward presented in the goal box. For
two groups, Groups 1 and 12, the reward was
1 and 12 food pellets, respectively, throughout training and testing. Just as Mollenauer
had found when rats were run at different levels of deprivation, reward magnitude also affected performance: Rats trained and tested
with 12 pellets ran markedly faster than did
those rewarded with 1 pellet.

The critical groups in this study are those
that were trained with either 12 or 1 pellet
and then shifted to the other reward magnitude for testing, Groups 12/1 and 1/12, respectively. Therefore, just as Mollenauer's
deprivation-shift study assessed control by deprivation state, this experiment evaluated the
influence of the reward on running speed by
shifting its magnitude. A comparison of Figures 12.1A and 12.1B reveals that these shifts
produced similar effects. An upshift in either
food deprivation in Group non/DEP or food
magnitude in Group 1/12 rapidly increased
the running speeds to the levels of Groups
DEP and 12, respectively. Correspondingly,
Groups dep/NON and 12/1 showed similar
profiles of reduced performance. Indeed, both
downshifts produced a negative contrast effect (see Flaherty, 1996, for a review), in
that Groups dep/NON and 12/1 ran slower
than did the animals trained and tested either
nondeprived in Group NON or with a low
reward magnitude in Group 1. It is clear,
therefore, that variations in reward magnitude
produce motivational-like shifts in performance, an observation that led S-R theorists
to assume that response habits were energized

not only by the current drive state but also by the incentive property of the reinforcer, a property that clearly had to be learned through experience with the reinforcer (Hull, 1952; Spence, 1956).

Once we allow that the reinforcer or outcome can exert a motivational influence, why do we need to assume that the motivational state induced, for example, by food deprivation has an independent, drive-like effect on performance? Just as a larger or more appetizing meal is a greater incentive, so perhaps a meal eaten in a state of hunger is also a greater incentive than is one consumed while sated. In other words, we can dispense with the whole concept of drive by assuming that primary biological motivational states act by modulating the incentive properties of the commodities and resources relevant to those states.

The development of motivational theory since the publication of Miller's (1951) chapter has been concerned primarily with the issue of how animals learn about the incentive properties of rewards and punishers, and how these properties exert their motivational influence on behavior. This being said, the study of motivation within experimental psychology has been largely neglected during the second half of twentieth century in favor of research on both general (Chaps. 1 and 2, this volume) and domain-specific learning processes (Chaps. 8 and 9, this volume). Unlike the neobehaviorist S-R theorists, contemporary students of learning have not, by and large, addressed the issue of how learning processes interact with motivational systems to generate behavior. It is true that we now know a great deal more about the mechanisms by which specific motivational systems, such as hunger (Chap. 15, this volume), thirst (Chap. 16, this volume), and fear (Chap. 13, this volume), control their consummatory behavior, feeding, drinking, freezing, and fleeing. Moreover, our understanding of the neurobiological systems engaged by rewards and reinforcers has also been transformed in the last few decades

(Chap. 14, this volume). What has been neglected, however, is the processes by which primary motivational states, such as hunger and thirst, interact with learning to regulate simple instrumental behavior. In other words, we have little understanding of what was happening during the first few postshift trials that led Mollenauer's and Franchina and Brown's rats to run faster when they were more hungry or when they received a larger reward and slower when they were less hungry or when they received a smaller reward. It is this issue that we address in the present chapter.

PAVLOVIAN INCENTIVE LEARNING

In a study of the motivation of drug taking, Ludwig, Wikler, Stark, and Lexington (1974) gave detoxified alcoholics the opportunity to press a button for pure alcohol; after every 15 presses a small quantity of alcohol was dispensed into a cup just below the button. In addition, the subjects were asked to rate their "craving" for alcohol periodically throughout the test period. The main variable in this study was the nature of the cues that were present prior to and during the test. The experimental group received powerful cues that presumably had been associated with alcohol consumption in the past. At the start of the session, they were given a small taste of their favorite liquor and, in addition, a quart bottle of this drink was placed in full view during the test. By contrast, the control group received only pure alcohol as the priming taste.

The presence of these alcohol-associated cues had a marked effect on performance; not only did the experimental subjects give much higher alcohol craving scores, but they also worked harder at the button-press response. Moreover, these two measures were highly related on an individual basis with a correlation of greater than 0.9 between the strength of the craving score and the level of instrumental performance for the alcohol reward. Thus, it would appear that stimuli associated with an incentive acquire the capacity to induce a craving for that commodity and to motivate behavior that gains access to it. We refer to this acquisition process as Pavlovian incentive learning because it depends on the Pavlovian contingency between the conditioned stimulus (CS), in this case the alcohol-associated cues, and the unconditioned stimulus (US) or primary incentive, the alcohol itself.

Motivational Conditioning

Although numerous authors have suggested that Pavlovian CSs acquire motivational properties (e.g., Berridge, 2000a; Bindra, 1974, 1978; Mowrer, 1960; Rescorla & Solomon, 1967; Toates, 1986), the most sophisticated account of Pavlovian conditioning that includes a motivational component is that developed by Konorski (1967). Konorski argued that Pavlovian conditioning comes in two forms: *consummatory* and *preparatory* conditioning (Chap. 1, this volume). Dickinson and Dearing (1979) developed a simplified version of Konorski's model, which is illustrated in Figure 12.2. Although this model

differs in many respects from the original theory (Konorski, 1967), we shall refer to it as Konorskian. Consummatory conditioning occurs when the form of the conditioned response reflects the specific sensory-perceptual properties of US. An example of this form of conditioning is Pavlov's classic procedure in which a signal, or CS, predicting a food US comes to elicit salivation in dogs. However, contemporary research on consummatory conditioning has predominantly employed procedures developed by Gormezano and his colleagues using the rabbit. For example, the appetitive jaw-movement conditioning reinforced by an intraoral fluid US or the defensive eye blink conditioned by an aversive orbital airpuff or shock US are examples of consummatory conditioning (Gormezano, 1972). Konorski assumed that consummatory conditioning reflects the formation of an association between the representation of the CS and a representation of the US that encodes its sensory and perceptual properties (see Figure 12.2). Activation of this US representation via the association elicits the consummatory conditioned responses.

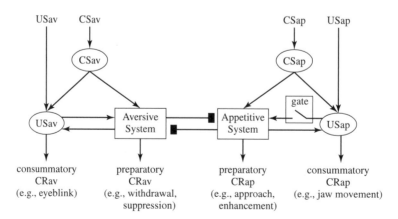

Figure 12.2   The Konorskian model of the stimulus representations and motivational systems mediating Pavlovian incentive learning (after Dickinson & Dearing, 1979).
NOTE: CSav: aversive conditioned stimulus; USav: aversive unconditioned stimulus; CRav: aversive conditioned response; CSap: appetitive conditioned stimulus; USap: appetitive unconditioned stimulus; CRap: appetitive conditioned response.

Konorski's (1967) second form of Pavlovian conditioning, which he designated as preparatory, reflects the acquisition of responses that are not specific to the particular US employed but, rather, are characteristic of the motivational class to which that US belongs. Examples of preparatory conditioning are CS-induced autonomic responses, such as changes in heart rate, and general behavioral responses, such as approach and withdrawal. Konorski assumed that these preparatory conditioned responses result from the activation of a motivational system by the CS and, moreover, that there are two routes by which this activation can occur. The first is via the US representation itself (see Figure 12.2). Indeed, within this model, it is the ability of the US representation to activate a motivational system that determines whether the US is motivationally potent.

Konorski (1967) also claimed that a CS could activate a motivational system through a direct association, thereby producing purely preparatory conditioning (see Figure 12.2). The basis of this claim is the observation that preparatory and consummatory conditioning can be dissociated under certain conditions. For example, when Vandercar and Schneiderman (1967) signaled mild eye-shock USs by a tone, this CS elicited both a conditioned eye blink and a heart rate change. Training with a longer CS-US interval, however, abolished the consummatory eye-blink conditioning without affecting the preparatory heart rate conditioning. This dissociation accords with Konorski's claim that long, tonic CSs, such as contextual stimuli, favor the preparatory form of conditioning, whereas both forms occur with short, phasic signals.

The reason for believing that preparatory conditioning engages motivational processes comes from evidence that preparatory CSs can modulate consummatory responding. Bombace, Brandon, and Wagner (1991) es-

tablished a relatively long auditory CS as a signal for a shock to the rear leg of a rabbit and a second, short visual stimulus as a CS for an eye-blink response. Bombace et al. were in a position to test the motivational property of the long auditory CS by presenting the visual CS embedded within the auditory stimulus. The critical finding was that the visual CS elicited a conditioned eye-blink response of greater amplitude when presented during the auditory stimulus.

The augmentation of the eye-blink response could not have reflected a simple response summation because the auditory CS, being both tonic and associated with a different, leg-shock US, did not elicit the eye-blink response. Rather, it appears that a preparatory CS motivates the performance of a consummatory response, and it is for this reason that Figure 12.2 shows not only a connection from the US representation to the motivational system but also a feedback connection from the motivational system. As a consequence of this feedback, exciting the motivational system by a preparatory CS augments activity in the US representation thereby enhancing the magnitude of any consummatory conditioned responses even when they are elicited by another CS.

Figure 12.2 illustrates just two motivational systems, an appetitive one and an aversive one. This structure therefore implies that different USs from the same affective class activate a common motivational system. We have already considered evidence for motivational transfer across aversive USs in the Bombace et al. (1991) study. A preparatory CS reinforced with a leg-shock US augmented a consummatory eye-blink response conditioned with an eye-shock reinforcer. It might be argued, however, that these two USs both elicit somatic pain and discomfort and therefore, not surprisingly, are mediated by a common system. Possibly more surprising is evidence from studies of transreinforcer blocking suggesting that the commonality between aversive reinforcers extends beyond those involving somatic pain.

Blocking refers to the observation that pretraining one CS often reduces conditioning to a second, added CS when a compound of these two stimuli is paired with the reinforcer (Kamin, 1969; see Chap. 2, this volume). The pretrained CS is said to block conditioning to the added CS. Whereas the standard blocking procedure employs the same reinforcer during pretraining and compound training, Bakal, Johnson, and Rescorla (1974) reported that pretraining with a foot-shock US blocked conditioning with a loud auditory US. Blocking is usually ascribed to the fact that only surprising or unexpected reinforcers support conditioning (Kamin, 1969; Rescorla & Wagner, 1972) and, as the pretrained CS predicts the reinforcer during compound training, little conditioning accrues to the added CS. Foot shock and a loud noise differ greatly in terms of their sensory-perceptual properties so that the transreinforcer blocking cannot have arisen from the prediction of these properties of the reinforcer. What they do have in common, however, is that they are aversive, and therefore transreinforcer blocking is usually taken as evidence that the two reinforcers activate a common motivational or reinforcement system.

Transreinforcer blocking also provides the best evidence for commonalities in appetitive motivation. The case for multiple motivational systems is particularly strong in the appetitive domain; Konorski (1967) certainly thought so. Not only are the various forms of appetitive consummatory conditioning—feeding, drinking, or courting—mediated by different US representations, which determine the form of these responses, but also each of these classes of consummatory behavior is modulated by its own motivational state. Even so, studies of transreinforcer blocking

suggest that these different forms of consummatory conditioning may well engage a common motivational system.

Ganesen and Pearce (1988) pretrained rats with either a water or food reinforcer before giving compound training with the other US. Conditioned approach to the food or water source, the magazine, during the added CS was blocked by pretraining with the alternative reinforcer. In other words, pretraining with the water reinforcer blocked conditioning with the food reinforcer and vice versa. Moreover, this transreinforcer blocking did not depend on the rats' being both thirsty and hungry throughout training. Following pretraining with the water reinforcer under the combined deprivation state, the pretrained CS blocked conditioning to the added CS with the food reinforcer even though the rats were only food-deprived during the compound conditioning. Nor did the effect depend on the two reinforcers' maintaining the same conditioned response: Blocking occurred even when the food and water were dispensed to different magazines.

This transreinforcer blocking effect is a dramatic demonstration of a commonality between the conditioning processes engaged by food and water reinforcers. In fact, Ganesen and Pearce interpreted their results in terms of the type of Konorskian model outlined in Figure 12.2 by assuming that CSs associated with food and water activate a common appetitive motivational system. In discussing such motivational interactions, however, it is important to distinguish between the commonality and interactions between *motivational systems* engaged by CSs and interactions between primary *motivation states,* such as the states of hunger and thirst induced by food and water deprivation. Whereas transreinforcer blocking suggests that food and water CSs activate a common appetitive system, there is good evidence that thirst actively inhibits feeding and food conditioned behavior. We return to this distinction between motivational systems and motivational states when discussing the issue of motivational control. Before doing so, however, we must consider why Dickinson and Dearing (1979) distinguished between the appetitive and aversive systems in their Konorskian model.

Appetitive-Aversive Interactions

Although the transreinforcer modulation and blocking establish motivational commonalities, it is equally clear that we must draw a distinction at least between appetitive and aversive systems. There is a wealth of evidence that CSs of one affective class, if anything, have an inhibitory influence on responses controlled by CSs of the opposite affective class (Dickinson & Pearce, 1977). This inhibitory interrelationship is most clearly illustrated by counterconditioning. In the first stage of a study by Lovibond and Dickinson (1982), an appetitive jaw-movement response was conditioned to a CS by pairing it with an intraoral sugar water US in rabbits. Once the jaw-movement response had been conditioned, the schedule was changed so that an aversive eye-shock US replaced the water US on half the trials. Consequently, the CS signaled the sugar water on half of the trials and the eye shock on the remaining trials during the counterconditioning stage.

The critical observation concerned the fate of the conditioned jaw movement response during counterconditioning. If concurrent aversive conditioning just serves to augment the general motivational potency of the CS, the appetitive jaw-movement response should, if anything, have been augmented. At variance with this prediction, however, the jaw-movement response was suppressed as the defensive eye-blink response was conditioned. It is unlikely that the inhibition of the

appetitive responding reflected a peripheral response interaction because Scavio (1974) had previously established that rabbits can blink and swallow at the same time without any interference. Consequently, a plausible interpretation of the counterconditioning of the appetitive response by the aversive US is that there are, at least, separate aversive and appetitive motivational systems; the former exerts an inhibitory influence, on the latter, an influence that is illustrated by the appropriate inhibitory connection in Figure 12.2.

Figure 12.2 also contains a reciprocal inhibitory connection from the appetitive to the aversive system, although the evidence for this connection is somewhat weaker. Lovibond and Dickinson (1982) were unable to countercondition an established defensive eye-blink response by pairing the CS with sugar water. However, this failure may have arisen from an inequality of the relative strength of the aversive and appetitive reinforcers because Scavio (1974) has reported such counterconditioning when the strength of the aversive conditioning was weakened by extinction. During extinction of the eye-blink response, the frequency of the defensive response declined more rapidly when the CS was paired with interoral water.[2] Therefore, on the basis of this and other evidence (Dickinson & Dearing, 1979; Dickinson & Pearce, 1977), we favor the view that the appetitive and aversive motivational systems exert a mutually inhibitory influence.

---

[2] Scavio (1987) himself has argued against the claim that appetitive CSs exert an inhibitory influence on defensive conditioning because prior appetitive conditioning has been observed to facilitate subsequent aversive conditioning (e.g., Dickinson, 1976; Scavio & Gormezano, 1980). However, this positive transfer may well reflect attentional/associability processes (see Chap. 2, this volume) rather than motivational interactions. The counterconditioning procedure, unlike a retardation test for inhibition, minimizes a role for attentional/associability processes.

As well as providing an explanation of counterconditioning, the opponent-process system offers an account of the properties of conditioned inhibitors. A conditioned inhibitor is a stimulus that acquires the capacity to inhibit the conditioned response elicited by an excitatory CS as a result of being paired with the omission of a predicted reinforcer. It has long been known that an inhibitory CS of one affective class appears to have some of the properties of an excitatory CS of the opposite affective class. Thus, a CS paired with the omission of an expected food reward, a so-called frustrative stimulus, is aversive in that rats will learned to escape from it (Daly, 1974). Correspondingly, a CS predicting the omission of an expected, aversive shock has rewarding properties in that the animal will preferentially perform responses that generate this CS (LoLordo, 1969). Moreover, by the transreinforcer blocking assay, conditioned exciters and inhibitors of opposite affective classes engage a common motivational system. A frustrative CS, pretrained to predict the absence of an appetitive food US, can block aversive conditioning with a shock US in rats (Dickinson & Dearing, 1979; Goodman & Fowler, 1983).

The Konorskian opponent-process model can explain these commonalities by assuming that the release of a motivational system from inhibition by the opponent system leads to a rebound excitation. Thus, for example, a CS for food excites the appetitive system, which in turn inhibits the aversive system. The presentation of an appetitive inhibitor then attenuates activation of the appetitive system, releasing the aversive system from inhibition and thereby producing rebound aversive excitation. This model therefore explains the commonalities of what have been called "hope" and "relief" and "fear" and "frustration" (Mowrer, 1960) by assuming that each pair of affective states is mediated by the same motivational system.

Motivational Control

Although the motivational impact of different appetitive CSs may well be mediated by a common system in the Konorskian model, we have already noted that different appetitive motivational states can exert inhibitory-like interactions. There is an extensive, classic literature on the effects of a so-called irrelevant drive within the context of general drive theory (see Bolles, 1975, for a review), and it is well known that dehydration actively inhibits feeding (e.g., Rolls & McFarland, 1973) and food seeking (e.g., Van Hemel & Myers, 1970). Indeed, the presence of the cues associated with feeding may actually be aversive when rats are thirsty (e.g., Pliskoff & Tolliver, 1960). The inhibitory interaction between hunger and thirst in the control of Pavlovian behavior is illustrated also in a series of studies by Ramachandran and Pearce (1987). The asymptotic level of magazine approach elicited by a CS paired with either food or water was reduced by the presence of the irrelevant motivational state—thirst in the case of the food reinforcer and hunger in the case of the water reinforcer. The suppression produced by the irrelevant deprivation state was motivational in origin because removal of the irrelevant state during an extinction test restored performance to the level observed in rats trained under the relevant state alone.

It might be thought that this motivational interaction is at variance with our conclusion that hunger- and thirst-relevant USs activate a common motivational system on the basis of the Ganesen and Pearce (1988) transreinforcer blocking effect. As we have noted, however, it is important to distinguish the interaction between motivational systems from the interaction between the mechanisms by which primary motivational states, such as hunger and thirst, modulate the capacity of relevant stimuli to activate these systems.

Ramachandran and Pearce (1987) themselves argued that the interaction between hunger and thirst does not occur at the level of the appetitive motivational systems within the Konorskian model but rather that it reflects the mechanism by which primary motivational states modulate the activation of specific US representations.

That there has to be some form of state modulation of a CS's capacity to activate the relevant US representation is required by the simple fact that the strength of appetitive conditioning depends directly on the deprivation state of the animal. To take but a couple of examples, the strength of consummatory responses—licking in the case of rats (DeBold, Miller, & Jensen, 1965) and jaw movement in the case of rabbits (Mitchell and Gormezano, 1970) both conditioned by an intraoral water US—was monotonically related to the degree of fluid deprivation. In order to accommodate control by primary motivational states within their Konorskian model, Dickinson and Dearing (1979) assumed that these states gate the capacity of an excited US representation to activate the common appetitive motivational system and thereby the motivational feedback on the US representation (see Figure 12.2).

Clearly, each gate has to be US-specific within this model, so that hydration modulates fluid representations and nutritional needs modulate food representations. The implication of the Ramachandran and Pearce (1987) results for the model, therefore, is not only that hunger enhances the activation of the appetitive motivational system by a nutritional US representation through the gating mechanism but also that thirst counteracts this enhancement and thereby reduces the motivational feedback upon the food US representation.

Indeed, studies of specific hungers (Chap. 15, this volume) suggest that US gating must be even more specific than a simple hunger-thirst distinction. For example, Davidson, Altizer, Benoit, Walls, and Powley (1997) exposed food-deprived rats to pairings of one CS with a carbohydrate US, sucrose pellets, and another with a fat US, peanut oil, before returning the animals to the nondeprived state for testing. During this test the CSs were presented in extinction so that performance would have been based solely on CS-US associations acquired during training. Prior to this test, one group was placed in a glucoprivic state, whereas a lipoprivic state was induced in another group by pharmacological manipulation. Importantly, the rats in the lipoprivic state showed more magazine approach during the peanut oil CS than during the sucrose CS, whereas the reverse pattern was observed in the glucoprivic state. This reinforcer specificity implies that there must be separate US gating for these two states and the relevant reinforcers.

Davidson (1993, 1997) would probably argue against this account of motivational control on the grounds that the behavioral control exerted by hunger induced by food deprivation has to be learned. It has long been known that deprivation states can be used as discriminative cues (Webb, 1955); for example, Davidson and his colleagues (Davidson, 1987; Davidson & Benoit, 1996; Davidson, Flynn & Jarrard, 1992) demonstrated that the level of food deprivation in rats rapidly acquires control over freezing when this state predicts the occurrence of foot shocks in a particular context. Moreover, Davidson (1993, 1997) drew an analogy between this form of motivational control and the conditional control exerted by so-called occasion setters in Pavlovian conditioning (see Chap. 1, this volume; Schmajuk & Holland, 1998). An occasion setter is a stimulus that signals when another Pavlovian CS is reinforced (or not reinforced); as a result of experience with this conditional contingency, the animal comes to respond (or not respond) to the CS only when the occasion setter is present.

Although it may well be the case that the control exerted by food deprivation over responses from a different motivational class, such as freezing, may well involve a form of conditional learning, the question at issue is whether such learning also mediates the control exerted by hunger over responses elicited by a CS for food. Davidson (1997) argues that it does. He described an experiment in which food-deprived rats were once again trained to approach a magazine into which sucrose pellets were delivered before the strength of the approach response was tested in an extinction test. Half of the rats were tested food-deprived, and the other half were tested undeprived. Importantly, the state of food deprivation on the test had no effect on the approach response unless the animals had previously eaten the sucrose pellets in the undeprived state. Only rats that had previously eaten the pellets when undeprived and were then tested in this state showed a reduced level of responding. Davidson (1997) interpreted this finding as evidence that motivational control of Pavlovian food seeking by hunger must be learned through experience with the food reinforcer in both the deprived and undeprived states. As this form of differential experience is assumed to be necessary for the acquisition of conditional control by an occasion setter, Davidson argued that hunger acts as an occasion setter that predicts when the approach response will be reinforced in the training context.

There are, however, reasons for questioning the generality of this finding. Indeed, one might think that Davidson et al.'s (1997) demonstration of reinforcer-specific control by lipoprivic and glucoprivic states is a demonstration of the direct impact of motivational states. It is always possible, however, that the conditional control by these states was acquired during the Pavlovian training under general food deprivation, which presumably involved both the gluco- and lipoprivic states. It should be noted, however, that their rats had never received prior experience with the sucrose pellets and the peanut oil in the absence of a nutritional need. Furthermore, whatever the source of motivational control was in the Davidson et al. study, it is well established that the induction of certain motivational states can have a direct impact on conditioned behavior even if the animals have never previously experienced this state.

A classic example is salt seeking under a sodium appetite. Following prior experience with a salty-flavored solution, the induction of a sodium appetite enhances the preference of rats for the salt-associated flavor. This preference is conditioned because the flavor solution is sodium free at test and, importantly, occurs even though the rats have no prior experience of a sodium deficiency (e.g., Berridge & Schulkin, 1989; Fudim, 1978). Therefore, the motivational state induced by a sodium need has a direct impact on a preference conditioned by a Pavlovian association with salt even though the animals have no prior experience of the sodium and flavor in the need state. Similarly, Krieckhaus (1970) had previously shown that rats in a sodium need for the first time will preferentially approach a source at which they have previously received salt while thirsty.

Even so, we still need an account of why the motivational control of food seeking in the Davidson et al. (1997) study required prior experience of the food in the undeprived state. In our laboratories we have repeatedly observed a direct impact of shifts in the level of food deprivation on the frequency of approach to a food source without prior experience of the food in the shifted state (e.g., Balleine, 1992). The reason for this discrepancy may well lie with the contingency controlling the approach behavior. Although students of conditioning often assume, as we have, that approach to a food source is a Pavlovian response (e.g., Holland, 1979), the relative contribution of Pavlovian and instrumental contingencies to this behavior may well vary with the specific procedure employed. A cornerstone of our motivational theory (discussed later) is that the process of motivational control differs when mediated by instrumental response-reinforcer and Pavlovian stimulus-reinforcer contingencies. Thus, it may well be that the instrumental relationship played a more significant role in the approach response in the Davidson et al. (1997) procedure, and that for this reason they failed to observe a direct impact of the shift in motivational state (discussed later).

Another problematic finding for a simple gating theory of motivation control arises from a study by Killcross and Balleine (1996) on the motivational control of latent inhibition. Latent inhibition refers to the retardation of conditioning that occurs when a CS is simply preexposed (Lubow & Moore, 1959; Chap. 2, this volume). What Killcross and Balleine found was a motivational specificity in latent inhibition. Their rats received preexposure to one CS under hunger and another under thirst before both CSs were reinforced with either food pellets or saline when the animals were concurrently food- and water-deprived. Importantly, the rate of conditioning with a particular reinforcer was retarded when the CS had been preexposed under the motivational state relevant to that reinforcer—hunger in the case of the food pellets and thirst in the case of the saline. The animals appeared to have learned during preexposure that a CS is unrelated to the class of reinforcers relevant to their current motivational state. At present, we can do no more than acknowledge that this form of learning is not readily explained by the simple version of the Konorskian model.

In conclusion, we assume that Pavlovian conditioned responses are directly modulated by primary motivational states, a modulation that is captured by their ability to gate the activation of the appetitive system by representations of the relevant reinforcers (Figure 12.2). Further evidence for this claim is to be found in studies of the motivational impact of Pavlovian CSs on instrumental behavior.

Pavlovian-Instrumental Transfer

We introduced the role of Pavlovian conditioning in motivation by reference to the Ludwig et al. (1974) study demonstrating that alcoholics worked harder for alcohol in the presence of alcohol-associated stimuli. To explain this potentiation in terms of the motivational properties of CSs, we must assume that these stimuli potentiate not only Pavlovian responses but also instrumental behavior, such as the button-push response by which the alcoholics self-administered the ethanol. In fact, the idea that a stimulus associated with a positive reinforcer or reward exerts a motivational effect on behavior originates with an early study by Estes (1943). He reported that a tone paired with food elevated lever pressing by rats that had been previously reinforced with the food reward even though this response had never been trained in the presence of the tone. One problem that has always bedeviled the interpretation of such Pavlovian-instrumental transfer concerns the extent to which the Pavlovian influence is due to the interaction between the responses elicited by the signal for the reward and the transfer response, in this case lever pressing. As we have already noted, a CS signaling the delivery of food elicits approach to the source of the food; therefore, the issue is whether the elevation of lever pressing by the tone represents a true motivational effect of the CS or simply a facilitatory interaction of the responses conditioned to the tone with the instrumental response of lever pressing, for example, by maintaining proximity to the lever.

Although response interactions can contribute to Pavlovian-instrumental transfer (e.g., Karpicke, Christoph, Peterson, & Hearst, 1977), it is also clear that not all examples of transfer can be reduced to this mechanism. For example, Lovibond (1983) conditioned a jaw-movement response to a CS by pairing it with infusions of a sucrose solution directly into the mouths of thirsty rabbits. In order to assess whether this CS modulated instrumental responding, the rabbits were also trained to press a lever for the intraoral sugar solution in separate sessions and then, for the first time, presented with the CS while they were working for the sugar. In agreement with Estes' observation, the CS elevated the rate of lever pressing. In this case, however, we can be confident that this transfer effect did not reflect an interaction between the Pavlovian conditioned jaw-movement response and the instrumental lever pressing because eliciting jaw movements directly by the presentations of the intraoral sugar solution suppressed lever pressing.

Reinforcer-Specificity of Transfer

Pavlovian-instrumental transfer suggests that activation of the appetitive system not only potentiates Pavlovian preparatory and consummatory responses but also enhances instrumental behavior. Given this claim, two questions arise within the framework of the Konorskian model (Figure 12.2). The first is whether the transfer is mediated by the activation of the appetitive system via the representation of the reinforcer or by direct activation by a purely preparatory CS. This distinction is important because it determines whether transfer is sensitive to primary motivational states. The second issue follows from the first; if the transfer effects are mediated by the US representation, are they sensitive to the similarity of the Pavlovian and instrumental reinforcers? In other words, if an animal is working instrumentally for a particular food, does the influence of a CS depend on whether it predicts the same food, a different food, or even a reinforcer from a different motivational category? We consider each of these issues in turn.

There is no doubt that transfer can be mediated by a representation of the Pavlovian reinforcer. Balleine (1994; see also Dickinson & Balleine, 1990) exposed thirsty rats to Pavlovian pairings of a CS with either a sucrose or a sodium chloride solution before switching the motivational state to hunger by depriving the animals of food and training them to lever press for food pellets. When the CSs were presented while the animals were lever pressing in extinction, the sucrose CS, but not the saline CS, elevated responding above the baseline level. However, this selective potentiation only occurred when the animals were hungry during the test. If they were water-deprived prior to the test, the sucrose and saline CSs produced comparable enhancements. This result shows that Pavlovian-instrumental transfer respects the relevance of the anticipated reinforcer to the motivational state of the animal on test. The sucrose solution, unlike the sodium chloride, is relevant to both hunger and thirst. Moreover, the reinforcer-specificity of the transfer could only have occurred if the motivational effect was mediated by the sucrose representation activated by the CS and modulated by the current motivation state of the animal.

Balleine (1994) also observed a similar selective transfer across the opposite motivational shift from hunger to thirst. In this case, the CS was associated with either the sucrose solution or food pellets under hunger before the rats were trained to lever press for water while thirsty. If tested thirsty, the sucrose CS elevated responding, whereas the pellet CS depressed responding below the baseline level, thereby demonstrating, once more, the inhibitory effect of thirst on the motivational effects of purely food-associated CS (as discussed earlier; Ramachandran & Pearce, 1987). Again, this selective transfer was not due to a difference in the general effectiveness of the reinforcers because the sucrose and pellet CSs produced comparable enhancement when lever pressing was tested under hunger.

Finally, it should be noted that sensitivity to the motivational state on test occurred even though the animals had never previously experienced the sucrose reinforcer in the test state. This finding serves to reinforce our conclusion in the preceding section that the control of the motivational effects of CSs does not depend on prior experience with the reinforcer in the test state and is, therefore, adequately modeled by the motivational gating of the activation of a general appetitive system by a relevant reinforcer representation.

In their study of alcoholics, Ludwig et al. (1974) noted a high correlation between ratings of the alcohol craving induced by the alcohol-associated cues and their capacity to motivate button pushing. This correlation accords with the reinforcer specificity observed in the Balleine (1994) transfer effects. The role of the US representation in the motivational influence of CSs enables such stimuli to induce a craving for alcohol in the alcoholics and, presumably, the sucrose solution in thirsty or hungry rats. We cannot assume from this conclusion, however, that these stimuli motivate instrumental behavior because the instrumental action gives access to the craved resource. Indeed, this cannot be the case in the transfer observed by Balleine (1994). The sucrose CS motivated lever pressing even when this response had been trained with very different outcomes from the sucrose solution, either food pellets or water.

In fact, when the commonality of the Pavlovian and instrumental reinforcers is put in conflict with the relevance of the Pavlovian

reinforcer to the test motivational state, it is the latter that determines transfer. In a study very similar to that of Balleine (1994), Dickinson and Dawson (1987a) also established the sucrose and pellets CSs while the animals were hungry. The only difference was that the rats were also trained to lever press for pellets at the same time as the Pavlovian conditioning. However, even though lever pressing was associated with pellets, it was the sucrose rather than pellet CS that potentiated lever pressing when the animals were tested in extinction while thirsty. The corresponding pattern of results was also seen when Dickinson and Balleine (1990) tested transfer across a thirst-to-hunger shift with sucrose and saline CSs. The sucrose CS sustained greater lever pressing on test even though this response was trained with the saline reinforcer. In these cases, therefore, the motivational impact of the CSs was general even though their influence was mediated by a US-specific representation.

In some circumstances, however, the transfer does depend on the relationship between the Pavlovian and instrumental reinforcers. Colwill and Motzkin (1994; see also Colwill & Rescorla, 1988) associated one CS with food pellets and another with a sucrose solution before training the hungry rats to lever press and chain pull for these two reinforcers. When the CSs were presented in an extinction test, the rats performed the instrumental response trained with the same reinforcer as the US more than that trained with the different reinforcer. It is far from clear, however, that this transfer reflects a motivational effect in that response rate in the presence of the CS associated with the instrumental reinforcer was no higher than the baseline rate in the absence of the CS. In other words, the differential transfer arose from the fact that the CS depressed the instrumental response trained with the different reinforcer. Colwill and Motzkin (1994) themselves favored an interpretation in terms of associative cuing of the responses by the CSs through their common reinforcers (Trapold & Overmier, 1972) rather than a motivational modulation of instrumental performance.

We therefore defend the claim that the motivational influence of an appetitive CS does not augment preferentially instrumental responses that share a common reinforcer but rather produces a general behavioral facilitation. This conclusion accords with a Konorskian model (Figure 12.2), which assumes that CSs for different appetitive reinforcers activate a common motivational system.

Conditioned Suppression

Finally, we should note one further prediction of the Konorskian model that concerns, in this case, the effect of aversive Pavlovian CSs on rewarded instrumental responding. Estes (Estes & Skinner, 1941) was again the first to investigate the effect of an aversive CS on instrumental behavior by demonstrating that a tone paired with an electric shock suppressed food-rewarded lever pressing by hungry rats. However, our favorite conditioned suppression study is that reported by Di Giusto, Di Giusto, and King (1974). They gave students pairings of a tone and a mild electric shock before introducing the instrumental task, in which the students could display pictures of art works by pressing a button. Presentations of the CS during instrumental performance suppressed button pressing. Importantly, this suppression was not accompanied by any change in muscle tension, suggesting that suppressive effects of the CS was not due to the elicitation of interfering behavior. Within the framework of the Konorskian model, conditioned suppression is mediated by a loss of appetitive motivation brought about by the inhibitory influence of the aversive motivational system.

Summary

In our introduction we described two motivational effects: the rapid adjustment of the running speed of rats for food rewards brought about by shifts in food deprivation (Mollenauer, 1971) and reward magnitude (Franchina & Brown, 1971). Moreover, we suggested that both these effects were mediated by variations in the incentive properties of the rewards. In this section, we have argued that these incentive properties act through Pavlovian learning and that the Konorskian model provides the machinery to explain this Pavlovian incentive learning. The initial approaches to the goal box and the receipt of food there would have established the stimuli of the runway as Pavlovian CSs capable of activating the appetitive system via a representation of the food reward. The activation of this system would then have either elicited the running as a Pavlovian preparatory approach response or potentiated running as an instrumental response through the transfer process. The fact that the level of appetitive consummatory conditioning is determined by the US magnitude (e.g., Sheafor & Gormezano, 1972) allows the Pavlovian process to explain why a shift in reward magnitude produces a motivational effect on running. The impact of deprivation shifts also follows directly from the fact that the activation of the appetitive system by the US representation is gated by the relevant primary motivational state. A prediction of this model of Pavlovian incentive learning is that consummatory appetitive responses should be elicited while the animal is running; indeed, thirsty rabbits showed a gradient of increasing conditioned jaw-movement responses as they approached the goal box of a runway for a water reward (Gormezano, 1980).

Another condition of Mollenauer's (1971) study suggested, however, that Pavlovian incentive learning does not provide an exhaustive account of the impact of motivational states on performance. In addition to the groups that received a shift in deprivation after 74 preshift training trials, she also tested a further set of groups, which experienced the deprivation shift after much more limited training: only 22 trials. The postshift running speeds of these groups are illustrated in Figure 12.1C. The important feature of these data is that more trials were required for the full impact of the motivational shifts to emerge. Whereas after extensive training the speeds of the shifted groups, Groups dep/NON and non/DEP, converged upon those of the non-shifted groups, Group NON and DEP, respectively, within two pairs of trials (Figure 12.1A), convergence required five or six trial pairs after the more limited training (Figure 12.1C). This latter performance profile reflects the operation of a second form of incentive learning that is mediated by the instrumental contingency between the response and reinforcer rather than the Pavlovian relationship between CS and reinforcer.

INSTRUMENTAL INCENTIVE LEARNING

In many situations a forager equipped only with Pavlovian incentive learning would face a dilemma. To shift paradigms, consider the case of a hypothetical castaway marooned on the proverbial desert island. Although this island is blessed with a fresh water supply, the only food source is an abundance of coconuts. Being from temperate latitudes, our castaway has no previous experience with coconuts; when motivated by hunger, however, he rapidly learns to puncture the shells for the milk and smash them open for the meat. One morning, however, our castaway wakes to find that the water source has failed, and he begins, for the first time, to experience increasing thirst.

Pavlovian incentive learning would, of course, focus behavior on coconuts even though the castaway has had no previous experience with them while thirsty. Past hunger-motivated foraging ensured that the coconut CS was associated with representations of both the milk and the meat. As a consequences, when tested in a state of thirst, coconuts would activate the appetitive system via the milk representation. We have no reason to believe, however, that this activation of the appetitive system would selectively motivate the appropriate instrumental response of piercing the shell rather than the inappropriate one of smashing it open. Recall that a CS paired with a sucrose solution under hunger potentiated food-reinforced instrumental responses when the rats were thirsty (Balleine, 1994; Dickinson & Dawson, 1987a).

Consequently, even though our castaway is thirsty instead of hungry, the sight and feel of the coconut should motivate not only actions that puncture the coconut but also those that smash it open with the consequent loss of the precious milk. Of course, once the two actions have been performed and produced their differential consequences, the castaway would rapidly learn to perform only the appropriate instrumental behavior. According to the Pavlovian account, however, the very first instrumental decision under thirst should not discriminate between the relevant and irrelevant actions. Consequently, Pavlovian incentive learning does not provide a solution to the dilemma of our thirsty castaway.

Surprisingly, and in accord with the Pavlovian account, thirsty rats do not always resolve this dilemma. Dickinson and Watt (Dickinson, 1997) trained hungry rats to lever press and chain pull concurrently with one action reinforced by a sucrose solution and the other by food pellets before testing their choice between these two actions when they were, for the first time, thirsty. This test was conducted in extinction to ensure that the choice between the two responses was not affected by differential reinforcement during the test itself. As in the case of our castaway, on the basis of Pavlovian incentive learning alone, these rats should not have preferred one action over the other on test, as they were both performed within the same Pavlovian context. Indeed, this is just what Dickinson and Watt found (see also Dickinson & Dawson, 1988, 1989). When tested thirsty, rats performed the pellet-trained response just as frequently as the one reinforced with the sucrose solution.[3]

The failure of these rats to solve the castaway's dilemma contrasts with the success of those in a very similar study by Shipley and Colwill (1996). Like the Dickinson and Watt animals, their hungry rats were also trained to lever press and chain pull for a sucrose solution and food pellets; in this case, however, the sucrose-trained action was preferred when the rats were tested thirsty in extinction. The important difference between the two studies the concentration of the sucrose solution. Dickinson and Watt (Dickinson, 1997) employed a concentrated 20% sucrose solution, whereas Shipley and Colwill (1996) used a more dilute 8% solution. Moreover, in an unpublished study from the Cambridge Laboratory, we have demonstrated that it is the concentration of the sucrose solution that determines the presence or absence of a preference for the sucrose-trained response. It is not that the concentrated solution is an ineffective reward when thirsty because rats will lever press and chain pull faster for this solution than for the food pellets (e.g., Dickinson & Dawson, 1988). Indeed, the concentrated 20% solution was employed in the experiments demonstrating that a sucrose CS trained under hunger potentiates instrumental responding under thirst (Balleine, 1994; Dickinson & Dawson, 1987a).

A possible reason why the concentration is important concerns the sucrose solution's similarity to water. As a result of their daily maintenance schedule, the rats were likely to have drunk water when thirsty before and therefore have had the opportunity to learn about its thirst-quenching properties. Whether or not the rats solve the castaway's dilemma then depends on whether this learning generalizes from water to the sucrose solution. Clearly, this generalization is more likely to have occurred for the weak sucrose solution employed by Shipley and Colwill than for the concentrated solution used by Dickinson and Watt. The implication of this analysis is that animals must learn about the relevance of the incentive properties of instrumental reinforcers to a particular motivational state before that state can control performance through an instrumental contingency.

In fact, Dickinson and Watt (Dickinson, 1997; see also Dickinson & Dawson, 1988,

---

[3]It should be noted that there are a number of successful demonstrations of an instrumental-irrelevant incentive effect. Dickinson and Dawson (1987b) trained one group to lever press for the sucrose solution and another group to press for the food pellets while the rats were hungry. When performance was subsequently assessed in extinction under thirst, the sucrose-trained group responded more than did the pellet-trained group. The important feature of this between-subject design is that the training contexts of the two groups were selectively associated with either the sucrose solution or the food pellets, so that the irrelevant incentive effect can be explained purely in terms of the Pavlovian incentive learning to the contextual stimuli.

The same analysis can be given of the classic irrelevant incentive effect reported by Krieckhaus and Wolf (1968), in which thirsty rats were trained to lever press for either a sodium solution or a nonsodium solution. Following the induction of a sodium need, rats trained with the sodium solution showed elevated responding in extinction. This selective enhancement of a sodium-trained responding was abolished, however, when the Pavlovian status of the context in which the sodium and nonsodium responses were tested was equated by giving concurrent training with the two responses in the same context (Dickinson, 1986).

1989) provided direct evidence for such learning. Prior to instrumental training in standard operant chambers, rats must learn that the rewards are available in the magazine and that they must collect them promptly once delivered. Consequently, Dickinson and Watt gave their rats a number of pretraining sessions in which the food pellets and the sucrose solution were delivered aperiodically in the absence of the opportunity to lever press and chain pull. These manipulanda were simply removed from the chamber during the pretraining sessions. For the group of rats already described, this pretraining occurred while they were hungry, as they were during instrumental training. By contrast, a second group of rats received this pretraining under water deprivation so that they had experience of the sucrose solution and food pellets while thirsty prior to instrumental training under hunger.[4] If these rats learned that the sucrose solution was more valuable than the food pellets when they were thirsty, they should have performed sucrose-trained response preferentially during the extinction test under thirst. This is just what Dickinson and Watt observed; at the outset of the test, the rats performed this response at over twice the rate of the pellet-trained response, but only if they had previously experienced the reinforcers when thirsty.

In summary, whether animals solve the castaway's dilemma depends on whether they have had prior experience with the rewards, or at least similar commodities, under thirst. If they have such experience, then animals are capable of using their knowledge of the instrumental response-reinforcer contingencies (see Colwill & Rescorla, 1986; Dickinson,

1994; Chap. 1, this volume) to select the action that in the past has yielded the reinforcer relevant to their current need state. The importance of this experience is that it allows the animal to learn about the incentive properties of the sucrose solution and the food pellets when thirsty. We refer to this form of learning as *instrumental incentive learning* because, though not itself instrumental, it is expressed in behavior through knowledge of the instrumental contingency between action and reinforcer.

Tolman's Cathexis Theory

The precursor to the concept of instrumental incentive learning is to be found in Tolman's (1949a, 1949b) cathexis theory of motivation (see Dickinson & Balleine, 1994). According to Tolman, instrumental performance is determined by the incentive value of the outcome of the instrumental action, or what he referred to as the goal-object. Moreover, Tolman argued that primary motivational states do not automatically confer value upon relevant outcomes; rather, both animals and humans must learn about relative incentive values in a particular motivational state through experience with the outcomes in that state. Therefore, unlike Pavlovian motivation, in which thirst automatically gates the activation of the appetitive system by a fluid US representation, an animal must learn about the incentive value of a fluid under water deprivation by actually drinking the solution when thirsty. Tolman's theory therefore anticipates the result found by Dickinson and colleagues (Dickinson & Dawson, 1988, 1989; Dickinson, 1997). Their rats failed to perform the action trained with the relevant sucrose solution when thirsty for the first time, which, according to Tolman, was because they had not formed a cathexis between thirst and the sucrose solution. When given the opportunity to do so by drinking the sucrose solution under water deprivation

[4]In fact, both groups of rats were placed on an alternating schedule of food and water deprivation during the pretraining; one group received the sucrose solution and food pellets on days when they were hungry, and the other group received them on days when they were thirsty.

during pretraining, the reinstatement of thirst on test conferred a positive incentive value on the solution and thereby motivated the appropriate instrumental behavior.

Tolman assumed that a cathexis is instantiated by the formation of a connection between the motivational state and the representation of the relevant outcome, which then allows the motivational state to activate the outcome representation and thereby confer incentive value upon the outcome. The Tolmanian concept of incentive learning therefore predicts an asymmetry in the impact of motivation shifts on performance, a prediction that was examined in Balleine's (1992) study of hunger shifts. Balleine trained rats to respond for either food pellets or a starch solution in a nondeprived state before testing their performance when food deprived in extinction. Cathexis theory predicts that the hungry rats should respond no more vigorously than would nondeprived animals unless they have previously experienced the foods when hungry. Without this experience, there would be no cathexis between the state of hunger and the representation of the food, so the induction of hunger could not enhance the incentive value of the food. In accord with this prediction, Balleine (1992) found that hungry and nondeprived rats pressed at the same low rate on test, but that this rate was elevated in hungry rats if they had received preexposure to the food when deprived.

In contrast to the role of incentive learning in motivational upshifts, cathexis theory predicts that a downshift should have an immediate impact on performance. Training the rats to respond while food-deprived should establish a connection between the state of hunger and the representation of the food reward that enables the induction of this state to endow the food with incentive value. Consequently, a downshift to the nondeprived state should produce an immediate loss of incentive

value by removing the activation of the reward representation by the hunger state. At variance with this prediction, however, Balleine (1992) found that a reduction in food deprivation had no impact on performance unless the animals had previously experienced the food in the nondeprived state. Following training under food deprivation with either the food pellets or the starch solution, nondeprived rats responded just as frequently as did deprived ones in an extinction test unless they had previously eaten the particular food reward in the sated state.

Therefore, simply experiencing a food in the hungry state is not sufficient to establish motivational control over its incentive value. This failure of cathexis theory prompted us to suggest that instrumental incentive learning consists of the interaction of two learning processes (Dickinson & Balleine, 1994). The first is the process by which an animal learns about the incentive value of an outcome through experience with it. We called this form of learning the determination process because it is this process that determines the incentive value of the outcome. Of course, one of the factors that determines the incentive value is the presence of a relevant motivational state so that it was the determination process that led Balleine's (1992) rats to respond more rapidly for food when hungry than when sated. However, a motivation state can determine an incentive value without acquiring control of that value. This point is illustrated by the fact that the incentive value generalized across shifts in motivational state in the Balleine (1992) study when the rats had no prior experience of the food rewards in the shifted state. The high incentive value established when rats were hungry during training generalized to the nondeprived state on test and maintained performance. Correspondingly, when the animals were trained nondeprived, the consequent low incentive value also controlled performance when the animals were tested hungry. For the motivational state to acquire control over incentive value, the animals had to receive prior experience with the outcome in the shifted state, and the acquisition of this motivational control over incentive value is the second component of the instrumental form of incentive learning.

In summary, motivational states serve two important functions in instrumental incentive learning. The first is that of *determining* the incentive value of an instrumental outcome, and the second is that of *controlling* the incentive value so that the value that controls performance at any given time depends on the current motivational state of the animal.

Motivational Control of Incentive Value

For Balleine's (1992) rats, motivational control required differential experience with the food in both the deprived and nondeprived states, and the necessity of differential experience suggested to us (Balleine, 2000; Dickinson & Balleine, 1994) that motivational states acquire control over instrumental incentive value through the normal discrimination learning processes underlying the acquisition of conditional control. As we have already noted, Davidson (1993, 1997) made this very claim in relation to the motivational control of Pavlovian conditioning, and we have already discussed the extensive evidence from his laboratory that deprivation states can acquire conditional control even over motivationally irrelevant responses. Although we take issue with his claim in respect to Pavlovian motivation, which we regard as being a direct form of control (as discussed earlier), we agree that the motivational control over the incentive value of instrumental outcomes depends on conditional learning.

The analogy between the acquisition of motivational control and standard conditional control is best illustrated by Bouton's (1993, 1994) account of the contextual control over

responding to a CS. Bouton argued that the context in which learning takes place acquires control over conditioned responding to a CS only when the CS has been both reinforced and extinguished so that its predictive status is ambiguous. Thus, just as the high incentive value of a food reward established by instrumental training under food deprivation generalizes to the nondeprived state, so conditioning in one context generalizes fully to a different context. By contrast, if conditioning in one context is followed by extinction in a second context, responding to the CS comes under contextual control. This control can be illustrated by a study in which Bouton and his colleagues (Bouton, Kenney, & Rosengard, 1990) used a drug-induced internal state, which is analogous to a motivational state, as the controlling context. Having been conditioned in a drug-free state, the CS was extinguished under a benzodiazepine agonist (BZ) before the rats were tested in the BZ and nondrug states. This two-state training induced control over responding by the BZ state in that the rats responded to the CS in the nondrug but not in the drugged state. This state-dependent control is, we argue, analogous to the control exerted by hunger over incentive value of food produced by experiencing the food in both the deprived and nondeprived states (Balleine, 1992).

If motivational states are in no way privileged in their acquisition of control over incentive value, artificially induced states should also readily acquire motivational control. The BZ state, in fact, provides an excellent model for testing this claim because it not only induces a highly discriminable internal state that can acquire conditional control over behavior but also enhances the rewarding property of foods in nondeprived rats (Balleine, Ball, & Dickinson, 1994). Therefore, in terms of the processes determining and controlling incentive value, the BZ state should function exactly like natural hunger according to incentive learning theory. Allowing animals to eat a particular food under a BZ agonist should not only enhance the incentive value of that food but also result in this enhancement's being conditional or dependent on the internal state induced by the drug when the animal has received experience with food in both the drugged and drug-free states.

To test this prediction, Balleine et al. (1994) trained nondeprived rats to lever press for food pellets before allowing them to eat the pellets under the influence of a BZ agonist in separate feeding cages. When the rats were returned to the operant chambers for an extinction test, these rats pressed more than did animals that had eaten the pellets following vehicle injections. Critically, however, this incentive-learning effect only emerged if the animals were tested in the state induced by an injection of the agonist. In other words, the motivational control exerted by the drug exactly paralleled that produced by food deprivation, although there was no transfer of control between these states (Balleine et al., 1994).

Thus, an internal, drug-induced state that does not mimic natural hunger can acquire control over the incentive value of the food in the way that parallels the control exerted by hunger. This result certainly suggests that the acquisition of control over incentive value is mediated by a general learning process rather than one specific to natural motivational states.

Determination of Incentive Value

Our analysis has done little so far to characterize the role of psychological states in motivational processes, whether it be in the determination of instrumental incentive value or in the activation of Pavlovian systems and their motivational feedback upon US representations (see Figure 12.2). This is not to say, however, that psychological states and reactions have no role in these processes. We have already noted that Ludwig et al. (1974) observed a correlation between the craving induced by alcohol-associated CSs and their motivational properties, and a number of authors have claimed a major role for affective experience by arguing that motivation is grounded on the hedonic reactions or, in other words, the pleasure elicited by rewards and appetitive USs (e.g., Cabanac, 1992; Toates, 1986).

Hedonics and Incentive Value

There are various reasons for believing that hedonics play an important role in motivation. The hedonic reaction to a stimulus, like the incentive value of a reward, is modulated by motivational states, a process that Cabanac refers to as *alliethesia*. For example, Cabanac (1971) asked human participants to make successive ratings of how much they liked a sweet-tasting glucose solution. Although these rating remained high for the group required to spit out the solution after each tasting, there was a progressive decline in the ratings when the solutions were swallowed. To what extent the differential hedonic evaluation depended on general nutritional state or specific satiety for the evaluated stimulus is unclear, although both processes probably play a role. There is ample evidence not only that a flavored food is rated as less pleasant shortly after a meal (e.g., Booth, Mather, & Fuller, 1982; Laeng, Berridge, & Butter, 1993) but also that consuming a particular food or fluid produces a flavor-specific reduction in hedonic ratings (see Hetherington, 1996; Hetherington & Rolls, 1996; Johnson & Vickers, 1993). Moreover, Gibson, and Desmond (1999) found that the hedonic evaluation of chocolate was in part determined by incentive learning. Chocolate was rated as more pleasant after it had been regularly eaten 2 hr rather than a few minutes following a meal when, presumably, the human participants were generally sated.

Assessment of taste reactivity in animals also suggests that hedonic evaluations are modulated by motivational state. Grill and Norgren (1978) reported that the very first intraoral infusion of a sucrose solution elicits a set of appetitive reactions by rats, such as rhythmic tongue protrusions and mouth movements, whereas a distasteful quinine solution elicits aversive reactions, such as gapes and head shakes. These basic patterns of affective reactions to tastes are exhibited by a wide range of species, including human infants and other primates (see Berridge, 2000b, for a review), and Berridge (1995, 2000a, 2000b) argued that they reflect an immediate and innate hedonic evaluation of the taste.

Taste reactivity can be dissociated from simple ingestion and rejection. Berridge (2000b) reviewed a number of brain lesions and pharmacological treatments that dissociate consumption and taste reactivity, but one particularly compelling example comes from a study of the suppression of sucrose drinking by different aversive consequences. Pelchat, Grill, Rozin, and Jacobs (1983) reduced the amount of a sucrose solution drunk by thirsty rats by pairing drinking of the solution with either foot shock or the induction of gastric malaise by an injection of lithium chloride (LiCl). Although both treatments were equally effective in suppressing intake, they had contrasting effects on the taste reactivity. Even though the rats would not drink the sucrose solution following the shock treatment, they still showed the full profile of appetitive taste reactivity with no aversive components. This pattern suggests that the rats still liked the sucrose solution but would not drink it because of its aversive consequences, much as we might avoid eating a favorite food if it regularly produces the pain of indigestion. By contrast, the LiCl treatment not only suppressed intake but also shifted the taste reactivity from the appetitive to the aversive pattern. This case is analogous to one in which we develop an aversion or disgust reaction to a food as a result of its association with nausea.

Studies of taste reactivity confirm that the hedonic reactions to food and fluid are modulated by motivational state. The taste reactivity patterns elicited by sugar solutions are augmented by hunger (e.g., Berridge, 1991; Cabanac & Lafrance, 1990, 1991; Grill, Roitman, & Kaplan, 1996), and those elicited by saline are enhanced by a sodium appetite (e.g., Berridge, Flynn, Schulkin, & Grill, 1984; Berridge & Shulkin, 1989). On the basis of these observations, we (Balleine & Dickinson, 1998a; Dickinson & Balleine, 1994, 2000) have suggested that the hedonic reactions elicited by an instrumental outcome determine the assignment of incentive value. Therefore, according to this account, hedonics serves as the interface between the cognitive representation of incentive value that controls the performance of instrumental actions and the basic neurobiological mechanism engaged by nutritional deficits and other motivational states.

The main prediction of the hedonic theory of incentive value is that any manipulation that alters the taste reactivity patterns elicited by a food or fluid should produce a concomitant change in the incentive value of that food or fluid. We have already noted in our discussion of motivational control that BZ agonists enhance the incentive value of food rewards (Balleine et al., 1994); therefore, it is instructive that these drugs also augment the appetitive taste reactivity patterns (e.g., Berridge & Peciña, 1995; Söderpalm & Berridge, 2000). Conversely, given that LiCl-induced aversions not only attenuate appetitive taste reactions but also induce aversive ones (e.g., Pelchat et al., 1983), this treatment should devalue foods and fluids with this taste, a prediction confirmed in numerous instrumental studies of outcome devaluation (e.g., Adams & Dickinson, 1981; Colwill & Rescorla, 1985).

Moreover, the hedonic theory predicts that the crucial event for outcome devaluation is experience with the devalued outcome rather than the conditioning of the aversion. This point is illustrated by a study in which we (Balleine & Dickinson, 1991) trained thirsty rats to lever press for a sucrose solution in a single session. We then devalued this outcome by injecting the rats with LiCl immediately following this session, which should have conditioned an aversion from the sucrose. According to the hedonic theory of incentive value, however, this aversion conditioning should not have been sufficient by itself to devalue the sucrose solution. In the absence of any reexposure to the sucrose following the aversion conditioning, our rats would not have had opportunity to learn about the change in their hedonic reactions to this outcome, and therefore their instrumental performance should have been controlled by the positive incentive value assigned to the sucrose solution during instrumental training. Indeed, we failed to detect any devaluation effect following this treatment; the pairing of the sucrose solution and the LiCl had no detectable effect on instrumental performance in a subsequent extinction test.[5]

In order to induce an outcome devaluation effect, we had to reexpose the rats to the sucrose solution in separate drinking cages between the aversion conditioning and testing. When we did so, the reexposed rats pressed less in the subsequent extinction test than did both nonreexposed animals and control rats that did not receive the aversion conditioning in the first place. Although the pairing of the sucrose and LiCl conditioned a latent

aversion from the solution, this aversion remained opaque to the cognitive system controlling lever pressing until the animals were reexposed to the sucrose solution. The reexposure then enabled the rats to experience the change in their hedonic evaluation following the aversion conditioning, and on the basis of this experience, they assigned a lower incentive value to the outcome.

The claim that outcome devaluation is based on the hedonic reactions elicited by the sucrose solution at the time of reexposure is supported by pharmacological manipulations of these reactions. Limebeer and Parker (2000) reported that the antiemetic and antinausea serotonin antagonist, ondansetron, reduces the aversive taste reactivity pattern elicited by a sweet solution after aversion conditioning without any detectable impact on its consumption. If outcome devaluation following aversion conditioning is due to experience of the aversive taste reactions during reexposure, administration of the antiemetic prior to reexposure should reduce the devaluation effect. This result was reported by Balleine, Garner, and Dickinson (1995). An aversion was conditioned from both a sucrose and sodium solution by following a single training session with LiCl. During this session one action delivered the sucrose solution, and the other delivered the saline. The rats then received a single exposure to both solutions, one under ondansetron and the other under vehicle. On test, our rats performed the response trained with the outcome reexposed under ondansetron in preference to the one trained with the outcome reexposed under the vehicle. State-dependency did not contribute to this preference, as its magnitude was unaffected by whether the antiemetic was administered prior to the test.

In summary, the conditions producing outcome devaluation by taste-aversion conditioning parallel those required for devaluation by motivational shifts. To recap, Balleine's

---

[5]Under certain conditions, an outcome devaluation effect can be observed after a single outcome-LiCl pairing in the absence of any reexposure to the outcome (Parades-Olay & Lopez, 2000; Rescorla, 1992, 1994). Balleine and Dickinson (1992) analyzed some of the conditions under which LiCl-induced outcome devaluation depends upon reexposure.

(1992) rats continued to respond at a high level even though they were not food-deprived unless they had previously experienced the food reward in the sated state. We interpret this persistence as evidence that performance was controlled by the positive incentive value assigned to the outcome during training under hunger. Similarly, instrumental performance following aversion conditioning alone was controlled by the positive incentive value of the sucrose generated by training the rats thirsty in the Balleine and Dickinson (1991) study. An outcome devaluation effect required that the animals had the opportunity to learn about the change in their hedonic reactions to the sucrose solution before the aversion conditioning reduced instrumental performance. The main difference between the two cases is that the reduction of incentive value produced by aversion conditioning does not readily come under the control of the animal's motivational state (Lopez, Balleine, & Dickinson, 1992b).

Finally, we should note an apparent challenge to the hedonic theory of incentive value. Dopamine antagonists attenuate instrumental performance for appetitive rewards (for reviews, see Beninger & Miller, 1998; Berridge & Robinson, 1998; Smith, 1995) but not for appetitive taste reactivity (Peciña, Berridge, & Parker, 1997). In this case, however, it is far from clear that the drug affects instrumental performance through the determination of incentive value. Dickinson, Smith, and Mirenowicz (2000) replicated the procedures that we had previously used to demonstrate a role for instrumental incentive learning in motivational control by hunger (Balleine, Davies, & Dickinson, 1995; Balleine & Dickinson, 1994) but substituted the dopamine antagonist for the state of satiety. The rats were trained to perform different instrumental actions for food pellets and a sucrose solution before one of the outcomes was reexposed under the drug and the other under the vehicle. If experienc-

ing a reward under a dopamine antagonist determines a lower incentive value, this reexposure should have produced a reduction in the subsequent performance of the associated action on test. However, Dickinson et al. (2000) could not detect any effect of the incentive learning treatment even when the animals were tested under the drug.

Rather than impacting upon instrumental incentive learning, dopamine antagonists may act through the Pavlovian form of incentive learning. Berridge and Robinson (1998; Robinson & Berridge, 1993) consistently argued that the dopamine system mediates the motivational properties of CSs. According to Berridge and Robinson, pairing a CS with an appetitive reinforcer endows the signal with incentive salience and the capacity to induce a state of wanting, which can be independent of the animal's liking for the reinforcer. Support for their claim comes from the observation that dopamine antagonists attenuated Pavlovian-instrumental transfer in rats at the doses that did not support instrumental incentive learning (Dickinson et al., 2000). Conversely, Wyvell and Berridge (2000) reported that a microinjection of a dopamine agonist into the nucleus accumbens of rats enhanced the potentiation of instrumental responding for sucrose pellets produced by an appetitive CS without affecting the appetitive and aversive taste reactivity profiles elicited by the intraoral infusion of a bitter-sweet sucrose-quinine solution. Therefore, it is likely that the effect of dopamine antagonists are mediated by the Pavlovian rather than the instrumental form of incentive learning and that the drug-induced reduction in simple instrumental performance reflects an attenuation of the motivational influence of contextual stimuli.

Representation of Incentive Value

Recall that the outcome devaluation produced by reexposure to a reward associated with gastric illness was ameliorated when an antiemetic was injected prior to reexposure but not when it was administered prior to the instrumental test (Balleine, Garner, & Dickinson, 1995). The finding that the antiemetic had no impact on the magnitude of the devaluation effect when administered prior to the instrumental extinction test has theoretical implications that go beyond the issue of state-dependency. If the control of instrumental action by incentive value depends on the reactivation of the hedonic response to the outcome at the time of performance, the presence of an antiemetic on test should have reduced the magnitude of the devaluation effect. The fact that it did not do so in the Balleine, Garner, and Dickinson (1995) study therefore suggests that once the assignment of incentive value has been made on the basis of hedonic evaluation, the representation of incentive value is relatively affect-free.

Moreover, in the case of foods at least, there is evidence that incentive value can be assigned to, or associated with, a purely sensory representation of the outcome. Balleine (2000) has recently reported an aversion-induced devaluation effect based entirely on the taste of the outcomes. The thirsty rats received a single training session in which one action was reinforced by an orange-flavored sucrose solution and the other by a grape-flavored solution. This session was then followed by a LiCl injection, which should have conditioned an aversion to both solutions. The animals then received reexposure to only one of the flavored solutions before a preference test between the two actions was conducted in extinction. In this test, the rats performed preferentially the action trained with the nonreexposed rather the reexposed outcome. Because the two outcomes differed only in their flavor, the selective devaluation effect implies that the incentive values of the outcomes were encoded in association with their gustatory representations.

Perhaps more surprising is the fact that state-specific incentive values are also encoded in association with outcome flavors. Once again, we (Balleine & Dickinson, 1998a) trained hungry rats to perform two actions for different outcomes, which in this case were a salty and a sour starch solution. In a second incentive-learning stage, the rats were given free access to one of the solutions for an hour. Presumably, the rats became sated on the starch during this reexposure and, as a consequence, experienced its flavor in association with reduced hedonic response to the starch solution. Therefore, we expected the rats to assign a low incentive value to the flavor conditional on being sated with starch. In accord with this prediction, the rats performed the action trained with the reexposed flavor at a reduced rate during an extinction test that followed satiation on the starch solution alone. It is important to note that this satiety was induced by prefeeding the rats for 1 hr with an unflavored starch solution and that the devaluation effect did not occur in the absence of the starch prefeeding.

The final strand of evidence for a sensory encoding of incentive value comes from studies of the role of insular cortex in incentive learning. The insular cortex contains the cortical representations of tastes in close association with visceral afferents; therefore, one might expect this region to be involved in incentive learning if the incentive value of a food outcome is bound to its flavor representation. To investigate the neurobiological encoding of incentive value, we (Balleine & Dickinson, 2000) lesioned the insular cortex before testing the rats in a standard incentive-learning paradigm. Once again, the hungry rats were trained to perform two actions for different outcomes, food pellets and a starch solution, before one of the outcomes was devalued by being reexposed in the nondeprived state. The control animals replicated the standard incentive-learning effect; when tested in the undeprived state, they performed the action trained with the devalued outcome less than that trained with the nondevalued outcome. Importantly, however, this difference was abolished following insular lesions.

It is not that the lesioned animals were insensitive to the rewarding properties of the foods, for their acquisition and performance of the instrumental actions were normal. Moreover, they were sensitive to the manipulation of motivational state in that they responded faster when food-deprived and actually receiving the food rewards. They could also discriminate between the two rewards in that they exhibited a specific satiety effect. Prefeeding one of the foods before an instrumental test session selectively reduced responding for the prefed food. However, if this test was conducted in extinction so that performance depended on the representation of the incentive values of the foods rather than on their immediate impact during the test session, the lesion abolished devaluation by specific satiety. Unlike the control animals, the lesioned rats performed the actions trained with the two foods at comparable levels.

Summary

In summary, our claim is that goal-directed instrumental action is motivated by the incentive value of the outcome that is encoded in association with a sensory/perceptual representation of the outcome. The assignment of a value to an outcome depends on the experience of the hedonic reactions elicited by that outcome—reactions that are modulated by the current motivational state. This process of assignment is the value-determination component of instrumental incentive learning. Finally, there is evidence that once an incentive value is assigned to an outcome representation, the capacity of that value to control action is relatively independent of the motivational and affective systems that determined the hedonic reactions to the outcome in the first place.

We must acknowledge, however, that this account is little more than descriptive, although Balleine (2000) has recently offered a mechanism for the determination of incentive value that employs a process of affective feedback.

Generality of Incentive Learning

Although the manipulation of hedonic evaluation by a variety of procedures—deprivation-induced motivational state changes, aversion conditioning, pharmacological treatments—establishes a role for incentive learning in instrumental motivation, this research has been conducted largely with food rewards and simple operant responses. Consequently, an important issue concerns the generality of incentive learning across both motivational systems and instrumental responses.

Motivational Generality

As we have already noted, some of the initial demonstrations of incentive learning involved shifts from hunger to thirst (Dickinson & Dawson, 1988, 1989). Moreover, changes in instrumental performance for fluid rewards brought about both by upshifts (Lopez & Paredes-Olay, 1999) and downshifts (Lopez, Balleine, & Dickinson, 1992a) in water deprivation depend on incentive learning. There is also evidence that incentive learning may play a role in sexual motivation. Everitt and Stacey (1987) trained male rats to press a lever to gain access to an estrous female before being castrated. This treatment, which reduces the level of circulating testosterone, impairs male sexual motivation. Nevertheless, the castrated animals, on being returned to the test chamber, initially pressed as rapidly as did intact rats. However, after only a single encounter with the female in their impotent state, the males reduced their rate of responding. The initial insensitivity of the female-seeking behavior to the reduction in testosterone suggests that instrumental performance was controlled by the high incentive value assigned to the female during precastration copulation and that this value continued to control postcastration performance until the male had an opportunity to learn about the female's low incentive value in his current state.

Finally, what is probably the very first demonstration of incentive learning established its role in the motivational control of avoidance behavior. Hendersen and Graham (1979) trained rats to avoid the onset of a heat source in a warm environment before testing them in extinction in either the same warm conditions or in a cold environment. The assumption behind the study was that avoidance was motivated by the warm conditions, so that reducing the ambient temperature would reduce the motivation for the avoidance response. In fact, the test temperature had no effect on performance unless the rats had previously experienced the heat source when cold. Given this incentive-learning treatment, which presumably allowed them to learn about the positive incentive value of the heat source when cold, the level of avoidance responding was subsequently reduced when tested under a low ambient temperature.

There is one case, however, in which a shift in motivational state does appear to have a direct impact on the incentive value of an instrumental outcome. Dickinson and Balleine (1990) trained thirsty rats to lever press and chain pull for a sucrose solution and for saline before testing performance in extinction when the animals were hungry. The rationale behind this motivation shift is that the incentive value of the sucrose, but not the saline, should have been maintained across the shift from thirst to hunger. The results of the test confirmed this prediction. The hungry animals performed the response trained with the sucrose more than that trained with the saline when they were tested hungry (but not when tested thirsty). The important point, however, is that this irrelevant incentive effect occurred even though

the rats had no previous experience with the two solutions when hungry and therefore had no opportunity to learn about their relative value in this state. Moreover, the design of the experiment precluded nonspecific, Pavlovian modulation of performance (discussed earlier) resulting from motivational conditioning to the context by testing both responses in the same context.

The immediate impact of a thirst-to-hunger shift stands in marked contrast to the absence of a direct effect for the opposite shift—from hunger to thirst—which requires incentive learning (Dickinson, 1997; Dickinson & Dawson, 1988, 1989). We suspect that the difference arises from the asymmetrical interaction between hunger and thirst. Whereas hungry rats are not concurrently thirsty, water-deprived animals have a nutritional deficit incurred by an active inhibition of food consumption. As noted earlier in our discussion of Pavlovian incentive learning, thirsty rats appear to be concurrently hungry so that experience with the sucrose solution and saline during the instrumental training under water deprivation may have allowed our rats to learn about the relative incentive values of the two solutions not only with respect to thirst but also with respect to hunger. In other words, the acquisition of motivational control over the incentive values of sucrose and saline may have occurred during the instrumental training in the Dickinson and Balleine (1990) study.

Whatever the merits of this particular explanation, it is clear that incentive learning makes an important contribution to the control of instrumental performance by a variety of motivational states and systems. What is equally clear, however, is that the role of incentive learning varies with the nature and extent of instrumental training.

Instrumental Generality

At the outset, we illustrated the influence of motivation with a demonstration by

Mollenauer (1971) that shifts in hunger had a rapid impact on running speed (Figure 12.1A), which, we suggested, reflected the effect of Pavlovian incentive learning to the runway cues. We have also noted, however, that the rapidity with which the rats adjusted to the shift in deprivation state varied with the amount of pretraining. The animals required more post-shift trials following limited (Figure 12.1C) rather than extensive training (Figure 12.1A). One explanation of the lag in adjusting to a deprivation shift following limited pretraining is that the animals required a number of experiences with the reward in the new deprivation state for instrumental incentive learning to change the incentive value of the food reward. This account implies, therefore, that the motivation of instrumental behavior changes with training from the instrumental to the Pavlovian form of incentive learning.

We have examined this possibility in an operant study in which hungry rats received either limited or extended training of lever pressing for a reward of food pellets (Dickinson, Balleine, Watt, Gonzalez, & Boakes, 1995). The animals then received an incentive-learning experience in which they were allowed to eat the pellets in separate feeding cages in either the deprived or undeprived state. Finally, we assessed performance during extinction when the rats were either hungry or sated on their maintenance diet. This study replicated the standard incentive-learning effect observed after limited training. The rats sated on test showed reduced performance only if they had previously eaten the food pellets in the undeprived state. By contrast—and in accordance with Mollenauer' results—after extended training the shift in motivation state had a direct impact on performance, which was not modulated by the incentive learning experience.

We (Dickinson et al., 1995) interpreted this change in motivational control in terms of the nature of the instrumental learning process that controls performance at different points in training. For outcome revaluation to be effective, instrumental performance must be controlled by an action-outcome (A-O) representation. In other words, a change in the incentive value of an outcome can only affect performance in an extinction test in which the outcome itself is not present, if performance is controlled by knowledge of the relationship by the action and the outcome. Therefore, the processes of instrumental incentive learning must operate throughout an A-O representation. There is evidence from other outcome devaluation studies, however, that instrumental responding can become autonomous of the current incentive value of the outcome with overtraining under the appropriate conditions (e.g., Adams, 1982), and one account of the development of behavioral autonomy with training is that it reflects a transition in the control of performance from a cognitive process based on the A-O representation to an S-R habit process (e.g., Dickinson, 1985, 1989).

This account is compatible with the change in motivational control observed by Dickinson et al. (1995). After limited training, the A-O representation mediates motivational control through the incentive value of the outcome acquired by the process of instrumental incentive learning. This process cannot operate, however, when the instrumental response becomes predominantly an S-R habit with overtraining. Therefore, after overtraining, the primary motivational influence is that mediated by Pavlovian incentive learning, which, we have argued, renders performance directly sensitive to shifts in motivational state. The same analysis can explain the contrasting patterns of postshift running speeds observed by Mollenauer (1971) after varying pretraining.

Finally, motivational control varies not only with the amount of instrumental training but also with the location of the instrumental action within an appetitive chain. In all the instrumental incentive learning studies we have considered so far, the target instrumental response, such as lever pressing or chain pulling, has acted as the first link in a behavioral chain that terminated in the opening of a flap door that gave access to the food magazine. In his initial incentive learning study, Balleine (1992) reported that flap opening, unlike lever pressing and chain pulling, did not require an incentive learning experience for motivational control and was directly affected by shifts in food deprivation. In other words, there was a motivational dissociation between the two responses. Rats that had been trained hungry but not received incentive learning pressed the lever frequently but did not enter the magazine when tested sated in extinction. The corresponding animals that were nondeprived during training pressed slowly but frequently entered the magazine when tested hungry.

In order to determine whether this variation in motivational control was a function of the response topography and manipulandum or the locus of the response in an appetitive chain, we (Balleine, Garner, Gonzalez, & Dickinson, 1995) locked the flap door of the chamber permanently open and trained our hungry rats to respond on a two-link chain schedule for food pellets. The response required in one link was lever pressing and in the other was chain pulling. When the rats were tested in extinction with both manipulanda present, the state of food deprivation had no impact on performance of the first-link response unless the animals had received previous experience with the food pellets in the undeprived state. Therefore, in replication of our previous findings, the motivational control of performance in the initial link of the instrumental chain depends on incentive learning. By contrast, performance of the terminal-link response was affected directly by the downshift in deprivation level.

It is clear, therefore, that processes of motivational control vary across the links of instrumental chains with terminal links being directly affected by motivational shifts and distal links being more dependent on incentive learning. The causes of this variation remain as yet unanalyzed, but the profile of motivational control suggests that terminal links, like overtrained responses, are more sensitive to Pavlovian influences.

SUMMARY AND CONCLUSIONS

In summary, our analysis of motivation vindicates Miller's (1951) original claim that acquired behavior is motivated by desires rather than drives and, moreover, that desires are learned even in the case of such basic biological commodities as food and water. Desires, however, come in two forms. The first is mediated by what we have called Pavlovian incentive learning. We have analyzed this incentive process in terms of a Konorskian model in which the CS activates an appetitive motivational system via a representation of the US or reinforcer with the Pavlovian desire arising from a feedback activation of this representation. These Pavlovian desires are modulated by two further processes or mechanisms. The first is engaged by primary motivational states. The presence of a motivational state, such as hunger or thirst, enhances or gates the capacity of an activated representation of a relevant US to excite the appetitive system and thereby the motivational impact of a CS. The second is an aversive system that serves to inhibit the appetitive system. This aversive system is embedded within a structure similar to that engaged by appetitive stimuli, and it modulates the performance of defensive Pavlovian behavior in a manner analogous to the appetitive case.

Whether Pavlovian desires are in fact desires of good standing is less clear, however.

As we have noted, there is evidence that CSs can induce craving, and Berridge has certainly characterized the state induced by a CS as one of wanting. Moreover, the motivational impact of a CS on instrumental behavior is modulated by the presence of the motivational state relevant to the US. What appears not to be the case, however, is that a CS acts by enhancing the desire for the outcome of the instrumental action in that the CS impacts on instrumental performance trained with a reinforcer relevant to a different motivational state. Rather, appetitive CSs appear to cause the Cartesian "agitation of spirits" that "dispose the body to movement," much as Hullian general drive was assumed to do.

Desires that function by specifying their objects as goals of instrumental action operate through a different form of incentive learning. Within this system, the desire is characterized as the incentive value of the instrumental outcome, which has to be learned through experience of the hedonic reactions elicited by the outcome. Primary motivational states play two roles within this form of incentive learning. First, they contribute to the determination of incentive value by altering the hedonic reactions elicited by the outcome; second, they can acquire control over incentive value so that the value controlling action is higher in the presence of relevant motivational state than in its absence.

Finally, although the Pavlovian and instrumental incentive learning are dissociable and have been treated separately in our analysis, they do, of course, function in parallel and in a dynamic interaction throughout the behavioral stream with the nature of the interaction varying with the status of the current action. Instrumental incentive learning can only motivate cognitively mediated, goal-directed actions but not S-R habits, which are primarily under the motivational influence of the Pavlovian form of incentive learning.

Miller (1951) concluded his chapter with the lament that "the theoretical and experimental work has a long way to go before it bridges completely the gap between the fundamental biological drives and the wonderfully complex web of socially learned motives that determine adult human behavior" (p. 469). That gap, of course, remains wide, but the recognition of the central role of incentive learning in the control of behavior by even the "fundamental biological drives" does provide the foundation for bridging this gap that was lacking 50 years ago.

REFERENCES

Adams, C. D. (1982). Variations in the sensitivity of instrumental responding to reinforcer devaluation. *Quarterly Journal of Experimental Psychology, 34B,* 77–98.

Adams, C. D., & Dickinson, A. (1981). Instrumental responding following reinforcer devaluation. *Quarterly Journal of Experimental Psychology, 33B,* 109–122.

Bakal, C. W., Johnson, R. D., & Rescorla, R. A. (1974). The effect of change in US quality on the blocking effect. *Pavlovian Journal of Biological Sciences, 9,* 97–103.

Balleine, B. (1992). Instrumental performance following a shift in primary motivation depends upon incentive learning. *Journal of Experimental Psychology: Animal Behavior Processes, 18,* 236–250.

Balleine, B. (1994). Asymmetrical interactions between thirst and hunger in Pavlovian-instrumental transfer. *Quarterly Journal of Experimental Psychology, 47B,* 211–231.

Balleine, B. (2000). Incentive processes in instrumental conditioning. In R. Mowrer & S. Klein (Eds.), *Handbook of contemporary learning theories* (pp. 307–366). Hillsdale, NJ: Erlbaum.

Balleine, B., Ball, J., & Dickinson, A. (1994). Benzodiazepine-induced outcome revaluation and the motivational control of instrumental action in rats. *Behavioral Neuroscience, 108,* 573–589.

Balleine, B., Davies, A., & Dickinson, A. (1995). Cholecystokinin attenuates incentive learning in rats. *Behavioral Neuroscience, 109,* 312–319.

Balleine, B., & Dickinson, A. (1991). Instrumental performance following reinforcer devaluation depends upon incentive learning. *Quarterly Journal of Experimental Psychology, 43B,* 279–296.

Balleine, B., & Dickinson, A. (1992). Signalling and incentive processes in instrumental reinforcer devaluation. *Quarterly Journal of Experimental Psychology, 45B,* 285–301.

Balleine, B., & Dickinson, A. (1994). Role of cholecystokinin in the motivational control of instrumental action in rats. *Behavioral Neuroscience, 108,* 590–605.

Balleine, B., & Dickinson, A. (1998a). The role of incentive learning in instrumental outcome revaluation by sensory-specific satiety. *Animal Learning and Behavior, 26,* 46–59.

Balleine, B., Garner, C., & Dickinson, A. (1995). Instrumental outcome devaluation is attenuated by the anti-emetic ondansetron. *Quarterly Journal of Experimental Psychology, 48B,* 235–251.

Balleine, B. W., & Dickinson, A. (1998b). Consciousness: The interface between affect and cognition. In J. Cornwell (Ed.), *Consciousness and human identity* (pp. 57–85). Oxford: Oxford University Press.

Balleine, B. W., & Dickinson, A. (2000). The effects of lesions of the insular cortex on instrumental conditioning: Evidence for a role in incentive learning. *Journal of Neuroscience, 20,* 8954–8964.

Balleine, B. W., Garner, C., Gonzalez, F., & Dickinson, A. (1995). Motivational control of heterogeneous instrumental chains. *Journal of Experimental Psychology: Animal Behavior Processes, 21,* 203–217.

Beninger, R. J., & Miller, R. (1998). Dopamine D1-receptors and reward-related incentice learning. *Neuroscience & Biobehavioral Reviews, 22,* 335–345.

Berridge, K. C. (1991). Modulation of taste affect by hunger, caloric satiety, and sensory-specific satiety in the rat. *Appetite, 16,* 103–120.

Berridge, K. C. (1995). Food reward: Brain substrates of wanting and liking. *Neuroscience and Biobehavioral Reviews, 20,* 1–25.

Berridge, K. C. (2000a). Reward learning: Reinforcement, incentives, and expectations. In D. L. Medin (Ed.), *The psychology of learning and motivation* (Vol. 40, pp. 223–278). New York: Academic Press.

Berridge, K. C. (2000b). Measuring hedonic impact in animals and infants: Microstructure of affective taste reactivity patterns. *Neuroscience and Biobehavioral Reviews, 24,* 173–198.

Berridge, K. C., Flynn, F. W., Schulkin, J., & Grill, H. J. (1984). Sodium depletion enhances salt palatability in rats. *Behavioral Neuroscience, 98,* 652–660.

Berridge, K. C., & Peciña, S. (1995). Benzodiazepines, appetite, and taste palatability. *Neuroscience and Biobehavioral Reviews, 19,* 121–131.

Berridge, K. C., & Robinson, T. E. (1998). What is the role of dopamine in reward: Hedonic impact, reward learning, or incentive salience? *Brain Research Reviews, 28,* 309–369.

Berridge, K. C., & Schulkin, J. (1989). Palatability shift of a salt-associated incentive during sodium depletion. *Quarterly Journal of Experimental Psychology, 41B,* 121–138.

Bindra, D. (1974). A motivational view of learning, performance, and behavior modification. *Psychological Review, 81,* 199–213.

Bindra, D. (1978). How adaptive behavior is produced: A perceptual-motivation alternative to response reinforcement. *Behavioral and Brain Sciences, 1,* 41–91.

Bolles, R. C. (1975). *Theory of Motivation.* New York: Harper & Row.

Bombace, J. C., Brandon, S. E., & Wagner, A. R. (1991). Modulation of a conditioned eyeblink response by a putative emotive stimulus conditioned with a hindleg shock. *Journal of Experimental Psychology: Animal Behavior Processes, 17,* 323–333.

Booth, D. A., Mather, P., & Fuller, J. (1982). Starch content of ordinary foods associatively conditions human appetite and satiation, indexed by intake and eating pleasantness of starched paired flavours. *Appetite, 3,* 163–184.

Bouton, M. E. (1993). Context, time, and memory retrieval in the interference paradigms of Pavlovian learning. *Psychological Bulletin, 114,* 80–99.

Bouton, M. E. (1994). Context, ambiguity, and classical conditioning. *Current Directions in Psychological Science, 3,* 49–53.

Bouton, M. E., Kenney, F. A., & Rosengard, C. (1990). State-dependent fear extinction with two benzodiazepine tranquilizers. *Behavioral Neuroscience, 104,* 44–55.

Cabanac, M. (1971). Physiological role of pleasure. *Science, 173,* 1103–1107.

Cabanac, M. (1992). Pleasure: The common currency. *Journal of Theoretical Biology, 155,* 173–200.

Cabanac, M., & Lafrance, L. (1990). Postingestive alliesthesia: The rat tells the same story. *Physiology and Behavior, 47,* 539–543.

Cabanac, M., & Lafrance, L. (1991) Facial consummatory responses support the ponderstat hypothesis. *Physiology and Behavior, 50,* 179–183.

Colwill, R. M., & Motzkin, D. K. (1994). Encoding of the unconditioned stimulus in Pavlovian conditioning. *Animal Learning and Behavior, 22,* 384–394.

Colwill, R. M., & Rescorla, R. A. (1985). Postconditioning devaluation of a reinforcer affects instrumental responding. *Journal of Experimental Psychology: Animal Behavior Processes, 11,* 120–132.

Colwill, R. M., & Rescorla, R. A. (1986). Associative structures in instrumental learning. In G. H. Bower (Ed.), *The psychology of learning and motivation* (Vol. 20, pp. 55–104). Orlando, FL: Academic Press.

Colwill, R. M., & Rescorla, R. A. (1988). Associations between the discriminative stimulus and the reinforcer in instrumental learning. *Journal of Experimental Psychology: Animal Behavior Processes, 14,* 155–164.

Crespi, L. P. (1942). Quantitative variation of incentive and performance in the white rat. *American Journal of Psychology, 55,* 467–517.

Daly, H. B. (1974). Reinforcing properties of escape from frustration aroused in various learning situations. In G. H. Bower (Ed.), *The psychology of learning and motivation* (Vol. 8, pp. 187–231). New York: Academic Press.

Davidson, T. L. (1987). Learning about deprivation intensity stimuli. *Behavioral Neuroscience, 101,* 198–208.

Davidson, T. L. (1993). The nature and function of interoceptive signals to feed: Towards integration of physiological and learning perspectives. *Psychological Review, 100,* 640–637.

Davidson, T. L. (1997). Hunger cues as modulatory stimuli. In N. A. Schmajuk & P. C. Holland (Eds.), *Occasion setting: Associative learning and cognition in animals* (pp. 223–248). Washington, DC: American Psychological Association.

Davidson, T. L., Altizer, A. M., Benoit, S. C., Walls, E. K., & Powley, T. L. (1997). Encoding and selective activation of "metabolic memories" in the rat. *Behavioral Neuroscience, 111,* 1014–1030.

Davidson, T. L., & Benoit, S. C. (1996). The learned function of food deprivation cues: A role for conditioned modulation. *Animal Learning and Behavior, 24,* 46–56.

Davidson, T. L., Flynn, F. W., & Jarrard, L. E. (1992). Potency of food deprivation intensity cues as discriminative stimuli. *Journal of Experimental Psychology: Animal Behavior Processes, 18,* 174–181.

DeBold, R. C., Miller, N. E., & Jensen, D. D. (1965). Effect of strength of drive determined by a new technique for appetitive classical conditioning of rats. *Journal of Comparative and Physiological Psychology, 59,* 102–108.

Descartes, R. (1911). Passions of the soul. In E. S. Haldane & G. R. T. Ross (Eds.), *The philosophical works of Descartes.* Vol. 1. Cambridge, UK: Cambridge University Press. (Original work published 1649.)

Dickinson, A. (1976). Appetitive-aversive interactions: Facilitation of aversive conditioning by prior appetitive training in the rat. *Animal Learning and Behavior, 4,* 416–420.

Dickinson, A. (1985). Actions and habits: The development of behavioural autonomy. *Philosophical Transactions of the Royal Society of London, 308B,* 67–78.

Dickinson, A. (1986). Re-examination of the role of the instrumental contingency in the sodium-appetite irrelevant incentive effect. *Quarterly Journal of Experimental Psychology, 38B,* 161–172.

Dickinson, A. (1989). Expectancy theory in animal conditioning. In S. B. Klein & R. R. Mowrer (Eds.), *Contemporary learning theories: Pavlovian conditioning and the status of traditional learning theories* (pp. 279–308). Hillsdale, NJ: Erlbaum.

Dickinson, A. (1994). Instrumental conditioning. In N. J. Mackintosh (Ed.), *Animal cognition and learning* (pp. 4–79). London: Academic Press.

Dickinson, A. (1997). Bolles' psychological syllogism. In M. E. Bouton & M. S. Fanselow (Eds.), *Learning, motivation, and cognition* (pp. 345–367). Washington, DC: American Psychological Association.

Dickinson, A., & Balleine, B. (1990). Motivational control of instrumental performance following a shift from thirst to hunger. *Quarterly Journal of Experimental Psychology, 42B,* 413–431.

Dickinson, A., & Balleine, B. (1994). Motivational control of goal-directed action. *Animal Learning & Behavior, 22,* 1–18.

Dickinson, A., & Balleine, B. W. (2000). Causal cognition and goal-directed action. In C. Heyes & L. Huber (Eds.), *The evolution of cognition* (pp. 185–204). Cambridge, MA: MIT Press.

Dickinson, A., Balleine, B., Watt, A., Gonzalez, F., & Boakes, R. A. (1995). Motivational control after extended instrumental training. *Animal Learning & Behavior, 23,* 197–206.

Dickinson, A., & Dawson, G. R. (1987a). Pavlovian processes in the motivational control of instrumental performance. *Quarterly Journal of Experimental Psychology, 39B,* 201–213.

Dickinson, A., & Dawson, G. R. (1987b). The role of the instrumental contingency in the motivational control of performance. *Quarterly Journal of Experimental Psychology, 39B,* 77–93.

Dickinson, A., & Dawson, G. R. (1988). Motivational control of instrumental performance: The role of prior experience of the reinforcer. *Quarterly Journal of Experimental Psychology, 40B,* 113–134.

Dickinson, A., & Dawson, G. R. (1989). Incentive learning and the motivational control of instru-

mental performance. *Quarterly Journal of Experimental Psychology, 41B,* 99–112.

Dickinson, A., & Dearing, M. F. (1979). Appetitive-aversive interactions and inhibitory processes. In A. Dickinson & R. A. Boakes (Eds.), *Mechanism of learning and motivation* (pp. 203–231). Hillsdale, NJ: Erlbaum.

Dickinson, A., & Pearce, J. M. (1977). Inhibitory interactions between appetitive and aversive stimuli. *Psychological Bulletin, 84,* 690–711.

Dickinson, A., Smith, J., & Mirenowicz, J. (2000). Dissociation of Pavlovian and instrumental incentive learning under dopamine antagonists. *Behavioral Neuroscience, 114,* 468–483.

Di Giusto, J. A., Di Giusto, E. L., & King, M. G. (1974). Heart rate and muscle tension correlates of conditioned suppression in humans. *Journal of Experimental Psychology, 103,* 515–521.

Estes, W. K. (1943). Discriminative conditioning, I: A discriminative property of conditioned anticipation. *Journal of Experimental Psychology, 32,* 150–155.

Estes, W. K., & Skinner, B. F. (1941). Some quantitative properties of anxiety. *Journal of Experimental Psychology, 29,* 390–400.

Everitt, B. J., & Stacey, P. (1987). Studies of instrumental behavior with sexual reinforcement in male rats (*Rattus novegicus*), II: Effects of preoptic area lesions, castration, and testosterone. *Journal of Comparative Psychology, 101,* 407–419.

Flaherty, C. F. (1996). *Incentive relativity.* New York: Columbia University Press.

Franchina, J. J., & Brown, T. S. (1971). Reward magnitude shift effects in rats with hippocampal lesions. *Journal of Comparative and Physiological Psychology, 76,* 365–370.

Fudim, O. K. (1978). Sensory preconditioning of flavors with formalin-produced sodium need. *Journal of Experimental Psychology: Animal Behavior Processes, 4,* 276–285.

Ganesen, R., & Pearce, J. M. (1988). Effects of changing the unconditioned stimulus on appetitive blocking. *Journal of Experimental Psychology: Animal Behavior Processes, 14,* 280–291.

Gibson, E. L., & Desmond, E. (1999). Chocolate craving and hunger state: Implications for the acquisition and expression of appetite and food choice. *Appetite, 32,* 219–240.

Goodman, J. H., & Fowler, H. (1983). Blocking and enhancement of fear conditioning by appetitive CSs. *Animal Learning and Behavior, 11,* 75–82.

Gormezano, I. (1972). Investigations of defensive and reward conditioning in the rabbit. In A. H. Black & W. F. Prokasy (Eds.), *Classical conditioning, II: Current research and theory* (pp. 151–181). New York: Appleton-Century-Crofts.

Gormezano, I. (1980). Pavlovian mechanisms of goal-directed behavior. In R. F. Thompson, L. H. Hicks, & V. B. Shvyrkov (Eds.), *Neural mechanisms of goal-directed behavior and learning* (pp. 39–56). New York: Academic Press.

Grill, H. J., & Norgren, K. C. (1978). The taste reactivity test, I: Mimetic responses to gustatory stimuli in neurologically normal rats. *Brain Research, 143,* 263–279.

Grill, H. J., Roitman, M. F., & Kaplan, J. M. (1996). A new taste reactivity analysis of the integration of taste and physiological state information. *American Journal of Physiology, 271,* R677–678.

Hendersen, R. W., & Graham, J. (1979). Avoidance of heat by rats: Effects of thermal context on the rapidity of extinction. *Learning and Motivation, 10,* 351–363.

Hetherington, M. M. (1996). Sensory-specific satiety and its importance in meal termination. *Neuroscience and Biobehavioral Reviews, 20,* 113–117.

Hetherington, M. M., & Rolls, B. J. (1996). Sensory-specific satiety: Theoretical issues and central characteristics. In E. D. Capaldi (Ed.), *Why we eat what we eat* (pp. 267–290). Washington, DC: American Psychological Association.

Holland, P. C. (1979). Differential effects of omission contingencies on various components of Pavlovian appetitive responding in rats. *Journal of Experimental Psychology: Animal Behavior Processes, 5,* 178–193.

Hull, C. L. (1943). *Principles of behavior.* New York: Appleton-Century-Crofts.

Hull, C. L. (1952). *A behavior system.* New Haven, CT: Yale University Press.

Johnson, J., & Vickers, Z. (1993). Effects of flavors and macronutrient composition of food servings on liking, hunger and subsequent intake. *Appetite, 21,* 25–39.

Kamin, L. J. (1969). Selective association and conditioning. In N. J. Mackintosh & W. K. Honig (Eds.), *Fundamental issues in associative learning* (pp. 42–64). Halifax, Nova Scotia: Dalhousie University Press.

Karpicke, J., Christoph, G., Peterson, G., & Hearst, E. (1977). Signal location and positive versus negative conditioned suppression in the rat. *Journal of Experimental Psychology: Animal behavior Processes, 3,* 105–118.

Killcross, S., & Balleine, B. (1996). Role of primary motivation in stimulus preexposure effects. *Journal of Experimental Psychology: Animal Behavior Processes, 22,* 32–42.

Konorski, J. (1967). *Integrative activity of the brain: An interdisciplinary approach.* Chicago: University of Chicago Press.

Krieckhaus, E. E. (1970). "Innate recognition" aids rats in sodium regulation, *Journal of Comparative and Physiological Psychology, 73,* 117–122.

Krieckhaus, E. E., & Wolf, G. (1968). Acquisition of sodium by rats: Interaction of innate mechanisms and latent learning. *Journal of Comparative and Physiological Psychology, 65,* 197–201.

Laeng, B., Berridge, K. C., & Butter, C. M. (1993). Pleasantness of a sweet taste during hunger and satiety: Effects of gender and "sweet tooth." *Appetite, 21,* 247–254.

Limebeer, C. L., & Parker, L. A. (2000). The antiemetic drug ondansetron interferes with lithium-induced conditioned rejection reactions, but not lithium-induced taste avoidance in rats. *Journal of Experimental Psychology: Animal Behavior Processes, 26,* 371–384.

LoLordo, V. M. (1969). Positive conditioned reinforcement from aversive situations. *Psychological Bulletin, 72,* 193–203.

Lopez, M., Balleine, B., & Dickinson, A. (1992a). Incentive learning and the motivational control of instrumental performance by thirst. *Animal Learning and Behavior, 20,* 322–328.

Lopez, M., Balleine, B., & Dickinson, A. (1992b). Incentive learning following reinforcer devaluation is not conditional upon motivational state during re-exposure. *Quarterly Journal of Experimental Psychology, 45B,* 265–284.

Lopez, M., & Paredes-Olay, C. (1999). Sensitivity of instrumental responses to an upshift in water deprivation, *Animal Learning and Behavior, 27,* 280–287.

Lovibond, P. F. (1983). Facilitation of instrumental behavior by a Pavlovian appetitive conditioned stimulus. *Journal of Experimental Psychology: Animal Behavior Processes, 9,* 225–247.

Lovibond, P. F., & Dickinson, A. (1982). Counterconditioning of appetitive and defensive CRs in rabbits. *Quarterly Journal of Experimental Psychology, 34B,* 115–126.

Lubow, R. E., & Moore, A. U. (1959). Latent inhibition: Effects of nonreinforced preexposure to the conditioned stimulus. *Journal of Comparative and Physiological Psychology, 52,* 415–419.

Ludwig, A. M., Wikler, A., Stark, L. H., & Lexington, K. (1974). The first drink: Psychobiological aspects of craving. *Archives of General Psychiatry, 30,* 539–547.

Miller, N. E. (1951). Learnable drives and reward. In S. S. Stevens (Ed.), *Handbook of experimental psychology* (pp. 435–472). New York: Wiley.

Mitchell, D. S., & Gormezano, I. (1970). Effects of water deprivation on classical appetitive conditioning of the rabbit's jaw movement response. *Learning and Motivation, 1,* 199–206.

Mollenauer, S. O. (1971). Shifts in deprivation level: Different effects depending on the amount of preshift training. *Learning and Motivation, 2,* 58–66.

Mowrer, O. H. (1960). *Learning theory and behavior.* New York: Wiley.

Parades-Olay, C., & Lopez, M. (2000). Comparison of the instrumental reinforcer devaluation effect in two strains of rats (Wistar and Lister). *Behavioural Processes, 50,* 165–169.

Peciña, S., Berridge, K. C., & Parker, L. A. (1997). Pimozide does not shift palatability: Separation of anhedonia from sensorimotor effects. *Pharmacology, Biochemistry and Behavior, 58,* 801–811.

Pelchat, M. L., Grill, H. J., Rozin, P., & Jacobs, J. (1983). Quality of acquired responses to taste by *Rattus norvegicus* depends upon type of associated discomfort. *Journal of Comparative and Psychology, 97,* 140–153.

Pliskoff, S., & Tolliver, G. (1960). Water-deprivation-produced sign reversal of a conditioned reinforcer based upon dry food. *Journal of the Experimental Analysis of Behavior, 3,* 323–329.

Ramachandran, R., & Pearce, J. M. (1987). Pavlovian analysis of interactions between hunger and thirst. *Journal of Experimental Psychology: Animal Behavior Processes, 13,* 182–192.

Rescorla, R. A. (1992). Depression of an instrumental response by a single devaluation of its outcome. *Quarterly Journal of Experimental Psychology, 44B,* 123–136.

Rescorla, R. A. (1994). A note of the depression of instrumental responding after one trial of outcome devaluation. *Quarterly Journal of Experimental Psychology, 47B,* 27–37.

Rescorla, R. A., & Solomon, R. L. (1967). Two-process learning theory: Relationship between Pavlovian conditioning and instrumental learning. *Psychological Review, 74,* 151–182.

Rescorla, R. A., & Wagner, A. R. (1972). A theory of Pavlovian conditioning: Variations in the effectiveness of reinforcement and nonreinforcement. In A. H. Black & W. F. Prokasy (Eds.), *Classical conditioning, II: Current research and theory* (pp. 64–99). New York: Appleton-Century-Crofts.

Robinson, T. E., & Berridge, K. C. (1993). The neural basis of of drug craving: An incentive-sensitization theory of addiction. *Brain Research Reviews, 18,* 247–291.

Rolls, B. J., & McFarland, D. J. (1973). Hydration releases inhibition of feeding produced by intracranial angiotensin. *Physiology and Behavior, 11,* 881–884.

Scavio, M. J., Jr. (1974). Classical-classical transfer: Effects of prior aversive conditioning in the rabbit. *Journal of Comparative and Physiological Psychology, 86,* 107–155.

Scavio, M. J., Jr. (1987). Appetitive-aversive interactions in rabbit conditioning preparations. In I. Gormezano, W. F. Prokasy, & R. F. Thompson, (Eds.), *Classical Conditioning* (pp. 319–338). Hillsdale, NJ: Lawrence Erlbaum Associates.

Scavio, M. J., Jr., & Gormezano, I. (1980). Classical-classical transfer: Effects of prior appetitive conditioning upon aversive conditioning in rabbits. *Animal Learning and Behavior, 8,* 218–224.

Schmajuk, N. A., & Holland, P. C. (1998). *Occasion setting: Associative learning and cognition in animals.* Washington, DC: American Psychological Association.

Sheafor, P. J., & Gormezano, I. (1972). Conditioning the rabbit's (*oryctolagus cuniculus*) jaw-movement response: US magnitude effects on URs, CRs, and pseudo-CRs. *Journal of Comparative and Physiological Psychology, 81,* 449–456.

Shipley, B. E., & Colwill, R. M. (1996). Direct effects on instrumental performance of outcome revaluation by drive shifts. *Animal Learning and Behavior, 24,* 57–67.

Smith, G. P. (1995). Dopamine and food reward. *Progress in Psychobiology and Physiological Psychology, 16,* 83–144.

Söderpalm, A. H. V., & Berridge, K. C. (2000). The hedonic impact and intake of food are increased by midazolam microinjections in the parabrachial nucleus. *Brain Research, 877,* 288–297.

Spence, K. W. (1956). *Behavior theory and conditioning.* New Haven, CT: Yale University Press.

Thorndike, E. L. (1911). *Animal intelligence: Experimental studies.* New York: Macmillan.

Toates, F. M. (1986). *Motivational systems.* Cambridge, UK: Cambridge University Press.

Tolman, E. C. (1949a). There is more than one kind of learning. *Psychological Review, 56,* 144–155.

Tolman, E. C. (1949b). The nature and function of wants. *Psychological Review, 56,* 357–369.

Trapold, M. A., & Overmier, J. B. (1972). The second learning process in instrumental learning. In A. H. Black & W. F. Prokasy (Eds.), *Classical conditioning, II: Current research and theory* (pp. 427–452). New York: Appleton-Century-Crofts.

Vandercar, D. H., & Schneiderman, N. (1967). Interstimulus interval functions in different response systems during classical conditioning. *Psychonomic Science, 9,* 9–10.

Van Hemel, P. E., & Myers, J. S. (1970). Control of food-motivated instrumental behavior in water-deprived rats by prior water and saline drinking. *Learning and Motivation, 1,* 86–94.

Webb, W. B. (1955). Drive stimuli as cues. *Psychological Reports, 1,* 287–298.

Wyvell, C. L., & Berridge, K. C. (2000). Intra-accumbens amphetamine increases the conditioned incentive salience of sucrose reward: Enhancement of reward "wanting" without enhanced liking or response reinforcement. *Journal of Neuroscience, 20,* 8122–8130.

CHAPTER 13

Emotional Plasticity

GLENN E. SCHAFE AND JOSEPH E. LeDOUX

EMOTION AND PLASTICITY

It is widely accepted that certain aspects of emotional expression are hardwired products of our evolutionary history. Indeed, the bodily response of a human to a sudden danger shares much in common with the bodily response of other mammals: Muscles tense; the heart races; hair stands on end; hormones surge. However, despite these similarities in expression, the things that trigger fear in people and other mammals do not necessarily overlap. This is in part due to differences in evolutionary history: Different species have been subject to different forms of predation, and their brains reflect this to some extent. But it is also due to the fact that emotion systems are incredibly plastic and are able to use information extracted from previous experiences to guide responses in current ones. A single encounter with a meaningless stimulus in an emotional situation can forever alter the way we act in the presence of that stimulus. In short, emotion systems respond in much the same way in different mammals. The things that trigger emotional responses in each species differ, however, and many of these triggers are learned rather than innate.

This work was supported in part by National Institutes of Health grants MH 46516, MH 00956, MH 39774, and MH 11902, and by a grant from the W. M. Keck Foundation to New York University.

In this chapter we describe the neural basis of emotional learning. We begin with a brief historical survey of efforts to pinpoint emotional circuits in the brain. We then turn to studies of the neural basis of fear, as work on this emotion system has been the most successful in identifying emotional circuits and their role in emotional learning.

IN SEARCH OF THE EMOTIONAL BRAIN

In the late 19th century pioneering neuroscientists identified regions of the neocortex involved in sensory perception and movement control. This prompted William James to ask whether emotions might be explained in terms of these known and localized functions or whether emotion was the business of a separate, yet undiscovered, brain system (James, 1890). Being a pragmatist, he proposed a theory of emotion based solely on known sensory and motor systems. Specifically, he argued that emotionally arousing stimuli are perceived by sensory cortex, which activates motor cortex to produce bodily responses appropriate to the emotionally arousing stimulus. Emotional feelings then result when our sensory cortex perceives the sensations that accompany bodily responses. Because different emotions involve different bodily responses, they have different sensory signatures and thus feel different. The essence of James' theory is captured by his often-stated conclusion that we do not run from a bear because we feel afraid, but instead we feel afraid because we run.

James' theory was quickly refuted by research showing that complete removal of the neocortex failed to disrupt the expression of emotional responses elicited by sensory stimuli; sensory and motor cortex could therefore not be the key (LeDoux, 1987). Subsequently, Cannon, Bard, Herrick, Hess, and Papez implicated the hypothalamus and related regions in the medial or old cortex in emotion, a trend that led to the view that the brain does indeed have special emotion system (LeDoux, 1987). This view ultimately culminated around mid-century in the famous and still popular *limbic system* theory of emotion.

The Limbic System: Is It Enough?

The limbic system concept, brainchild of Paul MacLean, was put forth in the context of an evolutionary explanation of mind and behavior (MacLean, 1949, 1952, 1970). It built upon the view, promoted by Herrick (1933) and Papez (1937), that the neocortex is a mammalian specialization; other vertebrates have primordial cortex, but only mammals were believed to have neocortex. And because thinking, reasoning, memory, and problem solving are especially well developed in mammals—and particularly in humans and other primates that have relatively more neocortical tissue—these cognitive processes must be mediated by the neocortex and not by the old cortex or subcortical brain areas. In contrast, the old cortex and related subcortical regions form the limbic system, which was said to mediate the evolutionarily older aspects of mental life and behavior: our emotions. In this way, cognition came to be thought of as the business of the neocortex and emotions of the limbic system.

The limbic system theory began to run into trouble almost immediately when it was discovered, in the mid-1950s, that damage to the hippocampus, an old cortical area and the centerpiece of the limbic system, led to severe deficits in a distinctly cognitive function, long-term memory (Scoville & Milner, 1957). This was incompatible with the original idea that the primitive architecture of the limbic system, and especially of the hippocampus, was poorly suited to participate in cognitive functions. Subsequently, in the late 1960s it was discovered that the equivalent of mammalian neocortex is present, though rudimentary, in nonmammalian vertebrates (Nauta & Karten, 1970; Northcutt & Kaas, 1995). As a result, the old/new cortex distinction broke down, challenging the evolutionary basis of the assignment of emotion to the old cortex (limbic system) and cognition to the neocortex (Swanson, 1983).

The limbic system itself has been a moving target. Within a few years after its inception, it expanded from the original notion of old cortex and related subcortical forebrain nuclei to include some areas of the midbrain, and even some regions of neocortex. Several attempts have been made to salvage the limbic system by defining it more precisely (Isaacson, 1982; Livingston & Escobar, 1971; Nauta, 1958; Swanson, 1983). Nevertheless, after half a century of debate and discussion, there are still no generally accepted criteria deciding which areas of the brain belong to the limbic system. Some have suggested that the concept be abandoned (Brodal, 1982; Kotter & Meyer, 1992; LeDoux, 1987, 1991).

Despite these difficulties, the limbic system continues to survive—both as an anatomical concept and as an explanation of emotions—in textbooks, research articles, and scientific lectures. This is in part attributable to the fact that both the anatomical concept and the emotional function it was supposed to mediate were defined so vaguely as to be irrefutable. For example, in most discussions of how the limbic system mediates emotion, the meaning of the term *emotion* is not defined. Reading between the lines, it seems that the authors are often referring to something akin to the common English-language use of the term, which is to say "feelings." However, a conception of emotion in terms of feelings is problematic because we have no way of knowing exactly what, if anything, animals other than humans experience subjectively. Further, the anatomical criteria for inclusion of brain areas in the limbic system remain undefined, and evidence that any limbic area, however defined, contributes to any aspect of any emotion has tended to validate the whole concept. For example, because the amygdala was one of the limbic areas, studies showing that the amygdala participates in fear were viewed as evidence that the limbic system theory was correct, even though many other limbic areas played little or no obvious role in fear or other emotions. Despite the numerous studies aimed at elucidating the role of limbic areas in emotion, there is still very little understanding of how our emotions might be the product of the limbic forebrain. Particularly troubling is the fact that one cannot predict, on the basis of the original limbic theory of emotion or any of its descendants, how specific aspects of emotion work in the brain. The explanations are all post hoc, concocted after the experiment to explain data. This problem is particularly apparent in recent work using functional imaging to study the human brain. Whenever a so-called emotional task is used, and a limbic area is activated, the activation is explained by reference to the fact that limbic areas mediate emotion. When a limbic area is activated in a cognitive task, it is often assumed that there must have been some emotional undertone to the task. We are, in other words, at a point where the limbic theory has become an off-the-shelf explanation of how the brain works. However,

this explanation is grounded in tradition rather than data. Deference to the concept is inhibiting creative thought about how mental life is mediated by the brain.

Although the limbic system theory is inadequate as an explanation of the specific brain circuits of emotion, MacLean's original ideas are insightful and quite interesting in the context of a general evolutionary explanation of emotion and the brain. In particular, the notion that emotions involve relatively primitive circuits that are conserved throughout mammalian evolution seems right on target. Further, the idea that cognitive processes might involve other circuits and might function relatively independent of emotional circuits, at least in some circumstances, also seems correct. These functional ideas are worth holding on to, even if we abandon the limbic system as an anatomical theory of the emotional brain.

LESS IS MORE: FEAR AS A MODEL

The limbic system theory failed in part because it attempted to account for all emotions at once and, in so doing, did not adequately account for any one emotion. In the 1980s researchers started taking another approach, focusing on one emotion—fear—and trying to understand it in depth.

Fear Conditioning

Much of what we have learned about the neural basis of fear has come from studies of fear conditioning, particularly in laboratory rats. In this paradigm, the animal is typically placed in an experimental chamber and is presented with an innocuous stimulus, such as a tone (the conditioned stimulus; CS) that is associated or paired with an aversive stimulus, such as a brief electric shock to the feet (the unconditioned stimulus; US). Before conditioning, the CS does not elicit defensive behavior. After a few CS-US pairings, however, the animal begins to exhibit a range of conditioned responses (CRs), both to the tone CS and to the context (i.e., the conditioning chamber) in which conditioning occurs. In rats, these responses include "freezing" or immobility (the rats' species-typical behavioral response to a threatening stimulus), autonomic and endocrine responses (such as changes in heart rate and blood pressure, defecation, and increased levels of circulating stress hormones), and other changes including the potentiation of reflexes such as the acoustic startle response (Blanchard & Blanchard, 1969; Davis, Walker, & Lee, 1997; Kapp, Frysinger, Gallagher, & Haselton, 1979; LeDoux, Iwata, Cicchetti, & Reis, 1988; Roozendaal, Koolhaas, & Bohus, 1991; Smith, Astley, Devito, Stein, & Walsh, 1980). Thus, as the result of simple associative pairing, the CS comes to elicit many of the same defensive responses that are elicited by naturally aversive or threatening stimuli (see Figure 13.1).

Fear conditioning was long a standard tool in behavioral psychology but had not been used much to study the brain. As we will see, some limbic areas turned out to be especially important in fear conditioning, namely the amygdala and hippocampus, but in a manner not anticipated by the limbic system theory.

Fear conditioning may in the end not tell us everything we would like to know about fear, especially human fear. For example, the neural circuits involved in responding to conditioned fear stimuli may participate in—but are probably not sufficient to account for—more complex aspects of fear-related behavior, especially responses that depend not on specific stimuli but on thoughts, such as the fear of failing, of being afraid, or of falling in love. Nevertheless, fear conditioning has been an excellent way to start understanding some basic facts about fear, especially how fear responses are coupled to specific stimuli that people and other animals encounter in their daily lives.

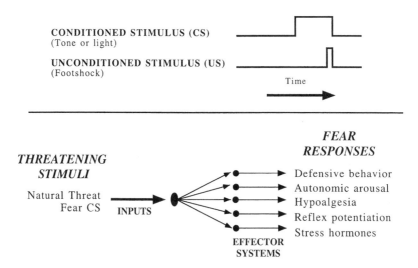

Figure 13.1   Pavlovian fear conditioning.
NOTE: Top: Fear conditioning involves the presentation of an initially innocuous stimulus, such as a tone (conditioned stimulus; CS), that is paired or associated with a noxious stimulus, such as a brief electric shock to the feet (unconditioned stimulus; US). Bottom: Before conditioning, the CS elicits little response from the animal. After conditioning, the CS elicits a wide range of behavioral and physiological responses that are characteristically elicited by naturally aversive or threatening stimuli.

Actually, fear conditioning is not the only means of studying fear behavior, and for a while it was not the primary task used. Through the 1970s researchers interested in fear often used so-called avoidance conditioning procedures, in which animals first undergo fear conditioning to stimuli associated with shock and then learn to perform behaviors that prevent exposure to shock (Goddard, 1964; Sarter & Markowitsch, 1985). This was particularly attractive because it was thought relevant to patients with pathological fear, who often go to great lengths to avoid situations that are likely to trigger anxiety responses. However, avoidance conditioning is more complex. It involves two kinds of learning: First, Pavlovian fear conditioning occurs to the stimuli present when shock occurs, and then the subject has to learn that if it performs certain responses in the presence of the conditioned fear stimuli, shock will be avoided (Mowrer, 1960). Imagine the difference between learning that some stimulus is dangerous and learning what to do to prevent encountering the danger; the first simply involves learning about stimuli, and the second involves response learning. This complexity was an impediment to the development of a clear understanding of the neural basis of fear through the use of studies of avoidance conditioning. This is not to say, however, that we have learned nothing about the neural substrates of instrumental fear learning tasks. Indeed, we return to this topic in a later section.

What makes fear conditioning so useful from a circuit-tracing point of view? For one thing, it is simple. All it takes to turn a meaningless stimulus, such as a tone, into a fear-arousing event is a few occurrences of the tone (often only one) at the same time as an aversive event, such as a mild shock to the skin. Also, it is versatile—just about any stimulus that predicts shock or other kinds of dangerous stimuli can serve as a conditioned fear stimulus. In addition, the learning is long lasting, maybe even permanent, and it can be done similarly in humans and rats, making it possible to study the rat brain for the purpose of understanding human fear. Further, the responses are hardwired and automatic. A rat does not have to learn to freeze or raise its blood pressure in the presence of dangerous stimuli. The brain is programmed by evolution to do these things. We have to learn what to be afraid of, but not how to act afraid. Implicit in all this is a strategy for figuring out the fear-processing circuit. All we have to do is trace the pathway forward from the input system (the sensory system that processes the conditioned stimulus, e.g., the tone) to the output system (the system that controls freezing or other hardwired responses). The fear-processing circuits, by this logic, should be located at the intersection of the input and output systems.

BASIC CIRCUITS

Using the input-output approach as a strategy, the neural circuitry underlying fear conditioning, particularly auditory fear conditioning, has been characterized in great detail. Early work aimed at defining the neural substrates of auditory fear conditioning, for example, simply started on the input side and, using targeted lesions, asked what parts of the auditory system were necessary for fear conditioning. Tract tracing studies then showed where in the brain the critical auditory nuclei projected. Then, additional lesion work asked whether those structures were critical for fear conditioning, and so forth. Using this systematic approach, it soon became clear that the amygdala was a critical locus of fear conditioning (see Figure 13.2).

The Input Pathways

The findings of the early anatomical and lesion-behavior work suggested that auditory

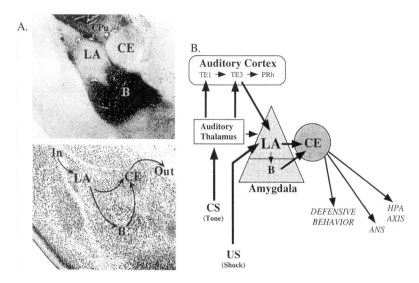

Figure 13.2   Anatomy of the fear system.
NOTE: (A). Top: Acetylcholinesterase (AChE) stain of the rat amygdala showing its major subdivisions, including the lateral nucleus (LA), the basal nucleus (B), and the central nucleus (CE). The caudate/putamen (CPu) lies just dorsal to the LA and CE. Bottom: Nissl stain of an adjacent section depicting information flow within the amygdala. Incoming sensory information first synapses in the LA. The LA, in turn, projects to both CE and B. The CE is the major output nucleus of the amygdala. (B). Auditory fear conditioning involves the transmission of CS sensory information from areas of the auditory thalamus and cortex to the LA, where it can converge with incoming somatosensory information from the foot-shock US. It is in the LA that alterations in synaptic transmission are thought to encode key aspects of the learning. During fear expression, the LA engages the CE, which projects widely to many areas of the forebrain and brainstem that control the expression of fear CRs, including freezing, HPA axis activation, and alterations in cardiovascular activity.

fear conditioning involves the transmission of CS information about the tone from cortical and subcortical areas of the auditory system to the lateral nucleus of the amygdala (LA), an area that is critical for fear conditioning. Cells in the LA receive monosynaptic projections from areas of the auditory thalamus and cortex, including the medial division of the thalamic medial geniculate body (MGm) and the posterior intralaminar nucleus (PIN), and also from cortical area TE3 (Bordi & LeDoux, 1992; Doron & Ledoux, 1999; LeDoux, Farb, & Romanski, 1991; LeDoux, Ruggiero, & Reis, 1985; McDonald, 1998; Romanski & LeDoux, 1993). Each of these pathways contains the excitatory neurotransmitter glutamate (Farb, Aoki, Milner, Kaneko,

& LeDoux, 1992; LeDoux & Farb, 1991). Electrophysiological studies have shown that the inputs from MGm/PIN and TE3 converge onto single cells in the LA (Li, Stutzmann, & LeDoux, 1996), and that these same cells are also responsive to the foot shock US (Romanski, Clugnet, Bordi, & LeDoux, 1993). Thus, individual cells in the LA are well suited to integrate information about the tone and shock during fear conditioning, suggesting that the LA is a critical locus of the cellular events underlying fear acquisition. Consistent with this notion, behavioral studies have demonstrated that acquisition of auditory fear conditioning is disrupted both by conventional electrolytic or neurotoxic lesions of LA and by reversible functional inactivation targeted to the LA (Campeau & Davis, 1995; LeDoux, Cicchetti, Xagoraris, & Romanski, 1990; Muller, Corodimas, Fridel, & LeDoux, 1997; Wilensky, Schafe, & LeDoux, 2000).

Pretraining lesions of MGm/PIN have also been shown to impair auditory fear conditioning (LeDoux, Iwata, Pearl, & Reis, 1986), but pretraining lesions of auditory cortex do not (LeDoux, Sakaguchi, & Reis, 1984; Romanski & LeDoux, 1992). Thus, the thalamic pathway between the MGm/PIN and the LA appears to be particularly important for auditory fear conditioning. This is not to say, however, that the cortical input to the LA is not essential. Indeed, the electrophysiological responses of cells in the auditory cortex are modified during fear conditioning (Edeline, Pham, & Weinberger, 1993). Further, when conditioning depends on the animal's ability to make fine discriminations between different auditory CSs, the auditory cortex appears to be required (Jarrell, Gentile, Romanski, McCabe, & Schneiderman, 1987).

The Output Pathways

The output pathways of the fear-conditioning system have also been well defined. The LA, for example, gives rise to connections to a variety of other amygdala regions, including the basal nucleus (B) and the central nucleus of the amygdala (CE; Pare, Smith, & Pare, 1995; Pitkänen, Savander, & LeDoux, 1997). However, damage confined only to the LA and CE disrupts auditory fear conditioning (Amorapanth, LeDoux, & Nader, 2000; Nader, Majidishad, Amorapanth, & LeDoux, 2001), suggesting that the direct connection from LA to CE is sufficient to mediate fear conditioning. The CE, in turn, projects to areas of the forebrain, hypothalamus, and brainstem that control behavioral, endocrine, and autonomic conditioned responses (CRs) associated with fear learn-ing. Projections from the CE to the midbrain periaqueductal gray, for example, have been shown to be particularly important for mediating behavioral and endocrine responses such as freezing and hypoalgesia (De Oca, DeCola, Maren, & Fanselow, 1998; Helmstetter & Landeira-Fernandez, 1990; Helmstetter & Tershner, 1994), while projections to the lateral hypothalamus have been implicated in the control of conditioned cardiovascular responses (Iwata, LeDoux, & Reis, 1986). Importantly, although lesions of these individual areas can selectively impair expression of individual CRs, damage to the CE interferes with the expression of all fear CRs (LeDoux, 2000). Thus, the CE is typically thought of as the principal output nucleus of the fear system that acts to orchestrate the collection of hardwired, and typically species-specific, responses that underlies defensive behavior.

SYNAPTIC PLASTICITY

The LA is not only the principle site of sensory input to the amygdala; it also appears to be an essential locus of plasticity during fear conditioning. For example, individual cells in the LA alter their response properties when CS and US are paired during fear conditioning (see Figure 13.3). Specifically, LA cells that are weakly responsive to auditory input initially respond vigorously to the same input after fear conditioning (Maren, 2000; Quirk, Armony, & LeDoux, 1997; Quirk, Armony, Repa, Li, & LeDoux, 1997; Quirk, Repa, & LeDoux, 1995). Thus, a change occurs in the function of LA cells as the result of training, a finding that has contributed to the view that neural plasticity in the LA encodes key aspects of fear learning and memory storage (Blair, Schafe, Bauer, Rodrigues, & LeDoux, 2001; Fanselow & LeDoux, 1999; Maren, 1999; Quirk, Armony, Repa, et al., 1997).

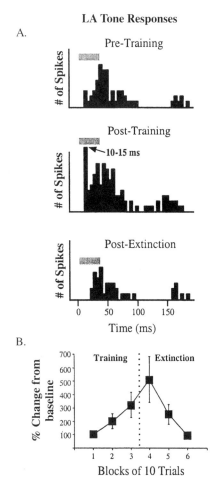

Figure 13.3 Plasticity in the LA during fear conditioning.

NOTE: Pairing of CS and US during fear conditioning leads to changes in the responsiveness of LA cells to auditory stimuli, as measured by electrophysiological recording of single cells in the LA. (A). Top: Prior to auditory fear conditioning, LA cells are weakly responsive to auditory stimuli. Middle: Immediately after conditioning, the same cells respond vigorously, especially in the first few milliseconds of the tone (arrow). Bottom: Tone conditioning of LA cells decreases with extinction. In each figure, the onset of the tone stimulus is depicted by a gray bar. (B). Change in firing rate of LA cells over the course of training and extinction. The values represent averaged responses of 16 cells within the first few milliseconds of the tone stimulus and are expressed as percentage change from preconditioning firing rates.

What mechanism may mediate the change that occurs in the LA as a result of conditioning? One of the leading candidates is *long-term potentiation* (LTP), an activity-dependent form of plasticity that was initially discovered in the hippocampus (Bliss & Lomø, 1973). LTP has been extensively studied using a number of different induction protocols. For example, in many LTP experiments application of high-frequency (or tetanic) stimulation to an afferent pathway leads to an amplification in neural responding (i.e., cell excitability) in the cells that are postsynaptic to that pathway. In other experiments LTP is induced by pairing stimulation of a weak afferent pathway with that of a strong input. After a few such pairings, the initially weak input becomes stronger. It is this latter protocol, so-called associative LTP, that is a particularly attractive candidate for a cellular mechanism of classical conditioning, including fear conditioning. Regardless of the induction protocol, the hallmark of LTP is the functional change in cell excitability that is observed after induction. This change is known to be dependent on Ca^{2+} entry into the postsynaptic cell. In some pathways, this increase in intracellular Ca^{2+} appears to be mediated by activity-dependent activation of the NMDA receptor during induction (Collingridge, Kehl, & McLennan, 1983; Malenka & Nicoll, 1993). In other pathways, LTP is NMDA receptor-independent, and instead Ca^{2+} entry through other types of receptor, such as the L-type voltage-gated calcium channel (VGCC), appears to be required (Grover & Teyler, 1990; Huang & Malenka, 1993). In still other pathways, both types of receptors appear to play important roles (Magee & Johnston, 1997).

LTP has been most extensively studied in the hippocampal formation. There, the relation between LTP and memory has remained controversial (Gallistel, 1995; Keith & Rudy,

1990; Shors & Matzel, 1997). One of main difficulties in determining the relation, if any, of LTP to memory in the hippocampus is the lack of a clear understanding of the relationship between specific hippocampal circuits and memory. In contrast, because the relation of specific circuits and synapses to memory formation has been established in the LA, it may in the end be easier to relate LTP to fear conditioning (Barnes, 1995; Eichenbaum, 1996; Stevens, 1998). Indeed, LTP has been demonstrated, both in vivo and in vitro, in each of the major sensory input pathways to the LA, including the thalamic and cortical auditory pathways (Chapman, Kairiss, Keenan, & Brown, 1990; Clugnet & LeDoux, 1989; Huang & Kandel, 1998; Maren & Fanselow, 1995; Rogan & LeDoux, 1995; Weisskopf, Bauer, & LeDoux, 1999). This includes tetanus-induced LTP, which appears to be NMDA receptor–dependent (Bauer, Schafe, & LeDoux, 2001; Huang & Kandel, 1998). Associative LTP has also been demonstrated in the LA. It is induced following pairing of subthreshold presynaptic auditory inputs with postsynaptic depolarizations of LA cells. This form of LTP is dependent on L-type VGCCs (Weisskopf et al., 1999). Further, fear conditioning itself has been shown to lead to electrophysiological changes in the LA in a manner that is very similar to those observed following artificial LTP induction, and these changes persist over days (McKernan & Shinnick-Gallagher, 1997; Rogan, Staubli, & LeDoux, 1997). Finally, associative LTP in the LA has been shown to be sensitive to the same contingencies as fear conditioning. That is, when presynaptic trains precede the onset of postsynaptic depolarizations 100% of the time, LTP is strong. However, if noncontingent depolarizations of the postsynaptic LA cell are interleaved within the same number of contiguous pairings, LTP is much weaker (Bauer, LeDoux, & Nader,

2001). Thus, the change in synaptic conductances within the LA depends on the contingency between pre- and postsynaptic activity rather than simply on temporal contiguity, and contingency rather than temporal pairing is known to be critical for associative learning, including fear conditioning (Rescorla, 1968).

Collectively, these findings are consistent with the hypothesis that fear conditioning is mediated by an associative LTP-like process in the LA (see Figure 13.4). Behavioral studies have also supported this notion. For example, fear conditioning, like LTP in the LA, has been shown to be impaired by pharmacological blockade of both NMDA receptors (Kim, DeCola, Landeira-Fernandez, & Fanselow, 1991; Miserendino, Sananes, Melia, & Davis, 1990; Rodrigues, Schafe, & LeDoux, 2001) and L-type VGCC (Bauer et al., 2001) receptors in the amygdala. Further, blockade of NMDA receptors has been shown to impair the conditioning-induced changes in single units in the LA that are observed after fear conditioning (Goosens & Maren, 2000). Thus, Ca^{2+} entry through both NMDA and L-type VGCCs in the LA appears to set in motion a process that is essential for both synaptic plasticity and memory formation.

MOLECULAR GLUE

At the same time that great strides were being made in elucidating the neuroanatomical pathways and cellular events that underlie fear conditioning in the LA, other research was uncovering the biochemical and molecular mechanisms involved in LTP, especially in the hippocampus. Thus, as data suggesting that an LTP-like process in the LA was involved in fear conditioning accumulated, one natural extension of these findings was to ask whether similar biochemical and molecular

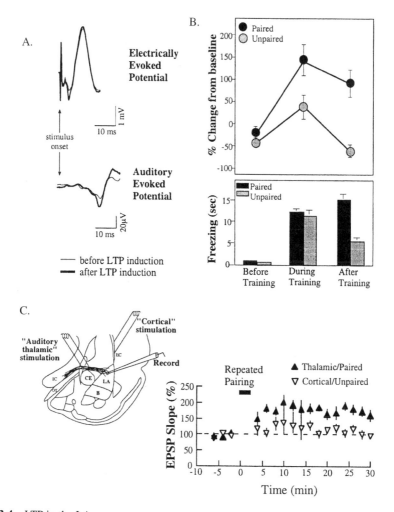

Figure 13.4   LTP in the LA.

NOTE: (A). Top: LTP is induced in the LA following high-frequency electrical stimulation of the MGm/PIN. The trace represents a stimulation-evoked field potential in the LA before and after LTP induction. Bottom: Following artificial LTP induction, processing of naturalistic auditory stimuli is also enhanced in the LA. The trace represents an auditory-evoked field potential in the LA before and after LTP induction. (B). Top: Fear conditioning leads to electrophysiological changes in the LA in a manner similar to LTP. The figure represents percentage change in the slope of the auditory-evoked field potential in the LA before, during, and after conditioning in both paired (black circles) and unpaired (gray circles) rats. Bottom: Freezing behavior across training and testing periods. Note that both paired (black bars) and unpaired (gray bars) groups show equivalent freezing behavior during training, but only the paired group shows an enhanced neural response. (C). Left: Associative LTP is induced in the amygdala slice by pairing trains of presynaptic stimulation of fibers coming from the auditory thalamus with depolarization of LA cells. Stimulation of fibers coming from cortical areas serves as a control for input specificity. Right: LTP induced by pairing as measured by the change in the slope of the EPSP over time. In this case, the thalamic pathway received paired stimulation (black triangles), whereas the cortical pathway received unpaired stimulation (i.e., trains and depolarizations, but in a noncontingent manner; white triangles). The black bar represents the duration of the pairing.

mechanisms were involved in fear conditioning (Schafe et al., 2001).

In the hippocampus, LTP is thought to involve the activation of a variety of protein kinase–signaling pathways by increases in intracellular Ca^{2+} at the time of induction. Many protein kinase–signaling pathways have been implicated in LTP, but two in particular have received much attention: the cAMP-dependent protein kinase (PKA) and the extracellular-regulated kinase/mitogen-activated protein kinase (ERK/MAPK; English & Sweatt, 1997; Huang, Li, & Kandel, 1994; Nguyen & Kandel, 1996). These kinases, when activated by increases in intracellular Ca^{2+} at the time of LTP induction, are thought to translocate to the cell nucleus, where they can engage activators of transcription, including the cAMP-response-element binding protein (CREB) and cAMP-response element (CRE) mediated gene expression (Impey et al., 1996; Impey, Obrietan, et al., 1998). The activation of CREB and CRE-mediated genes ultimately leads to the protein synthesis–dependent functional changes that are thought to underlie long-term synaptic plasticity and memory formation (Frank & Greenberg, 1994; Silva, Kogan, Frankland, & Kida, 1998; Stevens, 1994; Yin & Tully, 1996).

Many of these same intracellular proteins have also been implicated in amygdala LTP. For example, application of inhibitors of protein synthesis, PKA, or ERK/MAPK activation has been shown to impair LTP in the LA (Huang & Kandel, 1998; Huang, Martin, & Kandel, 2000; Schafe et al., 2000), and LTP-inducing stimulation of the LA has been shown to induce the phosphorylation of CREB, suggesting the involvement of CREB-mediated transcription (Huang et al., 2000).

Consistent with the notion that an LTP-like process underlies fear conditioning, a number of studies have demonstrated the involvement of intracellular processes such as PKA, MAPK, and CREB in fear conditioning. Many of these studies have used molecular genetic methods in which the molecules of interest have been manipulated in "knockout" or transgenic mouse lines (Abel et al., 1997; Bourtchuladze et al., 1994; Brambilla et al., 1997). Other recent studies have used pharmacological or viral transfection methods to examine the involvement of these molecules specifically in the amygdala. For example, studies have shown that infusions of drugs into the LA that specifically block RNA or protein synthesis or PKA activity impair the formation of fear memories (Bailey, Kim, Sun, Thompson, & Helmstetter, 1999; Schafe & LeDoux, 2000). Further, ERK/MAPK is activated in the LA following fear conditioning, and pharmacological blockade of this activation via localized infusions of ERK/MAPK inhibitors impairs fear conditioning (Schafe et al., 2000). Another recent study has shown that overexpression of the transcription factor CREB in the LA facilitates formation of fear memories (Josselyn et al., 2001). Thus, many of same biochemical signaling pathways and molecular events that are involved in LTP, both in the hippocampus and the amygdala, are also necessary for fear conditioning (see Figure 13.5).

We have now begun to identify the molecules in the amygdala that are involved in the formation of fear memory. But this is just the first step toward understanding how a fear memory is made. We must now ask a number of questions. For example, what neurotransmitter and neuromodulatory systems in the amygdala regulate the activation of these signaling proteins to promote fear-memory formation? What specific transcription factors and genes do these signaling pathways target in the nucleus of an amygdala cell to promote long-term formation of a fear memory? How might transcription of those genes and their respective proteins change the structure of the LA cell such that it now responds differently in the face of danger? Each of these questions awaits further examination.

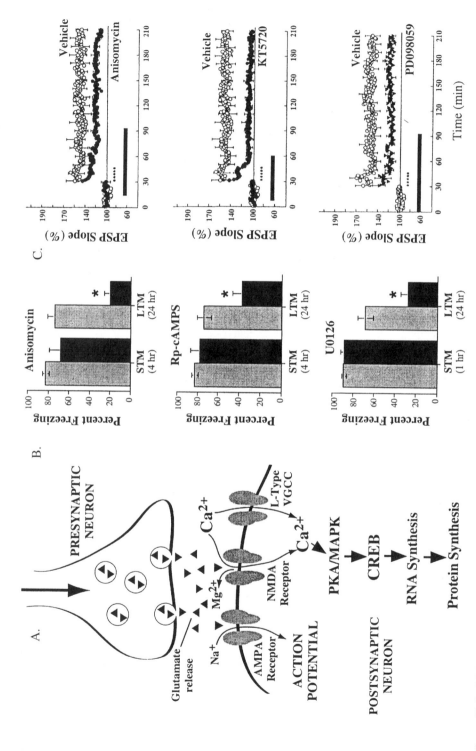

Figure 13.5 Molecular pathways underlying fear conditioning.

EXTENDED CIRCUITRY

Although the neural basis of fear conditioning is best understood for the acquisition and expression of fear responses to auditory stimuli, some progress has also been made in understanding the contribution of the amygdala and other brain areas to other fear-related behaviors, such as contextual fear, fear extinction, and instrumental fear learning.

Contextual Fear Conditioning

In a typical auditory fear conditioning experiment, the animal not only learns to fear the tone that is paired with the foot shock but also learns to fear the context in which conditioning occurs. Contextual fear may also be induced by the presentation of foot shocks alone within a novel environment. In the laboratory, fear to the context is measured by returning the rat to the conditioning chamber on the test day and measuring freezing behavior (Blanchard, Dielman, & Blanchard, 1968; Fanselow, 1980).

In comparison to that underlying auditory fear conditioning, the neural system underlying contextual fear has been less well characterized. Much of the work examining the neuroanatomical substrates of contextual fear has relied exclusively on lesion methods. As in auditory fear conditioning, however, the amygdala appears to play an essential role. For example, lesions of the amygdala, including the LA and B, have been shown to disrupt both acquisition and expression of contextual fear conditioning (Kim, Rison, & Fanselow, 1993; Maren, 1998; Phillips & LeDoux, 1992), as has reversible functional inactivation targeted to the LA (Muller et al., 1997). Contextual fear conditioning is also impaired by infusion of NMDA receptor antagonists, of RNA and protein synthesis inhibitors, and of inhibitors of PKA into the amygdala (Bailey et al., 1999; Goosens, Holt, & Maren, 2000; Kim et al., 1991a; Rodrigues et al., 2001), suggesting that essential aspects of the memory are encoded in the amygdala. At this time, however, few data allow us to distinguish between the involvement of different amygdala subnuclei in contextual fear.

The hippocampus has also been implicated in contextual fear conditioning, although its exact role has remained elusive. A number

---

Figure 13.5 (*Continued*)

NOTE: (A). In many pathways, LTP involves the release of glutamate and Ca^{2+} influx through either NMDA receptors or L-type VGCCs. The increase in intracellular Ca^{2+} leads to the activation of protein kinases, such as PKA and ERK/MAPK. Once activated, these kinases can translocate to the nucleus, where they activate transcription factors such as CREB. The activation of CREB by PKA and ERK/MAPK promotes CRE-mediated gene transcription and the synthesis of new proteins. (B). Fear memory formation in the amygdala has also recently been shown to require protein synthesis, PKA, and ERK/MAPK activation. In these studies, rats received intra-amygdala infusions of anisomycin (a protein synthesis inhibitor; Top), Rp-cAMPS (a PKA inhibitor; Middle), or U0126 (a MEK inhibitor, which is an upstream regulator of ERK/MAPK activation; Bottom) at or around the time of training and were assayed for both short-term memory (1–4 hr later) and long-term memory (24 hr later) of auditory fear conditioning. In each figure, vehicle-treated rats are represented by the gray bars, and drug-treated animals are represented by the black bars. $*p < 0.05$ relative to vehicle controls. (C). Amygdala LTP has recently been shown to require the same biochemical processes. In these studies, adapted from Huang, Martin, & Kandel (2000), amygdala slices were treated with either anisomycin (Top), KT5720 (a PKA inhibitor; Middle), or PD098059 (a MEK inhibitor; Bottom) prior to and during tetanus of the thalamic pathway. In each experiment, field recordings were obtained from the LA and expressed across time as a percentage of baseline.

SOURCE: Huang, Martin, & Kandel (2000). Copyright © 2000 by the Society for Neuroscience.

of studies have shown that electrolytic and neurotoxic lesions of the hippocampus disrupt contextual, but not auditory, fear conditioning (Kim & Fanselow, 1992; Kim et al., 1993; Maren, Aharonov, & Fanselow, 1997; Phillips & LeDoux, 1992). One view is that the hippocampus is necessary for forming a representation of the context in which conditioning occurs and for providing the amygdala with that information during training for CS-US integration and memory formation (Frankland, Cestari, Filipkowski, McDonald, & Silva, 1998; Phillips & LeDoux, 1992; Young, Bohenek, & Fanselow, 1994). In support of this view, the hippocampal formation has been shown to project to the basal nucleus of the amygdala (Canteras & Swanson, 1992), which provides a potential neuroanatomical substrate through which contextual fear associations can be formed (Maren & Fanselow, 1995). Alternatively, it may be the case that the hippocampus itself, in addition to the amygdala, undergoes plastic changes necessary for memory formation of contextual fear. For example, intrahippocampal infusion of the NMDA receptor antagonist APV impairs contextual fear conditioning (Stiedl, Birkenfeld, Palve, & Spiess, 2000; Young et al., 1994). These findings are consistent with a recent report that showed impaired contextual, but not auditory, fear conditioning in mice that lack the NR1 subunit of the NMDA receptor exclusively in area CA1 of the hippocampus (Rampon et al., 2000). Further, contextual fear conditioning leads to increases in the activation of ERK/MAPK and CRE-mediated gene expression in the hippocampus (Atkins, Selcher, Petraitis, Trzaskos, & Sweatt, 1998; Hall, Thomas, & Everitt, 2000; Impey, Smith, et al., 1998).

These findings add support to the notion that NMDA receptor-dependent plastic changes in the hippocampus, in addition to the amygdala, are required for contextual fear conditioning. However, the exact contribution of the these plastic changes to contextual fear conditioning remains unclear. For example, these studies cannot distinguish between a role for NMDA receptor-mediated plasticity in formation of contextual representations as opposed to a role in fear memory acquisition and storage. Clearly, more research is needed before a convincing picture of the role of the hippocampus in contextual fear conditioning emerges.

Extinction of Fear

Relative to what we have learned about fear acquisition, the neurobiological substrates of fear extinction have been less well defined. However, the medial prefrontal cortex (mPFC), and in particular the ventral mPFC, appears to play an important role. For example, selective lesions of the ventral mPFC retard the extinction of fear to an auditory CS while having no effect on initial fear acquisition (Morgan & LeDoux, 1995; Morgan, Romanski, & LeDoux, 1993; but see Gewirtz, Falls, & Davis, 1997). Further, neurons in the mPFC alter their response properties as the result of extinction (Garcia, Vouimba, Baudry, & Thompson, 1999; Herry, Vouimba, & Garcia, 1999). Interestingly, a recent study suggests that the mPFC may not be necessary for extinction per se, but rather in the long-term recall of extinguished fear. For example, rats with mPFC lesions are able to extinguish within a session but show impaired extinction between sessions (Quirk, Russo, Barron, & Lebron, 2000). Although additional work remains to be done, it seems likely that the mPFC exerts its effect on fear extinction by way of projections to the amygdala and other brainstem areas that control responding to fearful stimuli. In support of this hypothesis, infusions of NMDA receptor antagonists into the amygdala have been shown to impair fear extinction (Falls, Miserendino, & Davis, 1992). Additional experiments will be necessary to elucidate the exact contribution of connections between mPFC and the amygdala in extinction processes. Given its obvious clinical significance, this is a particularly important question.

Instrumental Fear Learning

In addition to its role in Pavlovian fear conditioning, the amygdala contributes to other fear-related aspects of behavior. For example, Pavlovian fear conditioning is useful for learning to detect a dangerous object or situation, but the animal must also be able to use this information to guide ongoing behavior that is instrumental in avoiding that danger. In some situations, the animal must learn to make a response (i.e., move away, press a bar, turn a wheel, etc.) that will allow it to avoid presentation of a shock or danger signal (so-called active avoidance). In other situations, the animal must learn *not* to respond (so-called passive avoidance).

The role of different amygdala nuclei, including the LA, CE, and B, in both fear conditioning and active avoidance learning has been examined by Amorapanth et al. (2000). In the first phase of training, rats received standard Pavlovian fear conditioning consisting of a tone paired with foot shock. In the second phase, they were trained in a traditional one-way active avoidance task, in which they were placed in one side of a two-compartment shuttle-box and presented with the aversive tone CS which was terminated only if the animal successfully moved into the adjoining chamber. The tone CS in this paradigm thus served as a negative reinforcer. Lesions of the LA impaired learning in both phases of the experiment. Lesions of the CE impaired only Pavlovian fear conditioning (i.e., the tone-shock association), and lesions of B impaired only the instrumental task (learning to move into the second compartment). Thus, different outputs of the LA appear to mediate reac-

tions and actions elicited by a fear-arousing stimulus. As outlined earlier in this chapter, direct projections from the LA to the CE appear to be sufficient for Pavlovian fear conditioning. Additionally, however, projections from the LA to B appear to be important for influencing ongoing behavior, specifically for reinforcing responses that are instrumental in avoiding a dangerous object or situation (see Figure 13.6).

These findings are in general agreement with those of a study that dissociated the involvement of B and CE in instrumental and Pavlovian aspects of fear conditioning, respectively (Killcross, Robbins, & Everitt, 1997). This is not to say, however, that the basal nucleus is a site of motor control or a locus of plasticity that underlies instrumental learning. Rather, the B likely guides fear-related behavior and reinforcement via its projections to nearby striatal regions that are known to be necessary for reinforcement learning, including active avoidance learning (Everitt, Cador, & Robbins, 1989; Everitt et al., 1999; Robbins, Cador, Taylor, & Everitt, 1989).

The amygdala also plays a role in passive avoidance learning, in which the rat learns, for example, not to cross through a doorway into a compartment that it previously received shock in or not to step down onto a platform that was previously electrified. Unlike Pavlovian fear conditioning, the amygdala does not appear to be a storage site for these inhibitory avoidance (IA) tasks (Wilensky et al., 2000). Rather, in IA the amygdala appears to modulate the strength of learning in other brain areas (McGaugh, 2000; McGaugh et al., 1993). In support of this view, lesions of the amygdala made after training, especially after a delay, result in partial retention of IA (Parent, Quirarte, Cahill, & McGaugh, 1995). Further, various pharmacological manipulations of the amygdala given immediately after training that affect neurotransmitter or

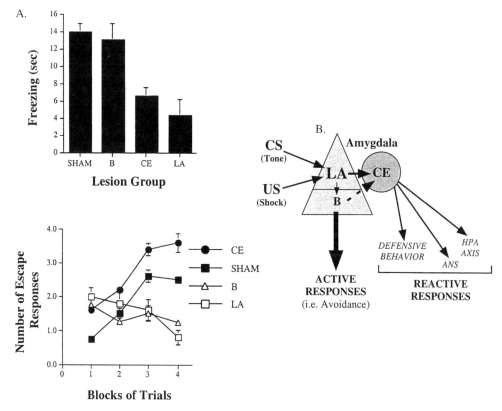

Figure 13.6 Active vs. reactive fear.

NOTE: (A). Top: Seconds freezing in rats given auditory fear conditioning after receiving selective lesions of different amygdala subnuclei. Auditory fear conditioning is impaired by lesions of the CE and LA, but spared by B lesions. Bottom: Number of escape responses across blocks of 5 trials during training in a one-way active avoidance task. Lesions of both LA and B impair this task, but lesions of CE do not. (B). The data are consistent with a model in which projections between LA and CE are sufficient for Pavlovian fear conditioning (reactive responses), whereas projections between LA and B are necessary for instrumental avoidance learning (active responses).

neurohormonal systems modulate the strength of IA. For example, immediate posttraining blockade of adrenergic or glucocorticoid receptors in the amygdala impairs memory retention of IA, whereas facilitation of these systems in the amygdala enhances acquisition and memory storage (McGaugh, 2000; McGaugh et al., 1993). The exact subnuclei in the amygdala that are critical for memory modulation remain unknown, as are the areas of the brain where these amygdala projections influence memory storage of IA. Candidate areas include the hippocampus and entorhinal and parietal cortices (Izquierdo et al., 1997).

HUMAN FEAR

Over the past several years there has been an explosion of interest in the role of the human amygdala in fear and fear learning. Deficits in the perception of the emotional meaning of faces, especially fearful faces, have been found in patients with amygdala damage (Adolphs, Tranel, Damasio, & Damasio,

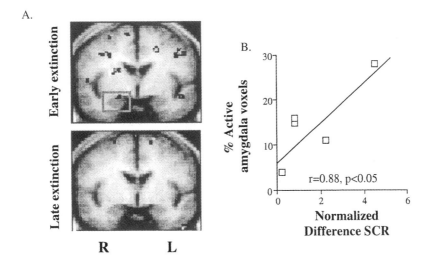

Figure 13.7   The human amygdala and fear conditioning.
NOTE: (A). Activation of the human amygdala, as measured by fMRI, increases as the result of fear conditioning. Top: Amygdala activity is high after training, especially on the right side of the brain (see box). Subjects were conditioned by pairing visual stimuli with a mild electric shock to the skin. Bottom: After extinction, amygdala activity is much lower. Images represent group average results. (B). Correlation between amygdala activation during training and psychophysiological measures of fear. Fear was assayed using the skin conductance response (SCR).
SOURCE: Adapted from *Neuron, 20,* LaBar, Gatenby, Gore, LeDoux, Phelps. Copyright 1998 with permission from Elsevier Science.

1995; Calder et al., 1996). Similar results were reported for detection of the emotional tone of voices (Scott et al., 1997). Further, damage to the amygdala (Bechara et al., 1995) or areas of temporal lobe including the amygdala (LaBar, LeDoux, Spencer, & Phelps, 1995) produce deficits in fear conditioning in humans. More recently, functional imaging studies have shown that the amygdala is activated more strongly in the presence of fearful and angry faces than in the presence of happy ones (Breiter et al., 1996), and that subliminal presentations of such stimuli lead to stronger activation than do freely seen ones (Whalen et al., 1998).

Fear conditioning in humans also leads to increases in amygdala activity, as measured by fMRI (Büchel, Morris, Dolan, & Friston, 1998; LaBar, Gatenby, Gore, LeDoux, & Phelps, 1998), and these effects also occur to subliminal stimuli (Morris, Öhman, & Dolan, 1998). In these studies, conditioning is typically accomplished by pairing the presentation of visual stimuli with either mild electric shock to the skin or an aversive high-amplitude (i.e., 100 dB or more) tone. Fear is measured by the change in skin conductance (see Figure 13.7). When the activity of the amygdala during fear conditioning is cross-correlated with the activity in other regions of the brain, the strongest relations are seen with subcortical (thalamic and collicular) rather than cortical areas, further emphasizing the importance of the direct thalamo-amygdala pathway in the human brain (Morris, Öhman, & Dolan, 1999). Other aspects of emotion and the human brain are reviewed in Phelps and Anderson (1997) and Davidson and Irwin (1999), as well as in Chapter 14, this volume.

Fear Conditioning and Psychopathology

In humans, we need to consider not only so-called "normal" fear but also pathologic conditions that occur in the form of fear or anxiety disorders. There is growing enthusiasm for the notion that fear learning processes similar to those occurring in fear conditioning experiments might be an important factor in certain anxiety disorders. Fear conditioning models of the posttraumatic stress syndrome and panic disorder (Goddard, Gorman, & Charney, 1998; Pitman, Shalev, & Orr, 2000) have recently been proposed by researchers in these fields.

Earlier in this century, the notion that conditioned fear contributes to phobias and related fear disorders gained popularity following John Watson's report of Little Albert, a boy who supposedly developed a conditioned phobia for rats when Watson sounded a loud noise in the presence of a rat (Watson & Rayner, 1920). However, this idea fell out of favor. For one thing, Watson's results were difficult to replicate. For another, laboratory fear conditioning, even in controlled animal studies, seemed to produce easily extinguishable fear, whereas clinical fear is difficult to treat. The notion arose that fear disorders involve a special kind of learning, called prepared learning, in which the CS is biologically significant rather than neutral (Marks, 1987; Öhman, 1993; Seligman, 1971). Although preparedness may indeed contribute to pathological fear, there is another factor to consider. As we have seen, easily extinguished fear can be converted into difficult-to-extinguish fear in rats with damage to the medial prefrontal cortex (Morgan et al., 1993). This suggests that alterations in the organization of the medial prefrontal regions might predispose certain people in some circumstances (such as stressful situations) to learn in a way that is difficult to extinguish (treat) under normal circumstances (LeDoux, 1996). These changes could come about because of genetic or experiential factors, or some combination of the two.

Much work is needed to understand more thoroughly the brain mechanisms of pathological fear and the ways in which it might be treated. The elucidation of the basic biology of fear reactions in animals should help facilitate progress on this important problem.

FEAR ITSELF

Consciousness is an important part of the study of emotion and other mental processes. Although we are far from solving what consciousness is, a number of theorists have proposed that it may be related to working memory, a serially organized mental workspace where things can be compared and contrasted and mentally manipulated (Baars, 1997; Baddley, 1998; Johnson-Laird, 1993; Kihlstrom, 1987; Kosslyn & Koenig, 1992; Marcel & Bisiach, 1988; Norman & Shallice, 1980; Shallice, 1988). A variety of studies of humans and nonhuman primates point to the prefrontal cortex, especially the dorsolateral prefrontal areas—as well as to the anterior cingulate and orbital cortical regions—as being involved in working memory (Braver, Cohen, Jonides, Smith, & Noll, 1997; Carter et al., 1998; Fuster, 1998; Goldman-Rakic, 1993). Immediately present stimuli and stored representations are integrated in working memory by way of interactions between prefrontal areas, sensory processing systems (which serve as short-term memory buffers, as well as perceptual processors), and the long-term explicit (declarative) memory system involving the hippocampus and related areas of the temporal lobe. In the case of an affectively charged stimulus, such as a trigger of fear, the same sorts of processes are called upon as for stimuli without emotional implications; in addition, however, working memory will become aware of the fact that the fear system of

FEARFUL FEELINGS?

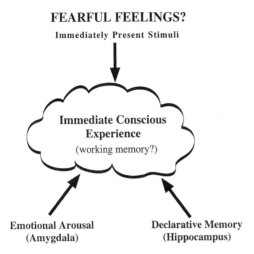

Immediately Present Stimuli

Immediate Conscious Experience
(working memory?)

Emotional Arousal
(Amygdala)

Declarative Memory
(Hippocampus)

Figure 13.8   How the brain might make fearful feelings.

NOTE: Conscious experience is often said to reflect the contents of working memory. In this sense, a conscious emotional experience may not be that different from any other conscious experience, differing only in the neural systems that provide the inputs to the working memory system. In the case of fearful feelings, the conscious emotion may be the result of some immediately present stimulus triggering long-term declarative memories (via the hippocampus) and amygdala activity at the same time. The simultaneous representation in working memory of these three active systems may contribute to what we experience as fear.

the brain has been activated (see Figure 13.8). When added to perceptual and mnemonic information about the object or event, this additional information could be the condition for the subjective experience of an emotional state of fear (LeDoux, 1996).

By way of projections to cortical areas, the amygdala can influence the operation of perceptual and short-term memory processes, as well as processes in higher order areas. Although the amygdala does not have extensive connections with the dorsolateral prefrontal cortex, it does communicate with the anterior cingulate and orbital cortex, two other components of the working memory network. In addition, however, the amygdala projects to

nonspecific systems involved in the regulation of cortical arousal and controls bodily responses (behavioral, autonomic, endocrine), which then provide feedback that can influence cortical processing indirectly. Thus, working memory receives a greater number of inputs, and receives inputs of a greater variety, in the presence of an emotional stimulus than in the presence of other stimuli. These extra inputs may be just what is required to add affective charge to working memory representations, and thus to turn subjective experiences into emotional experiences.

BEYOND FEAR

The degree to which findings on fear might apply to other emotions is not clear. The amygdala has been implicated in other emotions, including those involving positive affect (Aggleton, 1992, 2000), but it is not known whether the amygdala's involvement in different emotional processes is significant or spurious. Until other emotions are studied to the same extent that fear has been, it will not be possible to determine whether the amygdala plays a common or a different role in different emotions. Given the current enthusiasm for research on emotion within the neurosciences, we can look forward to rapid progress in characterizing the neural systems and mechanisms underlying other emotions in the coming years, and this will allow us to evaluate whether there is a specific emotion system in the brain or whether emotions are products of a variety of independent systems.

REFERENCES

Abel, T., Nguyen, P. V., Barad, M., Deuel, T. A., Kandel, E. R., & Bourtchouladze, R. (1997). Genetic demonstration of a role for PKA in the late phase of LTP and in hippocampus-based long-term memory. *Cell, 88*(5), 615–626.

Adolphs, R., Tranel, D., Damasio, H., & Damasio, A. R. (1995). Fear and the human amygdala, *Journal of Neuroscience, 15,* 5879–5891.

Aggleton, J. P. (1992). *The amygdala: Neurobiological aspects of emotion, memory, and mental dysfunction.* New York: Wiley-Liss.

Aggleton, J. P. (2000). *The amygdala: A functional analysis.* New York, Oxford University Press.

Amorapanth, P., LeDoux, J. E., & Nader, K. (2000). Different lateral amygdala outputs mediate reactions and actions elicited by a fear-arousing stimulus. *Nature Neuroscience, 3*(1), 74–79.

Atkins, C. M., Selcher, J. C., Petraitis, J. J., Trzaskos, J. M., & Sweatt, J. D. (1998). The MAPK cascade is required for mammalian associative learning. *Nature Neuroscience, 1*(7), 602–609.

Baars, B. J. (1997). In the theatre of consciousness. *Journal of Consciousness Studies, 4*(4), 292–309.

Baddley, A. (1998). Recent developments in working memory. *Current Opinion in Neurobiology, 8,* 234–238.

Bailey, D. J., Kim, J. J., Sun, W., Thompson, R. F., & Helmstetter, F. J. (1999). Acquisition of fear conditioning in rats requires the synthesis of mRNA in the amygdala. *Behavioral Neuroscience, 113*(2), 276–282.

Barnes, C. A. (1995). Involvement of LTP in memory: Are we "searching under the streetlight"? *Neuron, 15,* 751–754.

Bauer, E. P., LeDoux, J. E., & Nader, K. (2001). Fear conditioning and LTP in the lateral amygdala are sensitive to the same stimulus contingencies. *Nature Neuroscience, 4,* 687–688.

Bauer, E. P., Schafe, G. E., & LeDoux, J. E. (2001). N-Methyl-D-Aspartate receptors and L-type voltage-gated calcium channels contribute to long-term potentiation and different components of fear memory formation in the lateral amygdala. *Submitted for publication.*

Bechara, A., Tranel, D., Damasio, H., Adolphs, R., Rockland, C., & Damasio, A. R. (1995). Double dissociation of conditioning and declarative knowledge relative to the amygdala and hippocampus in humans. *Science, 269*(5227), 1115–1118.

Blair, H. T., Schafe, G. E., Bauer, E. P., Rodrigues, S. M., & LeDoux, J. E. (2001). *Synaptic plasticity in the lateral amygdala: A cellular hypothesis of fear conditioning. Learning and Memory* (in press).

Blanchard, R. J., & Blanchard, D. C. (1969). Crouching as an index of fear. *Journal of Comparative Physiological Psychology, 67,* 370–375.

Blanchard, R. J., Dielman, T. E., & Blanchard, D. C. (1968). Postshock crouching: Familiarity with the shock situation. *Psychonomic Science, 10,* 371–372.

Bliss, T. V. P., & Lomø, T. (1973). Long-lasting potentiation of synaptic transmission in the dentate area of the anaesthetized rabbit following stimulation of the perforant path. *Journal of Physiology, 232,* 331–356.

Bordi, F., & LeDoux, J. (1992). Sensory tuning beyond the sensory system: An initial analysis of auditory properties of neurons in the lateral amygdaloid nucleus and overlying areas of the striatum. *Journal of Neuroscience, 12*(7), 2493–2503.

Bourtchuladze, R., Frenguelli, B., Blendy, J., Cioffi, D., Schutz, G., & Silva, A. J. (1994). Deficient long-term memory in mice with a targeted mutation of the cAMP-responsive element-binding protein. *Cell, 79*(1), 59–68.

Brambilla, R., Gnesutta, N., Minichiello, L., White, G., Roylance, A. J., Herron, C. E., Ramsey, M., Wolfer, D. P., Cestari, V., Rossi-Arnaud, C., Grant, S. G., Chapman, P. F., Lipp, H. P., Sturani, E., & Klein, R. (1997). A role for the Ras signaling pathway in synaptic transmission and long-term memory. *Nature, 390,* 281–286.

Braver, T. S., Cohen, J. D., Jonides, J., Smith, E. E., & Noll, D. C. (1997). A parametric study of prefrontal cortex involvement in human working memory. *NeuroImage, 5*(1), 49–62.

Breiter, H. C., Etcoff, N. L., Whalen, P. J., Kennedy, W. A., Rauch, S. L., Buchner, R. L., Strauss, M. M., Hyman, S. E., & Rosen, B. R. (1996). Response and habituation of the human amygdala during visual processing of facial expression. *Neuron, 17,* 875–887.

Brodal, A. (1982). *Neurological anatomy.* New York: Oxford University Press.

Büchel, C., Morris, J., Dolan, R. J., & Friston, K. J. (1998). Brain systems mediating aversive conditioning: An event-related fMRI study. *Neuron, 20*(5), 947–957.

Calder, A. J., Young, A. W., Rowland, D., Perrett, D., Hodges, J. R., & Etcoff, N. L. (1996). Facial emotion recognition after bilateral amygdala damage: Differentially severe impairment of fear. *Cognitive Neuropsychology, 13,* 699–745.

Campeau, S., & Davis, M. (1995). Involvement of the central nucleus and basolateral complex of the amygdala in fear conditioning measured with fear-potentiated startle in rats trained concurrently with auditory and visual conditioned stimuli. *Journal of Neuroscience, 15,* 2301–2311.

Canteras, N. S., & Swanson, L. W. (1992). Projections of the ventral subiculum to the amygdala, septum, and hypothalamus: A PHAL anterograde tract-tracing study in the rat. *Journal of Comparative Neurology, 324,* 180–194.

Carter, C. S., Braver, T. S., Barch, D. M., Botvinick, M. M., Noll, D., & Cohen, J. D. (1998). Anterior cingulate cortex, error detection, and the online monitoring of performance. *Science, 280*(5364), 747–749.

Chapman, P. F., Kairiss, E. W., Keenan, C. L., & Brown, T. H. (1990). Long-term synaptic potentiation in the amygdala. *Synapse, 6,* 271–278.

Clugnet, M. C., & LeDoux, J. E. (1989). Synaptic plasticity in fear conditioning circuits: Induction of LTP in the lateral nucleus of the amygdala by stimulation of the medial geniculate body. *Journal of Neuroscience, 10*(8), 2818–2824.

Collingridge, G. L., Kehl, S. J., & McLennan, H. (1983). Excitatory amino acids in synaptic transmission in the Schaffer collateral-commissural pathway of the rat hippocampus. *Journal of Physiology, 334,* 33–46.

Davidson, R. J., & Irwin, W. (1999). The functional neuroanatomy of emotion and affective style. *Trends in Cognitive Sciences, 3*(11), 211–221.

Davis, M., Walker, D. L., & Lee, Y. (1997). Roles of the amygdala and bed nucleus of the stria terminalis in fear and anxiety measured with the acoustic startle reflex. Possible relevance to PTSD. *Annals of the New York Academy of Sciences, 821,* 305–331.

De Oca, B. M., DeCola, J. P., Maren, S., & Fanselow, M. S. (1998). Distinct regions of the periaqueductal gray are involved in the acquisition and expression of defensive responses. *Journal of Neuroscience, 18*(9), 3426–3432.

Doron, N. N., & Ledoux, J. E. (1999). Organization of projections of the lateral amygdala from auditory and visual areas of the thalamus in the rat. *Journal of Comparative Neurology, 412*(3), 383–409.

Edeline, J.-M., Pham, P., & Weinberger, N. M. (1993). Rapid development of learning-induced receptive field plasticity in the auditory cortex. *Behavioral Neuroscience, 107,* 539–551.

Eichenbaum, H. (1996). Learning from LTP: A comment on recent attempts to identify cellular and molecular mechanisms of memory. *Learning and Memory, 3*(2-3), 61–73.

English, J. D., & Sweatt, J. D. (1997). A requirement for the mitogen-activated protein kinase cascade in hippocampal long term potentiation. *Journal of Biological Chemistry, 272*(31), 19103–19106.

Everitt, B. J., Cador, M., & Robbins, T. W. (1989). Interactions between the amygdala and ventral striatum in stimulus-reward associations: Studies using a second-order schedule of sexual reinforcement. *Neuroscience, 30,* 63–75.

Everitt, B. J., Parkinson, J. A., Olmstead, M. C., Arroyo, M., Robledo, P., & Robbins, T. W. (1999). Associative processes in addiction and reward: The role of amygdala-ventral striatal subsystems. *Annals of the New York Academy of Sciences, 877,* 412–438.

Falls, W. A., Miserendino, M. J., & Davis, M. (1992). Extinction of fear-potentiated startle: Blockade by infusion of an NMDA antagonist into the amygdala. *Journal of Neuroscience, 12*(3), 854–863.

Fanselow, M. S. (1980). Conditional and unconditional components of postshock freezing. *Pavlovian Journal of Biological Science, 15,* 177–182.

Fanselow, M. S., & LeDoux, J. E. (1999). Why we think plasticity underlying Pavlovian fear conditioning occurs in the basolateral amygdala. *Neuron, 23*(2), 229–232.

Farb, C. R., Aoki, C., Milner, T., Kaneko, T., & LeDoux, J. (1992). Glutamate immunoreactive terminals in the lateral amygdaloid nucleus: A possible substrate for emotional memory. *Brain Research, 593,* 145–158.

Frank, D. A., & Greenberg, M. E. (1994). CREB: A mediator of long-term memory from mollusks to mammals. *Cell, 79*(1), 5–8.

Frankland, P. W., Cestari, V., Filipkowski, R. K., McDonald, R. J., & Silva, A. J. (1998). The dorsal hippocampus is essential for context discrimination but not for contextual conditioning. *Behavioral Neuroscience, 112*(4), 863–874.

Fuster, J. (1998). Linkage at the top. *Neuron, 21,* 1223–1229.

Gallistel, C. R. (1995). Is long-term potentiation a plausible basis for memory? In J. L. McGaugh, N. M. Weinberger, & G. Lynch (Eds.), *Brain and memory* (pp. 328–337). New York: Oxford University Press.

Garcia, R., Vouimba, R. M., Baudry, M., & Thompson, R. F. (1999). The amygdala modulates prefrontal cortex activity relative to conditioned fear. *Nature, 402*(6759), 294–296.

Gewirtz, J. C., Falls, W. A., & Davis, M. (1997). Normal conditioned inhibition and extinction of freezing and fear-potentiated startle following electrolytic lesions of medical prefrontal cortex in rats. *Behavioral Neuroscience, 111*(4), 712–726.

Goddard, A. W., Gorman, J. M., & Charney, D. S. (1998). Neurobiology of panic disorder. In J. F. Rosenblaum & M. H. Pollack (Eds.), *Panic disorder and its treatment.* New York: Dekker.

Goddard, G. (1964). Functions of the amygdala. *Psychological Review, 62,* 89–109.

Goldman-Rakic, P. S. (1993). Working memory and the mind. In W. H. Freeman (Ed.), *Mind and brain: Readings from Scientific American magazine* (pp. 66–77). New York: Freeman.

Goosens, K. A., Holt, W., & Maren, S. (2000). A role for amygdaloid PKA and PKC in the acquisition of long-term conditional fear memories in rats. *Behavioral Brain Research, 114*(1-2), 145–152.

Goosens, K. A., & Maren, S. (2000). NMDA receptors are necessary for the acquisition but not the expression of amygdaloid conditional unit activity and fear learning. *Society for Neuroscience Abstracts, Vol. 26.*

Grover, L. M., & Teyler, T. J. (1990). Two components of long-term potentiation induced by different patterns of afferent activation. *Nature, 347*(6292), 477–479.

Hall, J., Thomas, K. L., & Everitt, B. J. (2000). Rapid and selective induction of BDNF expression in the hippocampus during contextual learning. *Nature Neuroscience, 3*(6), 533–535.

Helmstetter, F. J., & Landeira-Fernandez, J. (1990). Conditional hypoalgesia is attenuated by naltrexone applied to the periaqueductal gray. *Brain Research, 537,* 88–92.

Helmstetter, F. J., & Tershner, S. A. (1994). Lesions of the periaqueductal gray and rostral ventromedial medulla disrupt antinociceptive but not cardiovascular aversive conditional responses. *Journal of Neuroscience, 14,* 7099–7108.

Herrick, C. J. (1933). The functions of the olfactory parts of the cerebral cortex. *Proceedings of the National Academy of Sciences, 19,* 7–14.

Herry, C., Vouimba, R. M., & Garcia, R. (1999). Plasticity in the mediodorsal thalamo-prefrontal cortical transmission in behaving mice. *Journal of Neurophysiology, 82*(5), 2827–2832.

Huang, Y. Y., & Kandel, E. R. (1998). Postsynaptic induction and PKA-dependent expression of LTP in the lateral amygdala. *Neuron, 21*(1), 169–178.

Huang, Y. Y., Li, X. C., & Kandel, E. R. (1994). cAMP contributes to mossy fiber LTP by initiating both a covalently mediated early phase and macromolecular synthesis-dependent late phase. *Cell, 79*(1), 69–79.

Huang, Y. Y., & Malenka, R. C. (1993). Examination of TEA-induced synaptic enhancement in area CA1 of the hippocampus: The role of voltage-dependent Ca^{2+} channels in the induction of LTP. *Journal of Neuroscience, 13*(2), 568–576.

Huang, Y. Y., Martin, K. C., & Kandel, E. R. (2000). Both protein kinase A and mitogen-activated protein kinase are required in the amygdala for the macromolecular synthesis-dependent late phase of long-term potentiation. *Journal of Neuroscience, 20*(17), 6317–6325.

Impey, S., Mark, M., Villacres, E. C., Poser, S., Chavkin, C., & Storm, D. R. (1996). Induction of CRE-mediated gene expression by stimuli that generate long-lasting LTP in area CA1 of the hippocampus. *Neuron, 16*(5), 973–982.

Impey, S., Obrietan, K., Wong, S. T., Poser, S., Yano, S., Wayman, G., Deloulme, J. C., Chan, G., & Storm, D. R. (1998). Cross talk between ERK and PKA is required for Ca^{2+} stimulation of CREB-dependent transcription and ERK nuclear translocation. *Neuron, 21*(4), 869–883.

Impey, S., Smith, D. M., Obrietan, K., Donahue, R., Wade, C., & Storm, D. R. (1998). Stimulation of cAMP response element (CRE)-mediated transcription during contextual learning. *Nature Neuroscience, 1*(7), 595–601.

Isaacson, R. L. (1982). *The limbic system.* New York: Plenum Press.

Iwata, J., LeDoux, J. E., & Reis, D. J. (1986). Destruction of intrinsic neurons in the lateral hypothalamus disrupts the classical conditioning of autonomic but not behavioral emotional responses in the rat. *Brain Research, 368*(1), 161–166.

Izquierdo, I., Quillfeldt, J. A., Zanatta, M. S., Quevedo, J., Schaeffer, E., Schmitz, P. K., & Medina, J. H. (1997). Sequential role of hippocampus and amygdala, entorhinal cortex and parietal cortex in formation and retrieval of memory for inhibitory avoidance in rats. *European Journal of Neuroscience, 9*(4), 786–793.

James, W. (1890). *Principles of psychology.* New York: Holt.

Jarrell, T. W., Gentile, C. G., Romanski, L. M., McCabe, P. M., & Schneiderman, N. (1987). Involvement of cortical and thalamic auditory regions in retention of differential bradycardia conditioning to acoustic conditioned stimuli in rabbits. *Brain Research, 412*, 285–294.

Johnson-Laird, P. N. (1993). A computational analysis of consciousness. In A. J. Marcel & E. Bisiach (Eds.), *Consciousness in contemporary science* (pp. 357–368). Oxford: Oxford University Press.

Josselyn, S. A., Shi, C., Carlezon, W. A., Jr., Neve, R. L., Nestler, E. J., & Davis, M. (2001). Long-term memory is facilitated by cAMP response-element binding protein overexpression in the amygdala. *Journal of Neuroscience, 21,* 2404–2412.

Kapp, B. S., Frysinger, R. C., Gallagher, M., & Haselton, J. R. (1979). Amygdala central nucleus lesions: Effect on heart rate conditioning in the rabbit. *Physiology and Behavior, 23*(6), 1109–1117.

Keith, J. R., & Rudy, J. W. (1990). Why NMDA-receptor-dependent long-term potentiation may not be a mechanism of learning and memory: Reappraisal of the NMDA-receptor blockade strategy. *Psychobiology, 18,* 251–257.

Kihlstrom, J. F. (1987). The cognitive unconscious. *Science, 237,* 1445–1452.

Killcross, S., Robbins, T. W., & Everitt, B. J. (1997). Different types of fear-conditioned behaviour mediated by separate nuclei within amygdala. *Nature, 388*(6640), 377–380.

Kim, J. J., DeCola, J. P., Landeira-Fernandez, J., & Fanselow, M. S. (1991). N-Methy-D-Aspartate receptor antagonist APV blocks acquisition but not expression of fear conditioning. *Behavioral Neuroscience, 105,* 126–133.

Kim, J. J., & Fanselow, M. S. (1992). Modality-specific retrograde amnesia of fear. *Science, 256,* 675–677.

Kim, J. J., Rison, R. A., & Fanselow, M. S. (1993). Effects of amygdala, hippocampus, and periaqueductal gray lesions on short- and long-term contextual fear. *Behavioral Neuroscience, 107,* 1–6.

Kosslyn, S. M., & Koenig, O. (1992). *Wet mind: The new cognitive neuroscience.* New York: Macmillan.

Kotter, R., & Meyer, N. (1992). The limbic system: A review of its empirical foundation. *Behavioural Brain Research, 52,* 105–127.

LaBar, K. S., Gatenby, J. C., Gore, J. C., LeDoux, J. E., & Phelps, E. A. (1998). Human amygdala activation during conditioned fear acquisition and extinction: A mixed-trial fMRI study. *Neuron, 20,* 937–945.

LaBar, K. S., LeDoux, J. E., Spencer, D. D., & Phelps, E. A. (1995). Impaired fear conditioning following unilateral temporal lobectomy in humans. *Journal of Neuroscience, 15*(10), 6846–6855.

LeDoux, J. E. (1987). Emotion. In F. Plum (Ed.), *Handbook of physiology: The nervous system, Vol. 5. Higher functions of the brain* (pp. 419–460). Bethesda: American Physiological Society.

LeDoux, J. E. (1991). Emotion and the limbic system concept. *Concepts in Neuroscience, 2,* 169–199.

LeDoux, J. E. (1996). *The emotional brain.* New York: Simon and Schuster.

LeDoux, J. E. (2000). Emotion circuits in the brain. *Annual Review of Neuroscience, 23,* 155–184.

LeDoux, J. E., Cicchetti, P., Xagoraris, A., & Romanski, L. M. (1990). The lateral amygdaloid nucleus: Sensory interface of the amygdala in fear conditioning. *Journal of Neuroscience, 10,* 1062–1069.

LeDoux, J. E., & Farb, C. R. (1991). Neurons of the acoustic thalamus that project to the amygdala contain glutamate. *Neuroscience Letters, 134,* 145–149.

LeDoux, J. E., Farb, C. R., & Romanski, L. M. (1991). Overlapping projections to the amygdala and striatum from auditory processing areas of the thalamus and cortex. *Neuroscience Letters, 134*(1), 139–144.

LeDoux, J. E., Iwata, J., Cicchetti, P., & Reis, D. J. (1988). Different projections of the central amygdaloid nucleus mediate autonomic and behavioral correlates of conditioned fear. *Journal of Neuroscience, 8,* 2517–2529.

LeDoux, J. E., Iwata, J., Pearl, D., & Reis, D. J. (1986). Disruption of auditory but not visual learning by destruction of intrinsic neurons in the rat medial geniculate body. *Brain Research, 371*(2), 395–399.

LeDoux, J. E., Ruggerio, D. A., & Reis, D. J. (1985). Projections to the subcortical forebrain from anatomically defined regions of the medial geniculate body in the rat. *Journal of Comparative Neurology, 242,* 182–213.

LeDoux, J. E., Sakaguchi, A., & Reis, D. J. (1984). Subcortical efferent projections of the medial geniculate nucleus mediate emotional responses conditioned by acoustic stimuli. *Journal of Neuroscience, 4*(3), 683–698.

Li, X. F., Stutzmann, G. E., & LeDoux, J. E. (1996). Convergent by temporally separated inputs to lateral amygdala neurons from the auditory thalamus and auditory cortex use different postsynaptic receptors: In vivo intracellular and extracellular recordings in fear conditioning pathways. *Learning and Memory, 3*(2-3), 229–242.

Livingston, K. E., & Escobar, A. (1971). Anatomical bias of the limbic system concept. *Archives of Neurology, 24,* 17–21.

MacLean, P. D. (1949). Psychosomatic disease and the "visceral brain": Recent developments bearing on the Papez theory of emotion. *Psychosomatic Medicine, 11,* 338–353.

MacLean, P. D. (1952). Some psychiatric implications of physiological studies on frontotemporal portion of limbic system (visceral brain). *Electroencephalography and Clinical Neurophysiology, 4,* 407–418.

MacLean, P. D. (1970). The triune brain, emotion and scientific bias. In F. O. Schmitt (Ed.), *The neurosciences: Second study program* (pp. 336–349). New York: Rockefeller University Press.

Magee, J. C., & Johnston, D. (1997). A synaptically controlled, associative signal for Hebbian plasticity in hippocampal neurons. *Science, 275*(5297), 209–213.

Malenka, R. C., & Nicoll, R. A. (1993). NMDA-receptor-dependent synaptic plasticity: Multiple forms and mechanisms. *Trends in Neurosciences, 16,* 521–527.

Marcel, A. J., & Bisiach, E. (1988). *Consciousness in contemporary science.* Oxford: Clarendon Press.

Maren, S. (1998). Overtraining does not mitigate contextual fear conditioning deficits produced by neurotoxic lesions of the basolateral amygdala. *The Journal of Neuroscience, 18*(8), 3088–3097.

Maren, S. (1999). Long-term potentiation in the amygdala: A mechanism for emotional learning and memory. *Trends in Neurosciences, 22*(12), 561–567.

Maren, S. (2000). Auditory fear conditioning increases CS-elicited spike firing in lateral amygdala neurons even after extensive overtraining.

European Journal of Neuroscience, 12(11), 4047–4054.

Maren, S., Aharonov, G., & Fanselow, M. S. (1997). Neurotoxic lesions of the dorsal hippocampus and Pavlovian fear conditioning in rats. *Behavioral Brain Research, 88*(2), 261–274.

Maren, S., & Fanselow, M. S. (1995). Synaptic plasticity in the basolateral amygdala induced by hippocampal formation stimulation *in vivo*. *Journal of Neuroscience, 15*(11), 7548–7564.

Marks, I. (1987). The development of normal fear: A review. *Journal of Child Psychology and Psychiatry, 28,* 667–697.

McDonald, A. J. (1998). Cortical pathways to the mammalian amygdala. *Prog. Neurobiology, 55,* 257–332.

McGaugh, J. L. (2000). Memory: A century of consolidation. *Science, 287*(5451), 248–251.

McGaugh, J. L., Introini-Collison, I. B., Cahill, L. F., Castellano, C., Dalmaz, C., Parent, M. B., & Williams, C. L. (1993). Neuromodulatory systems and memory storage: Role of the amygdala. *Behavioral Brain Research, 58,* 81–90.

McKernan, M. G., & Shinnick-Gallagher, P. (1997). Fear conditioning induces a lasting potentiation of synaptic currents in vitro. *Nature, 390,* 607–611.

Miserendino, M. J. D., Sananes, C. B., Melia, K. R., & Davis, M. (1990). Blocking of acquisition but not expression of conditioned fear-potentiated startle by NMDA antagonists in the amygdala. *Nature, 345,* 716–718.

Morgan, M. A., & LeDoux, J. E. (1995). Differential contribution of dorsal and ventral medial prefrontal cortex to the acquisition and extinction of conditioned fear in rats. *Behavioral Neuroscience, 109*(4), 681–688.

Morgan, M. A., Romanski, L. M., & LeDoux, J. E. (1993). Extinction of emotional learning: Contribution of medial prefrontal cortex. *Neuroscience Letters, 163,* 109–113.

Morris, J. S., Öhman, A., & Dolan, R. J. (1998). Conscious and unconscious emotional learning in the human amygdala. *Nature, 393*(6684), 467–470.

Morris, J. S., Öhman, A., & Dolan, R. J. (1999). A subcortical pathway to the right amygdala mediating "unseen" fear. *Procedures of the National Academy of Sciences, USA, 96*(4), 1680–1685.

Mowrer, O. H. (1960). *Learning theory and behavior*. New York: Wiley.

Muller, J., Corodimas, K. P., Fridel, Z., & LeDoux, J. E. (1997). Functional inactivation of the lateral and basal nuclei of the amygdala by muscimol infusion prevents fear conditioning to an explicit conditioned stimulus and to contextual stimuli. *Behavioral Neuroscience, 111*(4), 683–691.

Nader, K., Majidishad, P., Amorapanth, P., & LeDoux, J. E. (2001). Damage to the lateral and central, but not other, amygdaloid nuclei prevents the acquisition of auditory fear conditioning. *Learning and Memory, 8,* 156–163.

Nauta, W. J. H. (1958). Hippocampal projections and related neural pathway to the midbrain in the cat. *Brain, 81,* 319–341.

Nauta, W. J. H., & Karten, H. J. (1970). A general profile of the vertebrate brain, with sidelights on the ancestry of cerebral cortex. In F. O. Schmitt (Ed.), *The neurosciences: Second study program* (pp. 7–26). New York: Rockefeller University Press.

Nguyen, P. V., & Kandel, E. R. (1996). A macromolecular synthesis-dependent late phase of long-term potentiation requiring cAMP in the medial perforant pathway of rat hippocampal slices. *Journal of Neuroscience, 16*(10), 3189–3198.

Norman, D. A., & Shallice, T. (1980). Attention to action: Willed and automatic control of behavior. In R. J. Davidson, G. E. Schwartz, & D. Shapiro (Eds.), *Consciousness and self-regulation.* New York: Plenum, pp. 1–18.

Northcutt, R. G., & Kaas, J. H. (1995). The emergence and evolution of mammalian neocortex. *Trends in Neurosciences, 18,* 373–379.

Öhman, A. (1993). Fear and anxiety as emotional phenomena: Clinical phenomenology, evoluionary perspectives, and information-processing mechanisms. In M. Lewis & J. Haviland (Eds.), *Handbook of emotions* (pp. 511–536). New York: Guilford Press.

Papez, J. W. (1937). A proposed mechanism of emotion. *Archives of Neurology and Psychiatry, 79,* 217–224.

Pare, D., Smith, Y., & Pare, J. F. (1995). Intra-amygdaloid projections of the basolateral and basomedial nuclei in the cat: Phaseolus vulgaris-leucoagglutinin anterograde tracing at the light and electron microscopic level. *Neuroscience, 69*(2), 567–583.

Parent, M. B., Quirarte, G. L., Cahill, L., & McGaugh, J. L. (1995). Spared retention of inhibitory avoidance learning after posttraining amygdala lesions. *Behavioral Neuroscience, 109*(4), 803–807.

Phelps, E. A., & Anderson, A. K. (1997). Emotional memory: What does the amygdala do? *Current Biology, 7*(5), R311–R314.

Phillips, R. G., & LeDoux, J. E. (1992). Differential contribution of amygdala and hippocampus to cued and contextual fear conditioning. *Behavioral Neuroscience, 106*, 274–285.

Pitkänen, A., Savander, V., & LeDoux, J. E. (1997). Organization of intra-amygdaloid circuitries in the rat: An emerging framework for understanding functions of the amygdala. *Trends in Neurosciences, 20*(11), 517–523.

Pitman, R. K., Shalev, A. Y., & Orr, S. P. (2000). Posttraumatic stress disorder: Emotion, conditioning, and memory. In M. S. Gazzaniga (Ed.), *The new cognitive neurosciences* (pp. 1133–1147). Cambridge: MIT Press.

Quirk, G. J., Armony, J. L., & LeDoux, J. E. (1997). Fear conditioning enhances different temporal components of toned-evoked spike trains in auditory cortex and lateral amygdala. *Neuron, 19*, 613–624.

Quirk, G. J., Armony, J. L., Repa, J. C., Li, X.-F., & LeDoux, J. E. (1997). Emotional memory: A search for sites of plasticity. *Cold Spring Harbor Symposia on Biology, 61*, 247–257.

Quirk, G. J., Repa, C., & LeDoux, J. E. (1995). Fear conditioning enhances short-latency auditory responses of lateral amygdala neurons: Parallel recordings in the freely behaving rat. *Neuron, 15*(5), 1029–1039.

Quirk, G. J., Russo, G. K., Barron, J. L., & Lebron, K. (2000). The role of ventromedial prefrontal cortex in the recovery of extinguished fear. *Journal of Neuroscience, 20*(16), 6225–6231.

Rampon, C., Tang, Y. P., Goodhouse, J., Shimizu, E., Kyin, M., & Tsien, J. Z. (2000). Enrichment induces structural changes and recovery from nonspatial memory deficits in CA1 NMDAR1-knockout mice. *Nature Neuroscience, 3*(3), 238–244.

Rescorla, R. A. (1968). Probability of shock in the presence and absence of CS in fear conditioning. *Journal of Comparative Physiological Psychology, 66*, 1–5.

Robbins, T. W., Cador, M., Taylor, J. R., & Everitt, B. J. (1989). Limbic-striatal interactions in reward-related processes. *Neuroscience Biobehavioral Reviews, 13*, 155–162.

Rodrigues, S. M., Schafe, G. E., & LeDoux, J. E. (2001). Intraamygdala blockade of the NR2B subunit of the NMDA receptor disrupts the acquisition but not the expression of fear conditioning. *Journal of Neuroscience, 21*, 6889–6896.

Rogan, M. T., & LeDoux, J. E. (1995). LTP is accompanied by commensurate enhancement of auditory-evoked responses in a fear conditioning circuit. *Neuron, 15*, 127–136.

Rogan, M. T., Staubli, U., & LeDoux, J. (1997). Fear conditioning induces associative long-term potentiation in the amygdala. *Nature, 390*, 604–607.

Romanski, L. M., Clugnet, M. C., Bordi, F., & LeDoux, J. E. (1993). Somatosensory and auditory convergence in the lateral nucleus of the amygdala. *Behavioral Neuroscience, 107*(3), 444–450.

Romanski, L. M., & LeDoux, J. E. (1992). Equipotentiality of thalamo-amygdala and thalamo-cortico-amygdala circuits in auditory fear conditioning. *Journal of Neuroscience, 12*(11), 4501–4509.

Romanski, L. M., & LeDoux, J. E. (1993). Information cascade from primary auditory cortex to the amygdala: Corticocortical and corticoamygdaloid projections of temporal cortex in the rat. *Cerebral Cortex, 3*, 515–532.

Roozendaal, B., Koolhaas, J. M., & Bohus, B. (1991). Attenuated cardiovascular, neuroendocrine, and behavioral responses after a single footshock in central amygdaloid lesioned male rats. *Physiology and Behavior, 50*(4), 771–775.

Sarter, M. F., & Markowitsch, H. J. (1985). Involvement of the amygdala in learning and memory:

A critical review, with emphasis on anatomical relations. *Behavioral Neuroscience, 99,* 342–380.

Schafe, G. E., Atkins, C. M., Swank, M. W., Bauer, E. P., Sweatt, J. D., & LeDoux, J. E. (2000). Activation of ERK/MAP kinase in the amygdala is required for memory consolidation of pavlovian fear conditioning. *Journal of Neuroscience, 20*(21), 8177–8187.

Schafe, G. E., & LeDoux, J. E. (2000). Memory consolidation of auditory pavlovian fear conditioning requires protein synthesis and protein kinase A in the amygdala. *Journal of Neuroscience, 20*(18), RC96.

Schafe, G. E., Nader, K., Blair, H. T., & LeDoux, J. E. (2001). Memory consolidation of pavlovian fear conditioning: A cellular and molecular perspective. *Trends in Neurosciences, 24,* 540–546.

Scott, S. K., Young, A. W., Calder, A, J., Hellawell, D. J., Aggleton, J. P., & Johnson, M. (1997). Impaired auditory recognition of fear and anger following bilateral amygdala lesions. *Nature, 385,* 254–257.

Scoville, W. B., & Milner, B. (1957). Loss of recent memory after bilateral hippocampal lesions. *Journal of Neurology and Psychiatry, 20,* 11–21.

Seligman, M. E. P. (1971). Phobias and preparedness. *Behavior Therapy, 2,* 307–320.

Shallice, T. (1988). Information processing models of consiousness. In A. Marcel & E. Bisiach (Eds.), *Consciousness in contemporary science* (pp. 305–333). Oxford: Oxford University Press.

Shors, T. J., & Matzel, L. D.(1997). Long-term potentiation: What's learning got to do with it? *Behavioral and Brain Sciences, 20*(4), 597–613.

Silva, A. J., Kogan, J. H., Frankland, P. W., & Kida, S. (1998). CREB and memory. *Annual Review of Neuroscience, 21,* 127–148.

Smith, O. A., Astley, C. A., Devito, J. L., Stein, J. M., & Walsh, R. E. (1980). Functional analysis of hypothalamic control of the cardiovascular responses accompanying emotional behavior. *Federation Proceedings, 39*(8), 2487–2494.

Stevens, C. F. (1994). CREB and memory consolidation. *Neuron, 13*(4), 769–770.

Stevens, C. F. (1998). A million dollar question: Does LTP = memory? *Neuron, 20*(1), 1–2.

Stiedl, O., Birkenfeld, K., Palve, M., & Spiess, J. (2000). Impairment of conditioned contextual fear of C57BL/6J mice by intracerebral injections of the NMDA receptor antagonist APV. *Behavioral Brain Research, 116*(2), 157–168.

Swanson, L. W. (1983). The hippocampus and the concept of the limbic system. In W. Seifert (Ed.), *Neurobiology of the hippocampus* (pp. 3–19). London: Academic Press.

Watson, J. B., & Rayner, R. (1920). Conditioned emotional reactions. *Journal of Experimental Psychology, 3*(1), 1–14.

Weisskopf, M. G., Bauer, E. P., & LeDoux, J. E. (1999). L-Type voltage-gated calcium channels mediate NMDA-independent associative long-term potentiation at thalamic input synapses to the amygdala. *Journal of Neuroscience, 19*(23), 10512–10519.

Whalen, P. J., Rauch, S. L., Etcoff, N. L., McInerney, S. C., Lee, M. B., & Jenike, M. A. (1998). Masked presentations of emotional facial expressions modulate amygdala activity without explicit knowledge. *Journal of Neuroscience, 18,* 411–418.

Wilensky, A. E., Schafe, G. E., & LeDoux, J. E. (2000). The amygdala modulates memory consolidation of fear-motivated inhibitory avoidance learning but not classical fear conditioning. *Journal of Neuroscience, 20*(18), 7059–7066.

Yin, J. C., & Tully, T. (1996). CREB and the formation of long-term memory. *Current Opinion in Neurobiology, 6*(2), 264–268.

Young, S. L., Bohenek, D. L., & Fanselow, M. S. (1994). NMDA processes mediate anterograde amnesia of contextual fear conditioning induced by hippocampal damage: Immunization against amnesia by context preexposure. *Behavioral Neuroscience, 108,* 19–29.

CHAPTER 14

Anatomy of Motivation

ALAN G. WATTS AND LARRY W. SWANSON

INTRODUCTION

We are all familiar with the notion that much of our behavior has purpose and is directed toward specific goals. We often talk of being motivated or driven to perform particular acts. However, even though drive, instinct, and motivation are familiar terms in everyday speech, their use in a neuroscientific context—particularly when thinking about neural correlates—has always been controversial (for historical reviews, see Cofer, 1981; Pfaff, 1982). Although the most rigorous uses of the terms *drive* and *motivation* have been as intervening variables between stimulus and behavioral response, there has always been an attraction for designating particular brain regions as being responsible for putting the motivation into behavior. However, attempts at neuralizing drive and particularly motivation have often been criticized because it has been thought impossible to identify and measure the specific neural properties underlying these terms (for further discussion, see Hinde, 1970; Pfaff, 1982; Toates, 1986).

We have adopted a neural systems approach in this chapter that rather downplays the notion of associating what we commonly think of as motivation with specific neural mechanisms. Instead, we concentrate more on discussing which particular parts of the brain contribute to the expression of behaviors that have a motivated character and how the afferents and efferents of their constituent neurons are organized. The advantage of this approach is that it allows us to use the common experimental paradigm of identifying the neural substrates of specific behaviors by tracing how the information derived from sensory inputs critical to their expression is distributed within the brain (e.g., Risold, Thompson, & Swanson, 1997; Swanson & Mogenson, 1981; Watts, 2001). With the advent of sophisticated functional neuroanatomical methods, this approach has proved technically quite useful.

This chapter has five sections. In this introduction we briefly discuss the problems of reconciling the ever-increasing body of neuroanatomical data with the theoretical models of motivation derived from behavioral experiments. The second section considers the temporal organization of motivated behaviors, as this establishes the temporal constraints within which the various neural components must operate to control behaviors. This is followed in the third section by a description of the simple neural framework that we use to facilitate our understanding of how the various neural components that generate motivated behaviors are organized. In the next section we provide a more detailed description of the neuroanatomical organization of the structures that make up this framework. Most of the data we describe have been derived from the rat, which still remains the animal of choice for most behavioral and neuroanatomical studies. Finally, in the last section we use feeding and female reproductive function to illustrate how some these neural components operate to generate specific types of behavior.

Motivated Behaviors and Their Neuroanatomical Substrates

Motivated or goal-directed behaviors can be thought of at the simplest level as sets of striate muscle contractions that direct animals toward—or in some instances away from—a particular goal object. Interactions with these goal objects promote the survival of an individual or maintain sustainable numbers of individuals within a species. Classically, motivated behaviors consist of ingestive, thermoregulatory, defensive, and reproductive behaviors. Ingestive and thermoregulatory behaviors are the behavioral adjuncts of those physiological processes that maintain the stable composition of the animal's internal environment (i.e., homeostasis), whereas defensive and reproductive behaviors organize specific types of social interaction that are more concerned with individual security within the external environment and with survival of the species. To a large extent all these behaviors are accompanied by emotional affect and sets of sympathetic, parasympathetic, and neuroendocrine motor events that help adapt the internal environment to the consequences of the behavior. As their name suggests, motivated behaviors are those on which animals will expend energy or tolerate some discomfort in order to interact with specific goal objects. These qualities point to one of the defining features of the neural control of motivated behaviors: the existence of neural systems that assign hedonic values (reward or penalty/aversive) to objects encountered in the animal's environment.

In the past most descriptions of the neural circuits underlying motivated behaviors have concentrated on those sensory and motor functions involving the hypothalamus and hindbrain; little consideration was given to incorporating the types of higher order integrative processing executed by the cerebral hemispheres. For the most part this was simply because the data were inadequate for understanding how the brain was structured to perform these actions. In this respect, the truly enormous body of data that has emerged from the revolution in neuroanatomical methodology of the last 30 years has allowed advances in two directions. First, it has dramatically increased the complexity of how we view brain organization. For example, 30 years ago only about 75 different hypothalamic projections were recognized (of which about half have subsequently proved erroneous through the use of more sensitive techniques); today this number is at least 2,000, a 25-fold increase. Second, these data have provided the structural basis for clarifying many important issues; for example, although the cortex and the hypothalamus have for many years been viewed as being critical for generating motivated behaviors, the existence of direct hypothalamo-cortical interconnections has only been revealed in the last 15 years.

The ever-expanding neuroanatomical database is now providing a more solid foundation than ever before for understanding how different parts of the brain interact to control motivated behaviors. Increased knowledge of neural pathways means that we can now begin to incorporate into a control framework for motivated behaviors the circuits underlying a wider variety of neural functions than has previously been possible—for example, learning and memory mechanisms, circadian rhythms, arousal state control, and so on. In many respects our understanding of neural circuit architecture is now beginning to catch up with the experimental psychology of motivated behaviors. The type of neuroanatomical framework we present here reflects this ever-widening view. But the complexity of these neural connections also raises problems of comprehension; trying to reconcile the intricacies of neuroanatomy with data from behavioral neuroscience is not trivial. Centered around the functional schema described in the third section, this chapter aims to present a clear and hopefully digestible view of how the brain is organized to control the many neural control aspects of motivated behaviors, while at the same time providing a taste of the complexity afforded by current neuroanatomical data.

Theoretical Models of Motivation

The framework we use throughout this chapter is derived by merging our current understanding of rat brain circuitry (e.g., L. Swanson, 2000a; Watts, 2001) with what is essentially a Hullerian incentive model of motivation, where certain behaviors are selected at a particular time to reduce the level of associated drive states (for further discussion, see Berridge & Robinson, 1998; Bindra, 1978; Toates, 1986). Although the way the brain operates to control motivated behaviors is unquestionably far more complex than is accounted for by these rather simplistic types of model, they do have the advantage from a neuroanatomical standpoint of providing relatively simple and experimentally testable hypotheses for addressing the neuroanatomical organization of motivational systems.

Incentive models of behavior derive from the notion that at any one time the level (or intensity) of each drive state—and hence the probability that a particular behavior will be expressed—is dependent on the result of integrating four sets of inputs that project to those parts of the brain responsible for selecting the appropriate behavioral action (Figure 14.1). These inputs are information from systems that control behavioral state, interosensory information that encodes inter-

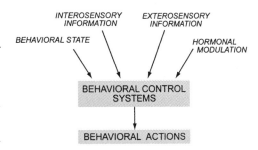

Figure 14.1   Four classes of inputs that influence how behavioral control systems generate motor actions.

nal state (e.g., hydration state, plasma glucose, leptin, gastric distension etc.), inputs that carry information from the neural processing of the classic sensory modalities (i.e., exterosensory information), and modulatory hormonal inputs such as the gonadal steroids that facilitate sexual behavior.

The integration of these inputs within the brain is central to the process of behavior (i.e., motor action) selection. This model (Figure 14.1) posits that at any one time a particular motivated behavior can be initiated when any one of these four sets of inputs predominates. For example, feeding can occur at one time because of strong signals encoding negative energy balance (interosensory information), but at another time because a highly desirable food object is encountered in the environment (exterosensory information), and yet at another time because of anticipatory signals generated from the circadian timing system (behavioral state). Similarly, a female rat may accept or reject the opportunity to mate because of varying circulating estrogen concentrations (hormonal modulation).

THE TEMPORAL ORGANIZATION OF MOTIVATED BEHAVIOR

Carefully describing the different motor acts that make up a behavior and how they are organized in time is one of the experimental foundations of ethology (e.g., Lorenz, 1950; Tinbergen, 1951). Over the years this approach has greatly facilitated our understanding of how particular neural structures contribute to each behavioral component; applied in this way, the approach defines neuroethology. A simple and useful scheme describing the temporal organization of motivated behavior was outlined by Wallace Craig in 1918 and has since been adopted and elaborated by a number of workers as a basis for investigating the various neural bases of motivated behaviors (e.g., Grill & Kaplan, 1990; L. Swanson & Mogenson, 1981). In this scheme, motivated behaviors are comprised of three phases, which, like many behavioral sequences or action patterns (Lashley, 1951), must be expressed in a specific temporal sequence for successful execution of the complete behavior (Figure 14.2).

In brief, motivated behaviors begin with the initiation of a procurement (or appetitive) phase in which the goal object is sought out. The behavioral motor events expressed during

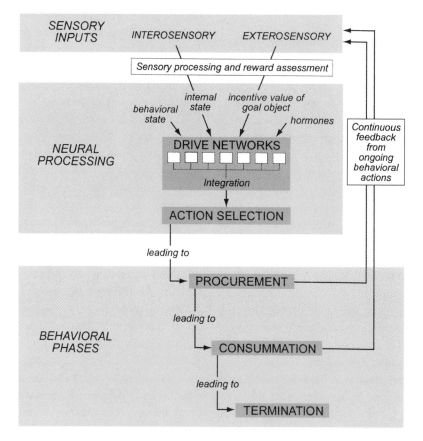

Figure 14.2   A schematic representation showing how the sensory inputs and neural processing that initiate the temporal sequence of motivated behaviors are organized.

NOTE: The four classes of inputs shown in Figure 14.1 are hypothesized to bias the level of drive within the neural networks responsible for controlling the motor events of specific behaviors. The resulting integration of the outputs from the drive networks by those regions of the brain responsible for action selection leads to the procurement phase of the chosen behavior. Continuous monitoring of the sensory consequences (feedback) of ongoing motor events constantly updates the status of the drive networks.

the procurement phase involve foraging behavior, are individualized for particular situations (e.g., courtship behaviors), can be quite complex, and are controlled by the forebrain. After the goal object has been located, the procurement phase is followed by a consummatory phase in which direct interaction with the goal object occurs (e.g., chewing, swallowing, mating). As the consummatory phase progresses, the nature of the information that is directed to the brain from both the internal and external environments changes in such a way that the ongoing behavior is eventually terminated, to be followed by the initiation of a new behavior.

The initiation of a motivated behavior develops from the continuous neural integration of the four types of information described in Figure 14.1. Conceptually, we can think of this integration as determining the ongoing value of the drive associated with a particular behavior. It is certainly not clear whether this drive value is a quantifiable physical property within neural networks, but in some instances the levels of neuropeptides or the degrees of neural activation (e.g., as revealed by immediate early gene activation) within some hypothalamic circuits appear to correlate with what might be envisaged as changes in drive state. As they continually decode the integrated outputs of competing drive networks, other neural circuits then select sets of motor actions for the most appropriate procurement phase to guide the animal toward the goal object (Figure 14.2).

Some of the most important processes for the development and expression of appropriate behaviors are reward/penalty functions and learning and memory processes; a previously rewarded or an aversive experience of a particular goal object as well as remembering where it is located and how to get there are clearly important considerations that must be included in the integrative process. We shall see that these highly complex cognitive functions can be conveniently categorized as ones that generate and control the neural representations of sensory objects. Critically, these processes are continually being revised and consolidated as the brain receives information about the consequences within the environment of the animal's motor actions (Figure 14.2). The continuous updating of these representations by new sensory information forms one of the fundamental neural functions for controlling motivated behaviors.

When the goal object has been located, the striate muscle contractions used during the subsequent consummatory phase may contain less of the nonstereotypic foraging behaviors and more reflex-stereotypic rhythmic movements than are generally seen during the procurement phase. These rhythmic movements allow the animal to interact directly with the goal object. Control mechanisms situated in the hindbrain and spinal cord are particularly important for some of these movements (Grill & Kaplan, 1990; Jean, 2001; Travers, Dinardo, & Karimnamazi, 1997). Others involve complex cortical processing, for example, the dexterous manipulation of food objects by the forelimbs and the control of tongue protrusion required for normal ingestive behaviors (Whishaw, 1990). How animals structure the interaction with the goal object during the consummatory phase (e.g., determine the duration and the amount consumed during a feeding episode, the duration of the intermeal interval, etc.) is an important function that once again arises from the ongoing complex dynamic interaction of sensory inputs and the central neural networks that control motor function.

As the consummatory phase continues, a variety of feedback signals are produced that increase the probability that the behavior will be terminated, most likely through the action of inhibitory networks that generate what we think of as satiety. Again, some of these signals are processed by brainstem mechanisms, whereas others involve cortical processing. However, termination may also arise from new exterosensory signals (e.g., the presence of a predator) that can at any time override an ongoing behavior, thus allowing the animal to switch immediately to another, more appropriate behavior (McFarland & Sibly, 1975).

A FRAMEWORK FOR CONSIDERING THE NEURAL CONTROL OF MOTIVATED BEHAVIORS

The theoretical framework that we use here as the basis for our examination of the neuroanatomy of motivated behaviors is illustrated in Figure 14.3. At this point it is important to note that this framework is a purely functional and not a neuroanatomical representation. For the moment, we only broadly consider the neuroanatomical components of these systems. We will be describing the nature and locations of the neuronal components of each system in more detail in the fourth section.

Figure 14.3 shows that at the simplest level the brain contains a series of networks to control the individual motor actions—neuroendocrine, sympathetic, parasympathetic, and behavioral—that constitute motivated behaviors. These can be broken down into four divisions and implement:

1. The transduction and processing of sensory signals (Figure 14.3a)
2. The control of behavioral state (Figure 14.3b)
3. The processing of the types of information concerned with generating neural representations of sensory objects (Figure 14.3c)
4. Motor control (Figure 14.3d)

In addition, this figure illustrates sets of motor feedback pathways and hormonal signals that interact with many different levels of the brain to influence behavioral and autonomic motor actions (Figure 14.3e).

Sensory Information

The neural systems that control motivated behaviors are regulated by a host of sensory inputs. These can be categorized either as interosensory signals that are used to encode internal state or as the exterosensory signals (the classic sensory modalities: smell, taste, temperature, tactile properties, and visual appearance) that are used to encode features of the animal's immediate environment, including potential goal objects. Each of these sensory modalities has specific receptors, transduction mechanisms, and labeled-line access to central processing networks across the whole neural axis (Figure 14.3a). Although a great deal of important sensory processing occurs within the cerebral hemispheres, particularly sensory cortex, some of the initial sensory processing that occurs subcortically has important implications for controlling motivated behaviors; for example, altered sensitivity to the taste of sodium occurs in the hindbrain of hyponatremic animals and is an important adjunct to increased sodium appetite (Jacobs, Mark, & Scott, 1988). Another example from the female rat is the way in which the somatosensory information responsible for lordosis is differentially interpreted by the hindbrain depending on the day of the rodent estrous cycle (Pfaff, 1999). The output of regions that process sensory information is directed to all of the other three network divisions (Figure 14.3a).

Behavioral State Control

Behavioral state provides the stage on which all motivated behaviors are expressed. The close interaction between those neural systems controlling behavioral state and the

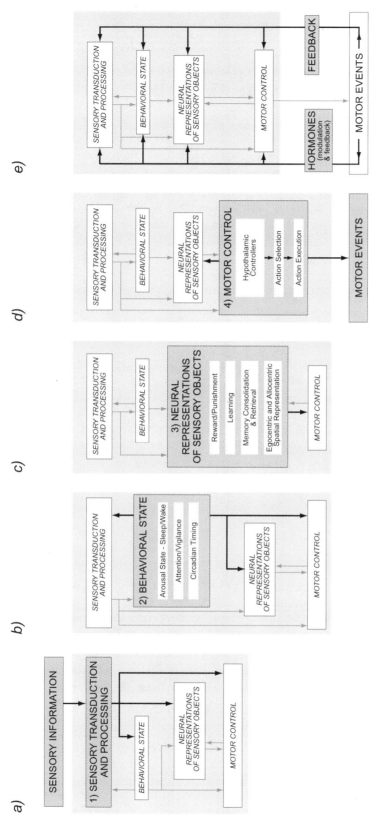

Figure 14.3 A hypothetical schema representing the interactions of four sets of neural networks responsible for controlling all the motor actions (behavioral, neuroendocrine, and autonomic) of motivated behaviors.

NOTE: These networks deal with the transduction and processing of sensory information (a); behavioral state, which involves the control of arousal state, attention and vigilance, and circadian timing (b); the neural representation of sensory objects, which comprise networks responsible for reward/punishment, learning, memory consolidation and retrieval, and the egocentric and allocentric spatial representation that are important for spatial awareness and navigation (c); and motor control (d). A fifth set of control inputs includes hormonal modulators and feedback signals (e).

569

expression of motivated behaviors is illustrated by the increased arousal that generally accompanies the execution of motivated behaviors and by the cessation of behavior during sleep.

At a first level of approximation, three interacting sets of neural circuits implement the actions of behavioral state on motor control networks (Figure 14.3b): networks responsible for controlling arousal state and sleep/wake status, circuits concerned with attention and vigilance control, and the circadian timing system that gives many biological processes a rhythm with a frequency of approximately 24 hours. Networks that control arousal and generate sleep/wake states include cholinergic and monoaminergic neurons in the midbrain and hindbrain (e.g., the locus coeruleus, raphe nuclei), GABAergic and cholinergic neurons in the basal forebrain, the GABAergic reticular nucleus of the thalamus, galanin/GABAergic neurons in the ventrolateral preoptic nucleus (VLPN), histaminergic neurons in the tuberomammillary nucleus (TM), and the recently identified hypocretin/orexin (H/OR) neurons in the lateral hypothalamic area (McCormick & Bal, 1997; Semba, 2000; Sherin, Elmquist, Torrealba, & Saper, 1998; Willie, Chemelli, Sinton, & Yanagisawa, 2001).

Changes in arousal state are reflected in alterations in vigilance that allow animals both to focus and to switch attention toward novel or familiar goal objects within the environment. The circuits responsible for controlling thalamo-cortical interactions play a central role in controlling attention and vigilance, and in particular involve the reticular nucleus of the thalamus (RT). This GABAergic cell group controls the flow of sensory information to and from the cortex and receives inputs from monoaminergic neurons in the midbrain and hindbrain and from cholinergic and GABAergic neurons in the basal forebrain. These circuits have close interactions with

the motor control mechanisms responsible for head direction and orienting responses by way of cerebral cortical and basal ganglia inputs.

Anticipation and the synchronization of various behavioral actions to particular times of the day are attributes of many motivated behaviors. These features are notably absent from animals with lesions in a small hypothalamic cell group called the suprachiasmatic nucleus (SCH). This small but densely packed cell group generates the timing signal that entrains virtually all neural activity within limits determined by the prevailing photoperiod (Moore, 1997).

The output of the neurons that control behavioral state is directed to all of the other three network divisions (Figure 14.3b).

Neural Representations of Sensory Objects

The brain contains a wide range of neural circuits that process sensory information in ways that develop what can be labeled as neural representations of sensory objects (Figure 14.3c). These highly complex cognitive networks take the information provided by sensory processing systems and generate, interpret, prioritize, store, and retrieve neural representations of sensory objects. Parts of the forebrain also produce emotional appraisals of this sensory information (LeDoux, 1996; Rolls, 1999a). Collectively, these systems are critical for controlling motivational behaviors, and they are the ones that we generally think of as being central for initiating voluntary behavior. For the most part their outputs are directed toward regions in the brain concerned with motor control (Figure 14.3c).

Motor Control

Motor Hierarchies

The three systems just described process information in ways that are not necessarily goal specific; in these systems the same neu-ral circuits are involved to some extent with *all* motivated behaviors. For example, the SCH provides circadian timing information for all neural functions. Similarly, the brain processes information for spatial navigation in the same parts of the cortical hemispheres regardless of whether the animal is looking for food, a mate, or shelter, although the *way* in which it is processed and the local neu-

ral topographic organization of information processing are likely to be different between goal objects (see, e.g., Risold & Swanson, 1996). On the other hand, when we begin to examine some of the components in the mo-tor control systems—notably in the hypotha-lamic controllers (Figures 14.3d and 14.4)—we find neurons associated with functions that are much more goal-specific and control par-ticular aspects of *individual* goal-associated

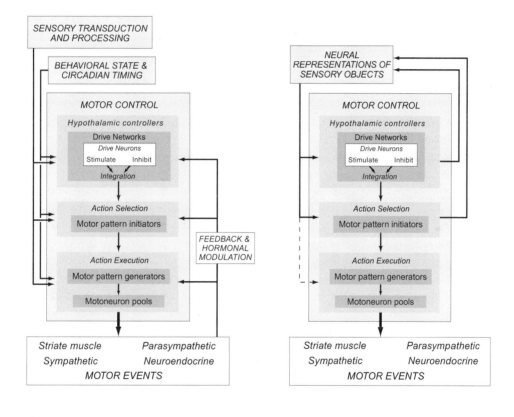

a)   b)

Figure 14.4   A hypothetical schema representing the neural components that control motor function. NOTE: At the top of the hierarchy are sets of hypothalamic controllers that are responsible for all the motor actions associated with specific types of motivated behaviors. Each controller is hypothesized to contain the sets of drive networks shown in Figure 14.2, which consist of neurons that either stimulate or inhibit specific motor actions. The integrated output of the drive networks then projects from the hypothalamic controllers to regions concerned with motor action selection, and from there to the networks that execute the motor actions. The figure also shows that the regions responsible for sensory processing and behavioral state appear to project to all levels of the motor control hierarchy (a), while those responsible for generating neural representations of sensory objects tend to project only to the upper levels of the hierarchy (b).

functions. For example, neurons in parts of the hypothalamus are concerned specifically with feeding or sexual behavior, but not with defensive or thermoregulatory behaviors. This is a defining feature of hypothalamic nuclei in the rostral behavior control column (L. Swanson, 2000a) that we will shortly consider in more detail.

At a first level of approximation, motor control systems function at three hierarchical levels (Figures 14.3d and 14.4):

1. *Hypothalamic controllers* each of which contains sets of drive networks whose output is integrated by nuclei in the behavior control column to set up and coordinate the specific motor events of a particular behavior.

2. *Action selection* occurs in regions that receive inputs from the hypothalamic controllers and is concerned with planning, selecting, and maintaining the sequences of motor actions appropriate for that behavior.

3. *Action execution* is accomplished by premotor/motor neuron networks that directly control the activity of effector systems such as striate and smooth muscle, the pituitary gland, and so on.

This hierarchical organization is consistent with the incentive/drive-reduction model outlined earlier, and it requires that the selection of motor programs for a particular motivated behavior be biased by the integrated output from different hypothalamic controllers. An important feature to note at this point is that this motor control hierarchy may also apply to autonomic as well as behavioral motor events. This property is explored more thoroughly in the section titled "Motor Outputs."

Critically, each of these three levels of motor control is regulated by inputs from the other network divisions illustrated in Figure 14.3, although the degree to which this occurs varies between networks. Thus, processed sensory information and inputs from the behavioral state networks are directed to all three levels of motor control: hypothalamic controllers, action selection, and action execution neurons (Figure 14.4a). On the other hand, it seems that little of the information generated by the neural representation of sensory objects directly reaches the neurons ultimately responsible for action execution (Figure 14.4b). For example, most of the output from orbitofrontal cortex does not reach the hindbrain, but instead targets other parts of the cortex, the hypothalamus, and the midbrain (Floyd, Price, Ferry, Keay, & Bandler, 2000; Öngur, An, & Price, 1998); similarly, nuclei in the amygdala (parts of which are concerned with emotional appraisals that generate aversive responses) project much more heavily to the hypothalamic controllers than to motor pattern generators and motor neurons in the hindbrain and spinal cord. All these regions tend to influence motor output indirectly by projecting to the upper parts of the motor control hierarchy.

Of paramount importance to the overall expression of motivated behaviors are the dynamic interactions between the separate hypothalamic controllers that control different behaviors. For example, the effects of negative energy balance are not limited only to increasing the drive to eat; they also reduce reproductive capacity (Schneider, Zhou, & Blum, 2000). Similarly, dehydration leads to severe anorexia in addition to increasing the drive to drink (Watts, 2001). This cross-behavioral coordination (Schneider and Watts, in press) is part of the mechanism that not only selects those motor actions with the highest behavioral priority but also suppresses those actions that may interfere with the expression of that behavior or may further exacerbate any physiologically challenged components. In the

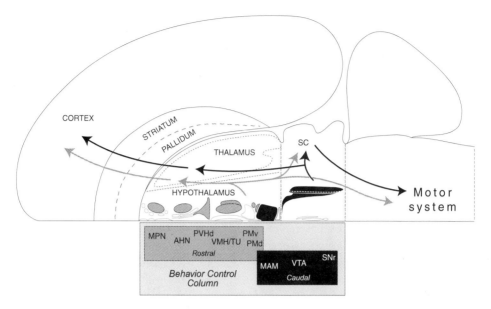

Figure 14.5   An overview of the behavior control column, with the rostral segment in gray and the caudal segment in black.

NOTE: Almost all of the nuclei in this column generate a dual, typically branched projection that descends to the motor system on one hand and ascends to thalamocortical loops on the other. Abbreviations: AHN, anterior hypothalamic nucleus; MAM, mammillary body; MPN, medial preoptic nucleus (lateral part in particular); PMd,v, premammillary nuclei, dorsal, ventral; PVHd, descending division of paraventricular nucleus; SC, superior colliculus, deeper layers; SNr, reticular substantia nigra; TH, dorsal thalamus; TU, tuberal nucleus; VMH, ventromedial nucleus; VTA, ventral tegmental area.

SOURCE: Adapted from Swanson (2000a).

section titled "Interactions between the Motor Control Networks of Different Motivated Behaviors," we see that this coordination most likely involves sensory and hormonal modulation acting together with the divergent neuroanatomical outputs of individual hypothalamic control networks.

Hypothalamic Controllers and Drive Networks

At the top of the control hierarchy for motivated behaviors is a series of motor controllers in the hypothalamus (Figures 14.3 and 14.4), the core of which is the behavior control column (Figure 14.5). This concept derives from a substantial body of connectional data reviewed by L. Swanson (2000a). The behavior control column consists of a series of nuclei in the medial zone of the hypothalamus and is topographically divided to control two fundamentally different aspects of motivated behaviors (Figure 14.5). The rostral segment of the behavior control column contains sets of neurons that organize the full spectrum of motor events—autonomic, neuroendocrine, and behavioral—associated with social and ingestive behaviors; neurons in the caudal behavior control column are important for organizing the various motor actions that comprise exploratory and foraging behavior, which in some ways can be regarded as a unique form of motivated behavior in which the goal object may be the pursuit of novelty (Hughes, 1997).

How hypothalamic controllers direct motivated behaviors is not clear. However, it is worth recalling that certain neuropeptides synthesized in the hypothalamus will either stimulate or inhibit different behaviors. These neurons might be thought of as contributing to networks that in a way embody the concept of drive for particular behaviors. In this form, these networks reprise the idea of discretely localized hypothalamic dual satiety and hunger centers popular during the 1950s and 1960s. Elaborating these pioneering studies during the past 30 years has replaced the idea of isolated centers with a scheme in which sets of more widely distributed but highly interconnected motor control networks direct the motor actions of specific behaviors.

As we discussed earlier, neuralizing drive has a controversial history. However, to help add function to the neuroanatomically based control column concept, it is useful to impute drives as being dynamic properties embedded within different sets of goal-specific neural networks at the level of the hypothalamic controllers (Figures 14.3d and 14.4). To function as behavior controllers, the control column nuclei must therefore either contain or receive direct projections from sets of drive neurons that either stimulate or inhibit particular behaviors (Figure 14.4). For example, neurons in the arcuate (for feeding) or median preoptic nuclei (for drinking) that project to the paraventricular nucleus might be considered in this category. As we discussed earlier, we are not suggesting that drive is necessarily a quantifiable entity within neural networks, but it is simply a useful correlate that helps us to dissect the functional organization of the hypothalamic controllers.

A fundamental property of drive networks—which derives from the dual-center concept originally elaborated by Stellar (1954)—is that the stimulation and inhibition of a behavior is mediated by *different* sets of neurons at the level of the hypothalamic controllers (Figure 14.4); it is not simply the result of increasing or decreasing the activity of a single command network. This type of organization is most apparent for those systems controlling feeding, where separate stimulatory and inhibitory peptidergic systems have been clearly identified (Watts, 2000, 2001; Woods, Seeley, Porte, & Schwartz, 1998), but it is less clear for the drive networks controlling other motivated behaviors.

Finally, in a way that reflects the idea of incentive models of motivation that we discussed earlier, the drive state within each of these networks can be increased or decreased by the inputs from sensory processing, behavioral state control, and object representational systems (Figure 14.4). At some stage the outputs of drive neurons are then integrated within behaviorally specific parts of the behavior control column and are then projected to the lower parts of the motor control hierarchy to bias the selection of a particular motor action (Figure 14.4).

Action Selection

Those parts of the brain concerned with the planning, selection, and moment-to-moment control of particular motor actions include the prefrontal, motor and other parts of the cortex (including the hippocampus; Oddie & Bland, 1998), the basal ganglia, parts of the lateral hypothalamus (including the subthalamic locomotor region), the mesencephalic locomotor region, the cerebellum, and the hindbrain. These regions control diverse motor actions ranging from precise manipulation of goal objects by the forelimbs (Iwaniuk & Whishaw, 2000; Rizzolatti & Luppino, 2001; Whishaw & Coles, 1996) to the types of syntactically organized sequences of movements best exemplified by grooming (Aldridge & Berridge, 1998; Berridge & Whishaw, 1992; Cromwell & Berridge, 1996). Like much of the circuitry concerned with sensory object representation, these regions, at least at a systems level, control motor actions that themselves are not necessarily goal-directed, but may instead be used for in a variety of behaviors to allow the animal to interact with different goal objects. Although these networks are topographically organized with regard to the mapping of pattern generation and the contractions of specific muscles (e.g., Fay & Norgren, 1997), they do not appear to be organized in the same goal-specific way seen in drive networks.

Regions controlling action selection must receive the integrated outputs from the hypothalamic controllers to organize the appropriate behavior (Figure 14.4). Although not well understood, complex sets of projections between the cerebral hemispheres, hypothalamus, and hindbrain are likely the key to this organizing and coordinating function (Risold et al., 1997; Saper, 1985; L. Swanson, 2000a).

Action Execution

Alpha-motor neurons in the ventral horn of the spinal cord and the corresponding cranial nerve nuclei are responsible for controlling the entire striate musculature and hence the expression of all behavior. In turn, sets of premotor networks directly control oscillatory and the more complex rhythmic patterns of motor neuron firing. Simple rhythmic movement patterns develop from an interaction between oscillatory rhythm generators, which directly involve the motor neurons, and networks of premotor central pattern generators located somewhat more distally in the spinal cord and brainstem (Rossignol, 1996). A critical feature of these pattern generators is that their ability to produce rhythmic output is endogenous (Arshavsky, Deliagina, & Orlovsky, 1997). In turn, pattern generator output is modulated further by afferents from those parts of the appropriate command networks in the diencephalon and telencephalon just discussed.

Though not as widely explored as in the striate muscle motor system, it appears that a similarly structured motor hierarchy—at least in principle—also controls the neuroendocrine, sympathetic, and parasympathetic motor functions that are coordinated with motivated behaviors. Here, the relevant motor neurons are located in periventricular zone of the hypothalamus (neuroendocrine motor system), hindbrain and sacral spinal cord (parasympathetic), and intermediolateral column of the thoracic and lumbar spinal cord (sympathetic).

Feedback and Hormonal Modulation

Feedback is a critical feature of behavioral motor control, and sensory signals encoding the magnitude and consequences of generated motor actions can control the length of a motivated behavioral episode. Temporally, these range from the long-term modulatory effects of hormones to the millisecond feedback required for adjusting limb movement (Ballermann, Tompkins, & Whishaw, 2000). For example, postabsorptive humoral feedback (e.g., increasing circulating cholecystokinin [CCK] or decreasing plasma osmolality) and interosensory signals (e.g., gastric distension, oropharyngeal metering) lead to the termination of ingestive behaviors and the subsequent behavioral refractoriness that we recognize as satiety. However, negative feedback control of this kind differs from other types of behavioral inhibition that are generated by the action of separate central inhibitory circuits (Watts, 2001).

Hormones have been known for many years as critical modulators of motivated behaviors, and they influence a variety of neural structures at all brain levels (Figure 14.3e). Consequently, they are integral components of any postulated motivated behavioral control mechanism. Another important feature of some hormones is that because signature secretory patterns often accompany specific behaviors, they can provide an important set of signals for cross-behavioral coordination, thus allowing the output of one behavior to influence another (Schneider & Watts, in press). We describe one example of this type of interaction later. The brain controls the secretion of some of these hormones—gonadal steroids, glucocorticoids, thyroid hormones—by way of trophic hormones released by the anterior pituitary gland. The neuroendocrine motor neurons responsible for these functions are located in the periventricular zone of the hypothalamus, and their afferent control is hierarchically organized in a manner not unlike that which controls the striate musculature.

With regard to ingestive behaviors, many hormones encode aspects of internal state (e.g., by acting as deficit signals), and their actions on neuronal networks can be categorized as feedback. However, other hormones do not act as feedback signals in the classic sense but operate more as permissive factors. Steroid hormones, particularly gonadal steroids, are important signals of this type.

NEUROANATOMY OF THE CONTROL SYSTEMS FOR MOTIVATED BEHAVIORS

The schemas illustrated in Figures 14.3 and 14.4 provide a multilevel operational framework for thinking about how the different neural systems are neuroanatomically organized to generate motivated behaviors. To consider these circuits and signals in more detail, we now turn our attention to the structure of the neural circuitry found at each of the functional levels shown in Figures 14.3 and 14.4. Because of the enormous volume of literature available, we do not attempt to describe the detailed neural architecture of all the components within each of the network divisions illustrated in Figure 14.3 but will instead high-light new findings and concepts for the most important neural groups. This means that we will tend to concentrate more on newly emerging concepts of hypothalamic and cerebral cortical control of motor functions rather than on tasks such as learning and memory, reward, or navigation, which are discussed comprehensively elsewhere (see each of the subsequent sections for additional references).

Throughout this and the following section we will primarily use, where appropriate, examples from ingestive and reproductive behaviors to illustrate the organization of motivational control circuitry. This is because these two behaviors have been very well studied over the past 30 years and because their neural substrates are becoming reasonably well understood from a neural systems perspective.

Sensory Information

Interosensory

Interosensory information affects all levels of the motivational control hierarchy (Figure 14.4a) in two fundamentally different ways: Information can be transmitted neurally or humorally.

Neural (See also the Section Titled "Interosensory Information"). Control systems receive a variety of neurally transmitted information from the viscera that can be classified in three principal ways: visceral sensation (e.g., gastric distension), cardiovascular information (e.g., cardiac output; blood gas composition, pressure, volume, and osmolality), and information related to energy balance (e.g., hepatic oxidation state). Visceral sensation is relayed by way of ascending fibers in the vagus nerve and sensory systems in the spinal cord. On the other hand, information related to cardiovascular function and energy balance is transduced by specialized receptors into neural signals that reach the brain by afferent fibers in the vagus and glossopharyngeal nerves. These afferents terminate in a topographic manner primarily in the caudal regions of the medial (m) part of the nucleus of the solitary tract (NTS; see Blessing, 1997, for a review).

Visceral sensory information processed in the caudal mNTS can affect the control hierarchy in two ways. First, it is relayed locally in the hindbrain (Herbert, Moga, & Saper, 1990) to influence motor (particularly autonomic) reflexes. In many respects the reflex release of pituitary hormones in response to visceral stimulation can be thought of in a similar way, since some hormone release (particularly adrenocortico-trophic hormone [ACTH], vasopressin, and oxytocin) is stimulated by direct and indirect projections from the mNTS to the neuroendocrine motor system (L. Swanson, 1987). Second, visceral sensory information is conveyed to the forebrain by direct and indirect catecholaminergic projections, which arise from the caudal NTS itself, as well as adrenergic and noradrenergic neurons in the ventral medulla and pons (Risold et al., 1997). The NTS also projects to the parabrachial nucleus (PB; Herbert et al., 1990), which in turn projects to the forebrain (Alden, Besson, & Bernard, 1994; Bernard, Alden, & Besson, 1993; Bester, Besson, & Bernard, 1997). Collectively, projections from the hindbrain target parts of the cortex, striatum (particular the striatal parts of the amygdala), pallidum (including the BST), and the hypothalamus, which then collectively can have important actions on the hypothalamic behavior controllers (Risold et al., 1997; L. Swanson, 2000a).

Humoral (See also the Section Titled "Interosensory Information"). Some parts of the control hierarchy receive interosensory information directly from the blood either in the form of metabolic substrates (glucose, free fatty acids) or hormones (e.g., insulin, leptin, glucocorticoid). This information accesses neural systems either by crossing the blood brain barrier to affect neuronal function directly or by way of projections from neurons in circumventricular organs that act as sensory transducers.

An example of a direct action is seen with those neurons in the hindbrain and hypothalamus that respond to fluctuating blood glucose levels by altering their output in a way that influences specific motor actions (Levin, Dunn-Meynell, & Routh, 1999). On the other hand, hormones directly influence the function of neurons that express specific hormone receptors. Although these receptors are expressed by many hypothalamic cell groups such as the arcuate (ARH) and ventromedial (VMH) nuclei, they are also found widely throughout the entire brain; for example, glucocorticoid receptors are found in the hippocampus and have significant effects on hippocampal neuronal function (de Kloet, Vreugdenhil, Oitzel, & Joels, 1998).

Those circumventricular organs important for controlling motivated behaviors are located in the hindbrain and hypothalamus. Of particularly significance are the subfornical organ (SFO), the vascular organ of the laminar terminalis (OVLT), both of which are located in the forebrain, and the area postrema (AP), which is located in the hindbrain. These structures are important because they lie outside the blood brain barrier and provide an interface between neurons and circulating substances that would normally not enter the brain. They also act as central osmoreceptors important for the generation of thirst.

From an anatomical perspective, circumventricular organs offer a rare opportunity to trace how sensory information known to trigger a specific behavior is distributed within the brain after it is transduced into neural signals. The SFO is perhaps the best studied from this perspective (L. Swanson, 1987). It contains receptors for angiotensin II (A-II) whose blood levels increase during hypovolemia to trigger three classes of motor actions that help protect the fluid compartment: A-II stimulates thirst (behavior) and vasopressin and glucocorticoid secretion (neuroendocrine), and activates the sympathetic motor output (autonomic). Interestingly, SFO efferents also contain A-II as a neurotransmitter and project quite specifically to those parts of the hypothalamic controllers most closely associated with the motor actions of thirst. These include the paraventricular nucleus (PVH), the lateral hypothalamic area (LHA), and supraoptic nucleus (L. Swanson, 1987). However, the SFO also projects outside the hypothalamus to other parts of the forebrain, including some of the bed nuclei of the stria terminalis (BST) and the infralimbic prefrontal cortex. These projections may be associated more with the cognitive aspects of thirst.

Exterosensory

All the classic exterosensory modalities play crucial roles in organizing motivated behaviors, although the extent to which any one predominates varies from behavior to behavior. To illustrate the organization of exterosensory pathways we describe how the information arising from one sensory modality—gustatory function, which is critically important for ingestive behaviors (Spector, 2000)—is distributed within the brain.

Gustatory.   Gustatory inputs from taste receptors in the tongue enter the brain through the facial, glossopharyngeal, and vagus nerves and terminate in the rostral zone of the mNTS. This part of the NTS has a variety of efferents (Norgen, 1984). One group provides inputs to the parvicellular and intermediate reticular formation (RF) of the hindbrain (Figure 14.6a), which in turn innervates the cell groups responsible for more reflex oromo-

tor functions that are important for moment-to-moment control during the consummatory phase of ingestive behaviors (Travers et al., 1997). Other gustatory neurons in the rostral part of the NTS generate ascending projections. The trajectory of ascending gustatory projections from the NTS then follows one of two pathways depending on the species (Figure 14.6; Norgen, 1984).

In the rat the gustatory part of the NTS (Figure 14.6a) projects to the PB, particularly to its medial division, from which two ascending gustatory pathways originate (Norgren, 1984). The first projects to some of the BST and to the medial part of the central nucleus of the amygdala (Alden et al., 1994; Bernard et al., 1993). After processing in the amygdala, gustatory information can then modulate hypothalamic function by way of projections back to the BST (Figure 14.6b), particularly its fusiform and oval nuclei, and from there to the hypothalamus (H.-W. Dong, Petrovich, Watts, & Swanson, 2001). The oval nucleus of the BST may also be an important point for the subcortical processing of information from main olfactory inputs (H.-W. Dong et al., 2001). The second pathway from the PB projects to the parvicellular part of the ventral posteriomedial nucleus of the thalamus, which then projects to the cortex, particularly the agranular insular region. In the primate (Figure 14.6a), however, gustatory-related pathways avoid the PB and project directly from the NTS to the thalamus, and from there to the insular cortex. Gustatory information also reaches the orbitofrontal cortex, where it is integrated with other types of sensory information and with reward-related signals (Rolls, 2000a; Schultz, Tremblay, & Hollerman, 2000). In both the primate and the rat, these cortical regions project back to the striatal amygdala and hypothalamus, particularly the LHA (Öngür, & Price, 1998; L. Swanson, 2000a), in a way that may offer a substrate for

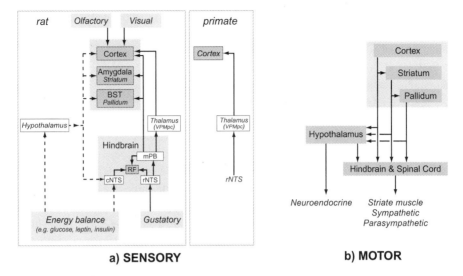

Figure 14.6 A summary of how gustatory inputs (solid lines) and inputs associated with relaying information about energy balance (dashed lines) are distributed within the rat and primate brains (a), and how outputs from the cerebral hemispheres (cortex, striatum, and pallidum) project to the hypothalamus, hindbrain, and spinal cord to control different classes of motor actions.

NOTE: Abbreviations: BST, bed nuclei of the stria terminalis; cNTS, caudal part of the nucleus of the solitary tract; rNTS, rostral part of the nucleus of the solitary tract; mPB, medial part of the parabrachial nucleus; RF, reticular formation; VPMpc, the parvicellular part of the ventral posterior medial nucleus of the thalamus.

incorporating cortically processed gustatory information into those parts of the ingestive-behavior drive networks that are located in the hypothalamus (Figure 14.6b).

Convergence of Information: Energy Balance and Taste

One important feature of the model we described earlier (Figure 14.2) is that interosensory and exterosensory information must at some point in the brain converge to bias the selection of appropriate motor actions. The arrangement of pathways associated with energy balance and gustatory processing offers some insight into how this might occur in the brain (Figure 14.6a).

As we just described, information about energy balance and taste are brought into the brain along distinct pathways. Gustatory information is first processed in the rostral

mNTS and from there is projected, at least in the rat, to the mPB. The only known projections from mPB to hypothalamus terminate in most lateral parts of the LHA (Bester et al., 1997), which current data do not implicate in the processing of energy balance information, but which do receive projections related to information from the main olfactory system (Risold et al., 1997). Some energy balance signals arrive at caudal regions of the mNTS by way of the vagal afferents, and humoral signals are transduced by receptors located in hindbrain and in hypothalamic regions, primarily the ARH. How and where might this information converge to account for changes in drive state that result in altered feeding?

The circuitry summarized in Figure 14.6a offers at least two possibilities. First, parts of the reticular formation concerned with

organizing orofacial aspects of ingestive behaviors receive inputs both from the caudal
NTS that processes visceral information and
from the rostral NTS and PB that process
gustatory information (Travers et al., 1997).
Convergence of information at this level may
account for the types of ingestive behavior that have a strong reflex component and
are expressed by decerebrate animals (Grill
& Kaplan, 1990). Second, projections from
those parts of the hypothalamus that are responsive to energy balance hormones (especially in the ARH) may influence cortical, striatal (amygdala), and pallidal (BST)
regions by way of direct ARH projections
(Broberger, Johansen, Johansson, Schalling,
& Hökfelt, 1998b), and from peptidergic neurons in the LHA that receive ARH efferents and project to the cerebral hemispheres
(see also the section titled "Example 1: Ingestive Behavior"). Information contained in
these inputs is likely reinforced by ascending catecholaminergic inputs from the hindbrain. This scheme shows that to influence
hypothalamic controllers, energy balance and
taste information most likely converge outside
the hypothalamus—probably in the cerebral
hemispheres and hindbrain—to be relayed
back to the behavior control column (Figure
14.6b). Based on currently known projections,
there does not appear to be a morphological

basis for a projection of gustatory information
directly into the control column nuclei.

Behavioral State Control: Arousal, Attention, and Circadian Timing

An animal's behavioral state is a central feature of motivated behavior and is determined
by the actions of three functional and interactive neural systems (Figures 14.7 and 14.8).
The first determines the sleep/wake status; the
second is the circadian timing system that provides many physiological and behavioral processes with an approximately 24-hour rhythm
that is coordinated with the local day/night
pattern; and the third system determines attention and vigilance states by controlling how
sensory information is directed to and from
the cortex, enabling animals to sharpen sensory receptive fields and to direct attention
toward salient sensory objects in the environment. As we discussed earlier, these behavioral state systems send efferents to all
other parts of the brain to influence all neural processes related to motivated behaviors
(Figure 14.3b). The detailed neuroanatomy
of these systems is highly complex, and here
we offer only a brief survey that focuses on
their organization as it relates to the forebrain
systems critical for controlling motivated
behaviors.

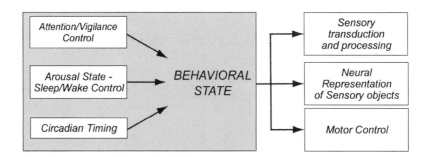

Figure 14.7   Behavioral state is generated by the interaction of networks that control attention and
vigilance, arousal state (including sleep/wake), and circadian timing.
NOTE: The output of behavioral state systems has a significant impact on the other three networks that
control motivated behaviors.

Arousal State Control

The arousal state of an animal is fundamental to behavioral expression, and the sleep/wake cycle is the major determinant for patterns of behavioral expression. Arousal states are initiated, maintained, and switched by distinct but interactive neural networks that have components situated throughout the brain. Three highly complex and interconnected neural systems located in the hindbrain, hypothalamus, and the basal forebrain appear to play key roles in controlling these aspects of arousal states (Figure 14.8a).

Hindbrain. Many neuroanatomical studies during the past 30 years have confirmed the existence of diffusely projecting monoaminergic and cholinergic neural systems that originate in the hindbrain. Clarifying the detailed projection patterns of these cell groups has revealed that they exhibit diversity in their physiology, projection patterns, and targets (Aston-Jones, Shipley, & Grzanna, 1995; B. Jones, 1995). Attention has focused on three sets of neurons in the hindbrain, notably the noradrenergic locus coeruleus (LC), the serotonergic raphe nuclei (RN), and cholinergic neurons confined to the peduncular pontine nucleus (PPN) and laterodorsal tegmental nucleus (LDT). Each of these nuclei exhibits firing patterns that closely correlate with arousal state (McGinty & Seigel, 1983), and their outputs are thought to be instrumental in controlling different sleep/wake states through projections both into the forebrain and into more caudal regions of the hindbrain and spinal cord (B. Jones, 1995).

Hypothalamus. A role for the hypothalamus in controlling arousal state was suspected during the earliest days of hypothalamic neurology (reviewed in Le Gros Clark, 1938). In particular, the observations of von

Economo (1931) and Ranson (1939) and the seminal lesion study of Nauta (1946) provided important data on the role of the hypothalamus in controlling arousal state.

Von Economo (1931) correlated the existence of tumors in the ventral transitional zone between the diencephalon and mesencephalon with encephalitis lethargica, in which patients develop hypersomnia, insomnia, inversion of sleep rhythms, and occasional narcolepsy. After observing the somnolegenic effects of lesions in the monkey lateral hypothalamus, Ranson (1939) concluded that the hypothalamus played an important role in maintaining wakefulness. Anticipating the widely projecting melanin-concentrating hormone (MCH) and H/OR lateral hypothalamic systems, he stated that "it is probable that the active hypothalamus not only discharges downward through the brain stem, spinal cord and peripheral nervous system into the body, but also upward into the thalamus and cerebral cortex," (p. 18). However, these long ascending and descending projections remained more or less unknown for at least another 30 years. Nauta (1946) showed that coronal transsections of the rat caudal hypothalamus were related to hypersomnolence, whereas similar lesions in the rostral hypothalamus were associated with hyposomnolence. He postulated that sleep was generated by the interaction of sleep-promoting and wake-promoting centers in the anterior and posterior hypothalamus, respectively.

In the years following Nauta's findings, little progress was made in clarifying the organization of hypothalamic sleep systems. However, this has changed dramatically in the past few years, and recent data have added a great deal to how we comprehend the structure of the hypothalamic systems that control arousal state. Three chemically defined systems in particular have emerged as central components of this hypothalamic arousal system: histaminergic neurons in the TM, H/OR

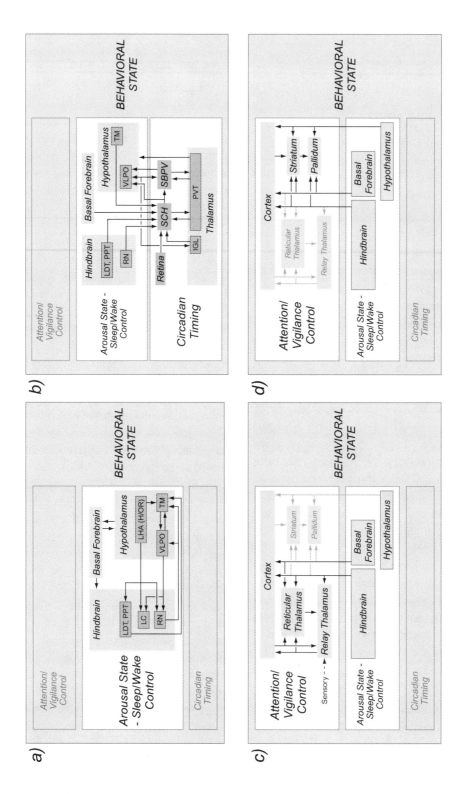

Figure 14.8 Schematic diagrams of the projections of regions involved with behavioral state control.

582

neurons found in tuberal levels of the lateral hypothalamus, and GABAergic/galanin neurons in the VLPO. These recent findings strongly suggest that these three sets of hypothalamic neurons control arousal states by forming a network with neurons in the basal forebrain and with monoaminergic and cholinergic neurons in the hindbrain (Figure 14.8a). In turn, this network affects sleep onset and wakefulness in way that generates a stable sleep/wake cycle when influenced by projections from the circadian timing system (Figure 14.8b; Kilduff & Peyron, 2000).

A. Tuberomammillary Nucleus. The TM contains all the histaminergic neurons in the brain (Panula, Pirvola, Auvinen, & Airaksinen, 1989) many of which are also GABAergic (Kohler, Swanson, Haglund, & Wu, 1985). The TM, a thin sheet of neurons that is located adjacent to the base of the brain, receives afferents from throughout the brain (Ericson, Blomqvist, & Kohler, 1991). Based on distribution of histaminergic fibers, TM neurons have widespread projections throughout the brain (Panula et al., 1989). There are at least three different histamine receptor subtypes, which have seven transmembrane domains and modulate neuronal cyclic AMP levels. Histamine is closely associated with controlling arousal state.

B. Lateral Hypothalamic Area. A recently identified cell group that appears to be closely associated with the control of arousal state consists of H/OR-containing neurons. The H/OR gene encodes two neuropeptides (H/OR 1 and 2) that are expressed in a set of neurons throughout a wide extent of the LHA caudal to the level of the PVH. Three important findings emphasize the central role played by H/OR neurons in promoting wakefulness: the tendency of H/OR knockout mice to show narcoleptic-like features (Chemelli et al., 1999), the fact that narcoleptic dogs have a mutation in the H/OR receptor 2 gene (Lin et al., 1999), and the report that the LHA of patients with narcolepsy show a dramatic loss of H/OR neurons (Thannickal et al., 2000).

H/OR neurons project widely within the brain and innervate regions from the frontal cortex to the spinal cord (Kilduff & Peyron, 2000; Peyron et al., 1998). Like VLPO efferents, H/OR neurons innervate the TM and the LC (Kilduff & Peyron, 2000; Peyron et al., 1998; Figure 14.8a). Indeed, H/OR projections to the LC are particularly striking and target the core of the nucleus rather than its shell. H/OR-containing fibers are also found in close apposition to cholinergic neurons in the PPN, LDT, and basal forebrain (Chemelli et al., 1999).

In accordance with its putative role in increasing arousal, H/OR strongly depolarizes target neurons and increases their intracellular calcium levels (de Lecea et al., 1998; van den Pol, Gao, Obrietan, Kilduff, & Belousov,

---

Figure 14.8 (*Continued*)

NOTE: Those regions concerned with arousal state and sleep/wake control are shown in (a); those responsible for circadian timing are shown in (b). Two systems involved with attention and vigilance are shown in (c) and (d): (c) shows the projections that influence thalamocortical oscillations; (d) represents the diffuse projections from the basal forebrain, and hindbrain that innervate the cerebral hemispheres that are thought to be important for mediating the influence of arousal state on attention and vigilance control. Abbreviations: H/OR, hypocretin/orexin; IGL, intergeniculate leaflet; LC, locus coeruleus, LDT, laterodorsal tegmental nucleus; LHA, lateral hypothalamic area; PPT, peduncular pontine nucleus; PVT, paraventricular nucleus of the thalamus; RN, raphe nuclei; SBPV, subparaventricular zone; SCH, suprachiasmatic nucleus; TM, tuberomammillary nucleus; VLPO, ventrolateral preoptic nucleus.

1998). In addition, application of H/OR1 to the LC suppresses REM sleep and increases wakefulness (Bourgin et al., 2000), and Fos expression is increased in H/OR neurons during both pharmacological- and behavioral-induced arousal (Scammell et al., 2000; Watts & Sanchez-Watts, 2000).

C. Ventrolateral Preoptic Nucleus. Although the preoptic region of the hypothalamus has long been associated with the regulation of sleep (von Economo, 1931; Nauta, 1946), identifying which of its component neurons were responsible for this function proved elusive for many years. Recent findings have focused attention on the VLPO, a small cell group located adjacent to the ventral surface of the hypothalamus that contains mostly galanin and GABA-expressing neurons (Sherin, Shiromani, McCarley, & Saper, 1996). Its importance for promoting sleep is shown by the fact that VLPO neurons preferentially show Fos expression during sleep (Sherin et al., 1996), while lesions of the VLPO significantly decrease the time spent in non-REM sleep (Lu, Greco, Shiromani, & Saper, 2000).

Critically, VLPO neurons project to three other cell groups heavily implicated in arousal state control (Figure 14.8a): the TM, the dorsal RN, and the LC (Sherin et al., 1998; Steininger et al., 2000). Interestingly, the strong GABAergic projection from the VLPO to the TM (Sherin et al., 1998; Sherin et al., 1996; Steininger et al., 2001) accords with Nauta's proposal for interconnected centers that are located in the rostral and caudal hypothalamus that respectively promote sleep or wakefulness (Nauta, 1946).

Basal Forebrain. The term *basal forebrain* (BF) is commonly used with reference to a collection of mainly cholinergic and GABAergic neurons that are distributed across the substantia innominata, medial septal nucleus/nucleus of the diagonal band, and magnocellular preoptic nucleus. They have for many years been variously associated with arousal state, learning and memory, and attention and vigilance control (Semba, 2000). In some ways BF neurons are similar to the monoaminergic neurons in the hindbrain discussed earlier in that they are chemically diverse and have wide-ranging projections throughout the brain (Semba, 2000). However, the degree of collateralization of BF neurons, though quite extensive locally (Zaborsky & Duque, 2000), is much more limited than is the case for monoaminergic neurons; each type of BF neuron has relatively limited projections.

Semba (2000) has proposed that BF efferents can be usefully placed into four functionally distinct systems:

1. Some descending cholinergic and GABAergic projections to hypothalamus and hindbrain may target neurons in the LHA and posterior hypothalamus and hindbrain (including the TM, LC, PPN, and RN) that control arousal state (Figure 14.8a), while others project to the SCH (Bina, Rusak, & Semba, 1993) and may be involved with circadian timing mechanisms (Figure 14.8b).

2. Mixed neurochemical (cholinergic, GABAergic, peptidergic, and possibly glutamatergic) projections to the entire cerebral cortex and reticular nucleus of the thalamus are in a position to influence cortical arousal and selective attention (Figure 14.8c).

3. Many cholinergic neurons in the substantia innominata project to the amygdala and may be involved with coordinating emotional appraisals with autonomic motor actions.

4. Some BF GABAergic neurons receive dopaminergic inputs from the nucleus accumbens and send descending projections

to the mediodorsal nucleus of the thalamus, hypothalamus, and ventral tegmental area. In this manner reward information encoded by dopaminergic neurons can be integrated by neurons important for motor control (Kalivas & Nakamura, 1999). Other BF neurons of this type may be concerned with regulating specific behaviors, such as those that are involved with the effects that the nucleus accumbens has on feeding behavior (Stratford & Kelley, 1997; Stratford, Kelley, & Simansky, 1999).

This type of representation emphasizes the complexity of BF function and shows the difficulty of trying to characterize it in terms of the schema presented in Figure 14.3. However, rather than considering BF neurons as a single entity, segregating the BF into the four functional groups just described shows that each fits more easily into this schema. Thus, BF group 1 neurons are related to arousal state functions; group 2 neurons are involved with the types of vigilance control described in the section titled "Attention and Vigilance Control"; group 3 may be involved with orchestrating the neural representations of sensory objects; and group 4 neurons seem to more related to integrating sensory object representation (e.g., reward function) with motor action selection.

Suprachiasmatic Nucleus and Circadian Timing

All physiological and behavioral rhythms that have a circadian period require the SCH for reliable timing. The effects of lesions have for the most part shown that the SCH is the only neural cell group that can act as a circadian generator. Lesion studies suggest that rather than acting as a switch that controls motor actions in a go/no-go manner, the SCH provides a timing signal that gates information flow to a variety of motor control networks (Watts,

1991). In this manner, animals with SCH lesions do not lose the ability to initiate motor actions; rather, they cannot organize these actions into circadian-defined temporal patterns and instead tend to express ultradian patterns of motor actions.

The SCH is a compact hypothalamic nucleus made up of small densely packed neurons located bilaterally at the base of the third ventricle (van den Pol, 1980). The vast majority of its neurons are GABAergic, although there is evidence for neurons that express excitatory neurotransmitters (Hermes, Caderre, Buijs, & Renaud, 1996; Sun, Rusak, & Semba, 2000). SCH neurons also express a variety of the neuropeptides, which are topographically expressed within the nucleus in a manner that is maintained by its efferent pathways (Leak & Moore, 2001; Watts & Swanson, 1987). These include vasopressin, vasoactive intestinal polypeptide (VIP), somatostatin, gastrin-releasing peptide, and, in the human, neurotensin (Mai, Kedziora, Teckhaus, & Sofroniew, 1991). Some studies have shown that these neuropeptides can influence the period of behavioral rhythms (Albers, Liou, Stopa, & Zoeller, 1991).

Compared to its contiguous regions, the SCH itself receives only a relatively sparse afferent input (Moga & Moore, 1997), perhaps reflecting the fact that its primary function is to generate a circadian timing signal that requires little influence from the rest of the brain. However, its pattern of afferents does emphasize the role of the photoperiod in entraining circadian rhythms as well as the importance of feedback from systems involved with controlling arousal state. One of its principal afferents is from the retina (Figure 14.8b), and this provides sensory information for entraining circadian rhythm generators to the prevailing photoperiod. Thus, some retino-geniculate fibers collateralize in the optic chiasm to innervate the SCH (Card & Moore, 1991). A secondary indirect photic input is provided by a projection from the intergeniculate leaflet of the lateral geniculate nucleus that contains neuropeptide Y (Card & Moore, 1991).

A second set of afferents derives from neurons that are concerned broadly with arousal state (Figure 14.8b). These include a histaminergic input from the rat TM (Panula et al., 1989), a cholinergic input from the basal forebrain, LDT, PPN (Bina et al., 1993), and a serotonergic input from the raphe magnus (Meyer-Bernstein & Morin, 1996). Apart from the TM, the other hypothalamic arousal state systems provide at the most only sparse inputs (Peyron et al., 1998). With regard to function, the serotonergic input is the best characterized and is thought to be involved with entrainment of rhythms to the local photoperiod (Meyer-Bernstein & Morin, 1996).

The major output from the SCH is to a rather poorly differentiated medial hypothalamic region called the subparaventricular zone (SBPV; Leak & Moore, 2001; Watts, 1991; Watts, Swanson, & Sanchez-Watts, 1987). The SBPV is delineated, at least in part, by vasopressin- and VIP-containing fibers originating in the dorsal and ventral SCH, respectively (Watts & Swanson, 1987). It begins at the dorsocaudal borders of the SCH and extends dorsally toward the PVH, before turning more caudally toward the dorsomedial nucleus (DMH), and finally ventrally to the cell-sparse region between the VMH and the ARH (Watts, 1991).

Other hypothalamic nuclei that receive significant direct inputs from the SCH include the anteroventral periventricular nucleus (AVPV) and the DMH, which contains a predominantly vasopressin-containing input from the SCH (R. H. Thompson & Swanson, 1998; Watts & Swanson, 1987). Neuroanatomical tracing techniques have demonstrated few SCH-derived terminals within the borders of the supraoptic, PVH, ARH, and VMH. However, electrophysiological data suggest that

the SCH may have direct interactions with neurons in some of these hypothalamic nuclei (Cui, Saeb-Parsy, & Dyball, 1997; Hermes et al., 1996; Saeb-Parsy et al., 2000). The paraventricular nucleus of the thalamus (PVT), which has bidirectional projections with the SCH, may be important for distributing circadian information more widely within the forebrain (Leak & Moore, 2001; Moga, Weis, & Moore, 1995; Watts et al., 1987).

There are no projections from the SCH timing system to the activating systems in the hindbrain, and only sparse projections to hypothalamic regions known to control arousal state directly. Thus, the SCH and SBPV send only meager inputs to the VLPO (Gaus & Saper, 1998; Novak & Nunuz, 2000) and no reported inputs to the TM (Watts et al., 1987); a recent report documented possible projections to the H/OR neurons in the LHA (Abrahamson, Leak, & Moore, 2001).

The SBPV duplicates much of the output from the SCH (Watts et al., 1987). In particular, the PVT, DMH, and AVPV receive strong projections from both the SCH and the SBPV (R. H. Thompson, Canteras, & Swanson, 1996; Watts, 1991; Watts et al., 1987), while SBPV projections to the VMH, lateral septum, and parts of the preoptic region are qualitatively stronger than are those from the SCH (Morin, Goodless-Sanchez, Smale, & Moore, 1994; Watts, 1991; Watts et al., 1987). The SBPV also receives a wider variety of afferents including some—like those from the lateral septal nuclei, ventral subiculum, and VMH—that do not directly innervate the SCH (Canteras, Simerly, & Swanson, 1994; Elmquist, Ahima, Elias, Flier, & Saper, 1998; Moga & Moore, 1997; Risold & Swanson, 1997). Lesion studies suggest that there is a functional topography within the SBPV. Thus, knife cuts made in the SBPV proximal to the SCH are more effective than are distal lesions at attenuating circadian-dependent gonadotropin secretion (Watts, Sheward, Whale,

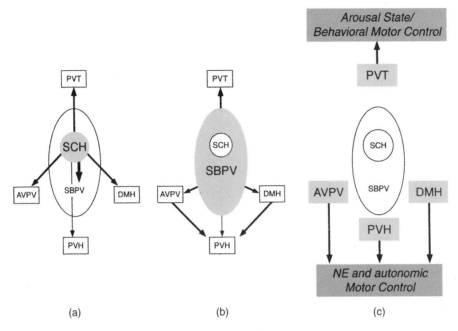

Figure 14.9   (a) The output of the suprachiasmatic nucleus (SCH) to target regions represented as a two-stage process that involves major inputs from the SCH to the subparaventricular zone (SBPV). (b) Important target regions from the SCH and SBPV include the anteroventral periventricular nucleus (AVPV), dorsomedial nucleus (DMH), paraventricular nucleus of the hypothalamus (PVH), and paraventricular nucleus of the thalamus (PVT). (c) In turn, the outputs of the AVPV, DMH, PVH, and PVT are each associated with specific motor functions.

& Fink, 1989), whereas ventral SBPV or dorsal SBPV lesions differentially attenuate body temperature and sleep/activity rhythms (Chou et al., 1999). Taken together, these findings suggest that at a first level of approximation, the SCH and SBPV (and perhaps the PVT) act in a two-stage process to integrate circadian signals with a variety of neural influences (Leak & Moore, 2001; Watts, 1991), which confers circadian rhythmicity to many physiologic and behavioral motor outputs (Figure 14.9).

Attention and Vigilance Control

By allowing animals to focus and switch attention between objects in the environment that have incentive salience, mechanisms that control vigilance states and develop selective attention play crucial roles in the execution of motivated behaviors. At the simplest level these motor actions are merely reflex-orienting movements developed in response to novel stimuli. In other cases, however, orienting responses involve directing the animal's attention toward objects that have acquired salience through reinforcement learning mechanisms. Studies suggest that these more complex attentional processes involve regions in the telencephalon such as the cortex, amygdala, and basal forebrain (Everitt & Robbins, 1997; Holland & Gallagher, 1999; Semba, 2000). Although detailed consideration of the neural systems implicated in these functions is beyond the scope of this chapter, we briefly describe the organization of the two systems concerned with processing sensory information in ways that affect vigilance and selective attention. First are the thalamic circuits that control sensory information flow to and from the cortex in a manner that focuses or sharpens certain sensory receptive fields while inhibiting others. Second are the networks that use processed sensory information to execute motor actions in a way that orients and maintains the animal's posture in a position toward one goal object at the expense of others.

The divergent projections of the subcortical arousal networks to both of these systems impart a mechanism for incorporating arousal state into attention processes (Figure 14.8c and 14.8d). By and large, most of the data that forms the basis for our understanding of selective attention and orienting responses relate to the visual system; in this respect, parts of the thalamus (particularly the pulvinar, which is especially well developed in the primate), the superior colliculus, and the motor cortices are all heavily implicated. However, all the other sensory modalities can also affect selective attention and orienting responses, but these are perhaps less well understood than for are those for visual processes.

The Control of Thalamo-Cortical Information Flow.   A process that is central to the control of selective attention is the ability of neural networks to highlight the receptive fields of certain sensory objects while at the same time inhibiting others. These networks also play important roles in managing how sensory information is processed during different arousal states. In addition, they have been implicated in the wider issue of how consciousness is generated (Llinas, Ribary, Canteras, & Pedroarena, 1998).

The most prominent and well studied system in this regard involves the RT, and lesion studies suggest that RT is involved with attentional orienting (Weese, Phillips, & Brown, 1999). The RT consists of GABAergic neurons that form a sheath around the core of thalamus. By virtue of its connections, it acts as an interface between the sensory parts of the thalamus and the cortex. Thalamic sensory relay neurons are glutamatergic and send their axons in a highly topographic manner to appropriate parts of sensory cortex. However, many of these axons have collaterals that innervate the RT. In turn, axons from RT neurons then project back onto the sensory relay neurons (Figure 14.8c). RT neurons also receive inputs from cortical efferents. Originally, it was thought that information processing in the RT was relatively homogenous, in that topographic sensory representation was relatively diffuse within the RT. However, recent studies have suggested that there is greater topography of sensory modalities in the RN than previously suspected (Guillery, Feig, & Lozsadi, 1998).

Arousal state has critical influences on how sensory information accesses the cortex, and this is mediated by cholinergic, serotonergic, and noradrenergic projections from basal forebrain, midbrain, and hindbrain cell groups (Figure 14.8c). These inputs modulate the firing patterns of RT neurons in a way that is dependent on arousal state to alter the transmission of sensory information to the cortex, and they produce the characteristic sleep/wake patterns of thalamo-cortical oscillations (Steriade, 2000).

Attention and Motor Control.   The role of telencephalic structures such as the amygdala, basal forebrain, and cortex in controlling attentional processes is highly complex (e.g., Everitt & Robbins, 1997; Holland & Gallagher, 1999; Semba, 2000), and it is beyond the scope of this chapter to describe the anatomy of these systems in any detail. However, what is clear is that attentional processes must involve motor cortical functions that control head, neck, and body positioning. To illustrate some of the neuroanatomical concepts involved with attentional processes of motivated behaviors, we will describe one example based on the organization of projections from the medial zone of the hypothalamus: how the pheromonal information important for initiating rodent reproductive behavior might be processed to affect head, neck, and body orientation.

Rodents use pheromones for orienting responses toward conspecifics in such a way as to begin the behavioral sequences that culminate with mating. Pheromones are transduced by receptors in the vomeronasal organ that project to the accessory olfactory bulb and then to the medial and posteriomedial cortical nuclei of the amygdala (L. Swanson & Petrovich, 1998). This pathway differs from that used by the types of olfactory stimuli detected by the primary olfactory system. In turn, pheromonal information is relayed in a topographic manner to the medial hypothalamus by substantial medial amygdalar projections to the anterior hypothalamic (AHN) and ventromedial nuclei (Figure 14.10), which with the dorsal premammillary nucleus (PMd) form a network in the rostral behavior control column that is intimately concerned with reproductive behaviors (Canteras & Swanson, 1992).

The neurons in this network provide two sets of outputs that may mediate pheromonal influences on the motor circuits required for attentional actions (Figure 14.10; see also the section titled "The Rostral Behavior Control Column"). The first set of outputs consists of descending projections to the periaqueductal gray (PAG) that have well documented actions in controlling the lordosis reflex in the female rat (Pfaff, 1999) and that might have a wider role in organizing the behavioral actions that occur before intromission. Second are projections to the rostral division of the nucleus reuniens (REr) and the ventral anteromedial nucleus of the thalamus (AMv). Information is relayed from these thalamic regions through extensive cortical projections both to the hippocampus and to the retrospenial area and the

frontal eye fields (Risold & Swanson, 1995). These cortical areas are important for controlling the eye-, neck-, and body-orienting movements by way of multiple projections to the superior colliculus and the PAG (Swanson, 2000a; Risold & L. Swanson, 1995).

Neural Representation of Sensory Objects

The brain's ability to manipulate information about objects in their sensory environment is a central feature of motivational control. These neural processes allow animals to form, retrieve, and update their appraisals of sensory space and objects within it. In turn, this type of processing gives animals the ability to generate behavioral motor programs that can, for example, anticipate energy deficits. The neural processing underlying these functions achieves a remarkable degree of sophistication in advanced vertebrates and is the subject of intense investigation.

The neural pathways mediating the interactions between the neural systems concerned with sensory object representation and the motor control networks (Figures 14.3c and 14.3d) are highly complex and not yet fully understood. However, the integrative operations that designate and coordinate these aspects of motivated behaviors most likely require sets of bidirectional connections between the hypothalamus and cortical structures, such as the prefrontal cortex and hippocampus, as well as subcortical regions in the basal ganglia (Öngür & Price, 1998, 2000; Risold et al., 1997; Saper, 1985; L. Swanson 2000a; L. Swanson & Petrovich, 1998).

The regions of the brain responsible for these functions include:

1. *Reward/punishment systems in the midbrain ventral tegmentum, amygdala, and parts of the cortex, particularly prefrontal regions.* Dopaminergic systems in the midbrain and their projections into various

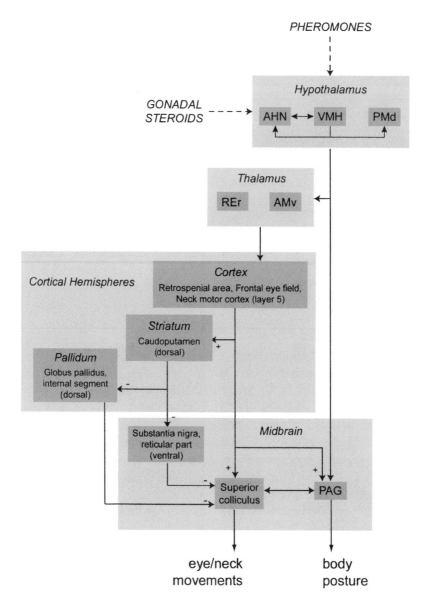

Figure 14.10 Projections from the hypothalamus, thalamus, and cortex to the midbrain thought to be involved with the head and body orientation.

NOTE: That the hypothalamic components can be influenced by pheromones and gonadal steroids implicates this circuit in the procurative phase of rodent reproductive behavior. Abbreviations: AHN, anterior hypothalamic nucleus; AMv, ventral part of the anteromedial nucleus of the thalamus; PAG, periaqueductal gray; PMd, dorsal premammillary nucleus; REr, rostral part of the nucleus reuniens; VMH, ventromedial nucleus of the hypothalamus.

SOURCE: Adapted from Risold and Swanson (1995); L. Swanson (2000a).

parts of the telencephalon have been strongly implicated in these processes (Rolls, 1999a, 2000a; Schultz et al., 2000).

2. *Systems in the hippocampus, parts of the parietal cortex, and other regions of the brain containing place and head-direction neurons.* These neurons fire preferentially in certain locales or head positions and are thought to be responsible for allocentric and egocentric spatial representation (Maguire et al., 1998; Taube, 1998). In this respect, territoriality is an important part of many motivated behaviors, and though not yet well understood, interactions between these systems and those parts of the hypothalamus responsible for controlling the locality aspects of motivated behaviors are likely to be important. Of particular interest in this regard is the fact that outputs from the ventral subiculum and lateral septal nuclei project topographically to the behavior control column (Risold & Swanson, 1996) and may provide a morphological substrate for the interaction of spatial information with the control of motivated behaviors to generate the types of motor responses required for territoriality.

3. *Learning and memory mechanisms in the cerebellum and in the cortical hemispheres.* Rolls (2000b) usefully divided cortical memory systems into four parts. The first is involved with representing the hedonic value of a stimulus and then learning stimulus-reinforcement associations. Neurons for this function are found in the amygdala and in the orbitofrontal cortex, which is particularly important in the primate for these processes. The second is concerned with learning invariant representations of a sensory object (e.g., recognizing that an object is a particular type of fruit). The temporal cortical visual areas are important here. The third part consists of short-term memory functions in the frontal and temporal cortices, and the fourth part consists of systems in the hippocampus that deal with episodic and spatial memory. Mechanisms in the cerebellum are responsible for the memory involved with Pavlovian conditioning of motor responses (R. F. Thompson & Kim, 1996).

Much exterosensory information is collectively processed through these networks, parts of which—particularly those responsible for reward/punishment and memory—assign what has been called *incentive value* to a goal object (Toates, 1986), which is effectively a measure of the reinforcement value of a goal object at a particular time. Whether incentive value is encoded by a quantifiable entity within a neural network or is an intervening variable between stimulus and response is not known.

Motor Control

Motor Hierarchies and the Triple Output of the Cerebral Hemispheres

For many years the established view of voluntary motor control has revolved dogmatically around the notion of loops and hierarchies located within a system composed of the cortex, thalamus, basal ganglia, cerebellum, brainstem, and spinal cord. Although this model is without question the foundation for virtually all our concepts of motor control, it is not without its problems, not least of which are the difficulties of nomenclature as well as the conspicuous absence of a role for the hypothalamus (L. Swanson, 2000a, 2000b).

Based mainly on traditional and molecular developmental data, L. Swanson (2000a) reconsidered this whole organization and proposed that many of the anomalies and confusions might be rationalized if we simply consider the constituents of the telencephalon—neocortex, hippocampus, basal ganglia, ventral forebrain, amygdala, septal complex, and BST—as being either cortical, striatal, or pallidal. Although this model is quite consistent with many well-accepted neuroanatomical and functional data (see L. Swanson, 2000a, for references), other aspects are more novel (e.g., L. Swanson & Petrovich, 1998). It states that the cortical part of the cerebral hemispheres includes the isocortex, neocortex, olfactory cortex, the hippocampus, and the cortical parts of the amygdala (L. Swanson & Petrovich, 1998); the striatum includes the caudate-putamen, the lateral septal complex, and the medial and central nuclei of the amygdala; whereas the pallidum includes the globus pallidus, the substantia innominata, the medial septum and the nucleus of the diagonal band, and BST (Table 14.1).

The fundamental output pattern of these components is then relatively simple and can be summarized as follows. The cerebral hemispheres generate a triple descending projection to the motor system, based on the classical isocortical-striatal-pallidal model (see Swanson, 2000a, for references), and the projections from structurally and functionally differentiated regions of the cerebrum (e.g., traditionally defined regions such as the amygdala and basal ganglia) are variations on this arrangement.

Thus, the adult minimal or prototypical circuit element (Figure 14.11) consists of:

1. An excitatory (glutamatergic) projection from cortex to the brainstem (recall that the brainstem part of the motor system, as defined here, includes the hypothalamus) and spinal cord motor system, with an excitatory collateral (Lévesque, Gagnon, Parent, & Deschênes, 1996a) to the striatum.

2. An inhibitory (GABAergic) projection from the striatum to the brainstem motor system, with an inhibitory collateral (Parent & Cicchetti, 1998) to the pallidum.

3. An inhibitory (GABAergic) projection from the pallidum to the brainstem motor system, with an inhibitory collateral (Parent & Cicchetti, 1998) to the thalamus. Functionally, the pallidal projection is disinhibitory (Roberts, 1976) because it is inhibited by the striatal input, which in turn is excited by the cortical input.

Figure 14.11 shows that the descending projection to the brainstem/spinal cord motor system from the isocortex arises primarily from layer 5, whereas the isocortical projection to thalamus arises predominantly from layer 6; cortical associational/commissural projections arise preferentially from supragranular layers 2 and 3 (see E. Jones, 1984; Lévesque, Charara, Gagnon, Parent, & Deschênes, 1996b).

Using these organizational principles, we now consider the various parts of this motor hierarchy in more detail.

Table 14.1   Simple Scheme for the Topographic Regionalization of the Basal Ganglia/Cerebral Nuclei.

	Dorsal	Ventral	Medial	Caudorostral
Striatum	Caudate Putamen	Nucleus accumbens Striatal fundus Olfactory tubercle	Lateral Septal Complex	Amygdala Medial nucleus Central nucleus Anterior nucleus Intercalated nuclei
Pallidum	Globus pallidus internal and external segments	Substantia innominata Magnocellular preoptic nucleus	Medial Septal/nucleus of the diagonal band	Bed nuclei of the stria terminalis

SOURCE: Adapted from Swanson (2000a).

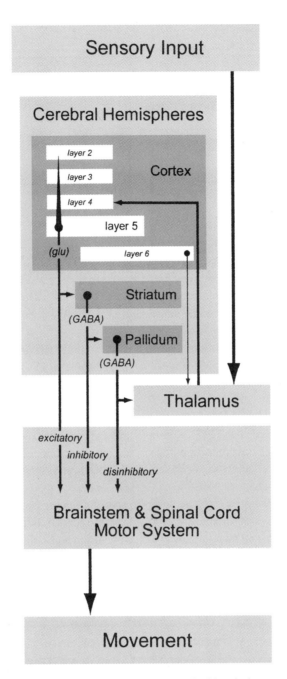

Figure 14.11 The triple cascading projection from the cerebral hemispheres to the brainstem motor system.

NOTE: This minimal or prototypical circuit element consists of a glutamatergic (glu) projection from layer 5 pyramidal neurons of the isocortex (or equivalent pyramidal neurons in allocortex), with a glutamatergic collateral to the striatum. These neurons receive part of their inputs from an apical dendrite that extends to cortical layer 2. The dual projection from layer 5 neurons appears to be excitatory. The striatum then generates a GABAergic projection to the motor system, with a GABAergic collateral to the pallidum. This dual striatal projection appears to be inhibitory. Finally, the pallidum generates a GABAergic projection to the brainstem motor system, with a GABAergic collateral to the dorsal thalamus. This dual pallidal projection can be viewed as disinhibitory because it is inhibited by the striatal input.

The Behavior Control Column and Drive Networks

Lesion and electrical stimulation experiments identified some time ago that the hypothalamus is a key structure for the expression of motivated behaviors. More recently, a wealth of neuropharmacological data has revealed that many neuropeptides have either stimulatory or inhibitory effects on particular motor functions. In turn, the fact that many of these neuropeptides are synthesized in hypothalamic neurons, which in some cases project extensively throughout the brain, has focused attention on this forebrain region as the key locus of specific drive network components.

To begin elaborating the structural principles underlying how the hypothalamus controls motivated behaviors, L. Swanson and his colleagues have over the past 15 years undertaken a systematic analysis of axonal projections from the medial half of the hypothalamus using more than 200 *Phaseolus vulgaris* leucoagglutinin injections (see L. Swanson, 2000a, for references). Collectively, these studies suggest that distinct cell groups in the hypothalamic medial zone form a *behavior control column* (Figure 14.5) at the top of the motor system hierarchy that we discussed in the section titled "Motor Hierarchies" (Figure 14.4). Synthesizing results from a wealth of studies that have measured the effects of lesions, electrical stimulations, and microinjections on behavior demonstrates that the behavior control column is functionally segregated in such a way as to control different classes of motivated behaviors. As discussed earlier, from the perspective of dissecting the functional organization of the behavior control column, it is useful to incorporate the idea that different sets of component neurons in the hypothalamic controllers either stimulate or inhibit specific behaviors in a manner that is consistent with their function as drive neurons (Figure 14.4).

Arranged from rostral to caudal, the behavior control column nuclei include the medial preoptic nucleus (MPN), AHN, the descending division of the PVH, the ventromedial nucleus (and adjacent tuberal nucleus), the PMd and ventral premammillary nuclei (PMv), and the mammillary body. Its rostral segment—the preoptic-premammillary part—plays a critical role in circuits regulating the four basic classes of goal-oriented behavior common to all animals: thermoregulatory, ingestive, reproductive, and defensive. The caudal segment—the mammillary-nigral part—plays a critical role in circuits underlying the expression of exploratory or foraging behavior.

Foraging Behavior and the Caudal Behavior Control Column.   When we examine the types of bodily movements required for exploratory and foraging behavior, we see that locomotion and the ability to orient the head and body toward salient environmental stimuli feature prominently. Based on connectional and physiological data, neurons in the mammillary body, substantia nigra (reticular part), and ventral tegmental area of the caudal behavior control column may be critically involved with both of these actions (Figure 14.5). Three observations support this assertion.

First, although the functional role of the ventral tegmental area is undoubtedly complex, there is little doubt that it is a critical component of the system that controls the expression of locomotor behavior (see C. Swanson & Kalivas, 2000).

Second, as we discussed earlier when considering the motor organization of selective attention (Figure 14.10), the reticular part of the substantia nigra plays a critical role in the expression of orienting movements of the eyes, head, and neck, and even of the upper limbs, by way of its massive projection to the deeper layers of the superior colliculus (Figure 14.12; e.g., Chevalier, Vacher,

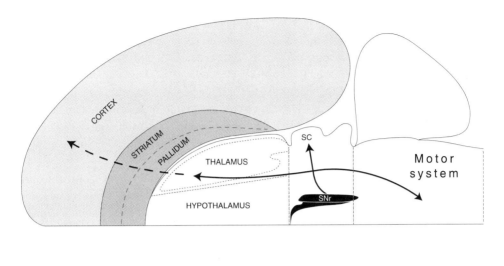

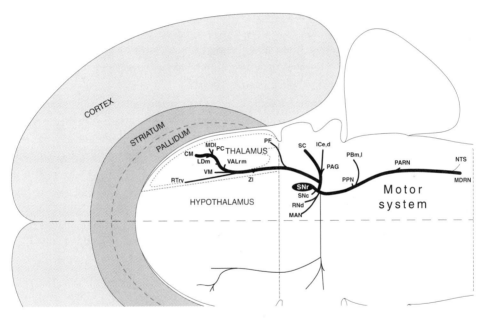

Figure 14.12   The outputs of the reticular part of the substantia nigra as an example of the projections of the caudal behavior control column.

NOTE: This nucleus sends projections to the thalamus, superior colliculus, and the motor system in the hindbrain. Outputs are summarized in the upper panel and shown in detail in lower panel. Abbreviations: CM, central medial nucleus; ICd,e, inferior colliculus, dorsal, external nuclei; LDm, lateral dorsal nucleus, medial region; MAN, medial accessory nucleus; MDl, mediodorsal nucleus, lateral part; MDRN, medullary reticular nucleus; NTS, nucleus solitary tract; PAG, periaqueductal gray; PARN, parvicellular reticular nucleus; PBm, parabrachial nucleus, medial division; PC, paracentral nucleus; PF, parafascicular nucleus; PPN, pedunculopontine nucleus/midbrain extrapyramidal area; RNd, red nucleus, dorsal region; RTrv, reticular nucleus thalamus, rostroventral region; SC, superior colliculus, deeper layers; SNr, substantia nigra, reticular parts; VALrm, ventral anterior lateral complex, rostromedial division; VM, ventral medial nucleus thalamus; ZI, zona incerta.

SOURCE: Adapted from L. Swanson (2000a).

Deniau, & Desban, 1985; Hikosaka & Wurtz, 1983; Stuphorn, Bauswein, & Hoffman, 2000; Werner, Hoffman, & Dannenberg, 1997).

Third, quite unexpected insights into the long enigmatic functions of the mammillary body have recently emerged (see Blair, Cho, & Sharp, 1998; Goodridge & Taube, 1997; Taube, 1998). Neurons in the mammillary body (and the anterior thalamic nuclei) display the features of head direction or compass cells, firing maximally when the animal's head is pointed in a certain direction within the environment. Interestingly, whereas neurons with this basic neurophysiological profile are present in the parietal cortex and subicular complex of the hippocampal formation, lesions there do not alter dramatically the physiological properties of head direction cells in the anterior thalamic nuclei. However, lesions in this part of the diencephalon abolish head direction responses in the subicular complex in the hippocampus. Preliminary evidence suggests that vestibular information about head orientation may be relayed by way of the dorsal tegmental nucleus to the mammillary body (and/or anterior thalamic nuclei), and then on to the subicular complex (Smith, 1997; Taube, 1998). It has been suggested that the mammillo-thalamic-cortical system containing head direction neurons is critically involved in elaborating a sense of direction (Taube, 1998).

It has long been known from developmental studies that individual neurons in the mammillary nuclei send a descending axon to the brainstem tegmentum as well as a collateral to the anterior thalamic nuclei (Canteras, Simerly, & Swanson, 1992; Fry & Cowan, 1972; Valverde, Garcia, López-Mascaraque, & De Carlos, 2000). This arrangement is also similar in principle to the caudally adjacent reticular part of the substantia nigra (Figure 14.12; Canteras & Swanson, 1992; Risold et al., 1997), which sends a branched projection to the brainstem motor system (includ-ing the deeper layers of the superior colliculus and reticular formation) and to the thalamus (Beckstead, 1983; Risold et al., 1997). Furthermore, it is similar to the adjacent ventral tegmental area, which sends projections to the brainstem motor system and thalamus, in addition to other sites (see Beckstead, Domesick, & Nauta, 1979; Swanson, 1982).

The Rostral Behavior Control Column. Evidence for the pivotal involvement of the nuclei in the rostral part of hypothalamic medial zone in motivated behavioral processes has a long history and is both considerable and compelling. However, in contrast to their established functional roles, only recently have researchers been able to construct a consolidated model for their connections that is compatible with their functions (L. Swanson, 2000a).

The overall pattern of efferents from the rostral behavior control column can be summarized as follows (Figure 14.13). Within the preoptic-premammillary segment all nuclei except the PVH generate a dual projection, with a primary branch descending to the hindbrain motor system and a secondary branch ascending to the thalamus (Risold et al., 1997). In principle, this is just like the projections of the caudally adjacent medial and lateral mammillary nuclei, which form the caudal medial zone of the hypothalamus. The efferents of the VMH illustrate this arrangement (Figure 14.14; see also the section on the ventromedial nucleus). Canteras et al. (1994) showed that the VMH has extensive connections within the striatum, pallidum, hypothalamus, dorsal thalamus, and hindbrain, which fits the generalized plan for the nuclei of the behavior control column. Finally, one of the defining features of the rostral behavior control column is the set of robust topographically organized inputs that they receive from cortical, striatal, and pallidal components (Figure 14.13; Risold & Swanson, 1996,

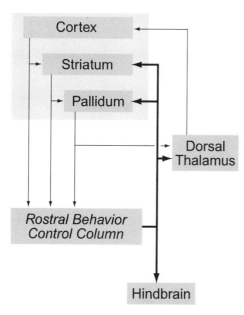

Figure 14.13 A schematic representation of the afferent and efferents pathways of the hypothalamic medial zone nuclei in the rostral part of the behavior control column.

NOTE: These nuclei receive inputs from the cerebral hemispheres by way of its triple descending output. Medial zone nuclei efferents have an ascending component to the dorsal thalamus, striatum, and pallidum. Descending projections are to the hindbrain.

1997). This system can be conceptualized using the triple output system described earlier (Figure 14.11).

The next section deals in more detail with the way in which some of these rostral behavior control column nuclei contribute to specific aspects of ingestive and reproductive behaviors.

SPECIFIC BEHAVIORS

Having just described the architecture of the components that make up the neural network divisions of the framework introduced in the third section, we now use ingestive and reproductive behaviors as examples to illustrate in more detail how we think that the neural components operate within the drive networks of the rostral behavior control column. Then we consider how the sensory inputs and the neural networks involved with these two behaviors might interact to mediate the effects that each behavior has on the other's expression.

Example 1: Ingestive Behavior

Techniques

Although the first clues to the role of the hypothalamus in energy balance were clinical data that correlated the location of hypothalamic tumors with obesity, the oldest experimental approaches measured the effects of targeted lesions or electrical stimulation on food intake. The first experimental use of lesions to address the central control of metabolism was reported by Hetherington and Ranson (1940), who produced adiposity in rats with lesions that involved the parts of the mediobasal hypothalamus. About 10 years later, the work of Anand and Brobeck (1951) helped conceptualize the dual-center control model (Stellar, 1954). Since that time lesions and focused electrical stimulation have been used extensively to plot the role of many different cell groups and fiber tracts throughout the brain in controlling ingestive behaviors.

A more recent approach for identifying neurons involved with generating feeding is to determine which are activated by a stimulus that alters feeding behavior. Although a number of markers are now being used in this respect, the transcription factor Fos is the most widely used, mostly because it is easily detected immunocytochemically. When researchers use this technique, the ARH, PVH, DMH, and VMH, as well as a number of brainstem sites, show increased Fos staining following stimuli such NPY injections into the brain or 2-deoxyglucose (2-DG) treatment

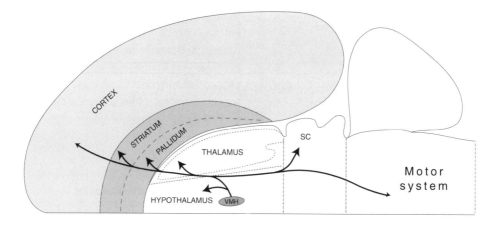

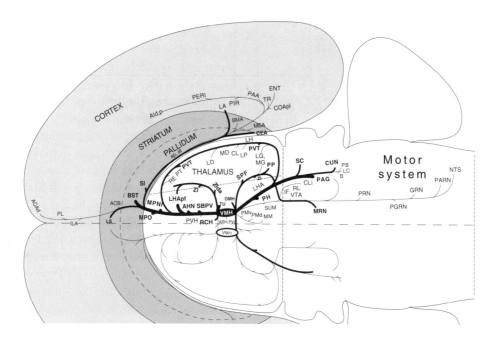

Figure 14.14   The efferents of the ventromedial nucleus of the hypothalamus as an example of the outputs from the rostral behavior control column.

NOTE: Efferents are summarized in the upper panel and shown in detail in lower panel. Abbreviations: ACAd, anterior cingulate area, dorsal part; ACB, nucleus accumbens; AHN, anterior hypothalamic nucleus; AIdp, agranular insular area, dorsal and posterior parts; ap, ansa peduncularis; ARH, arcuate nucleus; BMA, basomedial nucleus of the amygdala; BST, bed nuclei of the stria terminalis; CEA, central nucleus of the amygdala; CL, central lateral nucleus of the thalamus; COApl, cortical nucleus of the amygdala, posterior part, lateral zone; DMH, dorsomedial nucleus of the hypothalamus; ENT, entorhinal area; GRN, gigantocellular reticular nucleus; ILA, infralimbic area; LD, lateral dorsal nucleus of the thalamus; LG, lateral geniculate complex; LHApf, lateral hypothalamic area, perifornical part; LP, lateral posterior nucleus of the thalamus; LS, lateral septal nucleus; MD, mediodorsal nucleus of the thalamus; MEA, medial nucleus of the amygdala; MG, medial geniculate complex; MM, medial mammillary nucleus; MPNl, medial preoptic nucleus, lateral part; MPO, medial preoptic area; MRN, mesencephalic reticular nucleus; NTS, nucleus of the solitary tract; PAA, piriform-amygdaloid area; PARN, parvicellular reticular nucleus; PERI, perirhinal area; PGRN, paragigantocellular reticular nucleus;

(B. Li, Rowland, & Kalra, 1994; Minami et al., 1995; Ritter, Llewellyn-Smith, & Dinh, 1998).

A great deal of work over the past 30 years has measured the effects on food intake of neuropeptides that are either injected into the ventricles or targeted at specific structures. The attraction of these types of experiments is that they ostensibly help implicate neurons expressing these peptides with particular motor actions. However, in many instances the experimental design addresses only one aspect of feeding behaviors: how peptides alter food intake in simple environments where food is available with a minimum of procurement. These experiments have recently led to the generation of mice with targeted disruption of genes for neuropeptides, and their receptors that have shed further light on the neurochemical bases of ingestive behavior (e.g., Chemelli et al., 1999; Huszar et al., 1997; Palmiter, Erikson, Hollopeter, Baraban, & Schwartz, 1998; Shimada, Tritos, Lowell, Flier, & Maratos-Flier, 1998).

Collectively, the results from these types of techniques have focused attention on a restricted number of hypothalamic cell groups that appear to be intimately involved with regulating the motor responses to altered energy balance (Elmquist, Elias, & Saper, 1999; Schwartz, Woods, Porte, Seeley, & Baskin, 2000; Watts, 2000). Two of these—the VHM and PVH—are components of the rostral behavior control column, whereas two others—the ARH and DMH—are part of the periventricular zone of the hypothalamus that provides important modulatory humoral (ARH) or circadian (DMH) information into the appropriate control column nuclei. The final components in this hypothalamic feeding network are the retrochiasmatic area (RCH) and LHA. Although their function is less clear, they may be responsible, at least as far as the LHA is concerned, for integrating information from the cortical hemispheres into the control of ingestive behaviors. We see later that some of these nuclei may also act as part of an integrative network that helps mediate the interactions between energy balance and reproduction.

Sensory Systems

As we discussed earlier, the sensory inputs important for ingestive behaviors and energy metabolism can be categorized into intero- and exterosensory signals, and the integration of these signals with other systems in the brain eventually leads to the generation of appropriate sets of autonomic, neuroendocrine, and behavioral motor events (Figure 14.3). All the exterosensory modalities contribute to some extent to the organization of ingestive behaviors (Figure 14.15), but their relative importance varies depending on the species and the situation. However, the chemical senses—gustatory and olfactory—play particularly prominent roles in all vertebrates. A host of signals that are generated by digestion and subsequent cellular metabolism comprise the interosensory components

---

Figure 14.14 (*Continued*)   PH, posterior hypothalamic area; PIR, piriform area; PL, prelimbic area; PMd, premammillary nucleus, dorsal part; PMv, premammillary nucleus, ventral part; PP, peripeduncular nucleus; PRN, pontine reticular nucleus; PRT, pretectal area; PT, parataenial nucleus; PVH, paraventricular nucleus of the hypothalamus; PVi, periventricular nucleus of the hypothalamus, intermediate zone; PVT, paraventricular nucleus of the thalamus; RCH, retrochiasmatic area; RE, nucleus reuniens; SBPV, subparaventricular zone; SC, superior colliculus; SI, substantia innominata; SPF, subparafascicular nucleus; st, stria terminalis; TR, postpiriform transition area; TT, taenia tecta; TU, tuberal nucleus; VTA, ventral tegmental area; ZI, zona incerta; ZIda, zona incerta, dopaminergic group.
Source: Adapted from Canteras, Simerly, and Swanson (1994).

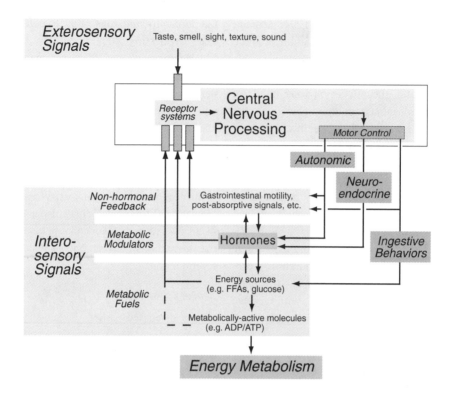

Figure 14.15   A schematic representation of the exterosensory and interosensory signals involved with regulating the motor events that control energy balance.

NOTE: Interosensory inputs can be categorized as nonhormonal feedback signals, hormones (metabolic modulators), and metabolic fuels. Autonomic motor actions regulate gastrointestinal, adrenal medullary, and pancreatic functions; neuroendocrine motor output controls glucocorticoid, thyroid, and growth hormones; and behavioral motor actions mediate eating, drinking, and specialized appetites. Abbreviations: ADP, adenosine diphosphate; ATP, adenosine triphosphate; CART, cocaine- and amphetamine-regulated transcript; CRH, corticotropin-releasing hormone; FFA, free fatty acid.

(Figure 14.15). Collectively, these signals relay information to the brain about internal states that are used to control a wide range of neuroendocrine, autonomic, and behavioral motor events associated with energy balance.

Timing is Everything.   The effects of these different sensory inputs on central networks are not temporally equal when it comes to regulating the motor events that make up ingestive behaviors. Some act quickly in a reflex manner to control the moment-to-moment actions within a meal (e.g., the processing of gustatory and oropharyngeal information in

the hindbrain); others act to control the duration of a single meal (e.g., vagal afferents); and others may have long-lasting effects on body weight (e.g., hormones) or food preference (e.g., conditioned taste aversion mediated by gustatory effects on learning mechanisms). These timing issues are determined in part by where sensory factors impact the neural hierarchies illustrated in Figure 14.4a.

Exterosensory Information.   All exterosensory modalities, but particularly the olfactory and gustatory information we described earlier, play key roles in organizing foraging behavior and food selection (Risold et al., 1997; Spector, 2000). In turn, these complex motor events require that before exterosensory information can affect the ingestive behavior motor networks to generate appropriate procurement actions, it must be processed by those parts of the brain—particularly the cortex—that assign reward value to a particular food item, that learn and remember its location in the environment, and that engage the appropriate navigational strategies for getting there (Rolls, 1999b, 2000a).

Interosensory Information. It is useful to place the interosensory signals that contribute to the central neural control of energy metabolism into three categories, each of which is influenced by centrally generated autonomic, neuroendocrine, and behavioral motor events. These categories are nonhormonal feedback signals, hormones (metabolic modulators), and metabolic fuels (Figure 14.15). The nature of these interosensory signals and how they impact the different network divisions within the brain (Figure 14.15) become important when we consider how energy balance impacts reproductive function, because some enable a significant degree of cross-talk between relevant neural circuits.

A. Metabolic Fuels. Energy expenditure is ultimately determined by the supply of ATP within all cells, which in turn is generated from fuel sources such as glucose and free fatty acids. Ingestive behaviors act directly to bring these fuels into the body in the form of food, which is digested in the gut, absorbed into the vasculature, and utilized in the tissues. In the body these fuels can act as important sensory signals to the brain following their transduction into neurally coded information either by peripherally located receptors, which generate vagal and splanchnic inputs to the NTS (Hevener,

Bergman, & Donovan, 2000) or by direct actions on central neurons (Levin et al., 1999). For example, glucoprivation of some hindbrain neurons leads relatively rapidly to feeding and hyperglycemia (Ritter, Bugarith, & Dinh, 2001; Ritter, Dinh, & Zhang, 2000), while reductions in levels of free fatty acids in the liver activate transduction mechanisms that are relayed to the NTS by the vagus nerve to trigger eating (Horn, Addis, & Friedman, 1999). Finally, there is strong evidence that the ATP/ADP ratio in the liver can be read directly as a behaviorally important sensory signal, although the effector transduction mechanisms are currently unclear (Friedman, 1995; Horn et al., 1999).

B. Hormones (Metabolic Modulators). Much of the ongoing management of fuel resources within the body is mediated by adrenaline, insulin, glucagon, leptin, and glucocorticoid. Secretion of these hormones is determined to a large extent by two sets of control mechanisms: first, by the sympathetic and neuroendocrine motor systems, and second, by fuels in the blood that act locally on the endocrine secretory cells themselves. However, at any particular time the relative importance of neural and peripheral control systems for each of these hormones is determined by a wide variety of factors including the rate of change of fuel levels in the blood and the time of day. To affect the three categories of ingestive motor actions (Figure 14.15), insulin, leptin, and glucocorticoid all target specific receptors expressed by restricted sets of neurons, particularly in the hypothalamus and hindbrain (Elmquist et al., 1999; Porte et al., 1998; Schwartz et al., 2000).

The hypothesis that insulin can target the brain directly to regulate feeding and metabolism was proposed over 20 years ago (Woods, Lotter, McKay, & Porte, 1979). Although its mechanism of action has proved difficult to elucidate, the fact that icv insulin reduces food intake—together with the identification of an active insulin transport mechanism across the blood brain barrier (Schwartz et al., 1991) and of specific insulin receptors in the brain, particularly in the ARH (Baskin, Figlewicz, Woods, Porte, & Dorsa, 1987; Marks, Porte, Stahl, & Baskin, 1990; J. Unger, Livingston, & Moss, 1991)—supports a central action of insulin. Recently, the finding in mice that targeted disruption of the neural but not the peripheral insulin receptor gene (NIRKO) is associated with increased body fat deposition and hyperphagia (at least in females) supports the view that insulin can act directly in the brain to regulate feeding and metabolism (Brüning et al., 2000).

The actions of leptin in the brain have been the focus of intense investigation over the past few years. Three findings have proved critical in this regard: that leptin infusions in the brain will reduce food intake (Campfield, Smith, Guisez, Devos, & Burn, 1995); that specific leptin receptors have been identified in the brain, particularly in the hypothalamus; and that leptin will specifically activate neurons in regions thought to be important for regulating metabolism, as evidenced by the increased expression of Fos (see Elmquist et al., 1999, for a review). Although chronic leptin administration reduces food intake (Campfield et al., 1995) and its plasma concentration increases following feeding in rats (Ahima, Pravakaran, & Flier, 1998), the evidence that leptin acts as a short-term satiety factor is not conclusive (Flier, 1998; R. Unger, 2000). Leptin is perhaps better considered as a longer-term hormonal feedback signal whose falling levels evident during negative energy balance target the ARH, for example, to initiate eating by both increasing the activity of NPY/agouti-related peptide (AGRP) neurons and decreasing activity in the pro-opiomelanocortin (POMC)/cocaine- and amphetamine-regulated transcript (CART) neurons. Each of these systems acts, at least

in part, by way of downstream NPY and melanocortin 4 (MC-4) receptor mechanisms in the LHA and PVH (Cowley et al., 1999; Cowley, Smart, Rubinstein, Cerdan, Diano, Horvath, Cone, & Low, 2001; Elmquist et al., 1999; Marsh et al., 1999; Schwartz et al., 2000).

Glucocorticoids have long been known to have important effects on metabolism. They are key regulators of glucose utilization and during negative energy balance can increase gluconeogenesis by increasing protein catabolism. Glucocorticoids can also affect many functions within the brain but are intimately involved with modulating the neural responses to stress (Sapolsky, Romero, & Munck, 2000; Watts, 1996). These effects are mediated by two types of receptors: mineralocorticoid receptors (MR), which are high-affinity low-capacity receptors, and glucocorticoid receptors (GR), which are lower-affinity high capacity receptors (de Kloet et al., 1998). With regard to the neural networks regulating ingestive behavior, elucidating how glucocorticoids are by themselves able to regulate ingestive behavior and metabolism has been confounded by the complex interrelationship between glucocorticoids, leptin, and insulin (Porte et al., 1998). Certainly the GR is expressed by virtually all nuclei implicated in controlling metabolism. But the fact that glucocorticoids will increase NPY levels in diabetic rats that lack insulin and leptin (Strack, Sebastian, Schwartz, & Dallman, 1995) suggests that glucocorticoids can act both by themselves and with insulin and leptin as important long-term modulators of neurons in the drive networks for ingestive behavior (Dallman et al., 1993).

C. Nonhormonal Feedback Signals. Feeding and digestion generate sets of feedback signals that act as satiety factors of varying duration to modulate all three of the brain's motor systems. For example, the entry of food into the stomach increases the fir-ing rate of gastric stretch receptors and ac-tivates CCK secretion from duodenum. Both of these negative feedback signals ultimately target neurons in the hindbrain and other brain sites to inhibit feeding and regulate associated autonomic motor actions.

Hypothalamic Control Networks

Arcuate Nucleus. The ARH is a peri-ventricular cell group located at the base of the third ventricle in the tuberal level of the hypothalamus. Although it is intimately re-lated to the median eminence and the con-trol of anterior pituitary hormone secretion, a wealth of data shows that it is a central com-ponent of the neural networks that regulate eating. It is a major target for the binding of leptin and insulin to the signaling forms of their respective receptors, and as such it con-stitutes an important site for endocrine signals to access hypothalamic networks. Many ARH neurons express leptin and insulin receptors, and manipulating circulating leptin alters the expression of neuropeptide genes in the ARH (Marks et al., 1990; Sahu, 1998; Schwartz et al., 1997).

Substantial evidence implicates many of the neuropeptides expressed by ARH neu-rons as critical determinants in the home-ostatic aspects of eating behavior; and in accordance with our model of drive net-works (Figure 14.4), some of these stimu-late eating, whereas others inhibit. Central injections of NPY (which is contained in a subpopulation of ARH neurons) increase food intake in a controlled environment (Clark, Kalra, & Kalra, 1985; Stanley & Leibowitz, 1985; Stanley, Magdalin, Seirafi, Thomas, & Leibowitz, 1993); elevated NPY mRNA occurs in the ARH following food restriction or dehydration (Brady, Smith, Gold, & Herkenham, 1990; Watts, Sanchez-Watts, & Kelly, 1999; Woods, Seeley, Porte, & Schwartz, 1998); and Y receptor antag-

onists block the feeding effects of NPY (Balasubramaniam, 1997). The endogenous MC-4 receptor antagonist, AGRP, is colocal-ized with NPY in the ARH and can stimu-late food intake when administered intraven-tricularly (Rossi et al., 1998). Furthermore, AGRP mRNA increases following starvation (Mizuno & Mobbs, 1999; Wilson et al., 1999), and targeted disruption of the MC-4 recep-tor is associated with obesity and hyperphagia (Huszar et al., 1997; Marsh et al., 1999).

ARH neurons also express neuropeptides that can inhibit food intake if administered directly into the brain. Two of them, d-MSH (a peptide derived from POMC) and CART, are coexpressed in the ARH (Elias et al., 1998a), and expression of both their genes decreases following starvation (Brady et al., 1990; Kristensen et al., 1998). Similarly, neu-rotensin is an anorexigenic peptide contained in ARH neurons whose gene expression is re-duced during negative energy balance (Watts et al., 1999). The ARH also contains a popu-lation of growth hormone releasing hormone (GHRH) neurons, some of which coexpress neurotensin (Sawchenko, Swanson, Rivier, & Vale, 1985). GHRH along with somatostatin regulates the secretion of growth hormone and thus the longer-term control of metabolism. In this manner the ARH can be considered as part of the neuroendocrine motor neuron network.

NPY/AGRP-containing ARH neurons project both to the PVH and to MCH-containing and H/OR-containing neurons in the LHA (Broberger, de Lecea, Sutcliffe, & Hokfelt, 1998a; Elias et al., 1998b; C. Li, Chen, & Smith, 2000). ARH projections to the LHA may provide a link between neurons directly engaged by hormones that signal changes in energy balance and neurons in the LHA projecting to those parts of the brain involved with the planning and execution of motivated behaviors (Elmquist et al., 1999; Risold et al., 1997; Sawchenko, 1998). Based on the presence of AGRP-immunoreactive fibers, ARH efferent connections apparently also target other parts of the brain implicated in regulating autonomic and behavioral aspects of feeding: the lateral septal nuclei, some parts of the BST and the amygdala, the parabrachial nucleus, and the medulla (Bagnol et al., 1999; Broberger et al., 1998b; Haskell-Luevano et al., 1999).

Paraventricular Nucleus. The PVH is a critical hypothalamic cell group that regulates many motor aspects of energy balance. It contains a prominent population of neuroendocrine CRH motor neurons that ultimately controls glucocorticoid secretion (Watts, 1996; Whitnall, 1993), as well as groups of thyrotropin-releasing hormone and somatostatin neuroendocrine neurons that are pivotally placed to regulate endocrine control of metabolism (Swanson, 1987). Injections of NPY or noradrenaline into the PVH stimulate feeding (Leibowitz, 1978; Stanley & Leibowitz, 1985), whereas food restriction increases NPY release in the PVH (Kalra, Dube, Sahu, Phelps, & Kalra, 1991). How these effects are mediated is unknown but most likely involves the extensive descending PVH projections to the PAG, PB, dorsal vagal complex, and preautonomic neurons in the hindbrain and spinal cord. In turn, the PVH receives leptin- and insulin-related viscerosensory information from the ARH and the DMH (Elmquist et al., 1999), as well as from ascending, predominantly monoaminergic inputs that relay the vagally mediated information from the viscera critical for coordinating feeding responses with peripheral requirements (Risold & Swanson, 1997; L. Swanson, 1987).

Lateral Hypothalamic Area. Of all the hypothalamic cell groups implicated in controlling ingestive behaviors, the multiple and complex roles of the LHA have been the most difficult to define. It is a large, generally ill-defined, and heterogenous collection of neurons that has connections extending throughout the brain. Its neurons project to and receive extensive inputs from the telencephalon, including parts of the isocortex and hippocampus, nucleus accumbens and substantia innominata, nuclei of the septal complex, amygdala, and BST (Öngür & Price, 2000; Risold & Swanson, 1997; Risold et al., 1997; Saper, 1985; L. Swanson, 1987, 2000a). In turn, it also has strong projections to the PAG, PB, and dorsal medulla (Kelly & Watts, 1998; Moga et al., 1990; Swanson, 1987), and to some parts of the periventricular hypothalamus that control neuroendocrine output (Larsen, Hay-Schmidt, & Mikkelsen, 1994; Swanson, 1987; Watts et al., 1999). These connections place the LHA in a prime position for incorporating the motivational aspects of ingestive behaviors (including behavioral state) into the motor patterns organized by the hypothalamus.

Under conditions of unrestricted feeding, the integrated output of LHA neurons tends to stimulate eating (Elmquist et al., 1999), the substrate of which probably includes the large population of MCH- and H/OR-containing neurons that have extensive projections throughout the brain (Bittencourt et al., 1992; Peyron et al., 1998; Shimada et al., 1998; Willie et al., 2001). However, its overall function is clearly not mandatory but apparently has a subtler and more modulatory nature (Bernardis & Bellinger, 1996; Sawchenko, 1998; Winn, 1995). This notion is supported by the fact that excitotoxic lesions in those parts of the LHA most closely related to feeding cause mild rather than catastrophic hypophagia and do not impede compensatory responses following food or water deprivation (Winn, 1995). Interestingly, however, these same LHA lesions do markedly attenuate compensatory ingestive responses to deficits originating internally—

that is, those that do not have the exterosensory components present with deprivation but instead are generated by direct manipulation of homeostatic variables (e.g., 2-DG treatment or colloid-induced hypovolemia; Winn, 1995). These data emphasize the idea that the LHA acts to coordinate signals derived from internal state variables (e.g., those originating the ARH, as discussed earlier) with those mechanisms originating in the telencephalon that are responsible for motivated anticipatory action (Elmquist et al., 1999; Winn, 1995).

Additional support for the LHA's complex role derives from two sets of data. First is the fact that glutamate mechanisms in the perifornical LHA specifically regulate feeding behavior (Stanley, Willett, Donias, Dee, & Duva, 1996). Second is the presence of at least two neuropeptides in normally fed animals (neurotensin and CART) that will inhibit eating if exogenously applied into the brain (Kristensen et al., 1998; Levine, Kneip, Grace, & Morley, 1983). In addition, during the development of dehydration-anorexia, there are increased levels of CRH and neurotensin (which are anorexic neuropeptides) in a subpopulation of LHA neurons that projects to the parabrachial nucleus (Kelly & Watts, 1998; Watts et al., 1999). Considered in this manner, it seems likely that the diverse neuropeptidergic output of the LHA—like that of the ARH—contributes to both the stimulatory and inhibitory networks, is differentially modulated by its array of afferents (Kelly & Watts, 1996; Swanson, 1987), and has the capacity to regulate feeding in a wide variety of circumstances.

Ventromedial Nucleus. Perhaps the most difficult nucleus to fit into an ingestive behavior control schema is the VMH. This large hypothalamic medial zone cell group is part of the rostral behavior control column (Figure 14.5) and consists of two well-defined subdivisions—the dorsomedial (dm) and ventrolateral parts (vl)—separated by a smaller central part. Early lesion studies identified the VMH as a pivotal component of the circuit that controlled eating behavior. During the 1950s it was considered the hypothalamic satiety center because large electrolytic lesions produced hyperphagia and obesity. However, the validity of these findings was questioned a few years later (Gold, 1973) on the grounds that more restricted lesions did not produce these effects, while lesions in the vicinity of the VMH may have compromised descending PVH projections that regulate autonomic functions leading to increased feeding (Berthould & Jeanrenaud, 1979; Gold, Sawchenko, DeLuca, Alexander, & Eng, 1980; Inoue & Bray, 1977; see Grossman, 1979, for a review). Since that time results using neuron-specific excitotoxic lesions have generally been equivocal and have failed to clarify the role of the VMH in the behavioral aspects of energy balance.

Most studies have reported that the VMH does not send significant projections to the PVH, and only sparse projections to the DMH (Figure 14.14; Canteras et al., 1994; Luiten, ter Horst, & Steffens, 1987; Sawchenko & Swanson, 1983; R. H. Thompson & Swanson, 1998). Furthermore, results from transneuronal viral tracers, which reveal neural projections across one or more synapses, have raised serious doubts about precisely how VMH neurons contribute to the sympathetic motor command circuit that is important for controlling energy metabolism (Strack, Sawyer, Hughes, Platt, & Loewy, 1989). Experiments using this technique have always conclusively failed to label VMH neurons following viral injections into peripheral targets such as the pancreas, stomach wall, or brown and white adipose tissue (Bamshad, Aoki, Adkison, Warren & Bartness, 1998; Jansen, Hoffman, & Loewy, 1997; Rinaman et al., 2000; Strack et al., 1989).

What is clear is that the VMHdm contains a significant number of leptin receptors and that some of these neurons project to parts of the hypothalamus concerned with circadian timekeeping (Elmquist et al., 1998). Lesions that include the VMH suppress the increase in diurnal activity induced by food deprivation (Challet, Le Maho, & Malan, 1995), and one of the most striking effects of temporary inactivation of the region including the VMH is a disruption to circadian-dependent spontaneous feeding where diurnal but not nocturnal food intake increases (Choi & Dallman, 1999; Choi, Wong, Yamat, & Dallman, 1998). Finally, the VMH contains glucose-sensing neurons that may contribute to a wider central glucose sensing network (Levin et al., 1999). Collectively, these data suggest that the VMH has at least two separate functions. One function of VMH neurons (particularly those in the VMHdm) may be to consolidate the circadian activity and feeding rhythms in the face of feedback from blood leptin and glucose alterations following a normal meal. The second, based on the evidence of its neural connections and its high levels of estrogen receptors (ER), particularly in the VMHvl, is concerned with regulating social behaviors, including female reproductive behaviors (discussed in the following sections).

Example 2: Reproduction

Those centrally regulated functions that contribute to successful reproduction culminate in a wide range of motor events that range from the complex social interactions of courtship and parental behaviors, through the behavioral acts associated with copulation, to neuroendocrine cycles and reflexes mediating ovulation and lactation. All of these neuroendocrine, autonomic, and behavioral motor processes must occur at the right time and in the correct sequence for successful reproduction. This means that the neural systems

concerned with reproduction offer an excellent insight for understanding how the forebrain coordinates all of these motor events (Figure 14.16). This section emphasizes how the coordinate control of the neuroendocrine system is an intimate part of the spectrum of motor events associated with motivated behaviors. Finally, the control of reproductive behaviors also offers a good example of how hormones can modulate behavioral processes in a manner that differs from the role that they play in controlling ingestive behaviors, in which they act primarily as feedback signals (Figure 14.15).

Controlling reproductive function involves a wide variety of neural and peripheral control systems that conform to the general schema illustrated in Figure 14.3. However, accounting for how this multiplicity of reproductive motor actions is controlled at the level of more detailed neural systems has proved difficult. With such complexity in mind, this section focuses on the neural control of three components of female rat reproductive function that are intimately involved with successful reproduction: luteinizing hormone (LH) pulsatility, which is the neuroendocrine motor pattern at the lowest hierarchical level of the gonadotropin secretory system; the phasic preovulatory release of LH from the anterior pituitary at proestrus that triggers ovulation; and lordosis, which is the female postural reflex essential for successful mating. These components have been particularly well studied with regard to circuits and mechanisms in the hypothalamus, and they therefore provide a good opportunity for looking at how different control networks might interact.

Sensory Inputs

Exterosensory Signals. Like the network controlling energy balance, those neural networks important for ovulation are influenced by internal and external sensory stimuli (Figure 14.16). Investigations into which

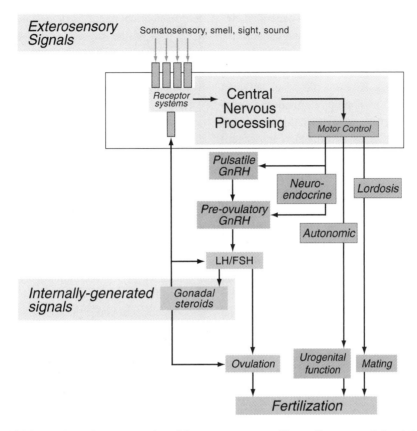

Figure 14.16   A schematic representation of the exterosensory and internally generated signals involved in regulating the motor events that control female reproductive functions in the rat.
NOTE: Somatosensory and olfactory inputs are key exterosensory inputs, while visual and auditory inputs play more subsidiary roles. Gonadal steroids are the internally generated permissive signals. Autonomic motor actions regulate urogenital functions; neuroendocrine motor output controls gonadotropin secretion from the anterior pituitary; and behavioral motor actions mediate lordosis. Abbreviations: FSH, follicle-stimulating hormone; GnRH, gonadotropin-releasing hormone; LH, luteinizing hormone.

exterosensory stimuli are important for reproduction have a long and distinguished history and have been central to formulating many of the main principles of neuroendocrinology and how hormones interact with the brain (Beach, 1948; Marshall, 1936; Pfaff, 1980; Tinbergen 1951).

Virtually all sensory modalities play critical roles in organizing reproductive behaviors. In rodents, olfaction plays a significant role in initiating sequences of reproductive events, whereas visual signals are clearly important in species that have complex courtship behaviors. Somatosensory signals are important for triggering postural reflexes, of which lordosis in rats is the best understood (Pfaff, 1980, 1999).

Internally Generated Signals.   Reproductive function differs from ingestive behaviors in that it does not contribute directly to bodily homeostasis. As such, there are no internally generated deficits or related interosensory signals that can trigger reproductive motor acts in the absence of the appropriate exterosensory stimuli. However, gonadal steroids are critical internally generated signals; without them reproduction cannot take place. Instead of acting as deficit signals, however, gonadal steroids act more as permissive factors that prime neuronal networks to respond in an appropriate manner to neurally generated (e.g., circadian timing) and exterosensory signals—particularly those generated by the presence of a conspecific. The way that estradiol mediates lordosis in the female rat by gating the flow of somatosensory information generated as she is mounted by the male is an excellent example of this type of priming (Pfaff, 1980, 1999).

Gonadal steroids also have profound effects on gonadotropin-releasing hormone (GnRH) release patterns (Herbison, 1998), which are the neuroendocrine motor events critical for reproduction. In spontaneous ovulating rodents such as the rat, estrogen acts throughout most of the estrous cycle as a negative feedback signal to the pituitary and the GnRH network to dampen release rates. However, as estrogen levels begin to rise on the evening before proestrus, this negative feedback switches to a potentiating signal that facilitates a robust GnRH surge that is timed by the SCH (Fink, 1988). Figure 14.16 illustrates in a simple manner how this information flow is organized to mediate the neuroendocrine (LH and FSH secretion), autonomic (urogenital function), and behavioral (lordosis) motor events of female reproductive behavior.

Motor Outputs

Neuroendocrine Motor Output and the Structure of Hypothalamic Control Networks. Up until this point, much of this chapter has concentrated on describing control networks concerned with the striate musculature and behavior. Because of the way that reproductive behaviors require coordination with other nonbehavioral motor actions, however, we now need to emphasize that the sympathetic, parasympathetic, and neuroendocrine motor systems are an intimate part of the overall pattern of motor events associated with motivated behaviors. The close interactions—particularly in the hypothalamus—between the cell groups involved with behavioral and neuroendocrine control are particularly striking. To illustrate the interactive nature of these control processes, this section incorporates a description of the organization of neural networks underlying gonadotropin secretion, which despite their importance for reproduction are not conventionally considered with motivated behavior control systems. We hope to emphasize that this should not be the case; the emerging concepts of forebrain neuroanatomy described earlier compel us in this more integrative direction. We begin by presenting a hierarchical model for the control of LH release as it relates to the overall control of reproductive behavior.

A. LH Pulsatility and Its Modulation. As discussed earlier, the idea of the hierarchical neural control of striate muscle contraction is the foundation of our understanding of behavioral motor control. However, to a lesser extent a hierarchical arrangement is also the best explanation for the control of autonomic, including neuroendocrine, motor events. In the neuroendocrine system, pulsatile hormone release is at the lowest level of this hierarchy and corresponds to the oscillatory motor patterns evident at the lowest hierarchical levels of the striate muscle control system (Rossignol, 1996). Like this system, the neuroendocrine motor system is modulated by a variety of inputs that coordinate neuroendocrine and behavioral motor actions.

Advances in two techniques over the past 25 years have allowed investigators to examine the release patterns of pituitary hormones in detail. The first has been the ever-increasing sensitivity of radioimmunoassay

(RIA) techniques, made possible largely through the generation of more specific antibodies. This has meant that frequent sampling of small blood volumes has greatly increased the temporal resolution of secretory patterns. The second is the application of sophisticated mathematical methods (e.g., spectral and deconvolution analyses) to expose underlying hormonal secretory patterns from the more noisy raw data derived from blood sample analysis (e.g., Hoeger, Kolp, Strobl, & Veldhuis, 1999). If we look at the temporal release pattern of almost any hormone into the blood using these techniques, we do not find release at a constant (tonic) rate; instead, hormone concentrations tend to vary in a series of quite well-defined pulses. The frequency of these pulses varies considerably between different hormonal systems, but for LH secretion in gonadectomized male and female rats this is between 20 and 30 min.

There is good reason to believe that the timing of anterior pituitary hormone pulsatility derives directly from the firing patterns of neuroendocrine motor neurons, which produce a pulsatile release pattern of neuroendocrine signals from their terminals in the median eminence. This has been elegantly revealed in the sheep, where it is possible to collect blood simultaneously from the hypophysial and systemic vasculatures (I. Clarke & Cummins, 1982). In this system, pulses of GnRH in hypophysial blood correlate very closely with pulses of LH in the general circulation.

Although a number of models have been proposed for explaining the neural basis of pulsatile LH release, the precise neural mechanism underlying GnRH pulsatility remains controversial. In one model the soma of GnRH neurons and their accompanying pulse generator are distinct entities located at different hypothalamic locations (Bourguignon et al., 1997a, 1997b; Maeda et al., 1995). Other evidence suggests that the pulse generator directly involves the soma of GnRH

motor neurons. Most compelling is the fact that a prototypical pulsatile GnRH release pattern is exhibited both by cultured neurons transfected with the GnRH gene (Wetsel et al., 1992) and by more physiologically derived in vitro preparations (Terasawa, Keen, Mogi, & Claude, 1999). Collectively, these data suggest that pulsatility is an emergent property of an interactive neuronal network (Leng & Brown, 1997). This network consists of GnRH motor neurons that have the ability to generate simple secretory oscillations, which are then coordinated, at least in the first instance, by proximal, possibly GABAergic and glutamatergic, premotor neurons (Figure 14.17a; Bourguignon et al., 1997a, 1997b; Brown, Herbison, Robinson, Marrs, & Leng, 1994; Herbison, 1998; Leng & Brown, 1997).

If pulsatility is the foundation of hormone secretion, then its modulation into more complex release patterns is the origin for many of the physiologically stimulated modes of anterior pituitary hormone secretion. These range from the different modes of ACTH and growth hormone release during stress and changes in arousal state, to the preovulatory surge of gonadotropins. Shaping pulsatile LH release into more complex secretory patterns most likely involves sets of afferents that originate more distally than do those responsible for generating basic pulsatility (Figure 14.17b). Many studies have shown that LH pulsatility can be modulated by pharmacological agents, thus implicating a variety of different transmitter systems, of which catecholamines and opiates are particularly prominent (Kalra et al., 1997). Collectively, these data show that a variety of neural inputs target both local premotor neurons and GnRH neurons themselves (Figure 14.17b) to alter LH pulsatility (Brown et al., 1994; Herbison, 1998). These inputs are important for two reasons. First, many (but not all) of these premotor neurons are estrogen-sensitive and are most likely critical for

Anatomy of Motivation

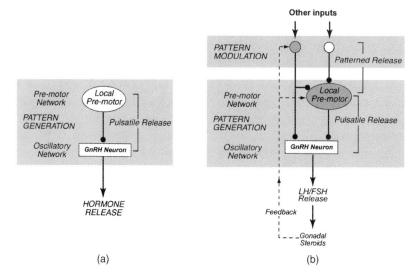

Figure 14.17 Two schematic diagrams illustrating the organization of the neural elements that control pulsatile (a) and more complex patterned gonadotropin secretion (b).
NOTE: In (a), pulsatile hormone release can be generated by the interaction of an oscillatory network consisting of the neuroendocrine motor neurons and local premotor neurons. In (b), more complex patterned release is generated by modulating pulsatile release by way of inputs from other sets of premotor neurons whose projections are directed either at the more local premotor neurons or at the local premotor neurons and the GnRH neurons. Some of these inputs are be estrogen-sensitive (gray shading) and are located more distal from the GnRH neurons. Abbreviations: FSH, follicle-stimulating hormone; GnRH, gonadotropin-releasing hormone; LH, luteinizing hormone.

mediating the effects of this gonadal steroid on the GnRH network (Herbison, 1998). Second, as discussed later, one of the ways by which systems concerned with controlling other motivated behaviors may modify reproductive competence is by altering the activity of the neural afferent systems that feed into the GnRH pattern generation system in the manner depicted in Figure 14.17b.

B. The Preovulatory Surge: Steroid Regulation and Circadian Timing. The fluctuating concentrations of LH seen during the rat estrous cycle that culminate in the LH surge seen on the afternoon of proestrus are the trigger for ovulation a few hours later. This preovulatory surge is formed by modulating underlying LH pulsatility. Detailed analyses of these patterns of hormone

release show that ovulation depends on the superimposition of a phasic pattern of release on the underlying pulsatility (Fox & Smith, 1985; Hoeger et al., 1999). In response to preceding increases in circulating estrogen, rat GnRH neurons are activated during the afternoon of proestrus to initiate a massive increase in GnRH release into the portal vasculature, which in turn is a major contributor to ovulation (Sarkar, Chiappa, Fink, & Sherwood, 1976). This patterning requires a circadian signal from the SCH that interacts in an estrogen-dependent manner with the network that generates pulsatility. Figure 14.18 uses the framework described in Figure 14.17 to outline schematically how these elements of neural pattern control might be organized to regulate circadian-dependent phasic gonadotropin release. This figure shows that two

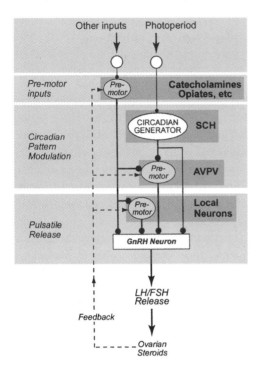

Figure 14.18 A schematic diagram, based on Figure 14.17, showing the organization of the neural components that are thought to mediate the preovulatory LH surge in rats.

NOTE: The pulsatile pattern of LH release generated by the GnRH network in Figure 14.17a is modulated by more complex sets of neural inputs to generate the surge, some of which are estrogen-sensitive (gray). These inputs include a circadian signal from the suprachiasmatic nucleus (SCH). The SCH projects to GnRH neurons and the anteroventral periventricular nucleus (AVPV), which, unlike the SCH, contains estrogen receptors. Other groups of premotor neurons are located both proximal (e.g., local GABAergic neurons) and distal (e.g., catecholaminergic neurons in the brainstem or opiate neurons in the arcuate nucleus) to GnRH neurons, some of which are estrogen-sensitive. Inputs that mediate the effects of energy balance on the preovulatory surge may do so by way of these premotor neurons.

sets of inputs are important for controlling the preovulatory LH surge, which in turn may be modulated by factors generated by changes in other homeostatic processes such as energy balance (Briski & Sylvester, 1998). First, pre-

motor inputs from catecholaminergic, opiate, and other peptidergic neurons are vital for the preovulatory surge and may well convey a variety of different types of information, including energy status, to the GnRH network. These inputs derive from a variety of sources within the forebrain and hindbrain and target both GnRH neurons as well as other more local premotor neurons (Figure 14.18; Herbison, 1998; Simonian, Spratt, & Herbison, 1999). However, by themselves these inputs are not sufficient to generate the preovulatory LH surge, and a second set of inputs influences preovulatory GnRH secretion by providing circadian timing signal from the SCH (Brown-Grant & Raisman, 1977; Wiegand & Terasawa, 1982; Wiegand, Terasawa, Bridson, & Goy, 1980).

Although there is evidence that the SCH provides a VIPergic input directly to GnRH neurons (van der Beek, Horvath, Wiegant, Van den Hurk, & Buijs, 1997), lesion data show that estrogen-stimulated phasic LH release in the female rat requires both the SCH and the AVPV to which vasopressin neurons in the SCH project (Watson, Langub, Engle, & Maley, 1995; Watts, 1991). The AVPV is sexually dimorphic in terms of its size, patterns of neuropeptide expression, and the density of its innervation from parts of the BST (Simerly, 1998; Simerly, McCall, & Watson, 1988). Critically, the AVPV also contains large numbers of estrogen and progesterone receptors, which is not the case for the SCH (Herbison, 1998). With respect to GnRH motor neurons, many studies have shown that they do not contain functional ERs, but some recent findings have begun to question this conclusion (Butler, Sjoberg, & Coen, 1999; Hrabovszky et al., 2000; Skynner, Sim, & Herbison, 1999).

Two sets of data suggest that the AVPV acts as a premotor neuroendocrine motor pattern generator of the type illustrated in Figure 14.17. First, it projects directly to GnRH neurons (Gu & Simerly, 1997). Second, small lesions of the AVPV as well as the region between the SCH and AVPV block both the preovulatory and the SCH-dependent release of LH (Wiegand & Terasawa, 1982; Wiegand et al., 1980). By virtue of its bidirectional neural connections with the ARH and the PVH, we will see that the AVPV may also be important for mediating some of the effects of changes in reproductive function on energy balance.

Lordosis.   Lordosis is an estrogen-gated postural reflex expressed by female rats that is essential for penile intromission. It is triggered by the somatosensory stimulation generated as the male mounts the female and is perhaps the best characterized motivated behavioral event in mammals (Pfaff, 1980, 1999). Because it is a reflex event, much of the sensory processing takes place in hindbrain and spinal motor pattern generators. However, estrogen's action occurs in the hypothalamus. An elegant series of experiments in the late 1970s and early 1980s identified one of the rostral behavior control column nuclei, the VMH, as the point where estrogen intervened in the sequence (Pfaff, 1980, 1999). For almost 30 years researchers have known that the VMH contains high numbers of ERs and that these are concentrated in its ventrolateral subdivision (Laflamme, Nappi, Drolet, Labrie, & Rivest, 1998; Pfaff, 1980; Shughrue, Lane, & Merchenthaler, 1997; Simerly, Chang, Muramatsu, & Swanson, 1990). Projections of the VMH to the PAG (Figure 14.14; Canteras et al., 1994) form part of the system that mediates estrogen's effects on lordosis (Pfaff, 1999). Interestingly, the pathway from the VMH to the PAG parallels VMH output to the thalamus (Figures 14.10 and 14.14), which may mediate the effects of pheromones on head-orienting responses required during earlier aspects of the mating sequence.

Interactions between the Motor Control Networks of Different Motivated Behaviors

Up to this point we have considered the organization of control networks for individual behaviors in relative isolation. However, an integral part of the overall control of motivated behaviors is how one behavior is favored at one time at the expense of another. This type of interaction must obviously occur over a variety of time scales, which range from the moment-to-moment selection of a particular behavior in a manner reminiscent of motivational timesharing described by McFarland and Sibly (1975), through the day-to-day homeostatic interactions of feeding and drinking (Watts, 2001), to the long-term interactions of behaviors (e.g., energy balance and reproduction that may occur over long breeding cycles; Schneider & Watts, in press). Although these types of interaction are of fundamental importance for animals, the neural mechanisms that are responsible can only begin to emerge as the types of neural circuit models that we described earlier are consolidated. With this in mind, this section describes a neural circuit model that accounts for how those systems controlling the motor aspects of reproduction and ingestive behaviors interact using the drive network and behavior control column concepts described earlier.

Whichever mechanisms mediate the interactions between the networks controlling energy balance and those controlling reproduction, at some stage there must be an exchange of information between the control networks responsible for specific ingestive or reproductive motor events. In this manner information about energy balance can, for example, influence the circuits controlling reproduction. These interactions may be mediated by the actions of hormones and sensory inputs that can directly influence both networks. A second mechanism may involve sets of projections

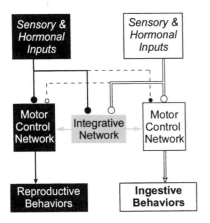

Figure 14.19   Interactions between the networks controlling energy balance and reproduction can be mediated in two ways.

NOTE: First, the diversity of hormone receptor expression shows that hormonal information that is primarily directed at one control network may also influence the other. In the figure the expression of gonadal steroid receptors is illustrated as open dots; leptin, insulin, and glucocorticoid receptors are shown as solid dots. The second mode of interaction utilizes the neural projections from an intermediate set of integrative nuclei that are responsive to both gonadal steroids and the hormones concerned with energy balance. In turn, the neural outputs of this integrative network target both the reproductive and ingestive behavior control networks.

from intermediate (integrative) cell groups that contain mixed populations of receptors and that have divergent sets of connections. These mechanisms are illustrated schematically in Figure 14.19.

Divergent Hormonal Information: Cross-Network Effects of Hormones

How Hormones Related to Energy Balance Can Affect the GNRH Network and Reproduction: Insulin and Leptin. Insulin is a hormone that is critical for the maintenance of energy balance, but it has effects also on reproductive function. In this regard, insulin appears to have a bimodal

effect on LH pulsatility. Insulin given systemically at doses sufficient to cause hypoglycemia has a suppressive effect on LH secretion (Medina et al., 1998). Other studies, however, suggest that the frequency of LH pulses in a number of species positively correlates with plasma insulin concentrations as levels fall (Q. Dong, Lazarus, Wong, Vellios, & Handelsman, 1991). This relationship may contribute significantly to reduced reproductive competence evident during diabetes or during starvation when insulin levels are low. However, the mode and site of action for these effects has been controversial and difficult to determine because insulin may act directly on neurons that control GnRH pulsatility, or it may affect these neurons indirectly through changes in glucose metabolism (Q. Dong et al., 1991). The fact that neural glucoprivation by 2-DG reduces LH pulsatility (Murahashi et al., 1996) illustrates the difficulty in assessing how insulin impacts LH secretion.

This situation may have been clarified by two sets of recent data suggesting that insulin can indeed act directly within the brain to facilitate LH pulsatility, this representing a hormonal signal that can affect both control networks. First, in male sheep, streptozotocin-induced diabetes reduces the frequency of LH pulses (Bucholtz et al., 2000), but this is subsequently reinstated by introcerebroventricular insulin at doses that affect neither peripheral insulin nor glucose concentrations (Tanaka et al., 2000). Second, mice that have functional disruption of the insulin receptor gene when it is expressed in the brain but not the periphery (NIRKO) show hypothalamic hypogonadism evidenced by a 60% reduction in males and a 90% reduction in females of circulating LH levels (Brüning et al., 2000). Interestingly, NIRKO mice are also obese, but increased food intake is only evident in female mice, suggesting that to control metabolism there are also interactions between those mechanisms controlling reproduction and neuronal insulin receptors. Although insulin receptors are expressed by neurons in the ARH, the location of the receptors responsible for these actions is currently unknown.

Fluctuating levels of leptin secretion have important consequences for controlling reproductive competence (Schneider et al., 2000). However, whether leptin achieves these effects by direct neuronal action or whether they occur indirectly by way of peripheral effects remains controversial (Schneider et al., 2000),

but there are potential neural substrates by which leptin might directly affect the GnRH network. Leptin receptors are strongly expressed by the PMv and the ARH, both of which have strong connections to the GnRH network and thus may affect GnRH release patterning. In addition, both nuclei project to the AVPV (Figure 14.20) and are in a position to exert leptin-sensitive effects on the preovulatory GnRH surge. Whether leptin receptor–containing neurons in the PMv or ARH specifically contribute to these projections has not been examined directly.

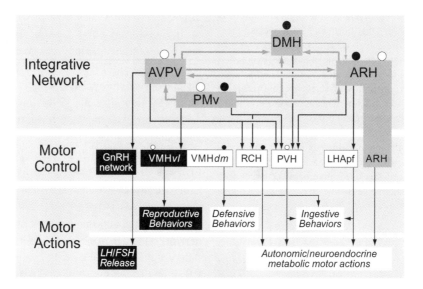

Figure 14.20   A schematic diagram of neural circuits that may help distribute information between different behavior control networks.

NOTE: Sets of neurons in the gonadotropin-releasing hormone (GnRH) network, ventromedial nucleus (VMH), retrochiasmatic area (RCH), paraventricular (PVH), perifornical part of the lateral hypothalamic area (LHApf), and arcuate nuclei (ARH) provide direct control for the motor functions for reproductive or ingestive behaviors. In turn, the ventrolateral part (vl) of the VMH controls female reproductive behaviors, and the dorsomedial (dm) part of the VMH appears to control defensive and some aspects of ingestive behavior. Collectively, these motor control cell groups are regulated by inputs from a higher-level intermediate integrative network. The receptor expression patterns and the connections from some neurons in the arcuate (ARH), anteroventral periventricular (AVPV), dorsomedial (DMH), and the ventral premammillary (PMv) nuclei provide evidence that they make up such an integrating network that can influence in a divergent manner the neurons in the reproductive and energy balance motor control networks. Functions concerned with integrative actions are shown in gray; those with reproductive function are shown in black; and those with ingestive behaviors and energy metabolism are shown in white. Cell groups that express gonadal steroid receptors are shown with black dots; cell groups that express receptors for hormones related to energy balance are shown with white dots.

Effects of Gonadal Steroids on Circuits Concerned with Energy Balance. Up to this point we have discussed how hormones concerned with energy balance affect the neural circuits controlling reproduction, but much evidence shows that gonadal steroids can have significant effects on networks concerned with energy balance. The fact that some aspects of eating patterns and metabolism are sexually dimorphic alludes to the effects of gonadal steroids on energy balance. Certainly the fact that eating disorders such as anorexia nervosa and bulimia are much more prevalent in females than in males underscores the clinical significance of sexual dimorphisms in the regulation of ingestive behaviors, although the neurobiological bases of these pathologies are virtually unknown. Furthermore, sex differences in the regulation of the hypothalamo-pituitary-adrenal axis that have implications for differences in energy metabolism and body form have been known for almost 40 years. These range from variations in resting circulating glucocorticoid levels to differential responses to stress.

The neural network illustrated in Figure 14.20 provides a basis for considering how energy balance can affect the GnRH network and for evaluating the effects of gonadal steroids on energy balance. A direct action of gonadal steroids on the circuits that regulate energy balance is suggested by the expression of ERs in the PVH (ERß) and ARH (ERd; Laflamme et al., 1999; Shughrue et al., 1997), a small proportion of which express NPY (Sar, Sahu, Crowley, & Kalra, 1990; Simonian et al., 1999). In most instances, however, specific data about which cell types are steroid-sensitive and about where they project are not available. Gonadal steroids may also act indirectly to alter the activity of afferent circuits into the drive networks for energy balance. These may involve AVPV, PMv, or catecholaminergic projections to the ARH and PVH and their constituent neurons concerned with regulating energy balance (Figure 14.20). Some of these effects may be mediated by steroid-sensitive afferents to CRH neuroendocrine motor neurons (Viau, Chu, Soriano, & Dallman, 1999), and by estrogen-mediated organizing effects on neural elements that contribute to HPA regulation (Patchev & Almeida, 1996; Viau, Soriano, & Dallman, 2001).

Divergent Neural Information Flow: Interactions between Control Networks

A number of hypothalamic nuclei may well form the type of integrative network that can facilitate information flow between the different types of motor control systems (Figure 14.19). This is because these cell groups contain mixed populations of hormone receptors and have robust connections to the neural networks responsible for controlling reproductive and ingestive behavioral motor actions. Four hypothalamic cell groups seem particularly well placed to function in this manner (Figure 14.20): the DMH, AVPV, ARH, and the PMv. Of these, the ARH and PMv express both gonadal steroid receptors and leptin or insulin receptors (Elias et al., 2000; Laflamme et al., 1998; Marks et al., 1990; Simerly et al., 1990). This property means that neurons in these nuclei are potentially regulated by the sets of hormones associated with reproduction and energy balance. On the other hand, neurons in the AVPV (gonadal steroid) and DMH (leptin) contain significant numbers of only one class of receptor, but they have afferent and efferent patterns that allow strong neural interactions with the more receptor-diverse ARH and PMv (Figure 14.20). Critically, each of these nuclei also has strong connections with other cell groups, such as the PVH or the GnRH network, that are responsible for controlling specific reproductive or metabolic motor actions. This type of intermediate integrative neural network may offer a model for understanding how the control networks for other motivated behaviors interact.

Dorsomedial Nucleus.   The DMH is a somewhat poorly defined nucleus that can be considered as part of the periventricular zone of the hypothalamus (R. H. Thompson & Swanson, 1998). It has long been associated with controlling ingestive behaviors (Bernardis & Bellinger, 1998) and appears to play an important role in the circadian control of corticosterone secretion (Buijs, Hermes, & Kalsbeek, 1998). With regard to reproductive function, electrical stimulation of the DMH blocks pulsatile LH release (Gallo, 1981) and is associated with some patterns of prolactin secretion (Gunnet & Freeman, 1985). The organization of both afferent and efferent DMH connections (Figure 14.20) suggests that it is well placed to act as part of a visceromotor (including neuroendocrine) pattern controller, particularly with regard to mediating circadian-related effects (Risold et al., 1997; R. H. Thompson & Swanson, 1998; Watts, 1991). Its major efferent connections are intrahypothalamic and target the AVPV, PVH, and ARH (Luiten et al., 1987; R. H. Thompson et al., 1996). However, the densest and best characterized DMH projection in terms of function is to the PVH, which is thought to be critical for mediating circadian effects on glucocorticoid secretion and may be responsible for some of leptin's actions on PVH function (Buijs et al., 1998; Elmquist et al., 1998).

Anteroventral Periventricular Nucleus. As we discussed earlier, the AVPV is a small periventricular nucleus located in the preoptic region. Because of its high levels of estrogen and progesterone receptors together with the sexual dimorphic expression of peptide and neurotransmitters (Simerly, 1998; Simerly et al., 1988), it plays a critical role in regulating the preovulatory gonadotropin surge (discussed earlier). However, three sets of efferent pathways may help mediate the influences of gonadal steroids on the ingestive behavior control networks (Figure 14.20; Gu et al., 1997). First, the AVPV provides strong atrial natriuretic peptide and neurotensin-containing projections to the PVH, particularly to its parvicellular parts (Moga & Saper, 1994; Standaert & Saper, 1988). Both of these neuropeptides can affect feeding behavior and those PVH regulated systems concerned with energy balance (Oliveira et al., 1997; Watts, 2001; Wiedemann, Jahn, & Kellner, 2000). Second, the AVPV projects to the DMH. Finally, it projects to the ARH. However, the significance of these projections with regard to reproductive behaviors and energy balance remains to be examined experimentally.

Arcuate Nucleus.   We already described how the NPY, AGRP, and d-MSH projections from the ARH to the PVH and LHA appear to be important for mediating hormonal effects on ingestive behaviors. However, the ARH has long been implicated with the regulation of ovulation, and the following results support the possibility that at least some of the effects of altered energy balance on GnRH release might be mediated by ARH neurons. First, both NPY and β-endorphin (which is synthesized from POMC) have major actions on GnRH release (Goodman, Parfitt, Evans, Dahl, & Karsch, 1995; Herbison, 1998; Kalra et al., 1997); second, POMC- and NPY-containing neurons in the ARH both express leptin receptors (Elmquist et al., 1999); and third, some NPY- and β-endorphin-containing neurons in the ARH project to the vicinity of GnRH cell bodies and terminals (C. Li, Chen, & Smith, 1999; Simonian et al., 1999). Given the complexity of neuropeptide signaling within the GnRH network (Herbison, 1998; Kalra et al., 1997) and given the diversity of hypothalamic and extrahypothalamic projections to the GnRH network, it is highly likely that these circuits represent at least part of the way that leptin can affect reproductive competence.

Ventral Premammillary Nucleus. The PMv is located in the caudal part of the hypothalamus immediately ventral to the fornix and lateral to the ARH and expresses both gonadal steroid and leptin receptors (Elias et al., 2000; Laflamme et al., 1998; Simerly et al., 1990). The PMv projects heavily to the PVH and ARH (Canteras et al., 1992; Luiten et al., 1987), placing it in a position to mediate some of the effects of gonadal steroids on energy balance. Its other major projections are to the VMHvl and the AVPV (Figure 14.20; Canteras et al., 1992; Luiten et al., 1987), which implicate it in the control of reproduction. In turn, the PMv receives strong projections from the posterodorsal part of the medial amygdala and the principal nucleus of the BST, both of which contain high levels of gonadal steroid receptors and are heavily implicated in olfactory-driven reproductive behaviors (Canteras, Simerly, & Swanson, 1995; Risold et al., 1997). The fact that leptin receptors are found in both the PMv and the VMH (albeit in rather lower abundance in the VMHvl than in the VMHdm; Elmquist, 1998) suggests that these two nuclei are able to mediate some of the effects of energy balance on reproductive behaviors (Figure 14.19).

CONCLUSION

The vast quantity of neuroanatomical data that is currently accumulating in the literature presents both an opportunity and a challenge for advancing our understanding of motivated behaviors. Simply handling the escalating volume of information on neural connections is a task on a scale similar to that currently being addressed in the field of genomics (Burns, 2001). The new discipline of neuroinfomatics presents similar technical challenges but potentially offers the types of rewards in terms of revolutionizing our understanding similar to those now emerging from human genome project. However, given the number of connections in the brain, along with the types of transmitters and neuromodulators that they use, the task of incorporating neuroanatomical information into an operational model of brain function perhaps presents an even more daunting challenge than that faced in genomics. In this chapter we attempted to begin amalgamating the type of information from each of these disciplines in a way that we believe is useful for understanding how the brain processes the information required for the many facets of motivated behavior. The challenge for the neuroanatomist is to explain and contextualize these data; for the experimental psychologist it is to move forward with the neuroanatomy to help understand how the brain functions.

REFERENCES

Abrahamson, E. E., Leak, R. K., & Moore, R. Y. (2001). The suprachiasmatic nucleus projects to posterior hypothalamic arousal systems. *Neuroreport, 12,* 435–440.

Ahima, R. S., Prabakaran, D., & Flier, J. S. (1998). Postnatal leptin surge and regulation of circadian rhythm of leptin by feeding. Implications for energy homeostasis and neuroendocrine function. *Journal of Clinical Investigation, 101,* 1020–1027.

Albers, H. E., Liou, S. Y., Stopa, E. G., & Zoeller, R. T. (1991). Interaction of colocalized neuropeptides: Functional significance in the circadian timing system. *Journal of Neuroscience, 11,* 846–851.

Alden, M., Besson, J. M., & Bernard, J. F. (1994). Organization of the efferent projections from the pontine parabrachial area to the bed nucleus of the stria terminalis and neighboring regions: A PHA-L study in the rat. *Journal of Comparative Neurology, 341,* 289–314.

Aldridge, J. W., & Berridge, K. C. (1998). Coding of serial order by neostriatal neurons: A "natural action" approach to movement sequence. *Journal of Neuroscience, 18,* 2777–2787.

Anand, B. K., & Brobeck, J. R. (1951). The localization of a feeding center in the hypothalamus. *Proceedings of the Society for Experimental Biology and Medicine, 77,* 323–324.

Arshavsky, Y. I., Deliagina, T. G., & Orlovsky, G. N. (1997). Pattern generation. *Current Opinion of Neurobiology, 7,* 781–789.

Aston-Jones, G., Shipley, M. T., & Grzanna, R. (1995). The locus coeruleus, A5 and A7 noradrenergic cell groups. In G. Paxinos (Ed.), *The rat nervous system* (pp. 183–214). San Diego, CA: Academic Press.

Bagnol, D., Lu, X.-Y., Kaelin, C. B., Day, H. E. W., Ollmann, M., Gantz, I., Akil, H., Barsh, G. S., & Watson, S. J. (1999). Anatomy of an endogenous antagonist: Relationship between agouti-related protein and proopiomelanocortin in brain. *Journal of Neuroscience, 19,* RC26 (1–7).

Balasubramaniam, A. (1997). Neuropeptide Y family of hormones: Receptor subtypes and antagonists. *Peptides, 18,* 445–457.

Ballermann, M., Tompkins, G., & Whishaw, I. Q. (2000). Skilled forelimb reaching for pasta guided by tactile input in the rat as measured by accuracy, spatial adjustments, and force. *Behavioral Brain Research, 109,* 49–57.

Bamshad, M., Aoki, V. T., Adkison, M. G., Warren, W. S., & Bartness, T. J. (1998). Central nervous system origins of the sympathetic nervous system outflow to white adipose tissue. *American Journal of Physiology, 275,* R291–R299.

Baskin, D. G., Figlewicz, D. P., Woods, S. C., Porte, D., Jr., & Dorsa, D. M. (1987). Insulin in the brain. *Annual Review of Physiology, 49,* 335–347.

Beach, F. A. (1948). *Hormones and Behavior.* Paul B. Hoebner Inc., New York.

Beckstead, R. M. (1983). Long collateral branches of substantia nigra pars reticulata axons to thalamus, superior colliculus and reticular formation in monkey and cat: Multiple retrograde neuronal labeling with fluorescent dyes. *Neuroscience, 10,* 767–779.

Beckstead, R. M., Domesick, V. B., & Nauta, W. J. H. (1979). Efferent connections of the substantia nigra and ventral tegmental area in the rat. *Brain Research, 175,* 191–217.

Bernard, J. F., Alden, M., & Besson, J. M. (1993). The organization of the efferent projections from the pontine parabrachial area to the amygdaloid complex: A *Phaseolus vulgaris* leucoagglutinin (PHA-L) study in the rat. *Journal of Comparative Neurology, 329,* 201–229.

Bernardis, L. L., & Bellinger, L. L. (1996). The lateral hypothalamic area revisited: Ingestive behavior. *Neuroscience and Biobehavioral Reviews, 20,* 189–287.

Bernardis, L. L., & Bellinger, L. L. (1998). The dorsomedial hypothalamic nucleus revisited: 1998 update. *Experimental Biology and Medicine, 218,* 284–306.

Berridge K. C., & Robinson, T. E. (1998). What is the role of dopamine in reward: Hedonic impact, reward learning, or incentive salience? *Brain Research Reviews, 28,* 309–369.

Berridge, K. C., & Whishaw, I. Q. (1992). Cortex, striatum and cerebellum: Control of serial order in a grooming sequence. *Experimental Brain Research, 90,* 275–290.

Berthoud, H. R., & Jeanrenaud, B. (1979). Acute hyperinsulinemia and its reversal by vagotomy after lesions of the ventromedial hypothalamus in anesthetized rats. *Endocrinology, 105,* 146–151.

Bester, H., Besson, J. M., & Bernard, J. F. (1997). Organization of efferent projections from the parabrachial area to the hypothalamus: A *Phaseolus vulgaris*-leucoagglutinin study in the rat. *Journal of Comparative Neurology, 383,* 245–281.

Bina K. G., Rusak, B., & Semba, K. (1993). Localization of cholinergic neurons in the forebrain and brainstem that project to the suprachiasmatic nucleus of the hypothalamus in rat. *Journal of Comparative Neurology, 335,* 295–307.

Bindra, D. (1978). How adaptive behavior is produced: A perceptual-motivational alternative to response reinforcement. *Behavioral and Brain Sciences, 1,* 41–91.

Bittencourt, J. C., Presse, F., Arias, C., Peto, C., Vaughan, J., Nahon, J. L., Vale, W.,

& Sawchenko, P. E. (1992). The melanin-concentrating hormone system of the rat brain: An immunization and hybridization histochemical characterization. *Journal of Comparative Neurology, 319,* 218–245.

Blair, H. T., Cho, J., & Sharp, P. E. (1998). Role of the lateral mammillary nucleus in the rat head direction circuit: A combined single unit recording and lesion study. *Neuron, 21,* 1387–1397.

Blessing, W. W. (1997). *The lower brainstem and bodily homeostasis.* New York: Oxford University Press.

Bourgin, P., Huitron-Resendiz, S., Spier, A. D., Fabre, V., Morte, B., Criado, J. R., Sutcliffe, J. G., Henriksen, S. J., & de Lecea, L. (2000). Hypocretin-1 modulates rapid eye movement sleep through activation of locus coeruleus neurons. *Journal of Neuroscience, 20,* 7760–7765.

Bourguignon, J. P., Gerard, A., Purnelle, G., Czajkowski, V., Yamanaka, C., Lemaitre, M., Rigo, J. M., Moonen, G., & Franchimont, P. (1997a). Duality of glutamatergic and GABAergic control of pulsatile GnRH secretion by rat hypothalamic explants: I. Effects of antisense oligodeoxynucleotides using explants including or excluding the preoptic area. *Journal of Neuroendocrinology, 9,* 183–191.

Bourguignon, J. P., Gerard, A., Purnelle, G., Czajkowski, V., Yamanaka, C., Lemaitre, M., Rigo, J. M., Moonen, G., & Franchimont, P. (1997b). Duality of glutamatergic and GABAergic control of pulsatile GnRH secretion by rat hypothalamic explants: II. Reduced NR2C- and GABAA-receptor-mediated inhibition at initiation of sexual maturation. *Journal of Neuroendocrinology, 9,* 193–199.

Brady, L. S., Smith, M. A., Gold, P. W., & Herkenham, M. (1990). Altered expression of hypothalamic neuropeptide mRNAs in food-restricted and food-deprived rats. *Neuroendocrinology, 52,* 441–447.

Briski, K. P., & Sylvester, P. W. (1998). Role of endogenous opiates in glucoprivic inhibition of the luteinizing hormone surge and fos expression by preoptic gonadotropin-releasing hormone neurones in ovariectomized steroid-primed female rats. *Journal of Neuroendocrinology, 10,* 769–776.

Broberger, C., de Lecea, L., Sutcliffe, J. G., & Hokfelt, T. (1998a). Hypocretin/orexin- and melanin-concentrating hormone-expressing cells form distinct populations in the rodent lateral hypothalamus: Relationship to the neuropeptide Y and agouti gene-related protein systems. *Journal of Comparative Neurology, 402,* 460–474.

Broberger, C., Johansen, J., Johansson, C., Schalling, M., & Hökfelt, T. (1998b). The neuropeptide Y/agouti gene-related protein (AGRP) brain circuitry in normal, anorectic, and monosodium glutamate-treated mice. *Proceedings of the National Academy of Sciences, USA, 95,* 15043–15048.

Brown, D., Herbison, A. E., Robinson, J. E., Marrs, R. W., & Leng, G. (1994). Modeling the luteinizing hormone-releasing hormone pulse generator. *Neuroscience, 63,* 869–879.

Brown-Grant, K., & Raisman, G. (1977). Abnormalities in reproductive function associated with the destruction of the suprachiasmatic nuclei in female rats. *Proceedings of the Royal Society of London, Series B: Biological Sciences, 198,* 279–296.

Brüning, J. C., Gautam, D., Burks, D. J., Gillette, J., Schubert, M., Orban, P. C., Klein, R., Krone, W., Muller-Wieland, D., & Kahn, C. R. (2000). Role of brain insulin receptor in control of body weight and reproduction. *Science, 289,* 2122–2125.

Bucholtz, D. C., Chiesa, A., Pappano, W. N., Nagatani, S., Tsukamura, H., Maeda, K. I., & Foster, D. L. (2000). Regulation of pulsatile luteinizing hormone secretion by insulin in the diabetic male lamb. *Biology of Reproduction, 62,* 1248–1255.

Buijs, R. M., Hermes, M. H. L. J., & Kalsbeek, A. (1998). The suprachiasmatic nucleus-paraventricular nucleus interactions: A bridge to the neuroendocrine and autonomic nervous system. *Progress in Brain Research, 119,* 365–382.

Burns, G. A. P. C. (2001). Knowledge mechanics and the neuroscholar project: A new approach to neuroscientific theory. In M. Arbib (Ed.), *Computing the brain: A guide to neuroinformatics.* San Diego: Academic Press, pp. 319–335.

Butler, J. A., Sjoberg, M., & Coen, C. W. (1999). Evidence for oestrogen receptor alpha-immunoreactivity in gonadotrophin-releasing hormone-expressing neurones. *Journal of Neuroendocrinology, 11,* 331–335.

Campfield, L. A., Smith, F. J., Guisez, Y., Devos, R., & Burn, P. (1995). Recombinant mouse OB protein: Evidence for a peripheral signal linking adiposity and central neural networks. *Science, 269,* 546–549.

Canteras, N. S., Simerly, R. B., & Swanson, L. W. (1992). The projections of the ventral premammillary nucleus. *Journal of Comparative Neurology, 324,* 195–212.

Canteras, N. S., Simerly, R. B., & Swanson, L. W. (1994). Organization of projections from the ventromedial nucleus of the hypothalamus: A *Phaseolus vulgaris*-leucoagglutinin study in the rat. *Journal of Comparative Neurology, 348,* 41–79.

Canteras, N. S., Simerly R. B., & Swanson, L. W. (1995). Organization of projections from the medial nucleus of the amygdala: A PHAL study in the rat. *Journal of Comparative Neurology, 360,* 213–245.

Canteras, N. S., & Swanson, L. W. (1992). The dorsal premammillary nucleus: An unusual component of the mammillary body. *Proceedings of the National Academy of Sciences, USA, 89,* 10089–10093.

Card, J. P., & Moore, R. Y. (1991). The organization of visual circuits influencing the circadian activity of the suprachiasmatic nucleus. In D. Klein, R. Y. Moore, & S. M. Reppert (Eds.), *The suprachiasmatic nucleus: The mind's clock* (pp. 51–76). New York: Oxford University Press.

Challet, E., Le Maho, Y., & Malan, A. (1995). Locomotor activity and utilization of energy reserves during fasting after ventromedial hypothalamic lesions. *Physiology and Behavior, 58,* 257–264.

Chemelli, R. M., Willie, J. T., Sinton, C. M., Elmquist, J. K., Scammell, T., Lee, C., Richardson, J. A., Williams, S. C., Xiong, Y., Kisanuki, Y., Fitch, T. E., Nakazato, M., Hammer, R. E., Saper, C. B., & Yanagisawa, M. (1999). Narcolepsy in orexin knockout mice:

Molecular genetics of sleep regulation. *Cell, 98,* 437–451.

Chevalier, G., Vacher, S., Deniau, J. M., & Desban, M. (1985). Disinhibition as a basic process in the expression of striatal functions, I: The striato-nigral influence on tecto-spinal/tecto-diencephalic neurons. *Brain Research, 334,* 215–226.

Choi, S., & Dallman, M. F. (1999). Hypothalamic obesity: Multiple routes mediated by loss of function in medial cell groups. *Endocrinology, 140,* 4081–4088.

Choi, S., Wong, L. S., Yamat, C., & Dallman, M. F. (1998). Hypothalamic ventromedial nuclei amplify circadian rhythms: Do they contain a food-entrained endogenous oscillator? *Journal of Neuroscience, 18,* 3843–3852.

Chou, T., Lu, J., Zhang, Y. H., Gaus, S., Elmquist, J. K., Shiromani, P., & Saper, C. B. (1999). Distinct lesions of the subparaventricular zone (SPZ) affect circadian rhythm of sleep versus temperature. *Society for Neuroscience Abstracts, 25,* 1370.

Clark, J. T., Kalra, P. S., & Kalra, S. P. (1985). Neuropeptide Y stimulates feeding but inhibits sexual behavior in rats. *Endocrinology, 117,* 2435–2442.

Clarke, I. J., & Cummins, J. T. (1982). The temporal relationship between gonadotropin releasing hormone (GnRH) and luteinizing hormone (LH) secretion in ovariectomized ewes. *Endocrinology, 111,* 1737–1739.

Cofer, C. N. (1981). The history of the concept of motivation. *Journal of the History of Behavioral Sciences, 17,* 48–53.

Cowley, M. A., Pronchuk, N., Fan, W., Dinulescu, D. M., Colmers, W. F., & Cone, R. D. (1999). Integration of NPY, AGRP, and melanocortin signals in the hypothalamic paraventricular nucleus, evidence of a cellular basis for the adipostat. *Neuron, 24,* 155–163.

Cowley, M. A., Smart, J. L., Rubinstein, M., Cerdan, M. G., Diano, S., Horvath, T. L., Cone, R. D., & Low, M. J. (2001). Leptin activates anorexigenic POMC neurons through a neural network in the arcuate nucleus. *Nature, 411,* 480–484.

Craig, W. (1918). Appetites and aversions as constituents of instincts. *Biological Bulletin, 34,* 91–107.

Cromwell, H. C., & Berridge, K. C. (1996). Implementation of action sequences by a neostriatal site: A lesion mapping study of grooming syntax. *Journal of Neuroscience, 16,* 3444–3458.

Cui, L. N., Saeb-Parsy, K., & Dyball, R. E. J. (1997). Neurones in the supraoptic nucleus of the rat are regulated by a projection from the suprachiasmatic nucleus. *Journal of Physiology (London), 502,* 149–159.

Dallman, M. F., Strack, A. M., Akana, S. F., Bradbury, M. J., Hanson, E. S., Scribner, K. A., & Smith, M. (1993). Feast and famine: Critical role of glucocorticoids with insulin in daily energy flow. *Frontiers in Neuroendocrinology, 14,* 303–347.

Dong, H.-W., Petrovich, G. D., Watts, A. G., & Swanson, L. W. (2001). The basic organization of the efferent projections of the oval and fusiform nuclei of the bed nuclei of the stria terminalis in the adult rat brain. *Journal of Comparative Neurology, 436,* 430–455.

Dong, Q., Lazarus, R. M., Wong, L. S., Vellios, M., & Handelsman, D. J. (1991). Pulsatile LH secretion in streptozotocin-induced diabetes in the rat. *Journal of Endocrinology, 131,* 49–55.

von Economo, C. (1931). *Encephalitis lethargica, its sequelae and treatment* (K.O. Newman, Trans.). London: Humphrey Milford.

Elias, C. F., Kelly, J. F., Lee, C. E., Ahima, R. S., Drucker, D. J., Saper, C. B., & Elmquist, J. K. (2000). Chemical characterization of leptin-activated neurons in the rat brain. *Journal of Comparative Neurology, 423,* 261–281.

Elias, C. F., Lee, C., Kelly, J., Aschkenasi, C., Ahima, R. S., Couceyro, P. R., Kuhar, M. J., Saper, C. B., & Elmquist, J. K. (1998a). Leptin activates hypothalamic CART neurons projecting to the spinal cord. *Neuron., 21,* 1375–1385.

Elias, C. F., Saper, C. B., Maratos-Flier, E., Tritos, N. A., Lee, C., Kelly, J., Tatro, J. B., Hoffman, G. E., Ollmann, M. M., Barsh, G. S., Sakurai, T., Yanagisawa, M., & Elmquist, J. K. (1998b). Chemically defined projections linking the mediobasal hypothalamus and the lateral hypothalamic area. *Journal of Comparative Neurology, 402,* 442–459.

Elmquist, J. K., Ahima, R. S., Elias, C. F., Flier, J. S., & Saper, C. B. (1998). Leptin activates distinct projections from the dorsomedial and ventromedial hypothalamic nuclei. *Proceedings of the National Academy of Sciences, USA, 95,* 741–746.

Elmquist, J. K., Elias, C. F., & Saper, C. B. (1999). From lesions to leptin: Hypothalamic control of food intake and body weight. *Neuron., 22,* 221–232.

Ericson, H., Blomqvist, A., & Kohler, C. (1991). Origin of neuronal inputs to the region of the tuberomammillary nucleus of the rat brain. *Journal of Comparative Neurology, 311,* 45–64.

Everitt, B. J., & Robbins, T. W. (1997). Central cholinergic systems and cognition. *Annual Review of Psychology, 48,* 649–684.

Fay, R. A., & Norgren, R. (1997). Identification of rat brainstem multisynaptic connections to the oral motor nuclei using pseudorabies virus, I: Masticatory muscle motor systems. *Brain Research Reviews, 25,* 255–275.

Fink, G. (1988). The G. W. Harris lecture. Steroid control of brain and pituitary function. *Quarterly Journal of Experimental Physiology, 73,* 257–293.

Flier, J. S. (1998). What's in a name? In search of leptin's physiologic role. *Journal of Clinical Endocrinology and Metabolism, 83,* 1407–1413.

Floyd, N. S., Price, J. L., Ferry, A. T., Keay, K. A., & Bandler, R. (2000). Orbitomedial prefrontal cortical projections to distinct longitudinal columns of the periaqueductal gray in the rat. *Journal of Comparative Neurology, 422,* 556–578.

Fox, S. R., & Smith, M. S. (1985). Changes in the pulsatile pattern of luteinizing hormone secretion during the rat estrous cycle. *Endocrinology, 116,* 1485–1492.

Friedman, M. I. (1995). Control of energy intake by energy metabolism. *American Journal of Clinical Nutrition, 62*(Suppl.), 1096S–1100S.

Fry, F. J., & Cowan, W. M. (1972). A study of retrograde cell degeneration in the lateral mammillary nucleus of the cat, with special reference to the role of axonal branching in the preservation of the cell. *Journal of Comparative Neurology, 144,* 1–24.

Gallo, R. V. (1981). Effect of electrical stimulation of the dorsomedial hypothalamic nucleus on pulsatile LH release in ovariectomized rats. *Neuroendocrinology, 32,* 134–138.

Gaus, S. E., & Saper, C. B. (1998). Efferent connections from the suprachiasmtic nucleus to the ventrolateral preoptic nucleus in the rat. *Society for Neuroscience Abstracts, 24,* 1920.

Gold, R. M. (1973). Hypothalamic obesity: The myth of the ventromedial nucleus. *Science, 182,* 488–490.

Gold, R. M., Sawchenko, P. E., DeLuca, C., Alexander, J., & Eng, R. (1980). Vagal mediation of hypothalamic obesity but not of supermarket dietary obesity. *American Journal of Physiology, 238,* R447–R453.

Goodman, R. L., Parfitt, D. B., Evans, N. P., Dahl, G. E., & Karsch, F. J. (1995). Endogenous opioid peptides control the amplitude and shape of gonadotropin-releasing hormone pulses in the ewe. *Endocrinology, 136,* 2412–2420.

Goodridge, J. P., & Taube, J. S. (1997). Interaction between the postsubiculum and anterior thalamus in the generation of head direction cell activity. *Journal of Neuroscience, 17,* 9315–9330.

Graybiel, A. M., & Kimura, M. (1995). Adaptive neural networks in the basal ganglia. In J. C. Houk, J. L. Davis, & D. G. Beiser (Eds.), *Models of information processing in the basal ganglia* (pp. 103–116). Cambridge, MA: MIT Press.

Grill, H. J., & Kaplan, J. M. (1990). Caudal brainstem participates in the distributed neural control of feeding. In E. M. Stricker (Ed.), *Neurobiology of food and fluid intake: Handbook of behavioral neurobiology* (Vol. 10, pp. 125–150). New York: Plenum Press.

Grossman, S. P. (1979). The biology of motivation. *Annual Review of Psychology, 30,* 209–242.

Gu, G. B., & Simerly, R. B. (1997). Projections of the sexually dimorphic anteroventral periventricular nucleus in the female rat. *Journal of Comparative Neurology, 384,* 142–164.

Guillery, R. W., Feig, S. L., & Lozsadi, D. A. (1998). Paying attention to the thalamic reticular nucleus. *Trends in Neuroscience, 21,* 28–32.

Gunnet, J. W., & Freeman, M. E. (1985). The interaction of the medial preoptic area and the dorsomedial-ventromedial nuclei of the hypothalamus in the regulation of the mating-induced release of prolactin. *Neuroendocrinology, 40,* 232–237.

Haskell-Luevano, C., Chen, P., Li, C., Chang, K., Smith, M. S., Cameron, J. L., & Cone, R. D. (1999). Characterization of the neuroanatomical distribution of agouti-related protein immunoreactivity in the rhesus monkey and the rat. *Endocrinology, 140,* 1408–1415.

Herbert, H., Moga, M. M., & Saper, C. B. (1990). Connections of the parabrachial nucleus with the nucleus of the solitary tract and the medullary reticular formation in the rat. *Journal of Comparative Neurology, 293,* 540–580.

Herbison, A. E. (1998). Multimodal influence of estrogen upon gonadotropin-releasing hormone neurons. *Endocrine Reviews, 19,* 302–330.

Hermes, M. L., Coderre, E. M., Buijs, R. M., & Renaud, L. P. (1996). GABA and glutamate mediate rapid neurotransmission from suprachiasmatic nucleus to hypothalamic paraventricular nucleus in rat. *Journal of Physiology (London), 496,* 749–757.

Hetherington, A. W., & Ranson, S. W. (1940). Hypothalamic lesions and adiposity in the rat. *Anatomical Record, 78,* 149–172.

Hevener, A. L., Bergman, R. N., & Donovan, C. M. (2000). Portal vein afferents are critical for the sympathoadrenal response to hypoglycemia. *Diabetes, 49,* 8–12.

Hikosaka, O., & Wurtz, R. H. (1983). Visual and oculomotor functions of monkey substantia nigra pars reticulata, IV: Relation of substantia nigra to superior colliculus. *Journal of Neurophysiology, 49,* 1285–1301.

Hinde, R. A. (1970). *Animal behaviour: A synthesis of ethology and comparative psychology.* New York: McGraw-Hill.

Hoeger, K. M., Kolp, L. A., Strobl, F. J., & Veldhuis, J. D. (1999). Evaluation of LH secretory dynamics during the rat proestrous LH surge. *American Journal of Physiology, 276,* R219–R225.

Holland, P. C., & Gallagher, M. (1999). Amygdala circuitry in attentional and representational processes. *Trends in Cognitive Science, 3,* 65–73.

Horn, C. C., Addis, A., & Friedman, M. I. (1999). Neural substrate for an integrated metabolic control of feeding behavior. *American Journal of Physiology, 276,* R113–R119.

Hrabovszky, E., Shughrue, P. J., Merchenthaler, I., Hajszan, T., Carpenter, C. D., Liposits, Z., & Petersen, S. L. (2000). Detection of estrogen receptor-beta messenger ribonucleic acid and 125I-estrogen binding sites in luteinizing hormone-releasing hormone neurons of the rat brain. *Endocrinology, 141,* 3506–3509.

Hughes, R. N. (1997). Intrinsic exploration in animals: Motives and measurement. *Behavioral Processes, 41,* 213–226.

Huszar, D., Lynch, C. A., Fairchild-Huntress, V., Dunmore, J. H., Fang, Q., Berkemeier, L. R., Gu, W., Kesterson, R. A., Boston, B. A., Cone, R. D., Smith, F. J., Campfield, L. A., Burn, P., & Lee, F. (1997). Targeted disruption of the melanocortin-4 receptor results in obesity in mice. *Cell., 88,* 131–141.

Inoue, S., & Bray, G. A. (1977). The effects of subdiaphragmatic vagotomy in rats with ventromedial hypothalamic obesity. *Endocrinology, 100,* 108–114.

Iwaniuk A. N., & Whishaw I. Q. (2000). On the origin of skilled forelimb movements. *Trends in Neuroscience, 23,* 372–376.

Jacobs, K. M., Mark, G. P., & Scott, T. R. (1988). Taste responses in the nucleus tractus solitarius of sodium-deprived rats. *Journal of Physiology (London), 406,* 393–410.

Jansen, A. S., Hoffman, J. L., & Loewy, A. D. (1997). CNS sites involved in sympathetic and parasympathetic control of the pancreas: A viral tracing. *Brain Research, 766,* 29–38.

Jean, A. (2001). Brain stem control of swallowing: Neuronal network and cellular mechanisms. *Physiological Reviews, 81,* 929–969.

Jones, B. (1995). Reticular formation: Cytoarchitecture, transmitters, and projections. In G. Paxinos (Ed.), *The rat nervous system* (pp. 155–172). San Diego, CA: Academic Press.

Jones, E. G. (1984). Laminar distribution of cortical efferent cells. In A. Peters & E. G. Jones (Eds.), *Cerebral cortex: Cellular components of the cerebral cortex* (Vol. 1, pp. 521–553). New York: Plenum Press.

Kalivas, P. W., & Nakamura, M. (1999). Neural systems for behavioral activation and reward. *Current Opinion in Neurobiology, 9,* 223–227.

Kalra, S. P., Dube, M. G., Sahu, A., Phelps, C. P., & Kalra, P. S. (1991). Neuropeptide Y secretion increases in the paraventricular nucleus in association with increased appetite for food. *Proceedings of the National Academy of Sciences, USA, 88,* 10931–10935.

Kalra, S. P., Horvath, T., Naftolin, F., Xu, B., Pu, S., & Kalra, P. S. (1997). The interactive language of the hypothalamus for the gonadotropin releasing hormone (GNRH) system. *Journal of Neuroendocrinology, 9,* 569–576.

Kelly, A. B., & Watts, A. G. (1996). The mediation of dehydration-induced peptidergic gene expression in the rat lateral hypothalamic area by forebrain afferent projections. *Journal of Comparative Neurology, 370,* 231–246.

Kelly, A. B., & Watts, A. G. (1998). The region of the pontine parabrachial nucleus is a major target of dehydration-sensitive CRH neurons in the rat lateral hypothalamic area. *Journal of Comparative Neurology, 394,* 48–63.

Kilduff, T. S., & Peyron, C. (2000). The hypocretin/orexin ligand-receptor system: Implications for sleep and sleep disorders. *Trends in Neuroscience, 23,* 359–365.

de Kloet, E. R., Vreugdenhil, E., Oitzl, M. S., & Joels, M. (1998). Brain corticosteroid receptor balance in health and disease. *Endocrine Reviews, 19,* 269–301.

Kohler, C., Swanson, L. W., Haglund, L., & Wu, J. Y. (1985). The cytoarchitecture, histochemistry and projections of the tuberomammillary nucleus in the rat. *Neuroscience, 16,* 85–110.

Kristensen, P., Judge, M. E., Thim, L., Ribel, U., Christjansen, K. N., Wulff, B. S., Clausen, J. T., Jensen, P. B., & Madsen, O. D. (1998). Hypothalamic CART is a new anorectic peptide regulated by leptin. *Nature, 393,* 72–76.

Laflamme, N., Nappi, R. E., Drolet, G., Labrie, C., & Rivest, S. (1998). Expression and neuropeptidergic characterization of estrogen receptors (ERalpha and ERbeta) throughout the rat brain:

Anatomical evidence of distinct roles of each subtype. *Journal of Neurobiology, 36,* 357–378.

Larsen, P. J., Hay-Schmidt, A., & Mikkelsen, J. D. (1994). Efferent connections from the lateral hypothalamic region and the lateral preoptic area to the hypothalamic paraventricular nucleus of the rat. *Journal of Comparative Neurology, 342,* 299–319.

Lashley, K. S. (1951). The problem of serial order in behavior. In L. A. Jeffress (Ed.), *Cerebral mechanisms in behavior* (pp. 112–136). New York: Wiley.

Leak, R. K., & Moore, R. Y. (2001). Topographic organization of suprachiasmatic nucleus projection neurons. *Journal of Comparative Neurology, 433,* 312–334.

de Lecea, L., Kilduff, T. S., Peyron, C., Gao, X., Foye, P. E., Danielson, P. E., Fukuhara, C., Battenberg, E. L., Gautvik, V. T., Bartlett, F. S., II, Frankel, W. N., van den Pol, A. N., Bloom, F. E., Gautvik, K. M., & Sutcliffe, J. G. (1998). The hypocretins: Hypothalamus-specific peptides with neuroexcitatory activity. *Proceedings of the National Academy of Sciences, USA, 95,* 322–327.

LeDoux, J. (1996). *The emotional brain.* New York: Simon and Schuster.

Le Gros Clark, W. E. (1938). Morphological aspects of the hypothalamus. In Le Gros Clark, W. E., Beattie, J., Riddoch, G., & Dott, N. M. (Eds.), *The hypothalamus. Morphological, functional, clinical and surgical aspects* (pp. 1–68). Edinburgh, UK: Oliver and Boyd.

Leibowitz, S. F. (1978). Paraventricular nucleus: A primary site mediating adrenergic stimulation of feeding and drinking. *Pharmacology, Biochemistry and Behavior, 8,* 163–75.

Leng, G., & Brown, D. (1997). The origins and significance of pulsatility in hormone secretion from the pituitary. *Journal of Neuroendocrinology, 9,* 493–513.

Lévesque, M., Charara, A., Gagnon, S., Parent, A., & Deschênes, M. (1996b). Corticostriatal projections from layer V cells in rat are collaterals of long-range corticofugal axons. *Brain Research, 709,* 311–315.

Lévesque, M., Gagnon, S., Parent, A., & Deschênes, M. (1996a). Axonal arborizations

of corticostriatal and corticothalamic fibers arising from the second somatosensory area in the rat. *Cerebral Cortex, 6,* 759–770.

Levin, B. E., Dunn-Meynell, A. A., & Routh, V. H. (1999). Brain glucose sensing and body energy homeostasis: Role in obesity and diabetes. *American Journal of Physiology, 276,* R1223–R1231.

Levine, A. S., Kneip, J., Grace, M., & Morley, J. E. (1983). Effect of centrally administered neurotensin on multiple feeding paradigms. *Pharmacology, Biochemistry, and Behavior, 18,* 19–23.

Li, B. H., Xu, B., Rowland, N. E., & Kalra, S. P. (1994). c-fos expression in the rat brain following central administration of neuropeptide Y and effects of food consumption. *Brain Research, 665,* 277–284.

Li, C., Chen, P., & Smith, M. S. (1999). Morphological evidence for direct interaction between arcuate nucleus neuropeptide Y (NPY) neurons and gonadotropin-releasing hormone neurons and the possible involvement of NPY Y1 receptors. *Endocrinology, 140,* 5382–5390.

Li, C., Chen, P. L., & Smith, M. S. (2000). Corticotropin releasing hormone neurons in the paraventricular nucleus are direct targets for neuropeptide Y neurons in the arcuate nucleus: An anterograde tracing study. *Brain Research, 854,* 122–129.

Lin, L., Faraco, J., Li, R., Kadotani, H., Rogers, W., Lin, X., Qiu, X., de Jong, P. J., Nishino, S., & Mignot, E. (1999). The sleep disorder canine narcolepsy is caused by a mutation in the hypocretin (orexin) receptor 2 gene. *Cell, 98,* 365–376.

Llinas, R., Ribary, U., Contreras, D., & Pedroarena, C. (1998). The neuronal basis for consciousness. *Philosophical Transactions of The Royal Society B. & Biological Sciences, 353,* 1841–1849.

Lorenz, K. (1950). The comparative method for studying innate behavior. *Symposium for the study of experimental biology, 4,* 221–268.

Lu, J., Greco, M. A., Shiromani, P., & Saper, C. B. (2000). Effect of lesions of the ventrolateral preoptic nucleus on NREM and REM sleep. *Journal of Neuroscience, 20,* 3830–3842.

Luiten, P. G., ter Horst, G. J., & Steffens, A. B. (1987). The hypothalamus: Intrinsic connections and outflow pathways to the endocrine system in relation to feeding and metabolism. *Progress in Neurobiology, 28,* 1–54.

Maeda, K., Tsukamura, H., Ohkura, S., Kawakami, S., Nagabukuro, H., & Yokoyama, A. (1995). The LHRH pulse generator: A mediobasal hypothalamic location. *Neuroscience and Biobehavioral Reviews, 19,* 427–437.

Maguire, E. A., Burgess, N., Donnett, J. G., Frackowiak, R. S., Frith, C. D., & O'Keefe, J. (1998). Knowing where and getting there: A human navigation network. *Science., 280,* 921–924.

Mai, J. K., Kedziora, O., Teckhaus, L., & Sofroniew, M. V. (1991). Evidence for subdivisions in the human suprachiasmatic nucleus. *Journal of Comparative Neurology, 305,* 508–525.

Marks, J. L., Porte, D., Jr., Stahl, W. L., & Baskin, D. G. (1990). Localization of insulin receptor mRNA in rat brain by in situ hybridization. *Endocrinology, 127,* 3234–3236.

Marsh, D. J., Hollopeter, G., Huszar, D., Laufer, R., Yagaloff, K. A., Fisher, S. L., Burn, P., & Palmiter, R. D. (1999). Response of melanocortin-4 receptor-deficient mice to anorectic and orexigenic peptides. *Nature Genetics, 21,* 119–122.

Marshall, F. H. A. (1936). Sexual periodicity and the causes which determine it. *Philosophical Transactions of the Royal Society, 226,* 423–456.

McCormick, D. A., & Bal, T. (1997). Sleep and arousal: Thalamocortical mechanisms. *Annual Review of Neuroscience, 20,* 185–215.

McFarland, D. J., & Sibly, R. M. (1975). The behavioural final common path. *Philosophical Transactions of The Royal Society B. Biological Sciences, 270,* 265–293.

McGinty, D. J., & Seigel, J. M. (1983). Sleep states. In E. Satinoff & P. Teitelbaum (Eds.), *Motivation* (Vol. 6, pp. 105–181). New York: Plenum Press.

Medina, C. L., Nagatani, S., Darling, T. A., Bucholtz, D. C., Tsukamura, H., Maeda, K., & Foster, D. L. (1998). Glucose availability modulates the timing of the luteinizing hormone surge in the ewe. *Journal of Neuroendocrinology, 10,* 785–792.

Meyer-Bernstein, E. L., & Morin, L. P. (1996). Differential serotonergic innervation of the suprachiasmatic nucleus and the intergeniculate leaflet and its role in circadian rhythm modulation. *Journal of Neuroscience, 16,* 2097–2111.

Minami, S., Kamegai, J., Sugihara, H., Suzuki, N., Higuchi, H., & Wakabayashi, I. (1995). Central glucoprivation evoked by administration of 2-deoxy-D-glucose induces expression of the c-fos gene in a subpopulation of neuropeptide Y neurons in the rat hypothalamus. *Molecular Brain Research, 33,* 305–310.

Mizuno, T. M., & Mobbs, C. V. (1999). Hypothalamic agouti-related protein messenger ribonucleic acid is inhibited by leptin and stimulated by fasting. *Endocrinology, 140,* 814–817.

Moga, M. M., Herbert, H., Hurley, K. M., Yasui, Y., Gray, T. S., & Saper, C. B. (1990). Organization of cortical, basal forebrain, and hypothalamic afferents to the parabrachial nucleus in the rat. *Journal of Comparative Neurology, 295,* 624–661.

Moga, M. M., & Moore, R. Y. (1997). Organization of neural inputs to the suprachiasmatic nucleus in the rat. *Journal of Comparative Neurology, 389,* 508–534.

Moga, M. M., & Saper, C. B. (1994). Neuropeptide-immunoreactive neurons projecting to the paraventricular hypothalamic nucleus in the rat. *Journal of Comparative Neurology, 346,* 137–150.

Moga, M. M., Weis, R. P., & Moore, R. Y. (1995). Efferent projections of the paraventricular thalamic nucleus in the rat. *Journal of Comparative Neurology, 359,* 221–238.

Moore, R. Y. (1997). Circadian rhythms: Basic neurobiology and clinical applications. *Annual Review of Medicine, 48,* 253–266.

Morin, L. P., Goodless-Sanchez, N., Smale, L., & Moore, R. Y. (1994). Projections of the suprachiasmatic nuclei, subparaventricular zone and retrochiasmatic area in the golden hamster. *Neuroscience, 61,* 391–410.

Murahashi, K., Bucholtz, D. C., Nagatani, S., Tsukahara, S., Tsukamura, H., Foster, D. L., & Maeda, K. I. (1996). Suppression of luteinizing hormone pulses by restriction of glucose avail-ability is mediated by sensors in the brain stem. *Endocrinology, 137,* 1171–1176.

Nauta, W. J. H. (1946). Hypothalamic regulation of sleep in rats: An experimental study. *Journal of Neurophysiology, 9,* 285–316.

Norgen, R. (1984). Taste: Central neural mecha-nisms. In I. Darien-Smith (Ed.), *Handbook of the physiology: The nervous system, III: Sen-sory processes* (pp. 1087–1128). Washington, DC: American Physiological Society.

Novak, C. M., & Nunez, A. A. (2000). A sparse projection from the suprachiasmatic nucleus to the sleep active ventrolateral preoptic area in the rat. *Neuroreport, 11,* 93–96.

Oddie, S. D., & Bland, B. H. (1998). Hippocampal formation theta activity and movement selection. *Neuroscience and Biobehavioral Reviews, 22,* 221–231.

Oliveira, M. H., Antunes-Rodrigues, J., Gutkowska, J., Leal, A. M., Elias, L. L., & Moreira, A. C. (1997). Atrial natriuretic peptide and feeding activity patterns in rats. *Brazilian Journal of Medical and Biological Research, 30,* 465–469.

Öngür, D., An, X., & Price, J. L. (1998). Pre-frontal cortical projections to the hypothalamus in macaque monkeys. *Journal of Comparative Neurology, 401,* 480–505.

Öngür, D., & Price, J. L. (2000). The organiza-tion of networks within the orbital and medial prefrontal cortex of rats, monkeys and humans. *Cerebral Cortex, 10,* 206–219.

Palmiter, R. D., Erickson, J. C., Hollopeter, G., Baraban, S. C., & Schwartz, M. W. (1998). Life without neuropeptide Y. *Recent Progress in Hormone Research, 53,* 163–199.

Panula, P., Pirvola, U., Auvinen, S., & Airaksinen, M. S. (1989). Histamine-immunoreactive nerve fibers in the rat brain. *Neuroscience, 28,* 585–610.

Parent, A., & Cicchetti, F. (1998). The cur-rent model of basal ganglia organization under scrutiny. *Movement Disorders, 13,* 199–202.

Patchev, V. K., & Almeida, O. F. (1996). Gonadal steroids exert facilitating and "buffering" effects on glucocorticoid-mediated transcriptional reg-ulation of corticotropin-releasing hormone and

corticosteroid receptor genes in rat brain. *Jour-nal of Neuroscience, 16,* 7077–7084.

Peyron, C., Tighe, D. K., van den Pol, A. N., de Lecea, L., Heller, H. C., Sutcliffe, J. G., & Kilduff, T. S. (1998). Neurons containing hypocretin (orexin) project to multiple neuronal systems. *Journal of Neuroscience, 18,* 9996–10015.

Pfaff, D. W. (1980). *Estrogens and brain function.* New York: Springer-Verlag.

Pfaff, D. W. (1982). Motivational concepts: Defini-tions and distinctions. In D. W. Pfaff (Ed.), *The physiological mechanisms of motivation.* New York: Springer-Verlag.

Pfaff, D. W. (1999). *Drive: Neurobiological and molecular mechanisms of sexual motivation.* Cambridge, MA: MIT Press.

Porte, D., Jr., Seeley, R. J., Woods, S. C., Baskin, D. G., Figlewicz, D. P., & Schwartz, M. W. (1998). Obesity, diabetes and the central nervous system. *Diabetologia, 41,* 863–881.

Ranson, S. W. (1939). Somnolence caused by hy-pothalamic lesions in the monkey. *Archives of Neurology and Psychiatry, 41,* 1–23.

Rinaman, L., Levitt, P., & Card, J. P. (2000). Progressive postnatal assembly of limbic-autonomic circuits revealed by central transneu-ronal transport of pseudorabies virus. *Journal of Neuroscience, 20,* 2731–2741.

Risold, P. Y., & Swanson, L. W. (1995). Evi-dence for a hypothalamothalamocortical circuit mediating pheromonal influences on eye and head movements. *Proceedings of the National Academy of Sciences, USA, 92,* 3898–3902.

Risold, P. Y., & Swanson, L. W. (1996). Struc-tural evidence for functional domains in the rat hippocampus. *Science, 272,* 1484–1486.

Risold, P. Y., & Swanson, L. W. (1997). Connec-tions of the rat lateral septal complex. *Brain Research Reviews, 24,* 115–196.

Risold, P. Y., Thompson, R. H., & Swanson, L. W. (1997). The structural organization of con-nections between the hypothalamus and cere-bral cortex. *Brain Research Reviews, 24,* 197–254.

Ritter, S., Bugarith, K., & Dinh, T. T. (2001). Im-munotoxic destruction of distinct catecholamine subgroups produces selective impairment of glucoregulatory responses and neuronal activation. *Journal of Comparative Neurology, 432,* 197–216.

Ritter, S., Dinh, T. T., & Zhang, Y. (2000). Localization of hindbrain glucoreceptive sites controlling food intake and blood glucose. *Brain Research, 856,* 37–47.

Ritter, S., Llewellyn-Smith, I., & Dinh, T. T. (1998). Subgroups of hindbrain catecholamine neurons are selectively activated by 2-deoxy-D-glucose induced metabolic challenge. *Brain Research, 805,* 41–54.

Rizzolatti, G., & Luppino, G. (2001). The cortical motor system. *Neuron, 31,* 889–901.

Roberts, E. (1976). Some thoughts about GABA and the basal ganglia. In M. D. Yahr (Ed.), *The basal ganglia.* New York: Raven Press. (pp. 191–203). Research Publications of the Association for Research in Nervous and Mental Diseases.

Rolls, E. T. (1999a). *The brain and emotion.* Oxford, UK: Oxford University Press.

Rolls, E. T. (1999b). Spatial view cells and the representation of place in the primate hippocampus. *Hippocampus, 9,* 467–480.

Rolls, E. T. (2000a). The orbitofrontal cortex and reward. *Cerebral Cortex, 10,* 284–294.

Rolls, E. T. (2000b). Memory systems in the brain. *Annual Review of Psychology, 51,* 599–630.

Rossi, M., Kim, M. S., Morgan, D. G., Small, C. J., Edwards, C. M., Sunter, D., Abusnana, S., Goldstone, A. P., Russell, S. H., Stanley, S. A., Smith, D. M., Yagaloff, K., Ghatei, M. A., & Bloom, S. R. (1998). A C-terminal fragment of Agouti-related protein increases feeding and antagonizes the effect of alpha-melanocyte stimulating hormone in vivo. *Endocrinology, 139,* 4428–4431.

Rossignol, S. (1996). Neural control of stereotypic limb movements. In L. B. Rowell & J. T. Shepard (Eds.), *Handbook of physiology, section 12. Exercise: Regulation and integration of multiple systems* (pp. 173–216). Bethesda, MD: American Physiological Society.

Saeb-Parsy, K., Lombardelli, S., Khan, F. Z., McDowall, K., Au-Yong, I. T., & Dyball, R. E. J. (2000). Neural connections of hypothalamic neuroendocrine nuclei in the rat. *Journal of Neuroendocrinology, 12,* 635–648.

Sahu, A. (1998). Evidence suggesting that galanin (GAL), melanin-concentrating hormone (MCH), neurotensin (NT), proopiomelanocortin (POMC) and neuropeptide Y (NPY) are targets of leptin signaling in the hypothalamus. *Endocrinology, 139,* 795–798.

Saper, C. B. (1985). Organization of cerebral cortical afferent systems in the rat, II: Hypothalamocortical projections. *Journal of Comparative Neurology, 237,* 21–46.

Sapolsky, R. M., Romero, L. M., & Munck, A. U. (2000). How do glucocorticoids influence stress responses? Integrating permissive, suppressive, stimulatory, and preparative actions. *Endocrine Reviews, 21,* 55–89.

Sar, M., Sahu, A., Crowley, W. R., & Kalra, S. P. (1990). Localization of neuropeptide-Y immunoreactivity in estradiol-concentrating cells in the hypothalamus. *Endocrinology, 127,* 2752–2756.

Sarkar, D. K., Chiappa, S. A., Fink, G., & Sherwood, N. M. (1976). Gonadotropin-releasing hormone surge in pro-oestrous rats. *Nature, 264,* 461–463.

Sawchenko, P. E. (1998). Toward a new neurobiology of energy balance, appetite, and obesity: The anatomists weigh in. *Journal of Comparative Neurology, 402,* 435–441.

Sawchenko, P. E., & Swanson, L. W. (1983). The organization of forebrain afferents to the paraventricular and supraoptic nuclei of the rat. *Journal of Comparative Neurology, 218,* 121–144.

Sawchenko, P. E., Swanson, L. W., Rivier, J., & Vale, W. W. (1985). The distribution of growth hormone releasing factor (GRF) immunoreactivity in the central nervous system of the rat: An immunohistochemical study using antisera directed against rat hypothalamic GRF. *Journal of Comparative Neurology, 237,* 100–115.

Scammell, T. E., Estabrooke, I. V., McCarthy, M. T., Chemelli, R. M., Yanagisawa, M., Miller, M. S., & Saper, C. B. (2000). Hypothalamic arousal regions are activated during modafinil-induced wakefulness. *Journal of Neuroscience, 20,* 8620–8628.

Schneider, J. E., & Watts, A. G. (In press). Energy balance, behavior and reproductive success. In

D. W. Pfaff & A. Etgen (Eds.), *Hormones, brain, and behavior.* San Diego, CA: Academic Press.

Schneider, J. E., Zhou, D., & Blum, R. M. (2000). Leptin and metabolic control of reproduction. *Hormones and Behavior, 37,* 306–326.

Schultz, W., Tremblay, L., & Hollerman, J. R. (2000). Reward processing in primate orbitofrontal cortex and basal ganglia. *Cerebral Cortex, 10,* 272–283.

Schwartz, M. W., Bergman, R. N., Kahn, S. E., Taborsky, G. J., Jr., Fisher, L. D., Sipols, A. J., Woods, S. C., Steil, G. M., & Porte, D., Jr. (1991). Evidence for entry of plasma insulin into cerebrospinal fluid through an intermediate compartment in dogs. Quantitative aspects and implications for transport. *Journal of Clinical Investigation, 88,* 1272–1281.

Schwartz, M. W., Seeley, R. J., Woods, S. C., Weigle, D. S., Campfield, L. A., Burn, P., & Baskin, D. G. (1997). Leptin increases hypothalamic pro-opiomelanocortin mRNA expression in the rostral arcuate nucleus. *Diabetes, 46,* 2119–2123.

Schwartz, M. W., Woods, S. C., Porte, D., Jr., Seeley, R. J., & Baskin, D. G. (2000). Central nervous system control of food intake. *Nature, 404,* 661–671.

Semba, K. (2000). Multiple output pathways of the basal forebrain: Organization, chemical heterogeneity, and roles in vigilance. *Behavioral Brain Research, 115,* 117–141.

Sherin, J. E., Elmquist, J. K., Torrealba, F., & Saper, C. B. (1998). Innervation of histaminergic tuberomammillary neurons by GABAergic and galaninergic neurons in the ventrolateral preoptic nucleus of the rat. *Journal of Neuroscience, 18,* 4705–4721.

Sherin, J. E., Shiromani, P. J., McCarley, R. W., & Saper, C. B. (1996). Activation of ventrolateral preoptic neurons during sleep. *Science, 271,* 216–219.

Shimada, M., Tritos, N. A., Lowell, B. B., Flier, J. S., & Maratos-Flier, E. (1998). Mice lacking melanin-concentrating hormone are hypophagic and lean. *Nature, 396,* 670–674.

Shughrue, P. J., Lane, M. V., & Merchenthaler, I. (1997). Comparative distribution of estrogen receptor-alpha and -beta mRNA in the rat central nervous. *Journal of Comparative Neurology, 388,* 507–525.

Simerly, R. B. (1998). Organization and regulation of sexually dimorphic neuroendocrine pathways. *Behavioral Brain Research, 92,* 195–203.

Simerly, R. B., Chang, C., Muramatsu, M., & Swanson, L. W. (1990). Distribution of androgen and estrogen receptor mRNA-containing cells in the rat brain: An in situ hybridization study. *Journal of Comparative Neurology, 294,* 76–95.

Simerly, R. B., McCall, L. D., & Watson, S. J. (1988). Distribution of opioid peptides in the preoptic region: Immunohistochemical evidence for a steroid-sensitive enkephalin sexual dimorphism. *Journal of Comparative Neurology, 276,* 442–459.

Simonian, S. X., Spratt, D. P., & Herbison, A. E. (1999). Identification and characterization of estrogen receptor alpha-containing neurons projecting to the vicinity of the gonadotropin-releasing hormone perikarya in the rostral preoptic area of the rat. *Journal of Comparative Neurology, 411,* 346–358.

Skynner, M. J., Sim, J. A., & Herbison, A. E. (1999). Detection of estrogen receptor alpha and beta messenger ribonucleic acids in adult gonadotropin-releasing hormone neurons. *Endocrinology, 140,* 5195–5201.

Smith, P. F. (1997). Vestibular-hippocampal interactions. *Hippocampus, 7,* 465–471.

Spector, A. C. (2000). Linking gustatory neurobiology to behavior in vertebrates. *Neuroscience and Biobehavioral Reviews, 24,* 391–416.

Standaert, D. G., & Saper, C. B. (1988). Origin of the atriopeptin-like immunoreactive innervation of the paraventricular nucleus of the hypothalamus. *Journal of Neuroscience, 8,* 1940–1950.

Stanley, B. G., & Leibowitz, S. F. (1985). Neuropeptide Y injected in the paraventricular hypothalamus: A powerful stimulant of feeding behavior. *Proceedings of the National Academy of Sciences, USA, 82,* 3940–3943.

Stanley, B. G., Magdalin, W., Seirafi, A., Thomas, W. J., & Leibowitz, S. F. (1993). The perifornical area—The major focus of (a) patchy distributed hypothalamic neuropeptide Y-sensitive feeding system(s). *Brain Research, 604,* 304–317.

Stanley, B. G., Willett, V. L., III, Donias, H. W., Dee, M. G., II, & Duva, M. A. (1996). Lateral hypothalamic NMDA receptors and glutamate as physiological mediators of eating and weight control. *American Journal of Physiology, 270,* R443–R449.

Steininger, T. L., Gong, H., McGinty, D., & Szymusiak, R. (2001). Subregional organization of preoptic area/anterior hypothalamic projections to arousal-related monoaminergic cell groups. *Journal of Comparative Neurology, 429,* 638–653.

Stellar, E. (1954). The physiology of emotion. *Psychological Reviews, 61,* 5–22.

Steriade, M. (2000). Corticothalamic resonance, states of vigilance and mentation. *Neuroscience, 101,* 243–276.

Strack, A. M., Sawyer, W. B., Hughes, J. H., Platt, K. B., & Loewy, A. D. (1989). A general pattern of CNS innervation of the sympathetic outflow demonstrated by transneuronal pseudorabies viral infections. *Brain Research, 491,* 156–162.

Strack, A. M., Sebastian, R. J., Schwartz, M. W., & Dallman, M. F. (1995). Glucocorticoids and insulin: Reciprocal signals for energy balance. *American Journal of Physiology, 268,* R142–R149.

Stratford, T. R., & Kelley, A. E. (1997). GABA in the nucleus accumbens shell participates in the central regulation of feeding behavior. *Journal of Neuroscience, 17,* 4434–4440.

Stratford, T. R., Kelley, A. E., & Simansky, K. J. (1999). Blockade of GABAA receptors in the medial ventral pallidum elicits feeding in satiated rats. *Brain Research, 825,* 199–203.

Stuphorn, V., Bauswein, E., & Hoffman, K.-P. (2000). Neurons in the primate superior colliculus coding for arm movements in gaze-related conditions. *Journal of Neurophysiology, 83,* 1283–1299.

Sun, X., Rusak, B., & Semba, K. (2000). Electrophysiology and pharmacology of projections from the suprachiasmatic nucleus to the ventromedial preoptic area in rat. *Neuroscience, 98,* 715–728.

Swanson, C. J., & Kalivas, P. W. (2000). Regulation of locomotor activity by metabotropic glutamate receptors in the nucleus accumbens and ventral tegmental area. *Journal of Pharmacology and Experimental Therapeutics, 292,* 406–414.

Swanson, L. W. (1982). The projections of the ventral tegmental area and adjacent regions: A combined fluorescent retrograde tracer and immunofluorescence study in the rat. *Brain Research Bulletin, 9,* 321–353.

Swanson, L. W. (1987). The hypothalamus. In A. Bjorklund, T. Hökfelt, & L. W. Swanson (Eds.), *Handbook of chemical neuroanatomy* (Vol. 5, pp. 1–124). Amsterdam: Elsevier.

Swanson, L. W. (2000a). Cerebral hemisphere regulation of motivated behavior. *Brain Research, 886,* 113–164.

Swanson, L. W. (2000b). What is the brain? *Trends in Neurosciences, 23,* 519–527.

Swanson, L. W., & Mogenson, G. J. (1981). Neural mechanisms for the functional coupling of autonomic, endocrine and somatomotor responses in adaptive behavior. *Brain Research, 228,* 1–34.

Swanson, L. W., & Petrovich, G. D. (1998). What is the amygdala? *Trends in Neurosciences, 21,* 323–331.

Tanaka, T., Nagatani, S., Bucholtz, D. C., Ohkura, S., Tsukamura, H., Maeda, K., & Foster, D. L. (2000). Central action of insulin regulates pulsatile luteinizing hormone secretion in the diabetic sheep model. *Biology of Reproduction, 62,* 1256–1261.

Taube, J. S. (1998). Head direction cells and the neurophysiological basis for a sense of direction. *Progress in Neurobiology, 55,* 225–256.

Terasawa, E., Keen, K. L., Mogi, K., & Claude, P. (1999). Pulsatile release of luteinizing hormone-releasing hormone (LHRH) in cultured LHRH neurons derived from the embryonic olfactory placode of the rhesus monkey. *Endocrinology, 140,* 1432–1441.

Thannickal, T. C., Moore, R. Y., Nienhuis, R., Ramanathan, L., Gulyani, S., Aldrich, M., Cornford, M., & Siegel, J. M. (2000). Reduced number of hypocretin neurons in human narcolepsy. *Neuron, 27,* 469–474.

Thompson, R. F., & Kim, J. J. (1996). Memory systems in the brain and localization of a memory. *Proceedings of the National Academy of Sciences, USA, 93,* 13438–13444.

Thompson, R. H., Canteras, N. S., & Swanson, L. W. (1996). Organization of projections from the dorsomedial nucleus of the hypothalamus—A PHA-L study in the rat. *Journal of Comparative Neurology, 376,* 143–173.

Thompson, R. H., & Swanson, L. W. (1998). Organization of inputs to the dorsomedial nucleus of the hypothalamus: A reexamination with Fluorogold and PHAL in the rat. *Brain Research Review, 27,* 89–118.

Tinbergen, N. (1951). *The study of instinct.* Oxford, UK: Oxford University Press.

Toates, F. (1986). *Motivational systems.* Cambridge, UK: Cambridge University Press.

Travers, J. B., Dinardo, L. A., & Karimnamazi, H. (1997). Motor and premotor mechanisms of licking. *Neuroscience and Biobehavioral Reviews, 21,* 631–647.

Unger, J. W., Livingston, J. N., & Moss, A. M. (1991). Insulin receptors in the central nervous system: Localization, signalling mechanisms and functional aspects. *Progress in Neurobiology, 36,* 343–362.

Unger, R. H. (2000). Leptin physiology: A second look. *Regulatory Peptides, 92,* 87–95.

Valverde, F., Garcia, C., López-Mascaraque, L., & De Carlos, J. A. (2000). Development of the mammillothalamic tract in normal and Pax-6 mutant mice. *Journal of Comparative Neurology, 419,* 485–504.

van den Pol, A. N. (1980). The hypothalamic suprachiasmatic nucleus of rat: Intrinsic anatomy. *Journal of Comparative Neurology, 191,* 661–702.

van den Pol, A. N., Gao, X. B., Obrietan, K., Kilduff, T. S., & Belousov, A. B. (1998). Presynaptic and postsynaptic actions and modulation of neuroendocrine neurons by a new hypothalamic peptide, hypocretin/orexin. *Journal of Neuroscience, 18,* 7962–7971.

van der Beek, E. M., Horvath, T. L., Wiegant, V. M., Van den Hurk, R., & Buijs, R. M. (1997). Evidence for a direct neuronal pathway from the suprachiasmatic nucleus to the gonadotropin-releasing hormone system: Combined tracing and light and electron microscopic immunocytochemical studies. *Journal of Comparative Neurology, 384,* 569–579.

Viau, V., Chu, A., Soriano, L., & Dallman, M. F. (1999). Independent and overlapping effects of corticosterone and testosterone on corticotropin-releasing hormone and arginine vasopressin mRNA expression in the paraventricular nucleus of the hypothalamus and stress-induced adrenocorticotropic hormone release. *Journal of Neuroscience, 19,* 6684–6693.

Viau, V., Soriano, L., & Dallman, M. F. (2001). Androgens alter corticotropin releasing hormone and arginine vasopressin mRNA within forebrain sites known to regulate activity in the hypothalamic-pituitary-adrenal axis. *Journal of Neuroendocrinology, 13,* 442–452.

Watson, R. E., Jr., Langub, M. C., Jr., Engle, M. G., & Maley, B. E. (1995). Estrogen-receptive neurons in the anteroventral periventricular nucleus are synaptic targets of the suprachiasmatic nucleus and peri-suprachiasmatic region. *Brain Research, 689,* 254–264.

Watts, A. G. (1991). The efferent projections of the suprachiasmatic nucleus: Anatomical insights into the control of circadian rhythms. In D. Klein, R. Y. Moore, & S. M. Reppert (Eds.), *The suprachiasmatic nucleus: The mind's clock* (pp. 77–104). New York: Oxford University Press.

Watts, A. G. (1996). The impact of physiological stimulation on the expression of corticotropin-releasing hormone and other neuropeptide genes. *Frontiers in Neuroendocrinology, 17,* 281–326.

Watts, A. G. (2000). Understanding the neural control of ingestive behaviors: Helping to separate cause from effect with dehydration-associated anorexia. *Hormones and Behavior, 37,* 261–283.

Watts, A. G. (2001). Neuropeptides and the integration of motor responses to dehydration. *Annual Reviews of Neuroscience, 24,* 357–384.

Watts, A. G., & Sanchez-Watts, G. (2000). Lateral hypothalamic fos expression is activated in hypocretin/orexin, but not CRH or melanin-concentrating hormone neurons after reversal of dehydration-anorexia. *Society for Neuroscience Abstracts, 26,* 2041.

Watts, A. G., Sanchez-Watts, G., & Kelly, A. B. (1999). Distinct and similar patterns of neuropeptide gene expression are present in rat hypothalamus following dehydration-induced anorexia or paired food restriction. *Journal of Neuroscience, 19,* 6111–6121.

Watts, A. G., Sheward, W. J., Whale, D., & Fink, G. (1989). The effects of knife cuts in the sub-paraventricular zone of the female rat hypothalamus on oestrogen-induced diurnal surges of plasma prolactin and LH, and on circadian wheel-running activity. *Journal of Endocrinology, 122,* 593–604.

Watts, A. G., & Swanson, L. W. (1987). Efferent projections of the suprachiasmatic nucleus, II: Studies using retrograde transport of fluorescent dyes and simultaneous peptide immunohistochemistry in the rat. *Journal of Comparative Neurology, 258,* 230–252.

Watts, A. G., Swanson, L. W., & Sanchez-Watts, G. (1987). Efferent projections of the suprachiasmatic nucleus, I: Studies using anterograde transport of *Phaseolus vulgaris* leucoagglutinin (PHA-L) in the rat. *Journal of Comparative Neurology, 258,* 204–229.

Weese, G. D., Phillips, J. M., & Brown, V. J. (1999). Attentional orienting is impaired by unilateral lesions of the thalamic reticular nucleus in the rat. *Journal of Neuroscience, 19,* 10135–10139.

Werner, W., Hoffman, K.-P., & Dannenberg, S. (1997). Anatomical distribution of arm-movement-related neurons in the primate superior colliculus and underlying reticular formation in comparison with visual and saccadic cells. *Experimental Brain Research, 115,* 206–216.

Wetsel, W. C., Valenca, M. M., Merchenthaler, I., Liposits, Z., Lopez, F. J., Weiner, R. I., Mellon, P. L., & Negro-Vilar, A. (1992). Intrinsic pulsatile secretory activity of immortalized luteinizing hormone-releasing hormone-secreting neurons. *Proceedings of the National Academy of Sciences, USA, 89,* 4149–4153.

Whishaw, I. Q. (1990). The decorticate rat. In B. Kolb & R. C. Tees (Eds.), *The cerebral cortex of the rat* (pp. 239–267). Cambridge, MA: MIT Press.

Whishaw, I. Q., & Coles, B. L. (1996). Varieties of paw and digit movement during spontaneous food handling in rats: Postures, bimanual coordination, preferences, and the effect of forelimb

cortex lesions. *Behavioral Brain Research, 77,* 135–148.

Whitnall, M. H. (1993). Regulation of the hypothalamic corticotropin-releasing hormone neurosecretory system. *Progress in Neurobiology, 40,* 573–629.

Wiedemann, K., Jahn, H., & Kellner, M. (2000). Effects of natriuretic peptides upon hypothalamo-pituitary-adrenocortical system activity and anxiety behaviour. *Experimental and Clinical Endocrinology and Diabetes, 108,* 5–13.

Wiegand, S. J., & Terasawa, E. (1982). Discrete lesions reveal functional heterogeneity of suprachiasmatic structures in regulation of gonadotropin secretion in the female rat. *Neuroendocrinology, 34,* 395–404.

Wiegand, S. J., Terasawa, E., Bridson, W. E., & Goy, R. W. (1980). Effects of discrete lesions of preoptic and suprachiasmatic structures in the female rat: Alterations in the feedback regulation of gonadotropin secretion. *Neuroendocrinology, 31,* 147–157.

Willie, J. T., Chemelli, R. M., Sinton, C. M., & Yanagisawa, M. (2001). To eat or sleep? The role of orexin in coordination of feeding and arousal. *Annual Review of Neuroscience, 24,* 429–458.

Wilson, B. D., Bagnol, D., Kaelin, C. B., Ollmann, M. M., Gantz, I., Watson, S. J., & Barsh, G. S. (1999). Physiological and anatomical circuitry between Agouti-related protein and leptin signaling. *Endocrinology, 140,* 2387–2397.

Winn, P. (1995). The lateral hypothalamus and motivated behavior: An old syndrome reassessed and a new perspective gained. *Current Directions in Psychological Science, 4,* 182–187.

Woods, S. C., Lotter, E. C., McKay, L. D., & Porte, D., Jr. (1979). Chronic intracerebroventricular infusion of insulin reduces food intake and body weight of baboons. *Nature, 282,* 503–505.

Woods, S. C., Seeley, R. J., Porte, D., Jr., & Schwartz, M. W. (1998). Signals that regulate food intake and energy homeostasis. *Science, 280,* 1378–1383.

Zaborsky, L., & Duque, A. (2000). Local synaptic connections of basal forebrain neurons. *Behavioral Brain Research, 115,* 143–158.

CHAPTER 15

Hunger and Energy Homeostasis

STEPHEN C. WOODS AND RANDY J. SEELEY

INTRODUCTION

In contemporary society, with abundant and readily available food, eating is such a commonplace behavior, and is such an integral part of social behavior, that many individuals normally pay little attention to its biological underpinnings. True, those who diet or count their calories are aware that such controls exist, and they often exert cognitive willpower in attempts to override their endogenous regulatory signals. Nonetheless, both a lack of sound knowledge and a wealth of misinformation concerning the controls over the ingestion of food abound in popular thought. The intent of this chapter is to describe what is known of the regulatory control and the measurement of food intake and to demonstrate how the controls over ingestion are normally integrated with the control of body weight (or, more specifically, body fat or adiposity).

We refer to "food" in this chapter as ingestible calories rather than as any substance that might be chewed and swallowed. Food is of course a primary reinforcer in that animals are genetically predisposed to receive reward value from it, particularly if insufficient food has been available in the immediate past. The energy content of food is the basis for this property and is necessary for life. Certain sensory qualities that reliably predict food energy also appear to act as primary reinforcers, such

as the sweet taste of saccharin or aspartame, and animals will readily learn responses to obtain them or make what appear to be unconditioned responses when they are presented. This is true even in very young individuals who have had little chance to make learned associations (Blass & Shah, 1995; Blass, Shide, & Weller, 1989; Ren, Blass, Zhou, & Dubner, 1997; Swithers, Westneat, & Hall, 1998). However, if these tastants are repeatedly dissociated from energy content, their reinforcement value wanes (R. Deutsch, 1974), implying that experience either greatly reduces an innate property or extinguishes a strong association. Food, along with water, another primary reinforcer, was pivotal in the original parametric descriptions of conditioning, in which Pavlov used food powder as an unconditioned stimulus to elicit salivation in his dogs and Skinner used food as a reinforcement in rats and pigeons. An important aspect of its reinforcing qualities is that food also elicits hedonic perceptions. Food is thus a powerful and critically important stimulus for both motivating and reinforcing behavior.

Humans (like the commonly studied laboratory rat) are classified as general omnivores, indicating that they consume, and are able to derive usable nutrients from, a broad range of possible foods. This simple fact has numerous complex implications. For one, the sensory systems that seek and identify foods must complement the potential diet and hence be sensitive to an equally broad range of sights, smells, and tastes. Likewise, the gastrointestinal system must possess a wide array of sensors, digestive enzymes, and other secretions to cope with whatever ingestants it encounters, and a system should exist for relaying information about the quantity and quality of foods being consumed to control circuits in the nervous system. Another consequence of being an omnivore is that a specialized learning system is required to facilitate remembering which specific foods are nutritious and which are not, and which are toxic or have other undesirable side effects. This learning mechanism must be able to associate cues that are present at the time the food is consumed with postingestive consequences that may occur several hours later. Finally, there must be a complex regulatory system to ensure that the best mix of possible nutrients is identified, consumed, stored, and meted to the various organ systems as needed.

MEALS

Another level of complexity relates to the processes of energy intake and energy expenditure. Energy is expended continuously by living organisms, and the rate of utilization and the mix of fuels vary with metabolic needs, physical activity, and other factors. Energy intake, on the other hand, is typically intermittent, occurring as discrete meals. When the energy content of food sources is high, and food is readily available, an animal need invest only a small proportion of its day in finding and eating food. Most of what is consumed in any given meal can then be stored until needed. Individuals living in such a luxurious world are often the subjects in laboratory investigations of the psychobiology of eating, but it should be recognized that conclusions based on such investigations are nec-

essarily limited. At the opposite end of the control system, the food source for some individuals has a relatively low energy content, necessitating long hours of grazing. Another commonly occurring factor is that food may not be readily available in ample quantities, necessitating a greater proportion of time foraging and perhaps necessitating a deviation from a preferred eating schedule to accommodate fewer but larger meals once an adequate food source is found. Yet another factor relates to the amount of energy that the body should normally store in an ideal world. Presumably, the amount reflects the interplay of those factors that ensure adequate energy when food is scarce and those that incapacitate the individual due to excessive storage. A control system that can integrate these numerous internal and external demands is necessarily complex.

For most general omnivores, a control system has evolved that accomplishes all of this while allowing a high degree of individual flexibility. Two basic features of this control system are critical for its success. The first basic feature is that the size of the energy storage organ (total adipose mass or body fat content in most instances), while genetically determined, has a wide range of latitude. In simple terms, as depicted in Figure 15.1, one's genetic heritage determines both an upper and a lower limit to what is acceptable. The environment in which an individual lives determines where within that range the individual will regulate its body fat content and hence its body weight. Although body fat content need not have absolute upper or lower limits for regulation to occur, there is strong evidence that such limits exist. For example, when the ventromedial hypothalamic (VMH) nuclei are destroyed, animals overeat until they reach a new, higher plateau of body weight, a plateau that they defend as long as the environment is constant (Hoebel & Teitelbaum, 1966). This suggests that the

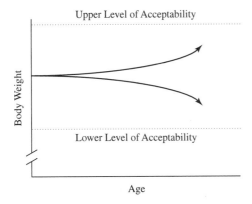

Figure 15.1   Theoretical depiction of how genetic factors provide upper and lower limits of body weight, whereas environmental factors account for much of the variance within those limits.

VMH normally helps determine the upper limit on body weight, and that other parts of the brain predominate and determine a higher boundary in its absence. When either normal control animals or obese VMH-lesioned animals are given bitter-tasting food as the only energy source, both groups eat less and lose weight. Importantly, both groups reduce their weight to the same absolute weight in this situation, suggesting that the VMH does not influence the lower boundary (Sclafani & Grossman, 1971; Sclafani, Springer, & Kluge, 1976). This model has several implications for the regulation of body weight. The first is that if an environment is relatively stable, an individual moves to the level of body fat that is appropriate for that environment and tends to stay there. Hence, if its body weight deviates slightly from time to time because of some situational event, it will always drift back when the opportunity arises. Likewise, if energy stores are experimentally or voluntarily moved off the regulated level, physiological regulatory systems will become activated, causing a net movement of body weight back toward the baseline (Woods & Seeley, 2000). In this regard the body can muster behavioral as well as metabolic adjustments to in-

gest or expend more or less energy (Keesey & Hirvonen, 1997). Hence, when an individual is living in a stable environment, it will appear to have what has been termed a set point. That is, whenever its body weight has been displaced away from its regulated level, it will return when conditions allow (Keesey & Hirvonen, 1997). As just described for animals with VMH lesions, this is the case regardless of the level of weight that is being maintained. Laboratory animals typically live in very stable environments because this is a prerequisite for good experimental control. Hence, the myth that animals have set points is probably an artifact of the laboratory setting. An important consideration is that the body weight of different individuals living in apparently comparable and stable environments varies considerably. Numerous experiments on humans and animals have led to the conclusion that this variation is genetically based (Bouchard, 1995; Bray & Bouchard, 1997; Reed, Bachmanov, Beauchamp, Tordoff, & Price, 1997; West, 1996), and the important implication is that there is considerable variability in the interaction of one's genes with specific environments.

   In the real world, individuals may go through long periods in which the available food varies in its palatability, energy content, or some other important parameter. Each of these would constitute a change in the environment, and each would be accompanied by an associated change in the regulated level of body weight. Analogously, an individual could be exposed to chronic stress or could be required to exercise more or less on a chronic basis, or live in a warmer or colder environment. Again, body weight will drift to a new level with each such environmental change and tend to remain there until conditions change again. On a practical level, humans are said to be experiencing an epidemic of obesity in that both the incidence and the severity of obesity are increasing

(Flegal, Carroll, Kuczmarski, & Johnson, 1998; Hill & Peters, 1998; Mokdad et al., 2000; Ogden et al., 1997). When one considers the correlated changes in food availability, food palatability, nutrient content, average exercise at work and home, and so on, the epidemic can be considered to be the natural consequence of an environment that has changed to favor more fat deposition in a species with a high average upper level of acceptable body fat.

The second basic feature of this integrated control system is that food intake is controlled not by when meals are initiated, but rather by how much is eaten once a meal is underway. When food is readily available, individuals could, in principle, eat whenever they choose. In such situations, most individuals tend to develop stable meal patterns. That is, they adopt a schedule that is relatively consistent from day to day, such as eating "three square meals a day." Individuals vary considerably in terms of the number and size of individual meals, yet most maintain stable body weights and daily caloric intakes. The ability to adopt a feeding schedule that meshes well with other demands and aspects of the environment is extremely adaptive. It allows optimal use of time for social activities, exercise, sleep patterns, and other behaviors.

Rats living in individual cages in a laboratory also develop stable feeding patterns, comparable in many ways to the patterns of humans. Most laboratory rats eat the largest meals of the day at highly predictable times, such as when the lights in the room go on or off, and smaller meals at other times (Alingh Prins, de Jong-Nagelsmit, Keijser, & Strubbe, 1986; Le Magnen & Tallon, 1966). Most also eat a relatively consistent number of meals each day. If constraints are imposed that make it more or less favorable to eat at certain times, that restrict the amount eaten at any given time, or that require considerable effort to gain access to food, the pattern changes

(see Woods, 1991; Woods & Strubbe, 1994). However, daily caloric intake and body weight remain remarkably constant. One reason is that the physiological controls over this system work primarily on meal termination rather than on meal initiation.

When food is being eaten, a wide array of sensory input impinges on the brain and provides information about the amount and quality of food that is available for consumption. This ranges from exteroceptive cues (seeing how much food is on one's plate), to the smell and taste of the food, to the physicochemical properties of the food (texture, osmolarity, macronutrient content), to the state of the gastrointestinal tract (degree of stomach distension). The brain in turn integrates all of this information and makes a decision about when the meal should end. Of particular importance, and as reviewed later, there is considerable evidence that as the gut (i.e., the stomach and small intestine) processes the food being consumed, specialized cells lining the gut secrete a number of peptides. Many of these peptides enter the blood as hormones and stimulate distant organs such as the liver and pancreas to secrete the appropriate mix of digestive enzymes and juices to break down the food into absorbable and usable molecules. Some of the same peptides double as signals to the nervous system and provide information about what and how much has been eaten. Hence, when brain activity based on some correlate of this peptidergic signal gets sufficiently high, heralding that a certain caloric load has been consumed, the nervous system sends signals to end the meal. Subjectively, individuals feel full or satiated, and they stop eating.

A key feature of this control mechanism is that other signals are continuously informing the nervous system about the amount of fat stored in the body (discussed later). These adiposity signals interact with the meal-generated signals in an important way. If an individual has lost some weight (i.e., has lost some body fat by drifting below the optimal weight for her or his environment), a smaller adiposity signal is generated and reaches the nervous system. One result of the reduced signal in the brain is that once the individual finds food and begins eating, he or she will be less sensitive to the satiating effect of the meal-generated peptides. The individual will thus eat larger meals and thereby tend to regain the lost weight. Analogously, when an individual has gained more weight than is appropriate for the environment, the elevated adiposity signal will render the nervous system more sensitive to meal-generated signals. In this way body weight tends to be maintained over long intervals, and this occurs independent of when meals are initiated or of their exact patterning (see reviews in M. W. Schwartz, Woods, Porte, Seeley, & Baskin, 2000; Woods & Seeley, 2000; Woods, Seeley, Porte, & Schwartz, 1998). This control system allows individuals to adopt whatever eating schedule best fits their environment. If food is available only at certain times (e.g., when a predator or social competitor is absent), individuals can eat at those times and adopt a schedule of fewer, larger meals each day.

Collier and his colleagues have investigated this phenomenon systematically. They refer to animals as economists in that they establish an eating pattern that optimizes ingesting sufficient calories to maintain body weight while minimizing the total daily time and effort necessary to obtain the calories (Collier, 1986; Collier, Johnson, Hill, & Kaufman, 1986; Mathis, Johnson, & Collier, 1995). Collier has found that individuals of most species adopt a schedule of eating a relatively large number of relatively small meals when food is readily available and easy to get. This is what happens in the typical laboratory setting where the prototypical rat resides in a small cage with abundant food that is always present. The rats adopt a pattern in which they eat up to 20 or more discrete meals each day.

The two largest meals occur close to the regular changing of the lights, and most meals (as well as the largest meals) occur in the dark phase because rats are nocturnal (Le Magnen & Tallon, 1966). That is, unless constrained to do otherwise, animals engage in food acquisition and intake, as well as general activity and most other behaviors, in a circadian pattern under the control of endogenous rhythms tied to the light/dark schedule.

When Collier required the rats to exert more effort to gain access to their food, a different pattern emerged. In variations of the paradigm, the animals might have to make a greater number of individual responses (e.g., lever presses), or to make a response that requires more effort (e.g., due to having a heavier load on the lever); but once the criterion is met, however, they can access the food bin and eat as much as they want. When they want to start another meal, they have to meet the requirement anew. Collier found that as the work to obtain access to food increases, animals of a wide range of species will readily adapt by eating more each time they eat and hence by not having to meet the work criterion too many times each day. Over a wide range of patterns, however, total daily caloric intake remained relatively constant, and body weight was essentially unchanged (Collier, 1986; Collier et al., 1986).

Analogously, if the amount of food that can be eaten in any one meal is limited, animals initiate more meals each day. When rats were administered a gut peptide that elicits sensations of satiation and causes them to eat smaller meals, they responded by eating more meals each day and maintaining their body weight (West, Fey, & Woods, 1984). Likewise, if physical constraints are put on the amount of food that can be easily processed by the gut at one time (e.g., by cutting the nerves that coordinate digestion, the vagus nerves), animals adapt by eating a large number of small meals (Inoue, Bray, & Mullen, 1978;

Snowden, 1970; Snowden & Epstein, 1970). There are two important points from this literature. The first is that when the environment permits, animals choose a meal pattern consisting of many small meals. One implication of this is that as meals increase in size, there are metabolic demands related to the processing of the food that are avoided whenever possible (Woods, 1991). The second is that if the environment precludes eating a large number of smaller meals, animals readily change their feeding schedule in order to ensure adequate caloric intake.

The dynamics, properties, and correlates of individual meals have been the subject of considerable investigation. An important consideration relates to what exactly constitutes a meal. Individuals with food that is freely available often snack by taking in small amounts of food between larger, discrete meals. To be considered a meal, a bout of ingestion must have a minimal size, and a certain amount of time must elapse after eating ceases before more eating occurs. That is, there is a minimum meal size and a minimum intermeal interval. When values for such parameters are set, computers attached to a rat's food cup can then be used to calculate meal patterns automatically (Kissileff, 1970; Kissileff, Klingsberg, & Van Itallie, 1980).

The meal pattern has been observed when rats eat solid or liquid food. However, when liquid foods such as sugar or milk solutions are the only source of available energy, and the rat derives its nourishment by licking at a drinking spout, finer analyses are possible. Analyzing the licks made as parameters are varied is called determining the microstructure of the meal, and considerable important information has been learned from such analyses (Davis & Smith, 1992). Licks are typically emitted at a highly stereotyped rate of between 6 to 7 licks per second in the rat. However, rather than being continuous throughout the duration of a meal, licking is interrupted

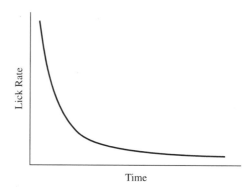

Figure 15.2   Idealized curve of lick rate of a rat consuming a palatable solution over the course of a single bout.

by short pauses between distinct bursts of activity. Longer pauses also occur, and they separate strings of bursts into clusters. The result of these patterns of licking behavior is an integrated licking rate that can be measured with great accuracy and that varies over a large range (Houpt & Frankmann, 1996). As depicted in Figure 15.2, when a rat is provided a sweet solution, licking starts at a high rate. This initial lick rate is linearly related to the concentration of the sweet solution and therefore is thought to be a direct reflection of the perceived palatability of a given solution. After this initial high rate, lick rate decreases over the course of the meal until it reaches zero. Interestingly, when postgastric feedback from the ingested food is minimized by opening up a fistula such that ingested food flows out of a tube in the animal's stomach rather than building up in the stomach and emptying into the intestine, lick rate remains elevated and the meal continues for a long interval. Consequently, the diminishing lick rate over time does not represent habituation or fatigue but rather reflects the postgastric actions of food to inhibit further intake (Davis & Smith, 1988).

One consequence of these observations is that microstructural analysis can be applied to determine the mechanism of action of drugs that alter food intake. For example, some dopamine receptor antagonists such as raclopride potently suppress food intake, and they do so by reducing initial lick rate rather than by increasing the rate of decline of licking during the meal (Schneider, Davis, Watson, & Smith, 1990). Consequently, this class of drugs might be influencing palatability directly or, possibly, some other aspect of hedonic value, such as the level of subjective utility (Shizgal, 1997). The point is that investigation of the microstructure of meals can be used to begin to understand how specific classes of drugs interact with food intake. Such analyses might also provide insight for understanding the relationship between addictive behaviors and food intake (e.g., Chap. 19, this volume; Woods & Ramsay, 2000).

MEAL INITIATION

The physiological factors that determine when a meal will begin are poorly understood at best. Historically, the prevailing belief was that meal initiation (and perhaps its subjective analogue, hunger) is regulated by changes in key metabolic parameters. Early in the last century, Cannon and his colleagues postulated that when the supply or level of some energy source in the body passed a low threshold, contractions of the stomach would be elicited, and these in turn would alert the brain to the dwindling resource. Based on this feedback, the individual would be compelled to seek and eat food (Cannon & Washburn, 1912). The concept of hunger pangs emanating from the stomach has considerable face validity and has persisted in common parlance despite a wealth of evidence indicating that, if anything, signals related to gastric contractions are more numerous and robust after rather than before meals. Further, individuals who are incapable of sensing stomach contractions experience apparently normal

hunger and meal initiation (Bash, 1939; M. I. Grossman, Cummins, & Ivy, 1947; Morgan & Morgan, 1940).

The most popular position concerning the cause of meal initiation was based on Mayer's glucostatic hypothesis. Early in the last century a decrease of blood glucose was considered to be a critical initiator of meals (Carlson, 1916), and this concept was formalized and popularized by Mayer (Mayer, 1955; Mayer & Thomas, 1967). In its original version, the glucostatic hypothesis stated that hunger and eating are initiated when blood glucose decreases to a threshold level and that meals are terminated when blood glucose returns to a higher and hence metabolically more secure level. Later versions of the hypothesis recognized the fact that individuals with insulin-deficiency diabetes mellitus have both elevated blood glucose and elevated hunger and food intake. Hence, the predominant incarnation of the hypothesis was that meal onset and offset are determined by the level of metabolic utilization of glucose by specific sensory cells located in the hypothalamus. These glucose-utilization-sensing cells were postulated by Mayer to be insulin-sensitive. Their characteristics were therefore hypothesized to represent to a better extent than most brain cells the ongoing metabolism of the whole body. It is now recognized that there are in fact glucose-sensitive neurons in many areas of the brain, including the hypothalamus, and that some of these in turn are sensitive to insulin as well (Levin, Dunn-Meynell, & Routh, 1999). There is also evidence that signals related to carbohydrate metabolism reach the brain from the liver, and there is compelling evidence that the level of circulating glucose is detected by sensory nerves located in the hepatic portal vein and that the signal is relayed to the brain via the vagus nerves (Hevener, Bergman, & Donovan, 2000). Hence, the sensory-neural apparatus exists that could enable fluctuations of glucose or its availability to control eating.

It is reasonable to speculate that the tendency to take food would be linked causally to the ebb and flow of metabolic fuels in the blood. That is, when readily available energy becomes relatively depleted from the blood, potentially threatening the ongoing activity of critical tissues, eating is initiated, and the circulating energy supply becomes repleted. Depletion-repletion logic has been applied successfully to the understanding of water and salt ingestion as they apply to the maintenance of blood volume and osmolarity (Flynn, 1999; Stricker & Sved, 2000). A key point, however, is that under usual circumstances, the supply of energy in the blood does not decrease to anywhere near the threshold necessary to trigger eating. Rather, individuals initiate meals even though ample circulating energy is readily available. The amount of cellular energy that can be derived from glucose can be rapidly decreased, either by administering drugs that deplete it from the blood (exogenous insulin: S. P. Grossman, 1986; Lotter & Woods, 1977; MacKay, Calloway, & Barnes, 1940) or drugs that prevent its cellular oxidation (e.g., 2-deoxy-D-glucose, or 2-DG: S. P. Grossman, 1986; G. P. Smith & Epstein, 1969). This creates a potentially threatening situation as the brain detects that its requisite fuel supply is dwindling. One result is that animals seek and ingest food (Langhans, 1996a), and this is also true of humans. Likewise, if cellular fat utilization is experimentally compromised (Langhans & Scharrer, 1987; Scharrer & Langhans, 1986), the integrity of the major user of energy from fat (the liver) is challenged, and critical neural messages are relayed to the brain from the liver. In this instance, animals also seek and ingest food (Langhans, 1996a, 1996b).

However, several observations argue against the notion that most meals are triggered in response to a depletion of metabolic substrates. Eating is in fact a relatively inefficient way to get calories into the blood rapidly. The digestion and absorption of fat are far too slow to be a factor. With regard to carbohydrates, unless pure glucose is available (which is rare in natural settings), foods must be processed and digested in the stomach, passed to the intestine where they are further processed, and then absorbed into the blood. This is also a relatively slow process. When the glucose supply to the brain is compromised by administering insulin systemically, or when the ability of the brain to utilize glucose is compromised by administering 2-DG, the initial compensatory response is increased glucagon and epinephrine secretion, hormones that rapidly increase blood glucose levels (Virally & Guillausseau, 1999). Hence, the first line of defense is a neuroendocrine mobilization of stored carbohydrate. Eating also occurs in this situation, but after a considerable lag (S. P. Grossman, 1986). In this light, the induced eating can be considered more as a hedge against future excursions of hypoglycemia than as a means of reversing the present one (see Ramsay, Seeley, Bolles, & Woods, 1996; Seeley, Ramsay, & Woods, 1997). In fact, Ritter and colleagues have found that rats will increase their food intake after administration of 2-DG even if food is not available until after the cellular effects of 2-DG have passed (Nonavinakere & Ritter, 1983). Pertinent to this, it would be maladaptive to require an individual to attain dangerously low levels of glucose prior to the initiation of every meal; nor is it clear what the consequences would be if glucose availability dipped to the threshold for initiating meals at a time when it was inconvenient or impossible to eat. It is now generally recognized that this protective system is probably activated to the point of initiating a meal only in extreme metabolic emergencies rather than as part of normal food intake regulation (Epstein, Nicolaidis, & Miselis, 1975; S. P. Grossman, 1986; Langhans, 1996a).

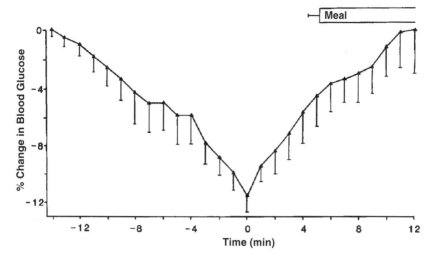

Figure 15.3   Data from Campfield & Smith (1986b, 1990b) depicting the levels of glucose in the blood prior to the initiation of a spontaneous meal.

Despite the contrary evidence, the glucostatic hypothesis has enjoyed tremendous popularity over the years. Renewed support for the hypothesis arose when it became possible to monitor blood glucose continuously by means of an indwelling intravenous catheter. Using this technique, Campfield and Smith (1986b, 1990b) observed that blood glucose starts to decrease a few minutes prior to the initiation of spontaneous meals in freely feeding rats (Figure 15.3). More recently, that group reported a similar phenomenon in humans (Campfield, Smith, Rosenbaum, & Hirsch, 1996). These are important observations because, at least in rats, every observed spontaneous meal was preceded by the small (approximately 12%) but reliable decline of plasma glucose (Campfield, Brandon, & Smith, 1985). The premeal decline of blood glucose reverses just prior to the actual initiation of eating, and if food is removed at that point (and no eating occurs), glucose returns to the baseline that was present before the decline began. Campfield and Smith have interpreted the premeal glucose decline as providing a signal that is monitored by the brain (Campfield & Smith, 1990a, 1990b; F. J. Smith & Campfield, 1993). When the parameters of the decline are perceived to be correct, a meal is initiated. If metabolic conditions preclude the decline meeting the correct criteria, no meal is initiated. In their schema, Campfield and Smith believe that the brain is the initiator of the decline of plasma glucose. Consistent with this, a small increase of plasma insulin which is dependent on an intact vagus nerve occurs at the start of the premeal decline of glucose (Campfield & Smith, 1986a, 1990a), and cutting the vagus disrupts the relationship between changes of glucose and the start of meals (Campfield & Smith, 1990a). This body of research suggests that small physiological fluctuations of glucose can provide important signals that the brain uses to help determine ingestive responses.

Analogous to decreases of blood glucose, other metabolic events occur prior to, and hence are predictive of, the onset of meals. Implanted thermistors allow body temperature to be monitored continuously in freely moving and feeding animals. Just prior to spontaneous meals, the body temperature of rats begins to increase (de Vries, Strubbe, Wildering, Gorter, & Prins, 1993). When the meal begins, temperature continues to increase and then declines as the meal is terminated. Likewise, metabolic rate as assessed by indirect calorimetry reportedly decreases prior to the start of spontaneous meals and increases as eating begins (Even & Nicolaidis, 1985; Nicolaidis & Even, 1984). All of these parameters (blood glucose, temperature, metabolic rate, and no doubt others as well) begin a gradual change 10 min to 15 min before meals begin, and all are therefore highly correlated with meal onset. With a slightly different time course, laboratory rats increase their activity (e.g., running in a wheel) prior to spontaneous meals (Aravich, Stanley, & Doerries, 1995; Rieg & Aravich, 1994; Sclafani & Rendel, 1978; Stevenson & Rixon, 1957). These phenomena have generally been viewed as supporting the hypothesis that animals eat because these changes are occurring (i.e., that the decrease of blood glucose or of metabolic rate, or the exercise-induced use of fuels, is causally related to meal onset). However, a compelling case can also be made that based on factors such as habit or opportunity, other factors determine when a meal is going to start, and that as part of the overall meal initiation process the brain elicits metabolic changes to prepare the body to receive the food (Woods & Ramsay, 2000; Woods & Strubbe, 1994). As an example, a premeal decline of blood glucose can limit the magnitude of the otherwise much larger postprandial increase of blood glucose. In this schema, individuals do not initiate meals because one or another tissue's supply of available energy is about to be compromised, but rather one eats in response to learned cues and various environmental or sensory stimuli. The timing of meals can therefore be quite idiosyncratic and dictated by an individual's lifestyle, convenience, and opportunity. This schema can account for the extreme variability of meal patterns among individuals in a society, but it cannot account, by itself, for the remarkable ability of individuals to maintain neutral energy balance and a constant level of adiposity.

To summarize, although it is possible that meal-related fluctuations in blood glucose and other parameters are the initiators and terminators of meals, the bulk of evidence is to the contrary. The brain and liver are quite efficient at controlling the provision of what is needed by various tissues, and as a result, adequate amounts of utilizable fuels (glucose and fats) are generally always available to tissues via the blood. Major fluctuations in the circulating levels of these fuels generally occur only during and after meals, as ingested energy passes from the gut into the circulation and from the circulation into tissues and energy storage organs. Decreases of plasma fuels below levels adequate to meet tissue requirements are rare in normal, free-feeding individuals, although they can be experimentally induced. Under usual circumstances, therefore, neither meal initiation nor meal termination is likely to occur as a response to fluctuations of metabolic fuels. Rather, meal initiation is based on idiosyncratic factors (such as habit and convenience), and meal termination is based, at least in part, on gastrointestinal peptides secreted during the ingestion of food, as discussed later.

LEARNING AND MEAL INITIATION

A key unanswered question concerns the factors that actually cause an individual to initiate a meal or to experience hunger. That is, if, under normal conditions, decreases of blood glucose or fats (or their correlated cellular utilization) do not cause an animal to initiate a meal, what stimuli do? Considerable evidence implicates environmental stimuli previously associated with the ingestion of calories as having fundamental importance (Sclafani, 1997; Warwick & Weingarten, 1996; Weingarten, 1983; Woods & Strubbe, 1994). Time of day is a particularly salient cue (Woods & Strubbe, 1994; see also Chap. 9, this volume). When food is amply and freely available, individuals tend to eat at the same time each day. If animals are fed only once a day at the same arbitrarily selected time each day, they are said to be meal-fed. If the amount of time allowed to feed is not too short, animals can maintain their body weight by eating very large meals once the food is available. When animals are initially put onto a meal-feeding schedule, their food intake during the meal increases over days and approaches asymptotic levels after around two weeks (Wiley & Leveille, 1970). As this occurs, meal-fed animals adopt a pattern in which they increase the synthesis and secretion of compounds that are important controllers of food intake and digestion at the specific time of day that food always becomes available (Woods et al., 1977). These time-dependent secretions are called cephalic because they are controlled by brain-originating signals rather than by signals such as glucose levels or gastric distension (Powley, 1977). In point of fact, any stimuli that reliably predict food availability can elicit cephalic responses, including time of day, the smell and taste of food, or totally arbitrary stimuli (Woods et al., 1977). Perhaps the best known example of a cephalic response is Pavlov's initial demonstration that dogs learn to secrete saliva and gastric juices when presented with a stimulus that predicts food in the mouth (Pavlov, 1927). Over the years, the secretion of many hormones (e.g., insulin: Steffens, 1976; Strubbe & Steffens, 1975; Woods & Kuskosky, 1976; Woods et al., 1977) and the synthesis and release of many brain neurotransmitters (e.g., neuropeptide Y; Yoshihara, Honma, & Honma, 1996a, 1996b) and

dopamine (Mark, Smith, Rada, & Hoebel, 1994) have been demonstrated to come under the control of stimuli that predict food and the opportunity to eat. In this way animals that anticipate eating an especially large meal are able to prepare the body to cope with the especially large influx of glucose and fats into the blood as the meal is digested and absorbed.

Animals readily learn associations based on the caloric content of food that they receive and the later presence of these cues in turn contributes to how much food is consumed during meals (Sclafani, 1997; Warwick & Schiffman, 1992). There is even evidence that the ability of satiation factors such as cholecystokinin (CCK; discussed later) to reduce meal size is modifiable by learning (Goodison & Siegel, 1995). Finally, the argument has been made that diurnal fluctuations of hormones and neurotransmitters that are important determinants of meals and meal size are in fact entrained to the time that animals normally eat the largest meals of the day (Woods & Strubbe, 1994). It is therefore reasonable to conclude that based upon an individual's history, idiosyncratic stimuli in the environment contribute to the timing of meals, and that associations based on the caloric (and nutrient) content of previously consumed foods contribute to how much is eaten (e.g., Altizer & Davidson, 1999; Davidson, Altizer, Benoit, Walls, & Powley, 1997; Sclafani, 1997; Warwick & Weingarten, 1996).

MEAL SIZE

The bottom line from the previous discussion is that the timing and frequency of meals are driven more by endogenous rhythms, past experience, and present opportunity than by immediate homeostatic need. Hence, given that caloric intake is normally very closely matched to caloric expenditure over long intervals, the regulation of energy homeostasis must be regulated by some factor other than meal onset or meal patterns. There is compelling evidence that this regulation occurs via control of how many calories are consumed once eating is underway. That is, energy homeostasis can be achieved independent of when meals are eaten as long as there is adequate control over meal size. Consistent with this, the amount of food consumed during individual meals is at least partly under the control of gut signals generated in response to the food being eaten (G. P. Smith & Gibbs, 1992, 1998); and there is further evidence that the sensitivity of the brain to these meal-generated signals is in turn determined in part by the size of the adipose mass. That is, when animals are administered compounds that indicate to the brain that body fat content has increased (leptin or insulin, as discussed later), they become far more sensitive to the meal-suppressing action of meal-generated signals such as CCK (Barrachina, Martinez, Wang, Wei, & Tache, 1997; Figlewicz et al., 1995; Matson, Reid, Cannon, & Ritter, 2000; Matson & Ritter, 1999; Matson, Wiater, Kuijper, & Weigle, 1997; Riedy, Chavez, Figlewicz, & Woods, 1995). The point is that an individual who has recently eaten insufficient food to maintain his or her weight will be less sensitive to meal-ending signals and, given the opportunity, will consume larger meals on the average. Analogously, an individual who has enjoyed excess food and consequently gained some weight will, as body fat increases, become more sensitive to meal-terminating signals.

In principle, signals indicating how much food (or how many calories) has been consumed at any point once a meal has started could originate in the mouth or esophagus (i.e., pregastric), in the stomach itself (gastric), in the upper small intestine (postgastric), or in the blood or liver or some other organ sensitive to the influx of calories into the body (postabsorptive). Although it is clear that signals emanating from each of these sites reach the central nervous system and could contribute to the cessation of a meal, numerous experiments have ruled out pregastric and gastric signals as having an exclusive role. For one thing, when animals sham feed such that ingested food drains out of the body at the esophagus or the stomach, enormous meals occur that appear to be limited only by the dehydration produced by the loss of fluids via the exteriorized catheter (Figure 15.4; Gibbs, Young, & Smith, 1973b; Young, Gibbs, Antin, Holt, & Smith, 1974). Consequently, without postgastric signals, stimulation from the mouth is insufficient to produce satiation. Another important observation is that when ingested food is limited to the stomach by means of an inflatable cuff placed around the pylorus that can prevent normal gastric emptying, meal size is normal (J. A. Deutsch, 1978; J. A. Deutsch & Gonzalez, 1980; J. A. Deutsch, Young, & Kalogeris, 1978). At first glance, such results would seem to indicate that signals from the stomach are sufficient to produce satiation. However, when the ingested food is not allowed to pass from the stomach to the small intestine, the volume of the stomach contents increases abnormally during meals and attains levels far larger than normally occur before the meal is stopped (Kaplan, Siemers, & Grill, 1994; Kaplan, Spector, & Grill, 1992). If the animal were relying solely on signals from the stomach, the prediction would be that it would eat a considerably smaller meal when gastric emptying is prevented (Seeley, Kaplan, & Grill, 1993). In fact, the collective data support a summative model whereby the animal uses both gastric and postgastric signals to determine when to stop the meal (Kaplan et al., 1994; Kaplan et al., 1992). Consistent with this, recent data indicate that for rats to make use of information from gastric distension, some of the ingested food must actually make it to critical

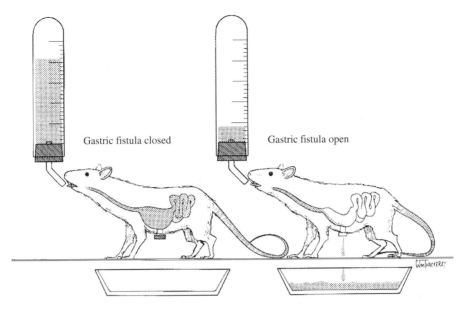

Figure 15.4   Sham-feeding rat where consumed fluid drains directly from the stomach when the gastric fistula is open and thereby minimizes gastric and postgastric feedback involved in meal termination.

receptors in the intestine (Phillips & Powley, 1996, 1998).

Gibbs, Young, and Smith (1973a) were the first to demonstrate unambiguously that certain meal-generated gut peptides are able to reduce meal size, and more recently G. P. Smith and Gibbs (1992) provided a theoretical framework to account for these observations. General omnivores such as humans and rats consume a wide spectrum of foods. Consistent with this, their digestive systems can draw on an analogously wide spectrum of digestive enzymes and secretions to customize the digestive process with what has actually entered the gut. This is accomplished via sensory receptors in the mouth and digestive tract that analyze what is consumed, that coordinate the precise blend of digestive juices to be added to the food, and that also control the speed with which the material moves through the system. Enteroendocrine cells lining the gut secrete compounds that signal distant organs such as the liver and exocrine pancreas to release the appropriate secretions into the

intestine. G. P. Smith and Gibbs (1992) postulated that some of these secreted compounds (mainly peptides) additionally stimulate sensory nerves passing to the brain and thereby provide a signal related to the number and type of calories being consumed. The brain consequently integrates this information with other controllers and determines when the meal will end. Hence, these peptides that stimulate the brain to terminate a meal are called satiety peptides, and they presumably contribute to the sensation of feeling full.

The best known of these meal-generated and meal size-controlling signals, CCK, is secreted from the intestines during meals, and there are specific receptors for it, among other places, on sensory fibers of the vagus nerve near the point where food passes from the stomach into the intestine (G. P. Smith et al., 1984). More precisely, these vagal nerve fibers contain CCK-A receptors (Corp, McQuade, Moran, & Smith, 1993; Mercer & Lawrence, 1992). Hence, during a meal, locally secreted CCK can stimulate these nerves via CCK-A receptors and thereby send a signal to the lower brainstem. Within the brain, these axons synapse with neurons controlling digestive reflexes and responses as well as with neurons passing anteriorly to the forebrain (see Moran & Schwartz, 1994; Rinaman et al., 1995). When CCK-A receptor antagonists are administered to animals prior to a meal, meal size is increased significantly (Hewson, Leighton, Hill, & Hughes, 1988; Moran, Ameglio, Peyton, Schwartz, & McHugh, 1993; Reidelberger & O'Rourke, 1989), implying that endogenous CCK normally reduces meal size. Consistent with this, exogenous CCK dose dependently decreases meal size when it is administered prior to a meal (Gibbs et al., 1973a, 1973b; Kulkosky, Breckenridge, Krinsky, & Woods, 1976; G. P. Smith & Gibbs, 1992, 1998). The importance of the CCK-to-vagus-to-brainstem circuitry is revealed when it is compromised at any level from the gut to the brainstem (Edwards, Ladenheim, & Ritter, 1986; Moran, Shnayder, Hostetler, & McHugh, 1988; G. P. Smith, Jerome, Cushin, Eterno, & Simansky, 1981; G. P. Smith, Jerome, & Norgren, 1985) because exogenous CCK no longer reduces meal size. Analogously, when this pathway is acutely compromised, there is an increase of meal size (Chavez, Kelly, York, & Berthoud, 1997; Kelly, Chavez, & Berthoud, 1999).

Several other points pertinent to satiety signals are important. The first is that the reduction of meal size elicited by exogenous CCK occurs at doses that do not create malaise or general incapability (see reviews in G. P. Smith & Gibbs, 1992, 1998). This is key because there may be myriad reasons why an individual would eat less food after being administered an exogenous drug. The fact that an individual who is nauseous or incapacitated eats less food is important, but it does not address the issue of homeostatic control based upon energy usage and needs (Woods et al., 1995).

Another key point is that the sensations elicited by CCK comprise but one portion or fraction of meal-related signals that influence meal size. Several other gut peptides have analogous actions although the routes by which their signals are passed to the brain differ. These include members of the bombesin family of peptides (gastrin-releasing peptide and neuromedin B in mammals; Gibbs, Fauser, Rowe, Rolls, & Maddison, 1979; G. P. Smith & Gibbs, 1998), glucagon (Geary, 1998; Salter, 1960), somatostatin (Lotter et al., 1981), amylin (Morley & Flood, 1991), enterostatin (Erlanson-Albertsson & York, 1997; Okada, York, Bray, & Erlanson-Albertsson, 1991; Shargill, Tsuji, Bray, & Erlanson-Albertsson, 1991), apolipoprotein A-IV (Fujimoto, Fukagawa, Sakata, & Tso, 1993; Fujimoto, Machidori, et al., 1993), and likely several others. An important consideration is that many gut peptides secreted during a meal induce satiety, whereas many others have no apparent effect on food intake. In contrast, not one has been reported to stimulate meal size. It is as if gut peptides can influence the size of meals in only one direction. Hence, any meal-size feedforward mechanism from the gut must use a different mechanism. This is consistent with the principle that meals, while supplying energy to the body, also pose a metabolic risk that is proportional to meal size (Woods & Strubbe, 1994). This is because the postprandial state is characterized by high levels of energy-rich fuels in the blood, and there is considerable evidence that numerous disorders are linked to these elevations, diabetes mellitus being the best known example. Having gut factors exert a tight control over how much is eaten at any one time is one reflection of the importance of limiting meal size. If an individual's environment dictates that it eat only occasional large meals (as opposed to numerous small ones), learning to secrete cephalic enzymes and other factors is a means of precluding the otherwise high excursions of blood fuels after the meal (Woods & Strubbe, 1994).

Other (nongut peptide) signals also help limit meal size, including the amount of distension or stretch in the stomach. Nerve endings on vagal sensory fibers in the muscle layers of the stomach are situated to function as tension or stretch receptors. Other branches of the same fibers have different kinds of sensory endings (Berthoud & Powley, 1992), implying that two or more kinds of sensory information can be integrated within single vagal neurons. Consistent with this anatomical observation, it was recently reported that vagal activity elicited by exogenous CCK combines synergistically with that caused by distension of either the stomach (G. J. Schwartz, McHugh, & Moran, 1993) or the intestine (G. J. Schwartz, Tougas, & Moran, 1995). The important point is that signals conveying information about numerous key parameters related to food intake converge in the vagus and are relayed directly to the brainstem (G. J. Schwartz & Moran, 1996; Wang, Martinez, Barrachina, & Tache, 1998). In addition to gastric stretch, these include information on the specific types and amounts of food being processed, on the relative amounts of water and solutes, on the possible presence of toxins in the food, and so on.

EATING AND THE REGULATION OF BODY WEIGHT

Body fat (adiposity) and food intake are closely interrelated. As a rule, if more calories are consumed than are necessary to maintain weight each day, stored energy in the form of body fat increases, and body weight goes up. The actual increase of stored calories is generally less than the increment of calories consumed in this situation because metabolic adjustments will occur to minimize the increment. Nonetheless, such weight gain is as inevitable as is the weight loss that occurs when individuals diet or have their food restricted. Everyday observations such as these imply that body weight (mainly body adiposity) is strictly a function of caloric intake. All else being equal, a change of daily caloric intake results in a consequent change in fat stores. Although such a relationship implies causality, the relationship between food intake and body fuel stores is more complex because causality appears to work in both directions. If otherwise weight-stable adults eat insufficient food for a period of time and consequently lose weight, they will likely overeat when ample food once again becomes available (or when the enthusiasm for dieting wanes). Likewise, if individuals consume excess calories to the point of weight gain for a prolonged interval, there will be an increasing tendency to eat less food and thus help return body weight and body fat stores to preintervention levels. This phenomenon need not rely on changes of caloric intake. For example, if fat stores are reduced by having fat surgically removed (lipectomy), individuals overeat and regain the lost weight if given a nutritionally complete diet (Faust, Johnson, & Hirsch, 1977). Viewed in this light, food intake would seem to be controlled by the amount of stored body fat. There are many reviews of these phenomena (Bray, 1976; Keesey, 1989; Keesey & Powley, 1986; Pinel, Assanand, & Lehman, 2000; M. W. Schwartz & Seeley, 1997; Woods et al., 1998). Understanding the causal factors that interrelate food intake and body adiposity is an important goal and the subject of considerable ongoing research.

The link between body fat and food intake was formalized a half century ago when Kennedy postulated that signals proportional to body fat influence the control of appetite and feeding by the brain (Kennedy, 1953). Thus, Kennedy's lipostatic hypothesis stated that adiposity is regulated by a negative feedback system in which food intake is controlled in part by the amount of total stored body fat. He envisioned a mechanism akin to a set point toward which body weight always converges following a deviation. Although the existence of a link between energy intake and body energy stores has never been questioned, an important issue over the intervening years has been the nature of the signal or signals that indicates how much fat is present in the body. Because body fat is stored in multiple depots dispersed widely throughout the body, a means of monitoring them all and integrating the information is required. One possibility is that sensory nerves could innervate, and hence provide information from, each fat depot, with the cumulated information from multiple sites integrated within the brain into a reliable total adiposity signal. However, adipose tissue is only sparsely innervated, and the majority of the fibers innervating fat depots are motor fibers that control the release of stored energy when it is acutely needed. A second possibility is that a single fat depot is sufficiently representative of all others that it serves as a bellwether. In this schema, the brain need receive a signal only from this sentinel depot. Even though different fat depots have quite different functions and secretions, such a depot could theoretically be located anywhere, including within the brain itself. Nicolaidis and his colleagues have hypothesized that specialized cells within the hypothalamus serve this function and influence all aspects of energy homeostasis (Even & Nicolaidis, 1985; Nicolaidis & Even, 1984). Unlike other brain cells, these neurons are postulated to share some properties with peripheral adipocytes, and in particular to be sensitive to insulin. As discussed earlier, many neurons in the ventral hypothalamus are insulin-sensitive in that their electrical activity varies with the local application of insulin and other metabolic signals (Levin et al., 1999; Oomura, 1976). There is also evidence for an energy-sensing receptor in the liver (or at least within the influence of the hepatic branches of the vagus nerves; Friedman, 1998; Langhans, 1996b). Although there seems little doubt that signals related both to stored energy and to ongoing energy utilization can arise in both the brain and the liver (and presumably other tissues as well), it is not clear how much they contribute to the normal control of meals. Further, there is compelling evidence for a third signaling pathway, one that influences overall energy homeostasis and that utilizes circulating hormones.

CIRCULATING ADIPOSITY SIGNALS

When two experimental animals are joined surgically at the flank such that a small proportion of the circulation exchanges between them (termed *parabiotic* animals), a dye administered into the blood of one can be detected in the blood of its partner. If two otherwise normal animals with similar body weight (either two lean or two obese rats or mice) are parabiotically joined, each eats normally and maintains its customary (presurgical) body weight. Hence, the parabiotic procedure itself is tolerated and both normal-weight and obese animals are able to maintain their body weight. When an obese animal is parabiotically joined with a lean partner, their respective body weights diverge. Although the obese partner may gain some weight, the lean partner becomes hypophagic and loses weight precipitously (Coleman, 1973; Hervey, 1952). Such experiments have been interpreted to indicate that a circulating signal proportional to body fat passes between the two partners. Because the obese partner has relatively more of this signal in its blood, sufficient signal passes into the blood of the lean partner to influence its behavior. Hence, the lean partner receives a false message that too much fat exists in its body, and it reduces its food intake and loses weight. Such experiments indicate that circulating signals have a powerful influence over eating behavior, and they imply that if the signal were identified and administered to an animal, it could provide an effective way to lose weight. The important conclusion is that signals proportional to body fat are found in the circulation. Such a cumulated signal presumably reflects the diverse fat depots and circumvents the need for direct neural signals.

Two peptide hormones fulfill the criteria to be adiposity signals: leptin, which is secreted from adipose tissue itself, and insulin, which is secreted from the B cells of the islets of Langerhans of the pancreas. Both are synthesized and secreted in direct proportion to the amount of fat in the body; both pass through the blood-brain barrier and thereby gain access to key regulatory areas; both influence food intake and body weight in predictable ways (M. W. Schwartz, Baskin, Kaiyala, & Woods, 1999; M. W. Schwartz & Seeley, 1997; M. W. Schwartz et al., 2000; Woods et al., 1998). Insulin is best known as a controller of blood glucose. When blood glucose increases, more insulin is secreted, enabling cells to take glucose up more rapidly, thus lowering blood glucose back to normal. These processes occur mainly during and after meals. Importantly, both basal insulin (the level in the absence of an obvious challenge) and insulin secreted in response to changes of glucose are directly proportional to body fat (Bagdade, Bierman, & Porte, 1967; B. D. Polonsky, Given, & Carter, 1988; K. S. Polonsky et al., 1988). Fatter individuals secrete more insulin during both basal and stimulated conditions than lean individuals, and insulin therefore reflects both acute metabolic needs and body fat content.

Leptin is secreted from adipocytes (Considine et al., 1996; Rosenbaum et al., 1996; Zhang et al., 1994) via a mechanism that is sensitive to ongoing metabolic activity of fat cells, in addition to fat content per se (Havel, 1999; Havel, Mundinger, & Taborsky,

1996). Hence, dissociations can occur between stored fat and leptin release, particularly when there is a rapid decrease of adipocyte glucose metabolism such as occurs in fasting (Ahren, Mansson, Gingerich, & Havel, 1997; Boden, Chen, Mozzoli, & Ryan, 1996; Wisse et al., 1999). In such instances, plasma leptin decreases more rapidly and to a greater degree than does body fat, but plasma leptin levels are a reliable indicator of body fat content among individuals who are weight-stable.

As a rule, peptides that are the size of insulin and leptin do not readily penetrate the blood-brain barrier. However, brain capillary cells express receptors that recognize insulin and leptin and transport them from the blood into the brain interstitial fluid (see reviews in M. W. Schwartz et al., 1991; M. W. Schwartz, Figlewicz, Baskin, Woods, & Porte, 1992; M. W. Schwartz et al., 1990), exposing brain cells to their actions. Receptors for insulin and leptin are expressed in brain regions that are important in the control of energy homeostasis, including several nuclei in the ventral hypothalamus (Baskin et al., 1990; Corp et al., 1986; Figlewicz et al., 1985; LeRoith, Rojeski, & Roth, 1988). The hypothalamic arcuate nuclei (ARC) have particularly high densities of insulin and leptin receptors, and the ARC is the location of at least two major types of neurons that potently influence food intake (discussed later). Hence, these cells have the capacity to detect and respond to both adiposity signals and are therefore also indirectly sensitive to body adiposity.

When exogenous insulin (Brief & Davis, 1984; Chavez, Kaiyala, Madden, Schwartz, & Woods, 1995; Chavez, Seeley, & Woods, 1995; McGowan, Andrews, Kelly, & Grossman, 1990; M. W. Schwartz, Minth, & Palmiter, 1994; van Dijk et al., 1997; Woods, 1996; Woods, Lotter, McKay, & Porte, 1979; Woods & Porte, 1983) or leptin (Campfield, Smith, Gulsez, Devos, & Burn, 1995; Seeley et al., 1996) is administered directly into the brain (into the ARC itself, into nearby ventral hypothalamus, or into the cerebrospinal fluid in the adjacent third cerebral ventricle), animals behave as if they are overweight; that is, they eat less food and lose weight. Conversely, when the functional levels of either insulin (McGowan, Andrews, & Grossman, 1992; Strubbe & Mein, 1977) or leptin (see M. W. Schwartz & Seeley, 1997; M. W. Schwartz et al., 2000; Woods et al., 1998) are low in the brain, animals overeat. Functional leptin deficiency exists in animals with mutations of either the leptin-synthesizing gene or the gene for the leptin receptor. In both instances the animals are hyperphagic and obese. Functional insulin deficiency occurs in insulin-deficiency diabetes. These individuals are hyperphagic but cannot become obese in the absence of peripheral insulin action. When insulin activity is lowered locally in the brain by administration of insulin antibodies, the animals are also hyperphagic and do become obese (McGowan et al., 1992; Strubbe & Mein, 1977). Analogously, mice with experimentally absent insulin receptors on brain cells (called neuronal insulin receptor knockout mice) also eat more and have a tendency to become obese (Brüning et al., 2000).

The important point is that both insulin and leptin are secreted in direct proportion to the amount of fat in the body, and both have access to receptors in areas of the brain that control energy homeostasis. When the levels of either hormone are increased or decreased locally in the brain, there are predictable changes of food intake and body weight. When the brains of animals are exposed to elevated levels of insulin or leptin, they behave as if they are overweight by reducing their food intake and losing body weight. Analogously, when they are exposed to decreased levels of insulin or leptin, the animals behave as if they are underweight, and they increase their food intake and gain weight.

Many other factors influence the amount of fat in the body. For example, the steroid hormone estrogen, which circulates in higher concentrations in females than in males, acts to reduce body fat. Ovariectomized female rats overeat and gain weight and then defend the elevated weight against imposed perturbations (Wade, Schneider, & Li, 1996). Restoring estrogen to these ovariectomized animals causes them to return to the lower, female-typical body weight. As might be expected, estrogen combines with CCK to reduce meal size (Asarian & Geary, 1999).

CENTRAL CONTROL SYSTEMS

Knowledge of the brain systems that regulate energy homeostasis, including food intake, is one of the fastest changing fields in all of science (Chap. 14, this volume). For this reason, any description must necessarily be considered a snapshot in time, one whose specifics will differ with each succeeding snapshot. Nonetheless, certain generalities can be made, and the model we present in the following paragraphs reflects these generalities. Time and considerably more research will reveal the accuracy of the model.

The modern era of how the brain controls food intake began when early investigations utilizing the stereotaxic apparatus identified two areas of the hypothalamus as having key roles. As discussed earlier, the VMH was considered to be the brain's satiety center because electrical stimulation there causes an animal engaged in a meal to stop eating, even if it is severely underweight (see the review of this early work in Stellar, 1954). When the VMH is lesioned, animals eat larger meals (and more total food each day), rapidly becoming obese. This phenomenon is already apparent at the first postlesion meal and continues until body weight stabilizes at the new, elevated plateau. After this dynamic phase of weight gain ends,

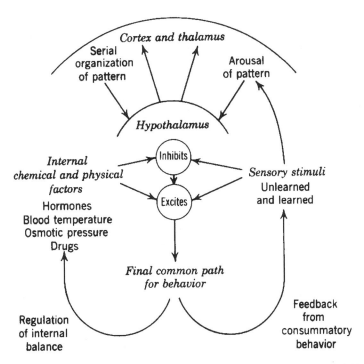

Figure 15.5 Figure depicting the dual-centers hypothesis from Stellar (1954).

the animals eat essentially normal amounts of food but maintain the elevated weight. Importantly, VMH-lesioned animals regulate their weight very well, albeit at an elevated level, because if their weight is displaced either upwards or downwards, they rapidly return to their prior obese state when given the opportunity (Hoebel & Teitelbaum, 1966). Analogously, the lateral hypothalamic area (LH) was considered the eating center of the brain because electrical stimulation there elicits voracious eating. If animals receive daily stimulation of the LH, they become obese. When the LH is lesioned, animals eat less food or stop eating altogether (depending on the extent of the lesion). These animals have to have food administered directly into their stomachs each day if they are to survive. Over time, they gradually begin eating again if highly palatable foods are offered (Teitelbaum, Cheng, & Rozin, 1969). Stellar (1954) reviewed this

early literature and recognized the fundamental importance of the hypothalamus to energy homeostasis (Figure 15.5).

The intervening decades have proven that this view of the central controls over eating is overly simplistic. For example, lesions of the VMH and LH do not necessarily result in changes of food intake. If a rat is made obese by overfeeding prior to receiving a lesion of the VMH, it does not overeat following the lesion but rather eats just enough to maintain its already-elevated body weight (Hoebel & Teitelbaum, 1966). Hence, there is no obligatory increase of food intake if the animal is already obese. Likewise, if a rat is food-restricted and loses considerable weight prior to receiving a small lesion of the LH, it need not become hypophagic after the lesion, but rather eats sufficient food to maintain its lowered weight (Powley & Keesey, 1970). In this light, the VMH can be considered an area of the brain that lowers the maximal weight that an individual will normally attain, whereas the LH can be considered an area that raises the minimal weight that an individual will defend.

Numerous other complexities have been revealed. Lesions of both the VMH and the LH have multiple consequences in addition to changing the average weight that the animal maintains. For example, VMH-lesioned animals have dysfunction of the hypothalamic-pituitary axis as well as a shift of autonomic tone throughout the body to favor parasympathetic actions (Bray, 1989). VMH-lesioned animals are said to be finicky in that they only overeat palatable foods and will not work hard to obtain their food. Animals with lesions of the LH are adipsic as well as aphagic. In fact, even though food intake may eventually return and appear quite normal, a deficit in water intake always remains. Animals with LH lesions also suffer from what has been termed *sensory neglect* in that they do not respond to sensory stimuli such as manipulation of the vibrissae or the smell of food with the same orienting responses that normal rats do (Zigmond & Stricker, 1973). In fact, if the LH is lesioned on only one side of the brain, the consequent sensory neglect is also unilateral. Therefore, although lesions of the LH may reveal something concerning the role of the LH in food intake, the ultimate interpretation must include

also an important role for a number of motor behaviors.

In the 1970s and 1980s, researchers began to understand the neuropharmacology of these systems. Manipulation of a number of neurotransmitter systems was found to have profound effects on food intake. For example, agents that increase serotonin or agonize serotonin receptors produce decreases in food intake (Hoebel, Hernandez, Schwartz, Mark, & Hunter, 1989). Complementing this was the finding that norepinephrine injected into a number of brain regions such as the LH produced profound increases in food and water intake (Leibowitz, 1985; Leibowitz, Roossin, & Roosinn, 1984). Another transmitter system that received intense scrutiny was dopamine. Dopamine receptor agonists increase food intake, and either dopamine receptor antagonists or pharmacological depletion of the dopamine system results in decreased food intake (Stricker & Zigmond, 1976). As with LH, it has been difficult to dissociate completely the role that dopamine plays in motor behavior from that involved in the motivation to ingest food.

The 1990s heralded in the age of neuropeptides. Perhaps most important were the discovery of leptin and the subsequent recognition that the arcuate nuclei were a major site in which adiposity is signaled to the brain. As depicted in Figure 15.6, the arcuate

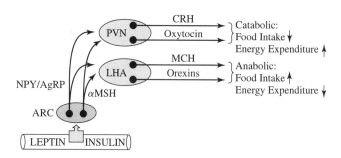

Figure 15.6   Idealized figure of a subset of the hypothalamic pathways implicated in the control of food intake and energy balance.

contains at least two major cell groups related to energy homeostasis, those that synthesize proopiomelanocortin (POMC) and those that synthesize neuropeptide Y (NPY) and agouti-related protein (AgRP). As seen in Figure 15.6, the arcuate is also a major site of receptors for both insulin and leptin such that it can be considered the major sense organ that detects the body's adiposity. When either insulin or leptin is administered into the brain, POMC neurons are activated, and they consequently release α-melanocyte stimulating hormone (αMSH) from the axon terminals in the paraventricular nuclei (PVN) and other sites. αMSH is an agonist at melanocortin-4 (MC4) receptors, and stimulation of these receptors by αMSH or other MC4 agonists reduces food intake, increases energy expenditure, and, if prolonged, induces a loss of body fat and body weight. This leptin/insulin → POMC neurons → MC4 receptors is an important catabolic pathway in the brain, and disruptions of it at any point result in severe obesity. This is a complex area of research, and recent reviews are found in M. W. Schwartz et al. (2000) and Woods and colleagues (Woods & Seeley, 2000; Woods et al., 1998).

In addition to stimulating POMC neurons, insulin and leptin simultaneously inhibit NPY/AgRP neurons in the arcuate nucleus. NPY and AgRP are both potent stimulants of food intake, and the prolonged administration of either results in hyperphagia and obesity via receptors in the LH and other areas. They represent the anabolic side of the central control of energy homeostasis. Hence, leptin and insulin simultaneously stimulate catabolic pathways and inhibit anabolic pathways. This dual control system is a key feature of the regulation of body weight. If an individual loses weight, the levels of insulin and leptin decrease in the blood, and a smaller signal consequently reaches the arcuate. The

result is less inhibition of the anabolic circuits and less stimulation of the catabolic circuits. The balance between the anabolic and catabolic circuits determines the individual's feeding behavior in response to changes in the level of adiposity (M. W. Schwartz et al., 2000; Woods & Seeley, 2000; Woods et al., 1998).

Anabolic Neurotransmitters and Circuits

The most investigated anabolic transmitter is NPY. Although NPY is made throughout the brain, NPY neurons in the ARC and other areas of the ventral hypothalamus are particularly important to energy homeostasis, especially their projections to the PVN and the LH. NPY neurons in the ARC respond to negative energy balance (i.e., to food deprivation or starvation) by synthesizing and releasing more NPY (Kalra, Dube, Sahu, Phelps, & Kalra, 1991; Sahu, Sninsky, Kalra, & Kalra, 1990; M. W. Schwartz, Sipols, et al., 1992). One consequence is increased feeding when food becomes available. Activation of hypothalamic NPY signaling occurs when insulin or leptin signaling is reduced, and the replacement of either insulin or leptin locally in the vicinity of the ARC prevents activation of the NPY system (M. W. Schwartz et al., 1996; Schwartz, Sipols, et al., 1992). Administration of exogenous NPY into the PVN or into the adjacent third cerebral ventricle elicits a rapid and robust increase in food intake (Clark, Kalra, Crowley, & Kalra, 1984; Sahu & Kalra, 1993; Seeley, Payne, & Woods, 1995; Stanley, Kyrkouli, Lampert, & Leibowitz, 1986; Stanley & Leibowitz, 1984) and decrease of energy expenditure (Billington, Briggs, Grace, & Levine, 1991; Billington, Briggs, Harker, Grace, & Levine, 1994). Repeated daily administration of NPY elicits sustained increases of food intake, body weight, and body adiposity (Stanley et al.,

1986). Reducing NPY synthesis locally in the ARC results in reduced food intake and body weight (Akabayashi, Wahlestedt, Alexander, & Leibowitz, 1994).

AgRP, the other transmitter made by NPY-synthesizing neurons in the ARC, is unique in being an endogenous antagonist (as opposed to agonist) at an important brain receptor. As discussed earlier, MC4 receptors in the PVN are activated by αMSH (Figure 15.6). Stated another way, αMSH is an agonist at MC4 receptors. AgRP acts at the same receptors to cause an opposite reaction. Hence, the administration of AgRP (or synthetic antagonists of the MC4 receptor) blocks the ability of αMSH or synthetic agonists to reduce food intake and body weight. Administration of AgRP by itself causes a potent and very long-lasting increase of food intake (Hagan et al., 2001; Hagan et al., 2000). In fact, rats given a single injection of AgRP still overeat one week later. The mechanisms of this long-term effect are completely unknown and may involve some sort of learning or neural plasticity.

The LH receives input from the ARC (and many other areas), and LH neurons synthesize and secrete transmitters that also have potent anabolic effects (Figure 15.6). Melanin concentrating hormone (MCH) and the orexins are the best known of these, and administration of exogenous MCH or orexins potently stimulates food intake and body weight, whereas animals that lack the ability to make or respond to these transmitters tend to be hyperphagic and to become obese. Table 15.1 lists brain transmitters that tend to have a net anabolic effect in the hypothalamus.

Catabolic Neurotransmitters and Circuits

As discussed earlier, considerable evidence implicates hypothalamic MC4 receptors as being important in mediating catabolic ef-

Table 15.1   Extracellular Signaling Molecules That Act in the Hypothalamus to Increase Food Intake or Body Weight.

Neuropeptide Y
Agouti-related peptide
Melanin concentrating hormone
Orexin A and B (hypocretins 1 and 2)
Ghrelin
Beacon
Norepinephrine
Galanin
Beta endorphin
Dynorphin
Corticosteron

fects. αMSH is the neurotransmitter that activates these receptors, and it is made from POMC in the arcuate nuclei (Figure 15.6). When administered into the third cerebral ventricle, αMSH (or other MC4 agonists) reduces food intake and body weight. POMC levels are reduced during negative energy balance (M. W. Schwartz et al., 1997) and increased during positive energy balance (Hagan et al., 1999). These changes are mediated by altered levels of leptin and insulin. Consistent with the model in Figure 15.6, leptin's ability to reduce food intake can be blocked by administering antagonists to the MC4 receptor (R. J. Seeley et al., 1997).

Numerous neurotransmitters in the hypothalamus appear to interact with and further the catabolic message delivered by the ARC POMC neurons. Of particular interest are several cell groups in the PVN. PVN neurons synthesize and secrete numerous catabolic transmitters throughout the brain. Perhaps the best known are corticotropin releasing hormone (CRH), thyrotropin releasing hormone (TRH), and oxytocin. Although each of these has numerous actions that are not directly related to energy homeostasis, administration of any of them into the brain reduces food intake. Table 15.2 lists several brain transmitters that have a net catabolic action.

Table 15.2 Extracellular Signaling Molecules That
Act in the Hypothalamus to Decrease Food Intake or
Body Weight.

Leptin
Insulin
Amylin (IAPP)
α-Melanocyte stimulating hormone
Corticotropin releasing hormone
Urocortin
Urocortin II
Neurotensin
Glucagon-like-peptide-1
Glucagon-like-peptide-2
Histamine
Serotonin
Oxytocin
Cocaine-amphetamine-related transcript peptide

SUMMARY OF HYPOTHALAMIC CIRCUITS

The model in Figure 15.6 places ARC anabolic and catabolic neurons at the hub of the system by which input from adiposity signals is transduced into behavioral and autonomic responses. The subsequent downstream neuronal events that control energy homeostasis are complex and diverse. However, two important areas are the nearby PVN and LH. Each of these pairs of hypothalamic nuclei receives rich inputs from both NPY/AgRP and POMC neurons in the ARC (Elmquist, Elias, & Saper, 1999; Elmquist, Maratos-Flier, Saper, & Flier, 1998), and each synthesizes several neuropeptides that are important in the energy balance equation. Because ablation of the PVN causes a chronic anabolic condition characterized by hyperphagia and obesity (see Bray, Fisler, & York, 1990), a rough generalization is that the PVN is a key component of the system that reduces energy intake and the amount of body fat. Analogously, the LH synthesizes several neuropeptides that cause a net anabolic response. Thus, regulation of activity of ARC neurons by input from adiposity signals alters feeding behavior

in part via changes in the output of catabolic second-order neurons in the PVN and anabolic second-order neurons in the LH. However, leptin and insulin receptors are present in the PVN and other areas, so some neuronal responses to input from these hormones are likely to be independent of the ARC. Moreover, LH neurons project dense fiber networks to the ARC that may have important effects on the output of NPY/AgRP and POMC neurons. A highly integrated and redundant neurobiological system is thus likely to mediate feeding responses to a change of energy balance.

Extrahypothalamic Controls over Food Intake

Although most research on the neural control of food intake has been lavished on the hypothalamus, it is clear that the control of food intake is accomplished by a distributed neural network. In particular, the traditional "hypothalamocentric" view of the control of food intake was challenged by work using the chronic decerebrate rat. Rather than make a focal lesion, Grill and his colleagues made a complete knife cut that separated the caudal brainstem and the motor neurons that controlled ingestion from all input from areas more rostral, including the entire hypothalamus (Grill & Norgren, 1978b). Despite receiving no input from the hypothalamus, these animals are capable of organizing ingestive bouts, and the sizes of these bouts are regulated by many of the same factors that are capable of regulating the sizes of ingestive bouts in intact rats without being able to respond to changes in overall energy balance (Grill & Miselis, 1981; Grill & Norgren, 1978a, 1978c, 1978d). Such data make a strong case for an independent role of the caudal brainstem in having the ability to integrate key sensory information about available energy (food) into ongoing ingestive motor behavior, and

subsequent research has pointed to a prominent role for both the nucleus of the solitary
tract and the parabrachial nucleus as being
particularly important in this integration. Information from these areas is then relayed to
appropriate motor neurons distributed from
the spinal cord to the midbrain. Current thinking is that hypothalamic nuclei exert their effects on food intake by means of potentiating
and depotentiating the signals sent to these
motor nuclei from integration areas of the
caudal brainstem.

Observations on the sufficiency of the
chronic decerebrate animal have led Smith to
conclude that the direct influences on food intake (i.e., those influences elicited directly by
food as it passes through the intestinal system)
interact uniquely with these caudal brainstem
circuits (G. P. Smith, 2000). In this schema,
the indirect influences on food intake, such as
learning and the availability of stored nutrients in the form of adipose tissue, are mediated
by forebrain circuits that include the hypothalamus, other limbic structures, and cortical
areas (see Figure 15.7).

Interaction of Adiposity Signals with Signals That Control Meal Size

A key question concerns how the various control systems are integrated in the control of

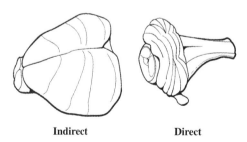

Indirect   **Direct**

Figure 15.7 Depiction of the neural substrates
that mediate either the direct or the indirect controllers of food intake.
SOURCE: Adapted from G. P. Smith (2000).

food intake. That is, what are the interrelationships among the systems that signal ingested calories and control meal size, those
that signal adiposity, and those hypothalamic neuropeptides and other neurotransmitters that receive other feeding-pertinent inputs
from throughout the brain? Some answers
are beginning to emerge. When rats have
free access to food and can eat whenever
they choose, they generally eat 10 to 12
meals a day, and most intake occurs during
the night (Kissileff & Van Itallie, 1982; Le
Magnen, 1969; Le Magnen & Tallon, 1966).
West et al. (1984) observed that when CCK
was administered to free-feeding rats at the
onset of each meal via an automated delivery
system over a 1-week interval, the size of each
meal was reduced. However, the rats maintained essentially normal total daily caloric intake and body weight because they increased
the number of times that they initiated meals
each day. This suggests that exogenous CCK,
by itself, is a relatively ineffective treatment
strategy for losing weight, at least over the
course of several days or a week. Nonetheless, rats without CCK-A receptors (Miyasaka
et al., 1994) gradually become obese over their
lifetimes (Kawano et al., 1992), suggesting
that an inability to terminate meals appropriately may contribute to a gradual expansion of
body fat (G. J. Schwartz, Whitney, Skogland,
Castonguay, & Moran, 1999). More to the
point, CCK and the adiposity hormones (insulin and leptin) have additive, or even synergistic effects, to reduce food intake. Rats
treated with very low doses of either exogenous insulin or leptin manifest a marked increase in the hypophagic response to a low
dose of CCK given once a day (Barrachina
et al., 1997; Figlewicz et al., 1995; Matson
et al., 1997; Riedy et al., 1995), and they
lose weight beyond that achieved by giving
these peptides by themselves (Matson et al.,
2000; Matson & Ritter, 1999). This observation suggests that the efficacy of CCK (and

presumably other signals that reduce meal size as well) is enhanced in the presence of elevated adiposity signaling in the brain. The infusion of a low dose of leptin directly into the brain also increases the sensitivity of the vagus nerve to gastric distension signals that reduce meal size (G. J. Schwartz & Moran, 1996), and leptin-induced anorexia is, in fact, characterized by consumption of smaller meals with no change of meal frequency (Flynn & Plata-Salaman, 1999). The effect of increased adiposity signaling to reduce energy intake may therefore depend largely on an increased response to signals that terminate meals. Analogously, small changes in the levels of either leptin or insulin change an animal's hedonic response to motivating signals (Figlewicz & Woods, 2000; Fulton, Woodside, & Shizgal, 2000), suggesting that the level of adiposity may have generalized actions on many brain systems.

These observations have important implications. When an individual goes on a diet and starts losing weight, there is a concomitant reduction of the secretion of adiposity signals and lower titers of these signals enter the brain. In and of itself, in fact, an acute fast is sufficient to reduce the transport of insulin (Strubbe, Porte, & Woods, 1988) or leptin (Karonen, Koistinen, Nikkinen, & Koivisto, 1998) into the brain. One consequence of reduced adiposity signaling is a reduced ability of meal-generated peptides such as CCK to terminate a meal, with the result that meals will tend to be larger until adiposity signaling (and body weight) is normalized. Likewise, individuals who overeat and gain weight will have increased adiposity signaling in the brain and will consequently tend to eat smaller meals, providing that they remain sensitive to adiposity signals. Hence, the net action of this control system is to oppose long-term changes of body weight, and it does so by changing the average size of meals. Note that individuals are still able to eat according to whatever

schedule best meets their lifestyles and environmental constraints; it is the meal size rather than the meal pattern that is controlled by this regulatory system.

An important unanswered question relates to what happens to this control system when the diet is changed. A strong case can be made that when individuals habitually consume diets rich in fat, they tend to become obese (Bray & Popkin, 1998; Lichtenstein et al., 1998; Popkin & Doak, 1998; Poppitt, 1995; Willett, 1998). This indicates that the normal feedback signaling system must become altered or insensitive on a high-fat diet. As the prevalence and associated morbidity of obesity continue to increase in modern society, the importance of understanding the interactions between diet and other environmental factors with the weight-regulatory system increases in parallel. Progress in the prevention and treatment of obesity will likely emerge from an improved understanding of these interactions.

REFERENCES

Ahren, B., Mansson, S., Gingerich, R. L., & Havel, P. J. (1997). Regulation of plasma leptin in mice: Influence of age, high-fat diet and fasting. *American Journal of Physiology, 273,* R113–R120.

Akabayashi, A., Wahlestedt, C., Alexander, J. T., & Leibowitz, S. F. (1994). Specific inhibition of endogenous neuropeptide Y synthesis in arcuate nucleus by antisense oligonucleotides suppresses feeding behavior and insulin secretion. *Brain Research, 21,* 55–61.

Alingh Prins, A., de Jong-Nagelsmit, A., Keijser, J., & Strubbe, J. H. (1986). Daily rhythms of feeding in the genetically obese and lean Zucker rats. *Physiology and Behavior, 38,* 423–426.

Altizer, A. M., & Davidson, T. L. (1999). The effects of NPY and 5-TG on responding to cues for fats and carbohydrates. *Physiology and Behavior, 65,* 685–690.

Aravich, P. F., Stanley, E. Z., & Doerries, L. E. (1995). Exercise in food-restricted rats produces 2DG feeding and metabolic abnormalities similar to anorexia nervosa. *Physiology and Behavior, 57,* 147–153.

Asarian, L., & Geary, N. (1999). Cyclic estradiol treatment phasically potentiates endogenous cholecystokinin's satiating action in ovariectomized rats. *Peptides, 20,* 445–450.

Bagdade, J. D., Bierman, E. L., & Porte, D., Jr. (1967). The significance of basal insulin levels in the evaluation of the insulin response to glucose in diabetic and nondiabetic subjects. *Journal of Clinical Investigation, 46,* 1549–1557.

Barrachina, M. D., Martinez, V., Wang, L., Wei, J. Y., & Tache, Y. (1997). Synergistic interaction between leptin and cholecystokinin to reduce short-term food intake in lean mice. *Proceedings of the National Academy of Science, USA, 94,* 10455–10460.

Bash, K. W. (1939). An investigation into a possible organic basis for the hunger drive. *Journal of Comparative Psychology, 28,* 109–134.

Baskin, D. G., Marks, J. L., Schwartz, M. W., Figewicz, D. P., Woods, S. C., & Porte, D., Jr. (1990). Insulin and insulin receptors in the brain in relation to food intake and body weight. In H. Lehnert, R. Murison, H. Weiner, D. Hellhammer, & J. Beyer (Eds.), *Endocrine and nutritional control of basic biological functions* (pp. 202–222). Stuttgart: Hogrefe & Huber.

Berthoud, H. R., & Powley, T. L. (1992). Vagal afferent innervation of the rat fundic stomach: Morphological characterization of the gastric tension receptor. *Journal of Comparative Neurology, 319,* 261–276.

Billington, C. J., Briggs, J. E., Grace, M., & Levine, A. S. (1991). Effects of intracerebroventricular injection of neuropeptide Y on energy metabolism. *American Journal of Physiology, 260,* R321–R327.

Billington, C. J., Briggs, J. E., Harker, S., Grace, M., & Levine, A. S. (1994). Neuropeptide Y in hypothalamic paraventricular nucleus: A center coordinating energy metabolism. *American Journal of Physiology, 266,* R1765–R1770.

Blass, E. M., & Shah, H. (1995). Pain-reducing properties of sucrose in human newborns. *Chemical Senses, 20,* 29–35.

Blass, E. M., Shide, D. J., & Weller, A. (1989). Stress-reducing effects of ingesting milk, sugars, and fats: A developmental perspective. *Annals of the New York Academy of Science, 575,* 292–305.

Boden, G., Chen, X., Mozzoli, M., & Ryan, I. (1996). Effect of fasting on serum leptin in normal human subjects. *Journal of Clinical Endocrinology and Metabolism, 81,* 3419–3423.

Bouchard, C. (1995). The genetics of obesity: From genetic epidemiology to molecular markers. *Molecular Medicine Today, 1,* 45–50.

Bray, G. A. (1976). *The obese patient.* Philadelphia: Saunders.

Bray, G. A. (1989). Autonomic and endocrine factors in the regulation of food intake. *International Journal of Obesity, 13*(3), 327–335.

Bray, G. A., & Bouchard, C. (1997). Genetics of human obesity: Research directions. *FASEB Journal, 11,* 937–945.

Bray, G. A., Fisler, J., & York, D. A. (1990). Neuroendocrine control of the development of obesity: Understanding gained from studies of experimental animal models. *Frontiers of Neuroendocrinology, 11,* 128–181.

Bray, G. A., & Popkin, B. M. (1998). Dietary fat does affect obesity. *American Journal of Clinical Nutrition, 68,* 1157–1173.

Brief, D. J., & Davis, J. D. (1984). Reduction of food intake and body weight by chronic intraventricular insulin infusion. *Brain Research Bulletin, 12,* 571–575.

Brüning, J. C., Gautam, D., Burks, D. J., Gillette, J., Schubert, M., Orban, P. C., Klein, R., Krone, W., Müller-Wieland, D., & Kahn, C. R. (2000). Role of brain insulin receptor in control of body weight and reproduction. *Science, 289,* 2122–2125.

Campfield, L. A., Brandon, P., & Smith, F. J. (1985). On-line continuous measurement of blood glucose and meal pattern in free-feeding rats: The role of glucose in meal initiation. *Brain Research Bulletin, 14,* 605–616.

Campfield, L. A., & Smith, F. J. (1986a). Blood glucose and meal initiation: A role for insulin? *Society for Neuroscience Abstracts, 12,* 109.

Campfield, L. A., & Smith, F. J. (1986b). Functional coupling between transient declines in blood glucose and feeding behavior: Temporal relationships. *Brain Research Bulletin, 17,* 427–433.

Campfield, L. A., & Smith, F. J. (1990a). Systemic factors in the control of food intake: Evidence for patterns as signals. In E. M. Stricker (Ed.), *Handbook of behavioral neurobiology: Vol. 10. Neurobiology of food and fluid intake* (pp. 183–206). New York: Plenum.

Campfield, L. A., & Smith, F. J. (1990b). Transient declines in blood glucose signal meal initiation. *International Journal of Obesity, 14*(Suppl. 3), 15–31.

Campfield, L. A., Smith, F. J., Gulsez, Y., Devos, R., & Burn, P. (1995). Mouse OB protein: Evidence for a peripheral signal linking adiposity and central neural networks. *Science, 269,* 546–549.

Campfield, L. A., Smith, F. J., Rosenbaum, M., & Hirsch, J. (1996). Human eating: Evidence for a physiological basis using a modified paradigm. *Neuroscience and Biobehavioral Reviews, 20,* 133–137.

Cannon, W. B., & Washburn, A. L. (1912). An explanation of hunger. *American Journal of Physiology, 29,* 441–454.

Carlson, A. J. (1916). *Control of hunger in health and disease.* Chicago: University of Chicago Press.

Chavez, M., Kaiyala, K., Madden, L. J., Schwartz, M. W., & Woods, S. C. (1995). Intraventricular insulin and the level of maintained body weight in rats. *Behavioral Neuroscience, 109,* 528–531.

Chavez, M., Kelly, L., York, D. A., & Berthoud, H. R. (1997). Chemical lesion of visceral afferents causes transient overconsumption of unfamilar high-fat diets in rats. *American Journal of Physiology, 272,* R1657–R1663.

Chavez, M., Seeley, R. J., & Woods, S. C. (1995). A comparison between the effects of intraventricular insulin and intraperitoneal LiCl on three measures sensitive to emetic agents. *Behavioral Neuroscience, 109,* 547–550.

Clark, J. T., Kalra, P. S., Crowley, W. R., & Kalra, S. P. (1984). Neuropeptide Y and human pancreatic polypeptide stimulate feeding behavior in rats. *Endocrinology, 115,* 427–429.

Coleman, D. L. (1973). Effects of parabiosis of obese with diabetes and normal mice. *Diabetologia, 9,* 294–298.

Collier, G. (1986). The dialogue between the house economist and the resident physiologist. *Nutrition and Behavior, 3,* 9–26.

Collier, G. H., Johnson, D. F., Hill, W. L., & Kaufman, L. W. (1986). The economics of the law of effect. *Journal of the Experimental Analysis of Behavior, 48,* 113–136.

Considine, R. V., Sinha, M. K., Heiman, M. L., Kriaucinas, A., Stephens, T. W., Nyce, M. R., Ohannesian, J. P., Marco, C. C., McKee, L. J., Bauer, T. L., & Caro, J. F. (1996). Serum immunoreactive-leptin concentrations in normal-weight and obese humans. *The New England Journal of Medicine, 334,* 292–295.

Corp, E. S., McQuade, J., Moran, T. H., & Smith, G. P. (1993). Characterization of type A and type B CCK receptor binding sites in rat vagus nerve. *Brain Research, 623,* 161–166.

Corp, E. S., Woods, S. C., Porte, D., Jr., Dorsa, D. M., Figlewicz, D. P., & Baskin, D. G. (1986). Localization of ^{125}I-insulin binding sites in the rat hypothalamus by quantitative autoradiography. *Neuroscience Letter, 70,* 17–22.

Davidson, T. L., Altizer, A. M., Benoit, S. C., Walls, E. K., & Powley, T. L. (1997). Encoding and selective activation of "metabolic memories" in the rat. *Behavioral Neuroscience, 111,* 1014–1030.

Davis, J. D., & Smith, G. P. (1988). Analysis of lick rate measures the positive and negative feedback effects of carbohydrates on eating. *Appetite, 11,* 229–238.

Davis, J. D., & Smith, G. P. (1992). Analysis of the microstructure of the rhthmic tongue movements of rats ingesting maltose and sucrose solutions. *Behavioral Neuroscience, 106,* 217–228.

de Vries, J., Strubbe, J. H., Wildering, W. C., Gorter, J. A., & Prins, A. J. A. (1993). Patterns of body temperature during feeding in rats under varying ambient temperatures. *Physiology and Behavior, 53,* 229–235.

Deutsch, J. A. (1978). The stomach in food satiation and the regulation of appetite. *Progress in Neurobiology, 10,* 135–153.

Deutsch, J. A., & Gonzalez, M. F. (1980). Gastric nutrient content signals satiety. *Behavioral and Neural Biology, 30,* 113–116.

Deutsch, J. A., Young, W. G., & Kalogeris, T. J. (1978). The stomach signals satiety. *Science, 201,* 165–167.

Deutsch, R. (1974). Conditioned hypoglycemia: A mechanism for saccharin-induced sensitivity to insulin in the rat. *Journal of Comparative and Physiological Psychology, 86,* 350–358.

Edwards, G. L., Ladenheim, E. E., & Ritter, R. C. (1986). Dorsomedial hindbrain participation in cholecystokinin-induced satiety. *American Journal of Physiology, 251,* R971–R977.

Elmquist, J. K., Elias, C. F., & Saper, C. B. (1999). From lesions to leptin: Hypothalamic control of food intake and body weight. *Neuron, 22,* 221–232.

Elmquist, J. K., Maratos-Flier, E., Saper, C. B., & Flier, J. S. (1998). Unraveling the central nervous system pathways underlying responses to leptin. *Nature Neuroscience, 1,* 445–450.

Epstein, A. N., Nicolaidis, S., & Miselis, R. (1975). The glucoprivic control of food intake and the glucostatic theory of feeding behavior. In G. J. Mogenson & F. R. Calaresci (Eds.), *Neural integration of physiological mechanisms and behavior* (pp. 148–168). Toronto: University Press.

Erlanson-Albertsson, C., & York, D. (1997). Enterostatin: A peptide regulating fat intake. *Obesity Research, 5,* 360–372.

Even, P., & Nicolaidis, S. (1985). Spontaneous and 2DG-induced metabolic changes and feeding: The ischymetric hypothesis. *Brain Research Bulletin, 15,* 429–435.

Faust, I. M., Johnson, P. R., & Hirsch, J. (1977). Adipose tissue regeneration following lipectomy. *Science, 197,* 391–393.

Figlewicz, D. P., Dorsa, D. M., Stein, L. J., Baskin, D. G., Paquette, T., Greenwood, M. R. C., Woods, S. C., & Porte, D., Jr. (1985). Brain and liver insulin binding is decreased in Zucker rats carrying the "fa" gene. *Endocrinology, 117,* 1537–1543.

Figlewicz, D. P., Sipols, A. J., Seeley, R. J., Chavez, M., Woods, S. C., & Porte, D. J. (1995). Intraventricular insulin enhances the meal-suppressive efficacy of intraventricular cholecystokinin octapeptide in the baboon. *Behavioral Neuroscience, 109,* 567–569.

Figlewicz, D. P., & Woods, S. C. (2000). Adiposity signals and brain reward mechanisms. *Trends in Pharmacological Sciences, 21,* 235–236.

Flegal, K. M., Carroll, M. D., Kuczmarski, R. J., & Johnson, C. L. (1998). Overweight and obesity in the United States: Prevalence and trends, 1960–1994. *International Journal of Obesity and Related Metabolic Disorders, 22,* 39–47.

Flynn, F. W. (1999). Brain tachykinins and the regulation of salt intake. *Annals of the New York Academy of Sciences, 897,* 432–435.

Flynn, M. C., & Plata-Salaman, C. R. (1999). Leptin (OB protein) and meal size. *Nutrition, 15,* 508–509.

Friedman, M. I. (1998). Fuel partitioning and food intake. *American Journal of Clinical Nutrition, 67*(Suppl. 3), 513S–518S.

Fujimoto, K., Fukagawa, K., Sakata, T., & Tso, P. (1993). Suppression of food intake by apolioprotein A-IV is mediated through the central nervous system in rats. *Journal of Clinical Investigation, 91,* 1830–1833.

Fujimoto, K., Machidori, H., Iwakiri, R., Yamamoto, K., Fujisaki, J., Sakata, T., & Tso, P. (1993). Effect of intravenous administration of apolipoprotein A-IV on patterns of feeding, drinking and ambulatory activity in rats. *Brain Research, 608,* 233–237.

Fulton, S., Woodside, B., & Shizgal, P. (2000). Modulation of brain reward circuitry by leptin. *Science, 287,* 125–128.

Geary, N. (1998). Glucagon and the control of meal size. In G. P. Smith (Ed.), *Satiation: From gut to brain* (pp. 164–197). New York: Oxford University press.

Gibbs, J., Fauser, D. J., Rowe, E. A., Rolls, E. T., & Maddison, S. P. (1979). Bombesin suppresses feeding in rats. *Nature, 282,* 208–210.

Gibbs, J., Young, R. C., & Smith, G. P. (1973a). Cholecystokinin decreases food intake in rats. *Journal of Comparative and Physiological Psychology, 84,* 488–495.

Gibbs, J., Young, R. C., & Smith, G. P. (1973b). Cholecystokinin elicits satiety in rats with open gastric fistulas. *Nature, 245,* 323–325.

Goodison, T., & Siegel, S. (1995). Learning and tolerance to the intake suppressive effect of cholecystokinin in rats. *Behavioral Neuroscience, 109,* 62–70.

Grill, H. J., & Miselis, R. R. (1981). Lack of ingestive compensation to osmotic stimuli in chronic decerebrate rats. *American Journal of Physiology, 240,* R81–R86.

Grill, H. J., & Norgren, R. (1978a). Chronically decerebrate rats demonstrate satiation but not bait shyness. *Science, 201,* 267–269.

Grill, H. J., & Norgren, R. (1978b). Neurological tests and behavioral deficits in chronic thalamic and chronic decerebrate rats. *Brain Research, 143,* 299–312.

Grill, H. J., & Norgren, R. (1978c). The taste reactivity test: I. Mimetic responses to gustatory stimuli in neurologically normal rats. *Brain Research, 143*(2), 263–279.

Grill, H. J., & Norgren, R. (1978d). The taste reactivity test: II. Mimetic responses to gustatory stimuli in chronic thalamic and chronic decerebrate rats. *Brain Research, 143,* 281–297.

Grossman, M. I., Cummins, G. M., & Ivy, A. C. (1947). The effect of insulin on food intake after vagotomy and sympathectomy. *American Journal of Physiology, 149,* 100–107.

Grossman, S. P. (1986). The role of glucose, insulin and glucagon in the regulation of food intake and body weight. *Neuroscience and Biobehavioral Reviews, 10,* 295–315.

Hagan, M., Rushing, P., Schwartz, M., Yagaloff, K., Burn, P., Woods, S., & Seeley, R. (1999). Role of the CNS melanocortin system in the response to overfeeding. *Journal of Neuroscience, 19,* 2362–2367.

Hagan, M. M., Benoit, S. C., Rushing, P. A., Pritchard, L. M., Woods, S. C., & Seeley, R. J. (2001). Immediate and prolonged patterns of agouti-related peptide-(83-132)-induced c-Fos activation in hypothalamic and extrahypothalamic sites. *Endocrinology, 142,* 1050–1056.

Hagan, M. M., Rushing, P. A., Pritchard, L. M., Schwartz, M. W., Strack, A. M., Van der Ploeg, H. T., Woods, S. C., & Seeley, R. J. (2000).

Long-term orexigenic effects of AgRP-(83-132) involve mechanisms other than melanocortin receptor blockade. *American Journal of Physiology, 279,* R47–R52.

Havel, P. J. (1999). Mechanisms regulating leptin production: Implications for control of energy balance. *American Journal of Clinical Nutrition, 70,* 305–306.

Havel, P. J., Mundinger, T. O., & Taborsky, G. J., Jr. (1996). Pancreatic sympathetic nerves contribute to increased glucagon secretion during severe hypoglycemia in dogs. *American Journal of Physiology, 270,* E20–E26.

Hervey, G. R. (1952). The effects of lesions in the hypothalalmus in parabiotic rats. *Journal of Physiology, 145,* 336–352.

Hevener, A. L., Bergman, R. N., & Donovan, C. M. (2000). Portal vein afferents are critical for the sympathoadrenal response to hypoglycemia. *Diabetes, 49,* 8–12.

Hewson, G., Leighton, G. E., Hill, R. G., & Hughes, J. (1988). The cholecystokinin receptor antagonist L364,718 increases food intake in the rat by attenuation of endogenous cholecystokinin. *British Journal of Pharmacology, 93,* 79–84.

Hill, J. O., & Peters, J. C. (1998). Environmental contributions to the obesity epidemic. *Science, 280,* 1371–1374.

Hoebel, B. G., Hernandez, L., Schwartz, D. H., Mark, G. P., & Hunter, G. A. (1989). Microdialysis studies of brain norepinephrine, serotonin, and dopamine release during ingestive behavior: Theoretical and clinical implications. *Annals of the New York Academy of Sciences, 575,* 171–191.

Hoebel, B. G., & Teitelbaum, P. (1966). Weight regulation in normal and hypothalamic hyperphagic rats. *Journal of Comparative and Physiological Psychology, 61,* 189–193.

Houpt, T. A., & Frankmann, S. P. (1996). TongueTwister: An integrated program for analyzing lickometer data. *Physiology and Behavior, 60,* 1277–1283.

Inoue, S., Bray, G. A., & Mullen, Y. S. (1978). Transplantation of pancreatic B-cells prevents development of hypothalamic obesity in rats. *American Journal of Physiology, 235,* E266–E271.

Kalra, S. P., Dube, M. G., Sahu, A., Phelps, C. P., & Kalra, P. (1991). Neuropeptide Y secretion increases in the paraventricular nucleus in association with increased appetite for food. *Proceedings of the National Academy of Sciences USA, 88,* 10931–10935.

Kaplan, J. M., Siemers, W., & Grill, H. J. (1994). Ingestion, gastric fill, and gastric emptying before and after withdrawal of gastric contents. *American Journal of Physiology, 267,* 1257–1265.

Kaplan, J. M., Spector, A. C., & Grill, H. J. (1992). Dynamics of gastric emptying during and after stomach fill. *American Journal of Physiology, 263,* R813–R819.

Karonen, S.-L., Koistinen, H. A., Nikkinen, P., & Koivisto, V. A. (1998). Is brain uptake of leptin in vivo saturable and reduced by fasting? *European Journal of Nuclear medicine, 25,* 607–612.

Kawano, K., Hirashima, T., Mori, S., Saitoh, Y., Kurosumi, M., & Natori, T. (1992). Spontaneous long-term hyperglycemic rat with diabetic complications: Otsuka Long-Evans Tokushima fatty (OLETF) strain. *Diabetes, 41,* 1422–1428.

Keesey, R. E. (1989). Physiological regulation of body weight and the issue of obesity. *Medical Clinics of North America, 73,* 15–27.

Keesey, R. E., & Hirvonen, M. D. (1997). Body weight set-points: Determination and adjustment. *Journal of Nutrition, 127,* 1875S–1883S.

Keesey, R. E., & Powley, T. L. (1986). The regulation of body weight. *Annual Review of Psychology, 37,* 109–133.

Kelly, L. A., Chavez, M., & Berthoud, H. R. (1999). Transient overconsumption of novel foods by deafferented rats: Effects of novel diet composition. *Physiology and Behavior, 65,* 793–800.

Kennedy, G. C. (1953). The role of depot fat in the hypothalamic control of food intake in the rat. *Proceedings of the Royal Society of London (Biology), 140,* 579–592.

Kissileff, H. R. (1970). Free feeding in normal and "recovered lateral" rats monitored by a pellet-detecting eatometer. *Physiology and Behavior, 5,* 163–173.

Kissileff, H. R., Klingsberg, G., & Van Itallie, T. B. (1980). Universal eating monitor for continuous recording of solid or liquid consumption in man. *American Journal of Physiology, 238,* R14–R22.

Kissileff, H. R., & Van Itallie, T. B. (1982). Physiology of the control of food intake. *Annual Review of Nutrition, 2,* 371–418.

Kulkosky, P. J., Breckenridge, C., Krinsky, R., & Woods, S. C. (1976). Satiety elicited by the C-terminal octapeptide of cholecystokinin-pancreozymin in normal and VMH-lesioned rats. *Behavioral Biology, 18,* 227–234.

Langhans, W. (1996a). Metabolic and glucostatic control of feeding. *Proceedings of the Nutrition Society, 55,* 497–515.

Langhans, W. (1996b). Role of the liver in the metabolic control of eating: What we know—and what we do not know. *Neuroscience and Biobehavioral Reviews, 20,* 145–153.

Langhans, W., & Scharrer, E. (1987). Role of fatty acid oxidation in control of meal pattern. *Behavioral and Neural Biology, 47,* 7–16.

Leibowitz, S. F. (1985). Brain monoamines and peptides: Role in the control of eating behavior. *Federation Proceedings, 45,* 1396–1403.

Leibowitz, S. F., Roossin, P., & Roosinn, M. (1984). Chronic norepinephrine injection into the hypothalamic paraventricular nucleus produces hyperphagia and increased body weight in the rat. *Pharmacology Biochemistry and Behavior, 21,* 801–808.

Le Magnen, J. (1969). Peripheral and systemic actions of food in the caloric regulation of intake. *Annals of the New York Academy of Science, 157,* 1126–1157.

Le Magnen, J., & Tallon, S. (1966). La periodicité spontanée de la prise d'aliments ad libitum du rat blanc (Natural periodicity of food intake in the white rat). *Journal de Physiologie, 58,* 323–349.

LeRoith, D., Rojeski, M., & Roth, J. (1988). Insulin receptors in brain and other tissues: Similarities and differences. *Neurochemistry International, 12,* 419–423.

Levin, B. E., Dunn-Meynell, A. A., & Routh, V. H. (1999). Brain glucose sensing and body energy homeostasis: Role in obesity and diabetes. *American Journal of Physiology, 276,* R1223–R1231.

Lichtenstein, A. H., Kennedy, E., Barrier, P., Danford, D., Ernst, N. D., Grundy, S. M.,

Leveille, G. A., Van Horn, L., Williams, C. L., & Booth, S. L. (1998). Dietary fat consumption and health. *Nutrition Reviews, 56,* S3–S19.

Lotter, E. C., Krinsky, R., McKay, J. M., Treneer, C. M., Porte, D., Jr., & Woods, S. C. (1981). Somatostatin decreases food intake of rats and baboons. *Journal of Comparative and Physiological Psychology, 95,* 278–287.

Lotter, E. C., & Woods, S. C. (1977). Injections of insulin and changes of body weight. *Physiology and Behavior, 18,* 293–297.

MacKay, E. M., Calloway, J. W., & Barnes, R. H. (1940). Hyperalimentation in normal animals produced by protamine insulin. *Journal of Nutrition, 20,* 59–66.

Mark, G. P., Smith, S. E., Rada, P. V., & Hoebel, B. G. (1994). An appetitively conditioned taste elicits a preferential increase in mesolimbic dopamine release. *Pharmacology Biochemistry and Behavior, 48,* 651–660.

Mathis, C. E., Johnson, D. F., & Collier, G. H. (1995). Procurement time as a determinant of meal frequency and meal duration. *Journal of the Experimental Analysis of Behavior, 63,* 295–311.

Matson, C. A., Reid, D. F., Cannon, T. A., & Ritter, R. C. (2000). Cholecystokinin and leptin act synergistically to reduce body weight. *American Journal of Physiology, 278,* R882–R890.

Matson, C. A., & Ritter, R. C. (1999). Long-term CCK-leptin synergy suggests a role for CCK in the regulation of body weight. *American Journal of Physiology, 276,* R1038–R1045.

Matson, C. A., Wiater, M. F., Kuijper, J. L., & Weigle, D. S. (1997). Synergy between leptin and cholecystokinin (CCK) to control daily caloric intake. *Peptides, 18,* 1275–1278.

Mayer, J. (1955). Regulation of energy intake and the body weight: The glucostatic and lipostatic hypothesis. *Annals of the New York Academy of Sciences, 63,* 14–42.

Mayer, J., & Thomas, D. W. (1967). Regulation of food intake and obesity. *Science, 156,* 328–337.

McGowan, M. K., Andrews, K. M., & Grossman, S. P. (1992). Chronic intrahypothalamic infusions of insulin or insulin antibodies alter body weight and food intake in the rat. *Physiology and Behavior, 51,* 753–766.

McGowan, M. K., Andrews, K. M., Kelly, J., & Grossman, S. P. (1990). Effects of chronic intrahypothalamic infusion of insulin on food intake and diurnal meal patterning in the rat. *Behavioral Neuroscience, 104,* 373–385.

Mercer, J. G., & Lawrence, C. B. (1992). Selectivity of cholecystokinin receptor antagonists, MK-329 and L-365,260 for axonally transported CCK binding sites in the rat vagus nerve. *Neuroscience Letters, 137,* 229–231.

Miyasaka, K., Kanai, S., Ohta, M., Kawanami, T., Kono, A., & Funakoshi, A. (1994). Lack of satiety effect of cholecystokinin (CCK) in a new rat model not expressing the CCK-A receptor gene. *Neuroscience Letters, 180,* 143–146.

Mokdad, A., H., Serdula, M. K., Dietz, W. H., Bowman, B. A., Marks, J. S., & Koplan, J. P. (2000). The continuing epidemic of obesity in the United States. *Journal of the American Medical Association, 284,* 1650–1651.

Moran, T. H., Ameglio, P. J., Peyton, H. J., Schwartz, G. J., & McHugh, P. R. (1993). Blockade of type A, but not type B, CCK receptors postpones satiety in rhesus monkeys. *American Journal of Physiology, 265,* R620–R624.

Moran, T. H., & Schwartz, G. J. (1994). Neurobiology of cholecystokinin. *Critical Reviews of Neurobiology, 9,* 1–28.

Moran, T. H., Shnayder, L., Hostetler, A. M., & McHugh, P. R. (1988). Pylorectomy reduces the satiety action of cholecystokinin. *American Journal of Physiology, 255,* R1059–R1063.

Morgan, C. T., & Morgan, J. D. (1940). Studies in hunger: II. The relation of gastric denervation and dietary sugar to the effect of insulin upon food intake in the rat. *Journal of General Psychology, 57,* 153–163.

Morley, J. E., & Flood, J. F. (1991). Amylin decreases food intake in mice. *Peptides, 12,* 865–869.

Nicolaidis, S., & Even, P. (1984). Mesure du métabolisme de fond en relation avec la prise alimentaire: Hypothese iscymétrique. *Comptes Rendus Academie de Sciences, Paris, 298,* 295–300.

Nonavinakere, V. K., & Ritter, R. C. (1983). Feeding elicited by 2-deoxyglucose occurs in the absence of reduced glucose oxidation. *Appetite, 4,* 177–185.

Ogden, C. L., Troiano, R. P., Briefel, R. R., Kuczmarski, R. J., Flegal, K. M., & Johnson, C. L. (1997). Prevalence of overweight among preschool children in the United States, 1971 through 1994. *Pediatrics, 99,* E1–E14.

Okada, S., York, D. A., Bray, G. A., & Erlanson-Albertsson, C. (1991). Enterostatin (Val-Pro-Asp-Pro-Arg), the activation peptide of procolipase, selectively reduces fat intake. *Physiology and Behavior, 49,* 1185–1189.

Oomura, Y. (1976). Significance of glucose, insulin, and free fatty acid on the hypothalamic feeding and satiety neurons. In D. Novin, W. Wyrwicka, & G. A. Bray (Eds.), *Hunger: Basic mechanisms and clinical implications* (pp. 145–157). New York: Raven Press.

Pavlov, I. P. (1927). *Conditioned reflexes.* London: Oxford University Press.

Phillips, R. J., & Powley, T. L. (1996). Gastric volume rather than nutrient content inhibits food intake. *American Journal of Physiology, 271,* R766–R769.

Phillips, R. J., & Powley, T. L. (1998). Gastric volume detection after selective vagotomies in rats. *American Journal of Physiology, 274,* R1626–R1638.

Pinel, J. P. J., Assanand, S., & Lehman, D. R. (2000). Hunger, eating and ill health. *American Psychologist, 55,* 1105–1116.

Polonsky, B. D., Given, E., & Carter, V. (1988). Twenty-four-hour profiles and pulsatile patterns of insulin secretion in normal and obese subjects. *Journal of Clinical Investigation, 81,* 442–448.

Polonsky, K. S., Given, B. D., Hirsch, L., Shapiro, E. T., Tillil, H., Beebe, C., Galloway, J. A., Frank, B. H., Karrison, T., & Van-Cauter, E. (1988). Quantitative study of insulin secretion and clearance in normal and obese subjects. *Journal of Clinical Investigation, 81,* 435–441.

Popkin, B. M., & Doak, C. (1998). The obesity epidemic is a worldwide phenomenon. *Nutrition Reviews, 56,* 106–114.

Poppitt, S. D. (1995). Energy density of diets and obesity. *International Journal of Obesity, 19*(Suppl.), S20–S26.

Powley, T. L. (1977). The ventromedial hypothalamic syndrome, satiety, and a cephalic phase hypothesis. *Psychological Review, 84,* 89–126.

Powley, T. L., & Keesey, R. E. (1970). Relationship of body weight to the lateral hypothalamic feeding syndrome. *Journal of Comparative and Physiological Psychology, 70,* 25–36.

Ramsay, D. S., Seeley, R. J., Bolles, R. C., & Woods, S. C. (1996). Ingestive homeostasis: The primacy of learning. In E. D. Capaldi (Ed.), *Why we eat what we eat* (pp. 11–27). Washington, DC: American Psychological Association.

Reed, D. R., Bachmanov, A. A., Beauchamp, G. K., Tordoff, M. G., & Price, R. A. (1997). Heritable variation in food preferences and their contribution to obesity. *Behavioral Genetics, 27,* 373–387.

Reidelberger, R. D., & O'Rourke, M. F. (1989). Potent cholecystokinin antagonist L-364,718 stimulates food intake in rats. *American Journal of Physiology, 257,* R1512–R1518.

Ren, K., Blass, E. M., Zhou, Q., & Dubner, R. (1997). Suckling and sucrose ingestion suppress persistent hyperalgesia and spinal Fos expression after forepaw inflammation in infant rats. *Proceedings of the National Academy of Science, USA, 94,* 1471–1475.

Riedy, C. A., Chavez, M., Figlewicz, D. P., & Woods, S. C. (1995). Central insulin enhances sensitivity to cholecystokinin. *Physiology and Behavior, 58,* 755–760.

Rieg, T. S., & Aravich, P. F. (1994). Systemic clonidine increases feeding and wheel running but does not affect rate of weight loss in rats subjected to activity-based anorexia. *Pharmacology Biochemistry and Behavior, 47,* 215–218.

Rinaman, L., Hoffman, G. E., Dohanics, J., Le, W. W., Stricker, E. M., & Verbalis, J. G. (1995). Cholecystokinin activates catecholaminergic neurons in the caudal medulla that innervate the paraventricular nucleus of the hypothalamus in rats. *Journal of Comparative Neurology, 360,* 246–256.

Rosenbaum, M., Nicolson, M., Hirsch, J., Heymsfield, S. B., Gallagher, D., Chu, F., & Leibel, R. L. (1996). Effects of gender, body composition, and menopause on plasma concentrations of leptin. *Journal of Clinical Endocrinology and Metabolism, 81,* 3424–3427.

Sahu, A., Sninsky, C. A., Kalra, P. S., & Kalra, S. P. (1990). Neuropeptide Y concentration in microdissected hypothalamic regions and in vitro release from the medial basal hypothalamus-preoptic area of streptozotocin-diabetic rats with and without insulin substitution therapy. *Endocrinology, 126,* 192–198.

Sahu, S., & Kalra, S. (1993). Neuropeptidergic regulation of feeding behavior. *Trends in Endocrinology and Metabolism, 4,* 217–224.

Salter, J. M. (1960). Metabolic effects of glucagon in the Wistar rat. *American Journal of Clinical Nutrition, 8,* 535–539.

Scharrer, E., & Langhans, W. (1986). Control of food intake by fatty acid oxidation. *American Journal of Physiology, 250,* R1003–R1006.

Schneider, L. H., Davis, J. D., Watson, C. A., & Smith, G. P. (1990). Similar effect of raclorpride and reduced sucrose concentration on the microstructure of sucrose sham feeding. *European Journal of Pharmacology, 186,* 61–70.

Schwartz, G. J., McHugh, P. R., & Moran, T. H. (1993). Gastric loads and cholecystokinin synergistically stimulate rat gastric vagal afferents. *American Journal of Physiology, 265,* R872–R876.

Schwartz, G. J., & Moran, T. H. (1996). Subdiaphragmatic vagal afferent integration of meal-related gastrointestinal signals. *Neuroscience and Biobehavioral Reviews, 20,* 47–56.

Schwartz, G. J., Tougas, G., & Moran, T. H. (1995). Integration of vagal afferent responses to duodenal loads and exogenous CCK in rats. *Peptides, 16,* 707–711.

Schwartz, G. J., Whitney, A., Skogland, C., Castonguay, T. W., & Moran, T. H. (1999). Decreased responsiveness to dietary fat in Otsuka Long-Evans Tokushima fatty rats lacking CCK-A receptors. *American Journal of Physiology, 277,* R1144–R1151.

Schwartz, M. W., Baskin, D. G., Bukowski, T. R., Kuijper, J. L., Foster, D., Lasser, G., Prunkard, D. E., Porte, D., Woods, S. C., Seeley, R. J., & Weigle, D. S. (1996). Specificity of leptin action on elevated blood glucose levels and hypotha-

lamic neuropeptide Y gene expression in *ob/ob* mice. *Diabetes, 45,* 531–535.

Schwartz, M. W., Baskin, D. G., Kaiyala, K. J., & Woods, S. C. (1999). Model for the regulation of energy balance and adiposity by the central nervous system. *American Journal of Clinical Nutrition, 69,* 584–596.

Schwartz, M. W., Bergman, R. N., Kahn, S. E., Taborsky, G. J., Jr., Fisher, L. D., Sipols, A. J., Woods, S. C., Steil, G. M., & Porte, D., Jr. (1991). Evidence for uptake of plasma insulin into cerebrospinal fluid through an intermediate compartment in dogs. *Journal of Clinical Investigation, 88,* 1272–1281.

Schwartz, M. W., Figlewicz, D. P., Baskin, D. G., Woods, S. C., & Porte, D., Jr. (1992). Insulin in the brain: A hormonal regulator of energy balance. *Endocrine Reviews, 13,* 387–414.

Schwartz, M. W., Minth, C. D., & Palmiter, R. (1994). A molecular mechanism for body weight regulation by insulin. *Diabetes, 43*(Suppl. 1), 88A.

Schwartz, M. W., & Seeley, R. J. (1997). The new biology of body weight regulation. *Journal of the American Dietetic Association, 97,* 54–58.

Schwartz, M. W., Seeley, R. J., Weigle, D. S., Burn, P., Campfield, L. A., & Baskin, D. G. (1997). Leptin increases hypothalamic proopiomelanocoritin (POMC) mRNA expression in the rostral arcuate nucleus. *Diabetes, 46,* 2119–2123.

Schwartz, M. W., Sipols, A. J., Kahn, S. E., Lattemann, D. P., Taborsky, G. J., Jr., Bergman, R. N., Woods, S. C., & Porte, D., Jr. (1990). Kinetics and specificity of insulin uptake from plasma into cerebrospinal fluid. *American Journal of Physiology, 259,* E378–E383.

Schwartz, M. W., Sipols, A. J., Marks, J. L., Sanacora, G., White, J. D., Scheurinck, A., Kahn, S. E., Baskin, D. G., Woods, S. C., Figlewicz, D. P., & Porte, D., Jr. (1992). Inhibition of hypothalamic neuropeptide Y gene expression by insulin. *Endocrinology, 130,* 3608–3616.

Schwartz, M. W., Woods, S. C., Porte, D. J., Seeley, R. J., & Baskin, D. G. (2000). Central nervous system control of food intake. *Nature, 404,* 661–671.

Sclafani, A. (1997). Learned controls of ingestive behaviour. *Appetite, 29,* 153–158.

Sclafani, A., & Grossman, S. P. (1971). Reactivity of hyperphagic and normal rats to quinine and electric shock. *Journal of Comparative and Physiological Psychology, 74,* 157–166.

Sclafani, A., & Rendel, A. (1978). Food deprivation-induced activity in dietary obese, dietary lean, and normal-weight rats. *Behavioral Biology, 24,* 220–228.

Sclafani, A., Springer, D., & Kluge, L. (1976). Effects of quinine adulterated diets on the food intake and body weight of obese and non-obese hypothalamic hyperphagic rats. *Physiology and Behavior, 16,* 631–640.

Seeley, R. J., Kaplan, J. M., & Grill, H. J. (1993). Effects of interrupting an intraoral meal on meal size and meal duration in rats. *Appetite, 20,* 13–20.

Seeley, R. J., Payne, C. J., & Woods, S. C. (1995). Neuropeptide Y fails to increase intraoral intake in rats. *American Journal of Physiology, 268,* R423–R427.

Seeley, R. J., Ramsay, D. S., & Woods, S. C. (1997). Regulation of food intake: Interactions between learning and physiology. In M. E. Bouton & M. S. Fanselow (Eds.), *Learning, motivation, and cognition: The functional behaviorism of Robert C. Bolles* (pp. 99–115). Washington, DC: American Psychological Association.

Seeley, R. J., van Dijk, G., Campfield, L. A., Smith, F. J., Nelligan, J. A., Bell, S. M., Baskin, D. G., Woods, S. C., & Schwartz, M. W. (1996). The effect of intraventricular administration of leptin on food intake and body weight in the rat. *Hormone and Metabolic Research, 28,* 664–668.

Seeley, R. J., Yagaloff, K., Fisher, S., Burn, P., Thiele, T., van Dijk, G., Baskin, D., & Schwartz, M. (1997). Melanocortin receptors in leptin effects. *Nature, 390,* 349.

Shargill, N. S., Tsuji, S., Bray, G. A., & Erlanson-Albertsson, C. (1991). Enterostatin suppresses food intake following injection into the third ventricle of rats. *Brain Research, 544,* 137–140.

Shizgal, P. (1997). Neural basis of utility estimation. *Current Opinions in Neurobiology, 7,* 198–208.

Smith, F. J., & Campfield, L. A. (1993). Meal initiation occurs after experimental induction of transient declines in blood glucose. *American Journal of Physiology, 265,* R1423–R1429.

Smith, G. P. (2000). The controls of eating: A shift from nutritional homeostasis to behavioral neuroscience. *Nutrition, 16,* 814–820.

Smith, G. P., & Epstein, A. N. (1969). Increased feeding in response to decreased glucose utilization in rat and monkey. *American Journal of Physiology, 217,* 1083–1087.

Smith, G. P., & Gibbs, J. (1992). The development and proof of the cholecystokinin hypothesis of satiety. In C. T. Dourish, S. J. Cooper, S. D. Iversen, & L. L. Iversen (Eds.), *Multiple cholecystokinin receptors in the CNS* (pp. 166–182). Oxford: Oxford University Press.

Smith, G. P., & Gibbs, J. (1998). The satiating effects of cholecystokinin and bombesin-like peptides. In G. P. Smith (Ed.), *Satiation: From gut to brain* (pp. 97–125). New York: Oxford Publishing Company.

Smith, G. P., Jerome, C., Cushin, B. J., Eterno, R., & Simansky, K. J. (1981). Abdominal vagotomy blocks the satiety effect of cholecystokinin in the rat. *Science, 213,* 1036–1037.

Smith, G. P., Jerome, C., & Norgren, R. (1985). Afferent axons in abdominal vagus mediate satiety effect of cholecystokinin in rats. *American Journal of Physiology, 249,* R638–R641.

Smith, G. P., Moran, T. H., Coyle, J. T., Kuhar, M. J., O'Donahue, T. L., & McHugh, P. R. (1984). Anatomic localization of cholecystokinin receptors to the pyloric sphincter. *American Journal of Physiology, 246,* R127–R130.

Snowden, C. T. (1970). Gastrointestinal sensory and motor control of food intake. *Journal of Comparative and Physiological Psychology, 71,* 68–76.

Snowden, C. T., & Epstein, A. N. (1970). Oral and intragastric feeding in vagotomized rats. *Journal of Comparative and Physiological Psychology, 71,* 59–67.

Stanley, B. G., Kyrkouli, S. E., Lampert, S., & Leibowitz, S. F. (1986). Neuropeptide Y chronically injected into the hypothalamus: A powerful neurochemical inducer of hyperphagia and obesity. *Peptides, 7,* 1189–1192.

Stanley, B. G., & Leibowitz, S. F. (1984). Neuropeptide Y injected into the paraventricular hypothalamus: A powerful stimulant of feeding behavior. *Proceedings of the National Academy of Sciences, USA, 82,* 3940–3943.

Steffens, A. B. (1976). Influence of the oral cavity on insulin release in the rat. *American Journal of Physiology, 230,* 1411–1415.

Stellar, E. (1954). The physiology of motivation. *Psychological Reviews, 101,* 301–311.

Stevenson, J. A. F., & Rixon, R. H. (1957). Environmental temperature and deprivation of food and water on the spontaneous activity of rats. *Yale Journal of Biology and Medicine, 29,* 575–584.

Stricker, E. M., & Sved, A. F. (2000). Thirst. *Nutrition, 16,* 821–826.

Stricker, E. M., & Zigmond, M. J. (1976). Recovery of function following damage to central catechoamine-conating neurons: A neurochemical model for the lateral hypothalamic syndrome. *Progress in Psychobiology and Physiological Psychology, 6,* 121–188.

Strubbe, J. H., & Mein, C. G. (1977). Increased feeding in response to bilateral injection of insulin antibodies in the VMH. *Physiology and Behavior, 19,* 309–313.

Strubbe, J. H., Porte, D. J., & Woods, S. C. (1988). Insulin responses and glucose levels in plasma and cerebrospinal fluid during fasting and refeeding in the rat. *Physiology and Behavior, 44,* 205–208.

Strubbe, J. H., & Steffens, A. B. (1975). Rapid insulin release after ingestion of a meal in the unanesthetized rat. *American Journal of Physiology, 229,* 1019–1022.

Swithers, S. E., Westneat, M. W., & Hall, W. G. (1998). Electromyographic analysis of oral habituation in rat pups. *Physiology and Behavior, 63,* 197–203.

Teitelbaum, P., Cheng, M. F., & Rozin, P. (1969). Stages of recovery and development of lateral hypothalamic control of food and water intake. *Annals of the New York Academy of Science, 157,* 849–860.

van Dijk, G., de Groote, C., Chavez, M., van der Werf, Y., Steffens, A. B., & Strubbe, J. H. (1997). Insulin in the arcuate nucleus reduces fat consumption in rats. *Brain Research, 777,* 147–152.

Virally, M. L., & Guillausseau, P. J. (1999). Hypoglycemia in adults. *Diabetes Metabolism, 25,* 477–490.

Wade, G. N., Schneider, J. E., & Li, H. Y. (1996). Control of fertility by metabolic cues. *American Journal of Physiology, 270,* E1–E19.

Wang, L., Martinez, V., Barrachina, M. D., & Tache, Y. (1998). Fos expression in the brain induced by peripheral injection of CCK or leptin plus CCK in fasted lean mice. *Brain Research, 791,* 157–166.

Warwick, Z. S., & Schiffman, S. S. (1992). Role of dietary fat in calorie intake and weight gain. *Neuroscience and Biobehavioral Reviews, 16,* 585–596.

Warwick, Z. S., & Weingarten, H. P. (1996). Flavor-postingestive consequence associations incorporate the behaviorally opposing effects of positive reinforcement and anticipated satiety: Implications for interpreting two-bottle tests. *Physiology and Behavior, 60,* 711–715.

Weingarten, H. P. (1983). Conditioned cues elicit feeding in sated rats: A role for learning in meal initiation. *Science, 220,* 431–433.

West, D. B. (1996). Genetics of obesity in humans and animal models. *Endocrinology and Metabolism Clinics of North America, 25,* 801–813.

West, D. B., Fey, D., & Woods, S. C. (1984). Cholecystokinin persistently suppresses meal size but not food intake in free-feeding rats. *American Journal of Physiology, 246,* R776–R787.

Wiley, J. H., & Leveille, G. A. (1970). Significance of insulin in the metabolic adaptation of rats to meal ingestion. *Journal of Nutrition, 100,* 1073–1080.

Willett, W. C. (1998). Dietary fat and obesity: An unconvincing relation. *American Journal of Clinical Nutrition, 68,* 1149–1150.

Wisse, B. E., Campfield, L. A., Marliss, E. B., Morais, J. A., Tenenbaum, R., & Gougeon, R. (1999). Effect of prolonged moderate and severe energy restriction and refeeding on plasma leptin concentrations in obese women. *American Journal of Clinical Nutrition, 70,* 321–330.

Woods, S. C. (1991). The eating paradox: How we tolerate food. *Psychological Reviews, 98,* 488–505.

Woods, S. C. (1996). Insulin and the brain: A mutual dependency. *Progress in Psychobiology and Physiological Psychology, 16,* 53–81.

Woods, S. C., Chavez, M., Park, C. R., Riedy, C., Kaiyala, K., Richardson, R. D., Figlewicz, D. P., Schwartz, M. W., Porte, D., & Seeley, R. J. (1995). The evaluation of insulin as a metabolic signal controlling behavior via the brain. *Neuroscience and Biobehavioral Reviews, 20,* 139–144.

Woods, S. C., & Kuskosky, P. J. (1976). Classically conditioned changes of blood glucose level. *Psychosomatic Medicine, 38,* 201–219.

Woods, S. C., Lotter, E. C., McKay, L. D., & Porte, D., Jr. (1979). Chronic intracerebroventricular infusion of insulin reduces food intake and body weight of baboons. *Nature, 282,* 503–505.

Woods, S. C., & Porte, D., Jr. (1983). The role of insulin as a satiety factor in the central nervous system. *Advances in Metabolic Disorders, 10,* 457–468.

Woods, S. C., & Ramsay, D. S. (2000). Pavlovian influences over food and drug intake. *Behavioral Brain Research, 110,* 175–182.

Woods, S. C., & Seeley, R. J. (2000). Adiposity signals and the control of energy homeostasis. *Nutrition, 16,* 894–902.

Woods, S. C., Seeley, R. J., Porte, D. J., & Schwartz, M. W. (1998). Signals that regulate food intake and energy homeostasis. *Science, 280,* 1378–1383.

Woods, S. C., & Strubbe, J. H. (1994). The psychobiology of meals. *Psychonomic Bulletin and Review, 1,* 141–155.

Woods, S. C., Vasselli, J. R., Kaestner, E., Szakmary, G. A., Milburn, P., & Vitiello, M. V. (1977). Conditioned insulin secretion and meal feeding in rats. *Journal of Comparative and Physiological Psychology, 91,* 128–133.

Yoshihara, T., Honma, S., & Honma, K. (1996a). Effects of restricted daily feeding on neuropeptide Y release in the rat paraventricular nucleus. *American Journal of Physiology, 270,* E589–E595.

Yoshihara, T., Honma, S., & Honma, K. (1996b). Prefeeding release of paraventricular neuropeptide Y is mediated by ascending noradrenergic neurons in rats. *American Journal of Physiology, 270,* E596–E600.

Young, R. C., Gibbs, J., Antin, J., Holt, J., & Smith, G. P. (1974). Absence of satiety during sham feeding in the rat. *Journal of Comparative and Physiological Psychology, 87*(5), 795–800.

Zhang, Y., Proenca, R., Maffei, M., Barone, M., Leopold, L., & Friedman, J. M. (1994). Positional cloning of the mouse obese gene and its human homologue. *Nature, 372,* 425–432.

Zigmond, M. J., & Stricker, E. M. (1973). Recovery of feeding and drinking by rats after after intraventricular 6-hydroxydopamine or lateral hypothalamic lesions. *Science, 182,* 717–720.

CHAPTER 16

Thirst and Water-Salt Appetite

NEIL E. ROWLAND

HISTORICAL PERSPECTIVE AND INTRODUCTORY CONCEPTS

Homeostasis

Maintenance of body fluids is one of the most vital functions of all animals. In the same way that the body is always oxidizing energy substrates, fluid is being lost continuously from our skin, lungs, and kidneys. For storing energy, the body has large and variable-sized stores such as fat cells (adipocytes), but it has no corresponding way to store fluids. Thus, the concerted action of both physiological and behavioral mechanisms in the service of body fluid balance is crucial.

The concept of *homeostasis*—the maintenance of physiological parameters within optimal ranges—is pivotal to any discussion of fluid balance. A basic homeostatic system has sensors for relevant physiological variables; set points (or *optimal values*) for those variables; and effector mechanisms, the actions of which change the value of the variables (Figure 16.1). These set points are usually genetically programmed. *Negative feedback systems* or devices detect the discrepancy or error between the actual and set-point values and generate proportional error signals that activate the effector mechanisms to reduce and eventually eliminate those errors. Because these effector mechanisms usually either have definite thresholds for activation or operate with

time delays (or both), homeostatic systems operate within set ranges. The thermostat and attached heating or cooling systems in a house work in this way. Most physiologists believe that some biological version of negative feedback operates for many regulated variables. Oatley (1973) was among the first to formalize a homeostatically based model for body fluid balance, incorporating two fluid compartments.

Body Fluid Compartments

Fluid is distributed nonuniformly throughout the body of a multicellular organism. Water accounts for approximately 60% of body weight of an adult human, and 75% in a newborn. This water is distributed into two major compartments: The intracellular fluid (ICF) compartment, which comprises the fluid inside all the body's cells, holds about 67% of total body water (40% of body weight), whereas the extracellular fluid (ECF) compartment holds half that amount (Table 16.1). Treating the ICF as a single compartment may seem confusing because it could be argued that each cell is a separate compartment; however, each cell is in constant exchange and communication with other cells via the ECF surrounding it. Dissolved substances (solutes) in different cell types usually differ in only minor ways, but the solutes in the ICF overall differ markedly from those in ECF. Solutes

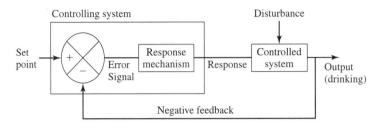

Figure 16.1 A simple negative feedback system believed to operate for homeostatic systems such as body fluid balance.
NOTE: The controlling system consists of a set point for a regulated variable and a means of comparing that set point with the actual value or feedback. Any difference constitutes an error signal that engages a response mechanism. That in turn drives a controlled system with an output (such as drinking behavior) that changes the current value of the variable.

generate an osmotic pressure that is proportional to the total number of particles in solution. At equilibrium, the osmotic pressures of ECF and ICF are the same, about 286 milliosmoles/l. ICF and ECF compartments are separated by cell membranes made of phospholipids. Such membranes, which separate all cells from their surroundings, allow passage of small, lipid-soluble (e.g., steroid) molecules. Most other substances rely on specialized channels or transporters if they are to enter or exit a cell; these channels are made of one or several proteins, the genes for which are expressed by that cell. *Ions* are charged particles, some of which are present in high concentrations that differ markedly between ICF and ECF (Table 16.1). These ions can move through cell membranes using either *ion channels* (which differ in their selectivity for one or more ion types) or *ion pumps*. These channels exist in both open (active) and closed (inactive) states. Ions flow through open ion channels down their own concentration gradients. In contrast, ion pumps use energy (e.g., via breakdown of ATP) to move ions against their concentration gradients. For example, the ATP-hydrolyzing enzyme that pumps three sodium (Na^+) ions out of the cell in exchange for two potassium (K^+) ions pumped into the cell is called the *Na^+, K^+-pump,* and is a key element in maintaining the very different concentrations of Na^+ and K^+ on either side of the cell membrane (Table 16.1).

The ECF is divided between interstitial fluid (ISF) and blood plasma at a ratio of about 3:1. These two compartments are separated by and exchange fluid across the walls of capillary blood vessels. The endothelial cells forming the walls of these capillaries generally do not form a tight seal, and small molecules can pass freely through these gaps in the walls. As a result of this movement, the chemical compositions of ISF and plasma are very similar, with the important exception that large soluble proteins such as albumin cannot fit through the gaps and so are trapped in the plasma.

Table 16.1 Body Fluid Compartments and Constituents in Adult Humans.

Property	Intracellular (ICF)	Extracellular (ECF)
Volume (% body weight)	~40%	~20%
Na^+ (meq/l)	12	145
K^+ (meq/l)	150	4
Ca^{++} (meq/l)	<.001	5
Cl^- (meq/l)	5	105
HCO_3^- (meq/l)	12	25
Phosphates (P_i, meq/l)	100	2

NOTE: ECF is ~75% interstitial fluid and ~25% plasma.
SOURCE: Adapted from Berne and Levy (1998).

The concentration of plasma proteins is ~70 g/l, which generates an osmotic pressure of ~0.8 milliosmoles/l.

In order to maintain the ICF and ECF fluid compartments in size and chemical content, a minimum of two parameters, which function effectively as the set points for these characteristics, must be regulated: the intracellular parameter of ionic composition and the extracellular parameter of absolute volume of fluid.

Intracellular Compartment

The first of these regulated parameters is ionic composition. Many cells have specialized water-transporting channels called *aquaporins* embedded in their membranes (Nielsen, Kwon, Frokiaer, & Knepper, 2000). Different variants or subtypes of aquaporin are expressed in different tissues. By regulating the abundance and fraction of active aquaporins, cells can become more or less permeable to water. When permeability (technically, the number of water molecules that can pass across an area of membrane per unit of time) is high, the forces of osmotic pressure will determine the flow of water between ICF and ECF compartments. Na^+ and chloride (Cl^-) ions are the major contributors to osmotic pressure outside cells (Table 16.1). K^+ and negatively charged ions (e.g., phosphates, proteins) are the major contributors to osmotic pressure inside cells. As previously noted, the osmotically effective concentration of these solutes inside the cell is 286 milliosmoles/l in humans (there are small differences between species). Equilibrium, by definition, occurs when the ECF also has an osmotic pressure of 286 milliosmoles/l and there is no net movement of water (or ions) across membranes. Note that *no net movement* is not synonymous with *no movement,* but means instead that the movements into and out of the cell are equivalent and thus functionally cancel each other out.

Most cells have a low resting permeability to sodium (Na^+) (i.e., their sodium channels are closed), and the addition of a solute (i.e., an osmotic load) such as NaCl to the ECF will differentially increase osmotic pressure in the ECF. As a result, water will flow out of cells and down its own concentration gradient until osmotic pressures are again equal on each side of the cell membrane. This results in *intracellular* (or simply *cellular*) *dehydration* because the net result is movement of water from ICF to ECF. Of course, this process results in a lower volume of fluid inside the cell, a concept to which we will return in the section "Drinking and Osmoreceptors."

Extracellular Compartment

The second of these regulated parameters is the absolute amount of fluid present in the ECF. ECF and its solutes may be lost (e.g., by loss of blood) without any change in osmotic pressure of the ECF. If we had only the mechanism that detects intracellular dehydration, no fluids would shift from the ICF. Thus, a mechanism that is responsive to ECF volume—specifically to *extracellular dehydration*—is necessary.

Systemic versus Peripheral Factors

Dry Mouth Theory

Both the intracellular and the extracellular parameters are internal or systemic, yet the psychological sensation of dehydration—thirst—has had a history of so-called peripheral theories, most notably that of dry mouth. W. B. Cannon (1919), a distinguished and influential physiologist of his time, asserted that "water supply is maintained because we avoid . . . the disagreeable sensations which arise . . . if the salivary glands . . . fail to pour out their watery secretion in sufficient amount . . . to keep moist the mouth and pharynx." In fact, Cannon presented very little scientific evidence in support of this theory, and Wolf (1958, p. 66) made the point that the weight of his evidence actually supported systemic or internal factors. The dry mouth theory, founded on reputation rather than data, sent many students down scientific dead ends for several decades. However, Cannon was correct in noting that dehydration does lead to a reduction of salivary flow and sensation of oropharyngeal (i.e., mouth and throat) dryness, which we now know is correlated with but not a cause of thirst.

The Rise of Systemic Theories

As early as 1867, Schiff (cited in Fitzsimons, 1979, p. 2) articulated the idea that thirst was a "general sensation arising from the lack of water in the blood" and was not attributable to dryness of the mouth. Consistent with this, Dupuytren (also during the 19th century) showed that the water intake induced in dogs by exposure to the sun was reduced by water infused intravenously, and Latta found that the burning thirst of patients with cholera was relieved by intravenous salt solution. In both of these cases, the fluid bypassed the mouth but clearly altered the sensation of thirst. Wolf (1958), in his pioneering monograph on thirst, attributes the work of Kerpel-Fronius in the 1930s as the first to indicate that thirst and water intake could arise from either intracellular or extracellular dehydration. The work that was most influential in finally turning the field away from unitary systemic theories was probably the paper entitled "Multiple Factors in Thirst," by E. F. Adolph, who spent a distinguished career studying a broad spectrum of physiological regulations (Adolph, Barker, & Hoy, 1954).

Double-Depletion Model

Extensive study on the intracellular and extracellular mechanisms continued during the next 20 years, culminating in a *double-depletion model* of thirst. Introduced by both

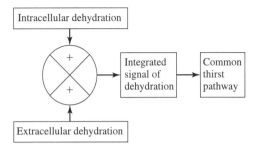

Figure 16.2 The double depletion model of thirst.

NOTE: This model hypothesizes that signals of intracellular and extracellular dehydration, arising as the error terms in Figure 16.1, are detected separately but are integrated or added to form a final thirst signal or common pathway.

Fitzsimons and Epstein in the proceedings of a 1971 conference on thirst (Epstein, Kissileff, & Stellar, 1973), this logic has dominated our conceptualization of fluid balance ever since. Because the behavior (intake of water) and the sensation (thirst) apparently do not discriminate between the intracellular and extracellular mechanisms, it is hypothesized that some integrator of these two signals of dehydration must impinge on a common pathway or thirst signal (Figure 16.2). The double-depletion model and its constituent processes are strictly homeostatic: Deficits are detected relative to set points, as in Figure 16.1. These models thus explain drinking in the context of error detection and error signals rising from dehydration.

Primary and Secondary Drinking

Notwithstanding the previous arguments, there are several situations in which water intake occurs in the absence of known systemic fluid deficits. One of these is adjunctive drinking (see "Adjunctive or Schedule-Induced Drinking" later in this chapter). Drinking that occurs after a spontaneous or small meal was also thought to fall into the category of drinking in the absence of deficit (see "Naturally

Occurring and Meal-Associated Drinking"). To clarify nomenclature, Fitzsimons (1972) introduced the terms *primary* and *secondary* drinking for water intake that either was or was not accompanied by known dehydration, respectively. Other terms that have been used include *regulatory* or *homeostatic,* and *nonregulatory* or *nonhomeostatic*.

Salt Appetite

The phenomenon of salt appetite is closely and inextricably tied to the regulation of ECF volume. Usually, the term *salt appetite* is used synonymously with *sodium appetite,* in large part because Na^+ is the principal cation of the ECF. Loss of ECF occurs concomitantly with loss of extracellular Na^+ (notice that this is the mirror image of the situation with Na^+ loads). Under natural conditions, appetite for Na^+ is especially prevalent in herbivores from environments with low concentrations of Na^+ in the soil. Perhaps the best-known example is the seeking of salt licks—mineral-rich deposits—by both wild and domestic animals. Denton (1982) has given a comprehensive account of many elaborate salt-seeking behaviors, and in some cases the appetite for Na^+ is confounded with need for other minerals. In the laboratory, it is possible to isolate the need for Na^+ from the need for other minerals, so I restrict my comments to this topic. The mechanisms of Na^+ appetite are discussed in a later section.

Neuroanatomy of Thirst

Several brain regions will be mentioned repeatedly in the following text, so it is useful to review these and associated abbreviations briefly before proceeding (see also the chapter by Watts and Swanson in this volume). Structures known as *circumventricular organs* play a pivotal role as interfaces between the peripheral circulation and the brain (Johnson &

Gross, 1993; Simon, 2000). In most of the brain, the endothelial cells (which comprise the walls of blood capillaries) and the overlying processes of *astrocytes* (a type of glial cell) form tight junctions that do not allow diffusion of small molecules. This configuration constitutes what is known as the *blood-brain barrier*. As is the case for individual cells, the only way that substances (other than lipid-soluble molecules such as steroid hormones) enter the brain is via active transport. In contrast, the circumventricular organs have so-called leaky or fenestrated capillaries, which allow diffusion of small molecules and thus have a less stringent blood-brain barrier. Principal among these are the *subfornical organ* (SFO) and the *organum vasculosum of the lamina terminalis* (OVLT), both located on the anterior wall of the third cerebral ventricle, and the *area postrema* (AP) located in the fourth ventricle. SFO and OVLT arise from a common embryological site at the rostral end of the neural tube. In adults, SFO and OVLT form the dorsal and ventral extremities, respectively, of a functionally related strip of midline hypothalamic tissue that includes the *median preoptic nucleus* (MnPO). These regions are interconnected very extensively and project to several other brain regions known to be involved in fluid balance (Lind, Van Hoesen, & Johnson, 1982; Miselis, 1981; and Oldfield, Hards, & McKinley, 1991, reviewed in Johnson & Gross, 1993). Two of these regions are the *supraoptic nuclei* (SON) and the *dorsolateral paraventricular nuclei* (PVN) of the hypothalamus, which together form the *magnocellular neurosecretory cell* (MNC) groups. Each is composed of approximately equal numbers of cells that are phenotypically characterized as manufacturing either of the peptide hormones vasopressin or oxytocin. Each of these cell types sends its axons to the posterior pituitary gland, where the axons release either vasopressin or oxytocin in an activity-dependent (i.e., neurosecretory) manner into the general blood circulation. These hormones are signals to specific target organs throughout the body, including the kidneys. The kidneys, of course, are the organs that produce urine, and the regulation of the amount and ionic content of urine is crucial to fluid balance.

Monographs and Sources

This chapter is fairly basic in its scope. As I noted earlier, Wolf's (1958) monograph was a landmark and contains many interesting historical and theoretical perspectives. Fitzsimons' (1979) monograph is essential reading for the serious student. It is a comprehensive and insightful analysis of the field at that time, and most of it is as true today as when it was written. Fitzsimons has contributed several major reviews on more selected topics, the most recent appearing in 1998 in *Physiological Reviews,* and this is also highly recommended. A recent chapter by Johnson and Thunhorst (1997) deals with central integration. Ramsay and Booth (1991) edited a volume devoted to thirst that contained many excellent chapters, several of which are cited herein. Grossman (1990) has written a very useful resource text on thirst and Na^+ appetite, which has been reviewed exhaustively by Denton (1982) and more briefly by Schulkin (1991).

DEHYDRATION AND WATER INTAKE

Intracellular Dehydration

Drinking and Osmoreceptors

All water-permeable cells change size in response to changes in concentration of impermeable solutes in the ECF. Some of these cells transduce the change in size caused by change in effective osmotic pressure into a biological

signal, such as released transmitter or altered neuronal firing rate; such cells are called *osmoreceptors.* In particular, MNCs studied in vitro, when exposed to hypertonic solutions, become depolarized through inactivation of cation channels (Bourque & Oliet, 1997). It is thus likely that osmoreceptors elsewhere also transduce ECF osmolality in a similar manner.

Mayer (cited in Wolf, 1958) was the first to show that the serum osmotic pressure in water-deprived animals was elevated, and suggested a central theory of thirst according to which osmotic change might be signaled to the brain to stimulate regulatory drinking. Gilman (1937) significantly advanced the understanding of osmotically stimulated thirst, showing in dogs that intravenous infusion of equal osmotic loads of different substances stimulated different intakes of water. Substances such as NaCl that are excluded from cells produced the most water intake, whereas partially permeable solutions such as urea produced smaller effects (Figure 16.3, Panel A) and fully permeable solutions such as glucose were ineffective dispogens. This key experiment showed that the critical stimulus to drinking is not the net osmotic load administered, but is related to the resultant level of cellular dehydration. Using gradual NaCl infusions in dogs and humans, and assuming that cells operate as perfect osmometers, Wolf (1958) estimated that the threshold for drinking corresponded to a 1–2% shrinkage of cell volume. Several authors (e.g., Corbit, 1965; Holmes & Gregersen, 1950) showed that the quantity of water consumed is a linear function of the total amount of NaCl administered.

One of the problems in interpreting the quantitative aspects of osmoregulatory drinking is that there is necessarily some delay between imposition of the stimulus and either the onset or completion of the drinking

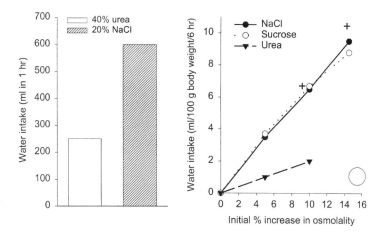

Figure 16.3 Characteristics of intracellular dehydration drinking.
NOTE: The left panel depicts data from Gilman's (1937) classic study in which dogs were infused with either hypertonic NaCl or isosmotic urea. The NaCl, which is trapped extracellularly, causes more cellular dehydration and drinking. The right panel depicts data derived from Fitzsimons' (1979) study of intracellular thirst in nephrectomized rats. Administration of either NaCl or sucrose cause dose-related water intake that approximates the amount needed to dilute the solute load to isotonicity (indicated by the crosses). Different subjects received different total loads, resulting in different initial increases in plasma osmolality. In contrast, isosmotic urea caused very little drinking, whereas cell permeable substances such as glucose and fructose caused no drinking (their data fall collectively inside the large circle at the lower right).

response, a delay during which some of the solute is excreted. The kidney is the principal organ of fluid and electrolyte excretion in mammals; a simplified diagram of its function is shown in Figure 16.4. In the case of NaCl infusion, the shift in fluid to the ECF (with or without drinking) will increase blood volume and cause the secretion of a hormone, *atrial natriuretic peptide,* from barosensitive cells in the heart (see the section on "Receptors for Extracellular Fluid Loss"). This peptide works in the kidney to cause a decrease in sodium reabsorption and thus an increase in natriuresis (sodium excretion).

In order to overcome any confound of sodium excretion on drinking (Fitzsimons, 1961, 1979) made a quantitative study of water intake in relation to intravenous NaCl loads in rats that had been nephrectomized (i.e., rats with their kidneys removed) so that they

could not excrete the load.[1] His result (Figure 16.3, Panel B) showed that the rats drank an amount of water to dilute the solute load precisely to isotonicity, reflecting perfect osmometric behavior. The fact that intact animals normally drink less than this reflects the rapid excretion of the NaCl load mentioned previously. To a first approximation, urinary excretion under these conditions is not dependent upon intake. Thus, as the delay

---

[1] After bilateral nephrectomy, rats remain in good condition for up to 24 hr after surgery if no food is allowed, at which time they should be euthanized. However, to have rats perform well in a behavioral study only a few hours after nephrectomy requires a very skilled surgeon, a suitably short-acting anesthetic, and the nonpainful intravenous route of NaCl infusion. As a result, few have tried to replicate Fitzsimons' study; using a considerably larger intravenous load, we found that some rats neared perfect osmometric behavior, whereas others drank much less (Rowland & Flamm, 1977).

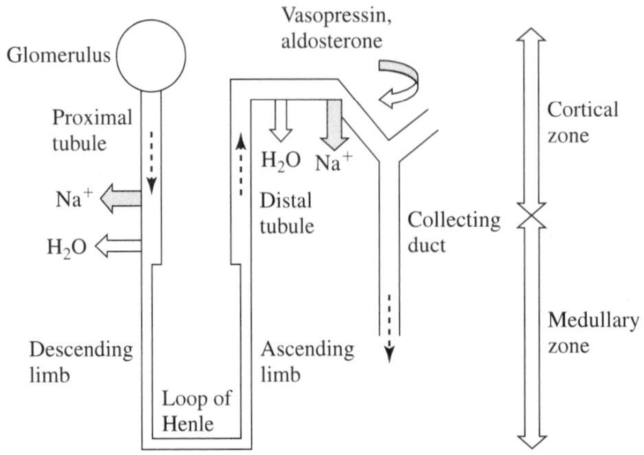

Figure 16.4   Schematic diagram of a juxtamedullary nephron of a typical mammalian kidney.
NOTE: In humans, each kidney contains about 1 million nephrons, some (as shown here) that form a loop spanning the cortical (outer) and medullary (inner) zones, and others with shorter loops just in the cortical zone. A protein-free filtrate of blood is formed by passage through "leaky" capillaries in the glomerulus and passes into the proximal tubule. The proximal tubule is highly permeable to water and other solutes, such as Na^+, that follow by osmosis. This constitutes obligatory fluid reabsorption and typically is >80% of the filtered volume. The filtrate (shown as dotted lines with arrow) then passes through the loop of Henle, which further concentrates Na^+ by a countercurrent mechanism. The distal tubule and collecting duct are relatively impermeable to water and Na^+ except under the action of vasopressin and aldosterone, respectively. Thus, vasopressin decreases the volume of fluid in the collecting duct, and aldosterone decreases its sodium concentration. Fluid at the end of the collecting duct is urine. Other hormones that stimulate Na^+ excretion include oxytocin and atrial natriuretic peptide (not shown).

between the imposition of the NaCl load and beginning to drink increases, the more of the load has been excreted, and the less water intake will be required (Corbit, 1965; Figure 16.5). In the earlier experiments in dogs, it was observed that some individuals consistently drank more than did others in response to a standard osmotic stimulus: The large and small drinkers were termed *minimal and maximal internal regulators,* respectively (Kanter, 1953; Holmes & Gregersen, 1950). Collectively, these observations emphasize a fundamental trade-off between natriuresis and water intake. Another aspect of this (which we will not discuss here) is *dehydration-associated anorexia.* Dehydrated animals that are unable to rehydrate because no suitable fluid is available show profound anorexia, which limits their further intake of solutes

until fluid can be located and consumed (Watts, 2000).

Vasopressin, Oxytocin, and Osmoreceptors

The nonapeptide vasopressin, also known as antidiuretic hormone, is one of the known major hormonal physiological regulators of body fluid homeostasis. In the previous section, it was noted that the MNCs, which secrete vasopressin into the circulation, are themselves capable of acting as osmometers. They also receive neuronal afferent information about osmolality from other locations, including the OVLT and the periphery (see the section on "Peripheral Osmoreception," as well as Bourque & Oliet, 1997 and Johnson & Thunhorst, 1997). In rats, as plasma osmolality rises, oxytocin neurons (which are found adjacent to vasopressin neurons in the MNCs)

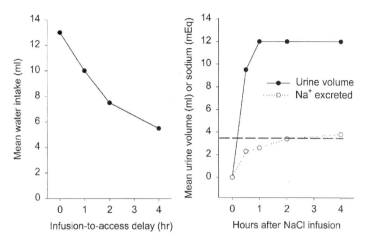

Figure 16.5 Effects of intravenous NaCl (1 ml of a 20% solution infused over ~5 min = 3.42 mEq/rat) on water intake (left) and urinary output (right panel).
NOTE: On the left, rats were given access to water for 1 hr either immediately after the infusion or after delays of 1–4 hr. Water intake clearly declines as delay increases. On the right is urinary excretion of the same load, with no water available to drink. The load is mainly excreted within 1 hr (dashed line = the load, i.e., 3.42 mEq).
SOURCE: Data redrawn from Corbit (1965).

are also activated and oxytocin is released into the bloodstream along with vasopressin. Oxytocin promotes sodium excretion by the kidney (Verbalis, Mangione, & Stricker, 1991).

Figure 16.4 summarizes the neuroendocrine regulation of urine production by the kidneys. To simplify, a kidney consists of thousands of individual functional units called *nephrons,* each of which filters blood plasma into tubes called *loops of Henle.* As this fluid flows through the tubes, both water and selected ions (we will mention only Na^+ here) can be reabsorbed through specific channels located in the tube walls. The greater the volume reabsorbed per unit of time, the lesser the volume that passes all the way through the tube to become urine; conversely, lesser reabsorption means more urine production. The final concentrations of many solutes in the urine are inversely related to this volume. At normal or resting plasma osmolality, the resulting concentration of vasopressin

in plasma produces a moderate level of urine flow. Increases in osmotic pressure elevate plasma concentrations of vasopressin and decrease urine production (a process called *antidiuresis*). Conversely, decreases in osmotic pressure decrease plasma vasopressin and increase urinary flow (a process called *diuresis;* Robertson, 1985).

The mechanism by which this occurs is as follows. The principal targets of vasopressin are Type 2 receptors (V2), which are located in the walls of the loop of Henle (Figure 16.4). Such stimulation of V2 receptors causes a rapid increase in the number of aquaporin (Subtype 2) channels on the surface of these cells (Nielsen et al., 2000). This in turn increases the permeability to—and thus reabsorption of—water in the distal tubules, causing the solutes in the tube and hence the urine to be more concentrated. The maximal concentration of urine thus achievable in rats is ~2,000 mOsm, more than 10 times isotonic. Furthermore, depending on the chemical nature of the solute load, the relative amount excreted after time t, and the net gain of water (calculated by subtracting urine volume from water consumption) at the same time t, there will be either a contraction or an expansion of ECF volume (Corbit, 1965; Wolf, 1958; p. 75). To summarize, the net result of the combined action of vasopressin and oxytocin on the kidneys will be excretion of a Na^+ load in a minimal volume of urine, and this hormonal response functionally reduces the volume of water that must eventually be consumed to restore osmotic homeostasis.

Evidence for Brain Osmoreceptors and Sodium Receptors

In classic studies on the secretion of antidiuretic hormone, E. B. Verney (1947) found that hyperosmolarity confined to the basal forebrain was sufficient to increase vasopressin secretion in dogs.[2] He also found that the osmotic threshold for this effect was 1–2%, very similar to that estimated for thirst (discussed previously). Are these brain osmoreceptors for vasopressin secretion the same as, or different from, those that produce drinking?

Andersson (1953), using goats as subjects, was the first to use chemical stimulation of the brain to address this question. He showed that injection of tiny amounts of hypertonic NaCl, but not equiosmolar glucose or sucrose, into the hypothalamus or ventricles of goats stimulated drinking and vasopressin secretion (Andersson, Olsson, & Warner, 1967). This demonstrates that local hyperosmolarity or hypernatremia is sufficient to induce drinking. In later studies using rats, criti-

cal osmoreceptor locations were mapped using intraparenchymal or tissue injections of NaCl; the results suggested that the medial or periventricular preoptic area is the most sensitive (Buggy, Hoffman, Phillips, Fisher, & Johnson, 1979; Peck & Blass, 1975). Studies using NaCl as a stimulus cannot discriminate between osmoreceptors or Na^+ receptors. McKinley, Denton, and Weisinger (1978) found that sugar solutions made up in artificial cerebrospinal fluid were effective osmotic stimuli but were less potent that equiosmolar Na^+ salts. On the basis of these and other data (reviewed by Johnson & Edwards, 1990), it is now believed that osmoreceptors and Na^+ receptors are separate entities. However, because Na^+ and the accompanying anion normally account for more than 90% of osmotic pressure in the ECF, "the distinction between an osmoreceptor and a sodium-sensitive receptor is unimportant from a practical point of view" (Fitzsimons, 1979, p. 189).

In vivo and in vitro electrophysiological studies have indicted the presence of either osmoreceptors or sodium sensors (or both) in the OVLT (Bourque & Oliet, 1997). Like the other circumventricular organs, the OVLT has a diminished blood-brain barrier, and it has become generally accepted that osmolar substances with otherwise poor penetration into brain may access parenchyma through the OVLT (Johnson & Thunhorst, 1997). Finally, although the emphasis in this section has been on osmoreception, water passage through aquaporins are also crucial. In this regard, Jung et al. (1994) reported that the mRNA for aquaporin Type 4 is expressed in brain in much higher concentrations than in other tissues, and that its distribution in brain is discrete. The highest levels are in cells lining the cerebral ventricles (ependyma) and in MNCs. They speculated that this aquaporin might be an osmoreceptive element that regulates water flow within the brain. Later, it was

---

[2]Verney's work predated considerably the development of radioimunoassays for quantitation of hormones. These studies instead used bioassays, in which the antidiuretic effect of a sample was estimated from inhibition of urine flow in a catheterized, water-loaded, anesthetized assay subject.

found that aquaporin 4 is expressed in glial cells rather than in neurons in the SON, and in ependymal cells in SFO and OVLT (Nielsen et al., 1997), leading to the proposal that an osmoreceptor complex may involve significant neuronal-glial interactions (Wells, 1998). Of additional interest is the idea that vasopressin not only stimulates aquaporins (and thus water flux) in the kidney (Figure 16.4) but also increases water flux in a preparation of brain cortex. It is known that hyperosmolality causes corelease of vasopressin into both plasma from the posterior pituitary and into brain parenchyma from intrinsic vasopressin axons (Ludwig et al., 1994). It is thus possible that brain vasopressin fibers modulate aquaporin-mediated water flux in glial cells, particularly in astrocytes (Niermann, Amiry-Maghaddam, Holthoff, Witte, & Ottersen, 2001). To a large extent, these and other recent findings reconcile the osmoreceptor versus sodium receptor debate, insofar as the same coordinated structural elements may serve both functions (Voisin, Chafke, & Bourque, 1999).

Lesions and Osmoregulatory Thirst

Experimental brain damage was one of the first methods used to localize osmoreceptors involved in thirst. Rats with large bilateral lesions of the lateral hypothalamus (LHA) stop eating and drinking; but if they are kept alive by force feeding during these initial stages, there is partial recovery of these functions (Epstein, 1971). Although the feeding aspects of this "lateral hypothalamic syndrome" have been the most widely studied, it is the drinking deficits that are the more persistent. Rats that have recovered spontaneous (but not completely normal) water intake fail to drink within 6 hr of acute injection of hypertonic NaCl, whereas neurologically intact controls drink copiously within 1 hr. The conclusion was that lateral hypothalamic lesions abolished the ability to respond to osmotic stimuli (Epstein, 1971). Rowland (1976a) noticed that LHA-lesion rats failing to drink within 6 hr of injection nonetheless showed an increase in water intake during the next 24 hr. Likewise, when the osmotic load was infused continuously for several days by intravenous or intragastric routes, such lesion rats increased their drinking, but only at night when they were eating (Rowland, 1976b). They also increased their drinking when NaCl was added to their food and decreased it when they were either infused with water or ate moistened food. Rats bearing excitotoxic lesions of the lateral hypothalamus, which damage intrinsic cells but leave intact fibers of passage, have similar deficits (Clark, Clark, Bartle, & Winn, 1991), as do rats with lesions of the zona incerta (Rowland, Grossman, & Grossman, 1979) or lateral preoptic area (Coburn & Stricker, 1978). In all of these cases, what is impaired is the ability to respond to a challenge of unnaturally rapid onset, rather than the ability to sense that challenge. Thus, the interpretation that these regions are essential to osmoregulatory drinking must be correspondingly modified. It should be noted that, after these delays in responding, the amount of water consumed is generally appropriate to that expected given the interim excretion of the load (Corbit, 1965, Figure 5): Using Kanter's (1953) terminology, these rats have become internal regulators par excellence.

A different type of osmoregulatory abnormality is seen after lesion of the anteroventral third ventricle, an area encompassing the OVLT and often including the ventral MnPO (Johnson & Edwards, 1990). Such lesions produce deficits in osmoregulatory drinking to hypertonic NaCl, and these rats maintain plasma sodium concentrations about 5% above normal (Buggy & Johnson, 1977), well in excess of the normal osmotic drinking threshold. The effective set point of the osmoregulatory mechanism has been elevated, suggesting that a primary (but probably not exclusive) osmoreceptive mechanism is located in this region.

Several studies have reported the distribution of Fos-immunoreactive (Fos-ir) cells in rat brain following injection or infusion of hypertonic NaCl (reviewed in Rowland, 1998). Fos is an inducible transcription factor that has been used as an indirect marker of cellular activation. Germane to the present discussion, hypertonic NaCl induced Fos-ir in neurons of the dorsal OVLT, a region outside the blood-brain barrier (Bisley, Rees, McKinley, Hards, & Oldfield, 1996). However, lesion of the MnPO, including this dorsal cap of the OVLT, produced only small decrements in Fos-ir induced by hypertonic NaCl in other brain regions, including MNCs of the SON and PVN (Xu & Herbert, 1995). This suggests that one or more alternative mechanisms may activate the latter areas either instead of or in addition to direct projections from osmoreceptors in the OVLT. Consistent with this, Han and Rowland (1996) found that low doses of NaCl induced little or no Fos-ir in the OVLT region, but gave a robust response in the SON and PVN.

All the structures we have considered thus far are in or near the hypothalamus, the region historically noted for its role in the maintenance of bodily homeostasis for temperature, energy, and drinking. Grill and Miselis (1981) showed that rats with of the brain at high level supracollicular transactions of the neuraxis failed to increase their water intake following injection of hypertonic saline or other dipsogenic stimuli. (Because such rats cannot seek out water in a normal way, water was delivered into the mouth from an intraoral catheter in these studies). This suggests that in contrast to feeding, for which hindbrain involvement can be shown using this preparation, drinking requires participation of forebrain sensors. Using the Fos-ir metric, Rinaman,

Stricker, Hoffman, and Verbalis (1997) have shown that forebrain structures are activated by hyperosmolarity in both infants and adults, whereas the activation of hindbrain regions seen in adults does not occur in infants. The authors suggest that the forebrain has an early-developing obligatory osmosensitive mechanism, whereas hindbrain activation reflects a later maturing influence of hyperosmolality (which is transduced in the forebrain) on functions such as cardiovascular control or dehydration anorexia. In contrast, Hostenbach and Cirello (1996) found that dual lesion of the OVLT and SFO led to a near total loss of the Fos-ir that normally is induced in the MNCs by intravenous infusions of hypertonic NaCl, but that Fos-ir was undiminished in hindbrain structures. They inferred that plasma osmolality affects hindbrain structures directly in the absence of input from forebrain osmoreceptor areas. It is difficult at this time to reconcile the different interpretations of these two studies, but neither ruled out a role for what is to be discussed in the next section, namely, the contribution of osmoreceptors outside of the brain.

Peripheral Osmoreception

The natural route by which solutes enter the body is through food in the gastrointestinal tract. The absorbed contents of the gastrointestinal tract drain into the hepatic portal vein and thence to the liver before entering the general circulation. To a systems analyst, it would make sense to have osmoreceptors in the liver or splanchnic (gut) regions because they would experience the earliest and undiluted effects of incoming osmotic loads. Indeed, in his pioneering work, Haberich (1968) proposed that such receptors would serve as "an advanced post in the 'dangerous' front line between the enteral and parenteral space of the body," (p. 1140). Despite several demonstrations that such peripheral receptors exist (e.g.,

Adachi, Niijima, & Jacobs, 1976; Haberich, 1968; Rogers, Novin, & Butcher, 1979) the field has been slow to accord them a prominent role in the control of drinking or vasopressin secretion (Johnson & Edwards, 1990).

To investigate peripheral mechanisms and how they communicate with the brain in more detail, Baertschi and his colleagues developed a protocol of brief intragastric infusion of hypertonic solutions in conscious rats at doses too low to cause measurable change in osmolality in the general circulation (Choi-Kwon & Baertschi, 1991; Choi-Kwon, McCarty, & Baertschi, 1991). NaCl, sucrose, and mannitol infused in this way all stimulated vasopressin secretion, but urea did not. This result is consistent with an earlier study in which dogs were given slow infusion of hypertonic NaCl into the hepatic portal vein (Chwalbinska-Moneta, 1979). This study also found a dose-related increase in plasma vasopressin that peaked ~4 min after the infusion started, with no change in systemic osmolality. In these studies, the investigators also cut sensory nerves that were likely to carry the osmotic information from the gut to the brain, holding that such nerve cuts should then abolish the vasopressin response to the infusion. Using this approach, the relevant osmoreceptors were localized to the mesentery of the upper small intestine or portal regions (or both), projecting to the brain via the splanchnic (rat) or vagus (dog) nerves.

The behavioral complement to these studies was reported using rats by Kraly et al. (1995a). Intragastric infusions of NaCl, as well as other osmotic substances, decreased latency to drink and increased the amount of water consumed, again without change in systemic osmolality. This drinking was abolished by cutting the hepatic branch of the vagus nerve, which carries sensory information from the liver to the brain.

King and Baertschi (1991, 1992) investigated the central pathway taken by this afferent signal by making various lesions in the central nervous system. They found specifically that noradrenergic projections from the subcoeruleus region in the hindbrain to the forebrain were responsible for initiating the vasopressin response. Because lesions of the MnPO also reduced vasopressin secretion to intragastric NaCl, the MnPO may be the principal forebrain target for the peripheral osmoreceptor information. Cunningham and Johnson (1989) have found deficits in drinking in rats with local destruction of norepinephrine axon terminals in the MnPO; unfortunately, intragastric NaCl was not tested in that study.

Recently, the problem has been examined using functional mapping with Fos. Carlson et al. (1997) found that low-dose intragastric saline infusions strongly stimulated Fos-ir in the SON and PVN, consistent with the increase in vasopressin secretion caused by these infusions. Fos was also induced in several hindbrain areas, including the caudal nucleus of the solitary tract. This area receives many types of visceral afferent, and so may be the first relay of peripheral osmoreceptors on their way to the forebrain MNCs, probably via the MnPO. Morita et al. (1997) reported complementary findings using hepatic portal infusion of hypertonic NaCl in rats, with the concurrent infusion of water into the vena cava to prevent systemic osmotic change. NaCl-induced Fos-ir was abolished by hepatic branch vagotomy. The evidence that these or other receptors are involved in drinking comes from studies of meal-associated drinking, and is reviewed later under "Naturally Occurring and Meal-Associated Drinking." At an evolutionary level of analysis, set points must have evolved for optimality, and it follows that a dehydrated brain will function suboptimally. It thus is to be expected that adaptations that avoid meal-related dehydration will have evolved, with prandial drinking prominent among these.

Extracellular Dehydration

Receptors for Extracellular Fluid Loss

Historical reports of intense thirst in humans after severe hemorrhage or illness such as cholera, both involving isotonic loss of vascular fluid, led to the concept of extracellular thirst. The lethargy animals often experience after rapid or large hemorrhage, however, may compromise the experimental method for behavioral studies. Fitzsimons (1961) introduced the use of the high–molecular weight colloid polyethylene glycol to produce slow onset hypovolemia (reduced blood volume; see Stricker, 1991, for review). When injected peripherally, this colloid sequesters isotonic fluid (ECF) at the injection site for several hours by disrupting the osmotic forces that normally cause capillary filtrate to return to the plasma. In contrast to hemorrhage, there is no loss of cells or protein from the blood stream, and animals are not behaviorally compromised. Another method of producing hypovolemia is the use of peritoneal dialysis with a high volume of isotonic glucose (Falk, 1966). This causes movement of Na^+ into the peritoneum and a reduction in plasma volume. Yet another method is injection of diuretic/natriuretic agents, to be discussed under "Sodium Depletion and Appetite."

Hypovolemia due to a rapid hemorrhage produces an initial drop in arterial blood pressure, followed by several physiological responses to restore that pressure. These responses are the activation of the sympathetic nervous system (through the secretion of norepinephrine), secretion of vasopressin from the posterior pituitary, and an increase in circulating angiotensin II (to be discussed shortly). Each of these three hormones constricts blood vessels and in turn elevates blood pressure. Unlike rapid hemorrhage, polyethylene glycol does not cause a marked drop in arterial blood pressure because the onset of hypovolemia is relatively slow and the above physiological reactions are able to take place more or less preventatively, rather than reactively.

The blood stream consists of high-pressure (arterial) and low-pressure (venous) regions, connected by capillaries throughout body tissues. Artery walls are relatively inelastic. In contrast, the venous walls are elastic, and as total blood volume increases or decreases the veins either expand or constrict to accommodate flow. The vena cava is the large vein that returns much of the blood to the atrium of the heart, and from there the blood passes through the pulmonary circulation. These low-pressure blood vessels in and near the heart are collectively called *cardiopulmonary vessels,* and their walls contain stretch-sensitive mechanoreceptors. As these vessels expand or constrict, the mechanoreceptors experience different degrees of stretch, and generate a proportional signal. The threshold decrease in blood volume or commensurate underfilling of low-pressure blood vessels is 8–10% for drinking (Fitzsimons, 1998) and vasopressin secretion (McKinley, 1985).

Direct evidence of the involvement of cardiopulmonary receptors in extracellular dehydration drinking comes from studies showing that damage to atrial receptors (or their efferents) in sheep and dogs decreased the drinking response (Quillen, Keil, & Reid, 1990; Zimmerman, Blaine, & Stricker, 1981). Inflation of a balloon—to generate an artificial signal of vascular filling at the junction of the right atrium and superior vena cava—decreased hypovolemic drinking in rats (Kaufman, 1984). These cardiopulmonary receptors send neural afferents to the brainstem nucleus of the solitary tract, and thence to the ventral medulla and rostrally to the lateral parabrachial nucleus and MNCs (Cravo, Morrison, & Reis, 1991; Johnson & Thunhorst, 1997).

Renin-Angiotensin Systems

Angiotensin II is one of the counterregulatory neurohormonal responses to hypovolemia. Because this peptide will be pivotal to our discussions of hypovolemic thirst and sodium appetite, this section will review the physiology and pharmacology of the angiotensin family.

Angiotensin II is an octapeptide formed by the cleavage of angiotensinogen by an acid protease enzyme, renin (Figure 16.6). The activity of renin normally is the rate-limiting step in this reaction, and, because angiotensin II is broken down rapidly by various peptidases, the concentration of angiotensin II in blood is closely correlated with renin activity. The term *renin-angiotensin system* refers to this entire biochemical cascade. Juxtaglomerular cells of the kidney are the principal source of renin in the blood stream. It is released from these cells into the circulation by a variety of stimuli, including reduced renal arterial pressure or stimulation of $\beta 1$ receptors by norepinephrine originating either in the circulation or released from renal sympathetic nerves. Both hypovolemia and administration of hypotensive agents cause rapid elevations of plasma renin activity and formation of angiotensin II. Angiotensin II (occasionally called angiotensin 1-8, referring to its eight amino acid sequence) is widely believed to be the most important signal molecule of this cascade, but there is evidence that the smaller fragments shown in Figure 16.6, including angiotensin 1-7, angiotensin 2-8 (also known as angiotensin III), and angiotensin IV, may have specific effects (Fitzsimons, 1998; Wright & Harding, 1994), but these are beyond the scope of the present treatment.

In addition to the well-known circulation-based renin-angiotensin system, it is now clear that many tissues (including the brain) have their own local systems (Ferguson & Washburn, 1998; Fitzsimons, 1998; Saavedra,

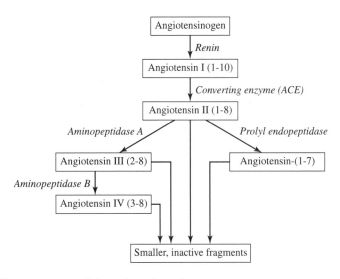

Figure 16.6 Key components of the renin angiotensin system.
NOTE: The precursor, angiotensinogen, is a large (453 amino acid) glycoprotein, from which the decapeptide angiotensin I is cleaved by renin. The activity of renin is the rate-limiting step in plasma. Angiotensin-converting enzyme (ACE, a dipeptidyl peptidase) cleaves it to the biologically active form angiotensin II. Various other peptidases cause the formation of the active angiotensin fragments shown, as well as smaller inactive fragments.

1999; Wright & Harding, 1994). Furthermore, the brain has a diffuse network of angiotensin-containing neurons and processes, and corresponding receptors for angiotensin II are found in many regions (Rowe, Saylor, & Speth, 1992; Saavedra, 1999).

There are two main subtypes of angiotensin II receptor, called AT_1 and AT_2, with at least two variants (A and B) of the AT_1 subtype. Prior to 1990, the best receptor-antagonists available were substituted peptide analogs of angiotensin II (e.g., sarile, saralasin), but these did not discriminate between AT_1 and AT_2 subtypes. The development of nonpeptide antagonists discriminated between the subtypes (Timmermans et al., 1993; Wright & Harding, 1994). The prototypical and most often used AT_1 antagonist is the orally active agent losartan (formerly known as DuP 753). The most widely used AT_2 antagonist is PD 123319. AT_1 receptors are found in several brain regions of adult rats, with the highest densities in the forebrain areas mentioned earlier: OVLT, SFO, SON, and PVN. AT_2 receptors are generally found in more caudal brain regions and apparently do not overlap markedly with the distribution of AT_1 (Rowe et al., 1992; Saavedra, 1999; Wright & Harding, 1994). AT_{1A} and AT_{1B} genes are differentially regulated and distributed in brain (AT_{1A} predominates over AT_{1B} except in pituitary), but no current pharmacological agents discriminate between these two receptors.

Another class of pharmacological agent that has been used in studies of fluid balance is the so-called *angiotensin-converting enzyme (ACE) inhibitors*. In reality, ACE is a dipeptidyl peptidase that, among other things, cleaves the decapeptide precursor angiotensin I into the angiotensin II (Figure 16.6). Work performed prior to about 1980 used peptide inhibitors such as SQ 20881; subsequently, orally active nonpeptide ACE inhibitors such as captopril became available. Based on studies showing opposite effects of low and high peripheral dosages of captopril on water intake, a spillover hypothesis that relies on partial permeability of the blood-brain barrier to captopril has become widely accepted (Elfont & Fitzsimons, 1983; Evered & Robinson, 1984). According to this hypothesis, captopril cannot cross the blood-brain barrier, and low dosages penetrate the circumventricular organs in concentrations insufficient to block the normally high ACE activity in these structures effectively. However, these low dosages fully block ACE in the periphery and so prevent circulating angiotensin I from being converted to angiotensin II. The resulting high plasma levels of angiotensin I are believed to penetrate (or spill over) into the circumventricular organs and to be converted locally to angiotensin II, because ACE is incompletely inhibited in these organs. In contrast, high dosages of captopril given peripherally are proposed to penetrate circumventricular organs in sufficient amounts to block local ACE activity completely. Therefore, when peripherally generated angiotensin I spills over into the SFO, it is not converted and thus remains inactive because angiotensin I does not activate angiotensin II receptors. Low doses of ACE inhibitors thus functionally increase (and high doses decrease) occupancy of angiotensin II receptors (most likely AT_{1A}) in the circumventricular organs.

Circulating Angiotensin II and Drinking

As reviewed by Fitzsimons (1979), Linazasoro, Jiminez-Diaz, and Castro Mendoza (1954) were the first to suspect that a hormonal factor of renal origin may participate in thirst, but they were unable to identify that factor. Fitzsimons (1969) showed that intraperitoneal injection of either crude or purified kidney extract promoted drinking in intact and (to an even greater degree) nephrectomized rats, and that intravenous infusion of renin had a similar action (Figure 16.7). He went on to show that intravenous infusion of angiotensin II had a

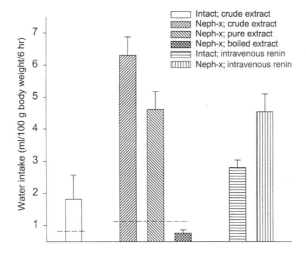

Figure 16.7 Classic demonstration of the dipsogenic potency of a kidney derived factor.
NOTE: Shown are the M (±SE) 6-hr water intakes of groups of either intact or bilaterally nephrectomized rats either injected intraperitoneally with various kidney extracts or infused intravenously with purified renin. All of these treatments, except for the extract which was boiled to denature proteins, caused water intake above baselines (dashed lines) and were more effective in nephrectomized than in intact (or sham operated) rats.
SOURCE: Drawn from data in Fitzsimons (1979, Table 7.3).

similar effect, and that renin is effective only because of the angiotensin II that it generates. The threshold intravenous infusion rate of exogenous angiotensin II required to elicit water intake in rats under optimal conditions is ~25 pmol/kg/min. This produces plasma levels of angiotensin II that lie between those found after 24 and 48 hr of fluid deprivation, and considerably lower than those achieved acutely after hyopvolemic treatments such as polyethylene glycol (Johnson & Thunhorst, 1997).

Does circulating angiotensin II affect the brain, and if so, what contribution does it make to hypovolemic thirst? Neither of these questions has a simple or as yet completely satisfactory answer. After intravenous injection of radioactively labelled angiotensin II, radioactivity is found in the circumventricular organs, indicating that angiotensin II can cross into the brain at sites with a diminished blood-brain barriers. Recent studies of induction of Fos-ir into the brain following intravenous in-

fusions of angiotensin II have found activation in the central or core regions of the SFO and OVLT, as well as in other discrete brain regions, including the MNCs (reviewed in Rowland, 1998). Simpson, Epstein, and Camardo (1978) showed that lesions of the SFO in rats completely abolished the dipsogenic effect of peripherally administered angiotensin II, and that this was selective insofar as many other types of thirst were either unaffected or only slightly disrupted (Hosutt, Rowland, & Stricker, 1981). The primacy of the SFO has also been found in studies measuring either Fos-ir or vasopressin secretion: Regarding the drinking response, lesions of the SFO completely abolish these responses to peripheral administration of angiotensin II (Simpson, Epstein, & Camardo, 1978). It is most likely that these effects are mediated by neural projections (some of which may take place via neurons using angiotensin as a transmitter) from the SFO to the MnPO, and thence to MNCs.

Peripheral Angiotensin II in Hypovolemic Drinking

Because hypovolemia stimulates production of angiotensin II, and exogenous angiotensin II is dipsogenic in all species that have been tested (Fitzsimons, 1979, 1998), it is logical to ask whether circulating angiotensin II contributes to hypovolemic drinking. As described previously, lesion of the SFO completely abolishes the dipsogenic action of peripherally administered angiotensin II. Injection of the AT_1 receptor antagonist losartan produced a complete block of both water intake and Fos-ir induced in brain by exogenous peripheral administration of angiotensin II (Fregly & Rowland, 1992; Rowland, Morien, & Fregly, 1996). This is strong indication that losartan's primary inhibitory effect is in the SFO, a region with very high AT_1 receptor density. It follows that if endogenous circulating angiotensin II is an important mediator of hypovolemic drinking, then either SFO lesion or losartan should likewise inhibit that drinking. This clearly is not the case: Drinking following administration of polyethylene glycol is unaffected by either SFO lesion (Hosutt et al., 1981) or losartan (Rowland et al., 1996). A similar point was made by Fitzsimons (1969), who showed that bilaterally nephrectomized rats that had no circulating angiotensin II nonetheless drank normally to polyethylene glycol. These and other results leave us with an apparent paradox: These hypovolemic treatments produce circulating levels of angiotensin II well above the dipsogenic threshold, yet interference with transduction of that angiotensin signal (presumably in the SFO) does not disrupt the drinking.

The resolution of this paradox seems to be that circulating angiotensin II interacts with cardiopulmonary stretch or other pressure-related signals to determine the drinking response. This has been shown most elegantly by Evered (1992), who used a high dose of captopril to block the production of endogenous angiotensin II following administration of a hypotensive agent (minoxidil). (The absence of an endogenous angiotensin II response to minoxidil renders the rats even more hypotensive than with minoxidil alone). Circulating angiotensin II was then replaced by intravenously infusing graded doses of exogenous angiotensin II to produce graded changes in blood pressure from hypotensive through hypertensive. Drinking was measured also in these studies, and the dipsogenic action of angiotensin II was found to be greatest when blood pressure was below normal. Of course, this is the normal condition under which renin is released from the kidney. It is reasonable to conclude that angiotensin II makes a partial contribution, along with cardiopulmonary input, to the drinking response to extracellular dehydration (Johnson & Thunhorst, 1997).

Vasopressin, the other peptide released during hypotension, does not induce drinking itself but does lower the threshold for osmoregulatory drinking (Szczepanska-Sadowska, Kozlowski, & Sobocinska, 1974).

Central Angiotensin and Drinking

Fitzsimons (1979) showed that injection of very small amounts of angiotensin II into the brain or cerebral ventricles also causes drinking. The SFO is one of the most sensitive sites in the brain for this effect, consistent with direct stimulation of angiotensin receptors that normally are engaged by the leaking of circulating angiotensin II across the blood-brain barrier. However, there are suggestions that the periperal and central sites may be different because drinking induced by cerebroventricular administration of angiotensin is not disrupted by SFO lesion. Moreover, Fos-ir is induced in a different population of SFO cells by central (versus peripheral) injection of angiotensin II (for reviews see Johnson & Thunhorst, 1997; Rowland, 1998). Of course, an important caveat is that ventricles are not the normal delivery route for endogenous angiotensin II. This, however, leads to questions: If angiotensin in the brain is involved in drinking, which angiotensinergic neurons are involved, and how is their activity regulated? This is an almost intractable problem because, if multiple or diffuse sites are involved, then the ventricular route of administration of angiotensin is the most pragmatic but does not exclude a role of receptors that normally are accessible to peripheral angiotensin II (i.e., in the circumventricular organs). Furthermore, because the amounts of angiotensin in brain are small, it has been difficult to accomplish direct measurements of angiotensin release in discrete sites during hypovolemia.

A contemporary approach has used targeted gene deletions or knockouts. Davisson et al. (2000) reported a complete absence of blood-pressure response after injection of angiotensin II into the cerebral ventricles of mice with targeted deletion of the AT_{1A} receptor gene. Water intake after central injection of angiotensin II was reduced in both AT_{1A} and AT_{1B} knockouts, but to a greater extent in those with the 1B gene deletion. This is the first evidence of a behavioral role for AT_{1B} receptors, but conflicts with conclusions based on the predominance of AT_{1A} receptor mRNAs in most brain regions and their selective up-regulation in SFO and OVLT by water deprivation in mice (Chen & Morris, 2001). Of course, studies like these still do not critically separate effects of centrally released from circulating angiotensin II, and thus any role of central angiotensin II in drinking remains poorly understood (Fitzsimons, 1998).

Additivity of Thirst

Direct measurements of body fluids during most naturally occurring states of dehydration indicate that both intracellular and extra-cellular depletions are involved; the double-depletion model, according to which these two signals are integrated, was introduced earlier in this chapter. Two general analytical approaches have been made to assess the respective roles of intra- and extracellular dehydration under these conditions: additive and subtractive.

Adding Primary Signals

Combination of hyperosmotic stimulation (NaCl injection) with hypovolemia (polyethylene glycol) can produce water intake greater than which either stimulus alone could induce, and in principle additive (reviewed in Fitzsimons, 1979; see also Figure 2). The difficulty with this approach is that the act of drinking itself produces short- and long-term satiating effects. In particular, hyponatremia caused by excessive water intake is known to inhibit water intake (e.g., Blass & Hall, 1976).

Salisbury and Rowland (1990) attempted to circumvent this problem by using a "sham-drinking" procedure. In this protocol, rats are fitted with indwelling gastric fistulas (flanged stainless steel shafts with a screw-in plugs) that can be opened during acute tests to allow ingested fluids to drain out with minimal absorption. We found, as have others, that water-deprived "sham-drinking" rats consume up to 100 ml in a 1-hr session—almost continuous drinking. This is presumably because the postingestive inhibitory effects of the behavior are absent. In our study, we went beyond fluid deprivation to study hypertonicity (NaCl), hypovolemia (polyethylene glycol), and their combination as dipsogenic treatments. As expected from the analysis of Fitzsimons (1979), in rats whose fistulas are closed (such that fluid was absorbed normally), the combination of NaCl and polyethylene glycol produced a drinking response that was additive of that produced by either treatment alone, approximating, in fact,

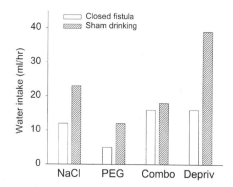

Figure 16.8 Effect of intracellular (4 mEq hypertonic NaCl) and extracellular (5-ml 20% polyethylene glycol, PEG 2 hr beforehand) dehydrations, and their combination on 1-hr water intake in rats with a gastric fistula closed (i.e., normal drinking) or with the fistula open (sham drinking).
NOTE: Drinking after the combination was additive of the component stimuli in closed- but not in open-fistula trials. Compared with 24-hr water deprivation (depriv), the combination caused approximately the same drinking in the closed-fistula trials, but much less on the open-fistula trials. That is, robust sham drinking occurred only in the deprived group.
SOURCE: Data redrawn from Salisbury and Rowland (1990).

that observed after 24-hr water deprivation (Figure 16.8). Unexpectedly, in sham-drinking trials with the fistula open, rats given the combination of NaCl and polyethylene glycol did not increase their intake over that observed in the closed-fistula condition; this result was remarkably different from the continuous sham-drinking in water-deprived rats. This remains the only published study, to my knowledge, that has used stimuli other than fluid deprivation to investigate the open-loop aspect of motivation to drink. The result raises interesting questions such as whether additive intake implies additive thirst. Further study is needed to resolve this issue.

Subtracting Primary Signals

The logic of this approach relies on the assumptions that (a) the amount of water consumed during a double-depletion state reflects an integrated thirst signal that is directly proportional to the physiological need, and (b) fluid intake proportionally decreases that need and thus the signal. Thus, either experimenter- or self-imposed (i.e., by the act of drinking) water loads should reverse the hyperosmotic signal but leave the volume depletion unchanged (at least initially). In contrast, isotonic NaCl loads should largely restore plasma volume but leave the osmotic signal unchanged. Ramsay, Rolls, and Wood (1977a, 1977b) examined the effects of water and isotonic NaCl loads on drinking after water deprivation in rats and dogs. In both species, they found that water loads attenuated drinking after 24-hr fluid deprivation by ~70%, while isotonic NaCl loads attenuated it by ~25%. It has been shown that most of the fluid deficit accrued during fluid deprivation is due to dry or hyperosmotic food intake during that time. Differences in food composition within a species, differences in intake between species, and the timing or duration of the deprivation may affect these relative percentages.

Fluid is being lost from the body continuously, for example in our breath and through our skin; fluid lost in this manner is often called *insensible water loss*. Some conditions increase that loss, the most common being elevation of body temperature (e.g., through exercise or exposure to high ambient temperature), which results in sweating or increased respiration, or both. This increased fluid loss is used for evaporative cooling, but the form of that fluid loss varies from species to species. For example, humans sweat and breathe heavily, dogs pant, and rats spread saliva on their skin using their forepaws. In each case, the result is a loss of hypotonic fluid, leading to both hypovolemia and hyperosmolarity (Nose, Sugimoto, Okuno, & Morimoto, 1987). As a result, drinking only water during thermal dehydration leads to osmotic dilution and satiation of thirst without full restoration of blood volume (involuntary dehydration; Greenleaf, 1992; Takamata, Mack, Gillen, & Nadel, 1997). This condition can be avoided by drinking hypotonic, electrolyte-containing fluids during thermal dehydration. The role of mineral (NaCl) appetite during hypovolemia will be discussed in more detail in a later section.

Naturally Occurring and Meal-Associated Drinking

The foregoing sections have dealt with what Fitzsimons (1979) called the primary stimuli of drinking, and their combinations. Secondary drinking was, for Fitzsimons, drinking in the absence of need. The body has minimal capacity to store fluids in excess of apparent set points, so that, unlike in the case of feeding and energy balance, there is no adaptive advantage to overconsuming or anticipating water need. Indeed, in hot or arid environments where water is scarce, an excursion to a fluid source shared by many species brings with it significant risks of predation. One might expect significant dehydration to accrue before such a potentially dangerous behavioral episode is triggered. Indeed, in laboratory rats, Marwine and Collier (1979) showed that imposition of a modest "foraging cost" on access to water produced a dramatic decline in the number of drinking episodes per day, and a reciprocal increase in the volume ingested at each episode.

In the standard, free-access "welfare state" of the laboratory, most of rats' water intake is in close temporal association with meals. With ad libitum access to dry rodent food, rats eat most of their 8–12 meals at night. Almost every meal is followed by a drinking bout, and some are either preceded by or interrupted for drinking; together, these types of bouts constitute prandial drinking. Fitzsimons and Le Magnen (1969) and Kissileff (1969) were

the first to develop protocols for quantitative continuous measurement of food and water intake, and they showed that the amount of water consumed with a meal was correlated with the size of that meal. Typical meals of rodent chow last ~10 min, at which time only a small fraction of the meal has entered the intestine and been absorbed. Thus, Fitzsimons and Le Magnen (1969) reasoned, prandial drinking occurs too soon to be in response to direct systemic dehydration, and therefore is probably anticipatory or learned (i.e., secondary). However, the subsequent work on peripheral osmoreception (discussed earlier) provides an alternative view. Kraly (1990; Kraly, Kim, & Tribuzio, 1995a, 1995b) showed that pharmacological antagonists of either histamine or angiotensin II receptors attenuated drinking associated with normal-sized meals. Plasma renin activity rises by the end of normal meals (Kraly et al., 1995b; Rowland, 1995). It appears that peripherally sensed osmoreceptive and angiotensin II signals occur during a meal, and so there is no longer a need to propose that this drinking is anticipatory.

In this regard, Starbuck and Fitts (1998, 2001) have shown that SFO lesions slow but do not abolish the appearance of drinking in rats after either dry meals or small intragastric NaCl loads. These authors note that it is not yet clear whether this reflects direct (humoral) or indirect (neural) activation of the SFO, or both. Kraly et al. (1995b) showed that both the increase in plasma renin near the end of a meal and postprandial drinking after a meal were attenuated by cutting the renal nerves. In contrast, slow intragastric infusions of NaCl that produced similar water intake did not increase plasma renin. Thus, something more than that simulated by infusions is taking place during meals, and Kraly suggests the difference lies in the preabsorptive stimuli (e.g., oral factors) associated with eating. Prandial drinking may then be a form of double-depletion thirst, with pre- and postabsorptive factors engaging angiotensin and peripheral osmoreceptors, respectively.

Adjunctive or Schedule-Induced Drinking

When rats or other animals (including humans) are in temporally predictable environments in which they can anticipate events, they often perform apparently purposeless adjunctive or stereotyped behaviors. One of the best studied of these is schedule-induced polydipsia, discovered by Falk (1969). In this protocol, hungry rats are given a small morsel of food at fixed intervals (e.g., every 30 sec); in the interpellet interval they quickly adopt adjunctive behaviors, the first of which is taking a draft of water. Each draft may be up to ~0.5 ml, so that during a session in which they receive 12 g food they may drink more than 100 ml water—far more than the ~12 ml that they normally would consume with a meal that size. Schedule-induced polydipsia has normally been considered secondary or nonhomeostatic drinking, but the resemblance to intrameal prandial drinking[3] is striking. The study of this behavior does not figure prominently in recent fluid-balance literature, but there are clinical correlates (Thompson, Edwards, & Baylis, 1991), which are useful in the study of obsessive-compulsive disorders.

---

[3]The dictionary definition of prandial is "of a meal," so prandial drinking is any drinking that *normally* occurs in temporal proximity to—including during—a meal (i.e., meal-associated). Confusingly, Epstein used the term *prandial drinking* to refer to the *abnormal* style of small drafts taken after almost every bite of dry food that is learned by rats to enable swallowing after total removal of their salivary glands and, with some similarities, in rats recovered from LHA lesions. I suggested using the term *intrameal prandial drinking* to distinguish this highly unusual mode of drinking during meals. From this perspective, adjunctive drinking is also a form of intrameal prandial drinking.

LIFESPAN ISSUES, INDIVIDUAL OR GENETIC DIFFERENCES, AND THIRST

Ontogeny

Infant mammals suckle and thereby affect body fluid status (Friedman, 1979); most, if not all, of their fluid needs are met in this way. Paque (1980) reported that human infants in a hot, arid climate (the Bedouin of the Sahara) are allowed to suckle very frequently, possibly an adaptation to match their continuous losses in sweat. However, in rats there is no evidence that experimental dehydration increases the amount or frequency of suckling behavior (see Hall, 1991, for review). Suckling is not simply an immature form of either eating or drinking, and it is more relevant to consider the ontogeny of water intake independent of the mother.

Most such studies of independent ingestion have been done in rats, whose young are motorically quite immature, necessitating the development of several ingenious testing procedures. These include intraoral infusion of water through a catheter inserted underneath the tongue or placing the rat pup on a moist surface (e.g., Bruno, 1981; Hall & Bryan, 1980; Wirth & Epstein, 1976). In each protocol, the pup can choose to ingest or refuse the fluid, and the usual measure of intake is weight gain during a session. The consensus (Hall, 1991) is that rat pups show robust independent drinking responses, reflective of operational sensory mechanisms, well before the time (14–21 days of age) that they would normally begin ingesting food and water independently. This time-frame corresponds to many developmental changes in the rat brain, including changes in the distribution of AT_1 and AT_2 receptors (Saavedra, 1999). As mentioned before, Rinaman et al. (1997) found induction of Fos-ir by hypertonic NaCl in the forebrain of both infant and adult rats, consistent with earlier findings by Hall (1989) using the 2-deoxyglucose method for mapping metabolic activity. Hall additionally examined the effects of extracellular dehydration and found only a few regions in common with areas activated by intracellular dehydration, but these included circumventricular sites. Most recently, Xu, Ross, and Johnson (2001) have shown in near-term sheep fetuses the presence of functional, albeit not completely mature, brain and behavioral (fetal swallowing activity) Fos-ir responses to hyperosmolality.

Aging

Studies comparing healthy humans of about 70 years of age with young adults have found dramatic deficits in both perceived intensity of thirst and the amount consumed to a given level of dehydration in the older group (Miescher & Fortney, 1989; Phillips et al., 1984, 1991). Dehydrating stimuli in these studies included water deprivation, heat exposure, and hypertonic NaCl, each causing comparable physiological changes in the two age groups. Thus, it seems that older people may have problems transducing the magnitude of dehydration.

We attempted to investigate the mechanism of this in aging rats (Rowland, Morien, Garcea, & Fregly, 1997). The robust declines in intake seen in humans were not observed in our rat population, with the exception of a decline in some forms of salt appetite. We also observed a 50% decline in the number of angiotensin receptors in the PVN at 20 months of age. Thus, the etiology of decreased thirst in aging humans remains unclear at this time.

Genetic and Individual Differences

In the section on osmoregulatory drinking, I noted that in some species it is possible to identify individuals that consume relatively small or large amounts of water in response to a given physiological stimulus, and that these have been characterized as internal and external regulators, respectively (Holmes & Gregersen, 1950). Such differences tend to be quite small in genetically homogeneous experimental subjects, such as rats of a given strain, and so have been little studied. Compared with rats of the Sprague-Dawley stock, rats of the Fischer 344 strain have lower meal-associated and extracellular dehydration drinking and also show more efficient reduction of water intake when water is added to the food (Rowland & Fregly, 1988a; see Walsh, 1980, for findings with other strains). Fischer 344 rats have some characteristics of internal regulators, although the physiological basis for this difference is unknown. We have also found differences between Long-Evans and Sprague-Dawley rats (Fregly, Paulding, & Rowland, 1990). The problem with these studies is that the differences ascribed to strain may also arise from batch to batch or among commercial suppliers. In a more general sense, then, no true control or comparison strain is available. Greater progress might be made by identification of inbred strains with definable genetic differences.

Brattleboro rats are homozygous for a defect in manufacture of vasopressin, and so are unable to retain fluid in their kidneys (i.e., they show polyuria). These animals consume as much as their body weight of water per day to keep up with this primary polyuria. However, this model is of limited usefulness for providing new insights on thirst. More promising is an inbred strain of mice (STR/N) that shows polydipsia but has normal levels of vasopressin. Compared with standard outbred mice, Fos-ir after water deprivation was comparable in the forebrain regions (OVLT, SFO, PVN), but only STR/N mice showed Fos-ir in the hindbrain NTS (Ueta, Yamashita, Kawata, & Koizomi, 1995). The recent development of mice with targeted gene deletions (e.g., as described previously in "Central Angiotensin and Drinking") also holds promise for new insights, although this field is in its infancy and the behavioral studies done to date generally have been very restricted in their scope.

SODIUM APPETITE

Sodium appetite is closely related to hypovolemic thirst: Because "pure" extracellular dehydration entails loss of volume and of isotonic extracellular electrolytes (prominently Na^+), rehydration requires Na^+ intake (Fitzsimons, 1998). Thus, some overlap of mechanism may be expected.

Most laboratory studies of Na^+ appetite have offered solutions of Na^+ salts, commonly NaCl. Anions other than Cl^- have occasionally been compared, and in almost every case it is the Na^+ rather than the anion that appears critical; thus I will not consider this further. Isotonic solutions are those with osmotic pressure equal to that of ECF; in the case of NaCl, each molecule gives rise to two ions in solution, each of which contributes to osmotic pressure; thus isotonic NaCl is approximately 0.15moles/l (M). Isotonic NaCl, sometimes simply called *saline*, is highly preferred to water under need-free conditions by many strains of rats and mice; that is, they find it palatable. However, motivation is clearly best assessed against an environmental hurdle, and most investigators use intake of unpleasantly concentrated (or hypertonic, e.g., ~0.5M) NaCl as a reliable index of Na^+ appetite in rodents. In keeping with this distinction, I will first discuss Na^+ preference and then Na^+ appetite and its mechanisms.

Sodium Preference and Preference-Aversion Curves

Taste preferences can be assessed in several ways. Key parameters of such tests are

- Whether only one fluid is available (as in one-bottle tests) or two or more fluids are available, either simultaneously or in rapid succession (as in two-bottle tests);
- Whether intake is limited, measured over a brief period of time (in which case postingestive effects are minimized), or assessed over a longer (e.g., 24-hr) period (in which case learning about postingestive effects may occur); and
- The physiological state of the organism, (e.g., fluid-deprived or non–fluid-deprived; in the former the organism is also hyperosmotic and hypovolemic at the start of testing).

Changing these parameters can certainly influence the outcome, and the parameters chosen depend in part on the experimental question (Grill, Spector, Schwartz, Kaplan, & Flynn, 1987). For example, Spector, Andrews-Labenski, and Letterio (1990) developed a brief-access, multisolution array for psychophysical testing of taste in the absence of postingestive effects. The main disadvantage here is that animals must be fluid deprived to motivate them to sample fluids. Procedurally simpler two-bottle intakes over 24-hr periods (Rowland & Fregly, 1988b) suffer from the disadvantage of postingestive factors as well as from the fact that most fluid bouts are prandial (Contreras & Smith, 1990), and so are not "pure" drinking.

At least in 24-hr tests, but often in short-term tests, too, many strains of adult rats in sodium balance show a preference for NaCl over water, beginning at a low-threshold concentration of approximately 0.05M NaCl. Preference typically reaches a maximum at isotonic (~0.15M); above this concentration, NaCl becomes progressively more aversive (Fitzsimons, 1979; Fregly & Rowland, 1985). Figure 16.9 shows an ideal preference-aversion function under need-free conditions, such as we typically observe in

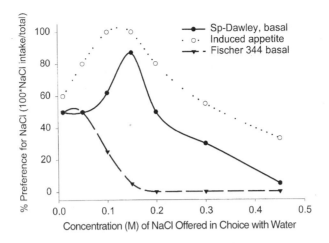

Figure 16.9 Schematic of preference/aversion curves for NaCl solutions of various concentrations offered in a 2-bottle choice with water.

NOTE: Preference = intake of NaCl/(intake of water + NaCl) is shown as a percentage. Many outbred strains such as Sprague-Dawley (solid line) are indifferent (i.e., they take about 50% from water and NaCl bottles) up to a preference threshold of ~0.05M. Above this they show an increasing preference, peaking at ~0.15M and at higher concentrations a progressive aversion, so that by 0.45M the intake of NaCl is minimal. In contrast, Fischer 344 rats show only an aversion even at isotonic solutions (dashed line). When a sodium appetite is induced in Sprague-Dawley and even Fischer 344 rats, their preference function is broadened at both low and high concentration ends.

Sprague-Dawley rats. This basic curve is affected in rats by gender, genetic, developmental, physiological, and experiential variables. There may additionally be some important species differences (Rowland & Fregly, 1988b).

Whenever an abnormal preference-aversion curve is observed, a search for mechanism is invited. Infant rats, tested using the independent ingestion protocols described in the section on ontogeny, show acceptance of much higher concentrations of NaCl than do adults (Leshem, 1999; Moe, 1986; Rowland, 1991). This can be ascribed largely to functional immaturity of the taste system (Formaker & Hill, 1990).

In adult rats, deviations from the basic preference-aversion curve are found in the Fischer 344 strain (Rowland & Fregly, 1988b; see Figure 16.10). Bernstein et al. (1991) have argued that this lack of salt preference in Fischer 344 rats may be caused by a different organization of their taste mechanisms for sodium, specifically, a greater number of functional amiloride-sensitive Na^+ channels in taste receptors.[4] Another interpretation is that postingestive consequences of NaCl may be in some way unpleasant for Fischer 344 rats, because their aversion to dilute NaCl develops only during the weaning period (N. E. Rowland, 1991). In contrast to need-free conditions, Fischer 344 rats consume high concentrations of NaCl when their appetite is stimulated by Na^+ depletion

---

[4]Amiloride is a pharmacological blocker of apical sodium channels and, in humans, prevents the sensation of saltiness. Electrophysiological studies of the whole chorda tympani nerve responses to application of NaCl to the tongue show that prior application of amiloride attenuates some but not all of that electrical response. This maximal reduction is referred to as the amiloride-sensitive component of the response.

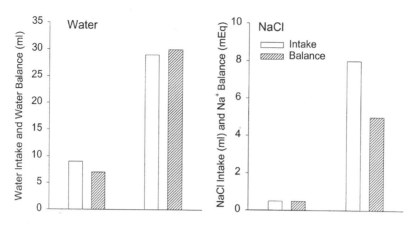

Figure 16.10   Intake and retention of water (left panels) and NaCl (right panels) in rats extracellularly dehydrated with polyethylene glycol (PEG, 5 ml 30%).
NOTE: The rats had continuous access to both water and 0.5M NaCl, but not food, for 18 hr after injection. The intakes and balances (= intake minus urinary excretion) are shown after 6 hr and 18 hr (data derived from Stricker, 1983). During the first 6 hr, rats consume water and very little NaCl, whereas in the next 12 hr they consume NaCl as well as water. They retain most of what they consume during this period of observation, and so go into positive fluid and sodium balance (most of this is sequestered as an edema at the PEG injection site).

(Rowland & Fregly, 1988b). This example further reinforces the point that Na^+ preference and appetite are separable.

Most physiological manipulations that increase Na^+ appetite broaden the basic NaCl preference-aversion function. This occurs by a shift in the preference threshold concentration to lower levels, to coincide with the detection threshold measured in psychophysical studies, and by an increase in the acceptance of hypertonic solutions (Figure 16.9). This bidirectional increase in Na^+ preference maximizes the rats' likelihood of being attracted to salt-containing commodities. The preference for Na^+ often is believed to be largely innate (Denton, 1982; Krieckhaus & Wolf, 1968), but consuming Na^+ salts when depleted has the potential to be reinforcing and increase later preference.

The converse can also occur. Devenport (1973) reported that Wistar rats, given a choice between water and 0.15M NaCl, showed the expected high preference (~75%) for NaCl. They were then presented, for 3 days, only 0.15M NaCl, which they consumed avidly. In a subsequent two-bottle test, they consumed a mean of only 26% from the NaCl bottle. This effect persisted for at least one week. In another type of two-bottle study, rats were first given 96 hr choices between water and progressively higher concentrations of NaCl (0.015–0.450M; an ascending series), and then returned using a descending series (Rowland & Fregly, 1990). This study was performed in Dahl "S" (salt-sensitive, inbred to develop hypertension on high-salt diets) and "R" (inbred to be resistant to hypertension on high-salt diets) strains. Both strains showed approximately twofold lower intake of NaCl during the descending series compared with the ascending series, an effect we have also seen in outbred rats. In each of these studies, exposure to NaCl has decreased subsequent two-bottle preference. Thus, the conditions under which preference can be altered by experience are poorly understood.

A different class of studies has examined whether physiological trauma in early life can affect NaCl preference later in life. Nicolaidis, Galaverna, and Metzler (1990) found that repeated hypovolemia produced with polyethylene glycol during pregnancy increased the need-free NaCl intake of the offspring measured at ~2 months of age. Galaverna, Nicolaidis, Yao, Sakai, and Epstein (1995) found a similar result when the mothers were repeatedly sodium depleted by injections of the diuretic/natriuretic agent furosemide, as did Leshem, Maroun, and Del Canho (1996) when pups themselves were acutely sodium depleted. Leshem (1999) has argued further that humans with increased sodium preference may have had analogous prenatal episodes of depletion—for example, if there was vomiting by the mother during pregnancy, or the infants were fed chronically with a low-sodium artificial milk.

Sodium Depletion and Appetite

Restricted sodium intake leads to a reduction in plasma volume and subsequent release of renal renin and an increase in levels of circulating angiotensin II (e.g., reviewed in Fitzsimons, 1979, 1998; Johnson & Thunhorst, 1997). One action of angiotensin II is to stimulate the synthesis and release of the steroid hormone aldosterone from the adrenal cortex. One of the primary actions of aldosterone is to promote the reabsorption of Na^+ (Figure 16.4) through epithelial Na^+-selective channels in cells of the renal collecting duct (Stockand, Edinger, Eaton, & Johnson, 2000). This in turn rapidly reduces urinary concentration of Na^+ to very low levels. Because of this very effective retention mechanism, simply feeding animals a low-Na^+ diet does not produce a rapid onset Na^+ deficit; and, although most forms of naturally occurring Na^+ appetite occur in this progressive way (Denton, 1982), it is poorly suited to mechanistic studies of Na^+ appetite in the laboratory. Jalowiec (1974) injected furosemide, a

diuretic/natriuretic (sodium-excretion) agent, in combination with a Na^+-free diet to produce a temporally well-defined and robust appetite in rats. This simple protocol has been used extensively since then.

The induced appetite has two characteristics that, aside from the fact that Na^+ rather than water is the variable of interest, distinguish it from thirst. The first is a delay of several hours between the onset of the physiological depletion and the onset of appetite. The second is that NaCl is often consumed in excess of need or persists beyond the apparent repletion of need.

Two principal hormones have been implicated in Na^+ appetite: angiotensin II and aldosterone. Epstein (1982) proposed that these two hormones acted synergistically to activate Na^+ appetite, a model that has proven a useful heuristic in studies in this area. Many hormones are surely involved (Denton, 1982; Schulkin, 1991), but this text considers only these two. Let us examine their hormonal profiles in relation to the induced appetite.

Onset of Sodium Appetite

Following administration in rats of the diuretic furosemide (also known as frusemide) and access to sodium-free food, induced appetite takes at least 3 hr to appear and up to 24 hr to develop fully (e.g., Jalowiec, 1974; Rowland & Morian, 1999). After 24 hr, rats consume large amounts (5–6 mEq) of hypertonic NaCl and very little water.

Following injection of a maximally effective dose of furosemide, rats excrete 1–2 mEq of Na^+ within 1 hr and, in the absence of Na^+ in their environment, little additional urinary Na^+ loss occurs during the next 24 hr. That is, in much the same way that injection of NaCl causes a rapid increase in plasma Na^+ concentration, so furosemide causes a rapid onset of depletion that reaches a maximal level within ~1 hr. At this time, plasma renin activity (and presumably angiotensin II) and aldosterone concentration are elevated above baseline, but aldosterone continues to rise for another few hours while renin activity seems to be maximal (Rowland & Morian, 1999). This suggests that the delay in the appetite may be related to the slower rise in aldosterone. However, infusions or injections of aldosterone are relatively ineffective in producing sodium appetite, even in conjunction with peripheral infusions of angiotensin II (Denton, 1982; Fregly & Rowland, 1985). In fact, Epstein (1982) specifically made the point that the proposed hormonal synergy was a central phenomenon, involving brain rather than circulating angiotensin II (discussed earlier in this chapter).

More recently, a protocol for rapid ($\sim$2-hr) onset of Na^+ appetite has been developed in which rats are treated with furosemide plus a low dose of captopril (see "Renin-Angiotensin Systems" ealier in this chapter for a discussion of this agent). Unlike after a 24-hr depletion period, these rats consume both water and NaCl, very much like the profile of intake after other hypovolemic stimuli such as polyethylene glycol (discussed shortly). This rapid-onset sodium appetite is abolished either by lesions of the SFO (Thunhorst, Beltz, & Johnson, 1999) or treatment with losartan (Thunhorst & Johnson, 1994) suggesting that circulating angiotensin II is crucial in this protocol (Thunhorst, 1996).

It should be noted that simulating this condition by long-term peripheral administration of angiotensin II produces mixed results (see Fitzsimons, 1998, for a full discussion), although cerebroventricular infusions are effective (Bryant, Epstein, Fitzsimons, & Fluharty, 1980). In both cases, however, the high water intakes that are also produced render it difficult to make the case for specificity. Chronic administration of low doses of ACE inhibitors such as captopril induce reliable Na^+ appetite in rats; this seems to be dependent on the previously mentioned spillover of peripher-

ally generated angiotensin I into the brain, and conversion to angiotensin II (Elfont, Epstein, & Fitzsimons, 1984).

Rats that are hypovolemic without Na^+ loss (e.g., after treatment with polyethylene glycol or peritoneal dialysis) likewise show an appetite for NaCl. Data for polyethylene glycol (Stricker, 1983) are shown in Figure 16.10. Compared with intake when only water is available after polyethylene glycol, rats drink much more isotonic NaCl, most likely because of the absence of osmotic dilution. In contrast, when hypertonic NaCl is available, intakes are smaller and occur only after a delay. Stricker (1983) analyzed the intakes of 0.5M NaCl and water over a 24-hr period following polyethylene glycol, and described three phases: The first lasted for $\sim$6 hr and only water was consumed; the second lasted $\sim$6 hr and an isotonic cocktail of NaCl and water was ingested; and the third lasted the remaining 12 hr, and salt intake predominated. Priming of the rat by feeding sodium-free food for a few days ahead of time abolished the first phase. This serves to illustrate a difference that is found when examining for enhanced intake of an already preferred (or at least neutral) NaCl solution compared with intake of a previously unacceptably concentrated solution.

Serotonergic mechanisms in the lateral parabrachial nucleus are inhibitory to this and other forms of extracellularly related Na^+ appetite. Thus, injection of the serotonin antagonist methysergide into this nucleus increases by about twofold the depletion-related NaCl intake (Menani, Thunhorst, & Johnson, 1996). It appears that the critical efferents involved in this effect are to the SFO (Menani, Colombari, Beltz, Thunhorst, & Johnson, 1998).

Adrenalectomy and Chronic Sodium Loss

Removal of the adrenal glands (the endogenous source of aldosterone) renders animals less able to retain the Na^+ filtered by the kidney. Richter (1936) was the first to demonstrate that adrenalectomized rats exhibit a strong and selective appetite for Na^+, without which they do not survive. Humans with uncorrected adrenal insufficiency also are known to show Na^+ cravings (reviewed in Denton, 1982; Rowland & Fregly, 1988b). Adrenalectomized rats are both hyponatremic and hypovolemic (e.g., Weisinger et al., 2000), showing that their appetite is associated with actual Na^+ depletion. Replacement injections in adrenalectomized rats of either aldosterone or deoxycorticosterone restore Na^+ retention and abolish their Na^+ appetite (Fregly & Rowland, 1985). Interestingly, while urinary Na^+ loss is continuous in untreated adrenalectomized rats, their intake of NaCl under conditions of continuous access is almost exclusively nocturnal (Rowland, Bellush, & Fregly, 1985; Weisinger et al., 2000). When the NaCl offered is hypertonic, it is often consumed in mixed bouts with water and in association with meals (Weisinger et al., 2000). Thus, adrenalectomized rats voluntarily sustain a relatively large daytime Na^+ deficit and a compensatory nocturnal surplus; the reasons for this nycthemeral (i.e., night/day) rhythm of intake are unknown, but pervade this and other aspects of fluid intake (e.g., Rowland, 1976a, 1976b; Rowland & Fregly, 1988b). However, with few exceptions (Rowland, Nicholson, & Smith, 1993), physiological and neural measurements relating to Na^+ intake typically have been made during the daytime when intake normally does not occur.

It is evident that one of the two previously discussed main hormones of Na^+ appetite, namely aldosterone, is not present after adrenalectomy. It then would be logical to ask whether the other candidate hormone, angiotensin II, might be the principal mechanism of Na^+ appetite in these animals. In support of this theory, peripheral administration of a high dose of captopril inhibited Na^+ appetite in adrenalectomized rats (Elfont & Fitzsimons, 1985). Similarly, in adrenalectomized rats, central administration of angiotensin II receptor antagonists reduces Na^+ appetite, consistent with (but not directly proving) the involvement of angiotensin II intrinsic to the brain (Galaverna et al., 1996; Sakai & Epstein, 1990). Moreover, in an important recent study, Weisinger et al. (2000) showed that peripheral administration of ZD 7155, an AT_1 receptor antagonist, abolished adrenalectomy-related Na^+ appetite. Adrenalectomized rats showed increased Fos-ir in the SFO, MnPO, and OVLT, and peripheral administration of ZD 7155 reversed this, but only in the SFO. Thus, there is evidence for involvement of both peripheral (via the SFO) and central angiotensin II in adrenalectomy-associated Na^+ appetite.

Mineralocorticoid-Induced Sodium Appetite

Restoration of normal levels of mineralocorticoids in adrenalectomized rats reverses their Na^+ loss and appetite. Administration of higher doses of mineralocorticoids to intact animals also increases Na^+ appetite and decreases secretion of renal renin, so peripheral angiotensin II is unlikely to be a contributing factor (Fitzsimons, 1979; Fregly & Rowland, 1985). As noted before, administration of exogenous aldosterone alone is not a very effective stimulus of Na^+ intake in rats, but coadministration with the glucocorticoid corticosterone produces a robust effect (Ma, McEwen, Sakai, & Schulkin, 1993).

Endogenous receptors for mineralocorticoids (MR, or type I) and glucocorticoids (GR, or type II) have similar in vitro affinities for both steroids (Monder & White, 1993). This raises an interesting problem: In rats, circulating concentrations of corticosterone normally exceed those of aldosterone by 2–3 orders of magnitude; how does this relatively tiny amount of aldosterone exert any effect?

The reason seems to be that MRs are coupled to an enzyme, 11β-hydroxysteroid dehydrogenase, that oxidizes corticosterone to 11-dehydrocorticosterone in rats (or cortisol to cortisone in humans). The latter metabolites do not occupy either MR or GR receptors, and thus 11-hydroxysteriod dehydrogenase effectively protects the MR from occupancy by glucocorticoids and allows it to respond to aldosterone. Glycyrrhizic acid, a constituent of licorice, is an inhibitor of 11-hydroxysteroid dehydrogenase, which thus allows corticosterone to occupy the MR. Consistent with this interpretation, rats given glycyrrhizic acid showed Na^+ appetite with corticosterone administration (Cooney & Fitzsimons, 1996).

The Na^+ appetite induced by systemic administration of exogenous corticosteroids is not rapid, often taking several days to become maximal. MR receptors in the brain underlie this effect. These receptors are found in highest concentrations in hippocampus, septum, and amygdala. Of these, the latter seems to be critical because electrolytic or cytotoxic lesions of the medial amygdala in rats abolish Na^+ appetite induced by corticosteroids (Schulkin, Marini, & Epstein, 1989; Zhang, Epstein, & Schulkin, 1993). The relatively slow onset of maximal mineralocorticoid-related Na^+ appetite is consistent with a mechanism involving transcription of target genes.

In studies of this proposed genomic mechanism, Sakai et al. (2000) induced a stable mineralocorticoid-related Na^+ appetite by daily injections of deoxycorticosterone to rats. This appetite was ~70% inhibited by cerebroventricular injection with antisense oligonucleotides to the MR, a procedure designed to halt translation of the mRNA for MR and so to decrease the number of available MRs. In contrast, administration of antisense oligonucleotides to the GR was ineffective. Bilateral administration into the amygdala of MR, but not GR, antisense oligonucleotides produced a similar inhibition of deoxycorticosterone-induced Na^+ appetite.

Sakai et al. (2000) also provided evidence for a nongenomic mechanism, showing that direct application of chemically reduced (tetrahydro) forms of aldosterone and corticosterone into the medial amygdala produced a small but rapid (<15 min) Na^+ appetite. This effect was site specific and was not affected by the classic (cytosolic) MR antagonist RU 28318. The synthetic enzymes for these tetrahydrocorticosteroids are found in the brain (Mellon & Deschepper, 1993), so an interesting possibility is that Na^+ deficiency induces production of these neurosteroids, which then play an immediate or longer-term role in Na^+ appetite.

Satiation of Sodium Appetite

It was noted that Na^+-depleted rats often ingest far more NaCl than their initial deficit. This may in part be because the provision of concentrated NaCl allows the rat to consume very large amounts in a short time. Tordoff, Schulkin, and Friedman (1987) showed that hepatic portal infusion of small amounts of hypertonic NaCl were able to reverse sodium appetite in rats depleted by furosemide treatment, whereas comparable infusions into the general circulation were without effect. Thus, the quantity of NaCl ingested is regulated in part by a postingestive mechanism if sufficient time is allowed to elapse.

Stricker (1991) has suggested that oxytocin may be involved in satiation of NaCl intake, at least in hypovolemia. Specifically, he suggests that hypovolemic rats first drink water, and that the ensuing drop in plasma osmolality enables Na^+ intake. As Na^+ is ingested, oxytocin levels increase and inhibit further intake. Because peripheral manipulation of oxytocin levels are ineffective, it was proposed that it must be release of oxytocin in the brain that is crucial to inhibition of Na^+ appetite. Unfortunately, direct measures of brain oxytocin are lacking; the most compelling data in support of this theory are that central administration of an oxytocin receptor antagonist increased angiotensin-related Na^+ appetite (Blackburn, Demko, Hoffman, Stricker, & Verbalis, 1992).

When salt and water intake occur together in excess of need, expansion of ECF volume occurs. This is a potent stimulus of release from the cardaic atria of a diuretic and natriuretic peptide hormone, atrial natriuretic peptide (discussed earlier). This and other members of this peptide family occur in brain, and may also have inhibitory actions on Na^+ appetite (Franci, 1997; Imura, Nakao, & Itoh, 1992).

SUMMARY AND CONCLUSIONS

Water and salt intakes provide the experimental psychologist with ideal models for the study of the physiological bases of motivated behaviors. Experimental procedures and rigorous controls, as well as identified dependent variables, are established in this area and can readily be applied to emerging applications such as the study of genetically modified animals and of newly discovered transmitters or neuromodulators.

Within this context, I have emphasized the double-depletion model of thirst, wherein both intra- and extracellular dehydration contribute to an integrated thirst signal; inclusion of peripheral osmoreceptors in this equation may allow us to explain meal-associated drinking. Likewise, for Na^+ appetite, both aldosterone and angiotensin II seem to be involved in a basic two-factor model. However, in each of these cases, although several brain structures have been implicated with consistency (OVLT, SFO, PVN), the detailed "wiring diagram" as well as the postulated integrators have proven refractory to our current methods of study.

Another area that is poorly understood from a mechanistic viewpoint is the relationship between candidate physiological signals and the structure (e.g., frequency, size) of drinking episodes under different environmental conditions, as well as the switching between drinking and other behaviors (including eating). However, insofar as psychologists often are seeking to understand human behavior, which certainly occurs in highly structured environments, it is important to understand this interaction between "physiological" and "ecological." It would also help to form a mechanistic link between proximal and distal explanations of behavior. The relatively small range of environmental commodities (i.e., water, salt) should make thirst and sodium appetite a particularly attractive model area for these types of study.

REFERENCES

Adachi, A., Niijima, A., & Jacobs, H. L. (1976). An hepatic osmoreceptor mechanism in the rat: Electro-physiological and behavioral studies. *American Journal of Physiology, 231,* 1043–1049.

Adolph, E. F., Barker, J. P., & Hoy, P. A. (1954). Multiple factors in thirst. *American Journal of Physiology, 178,* 538–562.

Andersson, B. (1953). The effect of injections of hypertonic NaCl solutions into different parts of the hypothalamus of goats. *Acta Physiologica Scandinavica, 28,* 188–201.

Andersson, B., Olsson, K., & Warner, R. G. (1967). Dissimilarities between the central control of thirst and the release of antidiuretic hormone (ADH). *Acta Physiologica Scandinavica, 71,* 57–64.

Berne, R. M., & Levy, M. N. (1998). *Physiology* (4th ed.). St. Louis, MO: Mosby.

Bernstein, I. L., Longley, A., & Taylor, E. M. (1991). Amiloride sensitivity of chorda tympani response to NaCl in Fischer 344 and Wistar rats. *American Journal of Physiology Regulatory Integrative and Comparative Physiology, 261,* R329–R333.

Bisley, J. W., Rees, S. M., McKinley, M. J., Hards, D. K., & Oldfield, B. J. (1996). Identification of osmoresponsive neurons in the forebrain of the rat: A Fos study at the ultrastructural level. *Brain Research, 720,* 25–34.

Blackburn, R. E., Demko, A. D., Hoffman, G. E., Stricker, E. M., & Verbalis, J. G. (1992). Central oxytocin inhibition of angiotensin-induced salt appetite in rats. *American Journal of Physiology Regulatory Integrative and Comparative Physiology, 263,* R1347–R1353.

Blass, E. M., & Hall, W. G. (1976). Drinking termination: Interactions among hydrational, orogastric, and behavioral controls in rats. *Psychological Review, 83,* 356–374.

Bourque, C. W., & Oliet, S. H. R. (1997). Osmoreceptors in the central nervous system. *Annual Review of Physiology, 59,* 601–619.

Bruno, J. P. (1981). Development of drinking behavior in perweanling rats. *Journal of Comparative and Physiological Psychology, 95,* 1016–1027.

Bryant, R. W., Epstein, A. N., Fitzsimons, J. T., & Fluharty, S. J. (1980). Arousal of a specific and persistent sodium appetite in the rat with continuous intracerebroventricular infusion of angiotensin II. *Journal of Physiology (London), 301,* 365–382.

Buggy, J., Hoffman, W. E., Phillips, M. I., Fisher, A. E., & Johnson, A. K. (1979). Osmosensitivity of rat third ventricle and interactions with angiotensin. *American Journal of Physiology Regulatory Integrative and Comparative Physiology, 236,* R75–R82.

Buggy, J., & Johnson, A. K. (1977). Preoptic-hypothalamic periventricular lesions: Thirst deficits and hypernatremia. *American Journal of Physiology Regulatory Integrative and Comparative Physiology, 233,* R44–R52.

Cannon, W. B. (1919). The physiological basis of thirst. *Proceedings of the Royal Society, 90,* 283–301.

Carlson, S. H., Beitz, A., & Osborn, J. W. (1997). Intragastric hypertonic saline increases vasopressin and central Fos immunoreactivity in conscious rats. *American Journal of Physiology Regulatory Integrative and Comparative Physiology, 272,* R750–R758.

Chen, Y., & Morris, M. (2001). Differentiation of brain angiotensin Type 1a and 1b receptor mRNAs. *Hypertension, 37,* 692–697.

Choi-Kwon, S., & Baertschi, A. J. (1991). Splanchnic osmosensation and vasopressin: Mechanisms and neural pathways. *American Journal of Physiology Endocrinology and Metabolism, 261,* E18–E25.

Choi-Kwon, S., McCarty, R., & Baertschi, A. J. (1991). Splanchic control of vasopressin secretion in conscious rats. *American Journal of Physiology Endocrinology and Metabolism, 259,* E19–E26.

Chwalbinska-Moneta, J. (1979). Role of hepatic portal osmoreception in the control of ADH release. *American Journal of Physiology Endocrinology and Metabolism, 236,* E603–E609.

Clark, J. M., Clark, A. J. M., Bartle, A., & Winn, P. (1991). The regulation of feeding and drinking in rats with lesions of the lateral hypothalamus made with N-methyl-D-aspartate. *Neuroscience, 45,* 631–640.

Coburn, P. C., & Stricker, E. M. (1978). Osmoregulatory thirst in rats after lateral preoptic lesions. *Journal of Comparative and Physiological Psychology, 92,* 350–361.

Contreras, R. J., & Smith, J. C. (1990). NaCl concentration alters temporal patterns of drinking and eating by rats. *Chemical Senses, 15,* 295–310.

Cooney, A. S., & Fitzsimons, J. T. (1996). Increased sodium appetite and thirst induced by the ingredients of liquorice, glycyrrhizic acid and glycyrrhetinic acid. *Regulatory Peptides, 66,* 127–133.

Corbit, J. D. (1965). Effect of intravenous sodium chloride on drinking in the rat. *Journal of Comparative and Physiological Psychology, 60,* 397–406.

Cravo, S. L., Morrison, S. F., & Reis, D. J. (1991). Differentiation of two cardiovascular regions within caudal ventrolateral medulla. *American Journal of Physiology Regulatory Integrative and Comparative Physiology, 261,* R985–R994.

Cunningham, J. T., & Johnson, A. K. (1989). Decreased norepinephrine on the ventral terminalis region is associated with angiotensin II drinking response deficits following local 6-hydroxydopamine injections. *Brain Research, 480,* 54–71.

Davisson, R. L., Oliverio, M. I., Coffman, T. M., & Sigmind, C. D. (2000). Divergent functions of angiotensin II receptor isoforms in the brain. *Journal of Clinical Investigation, 106,* 103–106.

Denton, D. A. (1982). *The hunger for salt.* Berlin: Springer.

Devenport, L. D. (1973). Aversion to a palatable saline solution in rats: interactions of physiology and experience. *Journal of Comparative and Physiological Psychology, 83,* 98–105.

Elfont, R. M., Epstein, A. N., & Fitzsimons, J. T. (1984). Involvement of the renin-angiotensin system in captopril-induced sodium appetite in the rat. *Journal of Physiology (London), 354,* 11–27.

Elfont, R. M., & Fitzsimons, J. T. (1983). Renin-dependence of captopril-induced drinking after ureteric ligation in the rat. *Journal of Physiology (London), 343,* 17–30.

Elfont, R. M., & Fitzsimons, J. T. (1985). The effect of captopril on sodium appetite in adrenalectomized and deoxycorticosterone-treated rats. *Journal of Physiology (London), 365,* 1–12.

Epstein, A. N. (1971). The lateral hypothalamic syndrome: Its implications for the physiological psychology of hunger and thirst. In E. Stellar & J. M. Sprague (Eds.), *Progress in physiological psychology* (Vol. 4, pp. 263–317). New York: Academic Press.

Epstein, A. N. (1982). Mineralocorticoids and cerebral angiotensin may act together to produce sodium appetite. *Peptides, 3,* 493–494.

Epstein, A. N., Kissileff, H. R., & Stellar, E. (Eds.). (1973). *The neuropsychology of thirst: New findings and advances in concepts.* Washington, DC: Winston.

Evered, M. D. (1992). Investigating the role of angiotensin II in thirst: Interactions between arterial pressure and the control of drinking. *Canadian Journal of Physiology and Pharmacology, 70,* 791–797.

Evered, M. D., & Robinson, M. M. (1984). Increased or decreased thirst caused by inhibition of angiotensin-converting enzyme in the rat. *Journal of Physiology (London),* 573–588.

Falk, J. L. (1966). Serial sodium depletion and NaCl solution intake. *Physiology and Behavior, 1,* 75–77.

Falk, J. L. (1969). Conditions producing psychogenic polydipsia in animals. *Annals of the New York Academy of Sciences, 157,* 569–589.

Ferguson, A. V., & Washburn, D. L. S. (1998). Angiotensin II: A peptidergic neurotransmitter in central autonomic pathways. *Progress in Neurobiology, 54,* 169–192.

Fitzsimons, J. T. (1961). Drinking by nephrectomised rats injected with various substances. *Journal of Physiology (London), 155,* 563–579.

Fitzsimons, J. T. (1969). The role of a renal thirst factor in drinking induces by extracellular stimuli. *Journal of Physiology (London), 201,* 349–368.

Fitzsimons, J. T. (1972). Thirst. *Physiological Reviews, 52,* 468–561.

Fitzsimons, J. T. (1979). *The physiology of thirst and sodium appetite.* Cambridge: Cambridge University Press.

Fitzsimons, J. T. (1998). Angiotensin, thirst, and sodium appetite. *Physiological Reviews, 78,* 583–686.

Fitzsimons, J. T., & LeMagnen, J. (1969). Eating as a regulatory control of drinking in the rat. *Journal of Comparative and Physiological Psychology, 67,* 273–283.

Formaker, B. K., & Hill, D. L. (1990). Alterations of taste perception in the developing rat. *Behavioral Neuroscience, 104,* 356–364.

Franci, C. R. (1997). Possible dual effects of endogenous ANP on water and sodium intake and role of AII. *Neuroscience and Biobehavioral Reviews, 21,* 525–529.

Fregly, M. J., Paulding, W., & Rowland, N. E. (1990). Comparison of the dipsogenic responsiveness of Long-Evans and Sprague-Dawley rats. *Physiology and Behavior, 47,* 1187–1192.

Fregly, M. J., & Rowland, N. E. (1985). Role of renin-angiotensin-aldosterone system in NaCl appetite of rats. *American Journal of Physiology*

Regulatory Integrative and Comparative Physiology, 248, R1–R11.

Fregly, M. J., & Rowland, N. E. (1992). Effect of DuP 753, a nonpeptide angiotensin II receptor antagonist, on the drinking responses to acutely administered dipsogenic agents in rats. *Proceedings of the Society for Experimental Biology and Medicine, 199,* 158–164.

Friedman, M. I. (1979). Effects of milk consumption and deprivation on body fluids of suckling rats. *Physiology and Behavior, 23,* 1029–1033.

Galaverna, O., Nicolaidis, S., Yao, S. Z., Sakai, R. R., & Epstein, A. N. (1995). Endocrine consequences of prenatal sodium depletion prepare rats for high need-free NaCl intake in adulthood. *American Journal of Physiology Regulatory Integrative and Comparative Physiology, 269,* R578–R583.

Galaverna, O., Polidori, C., Sakai, R. R., Lienard, F., Chow, S. Y., & Fluharty, S. J. (1996). Blockade of central angiotensin II type 1 and type 2 receptors suppresses adrenalectomy-induced NaCl intake in rats. *Regulatory Peptides, 66,* 47–50.

Gilman, A. (1937). The relation between blood osmotic pressure, fluid distribution, and voluntary water intake. *American Journal of Physiology, 120,* 323–328.

Greenleaf, J. E. (1992). Problem: Thirst, drinking behavior, and involuntary dehydration. *Medicine and Science in Sports and Exercise, 24,* 645–656.

Grill, H. J., & Miselis, R. R. (1981). Lack of ingestive compensation to osmotic stimuli in chronic decerebrate rats. *American Journal of Physiology Regulatory Integrative and Comparative Physiology, 240,* R81–R86.

Grill, H. J., Spector, A. C., Schwartz, G. J., Kaplan, J. M., & Flynn, F. W. (1987). Evaluating taste effects on ingestive behavior. In F. M. Toates & N. E. Rowland (Eds.), *Feeding and Drinking* (pp. 151–188). Amsterdam: Elsevier Science Publishers: Amsterdam.

Grossman, S. P. (1990). *Thirst and sodium appetite: Physiological basis.* San Diego: Academic Press.

Haberich, F. J. (1968). Osmoreception in the portal circulation. *Federation Proceedings, 27,* 1137–1141.

Hall, W. G. (1989). Neural systems for early independent ingestion: Regional metabolic changes during ingestive responding and dehydration. *Behavioral Neuroscience, 103,* 386–411.

Hall, W. G. (1991). The ontogeny of drinking. In D. J. Ramsay & D. A. Booth (Eds.), *Thirst: Physiological and psychological aspects* (pp. 35–52). London: Springer.

Hall, W. G., & Bryan, T. E. (1980). The ontogeny of feeding in rats: II. Independent ingestive behavior. *Journal of Comparative and Physiological Psychology, 94,* 746–756.

Han, L., & Rowland, N. E. (1996). Dissociation of Fos-like immunoreactivity in lamina terminalis and magnocellular hypothalamic nuclei induced by hypernatremia. *Brain Research, 708,* 45–49.

Holmes, J. H., & Gregersen, M. I. (1950). Observations on drinking induced by hypertonic solutions. *American Journal of Physiology, 162,* 326–337.

Holtzman, E., Braley, L. M., Menachery, A., Williams, G. H., & Hollenberg, N. K. (1989). Rate of activation of renon-angiotensin-aldosterone axis and sodium intake in rats. *American Journal of Physiology, Heart and Circulatory Physiology, 256,* H1311–H1315.

Hostenbach, S. L., & Ciriello, J. (1996). Effect of lesions of forebrain circumventricular organs on c-fos expression in the central nervous system to plasma hypernatremia. *Brain Research, 713,* 17–28.

Hosutt, J., Rowland, N., & Stricker, E. M. (1981). Impaired drinking responses of rats with lesions of the subfornical organ. *Journal of Comparative and Physiological Psychology, 95,* 104–111.

Imura, H., Nakao, K., & Itoh, H. (1992). The natriuretic peptide system in the brain: Implications in the central control of cardiovascular and neuroendocrine functions. *Frontiers in Neuroendocrinology, 13,* 217–249.

Jalowiec, J. E. (1974). Sodium appetite elicited by furosemide: Effects of differential dietary maintenance. *Behavioral Biology, 10,* 313–327.

Johnson, A. K., & Edwards, G. L. (1990). The neuroendocrinology of thirst: Afferent signaling and mechanisms of central integration. *Current topics in Neuroendocrinology, 10,* 149–190.

Johnson, A. K., & Gross, P. M. (1993). Sensory circumventricular organs and brain homeostatic pathways. *FASEB Journal, 7,* 678–686.

Johnson, A. K., & Thunhorst, R. L. (1997). The neuroendocrinology of thirst and salt appetite: Visceral sensory signals and mechanisms of central integration. *Frontiers in Neuroendocrinology, 18,* 292–353.

Jung, J. S., Bhat, R. V., Preston, G. M., Guggino, W. B., Baraban, J. M., & Agre, P. (1994). Molecular characterization of an aquaporin cDNA from brain: Candidate osmoreceptor and regulator of water balance. *Proceedings of the National Academy of Sciences USA, 91,* 13052–13056.

Kanter, G. S. (1953). Excretion and drinking after salt loading in dogs. *American Journal of Physiology, 174,* 89–94.

Kaufman, S. (1984). Role of right atrial receptors in the control of drinking in the rat. *Journal of Physiology (London), 349,* 389–396.

King, M. S., & Baertschi, A. J. (1991). A central neural pathway mediating splanchnic osmosensation. *Brain Research, 550,* 268–278.

King, M. S., & Baertschi, A. J. (1992). Ventral pontine catecholaminergic pathway mediates the vasopressin response to splanchnic osmostimulation in conscious rats. *Brain Research, 580,* 81–91.

Kissileff, H. R. (1969). Food associated drinking in the rat. *Journal of Comparative and Physiological Psychology, 67,* 284–300.

Kraly, F. S. (1990). Drinking elicited by eating. *Progress in Psychobiology and Physiological Psychology, 14,* 67–133.

Kraly, F. S., Kim, Y.-M., & Tribuzio, R. A. (1995a). Renal nerve transection inhibits drinking elicited by eating and by intragastric osmotic loads in rats. *Physiology and Behavior, 58,* 1129–1136.

Kraly, F. S., Tribuzio, R. A., Kim, Y.-M., Keefe, M. E., Braun, C. J., & Newman, B. H. (1995b). Angiotensin AT_1 and AT_2 receptors contribute to drinking elicited by eating in rats. *Physiology and Behavior, 58,* 1099–1109.

Kriekhaus, E. E., & Wolf, G. (1968). Acquisition of sodium by rats; interaction of innate mechanisms and latent learning. *Journal of Comparative and Physiological Psychology, 65,* 197–201.

Leshem, M. (1999). The ontogeny of salt hunger in the rat. *Neuroscience and Biobehavioral Reviews, 23,* 649–659.

Leshem, M., Maroun, M., & Del Canho, S. (1996). Sodium depletion and maternal separation in the suckling rat increase its salt intake when adult. *Physiology and Behavior, 59,* 199–204.

Linazasoro, J. M., Jimenez-Diaz, C., & Castro Mendoza, H. (1954). The kidney and thirst regulation. *Bulletin of the Institute of Medical Research, Madrid, 7,* 53–61.

Lind, R. W., Van Hoesen, G. W., & Johnson, A. K. (1982). An HRP study of the connections of the subfornical organ of the rat. *Journal of Comparative Neurology, 210,* 265–277.

Ludwig, M., Horn, T., Callahan, M. F., Grosche, I., Morris, M., & Landgraf, R. (1994). Osmotic stimulation of the supraoptic nucleus: Central and peripheral vasopressin release and blood pressure. *American Journal of Physiology, Endocrinology, and Metabolism, 266,* E351–E356.

Ma, L. Y., McEwen, B. S., Sakai, R. R., & Schulkin, J. (1993). Glucocorticoids facilitate mineralocorticoid-induced sodium intake in the rat. *Hormones and Behavior, 27,* 240–250.

Marwine, A. G., & Collier, G. C. (1979). The rat at the waterhole. *Journal of Comparative and Physiological Psychology, 93,* 392–402.

McKinley, M. J. (1985). Volume regulation of antidiuretic hormone secretion. In D. Ganten & D. W. Pfaff (Eds.), *Neurobiology of vasopressin* (pp. 61–100). Berlin: Springer.

McKinley, M. J., Denton, D. A., & Weisinger, R. S. (1978). Sensors for antidiuresis and thirst: Osmoreceptors or CSF-sodium detectors. *Brain Research, 141,* 89–103.

Mellon, S. H., & Deschepper, C. F. (1993). Neurosteroid biosynthesis: Genes of adrenal steroidogenic enzymes are expressed in the brain. *Brain Research, 629,* 83–291.

Menani, J. V., Colombari, D. S. A., Beltz, T. G., Thunhorst, R. L., & Johnson, A. K. (1998). Salt appetite: Interaction of forebrain angiotensinergic and hindbrain serotonergic mechanisms. *Brain Research, 801,* 29–35.

Menani, J. V., Thunhorst, R. L., & Johnson, A. K. (1996). Lateral parabrachial nucleus and serotonergic mechanisms in the control of salt appetite in rats. *American Journal of Physiology Regulatory Integrative and Comparative Physiology, 270,* R162–R168.

Miescher, E., & Fortney, S. (1989). Responses to dehydration and rehydration during heat exposure in young and older men. *American Journal of Physiology Regulatory Integrative and Comparative Physiology, 257,* R1050–R1056.

Miselis, R. R. (1981). The efferent projections of the subfornical organ of the rat: A circumventricular organ within a neural network subserving water balance. *Brain Research, 230,* 1–23.

Moe, K. E. (1986). The ontogeny of salt preference in rats. *Developmental Psychobiology, 19,* 185–196.

Monder, C., & White, P. C. (1993). 11β-hydroxysteroid dehydrogenase. *Vitamins and Hormones, 47,* 187–271.

Morita, H., Yamashita, Y., Nishida, Y., Tokuda, M., Hatase, O., & Hosomi, H. (1997). Fos induction in rat brain neurons after stimulation of the hepatoportal Na-sensitive mechanism. *American Journal of Physiology Regulatory Integrative and Comparative Physiology, 272,* R913–R923.

Nicolaidis, S., Galaverna, O., & Metzler, C. H. (1990). Extracellular dehydration during pregnancy increases salt appetite of offspring. *American Journal of Physiology Regulatory Integrative and Comparative Physiology, 258,* R281–R283.

Nielsen, S., Kwon, T.-H., Frokiaer, J., & Knepper, M. A. (2000). Key roles of renal aquaporins in water balance and water-balance disorders. *News in Physiological Sciences, 15,* 136–143.

Nielsen, S., Nagelhus, E. A., Amiry-Maghaddam, M., Bourque, C., Agre, P., & Ottersen, O. P. (1997). Specialized membrane domains for water transport in glial cells: High resolution immunogold cytochemistry of aquaporin-4 in rat brain. *Journal of Neuroscience, 17,* 171–180.

Niermann, H., Amiry-Maghaddam, M., Holthoff, K., Witte, O. W., & Ottersen, O. P. (2001). A novel role of vasopressin in the brain: Modulation of activity-dependent water flux in the neocortex. *Journal of Neuroscience, 21,* 3045–4051.

Nose, H., Sugimoto, E., Okuno, T., & Morimoto, T. (1987). Changes in blood volume and plasma sodium concentration after water intake in rats. *American Journal of Physiology Regulatory Integrative and Comparative Physiology, 253,* R15–R19.

Oatley, K. (1973). Simulation and theory of thirst. In A. N. Epstein, H. R. Kissileff, & E. Stellar (Eds.), *The neuropsychology of thirst: New findings and advances in concepts* (pp. 199–223). Washington, DC: Winston.

Oldfield, B. J., Hards, D. K., & McKinley, M. J. (1991). Projections from the subfornical organ to the supraoptic nucleus in the rat: Ultrastructural identification of an interposed synapse in the median preoptic nucleus using a combination of neuronal tracers. *Brain Research, 558,* 13–19.

Paque, C. (1980). Sahara Bedouins and the salt water of the Sahara: A model for salt intake. In M. R. Kare (Ed.), *Biological and behavioral aspects of salt intake* (pp. 31–47). New York: Academic Press.

Peck, J. W., & Blass, E. M. (1975). Localization of thirst and antidiuretic osmoreceptors by intracranial injection in rats. *American Journal of Physiology, 228,* 1501–1509.

Phillips, P. A., Bretherton, A. M., Johnson, C. I., & Gray, L. (1991). Reduced osmotic thirst in healthy elderly men. *American Journal of Physiology Regulatory Integrative and Comparative Physiology, 261,* R166–R172.

Phillips, P. A., Rolls, B. J., Ledingham, R. G. G., Forsling, M. L., Morton, J. J., Crowe, M. J., & Wollner, L. (1984). Reduced thirst after water deprivation in healthy elderly men. *New England Journal of Medicine, 311,* 753–759.

Quillen, E. W., Keil, L. C., & Reid, I. A. (1990). Effects of baroreceptor denervation on endocrine and drinking responses to caval constriction in dogs. *American Journal of Physiology Regulatory Integrative and Comparative Physiology, 259,* R618–R626.

Ramsay, D. J., & Booth, D. A. (Eds.). (1991). *Thirst: Physiological and psychological aspects.* London: Springer.

Ramsay, D. J., Rolls, B. J., & Wood, R. J. (1977a). Body fluid changes which influence drinking in the water deprived rat. *Journal of Physiology (London), 266,* 453–459.

Ramsay, D. J., Rolls, B. J., & Wood, R. J. (1977b). Thirst following water deprivation in dogs. *American Journal of Physiology Regulatory Integrative and Comparative Physiology, 232,* R93–R100.

Richter, C. P. (1936). Increased salt appetite in adrenalectomized rats. *American Journal of Physiology, 115,* 155–161.

Rinaman, L., Stricker, E. M., Hoffman, G. E., & Verbalis, J. G. (1997). Central c-fos expression in neonatal and adult rats after subcutaneous injection of hypertonic saline. *Neuroscience, 79,* 1165–1175.

Robertson, G. L. (1985). Osmoregulation of thirst and vasopressin secretion: Functional properties and their relationship to water balance. In R. W. Shrier (Ed.), *Vasopressin* (pp. 203–212). New York: Raven Press.

Rogers, R. C., Novin, D., & Butcher, L. L. (1979). Electrophysiological and neuroanatomical studies of hepatic portal osmo- and sodium-sensitive afferent projections within the brain. *Journal of the Autonomic Nervous System, 1,* 183–202.

Rowe, B. P., Saylor, D. L., & Speth, R. C. (1992). Analysis of angiotensin II receptor subtypes in individual rat brain nuclei. *Neuroendocrinology, 55,* 563–573.

Rowland, N. E. (1976a). Circadian rhythms and partial recovery of regulatory drinking in rats after lateral hypothalamic lesions. *Journal of Comparative and Physiological Psychology, 90,* 382–393.

Rowland, N. E. (1976b). Recovery of regulatory drinking following lateral hypothalamic lesions: Nature of residual deficits analyzed by NaCl and water infusions. *Experimental Neurology, 53,* 488–507.

Rowland, N. E. (1980). Impaired drinking to angiotensin II after subdiaphragmatic vagotomy in rats. *Physiology and Behavior, 24,* 1177–1180.

Rowland, N. E. (1991). Ontogeny of preference and aversion to salt in Fischer 344 rats and Syrian hamsters. *Developmental Psychobiology, 24,* 211–218.

Rowland, N. E. (1995). Neural activity and meal-associated drinking in rats. *Neuroscience Letters, 189,* 125–127.

Rowland, N. E. (1998). Brain mechanisms of mammalian fluid homeostasis: Insights from use of immediate early genes. *Neuroscience and Biobehavioral Reviews, 23,* 49–63.

Rowland, N. E., Bellush, L. L., & Fregly, M. J. (1985). Nycthemeral rhythms and sodium chloride appetite in rats. *American Journal of Physiology Regulatory Integrative and Comparative Physiology, 249,* R375–R378.

Rowland, N., & Flamm, C. (1977). Quinine drinking: More regulatory puzzles. *Physiology and Behavior, 18,* 1165–1170.

Rowland, N. E., & Fregly, M. J. (1988a). Behavioral and physiological aspects of body fluid homeostasis in Fischer 344 rats. *Physiology and Behavior, 42,* 499–505.

Rowland, N. E., & Fregly, M. J. (1988b). Sodium appetite: Species and strain differences and role of renin-angiotensin-aldosterone system. *Appetite, 11,* 143–178.

Rowland, N. E., & Fregly, M. J. (1990). Thirst and sodium appetite in Dahl rats. *Physiology and Behavior, 47,* 331–335.

Rowland, N., Grossman, S. P., & Grossman, L. (1979). Zona incerta lesions: Regulatory drinking deficits to intravenous NaCl, angiotensin, but not to salt in the food. *Physiology and Behavior, 23,* 745–750.

Rowland, N. E., & Morian, K. R. (1999). Roles of aldosterone and angiotensin in maturation of sodium appetite in furosemide-treated rats. *American Journal of Physiology Regulatory Integrative and Comparative Physiology, 276,* R1453–R1460.

Rowland, N. E., Morien, A., & Fregly, M. J. (1996). Losartan inhibition of angiotensin-related drinking and Fos immunoreactivity in hypertensive and hypotensive contexts. *Brain Research, 742,* 253–259.

Rowland, N. E., Morien, A., Garcea, M., & Fregly, M. J. (1997). Aging and fluid homeostasis in rats. *American Journal of Physiology Regulatory Integrative and Comparative Physiology, 273,* R1441–R1450.

Rowland, N. E., Nicholson, T. M., & Smith, J. C. (1993). Angiotensin-converting enzyme inhibition and Na appetite: Microbehavioral analysis and nycthemeral physiology. *American Journal of Physiology Regulatory Integrative and Comparative Physiology, 265,* R7–R13.

Saavedra, J. M. (1999). Emerging features of brain angiotensin receptors. *Regulatory Peptides, 85,* 31–45.

Sakai, R. R., & Epstein, A. N. (1990). Dependence of adrenalectomy-induced sodium appetite on the action of angiotensin II in the brain of the rat. *Behavioral Neuroscience, 104,* 167–176.

Sakai, R. R., Fine, W. B., Epstein, A. N., & Frankmann, S. P. (1987). Salt appetite is enhanced by one episode of sodium depletion in the rat. *Behavioral Neuroscience, 101,* 724–731.

Sakai, R. R., McEwen, B. S., Fluharty, S. J., & Ma, L. Y. (2000). The amygdala: Site of genomic and non-genomic arousal of aldosterone-induced sodium intake. *Kidney Inetrnational, 57,* 1337–1345.

Salisbury, J. J., & Rowland, N. E. (1990). Sham drinking in rats: Osmotic and volumetric manipulations. *Physiology and Behavior, 47,* 625–630.

Schulkin, J. (1991). *Sodium hunger: The search for a salty taste.* Cambridge: Cambridge University Press.

Schulkin, J., Marini, J., & Epstein, A. N. (1989). A role for the medial amygdala in mineralocorticoid-induced salt hunger. *Behavioral Neuroscience, 103,* 178–189.

Simon, E. (2000). Interface properties of circumventricular organs in salt and fluid balance. *News in Physiological Sciences, 15,* 61–67.

Simpson, J. B., Epstein, A. N., & Camardo, J. S. (1978). Localization of receptors for dipsogenic action of angiotensin II in the subfornical organ of rat. *Journal of Comparative and Physiological Psychology, 92,* 581–608.

Spector, A. C., Andrews-Labenski, J., & Letterio, F. C. (1990). A new gustometer for psychophysical taste testing in the rat. *Physiology and Behavior, 47,* 795–803.

Starbuck, E. M., & Fitts, D. A. (1998). Effects of SFO lesion or captopril on drinking induced by intragastric hypertonic saline. *Brain Research, 795,* 37–43.

Starbuck, E. M., & Fitts, D. A. (2001). Influence of the subfornical organ on meal-associated drinking in rats. *American Journal of Physiology Regulatory Integrative and Comparative Physiology, 280,* R669–R677.

Stockand, J. D., Edinger, R. S., Eaton, D. C., & Johnson, J. P. (2000). Toward understanding the role of methylation in aldosterone-sensitive Na$^+$ transport. *News in Physiological Sciences, 15,* 161–165.

Stricker, E. M. (1983). Thirst and sodium appetite after colloid treatment in rats: Role of renin-angiotensin-aldosterone system. *Behavioral Neuroscience, 97,* 725–737.

Stricker, E. M. (1991). Central control of water and sodium chloride intake in rats during hypovolemia. (pp. 194–203). In D. J. Ramsay & D. A. Booth (Eds.), *Thirst: Physiological and psychological aspects.* London: Springer.

Szczepanska-Sadowska, E., Kozlowski, S., & Sobocinska, J. (1974). Blood antidiuretic hormone level and osmotic reactivity of thirst mechanism in dogs. *American Journal of Physiology, 227,* 766–770.

Takamata, A., Mack, G. W., Gillen, C. M., & Nadel, E. M. (1994). Sodium appetite, thirst, and body fluid regulation in humans during rehydration without sodium replacement. *American Journal of Physiology Regulatory Integrative and Comparative Physiology, 266,* R1493–R1502.

Timmermans, P. B. M. W. M., Wong, P. C., Chiu, A. T., Herblin, W. F., Benfield, P., Carini, D. J., Lee, R. J., Wexler, R. R., Saye, J. M., & Smith, R. D. (1993). Angiotensin II receptors and angiotensin II receptor antagonists. *Pharmacological Reviews, 45,* 205–251.

Thompson, C. J., Edwards, C. R. W., & Baylis, P. H. (1991). Osmotic and non-osmotic regulation of thirst and vasopressin secretion in patients with compulsive water drinking. *Clinical Endocrinology, 35,* 221–228.

Thunhorst, R. L. (1996). Role of peripheral angiotensin in salt appetite of the sodium-deplete rat. *Neuroscience and Biobehavioral Reviews, 20,* 101–106.

Thunhorst, R. L., Beltz, T. G., & Johnson, A. K. (1999). Effects of subfornical organ lesions on acutely induced thirst and salt appetite.

American Journal of Physiology Regulatory Integrative and Comparative Physiology, 277, R56–R65.

Thunhorst, R. L., & Johnson, A. K. (1994). Renin-angiotensin, arterial blood pressure, and salt appetite in rats. *American Journal of Physiology Regulatory Integrative and Comparative Physiology, 266,* R458–R465.

Tordoff, M. G., Schulkin, J., & Friedman, M. I. (1987). Further evidence for hepatic control of salt intake in rats. *American Journal of Physiology Regulatory Integrative and Comparative Physiology, 253,* R444–R449.

Ueta, Y., Yamashita, H., Kawata, M., & Koizumi, K. (1995). Water deprivation induces regional expression of c-fos protein in the brain of inbred polydipsic mice. *Brain Research, 677,* 221–228.

Verbalis, J. G., Mangione, M. P., & Stricker, E. M. (1991). Oxytocin produces natriuresis in rats at physiological plasma concentration. *Endocrinology, 128,* 1317–1322.

Verney, E. B. (1947). The antidiuretic hormone and the factors which determine its release. *Proceedings of the Royal Society, London, series B, 135,* 26–106.

Voisin, D. L., Chafke, Y., & Bourque C. W. (1999). Coincident detection of CSF Na$^+$ and osmotic pressure in osmoregulatory neurons of the supraoptic nucleus. *Neuron, 24,* 453–460.

Walsh, L. L. (1980). Differences in food, water, and food-deprivation water intake in 16 strains of rats. *Journal of Comparative and Physiological Psychology, 94,* 775–781.

Watts, A. G. (2000). Understanding the neural control of ingestive behaviors: Helping to separate cause from effect with dehydration-associated anorexia. *Hormones and Behavior, 37,* 261–283.

Weisinger, R. S., Burns, P., Colvill, L. M., Davern, P., Giles, M. E., Oldfield, B. J., & McKinley, M. J. (2000). Fos immunoreactivity in the lamina terminalis of adrenalectomized rats and effects of angiotensin II type 1 receptor blockade or deoxycorticosterone. *Neuroscience, 98,* 167–180.

Weisinger, R. S., Denton, D. A., Di Nicolantonio, R., Hards, D. K., McKinley, M. J., Oldfield, B., & Osborne, P. G. (1990). Subfornical organ lesion decreases sodium appetite in the sodium-depleted rat. *Brain Research, 526,* 23–30.

Wells, T. (1998). Vesicular osmometers, vasopressin secretion and aquaporin-4: A new mechanism for osmoreception? *Molecular and Cellular Endocrinology, 136,* 103–107.

Wirth, J. B., & Epstein, A. N. (1976). The ontogeny of thirst in the infant rat. *American Journal of Physiology, 230,* 188–198.

Wolf, A. V. (1958). *Thirst.* Springfield, IL: Thomas.

Wright, J. W., & Harding, J. W. (1994). Brain angiotensin receptor subtypes in the control of physiological and behavioral responses. *Neuroscience and Biobehavioral Reviews, 18,* 21–53.

Xu, Z., & Herbert, J. (1995). Regional suppression by lesions in the anterior third ventricle of *c-fos* expression induced by either angiotensin II or hypertonic saline. *Neuroscience, 67,* 135–147.

Xu, Z., Ross, M. G., & Johnson, A. K. (2001). Intracerebroventricular carbachol induces FOS immuno-reactivity in lamina terminalis neurons projecting to the supraoptic nucleus. *Brain Research, 895,* 104–110.

Zhang, D., Epstein, A. N., & Schulkin, J. (1993). Medial region of the amygdala: Involvement in adrenal-steroid-induced salt appetite. *Brain Research, 600,* 20–26.

Zimmerman, M. B., Blaine, E. H., & Stricker, E. M. (1981). Water intake in hypovolemic sheep: Effects of crushing the left atrial appendage. *Science, 211,* 489–491.

CHAPTER 17

Reproductive Motivation

DONALD W. PFAFF AND ANDERS ÅGMO

The study of reproductive behavior and its control through the action of hormones has revealed general principles that apply to the hormonal control of other motivational states. For example, the hormones that control reproductive behavior in the female rat act on targets in the membranes and in the nuclei of specific, highly localized neurons to change the animal's motivational state. *Motivational states* are states of the central nervous system that determine how an animal will react to a fixed stimulus under constant environmental circumstances. A change in motivational state leads to the disappearance of whole classes of reactions and to the appearance of new classes of reactions to the same set of eliciting or provoking stimuli. These changes often occur in the absence of changes in the environment.

A representative reaction in the female rat, which serves as a barometer of her sexual motivation, is *lordosis behavior*. It consists of an arching of the back, which elevates the genitalia, and a diversion of the tail. These movements make it possible for penile insertion by a mounting male. This mounting is usually the consequence of a complex, often lengthy sequence of actions initiated by the female when her hormonal conditional has brought her into a state of reproductive readiness—both physiological and behavioral. The lor-

dosis reaction makes fertilization and reproduction possible.

For much of this chapter we focus on the neurobiology of the lordosis reaction and the effects of hormones on this neurobiology, because so much is known about this neural circuit and the mechanisms by which hormones affect its functioning. This circuit and the simple behavior it mediates has been subject to such intensive study because it is assumed to be representative of many other circuits mediating other simple components of complex motivated behaviors. All these components are under coordinative control by both hormones and environmental stimuli. This functionally cohesive coordinative control by processes in the central nervous system constitutes the central states that we call motivational states.

Because of a large number of strategic advantages inherent in studying hormone-controlled behaviors, tremendous progress has been made in determining their endocrine, neural, and genetic mechanisms. Some of these data are reviewed in the next section ("Reproductive Behaviors"). The very ability of specific hormones to facilitate reproductive behavioral responses to constant stimuli under fixed environmental conditions proves the existence of an underlying hormone-dependent motivational change. These are treated in the section titled "Reproductive Motivation," Section II. Because a significant component of a motivational mechanism devolves upon elementary arousal of brain and behavior, hormonal and neural influences on arousal components are introduced in the final section, "Arousal as Part of Reproductive Motivation."

Logically, we study reproductive behavior and infer motivational changes; and, when analyzing motivational changes, we invoke arousal. In terms of the temporal order of events, however, the elevated arousal probably comes first, followed by evidence of heightened sexual motivation, followed in turn by actual mating behaviors.

REPRODUCTIVE BEHAVIORS

Key hormonal players in the female are the steroids estradiol and progesterone, produced in the ovaries. They are under the control of protein hormones coming from the pituitary (luteinizing hormone and follicle-stimulating hormone). These in turn are controlled by the neuropeptide LHRH (also called GnRH) coming from the hypothalamus.

All hormone/behavior phenomena are subject to certain principles that appear to apply across a wide range of vertebrate forms (Pfaff, 1999). First, the assertion of efficacy: In a variety of vertebrate animals, sex steroid hormones, working through specific neuronal groups, promote behaviors associated with mating.

Second, for stimulating behavior as well as for facilitating pituitary hormone release, the rates of onset of hormone treatments, along with the durations and other temporal features of hormone administration, are all important. In males, androgens must be circulating at high levels for long periods to be effective. In females, estrogens are never absent and their effects seem to build up, working through very

fast membrane mechanisms as well as very slow nuclear mechanisms, to achieve their overall results. In contrast, a rapid increase in progesterone will facilitate both female reproductive behavior and the ovulatory release of luteinizing hormone (LH) from the pituitary in estrogen-primed animals; but a longer duration of progesterone action without a sudden increase will inhibit both lordosis behavior and the ovulatory release of luteinizing hormone from the pituitary.

Not only the presence and the duration of hormone treatment but also the order of appearance of hormones in the brain can be important for stimulating reproductive behavior. Progesterone by itself is not effective. Following a period of estrogen exposure of at least 24 hr (but preferably 48 or 72 hr), however, progesterone can greatly amplify the effect of estrogen on female-typical behaviors and LH release. Gene expression for the progesterone receptor is required for this effect. Gene knockout data, antisense DNA data, and progesterone receptor blocker data all agree on this point.

Finally, when the steroid sex hormones themselves are administered by injection or other routes, their metabolites also can be important for triggering reproductive behavior. Testosterone can act in its own chemical form, but also can be converted to dihydrotesterone or, by a different chemical reaction, to estradiol. The case of progesterone is similarly complicated. Progesterone itself can operate through the progesterone receptor, which goes from the cytoplasm of the nerve cell into its nucleus and affects gene expression. Metabolized, progesterone can operate in the brain by affecting transmission through cell membrane receptors for an inhibitory transmitter, GABA.

Because of the specificity of estrogenic actions on behavior through neural mechanisms, and because of the relative simplicity of certain female-typical mating behavior responses, the greatest progress has been made using female-typical behaviors as endpoints (Pfaff, 1999). Relying heavily on this reference and on a voluminous literature covering this and closely related subjects (e.g., Becker, Breedlove, & Crews, 1992; Conn & Freeman, 1999; Knobil & Neill, 1994; Meisel & Sachs, 1994), we review first the neural and genetic mechanisms underlying the production of normal female-typical sexual behavior.

Neural Circuitry Responsible for Producing the Behavior

The neural circuit for female rat lordosis behavior has been presented in detail (Pfaff, 1999). Because the evidence establishing this circuit has been published in extenso, only a few of the main points will be illustrated here.

Lordosis is triggered by cutaneous stimulation on the flanks of female rats followed by pressure on the posterior rump, tail base, and perineum. This pressure, which is applied by the male rat during natural mating behavior, is necessary and sufficient for lordosis to occur. Such cutaneous stimulation as applied by the male rat, leading to lordosis, can cause a barrage of action potentials from most of the cutaneous mechanoreceptive unit types in the dorsal root ganglia of the female. However, among all primary sensory neurons, only pressure units and Type I units give sustained responses to a lordosis-triggering type of cutaneous pressure stimulation. These types of sensory units have requirements that most closely fit the pattern of stimulus requirements for lordosis behavior as a whole. In order to evoke lordosis behavior, summation across pressure units certainly occurs and summation with other unit types may also be involved. If any single chain of events plays a central role in the behavior, however, it is that pressure on the crucial skin areas deforms a special class of cutaneous recep-

tors called Ruffini endings, thereby activating pressure units. Determining precise stimulus requirements for the lordosis circuit to function was important because the specificity of the behavioral result depends not only on hormone action and gene transcription but also on the exact nature of the sensory input.

Behaviorally important sensory information triggers massive discharges in neurons deep in the dorsal horn of the rat spinal cord. However, local spinal circuits alone are not sufficient for lordosis behavior. Instead, a long circuit comprising ascending sensory information and descending neuronal facilitation from supraspinal nerve-cell groups are required for lordosis behavior. The critical ascending and descending pathways run in the anterolateral columns of the spinal cord. The behaviorally important targets of the ascending fibers in lordosis behavior circuitry are in the medullary reticular formation and the lateral vestibular nucleus. Some of these fibers also make it to the midbrain central gray. Ascending sensory terminations in the brainstem do not immediately control descending neurons in a simple and direct manner. That is, it appears that the subsequent descending facilitation of lordosis behavior by brainstem neurons is not simply the result of a spinal-brainstem-spinal reflex, but rather has a tonic nature that reflects, in part, durable estrogenic influences originating in the hypothalamus.

At the top of the circuitry that facilitates lordosis behavior are the nerve cells in and immediately surrounding the ventromedial nucleus of the hypothalamus. Lesions or pharmacologic blockage of these cells leads to a loss of lordosis behavior. Electrical stimulation of these cells leads to lordosis facilitation. No other lesion or electrical-stimulation sites in the forebrain can account for the facilitation of lordosis behavior. Therefore, among all telencephalic and diencephalic sites, the main source of lordosis behavior facilitation must be ventromedial hypothalamic neurons.

The organization of axons descending from the hypothalamus has begun to be sorted out. Those related to lordosis behavior descend from the ventromedial hypothalamus, either through a medial periventricular trajectory or through a lateral sweeping trajectory, back to the midbrain reticular formation and periaqueductal gray. Those axons descending through a lateral sweeping trajectory make a larger quantitative contribution to lordosis. Neurons in the central gray send axons descending into the medullary reticular formation. The descending central gray signal activates medullary reticulospinal neurons as they synergize with lateral vestibulospinal neurons to control the deep back muscles that execute lordosis.

This midbrain central gray module is crucial. Electrical stimulation of the midbrain central gray facilitates lordosis, and central gray lesions disrupt it. The physiology of central gray neurons also allows us to understand how a strong somatosensory stimulus from the male, which ordinarily would be treated as noxious, can lead to a reproductive behavior. The same subregions of the central gray of the midbrain that are important for lordosis behavior, when activated, will lead to a decrease in pain—that is, they cause stimulus-dependent analgesia. Thus we can see how their activation by hormone-dependent inputs from the hypothalamus, as well as by perineal stimuli from the male, actually permits the lordosis response to occur.

The synergizing input from the lateral vestibular nucleus is also important, as lesions there will reduce lordosis in proportion to the number of vestibulospinal cells destroyed, and electrical stimulation of the lateral vestibular nucleus will facilitate lordosis. The lateral vestibulospinal tract from the lateral vestibular nucleus and the lateral reticulospinal tract from the medullary reticular formation are the descending pathways that facilitate lordosis. They enhance the through-put from behaviorally adequate sensory stimulation to the deep back muscle motor neurons. These descending systems themselves and the muscle groups that execute lordosis behavior have physiological properties absolutely congruent with the requirements of lordosis behavior as a whole.

The deep back muscles, called lateral longissimus and transversospinalis, are attached dorsally to the spinal column so that when they contract, the spinal column will be bent "concave up." Consequently, these muscles are perfectly positioned to execute the vertebral dorsiflexion (arching of the back) of lordosis. Thus, these muscles are responsible for the rump elevation, the most crucial component of lordosis behavior, which allows fertilization by the male. These muscles are anatomically connected to the skeleton so as to be physically competent to execute the lordosis response, and they are electrically active during the initiation of lordosis behavior. Bilateral electrical stimulation of the lateral longissimus or transversospinalis muscles produces vertebral dorsiflexion. Ablation of these muscles reduces lordosis strength.

The motor neurons for these muscles lie on the medial and ventral sides of the ventral horn. They can be found at spinal levels receiving dorsal roots from thoracic level 12 through sacral level 1—that is, just anterior to, in, and just posterior to the lumbar enlargement. As a result of the contraction of these muscles, lordosis behavior is displayed.

Genetic Mechanisms Mediating the Effects of Hormones on Behavior

Hormone Effects on Gene Expression

Hormones influence genes, and those gene products influence behavior (Pfaff, 1999). Thus, part of the way in which sex steroid hormones influence behavior is through genetic alterations. Different genes are turned on by estrogens in different neurons, and their respective gene products have different biochemical functions within those neurons.

Perhaps one of the best examples of this causal relation is the effect of estrogen on the gene for the progesterone receptor. Not only does estrogen administration induce the binding of radioactive progesterone in the hypothalamus, but also it causes an increase in the messenger RNA for the progesterone receptor. This effect occurs in females but not in males, and is restricted to brain regions related to reproductive behaviors. The effect of estrogen really is transcriptional, as shown by the use of neurotropic viral vectors for in vivo promoter analysis (a technique by which the ability of the progesterone receptor-gene promoter to respond is tested in normal neurons). In fact, estrogen induces the progesterone receptor in the very cells in the hypothalamus needed for reproductive behavior. Since the progesterone receptor itself is a genetic transcription factor, these experiments represent the first example of the induction of a specific transcription factor key for the performance of a specific behavior. Both antisense DNA and genetic knockout technology show that gene expression for the progesterone receptor is, in its turn, necessary for normal hormone-driven reproductive behavior.

Likewise, estrogen induces expression of the gene for the opioid peptide enkephalin, whose messenger RNA levels are strongly correlated with the performance of female rat reproductive behavior. In the ventromedial hypothalamus (VMH), enkephalin mRNA fluctuates during the normal estrous cycle, suggesting that enkephalin gene expression is important for the performance of lordosis. Again, the use of a viral vector for in vivo promoter analysis shows not only that the enkephalin gene promoter directs expression of a reporter gene correctly in the brain, but also that it is turned on by estrogen. Since the normal receptor for enkephalin, the delta opioid receptor, is also increased by estradiol, the enkephalin effect and the receptor effect should multiply each other. Again, the parallelisms between gene expression and behavior are striking: Enkephalin induction occurs in females to a greater extent than in males and is strongest in the parts of the brain mediating female reproductive behavior.

This genomic action of estrogen on enkephalin in ventromedial hypothalamic neurons appears to produce a partial analgesia, allowing the female to tolerate strong cutaneous and visceral stimuli from the male (Bodnar, Commons, & Pfaff, 2001). VM hypothalamic projections in the lordosis circuit to ventral periaqueductal gray would be most important in this regard.

Gene Effects on Behavior

It is widely recognized that causal relations between genes and the behaviors of higher animals will be difficult to discern for a variety of reasons. Among them are the pleiotropy of gene actions (one gene, several functions), redundancies among the functions of different genes, and variations in penetrance (Pfaff, Berrettini, Joh, & Maxson, 1999). Quantitative relations between genes and behaviors appear to be neither linear nor modular. With respect to reproductive behavior, genetic influences may be indirect (e.g., witness their effects on sexual differentiation); or they may be direct, as from their induction during adulthood in the very neurons that execute sex behavior (mentioned previously). Two successful approaches to demonstrating influences of specific genes on reproductive behavior have used mice with gene knockouts following homologous recombination and local CNS application of antisense DNA (see the chapter by Louis Matzel in this volume).

Gene Knockout Discoveries.   Preparation of mice lacking the function of a normal, classical, estrogen receptor (ER-α) gene permitted a thorough assessment of the contribution of that gene to female mouse reproductive behavior. The answer was clear (Ogawa, Taylor, Lubahn, Korach, & Pfaff, 1996): Estrogen receptor knockout (ERKO) female mice simply would not show lordosis. There were at least three reasons for the absence of this behavior. First, ERKO females were treated as males by would-be stud males, with aggression following rapidly. Second, the ERKO females did not permit full mounts by stud males. Third, even if cutaneous stimulation as should lead to lordosis was applied forcefully, the response by ERKO females was reduced (Ogawa et al., 1996). Subsequent work with β-ER knockout and double-knockout females and males (Ogawa, Lubahn, Korach, & Pfaff, 1997; Ogawa et al., 1999, 2000) revealed that different patterns of ER gene expression are required for different patterns of behavior.

Antisense DNA Evidence.   How might the behavioral importance of the induction of the progesterone receptor gene by estrogen in hypothalamic neurons be experimentally tested? Ogawa, Olazabal, Pahar, and Pfaff (1994) microinjected antisense DNA (which blocks protein production from mRNA) directed against progesterone-receptor mRNA among ventromedial hypothalamic neurons, and compared the behavioral results following microinjection of a DNA "scrambled sequence" control (nucleotide base composition held constant but genetic information destroyed). Not only was lordosis behavior significantly reduced by the antisense DNA and not by the control DNA, but also courtship behaviors, known to depend heavily on progesterone, were reduced to 20% of their normal frequency. In this and many other antisense DNA experiments, the recovery, with time, of the behaviors affected indicated that the antisense effect was not due to a neuronal lesion.

Summary of Neural and Genetic Mechanisms for Producing Female-Typical Sexual Behavior

Estrogens circulating in the blood enter the brain and are retained in a small number of neurons having nuclear proteins that are estrogen receptors. These proteins are *transcription factors*—that is, they bind to chromosomes at sites that control the transcription of a structural gene, thereby controlling the extent to which the protein for which that gene codes is produced. The ability of the transcription factor to control transcription depends on the extent to which estrogen binds to it. When estrogens bind to the ligand-binding region of the transcription factor, the resulting molecular complex binds to the chromosome and turns on the transcription of a small number of genes whose protein products are important for female-typical behaviors. Consequently, a neural circuit that stretches all the way from the lumbar spinal cord to the basal forebrain is activated. When the female receives the appropriate cutaneous stimuli from the male, mating behavior ensues.

REPRODUCTIVE MOTIVATION

What concepts and underlying mechanisms explain the ability of hormones to facilitate reproductive behavior responses (compared to the hormone-free state) when all other variables are held constant? That is, why does the animal without sex hormones demonstrate no response to a given stimulus under given environmental conditions, whereas the steroid hormone–treated animal demonstrates robust reproductive behavior in response to that same given stimulus under the same environmental conditions? The logically required explanation is a change created by the hormone administration in an underlying, intervening variable: sexual motivation.

How can this be? Is lordosis behavior, for example, a motivated behavior, or is it only a reflexive behavior? This is a false dichotomy, for two reasons. First, in the history of neurophysiology, we have tended to apply the term *reflexive* to those mechanisms we have worked out, no matter how highly integrated they are. Second, although lordosis behavior is relatively simple, it is a forebrain-controlled social behavior that controls reproduction and integrates biologically adaptive behavior with gamete production and release. Indeed, it has been shown by direct, formal assay (reviewed in Pfaff, 1982) that estrogen administration does elevate sexual motivation in that females will work to approach stud males. The zeal with which reproductively competent males seek out females is even more obvious.

Another type of behavioral change that can be distinguished from motivational influence includes changes brought about by certain drugs, such as dopamine-induced stereotyped behaviors. In that general case, however, the causative agent is an exogenous pharmaceutical compound. In contrast, true motivational changes are due to natural substances whose fluctuating levels in the body reflect naturally altered physiological states.

Drives and Incentive

Two conditions, one external, the other internal, are necessary for the expression of sexual behavior. The external condition is the presence of a suitable mate; the internal condition is a propensity to respond to cues from the mate that are sufficient for activating behavior. In the case of lordosis, the cue includes mechanical stimulation provided by the mate. The propensity to respond to cues emitted by the potential mate is frequently called *motivation*. Supposing that both conditions are satisfied and that behavior is activated, a two-component process occurs, one component being operant and the other be-

ing respondent (in Skinnerian terms). The operant or "appetitive" component is approach to the mate and establishment of initial contact. The ensuing "consummatory" component consists of a series of sex-specific, highly stereotyped responses. Both kinds of response are probably equally dependent on the propensity to respond to the mate; that is, the likelihood of their occurrence or their intensity (or both) is determined by motivation. More generally, the concept of motivation is central in the analysis of behavioral activation (Gallistel, 1980). Consequently, it is impossible to understand sexual behavior without taking motivation into account.

Considering the fundamental importance of motivation, it is not surprising that there are many quite different theoretical approaches to it. Here, we will make only brief mention of those that have had some influence on analyses of sexual motivation. The most important source of inspiration for experimental studies of sexual motivation was for many years neobehavioristic learning theory. Although not primarily concerned with problems of motivation, the concept of *drive* was of basic importance to this group of theories. Following the original proposal (Woodworth, 1918), drive was regarded as a mechanism that energizes behavior. In addition, other processes determining the direction of behavior were required. Many different hypotheses concerning the behavioral manifestations of drive have been proposed (for a review, see Young, 1961); the most explicit were probably those of Hull (1943). As will be shown later, the Hullian concept of drive and its relationship to behavior was and continues to be the (frequently implicit) theoretical basis for many studies of sexual motivation. Another source of inspiration for studies of sexual motivation has come from ethology. Perhaps the most well-known ethological motivation theory is Lorenz's hydraulic model (Lorenz, 1950).

During recent years it has become increasingly apparent that incentive motivational theory as formulated by Bindra (1974, 1976, 1978) can be highly useful for the understanding of sexual motivation (Ågmo, 1999; Stewart, 1995). This is associated with the wider acceptance of the fact that sexual motivation cannot be adequately assessed by looking only upon the execution of sexual reflexes (i.e., copulatory behavior). Behavioral events immediately preceding and following actual copulation must be included in a complete analysis of sexual motivation. To that end, incentive motivational theory is most useful. Furthermore, sexual motivation is unlike other primary or biological motives in that it is not generated by organismic need. For example, hunger and thirst are associated with requirements for energy and maintenance of constant concentrations of electrolytes. The urge to satisfy these needs is a function of deprivation (but see, in this volume, the chapter on hunger by Woods and Seeley), and absence of satisfaction will eventually become life threatening. This is not the case with sex. It makes no sense to talk about sexual deprivation in the same way that we talk about deprivation of food or water. Long ago it was argued that sexual motivation is not activated by any need but by the presence of the adequate stimulus, normally a mate (Beach, 1956); this is exactly what incentive motivation theory maintains (Bindra, 1974, 1976, 1978). It is, then, quite natural that this theory has been used in analyses of sexual motivation, given the appropriate hormonal drive.

Despite the fact that psychoanalytic motivation theory has had only marginal impact on experimental studies of sexual motivation, it cannot be ignored. Some of its terms, such as *libido,* have infected the experimental literature. The empirical content of the term is unclear, but as it was employed in the original work (Freud, 1905) it seems to refer to at least two things: First an internal process, *die Ichlibido* (the I libido), an excitation stemming not only from the genitals but also from other parts of the body; second, *die Objektlibido* (the object libido), an excitation stemming from sexually charged objects in the environment. Apparently the objects are arbitrary, but it is not clear how they acquire their sexual charge. Nevertheless, these basic Freudian concepts coincide quite nicely with basic principles of incentive motivation theory. The I libido, as an internal process, is similar to Bindra's (1974) central motive state, whereas the object libido is the result of an incentive stimulus acting in concert with the central motive state. There is thus no contradiction between modern incentive motivation theory and classic psychoanalytic theory.

Because most of the experimental studies of sexual motivation have employed rats, many examples will be based on data from this species. At the end of this section, however, there will be a short discussion of how motivational concepts have been employed in experimental studies of human sexuality. For this reason, as we proceed now with the analysis of female and male sexual motivation in the rat, we will discuss each sex separately.

In the Female

Copulatory Behavior (Lordosis) as a Motivational Phenomenon

Actual copulation can be considered a sequence of rather stereotyped reflexes that engage mainly the striated muscles. In the rat, as in most rodents and many other mammals, the essential behavior pattern is the lordosis response. As described previously, it appears that mechanical stimulation of the flanks or genital region (or both) is a necessary and sufficient stimulus for activation of all components of lordosis (Pfaff, Montgomery, & Lewis, 1977).

The *lordosis quotient* (Kuehn & Beach, 1963), the proportion of mounts producing a clear cut lordosis, has become the standard measure of female sexual behavior. Usually a female is exposed to a fixed number of mounts, 10 being the favorite, and the number of lordosis responses obtained is divided by the number of mounts. It constitutes a measure of the probability that a mount will activate the lordosis reflex. The lordosis quotient has been employed as a measure of female rat sexual motivation in a large number of studies. A crucial question in this context is whether the lordosis quotient can be considered an accurate indicator of the intensity of sexual motivation or drive. Within the ethological tradition it would be perfectly legitimate to consider the lordosis quotient an indicator of motivation. The lordosis reflex fulfills the criteria for a *fixed action pattern* (as the term was used within classical ethology; see, e.g., Schleidt, 1974). It is quite stereotyped, is present in most individuals of the species without prior learning, and is elicited by specific stimuli (sign stimuli). According to Lorenz's hydraulic model (Lorenz, 1950), the ease by which a particular sign stimulus releases a fixed action pattern is determined by the intensity of motivation or drive. The ease of activation of a fixed action pattern is exactly what the lordosis quotient measures. Hence, it is a good measure of motivation or drive. The same holds for Hullian motivation theory. Hull (1943) makes no distinction between learned responses ($_sH_R$) and unlearned (inherited) responses ($_sU_R$) with regard to how their probability of occurrence is determined by motivation. In fact, Hull (1943) uses some of Beach's data (Beach, 1942) on sex behavior as supportive of his Postulate 7, in which he establishes a multiplicative relationship between intensity of drive and habit (implicitly including $_sU_R$ in addition to the explicit $_sH_R$). Thus, provided that the stimulus situation is maintained constant, the probability of occur-

rence of lordosis should be determined entirely by the intensity of drive.

Incentive motivational theory is not directly applicable to the analysis of ease of activation of reflexes or fixed action patterns. Nevertheless, we must accept that the lordosis quotient, culminating in the female's courtship behaviors and beginning her maternal labors, is a legitimate measure of sexual motivation, at least according to two major behavior theories.

In addition, to determine the simple presence or absence of lordosis, it is possible to evaluate its intensity. Some researchers have used rating scales (Hardy & DeBold, 1972); others have measured the duration of lordosis (Caggiula et al., 1979; Hardy & DeBold, 1971; Williams, 1987). It is difficult to see how any of these measures provides information concerning motivation not contained in the lordosis quotient. Their use seems, in fact, entirely unjustified in studies of motivation. Quite complicated methods for determining the stimulus intensity required for elicitation of lordosis combined with the rating of the intensity of female response were proposed many years ago (Ball, 1937; Hemmingsen, 1933). Their use and interpretation are difficult, and they have rarely been employed.

Paced Mating and Female Sexual Motivation

In most studies of female sexual behavior, tests are performed in a small enclosure. This situation is highly artificial. In the wild or in seminatural conditions, a very important feature of sexual interaction is that the female escapes from the male after almost every sexual event (Calhoun, 1962; McClintock & Adler, 1978; Robitaille & Bouvet, 1976; Steiniger, 1950; Telle, 1966). She disappears in a burrow or some other place not accessible to males, and several males will wait at the entrance until the female decides to reappear. Thus, the female decides the pace of sexual interaction whenever she has the opportunity to do so. In the standard laboratory test she lacks this opportunity, because of the small space and the absence of opportunity to escape from the male. However, a situation can be arranged in which the female can easily escape from the male and thereby control sexual interactions. One possibility is to tether the male in a specific area of the mating environment (e.g., Ågmo & Soria, 1997; Brandling-Bennett, Blasberg, & Becker, 1999; W. J. Jenkins & Becker, 2001). Another is to divide the testing arena into two or more compartments such that the female can move around freely through small openings but the male is confined to one compartment simply because his larger size prevents him from passing through the openings (e.g., Coopersmith, Candurra, & Erskine, 1996; Erskine, Kornberg, & Cherry, 1989; Paredes & Alonso, 1997; Yang & Clemens, 1998). This kind of sexual interaction is usually called *paced mating*. Here, the female can display a larger range of behaviors than is possible in the standard mating arena. Some of these behaviors might be assumed to exquisitely represent sexual motivation defined in a broader sense than is possible when lordosis behavior is the subject of study.

The first study employing a procedure with an escape possibility for the female was performed by Peirce and Nuttall (1961). They reported that the duration of the females' escape periods was directly proportional to the amount of sexual stimulation received. Thus, escape was absent or short after the female received a simple mount, somewhat longer after an intromission (penile insertion), and quite long after an ejaculation. This observation has been replicated many times and in different pacing procedures (e.g., Erskine, 1985; Krieger, Orr, & Perper, 1976). It is evident that the duration of escape (frequently called the *return latency*) is determined by the amount of genital stimulation received by the fe-

male (Bermant & Westbrook, 1966; Erskine, 1992).

Can the return latency be considered an indicator of sexual motivation? Hullian theory could be applied, provided the concept of reactive inhibition is added. The execution of the $_sU_R$ lordosis should generate reactive inhibition of an amount determined by the quantity of work associated with its execution (Postulate 8), and the reactive inhibition should be subtracted from current level of drive. It is reasonable to assume that the amount of work by the female is larger when the male ejaculates than when he intromits, which in turn is larger than when only a mount is received. Thus, the quantity that must be subtracted from the drive increases with the amount of sexual stimulation obtained. The result should be increased return latency. This prediction coincides with available data.

According to incentive motivational theory, a withdrawal response (female escape from the male) is activated by a negative incentive (i.e., a stimulus having aversive properties). The duration of the withdrawal response (the return latency) should then be a measure of the male's aversive properties. These properties must have been acquired through association with the aversive components of copulation. That copulation contains an aversive element was originally proposed by Peirce and Nuttall (1961), and this notion has received experimental support in subsequent studies (e.g., van der Schoot, von Ophemert, & Baumgarten, 1992). However, before escape occurs, the female must approach the male and copulate with him. At the moment of approach the male is, by definition, a positive incentive. Then, after a sexual interaction, the male is transformed into a negative incentive producing withdrawal. This situation, in which a constant stimulus suddenly changes its valence from positive to negative because of interaction with that stimulus, is problematic for incentive motivational theory. To explain the process satisfactorily, additional assumptions need to be made.

It seems that paced mating is a procedure not ideal for estimating female sexual motivation because of the complex interplay of approach and avoidance. The lordosis quotient is devoid of all of the problems of interpretation associated with paced mating, and thus is a simpler measure of female sexual motivation.

Another way to approach the problem of female motivation is the use of bilevel observation chambers. These chambers were designed with the purpose of assuring a perpendicular view of the female, thereby facilitating the observation of lordosis (Mendelson & Gorzalka, 1987). Therefore, they are quite narrow and the total surface available for movement is not larger than in most standard observation arenas. Because of the restricted floor area, the experimental subjects are forced to move from one level to another. The advantage of this chamber over a traditional one is probably that ambulatory activity is easily quantified as the number of level changes. The procedure has been employed in studies of paced mating (Pfaus, Smith, Byrne, & Stephens, 2000; Pfaus, Smith, & Coopersmith, 1999). Pacing consists of the female's running from one level to another with the male behind, exactly as she might run in circles in any standard observation arena. Results from such a procedure are difficult to interpret strictly in terms of sexual motivation, itself.

Responses

Several kinds of operant tasks have been used in the study of female sexual motivation. Runways, mazes, obstruction boxes, and Skinner boxes seem to have been particularly popular (Bermant, 1961; Bermant & Westbrook, 1966; Matthews et al., 1997; Meyerson & Lindström, 1973). Running speed or response rate has usually been recorded after the learn-

ing of the response has reached asymptotic levels. The assumption underlying these procedures is obviously that the intensity of the instrumental response is determined by the intensity of sexual motivation. This is perfectly in line with Hullian reasoning. It is also coincident with an incentive motivational approach. The larger the impact of the incentive, the larger the intensity of the operant response (see the chapter by Gould on "Instinctive Learning," in this volume).

One serious disadvantage of operant responses is that they might be most sensitive to changes in motor functions. Whereas lordosis is a very robust motor pattern, operants may easily be disturbed. Any experimental manipulation having effects on motor functions could modify operant behavior, not as a consequence of actions on motivation, but because of undesired motor actions. Furthermore, any intervention that affects learning and memory could give rise to false interpretations of changes in the rate of execution of the operant. Although attractive because of the apparent straightforwardness, results from operant procedures should be employed with utmost caution and with appropriate controls fully reported.

A different kind of operant response is required in preference tests of different kinds. Here, sexual interaction has been eliminated and the tests simply quantify approach behavior. The female is allowed to choose between two or more stimuli, one of which normally is a sexually active male or the odor of a sexually active male, and the other, a neutral social stimulus such as a castrated male or a nonreceptive female (or odors of either of these; Brown, 1978; Kinsley & Bridges, 1990; White, Fischer, & Meunier, 1984). The response frequently is simple approach; that is, no learning is required. The critical variable is usually the time spent in the vicinity of the target stimulus. This kind of procedure circumvents the problems associated with learned instrumental responses and substantially reduces the potential impact of motor disturbances. Response speed or rate is rarely (if ever) used, and the motor abilities required for moving close to the stationary target stimulus are not exacting. The intensity of the response (moving toward and then staying close to the stimulus) is directly determined by the strength of drive in the Hullian system and by the value of the incentive in the incentive motivational system. It constitutes, then, an almost ideal measure of sexual motivation. An additional advantage is that the behavior studied is operant in contrast to the respondent behavior of lordosis.

A case of learned operant response is the conditioned place preference shown to occur when a female has been allowed to copulate in a specific environment. At a test in the absence of copulation, the female will prefer the environment where she previously copulated over an environment in which no sexual activity occurred (Oldenburger, Everitt, & de Jonge, 1992). The rather trivial conclusion is that a female can localize an environment where she previously has found a mate. This does not seem to be an interesting measure of sexual motivation. Instead of being made to copulate in a particular environment, the female can be put into that environment just after receiving an ejaculation. On other occasions, she is put into another environment without preceding sexual activity. If the female is allowed to pace sexual interaction, she will show a preference for the environment associated with sex (Paredes & Vázquez, 1999). If she cannot pace copulation, no preference is shown. The affective consequences of copulation can be supposed to influence sexual motivation on future occasions, although how is not known.

The Problem of Proceptive Behaviors

A highly receptive female rat displays a series of stereotyped sexual behaviors in addition to lordosis. Most evident among these are ear-wiggling and hopping-darting. These behaviors were termed *proceptive* (Beach, 1976), and their function is supposed to enhance sexual excitation in the male. Proceptive behaviors have sometimes been quantified and employed as indicators of sexual motivation. The stimuli capable of eliciting these behaviors are not known, but it is most likely that they emanate from the male. Whether proceptive behaviors depend on the intensity of sexual motivation is not precisely known. However, there is an inverse relationship between proceptivity and receptivity under some circumstances. Lesion of the medial preoptic area facilitates lordosis but abolishes proceptive behaviors (Hoshina, Takeo, Nakano, Sato, & Sakuma, 1994; Whitney, 1986). Thus, if sexual motivation is somehow related to the willingness to engage in sexual behavior, proceptive behaviors cannot be indicators of motivation, independently of theoretical inclination.

Summary

As should be evident from the preceding discussion, the lordosis quotient, in all its simplicity, is a good and reliable indicator of female sexual motivation. The intensity of approach behavior toward a sexually relevant stimulus also seems to be a convenient measure of motivation. The use of both lordosis and the approach response covers the consummatory as well as the appetitive parts of female sexual behavior and motivation. In an ideal study, they should be employed in concert. Our extensive mechanistic knowledge concerning the consummatory component of female sexual motivation, or drive, has been presented earlier in this chapter. Regarding the neurobiological mechanisms behind the appetitive component, all that can be stated is that our knowledge is scant. It is clear, however, that gonadal hormones are essential.

In the Male

Copulation as an Indicator of Motivation

In the male, the basic sexual behavior pattern is to mount with pelvic thrusting, with or without penile insertion. Successful vaginal penetration also requires erection, a process dependent on the autonomic nervous system and contraction of the penile striated muscles, notably the ischiocavernosus. The motor pattern associated with pelvic thrusting has been described in certain detail (Beyer, Contreras, Larsson, Olmedo, & Moralí, 1981, 1982; Moralí & Beyer, 1992), but the neural control is badly understood despite some intents to unravel it (Hernández-González, Guevara, Cervantes, Moralí, & Corsi-Cabrera, 1998; Hernández-González, Guevara, Moralí, & Cervantes, 1997). The role of the penile muscles during spontaneous erection and *in copula* has been elucidated in some detail (Bernabé, Rampin, Sachs, & Giuliano, 1999; Giuliano et al., 1994; Holmes, Chapple, Leipheimer, & Sachs, 1991). Furthermore, promising advances have been made in the understanding of central nervous and peripheral autonomous control of erection, including the actions of androgens on the autonomic nervous system (Giuliano, Rampin, Bernabé, & Rousseau, 1995; Giuliano et al., 1996; Keast, 1998; Keast & Gleeson, 1998; Keast & Saunders, 1998; Tang, Rampin, Giuliano, & Ugolini, 1999).

The occurrence of mount with pelvic thrusting should constitute a measure of sexual motivation in the same way that the basic sexual behavior pattern in the female, lordosis, does. This was in fact suggested many years ago (Beach, 1956). However, most studies of male sexual behavior and motivation include the entire copulatory sequence: mounts, vaginal penetrations (intromissions), and ejaculation. Several of the standard measures of male sexual behavior are determined by the ease with which the ejaculatory reflex is activated. Whether this depends on the intensity of motivation or on some other factor is unknown. Beach (1956) considered the intromission and ejaculation mechanism to be separate from motivation, and most researchers seem to follow this distinction. Moreover, factor analytic studies of parameters of male sexual behavior have confirmed that the activation of behavior (mount and intromission latencies) are quite independent of the ease of achievement of ejaculation (including intromission behavior; Pfaus, Mendelson, & Phillips, 1990; Sachs, 1978). One reason for this could be that intromission/erection and ejaculation are partly dependent on the autonomic nervous system. Nothing is known concerning the interrelationship between motivation or drive and autonomic reflexes; still less is known about responses' being a compound of autonomic and somatic activity, as is the case for intromission and ejaculation. These considerations support Beach's (1956) notion that the occurrence of mount with pelvic thrusting, a purely somatic event, could be determined by motivation, whereas other factors determine the rest of sexual behavior. However, the use of mounting as an indicator of sexual motivation is not uncomplicated. During the normal sequence of copulation the occurrence of mounting is influenced by intromissions and still more by ejaculation. The latter events exert an inhibitory effect on subsequent mounting. This is easily illustrated by the fact that rats unable to achieve intromission because of reduced sensitivity of the glans penis show greatly enhanced mounting behavior (Dahlöf & Larsson, 1978; Contreras & Ågmo, 1993; Larsson & Södersten, 1973) and that ejaculation suppresses mounting for several minutes. To circumvent these problems, intromission can be prevented. The female's vagina may be closed or the male's penis anesthetized. In both cases, intromissions are almost completely eliminated. Curiously enough, this procedure has rarely been used (see, however, Clark, Smith, & Davidson, 1984).

Mounting is undoubtedly a fixed action pattern, and provided that the appropriate sign stimulus (a receptive female) is held constant, it should be entirely dependent on motivation. It is also an $_SU_R$, so the foregoing argument should be applicable to the Hullian drive concept. Moreover, an incentive motivational approach would accept the initiation of mounting as a good indicator of the female's incentive value. However, the entire sequence of male sexual behavior is a mixture of excitatory and inhibitory processes, as is paced mating in the female, and cannot provide any accurate information about motivation.

Operant Responses as Indicators of Sexual Motivation

In males as well as in females, numerous operant procedures have been employed for evaluating sexual motivation. The earliest studies used the once-famous Columbia Obstruction Box, a procedure in which males had to traverse an electrified grid in order to gain access to and copulate with a receptive female (T. N. Jenkins, Warner, & Warden, 1926; Moss, 1924; Nissen, 1929; Warden & Nissen, 1928). The intensity of the operant response (approach to a female) should be determined by the intensity of motivation, according to both Hullian and incentive theories. However, the Columbia Obstruction Box situation was highly complex because an opposite operant response—avoidance of pain associated with electric shock—counteracted the approach response. Presumably, whether a male passed was determined by the sum of the approach and the avoidance motives. Thus, results from this kind of procedure are inevitably confounded. Was a change in behavior produced by modified approach (sexual motivation) or by modified avoidance? Because of this problem of interpretation,

procedures involving aversive stimuli were rapidly abandoned.

Runways, mazes, and Skinner boxes of different kinds have also been used, the logic behind these being the same as that for females (Denniston, 1954; Everitt, Fray, Kostarczyk, Taylor, & Stacey, 1987; Jowaisas, Taylor, Dewsbury, & Malagodi, 1971; Kagan, 1955; Sheffield, Wulff, & Backer, 1951; Whalen, 1961). In some cases copulation with the female was the reward, but in others sexual activity was limited to the mounting of a female with closed vagina. This amount of sexual contact promoted learning as much as complete copulation. In more recent studies, sexual interaction has been completely eliminated. The male is offered only the possibility to see, hear, and smell a receptive female. This is quite sufficient for producing improved performance in a runway (López & Ettenberg, 2000; López, Olster, & Ettenberg, 1999).

Many of the older studies were focused on testing the hypothesis that reinforcement was always associated with need reduction. Therefore, they concentrated on the *acquisition* of the operant response. This is quite irrelevant to the problem of motivation, in which variations in drive will be manifest only when performance of the learned response has reached asymptotic levels. The more recent studies evaluate speed of running in a straight runway, and, provided that the acquisition phase is left behind, this should represent Hullian drive. It is also evident that running speed is a good measure of the incentive motivational properties of the female.

The bilevel chamber used to evaluate sexual motivation in the female, as mentioned earlier (Mendelson & Gorzalka, 1987), has also been used for this purpose with the male (Mendelson & Pfaus, 1989; van Furth & van Ree, 1996b; van Furth & van Ree, 1994; van Furth, Wolterink, & van Ree, 1995). The response that is suggested to represent motivation is the male rat's conditioned ambulatory activity preceding the presentation of a receptive female. It is conditioned because males having experienced copulation in the chamber show higher activity than inexperienced males, and only males with sexual experience are employed. However, ambulatory activity is usually not considered a sexual response. At most, it could be supposed to represent some general state of arousal or, in Hullian terms, the many unspecific drives active at any moment. An additional complication stems from the fact that exposure to a nonreceptive female during training leads to as much activity as exposure to a receptive female (van Furth & van Ree, 1996a). It is, therefore, far from evident that the increased ambulatory activity by itself has any specifically sexual meaning at all.

As with the female, several kinds of preference tests have been employed with the male. In one procedure, the experimental subject is placed in a large, open field, at the circumference of which different incentive animals are located, normally behind a wire mesh (Hetta & Meyerson, 1978). The time spent by the experimental subject in the vicinity of the various incentives is the measure of motivation. As already mentioned, the intensity of approach behavior clearly represents motivation from an incentive motivational and from a Hullian point of view.

In light of the many advantages of this type of procedure, it is surprising that they have been little employed in the analysis of basic mechanisms of sexual motivation. Only a few studies have basically addressed the problem of sexual differentiation (Eliasson & Meyerson, 1981; Merkx, 1983, 1984; Merkx, Slob, & van der Werff ten Bosch, 1987, 1988; Vega-Matuszczyk, Appa, & Larsson, 1994; Vega-Matuszczyk & Larsson, 1993, 1994), and one has been a simple study on the role of serotonin (Vega-Matuszczyk, Larsson, & Erikson, 1998). Living incentives

have been replaced by odors in some studies (Brown, 1978; Carr, Loeb, & Dissinger, 1965; Carr, Loeb, & Wylie, 1966; Carr, Wylie, & Loeb, 1970; Landauer, Wiese, & Carr, 1977); however, these studies were complicated by the fact that sexual experience seems necessary if males are to show preference for the odor of receptive females. Except for demonstrating the role of gonadal hormones, these studies have not contributed much to our understanding of sexual motivation, per se.

Place preference procedures have been employed in studies of male sexual motivation. Sometimes males were allowed to copulate with females in a particular environment, and later displayed preference for that environment (Everitt, 1990; Hughes, Everitt, & Herbert, 1990; Mehrara & Baum, 1990; Miller & Baum, 1987). As was the case for the female, this shows only that a male is able to remember a place where receptive females may be found, a parallel to foraging behavior having little relevance for studies of motivation (Spiteri, Le Pape, & Ågmo, 2000). In other studies the male has been placed in a particular environment immediately after ejaculation (Ågmo & Berenfeld, 1990). Here, the affective consequences of copulation became associated to the environmental cues. Interestingly, the positive effect associated with sexual behavior can be abolished by infusion of an opiate antagonist into the medial preoptic area (Ågmo & Gómez, 1993). It is unclear how these aftereffects of copulation influence sexual motivation.

Summary

The consummatory component of male sexual motivation—mounting—can be studied in tests in which intromission is prevented through the use of females with closed vaginas. The appetitive component—approach—is most conveniently studied in preference tests where living animals are employed as incentives. The many other procedures used should be avoided because their interpretation in terms of motivation is unclear.

In applying these rather stringent criteria, we are forced to conclude that the number of studies having adequately addressed the problem of sexual motivation is small indeed. The only thing that can be concluded at present is that sexual motivation in the male, exactly as in the female, is strictly dependent on gonadal hormones. The brain structures and neurotransmitters involved are unclear. A strong case could be made for the medial preoptic area as a critical structure (see Paredes & Baum, 1997, for a review), and some data indicate that noradrenergic α_2 antagonists stimulate sexual motivation (Bidtnes, Bals, Viitamaa, & Ågmo, in press; Clark, Smith, & Davidson, 1984).

From Rats to Men and Women. Sexual motivation in the human has been the subject of much discussion, both within and outside science. An exhaustive discussion of the subject is far beyond the scope of the present contribution. Nevertheless, it might be worthwhile to point out some similarities (cf. Pfaff, 1999, Chapter 8). Outstanding among these is probably the importance of gonadal hormones. Although it sometimes is maintained that human sexuality is less dependent on hormones than is sexuality in other animals, the truth of this idea is far from clear. Castration in the male leads to an almost total absence of sexual activity and desire (Bremer, 1958). Similar effects are obtained with treatment with androgen antagonists. In women, ovariectomy and menopause seem to have slight influences on sexual activity and desire, but adrenalectomy and consequent loss of androgens is frequently associated with a significant reduction of sexual activity (Alexander, Sherwin, Bancroft, & Davidson, 1990; Sherwin, Gelfand, & Brender, 1985), which can be restored by androgen treatment. Although the specific hormone may not be the same in rats

and humans, the principle of hormone dependency seems equally applicable.

Another similarity concerns the importance of the preoptic area, damage to which reduces sexual activity and motivation both in male rats and in men (Meisel & Sachs, 1994). The role of α_2 antagonists seems also to be rather similar; they have, as mentioned, profound facilitative effects on sexual motivation in rats and (purportedly) in men and women as well (Segraves, 1991).

This very short outline of similarities between rodents and humans should make it evident that the study of the former can provide us with valuable information concerning the latter. Considering the great importance of adequate sexual functioning for quality of life and the surprisingly high incidence of sexual dysfunction (Bortolotti, Parazzini, Colli, & Landoni, 1997; Dunn, Croft, & Hackett, 1998; Rosen & Leiblum, 1995; Spector & Carey, 1990), whether due to impotence in the male or hypoactive sexual desire in the female, it becomes evident that an increased knowledge of the basic neurobiological mechanisms of sexual motivation could offer a significant contribution to human well being.

AROUSAL AS PART OF REPRODUCTIVE MOTIVATION

If a motivated behavioral response is viewed as a vector, the amplitude (of the vector) depends on arousal. Dealing with mechanisms of arousal opens up a risky but new and exciting area of study.

Arousal of Brain and Behavior

At least two definitional problems are apparent when one is approaching brain mechanisms of arousal. First, although analysis of human behavior makes it obvious that elementary arousal of the brain is required for any higher cognitive or emotional function, the apparent difficulty of achieving intuitive definitions of arousal in mouse behavior has caused neurobiologists to discard the subject. We shall review an operational definition later. Second, some experimenters treated arousal as a monolithic function entirely in the service of the activation of forebrain circuits and motor responses, whereas other researchers argued that arousal does not exist as such because they viewed it as subdivided neurochemically, neurophysiologically, and functionally. In this chapter, relying heavily on a recent treatment (Pfaff, Frohlich, & Morgan, 2001), we take a thoroughly quantitative approach that avoids extreme categorizations and is based in neurobiology.

From both a neuroanatomical and a behavioral perspective, arousal systems form such an important part of mammalian brain activity that a clear definition is required. We are best served by an objective operational definition; that is, an animal that is more aroused, by definition, shows (a) greater alertness to sensory stimuli; (b) greater motor activity; and (c) greater emotional reactivity.

A tremendous argument in the literature arose between those who considered arousal to be a unitary product of ascending reticular activating systems (Hebb, 1955) versus those who considered the arousal functions so fragmented as to be useless and nonexistent (Robbins & Everitt, 1996). This donnybrook yielded a false dichotomy; avoiding it requires a quantitative, statistical approach. Comparing the responses of 48 mice across a variety of tasks that tap the three elements of the operational definition of arousal given earlier, we constructed an interresponse correlational matrix. From that matrix we used the numerical data for both factor analysis and cluster analysis (Frohlich, Morgan, Ogawa, Burton, & Pfaff, 2001). The "one-factor solution" represents the percentage of variance accounted for by general arousal. Clearly, in this and

subsequent experiments that replicated these results, general arousal is an important behavioral feature, explaining between 29% and 39% of the data. In addition, however, specific arousal factors are required to account for all the rest of the variance (Frohlich et al., 2001).

Matching the mathematical approach to a general arousal function is the neuroanatomical delineation of the brainstem arousal system. A crescent of neurons along the bottom (ventral portion) of the medullary reticular formation includes large numbers of multimodal responding neurons perfectly adjusted in their physiology to underlie general arousal. As one moves forward (anterior) in the brainstem reticular formation, reticular neurons near the midline include many such nonspecifically responding neurons, which bring in auditory and vestibular responses (Lindsley, 1951, 1960; Peterson & Abzug, 1975). The massive brainstem area and large numbers of neurons devoted to these arousal functions apparently make them the neurobiological correlate of the generalized arousal behavior mentioned previously.

The dominating feature of brainstem arousal systems is that they are not allowed to fail: Failure would be catastrophic, so the system must be structured as to forestall failure. Therefore, in terms of neuroanatomical pathways and neurochemical mechanisms, we must expect (a) massive redundancy, and (b) modulatory influences, rather than dichotomous turning on and turning off. The specific and differential effects of hormonal and genetic manipulations referred to later in this section are consistent with this requirement. Hormonal and genetic influences referred to later likely reach ascending arousal systems at different points of the neuraxis.

The neuroanatomical, neurophysiological, and behavioral data quoted previously lead to a "bottom-up" approach to the function of brain arousal; and the hormonal and genetic mechanisms we shall introduced shortly speak of the same. These are opposed to "top-down" approaches. Even the best of them invoke *dei ex mechani* such as "distributed reentrant networks" (Edelman & Tononi, 2000). This suggestion lacks specificity because almost any neural network can be so characterized. Instead, a direct, frontal, neurobiological approach proposes a functional pyramid: Arousal crescent neurons necessary but not sufficient for awareness, in turn necessary but not sufficient for alertness, in turn necessary but not sufficient for attention. The protocol for testing this proposal would seek hierarchical neuroanatomical and electrophysiological relations among the relevant brainstem neurons and parallel hierarchical relations among relevant hormonally mechanical genes.

Hormonal Influences

Estrogens obviously elevate the arousal state of female rats (Pfaff, 1980). Females ready to mate display heightened muscular tension throughout their bodies, evident as well in rapid alternating movements and rapid locomotor movements. The robust elevations of locomotor activities in rats and mice following estrogen treatment give additional evidence of heightened arousal (Garey, Morgan, Frohlich, McEwen, & Pfaff, 2001; Wade & Zucker, 1970). Moreover, estrogen administration increases the emotional reactivity of female mice evident not only in their responses to anxiety-producing situations but also in fear conditioning (Morgan & Pfaff, 2001). The emotional effects of estrogens can be seen in part through the fact that estrogen administration has an antidepressant effect both in experimental animals and in humans (Rachman, Unnerstall, Pfaff, & Cohen, 1998; Rubinow, Schmidt, & Roca, 1998). While some of these estrogenic effects could depend on the arousal crescent of neurons in the hindbrain, the actions on fear and mood are most easily conceived of as occurring in the amyg-

dala. Furthermore, actions through the ER-β gene product in the dorsal raphe nucleus of the midbrain (Alves et al., 2000; Bethea, 1993) could account for elevated mood, through serotonergic mechanisms.

Thus, both from the natural behavior of the animal and from formal assays, it appears that estrogens heighten general arousal. On one hand, this permits elevated locomotion; on the other hand, it leads to greater fear and anxiety. There are circumstances in which the fear would actually block the locomotor effect. In summary, moreover, stepping back from the data, there must be even more to the hormone effect, in order to deal with two potential paradoxes: (a) In behavioral assays, even as estrogens can heighten fear, they can also act as antidepressants; and (b) in molecular assays, even as estrogens can elevate arousal, they also facilitate transcription of the oxytocin and oxytocin receptor genes (Bale & Dorsa, 1997; Dellovade, Zhu, & Pfaff, 1999), which can have an anxiolytic effect. Furthermore, estrogen administration can turn on both enkephalin (Romano, Harlan, Shivers, Howells, & Pfaff, 1988; Romano, Mobbs, Lauber, Howells, & Pfaff, 1990; Romano, Mobbs, & Pfaff, 1989) and opioid receptor (Quinones-Jenab et al.) genes, which can exert a partial analgesia (Bodnar, Commons, & Pfaff, 2001). Therefore, we must conclude that estrogens both heighten arousal and facilitate molecular mechanisms that would ameliorate certain consequences of pain, fear, or anxiety. In mouse systems, the hormone seems to provide both for greater behavioral responsiveness and for the *balancing* mechanisms of anxiolysis and analgesia. Another way of summarizing this mixture of molecular and behavioral information is to say that estrogen entering the brain makes the animal ready to respond either by attentive, vigorous, and emotionally reactive behaviors, *or* by more relaxed, balanced responses. The nature of the stimuli and environmental circumstances imposed will determine which side of the hormone effect predominates.

Thyroid hormones, as well, influence states of arousal. In human patients, hyperthyroid conditions are associated with tenseness and irritability; hypothyroid conditions, in contrast, are associated with sluggishness. In fact, thyroid hormone administration can be used as adjunct therapy with antidepressants (Haggerty & Prange, 1995; Hendrick, Altshuler, & Whybrow, 1998). Because thyroid hormone receptor genes are expressed widely along the neuraxis in rats (Bradley, Towle, & Young, 1992) and mice (Kia, Krebs, Koibuchi, Chin, & Pfaff, 2001), these hormones could impact ascending arousal pathways at many points. It is clear from objective statistical analysis that estrogens and thyroid hormones are not acting in the same way, because in some assays that tap the operational features described previously [Jonathan Frohlich et al. (manuscript in preparation)] the two hormone conditions are significantly different from each other.

Genetic Influences

For a bottom-up approach to arousal, we must think of the potential sites of genetic and hormonal influences from the medullary reticular formation ascending into the forebrain. From the genes studied so far it is clear that ERα and ERβ are not identical to each other in their effects, nor are they the same as TRα or TRβ. All of these genes have different actions from the one coding for the opioid peptide enkephalin. It can be expected that genetic influences impacting generalized arousal would be manifest in the lower brainstem—the arousal crescent of neurons in the medullary reticular formation mentioned earlier. In contrast, highly specific and particular influences of these genes for hormones on behavior should arise from fore-

brain sites devoted to those particular behavioral functions.

For example, the effects of estrogen on locomotor activity clearly depend upon expression of the ERα gene and not the ERβ [Ogawa, ms. submitted]. This genetic influence serves the locomotion-producing effects of estrogens on preoptic neurons (Fahrbach, Meisel, & Pfaff, 1985). It could additionally depend on the effects of estrogens liganded to the ERα in noradrenergic neurons of the cell group A1, influencing generalized arousal states. Finally, although our results with ER knockout mice are most easily interpreted in terms of nuclear receptors, the possible participation of nongenomic mechanisms should not be ignored. Rapid membrane actions of estrogens have been reported (reviewed in Kelly, 2001) and may be relevant for reproductive behavior and sexual arousal (Becker & Beer, 1986; Becker, Rudick, & Jenkins, 2001; Mermelstein, Becker, & Surmeier, 1996).

In dramatic contrast, genes for a different kind of nuclear receptor—thyroid hormone receptors TRα and TRβ—have a different spectrum of actions on arousal (Vasudevan, Zhu, Koibuchi, Chin, & Pfaff, 2000). TRα knockout mice showed significantly lower acoustic startle responses and tactile startle responses. In contrast, the deletion of the TRβ gene did not have these effects, but TRβ knockout mice showed less anxiety. They entered the open arms of the elevated plus maze more frequently and spent more time in the lighted compartment of the dark-light transition test than β wild-type animals. In still another contrast to estrogenic activities, the deletion of either the TRα1 gene or TRβ had no effect on fear learning, implying that these thyroid-related genes affect anxiety but not fear. Because startle responses depend acutely on rhombencephalic neuronal groups, TR gene expression in the hindbrain is likely to be crucial for this genetic influence.

Still another spectrum of genetic influences is seen when measuring the behaviors of enkephalin knockout animals (Ragnauth et al., 2001). The loss of the gene for this opioid peptide yielded mice that could comprise a new genetic model of chronic fear and anxiety. Responses to a fear-learning situation were elevated and measurements of anxiety were heightened. This is a significantly different pattern of behavior than either of those measured following the loss of genes for nuclear receptors. The phenotype of the enkephalin knockout mouse, coupled with the neuropharmacologic data from the lab of Kang and Wilson (Kang, Wilson, Bender, Glorioso, & Wilson, 1998; Kang, Wilson, & Wilson, 1999), make it highly likely that enkephalin gene expression in the amygdala is centrally involved in this set of results.

In all of these cases, genetic manipulations *modulate* arousal responses selectively, but do not make them simply appear or disappear. The arousal functions are too crucial for gross alterations of the latter sort. Thus, operationally defined, quantitative measurements of arousal and their concrete, physical, corresponding mechanisms, will continue to be required during further explorations of the genetics of arousal pathways.

REFERENCES

Ågmo, A. (1999). Sexual motivation: An inquiry into events determining the occurrence of sexual behavior. *Behavioural Brain Research, 105,* 129–150.

Ågmo, A., & Berenfeld, R. (1990). Reinforcing properties of ejaculation in the male rat: Role of opioids and dopamine. *Behavioral Neuroscience, 104,* 177–182.

Ågmo, A., & Gómez, M. (1993). Sexual reinforcement is blocked by infusion of naloxone into the medial preoptic area. *Behavioral Neuroscience, 107,* 812–818.

Ågmo, A., & Soria, P. (1997). GABAergic drugs and sexual motivation, receptivity and exploratory behaviors in the female rat. *Psychopharmacology, 129,* 372–381.

Alexander, G. M., Sherwin, B. B., Bancroft, J., & Davidson, D. W. (1990). Testosterone and sexual behavior in oral contraceptive users and nonusers: A Prospective study. *Hormones and Behavior, 24,* 388–402.

Alves, S., McEwen, B., Hayashi, S., Korach, K., Pfaff, D., & Ogawa, S. (2000). Estrogen-regulated progestin receptors are found in the midbrain raphe but not hippocampus of estrogen receptor alpha (ERα) gene disrupted mice. *Journal of Comprehensive Neurology, 427*(2), 185–195.

Bale, T. L., & Dorsa, D. M. (1997). Cloning, novel promoter sequence, and estrogen regulation of a rat oxytocin receptor gene. *Endocrinology, 138,* 1151–1158.

Ball, J. (1937). A test for measuring sexual excitability in the female rat. *Comparative Psychology Monographs, 14,* 1–37.

Beach, F. A. (1942). Arousal, maintenance, and manifestation of sexual excitement in male animals. *Psychosomatic Medicine, 4,* 173–198.

Beach, F. A. (1956). Characteristics of masculine "sex drive." In M. R. Jones (Ed.), *Nebraska symposium on motivation* (pp. 1–32). Lincoln, NE: University of Nebraska Press.

Beach, F. A. (1976). Sexual attractivity, proceptivity, and receptivity in female mammals. *Hormones and Behavior, 7,* 105–138.

Becker, J. B., & Beer, M. E. (1986). The influence of estrogen on nigrostriatal dopamine activity: Behavioral and neurochemical evidence for both pre- and postsynaptic components. *Behavior and Brain Research, 19,* 27–33.

Becker, J. B., Breedlove, S. M., & Crews, D. (1992). *Behavioral endocrinology.* Cambridge: MIT Press.

Becker, J. B., Rudick, C. N., & Jenkins, W. J. (2001). The role of dopamine in the nucleus accumbens and striatum during sexual behavior in the female rat. *Journal of Neuroscience, 21*(9), 3236–3241.

Bermant, G. (1961). Response latencies of female rats during sexual intercourse. *Science, 133,* 1771–1773.

Bermant, G., & Westbrook, W. H. (1966). Peripheral factors in the regulation of sexual contacts in female rats. *Journal of Comparative and Physiological Psychology, 61,* 244–250.

Bernabé, J., Rampin, O., Sachs, B. D., & Giuliano, F. (1999). Intracavernous pressure during erection in rats: An integrative approach based on telemetric recording. *American Journal of Physiology: Regulatory, Integrative and Comparative Physiology, 45,* R441–R449.

Bethea, C. L. (1993). Colocalization of progestin receptors with serotonin in raphe neurons of macaque. *Neuroendocrinology, 57,* 1–6.

Beyer, C., Contreras, J. L., Larsson, K., Olmedo, M., & Moralí, G. (1981). Effects of castration and sex steroid replacement on the motor copulatory pattern of the male rat. *Physiology and Behavior, 27,* 727–730.

Beyer, C., Contreras, J. L., Larsson, K., Olmedo, M., & Moralí, G. (1982). Patterns of motor and seminal vesicle activities during copulation in the male rat. *Physiology and Behavior, 29,* 495–500.

Bidtnes, V., Bals, M., Viitamaa, T., & Ågmo, A. (in press). The adrenergic α_2 antagonist atipamezole enhances sexual incentive motivation in the male rat whereas yohimbine is ineffective. *Society for Neuroscience Abstracts.*

Bindra, D. (1974). A motivational view of learning, performance, and behavior modification. *Psychological Review, 81,* 199–213.

Bindra, D. (1976). *A theory of intelligent behaviour.* New York: Wiley.

Bindra, D. (1978). How adaptive behaviour is produced: A perceptual-motivational alternative to response reinforcement. *Behavioral and Brain Sciences, 1,* 41–52.

Bodnar, R., Commons, K., & Pfaff, D. W. (2001). *Central neural states relating sex and Pain* (in press). Baltimore: Johns Hopkins University Press.

Bortolotti, A., Parazzini, F., Colli, E., & Landoni, M. (1997). The epidemiology of erectile dysfunction and its risk factors. *International Journal of Andrology, 20,* 323–334.

Bradley, D. J., Towle, H. C., & Young, W. S., III. (1992). Spatial and temporal expression of α and β thyroid hormone receptor mRNAs, including the β_2 subtype, in the developing mammalian nervous system. *Journal of Neuroscience, 12,* 2288–2302.

Brandling-Bennett, E. M., Blasberg, M. E., & Becker, J. B. (1999). Paced mating behavior in female rats in response to different hormone priming regimens. *Hormones and Behavior, 35,* 144–154.

Bremer, J. (1958). *A sexualization: A follow-up study of 244 cases.* Oslo: Oslo University Press.

Brown, R. E. (1978). Hormonal control of odor preferences and urine-marking in male and female rats. *Physiology and Behavior, 20,* 21–24.

Caggiula, A. R., Herndon, J. G., Jr., Scanlon, R., Greenstone, D., Bradshaw, W., & Sharp, D. (1979). Dissociation of active from immobility components of sexual behavior in female rats by central 6-hydroxydopamine: Implications for CA involvement in sexual behavior and sensorimotor responsiveness. *Brain Research, 172,* 505–520.

Calhoun, J. B. (1962). *The ecology and sociology of the Norway rat.* Washington, DC: Government Printing Office.

Carr, W. J., Loeb, L. S., & Dissinger, M. L. (1965). Responses of rats to sex odors. *Journal of Comparative and Physiological Psychology, 59,* 370–377.

Carr, W. J., Loeb, L. S., & Wylie, N. R. (1966). Responses to feminine odors in normal and castrated male rats. *Journal of Comparative and Physiological Psychology, 62,* 336–338.

Carr, W. J., Wylie, N. R., & Loeb, L. S. (1970). Responses of adult and immature rats to sex odors. *Journal of Comparative and Physiological Psychology, 72,* 51–59.

Clark, J. T., Smith, E. R., & Davidson, J. M. (1984). Enhancement of sexual motivation in male rats by yohimbine. *Science, 225,* 847–849.

Conn, P. M., & Freeman, M. E. (1999). *Neuroendocrinology in physiology and medicine.* Totowa, NJ: Humana Press.

Contreras, J. L., & Ågmo, A. (1993). Sensory control of the male rat's copulatory thrusting patterns. *Behavioral and Neural Biology, 60,* 234–240.

Coopersmith, C., Candurra, C., & Erskine, M. S. (1996). Effects of paced mating and intromissive stimulation on feminine sexual behavior and estrus termination in the cycling rat. *Journal of Comparative Psychology, 110,* 176–186.

Dahlöf, L. G., & Larsson, K. (1978). Copulatory performance of penile desensitized male rats as a function of prior social and sexual experience. *Behavioral Biology, 24,* 492–497.

Dellovade, T. L., Zhu, Y. S., & Pfaff, D. W. (1999). Thyroid hormones and estrogen affect oxytocin gene expression in hypothalamic neurons. *Journal of Neuroendocrinology, 11,* 1–10.

Denniston, R. H. (1954). Quantification and comparison of sex drives under various conditions in terms of learned responses. *Journal of Comparative and Physiological Psychology, 47,* 437–440.

Dunn, K. M., Croft, P. R., & Hackett, G. I. (1998). Sexual problems: A study of the prevalence and need for health care in the general population. *Family Practice, 15,* 519–524.

Edelman, G. M., & Tononi, G. (2000). *A universe of consciousness: How matter becomes imagination.* New York: Basic Books.

Eliasson, M., & Meyerson, B. (1981). Development of sociosexual approach behavior in male laboratory rats. *Journal of Comparative and Physiological Psychology, 95,* 160–165.

Erskine, M. S. (1985). Effects of paced coital stimulation on estrus duration in intact cycling rats and ovariectomized and ovariectomized-adrenalectomized hormone-primed rats. *Behavioral Neuroscience, 99,* 151–161.

Erskine, M. S. (1992). Pelvic and pudendal nerves influence the display of paced mating behavior in response to estrogen and progesterone in the female rat. *Behavioral Neuroscience, 106,* 690–697.

Erskine, M. S., Kornberg, E., & Cherry, J. A. (1989). Paced copulation in rats: Effects of intromission frequency and duration on luteal activation and estrus length. *Physiology and Behavior, 45,* 33–39.

Everitt, B. J. (1990). Sexual motivation: A neural and behavioral analysis of the mechanisms underlying appetitive and copulatory responses of male rats. *Neuroscience and Biobehavioral Reviews, 14,* 217–232.

Everitt, B. J., Fray, P., Kostarczyk, E., Taylor, S., & Stacey, P. (1987). Studies of instrumental behavior with sexual reinforcement in male rats (*Rattus norvegicus*): I. Control by brief visual stimuli paired with a receptive female. *Journal of Comparative Psychology, 101,* 395–406.

Fahrbach, S. E., Meisel, R. L., & Pfaff, D. W. (1985). Preoptic implants of estradiol increase wheel running but not the open field activity of female rats. *Physiology and Behavior, 35,* 985–992.

Freud, S. (1905). *Drei abhandlungen zur sexualtheorie.* Leipzig: F. Deuticke.

Frohlich, J., Mogan, M., Ogawa, S., Burton, L., & Pfaff, D. W. (2001). Statistical analysis of measures of arousal in ovariectomized female mice. *Hormones and Behavior, 39,* 39–47.

Gallistel, C. R. (1980). The organization of action: A new synthesis. Hillsdale, NJ: Erlbaum.

Garey, J., Morgan, M. A., Frohlich, J., McEwen, B. S., & Pfaff, D. W. (2001). Effects of the phytoestrogen coumestrol on locomotor and fear-related behaviors in female mice. *Hormones and Behavior* (in press).

Giuliano, F., Bernabé, J., Rampin, O., Courtois, F., Benoit, G., & Rosseau, J. P. (1994). Telemetric monitoring of intracavernous pressure in freely moving rats during copulation. *Journal of Urology, 152,* 1271–1274.

Giuliano, F., Rampin, O., Bernabé, J., & Rousseau, J. P. (1995). Neural control of penile erection in the rat. *Journal of the Autonomic Nervous System, 55,* 36–44.

Giuliano, F., Rampin, O., Brown, K., Courtois, F., Benoit, G., & Jardin, A. (1996). Stimulation of the medial preoptic area of the hypothalamus in the rat elicits increases in intracavernous pressure. *Neuroscience Letters, 209,* 1–4.

Haggerty, J. J., & Prange, A. J. (1995). Borderline hypothyrodism and depression. *Annual Review of Medicine, 46,* 37–46.

Hardy, D. F., & DeBold, J. F. (1971). The relationship between levels of exogenous hormones and the display of lordosis by the female rat. *Hormones and Behavior, 2,* 287–297.

Hardy, D. F., & DeBold, J. F. (1972). Effects of coital stimulation upon behavior of the female rat. *Journal of Comparative and Physiological Psychology, 78,* 400–408.

Hebb, D. O. (1955). Drives and the CNS. *Psychological Review, 62,* 243–254.

Hemmingsen, A. M. (1933). Studies on the oestrus-producing hormone (oestrin). *Skandinavischer Archiv für Physiologie, 65,* 97–250.

Hendrick, V., Altshuler, L., & Whybrow, P. (1998). Psychoneuroendocrinology of mood disorders. The hypothalamic-pituitary-thyroid-axis. *Psychiatric Clinic of North America, 21*(2), 277–292.

Hernández-González, M., Guevara, M. A., Cervantes, M., Moralí, G., & Corsi-Cabrera, M. (1998). Characteristic frequency bands of the cortico-frontal EEG during the sexual interaction of the male rat as a result of factorial analysis. *Journal de Physiologie (Paris), 92,* 43–50.

Hernández-González, M., Guevara, M. A., Moralí, G., & Cervantes, M. (1997). Subcortical multiple unit activity changes during rat male sexual behavior. *Physiology and Behavior, 61,* 285–291.

Hetta, J., & Meyerson, B. J. (1978). Sexual motivation in the male rat: A methodological study of sex-specific orientation and the effects of gonadal hormones. *Acta Physiologica Scandinavica, 453*(Suppl.), 1–67.

Holmes, G. M., Chapple, W. D., Leipheimer, R. E., & Sachs, B. D. (1991). Electromyographic analysis of male rat perineal muscles during copulation and reflexive erections. *Physiology and Behavior, 49,* 1235–1246.

Hoshina, Y., Takeo, T., Nakano, K., Sato, T., & Sakuma, Y. (1994). Axon-sparing lesion of the preoptic area enhances receptivity and diminishes proceptivity among components of female rat sexual behavior. *Behavioural Brain Research, 61,* 197–204.

Hughes, A. M., Everitt, B. J., & Herbert, J. (1990). Comparative effects of preoptic area infusions of opioid peptides, lesions and castration on sexual behaviour in male rats: Studies of instrumental behaviour, conditioned place preference and partner preference. *Psychopharmacology, 102,* 243–256.

Hull, C. L. (1943). *Principles of behavior.* New York: Appleton-Century-Crofts.

Jenkins, T. N., Warner, L. H., & Warden, C. J. (1926). Standard apparatus for the study of animal motivation. *Journal of Comparative Psychology, 6,* 361–382.

Jenkins, W. J., & Becker, J. B. (2001). Role of the striatum and nucleus accumbens in paced copulatory behavior in the female rat. *Behavioural Brain Research, 121,* 119–129.

Jowaisas, D., Taylor, J., Dewsbury, D. A., & Malagodi, E. F. (1971). Copulatory behavior of male rats under an imposed operant requirement. *Psychonomic Science, 25,* 287–290.

Kagan, J. (1955). Differential reward value of incomplete and complete sexual behavior. *Journal of Comparative and Physiological Psychology, 48,* 59–64.

Kang, W., Wilson, M. A., Bender, M. A., Glorioso, J. C., & Wilson, S. P. (1998). *Brain Research, 792,* 133–135.

Kang, W., Wilson, S. P., & Wilson, M. A. (1999). *Neuropsychopharmacology, 22,* 77–88.

Kato, A., & Sakuma, Y. (2000). Neuronal activity in female rat preoptic area associated with sexually motivated behavior. *Brain Research, 862* (1/2), 90–102.

Keast, J. R. (1991). The autonomous nerve supply of male sex organs: An important target of circulating androgens. *Behavioural Brain Research, 105,* 81–92.

Keast, J. R., & Gleeson, R. J. (1998). Androgen receptor immunoreactivity is present in primary sensory neurons of male rats. *Neuroreport, 9,* 4137–4140.

Keast, J. R., & Saunders, R. J. (1998). Testosterone has potent, selective effects on the morphology of pelvic autonomic neurons which control the bladder, lower bowel and internal reproductive prgans of the male rat. *Neuroscience, 85,* 543–556.

Kelly, M. (2001). In D. W. Pfaff (Ed.), *Hormones, brain, and behavior.* San Diego: Academic Press.

Kia, H. K., Krebs, C. J., Koibuchi, N., Chin, W. W., & Pfaff, D. W. (2001). Expression of estrogen and thyroid hormone receptors in individual hypothalamic neurons. *Journal of Comparative Neurology.*

Kinsley, C. H., & Bridges, R. S. (1990). Morphine treatment and reproductive condition alter olfactory preferences for pup and adult male odors in female rats. *Developmental Psychobiology, 23,* 331–347.

Knobil, E., & Neill, J. (1994). *The physiology of reproduction* (2nd ed.). New York: Raven.

Krieger, M. S., Orr, D., & Perper, T. (1976). Temporal patterning of sexual behavior in the female rat. *Behavioral Biology, 18,* 379–386.

Kuehn, R. E., & Beach, F. A. (1963). Quantitative measurement of sexual receptivity in female rats. *Behaviour, 21,* 282–299.

Landauer, M. R., Wiese, R. E., & Carr, W. J. (1977). Responses of sexually experienced and naive male rats to cues from receptive vs. nonreceptive females. *Animal Learning and Behavior, 5,* 398–402.

Larsson, K., & Södersten, P. (1973). Mating in male rats after section of the dorsal penile nerve. *Physiology and Behavior, 10,* 567–571.

Leung, C. G., & Mason, P. (1999). Physiological properties of raphe magnus neurons during sleep and waking. *Journal of Neurophysiology, 81*(2), 584–595.

Lindsley, D. B. (1951). Emotion. In S. S. Stevens (Ed.), *Handbook of experimental psychology* (pp. 473–516). New York: Wiley.

Lindsley, D. B. (1960). Attention, consciousness, sleep and wakefulness. In J. Field (Ed.), *Handbook of physiology: Neurophysiology III* (pp. 1553–1593). Washington, DC: American Physiological Society.

Lorenz, K. (1950). The comparative method in studying innate behavior patterns. *Symposium of the Society for Experimental Biology, 4,* 221–268.

López, H. H., & Ettenberg, A. (2000). Haloperidol challenge during copulation prevents subsequent increase in male sexual motivation. *Pharmacology Biochemistry and Behavior, 67,* 387–393.

López, H. H., Olster, D. H., & Ettenberg, A. (1999). Sexual motivation in the male rat: The role of primary incentives and copulatory experience. *Hormones and Behavior, 38,* 176–185.

Matthews, T. J., Grigore, M., Tang, L., Doat, M., Kow, L. M., & Pfaff, D. W. (1997). Sexual reinforcement in the female rat. *Journal of the Experimental Analysis of Behavior, 68,* 399–410.

McClintock, M. K., & Adler, N. T. (1978). The role of the female during copulation in wild and domestic Norway rats *(Rattus norvegicus). Behaviour, 67,* 67–96.

Mehrara, B. J., & Baum, M. J. (1990). Naloxone disrupts the expression but not the acquisition by male rats of a conditioned place preference response for an estrous female. *Psychopharmacology, 101,* 118–125.

Meisel, R. L., & Sachs, B. D. (1994). The physiology of male sexual behavior. In E. Knobil & J. D. Neill (Eds.), *The physiology of reproduction* (2nd ed; pp. 3–105). New York: Raven Press.

Mendelson, S. D., & Gorzalka, B. B. (1987). An improved chamber for the observation and analysis of the sexual behavior of the female rat. *Physiology and Behavior, 39,* 67–71.

Mendelson, S. D., & Pfaus, J. G. (1989). Level searching: A new assay of sexual motivation in the male rat. *Physiology and Behavior, 45,* 337–341.

Mermelstein, P. G., Becker, J. B., & Surmeier, D. J. (1996). Estrogen reduces calcium currents in rat neostriatal neurons via a membrane receptor. *Journal of Neuroscience, 16,* 595–604.

Merkx, J. (1983). Sexual motivation of the male rat during the oestrus cycle of the female rat. *Behavioural Brain Research, 7,* 229–237.

Merkx, J. (1984). Effect of castration and subsequent substitution with testosterone, dihydrotestosterone and oestradiol on sexual preference behaviour in the male rat. *Behavioral Brain Research, 11,* 59–65.

Merkx, J., Slob, A. K., & van der Werff ten Bosch, J. J. (1987). Attractivity of male rats induced by estradiol and progesterone. *Physiology and Behavior, 40,* 737–740.

Merkx, J., Slob, A. K., & van der Werff ten Bosch, J. J. (1988). The role of the preputial glands in sexual attractivity of the female rat. *Physiology and Behavior, 42,* 59–64.

Meyerson, B. J., & Lindström, L. H. (1973). Sexual motivation in the female rat: A methodological study applied to the investigation of the effect of estradiol benzoate. *Acta Physiologica Scandinavica, 389*(Suppl.), 1–80.

Miller, R. L., & Baum, M. J. (1987). Naloxone inhibits mating and conditioned place preference for an estrous female in male rats soon after castration. *Pharmacology Biochemistry and Behavior, 26,* 781–789.

Moralí, G., & Beyer, C. (1992). Motor aspects of masculine sexual behavior in rats and rabbits. *Advances in the Study of Behavior, 21,* 201–238.

Morgan, M. A., & Pfaff, D. W. (2001). Effects of estrogen level on activity and fear-related behaviors in mice. *Hormones and Behavior.*

Moss, F. A. (1924). Study of animal drives. *Journal of Experimental Psychology, 7,* 165–185.

Nissen, H. W. (1929). The effects of gonadectomy, vasotomy, and injections of placental and orchic extracts on the sex behavior of the white rat. *Genetic Psychology Monographs, 5,* 455–547.

Ogawa, S., Chan, J., Chester, A. C., Gustafsson, J.-A., Korach, K. S., & Pfaff, D. W. (1999). *Proceedings of the National Academy of Science, USA, 96,* 12887–12892.

Ogawa, S., Chester, A. E., Hewitt, S. C., Walker, V. R., Gustafsson, J.-A., Smithies, O., Korach, K. S., & Pfaff, D. W. (2000). Abolition of male sexual behaviors in mice lacking estrogen receptors a and b (abERKO). *Proceedings of the National Academy of Sciences, USA, 97*(26), 14737–14741.

Ogawa, S., Lubahn, D. B., Korach, K. S., & Pfaff, D. W. (1997). Behavioral effects of estrogen receptor gene disruption in male mice. *Proceedings of the National Academy of Sciences, USA, 94,* 1476–1481.

Ogawa, S., Olazabal, U. E., Parhar, I. S., & Pfaff, D. W. (1994). Effects of intrahypothalamic administration of antisense DNA for progesterone receptor mRNA on reproductive behavior and progesterone receptor immunoreactivity in female rat. *Journal of Neuroscience, 14,* 1766–1774.

Ogawa, S., Taylor, J., Lubahn, D. B., Korach, K. S., & Pfaff, D. W. (1996). Reversal of sex roles in genetic female mice by disruption of estrogen receptor gene. *Neuroendocrinology, 64,* 467–470.

Oldenburger, W. P., Everitt, B. J., & de Jonge, F. H. (1992). Conditioned place preference induced by sexual interaction in female rats. *Hormones and Behavior, 26,* 214–228.

Paredes, R. G., & Alonso, A. (1997). Sexual behavior regulated (paced) by the female induces conditioned place preference. *Behavioral Neuroscience, 111,* 123–128.

Paredes, R. G., & Baum, M. J. (1997). Role of the medial preoptic area/anterior hypothalamus in the control of masculine sexual behavior. In R. C. Rosen, C. R. Davis, & H. J. Ruppel, Jr. (Eds.), *Annual review of sex research* (pp. 68–101). Society for the Scientific Study of Sexuality.

Paredes, R. G., & Vázquez, B. (1999). What do female rats like about sex? Paced mating. *Behavioral Brain Research, 105,* 117–127.

Peirce, J. T., & Nuttall, R. L. (1961). Self-paced sexual behavior in the female rat. *Journal of Comparative and Physiological Psychology, 54,* 310–313.

Peterson, B. W., & Abzug, C. (1975). Properties of projections from vestibular nuclei to medial reticular formation in the cat. *Journal of Neurophysiology, 38*(6), 1421–1435.

Pfaff, D. W. (1980). *Estrogens and Brain Function.* New York: Springer Verlag.

Pfaff, D. W. (1982). Neurobiological mechanisms of sexual motivation. In D. W. Pfaff (Ed.), *The physiological mechanisms of motivation* (pp. 287–317). New York: Springer.

Pfaff, D. W. (1999). *Drive: Neural and molecular mechanisms for sexual motivation.* Cambridge: MIT Press.

Pfaff, D. W., Berrettini, W., Joh, T., & Maxson, S. (Eds.). (1999). *Genetic influences on neural and behavioral functions.* Boca Raton, FL: CRC Press.

Pfaff, D. W., Frohlich, J., & Morgan, M. (2001). *Hormonal and genetic influences on arousal, sexual and otherwise.* Manuscript submitted for publication.

Pfaff, D. W., Montgomery, M., & Lewis, C. (1977). Somatosensory determinants of lordosis in female rats: Behavioral definition of the estrogen effect. *Journal of Comparative and Physiological Psychology, 91,* 134–145.

Pfaus, J. G., Mendelson, S. D., & Phillips, A. G. (1990). A correlational and factor analysis of anticipatory and consummatory measures of sexual behavior in the male rat. *Psychoneuroendocrinology, 15,* 329–340.

Pfaus, J. G., Smith, W. J., Byrne, N., & Stephens, G. (2000). Appetitive and consummatory sexual behaviors of female rats in bilevel chambers: II. Patterns of estrus termination following vaginocervical stimulation. *Hormones and Behavior, 37,* 96–107.

Pfaus, J. G., Smith, W. J., & Coopersmith, C. B. (1999). Appetitive and consummatory sexual behaviors of female rats in bilevel chambers: I. A correlational and factor analysis and the effects of ovarian hormones. *Hormones and Behavior, 35,* 224–240.

Quinones-Jenab, V., Jenab, S., Ogawa, S., Inturrisi, C., & Pfaff, D. W. (1997). Estrogen regulation of mu-opioid receptor mRNA in the forerain of female rats. *Molecular Brain Research, 47,* 134–138.

Rachman, I. M., Unnerstall, J. R., Pfaff, D. W., & Cohen, R. S. (1998). Estrogen alters behavior and forebrain c-fos expression in ovariectomized rats subjected to the forced swim test. *Proceedings of the National Academy of Sciences, USA, 95,* 13941–13946.

Ragnauth, A., Schuller, A., Morgan, M., Chan, J., Ogawa, S., Bodnar, R. J., Pintar, J., & Pfaff, D. W. (2001). Female preproenkephalin knockout mice display altered emotional responses. *Proceedings of the National Academy of Sciences, USA, 98*(4), 1958–1963.

Robbins, T. W., & Everitt, B. J. (1996). Arousal systems and attention. In *Handbook of cognitive neuroscience* (pp. 703–720). Cambridge: MIT Press.

Robitaille, J. A., & Bouvet, J. (1976). Field observations on the social behaviour of the Norway rat, *Rattus norvegicus* (Berkenhout). *Biology of Behaviour, 1,* 289–308.

Romano, G. J., Harlan, R. E., Shivers, B. D., Howells, R. D., & Pfaff, D. W. (1988). Estrogen increases proenkephalin messenger ribonucleic acid levels in the ventromedial hypothalamus of the rat. *Molecular Endocrinology, 2,* 1320–1328.

Romano, G. J., Mobbs, C. V., Lauber, A., Howells, R. D., & Pfaff, D. W. (1990). Differential regulation of proenkephalin gene expression by estrogen in the ventromedial hypothalamus of male and female rats: Implications for the molecular basis of a sexually differentiated behavior. *Brain Research, 536,* 63–68.

Romano, G. J., Mobbs, C. B., & Pfaff, D. W. (1989). Estrogen regulation of proenkephalin gene expression in the ventromedial hypothalamus of the rat: Temporal qualities and synergism with progesterone. *Molecular Brain Research, 5,* 51–58.

Rosen, R. C., & Leiblum, S. R. (1995). Hypoactive sexual desire. *Psychiatric Clinics of North America, 18,* 107–121.

Rubinow, D. R., Schmidt, P. J., & Roca, C. A. (1998). Estrogen Serotonin–interactions–implications for affective regulation. *Biological Psychiatry, 44,* 839–850.

Sachs, B. D. (1978). Conceptual and neural mechanisms of masculine copulatory behavior. In T. E. McGill, D. A. Dewsbury, & B. D. Sachs (Eds.), *Sex and behavior: Status and prospectus* (pp. 267–295). New York: Plenum.

Schleidt, W. M. (1974). How "fixed" is the fixed action pattern? *Zeitschrift für Tierpsychologie, 36,* 184–211.

Segraves, R. T. (1991). Pharmacological enhancement of human sexual behavior. *Journal of Sex Education and Therapy, 17,* 283–289.

Sheffield, F. D., Wulff, J. J., & Backer, R. (1951). Reward value of copulation without sexual drive reduction. *Journal of Comparative and Physiological Psychology, 44,* 3–8.

Sherwin, B. B., Gelfand, M. M., & Brender, W. (1985). Androgen enhances sexual motivation in females: A prospective, crossover study of sex steroid administration in the surgical menopause. *Psychosomatic Medicine, 47,* 339–351.

Spector, I., & Carey, M. (1990). Incidence and prevalence of the sexual dysfunctions: A critical review of the empirical literature. *Archives of Sexual Behavior, 19,* 389–408.

Spiteri, T., Le Pape, G., & Ågmo, A. (2000). What is learned during place preference conditioning? A comparison of food- and morphine-induced reward. *Psychobiology, 28,* 367–382.

Steiniger, F. (1950). Beiträge zur Soziologie und sonstigen Biologie der Wanderratte. *Zeitschrift für Tierpsychologie, 7,* 356–379.

Stewart, J. (1995). How does incentive motivational theory apply to sexual behavior? In J. Bancroft (Ed.), *The pharmacology of sexual function and dysfunction* (pp. 3–11). Amsterdam: Elsevier.

Takeo, T., & Sakuma, Y. (1995). Diametrically opposite effects of estrogen on the excitability of female rat medial and lateral preoptic neurons with axons to the midbrain locomotor region. *Neuroscience Research, 22*(1), 73–80.

Tang, Y., Rampin, O., Giuliano, F., & Ugolini, G. (1999). Spinal and brain circuits to motoneurons of the bulbospongiosus muscle: Retrograde transneuronal tracing with rabies virus. *Journal of Comparative Neurology, 414,* 167–192.

Telle, H. J. (1966). Beitrag zur Kenntnis der Verhaltensweise von Ratten, vergleichend dargestellt bei *Rattus norvegicus* und *Rattus rattus. Zeitschrift für angewandte Zoologie, 53,* 129–196.

van der Schoot, P., von Ophemert, J., & Baumgarten, R. (1992). Copulatory stimuli in rats induce heat abbreviation through effects on genitalia but not through effects on central nervous mechanisms supporting the steroid hormone-induced sexual responsiveness. *Behavioural Brain Research, 49,* 213–223.

van Furth, W. R., & van Ree, J. M. (1994). Endogenous opioids are differentially involved in appetitive and consummatory aspects of sexual behavior of male rats. *American Journal of Physiology: Regulatory, Integrative and Comparative Physiology, 266,* R606–R613.

van Furth, W. R., & van Ree, J. M. (1996a). Appetitive sexual behavior in male rats: I. The role of olfaction in level-changing behavior. *Physiology and Behavior, 60,* 999–1005.

van Furth, W. R., & van Ree, J. M. (1996b). Appetitive sexual behavior in male rats: II. Sexual reward and level-changing behavior. *Physiology and Behavior, 60,* 1007–1012.

van Furth, W. R., Wolterink, G., & van Ree, J. M. (1995). Regulation of masculine sexual behavior: Involvement of brain opioids and dopamine. *Brain Research Reviews, 21,* 162–184.

Vasudevan, N., Zhu, Y.-S., Koibuichi, Chin, W. W., & Pfaff, D. W. (2000). Differential crosstalk between estrogen receptor α and β and the thyroid hormone receptor results in flexible regulation of the consensus ERE. *Society for Neuroscience Abstracts, 26,* 1105.

Vega-Matuszczyk, J., Appa, R. S., & Larsson, K. (1994). Age-dependent variations in the sexual preference of male rats. *Physiology and Behavior, 55,* 827–830.

Vega-Matuszczyk, J., & Larsson, K. (1993). Sexual orientation and sexual motivation of the adult male rat. *Physiology and Behavior, 53,* 747–750.

Vega-Matuszczyk, J., & Larsson, K. (1994). Experience modulates the influence of gonadal hormones on sexual orientation of male rats. *Physiology and Behavior, 55,* 527–531.

Vega-Matuszczyk, J., Larsson, K., & Erikson, E. (1998). The selective serotonin reuptake inhibitor fluoxetine reduces sexual motivation in male rats. *Pharmacology Biochemistry and Behavior, 60,* 527–532.

Wade, G. N., & Zucker, I. (1970). Modulation of food intake and locomotor activity in female rats by diencephalic hormone implants. *Journal of Comparative and Physiological Psychology, 72,* 328–336.

Warden, C. J., & Nissen, H. W. (1928). An experimental analysis of the obstruction method for measuring animal drives. *Journal of Comparative Psychology, 8,* 325–342.

Whalen, R. E. (1961). Effects of mounting without intromission and intromission without ejaculation on sexual behavior and maze learning. *Journal of Comparative and Physiological Psychology, 54,* 409–415.

White, P. J., Fischer, R. B., & Meunier, G. F. (1984). The ability of females to predict male status via urinary odors. *Hormones and Behavior, 18,* 491–494.

Whitney, J. F. (1986). Effect of medial preoptic lesions on sexual behavior of female rats is determined by test situation. *Behavioral Neuroscience, 100,* 230–235.

Williams, C. L. (1987). Estradiol facilitates lordosis and ear wiggling of 4- to 6-day old rats. *Behavioral Neuroscience, 101,* 718–723.

Woodworth, R. S. (1918). *Dynamic psychology.* New York: Columbia University Press.

Yang, L. Y., & Clemens, L. G. (1998). Influence of male-related stimuli on female postejaculatory refractory period in rats. *Physiology and Behavior, 63,* 675–682.

Young, P. T. (1961). *Motivation and emotion: A survey of the determinants of human and animal activity.* New York: Wiley.

CHAPTER 18

Social Behavior

L. ELIZABETH CRAWFORD, BARBARA LUKA, AND JOHN T. CACIOPPO

Not only is the human brain an information-processing organ, but it also perceives individuals, social hierarchies, and coalitions; infers traits, intentions, and emotions; communicates and obfuscates one's mental contents; and forms relationships, unions, and alliances. Sociality is such a fundamental component of human nature that it is perceived in the orchestrated movements of simple objects. Heider and Simmel (1944), for instance, produced a short film of the movement of a small triangle, a small circle, and a large triangle around and into a large rectangle. Although the animated film consisted only of these geometric shapes, everyone who viewed the film "saw" a social drama. A representative participant described the film as follows:

> "I saw a box, like a room, that had an opening to it. There was a large triangle chasing around a smaller triangle, and a circle . . . got into the box, or the room, and hid. And then the big triangle chased the little triangle around. Finally he went in, got inside the box to go after the circle, and the circle was scared of him . . . but maneuvered its way around and was able to get out of the opening, and they shut it on him. And the little circle and the little triangle were happy that they got that, the big one, caught. And they went off on their way, and the big triangle got upset and started breaking the box open." (Adolphs, 1999, p. 473)

The unanimous perception of a social interaction by viewers who know that the geometric shapes have no social life is all the more extraordinary when one contrasts this with the description given by S. M., a patient with bilateral calcification of the amygdala:

> "OK, so, a rectangle, two triangles, and a small circle. Let's see, the triangle and the circle went inside the rectangle, and then the other triangle went in, and then the triangle and the circle went out and took off, left one triangle there. And then the two parts of the rectangle made like an upside-down V, and that was it." (Adolphs, 1999, p. 473)

S. M. described the movement of the shapes and breaking of the box accurately—possibly more accurately than did those with intact brains—but did not perceive the movement as social interaction. The human brain is so fundamentally social that it takes a broken one to remind us just how automatic social perception and construal can be.

The first reported social psychology experiment (Triplett, 1898) asked, in the words of Allport (1985, p. 39), "What change in an individual's normal solitary performance occurs when other people are present?" Notable about this description, coming from one of the founders of social psychology, is the implied association of *normal* with *solitary*. The same implication can be gleaned from the field of experimental psychology, where the isolated mind has been the modal subject of research. Given the research questions of experimental psychology, this isolation may be necessary in order to limit the contamination of uncontrollable social factors, and the three editions of the *Stevens' Handbook* offer a testament to how much has been learned about mind, brain, and behavior through this approach. Social psychology, included in the *Stevens' Handbook* for the first time in this edition, offers an important complementary perspective on the human mind.

A primary aim of social psychology is to understand the interplay between individuals and their social contexts. This goal requires social psychology to span levels of analysis. At the social level, it examines how the behavior and attitudes of individuals are influenced by social factors such as norms, self-identity, and relationships with others. At the cognitive level, it addresses how the individual interprets, evaluates, and ascribes meaning to the social world. At the biological level, social psychology understands individuals as biological entities whose physiology influences—and is influenced by—social life. The historical development of social psychology mirrors these levels. In the early part of the 20th century it focused largely on how the presence of others (real or imagined) affected the individual's thought and behavior (Allport, 1985). Following the cognitive revolution, social psychology shifted its focus to the cognitive underpinnings of social thought. Currently, as with cognitive science in general, social psychology is being increasingly integrated with a neuroscience approach, leading to advances in our understanding of the operation of certain brain structures (Adolphs, 1999; Cacioppo et al., in press) and in how social and emotional factors affect gene expression, cardiovascular functioning, and immune

activity (Cacioppo, Berntson, Sheridan, & McClintock, 2000).

The purpose of this chapter is to give the reader a sense of where empirical social psychology has been and where it is heading. We cover several of the central topics in experimental social psychology, including motivation, emotion, attitudes, social influence, the self, and social cognition. In the process, we review many of psychology's classic studies. In keeping with the increasingly cross-disciplinary nature of psychological research, we also briefly address current research applying neuroscientific approaches to these topics.

SELF AS A SOCIAL CONSTRUCT

One's representation of oneself is a powerful regulator of cognition, motivation, emotion, and behavior. In this section we review the experimental literature regarding the ways in which knowledge of the self and its place in a social context influences cognition and behavior. We also review research that addresses how self-esteem is maintained and constructed. The following sections introduce the structure of self-knowledge, strategies for exercising resilience in the face of challenges to a self-view, and how the structures of self-knowledge are rooted in cultural context. The experimental literature reveals the self to be a dynamic social construct, one which shapes action and behavior but which is itself shaped by memory, experience, culture, and biology.

The Structure and Influence of Self-Knowledge

Knowledge of the self is not viewed as a coherent and unified concept, but rather as a loose collection of information about one's own traits, values, experiences, and behaviors. The units of this knowledge have been termed self-schemas, representations of the self that organize and guide the processing of information relevant to the self (Markus, 1977). A self-schema may capture general traits (e.g., I am brave) as well as knowledge about specific events (e.g., I risked my life to save a child from a burning building). Self-schemas provide a basis for predicting behavior and overriding or resisting information that contradicts the self-schema (Markus, 1977; Markus & Nurius, 1986). Self-schemas are dynamic and evolving: When a social need arises, self-schemas can be revised and expanded to include new characteristics.

Self-schemas provide elaborate and accessible knowledge to facilitate transactions with the physical and social environment. Individuals who possess self-schemas that weight heavily a given attribute remember a greater number of characteristics and endorse more qualities related to that attribute, require shorter processing times for self-descriptive judgments of the attribute, are more confident of their judgments pertinent to that attribute, and are able to supply more examples of past behavior related to that attribute (Markus, Crane, Bernstein, & Siladi, 1982). Such individuals are also more likely to discount information that contradicts the valued attribute (Markus, 1977; for reviews, see also Fiske & Taylor, 1991; Kihlstrom & Cantor, 1988; Kihlstrom et al., 1988; Kihlstrom & Klein, 1994). In this way, self-schemas serve a memory-saving function similar to knowledge-based schemas in domains of expertise (Chase & Simon, 1973; Markus, Smith, & Moreland, 1985).

A substantial body of research demonstrates that information about the self is processed differently than are other types of information. A primary example of this preferential treatment for the self is the case of *self-referential memory,* in which the self improves encoding and recall for self-relevant dimensions. Studies of self-referential memory find that information coded with respect

to the self is more easily recalled than is information associated with others. In a typical self-referential memory paradigm, participants review a word list, evaluating each word with respect to a given characteristic such as word meaning, word length, and applicability of the word to oneself or to another individual. These various encoding conditions influence participants' performance on a subsequent, unexpected free recall test, and participants have better memory for words encoded with respect to the self than in any other condition (Greenwald & Banaji, 1989; Klein & Kihlstrom, 1986; Rogers, Kuiper, & Kirker, 1977; Rogers, Rogers, & Kuiper, 1979). Researchers have attributed these findings to depth of processing, in which self-relevant information receives more attention and is processed more deeply (Greenwald & Pratkanis, 1984; Rogers, 1981), and to structure in memory, in which self-representations provide a more elaborated and organized network of associations (Kihlstrom & Klein, 1997; Klein & Kihlstrom, 1986).

Individuals use their own standards for themselves to process information about and to evaluate the behavior of others (Lewicki, 1983, 1984). They do this by using their own self-schemas to interpret the behavior of others or to infer causal structure and motivations for others' behavior (Carpenter, 1988; Dunning & Hayes, 1996; Markus et al., 1985; for a review, see also Kihlstrom et al., 1988). For example, in a study by Dunning and Hayes, participants reported that they judged the behavior of others in comparison to their own behavior, and they were also quicker to respond to questions about their own behavior if they had just evaluated the behavior of someone else. Such self-focused processing may be motivated by cognitive efficiency rather than egocentrism: It is fast and efficient to use the motivated and richly elaborated schemas that self-representations keep active, rather than to infer and reconstruct an alternative—perhaps inaccurate, ill-informed, or poorly motivated—schema that is attributed to another individual.

Self Schemas in Social Context

Self-schemas, like schemas studied in cognitive psychology, influence information processing. However, the self is not simply a knowledge structure; it is also a social entity that is partly determined by its relation to others. Because of the sensitivity of self-schemas to social context, self-schemas can appear quite labile or even contradictory when compared across situations (L. Ross & Nisbett, 1991), depending upon the social ground to which the self is compared. For example, sex and ethnicity can become salient with respect to the composition of the social contrast set. In spontaneous self-descriptions, children were more likely to mention their sex (McGuire, McGuire, & Winton, 1979) or their ethnicity (McGuire, McGuire, Child, & Fujioka, 1978) when their category membership represented a minority within their family or their classroom.

Individuals identify themselves with respect to a variety of groups based on sex, gender, and religion, as well as social, political, or consumerist affiliations. By identifying themselves as members of these larger groups, individuals extend their definitions of self beyond their personal identities (Tajfel & Turner, 1986; Turner, 1985). Reaping the benefits of membership in these various groups requires that individuals deindividuate and depersonalize aspects of their sense of self in order to maximize their similarity with others. Their evaluations of themselves are then linked to the reputation and outcomes of the group (Luhtanen & Crocker, 1992).

Just as people have the need to integrate themselves with the group to recognize the similarities shared with the other members, people also have the simultaneous need to individuate themselves within the group to recognize themselves as unique, even within a context of general similarity. The tension between the sense of validation that comes with group membership and the need for a personal identity apart from a social identity is addressed by models of identity such as uniqueness theory (Snyder & Fromkin, 1980), models of individuation (e.g., Codol, 1984; Lemaine, 1974; Maslach, 1974; Ziller, 1964), and optimal distinctiveness theory (Brewer, 1991).

Self-Regulation

Self-knowledge provides the regulatory control that enables decision making and action. Self-knowledge allows one to act as an agent, to predict and control one's behavior and guide oneself toward a goal. Self-knowledge provides the power to change one's behavior and regulate oneself in order to obtain a desired result. Self-regulation, in combination with a model for a desired future self, is crucial in this process.

Self-regulation is the executive control of desires, beliefs, thoughts, and goals. A simple example of self-regulation is skipping dessert in order to lose weight. One forfeits an immediate gratification to enjoy a greater delayed reward. Self-regulation is an effortful process that consumes cognitive resources, resulting in decreased performance on concurrent tasks (Gilbert, Krull, & Pelham, 1988). Self-regulation is also associated with increases in physiological arousal (e.g., Gross & Levenson, 1993) and decreases in physical stamina (Muraven, Tice, & Baumeister, 1998). Models of self-regulation have been adapted from feedback loops that modify present behavior to minimize discrepancies with the goal behavior (Carver & Scheier, 1981; Scheier & Carver, 1982). Recent work in self-regulation relates executive control to mental models for one's own goals compared to the goals of others who are close (Moretti

& Higgins, 1999). Self-regulation is also fundamental in explaining motivations for self-improvement (Banaji & Prentice, 1994), and models of self-control and willpower (Metcalfe & Mischel, 1999).

These studies support the role that self-regulation has in directing and enacting motivation, but self-regulation has itself been shown to be mediated by a number of other cognitive constructs. Emotion, for example, plays an influential role in self-regulation. Emotional distress can precipitate regulatory failure by reducing motivation; in some cases, however, distressing emotions such as guilt can strengthen regulatory control by focusing attention on aversive outcomes and the consequences of regulatory failure (Heatherton & Baumeister, 1996; Tangney & Fischer, 1995). The role of emotion is especially clear in the context of goal attainment. Because so much time is spent working toward a goal without actually reaching the goal, emotional involvement maintains a state of interest in individuals while they strive toward the reward. Seeing improvement provides an incentive to enjoy the processing of moving toward the goal; the rate of improvement modulates the motivation to pursue the endeavor (Cacioppo & Gardner, 1999; Carver & Scheier, 1990).

Self-regulation has high cognitive costs, but the payoffs are also high. Discipline and delayed gratification can produce long-term rewards. For example, in studies of preschool children, willingness to wait to receive larger rewards (exercising self-regulation in the form of delayed gratification) was correlated with higher ratings of academic and social performance 10 years later (Mischel, 1988; Mischel, Shoda, & Peake, 1988; Mischel, Zeiss, & Zeiss, 1974).

Resilience of Self-Esteem

Self-esteem is a global evaluation of one's worthiness or goodness (Rosenberg, 1965).

When faced with challenges to their self-esteem, individuals exercise a variety of strategies to regulate their self-evaluation and their resulting feelings of self-esteem. Much of this research has been conducted in the domain of social comparison theory, which finds that individuals strive to enhance the self by upward comparison, focusing on improvements against a superior, and by downward comparison, focusing on the advantages of the self over others who are not as prosperous or skilled (Festinger, 1954; Gibbons & Gerrard, 1991; Wills, 1981; J. Wood & Taylor, 1991).

Self-Serving Strategies

Research on self-esteem has shown that normal individuals (who are neither depressed nor egomaniacal) invest a surprising amount of cognitive effort maintaining a positive—rather than realistic or accurate—view of the self (Kunda, 1990; Taylor & Brown, 1988). A variety of studies provide support for the view that normal individuals develop and preserve an illusion of superiority. For example, individuals view their own strengths and abilities as rare or unique, while viewing their faults or weaknesses as fairly common or unremarkable (Campbell, 1986; Goethals, Messick, & Allison, 1991; Marks, 1984). Individuals also identify positive traits as being more characteristic of themselves than are negative traits, recall positive information about themselves more easily than they do negative information, recall successes more often than they do failures, and recall their performance on tasks as better than it actually was (Brown, 1986; Crary, 1966; Kuiper, Olinger, MacDonald, & Shaw, 1985; Silverman, 1964). Individuals have unrealistically positive self-views, exaggerated feelings of control over events, and inflated optimism about the future (Taylor & Brown, 1988). This provides a reassuring sense of well-being that allows individuals to be more resilient in the face of obstacles, setbacks, and failures, and allows them to be happier, more optimistic, and more willing to undertake new challenges.

Similar self-enhancement strategies may be enacted by members of stigmatized groups. In order to preserve a healthy sense of self-esteem in hostile contexts, stigmatized individuals may attribute negative feedback that they receive as arising from prejudice toward the group, mitigating a more personal insult. For example, after receiving negative feedback from a male evaluator, women who had previously been given evidence that the evaluator was sexist were less likely to experience a decrease in self-esteem than were women who had received no information about the evaluator (Crocker, Voelkl, Testa, & Major, 1991). They may also compare personal outcomes with those of other in-group members, rather than with the relatively advantaged out group, and may selectively devalue characteristics of the out group that they do not share and instead value characteristics on which their group excels (Crocker & Major, 1989).

Self-esteem can also work as a mediating factor in the exercise of self-knowledge. Individuals may have similar self-schemas and yet behave very differently in social contexts because of the mediating role of self-esteem in the expression of behavior (although the self-knowledge of individuals with low self-esteem is less stable and less internally consistent; Campbell, 1990). These differences can be understood by considering the motivations and coping strategies of individuals having varying levels of self-esteem (Blaine & Crocker, 1993).

For example, individuals with high self-esteem respond to failure by focusing on their personal strengths, while individuals with low self-esteem respond to failure by focusing on negative emotions such as humiliation and by overgeneralizing the implications of failure (Brown & Dutton, 1995; Brown & Smart, 1991; Dodgson & Wood, 1998). In-

dividuals with high self-esteem have different strategies for maintaining self-worth compared to individuals with low self-esteem, for example, by using relationship bonds to strengthen self-affirmation rather than by distancing oneself from one's partner (Murray, Holmes, MacDonald, & Ellsworth, 1998; J. Wood, Giordano-Beech, Taylor, Michela, & Gaus, 1994). Individuals with high or low self-esteem vary also in the their ratings of self-confidence. In a self-descriptive rating task, individuals with high self-esteem were more confident and made self-descriptive, but not other-descriptive, ratings more quickly than did low self-esteem individuals (Baumgardner, 1990). These studies indicate that strategies for regaining and maintaining self-esteem may become habitual and that interventions can be created to break the cycle of behaviors that limit valuations of the self.

Self Complexity

Research on self-schemas demonstrates that individuals are able to recognize and describe aspects of themselves that they find most meaningful. Recognizing oneself as possessing a complex variety of traits and social roles provides a broad and resilient structure to self-knowledge. High self-complexity has been shown to mitigate the consequences of stressful events, promoting benefits such as reduced health problems and reduced vulnerability to depression (Linville, 1987; Linville & Clark, 1989). Individuals who establish their self-definition in a more restricted range of traits and social roles may also experience greater instability in mood (Niedenthal, Setterlund, & Wherry, 1992). These distinctions emerge only when the self is confronted with challenges or threats to self-esteem.

Self-Enhancement, Self-Verification, and Self-Affirmation

Individuals work to enhance their self-evaluations (Greenwald, 1980; Steele, 1988;

Tesser, 1988). An individual's behavioral strategies and interpretation of events can be influenced by his or her desire to verify or confirm central aspects of a self-schema (Lecky, 1945). This type of self-enhancement can be seen as beneficial in predictable circumstances because having a high regard for the self motivates persistence and resilience in the face of failure.

There are times, however, when individuals prefer accurate feedback even if the evaluation is not self-enhancing. People seek out self-verification rather than self-affirmation because it is more useful, and less painful in the long term, to have a realistic sense of self rather than completely unfounded self-enhancement and unconditional positive self-regard (Swann, 1987, 1990; Swann & Read, 1981). One needs at least a somewhat realistic assessment of oneself, for example, in order to form accurate representations, effective expectancies of and goals for social interaction, and accurate interpersonal communication. The degree to which individuals enhance or verify the self depends on the context of social relationships. A casual dating relationship, in which one still sees oneself as independent, maximizes one's interest in receiving self-enhancing appraisals, whereas committed relationships maximize one's interest in receiving self-verifying or accurate appraisals, which in turn fosters communication, improvement, and stability (Murray, Holmes, & Griffin, 1996; Pelham & Swann, 1989; Swann, de la Ronde, & Hixon, 1994).

Self-Evaluation Maintenance

The self is not autonomous but is dependent on one's evaluation of others, especially those close to oneself. The self-evaluation maintenance model (SEM) was developed in order to explain the interaction between self-schemas, self-esteem, and the performance of close others (individuals who are either important to

the self or similar to the self; Pleban & Tesser, 1981; Tesser, 1988; Tesser & Martin, 1996; Tesser, Pilkington, & McIntosh, 1989).

The earliest version of the SEM assumed that individuals enjoy a boost in self-appraisal if they perform better than others in a domain that was central to their self-schema and reciprocally, that they would be least threatened if they performed worse than others in a domain that was irrelevant to their self-schema (Tesser, 1988). In addition, if the domain is not relevant to one's self-definition, superior performance by an individual close to oneself may enhance one's view of self. This process of *"reflection,"* or basking in glory of another, is evident in the number of undergraduates who wear clothing bearing their team logo the day after a university team victory in contrast to a team defeat (Cialdini et al., 1976). The process of reflection boosts one's social, collective self. The personal relationship with the other is also important, and the SEM model predicts that being outperformed by close others, in contrast to strangers, is more troubling when the task dimension is central to one's self-definition.

Subsequent recent research has expanded and modified the original SEM model to explain how one's own failure can result in vicarious self-enhancement if a close other succeeds. If the domain in which a close other outperforms oneself is a highly relevant domain, one's self-view can be threatened; but if one sees the potential for the self to improve performance, then success of a close other can be inspirational (Lockwood & Kunda, 1997).

Conflicts of Self-Presentation

Despite the wealth of strategies available to manipulate one's own self-esteem, there are still times when performance does not always reach expectations. When one does not live up to one's own expectations or those of close others, such mismatches can lead to anxiety or depression, and, in some cases, to seemingly self-destructive behavior. It is possible to explain some of these behaviors by examining the organization of self-knowledge and the motivations for self-consistency and self-presentation.

Self-Guides and Self-Discrepancy

Self-guides form the basis of standards for a possible future self. Individuals can evaluate their current self-schemas and develop schemas for future selves that represent how they ideally want to be or how they feel they ought to be. These two self-guides, the *ideal self* and the *ought self,* affect behavior through different causal motives (E. Higgins, 1987).

In the construction of the ideal self, the primary motivation is an approach goal, focusing on a positive outcome and working toward a desired benefit. A case in point, for example, is an individual who wants to quit smoking to gain feelings of control and freedom from chemical dependence. When people fall short of their expectations for an ideal self, the predicted affective reaction is depression (E. Higgins, Klein, & Strauman, 1985, 1987; E. Higgins, Strauman, & Klein, 1986; E. Higgins, Vookles, & Tykocinski, 1992). In contrast, when the standard of comparison is the ought self, the primary motivation is usually a prevention goal of avoiding an unwelcome outcome. For example, if a doctor exhorts someone to quit smoking because of the serious health risks, the doctor is creating a prevention focus based on what the individual ought to be doing. When one's basis of comparison is the ought self, predicted affective response to a discrepancy between the current and ought selves is anxiety (E. Higgins et al., 1985, 1987; E. Higgins et al., 1986; E. Higgins et al., 1992). An interesting implication is that individuals with similar goals and self-schemas may nevertheless differ in their motivations and emotional responses because they differ in promotion or prevention focus.

Tradeoffs between Linked Positive and Negative Outcomes

When faced with failure, individuals sometimes try to change the meaning of the failure and try to find more palatable interpretations of events that threaten their self-esteem and feelings of personal control. There are many strategies for coping with failure that seem to have paradoxical motives. Two very common strategies are perseveration and self-handicapping. Both strategies depend on interpersonal motivation and reflect a concern with how one appears to others.

In the case of perseveration, or excessive persistence, individuals continue a deleterious behavior because they focus on the amount invested or the shame of withdrawal rather than focusing on the cost of continuing the current action. The momentum of the situation, commitment to initial course of action, feelings of personal responsibility, or attention to sunk costs all extend an individual's interest in continuing self-defeating behavior (Staw, 1976). Self-presentation also influences one's willingness to persist in disadvantageous behavior. Losing face or fear of hearing others say "I told you so" encourages perseveration (Brockner, Shaw, & Rubin, 1979; Teger, 1980), whereas an awareness of the dangers of persistence and knowledge that others would be accepting reduces perseverative behavior (Brockner, Rubin, & Lang, 1981).

There are situations in which even the potential for failure may trigger defensive behaviors that have destructive outcomes. In the case of self-handicapping, individuals betray their unrealized potential in return for a false sense of security. If an individual performs poorly after not trying very hard, his or her self-esteem is not as threatened because the failure can be attributed to causes other than lack of ability (Jones & Berglas,

1978; Jones, Rhodewalt, Berglas, & Skelton, 1981). Underachievement, withholding effort, inadequate preparation, and even substance abuse may be interpreted as strategic self-handicapping (Feick & Rhodewalt, 1997; Ferrari & Tice, 2000; R. Higgins & Berglas, 1990; Zuckerman, Kieffer, & Knee, 1998). Sacrificing the quality of one's performance is only a painful intermediate goal on the route to achieving a larger more acceptable goal— that is, to buffer the interpretation of what is perceived to be unavoidable failure.

The presentation of the self to others plays an influential role in self-handicapping. Individuals do self-handicapping behaviors only if these behaviors may become known to others (Kolditz & Arkin, 1982). Self-esteem may also play a moderating role in self-handicapping. Tice (1991) suggested that people with high and low self-esteem self-handicap for different reasons: People with high self-esteem do so to enhance success, whereas people with low self-esteem do so to protect themselves against the threatening implications of failure.

Perseveration and self-handicapping begin with the exercise of beneficial behaviors: judicious persistence and a willingness to accept short-term discomfort for the sake of a larger goal. These are both laudable exercises in self-regulation, but both of these strategies, taken to the extremes of perseveration and self-handicapping, become impediments to adaptive coping and threats to positive self-regard.

The Embedded Self: Cross-Cultural Models

Nearly all of the research presented in this section has been conducted using American undergraduate students as participants. This provides a starting point for research on the self, but it cannot be assumed that these findings may be extrapolated to other populations or contexts.

In an influential paper, Triandis (1989) described cross-cultural differences in the emphasis placed on certain aspects of the self. In particular, he contrasted individualist cultures, which emphasize independence and individual achievement, with collectivist cultures, which emphasize conformity, relations with others, and striving to meet the goals of the group. American culture has been characterized by an independent view of self, compared to the emphasis of interdependent views of self among age-matched peers in China (Morris & Peng, 1994), India (Markus & Kitayama, 1991; Miller, 1984), and Japan (Cousins, 1989; Markus & Kitayama, 1991). The imperative of the independent self is to achieve independence and understand oneself as a unique individual, whereas the imperative of the interdependent self is to maintain relationships with others.

These different construals of the self have consequences for cognition. For example, when students from America and India were asked to judge the similarity of self to another and that other to self, American students rated the other as more similar to self than self to other, implying that their own self concepts were more elaborated or more salient (Holyoak & Gordon, 1983; Tversky, 1977). Indian students, in contrast, did not fall prey to this egocentric bias (Markus & Kitayama, 1991). In addition, consistent with their emphasis on independence, American students generally overestimate the role that dispositional factors (and underestimate the role that situational factors) play in determining the behavior of others, a bias known as the *fundamental attribution error.* In contrast, Japanese and Korean students are less susceptible to the fundamental attribution error than are American students, suggesting that they better appreciate the individual's relation to context (Choi & Nisbett, 1998; Fiske, Kitayama, Markus, & Nisbett, 1998; Sampson, 1988, 1989). In addition, when

Shweder and Bourne (1984) asked Indian and American participants to describe acquaintances, they found that Indian participants included more descriptions of situations and relationships than did American participants.

The independent and interdependent construals of the self have implications for the self-enhancement strategies described earlier. People in collectivist and individualist cultures differ in the management of and apparent need for self-esteem. Whereas some have argued for a basic human need for positive self-regard (Brown, 1998), others have noted the absence of such a need in Japanese culture (Heine et al., 1999). Thus, Japanese do not use many of the self-enhancement strategies commonly found among North Americans, leading Heine et al. to conclude, "we are unable to find clear and consistent evidence of any self-esteem maintenance strategies within the Japanese psychological literature" (p. 780).

In much of the cross-cultural literature, between-group differences have often been described as a contrast between Western and Eastern representations of the self, but it may be wise to extend the research samples before such broad labels are applied. The influence of culture may represent variations of degree, or simply greater attention to different perspectives toward the self that are present cross-culturally. For example, some have emphasized that aspects of the self, such as the private, public, and collective self, are present in all cultures, but are activated differentially by the contexts required in the culture (Triandis, 1989).

The notion of self-construal introduced at the outset of this section plays an important role in exploring proposed cross-cultural differences. One's self-representation can be construed in different social contexts as personal (emphasizing the individuated or autonomous nature of the self), relational (emphasizing dyadic relationships with close others), or collective (emphasizing one's membership and identification with a larger social group), and an experimental task may prime different self-construals (Brewer & Gardner, 1996). The dynamic nature of self-construals can begin to explain why individuals in different cultures might respond in very different ways to a reputedly identical task, not because a sense of self is so different across cultures, but rather because the experimental task may evoke different affiliations, alliances, and motivations across cultures. Within each culture and each social context, individuals may differentially activate personal, relational, or collective construals of the self.

It is important to keep in mind these qualifications to cross-cultural comparisons. Even cultural definitions of self can be very quickly revised when cultural values shift and individuals within the culture reprioritize their concerns, from valuing societal obligation, for example, to a greater interest in self-fulfillment and personal autonomy. In the context of global communication and international exchange, a new cultural sense of self can be recreated within a few generations. For example, a pressure for self-definition and individualistic expression during adolescence is a relatively recent development in American culture (Baumeister, 1986, 1987, 1998; Baumeister & Tice, 1986). The influence of zeitgeist and romantic historicism should also be acknowledged, in which each culture tends to describe its ideal self in glowing terms of the day, and the social complexities of the past become simplified, and either idealized or vilified.

SOCIAL COGNITION

Social cognition examines the cognitive underpinnings of social thought. This approach, having gained wide acceptance in the 1980s on the heels of the cognitive revolution, is now fully established as a subfield of social psychology. Rather than a content area, social cognition is a research approach that has been used to study several topics in social psychology, including impression formation, stereotyping, personality, attribution, social communication, affect, judgment processes, and the self (Devine, Hamilton, & Ostrom, 1994). Thus, much of what was reviewed in the preceding section could fall under the rubric of social cognition. Here we review topics in social cognition research that have dominated theory and research, including processing heuristics, social concepts and stereotypes, and the role of automatic processes. We also consider the limitations of a strictly cognitive approach and discuss the importance of integrating social cognition with affective and motivational processes in the study of social processes and behavior.

A major focus of social cognition research is how people navigate the complex situations necessary for social interaction. These situations require people to encode and store social information and produce social inferences. As in cognitive psychology, social cognition has revealed persistent and systematic deviations from normative models of information integration and judgment (Nisbett & Ross, 1980). In part, these biases result from reliance on cognitive structures such as categories, scripts, schemas, or frames. In addition, they reveal the use of heuristics: simple, efficient strategies to produce judgments that may not be perfectly accurate but are often serviceable given typical conditions. In the following sections we consider the effects of processing strategies and knowledge structures on social judgments.

Heuristics: Simple Processing Strategies

Two processing heuristics that have garnered attention in social psychology are the representativeness and availability heuristics (for reviews of others, see Kunda, 1999). The availability heuristic uses the subjective sense of availability (i.e., the ease with which a thought or memory is accessed) as an indicator of the frequency or probability of objective events. Thus, because we easily recall frequent and vivid accounts of homicide from the evening news, homicide is incorrectly judged to be more prevalent than stomach cancer (Slovic, Fischhoff, & Lichtenstein, 1982). Relying on the availability heuristic can also produce egocentric biases. Because an individual's own actions are more available in memory than are the actions of others, each individual participating in an interaction may believe that he or she contributed more to a joint effort than did the other partner (M. Ross & Sicoly, 1979). Use of the availability heuristic may also account for the fundamental attribution error, the tendency to attribute one's own behavior to situational factors and others' behavior to stable personality factors. Because individuals can observe the external forces that cause their own behavior but often do not see what precipitates the behavior of others, they are more likely to perceive the behavior of others as internally motivated and less susceptible to external influences (Nisbett & Ross, 1980). Although use of the availability heuristic may lead to biased judgments under controlled testing conditions, availability may serve as a reasonable estimate of frequency information because common items are generally more accessible in memory.

In addition to biasing judgments about individuals, the availability heuristic may contribute to the development of beliefs about social groups. For example, Hamilton and Gifford (1976) showed that people tend to overestimate the occurrence of negative behaviors by minorities. They argued that both negative behaviors and minority status are distinctive and thus that the combination of negative behavior and minority status is especially available in memory. As a result, under conditions that equated the percentage of majority and minority group members who exhibited negative behaviors, participants perceived an illusory correlation between minority status and behavior: They believed that minorities were disproportionately responsible for negative acts.

Cognition in social life also employs the representativeness heuristic. In this strategy, people rely on an individual's representativeness of, or similarity to, a social category to judge the probability that the individual belongs to that category, often ignoring relevant information about prior probabilities. Use of this heuristic can produce patently incorrect responses, as in the *conjunction fallacy*. A classic example of the conjunction fallacy is the target Linda, described as an outspoken, bright activist who majored in philosophy, who is judged more likely to be a feminist bank teller than to be a bank teller. The probability of the conjoint event (feminist bank teller) is judged to be higher than the probability of one constituent event (bank teller) because the description of Linda is more representative of feminist bank tellers than of bank tellers (Kahneman, Slovic, & Tversky, 1982). In some cases, representativeness leads people to ignore population base rates that should, by normative standards, inform their judgments. For example, knowing the prevalence of social categories in the population can help determine the likelihood that any individual belongs to a given category, but people have been shown to ignore knowledge about base rates and focus instead on ways in which the individual is similar to, or represents, the target category (Kahneman et al., 1982). People may ignore base rates when predicting behavior. For example, Nisbett and Borgida (1975) showed that knowing the base rate of helping behavior had no effect on participants' predictions about the helping behavior of particular individuals. Base rates are given more consideration when the individuating information is less diagnostic or less causally related to

the judgment (Ajzen, 1977; Ginosar & Trope, 1980).

In addition to using processing strategies such as the representativeness and availability heuristics, people simplify processing by relying on prior knowledge. Knowledge structures such as schemas, concepts, and categories are used to organize, interpret, and remember information, including social information. Schemas of types of people (e.g., athletes), specific individuals (e.g., a significant other), social events (e.g., job interviews), and social roles (e.g., the parenting role) contain knowledge and expectations that guide behavior and thought in social situations. They act as filters by determining what draws attention, what is encoded in memory, and what is retrieved. When information is lacking, they offer a way to fill in the gaps with schema-driven inferences.

Several theories in social and cognitive psychology claim that people fall back on processing heuristics or prior knowledge when they are unmotivated or unable to engage in more effortful, detailed processing. The elaboration likelihood model of attitude change (ELM), for instance, posits that people seek to hold veridical beliefs and opinions, but that various factors influence whether they engage in extensive issue-relevant thinking to achieve that goal (central route) or rely on cues, conditioning histories, or heuristic processes (peripheral route; Petty & Cacioppo, 1981, 1986). According to the ELM, people are more likely to travel the central route to beliefs and attitudes when accuracy is especially important or when the information to be judged is personally relevant. Because elaboration requires cognitive work, it is less likely to occur when people are cognitively busy. In addition, the ELM predicts that people are more likely to travel the peripheral route when they are unable to engage in issue-relevant thinking, as when they know nothing about the issue. Although the ELM was originally developed to account for information process-ing in attitude change, it and related mod-els, such as the continuum model (Fiske & Neuberg, 1990) and the dual-process model (Brewer, 1988), apply to the role of social con-cepts in information processing.

Drawing on the ELM, the following sec-tions consider how motivation, cognitive load, and other factors mediate the use of con-cepts in social cognition. Although there are many kinds of social concepts, we focus on stereotypes because in addition to generating enormous interest in recent years, research on stereotypes addresses all of the major issues in current social cognition research.

Social Concepts: Stereotypes

Stereotypes can be thought of as cognitive structures that contain knowledge and ex-pectations about the members of a group. *Stereotyping* refers to the process of apply-ing those group-level beliefs to an individual group member. As primary examples, cate-gories of race and gender have been shown to have powerful effects on how social infor-mation is construed (Duncan, 1976; Locksley, Borgida, Brekke, & Hepburn, 1980; Sagar & Schofield, 1980). For instance, social cate-gories generally lead individuals to see the members of an out group as being less vari-able, or more homogenous, than they actually are, whereas members of an in group are per-ceived as less homogenous than they actually are (Tajfel & Turner, 1986). This may occur because individuals have more experience with members of their in group and thus are more frequently reminded of the differences among in group members (Linville, Fischer, & Salovey, 1989). Complex representations of an in group may increase sensitivities to sub-categories within the group and may make one's own in group seem more variable (Park, Ryan, & Judd, 1992; see also Simon, 1992, for interesting exceptions). An implication of

the out-group homogeneity effect is that par-ticipants are more likely to generalize from an individual to the group if the group is an out group rather than the participants' own group, and vice versa (Quattrone & Jones, 1980).

Consistent with the ELM, perceivers rely on stereotypes less when they are especially motivated to engage in effortful processing about individuals. When the situation requires accurate as opposed to immediate judgments, as Fisk and Neuberg (1990) argued, individ-uating information plays a relatively larger role than category information does in de-termining impressions of targets. In addition, Bodenhausen (1990) found that participants were more likely to use stereotypes at times of low circadian arousal, presumably because either motivation or cognitive resources were low.

The amount of available cognitive re-sources is an influential factor mediating stereotype effects. Under conditions of dis-traction, information overload, and high task complexity, people are more likely to rely on stereotypes to process social information (Petty, Wells, & Brock, 1976). Stereotyping may offer people a way to simplify informa-tion processing and thereby free up cognitive resources. Support for this "cognitive miser" view comes from a study by Macrae, Milne, and Bodenhausen (1994), in which partici-pants formed impressions of targets while si-multaneously monitoring spoken prose. Ac-tivating stereotype labels improved memory for the prose as well as memory for tar-get attributes that were consistent with the stereotype. Macrae et al. (1994) concluded that stereotype activation, like categorization generally, simplifies processing, thus leaving more cognitive resources available for other tasks.

The amount of available cognitive re-sources may also determine how the perceiver processes information that is consistent or inconsistent with the stereotypes. Research on stereotype-consistent information has shown that individuals are more likely to encode information that is consistent with a stereotype than information that is irrelevant (Bodenhausen, 1988; Rothbart, Evans, & Fulero, 1979) and that they tend to process consistent information more quickly (Dovidio, Evans, & Tyler, 1986; Macrae, Bodenhausen, Milne, Thorn, & Castelli, 1997). The reaction to inconsistent information depends on cognitive load. If cognitive resources are available, inconsistent information may attract more attention as the perceiver attempts to resolve the inconsistency. In some cases, this attempt to resolve the inconsistency leads the information to be altered or discounted in such a way that the stereotype is preserved (Kunda & Oleson, 1995). In contrast, if the perceiver is cognitively busy or rushed, inconsistent information may be ignored altogether (Stangor & Duan, 1991). By treating stereotype-consistent information preferentially and by assimilating or discounting inconsistent information, stereotypes can be maintained, even in the face of disconfirming information.

In addition to the motivation and cognitive resources of the perceiver, characteristics of the target also affect whether stereotyping will occur. Reliance on stereotypes, and on prior knowledge more generally, is greater when perceivers must produce judgments based on limited or ambiguous information. When information about a target is ambiguous, perceivers are more likely to go beyond the information given, filling in the blanks with prior category knowledge. This occurs in judgments about physical as well as social characteristics. For example, Nelson, Biernat, and Manis (1990) asked participants to judge the heights of photographed targets and found that estimates were biased by the gender of the targets. They also found that the category effects were stronger when the targets were seated, and thus when their heights

were more difficult to judge. As the ambiguity of the stimulus increased, the reliance on stored knowledge about the heights of men and women increased. Although relying on prior knowledge produces bias in judgments, referring to category knowledge when new information is ambiguous is a rational strategy in Bayesian terms (Huttenlocher, Hedges, & Vevea, 2000). Findings such as these are consistent with the view that stereotyping may be a consequence of an adaptive cognitive mechanism.

The studies just reviewed show that in social judgment situations stereotypes are employed when effortful thinking is low and that stereotypes can also bias information processing when elaboration increases. These studies also suggest that stereotypes can be ignored when individuating information is present, cognitive load is low, and motivation for accuracy is high. That is, stereotypes are more likely to be recruited when needed. However, in the past 15 years, several studies have suggested that stereotyping and other social-cognitive processes may be automatic, occurring outside of awareness, intention, or control. Thus, they are not mediated by the perceiver's processing goals, the stimulus context, or the availability of cognitive resources, and they are obligatory. In contrast, "controlled" processes are intentional, controllable, effortful, and available to consciousness. As Macrae et al. (1997) noted, few psychological processes fit the stringent definition of *automaticity*. A major research question in social categorization is the degree to which stereotyping is an automatic process. In the following sections we discuss evidence for the automaticity of stereotyping and its relation to prejudiced social behavior, as well as the counter-evidence that qualifies such claims of automaticity. We further consider the question of whether, once activated, stereotypes can be consciously deactivated.

Automatic Stereotyping

Devine (1989) distinguished between stereotype activation, which she argued is an automatic information-processing operation, and stereotype application, which she contended was a controlled information-processing operation. If stereotype activation is automatic, it should be able to operate without conscious awareness. Several studies have supported the claim that stereotypes and other social concepts can be activated unconsciously through the use of subliminal primes. In an early study that examined subliminal activation of trait concepts, Bargh and Pietromonaco (1982) primed the trait "hostile" by presenting words associated with hostility at a rate too fast for the words to be consciously recognized. Participants who received the hostile primes subsequently rated a target as more hostile than did control participants. Devine extended this paradigm to the study of racial stereotypes. Using subliminally presented words associated with the African American stereotype (ghetto, lazy, jazz), she found that participants who had been primed with these words judged a subsequent race-unspecified target to be more hostile than did control participants. Although Devine interpreted these findings as evidence for unconscious stereotype activation, a more conservative interpretation is that the concept of hostility was activated by the negative words used in the priming manipulation. The studies by Bargh and Pietromonaco and by Devine supported one tenet of automaticity by showing that it was possible for traits such as hostility to be activated outside of conscious awareness. Importantly, these studies also showed that the unconscious activation of traits has consequences for social judgment.

If stereotypes operate automatically, they should also operate independent of the perceiver's goals and intentions. Devine's (1989) study offers some support for this. The priming effects observed were independent of participants' explicit beliefs about African Americans, as measured by the Modern Racism Scale. She argued that even those who do not endorse the negative stereotype of African Americans are susceptible to its effects, and she concluded that "automatic stereotype activation is equally strong and equally inescapable for high- and low-prejudice subjects" (Devine, 1989, p. 15).

Devine showed that the concept of hostility can be activated by presenting words associated with the negative African American stereotype. However, an important question that this study did not address is whether the negative stereotype is automatically activated under more natural conditions, such as when the perceiver encounters an African American. Under these conditions, do people spontaneously activate the negative stereotype of African Americans? Some results suggest that they do. Bargh, Chen, and Burrows (1996) presented images of African American or Euro-American faces outside of conscious awareness and found that viewing African American faces activated the stereotype of hostility in Euro-American participants. Bargh et al. also showed that after being primed with African American faces, Euro-American participants exhibited more hostile reactions to a bogus computer failure. These results indicate that African American faces may suffice to unconsciously activate a negative stereotype. In addition, this study showed that once the stereotype was activated, it affected not only judgments about ambiguous targets but also the behavior of the participants themselves.

A hallmark of automatic processes is that they operate even when few cognitive resources are available. Thus, if stereotypes are activated automatically, their activation should not be affected by degree of cognitive load. Macrae et al. (1994) reported evidence of stereotype activation in response to subliminal primes while participants were under conditions of at least moderate cognitive load (Pratto & Bargh, 1991). The studies just described indicate that stereotyping may operate without awareness or intention, and may not require cognitive resources to do so. However, several other studies have challenged the claim of automaticity in stereotyping and prejudice. These studies, reviewed next, indicate that stereotyping is mediated by cognitive load as well as the perceiver's motivation and degree of self-avowed prejudice.

Automaticity under Control

In contrast to the definition of automaticity, there is evidence that stereotype activation may depend on the available cognitive resources. For example, there is some evidence that cognitive load can disrupt stereotype activation, at least with certain kinds of stereotypes (Gilbert & Hixon, 1991). In addition, the spontaneous activation of some stereotypes may be disrupted if other stereotypes are already activated. To investigate this, Macrae, Bodenhausen, and Milne (1995) activated either the Chinese stereotype by showing a Chinese woman eating noodles or activated the woman stereotype by showing the same woman applying makeup. A subsequent word identification task included words associated with both stereotypes. Results showed that relative to controls, those who were primed with the concept "woman" had faster reaction times to woman-associated words and slower reaction times to Chinese-associated words, whereas those who were primed with the Chinese stereotype showed the opposite pattern. These findings suggest that whether or not a particular stereotype is activated may depend on prior activation of other stereotypes. In contrast to the strict definition of automaticity, these results also indicate that the activation of any particular stereotype is not obligatory, but depends on the context of the target and the cognitive state of the perceiver.

Further evidence for controlled processing in stereotyping is suggested by studies showing that the perceiver's own motivations can mediate the activation or inhibition of stereotypes. Stereotypes may be inhibited when it is advantageous for the perceiver to do so. For example, Sinclair and Kunda (1999) found that participants were more likely to inhibit the negative stereotype of African Americans when an African American evaluator had recently praised them but were more likely to activate the stereotype when they had been criticized. Sinclair and Kunda argued that, in this case, people are motivated to activate stereotypes selectively because doing so allows these individuals to discount the criticism but validate the praise. These findings imply that stereotype activation has a strategic component.

The perceiver's mood or feelings of threat and security may influence whether they think of others in a stereotyped manner. Fein and Spencer (1997) found that participants who experienced a threat to their self-image were more likely to employ negative stereotypes in their judgments of others than were those whose self-image was affirmed. Among the participants who experienced the self-image threat, those who judged a member of a stereotyped group showed greater self-esteem after this judgment than did those who judged a member of a nonstereotyped group. The results indicate that stereotyping others may serve to maintain one's own positive self-image.

In addition, it has been shown that affective states influence cognitive processes in general and stereotyping in particular. Both anxiety and happiness tend to produce greater reliance on cognitive shortcuts, whereas sadness tends to have the opposite effect (Bless et al., 1996). Similar findings have been found in studies of stereotyping. Bodenhausen, Kramer, and Suesser (1994) induced a happy mood in participants, followed by an allegedly unrelated task in which participants judged the guilt or innocence of targets suspected of violence or academic fraud. The degree to which judgments were affected by the targets' social group membership was influenced by the mood-induction manipulation. Those who were induced to have a positive mood showed stronger stereotype effects than did controls. Other studies have shown that inducing either a positive or negative mood can decrease sensitivity to the variability of group members (Stroessner & Mackie, 1992). These findings suggest that the degree of stereotyping depends on the affective state of the perceiver.

Finally, subsequent research has called into question Devine's conclusion that prejudiced and nonprejudiced participants are equally susceptible to stereotyping. Further studies that activated stereotypes by using neutral primes—such as faces, rather than the negative word primes that Devine (1989) employed—have shown that people who express egalitarian, nonprejudiced views on the Modern Racism Scale are also less likely to activate negative stereotypes (Wittenbrink, Judd, & Park, 1997).

Stereotypes exhibit some, but not all, characteristics of automatic processes. This has led Fazio and Dunton (1997) to describe stereotyping as "conditionally automatic." Activation of stereotypes may depend on the types of primes used, such as faces or negative word associates, as well as participants' cognitive load, affective and motivational states, and degree of prejudice as assessed by more explicit measures. It is certainly possible to activate stereotypes outside of conscious awareness through the use of word associations. If enough negative word associates are presented, negative stereotypes can be activated even in people who do not ascribe to them. In addition, stereotype activation may depend on the particular stereotype being activated. Some stereotypes, such as the African American stereotype, may be chronically accessi-

ble, whereas other less common stereotypes may require more effort to activate, such as the stereotype of grandmothers.

One of the reasons automaticity has attracted attention in stereotyping research, and in social psychology more generally, is that it suggests that people have less control over their own thoughts and behavior than they believe. Automatic stereotyping is especially disturbing because it produces results that, for many people, are inconsistent with their explicit social ideals. If one is motivated to live by such egalitarian ideals, how can one fight unconscious racism in order to meet this goal? Given that stereotypes sometimes become activated in the minds of people who believe themselves to be nonprejudiced, one might try to make a conscious effort to suppress stereotypes before they affect judgments or behavior.

Stereotype suppression may seem to be a way to avoid prejudice, but it comes at a cost (Wegner, 1989). Suppressing stereotypes can produce a subsequent rebound in stereotype activation once the purposeful suppression has ceased, and this rebound has behavioral consequences. Macrae et al. (1994) asked participants to write about the typical day of a target person. Although the target was a member of a despised group (skinheads), some participants were urged to suppress their stereotypes of skinheads and not let them affect their responses on the task. Those who had been told to suppress the stereotype produced descriptions that were less stereotypical, suggesting that the instructions to suppress stereotypes were effective. Participants were then led to another room where they expected to meet the target person. The target was not there, but a jacket was left on one of the chairs to indicate where the target was seated. The participant was invited to sit down, and their choice of where to sit was recorded. Those participants who had suppressed stereotypes chose to sit further from the target's chair than did controls. Thus, in the behavioral component of the study, stereotype suppressors maintained greater social distance from the target individual than did nonsuppressors. The results suggest that the strategy of suppressing stereotypes in order to avoid prejudice may backfire.

Effects of Being Stereotyped

One important difference between cognitive psychology and social psychology is that the latter is concerned with the psychological processes of both the perceiver and target. Members of stereotyped groups often feel that their own failures or incompetence reflect not only on themselves but also on the group that they represent. This has been posited to produce fear and anxiety known as *stereotype threat* (Steele, 1997). For example, in one study African American and Euro-American students were given a verbal ability test under conditions that either did or did not evoke stereotype threat. Participants in the stereotype threat condition were told that the test would assess their intellectual ability; others were told that the test was still in development and would not assess their ability. Euro-American students did not score differently under these conditions, but African American students showed decreased performance under stereotype threat conditions. On a subsequent indirect test of stereotype activation, it was found that believing that intellect was being evaluated led African American students, but not Euro-American students, to increase activation of the stereotype of African Americans. Decreased performance due to stereotype threat has also been shown to occur for Euro-Americans when evaluated for natural athletic ability (Stone, Lynch, Sjomeling, & Darley, 1999) and for women when evaluated for mathematical ability (Spencer, Steele, & Quinn, 1999). An alternative explanation attributes these effects to expectations based on social identity rather than anxiety due to stereotype threat. Evidence for this view comes from findings that in some cases a stereotype may lead to improvements in performance. Asian American women show decreased performance on a math task when their gender identity is activated but improved performance when their ethnic identity is activated (Shih, Pittinsky, & Ambady, 1999). These participants appeared to be meeting the expectations of the stereotypes of women (poor at math) and Asians (good at math) depending on which aspect of their identity was made salient.

Stereotype activation can affect behavior of the perceiver, which in turn affects the person being perceived. For example, the studies by Bargh (Bargh et al., 1996; Bargh & Pietromonaco, 1982) reviewed earlier show that activating the African American stereotype can lead participants to behave in a more hostile manner. If upon meeting an African American, a Euro-American individual is more hostile because of automatic stereotype activation, the African American individual is likely to respond with increased hostility. Because the stereotype activation was unconscious, the Euro-American individual will not realize that his or her own hostility is increasing the hostility of the interaction, and thus may interpret the exchange as a confirmation of the negative stereotype. In this way, cognitive processes such as stereotype activation can produce behavioral confirmations that have important social consequences.

The "Social" in Social Cognition

In the past 20 years most research in social cognition has been based on a domain-general assumption that the same cognitive principles operate in social and nonsocial thought. Thus, social cognition has adopted many of the theories, methodologies, and debates of cognitive psychology. For example, extending earlier work by Rosch (Rosch & Lloyd, 1978), some have argued for a basic level in social categories (Brewer, Dull, & Lui, 1981; Cantor & Mischel, 1979). In addition, the field of social cognition has inherited cognitive psychology's theories and disagreements about representation. There is a general consensus that social concepts are not, as the classical view would have it, defined by sets of necessary and sufficient conditions for membership. Instead, some have taken a prototype, or abstraction-based, view of social concepts. For example, Park and Hastie (1987) have shown that people form abstractions from their experiences with a set of people and use these abstractions in social judgment. Alternatively, there is evidence that judgments about a group are affected by recent exposure to particular exemplars. These results are thought to support an exemplar account in which a category consists of specific instances that are stored in memory (Schwarz & Bless, 1992). Recently, associative network models have entered the social domain as well (Thagard & Kunda, 1998). Finally, theory theories, which represent concepts with causal theories, have been used to address conceptual combination in the social domain (Kunda, Miller, & Claire, 1990; Wittenbrink, Park, & Judd, 1998).

By applying cognitive psychology to social experience, early social cognition research offered a powerful new way to understand social phenomenon. The only drawback was that in many respects this approach neglected many social and emotional aspects of social experience and, in so doing, became isolated from other research in social psychology. In the 1985 edition of the *Handbook of Social Psychology,* Markus and Zajonc (1985, pp. 213–214) described social cognition as "a concerted effort to see if one could parsimoniously explain all the variance in cognitive terms *without* invoking such concepts as motives, values, affect, emotions, goals, incentives, fears, or rewards." They predicted that this restricted focus on cold cognition would be short-lived and destined to be replaced by an approach that addressed a wider range of these social and emotional factors.

Recent work has shown that social cognition is warming up. Many of the studies reviewed here assessed not only activation of concepts, but also the perceiver's motivations and impact of individual differences in prejudicial attitudes. Furthermore, it is becoming increasingly clear that social cognition must be integrated with the study of affect. More recent work, especially work on automaticity, assumes an integration of knowledge and feelings about a group. These developments not only distinguish social cognition from cognitive psychology but also keep social cognition relevant to the broader interests of social psychology.

ATTITUDES, PERSUASION, AND SOCIAL INFLUENCE

One of social psychology's primary contributions has been to show how social forces influence the behavior and attitudes of individuals. These forces may be so subtle that they are barely noticed, such as the social norms that dictate how close we stand to each other while talking, or they may be obnoxiously intrusive, such as a flashing banner advertisement on a Web page. Social influences on behavior are reviewed in the following section. We begin by examining why people conform, comply with requests, and obey orders. We then turn to social influences on attitudes, focusing in particular on the attempt to change people's attitudes through persuasion.

Conformity

One of the strongest social influences on behavior is the tendency to conform to social norms. Conformity carries negative connotations in Western culture (Markus, Kitayama, & Heiman, 1996), and there are many disturbing accounts of its harmful consequences; however, conformity is a normal part of social life that serves important social and psychological functions. In general, conforming behavior stems from either informational or normative social influences.

When uncertain about how to act, people often use the behavior of other people as a guide for their own behavior. This informational social influence offers people a way to manage ambiguous situations. A famous example of informational social influence comes from an early study by Sherif and Murphy (1936). In this study, participants experienced the autokinetic effect in which a stable point of light in a dark room appears to move. Participants first judged how far the light moved while they were alone, then while they were in groups, and then while they were alone again. In the first alone condition, participants' reports varied widely, with some participants seeing very little movement on average and others seeing a lot of movement. In the group condition, however, participants' judgments tended to converge on an intermediate and limited range of estimates. Participants were using the judgment of the group as a reference point for estimating the movement of the light. When participants were subsequently tested while alone, they retained the standards set by the group and did not return to their initial set points. Thus, conformity in this experiment did not seem to stem from the desire to respond in an acceptable way in front of the group (public compliance) but rather from a change in participants' beliefs about how far the light moved (private acceptance). As the informational model of conformity suggests, people are most likely to conform when they are uncertain, when the task is difficult, or when they are made to doubt their own competence (Coleman, Blake, & Mouton,

1958; Hochbaum, 1954; Tesser, Campbell, & Mickler, 1983).

In addition to its informational aspects, conforming serves social and psychological functions. Conforming leads to social acceptance; conversely, failure to conform can lead to disapproval or rejection (Schachter, 1951). Even when the group consists of strangers, people will often conform to it rather than risk disapproval (Tanford & Penrod, 1984). This was demonstrated by Asch's (1955) classic studies of group effects on judgments of line lengths. In these experiments, a participant was placed in a group of confederates, and members of the group were asked which of a set of lines was the same length as a standard line. Although the correct answer was obvious, when all of the confederates chose the same incorrect answer, the participant also chose that answer on about one third of the trials. Postexperimental interviews revealed that participants did not misperceive the length of the lines but went along with the group because they were afraid of looking foolish. In addition to this normative conformity, Asch also observed information-based conformity. The information of the group response was powerful enough to override some individual's judgments, leading them to report that they thought there must be something wrong with their eyes.

Additional studies have determined the conditions under which people are most likely to conform for social acceptance. Group cohesion is an important factor: People are less likely to conform when at least one other nonconformist is in the group (Nemeth & Chiles, 1988). People are also more likely to conform when their responses are public rather than private (Deutsch & Gerard, 1955). In addition, conformity increases with group size up to about four group members (Latane, 1981; Tanford & Penrod, 1984). Conformity also increases if the group is interdependent, that is, if they are trying to achieve a common goal for which they will all be rewarded (Deutsch & Gerard, 1955) or if the individual likes the group (Dittes & Kelly, 1956).

Several researchers have documented personality factors that make individuals more or less likely to conform. In general, people with low self-esteem or high need for approval from others are more subject to normative conformity (Crutchfield, 1955). Women are thought to be more subject to social influence than are men (Cooper, 1979; Nord, 1968), although Eagly and Carli (1981) argued that the gender difference is small and results from men's greater resistance to conformity in public responses (Eagly, Wood, & Fishbaugh, 1981).

Compliance and Obedience

Some social influences of conformity are quite indirect, such as the group influences just reviewed. Other social influences are quite direct, such as overt encouragement, suggestions or orders from authority figures. Studies of obedience and compliance have examined the social factors that influence how individuals respond to such requests. Milgram's (1963) initial obedience experiment revealed that people who thought they were participating in a study of learning were far more likely than expected to give what they believed were increasingly painful shocks to another participant who made repeated mistakes on a memorization task. Participants exhibited signs of extreme stress, and many protested; when prompted by the experimenter, however, 65% of participants continued through all 37 levels of shock, reaching the maximum shock on the generator before the experiment was ended. The remaining 35% of participants began to defy the experiment only at the 25th shock level (labeled "300 volts, Intense shock"), which was the level at which the confederate in the next room began pounding on the wall. Several factors

may have contributed to the unexpected obedience, including the authority of the experimenter (a scientist in a Yale laboratory), uncertainty about what behavior is appropriate in the novel situation of psychology experiments, and the absence of other participants to offer behavioral guidance. Subsequent variations on this experiment showed that obedience decreased when the experimenter's authority was undermined or when the participant observed another participant disobey the experimenter (Blass, 1991).

Since Milgram's (1963) initial experiments, a variety of other social factors have been shown to affect people's compliance (Cialdini, 1993; Cialdini & Trost, 1998). These factors can be grouped into three categories: aspects of the person making the request, aspects of the requested person, and aspects of their relationship. For example, if the person making the request is imbued with authority, people are more likely to acquiesce (Blass, 1991). In addition, people are more likely to comply if doing so is consistent with their own prior behavior (Pliner, Hart, Kohl, & Saari, 1974), or if doing so reciprocates a prior gift or favor given by the person making the request (Berry & Kanouse, 1987). All these factors are engaged by various social control techniques such as the "foot in the door" sales tactic in which the salesperson initially makes a small request and then increases the demand after the customer has made a commitment to comply (Beaman, Cole, Preston, Kentz, & Mehrkens Steblay, 1983).

Research on obedience and compliance has demonstrated that social situations are powerful determinants of the behavior of individuals, even if this behavior is inconsistent with their own values. Another important finding from this work is that the folk theories that people hold about obedience are often inaccurate. That is, people fail to predict accurately the extent to which others will obey, and they do not seem to understand the power of situational and social forces to determine behavior. This combination of susceptibility and inaccurate beliefs about the causes of social behavior underscores the importance of empirically investigating the sources and mechanisms of social control (cf. Nisbett & Wilson, 1977).

Historically, obedience to authority, threat of physical force, and intimidation have been common means to achieve social control by controlling individual behavior. A more common approach to social control in contemporary society is to influence people's behavior indirectly by altering their attitudes. Although this may be the dominant approach to social control in our time, McGuire (1985) argues that it has not always been. According to McGuire, although persuasion has been practiced throughout history, it has had been a primary means of social influence in only four eras: the Periclean Hellenic period, the last decades of the Roman republic, the humanistic Renaissance, and the current era of mass media. Only in these eras "has persuasion played so central an economic, social, and political role as to have become not just an art but an essential craft in whose rules of thumb the elite youth were trained and a recognized science with a systemized body of theory developed by savants" (McGuire, 1985, p. 233). Persuasion has become an essential craft and a big business, not because changing attitudes themselves are socially important, but because changing attitudes are thought to produce consequential changes in behavior, such as purchasing and voting decisions.

Attitude Function, Structure, and Formation

An *attitude* is an enduring positive or negative feeling toward some entity or issue. One can hold an attitude about almost anything, including concrete particulars (the cake you had on your birthday), categories (cake in general), abstract ideas (aging), or issues (mandatory retirement). In attitude research, commonly studied attitude objects include social policies, social entities such as groups or individuals, and behaviors. In this section we first review the components, functions, and development of attitudes themselves. We then turn to the topic of persuasion and the factors that determine whether attempts at persuasion will be effective.

The study of attitudes and social influence is central to research in social psychology. Allport (1935, p. 798) wrote that the attitude construct is "the most distinctive and indispensable concept in social psychology." Attitudes are important for several reasons. They are a pervasive aspect of mental and social life that influences perceptions and representations of quotidian events. They also influence behavior and decision making, at least under some conditions. Attitudes therefore determine not only purchasing and voting choices, but also other decisions that have far-reaching social, political, and economic consequences. Attitudes also serve as summary guides for knowledge about and reactions to classes of stimuli, and they reduce the effort and stress of decision making. Thus, understanding how attitudes are formed, how they function, and how they can be manipulated should therefore be of interest to cognitive as well as social psychologists.

Early researchers of attitude function posited that attitudes serve psychological needs (Katz, 1960). Various delineations of these functions have been proposed, but the current claim is that the primary function of attitudes is object appraisal (Eagly & Chaiken, 1998; Fazio, 1989; Greenwald, 1989). Attitudes allow people to determine efficiently whether the attitude object is good or bad with respect to the individual's interests. Additionally, attitudes have been characterized as serving three other functions: value-expressive, ego-defensive, and social adjustment. Attitudes serve the value-expressive function by giving the individual a way to satisfy his or her desire to express core values and aspects of self and thus to establish a clear self-concept (Katz, 1960). They serve the ego-defensive function, in keeping with the psychoanalytic tradition, by acting as defense mechanisms, as when people project negative feelings about the self onto racial out groups and thus are protected from threats to self-esteem. Finally, attitudes serve the social adjustment function (Smith, Bruner, & White, 1956) by contributing to social relationships. Adopting the attitudes of others tends to establish a positive relationship with those others, whereas expressing differing attitudes tends to diminish those relationships.

In order to predict better how attitudes may be changed or when they guide behavior, researchers have attempted to understand the structure of attitudes and attitudinal systems. One early approach was to divide attitudes and attitude-based responses into their cognitive, affective, and behavioral components (Katz & Stoteland, 1959; Rosenberg & Hovland, 1960). The cognitive component includes thoughts, beliefs, or knowledge about an attitude object, such as your knowledge about the ingredients of your mother's cookies. The affective component includes emotions that have been associated with the attitude object, such as the feelings you have had while eating your mother's cookies. The behavioral component includes associations between behavior, or behavioral intentions, and the attitude object, such as the action of eating your mother's cookies.

These different structural components of attitudes correspond generally to different means of attitude formation. For example, attitudes may develop from cognitive processing. This was assumed in earlier research on message-based persuasion, which argued that attitude change depends on attending to and comprehending the content of the persuasive message (Hovland, Janis, & Kelly, 1953). The hard sell approach in advertising attempts to change attitudes by giving people information about the attitude object, such as presenting a comparison chart listing features and prices of various computer systems. In addition, people may develop attitudes based on their knowledge of others' positive or negative experiences with the attitude object. This observational learning is tapped by advertisements that show an individual experiencing a positive outcome as a result of using some product (Petty & Cacioppo, 1981). Thus, individuals may develop a positive attitude about some model of car because they know about its amenities and low price and because they know someone who has one and likes it.

However, one may also develop a positive attitude toward a car (or any other object) because of the emotional experiences associated with it. Several studies have shown that pairing a neutral stimulus, such as words or slogans, with a pleasant or unpleasant unconditioned stimulus, such as shock, can lead people to develop more positive or negative attitudes toward the stimulus (Cacioppo, Uchino, et al., 1992; Staats, Staats, & Crawford, 1962). Additional studies have shown that attitudes can be conditioned outside of conscious awareness. Krosnick, Betz, Jussim, and Lynn (1992) showed photos of a person engaged in various activities. In one condition, these photos appeared immediately after subliminal presentation of photos that were known to produce positive or negative affect. The pairing affected participants' attitudes toward the person in the test pictures. The affective focus is stressed by Zajonc, who argued that attitudes stem from largely automatic affective responses toward some object that can emerge with little cognitive involvement, as may occur in mere exposure (Kunst-Wilson & Zajonc, 1980; Zajonc, 1980). In addition, attitudes are learned instrumentally from the experiences of reward and punishment. Children win approval by expressing attitudes that others hold, and thus they tend to develop approved attitudes. Studies have shown that attitudinal responses can be instrumentally conditioned during conversation. Attitudes that are rewarded with praise by an interviewer are expressed more (Hildum & Brown, 1956), and such conditioning affects attitudes when measured one week later (Insko, 1965).

Finally, attitudes may be derived from behavior. People will infer their attitudes from observations of their own behaviors as long as they attribute their behaviors to their own choices (Bem, 1972). In addition, attitudes that are discrepant with behavior may also be adjusted to better fit that behavior. This issue is discussed further in the section on cognitive consistency models of attitudes.

In addition to these cognitive, affective, and behavioral means of attitude formation, there are other sources of attitudes. For example, some research suggests that attitudes may have a genetic component (Hershberger, Lichtenstein, & Knox, 1994), namely, that through evolution humans have developed certain attitudes as adaptations to their environment (Buss & Schmitt, 1993). The various means of attitude formation described here are not exclusive, and a given attitude can be subject to multiple attitudinal influences (Cacioppo, Marshall-Goodell, Tassinary, & Petty, 1992; Tesser & Martin, 1996; T. Wilson, Lindsey, & Schooler, 2000; Zanna & Rempel, 1988). One of the interesting consequences of these myriad sources of an attitude is that individuals can be of two minds at once about an attitude object (Cacioppo & Berntson, 2001; T. Wilson et al., 2000). Cognitive consistency theorists were the first to entertain such a notion. We consider their perspective next.

Cognitive Consistency

The separation of attitudes into cognitive, affective, and behavioral components was thought to be useful not only for describing the different means of attitude formation but also for describing how these components are intertwined. The connections between cognition, affect, and behavior have been addressed by consistency theories of attitude. The basic claim of cognitive consistency theories is that people are motivated to achieve and maintain consistency in their behavior, knowledge, and attitudes, and that inconsistency in the cognitive representation leads to additional alterations in those representations (Festinger, 1957; Heider, 1958; Osgood & Tannenbaum, 1955). Feeling inconsistent attitudes simultaneously or behaving in a way that contradicts one's attitudes, for instance, can create an unstable and unpleasant state that motivates people to change in order to restore balance.

Several consistency theories, such as balance theory (Heider, 1958) and congruity theory (Osgood & Tannenbaum, 1955), have argued that humans seek internal consistency. The most influential consistency theory, however, is Festinger's (1957) cognitive dissonance theory. As in the balance and congruity theories, cognitive dissonance theory describes elements as "consistent" when one follows from the other (e.g., I like my pets and care for my pets) and "inconsistent" when knowledge of one predicts the opposite of the other (e.g., I travel for extended periods and neglect my pets). In addition, two elements may be irrelevant if knowledge of one tells you nothing about what to expect of the other (e.g., I like pets; airfare to Egypt is low). Cognitive dissonance occurs when elements are inconsistent and no "neutralizing" cognitions are available. For example, if one behaves in a way that is inconsistent with one's attitudes, dissonance is neutralized if the individual believes he or she had no choice in the behavior (Linder, Cooper, & Jones, 1967; Sherman, 1970), if the individual is able to deny the behavior (J. Brehm & Cohen, 1962; Riess

& Schlenker, 1977), or if the behavior did not harm anybody any other parties (Calder, Ross, & Insko, 1973; Collins & Hoyt, 1972; Goethals & Cooper, 1975). Dissonance occurs when one feels responsible for an action that is personally significant and leads to predictable negative consequences.

People are motivated to reduce cognitive dissonance because it is unpleasant (Elliot & Devine, 1994; Losch & Cacioppo, 1990). Zanna and Cooper (1974) argued that cognitive dissonance is an arousing state and that attitudes change in order to decrease arousal. In a test of this hypothesis, Losch and Cacioppo found that cognitive dissonance was associated with increased sympathetic tonus, but they also demonstrated that the resulting attitude change was driven by negative affect rather than feelings of arousal. Elliot and Devine (1994) conceptually replicated these findings in a study of dissonance reduction in which each student wrote an essay supporting the contrary of his initial position on a personally important issue. When the students were unable to engage in dissonance reduction, they reported more emotional discomfort than when they were able to do so.

As with all consistency theories, dissonance theory predicts that there are multiple ways of restoring consonance, and which means are employed depends on which are the least resistant to change. To restore cognitive consistency, a person can change one of the dissonant elements, add new elements that are consonant, or reduce the personal importance of the elements (Festinger, 1957). In addition, engaging in self-affirmation can reduce the effects of cognitive dissonance, suggesting that self-affirmation may be another means of dissonance reduction (Steele, 1988).

Dissonance theory still attracts attention because it makes such counterintuitive predictions about attitude change. Most notably, low compensation, mild threat, and high effort were predicted to have stronger effects on attitude change, but dissonance theory explains why the surprising opposite is found: High compensation, strong threat, or low effort actually tend to inhibit attitude change. In a classic study, Festinger and Carlsmith (1959) had participants perform several tedious tasks and then offered each participant either one or twenty dollars to convince a waiting participant that the tasks were interesting and fun. All participants then rated how interesting they found the task. A basic prediction of cognitive dissonance theory is that after people lie about the task, they will then rate it as more interesting in order to reduce cognitive dissonance. Festinger and Carlsmith predicted that it would be easier for participants to rationalize their actions when they were paid twenty dollars than when they were paid only one dollar, and thus cognitive dissonance would be stronger in the low-compensation case. Consistent with this prediction, they found that those who received low compensation rated the task as more interesting than did those who received high compensation. Although an instrumental view of attitudes would suggest that stronger rewards lead to greater attitude change, cognitive dissonance theory predicts the opposite under certain conditions.

An alternative to cognitive dissonance theory is impression management theory. This theory argues that people are motivated to ensure that others see them favorably and that people sometimes develop new attitudes or change their existing attitudes in order to make a good impression on others (Arkin, 1981; Baumeister, Cooper, & Skib, 1979). Whereas cognitive dissonance theory argues that people change attitudes because of an internal tension, impression management theory argues that whether people need to be internally consistent, the outward appearance of inconsistency can undermine social approval (Schlenker & Forsyth, 1980; Tedeschi, Schlenker, & Bonoma, 1971). As a result, people are motivated to reduce public inconsistency by expressing attitudes that are consistent with their public behavior.

Belief Structure

Early research on the cognitive and logical bases of attitudes argued that attitudes arise from systems of beliefs, and that in order to change an attitude, it is necessary to change beliefs. Within this theory, belief systems are viewed as interconnected syllogistic networks (McGuire, 1960; Wyer, 1974; Wyer & Goldberg, 1970). These networks may have a vertical structure, as when beliefs serve as premises for an inferred conclusion, or horizontal structure, as when the same conclusion can follow from multiple syllogisms. Belief structures that have an extensive horizontal structure are less susceptible to change because many syllogisms must be violated before the conclusion is no longer valid. Several syllogistic models of belief structure and change have been proposed to predict the probability that people will draw certain conclusions, given the probabilities that they associate with given premises (McGuire, 1960; Wyer, 1974; Wyer & Goldberg, 1970). This work has revealed the operation of both cognitive and affective factors. McGuire (1960), for instance, argued that in addition to the logical consistency of the arguments, conclusions are affected also by their hedonic consistency, or the degree to which the arguments are consistent with what the individual desires. Prone to "wishful thinking," people tend to overestimate the probability of conclusions that are desirable and underestimate the probability of conclusions that are undesirable. In an illustrative study, McGuire had participants estimate the probability and desirability of the premises and conclusions comprising several syllogisms. He found evidence that both logical and hedonic factors influenced estimates of conclusion probabilities. Further studies have shown that hedonic factors are relatively more important for participants who are less

intelligent or less educated (Dillehay, Insko, & Smith, 1966; Watts & Holt, 1970). The early demonstration in the attitudes domain of cognitive and affective processes working hand in glove to produce mentation and behavior is noteworthy in light of attempts in the past two decades to show the independence of affect and cognition (Zajonc, 1980).

Persuasion

An enormous amount of research has been conducted to determine how attitudes change in response to persuasive appeals (e.g., a political speech, or the presence of a swoosh logo on the jerseys of professional athletes). The ELM (Petty & Cacioppo, 1981, 1986), described earlier in the discussion of social stereotypes, was developed as an overarching framework to synthesize the various and often conflicting results in persuasion research. As noted, the ELM proposes two routes to attitude change. The first is a central route, which is used when an individual gives thoughtful consideration to presented information. This increased scrutiny need not be dispassionate or veridical, however. Prior attitudes, for instance, can bias information processing (e.g., Cacioppo & Petty, 1979; Pomerantz, Chaiken, & Tordesillas, 1995). In contrast, the second route is a peripheral route, whereby rather than scrutinize the message content or engage in issue-relevant thinking, the individual is influenced by a peripheral cue such as the attractiveness or celebrity of the person delivering the message (e.g., Puckett, Petty, Cacioppo, & Fischer, 1983). The ELM postulates that people are motivated to form accurate attitudes, but that the degree of elaboration, or issue-relevant thinking, in which they engage can vary across individuals and situations. Thus, three variables interact to determine the effectiveness of any attempt at persuasion: the message content, the peripheral cues, and elaboration likelihood (Petty & Cacioppo, 1986).

The degree of elaboration that people use to process a message depends on several factors, including how distracted they are (Petty et al., 1976), how knowledgeable they are (W. Wood, Kallgren, & Preisler, 1985), and how they tend to engage in effortful thought (need for cognition, or NFC; cf. Cacioppo, Petty, Feinstein, & Jarvis, 1996). When elaboration is low, people are less affected by the quality of the arguments in the message and more affected by peripheral cues. Peripheral cues may include anything apart from the content of the arguments that might indicate whether the message is agreeable or not. Credibility, likeability, and attractiveness of the source have been shown to serve as powerful cues (Chaiken, 1980; Petty, Cacioppo, & Goldman, 1981), and advertisements commonly use spokespeople that have these features. In addition, the number of arguments contained in a message may serve as a cue to argument strength (Petty & Cacioppo, 1984).

Consequences of Routes to Persuasion

The ELM provided clarity to a field that had been muddied with inconsistent findings and questions about whether attitudes predicted behavior. These inconsistencies were resolved by showing that factors such as the source, message, recipient, and modality did not exert main effects on persuasion but rather that their effects depended on processing routes. Not only did the ELM specify the conditions under which a single variable (e.g., source credibility) acted in a particular way (e.g., as a persuasion cue), but it also specified differential consequences of beliefs and attitudes achieved through the central versus peripheral route: Attitudes formed via the central route were predicted to be more persistent, resistant to counterpersuasion, and predictive of behavior than were attitudes formed via the peripheral route (Petty & Cacioppo, 1981, 1986).

Attitudes, Persuasion, and Behavior

The relation between attitudes and behavior is a critically important issue in research on attitudes and persuasion. Originally, social psychologists defined attitudes as behavioral tendencies, thus assuming that attitudes predicted behavior (Allport, 1924). The attitude-behavior link appeared to be violated in LaPiere's (1934) famous demonstration that when asked over the phone whether they would offer service to a Chinese couple, many businesses said they would not, but when confronted with Chinese customers, most had offered the service (Wicker, 1969). Although the attitude behavior mismatch was probably exaggerated by the design of this study, which did not ensure that the individuals who responded to the attitude question were the same individuals who met the Chinese couple, it prompted a surge of research on the link between attitudes and behaviors. Several additional studies have shown that even within the same individuals, attitudes do not always predict behavior, thus calling into question the value of the attitude construct itself (Ajzen & Fishbein, 1977).

The attitude-behavior link depends both on the attitudes themselves and on the situation. Behavior is constrained by situations, and if the situation limits the range of behaviors but not the range of attitudes, there will be a mismatch between attitudes and behavior (Ajzen & Fishbein, 1977; Fazio & Roskos-Ewoldsen, 1994). However, the degree to which situations constrain the behavioral expression of attitudes may be limited by the tendency for people to seek situations in which attitudes and behavior can peacefully coincide, and being in these situations may strengthen the attitude (DeBono & Snyder, 1995). Thus, situations constrain attitudes, but attitudes may determine which situations are chosen.

The relation between behavior and the central and peripheral routes to persuasion was examined in a study of voting behavior

(Cacioppo, Petty, Kao, & Rodriguez, 1986). It was predicted that individuals higher in NFC (an index of individual differences in enjoyment of and willingness to engage in effortful thought) would rely more on central processing routes, and that this would have implications for their behavior. In this study, students who were high or low in NFC listened to either strong or weak arguments for a tuition increase. Those who heard weak arguments generated more unfavorable thoughts than did those who heard strong ones, and this difference was greater for the high-NFC group than for the low-NFC group. In addition, argument quality had a stronger impact on the subsequent attitudes of the high-NFC group than of the low. In a separate study of voting behavior, it was found that the pre-election attitudes were a better predictor of subsequently reported voting behavior for high-relative to low-NFC participants. These findings were consistent with the ELM's prediction that attitudes formed through effortful elaboration are more predictive of behavior than are those formed through more heuristic processes.

Several features of attitudes also determine whether they will predict behavior. For example, attitudes formed out of experience are more likely to predict behavior than are those formed indirectly. In addition, attitude strength is an important factor. Stronger attitudes are more likely to predict behavior (Petkova, Ajzen, & Driver, 1995). "Strength" may refer to extremity or intensity (how strong one's emotional response is to some attitude object), the attitude's importance to the individual, knowledge (how much is known about the attitude object) and accessibility (how easily the attitude or the attitude object comes to mind; Crano, 1995; Kraus, 1995; Krosnick, Boninger, Chuang, Berent, & Carnot, 1993). Another determinant of the attitude-behavior link is attitude specificity. The attitude and behavior link is strongest when attitude and behavior are assessed at comparable levels of specificity. In LaPiere's (1934) study, the attitude and behavior were assessed at different levels: The questionnaire asked how the managers felt about serving Chinese couples in general, but the behavior was a response to a particular Chinese couple (Fazio & Roskos-Ewoldsen, 1994).

Attitudes toward stimuli provide evaluations of desirability for a given outcome. The strength of attitudes sets priorities and goals. In the following section we discuss how motivation and emotion energize and direct social behavior toward desired goals and away from aversive outcomes.

THE AFFECT SYSTEM: ENERGIZING AND DIRECTING BEHAVIOR

The terms *"motivation"* and *"emotion"* both share an etymology in the Latin root "movere," meaning "to move." In social contexts, motivations and emotions guide and direct human interaction, moving individuals toward situations that are desirable or appetitive, and away from situations that are unappealing, threatening, or aversive. In the following section we discuss social motivations such as the desire to belong to a group, how the presence of a group influences individual behavior, and the contrast between internally motivated and externally motivated goals. In the subsequent section we review the adaptive value of emotions in guiding behavior, with special attention to various models of emotion.

Social Motivation

Motivation in its broadest sense has been used in the psychological literature to explain action and reaction in animal behavior. Motivations are what impel an animal to act, to move toward or away from presented stimuli.

When applied to a human context, the term *motivation* encompasses both a disposition toward a goal and any goal-directed behavior. In this section, the use of the term highlights the social motivations of people interacting within complex cultural and communicative contexts.

One class of social motivations begins at the level of the individual, that is, with a particular individual holding the goal of initiating and maintaining contact with other individuals. Individual motivations include desires for attachment and belonging, as well as desires to avoid exclusion from the social group. These types of individual motivations are subsumed under the topic of affiliation and social embeddedness.

A second class of social motivations is forged from collaborative processes between two (or more) individuals in a group. In some instances, when an individual attempts to merge with a group, the desires of the individual are adapted or refined to meet the needs of the other group members. Ways in which the group can influence the motivation of an individual include effects such as social facilitation and social loafing. (Related issues such as conformity are addressed in the section on persuasion.) In other instances, as social groups form, the involvement of the individual interacts with the goals of others, for example, in assertions of cooperation and responsibility toward others, expectations and accountability, and helping or altruism. These types of motivations are subsumed under the umbrella of group dynamics.

Individuals do not always meet their goals, either because of limitations imposed by membership in a group or by other situational factors, so a third class of motivations arise as individuals develop patterns of responses to challenge and failure. These types of motivations include the topics of reactance, control, learned helplessness, intrinsic and extrinsic motivation, and mastery, which will be collectively addressed under the heading of control.

Affiliation and Embeddedness

People are motivated to be part of a group and to achieve a station in the social hierarchy where they can maintain a balance of contribution and personal benefit. Among the motivations driving social behavior, therefore, are affiliative motivations such as attachment and belonging, and aversive or avoidant motivations such fear of social ostracism or anxiety about exclusion from the group.

Attachment

Attachment is a lasting affective relationship between an infant and a caregiver (Bowlby, 1969). It is a social, biologically mediated need that usually motivates an individual during infancy to bond with a parent. A reciprocal type of attachment motivates the caregiver to bond with the infant. Evolutionarily, such biological safeguards would ensure both survival and reproductive advantages to the infants.

Behaviorist explanations of mother-infant bonding explained attachment as resulting from positive associations with the mother during feeding, but Harlow's (1958, 1961) experiments raising infant monkeys in isolation demonstrated that the need for social attachment and the reassurance of physical contact is independent of the satisfaction of basic physical drives such as satisfying hunger or thirst. In these experiments, Harlow provided infant monkeys with two types of "surrogate" mothers, one made of wire and one made of a padded wooden frame. Even in conditions where the wire surrogate mother provided milk for the infant (by means of a bottle attached to the wire frame), the infant preferred physical contact with the soft-covered surrogate, clinging to it, rubbing its face against it, and running to it when the infant was startled. Even though the soft-covered surrogate mother did not provide interactive or affirmative social responses, the infants were physically healthier if they were allowed contact with the soft surrogate mothers. Recent research confirms the need for touch in human infants, showing that infants born prematurely have a higher survival rate and tend to gain weight more quickly if they are touched or held (Field, 1995; Harrison, 2000; Reite, 1990). Furthermore, lack of attachment is linked to a variety of ill effects on health, adjustment, and well-being (Maestripieri, 2001).

Attachment is important not only to ensure the physical health of infants but also to provide a basis of social safety in which the infant could can learn adaptive, nonthreatening ways to explore the environment, eventually developing self-confidence, autonomy, and a style of interacting in the world. In order to investigate caregiver-child interactions, Ainsworth et al. (1978) developed the strange situation procedure, in which an infant or toddler is left in the care of concerned but unfamiliar adults while the caregiver leaves the room for a short period of time. Experimenters observe the child and note his or her responses, which might include sadness, anxiety, or fear as the caregiver leaves, happier behavior when the caregiver returns, and more confident and active exploration of the environment in the presence of the caregiver. This controlled setting provided an experimental means to compare different types of attachment styles. Through this research, three fundamental attachment styles were analyzed: secure, avoidant, and anxious/ambivalent (Ainsworth, Blehar, Waters, & Wall, 1978). The secure attachment style was defined as most supportive or beneficial to infant development, but subsequent research on parenting styles and other environmental factors has indicated that infants exhibiting avoidant or anxious attachment styles may be exercising adaptive mechanisms that help

them to survive in a more hostile or insensitive environment (Hinde, 1982; Lamb, Thompson, Gardner, & Charnov, 1985).

Extending Attachment Theory to Adult Behaviors

The patterns of attachment acquired during infancy may become incorporated into mental models of the self and therefore correlate to the attachment styles that the individual exercises in bonding relationships in adulthood (Hazan & Shaver, 1987, 1994a, 1994b; Shaver, Hazan, & Bradshaw, 1988). Emotions such as romantic love provide the motivational basis that maintains the pair bond (Shaver et al., 1988). Many of these attachment motivations may be mediated by neurochemical responses between parents and offspring or between pair-bonding adults, if the research using prairie voles as an animal model for attachment can be extended to nonhuman and human primates (Insel, 1997; Young, Wang, & Insel, 1998). This research has not yet been extended to humans, but pheromone research in nursing mothers suggest a possible neurobiological contribution to social attachment in humans (McClintock, 1998).

Belonging

In addition to being motivated to form close familial attachments with other individuals, people seem to seek affiliations, alliances, and social identities. Early research in social psychology found that the mere presence of others can be comforting and that human companionship is preferred more when an individual is facing a potentially frightening event (Schachter, 1959). People also seem to be motivated to feel a sense of belonging to larger social groups or other affiliative social networks. Baumeister and Leary (1995) suggested that the definition of belonging necessarily includes frequent personal contacts, free from conflict and negative affect, and a perceived bond marked by stability, affective concern, and a sense of connected future. This definition of belongingness extends beyond perfunctory social contact and, importantly, requires a degree of emotional involvement and responsibility or concern for the welfare of others. The social bond, however lax or strong it may be, must be mutual in order to fulfill an individual's social motivation. If the bond is unilateral or is not equally reciprocal, the individual's sense of belongingness may not be fulfilled. Recent studies on the association between social support and physiological functioning (for a review, see Uchino, Cacioppo, & Keicolt-Glaser, 1996) also underscore the important role of belongingness.

Further support for the importance of belongingness is found in the research on in groups and out groups. People feel positively toward members of their own in group and will treat in-group members preferentially (Tajfel, 1982). In-group biases are pervasive, influential, and, sometimes, unconscious. What is most surprising about the in-group effect is that it takes so little to define an in group. Even in the blatantly arbitrary case of random assignment to a group, an individual's self-identification and sense of belongingness will solidify a group identity, including the projection of animosity toward the arbitrarily-defined out group, with very enduring effects in some circumstances. This was demonstrated early in social research in the now classic Robbers Cave study, in which the organizers of a boys' summer camp randomly assigned the camp participants to one of two groups. The group differences existed in name only, but the social division and the persistent animosity that developed between the two groups extended well beyond the duration of the summer camp (Sherif, Harvey, White, Good, & Sherif, 1961). This research and the volumes of research that have accrued since then on in-group influences indicate that the sense of belongingness provided by group membership can supercede any other functional needs for which the group may have been originally formed.

Social Exclusion as a Basis for Anxiety

As noted in an epithet attributed to the economist John Maynard Keynes (1936), "In the long run, we are all dead." Because humans have consciously accessible long-term memories and the ability to represent future possible scenarios, individuals eventually come to acknowledge their own mortality. This individual realization contradicts a necessarily strong evolutionary drive for survival, and the contradiction of the desire for life and the knowledge of inescapable death have been hypothesized, within the paradigm of terror management theory, to form the basis of a deep state of anxiety, which people are constantly, unconsciously, seeking to redress (Greenberg et al., 1990; Pyszczynski, Greenberg, & Solomon, 1999; Rosenblatt, Greenberg, Solomon, Pyszczynski, & Lyon, 1989). The data supporting terror management theory can be redescribed in the context of social isolation, where the basis of fear of death is separation from friends and family, a very deep-seated and unconscious form of social exclusion (Barden, Garber, Leiman, Ford, & Masters, 1985; Leary, 1990).

Terror management theory is controversial, but the prevalence of conscious, immediate forms of social anxiety, such as fears of doing something socially inappropriate or publicly embarrassing, is a negative and painful mental state that is felt by all individuals at some time. These painful experiences can have beneficial effects because they play a role in social reinforcement and maintaining group cohesion, and they foster balance between the motivation to pursue self-interests and the motivation to pursue collective interests. The uncomfortable emotional state of anxiety interrupts the individual's behavior and focuses the individual's attention on his or her current action, inducing a comparison between current behavior to expected social norms and potential future states of social disapproval for aberrant behavior, which in turn motivates a search for alternative, more socially approved behaviors (Baumeister & Tice, 1990). The social function of this form of anxiety is an aspect of self-monitoring and self-presentation as discussed previously in the section on self. Disappointing one's close others may also lead to the experience of other corrective motivations in the form of social emotions, such as guilt, remorse, or shame. The development of these complex social emotions seems to support the case that social isolation is one of the deepest human fears.

Group Dynamics

Individuals feel drawn to belong in groups, but the presence of others affects the behavior of the individual in a variety of ways. In this section we briefly discuss a few of these effects: social facilitation and inhibition, and expectations and accountability.

Social Facilitation

Sometimes the presence of a group or an audience can impel individuals to try their best. This topic, in fact, is the basis for one of the first articles published in the field of social psychology: In 1898, Triplett published a study in the *American Journal of Psychology* noting that competition among sports cyclists improved individual performance (Triplett, 1898). This initial paper was followed shortly by a study of children engaging in a task of reeling in a fishing line. Tripplet found that children reeled in fishing line faster when performing the task with other children compared to performing the task alone. Subsequent research found that fellow participants or an audience did not always exert a positive influence on individual behavior. The pres-

ence of others sometimes improved and sometimes impaired performance. Zajonc (1965) provided an explanation for these conflicting results in his social facilitation theory, which posited that the presence of others facilitated performance on simple tasks and impaired performance on complex tasks. He further argued that social facilitation was not uniquely human, and there is now a large literature supporting this effect across cultures and species. There is less agreement, however, about the mechanism underlying social facilitation in humans. Although Zajonc reasoned that the effect was mediated by arousal, other explanations, such as evaluation apprehension (Cottrell, Wack, Sekerak, & Rittle, 1968; Henchy & Glass, 1968; Seta, Crisson, Seta, & Wang, 1989; Seta & Hassan, 1980) and distraction-conflict (Baron, 1986; Mansted & Semin, 1980), have also been proposed.

Social Loafing

Even before the publication of Triplett's study, researchers noted that groups may have a variable influence on individual behavior. In a study that actually predated Triplett's report, but which was not published until later, Rigelmann (reported in Kravitz & Martin, 1986) found that individuals in a rope-pulling task pulled less hard when working as members of a group than when they were pulling as individuals. This observation eventually became incorporated into a literature on social loafing, in which individuals apparently lose motivation in the presence of a group (Latane, Williams, & Harkins, 1979). Harkins and Szymanski (1988, 1989) found that individuals tried to match their behavior to the believed standard of the group and did not strive beyond that standard. In the case of social loafing, the individual conserves his own energy, enjoying the benefits of group success without overexerting himself. The individual becomes a "free rider." There is also social pressure to maintain a reduced effort within a group, because any individual contributing comparatively more than his peers will be viewed as a "sucker," foolishly carrying more than his own weight.

Social loafing was thought to be a purely motivational issue, but recent research has explored the role of disinterest and attention in social loafing. If individuals are able to make the personal, social, or collective standards of the group more salient, they become more engaged in the group effort. For example, Williams, Harkins, and Latane (1981) found that if information about the output of each individual in the group is made known to the other group members, social loafing disappears, implying that self-presentational goals become foremost. Harkins and Jackson (1985), however, found that if a task engages an individual's interest, social loafing disappears. Harkins and Petty (1982) found that individuals do not loaf when they believe that they can make a unique contribution to the group.

Intrinsic motivation also mitigates social loafing. Petty, Cacioppo, and Kasmer (1987; cited in Cacioppo et al., 1996) reasoned that if individuals high in NFC—that is, individuals who tend to engage in and enjoy effortful thinking (Cacioppo & Petty, 1982)—are more intrinsically motivated to engage in effortful cognitive endeavors, then they should be less likely to loaf socially on a cognitive task than would individuals low in NFC. To test this hypothesis, participants performed a brainstorming task (generating uses for objects) after they were led to believe that they were individually responsible or that they were part of a group that was responsible for performing the task. Results revealed a significant interaction showing that participants low in NFC generated fewer ideas under group than under individual conditions (i.e., they socially loafed), whereas individuals high in NFC generated equally high numbers of ideas regardless of social condition. For compari-

son purposes, another group of participants performed a physical task (screwing and unscrewing bolts and nuts) under individual or group instructions. Results revealed only a significant main effect for the social condition group, showing greater loafing by participants high and low in NFC. Thus, only participants high in NFC working on cognitively challenging tasks failed to show the motivational deficit that usually results from shared responsibility. The beneficial effects of such types of intrinsic motivation are further addressed later.

Control

Action toward a goal may not always be successful or unimpaired. Motivations for competence and control provide explanations that relate actions and efforts toward goals, even when those goals are thwarted or progress toward a goal is impeded.

Control Motivation

Control is the perception or belief that one can influence potential outcomes. If an individual cannot control the outcome of an event, there may be an option to exercise a secondary form of control, such as redefining the desired outcome or devaluing the perceived need for an unattainable goal (Folkman, 1984). Secondary forms of control may not be as initially gratifying, but the redefinition of a goal permits an active coping strategy that allows the continued motivational interest to be maintained.

If an individual has had previous experience with a similar situation that was at least moderately challenging and rewarding, control motivations will be activated, and the individual will have some expectation to succeed in the current task. However, if an individual is engaged only in endeavors that are not rewarding, such as performing tasks that are either too easy or are impossible, need for control will not be activated, and motivation will not be engaged (J. Brehm, 1993).

The feeling of control can be such a motivating force that individuals can create illusions of control. For example, the statistical odds of winning a raffle or lottery are defined by the parameters of the design of the lottery, such as number of tickets purchased and the method of randomly drawing a single winner, yet some individuals believe that they will have a better chance of winning if they pick the lottery numbers themselves compared to being randomly assigned a number, even though the statistical odds of winning are unchanged by this manipulation (Langer, 1975).

If one is deprived of an aspect of control, the state of deprivation itself is an uncomfortable and motivating state. Reactance theory describes the motivation to regain control over the environment. When an established freedom is threatened, individuals react and are motivated to regain and reinstate the freedom. When freedom is lost, there is an increased interest or valuation of lost freedom (J. Brehm, 1966; S. Brehm & Brehm, 1981). The motivation for control has been found in children as young as two years old (S. Brehm & Weinraub, 1977), as well as in animals (Kavanau, 1967).

It is important to note the wide range of individual differences in the amount of control people require to feel secure in a given context (Burger, 1993). These individual differences highlight the complementary roles of emotion and cognition in determining social motivation. The role of emotion is important because the impetus for behavior lies in the assessment or evaluation of a situation. The role of cognition is important because the evaluation of a situation requires the faculties of learning, memory, affective judgments, and decision making. People have the ability to choose their own goals, revalue selected goals, and redefine what it means to be successfully moving toward a goal. The interaction of these

factors makes the context of human social interaction especially complex.

Learned Helplessness

Having control over a social situation or environment is not always possible. In many situations, social or otherwise, individuals are faced with uncomfortable circumstances over which they seem to have no control. Inducing control-deprived situations in humans in a laboratory setting would likely be either ineffective or unethical, so research in this area of social motivation has been inspired by investigations of the behavior of nonhuman animals. An influential line of research investigated the circumstances that lead to a loss of motivation. In these experiments, dogs were exposed to inescapable electric shocks. Later, the dogs were placed in a new situation in which they could engage in behavior that would stop the shocks from occurring. However, because they had been helpless in the earlier trials of the experiment, the dogs did not try to escape or engage in avoidance behaviors (Abramson, Seligman, & Teasdale, 1978; Seligman, 1975). Research on learned helplessness has been very influential, especially in extending to models of human depression. This productive line of investigation has also developed into an exploration of models of successful coping, or "learned optimism" (Seligman & Csikszentmihalyi, 2000; Seligman, Reivich, Jaycox, & Gillham, 1995).

Some research has questioned whether the earliest investigations on adult domesticated animals in a laboratory setting would extend to humans in social developmental contexts (Wortman & Brehm, 1975). There was even some question whether the findings would generalize to other nonhuman animals in natural settings: "Anyone who is familiar with the inventiveness of animals in their natural habitat would also have had doubts about the [learned helplessness] model; trying to keep raccoons out of the trash or squirrels out of the bird feeders can be a sobering experience" (J. Brehm, 1993, p. 9). The data produced by research in the area of learned helplessness may also be open to alternative explanations, including motivations other than helplessness or by conflicting motivations, such a being in a state of maximal uncertainty, in which case the uncertainty would extinguish motivation, not a perceived lack of control.

Other researchers have noted that a lack of motivation can be adaptive. Klinger (1975) observed that disengagement from an unproductive effort avoids increased arousal and increased psychological stress. The defining issue then becomes at what level a threshold of effort is established. If motivation is extinguished early, then learning is arrested prematurely, but if an individual perseverates in an ineffective effort, then more beneficial strategies may be ignored.

Intrinsic and Extrinsic Motivation

Intrinsic and extrinsic motivation describes one's perspective, orientation, or motive for engaging in a task. When individuals engage in activities of variable duration, such as preparing a meal, finishing college, or raising a child, individuals may be most motivated by *extrinsic* forces (attaining the final goal), or they may be motivated by *intrinsic* enjoyment of the process itself. The value of extrinsic motivations, formed through the external contingencies of rewards and punishments, has clear parallels in animal models, but intrinsic motivation may play a larger role in human motivation, recruiting the cognitive services of memory, planning, and decision making in the service of emotional gratification. Feelings of competence, self-determination, control, and effectiveness are emotional states that are rewards in themselves, providing the basis for persisting in the pursuit of long-term goals (Deci, 1975; Deci & Ryan, 1985; Diener & Dweck, 1978; Dweck, 1975,

1999; Dweck & Leggett, 1988; Sansone & Harackiewicz, 2000; White, 1959; Woodworth, 1921), as are novelty, creativity, entertainment value, and the satisfaction of curiosity (Amabile, 1979, 1983; Csikszentmihalyi, 1975, 1991). This area of research established the basis for theories of intrinsic motivation.

Both extrinsic and intrinsic motivations can be simultaneously active. An interesting finding in this context is that intrinsic motivation can be dampened or extinguished if the extrinsic motivation is made most salient (Lepper & Greene, 1978). Thus, a task that is intrinsically enjoyable can be made less interesting if the exterior rewards offered for engaging in the activity are disproportionately high, as found in studies of college students (Deci, 1971) and in studies with preschool children (Lepper, Greene, & Nisbett, 1973). This overjustification effect has been extended to describe the aversive influences of other external constraints, such as lack of choice, surveillance, or deadlines (for a review, see Boggiano & Pittman, 1992). Levels of self-esteem, perhaps relating to attachment styles, also interact with motivational strategies. Secure or self-confident individuals, for instance, may be less easily deterred by exterior pressures or initial failures (Dweck, 1999).

Effectance/Mastery

One of the earliest and most influential papers on social motivation was a response to the drive-reduction theories of behaviorism and the unconscious motivations proposed by psychoanalytic theory. In "Motivation Reconsidered," White (1959, p. 297) proposed the notion of competence, which he defined as "the organism's capacity to interact effectively with its environment." This drive for competence, which inspired effectance theory, is a proactive control motivation with the intrinsic rewards of mastery and growth.

In adult development this concept has been extended to describe a mastery-focus for personal improvement (Elliot & Harackiewicz, 1994).

Motivations are often successful because they work in the face of failure. This question becomes most salient in the context of child development, where the infant's initial attempts, such as reaching, standing up, or walking, for example, are certainly not successful, but the behavioral efforts are not extinguished. For this reason, White's work on effectance motivation has been especially influential in developmental psychology. Effectance motivation and mastery motivation have been used to evaluate and classify different styles for the way infants explore and make sense of their world, by manipulating external objects, responding to individuals, and reacting to obstacles and impairments to their interactive goals (Caplovitz, Barrett, & Morgan, 1995; MacTurk, Morgan, & Jennings, 1995). Recent research in this area of mastery motivation focuses on the role of constituent processes such as the selection of goals, engagement, and interest, as well as individual differences in these approaches (MacTurk & Morgan, 1995). The reader may also recognize that social motivation is an underpinning of theories of the self and self-regulation (reviewed earlier), as discrepancies between actual and desired states have both social causes and social consequences.

Caveats Regarding Human and Nonhuman Animal Models

Numerous behaviors that encompass social motivations have been studied in nonhuman species. Some basic social motivations, such as attachment, dominance hierarchies, cooperation, group dynamics, and social facilitation, are clearly evident in nonhuman species (Carter, Lederhendler, & Kirkpatrick, 1997). In addition, motivation for control is attributed to dogs based on studies of learned helplessness (Seligman, 1975) and to white footed mice based on observational studies (Kavanau, 1967). Whether human-like social motivations and emotions can be found in various nonhuman species depends on the social complexity and representational capacity of the species. Although it might seem reasonable to assume that species that are closest to each other genetically would also have similar social motivations and emotions, often this is not the case. For example, prairie voles (*Microtus ochrogaster*) are extremely social and form monogamous pair bonds, whereas the closely related montane voles (*Microtus montanus*) live in relative isolation and are not monogamous. Thus, phylogenetic similarity does not imply similarity in social behavior. Social behavior is not unique in this regard. No single species provides the best animal model for all physiological questions, either.

The effects of complex cognition, higher order reasoning, and language on social motivation shape not only phylogenetic gradations in motivational theory, but also ontological gradations. In a developmental continuum, some aspects of social motivation, such as early attachment, may be heavily predetermined by biology, whereas other aspects depend more heavily on learning and memory and emerge later in development. These caveats about phylogeny and ontogeny also extend to the following section on emotions, in which emotions such as embarrassment and shame may have less direct analogs in nonhuman animals than do fear and disgust.

Emotion

We noted in the prior section that motivations are often successful because they work in the face of failure feedback. Success feedback tends to be associated with positive emotional states, and failure feedback tends to be associated with negative emotional states.

Interestingly, in this context negative emotions have also been associated with increased attentional and more effortful cognitive processing as individuals attempt to resolve, adapt, or respond to the negative circumstance, whereas positive emotions have been associated with relatively little change in attentional or cognitive processing as individuals try to maintain the status quo (cf. Cacioppo & Gardner, 1999). The affect system evolved to differentiate hostile from hospitable stimuli and to foster adaptive movement and action in an organism's ecological niche.

The etymological relationship of emotion and movement is more than a linguistic accident. Emotions direct attention to goal-relevant information in a context. They guide and organize behavior toward goals, and they serve to develop a hierarchy of attention that prioritizes goals (Bower, 1992; Frijda, 1986; Karniol & Ross, 1996; Stein & Levine, 1989). Emotions are also evolutionarily adaptive (Bateson, Klopfer, & Thompson, 1993; Lazarus, 1991). Furthermore, it is no physiological accident that the hormonal systems of emotion are the same as those for motivating action (Bateson et al., 1993). The extensive neocortex in humans supports the intervention of prospective imagery, counterfactual reasoning, and conscious decision making, decoupling a stimulus and response (Cannon, 1927; Damasio, 2000; Lane, 2000).

As a term, *emotion* is not easily defined, although it can be described on the basis of a number of salient characteristics. Two of these characteristics were just mentioned: the adaptive value of emotions and the relation of emotions in directing behavior toward goals. Five additional characteristics or components of emotion include the basis of emotions in physiology; the subjective, experiential nature of emotions; the motivational nature of emotions to engage behavior; the influence of emotional arousal on cognition and attention; and the expressive, social role of emotions.

The emotion *fear* is often singled out to exemplify how emotion motivates action in a way that is evolutionarily advantageous (Le Doux, this volume). Consider the case of two friends hiking in a wooded area, and one suddenly notices a well-camouflaged, deadly snake about to strike. The person freezes instantly in terror, eyes riveted on the snake, and an unmistakable display of fear appears automatically on the face. The companion notices the sudden change in posture and expression, follows the person's directed gaze, and takes action against the snake so that both individuals are safe. The fear expression and the behavior of freezing are survival-enhancing, automatic responses to terror, and they can be observed in nonhuman animals as well. The perception and comprehension of emotions by others is a secondarily adaptive characteristic that also enhances survival of the species. Both companions continue on the trail with a heightened state of vigilance, avoiding future threatening encounters.

This example emphasizes several of the relevant dimensions of emotion. Emotions can have a positive valence (e.g., happiness, pride, satisfaction, enthusiasm), which generally motivates approach behaviors and the maintenance of the status quo, or emotions can have a negative valence (e.g., fear, sadness, anger, disgust), which usually activates avoidance behaviors. Emotions also have different degrees of intensity, or levels of arousal, from contentment to ecstasy, or timidity to terror. The example also emphasizes the physiology of emotion. The physiology of fear is especially well investigated because a great deal of the physiology of human fear is shared with nonhuman animals. The example also emphasizes the interaction of emotion with cognition and behavior. Processes of learning and memory, conscious and unconscious, were triggered by both individuals in this encounter, and the behavior of both individuals, such as sensitivity to environmental cues, will be modified due to this experience. Finally, the example emphasizes the social aspect of emotion. Emotion seems to be a conscious, subjective feeling state, the mental experience of one individual, but the expression of emotion is developed in a social context. There are obvious examples of the social benefits of emotional displays, such as warning others of potential threats, but there are also more subtle but still evolutionarily powerful examples of bonding emotions, including social empathy and nurturance, which establish social relationships and kinship groups and ensure the survival and future parenting abilities of the offspring. All of these characteristics of emotion are important to establishing a comprehensive definition of emotion, but no single area of emotion research has been able to encompass all of these features. Rather, different areas of research on emotion focus attention on certain characteristics that address the role of emotions in diverse contexts.

Much of the experimental research in emotion has been directed toward developing models of emotion, and the characteristics of emotion just exemplified recur in the description of these models. Early models of emotion—somatic models developing during the 19th century—were influenced by medical research and animal physiology and focused on the physical description of emotional states. Although this approach was found to be incomplete, no single model of emotion currently dominates emotion research. Rather, three different classes of models have been developed to explain different aspects of emotional processes: (a) models of basic emotions that address the cross-cultural or universal aspects of emotion while retaining a focus on physiology and the sensory experience and expression of emotion; (b) models of affective space that focus on the linguistic description of emotion, using statistical methods to investigate the similarities of various emotional experiences; and (c) models of the

affect system, which focus on the production system—neural and conceptual—that underlies emotional feelings and treats feelings as the output of a set of elementary information-processing operations that involve the appetitive and aversive motivational systems. The models of emotion reviewed here are developed for different descriptive purposes, so various models need not be held in opposition but rather should be seen as describing the same phenomenon at different levels of analysis. Emotion theory can be seen as analogous to astronomical theory, whereby an emotional state can be conceived as a metaphorical star in a galaxy and models of basic emotions describe the behavior of individual stars in a galaxy. In contrast, models of the affect system, such as the evaluative space model (ESM), describe the general characteristics of various types of galaxies. Which model is used for a type of experimental research depends on the level of description under investigation. In the following section we investigate four classes of emotion models: somatovisceral models, models of basic emotion, circumplex models of emotion, and models of affective space.

Somatovisceral Activation and Emotion

Early models of emotion were influenced by both science and philosophy. The philosophical roots of these theories grew from an approach popularized by Descartes, which distinguished the ethereal aspects of the mind with the physical aspects of the body. Through this dichotomy, human intelligence and reason were identified as properties of the mind, while emotional passions such as fear and anger were observed in nonhuman animals and thus were identified as properties of the physical body. Emotions co-occurred with—and in fact were defined by—the physiological symptoms experienced during passionate states of feeling.

Darwin's (1872) text, *The Expression of Emotion in Man and Animals,* strengthened the ties between emotions and the body, emphasizing the common physical characteristics of emotional displays in humans and nonhuman animals. The somatic theory of emotions entered the archives of psychological research through the influential writings of William James in his essay (1884), "What Is an Emotion?" in which he proposed that a somatic state is a determinant of emotional experience and that feeling states are not only associated with, but are caused by, the perception of specific patterns of somatovisceral activation. In this model, feeling states are associated with a common set of physiological responses, and each constellation of responses defines a discrete emotion. This hypothesis became known as James-Lange theory of emotion, but it quickly came under fire for a number of reasons. First, the James-Lange theory did not elaborate this hypothesis in detail; for example, it did not specify which physiological patterns corresponded to which emotions, nor did it explain why a given physiological pattern should instantiate one emotion rather than another. Second, the same discrete emotion (e.g., fear) could be associated with different patterns of physiological activation across contexts (e.g., viewing versus imagining fearful stimuli), and different discrete emotions could be associated with the same pattern of physiological activation (for a review, see Cacioppo, Berntson, Larsen, Poehlmann, & Ito, 2000). Early work by Cannon (Cannon, Newton, Bright, Menkin, & Moore, 1929) and Bard (1934) indicated that dogs whose spinal columns had been severed and therefore could not detect peripheral somatic sensations still demonstrated responses of fear and anger. Cannon (1927) further argued that even in healthy individuals whose nervous systems are still intact, the viscera do not provide an adequate level of neurological input to the

brain for the somatosensory model of emotion to be correct.

The evidence against the James-Lange hypothesis appears compelling, but the hypothesis has continued to garner research attention because it is axiomatic that somatovisceral activation contributes to emotional experience (e.g., Levenson, Ekman, & Friesen, 1990). The role of somatovisceral input in the context of many-to-many mappings among patterns of physiology and emotional states is specified in the somatoviceral afference model of emotion (SAME; Cacioppo, Berntson, & Klein, 1992; Cacioppo et al., 2000). The SAME, which draws parallels between visual information processing in the ambiguous visual illusions and somatovisceral information processing in discrete emotions, specifies psychological and physiological conditions under which a given somatovisceral pattern can be reported as discrete emotional experiences, and how different somatovisceral patterns can produce the same emotional experience. The important point here is that the SAME provides a role for somatovisceral input in emotion even when visceral reactions are undifferentiated.

Darwin's observational data regarding the commonality of the expression of emotion in human and nonhuman animals suggested a set of basic emotions each with an innate motor program. Human and nonhuman animals do seem to share some aspects of emotional expression, especially with respect to fear behaviors, which might imply common neurological substrates for emotional expression. Furthermore, some facial expressions such as disgust at the presentation of undesirable tastes are observed even in newborns, implying that some facial expressions are innate rather than socially acquired. The smiling expressions of pleasure found in children who have been blind since birth provide further support for this notion (Ekman, 1971).

Certainly not all human emotions have parallels in animal models or have distinctive facial expressions. Pleasure, satisfaction, and pride, for example, would all be indistinguishable from a more general description of happiness. The expression "happiness" is applied to a broader range of contexts, and each of the related terms can be defined with respect to happiness. Happiness is therefore considered to be a more basic emotion than pleasure, satisfaction, and pride. More socially complex emotions are exhibited later in childhood development, such as remorse, shame, or embarrassment. These emotions are considered to be secondary in comparison to emotions such as sadness, which have recognizable facial and behavioral displays that are spontaneously expressed very early in life and recognizable across cultures. Criteria such as these define the constellation of basic emotions. Although different theorists disagree on the thresholds of the criteria for basic emotions and therefore endorse slightly different lists of which emotions are basic, a proposed list developed in Ekman's cross-cultural research is generally accepted and includes the emotions of happiness, sadness, fear, anger, disgust, and surprise (Ekman, 1973, 1992; Izard, 1991; Oatley, 1992; Tomkins, 1962, 1963).

Theories of basic emotions, such as Tomkins' (1962) theory of individual emotions, endorsed the idea that each basic emotion could be identified with discrete neurological substrates, a refined theory of the physiology of emotions. Animal models did seem to provide support for neurological specialization for responses such as fear, which involve the amygdala (cf. LeDoux, 1995). Although the neural and neurochemical pathways of emotional processing are beyond the scope of this chapter, current modular theories emphasize various regions of the brain rather than the somatic perceptions of emotions (cf. Adolphs & Damasio, 2001). Modular processing theories of discrete emotion presuppose that a neurological or neurochemical subsystem that mediates one emotion may not be activated during the expression of other emotions but that the same subsystem may mediate other aspects of nonemotional processing (cf. Le Doux, this volume).

A second broad class of theories of discrete emotions in social psychology are appraisal theories. Pioneered by Arnold (1945) and Lazarus (1966), discrete emotions are depicted as elicited and differentiated by an individual's interpretation or evaluation of important events or situations. A stimulus perceived to block progress toward an important goal elicits anger, for instance. The focus of appraisal theories, therefore, is to identify the dimensions or criteria that predict the various discrete emotions. For recent developments in appraisal measures, methods, and models, see Scherer, Schorr, and Johnstone (2001).

Emotion as Affective Space

The birth of a child, children opening holiday gifts, commuting along congested highways, the loss of a loved one, and threats to personal property or national security are illustrative of emotionally provocative events in quotidian life. Communications, whether verbal or nonverbal, are rich in affective signals. Affective states ranging from discrete emotions (e.g., anger) to general moods (e.g., irritable) influence and are influenced by interpersonal interactions. For these reasons, social psychologists have long been interested in moods and emotions. One approach is to study moods and emotions as they are seen through the language of feelings. This clearly provides a limited view of affect and emotion, but the view is nevertheless important to consider if a general theory of affect and emotion is to be developed (Cacioppo & Gardner, 1999).

In early work on the conceptual organization of emotion, bipolar rating scales such as "good/bad," "slow/fast," and "large/small" were used to quantify people's responses to emotional descriptors (Allport, 1935;

Thurstone, 1928, 1931). Wundt's (1902) pioneering work in this area led him to classify subjective experience along three primary dimensions: quality, activity, and excitement. These dimensions became the inspiration for subsequent research on semantic space, largely conducted by Osgood and colleagues, who sought to map the psychological representations of meaning (Osgood, 1976). Participants in Osgood's surveys were asked to rate descriptors, which were usually single nouns or phrases, using up to 76 different dimensional scales, such as hard/soft and slow/fast. By comparing the profiles of various descriptors, the descriptors could be ranked in affective space according to the dimensional scales of relevance (Osgood, Suci, & Tannenbaum, 1957). The averaged rating values for each descriptor would be arranged in a matrix, which would show the semantic difference between each descriptor, as well as the points at which various terms would cluster based on similarity of meaning. Osgood and colleagues consistently found that the three major factors that emerged in these studies were valence (pleasant/unpleasant), arousal (calm/excited), and potency or control (strong/weak; Osgood, 1969; Osgood et al., 1957). The vigor of a response (the arousal level) was understood in behaviorist terms as a nonspecific energizing force, a measure of the intensity or strength of the approach or withdrawal response (Hull, 1943). This conception of vigor, drive, or arousal inspired the development of activation theory in the late 1950s and early 1960s. Activation theory emphasized the energizing, activating, and motivating influences of emotions on behavior (Duffy, 1957; Lindsley, 1951; Malmo, 1959).

Current models of affective space continue to demonstrate the salience of the dimensions of valence and arousal (cf. the motivation-emotion circumplex model of Lang, Bradley, & Cuthbert, 1990). Alternatives, such as the circumplex models of Russell (1980) and

the dual bipolar dimensions of Watson and Tellegen (1985) and Watson, Wiese, Vidya, and Tellegen (1999), are also based on data collected from bipolar ratings of emotional terms. Descriptors that are on opposite sides of the circumplex (separated by $180°$) have a negative correlation. Descriptors that are separated by $90°$ on the circle have a correlation near zero (Larsen & Diener, 1992). One property of the circumplex models of affect is that no dimension can be assumed as more basic than another. An interesting variation incorporates an additional dimension to represent the intensity of the affective state, for example, by being able to represent a gradient of anger that describes degrees of intensity from mild irritation to blind rage. This alternative conical-shaped model provides a useful comparison and allows the description of a greater range of affect space (Daly, Lancee, & Polivy, 1983).

Research on the structure of affective words has also revealed that regardless of the language or the linguistic descriptors used for anchor points on the rating scales, affective space is not homogeneous. For instance, there are consistently higher arousal ratings for negative and positive stimuli than for neutral stimuli and slightly higher arousal ratings of negative stimuli than of positive stimuli (Ito, Cacioppo, & Lang, 1998). The generality of this effect across stimuli and studies suggests that these structural features may reflect underlying properties of emotional experiences or, at least, of their representation.

Emotional experiences, or, more specifically, the structure of the representation of those experiences, may not be particularly informative about the elementary operations that conspired to produce these experiences (Cacioppo, Gardner, & Berntson, 1997). Research on appetitive and aversive motivational systems in animals and on the neural substrates of affective processes in the neurosciences, therefore, may reveal details about the structure and operation of the affect system that is not discernible from verbal reports or language processes. This notion of complementing literatures, at least, was the inspiration for the ESM (Cacioppo & Berntson, 1994; Cacioppo et al., 1997). The model posits that early positive and negative evaluative processing are distinguishable (stochastically and functionally independent) and that the antagonistic outputs of these systems are combined to produce an approach/withdrawal tendency and a correspondingly bipolar affective response (e.g., feeling, emotional percept) for helping to guide current and future responses toward the stimulus. The underlying appetitive and aversive activation functions (i.e., positivity and negativity, respectively) are also conceived as having distinct activation functions, with the offset higher for positivity than for negativity (fostering exploratory behavior in neutral environments) and the slope (i.e., bias) of the activation function higher for negativity than for positivity (fostering survival in a sometimes dangerous world). Activation of these underlying systems are posited to relate differentially to ambivalence (corollary of ambivalence asymmetries), have distinguishable antecedents (heteroscedacity principle), and tend to gravitate from a bivariate toward a bipolar structure when the underlying beliefs are the target of deliberation or a guide for behavior (principle of motivational certainty).

Whereas a bipolar model allows only for reciprocal activation between positivity and negativity, the ESM posits multiple modes of activation of the motivational substrates: (a) reciprocal activation occurs when a stimulus has opposing effects on the activation of positivity and negativity; (b) uncoupled activation occurs when a stimulus affects only positive or only negative evaluative activation; and (c) nonreciprocal activation occurs when a stimulus increases (or decreases) the activation of both positivity and negativity (Cacioppo & Berntson, 1994; Cacioppo et al., 1999). Thus, the bivariate model of evaluative space does not reject reciprocal activation but rather subsumes it as one of the three possible modes of activation and explores the antecedents for each mode of evaluative activation. Evidence for the existence of multiple modes of evaluative activation has been observed across all levels of analysis (Cacioppo & Berntson, 1994). For instance, food restriction alters neurochemical effects underlying approach behavior in an uncoupled fashion, and morphine has reciprocal effects on neurochemical processes underlying approach and withdrawal behavior (Hoebel, Rada, Mark, & Pothos, 1999). The separable activation of positivity and negativity at the verbal level is evident in a study by Goldstein and Strube (1994) in which self-reported positive and negative affect were collected from students at the beginning and end of three consecutive class periods. Whereas a bipolar model would predict reciprocal activation of positive and negative affect, as evidenced by negative within-participant correlations between the intensity of positive and negative reactions on a particular day, the reactions were in fact uncorrelated. Moreover, exam feedback activated positivity and negativity differently. Students who scored above the mean on the exam showed an increase in positive affect relative to their beginning-of-class level, whereas their level of negative affect remained unchanged within the class period. Similarly, students who scored below the mean on the exam showed an increase in negative affect, but no change in positive affect within the class period.

The models of affective structure reviewed in this section have contested for years whether affective space is bipolar or bivariate. According to the ESM, the question should be under what conditions it is bipolar or bivariate.

Building on work in animal learning and the neurosciences, the ESM predicts conditions in which affective space is organized in a circumplex structure and those in which the circumplex structure will be violated (Cacioppo, Gardner, & Berntson, 1999).

MULTIPLE INTEGRATIVE LEVELS OF ANALYSIS

Complex human behavior is multiply determined (Cacioppo & Berntson, 1992). The study of the individual may therefore be incomplete without considering the independent, interactive, and reciprocal effects of biological, cognitive, and social factors (Cacioppo, Berntson, Sheridan, & McClintock, 2000). Food intake is influenced by the presence of others as well as by hunger. A simple judgment of spatial distance depends not only on perception and measurement but also on social context. The judgments of individuals are affected, sometimes quite dramatically, by whether the judgments are made alone or in groups, by the participant's relationship to others in the group, and by the behavior of others in the group (Pickett, 2001; Sherif & Murphy, 1936).

Isolated studies of each of the determinants will yield comprehensive theories of complex human behavior only if these factors operate in an additive fashion. In fact, however, complex human behavior is often nonadditively determined, which means that the properties of the whole are not readily predicted by the properties of the parts (Cacioppo & Berntson, 1992). For example, in an investigation of amphetamine on primate behavior, Haber and Barchas (1983) found no main effect of amphetamine but instead found that amphetamine interacted with individuals' ranking in the social hierarchy: Those that were higher ranking became more dominant after receiving the drug, and those that

were lower ranking became more submissive. Thus, the effects of a biological intervention (amphetamine) could not have been discerned regardless of the accuracy or specificity of the physiological assessments without also considering social factors. There are also mutual influences between social and nonsocial factors, as specified by the principle of reciprocal determinism (Cacioppo & Berntson, 1992). For example, just as poor health may limit an individual's opportunities for social interaction, a lack of social interaction can have deleterious effects on health (Uchino et al., 1996). Consideration of the independent, interactive, and reciprocal effects of social factors can provide a more complete depiction of the human mind and body.

Traditionally, questions about the mind, brain, or body have been examined from a single perspective. Within social psychology (as exemplified in this chapter), for example, stereotyping and prejudice were originally investigated from the perspective of social psychology by examining social behavior, such as in Sheriff et al.'s (1961) study of the competition and animosity that developed between two teams of boys at a summer camp. This perspective was expanded by the cognitive revolution and the subsequent rise of social cognition, which led to an understanding of how simple cognitive mechanisms, such as the increased availability in memory of salient negative traits and behaviors associated with minority group members, could lead to the formation of prejudice (Hamilton & Gifford, 1976) or the automatic activation of an existing stereotype (Devine, 1989). The cognitive approach also produced important findings about how prior prejudices influence subsequent information processing in self-affirming ways. Currently, with the increasing availability of event-related potentials and functional magnetic resonance imaging technology, psychologists and neuroscientists are now teaming up to examine the neural substrates of prejudice (Cacioppo & Berntson, 2001; Phelps et al., 2000). These developments promise to enrich our understanding of stereotypes and prejudice, and they demonstrate how the complex questions of social psychology are now being addressed through multiple approaches. This integration of a social perspective with cognitive and neuroscientific approaches has the potential to yield more comprehensive theories of complex social behaviors as more influences on social behavior (e.g., genetic, hormonal, attentional, memorial, social, cultural) are considered.

The crossing of disciplinary boundaries also leads to the formation of new questions. For example, studies relating brain injury to social deficits have shown that the amygdala and ventromedial frontal cortices may be critical brain structures guiding social cognition, emotion, and behavior (Adolphs, 1999; Damasio, 1994). Damasio, for instance, described the neurological case of Elliot, a businessman who developed a brain tumor in the midline area just above the nasal cavities. The tumor had grown to the size of a small orange when it was removed along with the damaged areas of the frontal lobes. Testing of Elliot revealed that his intelligence, attention, and memory were unaffected. Elliot, however, had lost the ability to experience emotion and, therefore, to learn from his mistakes. Damasio observed that Elliot had no emotional guidance to help him select among alternatives in his life, and he had no emotional response to good decisions or to bad ones with which to foster learning or decision making. This work has cast a new light on the role of emotion in intelligence, decision making, and social behavior.

The call for multilevel, integrative analyses stands in sharp contrast to recent arguments for a reductionist approach that restricts its focus to the biological determinants of behavior (e.g., E. Wilson, 1998). Biologists, however,

are also beginning to call for multilevel integrative research to better understand gene-behavior relationships (Lewontin, 2000). Indeed, burgeoning research fields such as social neuroscience, psychoneuroimunology, and behavioral endocrinology are expanding the range of theoretical explanation. Although these approaches consider the ways in which biology determines behavior, they also place due emphasis on how social experience determines gene expression; disease susceptibility and recovery; and autonomic, neuroendocrine, and immune activity. People are born with a set of master genes that work throughout the life span to determine the production of proteins that influence development and behavior. When these proteins are produced, the gene is said to be expressed. In the scientific literature and the popular media, much attention has been paid to the significant role that genes have in determining our behavior and personalities, and there is substantial evidence from studies of twins reared apart that socially relevant traits such as extraversion and emotional stability have a substantial heritable component (e.g., McCartney, Harris, & Bernieri, 1990). However, recent findings have shown how experience, particularly social experiences such as early nurturing, can influence gene expression, effectively determining which genes are turned on or off. For example, laboratory rats have been bred in ways that produce certain characteristics. High-reactive strains of rats have a lower threshold for stress reactions, show larger responses to stressors and are generally less nurturing, whereas low-reactive strains are generally less reactive and display more nurturing behaviors. Although these predispositions are clearly determined by genetic pedigree, early experience strongly determines the reactivity of developing offspring. By manipulating maternal nurturance or by cross-fostering low or high reactive pups with low or high reactive mothers, Meany and colleagues have shown that nurturance, in the form of licking, increases the number of glucocorticoid receptor binding sites in the hippocampus and frontal cortex and lowers HPA reactivity in adulthood (Anisman, Zaharia, Meany, & Merali, 1998; Meany et al., 1996). As adults, the offspring of mothers that exhibited more licking, grooming, and nurturing of pups during the first 10 days of life not only were characterized by reduced adrenocorticotropic hormone and corticosterone responses to acute stress but also, as mothers, tended to lick and groom their pups more often (Liu et al., 1997).

A set of master genes was thought to activate the DNA necessary to produce the appropriate proteins for development and behavior (Crick, 1970). The architects of the construction of development and behavior were conceived as the forces of evolution operating over millennia, and the builders were thought to be encapsulated within each living cell far from the reach of personal ties or social influences. However, the social context has been shown to influence DNA to RNA transcription (Wu et al., 1999) as well as RNA to protein translation (e.g., Cacioppo et al., 2000). Moreover, recent work in molecular biology has revealed that the proteins produced when genes are expressed operate quite differently depending on their shape or structure (i.e., protein folding) and that the environment determines protein folding (Lewontin, 2000).

An implication of this work is that the social environment and social behavior will contribute to the empirical data and theoretical components needed for a comprehensive understanding of human behavior (Cacioppo, Berntson, Sheridan, & McClintock, 2000). Although still emergent, we anticipate that research spanning biological, cognitive, and social levels of analysis will enrich our understanding of social behavior by the time the next edition of the *Stevens' Handbook* is prepared.

REFERENCES

Abramson, L. Y., Seligman, M. E., & Teasdale, J. D. (1978). Learned helplessness in humans: Critique and reformulation. *Journal of Abnormal Psychology, 87*(1), 49–74.

Adolphs, R. (1999). Social cognition and the human brain. *Trends in Cognitive Sciences, 3*(12), 469–479.

Adolphs, R., & Damasio, A. R. (2001). The interaction of affect and cognition: A neurobiological perspective. In J. P. Forgas (Ed.), *Handbook of affect and social cognition* (pp. 27–49). Mahwah, NJ: Erlbaum.

Ainsworth, M. D. S., Blehar, M. C., Waters, E., & Wall, S. (1978). *Patterns of attachment. A psychological study of the strange situation*. Hillsdale, NJ: Erlbaum.

Ajzen, I. (1977). Intuitive theories of events and the effects of base-rate information on prediction. *Journal of Personality and Social Psychology, 35*(5), 303–314.

Ajzen, I., & Fishbein, M. (1977). Attitude-behavior relations: A theoretical analysis and review of empirical research. *Psychological Bulletin, 84*(5), 888–918.

Allport, F. H. (1924). *Social Psychology*. Boston: Houghton Mifflin.

Allport, G. W. (1935). Attitudes. In C. Murchison (Ed.), *Handbook of social psychology* (Vol. 2). Worcester, MA: Clark University Press.

Allport, G. W. (1985). The historical background of social psychology. In G. Lindzey & E. Aronson (Eds.), *The handbook of social psychology* (Vol. 1, pp. 1–46). New York: Random House.

Amabile, T. M. (1979). Effects of external evaluation on artistic creativity. *Journal of Personality and Social Psychology, 37*, 221–233.

Amabile, T. M. (1983). *The social psychology of creativity*. New York: Springer-Verlag.

Anisman, H., Zaharia, M. D., Meany, M. J., & Merali, Z. (1998). Do early-life events permanently alter behavioral and hormonal responses to stressors? *International Journal of Developmental Neuroscience, 16*, 149–164.

Arkin, R. M. (1981). Self-presentation styles. In J. T. Tedeschi (Ed.), *Impression management:*

Theory and social psychological research (pp. 311–333). New York: Academic Press.

Arnold, M. B. (1945). Physiological differentiation of emotional states. *Psychological Review, 52,* 35–48.

Asch, S. E. (1955). Opinions and social pressure. *Scientific American, 193*(5), 31–35.

Banaji, M. R., & Prentice, D. A. (1994). The self in social contexts. *Annual Review of Psychology, 45,* 297–332.

Bard, P. (1934). On emotional expression after decortication with some remarks on certain theoretical views, Part II. *Psychological Review, 41,* 424–449.

Barden, R. C., Garber, J., Leiman, B., Ford, M. E., & Masters, J. C. (1985). Factors governing the effective remediation of negative affect and its cognitive and behavioral consequences. *Journal of Personality and Social Psychology, 49,* 1040–1053.

Bargh, J. A., Chen, M., & Burrows, L. (1996). Automaticity of social behavior: Direct effects of trait construct and stereotype activation on action. *Journal of Personality and Social Psychology, 71*(2), 230–244.

Bargh, J. A., & Pietromonaco, P. (1982). Automatic information processing and social perception: The influence of trait information presented outside of conscious awareness on impression formation. *Journal of Personality and Social Psychology, 43*(3), 437–449.

Baron, R. S. (1986). Distraction-conflict theory: Progress and problems. In L. Berkowitz (Ed.), *Advances in experimental social psychology* (Vol. 19, pp. 1–40). New York: Academic Press.

Bateson, P. P. G., Klopfer, P. H., & Thompson, N. S. (Eds.). (1993). *Behavior and evolution. Perspectives in ethology* (Vol. 10). New York: Plenum Press.

Baumeister, R. F. (1986). *Identity: Cultural change and the struggle for self.* New York: Oxford University Press.

Baumeister, R. F. (1987). How the self became a problem: A psychological review of historical research. *Journal of Personality and Social Psychology, 52*(1), 163–176.

Baumeister, R. F. (1998). The self. In D. T. Gilbert, S. T. Fiske, & G. Lindzey (Eds.), *The handbook of social psychology* (Vol. 1, pp. 680–740). Boston: Mcgraw-Hill.

Baumeister, R. F., Cooper, J., & Skib, B. A. (1979). Inferior performance as a selective response to expectancy: Taking a dive to make a point. *Journal of Personality and Social Psychology, 37*(3), 424–432.

Baumeister, R. F., & Leary, M. R. (1995). The need to belong: Desire for interpersonal attachments as a fundamental human motivation. *Psychological Bulletin, 117*(3), 497–529.

Baumeister, R. F., & Tice, D. M. (1986). How adolescence became the struggle for self: A historical transformation of psychological development. In J. Suls & A. G. Greenwald (Eds.), *Psychological perspectives on the self* (Vol. 3, pp. 183–201). Hillsdale, NJ: Erlbaum.

Baumeister, R. F., & Tice, D. M. (1990). Anxiety and social exclusion. *Journal of Social and Clinical Psychology, 9,* 165–195.

Baumgardner, A. H. (1990). To know oneself is to like oneself: Self-certainty and self-affect. *Journal of Personality and Social Psychology, 58*(6), 1062–1072.

Beaman, A. L., Cole, C. M., Preston, M., Kentz, B., & Mehrkens Steblay, N. (1983). Fifteen years of foot-in-the-door research: A meta-analysis. *Personality & Social Psychology Bulletin, 9*(2), 181–196.

Bem, D. J. (1972). Self-perception theory. In L. Berkowitz (Ed.), *Advances in experimental social psychology* (Vol. 6, pp. 2–62). New York: Academic Press.

Berry, S. H., & Kanouse, D. E. (1987). Physician response to a mailed survey: An experiment in timing of payment. *Public Opinion Quarterly, 51*(1), 102–114.

Blaine, B., & Crocker, J. (1993). Self-esteem and self-serving biases in reactions to positive and negative events: An integrative review. In R. F. Baumeister (Ed.), *Self-esteem: The puzzle of low self-regard* (pp. 55–85). New York: Plenum Press.

Blass, T. (1991). Understanding behavior in the Milgram obedience experiment: The role of personality, situations, and their interactions. *Journal of Personality and Social Psychology, 60*(3), 398–413.

Bless, H., Clore, G. L., Schwarz, N., Golisano, V., Rabe, C., & Wolk, M. (1996). Mood and the use of scripts: Does a happy mood really lead to mindlessness? *Journal of Personality and Social Psychology, 71*(4), 665–679.

Bodenhausen, G. V. (1988). Stereotypic biases in social decision making and memory: Testing process models of stereotype use. *Journal of Personality and Social Psychology, 55*(5), 726–737.

Bodenhausen, G. V. (1990). Stereotypes as judgmental heuristics: Evidence of circadian variations in discrimination. *Psychological Science, 1*(5), 319–322.

Bodenhausen, G. V., Kramer, G. P., & Suesser, K. (1994). Happiness and stereotypic thinking in social judgment. *Journal of Personality and Social Psychology, 66*(4), 621–632.

Boggiano, A. K., & Pittman, N. L. (1992). *Achievement and motivation: A social-developmental perspective.* New York: Cambridge University Press.

Bower, G. H. (1992). How might emotions affect learning? In S. Christianson (Ed.), *The handbook of emotion and memory: Research and theory* (pp. 3–31). Hillsdale, NJ: Erlbaum.

Bowlby, J. (1969). *Attachment.* New York: Basic Books.

Brehm, J. W. (1966). *A theory of psychological reactance.* New York: Academic Press.

Brehm, J. W. (1993). Control, its loss, and psychological reactance. In G. Weary, F. Gleicher, & K. L. Marsh (Eds.), *Control motivation and social cognition* (pp. 3–30). New York: Springer-Verlag.

Brehm, J. W., & Cohen, A. R. (1962). *Explorations in cognitive dissonance.* New York: Wiley.

Brehm, S. S., & Brehm, J. W. (1981). *Psychological reactance: A theory of freedom and control.* New York: Academic Press.

Brehm, S. S., & Weinraub, M. (1977). Physical barriers and psychological reactance: 2-yr-olds' responses to threats to freedom. *Journal of Personality and Social Psychology, 35*(11), 830–836.

Brewer, M. B. (1988). A dual process model of impression formation. In T. K. Srull & R. S. Wyer, Jr. (Eds.), *Advances in social cognition* (Vol. 1, pp. 1–36). Hillsdale, NJ: Erlbaum.

Brewer, M. B. (1991). The social self: On being the same and different at the same time. *Personality and Social Psychology Bulletin, 17*(5), 475–482.

Brewer, M. B., Dull, V., & Lui, L. (1981). Perceptions of the elderly: Stereotypes as prototypes. *Journal of Personality and Social Psychology, 41*(4), 656–670.

Brewer, M. B., & Gardner, W. (1996). Who is this "We"? Levels of collective identity and self-representations. *Journal of Personality and Social Psychology, 71*(1), 83–93.

Brockner, J., Rubin, J. Z., & Lang, E. (1981). Face-saving and entrapment. *Journal of Experimental Social Psychology, 17*(1), 68–79.

Brockner, J., Shaw, M. C., & Rubin, J. Z. (1979). Factors affecting withdrawal from an escalating conflict: Quitting before it's too late. *Journal of Experimental Social Psychology, 15*(5), 492–503.

Brown, J. D. (1986). Evaluations of self and others: Self-enhancement biases in social judgments. *Social Cognition, 4*(4), 353–376.

Brown, J. D. (1998). *The self.* New York: McGraw-Hill.

Brown, J. D., & Dutton, K. A. (1995). The thrill of victory, the complexity of defeat: Self-esteem and people's emotional reactions to success and failure. *Journal of Personality and Social Psychology, 68*(4), 712–722.

Brown, J. D., & Smart, S. A. (1991). The self and social conduct: Linking self-representations to prosocial behavior. *Journal of Personality and Social Psychology, 60*(3), 368–375.

Burger, J. M. (1993). Individual differences in control motivation and social information processing. In G. Weary, F. Gleicher, & K. Marsh (Eds.), *Control motivation and social cognition* (pp. 203–219). New York: Springer-Verlag.

Buss, D. M., & Schmitt, D. P. (1993). Sexual Strategies Theory: An evolutionary perspective on human mating. *Psychological Review, 100*(2), 204–232.

Cacioppo, J. T., & Berntson, G. C. (2001). The affect system and racial prejudice. In J. A. Bargh & D. K. Apsley (Eds.), *Unraveling the complexities of social life: A festschrift in honor of Robert B. Zajonc* (pp. 95–110). Washington, DC: American Psychological Association.

Cacioppo, J. T., & Berntson, G. G. (1992). The principles of multiple, nonadditive, and reciprocal determinism: Implications for social psychological research and levels of analysis. In D. N. Ruble & P. R. Costanzo (Eds.), *The social psychology of mental health: Basic mechanisms and applications* (pp. 328–349). New York: Guilford Press.

Cacioppo, J. T., & Berntson, G. G. (1994). Relationship between attitudes and evaluative space: A critical review, with emphasis on the separability of positive and negative substrates. *Psychological Bulletin, 115*(3), 401–423.

Cacioppo, J. T., Berntson, G. G., Adolphs, R., Carter, C. S., Davidson, R. J., McClintock, M. K., McEwen, B. S., Meaney, M. J., Schacter, D. L., Sternberg, E. M., Suomi, S. S., & Taylor, S. E. (in press). *Foundations in social neuroscience.* Cambridge, MA: MIT Press.

Cacioppo, J. T., Berntson, G. G., & Klein, D. J. (1992). What is an emotion? The role of somatovisceral afference, with special emphasis on somatovisceral "illusions." In M. S. Clark (Ed.), *Emotion and social behavior* (pp. 63–98). Newbury Park, CA: Sage Publications.

Cacioppo, J. T., Berntson, G. G., Larsen, J. T., Poehlmann, K. M., & Ito, T. A. (2000). The psychophysiology of emotion. In R. Lewis & J. M. Haviland-Jones (Eds.), *The handbook of emotion* (2nd ed., pp. 173–191). New York: Guilford Press.

Cacioppo, J. T., Berntson, G. G., Sheridan, J. F., & McClintock, M. K. (2000). Multilevel integrative analyses of human behavior: Social neuroscience and the complementing nature of social and biological approaches. *Psychological Bulletin, 126*(6), 829–843.

Cacioppo, J. T., Ernst, J. M., Burleson, M. H., McClintock, M. K., Malarkey, W. B., Hawkley, L. C., Kowalewski, R. B., Paulsen, A., Hobson, J. A., Hugdahl, K., Spiegel, D., & Berntson, G. G. (2000). Lonely traits and concomitant physiological processes: The MacArthur Social Neuroscience Studies. *International Journal of Psychophysiology, 35,* 143–154.

Cacioppo, J. T., & Gardner, W. L. (1999). Emotions. *Annual Review of Psychology, 50,* 191–214.

Cacioppo, J. T., Gardner, W. L., & Berntson, G. G. (1997). Beyond bipolar conceptualizations and measures: The case of attitudes and evaluative space. *Personality and Social Psychology Review, 1*(1), 1993–1925.

Cacioppo, J. T., Gardner, W. L., & Berntson, G. G. (1999). The affect system has parallel and integrative processing components: Form follows function. *Journal of Personality and Social Psychology, 76*(5), 839–855.

Cacioppo, J. T., Marshall-Goodell, B. S., Tassinary, L. G., & Petty, R. E. (1992). Rudimentary determinants of attitudes: Classical conditioning is more effective when prior knowledge about the attitude stimulus is low than high. *Journal of Experimental Social Psychology, 28*(3), 207–233.

Cacioppo, J. T., & Petty, R. E. (1979). Effects of message repetition and position on cognitive response, recall, and persuasion. *Journal of Personality and Social Psychology. 37*(1), 97–109.

Cacioppo, J. T., & Petty, R. E. (1982). The need for cognition. *Journal of Personality and Social Psychology, 42*(1), 116–131.

Cacioppo, J. T., Petty, R. E., Feinstein, J. A., & Jarvis, W. B. G. (1996). Dispositional differences in cognitive motivation: The life and times of individuals varying in need for cognition. *Psychological Bulletin, 119*(2), 197–253.

Cacioppo, J. T., Petty, R. E., Kao, C. F., & Rodriguez, R. (1986). Central and peripheral routes to persuasion: An individual difference perspective. *Journal of Personality and Social Psychology, 51*(5), 1032–1043.

Cacioppo, J. T., Uchino, B. N., Crites, S. L., Snydersmith, M. A., Smith, G., Berntson, G. G., & Lang, P. J. (1992). Relationship between facial expressiveness and sympathetic activation in emotion: A critical review, with emphasis on modeling underlying mechanisms and individual differences. *Journal of Personality and Social Psychology, 62*(1), 110–128.

Calder, B. J., Ross, M., & Insko, C. A. (1973). Attitude change and attitude attribution: Effects of incentive, choice, and consequences. *Journal* of Personality and Social Psychology, 25(1), 84–99.

Campbell, J. D. (1986). Similarity and uniqueness: The effects of attribute type, relevance, an individual differences in self-esteem and depression. Journal of Personality and Social Psychology, 50, 281–294.

Campbell, J. D. (1990). Self-esteem and clarity of the self-concept. Journal of Personality and Social Psychology, 59(3), 538–549.

Cannon, W. B. (1927). The James-Lange theory of emotions: A critical examination and an alternative theory. American Journal of Psychology, 39, 106–124.

Cannon, W. B., Newton, H. F., Bright, E. M., Menkin, V., & Moore, R. M. (1929). Some aspects of the physiology of animals surviving complete exclusion of sympathetic nerve impulses. American Journal of Physiology, 89, 84–107.

Cantor, N., & Mischel, W. (1979). Prototypicality and personality: Effects on free recall and personality impressions. Journal of Research in Personality, 13(2), 187–205.

Caplovitz Barrett, K., & Morgan, G. A. (1995). Continuities and discontinuities in mastery motivation during infancy and toddlerhood: A conceptualization and review. In R. H. MacTurk & G. A. Morgan (Eds.), Mastery motivation: Origins, conceptualizations, and applications (pp. 57–93). Norwood, NJ: Ablex Publishing.

Carpenter, S. L. (1988). Self-relevance and goal-directed processing in the recall and weighting of information about others. Journal of Experimental Social Psychology, 24(4), 310–332.

Carter, C. S., Lederhendler, I. I., Kirkpatrick, B. (1997). The integrative neurobiology of affiliation. New York: New York Academy of Sciences.

Carver, C. S., & Scheier, M. F. (1981). The self-attention-induced feedback loop and social facilitation. Journal of Experimental Social Psychology, 17(6), 545–568.

Carver, C. S., & Scheier, M. F. (1990). Origins and functions of positive and negative affect: A control-process view. Psychological Review, 97(1), 19–35.

Chaiken, S. (1980). Heuristic versus systematic information processing and the use of source versus message cues in persuasion. Journal of Personality and Social Psychology, 39(5), 752–766.

Chase, W. G., & Simon, H. A. (1973). The mind's eye in chess. In W. G. Chase (Ed.), Visual information processing (pp. 215–281). New York: Academic Press.

Choi, I., & Nisbett, R. E. (1998). Situational salience and cultural differences in the correspondence bias and actor-observer bias. Personality and Social Psychology Bulletin, 24(9), 949–960.

Cialdini, R. B. (1993). Influence: Science and practice. New York: HarperCollins.

Cialdini, R. B., Borden, R. J., Thorne, A., Walker, M. R., Freeman, S., & Sloan, L. R. (1976). Basking in reflected glory: Three (football) field studies. Journal of Personality and Social Psychology, 34(3), 366–375.

Cialdini, R. B., & Trost, M. R. (1998). Social influence: Social norms, conformity and compliance. In D. T. Gilbert & S. T. Fiske (Eds.), The handbook of social psychology (Vol. 2, pp. 151–192). Boston: Mcgraw-Hill.

Codol, J. P. (1984). Social differentiation and non-differentiation. In H. Tajfel, C. Fraser, & J. M. F. Jaspars (Eds.), The social dimension (pp. 314–337). Cambridge, UK: Cambridge University Press.

Coleman, J. F., Blake, R. R., & Mouton, J. S. (1958). Task difficulty and conformity pressures. Journal of Abnormal and Social Psychology, 57, 120–122.

Collins, B. E., & Hoyt, M. F. (1972). Choice, aversive consequences, and the "truth-telling" potential of the situation as integrating concepts in forced compliance. Psychological Reports, 30(3), 875–885.

Cooper, H. M. (1979). Statistically combining independent studies: A meta-analysis of sex differences in conformity research. Journal of Personality and Social Psychology, 37(1), 131–146.

Cottrell, N. B., Wack, D. L., Sekerak, G. J., & Rittle, R. H. (1968). Social facilitation of dominant responses by the presence of an audience and the mere presence of others. Journal of Personality and Social Psychology, 9, 245–250.

Cousins, S. D. (1989). Culture and self-perception in Japan and the United States. *Journal of Personality and Social Psychology, 56,* 124–131.

Crano, W. D. (1995). Attitude strength and vested interest. In R. E. Petty & J. A. Krosnick (Eds.), *Attitude strength: Antecedents and consequences* (pp. 131–157). Mahwah, NJ: Erlbaum.

Crary, W. G. (1966). Reactions to incongruent self-experiences. *Journal of Consulting Psychology, 30,* 246–252.

Crick, F. (1970). Central dogma of molecular biology. *Nature, 227*(258), 561–563.

Crocker, J., & Major, B. (1989). Social stigma and self-esteem: The self-protective properties of stigma. *Psychological Review, 96*(4), 608–630.

Crocker, J., Voelkl, K., Testa, M., & Major, B. (1991). Social stigma: The affective consequences of attributional ambiguity. *Journal of Personality and Social Psychology, 60*(2), 218–228.

Crutchfield, R. S. (1955). Conformity and character. *American Psychologist, 10,* 191–198.

Csikszentmihalyi, M. (1975). *Beyond boredom and anxiety: The experience of play in work and games.* San Francisco: Jossey-Bass.

Csikszentmihalyi, M. (1991). *Flow: The psychology of optimal experience.* New York: HarperPerennial.

Daly, E. M., Lancee, W. J., & Polivy, J. (1983). A conical model for the taxonomy of emotional experience. *Journal of Personality and Social Psychology, 45,* 443–457.

Damasio, A. R. (1994). Descartes' error: Emotion, reason, and the human brain. New York: G. P. Putnam.

Damasio, A. R. (2000). A second chance for emotion. In R. D. Lane & L. Nadel (Eds.), *Cognitive neuroscience of emotion* (pp. 12–23). New York: Oxford University Press.

Darwin, C. (1872). *The expression of emotion in man and animals.* London: Murray.

DeBono, K. G., & Snyder, M. (1995). Acting on one's attitudes: The role of a history of choosing situations. *Personality and Social Psychology Bulletin, 21*(6), 620–628.

Deci, E. L. (1971). Effects of externally mediated rewards on intrinsic motivation. *Journal of Personality and Social Psychology, 18,* 105–115.

Deci, E. L. (1975). *Intrinsic motivation.* New York: Plenum Press.

Deci, E. L., & Ryan, R. M. (1985). *Intrinsic motivation and self-determination in human behavior.* New York: Plenum Press.

Descartes, R. (1647). The passions of the soul. In J. Cottingham, R. Stoothoff, & D. Murdoch (Eds.) *The philosophical writings of Descartes, Vol. .* Cambridge England: Cambridge University Press (1985).

Deutsch, M., & Gerard, H. B. (1955). A study of normative and informational social influences upon individual judgment. *Journal of Abnormal and Social Psychology, 51,* 629–636.

Devine, P. G. (1989). Stereotypes and prejudice: Their automatic and controlled components. *Journal of Personality and Social Psychology, 56*(1), 5–18.

Devine, P. G., Hamilton, D. L., & Ostrom, T. M. (Eds.). (1994). *Social cognition: Impact on social psychology.* San Diego, CA: Academic Press.

Diener, C. I., & Dweck, C. S. (1978). An analysis of learned helplessness: Continuous changes in performance, strategy, and achievement cognitions following failure. *Journal of Personality and Social Psychology, 36*(5), 451–462.

Dillehay, R. C., Insko, C. A., & Smith, M. B. (1966). Logical consistency and attitude change. *Journal of Personality and Social Psychology, 3,* 646–654.

Dittes, J. E., & Kelly, H. H. (1956). Effects of different conditions of acceptance upon conformity to group norms. *Journal of Abnormal and Social Psychology, 53,* 100–107.

Dodgson, P. G., & Wood, J. V. (1998). Self-esteem and the cognitive accessibility of strengths and weaknesses after failure. *Journal of Personality and Social Psychology, 75*(1), 178–197.

Dovidio, J. F., Evans, N., & Tyler, R. B. (1986). Racial stereotypes: The contents of their cognitive representations. *Journal of Experimental Social Psychology, 22*(1), 22–37.

Duffy, E. (1957). The psychological significance of the concept of "arousal" and "activation." *Psychological Review, 64,* 265–275.

Duncan, B. L. (1976). Differential social perception and attribution of intergroup violence: Testing the lower limits of stereotyping of blacks. *Journal of Personality and Social Psychology, 34*(4), 590–598.

Dunning, D., & Hayes, A. F. (1996). Evidence for egocentric comparison in social judgment. *Journal of Personality and Social Psychology, 71*(2), 213–229.

Dweck, C. S. (1975). The role of expectations and attributions in the alleviation of learned helplessness. *Journal of Personality and Social Psychology, 31*(4), 674–685.

Dweck, C. S. (1999). *Self-theories: Their role in motivation, personality, and development.* Philadelphia, PA: Psychology Press.

Dweck, C. S., & Leggett, E. L. (1988). A social-cognitive approach to motivation and personality. *Psychological Review, 95*(2), 256–273.

Eagly, A. H., & Carli, L. L. (1981). Sex of researchers and sex-typed communications as determinants of sex differences in influenceability: A meta-analysis of social influence studies. *Psychological, 90*(1), 1–20.

Eagly, A. H., & Chaiken, S. (1998). Attitude structure and function. In D. T. Gilbert & S. T. Fiske (Eds.), *The handbook of social psychology* (Vol. 2, pp. 269–322). Boston: Mcgraw-Hill.

Eagly, A. H., Wood, W., & Fishbaugh, L. (1981). Sex differences in conformity: Surveillance by the group as a determinant of male nonconformity. *Journal of Personality and Social Psychology, 40*(2), 384–394.

Ekman, P. (1971). Universals and cultural differences in facial expressions of emotion. In J. Cole (Ed.), *Nebraska Symposium on Motivation,* Vol. 20 (pp. 207–283). Lincoln: University of Nebraska Press.

Ekman, P. (Ed.). (1973). *Darwin and facial expression.* New York: Academic Press.

Ekman, P. (1992). An argument for basic emotions. *Cognition and Emotion, 6,* 169–200.

Elliot, A. J., & Devine, P. G. (1994). On the motivational nature of cognitive dissonance: Dissonance as psychological discomfort. *Journal of Personality and Social Psychology, 67*(3), 382–394.

Elliot, A. J., & Harackiewicz, J. M. (1994). Goal setting, achievement orientation, and intrinsic motivation: A mediational analysis. *Journal of Personality and Social Psychology, 66*(5), 968–980.

Fazio, R. H. (1989). On the power and functionality of attitudes: The role of attitude accessibility. In A. R. Pratkanis & S. J. Breckler (Eds.), *Attitude structure and function. The third Ohio State University volume on attitudes and persuasion* (pp. 153–179). Hillsdale, NJ: Erlbaum.

Fazio, R. H., & Dunton, B. C. (1997). Categorization by race: The impact of automatic and controlled components of racial prejudice. *Journal of Experimental Social Psychology, 33*(5), 451–470.

Fazio, R. H., & Roskos-Ewoldsen, D. R. (1994). Acting as we feel: When and how attitudes guide behavior. In S. Shavitt & T. C. Brock (Eds.), *Persuasion: Psychological insights and perspectives* (pp. 71–93). Boston: Allyn & Bacon.

Feick, D. L., & Rhodewalt, F. (1997). The double-edged sword of self-handicapping: Discounting, augmentation, and the protection and enhancement of self-esteem. *Motivation and Emotion, 21*(2), 147–163.

Fein, S., & Spencer, S. J. (1997). Prejudice as self-image maintenance: Affirming the self through derogating others. *Journal of Personality and Social Psychology, 73*(1), 31–44.

Ferrari, J. R., & Tice, D. M. (2000). Procrastination as a self-handicap for men and women: A task-avoidance strategy in a laboratory setting. *Journal of Research in Personality, 34*(1), 73–83.

Festinger, L. (1954). A theory of social comparison processes. *Human Relations, 7,* 117–140.

Festinger, L. (1957). *A theory of cognitive dissonance.* Evanston, IL: Row Peterson.

Festinger, L., & Carlsmith, J. M. (1959). Cognitive consequences of forced compliance. *Journal of Abnormal and Social Psychology, 58,* 203–210.

Field, T. M. (1995). *Touch in early development.* Mahwah, NJ: Erlbaum.

Fiske, A. P., Kitayama, S., Markus, H. R., & Nisbett, R. E. (1998). The cultural matrix of social psychology. In D. T. Gilbert, S. T. Fiske, & G. Lindzey (Eds.), *The handbook of social psychology,* Vol. 2, (pp. 915–981). New York: McGraw Hill.

Fiske, S. T., & Neuberg, S. L. (1990). A continuum model of impression formation, from category-based to individuating processes: Influences of information and motivation on attention and interpretation. In M. P. Zanna (Ed.), *Advances in experimental social psychology* (Vol. 23, pp. 1–74). San Diego, CA: Academic Press.

Fiske, S. T., & Taylor, S. E. (1991). *Social cognition.* New York: Mcgraw-Hill.

Folkman, S. (1984). Personal control and stress and coping processes: A theoretical analysis. *Journal of Personality and Social Psychology, 46,* 839–825.

Frijda, N. H. (1986). *The emotions.* Cambridge, UK: Cambridge University Press.

Gibbons, F. X., & Gerrard, M. (1991). Downward comparison and coping with threat. In J. Suls & T. A. Wills (Eds.), *Social comparison: Contemporary theory and research* (pp. 317–345). Hillsdale, NJ: Erlbaum.

Gilbert, D. T., & Hixon, J. G. (1991). The trouble of thinking: Activation and application of stereotypic beliefs. *Journal of Personality and Social Psychology, 60*(4), 509–517.

Gilbert, D. T., Krull, D. S., & Pelham, B. W. (1988). Of thoughts unspoken: Social inference and the self-regulation of behavior. *Journal of Personality and Social Psychology, 55*(5), 685–694.

Ginosar, Z., & Trope, Y. (1980). The effects of base rates and individuating information on judgments about another person. *Journal of Experimental Social Psychology, 16*(3), 228–242.

Goethals, G. R., & Cooper, J. (1975). When dissonance is reduced: The timing of self-justificatory attitude change. *Journal of Personality and Social Psychology, 32*(2), 361–367.

Goethals, G. R., Messick, D. M., & Allison, S. T. (1991). The uniqueness bias: Studies of constructive social comparison. In J. Suls & T. A. Wills (Eds.), *Social comparison: Contemporary theory and research* (pp. 149–176). Hillsdale, NJ: Erlbaum.

Goldstein, M. D., & Strube, M. J. (1994). Independence revisited: The relation between positive and negative affect in a naturalistic setting. *Personality and Social Psychology Bulletin, 20*(1), 57–64.

Greenberg, J., Pyszczynski, T., Solomon, S., Rosenblatt, A., Veeder, M., Kirkland, S., & Lyon, D. (1990). Evidence for terror management theory, II: The effects of mortality salience on reactions to those who threaten or bolster the cultural worldview. *Journal of Personality and Social Psychology, 58*(2), 308–318.

Greenwald, A. G. (1980). The totalitarian ego: Fabrication and revision of personal history. *American Psychologist, 35*(7), 603–618.

Greenwald, A. G. (1989). Why are attitudes important? In A. R. Pratkanis & S. J. Breckler (Eds.), *Attitude structure and function* (pp. 1–10). Hillsdale, NJ: Erlbaum.

Greenwald, A. G., & Banaji, M. R. (1989). The self as a memory system: Powerful, but ordinary. *Journal of Personality and Social Psychology, 57*(1), 41–54.

Greenwald, A. G., & Pratkanis, A. R. (1984). The self. In R. S. Wyer, Jr., & T. K. Srull (Eds.), *Handbook of social cognition* (pp. 129–178). Hillsdale, NJ: Erlbaum.

Gross, J. J., & Levenson, R. W. (1993). Emotional suppression: Physiology, self-report, and expressive behavior. *Journal of Personality and Social Psychology, 64*(6), 970–986.

Haber, S. N., & Barchas, P. R. (1983). The regulatory effect of social rank on behavior after amphetamine administration. In P. R. Barchas (Ed.), *Social hierarchies: Essays toward a sociophysiological perspective* (pp. 119–132). Westport, CT: Greenwood Press.

Hamilton, D. L., & Gifford, R. K. (1976). Illusory correlation in interpersonal perception: A cognitive basis of stereotypic judgments. *Journal of Experimental Social Psychology, 12*(4), 392–407.

Harkins, S. G., & Jackson, J. M. (1985). The role of evaluation in eliminating social loafing. *Personality and Social Psychology Bulletin, 11*(4), 457–465.

Harkins, S. G., & Petty, R. E. (1982). Effects of task difficulty and task uniqueness on social loafing. *Journal of Personality and Social Psychology, 43*(6), 1214–1229.

Harkins, S. G., & Szymanski, K. (1988). Social loafing and self-evaluation with an objective standard. *Journal of Experimental Social Psychology, 24*(4), 354–365.

Harkins, S. G., & Szymanski, K. (1989). Social loafing and group evaluation. *Journal of Personality and Social Psychology, 56*(6), 934–941.

Harlow, H. F. (1958). The nature of love. *American Psychologist, 13,* 679–685.

Harlow, H. F. (1961). The development of affectional patterns in infant monkeys. In B. M. Foss (Ed.), *Determinants of infant behaviour* (pp. 75–88). London: Methuen/Wiley.

Harrison, L. L. (2000). Psychologic and behavioral effects of gentle human touch on preterm infants. *Research in Nursing and Health, 23*(9-6), 435–446.

Hazan, C., & Shaver, P. (1987). Romantic love conceptualized as an attachment process. *Journal of Personality and Social Psychology, 52*(3), 511–524.

Hazan, C., & Shaver, P. R. (1994a). Attachment as an organizational framework for research on close relationships. *Psychological Inquiry, 5*(1), 1–22.

Hazan, C., & Shaver, P. R. (1994b). Deeper into attachment theory. *Psychological Inquiry, 5*(1), 68–79.

Heatherton, T. F., & Baumeister, R. F. (1996). Self-regulation failure: Past, present, and future. *Psychological Inquiry, 7*(1), 90–98.

Heider, F. (1958). *The psychology of interpersonal relations.* New York: Wiley.

Heider, F., & Simmel, M. (1944). An experimental study of apparent behavior. *American Journal of Psychology, 57,* 243–259.

Heine, S. H., Lehman, D. R., Markus, H. R., & Kitayama, S. (1999). Is there a universal need for positive self-regard? *Psychological Review, 106*(4), 766–794.

Henchy, T., & Glass, D. C. (1968). Evaluation apprehension and the social facilitation of dominant and subordinate responses. *Journal of Personality and Social Psychology, 10,* 446–454.

Hershberger, S. L., Lichtenstein, P., & Knox, S. S. (1994). Genetic and environmental influences on perceptions of organizational climate. *Journal of Applied Psychology, 79*(1), 24–33.

Higgins, E. T. (1987). Self-discrepancy: A theory relating self and affect. *Psychological Review, 94*(3), 319–340.

Higgins, E. T., Klein, R., & Strauman, T. (1985). Self-concept discrepancy theory: A psychological model for distinguishing among different aspects of depression and anxiety. *Social Cognition, 3*(1), 51–76.

Higgins, E. T., Klein, R. L., & Strauman, T. J. (1987). Self-discrepancies: Distinguishing among self-states, self-state conflicts, and emotional vulnerability. In K. Yardley & T. Honess (Eds.), *Self and identity: Psychosocial perspectives.* Chichester, UK: Wiley.

Higgins, E. T., Strauman, T., & Klein, R. (1986). Standards and the process of self-evaluation: Multiple affects from multiple stages. In R. M. Sorrentino & E. T. Higgins (Eds.), *Handbook of motivation and cognition: Foundations of social behavior* (pp. 23–63). New York: Guilford Press.

Higgins, E. T., Vookles, J., & Tykocinski, O. (1992). Self and health: How "patterns" of self-beliefs predict types of emotional and physical problems. *Social Cognition, 10*(1), 125–150.

Higgins, R. L., & Berglas, S. (1990). The maintenance and treatment of self-handicapping: From risk-taking to face-saving—and back. In R. L. Higgins (Ed.), *Self-handicapping: The paradox that isn't. The Plenum series in social/clinical psychology* (pp. 187–238). New York: Plenum Press.

Hildum, D. C., & Brown, R. W. (1956). Verbal reinforcement and interviewer bias. *Journal of Abnormal and Social Psychology, 53,* 108–111.

Hinde, R. A. (1982). Attachment: Some conceptual and biological issues. In J. Stevenson-Hinde & C. Murray Parkes (Eds.), *The place of attachment in human behavior* (pp. 60–78). New York: Basic Books.

Hochbaum, G. M. (1954). The relation between group members' self-confidence and their reactions to group pressure to conformity. *American Sociological Review, 19,* 678–687.

Hoebel, B. G., Rada, P. V., Mark, G. P., & Pothos, E. N. (1999). Neural systems for reinforcement and inhibition of behavior: Relevance to eating, addiction, and depression. In D. Kahneman & E. Diener (Eds.), *Well-being: The foundations of hedonic psychology* (pp. 558–572). New York: Russell Sage Foundation.

Holyoak, K. J., & Gordon, P. C. (1983). Social reference points. *Journal of Personality and Social Psychology, 44*(5), 881–887.

Hovland, C. I., Janis, I. L., & Kelly, H. H. (1953). *Communication and persuasion: Psychological studies of opinion change*. New Haven, CT: Yale University Press.

Hull, C. L. (1943). *Principles of behavior*. New York: Appleton-Century-Crofts.

Huttenlocher, J., Hedges, L. V., & Vevea, J. L. (2000). Why do categories affect stimulus judgment? *Journal of Experimental Psychology: General, 129*(2), 220–241.

Insel, T. R. (1997). A neurobiological basis of social attachment. *American Journal of Psychiatry, 154*(6), 726–735.

Insko, C. A. (1965). Verbal reinforcement of attitude. *Journal of Personality and Social Psychology, 2,* 621–623.

Ito, T. A., & Cacioppo, J. T. (1997). The psychophysiology of utility appraisals. In D. Kahneman, E. Diener, & N. Schwarz (Eds.), *Well-being: The foundations of hedonic psychology* (pp. 470–488). New York: Russell Sage Foundation.

Ito, T. A., Cacioppo, J. T., & Lang, P. J. (1998). Eliciting affect using the International Affective Picture System: Trajectories through evaluative space. *Personality and Social Psychology Bulletin, 24*(8), 855–879.

Izard, C. E. (1991). *The psychology of emotions*. New York: Plenum.

James, W. (1884). What is an emotion? *Mind, 9,* 188–205.

Jones, E. E., & Berglas, S. (1978). Control of attributions about the self through self-handicapping strategies: The appeal of alcohol and the role of underachievement. *Personality and Social Psychology Bulletin, 4*(2), 200–206.

Jones, E. E., Rhodewalt, F., Berglas, S., & Skelton, J. A. (1981). Effects of strategic self-presentation on subsequent self-esteem. *Journal of Personality and Social Psychology, 41*(3), 407–421.

Kahneman, D., Slovic, P., & Tversky, A. (1982). *Judgment under uncertainty: Heuristics and biases.* Cambridge, UK: Cambridge University Press.

Karniol, R., & Ross, M. (1996). The motivational impact of temporal focus: Thinking about the future and the past. *Annual Review of Psychology, 47,* 593–620.

Katz, D. (1960). The functional approach to the study of attitudes. *Public Opinion Quarterly, 24,* 163–204.

Katz, D., & Stoteland, E. (1959). A preliminary statement to a theory of attitude structure and change. In S. Koch (Ed.), *Psychology: A study of a science* (Vol. 3, pp. 423–475). New York: McGraw-Hill.

Kavanau, J. L. (1967). Behavior of captive white-footed mice. *Science, 155*(3770), 1632–1639.

Keynes, J. M. (1936). *The general theory of employment, interest and money.* New York: Harcourt Brace.

Kihlstrom, J. F., & Cantor, N. (1988). Mental representations of the self. In L. Berkowitz (Ed.), *Advances in experimental social psychology* (Vol. 21, pp. 2–48). New York: Academic Press.

Kihlstrom, J. F., Cantor, N., Albright, J. S., Chew, B. R., Klein, S. B., & Niedenthal, P. M. (1988). Information processing and the study of the self. In L. Berkowitz (Ed.), *Advances in experimental social psychology* (Vol. 21, pp. 145–180). New York: Academic Press.

Kihlstrom, J. F., & Klein, S. B. (1994). The self as a knowledge structure. In R. S. J. Wyer & T. K. Srull (Eds.), *Handbook of social cognition* (pp. 153–208). Hillsdale, NJ: Erlbaum.

Kihlstrom, J. F., & Klein, S. B. (1997). Self-knowledge and self-awareness. In J. G. Snodgrass & R. L. Thompson (Eds.), *The self across psychology: Self-recognition, self-awareness, and the self concept* (pp. 5–17). New York: New York Academy of Sciences.

Klein, S. B., & Kihlstrom, J. F. (1986). Elaboration, organization, and the self-reference effect in memory. *Journal of Experimental Psychology: General, 115*(1), 26–38.

Klinger, E. (1975). Consequences of commitment to and disengagement from incentives. *Psychological Review, 82*(1), 1–25.

Kolditz, T. A., & Arkin, R. M. (1982). An impression management interpretation of the self-handicapping strategy. *Journal of Personality and Social Psychology, 43*(3), 492–502.

Kraus, S. J. (1995). Attitudes and the prediction of behavior: A meta-analysis of the empirical literature. *Personality and Social Psychology Bulletin, 21*(1), 58–75.

Kravitz, D., & Martin, B. (1986). Ringelmann rediscovered: The original article. *Journal of Personality and Social Psychology, 50,* 936–941.

Krosnick, J. A., Betz, A. L., Jussim, L. J., & Lynn, A. R. (1992). Subliminal conditioning of attitudes. *Personality and Social Psychology Bulletin, 18*(2), 152–162.

Krosnick, J. A., Boninger, D. S., Chuang, Y. C., Berent, M. K., & Carnot, C. G. (1993). Attitude strength: One construct or many related constructs? *Journal of Personality and Social Psychology, 65*(6), 1132–1151.

Kuiper, N. A., Olinger, L. J., MacDonald, M. R., & Shaw, B. F. (1985). Self-schema processing of depressed and nondepressed content: The effects of vulnerability to depression. *Social Cognition, 3*(1), 77–93.

Kunda, Z. (1990). The case for motivated reasoning. *Psychological Bulletin, 108*(3), 480–498.

Kunda, Z. (1999). Social cognition: Making sense of people. Cambridge, MA: The MIT Press.

Kunda, Z., Miller, D. T., & Claire, T. (1990). Combining social concepts: The role of causal reasoning. *Cognitive Science, 14*(4), 551–577.

Kunda, Z., & Oleson, K. C. (1995). Maintaining stereotypes in the face of disconfirmation: Constructing grounds for subtyping deviants. *Journal of Personality and Social Psychology, 68*(4), 565–579.

Kunst-Wilson, W. R., & Zajonc, R. B. (1980). Affective discrimination of stimuli that cannot be recognized. *Science, 207*(4430), 557–558.

Lamb, M. E., Thompson, R. A., Gardner, W., & Charnov, E. L. (1985). *Infant-mother attachment: The origins and developmental significance of individual differences in Strange Situation-behavior* (Vol. 7). Hillsdale, NJ: Erlbaum.

Lane, R. D. (2000). Neural correlates of conscious emotional experience. In R. D. Lane & L. Nadel (Eds.), *Cognitive neuroscience of emotion. Series in affective science* (pp. 345–370). New York: Oxford University Press.

Lang, P. J., Bradley, M. M., & Cuthbert, B. N. (1990). Emotion, attention, and the startle reflex. *Psychological Review, 97*(3), 377–395.

Langer, E. J. (1975). The illusion of control. *Journal of Personality and Social Psychology, 32*(2), 311–328.

LaPiere, R. T. (1934). Attitudes versus actions. *Social Forces, 13,* 230–237.

Larsen, R. J., & Diener, E. (1992). Promises and problems with the circumplex model of emotion. In M. S. Clark (Ed.), *Review of personality and social psychology: Emotion* (Vol. 13, pp. 25–59). Newbury Park, CA: Sage.

Latane, B. (1981). The psychology of social impact. *American Psychologist, 36*(4), 343–356.

Latane, B., Williams, K., & Harkins, S. (1979). Many hands make light the work: The causes and consequences of social loafing. *Journal of Personality and Social Psychology, 37*(6), 822–832.

Lazarus, R. S. (1966). *Psychological stress and the coping process.* New York: McGraw-Hill.

Lazarus, R. S. (1991). *Emotion and adaptation.* Oxford, UK: Oxford University Press.

Leary, M. R. (1990). Responses to social exclusion: Social anxiety, jealousy, loneliness, depression, and low self-esteem. *Journal of Social and Clinical Psychology, 9,* 221–229.

Lecky, P. (1945). *Self-consistency: A theory of personality.* New York: Island Press.

LeDoux, J. E. (1995). Emotion: Clues from the brain. *Annual Review of Psychology, 46,* 209–235.

Lemaine, G. (1974). Social differentiation and social originality. *European Journal of Personality and Social Psychology, 49*(4), 17–52.

Lepper, M. R., & Greene, D. (Eds.). (1978). *The hidden costs of rewards: New perspectives on the psychology of human motivation.* Hillsdale, NJ: Erlbaum.

Lepper, M. R., Greene, D., & Nisbett, R. E. (1973). Undermining children's intrinsic interest with extrinsic rewards: A test of the "overjustification" hypothesis. *Journal of Personality and Social Psychology, 31,* 129–137.

Levenson, R. W., Ekman, P., & Friesen, W. V. (1990). Voluntary facial action generates emotion-specific autonomic nervous system activity. *Psychophysiology, 27,* 363–384.

Lewicki, P. (1983). Self-image bias in person perception. *Journal of Personality and Social Psychology, 45,* 384–393.

Lewicki, P. (1984). Self-schema and social information processing. *Journal of Personality and Social Psychology, 47*(6), 1177–1190.

Lewontin, R. (2000). *The triple helix.* Cambridge, MA: Harvard University Press.

Linder, D. E., Cooper, J., & Jones, E. E. (1967). Decision freedom as a determinant of the role of incentive magnitude in attitude change. *Journal of Personality and Social Psychology, 6*(3), 245–254.

Lindsley, D. B. (1951). Emotion. In S. S. Stevens (Ed.), *Handbook of experimental psychology* (pp. 473–516). New York: Wiley.

Linville, P. W. (1987). Self-complexity as a cognitive buffer against stress-related illness and depression. *Journal of Personality and Social Psychology, 52*(4), 663–676.

Linville, P. W., & Clark, L. F. (1989). Can production systems cope with coping? *Social Cognition, 7*(2), 195–236.

Linville, P. W., Fischer, G. W., & Salovey, P. (1989). Perceived distributions of the characteristics of in-group and out-group members: Empirical evidence and a computer simulation. *Journal of Personality and Social Psychology, 57*(2), 165–188.

Liu, D., Diorio, J., Tannenbaum, B., Caldji, C., Francis, D., Freedman, A., Sharma, S., Pearson, D., Plotsky, P. M., & Meany, M. J. (1997). Maternal care, hippocampal glucocorticoid receptors, and hypothalamic-pituitary-adrenal responses to stress [see comments]. *Science, 277*(5332), 1659–1662.

Locksley, A., Borgida, E., Brekke, N., & Hepburn, C. (1980). Sex stereotypes and social judgment. *Journal of Personality and Social Psychology, 39*(5), 821–831.

Lockwood, P., & Kunda, Z. (1997). Superstars and me: Predicting the impact of role models on the self. *Journal of Personality and Social Psychology, 73*(1), 91–103.

Losch, M. E., & Cacioppo, J. T. (1990). Cognitive dissonance may enhance sympathetic tonus, but attitudes are changed to reduce negative affect rather than arousal. *Journal of Experimental Social Psychology, 26*(4), 289–304.

Luhtanen, R., & Crocker, J. (1992). A collective self-esteem scale: Self-evaluation of one's social identity. *Personality and Social Psychology Bulletin, 18*(3), 302–318.

Macrae, C. N., Bodenhausen, G. V., & Milne, A. B. (1995). The dissection of selection in person perception: Inhibitory processes in social stereotyping. *Journal of Personality and Social Psychology, 69*(3), 397–407.

Macrae, C. N., Bodenhausen, G. V., Milne, A. B., Thorn, T. M. J., & Castelli, L. (1997). On the activation of social stereotypes: The moderating role of processing objectives. *Journal of Experimental Social Psychology, 33*(5), 471–489.

Macrae, C. N., Milne, A. B., & Bodenhausen, G. V. (1994). Stereotypes as energy-saving devices: A peek inside the cognitive toolbox. *Journal of Personality and Social Psychology, 66*(1), 37–47.

MacTurk, R. H., & Morgan, G. A. (Eds.). (1995). *Mastery motivation: Origins, conceptualizations, and applications.* Norwood, NJ: Ablex Publishing.

MacTurk, R. H., Morgan, G. A., & Jennings, K. D. (1995). The assessment of mastery motivation in infants and young children. In R. H. MacTurk & G. A. Morgan (Eds.), *Mastery motivation: Origins, conceptualizations, and applications.* Norwood, NJ: Ablex Publishing.

Maestripieri, D. (2001). Biological bases of maternal attachment. *Current Directions in Psychological Science, 10,* 79–83.

Malmo, R. B. (1959). Activation: A neuropsychological dimension. *Psychological Review, 66,* 367–368.

Mansted, A. S. R., & Semin, G. (1980). Social facilitation effects: Mere enhancement of dominant responses? *British Journal of Social and Clincal Psychology, 19,* 119–136.

Marks, G. (1984). Thinking one's abilities are unique and one's opinions are common. *Personality and Social Psychology Bulletin, 10*(2), 203–208.

Markus, H. R. (1977). Self-schemata and processing information about the self. *Journal of Personality and Social Psychology, 35*(2), 63–78.

Markus, H. R., Crane, M., Bernstein, S., & Siladi, M. (1982). Self-schemas and gender. *Journal of Personality and Social Psychology, 42*(1), 38–50.

Markus, H. R., & Kitayama, S. (1991). Culture and the self: Implications for cognition, emotion, and motivation. *Psychological Review, 98*(2), 224–253.

Markus, H. R., Kitayama, S., & Heiman, R. J. (1996). Culture and "basic" psychological principles. In E. T. Higgins & A. W. Kruglanski (Eds.), *Social psychology: Handbook of basic principles* (pp. 857–913). New York: Guilford Press.

Markus, H. R., & Nurius, P. (1986). Possible selves. *American Psychologist, 41*(9), 954–969.

Markus, H. R., Smith, J., & Moreland, R. L. (1985). Role of the self-concept in the perception of others. *Journal of Personality and Social Psychology, 49*(6), 1494–1512.

Markus, H. R., & Zajonc, R. B. (1985). The cognitive perspective in social psychology. In G. Lindzey & E. Aronson (Eds.), *Handbook of Social Psychology* (3rd ed., Vol. 1, pp. 137–230). New York: Random House.

Maslach, C. (1974). Social and personal bases of individuation. *Journal of Personality and Social Psychology, 29*, 411–425.

McCartney, K., Harris, M. J., & Bernieri, F. (1990). Growing up and growing apart: A developmental meta-analysis of twin studies. *Psychological Bulletin, 107*(2), 226–237.

McClintock, M. K. (1998). On the nature of mammalian and human pheromones. *Annals of the New York Academy of Sciences, 855*, 390–392.

McGuire, W. J. (1960). A syllogistic analysis of cognitive relationships. In C. I. Hovland & M. J. Rosenberg (Eds.), *Attitude organization and change* (pp. 65–111). New Haven, CT: Yale University Press.

McGuire, W. J. (1985). Attitudes and attitude change. In G. Lindzey & E. Aronson (Eds.), *Handbook of social psychology* (3rd ed., Vol. 2, pp. 233–246). New York: Random House.

McGuire, W. J., McGuire, C. V., Child, P., & Fujioka, T. (1978). Salience of ethnicity in the spontaneous self-concept as a function of one's ethnic distinctiveness in the social environment. *Journal of Personality and Social Psychology, 36*(5), 511–520.

McGuire, W. J., McGuire, C. V., & Winton, W. (1979). Effects of household sex composition on the salience of one's gender in the spontaneous self-concept. *Journal of Experimental Social Psychology, 15*(1), 77–90.

Meany, M. J., Bhatnagar, S., Larocque, S., McCormick, C. M., Shanks, N., Sharma, N., Smythe, J., Viau, V., & Plotsky, P. M. (1996). Early environment and the development of individual differences in the hypothalamic-pituitary-adrenal stress response. In C. R. Pfeffer (Ed.), *Severe stress and mental disturbance in children* (pp. 85–127). Washington, DC: American Psychiatric Press.

Metcalfe, J., & Mischel, W. (1999). A hot/cool-system analysis of delay of gratification: Dynamics of willpower. *Psychological Review, 106*(1), 3–19.

Milgram, S. (1963). Behavioral study of obedience. *Journal of Abnormal and Social Psychology, 67*(4), 371–378.

Miller, J. G. (1984). Culture and the development of everyday social explanation. *Journal of Personality and Social Psychology, 46*, 961–978.

Mischel, W. (1988). Processes in delay of gratification. In L. Berkowitz (Ed.), *Advances in experimental social psychology* (Vol. 7, pp. 249–292). San Diego, CA: Academic Press.

Mischel, W., Shoda, Y., & Peake, P. K. (1988). The nature of adolescent competencies predicted by preschool delay of gratification. *Journal of Personality and Social Psychology, 54*(4), 687–696.

Mischel, W., Zeiss, R., & Zeiss, A. (1974). Internal-external control and persistence: Validation and implications of the Stanford Preschool Internal-External Scale. *Journal of Personality and Social Psychology, 29*(2), 265–278.

Moretti, M. M., & Higgins, E. T. (1999). Internal representations of others in self-regulation: A new look at a classic issue. *Social Cognition, 17*(2), 186–208.

Morris, M. W., & Peng, K. (1994). Culture and cause: American and Chinese attributions for social and physical events. *Journal of Personality and Social Psychology, 21*, 262–283.

Muraven, M., Tice, D. M., & Baumeister, R. F. (1998). Self-control as a limited resource: Regulatory depletion patterns. *Journal of Personality and Social Psychology, 74*(3), 774–789.

Murray, S. L., Holmes, J. G., & Griffin, D. W. (1996). The benefits of positive illusions: Idealization and the construction of satisfaction in close relationships. *Journal of Personality and Social Psychology, 70*(1), 79–98.

Murray, S. L., Holmes, J. G., MacDonald, G., & Ellsworth, P. C. (1998). Through the looking glass darkly? When self-doubts turn into relationship insecurities. *Journal of Personality and Social Psychology, 75*(6), 1459–1480.

Nelson, T. E., Biernat, M. R., & Manis, M. (1990). Everyday base rates (sex stereotypes): Potent and resilient. *Journal of Personality and Social Psychology, 59*(4), 664–675.

Nemeth, C., & Chiles, C. (1988). Modelling courage: The role of dissent in fostering independence. *European Journal of Social Psychology, 18*(3), 275–280.

Niedenthal, P. M., Setterlund, M. B., & Wherry, M. B. (1992). Possible self-complexity and affective reactions to goal-relevant evaluation. *Journal of Personality and Social Psychology, 63*(1), 5–16.

Nisbett, R. E., & Borgida, E. (1975). Attribution and the psychology of prediction. *Journal of Personality and Social Psychology, 32*(5), 932–943.

Nisbett, R. E., & Ross, L. (1980). *Human inference: Strategies and shortcomings of social judgment.* Englewood Cliffs, N.J.: Prentice-Hall.

Nisbett, R. E., & Wilson, T. D. (1977). Telling more than we can know: Verbal reports on mental processes. *Psychological Review, 84*(3), 231–259.

Nord, W. R. (1968). Social exchange theory: An integrative approach to social conformity. *Psychological Bulletin, 71*(3), 174–208.

Oatley, K. (1992). *Best laid schemes: The psychology of emotions.* Cambridge, UK: Cambridge University Press.

Osgood, C. (1969). The nature and measurement of meaning. In J. G. Snider & C. E. Osgood (Eds.), *Semantic differential technique* (pp. 3–41). Chicago: Aldine.

Osgood, C. (1976). *Focus on meaning, Vol. 1: Explorations in semantic space.* The Hague, Netherlands: Mouton.

Osgood, C., Suci, G., & Tannenbaum, P. (1957). *The measurement of meaning.* Urbana: University of Illinois.

Osgood, C. E., & Tannenbaum, P. H. (1955). The principle of congruity in the prediction of attitude change. *Psychological Review, 62*, 42–55.

Park, B., & Hastie, R. (1987). Perception of variability in category development: Instance- versus abstraction-based stereotypes. *Journal of Personality and Social Psychology, 53*(4), 621–635.

Park, B., Ryan, C. S., & Judd, C. M. (1992). Role of meaningful subgroups in explaining differences in perceived variability for in-groups and out-groups. *Journal of Personality and Social Psychology, 63*(4), 553–567.

Pelham, B. W., & Swann, W. B. (1989). From self-conceptions to self-worth: On the sources and structure of global self-esteem. *Journal of Personality and Social Psychology, 57*(4), 672–680.

Petkova, K. G., Ajzen, I., & Driver, B. L. (1995). Salience of anti-abortion beliefs and commitment to an attitudinal position: On the strength, structure, and predictive validity of anti-abortion attitudes. *Journal of Applied Social Psychology, 25*(6), 463–483.

Petty, R. E., & Cacioppo, J. T. (1981). *Attitudes and persuasion—classic and contemporary approaches.* Dubuque, IA: W.C. Brown.

Petty, R. E., & Cacioppo, J. T. (1984). The effects of involvement on responses to argument quantity and quality: Central and peripheral routes to persuasion. *Journal of Personality and Social Psychology, 46*(1), 69–81.

Petty, R. E., & Cacioppo, J. T. (1986). *Communication and persuasion: Central and peripheral routes to attitude change.* New York: Springer-Verlag.

Petty, R. E., Cacioppo, J. T., & Goldman, R. (1981). Personal involvement as a determinant of argument-based persuasion. *Journal of Personality and Social Psychology, 41*(5), 847–855.

Petty, R. E., Cacioppo, J. T., & Kasmer, J. A. (1987). The role of affect in the elaboration likelihood model of persuasion. In L. Donohew, H. E. Sypher, & E. T. Higgins (Eds.), *Communication, social cognition, and affect* (pp. 117–146). Hillsdale, NJ: Erlbaum.

Petty, R. E., Wells, G. L., & Brock, T. C. (1976). Distraction can enhance or reduce yielding to propaganda: Thought disruption versus effort justification. *Journal of Personality and Social Psychology, 34*(5), 874–884.

Phelps, E. A., O'Connor, K. J., Cunningham, W. A., Funayama, E. S., Gatenby, J. C., Gore, J. C., & Banaji, M. R. (2000). Performance on indirect measures of race evaluation predicts amygdala activation. *Journal of Cognitive Neuroscience, 12*(5), 729–738.

Pickett, C. L. (2001). The effects of entitativity beliefs on implicit comparisons between group members. *Personality and Social Psychology Bulletin, 27,* 515–525.

Pleban, R., & Tesser, A. (1981). The effects of relevance and quality of another's performance on interpersonal closeness. *Social Psychology Quarterly, 44*(3), 278–285.

Pliner, P., Hart, H., Kohl, J., & Saari, D. (1974). Compliance without pressure: Some further data on the foot-in-the-door technique. *Journal of Experimental Social Psychology, 10*(1), 17–22.

Pomerantz, E. M., Chaiken, S., & Tordesillas, R. S. (1995). Attitude strength and resistance processes. *Journal of Personality and Social Psychology, 69*(3), 408–419.

Pratto, F., & Bargh, J. A. (1991). Stereotyping based on apparently individuating information: Trait and global components of sex stereotypes under attention overload. *Journal of Experimental Social Psychology, 27*(1), 26–47.

Puckett, J. M., Petty, R. E., Cacioppo, J. T., & Fischer, D. L. (1983). The relative impact of age and attractiveness stereotypes on persuasion. *Journal of Gerontology, 38*(3), 340–343.

Pyszczynski, T., Greenberg, J., & Solomon, S. (1999). A dual-process model of defense against conscious and unconscious death-related thoughts: An extension of terror management theory. *Psychological Review 106*(4), 835–845.

Quattrone, G. A., & Jones, E. E. (1980). The perception of variability within in-groups and out-groups: Implications for the law of small numbers. *Journal of Personality and Social Psychology, 38*(1), 141–152.

Reite, M. (1990). Touch, attachment, and health: Is there a relationship? In K. E. Barnard & T. B. Brazelton (Eds.), *Touch: The foundation of experience: Full revised and expanded proceedings of Johnson & Johnson Pediatric Round Table X. Clinical infant reports* (pp. 195–225). Madison, CT: International Universities Press.

Riess, M., & Schlenker, B. R. (1977). Attitude change and responsibility avoidance as modes of dilemma resolution in forced-compliance situations. *Journal of Personality and Social Psychology, 35*(1), 21–30.

Rogers, T. B. (1981). A model of the self as an aspect of human information processing. In N. Cantor & J. F. Kihlstrom (Eds.), *Personality, cognition, and social interaction* (pp. 193–214). Hillsdale, NJ: Erlbaum.

Rogers, T. B., Kuiper, N. A., & Kirker, W. S. (1977). Self-reference and the encoding of personal information. *Journal of Personality and Social Psychology, 35*(9), 677–688.

Rogers, T. B., Rogers, P. J., & Kuiper, N. A. (1979). Evidence for the self as a cognitive prototype: The "false alarms effect." *Personality and Social Psychology Bulletin, 5*(1), 53–56.

Rosch, E., & Lloyd, B. B. (1978). *Cognition and categorization.* Hillsdale, NJ: Erlbaum.

Rosenberg, M. (1965). *Society and the adolescent self-image.* Princeton, NJ: Princeton University Press.

Rosenberg, M. J., & Hovland, C. I. (1960). Cognitive, affective, and behavioral components of attitudes. In C. I. Hovland & M. J. Rosenberg (Eds.), *Attitude organization and change: An analysis of consistency among attitude components* (pp. 1–14). New Haven, CT: Yale University Press.

Rosenblatt, A., Greenberg, J., Solomon, S., Pyszczynski, T., & Lyon, D. (1989). Evidence for terror management theory, I: The effects of mortality salience on reactions to those who violate or uphold cultural values. *Journal of Personality and Social Psychology, 57*(4), 681–690.

Ross, L., & Nisbett, R. E. (1991). *The person and the situation: Perspectives of social psychology.* New York: Mcgraw-Hill.

Ross, M., & Sicoly, F. (1979). Egocentric biases in availability and attribution. *Journal of Personality and Social Psychology, 37*(3), 322–336.

Rothbart, M., Evans, M., & Fulero, S. (1979). Recall for confirming events: Memory processes and the maintenance of social stereotypes. *Journal of Experimental Social Psychology, 15*(4), 343–355.

Russell, J. A. (1980). A circumplex model of affect. *Journal of Personality and Social Psychology, 39,* 1161–1178.

Sagar, H. A., & Schofield, J. W. (1980). Racial and behavioral cues in Black and White children's perceptions of ambiguously aggressive acts. *Journal of Personality and Social Psychology, 39*(4), 590–598.

Sampson, E. E. (1988). The debate on individualism: Indigenous psychologies of the individual and their role in personal and societal functioning. *American Psychologist, 43*(1), 15–22.

Sampson, E. E. (1989). The challenge of social change for psychology: Globalization and psychology's theory of the person. *American Psychologist, 44*(6), 914–921.

Sansone, C., & Harackiewicz, J. M. (2000). *Intrinsic and extrinsic motivation: The search for optimal motivation and performance.* San Diego, CA: Academic Press.

Schachter, S. (1951). Deviation, rejection, and communication. *Journal of Abnormal and Social Psychology, 46,* 190–207.

Schachter, S. (1959). *The psychology of affiliation.* Stanford, CT: Stanford University Press.

Scheier, M. F., & Carver, C. S. (1982). Self-consciousness, outcome expectancy, and persistence. *Journal of Research in Personality, 16*(4), 409–418.

Scherer, K. R., Schorr, A., & Johnstone, T. (Eds.). (2001). *Appraisal processes in emotion.* New York: Oxford University Press.

Schlenker, B. R., & Forsyth, D. R. (1980). Effects of choice, responsibility, and anonymity on attitudes following attitude-consistent behavior. *Journal of Psychology, 105*(1), 75–82.

Schwarz, N., & Bless, H. (1992). Constructing reality and its alternatives: An inclusion/exclusion model of assimilation and contrast effects in social judgment. In L. L. Martin & A. Tesser (Eds.), *The construction of social judgments* (pp. 217–245). Hillsdale, NJ: Erlbaum.

Seligman, M. E. P. (1975). *Helplessness: On depression, development, and death.* San Francisco, CA: Freeman.

Seligman, M. E. P., & Csikszentmihalyi, M. (2000). Positive psychology: An introduction. *American Psychologist, 55*(1), 5–14.

Seligman, M. E. P., Reivich, K., Jaycox, L., & Gillham, J. (1995). *The optimistic child.* Boston: Houghton Mifflin.

Seta, J. J., Crisson, J. E., Seta, C. E., & Wang, M. A. (1989). Task performance and perceptions of anxiety: Averaging and summation in an evaluative setting. *Journal of Personality and Social Psychology, 56,* 387–396.

Seta, J. J., & Hassan, R. K. (1980). Awareness of prior success or failure: A critical factor in task performance. *Journal of Personality and Social Psychology, 39,* 70–76.

Shaver, P., Hazan, C., & Bradshaw, D. (1988). Love as attachment. In R. J. Sternberg & M. L. Barnes (Eds.), *The psychology of love* (pp. 68–99). New Haven, CT: Yale University Press.

Sherif, M., Harvey, O. H., White, B. J., Good, W. R., & Sherif, C. W. (1961). *The Robbers Cave experiment: Intergroup conflict and cooperation.* Norman: University of Oklahoma Institute of Intergroup Relations.

Sherif, M., & Murphy, G. (1936). *The psychology of social norms.* New York: Harper.

Sherman, S. J. (1970). Effects of choice and incentive on attitude change in a discrepant behavior situation. *Journal of Personality and Social Psychology, 15*(3), 245–252.

Shih, M., Pittinsky, T. L., & Ambady, N. (1999). Stereotype susceptibility: Identity salience and shifts in quantitative performance. *Psychological Science, 10*(1), 80–83.

Shweder, R. A., & Bourne, E. J. (1984). Does the concept of the person vary cross culturally? In R. A. Shweder & R. A. Levine (Eds.), *Cul-*

ture theory: Essays on mind, self, and emotion (pp. 158–199). Cambridge, England: Cambridge University Press.

Silverman, I. (1964). Self-esteem and differential responsiveness to success and failure. *Journal of Abnormal and Social Psychology, 69,* 115–119.

Simon, B. (1992). Intragroup differentiation in terms of ingroup and outgroup attributes. *European Journal of Social Psychology, 22*(4), 407–413.

Sinclair, L., & Kunda, Z. (1999). Reactions to a Black professional: Motivated inhibition and activation of conflicting stereotypes. *Journal of Personality and Social Psychology, 77*(5), 885–904.

Slovic, P., Fischhoff, B., & Lichtenstein, P. (1982). Facts versus fears: Understanding perceived risk. In D. Kahneman, P. Slovic, & A. Tversky (Eds.), *Judgment under uncertainty: Heuristics and biases* (pp. 436–489). New York: Cambridge University Press.

Smith, M. B., Bruner, J. S., & White, R. W. (1956). *Opinions and personality.* New York: Wiley.

Snyder, C. R., & Fromkin, H. L. (1980). *Uniqueness: The human pursuit of difference.* New York: Plenum Press.

Spencer, S. J., Steele, C. M., & Quinn, D. M. (1999). Stereotype threat and women's math performance. *Journal of Experimental Social Psychology, 35*(1), 4–28.

Staats, A. W., Staats, C. K., & Crawford, H. L. (1962). First order conditioning of meaning and the parallel conditioning of a GSR. *Journal of General Psychology, 67,* 159–167.

Stangor, C., & Duan, C. (1991). Effects of multiple task demands upon memory for information about social groups. *Journal of Experimental Social Psychology, 27*(4), 357–378.

Staw, B. M. (1976). Knee-deep in the Big Muddy: A study of escalating commitment to a chosen course of action. *Organizational Behavior and Human Decision Processes, 16*(1), 27–44.

Steele, C. M. (1988). The psychology of self-affirmation: Sustaining the integrity of the self. In L. Berkowitz (Ed.), *Advances in experimental social psychology, Vol. 21: Social psychological studies of the self: Perspectives and programs* (pp. 261–302). San Diego, CA: Academic Press.

Steele, C. M. (1997). A threat in the air: How stereotypes shape intellectual identity and performance. *American Psychologist, 52*(6), 613–629.

Stein, N. L., & Levine, L. J. (1989). The causal organisation of emotional knowledge: A developmental study. *Cognition and Emotion, 3*(4), 343–378.

Stone, J., Lynch, C. I., Sjomeling, M., & Darley, J. M. (1999). Stereotype threat effects on Black and White athletic performance. *Journal of Personality and Social Psychology, 77*(6), 1213–1227.

Stroessner, S. J., & Mackie, D. M. (1992). The impact of induced affect on the perception of variability in social groups. *Personality and Social Psychology Bulletin, 18*(5), 546–554.

Swann, W. B. (1987). Identity negotiation: Where two roads meet. *Journal of Personality and Social Psychology, 53*(6), 1038–1051.

Swann, W. B. (1990). To be adored or to be known? The interplay of self-enhancement and self-verification. In E. T. Higgins & R. M. Sorrentino (Eds.), *Handbook of motivation and cognition: Foundations of social behavior* (Vol. 2, pp. 408–448). New York: Guilford Press.

Swann, W. B., & Read, S. J. (1981). Self-verification processes: How we sustain our self-conceptions. *Journal of Experimental Social Psychology, 17*(4), 351–372.

Swann, W. B., de la Ronde, C., & Hixon, J. G. (1994). Authenticity and positivity strivings in marriage and courtship. *Journal of Personality and Social Psychology, 66*(5), 857–869.

Tajfel, H. (1982). Social psychology of intergroup relations. *Annual Review of Psychology, 33,* 1–39.

Tajfel, H., & Turner, J. C. (1986). The social identity theory of intergroup behavior. In S. Worchel & W. G. Austin (Eds.), *The social psychology of intergroup relations* (2nd ed., pp. 7–24). Pacific Grove, CA: Brookes/Cole.

Tanford, S., & Penrod, S. (1984). Social inference processes in juror judgments of multiple-offense trials. *Journal of Personality and Social Psychology, 47*(4), 749–765.

Tangney, J. P., & Fischer, K. W. (Eds.). (1995). *Self-conscious emotions: The psychology of shame, guilt, embarrassment, and pride.* New York: Guilford Press.

Taylor, S. E., & Brown, J. D. (1988). Illusion and well-being: A social psychological perspective on mental health. *Psychological Bulletin, 103*(2), 193–210.

Tedeschi, J. T., Schlenker, B. R., & Bonoma, T. V. (1971). Cognitive dissonance: Private ratiocination or public spectacle? *American Psychologist, 26*(8), 685–695.

Teger, A. I. (1980). *Too much invested to quit.* New York: Pergamon Press.

Tesser, A. (1988). Toward a self-evaluation maintenance model of social behavior. In L. Berkowitz (Ed.), *Advances in experimental social psychology, Vol. 21: Social psychological studies of the self: Perspectives and programs* (pp. 181–227). San Diego, CA: Academic Press.

Tesser, A., Campbell, J., & Mickler, S. (1983). The role of social pressure, attention to the stimulus, and self-doubt in conformity. *European Journal of Social Psychology, 13*(3), 217–233.

Tesser, A., & Martin, L. (1996). The psychology of evaluation. In E. T. Higgins & A. W. Kruglanski (Eds.), *Social psychology: Handbook of basic principles* (pp. 400–432). New York: Guilford Press.

Tesser, A., Pilkington, C. J., & McIntosh, W. D. (1989). Self-evaluation maintenance and the mediational role of emotion: The perception of friends and strangers. *Journal of Personality and Social Psychology, 57*(3), 442–456.

Thagard, P., & Kunda, Z. (1998). Making sense of people: Coherence mechanisms. In S. J. Read & L. C. Miller (Eds.), *Connectionist models of social reasoning and social behavior* (pp. 3–26). Mahwah, NJ: Erlbaum.

Thurstone, L. L. (1928). Attitudes can be measured. *American Journal of Sociology, 33,* 529–554.

Thurstone, L. L. (1931). The measurement of social attitudes. *Journal of Abnormal and Social Psychology, 26,* 249–269.

Tice, D. M. (1991). Esteem protection or enhancement? Self-handicapping motives and attributions differ by trait self-esteem. *Journal of Personality and Social Psychology, 60*(5), 711–725.

Tomkins, S. S. (1962). *Affect, imagery, conscious-*

ness, Vol. I: The positive affects. New York: Springer-Verlag.

Tomkins, S. S. (1963). *Affect, imagery, consciousness, Vol. II: The negative affects.* New York: Springer-Verlag.

Triandis, H. C. (1989). The self and social behavior in differing cultural contexts. *Psychological Review, 96*(3), 506–520.

Triplett, N. (1898). The dynamogenic factors in pacemaking and competition. *American Journal of Psychology, 9,* 507–533.

Turner, J. C. (1985). *Rediscovering the social group: A self-categorization theory.* New York: Blackwell.

Tversky, A. (1977). Features of similarity. *Psychological Review, 84*(4), 327–352.

Uchino, B. N., Cacioppo, J. T., & Keicolt-Glaser, J. K. (1996). The relationship between social support and physiological processes: A review with emphasis on underlying mechanisms and implications for health. *Psychological Bulletin, 119*(3), 488–531.

Watson, D., & Tellegen, A. (1985). Toward a consensual structure of mood. *Psychological Bulletin, 98,* 219–235.

Watson, D., Wiese, D., Vidya, J., & Tellegen, A. (1999). The two general activation systems of affect: Structural findings, evolutionary considerations, and psychobiolobical evidence. *Journal of Personality and Social Psychology, 76,* 820–838.

Watts, W. A., & Holt, L. E. (1970). Logical relationships among beliefs and timing as factors in persuasion. *Journal of Personality and Social Psychology, 16*(4), 571–582.

Wegner, D. M. (1989). *White bears and other unwanted thoughts: Suppression, obsession, and the psychology of mental control.* New York: Penguin Books.

White, R. W. (1959). Motivation reconsidered: The concept of competence. *Psychological Review, 66,* 297–333.

Wicker, A. W. (1969). Attitudes versus actions: The relationship of verbal and overt behavioral responses to attitude objects. *Journal of Social Issues, 25,* 41–78.

Williams, K., Harkins, S. G., & Latane, B. (1981). Identifiability as a deterrant to social loafing: Two cheering experiments. *Journal of Personality and Social Psychology, 40*(2), 303–311.

Wills, T. A. (1981). Downward comparison principles in social psychology. *Psychological Bulletin, 90*(2), 245–271.

Wilson, E. O. (1998). *Consilience.* New York: Knopf.

Wilson, T. D., Lindsey, S., & Schooler, T. Y. (2000). A model of dual attitudes. *Psychological Review, 107*(1), 101–126.

Wittenbrink, B., Judd, C. M., & Park, B. (1997). Evidence for racial prejudice at the implicit level and its relationship with questionnaire measures. *Journal of Personality and Social Psychology, 72*(2), 262–274.

Wittenbrink, B., Park, B., & Judd, C. M. (1998). The role of stereotypic knowledge in the construal of person models. In C. Sedikides & J. Schopler (Eds.), *Intergroup cognition and intergroup behavior* (pp. 177–202). Mahwah, NJ: Erlbaum.

Wood, J. V., Giordano-Beech, M., Taylor, K. L., Michela, J. L., & Gaus, V. (1994). Strategies of social comparison among people with low self-esteem: Self-protection and self-enhancement. *Journal of Personality and Social Psychology, 67*(4), 713–731.

Wood, J. V., & Taylor, K. L. (1991). Serving self-relevant goals through social comparison. In J. Suls & T. A. Wills (Eds.), *Social comparison: Contemporary theory and research* (pp. 23–49). Hillsdale, NJ: Erlbaum.

Wood, W., Kallgren, C. A., & Preisler, R. M. (1985). Access to attitude-relevant information in memory as a determinant of persuasion: The role of message attributes. *Journal of Experimental Social Psychology, 21*(1), 73–85.

Woodworth, R. S. (1921). *Psychology: A study of mental life.* New York: Henry Holt.

Wortman, C. B., & Brehm, J. W. (1975). Responses to uncontrollable outcomes: An integration of reactance theory and learned helplessness. In L. Berkowitz (Ed.), *Advances in experimental social psychology* (Vol. 8, pp. 277–336). New York: Academic Press.

Wu, H., Wang, J., Cacioppo, J. T., Glaser, R., Kiecolt-Glaser, J. K., & Malarkey, W. B. (1999). Chronic stress associated with spousal caregiving of patients with Alzheimer's dementia is associated with downregulation of B-lymphocyte GH mRNA. *Journals of Gerontology, Series A: Biological Sciences and Medical Sciences, 54*(4), M212–M215.

Wundt, W. M. (1902). *Grundzüge der physiologischen Psychologie,* (Principles of Physiological Psychology) (5th ed., Vol. 3). Leipzig, Germany: W. Engelmann.

Wyer, R. S. (1974). Some implications of the "Socratic effect" for alternative models of cognitive consistency. *Journal of Personality, 42*(3), 399–419.

Wyer, R. S., Jr., & Goldberg, L. (1970). A probabilistic analysis of the relationships among belief and attitudes. *Psychological Review, 77*(2), 100–120.

Young, L. J., Wang, Z., & Insel, T. R. (1998). Neuroendocrine bases of monogamy. *Trends in Neurosciences, 21*(2), 71–75.

Zajonc, R. B. (1965). Social facilitation. *Science, 149,* 269–274.

Zajonc, R. B. (1980). Feeling and thinking: Preferences need no inferences. *American Psychologist, 35*(2), 151–175.

Zanna, M. P., & Cooper, J. (1974). Dissonance and the pill: An attribution approach to studying the arousal properties of dissonance. *Journal of Personality and Social Psychology, 29*(5), 703–709.

Zanna, M. P., & Rempel, J. K. (1988). Attitudes: A new look at an old concept. In D. Bar-Tal & A. W. Kruglanski (Eds.), *The social psychology of knowledge* (pp. 315–334). Cambridge, UK: Cambridge University Press.

Ziller, R. C. (1964). Individuation and socialization. *Human Relations, 17,* 341–360.

Zuckerman, M., Kieffer, S. C., & Knee, C. R. (1998). Consequences of self-handicapping: Effects on coping, academic performance, and adjustment. *Journal of Personality and Social Psychology, 74*(6), 1619–1628.

CHAPTER 19

Addiction

ROY A. WISE

Addiction is a term that has broad general meaning, having been used in connection with obesity, sexual behavior, gambling, drugs of abuse, and an increasing list of motivated behaviors (Orford, 2001). There are multiple definitions of the term, and whether a given substance or event is deemed addictive depends largely on the definition selected. There is, perhaps, as much controversy about the definition of addiction as there is about the nature of addiction. The present chapter deals with the topic from the viewpoint of addiction to drugs.

DEFINITIONS AND TERMS

Addiction

Even the special case of drug addiction is not well defined. While it is generally accepted that cocaine and heroin are strongly addictive and that alcohol can be, there is still disagreement about whether such drugs as nicotine, caffeine, or cannabis should be seen in the same light. The lack of a satisfactory scientific definition leaves such questions unresolved. The various committees of such groups as the World Health Organization (Edwards, Arif, & Hodgson, 1981) and the American Psychiatric Association (1987, 1994) regularly revise their opinions and craft them, understandably, in language that is more sensitive to political and public health pressures than to scientific precision.

The dictionary definitions of addiction identify it as a "state of being given up to some habit." Although the concept of habit—once the dominant concept in psychological theory—is central to all definitions of addiction, most specialist definitions involve attempts to distinguish addictions from the habits of everyday life. Thus, recent specialist definitions invoke the qualifier that addiction is a *compulsive* habit having harmful health and social consequences (Cottler, 1993; Leshner, 1999; Rounsaville, Bryant, Babor, Kranzler, & Kadden, 1993). Historically, the compulsive nature of drug self-administration in addicts has been attributed to drug *dependence* and its correlated phenomenon drug *tolerance*.

Tolerance

Tolerance refers to a progressive loss of sensitivity to one or more effects of a drug as a result of prior drug experience. In part, tolerance is assumed to reflect a variety of drug-opposite neural adaptations that bias the body against the actions of the drug (Collier, 1968, 1980; D. B. Goldstein & Goldstein, 1961; Jaffe & Sharpless, 1968). In part, tolerance reflects drug-opposite conditioned responses to the environment where the drug is given (Siegel, 1976; Stewart & Eikelboom, 1987).

In keeping with Pavlovian theory, these drug-opposite reactions to environmental stimuli appear to reflect association of the injection environment with the preinjection (withdrawal) state of the animal (Eikelboom & Stewart, 1979).

Dependence

Although the measurable signs of tolerance and dependence can be dissociated (e.g., Aley & Levine, 1997; Kishioka, Paronis, & Woods, 2000; Perkins et al., 2001), they are two sides of the same coin conceptually and mechanistically. Dependence develops during periods of drug intoxication and is revealed by withdrawal symptoms in periods of drug abstinence. Withdrawal symptoms reflect organ or mood responses that are opposite to those caused by the drug in question; thus the classic withdrawal symptom associated with sedative drugs is insomnia. Opiates cause pupillary constriction and constipation, whereas opiate withdrawal causes pupillary dilation and diarrhea. Psychomotor stimulants cause agitation and alertness and suppress appetite; their withdrawal causes fatigue and depression along with increased appetite.

Habit

Habit is a term familiar to the experimental psychologist but avoided by many addiction specialists. There are various reasons for this. If we define addiction as a subclass of habit, we de-mystify it more than many would like. Antismoking activists argue that addiction to nicotine is much *more* than simply a habit. Representatives of the tobacco industry, on the other hand, would like to claim that nicotine self-administration, like caffeine consumption, is *merely* a habit and, by implication, not an addiction (J. H. Robinson & Pritchard, 1995). The truth is that habit is at the core of all addictions and that addictions come in a variety of strengths and with a variety of characteristics and side effects. Is an addiction merely a *very strong* habit, a *compulsive* habit? The objective definitions and quantification of "very strong" and "compulsive" are obviously problematic.

Sensitization

While repeated use of some drugs can, under some circumstances, lead to drug tolerance (and associated dependence), repeated use of addictive drugs can also, under other circumstances, cause the opposite effect: sensitization to effects of the drug (Babbini & Davis, 1972; Downs & Eddy, 1932; Ellinwood & Kilbey, 1975; Post & Kopanda, 1976; Segal & Mandell, 1974). This is most evident with the psychomotor stimulant effects of amphetamine and cocaine; these substances induce locomotion and stereotyped movements in laboratory animals, and repeated intermittent injections of these agents become increasingly effective in this regard (T. E. Robinson & Becker, 1986). Low doses of opiates also cause locomotion, and the locomotor response to opiates not only sensitizes like those of amphetamine and cocaine (Babbini & Davis, 1972) but also cross-sensitizes with those of cocaine and amphetamine. That is, repeated exposure to cocaine or amphetamine sensitizes animals to the subsequent locomotor stimulating effects of opiates (DuMars, Rodger, & Kalivas, 1988; Stewart & Vezina, 1987) and exposure to morphine sensitizes animals to the subsequent locomotor stimulating effects of cocaine (Vezina, Giovino, Wise, & Stewart, 1989). As with the phenomenon of tolerance, sensitization seems to develop in part because of neuroadaptations induced by the pharmacological consequences of the drug but also in part because of the learned association of the drug with the environment in which the animal normally receives the drug (T. E. Robinson, Browman, Crombag, & Badiani, 1998; Tilson & Rech, 1973).

Reinforcement

Most behavioral pharmacologists and many physiological psychologists are content to identify the addictive properties with the reinforcing properties of drugs (Schuster & Thompson, 1969; Thompson, 1968). The concept of reinforcement arose first in the study of classical conditioning; in 1903 Pavlov (cited in Pavlov, 1928) used the term to denote the strengthening of a conditioned response by occasional re-pairing of a conditioned stimulus with an unconditioned stimulus. For Pavlov, a conditioned stimulus is reinforced; an unconditioned stimulus is the reinforcer; and the pairing of the conditioned stimulus with the unconditioned stimulus is the reinforcement. Skinner and Thorndike each adapted Pavlov's term to instrumental behavior. Just as Pavlov had used it to imply the strengthening of associations between stimuli, so Thorndike (1933) used it to imply the strengthening or "stamping in" (Thorndike, 1898) of associations between a stimulus and a response. Skinner (1933) used it to imply the strengthening of the association between an act and its consequences, without presuming that the act was elicited by any particular stimulus.

Reinforcement comes in two varieties, positive and negative. A positive reinforcer is a stimulus or event whose *onset* increases the probability of the responses that it reliably follows. A negative reinforcer is a stimulus or event whose *offset* increases the probability of the responses that it reliably follows. In the context of addiction, drugs might be reinforcing because of the states of intoxication that they induce, because of the states of withdrawal distress that they alleviate, or both.

Reward

J. Olds and Milner (1954) discovered that direct electrical stimulation of the brain could be reinforcing. Subsequent workers have found that such stimulation not only reinforces the responses that precede it but also "primes" the recurrence of such responses during periods when they are not occurring spontaneously (Deutsch & Howarth, 1963; Gallistel, 1966). The classic example of priming is the induction of the strong craving for (and ingestion of) peanuts or potato chips that can be induced by the halfhearted tasting of an initial nut or chip. The priming effect of hypothalamic brain stimulation contributes greatly to the compulsive nature of intracranial self-stimulation (Howarth & Deutsch, 1962), and where Skinner advocated the term *reinforcement* to avoid the surplus meaning of the term *reward* and its implication of subjective pleasure, physiological psychologists have used the term *reward* to avoid the implication that the only significant effect of the stimulation is to stamp in a response habit (Wise, 1989). They use the term *reward* to encompass both the reinforcing (retroactive in the sense that they act on the memory trace of the prior response) and the priming (proactive in that they affect the vigor of the *next* response) effects of the stimulation. The proactive effects of reward presentation can also be viewed as incentive-motivational effects in that it is exposure to the incentive that energizes subsequent responding.

Incentive Motivation

The notion of incentive motivation was formulated to explain the apparent control of behavior by the expectancy of rewards that have yet to be earned (Bindra, 1978; Spence, 1956). The notion is a simple one; it posits that stimuli associated with the incentive come to invigorate the behavior in much the same way as would the incentive itself, were it immediately available to the senses. Incentive-motivational states are states of activation and response-readiness induced by sensed incentives or by stimuli that have been previously associated with such incentives. A classic example is the waiting dog's burst of excitement when its owner finally turns from some other activity to ask, "Do you want to go for a walk?" The transition from quiet waiting to tail- and rump-wagging, scampering, and jumping is a case of incentive motivation. We can only speculate that it is motivation *for* the incentive, but we know by observation that it is motivation *induced by* a stimulus associated with the incentive.

ANIMAL MODELS

A variety of animal models are used to reflect aspects of the human phenomenon of addiction. Although there are many reports of self-intoxication in lower animals (Siegel, 1976) and although lower animals can become addicted to many of the drugs abused by humans (Collins, Weeks, Cooper, Good, & Russell, 1984), addiction is, nonetheless, a uniquely human phenomenon. Only humans have the mastery of fire necessary for the smoking of drugs or drug-containing plant substances; only humans have the mastery of syringe and needle necessary for intravenous injections; only humans have the mastery of chemical purification and synthesis necessary to produce highly concentrated synthetic drugs or plant extracts; only humans have the mastery of cork and bottle to preserve alcohol for use over the long periods when fermenting plants are out of season. Addiction to drugs would not have arisen in the absence the human ability to self-administer highly concentrated substances on a regular basis and by a route of administration that quickly carries drug to the brain.

Intravenous Drug Self-Administration

Intravenous drug self-administration (Weeks, 1962) is a model based on instrumental con-ditioning (Griffiths, Brady, & Bradford, 1979; Johanson, 1978; Thompson, 1968) and is the model of addiction with the greatest face validity. Usually, animals are trained to lever press for intravenous injections much as rats were trained to lever press and pigeons trained to key peck for food by Skinner and his students. Rats, dogs, and primates have been used most widely, and they readily learn to self-administer the various drugs that are self-administered by humans (Collins et al., 1984). Laboratory animals learn to self-administer amphetamine, cocaine, and heroin to the point of death (Bozarth & Wise, 1985; Johanson, Balster, & Bonese, 1976) or physical dependence (Deneau, Yanagita, & Seevers, 1969; Goldberg, Woods, & Schuster, 1969) if given unlimited access to the drug by the intravenous route of administration.

In general, the drugs that are most addictive for humans are the most addictive for lower animals. This generalization must be qualified in the cases of intravenous nicotine, cannabis, and alcohol, which are marginally self-administered, if at all, by most laboratory animals. Our ability to train laboratory animals to take nicotine or cannabis by smoking is limited, of course (Jarvik, 1964), and much of the control that these drugs exert over human behavior is thought to result from the fact that smoked drugs reach the brain much more quickly than do drugs taken orally or even intravenously. Although rats and squirrel monkeys can be trained to self-administer intravenous nicotine (Corrigall & Coen, 1989; Goldberg, Spealman, Risner, & Henningfield, 1983) and cannabis (Tanda, Munzar, & Goldberg, 2000), they do not do so nearly as avidly as they self-administer amphetamine, cocaine, or heroin. Intravenous self-administration of alcohol has also been reported (Woods, Ikomi, & Winger, 1971), but in most animal models the oral route of administration is used. Alcohol is usually avoided by laboratory animals (Lester, 1966; Mello,

1973) unless its taste is masked (Macenski & Meisch, 1994; Samson, 1986) or unless susceptible strains are bred (Eriksson, 1968; Li et al., 1988; Mardones & Segovia-Riquelme, 1983) or selected (Phillips, Feller, & Crabbe, 1989) for unusual alcohol preference.

Self-administration of intravenous morphine, heroin, amphetamine, or cocaine offers the animal models that have the greatest commonality with major human addictions. The intravenous route of administration of these drugs clearly puts both humans and lower mammals at great risk of addiction, and it is by this route of administration that animals will self-administer these drugs to the point of death or physical dependence. Although human addiction to cocaine involves the smoking of free-base or crack cocaine more frequently than it involves intravenous injection, the two routes of administration produce self-administration that is comparably compulsive, presumably because they deliver the drug to the brain in comparable concentration and with much greater speed than occurs with intranasal (snorting) or oral administration (Fischman & Schuster, 1982; Paly, Jatlow, Van Dyke, Jeri, & Byck, 1982).

The intravenous drug self-administration model was developed to measure drug reinforcement, but the response rates that are the usual dependent variables in self-administration experiments reflect much more than just the "stamping in" of memory traces and response habits that were originally intended by that term. Most studies deal with the maintenance of self-administration habits that are already well established. Acquisition studies—studies of the ability of drug reinforcement to establish a new response habit—are infrequent for a variety of reasons. First, they require large numbers of animals because of the considerable between-subjects variability. Second, they are wasteful of animals—particularly when primates are involved—unless the animals, once trained, are tested

further in studies of response maintenance or willingness to continue to work when other drugs are substituted for the training drug. Third and perhaps most important, the rate of acquisition of a response habit is affected by more factors than simply the strength of reinforcement. For example, whereas Lewis rats tend to learn to take intravenous cocaine compulsively within a few hours of exposure, Fischer rats may take weeks before learning the same habit (Kosten, Miserendino, Chi, & Nestler, 1994; Leeb & Wise, 1993; Ranaldi et al., 2001). This is apparently not, however, because the drug is less reinforcing for the Fischer rat. The Fischer rat is slower to make the initial lever presses that first expose it to the reinforcing effects of cocaine. With extended opportunity, nonetheless, Fischer rats can be trained to respond for the drug, and they reach asymptotic rates of lever pressing with approximately the same number of reinforced responses (simply taking much longer to achieve that number) as do Lewis rats. When their habit stabilizes, their hourly intake is similar to that of the faster-learning Lewis rats. The Fischer rat is simply less active in the test box—its baseline lever-pressing rate is much lower—than the Lewis rat. Thus, despite apparently similar sensitivity to the reinforcing effects of the drug, acquisition of drug habits can differ widely between strains and individuals.

Finally, although the self-administration model is useful in determining that a drug *is* reinforcing, it is not a particularly useful model for determining the *strength* of drug reinforcement. Nor is it a good model for determining the relative reinforcing effectiveness of *different* drugs. Different drugs have different side effects, many of which can alter the rat's performance and its rate of habit acquisition.

Thus, the self-administration model is usually used to study the *maintenance* rather than the acquisition of drug-seeking habits. Here, at least when response requirements are low (a fixed ratio-1—FR-1—schedule of reinforcement is frequently used), the rate of responding offers a measure of drug satiety or drug satisfaction rather than a measure of the strength of drug reinforcement. Well-trained animals that earn intravenous psychomotor stimulants or opiates for each lever press (FR-1) self-administer these drugs at very reliable rates, with significant but reliable pauses between responses (Gerber & Wise, 1989; Pickens & Harris, 1968; Pickens & Thompson, 1968). When rewarded for each lever press, this is a model that tells us more about when the animal is motivated for more drug than about how much the animal is motivated for a drug. The model is thus useful for those who are concerned with inferences about the points in time when drug *craving* arises.

With the psychomotor stimulants and opiates, the time of initiation of a drug-seeking lever press (the few seconds prior to a response or a move toward the lever) is well predicted by the level of the drug in the blood (Yokel & Pickens, 1973, 1974) or by the correlated extracellular level of the neurotransmitter dopamine (Ranaldi, Pocock, Zereik, & Wise, 1999; Wise, Leone, Rivest, & Leeb, 1995; Wise, Newton, et al., 1995), on which the reinforcing efficacy of cocaine (de Wit & Wise, 1977; Risner & Jones, 1980) and amphetamine (Risner & Jones, 1976; Yokel & Wise, 1975, 1976) are known to depend. Cocaine, amphetamine, heroin, nicotine, alcohol, phencyclidine, and cannabis each elevate extracellular levels of brain dopamine (Church, Justice, & Byrd, 1987; Di Chiara & Imperato, 1988; Gerhardt, Pang, & Rose, 1987; Ng et al., 1988; Zetterström, Sharp, Marsden, & Ungerstedt, 1983), as do the natural pleasures of life (Fiorino, Coury, & Phillips, 1997; Hernandez & Hoebel, 1988). Cocaine does so by blocking the reuptake of spontaneously released dopamine (Heikkila, Orlansky, & Cohen, 1975). Amphetamine

does so by causing dopamine-containing neurons to release dopamine even in the absence of neural impulses (Heikkila, Orlansky, Mytilineou, & Cohen, 1975). Nicotine acts directly on dopamine-containing neurons to trigger nerve impulses (Grenhoff, Aston-Jones, & Svensson, 1986; Mereu et al., 1987) and thus to induce distal dopamine release. Heroin and morphine also increase dopaminergic cell firing and distal dopamine release, but they do so, at least in part, by inhibiting neighboring GABAergic neurons that normally hold dopaminergic neurons under inhibitory control (Johnson & North, 1992). Thus, the opiates disinhibit the dopaminergic system rather than stimulating it directly. Alcohol (Gessa, Muntoni, Collu, Vargiu, & Mereu, 1985) and cannabis (French, 1997) also increase the firing of dopaminergic cells and increase dopamine release; in these cases the mechanisms of dopaminergic cell activation are not yet known.

By whatever mechanism, these substances all elevate dopamine levels. Once an animal has self-intoxicated, it appears to have elevated dopamine levels that determine when the experienced animal will respond for more cocaine, amphetamine, or heroin. The probability of responding is high when the drug is first made available to a trained animal, and a low priming dose of these drugs elevates both dopamine levels and the probability of responding even more. Once drug-induced dopamine levels are elevated to two or three times normal values, however, the probability that the animal will respond again decreases, falling to near zero. Subsequent lever pressing becomes increasingly probable only when the previous injections are partially metabolized and dopamine levels fall again to below about 200% of normal (Ranaldi et al., 1999; Wise, Newton, et al., 1995). Dopamine level probably acts more as an occasion setter than as a literal stimulus for responding; it appears that the dopamine level in the nucleus accumbens determines when the drug will again be re-inforcing. The experienced animal appears to learn not to respond when already intoxicated; responding under the condition of high dopamine appears to extinguish as if the reward system were saturated such that additional drug did not, for the moment, produce additional reward.

Analysis of interresponse time distributions over the course of training indicates two phases of learning. In initial trials, responding is erratic, sometimes with only a few minutes and sometimes as much an hour between responses (Figure 19.1). As learning progresses, mean interresponse times decrease dramatically, and an approximately normal distribution of interresponse times develops. The animal learns first not to wait long intervals between responses. Rats responding for intravenous cocaine injections of 1 mg/kg/injection learn within a few days to respond regularly at 5 min to 6 min intervals, rarely waiting 8 min or longer. Short interresponse times—times of 3 min or less—drop out more slowly, disappearing only after two to four weeks of training. This slow loss of short interresponse times does not appear to reflect any aversion, but rather insensitivity, to the high drug levels and high extracellular dopamine levels that result from short interresponse times. If high drug levels were aversive, animals should learn to avoid short interinjection intervals much earlier. Moreover, animals tested in choice paradigms show preferences for high doses (Iglauer, Llewellyn, & Woods, 1976; Johanson & Schuster, 1975). Thus it appears that cocaine is simply no longer reinforcing when dopamine levels are abnormally high. Just as animals trained with 1 mg/kg-injections of cocaine learn not to

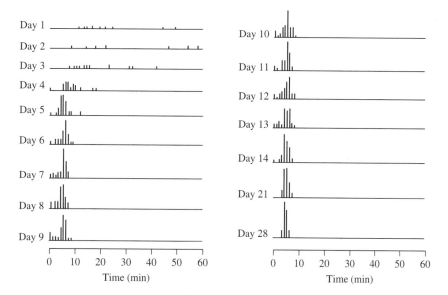

Figure 19.1 Interresponse time histograms for four weeks of intravenous cocaine self-administration sessions.

NOTE: The distribution of interresponse times normalizes as the animal acquires the response habit. In the well-trained animal (Day 28) the mean interresponse time is between 5 min and 6 min for unit doses of 1 mg/kg of cocaine. Note that the variance narrows first when unusually long interresponse times drop out (Days 3, 4, 5) and narrows further later (Week 3, 4) when unusually short interresponse times drop out. The slow dropout of short interresponse times suggests that the drug is unrewarding but not punishing when one injection is taken quickly after another.

respond in less than 4 min from the last injection when dopamine levels are still elevated, so do animals trained with heroin at 0.1 mg/kg/injection and animals trained with amphetamine at 0.25 mg/kg/injection learn not to respond in less than 20 min or 30 min, respectively, of their last injections (when *their* dopamine levels are similarly elevated). In each case this is the time it takes the last dose to be metabolized back to about 200% of normal, where the well-trained animal regularly responds for these drugs (Wise, 1999).

Because the FR-1 schedule of reinforcement does not appear to reflect the strength of drug reinforcement in a straightforward way—animals that press less for high doses nonetheless prefer them—other schedules of reinforcement have drawn recent interest (Arnold & Roberts, 1997; Olmstead, Parkinson, Miles, Everitt, & Dickinson, 2000). Low-density reinforcement schedules that generate high rates of responding are frequently used to demonstrate drug reinforcement in primates that have a history of self-administration of other drugs (Goldberg, Kelleher, & Morse, 1975). High rates of responding, sensitive to changes in dose and to the substitution of saline for the rewarding drug, establish that it is the pharmacology of the new drug rather than an elevated baseline of habitual responding established by previous drugs that controls the behavior.

Problems of baseline operant rate have become significant for those who work with rodents as well; here the concern is for more efficient methods of testing groups of animals. When baseline rates of the operant are low (as, for example, when animals are trained to press a lever situated well above the floor), the training of animals becomes time-consuming, particularly with rat strains like the Fischer 344 and mouse strains like the A/J or DBA strains, which are typically timid and slow learners. One way to train animals quickly is to use an operant that has a high initial (baseline) rate, such as nose poking into a small hole in the wall of the test chamber (Ross & Malmo, 1979) or lever pressing with levers that are large, light, and low to the floor (J. Olds, 1958a). Although animals are easier to train in such cases, discriminating drug-reinforced responding from spontaneous responding becomes more problematic. The nose-poke response is particularly problematic because forward movement is an unconditioned response to both drug (Wise & Bozarth, 1987) and brain stimulation (Glickman & Schiff, 1967) rewards, and it is not clear how to discriminate unconditioned forward movements from those that have developed purely as a result of instrumental reinforcement. How can we know whether the second nose poke was an instrumental response for the second reinforcement and not the result of an unconditioned forward movement triggered by the first reinforcement?

One popular—but often underanalyzed—approach to dealing with the problem of discriminating instrumental from spontaneous responding is the use of the two-lever (or, in the case of nose poking, the two-hole) control. Here two manipulanda are available, and responding on only one of the two is reinforced. If the animal discriminates between the two levers and responds only on the one that triggers reinforcement (the so-called "active" lever), it is clear that the behavior is instrumental and results from the contingency between response and reinforcement and is not simply a result of the activating effects of the drug. The converse, however, is not necessarily true. Responding on the "inactive" lever is frequently, but erroneously, interpreted as a simple reflection of drug-induced activation. It is well established, however, that animals will respond to a new manipulandum in proportion to its similarity to one on which responding has previously been reinforced (Guttman & Kalish, 1956). In the early stages, at least, responding on the inactive lever in a two-lever test chamber tends to reflect generalization from the similar, reward-associated, active lever. If reinforcement is terminated in such an apparatus, animals increase their responding on the alternate, previously nonreinforcing manipulandum as well as on the previously reinforcing one. Only after a number of trials does the animal learn to discriminate between the two levers, and even then responding on the inactive lever is not completely extinguished. Thus, if a within-subjects design must be used to assess drug-induced general activation, it should assess general activation by measurement of nonrewarded responses on a control manipulandum that is dissimilar from the one that the animal has been trained to use.

A better control for drug-induced general activation is a yoked control, in which the same drug injections are given to two animals with access to identical manipulanda. The executive animal is allowed to earn response-contingent reinforcement that is given equally to both the executive and the yoked partner, and the comparable response of the yoked partner is recorded but has no scheduled consequence for either animal. Thus the yoked partner receives the same amount of drug and the same pattern of drug delivery, but the timing of injections is random with respect to the yoked animal's behavior. Any lever pressing above baseline that occurs in the yoked animal can be attributed to nonspecific activation by the drug, whereas any difference in the responding of the executive animal and its yoked partner reflects the if-and-only-if contingency that controls the contiguity of the injections with the executive's responses.

In attempts to determine how much an animal wants the next injection rather than simply *when* the animal wants the next injection, some workers have turned to more complex paradigms such as the progressive ratio paradigm. Progressive ratio schedules demand incrementally more responses for successive injections. Eventually, the animal on a progressive ratio schedule reaches a break point where it ceases to respond further. This is often taken to reflect the maximum price that the animal is willing to pay for the next injection (Hodos, 1961). Progressive ratio studies suggest that the reinforcing value of intravenous drugs generally increases with drug dose, and this is consistent with the behavior of animals given a choice between two doses (Iglauer et al., 1976; Johanson & Schuster, 1975).

Comparisons of progressive ratio responding for cocaine and heroin (Arnold & Roberts, 1997), however, reveal that break points are not necessarily a good index of the animal's relative motivations for different drugs. The way that the progressive ratio testing is done can be more important than the drug itself in determining what ratio an animal will reach for a given dose of a given drug. If the session begins with a low response requirement and approaches higher requirements gradually within each session, animals reinforced with cocaine will continue to respond despite high response requirements. Such animals will not, however, initiate responding for high ratios when not intoxicated at the beginning of a session. The cocaine-reinforced animal appears strongly motivated for the *next* injection but not strongly motivated for the *first* injection in a session. In contrast, animals reinforced with heroin will initiate responding despite initially high requirements but will not work up to high requirements if they have to start over at the beginning of each session. Animals reinforced with heroin stop at low ratios if they must first work through the low ratios that are necessary for the cocaine-reinforced animal. The heroin-reinforced animal appears strongly motivated for the first injection but is not so strongly motivated for, say, the fifth injection of a given session (Arnold & Roberts, 1997). This limits the utility of the otherwise face-valid progressive ratio approach to comparing drug reinforcement across drugs or doses.

Three major factors can be seen to control intravenous self-administration of cocaine, amphetamine, or heroin in laboratory animals having easy access to the drug. First, although initial self-administration is accidental in laboratory animals and is motivated by a variety of personal decisions in humans, continued and increasingly compulsive drug use is the result of drug *reinforcement*. The lever on which the animal responds and the cigarette or syringe the human uses have no unconditioned motivational significance, apart from novelty (Sokolov, 1963). Drug reinforcement establishes the self-administration habit and the learned significance of the incentives that sequentially guide the individual through the instrumental response sequence. Second, *incentive motivation*—the motivational arousal caused by the drug-associated stimuli—can energize the first response in a session or the next response in a session. Incentive-motivational stimuli can trigger the focusing of attention on drug-associated stimuli and thus precipitate the transition from other behaviors to drug-oriented behaviors. Either the presentation of drug-associated stimuli or a small unearned injection of the drug itself has high probability of turning the attention of the animal to the operant manipulandum that is associated with drug injections. Once instrumental responding begins, the priming value of the drug reward (some combination of dose, concentration, speed of injection) controls the initial behavior of the animal. The rate of learning of a drug-naive animal, the rate of responding on a low-density reinforcement schedule, and the rate of responding in the early loading phase of a self-administration session are each reasonably proportional to the rewarding drug dose until such time as the animal reaches and maintains an intoxicated state. Once the animal becomes intoxicated, responding comes largely under control of a third factor: drug *satiety*. Here, response rate is regulated by the blood level of drug and by its neurochemical correlates. In this third phase—the maintenance phase—of self-administration the effectiveness of incentive and reinforcement factors fluctuates with the state of intoxication, decreasing in periods of intoxication only to intensify as the previous injection is metabolized.

Drug self-administration can be studied under even more complex schedules of reinforcement. One second-order or chain schedule of interest involves two manipulanda (Hawkins & Pliskoff, 1964; Olmstead et al., 2000). The animal must respond on the first manipulandum to earn access to the second, and must respond on the second to earn units of reinforcement. Responding on the first manipulandum offers a model of drug *seeking*, whereas responding on the second offers a relatively unconfounded model of drug *taking*. The first is seen as a more *instrumental* response, and the second is seen as a more *consummatory* response (Craig, 1918; Sherrington, 1906). Studies in which instrumental and consummatory responses are differentiated—and in which discrete trials are separated and initiated by earned or unearned priming injections—confirm that cocaine self-administration in well trained animals (a) is self-limited by a satiety factor (where each injection appears to alleviate, until it is partly metabolized, the motivation further responding), (b) is stimulated when low (priming) levels of drugs remain in the system, and (c) reflects the consequences of a reinforcement factor—giving rise to increasing rates of seeking responses in response to increasing doses of drug—that is evident only after the satiating effects of the last dose have dissipated (Olmstead et al., 2000).

Reinstatement

One of the prominent characteristics of drug addiction is the high probability of relapse even after prolonged periods of self-imposed drug abstinence. This cannot be well modeled in lower animals because lower animals do not self-impose abstinence from compulsively self-administered drugs. Thus, although it is possible to model the effects of incarceration—experimenter-imposed abstinence—it is not possible to model the attempts of the human addict to give up a habit because of its perceived long-term consequences.

Animal models can be used, however, to model the reinstatement of *extinguished* habits, a condition rarely experienced by human addicts. Here the animal is trained to self-administer the drug and then subjected to extinction conditions in which the habit is practiced in the absence of reinforcement. After the response habit has essentially died out (some degree of weak tendency to perform the once-rewarded response always remains), treatments can be tested for their ability to reinstate the still-unreinforced response habit. Predictably, response-independent injections of the training drug or a related drug are effective (de Wit & Stewart, 1981, 1983; Gerber & Stretch, 1975). Environmental stimuli that have been paired with drug injections (Meil & See, 1996), and various stressors (Erb, Shaham, & Stewart, 1996; Shaham & Stewart, 1995; Shalev, Highfield, Yap, & Shaham, 2000) have also been shown to reinstate extinguished drug-seeking habits. If the habit is again rewarded by response-reinforcement drug injections, reinstatement occurs essentially immediately after the first earned injection.

Self-Administration by Other Routes

The oral self-administration of drugs is also well studied. In the case of alcohol, oral self-administration models the human use of the drug. However, oral self-administration of alcohol is a disappointing model in lower animals, most of which eschew the drug, presumably because of its aversive taste (Cicero, 1980; Macenski & Meisch, 1994;

Mello, 1973). Lower animals can be coerced to drink alcohol by a variety of methods (Falk, Samson, & Winger, 1972; Freund, 1973; D. B. Goldstein & Pal, 1971; Hyytia & Sinclair, 1989), but voluntary self-administration in lower animals rarely results in sufficient intake to produce intoxication. The effects of taste can be overcome in laboratory animals, as in humans, by masking it in sweet solutions; such masking can then be progressively decreased until the animals appear to be drinking the alcohol for its pharmacological effects (Tolliver, Sadeghi, & Samson, 1988). Without such masking, significant alcohol consumption can be seen in some selected strains of rodents, and there are strong efforts to understand genetic contributions to alcohol preference (Crabbe, Belknap, & Buck, 1994).

Other drugs are also self-administered by the oral route, but this route of administration has obvious drawbacks. First, alcohol aside, oral self-administration does not model the prototypical human addictions (save, perhaps, caffeine: Gilbert, 1976). Second, oral drug self-administration is often studied in the absence of measured instrumental behavior. Even if animals are required to make an arbitrary instrumental response for access to a drug solution, the fact that the temperature of fluids is itself a reinforcer, and one that varies with the state of hydration (Freed & Mendelson, 1974; Gold, Kapatos, Prowse, Quackenbush, & Oxford, 1973; Mendelson & Chillag, 1970), suggests that drug reinforcement in this preparation is seriously confounded with other motivational variables.

Conditioned Place Preference

The conditioned place preference model involves Pavlovian rather than instrumental conditioning. Here the animal is exposed to two test chambers, one in which it receives drug injections and one in which it receives placebo injections. After 1 to 10 conditioning sessions, the animal is given free access to the two compartments, and its relative preference for the drug-associated compartment is taken as a measure of drug reinforcement (Bozarth, 1987). This is a useful paradigm in that it requires less surgical preparation and less time-consuming training than is required in the self-administration model, and conditioned place preference is an interesting paradigm theoretically because it involves stimulus rather than response learning. It is a Pavlovian paradigm in that a conditioned stimulus—the chamber—is paired with an unconditioned stimulus—the drug—without any contingency on the animal's behavior rather than an instrumental paradigm in which the drug is given if and only if the animal performs some arbitrary act.

Even though the conditioned place preference paradigm involves Pavlovian rather than instrumental reinforcement, the same brain mechanisms seem to be involved in the rewarding effects of drugs in the two paradigms. In each case where central injections have been used for self-administration and for conditioned place preference, the same effective brain sites and the same receptor subtypes have been identified. For example, mu and delta opioids each induce conditioned place preferences (Bals-Kubik, Ableitner, Herz, & Shippenberg, 1993) and intracranial self-administration (Devine & Wise, 1994) when injected into the ventral tegmental area. Amphetamine induces conditioned place preference (Carr & White, 1983) and intracranial self-administration (Hoebel et al., 1983) when injected into the nucleus accumbens. Although Skinner (1935) and others have argued that instrumental and Pavlovian reinforcements involve fundamentally different phenomena, the sites, drugs, and doses effective in the one paradigm have not yet, despite several opportunities, been dissociated from those effective in the other paradigm. Thus there is growing credibility for the hypothesis that the reinforcement of stimulus as-sociations in place preference learning and of response habits in instrumental learning involves common or overlapping brain mechanisms (Wise, 1989).

Reward Potentiation

Addictive drugs are not only rewarding in their own right; they can enhance the rewarding effects of other stimuli. Although there is little objective evidence to confirm this suggestion, many feel that alcohol and cannabis enhance the reinforcing effects of food and that low levels can enhance the reinforcing effects of sexual interaction. Clearly, amphetamine, cocaine, heroin, morphine, nicotine, phencyclidine, and cannabis can enhance the rewarding effects of direct electrical stimulation of the medial forebrain bundle and related components of brain reward circuitry (Wise, 1996).

Drug-potentiation of brain stimulation reward offers a particularly useful model because brain stimulation reward lends itself to quantitative analysis and because it illustrates two important motivational influences on instrumental behavior. Rewarding electrical stimulation of the brain—lateral hypothalamic stimulation is best characterized—influences operant behavior from both the Pavlovian and the Skinnerian perspectives. Lateral hypothalamic stimulation is reinforcing in that it "stamps in"—as do drugs of abuse—the response habits (presumably by stamping in the residual brain activity or memory trace associated with the response-reinforcement contingency: Landauer, 1969; Pfaff, 1969) that it reliably follows. Although there is response generalization such that the animal does not always press the lever in exactly the same way, in point of fact a given animal does tend to press the lever in a stereotyped manner with the same paw or with approximately the same snout movement or the same rearing and falling action each time.

Thus what is "reinforced" from the instrumental paradigm is a fairly stereotyped response tendency. Should the lever be withdrawn from the cage, however, such that the animal cannot perform the normal lever press, the animal initiates a variety of other behaviors oriented toward the lever or the place where the lever was withdrawn.

The stimulation need not be given in a response-contingent manner to evoke motivated behavior. A free priming train of stimulation pulses, given at a time when the animal is not lever pressing or even near the lever, will usually trigger reinitiation of lever pressing in a well-trained animal. This is the second motivational influence of the stimulation. This priming effect of stimulation is viewed as incentive motivational in that it involves arousal and response selection that is triggered by the reinforcer itself or by stimuli associated with the reinforcer. The attempt to gain access to the withdrawn lever that was just mentioned is also an incentive-motivational response.

The priming and the reinforcing effects of rewarding brain stimulation are dissociable effects of the same stimulation and serve as models of the priming and reinforcing effects that are not so easily studied with natural reinforcers such as peanuts and popcorn. When the stimulation is given in a response-independent manner, its motivational effectiveness decays in seconds or tens of seconds (Gallistel, 1969; Howarth & Deutsch, 1962). How fast the animal runs down an alley after priming stimulation depends not only on the strength of the stimulation but also quite strongly on the delay between the time the stimulation is given and the time when the door to the alley is opened. A minute or two after priming stimulation has been given, the animal will run as if there had been no priming. In contrast, the effectiveness of response-contingent stimulation does not decay over hours or even a few days. How fast the animal runs down an alley depends not only

on the strength of any priming stimulation that is given but also on the strength of the half-dozen or so most recent earned stimulations. The animal remembers for days the strength of the last response-dependent stimulation but not the strength of the last response-independent (priming) stimulation (Gallistel, Stellar, & Bubis, 1974).

The distinction between the priming and the reinforcing effects of brain stimulation reward is important because it illustrates two analogous effects of drug reward. Drugs of abuse can serve as incentive-motivational priming stimuli, to initiate drug seeking when the animal is otherwise engaged, and it can serve as a reinforcer to maintain responding when it is in progress.

The strength of brain stimulation reward is quantified in much the same manner as is the strength of a drug effect in classic pharmacology. Behavior is assessed as a function of a range of reward strengths, from subthreshold strengths that do not maintain the behavior to suprathreshold strengths sufficient to maintain it at maximal rates. Reward strength varies with the intensity, the frequency, and the duration of the alternating current that is used, and also with the duration of the stimulation trains that serve as the units of reward (Frank, Martz, & Pommering, 1988; Gallistel, Shizgal, & Yeomans, 1981). Typical parameters might be $500 \mu A$ of 0.1 ms rectangular pulses administered at 50 Hz for 0.5 s following each lever press. The favored parameter for varying the strength of the stimulation is the pulse frequency, which is varied in equal log units over the range of 20 Hz to 200 Hz. Drug potentiation of brain stimulation reward is then quantified as the number of log units that a given dose of a given drug shifts this rate-frequency function to the left. Inasmuch as each 0.1-ms stimulation pulse is long enough to cause one but only one action potential in each axon within the stimulation field, the stimulation frequency needed for a given level of reward is proportional to the required number of action potentials in the reward system. A drug treatment that doubles the number of pulses required for a given level of reward can be assumed to have reduced by half the rewarding impact of the original stimulation (Gallistel, 1987).

The potentiation of brain stimulation reward by drugs of abuse clearly involves summation of the rewarding effect of the stimulation with a reward-associated effect of the drug. When the rate of responding for brain stimulation reward is plotted against the frequency of stimulation, a function is generated that is very similar in form to the traditional dose-response function in classic pharmacology. At low stimulation frequencies, response rates are nil, the same as if no stimulation is given. At high stimulation frequencies, response rates are high but asymptotic: Above some "dose" of stimulation, performance does not improve further. Between these extremes, there is a range of stimulation frequencies over which response rate increases in proportion to increases in frequency. This curve is the rate-frequency curve of self-stimulation, the analog of the dose-response curve in pharmacology.

The rate-frequency curve is shifted to the right by decreases in stimulation intensity that—by restricting the effective range of current from the electrode tip (Fouriezos & Wise, 1984; Wise, 1972)—make each stimulation pulse less effective. Similarly, the rate-frequency curve is shifted to the right by dopamine antagonists (Franklin, 1978; Gallistel & Karras, 1984), drugs that attenuate the rewarding effects (Fouriezos & Wise, 1984; Franklin & McCoy, 1979) of the stimulation. Thus reward-antagonists shift the rate-frequency curve to the right just as drug antagonists shift a drug's dose-effect curve to the right. The curve is shifted to the left by dopamine agonists (Franklin, 1978; Gallistel & Freyd, 1987), which include most drugs of abuse (Wise, 1996). A dose of dopamine antagonist that shifts the curve to the right neutralizes the effects of a dose of a dopamine agonist that shifts the curve an equal number of log units to the left (Figure 19.2; Gallistel & Karras, 1984). The fact that they shift the rate-frequency function to the left favors the assumption that the enhancement of brain stimulation reward reflects activation of the same brain mechanism as is responsible for the direct rewarding effects of the drugs. The drugs that shift the rate-frequency function to the left include amphetamine, cocaine, morphine, heroin, nicotine, phencyclidine, and cannabis, drugs that are self-administered in their own right (Carlezon & Wise, 1996a, 1996b; Deneau et al., 1969; Pickens & Harris, 1968; Pickens & Thompson, 1968; Tanda et al., 2000; Woods & Schuster, 1971).

Confidence in the interpretation that the rewarding actions of drugs of abuse—rather than some other action, such as a general arousal action or an anxiolytic action—comes from the observation that changes in the response requirements (more weight or less weight on the lever, incline to the runway, sedative drug treatment) cause upward or downward shifts of asymptotic performance rather than left or right shifts in the ascending limb of the curve (Edmonds & Gallistel, 1974). Some drugs can both decrease the rewarding impact of the stimulation and depress asymptotic performance; when they do so, the two effects can sometimes be dissociated by a second drug that restores the rewarding efficacy of the stimulation (leftward shift in the function) without restoring the response capacity (upward shift in the function) of the animal (Franklin, 1978; Rompré & Wise, 1989).

An addictive drug's ability to potentiate the rewarding effects of lateral hypothalamic brain stimulation is a hybrid paradigm, a mix of Pavlovian and Skinnerian features. The brain stimulation reward is given in the

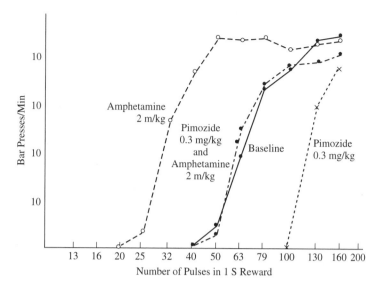

Figure 19.2   Reward antagonist and reward synergist effects of drugs on intracranial self-stimulation.
NOTE: Reward strength is an increasing function of the number of 0.1 ms pulses in a 1-s train of rewarding
stimulation. Pimozide at 0.3 mg/kg halved the effectiveness of stimulation (doubled the number of pulses
per reward required to maintain normal responding); amphetamine at 2 mg/kg doubled the effectiveness
of stimulation (halved the number of pulses per reward required to maintain normal responding). The
drug and dose that antagonized brain stimulation reward was completely offset by the drug and dose that
synergized with brain stimulation reward.
SOURCE: After Gallistel and Karras (1984), by permission.

Skinnerian way, where the animal receives
the stimulation if and only if it makes a required response, *after* the behavior of interest.
The rewarding drug is given in the Pavlovian
way, as scheduled by the experimenter, *prior
to* the experimental observations of interest.
The contribution of the rewarding drug is
not response-dependent except inasmuch as it
may interact in a neuromodulatory way with
the response-contingent impact of the stimulation. Rewarding drugs may also enhance
or substitute for the priming effect of stimulation.

Although the ability of drugs of abuse to
potentiate the rewarding effects of hypothalamic (and presumably other) brain stimulation has less face validity, it has the strong
advantage over other paradigms that it offers
a ratio scale measure of the rewarding effi-

cacy of a given dose of a given drug (Gallistel,
1987; Gallistel et al., 1981; Miliaressis,
Rompré, Laviolette, Philippe, & Coulombe,
1986). Measures of drug reward based on
other paradigms offer ordinal scales at best.

Conditioned Reinforcement

Stimuli associated with drug injections
can become conditioned reinforcers. Drug-
conditioned reinforcers can establish response
habits of their own and can prolong extinction
of habits learned under primary reinforcement
(Davis & Smith, 1976). This reflects a drug-
like action of drug-associated stimuli.

Although conditioned reinforcement reflects a drug-like effect of the conditioned
stimulus, consistent with Pavlovian theory,
not all drug-conditioning studies reveal

drug-like conditioned effects. Conditioned stimuli in drug experiments are drug-opposite (Siegel, 1976) when the primary association that is formed is between the stimuli and the abstinence symptoms that precede regular drug injections (Eikelboom & Stewart, 1979). Drug-opposite abstinence effects can be conditioned to, among other things, the time of day just prior to when injections have regularly occurred (Eikelboom & Stewart, 1981). Conditioned withdrawal signs (Wikler & Pescor, 1967) or conditioned drug-like effects (Childress, Ehrman, McLellan, & O'Brien, 1988; Meil & See, 1996; Tilson & Rech, 1973) have each been postulated to precipitate drug craving and drug seeking (Childress et al., 1999; Jaffe, Cascella, Kumor, & Sherer, 1989; Stewart, de Wit, & Eikelboom, 1984).

THE RELATIVE IMPORTANCE OF POSITIVE AND NEGATIVE REINFORCEMENT

Two questions remain open: to what degree the compulsive nature of drug seeking in addicts depends on the inherent rewarding properties of the drugs that can be seen in normal individuals and to what degree it depends on the ability of the drug to alleviate drug-opposite withdrawal states that develop only after adaptation to and withdrawal from the drug in question. It seems self-evident that if a drug is habit forming for individuals that have never experienced that drug or similar drugs before—if the drug has positive reinforcing effects sufficient to explain acquisition of the drug self-administration habit—then such reinforcing effects probably contribute importantly to the maintenance of the self-administration habit. It seems equally self-evident that if aversive withdrawal symptoms result from termination of the use of a drug of abuse, and if the drug has the capacity to medi-

cate these symptoms, negative reinforcement, too, will contribute to self-administration of the drug. What remains unclear is the degree to which positive or negative reinforcement is a necessary or sufficient condition for drug self-administration to progress from what is questionably labeled recreational drug taking to what is objectively labeled compulsive drug taking.

The Negative Reinforcement View

Traditional dependence theory (Collier, 1968, 1980; Dole & Nyswander, 1965, 1967; D. B. Goldstein & Goldstein, 1961; Himmelsbach, 1943; Jellenek, 1960; Lindesmith, 1947; Tatum, Seevers, & Collins, 1929) is a negative-reinforcement point of view. It allows for peer pressure, thrill seeking, or simple accident to explain initial drug taking but argues that once an addictive drug has been used for a significant period of time the body adapts to the drug, desensitizing the individual such that stronger doses are needed to obtain the original effect, and creating an acquired need state in which the drug is required to maintain the state of homeostatic equilibrium that existed before drug use began. Dependence theory is an *opponent process* theory, suggesting that bodily counteradaptations to the drug—which make the drug less reinforcing and which shift bodily or system homeostasis in the opposite direction to the drug effect—differentiates the individual whose drug use is volitional from the individual whose drug use is compulsive.

One source of the hypothesis that compulsive drug use is motivated by the need to medicate withdrawal stress is the verbal reports of some addicts. Such claims may be self-serving, since the addict is often reporting to a physician from whom the addict may want a prescription, and they are difficult to validate objectively. Moreover, such claims are informed at least in part by the wide circulation and acceptance of dependence theory in Western culture. Dependence theory originated in the opiate and alcohol literatures and was the basis for the methadone maintenance therapy that has been found useful in treating heroin addiction. Methadone maintenance programs use the slower and longer acting opiate methadone in an attempt to medicate heroin's withdrawal symptoms without inducing the euphoria associated with the faster acting drug heroin (Dole & Nyswander, 1965). One argument for the importance of self-medication of withdrawal distress is that methadone-treated addicts have just as much difficulty terminating treatment as they had attempting to terminate heroin addiction. The argument here is that if medication of withdrawal symptoms were not important, it should not be difficult to discontinue use of a medication that only alleviates withdrawal distress. The weakness of this argument is that methadone has not only the ability to alleviate withdrawal distress but also the ability to establish self-administration in previously naive subjects (Werner, Smith, & Davis, 1976).

The withdrawal syndrome associated with opiates is similar in many of its symptoms to the withdrawal syndromes of other depressant drugs including alcohol, barbiturates, and benzodiazepines (Kalant, 1977). These drugs produce cross-tolerance and are effective at relieving the withdrawal symptoms associated with each other (Le, Khanna, Kalant, & Grossi, 1986). Despite minor differences, the similarities in the dependence syndromes encourage the view that a common mechanism underlies addiction to these four depressant drug types. The symptoms associated with withdrawal from stimulant drugs such as cocaine, amphetamine, or nicotine are similar to each other but quite different from those of depressant drugs (Hatsukami, Hughes, Pickens, & Svikis, 1984; Jones, 1984; Shiffman & Jarvik, 1976; Weddington et al., 1991). Whereas withdrawal from the depres-

sant classes involves restlessness and excitability, withdrawal from the stimulant classes involves drowsiness and depression. There is no obvious common denominator, and thus no obvious common mechanism, for the classic depressant and stimulant withdrawal symptoms (Wise, 1987b).

A major problem for dependence theory has been evidence that the time of peak withdrawal distress does not necessarily correspond with the time of peak compulsion to take drugs. A particularly striking example is seen in alcohol-dependent monkeys (Woods et al., 1971) and alcoholic humans (Mello & Mendelson, 1972). Here, dependent individuals are seen to refrain from alcohol self-administration during periods of peak withdrawal distress only to take up alcohol self-administration again after withdrawal distress has largely dissipated.

Another development within dependence theory was to posit some form of dependence simply from evidence that self-administration of a given drug developed a compulsive character over time. Dependence that was based on the criterion of *compulsive* drug use— rather than on the criterion of objective somatic symptoms—was designated psychic or psychological dependence (Eddy, Halbach, Isbell, & Seevers, 1965). The circularity of this definition is obvious, and its inadequacy led to even more subjective definitions of dependence (Edwards et al., 1981). With the increasingly subjective and circular definitions of dependence, classic dependence theory lost favor among addiction specialists in the 1980s and 1990s.

The Positive Reinforcement View

With the discovery that rats would learn to lever press for direct electrical stimulation of the brain (J. Olds & Milner, 1954), physiological psychologists began to characterize a system in the brain that appears to mediate positive reinforcement (M. E. Olds & Olds, 1963). Rats learn quickly to lever press for stimulation of the lateral hypothalamus and related structures along the medial forebrain bundle and will lever press for such stimulation for hours or days, sometimes at rates of several thousand lever presses per hour (J. Olds, 1958b). With limited periods of access to the choice between food and stimulation, rats will self-stimulate to the neglect of feeding, losing over 10% of their body weight in the first four days of consecutive testing (Routtenberg & Lindy, 1965). Hungry rats will accept higher levels of painful foot shock to gain access to the stimulation than to gain access to food; female rats will accept more shock to get stimulation than to retrieve their own pups (J. Olds, 1961). However, this stimulation appears to be a positive reinforcer in that the stimulation satisfies no obvious need state of the animal. Although the stimulation is more rewarding in chronically weight-reduced animals, it is insensitive to acute food deprivation (Carr & Wolinsky, 1993) and is not affected by deprivation of the stimulation itself (J. Olds, 1958a).

Soon after the discovery of brain stimulation reward, methods were developed to allow animals to self-administer intravenous drugs (Weeks, 1962). It was quickly found that rats and monkeys will self-administer psychomotor stimulants and opiates as avidly and in much the same way as they will self-administer lateral hypothalamic brain stimulation (Pickens & Harris, 1968). The parallel was quickly drawn between self-stimulation and amphetamine self-administration: In each case the behavior is characterized by sequential periods of intake and abstinence; the periods of abstinence are unpredictable in length; and periods of spontaneous abstinence will be terminated and periods of intake initiated if the animal is given a priming administration of the reward (Pickens & Harris, 1968).

Investigations into the brain mechanisms of drug reward and brain stimulation reward have largely confirmed deeper similarities between the two behaviors; intravenous amphetamine, cocaine, heroin, and nicotine each appear to activate pharmacologically the same reward circuitry that is activated electrophysiologically by hypothalamic brain stimulation (Wise, 1989). The circuitry has as its best characterized link the mesolimbic dopamine system, a system of fibers projecting primarily from the ventral tegmental area to the nucleus accumbens. Blockade of dopamine receptors or lesions of nucleus accumbens prevents or attenuates the rewarding effects of hypothalamic brain stimulation (Fibiger, Carter, & Phillips, 1976; Fouriezos & Wise, 1976; Franklin & McCoy, 1979), intravenous amphetamine (Lyness, Friedle, & Moore, 1979; Yokel & Wise, 1975), intravenous cocaine (de Wit & Wise, 1977), and intravenous nicotine (Corrigall, Franklin, Coen, & Clarke, 1992). Amphetamine, cocaine, morphine, heroin, nicotine, ethyl alcohol, cannabis, and phencyclidine each elevate nucleus accumbens dopamine levels (Di Chiara & Imperato, 1988; Gerhardt et al., 1987; Ng Cheong Ton et al., 1988; Zetterström et al., 1983). Amphetamine does so by causing direct release of dopamine from terminals (Heikkila, Orlansky, Mytilineou, et al., 1975), while cocaine (Heikkila, Orlansky, & Cohen, 1975) and phencyclidine (Gerhardt et al., 1987) do so by blocking the reuptake of spontaneously released dopamine. Nicotine stimulates the dopamine system by acting on nicotinic receptors on the dopaminergic cells themselves (Clarke & Pert, 1985); morphine and heroin increase dopaminergic cell firing by inhibiting GABAergic neurons that normally hold their dopaminergic neighbors under inhibitory control (Johnson & North, 1992). It is not yet known how cannabis or alcohol activates the system, but each increases firing of the dopaminergic neurons (French, 1997; Mereu et al., 1987).

As mentioned earlier, when rats are allowed to self-administer cocaine (Hurd, Weiss, Koob, Anden, & Ungerstedt, 1989; Pettit, & Justice, 1989; Wise, Newton, et al., 1995), amphetamine (Ranaldi et al., 1999), or heroin (Wise, Leone, et al., 1995), they do so with regularity and at a rate that elevates dopamine levels in the nucleus accumbens to two or three times normal. Once dopamine levels are elevated, self-administration rates are regular, and the timing of each response is predictable from the fall of dopamine levels to about twice normal values; when dopamine levels fall to this point, the animal usually responds for additional drug. The probability that the animal will respond again within the next few seconds is high when dopamine levels are normal and higher when dopamine levels are slightly elevated by previous injections, and they fall to nil when dopamine levels are three or four times normal. Thus, it appears that drug craving is highest when low levels of the drug are present. Indeed, priming injections of cocaine are known to cause cocaine craving in humans (Jaffe et al., 1989), and cocaine or amphetamine are known to cause cocaine or amphetamine seeking in laboratory animals (Pickens & Harris, 1968; Pickens & Thompson, 1971), just as priming by brain stimulation reward causes brain stimulation reward seeking in laboratory animals (Wetzel, 1963).

That these various addictive drugs each activate the mechanism presumed to mediate the positive reinforcing effects of hypothalamic brain stimulation raises two important issues. First, is there a common denominator between the habit-forming actions of stimulant and depressant drugs? Second, to what extent are the habit-forming effects of these drugs related to positive reinforcement and relatively independent of their ability to alleviate withdrawal distress? Several studies have demon-

strated the ability of opiates to establish compulsive self-administration in the absence of classic dependence signs (e.g., Deneau et al., 1969; Woods & Schuster, 1971). Moreover, morphine and mu and delta opioids are self-administered into the ventral tegmental area (Bozarth & Wise, 1981; Devine & Wise, 1994; Welzl, Kuhn, & Huston, 1989), origin of the mesolimbic dopamine system, where such injections cause no signs of physical dependence (Bozarth & Wise, 1984), and where the rewarding potency of the various agents is proportional to their ability to activate the dopamine system (Devine, Leone, Pocock, & Wise, 1993). Although these injections—and, indeed, days of continuous infusion of even higher doses into this brain region—do not produce signs of physical dependence, similar injections of opiates into other brain regions do establish obvious physical dependence (Bozarth & Wise, 1984; Harris & Aston-Jones, 1994; Tremblay & Charton, 1981; Wei, 1981; Wei, Loh, & Way, 1973; Weh, Sigel, & Way, 1975). Similarly, self-administration of intravenous amphetamine or cocaine for limited periods each day is compulsive, occurring with rigid regularity and to the exclusion of other behaviors, yet it does not produce obvious signs of tolerance or physical dependence (Deneau et al., 1969; Pickens & Harris, 1968).

These findings suggest that at least some addictive drugs are powerful positive reinforcers and that the positive reinforcing actions of the drugs are the common denominator accounting for the addictive properties of both stimulant and depressant classes. Moreover, by definition, the positive reinforcing actions of the drugs in animal models account for the initial development of drug-seeking habits and for the rapid reinstatement of such habits after long periods of drug abstinence. This raises the question of the relative contributions of positive and negative reinforcement mechanisms in addiction (Wise, 1988). The positive reinforcing effects of amphetamine, cocaine, and heroin appear to be sufficient to establish compulsive drug-seeking habits. Compulsive self-administration of these drugs can be established in daily sessions of four or fewer hours, such that intoxication is not continuous around the clock; continuous intoxication appears to be a necessary condition for the development of physical dependence, at least in the case of alcohol (Falk et al., 1972; Freund, 1969; D. B. Goldstein & Pal, 1971). The apparent strength of the stimulants and opiates as positive reinforcers, like the strength of brain stimulation reward as a positive reinforcer, thus seems sufficient to explain the development and maintenance of compulsive self-administration. This fact adds to the reasons for questioning the importance of negative reinforcement—the reinforcement attendant on alleviation of withdrawal distress—in the critical stages of the addiction process.

The Two-Factor Perspective

Researchers often ask why advocates of positive and negative reinforcement models cannot both be correct, with the positive hedonic effects of the drug being one factor and the drug's ability to alleviate withdrawal distress being another. It seems self-evident that if the drug is able to serve both functions, each function must contribute something to drug taking in the addicted individual. If the addict takes drug primarily to "get high," alleviation of some form of hangover should be an added benefit. If the addict takes a drug primarily to alleviate hangover and, in the process, experiences pleasant intoxication, each factor should again contribute to continued drug taking. Moreover, whereas positive reinforcement may be more important in the earlier stages of addiction, negative reinforcement could become important for maintaining drug-seeking in longstanding addicts who

claim that they no longer feel any euphoric response to their drug. Although addiction theorists may be reluctant to accept a two-factor explanation of drug taking, such an explanation is widely accepted by addicts, clinicians, and distant observers. Why must positive and negative reinforcement models be seen as mutually exclusive possibilities?

Although the idea that positive and negative reinforcement each contribute to addiction seems reasonable from a clinical perspective, it is difficult to reconcile with a postulated mechanism. Positive and negative reinforcement are mechanistic opposites, and they are associated with several correlated opposites. Positive reinforcement theories hold that the pharmacological actions of the drug (Jaffe et al., 1989; Stewart & Eikelboom, 1987; Wise, 1999) and the drug-like actions of associated stimuli (Ehrman, Robbins, Childress, & O'Brien, 1992; Meil & See, 1996) stimulate craving. Negative reinforcement theories hold that drug-opposite responses in the brain (Dackis & Gold, 1985; Koob, Stinus, Le Moal, & Bloom, 1989; Solomon & Corbit, 1973) and withdrawal-associated environmental cues (Wikler & Pescor, 1967) stimulate craving. Positive reinforcement theories hold that drug experience is associated with sensitization to the rewarding effects of addictive drugs (Horger, Giles, & Schenk, 1992; Horger, Shelton, & Schenk, 1990; Lett, 1989; Piazza, Deminiere, Le Moal, & Simon, 1990; Robinson & Berridge, 1993; Shippenberg, Heidbreder, & Lefevour, 1996); negative reinforcement theories hold that tolerance to the reinforcing properties of the drug develops and locks the addict in compulsive drug-seeking patterns (Solomon & Corbit, 1973; Koob et al., 1989). The negative reinforcement view is an *opponent process* view (Solomon & Corbit, 1973), positing drug-opposite neuroadaptations as the cause of addiction; the positive reinforcement view is a *proponent process* view (Stewart & Wise,

1992), positing drug-like effects as the primary source of drug craving.

It is now widely accepted that the negative reinforcement conferred by alleviation of somatic withdrawal distress is not critical for alcoholism (Mello & Mendelson, 1972; Woods et al., 1971) or heroin addiction (Bozarth & Wise, 1984; Deneau et al., 1969; Woods & Schuster, 1968). Although somatic withdrawal distress is clearly evident, and although considerably lesser degrees of somatic distress can also be identified with cocaine (Jones, 1984), cannabis (Jones, 1980), and nicotine (Hughes & Hatsukami, 1986; Malin et al., 1992) withdrawal, such dependence does not appear to be necessary or sufficient to motivate compulsive drug self-administration. The mechanisms of opiate reinforcement and of opiate somatic withdrawal symptoms can be dissociated (Bozarth & Wise, 1984), and use of other drugs that are associated with pronounced withdrawal syndromes—anticholinergics, chlorpromazine, and imipramine—can be given up without great difficulty (Jaffe, 1985). The somatic withdrawal symptoms associated with opiates have been likened in severity to a bad case of influenza (Peele & Brodsky, 1975), certainly a sufficient reason to take a medication such as aspirin but not an obviously sufficient reason to suffer the loss of employment, loss of family, loss of health, or incarceration that are frequently part and parcel of the lives of addicts.

Although contemporary theory does not attribute addiction to the alleviation of somatic withdrawal signs—many of which are associated with counteradaptations of the autonomic nervous system (Echenhoff & Oech, 1960; Martin, 1967; Wei, Tseng, Loh, & Way, 1974)—an interesting possibility is that drug-opposite adaptations within the reward circuitry itself may contribute to the compulsive nature of addiction (Dackis & Gold, 1985; Koob & Bloom, 1988; Leith & Barrett, 1976).

In this view, counteradaptations to the reward-inducing actions of the drug in the mesolimbic dopamine system (Dackis & Gold, 1985) itself or in other elements of the reward circuitry (Frank et al., 1988; Kokkinidis & McCarter, 1990; Kokkinidis, Zacharko, & Predy, 1980; Koob & Bloom, 1988; Leith & Barrett, 1976) within which dopamine plays a critical role cause a behavioral depression that can be overcome by ever increasing doses of addictive drugs. Indeed, extracellular dopamine levels are depleted during withdrawal from amphetamine, cocaine, morphine, and alcohol (Parsons, Smith, & Justice, 1991; Robertson, Leslie, & Bennett, 1991; Rossetti, Hmaidan, & Gessa, 1992). The minimal levels of stimulation current needed to sustain lateral hypothalamic self-stimulation increase during withdrawal from amphetamine (Kokkinidis et al., 1980; Leith & Barrett, 1976) or cocaine (Frank et al., 1988; Kokkinidis & McCarter, 1990; Markou & Koob, 1991). Moreover, electrophysiological and neurochemical changes within the reward circuitry follow chronic cocaine or morphine treatments (Nestler, 1997; Nestler & Aghajanian, 1997; White & Kalivas, 1998).

Thus, the possibility that neuroadaptations in the reward circuitry—quite independent of those in the autonomic systems associated with classic somatic withdrawal symptoms—desensitize the animal to addictive drugs, accounting for tolerance to their habit-forming (but not their somatic) effects, has attracted considerable recent attention (Dackis & Gold, 1985; Frank et al., 1988; Kokkinidis & McCarter, 1990; Kokkinidis et al., 1980; Leith & Barrett, 1976; Markou & Koob, 1991). This possibility has revitalized dependence theory, offering a variant that sidesteps the major arguments against the earlier, classic, view.

Can the newer versions of opponent process theory be reconciled with the positive-reinforcement, proponent process view? Not without difficulty. The counteradaptations associated with tolerance and elevation of reward thresholds are still opposite in direction from the proponent processes that have been shown to be the powerful stimuli for drug craving and drug seeking (de Wit & Stewart, 1981, 1983; Ehrman et al., 1992; Jaffe et al., 1989; Pickens & Harris, 1968; Stewart & Wise, 1992). These counteradaptations are still opposite to the sensitization that increases the risk of addiction in subsequently tested animals (Horger et al., 1992, 1990; Lett, 1989; Piazza et al., 1990; Shippenberg et al., 1996). Finally, the opponent process neuroadaptations that have been demonstrated to date do not last long enough to represent correlates of the long-term vulnerability to relapse that characterizes human addiction.

Rather than the drug-opposite neuroadaptations that are associated with drug tolerance, it is the drug-similar neuroadaptations that are associated with drug sensitization and conditioned drug effects that tend to correlate with the long-term vulnerability to relapse. Sensitization to psychomotor stimulants can last for most, if not all, of an animal's remaining lifetime (Robinson & Becker, 1986), and the search for neuroadaptations underlying sensitization is beginning to uncover adaptations with time courses that are longer than the three days or so of reward threshold elevation or the week or so of dopamine depletion that is associated with stimulant withdrawal. Of particular interest is the transcription factor ΔFosB, which is induced as part of the intracellular signaling cascade in the medium spiny neurons of nucleus accumbens. Unlike most transcription factors, ΔFosB accumulates during and following a series of chronic cocaine injections and remains in place for weeks (Nestler, 1997). Experimental induction of this Fos-related antigen in adult transgenic mice renders these animals supersensitive to cocaine (Kelz et al., 1999), and the accumulation of this transcription factor is

thought to be related to the mechanisms of the neuroadaptations that underlie learning and memory (Kelz & Nestler, 2000; Nestler, Kelz, & Chen, 1999).

COGNITIVE FACTORS IN ADDICTION THEORY

Many discussions of addiction involve subjective terms from the everyday vernacular. In part this is due to the broad interest in addiction. Although such terms are difficult to quantify for scientific use, in some cases the use of subjective terms appears, for the moment, to have some heuristic value. For the most part, however, the subjective correlates of the various phases of addiction—rather than drug-seeking behavior—continue to be mysteries requiring explanation and do not serve as useful explanations of drug-seeking behavior.

Craving

The addiction literature is rife with the term *craving*. The term arises both from self-reports in humans and from inferences from the observation of drug-trained habits in laboratory animals. Inasmuch as the subjective states of animals cannot be known directly, and inasmuch as the only evidence from which it can be inferred is the behavior that it is invoked to explain, the value of the subjective label has been questioned by many. The term is conceptually useful, however, as a temporal marker of motivational change.

The addict who seeks treatment approaches the therapist as an ally and considers, for the moment at least, that the drug is the enemy. The addict in relapse, on the other hand, sees the drug as the friend and the therapist as the enemy. The onset of craving is the best available marker for the transition between these mindsets. The onset of craving antedates the onset of drug seeking and thus gives the addict a warning that help is needed. Often, the addict can be talked down from the transition to a mental set that would otherwise lead to relapse.

In laboratory animals, the onset of craving is not directly known; however the concept of craving focuses experimental attention on the important neuronal and bodily events occurring just prior to drug-seeking episodes. Drug seeking in laboratory animals is predicted by drug levels in the blood (Yokel & Pickens, 1973, 1974), dopamine levels in nucleus accumbens (Ranaldi et al., 1999; Wise, Newton, et al., 1995), and the firing of ventral tegmental (Kiyatkin & Rebec, 2001) and nucleus accumbens (Carelli & Deadwyler, 1994; Carelli, Ijames, Konstantopoulos, & Deadwyler, 1999; Carelli, King, Hampson, & Deadwyler, 1993; Chang, Janak, & Woodward, 1998; Lee, Criado, Koob, & Henriksen, 1999; Peoples, Uzwiak, Gee, & West, 1997; Peoples & West, 1996) neurons just prior to drug seeking.

Wanting versus Liking

The traditional terms for the excitement and focusing of attention that precedes an instrumental act and the events that accompany the receipt of the earned reward are *incentive motivation* and *reinforcement*. The former term is rarely familiar to the broad range of interested readers, and the latter term is not usually known by its formal definition. The terms *wanting* and *liking* have been recently used (T. E. Robinson & Berridge, 1993, 2001) to draw attention to the subjective states associated with these two terms and the functional distinction between them. The terms are effective in that they clearly identify and dissociate for the nonspecialist the state of the animal prior to the response and reward from the state that follows the receipt of drug reward. The terms may be misleading, however,

if one assumes a causal relationship between the subjective states and either the behavior or the habit-forming consequence of response-contingent reinforcement.

There is reason to question whether addicts are consciously aware of the factors that initiate drug seeking or that increase the probability of repeating a drug-reinforced act. How predictive of behavior are subjective ratings of wanting and liking? The subjective euphoria associated with intravenous injections of cocaine and nicotine undergo within-session tolerance; successive injections in a series are progressively less pleasant (Foltin & Fischman, 1991; Henningfield, 1984). There is no such within-session tolerance to the control of behavior by intravenous cocaine or nicotine; these drugs sustain behavior at a constant rates with little variation for hours (Goldberg et al., 1983; Pickens & Thompson, 1968). Thus, within-session tolerance dissociates subjective pleasure from objective reinforcement. This fact suggests that objective reinforcement is not a conscious phenomenon, but rather is merely the closest conscious correlate that the addict can identify and report.

Other Mental Correlates

One of the issues that surrounds discussions of drug craving, desire, or wanting is the degree to which the addict is aware of his or her own motivations. Tiffany, who has done much to develop objective tools for rating subjective drug cravings, has suggested that compulsive drug use is largely an automatic performance—which earlier theorists might well have termed a habit—and that it is not well correlated with verbal reports of drug cravings, desires, or urges (Tiffany, 1990; Tiffany & Carter, 1998). Berridge and Robinson (1995) also dilute the potential significance of the notion that subjective urges play a causal role in compulsive drug use, by redefining "wanting" to denote a "precon-scious" psychological process that "can cause conscious desire" but is not identical *to* con-scious desire. The major problem with cogni-tive theories of addiction is that they gain their popularity from the use of terms that suggest conscious subjective awareness of the causes of the addict's behavior, yet the knowledge-able theorist finds it necessary to deny such awareness despite the use of terms that imply it. Most clinicians and many addicts are quite convinced that the subjective explanations of addicts have little more than face validity to recommend them. In any case, although there is an increasing tendency to attach cognitive labels to the state of mind at the time of drug seeking, there are at the same time seri-ous attempts to play down conscious motiva-tions and posit unconscious or "preconscious" automatized actions that are hard to differ-entiate from reflex-like, reinforcement-based habits.

ADDICTION AND MOTIVATION

Addiction shares many characteristics of nor-mal, biologically primitive, species-typical motivated behaviors such as feeding and drinking. Most important, drugs, like food or water, can serve as reinforcers of instrumental behavior. For the most part, drug reinforcers establish and sustain instrumental habits in ways similar to those of food reinforcers (Johanson, 1978; Malmo, 1975; Weingarten & Elston, 1990; Wise, 1996; Woods & Schuster, 1971). However, these similarities notwithstanding, drugs and rewarding brain stimulation each differ from traditional re-inforcers in certain important ways (Trowill, Panksepp, & Gandelman, 1969; Wise, 1987a). Intravenous drug rewards and intracranial stimulation rewards are each unsensed incen-tives, detected not by sight, not by hearing, not by smell, not by touch, and not, until they

diffuse into the saliva, by taste. Thus, they are incentives that the animal cannot localize in external space. News of these incentives arrives in the central nervous system in two ways: directly, via the circulation, and indi-rectly, by way of environmental stimuli that have been paired with them in the past.

The fact that most drug rewards are usu-ally not directly available to the senses poses two interesting issues for addiction and moti-vation specialists. First, it confounds the inter-pretation of conditioned place preference con-ditioning within the framework of Pavlovian conditioning. In traditional Pavlovian theory, a conditioned stimulus (CS) gains the abil-ity to elicit some of the unconditioned re-sponses to the unconditioned stimulus with which the CS is paired. Although it is true that not all conditioned responses resem-ble their unconditioned cousins (consider, e.g., the unconditioned jumping and running and the conditioned freezing in response to foot shock), the hyperlocomotion associated with psychomotor stimulants has been inter-preted in this way. In the conditioned place preference paradigm, the CS gains the abil-ity to elicit *approach responses,* the pre-sumed common denominator of all positive reinforcers (Schneirla, 1959). However, in the case of the conditioned place preference experiment one cannot attribute the drug-induced locomotion to an approach tendency. Because the drug is not localized in ex-ternal space, there can be no approach to the unconditioned stimulus—the Pavlovian reinforcer—itself. The drug is not yet sensed when it remains external to the animal, where it might otherwise be localized and ap-proached. If we do not accept the stimu-lus substitution notion from classic Pavlovian theory, however, how do we interpret the un-conditioned hyperlocomotion that is common to most drugs of abuse? We might lean to-ward the conclusion that the laboratory ani-mal *would* approach the drug itself repeatedly if the drug were externally available, but such assumptions undermine the power of the original hypothesis.

The fact that reinforcing drugs are not directly available to the senses raises another significant issue. Electrophysiological recording studies have shown that dopaminergic cells of the ventral tegmental area—the cells presumed critical to a wide range of reinforcers—discharge more reliably in response to stimuli that predict reward than in response to the rewarding substance itself (Schultz, 1997). When first exposed to a test situation, midbrain dopaminergic neurons are activated when a monkey finds a piece of apple in a cup behind a door. With repeated experience, however, the response to the apple itself is lost, and the same cell comes to discharge in response to the click as the latch on the door is released (Ljungberg et al., 1992). The interpretation has been that the neuron is more involved with the *prediction* of reward than with the *receipt* of reward (Schultz & Dickenson, 2000).

The suggestion that the dopaminergic neuron responds initially to the *receipt* of reward but responds after conditioning to the *anticipation* of reward is called into question by the fact that even food is identified largely through the association of its sensory properties with its postingestive consequences (Capaldi & Powley, 1990; Le Magnen, 1959; Sclafani & Ackroff, 1994; Tordoff, 1991). Although some tastes are innately preferred (Sclafani & Ackroff, 1994; Weingarten & Kulikovsky, 1989), even these must be associated with shape, texture, color, and so on before, for example, a piece of apple is recognized by a primate as a foodstuff. Most food stimuli should thus not be identified as unconditioned rewards. Rather, they are nutrient-associated sensory stimuli that predict the postingestive consequences that serve to reinforce learning. The sight of the piece of apple, the feel of the apple, and perhaps even

much of the discriminative taste of the apple is a conditioned stimulus predicting reward just as is the click that precedes the delivery of the apple in the Ljungberg (1992) paradigm. In this sense the dopaminergic neurons are always responding to the sensory predictors (taste as well as smell, touch, sight, and sound) of the postingestional effects that are the ultimate reward of food. It should then not be surprising that dopaminergic neurons and their target neurons appear to be most responsive to events just prior to injection rather than to injections themselves. The human response to cash is a response well in advance of the primary rewards that cash can purchase; nonetheless, it is clearly considered the receipt of a reward. In any case, notwithstanding the fact that injected drugs can serve as discriminative stimuli (Colpaert & Slangen, 1982), it is only external drug-predictive cues that can attract the attention and guide the behavior of the animal in space.

A major issue in addiction theory is whether addiction is qualitatively or quantitatively different from a healthy habit such as eating an apple a day. To be sure, it is quantitatively different from many food-related habits, but it is not clear that it is different from the ritualized and excessive eating to the point of obesity that can sometimes be focused on a particular foodstuff such as ice cream or chocolate (Weil & Rosen, 1993). Definitions of addiction stress the compulsive nature of the habits associated with addiction, but the term *compulsive* is difficult to define objectively, and compulsive eating or compulsive masturbation or copulation are not excluded by such definitions. With the decline of dependence theory, the attempt to differentiate addiction from other habits has required the use of further qualifiers such as "despite harmful consequences" or "even in the face of negative health and social consequences." These qualifiers do not differentiate compulsive drug self-administration from compulsive eating or compulsive gambling (Orford, 2001). Thus, the American Psychiatric Association has given up the attempt to define addiction and has moved progressively to diagnostic categories of "Substance-Induced Disorders" (APA, 1987) and now "Substance Dependence" (APA, 1994). Suits brought against tobacco vendors in the United States tend to hinge on the issue of whether cigarettes are addictive or "merely" habit forming (J. H. Robinson & Pritchard, 1995). Our inability to differentiate the habits we term "addictions" from other habits—for example, to differentiate cannabis habits from chocolate habits or nicotine habits from caffeine habits—makes this defense effective.

The failure to find an objective definition of addiction—a definition that not only specifies what characteristics qualify a habit for the label addiction but also what characteristics rule out a habit as reflecting addiction—leaves open the question of whether the brain mechanisms of addiction can be differentiated from those of lesser habits. Addictive drugs clearly activate the mesolimbic link in brain reward circuitry more strongly than do more natural reinforcers such as food or sex. Thus, it seems clear that the major addictive drugs—at adequate doses and via adequate routes of administration—are quantitatively different from more natural reinforcers such as food and sex. Drugs of abuse taken intravenously or by smoking should also have shorter delays of reinforcement than do foods, for example. Again, this argues for quantitative difference. On what grounds can it be suggested that they are also *qualitatively* different?

One suggestion is that drug reinforcers are qualitatively different from natural reinforcers because they cause neuroadaptations that alter drug sensitivity. Amphetamine, cocaine, and morphine clearly do alter electrophysiological and neurochemical aspects of brain function (Nestler, 2001; White & Kalivas,

1998), but repeated stress appears to have similar effects involving the same mechanisms (Antelman, Eichler, Black, & Kocan, 1980; Kalivas & Duffy, 1989). Some of the neuroadaptations alter neuronal function in the reward circuitry itself, presumably accounting for changes in sensitivity to the habit-forming effects of the drug (Horger et al., 1992, 1990; Lett, 1989; Piazza et al., 1990; Shippenberg et al., 1996). It remains to be explained, however, how such neuroadaptations might selectively enhance sensitivity to drug reinforcers without enhancing sensitivity to other rewards that activate the same circuitry. Indeed, stress cross-sensitizes animals to drugs of abuse and also activates the mesolimbic and mesocortical dopamine systems (Kalivas & Duffy, 1989, 1995; Sorg & Kalivas, 1991; Thierry, Tassin, Blanc, & Glowinski, 1976). The repeated stress of thrill seeking should cause neuroadaptations quite similar to those caused by the repeated stress of stimulant injections. It is difficult to imagine that any neuroadaptations other than those associated with the specific learning of drug-seeking habits and the specific memories of drug reinforcement might divert the attention of the addict selectively toward drugs and away from the traditional pleasures of life.

CONCLUSIONS: TRENDS AND NEW DIRECTIONS

Dependence Theory: The Medical Model

Dependence theory remains the dominant theory of addiction in society at large and continues to be advanced in various forms by serious specialists. Some theorists hold that addicts take drugs as self-medication for pre-existing conditions such as depression or anxiety; such conditions are thought to reflect genetic factors, environmental factors, or both.

Some hold that self-medication of withdrawal distress is a major contribution to the compulsive nature of drug self-administration, particularly in long-term addicts who claim no longer to feel any euphoric response to their drug regimen; one possibility is that such self-medication plays a significant role in some human addictions but a minor role, if any, in the addiction of lower animals (Wise, 1999). Methadone maintenance therapy for heroin addiction, which is clearly effective in alleviating the various individual and societal costs of heroin addiction (Barthwell, Senay, Marks, & White, 1989; Bell, Mattick, Hay, Chan, & Hall, 1997; Caplehorn, Dalton, Cluff, & Petrenas, 1994; A. Goldstein & Herrera, 1995), is based on the assumption that medicating withdrawal distress is essential for dealing with hard-core heroin addiction.

Reinforcement Theory

Reinforcement theory is generally accepted as the explanation for acquisition of drug self-administration habits and for rapid reinstatement of such habits after periods of abstinence. Reinforcement theory encourages the view that regardless of preexisting conditions or genetic susceptibility, all mammals exposed to significant doses by intravenous injection are at risk for addiction to heroin, cocaine, or amphetamine and that most, if not all, humans exposed to significant doses are at risk for addiction to nicotine, heroin, or freebase cocaine taken by smoking.

Incentive Theory

Incentive-motivational theory is closely linked to reinforcement theory in that incentive-motivational stimuli are established by their association with primary reinforcement. Incentive-motivational theory stresses the importance of stimuli present prior to drug ingestion, both for energizing and for guiding drug-seeking behavior. Incentive motivation is the formal name for situationally based craving or wanting, two popular terms that are responsible for bringing incentive-motivational theory to the attention of a broad audience in the last decade.

Neuroadaptation

The realization that all mammals are vulnerable to drug self-administration habits, self-administering the range of substances abused by humans and doing so in approximate proportion to the degree of compulsiveness of human self-administration, has focused attention on the biological basis of addiction. The compulsive nature of stimulant self-administration has drawn attention away from the effects of drugs on the autonomic nervous system, and the common actions of stimulants and brain stimulation reward have focused attention on the effects of addictive drugs in the brain. The search for biological correlates of addiction has led to the characterization of several alterations of function within the reward system itself, some that enhance the effectiveness of the drug and some that antagonize the effectiveness of the drug.

The Possible Fate of the Habit Concept in the Study of Addiction

The current trend is to find ways to differentiate compulsive drug-seeking habits from other habits. Partly, this is because of the legal contests over the addictive nature of nicotine. The fate of the notion that habit is the core of addiction is not clear, but the reasons for abandoning the term *habit* are less scientific than political. It remains to be proven that addiction is more than a very strong habit directed toward a harmful and socially unacceptable reinforcer.

REFERENCES

Aley, K. O., & Levine, J. D. (1997). Dissociation of tolerance and dependence for opioid peripheral antinociception in rats. *Journal of Neuroscience, 17,* 3907–3912.

American Psychiatric Association. (1987). *Diagnostic and statistical manual of mental disorders.* Washington, DC: Author.

American Psychiatric Association. (1994). *Diagnostic and statistical manual of mental disorders.* Washington, DC: Author.

Antelman, S. M., Eichler, A. J., Black, C. A., & Kocan, D. (1980). Interchangeability of stress and amphetamine in sensitization. *Science, 207,* 329–331.

Arnold, J. M., & Roberts, D. C. (1997). A critique of fixed and progressive ratio schedules used to examine the neural substrates of drug reinforcement. *Pharmacology Biochemistry and Behavior, 57,* 441–447.

Babbini, M., & Davis, W. M. (1972). Time-dose relationships for locomotor activity effects of morphine after acute or repeated treatment. *British Journal of Pharmacology, 46,* 213–224.

Bals-Kubik, R., Ableitner, A., Herz, A., & Shippenberg, T. S. (1993). Neuroanatomical sites mediating the motivational effects of opioids as mapped by the conditioned place preference paradigm in rats. *Journal of Pharmacology and Experimental Therapeutics, 264,* 489–495.

Barthwell, A., Senay, E., Marks, R., & White, R. (1989). Patients successfully maintained with methadone escaped human immunodeficiency virus infection. *Archives of General Psychiatry, 46,* 957–958.

Bell, J., Mattick, R., Hay, A., Chan, J., & Hall, W. (1997). Methadone maintenance and drug-related crime. *Journal of Substance Abuse, 9,* 15–25.

Berridge, K. C., & Robinson, T. E. (1995). The mind of an addicted brain: Neural sensitization of wanting and liking. *Current Directions in Psychological Science, 4,* 71–76.

Bindra, D. (1978). How adaptive behavior is produced: A perceptual-motivational alternative to response-reinforcement. *Behavioral and Brain Sciences, 1,* 41–91.

Bozarth, M. A. (1987). Conditioned place preference: A parametric analysis using systemic heroin injections. In M. A. Bozarth (Ed.), *Methods of assessing the reinforcing properties of abused drugs* (pp. 241–274). New York: Springer.

Bozarth, M. A., & Wise, R. A. (1981). Intracranial self-administration of morphine into the ventral tegmental area in rats. *Life Sciences, 28,* 551–555.

Bozarth, M. A., & Wise, R. A. (1984). Anatomically distinct opiate receptor fields mediate reward and physical dependence. *Science, 224,* 516–518.

Bozarth, M. A., & Wise, R. A. (1985). Toxicity associated with long-term intravenous heroin and cocaine self-administration in the rat. *Journal of the American Medical Association, 254,* 81–83.

Capaldi, E. D., & Powley, T. L. (1990). *Taste, experience, and feeding.* Washington, DC: American Psychological Association.

Caplehorn, J. R., Dalton, M. S., Cluff, M. C., & Petrenas, A. M. (1994). Retention in methadone maintenance and heroin addicts' risk of death. *Addiction, 89,* 203–209.

Carelli, R. M., & Deadwyler, S. A. (1994). A comparison of nucleus accumbens neuronal firing patterns during cocaine self-administration and water reinforcement in rats. *Journal of Neuroscience, 14,* 7735–7746.

Carelli, R. M., Ijames, S., Konstantopoulos, J., & Deadwyler, S. A. (1999). Examination of factors mediating the transition to behaviorally correlated nucleus accumbens cell firing during cocaine self-administration sessions in rats. *Behavioral Brain Research, 104,* 127–139.

Carelli, R. M., King, V. C., Hampson, R. E., & Deadwyler, S. A. (1993). Firing patterns of nucleus accumbens neurons during cocaine self-administration in rats. *Brain Research, 626,* 14–22.

Carlezon, W. A., Jr., & Wise, R. A. (1996a). Microinjections of phencyclidine (PCP) and related drugs into nucleus accumbens shell potentiate lateral hypothalamic brain stimulation reward. *Psychopharmacology, 128,* 413–420.

Carlezon, W. A., Jr., & Wise, R. A. (1996b). Rewarding actions of phencyclidine and related drugs in nucleus accumbens shell and frontal cortex. *Journal of Neuroscience, 16,* 3112–3122.

Carr, G. D., & White, N. M. (1983). Conditioned place preference from intra-accumbens but not intra-caudate amphetamine injections. *Life Science, 33,* 2551–2557.

Carr, K. C., & Wolinsky, T. D. (1993). Chronic food restriction and weight loss produce opioid facilitation of perifornical hypothalamic self-stimulation. *Brain Research, 607,* 141–148.

Chang, J. Y., Janak, P. H., & Woodward, D. J. (1998). Comparison of mesocorticolimbic neuronal responses during cocaine and heroin self-administration in freely moving rats. *Journal of Neuroscience, 18,* 3098–3115.

Childress, A. R., Ehrman, R., McLellan, A. T., & O'Brien, C. P. (1988). Conditioned craving and arousal in cocaine addiction: A preliminary report. *Problems of Drug Dependence 1987, NIDA Research Monograph (ADM), 88-1564,* 74–80.

Childress, A. R., Mozley, P. D., McElgin, W., Fitzgerald, J., Reivich, M., & O'Brien, C. P. (1999). Limbic activation during cue-induced cocaine craving. *American Journal of Psychiatry, 156,* 11–18.

Church, W. H., Justice, J. B., Jr., & Byrd, L. D. (1987). Extracellular dopamine in rat striatum following uptake inhibition by cocaine, nomifensine and benztropine. *European Journal of Pharmacology, 139,* 345–348.

Cicero, T. J. (1980). Animal models of alcoholism. In K. Eriksson, J. D. Sinclair, & K. Kiianmaa (Ed.), *Animal models in alcohol research* (pp. 99–118). New York: Academic.

Clarke, P. B. S., & Pert, A. (1985). Autoradiographic evidence for nicotine receptors on nigrostriatal and mesolimbic dopaminergic neurons. *Brain Research, 348,* 355–358.

Collier, H. O. J. (1968). Supersensitivity and dependence. *Nature, 220,* 228–231.

Collier, H. O. J. (1980). Cellular site of opiate dependence. *Nature, 283,* 625–629.

Collins, R. J., Weeks, J. R., Cooper, M. M., Good, P. I., & Russell, R. R. (1984). Prediction of abuse liability of drugs using IV self-administration by rats. *Psychopharmacology, 82,* 6–13.

Colpaert, F. C., & Slangen, J. L. (Eds.). (1982). *Drug discrimination: Applications in CNS pharmacology.* Amsterdam: Elsevier.

Corrigall, W. A., & Coen, K. M. (1989). Nicotine maintains robust self-administration in rats on a limited-access schedule. *Psychopharmacology, 99,* 473–478.

Corrigall, W. A., Franklin, K. B. J., Coen, K. M., & Clarke, P. (1992). The mesolimbic dopaminergic system is implicated in the reinforcing effects of nicotine. *Psychopharmacology, 107,* 285–289.

Cottler, L. B. (1993). Comparing DSM-III-R and ICD-10 substance use disorders. *Addiction, 88,* 689–696.

Crabbe, J. C., Belknap, J. K., & Buck, K. J. (1994). Genetic animal models of alcohol and drug abuse. *Science, 264,* 1715–1723.

Craig, W. (1918). Appetites and aversions as constituents of instincts. *Biological Bulletin, 34,* 91–107.

Dackis, C. A., & Gold, M. S. (1985). New concepts in cocaine addiction: The dopamine depletion hypothesis. *Neuroscience and Biobehavioral Reviews, 9,* 469–477.

Davis, W. M., & Smith, S. G. (1976). Role of conditioned reinforcers in the initiation, maintenance and extinction of drug-seeking behavior. *Pavlovian Journal of Biological Science, 11,* 222–236.

Deneau, G., Yanagita, T., & Seevers, M. H. (1969). Self-administration of psychoactive substances by the monkey: A measure of psychological dependence. *Psychopharmacologia, 16,* 30–48.

Deutsch, J. A., & Howarth, C. I. (1963). Some tests of a theory of intracranial self-stimulation. *Psychological Review, 70,* 444–460.

Devine, D. P., Leone, P., Pocock, D., & Wise, R. A. (1993). Differential involvement of ventral tegmental mu, delta, and kappa opioid receptors in modulation of basal mesolimbic dopamine release: *In vivo* microdialysis studies. *Journal of Pharmacology and Experimental Therapeutics, 266,* 1236–1246.

Devine, D. P., & Wise, R. A. (1994). Self-administration of morphine, DAMGO, and DPDPE into the ventral tegmental area of rats. *Journal of Neuroscience, 14,* 1978–1984.

de Wit, H., & Stewart, J. (1981). Reinstatement of cocaine-reinforced responding in the rat. *Psychopharmacology, 75,* 134–143.

de Wit, H., & Stewart, J. (1983). Drug reinstatement of heroin-reinforced responding in the rat. *Psychopharmacology, 79,* 29–31.

de Wit, H., & Wise, R. A. (1977). Blockade of cocaine reinforcement in rats with the dopamine receptor blocker pimozide but not with the noradrenergic blockers phentolamine or phenoxybenzamine. *Canadian Journal of Psychology, 31,* 195–203.

Di Chiara, G., & Imperato, A. (1988). Drugs abused by humans preferentially increase synaptic dopamine concentrations in the mesolimbic system of freely moving rats. *Proceedings of the National Academy of Sciences (USA), 85,* 5274–5278.

Dole, V. P., & Nyswander, M. (1965). A medical treatment for diacetylmorphine (heroin) addiction. *Journal of the American Medical Association, 193,* 646–650.

Dole, V. P., & Nyswander, M. (1967). Heroin addiction: A metabolic disease. *Archives of Internal Medicine, 120,* 19–24.

Downs, A. W., & Eddy, N. B. (1932). The effect of repeated doses of cocaine on the dog. *Journal of Pharmacology and Experimental Therapeutics, 46,* 195–198.

DuMars, L. A., Rodger, L. D., & Kalivas, P. W. (1988). Behavioral cross-sensitization between cocaine and enkephalin in the A10 dopamine region. *Behavioural Brain Research, 27,* 87–91.

Echenhoff, J., & Oech, S. (1960). Effects of narcotics upon respiration and circulation in man: A review. *Clinical and Pharmacological Therapy, 1,* 483–524.

Eddy, N. B., Halbach, H., Isbell, H., & Seevers, M. H. (1965). Drug dependence: Its significance and characteristics. *Bulletin of the World Health Organization, 32,* 721–733.

Edmonds, D. E., & Gallistel, C. R. (1974). Parametric analysis of brain stimulation reward in the rat: III. Effect of performance variables on the reward summation function. *Journal of Comparative and Physiological Psychology, 87,* 876–883.

Edwards, G., Arif, A., & Hodgson, R. (1981). Nomenclature and classification of drug- and alcohol-related problems: A WHO memorandum. *Bulletin of the World Health Organization, 59,* 225–242.

Ehrman, R. N., Robbins, S. J., Childress, A. R., & O'Brien, C. P. (1992). Conditioned responses to cocaine-related stimuli in cocaine abuse patients. *Psychopharmacology, 107,* 523–529.

Eikelboom, R., & Stewart, J. (1979). Conditioned temperature effects using morphine as the unconditioned stimulus. *Psychopharmacology, 61,* 31–38.

Eikelboom, R., & Stewart, J. (1981). Temporal and environmental cues in conditioned hypothermia and hyperthermia associated with morphine. *Psychopharmacology, 72,* 147–153.

Ellinwood, E. H., & Kilbey, M. M. (1975). Amphetamine stereotypy: The influence of environmental factors and prepotent behavioral patterns on its topography and development. *Biological Psychiatry, 10,* 3–16.

Erb, S., Shaham, Y., & Stewart, J. (1996). Stress reinstates cocaine-seeking behavior after prolonged extinction and a drug-free period. *Psychopharmacology, 128,* 408–412.

Eriksson, K. (1968). Genetic selection for voluntary alcohol consumption in the albino rat. *Science, 159,* 739–741.

Falk, J. L., Samson, H. M., & Winger, G. (1972). Behavioural maintenance of high concentrations of blood ethanol and physical dependence in the rat. *Science, 177,* 811–813.

Fibiger, H. C., Carter, D. A., & Phillips, A. G. (1976). Decreased intracranial self-stimulation after neuroleptics or 6-hydroxydopamine: Evidence for mediation by motor deficits rather than by reduced reward. *Psychopharmacology, 47,* 21–27.

Fiorino, D. F., Coury, A., & Phillips, A. G. (1997). Dynamic changes in nucleus accumbens dopamine efflux during the Coolidge effect in male rats. *Journal of Neuroscience, 17,* 4849–4855.

Fischman, M. W., & Schuster, C. R. (1982). Cocaine self-administration in humans. *Federation Proceedings, 41,* 241–246.

Foltin, R. W., & Fischman, M. W. (1991). Smoked and intravenous cocaine in humans: Acute tolerance, cardiovascular and subjective effects.

Journal of Pharmacology and Experimental Therapeutics, 257(1), 247–261.

Fouriezos, G., & Wise, R. A. (1976). Pimozide-induced extinction of intracranial self-stimulation: Response patterns rule out motor or performance deficits. *Brain Research, 103,* 377–380.

Fouriezos, G., & Wise, R. A. (1984). Current-distance relation for rewarding brain stimulation. *Behavioural Brain Research, 14,* 85–89.

Frank, R. A., Martz, S., & Pommering, T. (1988). The effect of chronic cocaine on self-stimulation train-duration thresholds. *Pharmacology Biochemistry and Behavior, 29,* 755–758.

Franklin, K. B. J. (1978). Catecholamines and self-stimulation: Reward and performance effects dissociated. *Pharmacology Biochemistry and Behavior, 9,* 813–820.

Franklin, K. B. J., & McCoy, S. N. (1979). Pimozide-induced extinction in rats: Stimulus control of responding rules out motor deficit. *Pharmacology Biochemistry and Behavior, 11,* 71–75.

Freed, W. J., & Mendelson, J. (1974). Airlicking: Thirsty rats prefer a warm dry airstream to a warm humid airstream. *Physiology and Behavior, 12,* 557–561.

French, E. D. (1997). Δ9 Tetrahydrocannabinol excites rat VTA dopamine neurons through activation of cannabinoid CB1 but not opioid receptors. *Neuroscience Letters, 226,* 159–162.

Freund, G. (1969). Alcohol withdrawal syndrome in mice. *Archives of Neurology, 21,* 315–320.

Freund, G. (1973). Alcohol, barbiturate and bromide withdrawal syndrome in mice. *Annals of the New York Academy of Sciences, 215,* 224–234.

Gallistel, C. R. (1966). Motivating effects in self-stimulation. *Journal of Comparative and Physiological Psychology, 62,* 95–101.

Gallistel, C. R. (1969). The incentive of brain-stimulation reward. *Journal of Comparative and Physiological Psychology, 69,* 713–721.

Gallistel, C. R. (1987). Determining the quantitative characteristics of a reward pathway. In R. M. Church, M. L. Commons, J. R. Stellar, & A. R. Wagner (Eds.), *Biological determinants of reinforcement* (pp. 1–30). Hillsdale, NJ: Erlbaum.

Gallistel, C. R., & Freyd, G. (1987). Quantitative determination of the effects of catecholaminergic agonists and antagonists on the rewarding efficacy of brain stimulation. *Pharmacology Biochemistry and Behavior, 26,* 731–741.

Gallistel, C. R., & Karras, D. (1984). Pimozide and amphetamine have opposing effects on the reward summation function. *Pharmacology Biochemistry and Behavior, 20,* 73–77.

Gallistel, C. R., Stellar, J. R., & Bubis, E. (1974). Parametric analysis of brain stimulation reward in the rat: I. The transient process and the memory-containing process. *Journal of Comparative and Physiological Psychology, 87,* 848–859.

Gallistel, C. R., Shizgal, P., & Yeomans, J. (1981). A portrait of the substrate for self-stimulation. *Psychological Review, 88,* 228–273.

Gerber, G. J., & Stretch, R. (1975). Drug-induced reinstatement of extinguished self-administration behavior in monkeys. *Pharmacology Biochemistry and Behavior, 3,* 1055–1061.

Gerber, G. J., & Wise, R. A. (1989). Pharmacological regulation of intravenous cocaine and heroin self-administration in rats: A variable dose paradigm. *Pharmacology Biochemistry and Behavior, 32,* 527–531.

Gerhardt, G. A., Pang, K., & Rose, G. M. (1987). In vivo electrochemical demonstration of the presynaptic actions of phencyclidine in rat caudate nucleus. *Journal of Pharmacology and Experimental Therapeutics, 241,* 714–721.

Gessa, G. L., Muntoni, F., Collu, M., Vargiu, L., & Mereu, G. (1985). Low doses of ethanol activate dopaminergic neurons in the ventral tegmental area. *Brain Research, 348,* 201–204.

Gilbert, R. M. (1976). Caffeine as a drug of abuse. In R. J. Gibbons, Y. Israel, H. Kalant, & R. E. Popham (Eds.), *Research advances in alcohol and drug problems* (pp. 49–176). New York: Wiley.

Glickman, S. E., & Schiff, B. B. (1967). A biological theory of reinforcement. *Psychological Review, 74,* 81–109.

Gold, R. M., Kapatos, G., Prowse, J., Quackenbush, P. M., & Oxford, T. W. (1973). Role of water temperature in the regulation of water intake. *Journal of Comparative and Physiological Psychology, 85,* 52–63.

Goldberg, S. R., Kelleher, R. T., & Morse, W. H. (1975). Second-order schedules of drug injection. *Federation Proceedings, 34,* 1771–1776.

Goldberg, S. R., Spealman, R. D., Risner, M. E., & Henningfield, J. E. (1983). Control of behavior by intravenous nicotine injections in laboratory animals. *Pharmacology Biochemistry and Behavior, 19,* 1011–1020.

Goldberg, S. R., Woods, J. H., & Schuster, C. R. (1969). Morphine: Conditioned increases in self-administration in rhesus monkeys. *Science, 166,* 1306–1307.

Goldstein, A., & Herrera, J. (1995). Heroin addicts and methadone treatment in Albuquerque: A 22-year follow-up. *Drug and Alcohol Dependence, 40,* 139–150.

Goldstein, D. B., & Goldstein, A. (1961). Possible role of enzyme inhibition and repression in drug tolerance and addiction. *Biochemical Pharmacology, 8,* 48.

Goldstein, D. B., & Pal, N. (1971). Alcohol dependence produced in mice by inhalation of ethanol: Grading the withdrawal reaction. *Science, 172,* 288–290.

Grenhoff, J., Aston-Jones, G., & Svensson, T. H. (1986). Nicotinic effects on the firing pattern of midbrain dopamine neurons. *Acta Physiologica Scandanavica, 128,* 351–358.

Griffiths, R. R., Brady, J. V., & Bradford, L. D. (1979). Predicting the abuse liability of drugs with animal drug self-administration procedures: Psychomotor stimulants and hallucinogens. In T. Thompson & P. B. Dews (Eds.), *Advances in behavioral pharmacology* (pp. 163–208). New York: Academic Press.

Guttman, N., & Kalish, H. I. (1956). Discriminability and stimulus generalization. *Journal of Experimental Psychology, 51,* 79–88.

Harris, G. C., & Aston-Jones, G. (1994). Involvement of D2 dopamine receptors in the nucleus accumbens in the opiate withdrawal syndrome. *Nature, 371,* 155–157.

Hatsukami, D. K., Hughes, J. R., Pickens, R. W., & Svikis, D. (1984). Tobacco withdrawal symptoms: An experimental analysis. *Psychopharmacology, 84,* 231–236.

Hawkins, T. D., & Pliskoff, S. S. (1964). Brain stimulation intensity, rate of self-stimulation and reinforcement strength: An analysis through chaining. *Journal of the Experimental Analysis of Behavior, 7,* 285–288.

Heikkila, R. E., Orlansky, H., & Cohen, G. (1975). Studies on the distinction between uptake inhibition and release of (^{3}H)dopamine in rat brain tissue slices. *Biochemical Pharmacology, 24,* 847–852.

Heikkila, R. E., Orlansky, H., Mytilineou, C., & Cohen, G. (1975). Amphetamine: Evaluation of *d*- and *l*-isomers as releasing agents and uptake inhibitors for ^{3}H-dopamine and ^{3}H-norepinephrine in slices of rat neostriatum and cerebral cortex. *Journal of Pharmacology and Experimental Therapeutics, 194,* 47–56.

Henningfield, J. E. (1984). Behavioral pharmacology of cigarette smoking. *Advances in Behavioral Pharmacology, 4,* 131–210.

Hernandez, L., & Hoebel, B. G. (1988). Food reward and cocaine increase extracellular dopamine in the nucleus accumbens as measured by microdialysis. *Life Sciences, 42,* 1705–1712.

Himmelsbach, C. K. (1943). Morphine, with reference to physical dependence. *Federation Proceedings, 2,* 201–203.

Hodos, W. (1961). Progressive ratio as a measure of reward strength. *Science, 134,* 943–944.

Hoebel, B. G., Monaco, A. P., Hernandez, L., Aulisi, E. F., Stanley, B. G., & Lenard, L. (1983). Self-injection of amphetamine directly into the brain. *Psychopharmacology, 81,* 158–163.

Horger, B. A., Giles, M. K., & Schenk, S. (1992). Preexposure to amphetamine and nicotine predisposes rats to self-administer a low dose of cocaine. *Psychopharmacology, 107,* 271–276.

Horger, B. A., Shelton, K., & Schenk, S. (1990). Preexposure sensitizes rats to the rewarding effects of cocaine. *Pharmacology Biochemistry and Behavior, 37,* 707–711.

Howarth, C. I., & Deutsch, J. A. (1962). Drive decay: The cause of fast "extinction" of habits learned for brain stimulation. *Science, 137,* 35–36.

Hughes, J. R., & Hatsukami, D. (1986). Signs and symptoms of tobacco withdrawal. *Archives of General Psychiatry, 43,* 289–294.

Hurd, J. L., Weiss, F., Koob, G. F., Anden, N.-E., & Ungerstedt, U. (1989). Cocaine reinforcement and extracellular dopamine overflow in rat nucleus accumbens: An in vivo microdialysis study. *Brain Research, 498,* 199–203.

Hyytia, P., & Sinclair, J. D. (1989). Demonstration of lever pressing for oral ethanol by rats with no prior training or experience. *Alcohol, 6,* 161–164.

Iglauer, C., Llewellyn, M. E., & Woods, J. H. (1976). Concurrent schedules of cocaine injection in rhesus monkeys: Dose variations under independent and non-independent variable-interval procedures. *Pharmacological Reviews, 27,* 367–383.

Jaffe, J. H. (1985). Drug addiction and drug abuse. In A. G. Gilman, L. S. Goodman, & A. Gilman (Eds.), *The pharmacological basis of therapeutics* (pp. 532–581). New York: Macmillan.

Jaffe, J., Cascella, N. G., Kumor, K. M., & Sherer, M. A. (1989). Cocaine-induced cocaine craving. *Psychopharmacology, 97,* 59–64.

Jaffe, J. H., & Sharpless, S. K. (1968). Pharmacological denervation supersensitivity in the central nervous system: A theory of physical dependence. In A. H. Wikler (Ed.), *The addictive states* (pp. 226–246). Baltimore: Williams and Wilkins.

Jarvik, M. E. (1964). Tobacco smoking in monkeys. *Annals of the New York Academy of Sciences, 142,* 280–294.

Jellinek, W. M. (1960). *The disease concept of alcoholism.* New Haven, CT: Hillhouse Press.

Johanson, C. E. (1978). Drugs as reinforcers. In D. E. Blackman & D. J. Sanger (Eds.), *Contemporary research in behavioral pharmacology* (pp. 325–390). New York: Plenum Press.

Johanson, C. E., Balster, R. L., & Bonese, K. (1976). Self-administration of psychomotor stimulant drugs: The effects of unlimited access. *Pharmacology Biochemistry and Behavior, 4,* 45–51.

Johanson, C. E., & Schuster, C. R. (1975). A choice procedure for drug reinforcers: Cocaine and methylphenidate in the rhesus monkey. *Journal of Pharmacology and Experimental Therapeutics, 193,* 675–688.

Johnson, S. W., & North, R. A. (1992). Opioids excite dopamine neurons by hyperpolarization of local interneurons. *Journal of Neuroscience, 12,* 483–488.

Jones, R. T. (1980). Human effects: An overview. In R. C. Petersen (Ed.), *Marijuana research findings: 1980 (National Institute on Drug Abuse Research Monograph 31)* (pp. 54–80). Washington, DC: U.S. Government Printing Office.

Jones, R. T. (1984). The pharmacology of cocaine. In J. Grabowski (Ed.), *Cocaine: Pharmacology, effects, and treatment of abuse (National Institute on Drug Abuse Research Monograph 50)* (pp. 34–53). Washington, DC: U.S. Government Printing Office.

Kalant, H. (1977). Comparative aspects of tolerance to, and dependence on, alchohol, barbiturates, and opiates. In M. M. Gross (Ed.), *Alcohol intoxication and withdrawal* (pp. 169–186). New York: Plenum.

Kalivas, P. W., & Duffy, P. (1989). Similar effects of daily cocaine and stress on mesocorticolimbic dopamine neurotransmission in the rat. *Biological Psychiatry, 25,* 913–928.

Kalivas, P. W., & Duffy, P. (1995). Selective activation of dopamine transmission in the shell of the nucleus accumbens by stress. *Brain Research, 675,* 325–328.

Kelz, M. B., Chen, J., Carlezon, W. A., Whisler, K., Gilden, L., Bechmann, A. M., Steffen, C., Zhang, Y.-J., Marotti, L., Self, D. W., Tkatch, T., Baranauskas, G., Surmeier, D. J., Neve, R. L., Duman, R. S., Picciotto, M. R., & Nestler, E. J. (1999). Expression of the transcription factor DFosB in the brain controls sensitivity to cocaine. *Nature, 401,* 272–276.

Kelz, M. B., & Nestler, E. J. (2000). deltaFosB: A molecular switch underlying long-term neural plasticity. *Current Opinion in Neurology, 13,* 715–720.

Kishioka, S., Paronis, C. A., & Woods, J. H. (2000). Acute dependence on, but not tolerance to, heroin and morphine as measured by respiratory effects in rhesus monkeys. *European Journal of Pharmacology, 398,* 121–130.

Kiyatkin, E. A., & Rebec, G. V. (2001). Impulse activity of ventral tegmental area neurons during heroin self-administration in rats. *Neuroscience, 102,* 565–580.

Kokkinidis, L., & McCarter, B. D. (1990). Post-cocaine depression and sensitization of brain-stimulation reward: Analysis of reinforcement and performance effects. *Pharmacology Biochemistry and Behavior, 36,* 463–471.

Kokkinidis, L., Zacharko, R. M., & Predy, P. A. (1980). Post-amphetamine depression of self-stimulation responding from the substantia nigra: Reversal by tricyclic antidepressants. *Pharmacology Biochemistry and Behavior, 13,* 379–383.

Koob, G. F., & Bloom, F. E. (1988). Cellular and molecular mechanisms of drug dependence. *Science, 242,* 715–723.

Koob, G. F., Stinus, L., Le Moal, M., & Bloom, F. E. (1989). Opponent process theory of motivation: Neurobiological evidence from studies of opiate dependence. *Neuroscience and Biobehavioral Reviews, 13,* 135–140.

Kosten, T. A., Miserendino, M. J. D., Chi, S., & Nestler, E. J. (1994). Fischer and Lewis rat strains show differential cocaine effects in conditioned place preference and behavioral sensitization but not in locomotor activity or conditioned taste aversion. *Journal of Pharmacology and Experimental Therapeutics, 269,* 137–144.

Landauer, T. K. (1969). Reinforcement as consolidation. *Psychological Review, 76,* 82–96.

Le, A. D., Khanna, J. M., Kalant, H., & Grossi, F. (1986). Tolerance to and cross-tolerance among ethanol, pentobarbital and chlordiazepoxide. *Pharmacology Biochemistry and Behavior, 24,* 93–98.

Lee, R. S., Criado, J. R., Koob, G. F., & Henriksen, S. J. (1999). Cellular responses of nucleus accumbens neurons to opiate-seeking behavior: I. Sustained responding during heroin self-administration. *Synapse, 33,* 49–58.

Leeb, K., & Wise, R. A. (1993). Acquisition of intravenous heroin self-administration in Lewis and Fischer rats. *Society for Neuroscience Abstracts, 19,* 1025.

Leith, N. J., & Barrett, R. J. (1976). Amphetamine and the reward system: Evidence for tolerance and post-drug depression. *Psychopharmacologia, 46,* 19–25.

Le Magnen, J. (1959). Effects des administrations post-prandiales de glucose sur l'établissement des appétits. *Comptes Rendus des Seances ce la Societe de Biologie (Paris), 153,* 212–215.

Leshner, A. I. (1999). Science-based views of drug addiction and its treatment. *Journal of the American Medical Association, 282,* 1314–1316.

Lester, D. (1966). Self-selection of alcohol by animals, human variation and the etiology of alcoholism: A critical review. *Quarterly Journal of Studies on Alcohol, 27,* 395–438.

Lett, B. T. (1989). Repeated exposures intensify rather than diminish the rewarding effects of amphetamine, morphine, and cocaine. *Psychopharmacology, 98,* 357–362.

Li, T. K., Lumeng, L., McBride, W. J., Murphy, J. M., Froehlich, J. C., & Morzorati, S. (1988). Pharmacology of alcohol preference in rodents. *Advances in Alcohol and Substance Abuse, 7,* 73–86.

Lindesmith, A. R. (1947). *Opiate addiction.* Bloomington, IN: Principia Press.

Ljungberg, T., Apicella, P., & Schultz, W. (1992). Responses of monkey dopamine neurons during learning of behavioral reactions. *Journal of Neurophysiology, 67,* 145–163.

Lyness, W. H., Friedle, N. M., & Moore, K. E. (1979). Destruction of dopaminergic nerve terminals in nucleus accumbens: Effect on d-amphetamine self-administration. *Pharmacology Biochemistry and Behavior, 11,* 553–556.

Macenski, M. J., & Meisch, R. A. (1994). Oral drug reinforcement studies with laboratory animals: Applications and implications for understanding drug-reinforced behavior. *Current Directions in Psychological Science, 3,* 22–27.

Malin, D. H., Lake, J. R., Newlin-Maultsby, P., Roberts, L. K., Lanier, J. G., Carter, V. A., Cunningham, J. S., & Wilson, O. B. (1992). Rodent model of nicotine abstinence syndrome. *Pharmacology Biochemistry and Behavior, 43,* 779–784.

Malmo, R. B. (1975). *On emotions, needs, and our archaic brain.* New York: Holt, Rinehart and Winston.

Mardones, J., & Segovia-Riquelme, N. (1983). Thirty two years of selection of rats by ethanol preference: UChA and UChB strains. *Neurobehavioral Toxicology and Teratology, 5,* 171–178.

Markou, A., & Koob, G. F. (1991). Postcocaine anhedonia: An animal model of cocaine withdrawal. *Neuropsychopharmacology, 4,* 17–26.

Martin, W. R. (1967). Opioid antagonists. *Pharmacological Reviews, 19,* 464–521.

Meil, W. M., & See, R. E. (1996). Conditioned cued responding following prolonged withdrawal from self-administered cocaine in rats: An animal model of relapse. *Behavioral Pharmacology, 7,* 754–763.

Mello, N. K. (1973). A review of methods to induce alcohol addiction in animals. *Pharmacology Biochemistry and Behavior, 1,* 89–101.

Mello, N. K., & Mendelson, J. H. (1972). Drinking patterns during work-contingent and noncontingent alcohol acquisition. *Psychosomatic Medicine, 34,* 139–164.

Mendelson, J., & Chillag, D. (1970). Tongue cooling: A new reward for thirsty rodents. *Science, 170,* 1418–1419.

Mereu, G., Yoon, K.-W. P., Boi, V., Gessa, G. L., Naes, L., & Westfall, T. C. (1987). Preferential stimulation of ventral tegmental area dopaminergic neurons by nicotine. *European Journal of Pharmacology, 141,* 395–400.

Miliaressis, E., Rompré, P.-P., Laviolette, L. P., Philippe, L., & Coulombe, D. (1986). The curve-shift paradigm in self-stimulation. *Physiology and Behavior, 37,* 85–91.

Nestler, E. J. (1997). Molecular mechanisms of opiate and cocaine addiction. *Current Opinion in Neurobiology, 7,* 713–719.

Nestler, E. J. (2001). Molecular basis of long-term plasticity underlying addiction. *Nature Reviews Neuroscience, 2,* 119–128.

Nestler, E. J., & Aghajanian, G. K. (1997). Molecular and cellular basis of addiction. *Science, 278,* 58–63.

Nestler, E. J., Kelz, M. B., & Chen, J. (1999). DeltaFosB: A molecular mediator of long-term neural and behavioral plasticity. *Brain Research, 835,* 10–17.

Ng Cheong Ton, J. M., Gerhardt, G. A., Friedemann, M., Etgen, A., Rose, G. M., Sharpless, N. S., & Gardner, E. L. (1988). The effects of Δ^9-tetrahydrocannabinol on potassium-evoked release of dopamine in the rat caudate nucleus: An in vivo electrochemical and in vivo dialysis study. *Brain Research, 451,* 59–68.

Olds, J. (1958a). Satiation effects in self-stimulation of the brain. *Journal of Comparative and Physiological Psychology, 51,* 675–678.

Olds, J. (1958b). Self-stimulation of the brain. *Science, 127,* 315–324.

Olds, J. (1961). Differential effects of drives and drugs on self-stimulation at different brain sites. In D. E. Sheer (Ed.), *Electrical stimulation of the brain* (pp. 350–370). Austin: University of Texas Press.

Olds, J., & Milner, P. M. (1954). Positive reinforcement produced by electrical stimulation of septal area and other regions of rat brain. *Journal of Comparative and Physiological Psychology, 47,* 419–427.

Olds, M. E., & Olds, J. (1963). Approach-avoidance analysis of rat diencephalon. *Journal of Comparative Neurology, 120,* 259–295.

Olmstead, M. C., Parkinson, J. A., Miles, F. J., Everitt, B. J., & Dickinson, A. (2000). Cocaine-seeking by rats: Regulation, reinforcement and activation. *Psychopharmacology, 152,* 123–131.

Orford, J. (2001). Addiction as excessive appetite. *Addiction, 96,* 15–31.

Paly, D., Jatlow, P., Van Dyke, C., Jeri, F. R., & Byck, R. (1982). Plasma cocaine concentrations during cocaine paste smoking. *Life Sciences, 30,* 731–738.

Parsons, L. H., Smith, A. D., & Justice, J. B. (1991). Basal extracellular dopamine is decreased in the rat nucleus accumbens during abstinence from chronic cocaine. *Synapse, 9,* 60–65.

Pavlov, I. P. (1928). *Lectures on conditioned reflexes.* New York: International.

Peele, S., & Brodsky, A. (1975). *Love and addiction.* Scarborough, Ontario: New American Library of Canada.

Peoples, L. L., Uzwiak, A. J., Gee, F., & West, M. O. (1997). Operant behavior during sessions of intravenous cocaine infusion is necessary and sufficient for phasic firing of single nucleus accumbens neurons. *Brain Research, 757,* 280–284.

Peoples, L. L., & West, M. O. (1996). Phasic firing of single neurons in the rat nucleus accumbens correlated with the timing of intravenous cocaine self-administration. *Journal of Neuroscience, 16,* 3459–3473.

Perkins, K. A., Gerlach, D., Broge, M., Grobe, J. E., Sanders, J., Fonte, C., Vender, J., Cherry, C., & Wilson, A. (2001). Dissociation of nicotine tolerance from tobacco dependence in humans. *Journal of Pharmacology and Experimental Therapeutics, 296,* 849–856.

Pettit, H. O., & Justice, J. B. (1989). Dopamine in the nucleus accumbens during cocaine self-administration as studied by in vivo microdialysis. *Pharmacology Biochemistry and Behavior, 34,* 899–904.

Pfaff, D. (1969). Parsimonious biological models of memory and reinforcement. *Psychological Review, 76,* 70–81.

Phillips, T. J., Feller, D. J., & Crabbe, J. C. (1989). Selected mouse lines, alcohol and behavior. *Experientia, 45,* 805–827.

Piazza, P. V., Deminiere, J. M., Le Moal, M., & Simon, H. (1990). Stress- and pharmacologically-induced behavioral sensitization increases vulnerability to acquisition of amphetamine self-administration. *Brain Research, 514,* 22–26.

Pickens, R., & Harris, W. C. (1968). Self-administration of d-amphetamine by rats. *Psychopharmacologia, 12,* 158–163.

Pickens, R., & Thompson, T. (1968). Cocaine-reinforced behavior in rats: Effects of reinforcement magnitude and fixed-ratio size. *Journal of Pharmacology and Experimental Therapeutics, 161,* 122–129.

Pickens, R., & Thompson, T. (1971). Characteristics of stimulant reinforcement. In T. Thompson & R. Pickens (Eds.), *Stimulus properties of drugs* (pp. 177–192). New York: Appleton-Century-Crofts.

Post, R. M., & Kopanda, R. T. (1976). Cocaine, kindling, and psychosis. *American Journal of Psychiatry, 133,* 627–634.

Ranaldi, R., Bauco, P., McCormick, S., Cools, A. R., & Wise, R. A. (2001). Equal sensitivity to cocaine reward in addiction-prone and addiction-resistant rat genotypes. *Behavioural Pharmacology,* in press.

Ranaldi, R., Pocock, D., Zereik, R., & Wise, R. A. (1999). Dopamine fluctuations in the nucleus accumbens during maintenance, extinction, and reinstatement of intravenous D-amphetamine self-administration. *Journal of Neuroscience, 19,* 4102–4109.

Risner, M. E., & Jones, B. E. (1976). Role of noradrenergic and dopaminergic processes in amphetamine self-administration. *Pharmacology Biochemistry and Behavior, 5,* 477–482.

Risner, M. E., & Jones, B. E. (1980). Intravenous self-administration of cocaine and norcocaine by dogs. *Psychopharmacology, 71,* 83–89.

Robertson, M. W., Leslie, C. A., & Bennett, Jr., J. P. (1991). Apparent synaptic dopamine deficiency induced by withdrawal from chronic cocaine treatment. *Brain Research, 538,* 337–339.

Robinson, J. H., & Pritchard, W. S. (1995). Differentiating habits and addictions: The evidence that nicotine is not "addictive." In P. B. S. Clarke, M. Quik, F. Adlkofer, & K. Thurau (Eds.), *Effects of nicotine on biological systems II* (pp. 273–278). Basel: Birkhäuser.

Robinson, T. E., & Becker, J. B. (1986). Enduring changes in brain and behavior produced by chronic amphetamine administration: A review and evaluation of animal models of amphetamine psychosis. *Brain Research Reviews, 11,* 157–198.

Robinson, T. E., & Berridge, K. C. (1993). The neural basis of drug craving: An incentive-sensitization theory of addiction. *Brain Research Reviews, 18,* 247–292.

Robinson, T. E., & Berridge, K. C. (2001). Incentive-sensitization and addiction. *Addiction, 96,* 103–114.

Robinson, T. E., Browman, K. E., Crombag, H. S., & Badiani, A. (1998). Modulation of the induction or expression of psychostimulant surrounding drug administration. *Neuroscience and Biobehavioral Reviews, 22,* 347–354.

Rompré, P.-P., & Wise, R. A. (1989). Opioid-neuroleptic interaction in brain stem self-stimulation. *Brain Research, 477,* 144–151.

Ross, A. R., & Malmo, R. B. (1979). Cardiovascular response to rewarding brain stimulation. *Physiology and Behavior, 22,* 1005–1013.

Rossetti, Z. L., Hmaidan, Y., & Gessa, G. L. (1992). Marked inhibition of mesolimbic dopamine release: A common feature of ethanol, morphine, cocaine, and amphetamine abstinence in rats. *European Journal of Pharmacology, 221,* 227–234.

Rounsaville, B. J., Bryant, K., Babor, T., Kranzler, H., & Kadden, R. (1993). Cross system agreement for substance use disorders: DSM-III-R, DSM-IV and ICD-10. *Addiction, 88,* 337–348.

Routtenberg, A., & Lindy, J. (1965). Effects of the availability of rewarding septal and hypothalamic stimulation on bar pressing for food under conditions of deprivation. *Journal of Comparative and Physiological Psychology, 60,* 158–161.

Samson, H. H. (1986). Initiation of ethanol reinforcement using a sucrose-substitution procedure in food- and water-sated rats. *Alcohol Clinical and Experimental Research, 10,* 436–442.

Schneirla, T. C. (1959). An evolutionary and developmental theory of biphasic processes underlying approach and withdrawal. In M. R. Jones (Ed.), *Nebraska symposium on motivation* (pp. 1–42). Lincoln: University of Nebraska Press.

Schultz, W. (1997). A neural substrate of prediction and reward. *Science, 275,* 1593–1599.

Schultz, W., & Dickenson, A. (2000). Neuronal coding of prediction errors. *Annual Review of Neuroscience, 23,* 473–500.

Schuster, C. R., & Thompson, T. (1969). Self-administration of and behavioral dependence on drugs. *Annual Review of Pharmacology, 9,* 483–502.

Sclafani, A., & Ackroff, K. (1994). Glucose-and fructose-conditioned flavor preferences in rats: Taste versus postingestive conditioning. *Physiology and Behavior, 56,* 399–405.

Segal, D. S., & Mandell, A. J. (1974). Long-term administration of d-amphetamine: Progressive augmentation of motor activity and stereotypy. *Pharmacology Biochemistry and Behavior, 2,* 249–255.

Shaham, Y., & Stewart, J. (1995). Stress reinstates heroin-seeking in drug-free animals: An effect mimicking heroin, not withdrawal. *Psychopharmacology, 119,* 334–341.

Shalev, U., Highfield, D., Yap, J., & Shaham, Y. (2000). Stress and relapse to drug seeking in rats: Studies on the generality of the effect. *Psychopharmacology, 150,* 337–346.

Sherrington, C. S. (1906). *The integrative action of the nervous system.* New Haven, CT: Yale University Press.

Shiffman, S. M., & Jarvik, M. E. (1976). Smoking withdrawal symptoms in two weeks of abstinence. *Psychopharmacology, 50,* 35–39.

Shippenberg, T. S., Heidbreder, C., & Lefevour, A. (1996). Sensitization to the conditioned rewarding effects of morphine: Pharmacology and temporal characteristics. *European Journal of Pharmacology, 299,* 33–39.

Siegel, S. (1976). Morphine analgesic tolerance: Its situation specificity supports a Pavlovian conditioning model. *Science, 193,* 323–325.

Skinner, B. F. (1933). The rate of establishment of a discrimination. *Journal of General Psychology, 9,* 302–350.

Skinner, B. F. (1935). Two types of conditioned reflex and a pseudotype. *Journal of General Psychology, 12,* 66–77.

Sokolov, Y. N. (1963). *Perception and the conditioned reflex.* Oxford, UK: Pergamon.

Solomon, R. L., & Corbit, J. D. (1973). An opponent-process theory of motivation: II. Cigarette addiction. *Journal of Abnormal Psychology, 81,* 158–171.

Sorg, B. A., & Kalivas, P. W. (1991). Effects of cocaine and footshock stress on extracellular dopamine levels in the ventral tegmentum. *Brain Research, 559,* 29–36.

Spence, K. W. (1956). *Behavior Theory and Conditioning.* Yale University Press, New Haven.

Stewart, J., de Wit, H., & Eikelboom, R. (1984). Role of unconditioned and conditioned drug effects in the self-administration of opiates and stimulants. *Psychological Review, 91,* 251–268.

Stewart, J., & Eikelboom, R. (1987). Conditioned drug effects. In L. L. Iversen, S. D. Iversen, &

S. H. Snyder (Ed.), *Handbook of psychopharmacology* (pp. 1–57). New York: Plenum.

Stewart, J., & Vezina, P. (1987). Environment-specific enhancement of the hyperactivity induced by systemic or intra-VTA morphine injections of rats pre-exposed to amphetamine. *Psychobiology, 15,* 144–153.

Stewart, J., & Wise, R. A. (1992). Reinstatement of heroin self-administration habits: Morphine prompts and naltrexone discourages renewed responding after extinction. *Psychopharmacology, 108,* 79–84.

Tanda, G., Munzar, P., & Goldberg, S. R. (2000). Self-administration behavior is maintained by the psychoactive ingredient of marijuana in squirrel monkeys. *Nature Neuroscience, 3,* 1073–1074.

Tatum, A. L., Seevers, M. H., & Collins, K. H. (1929). Morphine addiction and its physiological interpretation based on experimental evidence. *Journal of Pharmacology and Experimental Therapeutics, 36,* 447–475.

Thierry, A. M., Tassin, J. P., Blanc, G., & Glowinski, J. (1976). Selective activation of the mesocortical DA system by stress. *Nature, 263,* 242–244.

Thompson, T. (1968). Drugs as reinforcers: Experimental addiction. *International Journal of the Addictions, 3,* 199–206.

Thorndike, E. L. (1898). Animal intelligence: An experimental study of the associative processes in animals. *Psychological Monographs, 8,* 1–109.

Thorndike, E. L. (1933). A theory of the action of the after-effects of a connection upon it. *Psychological Review, 40,* 434–439.

Tiffany, S. T. (1990). A cognitive model of drug urges and drug-use behavior: Role of automatic and nonautomatic processes. *Psychological Review, 97,* 147–168.

Tiffany, S. T., & Carter, B. L. (1998). Is craving the source of compulsive drug use? *Journal of Psychopharmacology, 12,* 23–30.

Tilson, H. A., & Rech, R. H. (1973). Conditioned drug effects and absence of tolerance to *d*-amphetamine induced motor activity. *Phar-*

macology Biochemistry and Behavior, 1, 149–153.

Tolliver, G. A., Sadeghi, K. G., & Samson, H. H. (1988). Ethanol preference following the sucrose-fading initiation procedure. *Alcohol, 5,* 9–13.

Tordoff, M. G. (1991). Metabolic basis of learned flavor preferences. In M. I. Friedman, M. G. Tordoff, & M. R. Kare (Eds.), *Chemical senses: Appetite and nutrition* (pp. 239–260). New York: Dekker.

Tremblay, E. C., & Charton, G. (1981). Anatomical correlates of morphine-withdrawal syndrome: Differential participation of structures located within the limbic system and striatum. *Neuroscience Letters, 23,* 137–142.

Trowill, J. A., Panksepp, J., & Gandelman, R. (1969). An incentive model of rewarding brain stimulation. *Psychological Review, 76,* 264–281.

Vezina, P., Giovino, A. A., Wise, R. A., & Stewart, J. (1989). Environment-specific cross-sensitization between the locomotor activating effects of morphine and amphetamine. *Pharmacology Biochemistry and Behavior, 32,* 581–584.

Weddington, W. W., Brown, B. S., Cone, E. J., Haertzen, C. A., Dax, E. M., Herning, R. I., & Michaelson, B. S. (1991). Changes in mood, craving and sleep during acute abstinence reported by male cocaine addicts. *NIDA Research Monographs, 105,* 453–454.

Weeks, J. R. (1962). Experimental morphine addiction: Method for automatic intravenous injections in unrestrained rats. *Science, 138,* 143–144.

Wei, E. T. (1981). Enkephalin analogs and physical dependence. *Journal of Pharmacology and Experimental Therapeutics, 216,* 12–18.

Wei, E. T., Loh, H. H., & Way, E. L. (1973). Brain sites of precipitated abstinence in morphine-dependent rats. *Journal of Pharmacology and Experimental Therapeutics, 185,* 108–115.

Wei, E. T., Sigel, S., & Way, E. L. (1975). Regional sensitivity of the rat brain to the inhibitory effects of morphine on wet shake behavior. *Journal of*

Pharmacology and Experimental Therapeutics, 193, 56–63.

Wei, E. T., Tseng, L. F., Loh, H. H., & Way, E. L. (1974). Similarity of morphine abstinence signs to thermoregulatory behaviour. *Nature, 247,* 398–399.

Weil, A., & Rosen, W. (1993). *From chocolate to morphine.* New York: Houghton Mifflin.

Weingarten, H. P., & Elston, D. (1990). The phenomenology of food craving. *Appetite, 15,* 231–246.

Weingarten, H. P., & Kulikovsky, O. T. (1989). Taste-to-postingestive consequence conditioning: Is the rise in sham feeding with repeated experience a learning phenomenon? *Physiology and Behavior, 45,* 471–476.

Welzl, H., Kuhn, G., & Huston, J. P. (1989). Self-administration of small amounts of morphine through glass micropipettes into the ventral tegmental area of the rat. *Neuropharmacology, 28,* 1017–1023.

Werner, T. E., Smith, S. G., & Davis, W. M. (1976). A dose-response comparison between methadone and morphine self-administration. *Psychopharmacologia, 47,* 209–211.

Wetzel, M. C. (1963). Self-stimulation aftereffects and runway performance in the rat. *Journal of Comparative and Physiological Psychology, 56,* 673–678.

White, F. J., & Kalivas, P. W. (1998). Neuroadaptations involved in amphetamine and cocaine addiction. *Drug and Alcohol Dependence, 51,* 141–153.

Wikler, A., & Pescor, F. (1967). Classical conditioning of a morphine abstinence phenomenon, reinforcement of opioid drinking behavior, and "relapse" in morphine-addicted rats. *Psychopharmacologia, 10,* 255–284.

Wise, R. A. (1972). Spread of current from monopolar stimulation of the lateral hypothalamus. *American Journal of Physiology, 223,* 545–548.

Wise, R. A. (1987a). Intravenous drug self-administration: A special case of positive reinforcement. In M. A. Bozarth (Ed.), *Methods of assessing the reinforcing properties of abused brugs* (pp. 117–141). New York: Springer.

Wise, R. A. (1987b). The role of reward pathways in the development of drug dependence. *Pharmacology and Therapeutics, 35,* 227–263.

Wise, R. A. (1988). The neurobiology of craving: Implications for understanding and treatment of addiction. *Journal of Abnormal Psychology, 97,* 118–132.

Wise, R. A. (1989). The brain and reward. In J. M. Liebman & S. J. Cooper (Eds.), *The neuropharmacological basis of reward* (pp. 377–424). Oxford, UK: Oxford University Press.

Wise, R. A. (1996). Addictive drugs and brain stimulation reward. *Annual Review of Neuroscience, 19,* 319–340.

Wise, R. A. (1999). Cognitive factors in addiction and nucleus accumbens function: Some hints from rodent models. *Psychobiology, 27,* 300–310.

Wise, R. A., & Bozarth, M. A. (1987). A psychomotor stimulant theory of addiction. *Psychological Review, 94,* 469–492.

Wise, R. A., Leone, P., Rivest, R., & Leeb, K. (1995). Elevations of nucleus accumbens dopamine and DOPAC levels during intravenous heroin self-administration. *Synapse, 21,* 140–148.

Wise, R. A., Newton, P., Leeb, K., Burnette, B., Pocock, P., & Justice, J. B. (1995). Fluctuations in nucleus accumbens dopamine concentration during intravenous cocaine self-administration in rats. *Psychopharmacology, 120,* 10–20.

Woods, J. H., Ikomi, F., & Winger, G. (1971). The reinforcing properties of ethanol. In M. K. Roach, W. M. Creaven, & P. J. Creaven (Eds.), *Biological aspects of alcoholism* (pp. 371–388). Austin: University of Texas Press.

Woods, J. H., & Schuster, C. R. (1968). Reinforcement properties of morphine, cocaine, and SPA as a function of unit dose. *International Journal of the Addictions, 3,* 231–237.

Woods, J. H., & Schuster, C. R. (1971). Opiates as reinforcing stimuli. In T. Thompson & R. Pickens (Eds.), *Stimulus properties of drugs* (pp. 163–175). New York: Appleton, Century, Crofts.

Yokel, R. A., & Pickens, R. (1973). Self-administration of optical isomers of amphetamine and methylamphetamine by rats. *Journal of Pharmacology and Experimental Therapeutics, 187,* 27–33.

Yokel, R. A., & Pickens, R. (1974). Drug level of *d*- and *l*-amphetamine during intravenous self-administration. *Psychopharmacologia, 34,* 255–264.

Yokel, R. A., & Wise, R. A. (1975). Increased lever-pressing for amphetamine after pimozide in rats: Implications for a dopamine theory of reward. *Science, 187,* 547–549.

Yokel, R. A., & Wise, R. A. (1976). Attenuation of intravenous amphetamine reinforcement by central dopamine blockade in rats. *Psychopharmacology, 48,* 311–318.

Zetterström, T., Sharp, T., Marsden, C. A., & Ungerstedt, U. (1983). *In vivo* measurement of dopamine and its metabolites by intracerebral dialysis: Changes after d-amphetamine. *Journal of Neurochemistry, 41,* 1769–1773.

Author Index

Bauco, P., 805
Baudonniere, P., 416
Baudry, M., 141, 213, 548
Bauer, E. P., 541, 543, 545
Bauer, P. J., 422
Bauer, T. L., 649
Baum, M. J., 723–724
Baumeister, R. F., 740–741, 746, 761, 766, 768
Baumgardner, A. H., 742
Baumgarten, R., 718
Bauswein, E., 596
Baxter, D. A., 161–162
Baxter, M. G., 118
Bayley, H., 173–174
Baylis, P. H., 690
Beach, C. M., 454, 607
Beach, F. A., 716–717, 720–721
Beaman, A. L., 757
Bear, M. F., 137, 163, 168
Beard, B. L., 268–269
Beattie, E. C., 164
Beauchamp, G. K., 635
Bechara, A., 551
Bechmann, A. M., 822
Becker, J. B., 711, 718, 727, 822
Becker, L., 314
Becker, L. E., 164
Becker, S., 123
Beckstead, R. M., 596
Bedford, F. L., 265, 278
Bednekoff, P. A., 315
Beebe, C., 649
Beeghly-Smith, M., 420
Beer, M. E., 727
Behr, M. J., 413
Beiko, J., 227
Beiser, D. G., 117
Beitz, A., 681
Belknap, J. K., 811
Bell, J., 827
Bell, S. M., 649
Bellinger, L. L., 604, 616
Bellman, R. E., 105, 113
Bellush, L. L., 697
Belousov, A. B., 583
Beltz, T. G., 696
Bem, D. J., 760
Bender, M. A., 728
Beneviste, S., 469, 477
Benfield, P., 684
Benigni, L., 420
Beninger, R. J., 114, 521

Benke, T. A., 163
Benkovic, S., 225, 230
Bennett, A. T. D., 314, 333
Bennett, C. H., 58
Bennett, J. P., Jr., 821
Bennett, P. J., 262, 273
Bennett, R. G., 268–269, 290
Benoit, G., 721
Benoit, S. C., 507–509, 643, 654
Benowitz, L. I., 223
Benson, J. B., 396
Bentley, D. R., 246
Berardi, N., 270
Berenfeld, R., 723
Berent, M. K., 764
Berger, S. A., 421
Berglas, S., 744–745
Bergles, D. E., 160
Bergman, R. N., 601–602, 639, 649
Bergold, P. J., 173–174
Berkeley, G., 55
Berkemeier, L. R., 599, 603
Berlie, J., 69, 79
Bermant, G., 718–719
Bermudez-Rattoni, F., 82
Bernabé, J., 721
Bernard, A., 224
Bernard, J. F., 577–579
Bernardis, L. L., 604, 616
Berne, R. M., 670
Bernhardt, J., 165
Bernier, L., 164, 170
Bernieri, F., 780
Bernstein, I. L., 693
Bernstein, S., 739
Bernstein Ratner, N., 454
Berntson, G. C., 760
Berntson, G. G., 738, 759, 775, 777–781
Berrettini, W., 713
Berridge, K. C., 114, 123, 497, 502, 508, 518–519, 521, 527, 565, 574, 820, 823
Berry, D. A., 105
Berry, S. H., 757
Bertenthal, B. I., 418
Berthier, N. E., 116, 181
Berthoud, H. R., 605, 646–647
Berthoz, A., 345
Bertoncini, J., 451, 455
Bertsekas, D., 104, 111, 114

Besson, J. M., 577–579
Best, M. R., 71
Bester, H., 577, 579
Bethea, C. L., 726
Betts, S. L., 9–10
Betz, A. L., 759
Bever, T. G., 458
Beyer, C., 721
Bhalla, U. S., 168, 173
Bhat, R. V., 678
Bhatnagar, S., 781
Bhatt, R. S., 402
Bi, G.-q., 178–179
Bidoleau, I., 66
Bidtnes, V., 724
Bidwell, N. J., 336
Bieback, H., 387
Biegler, R., 325, 344
Bienenstock, E., 273
Bierman, E. L., 649
Biernat, M. R., 750
Bierwisch, M., 461
Bijeljac-Babic, R., 451
Billington, C. J., 653
Bina, K. G., 584, 586
Bindra, D., 502, 565, 716, 803
Birkenfeld, K., 548
Biró, S., 418, 462
Bisch, S., 336, 339
Bisiach, E., 552
Bisley, J. W., 680
Bittencourt, J. C., 604
Bitterman, M. E., 252, 254
Black, C. A., 826
Blackburn, R. E., 699
Blaine, B., 742
Blaine, E. H., 682
Blair, H. T., 541, 545, 596
Blaisdell, A. P., 63, 71, 375
Blake, R. R., 756
Blanc, G., 826
Blanchard, D. C., 538, 547
Blanchard, R. J., 538, 547
Bland, B. H., 215, 227, 574
Blasberg, M. E., 718
Blass, E. M., 633, 678, 687
Blass, T., 757
Blazis, D. E. J., 116
Blehar, M. C., 766
Blendy, J. A., 137, 142, 175–176, 545
Blesbois, E., 51
Bless, H., 752, 755

Subject Index

Abeki fruit, 353
ACE (angiotensin-converting)
 enzymes, 683–684
ACh, 118
Acquired equivalence, 38
ACTH (adrenocorticotropic
 hormone), 577, 781
Active avoidance, 549
Addiction, 105
 animal models:
  conditioned place
   preference, 811–812, 824
  conditioned reinforcement,
   815–816
  drug-induced general
   activation, 809
  instrumental vs.
   spontaneous responding,
   808
  intravenous drug
   self-administration,
   804–810
  oral self-administration,
   804, 810
  progressive ratio testing,
   809–810
  reinstatement, 810–811
  reward potentiation,
   812–815
 cognitive factors in theory of:
  automatic performance,
   823–824
  craving, 822–823
  wanting vs. liking, 823
 compulsion, 825–826
 definition, 801
 dependence, 802
 dopamine role in, 806
 drug sensitization, 802

food as, 825–826
habit, 802, 810, 826–827
incentive motivation,
 803–804, 810
maintenance, 805–806
methadone maintenance
 therapy, 817, 827
motivation and, 824–826
neuroadaptation, 827
reinforcement, 803, 805,
 808–810
reinforcement types in:
 negative, 816–817
 positive, 817–820
 two factor perspective,
  820–822
reward, 803, 825
satiety, 810
sex as, 825–826
theories:
 dependence, 817, 826–827
 incentive-motivational, 827
 opponent process, 816,
  820
 proponent process,
  820–821
 reinforcement, 827
 tolerance, 801–802, 823
Adenosine diphosphate (ADP),
 600–601
Adenosine triphosphate (ATP),
 600–601, 670
Adenylate cyclase, 168, 181
Adipocytes, 649, 669
Adiposity, 597, 633, 642
Adipsia, 652
Adrenalectomy, 724
Adrenal glands, 696–697
African-Americans, 750–754

Agency, 414, 416–419, 422,
 424, 427
Aging, 365, 691
Albumin, 670
Alcohol:
 addictive nature of, 801
 dependence theory, 817
 physical dependence, 820
 reward circuitry, 818
 self-administration by
  laboratory animals,
  804–806, 811
 withdrawal, 817, 821
Aldosterone, 695–697
Alliethesia, 518
Allophones, 450
Alzheimer's disease, 224–226
Ambiguity, 447
American culture, 745–746
American English, 455
American Sign Language
 (ASL), 484
Amiloride, 693
Amnesia, 267, 280
AMPA, 136–137, 160–161,
 163, 165, 168, 171,
 205–207, 210, 214
Amphetamine:
 brain function, 826
 conditioned place preference,
  812
 reward potentiation, 812,
  818–820
 self-administration by
  laboratory animals,
  804–804, 808, 810
 sensitization in use of, 802
 social hierarchy and, 779
 withdrawal symptoms, 817

877